CASES IN THE ENVIRONMENT OF BUSINESS

THE IVEY CASEBOOK SERIES
A SAGE Publications Series

Series Editor
Paul W. Beamish
Richard Ivey School of Business
The University of Western Ontario

Books in This Series

CASES IN BUSINESS ETHICS
Edited by David J. Sharp

CASES IN ENTREPRENEURSHIP
The Venture Creation Process
Edited by Eric A. Morse and Ronald K. Mitchell

CASES IN OPERATIONS MANAGEMENT
Building Customer Value Through World-Class Operations
Edited by Robert D. Klassen and Larry J. Menor

CASES IN ORGANIZATIONAL BEHAVIOR
Edited by Gerard H. Seijts

CASES IN THE ENVIRONMENT OF BUSINESS
International Perspectives
Edited by David W. Conklin

Forthcoming

CASES IN GENDER AND DIVERSITY IN ORGANIZATIONS
Edited by Alison M. Konrad

DAVID W. CONKLIN
The University of Western Ontario

CASES IN THE ENVIRONMENT OF BUSINESS
International Perspectives

SAGE Publications
Thousand Oaks ▪ London ▪ New Delhi

CONTENTS

INTRODUCTION TO THE IVEY CASEBOOK SERIES

As the title of this series suggests, these books all draw from the Ivey Business School's case collection. Ivey has long had the world's second largest collection of decision-oriented, field-based business cases. Well more than a million copies of Ivey cases are studied every year. There are more than 2,000 cases in Ivey's current collection, with more than 6,000 in the total collection. Each year approximately 200 new titles are registered at Ivey Publishing (www.ivey.uwo.ca/cases), and a similar number are retired. Nearly all Ivey cases have teaching notes available to qualified instructors. The cases included in this volume are all from the current collection.

The vision for the series was a result of conversations I had with Sage's Senior Editor, Al Bruckner, starting in September 2002. Over the subsequent months, we were able to shape a model for the books in the series that we felt would meet a market need.

Each volume in the series contains text and cases. "Some" text was deemed essential in order to provide a basic overview of the particular field and to place the selected cases in an appropriate context. We made a conscious decision to not include hundreds of pages of text material in each volume in recognition of the fact that many professors prefer to supplement basic text material with readings or lectures customized to their interests and to those of their students.

The editors of the books in this series are all highly qualified experts in their respective fields. I was delighted when each agreed to prepare a volume. We very much welcome your comments on this casebook.

—Paul W. Beamish
Series Editor

PREFACE

A central purpose of this book is to extend the geographical scope of analysis beyond a particular nation's borders. Business decisions and profitability depend on international environmental forces and differ among countries. The relevant environment of business has become the global environment, and so the cases in this book involve students in managerial decisions in an international context.

ACKNOWLEDGMENTS

I would like to thank the numerous individuals and institutions involved in the production of the cases that have made this book possible, including the following:

Case Authors

W. Aldridge	J. Dietz
S. Algar	E. Dolansky
A. W. Andron	D. Eaton
P. W. Beamish	J. A. Erskine
L. A. Beer	D. Everatt
J.-P. Bonardi	T. S. Frost
Y. Boshyk	J. Gandz
C. Bouquet	T. Gleave
D. Cadieux	A. Goerzen
D. D. Campbell	T. Hunter
B. Cheng	A. Inkpen
J. Chung	K. Johnston
A. Davenport	D. Jones
C. Dhanaraj	B. Judiesch

J. R. Kennedy

Y. S. Kim

J. Knowles

G. Kudar

V. Kumar

D. J. Lecraw

M. Martin

H. Minhas

M. H. Moffett

A. Morrison

R. C. Nelson

H. Ngo

E. Ossowski

A. Phatak

K. Ramaswamy

M. Siwak

M. Smith

A. K. Sundaram

C. W. Tan

J. Thompson

M. Trudeau

T. Tsai

A. Wali

S. Weeks

X. Zhang

Institutional Contributors

Richard Ivey School of Business, The University of Western Ontario, London, Canada
Thunderbird, The American Graduate School of International Management, Arizona, United States

Many colleagues have contributed to the development of the themes in this book, and I would like in particular to thank those who wrote cases. Thunderbird University kindly gave permission to include cases written by their professors. Ivey Publishing provided ongoing assistance in editing and compiling cases.

I would also like to thank Al Bruckner, Senior Acquisitions Editor, Sage Publications, for providing ongoing advice, together with anonymous referees.

INTRODUCTION

In discussing the cases in this book, students will participate in managerial decisions in an international context. Most cases deal with a variety of environmental forces, but generally a single set of forces plays a predominant role. In view of this, the cases are divided in accordance with the following themes.

1. **Industry structure:** Management must react to the strategies and bargaining strength of customers, suppliers, and competitors, and these vary from one country to another. To a major degree, profitability depends on the development of unique value-added attributes in the context of substitutes and potential market entrants. With the 21st century, the nature and structure of the firm is changing dramatically in response to new outsourcing opportunities and the shift of labor-intensive activities to low-wage countries. For an increasing number of firms, the analysis of industry structure must be undertaken from a global perspective.

2. **Macroeconomic forces:** Management must formulate country strategies in light of each country's income levels and growth rates, foreign exchange rates, inflation rates, interest rates, and unemployment rates.

3. **Political forces:** Management must respond to each country's regulations, financial incentives, tax regimes, foreign investment restrictions, and international trade and investment agreements.

4. **Societal forces:** Labor and environmental practices differ among countries, and so do commonly accepted ethical standards. Consequently, management and boards of directors must confront varying public attitudes toward appropriate corporate behavior and social responsibility. For many products and services, consumer preferences and demographic trends also differ among countries and so play a role in the development of national strategies and practices.

5. **Technological forces:** Strategies must be congruent with a nation's technological infrastructure and the pace and direction of technological changes. Of particular importance is the ability to adopt Internet and e-business strategies in each country where the firm operates.

Cases are grouped under the above themes. However, although one set of forces plays a predominant role in the decisions of each case, most cases do entail more than this single set of forces. The following matrix, Table 0.1, suggests the scope of each case. A double check mark indicates the predominant set of forces, whereas a single check mark indicates additional forces that also play a significant role in management decisions. Instructors may wish to alter the order in which cases are studied or may wish to choose a selection of cases based on this matrix.

Case Title	Industry Structure	Macroeconomic Forces	Political Forces	Societal Forces	Technological Forces
Samsung and the Theme Park Industry in Korea, Ivey Case #9A96M006	✓✓			✓	
PharmaPlus in Hungary, Ivey Case #9A98G002	✓✓			✓	
Singapore International Airlines: Preparing for Turbulence Ahead, Thunderbird Case #A09040013	✓✓		✓	✓	
Swatch and the Global Watch Industry, Ivey Case #9A99M023	✓✓				✓
Whirlpool Corporation's Global Strategy, Thunderbird Case #A07000013	✓✓				
Wal-Mart Stores Inc.: Dominating Global Retailing, Thunderbird Case #A09040012	✓✓			✓	
The Global Branding of Stella Artois, Ivey Case #9B00A019	✓✓			✓	
A Global Manager's Guide to Currency Risk Management, Thunderbird Case #B06030006		✓✓			
Chauvco Resources Ltd.: The Argentina Decisions, Ivey Case #9A95H003	✓	✓✓	✓		✓
Crisis in Japan, Ivey Case #9B02M024		✓✓	✓		
Procter & Gamble in Eastern Europe, Ivey Case #9A97H001		✓✓	✓	✓	
Bank Vozrozhdeniye (V.Bank), Ivey Case #9A99M008	✓	✓✓	✓		
ING and Global Financial Integration, Ivey Case #9A99M022	✓	✓✓		✓	✓
Mekong Corporation and the Viet Nam Motor Vehicle Industry, Ivey Case #9A96H002	✓		✓✓		✓
Thai Telecoms in the New Economy: Privatization & Liberalization, Ivey Case #9B01M064		✓	✓✓		✓
Lucent in India, Ivey Case #9B01M047		✓	✓✓		✓
Citigroup in Post-WTO China, Ivey Case #9B02M012	✓		✓✓		✓
Point Lisas Industrial Estate: Trinidad, Ivey Case #9A99M099			✓✓	✓	
Dell's Dilemma in Brazil: Negotiating at the State Level, Thunderbird Case #A03030021			✓✓		✓
Enron and the Dabhol Power Company, Thunderbird Case #A07020008			✓✓		
Bombardier Versus Embraer: Charges of Unfair Competition, Ivey Case #9A99M004	✓		✓✓		✓

Table 0.1   Prominent Environmental Forces in Each Case *(Continued)*

Case Title	Industry Structure	Macroeconomic Forces	Political Forces	Societal Forces	Technological Forces
John McCulloch—United Beef Packers, Ivey Case #9B03C022				✓✓	
NES China: Business Ethics (A), Ivey Case #9B01C029			✓	✓✓	
NES China: Business Ethics (B), Ivey Case #9B01C030			✓	✓✓	
Textron Ltd., Ivey Case #9B01M070	✓			✓✓	
Note on the Pollution Problem in the Mexico-U.S. Border Region, Ivey Case #9A98H001			✓	✓✓	
Planet Starbucks (A), Thunderbird Case #A09030007	✓			✓✓	
Siam Canadian Foods Co., Ltd., Ivey Case #9A97G003	✓		✓	✓✓	
Royal Trustco, Ivey Case #9A94H004	✓		✓	✓✓	
Privatizing Poland's Telecom Industry: Opportunities and Challenges in the New Economy and E-Business, Ivey Case #9B00M023	✓	✓	✓	✓	✓✓
Malaysia's Multimedia Development Corporation, Ivey Case #9A98G001			✓		✓✓
Global Warming and the Kyoto Protocol: Implications for Business, Ivey Case #9B01M071			✓	✓	✓✓
Enron Wind Corporation: Challenges and Opportunities in the 21st Century, Ivey Case #9B01M069			✓	✓	✓✓
Eurograin (Philippines) and Hybrid Corn, Ivey Case #9A97G006	✓		✓	✓	✓✓
Shire Pharmaceuticals Group's Acquisition of BioChem Pharma: Broadening Product Portfolio and Achieving Economies of Scale in Pharmaceuticals, Ivey Case #9B03M034	✓		✓		✓✓
GM in China, Ivey Case #9B05M007	✓	✓	✓	✓	✓
Intel's Site Selection Decision in Latin America, Thunderbird Case #A03990016	✓	✓	✓	✓	✓
The Acer Group's China Manufacturing Decision, Ivey Case #9A99M009	✓	✓	✓	✓	✓

Table 0.1   Prominent Environmental Forces in Each Case

Note: ✓✓ indicates predominant set of forces; ✓ indicates additional significant forces.

Of importance are the interactions among the environmental forces. Furthermore, broadening the scope of environmental forces to a global rather than a domestic context leads to cross-country comparisons that add complexity to the subject matter, enrich analytical theories, and heighten the interest of students.

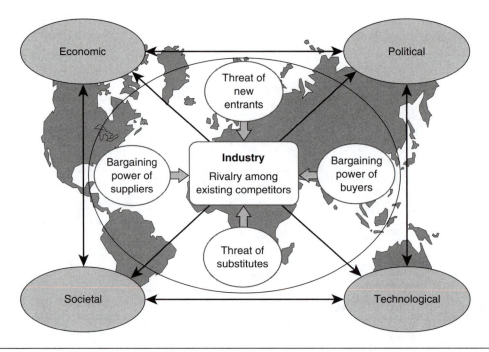

Diagram 0.1 Forces Acting on Business

Diagram 0.1 illustrates the need to consider environmental interactions in the global context. These interactions create a set of risks and opportunities that are unique in each country and that must be evaluated in formulating trade and investment decisions.

Some cases quickly become outdated. A valuable solution is to provide supplementary materials such as media reports and analysts' commentaries that discuss recent developments. For example, the "Chauvco Resources Ltd.: The Argentina Decisions" case can be supplemented with information concerning the post-2000 economic crisis and with a discussion of why macroeconomic policies failed after the 1995 situation described in the case. In this way, cases can be updated regularly.

To the memory of Saint Josemaría Escrivá, whose life and writings have inspired the creation of business schools throughout the world and have led managers to recognize personal responsibilities in business leadership.

1

THE DEPENDENCE
OF PROFITABILITY ON
INDUSTRY STRUCTURE

The cases in this chapter illustrate the ways that microeconomic forces and industry structure influence management decisions. Determining the prices to be charged and quantities to be produced requires that management understand customer, supplier, and competitor strategies, and these market realities vary among countries. Conceptual frameworks used in analyzing industry structure include Michael Porter's (1979) "five forces model," through which each industry can be analyzed from the perspective of the rivalry among existing competitors, the threat of new entrants, the bargaining power of buyers, the threat of substitutes, and the bargaining power of suppliers. A sixth force, the impacts of complementors, can be added to this model. Elements of microeconomic theory and game theory are analytical tools that help in the examination of how a change in price will affect sales volumes and hence revenue, costs, and profits.

Industry structures may differ significantly from one country to another, and these differences may provide a rationale for international investment. In particular, international investment can enable a firm to increase its profitability by shifting from a market where it has no significant competitive advantage to a market where its activities are unique. Strong competitors can limit expansion opportunities in a firm's home country, whereas the firm may benefit from a monopoly position if it invests in a foreign market. Differences in industry structures among countries can result from any of the environmental forces: for example, levels of economic development, types of political regulations, preferences of consumers, or stages of technologies. As Douglass North (1990) has discussed, many of a country's institutions can shape an industry's international competitiveness. Consequently, governments often seek to affect an industry structure, through a variety of programs and policies.

Some industry structures can lead to a "game" among participants in the sense that the actions of one participant will affect the profitability of other participants. Decisions must

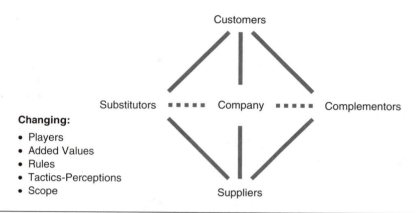

Diagram 1.1   The Value Net

be undertaken based on an evaluation of a series of possible outcomes, where each outcome depends on the reaction of others in the industry. From this perspective, Brandenburger and Nalebuff (1995) have suggested a useful framework for the analysis of an industry (see Diagram 1.1).

Participants may alter potential outcomes by changing the industry structure in a variety of ways. In particular, Brandenburger and Nalebuff (1995) suggest that each corporation should use what they refer to as "PARTS as a comprehensive, theory-based set of levers" to help generate strategies. Each letter in the phrase "PARTS" represents a lever for changing the industry structure. A firm may threaten to change the number of players (P) by indicating that it intends to enter an industry. The mere threat may result in the firm receiving a benefit, thereby altering the allocation of the value added among the participants. A firm may change the "added values" (A) by lowering the added value of others, as well as by increasing its own added value. A firm may change the rules (R), for example, by developing new pricing policies. A firm may change tactics (T) in ways that alter other players' perceptions and therefore their decisions. A firm may change the scope (S) of the game by severing linkages with other companies or building new alliances. Unlike Porter's (1979) five forces, which analyze an existing industry structure, this game theory approach examines ways to change the industry structure.

The concept of an industry as a "value chain" involves the analysis of the relative attractiveness of alternative business activities required in the process of creating products or services, where each link adds a certain value within the "chain." The "creative web" concept suggests perspectives and practices necessary to stimulate the innovation process among firms that are separate corporations but that work together within a value chain (Conklin & Tapp, 2000). Many organizational structures in the 21st century will rest on cooperation as well as competition. A set of corporations will work together to expand the value that is added by their group. Although the group as a whole faces competition from other groups, the organizational dynamic within each group seeks to improve the outcomes for all participants. The analysis of the creative web builds on the game theory framework, in that it focuses on the ways in which individual corporations may affect the success of each other. However, it sees this relationship as one where the objective is for all participants to win through innovation that increases the web's value added, enabling all participants to increase their financial gain. Outsourcing of various activities to other firms and shifting some activities to lower-cost countries extends this concept of the creative web.

To evaluate the international competitiveness of a potential investment location for a specific industry or for a specific activity within the industry, Michael Porter's (1990) "diamond framework" is helpful. Countries differ in regard to factor conditions, demand conditions, rivalry among competitors, and related and supporting industries. These features, together with the role of government and of chance, may combine to create a competitive advantage in a region or country for certain types of activities that may then develop as a "cluster" of firms. Business investment decisions can be strengthened through such an analysis of industry/country competitiveness. New international trade and investment agreements can radically alter this "diamond," changing an industry/country competitive advantage. Trade and investment agreements, together with an industry structure of a value chain or a creative web, can facilitate the location of separable activities in different countries. Each of these countries may offer a competitive advantage for a specific type of activity, leading to the concept of an activity/country competitive advantage.

SAMSUNG AND THE THEME PARK INDUSTRY IN KOREA

The management of the Samsung Group has to decide whether to enter the Korean theme park industry. The case focuses on three main issues in the context of the entry decision: (a) the underlying forces that shape industry structure, competitive interaction, and profits; (b) the impact of globalization on industry structure; and (c) the relationship between a firm's resources and its strategy. Porter's (1979) five forces model is used to analyze the impact of the competitive forces on profitability.

PHARMAPLUS IN HUNGARY

Hungary had strict laws defining what could be sold in a pharmacy and a "druggery" (which were two separate entities), yet PharmaPlus was attempting to combine the two within a single store. Management of PharmaPlus faced opposition from the regulatory body of pharmacists that had authority over each pharmacy's operations. The case deals with issues of lobbying stakeholders who have power, finding a sustainable competitive advantage in a market with many competitors that has never seen this type of business, and exploring potential international expansion in the context of Hungary entering the European Union (EU).

SINGAPORE INTERNATIONAL AIRLINES: PREPARING FOR TURBULENCE AHEAD

By 2004, Singapore International Airlines (SIA) enjoyed a run of exemplary profitability and service performance. It had built its strategy around the principles of a differentiated positioning using its brand image, geographic location, and outstanding service as the cornerstones of its strategy. The case offers enough data to launch into a rich discussion of the industry factors that drive profitability and complements it with an in-depth look at the model of strategy that SIA had built to compete in the airline business. In recent years, there have been many environmental shocks, such as severe acute respiratory syndrome (SARS), that have challenged the continued viability of the model. The company entered into an equity alliance with Virgin that has destroyed significant value. It found itself challenged by the entry of many low-cost airlines in its home market. The case closes with a decision that SIA needed to make about how it would address the onset of low-cost competitors and whether it would make sense to move away from its differentiated premium approach.

SWATCH AND THE GLOBAL WATCH INDUSTRY

The efforts of Swatch to reposition itself in the increasingly competitive global watch industry are reviewed in this case. Extensive information on the history and structure of the global watch industry is provided, and the shrinking time horizons decision makers face in formulating strategy and in responding to changes in the industry are highlighted. In particular, the case discusses how technology and globalization have changed industry dynamics and have caused companies to reassess their sources of competitive advantage. Like other companies, Swatch faced the difficult task of deciding whether to emphasize product breadth or focus on a few key global brands. It also had to decide whether to shift manufacturing away from Switzerland to lower-cost countries such as India.

WHIRLPOOL CORPORATION'S GLOBAL STRATEGY

This case deals with Whirlpool Corporation (Whirlpool) and its global expansion, which was driven by Whirlpool's objective of becoming the world market leader in home appliances. By the mid-1990s, serious problems had emerged in Whirlpool's international operations. In 1995, Whirlpool's European profit fell by 50%, and in 1996, the company reported a $13 million loss in Europe. In Asia, the situation was even worse. Although the region accounted for only 6% of corporate sales, Whirlpool lost $70 million in Asia in 1996 and $62 million in 1997. In Brazil, Whirlpool found itself a victim in 1997, and again in 1998, of spiraling interest rates. This case examines the concepts of global industry and global strategy and the related question of how globalization affects competition. The appliance industry produces products that are used in every country. Is it a global industry? Will the industry evolve like the automobile industry to the point that there are a small number of international firms present in all major markets? Or will the industry remain a collection of local industries?

WAL-MART STORES INC.: DOMINATING GLOBAL RETAILING

The case explores the fundamental features of the business model that Wal-Mart has been adopting, both in the United States and abroad. It places particular emphasis on the company's supplier management approaches, supplier strategies in doing business with

Wal-Mart, and the company's track record in international operations. It offers insights into the ways in which Wal-Mart's suppliers can design their own strategies to ensure continued viability amid significant pricing pressure from the retail giant. It closes with important questions about the continued success of the company in the face of allegations of labor violations, increasing competition in foreign markets, and the likelihood of a supplier push-back against Wal-Mart's continued pressure to bring down its prices. The major objectives of this case are to illustrate the fundamental concepts of competitive advantage and how it is built and nurtured, explore issues of sustainability, look at Wal-Mart's strategies of supplier relationship management and the consequences of its restrictive practices in managing its supplier network, and examine the transferability of homegrown sources of competitive advantage to foreign locations.

THE GLOBAL BRANDING OF STELLA ARTOIS

Interbrew had developed into the world's fourth largest brewer by acquiring and managing a large portfolio of national and regional beer brands in markets around the world. Recently, senior management had decided to develop one of its premium beers, Stella Artois, as a global brand. The early stages of Interbrew's global branding strategy and tactics are examined, enabling students to consider these concepts in the context of a fragmented but consolidating industry.

SAMSUNG AND THE THEME PARK INDUSTRY IN KOREA

*Prepared by Charles Dhanaraj and Young Soo Kim
under the supervision of Professor Paul Beamish*

Copyright © 1996, Ivey Management Services and Samsung HRDC   Version: (A) 2002-11-22

SAMSUNG has the right to reproduce and use this case for its educational purposes.

In October 1994, Her Tae-Hak, President of Samsung's Joong-Ang Development Company, was driving to his office, past the "Yongin Farmland" (Farmland), an amusement complex sprawling over 3,700 acres in the Yongin valley. Her was spearheading a major drive within the company to position the theme park as one of the world's leading vacation resort towns. His master plan called for an investment of about US$300 million over the next five years, to be internally funded by the Samsung Group. Despite the booming Korean economy and the increasing demands for leisure attractions, the global competitive environment of the theme park industry raised several concerns. Should Samsung invest in such an aggressive expansion plan for Farmland? Was this an attractive industry for investment? Her was scheduled for a meeting with the Chairman of the Samsung Group for a formal presentation of the proposal at the end of the month.

THE GLOBAL THEME PARK INDUSTRY

The early 1990s saw the emergence of theme parks as a major source of family entertainment, not just in the United States but around the world. The earliest evidence of a business where people "paid money to be terrified" was in the early 1600s when several Russians operated a sled ride with a 70-foot vertical drop. In the late 1800s, several theme parks were set up in Coney Island (New York) in the United States. The first roller coaster was set up in 1884, followed by an indoor amusement park, Sealion Park. In the 1930s, the amusement industry had to contend with alternative entertainment offered by the movie houses as well as setbacks due to economic depression. However, with the Disneyland Park opening in 1955 in California, the industry was revived and Walt Disney was credited with raising the profile, as well as the profitability, of the industry to a new height.

There was a variety of parks and attractions, each with a different approach to drawing crowds and showing them a good time:

- **Cultural and Education Parks** were a remnant of the old-fashioned type of European park. Such parks featured formal greens, gardens, and fountains. Generally they incorporated historical and educational exhibits.
- **Outdoor Amusement Parks** were small parks that served a metropolitan or regional market. These parks featured traditional thrill rides, carnival midways, and some entertainment. Most amusement parks did not have a theme to the architecture, rides, and entertainment.
- **Theme Parks** were generally family-oriented entertainment complexes that were built around a theme. Theme parks were larger and had a greater variety of rides and attractions than amusement parks.
- **Water Theme Parks** were a recent phenomenon, a special type of theme parks centered on water activities. Large water parks featured wave action pools, river rides, steep vertical drop slides, and a variety of twisting flume slides.

Most of the theme parks were members of the International Association of Amusement Parks and Attractions, which tracked the attendance at various theme parks. In 1993, North American parks accounted for 48 per cent of the worldwide attendance, Asian parks 33 per cent, European parks 14 per cent, and Central and South American parks four per cent (see Table 1).

North America

The Walt Disney Company was the largest park chain in the world with three major theme parks in the United States. Time Warner's Six Flags Corporation was the second largest with seven parks spread out in the United States. Paramount, Anheuser Busch and Cedar Fair were some of the other conglomerates who owned theme parks. In mid-1993, Paramount bought Canada's Wonderland theme park originally developed by Taft Broadcasting Company in 1981. Despite the mature nature of the industry in the United States, a number of theme parks were investing heavily in upgrading their facilities, and extending the theme parks' services.

Europe

In 1980, Alton Towers, a 60-year-old park in North Staffordshire (England), comprised primarily of historic gardens, repositioned itself as a theme park by adding a roller coaster and some other attractions. The park was extremely successful within a very short span of time. The success of Alton Towers led to a number of new theme parks in the late 1980s and the early 1990s, including Blackpool Pleasure Beach (England) that featured the world's tallest roller coaster. In France alone, three major theme parks emerged in the early 1990s: Walt Disney's $3 billion Euro Disney, the $150 million Parc Asterix located northeast of Paris, and the $110 million Big Bang Schtroumpf (Smurfs) theme park just north of Metz. Six Flags Corporation and Anheuser-Busch both recently opened new theme parks in Spain coinciding with the 1992 Barcelona Olympics.

Rank	Park & Location	Attendance (in millions)
1	Tokyo (Japan) DISNEYLAND	16.030
2	MAGIC KINGDOM of Walt Disney World, Florida, United States	11.200
3	DISNEYLAND, Anaheim, California, United States	10.300
4	JAYA ANCOL DREAMLAND, Jakarta, Indonesia	9.800
5	EPCOT at Walt Disney World, Florida, United States	9.700
6	EURO DISNEYLAND, Morne La Voltee, France	8.800
7	YOKOHAMA (Japan) HAKKEIJIMA SEA PARADISE, Japan	8.737
8	DISNEY-MGM STUDIOS, Walt Disney World, Florida, United States	8.000
9	UNIVERSAL STUDIOS FLORIDA, Orlando, Florida, United States	7.700
10	BLACKPOOL (England) PLEASURE BEACH, England	7.000
11	YONGIN FARMLAND, Kyonggi-Do, South Korea	6.071
12	UNIVERSAL STUDIOS HOLLYWOOD, California, United States	4.600
13	SEA WORLD OF FLORIDA, Florida, United States	4.600
14	LOTTE WORLD, Seoul, South Korea	4.433
15	CHAPULTEPEC, Mexico City, Mexico	4.200
16	HUIS TEN BOSCH, Sosebo, Japan	3.902
17	TOSHIMAEN AMUSEMENT PARK, Tokyo, Japan	3.800
18	KNOTT'S BERRY FARM, Fuona Park, California, United States	3.800
19	SEA WORLD OF CALIFORNIA, San Diego, California, United States	3.700
20	BUSCH GARDENS, Tampa, Florida, United States	3.700
21	CEDAR POINT, Sandusky, Ohio, United States	3.600
22	SIX FLAGS MAGIC MOUNTAIN, Valencia, Calif, United States	3.500
23	SEOUL LAND, Seoul, South Korea	3.311
24	PARAMOUNT'S KING'S ISLAND, Ohio, United States	3.300
25	OCEAN PARK, Hong Kong	3.200
26	SIX FLAGS GREAT ADVENTURE, Jackson, New Jersey, United States	3.200
27	SANTA CRUZ BEACH BOARDWALK, California, United States	3.100
28	NAGASHIMA SPA LAND, Kuwona, Japan	3.008
29	TIVOLI GARDENS, Copenhagen, Denmark	3.000
30	SIX FLAGS OVER TEXAS, Arlington, Texas, United States	3.000
31	ALTON TOWERS, North Staffordshire, United Kingdom	3.000
32	SIX FLAGS GREAT AMERICA, Gumee, Illinois, United States	2.900
33	PARAMOUNT CANADA'S WONDERLAND, Maple, Canada	2.850
34	TAKARAZUKA (Japan) FAMILY LAND	2.796
35	SIX FLAGS OVER GEORGIA, Atlanta, United States	2.600
36	DE EFTELING, The Netherlands	2.550
37	PLAYCENTER, São Paulo, Brazil	2.500
38	DUNIA FUNTASI, Jakarta, Indonesia	2.500
39	PARAMOUNT'S GREAT AMERICA, California, United States	2.500
40	KNOTT'S CAMP SNOOPY, Bloomington, Minnesota, United States	2.500
41	EUROPA PARK, Germany	2.450
42	KORAKUEN, Tokyo, Japan	2.423
43	PARAMOUNT'S KINGS DOMINION, Virginia, United States	2.400
44	SIX FLAGS ASTROWORLD, Houston, Texas, United States	2.400
45	PLAYCENTER, São Paulo, Brazil	2.400
46	BUSCH GARDENS THE OLD COUNTRY, Virginia, United States	2.300
47	DAKKEN, Klampenborg, Denmark	2.300
48	LISEBERG, Gothenburg, Sweden	2.200
49	TOEI UZUMASA EIGAMURA, Kyoto, Japan	2.146
50	BEIJING (China) AMUSEMENT PARK	2.050

Table 1   Top 50 Amusement/Theme Parks Worldwide (1994)

Source: Amusement Business.

Asia

Tokyo Disneyland was opened in 1983 by Walt Disney as a joint venture with the Oriental Land Company (OLC). The success of Tokyo Disneyland set off a wave of theme park developments in Asia. OLC and Disney had agreed to open a second theme park, "Tokyo Disney Sea" in 2001. Ocean Park in Hong Kong, started in 1977, was the largest water park in Asia with an annual attendance of 3.2 million. Jaya Ancol Dreamland, located in North Jakarta, Indonesia, was one of the largest recreation complexes in south east Asia. Dreamland had a theme park (Dunia Fantasi), a waterpark complex, an oceanarium, a golf course, a beach and several hotels. China was a major growth market. Beijing Amusement Park, started in 1981, reported that between 1990 and 1993 revenues increased over 2,000 per cent and earnings before interest and taxes were up 200 per cent. Over the next five years, six regional theme parks were to be developed with a total investment of over $100 million.

FINANCIAL ISSUES

The theme park business required a large-scale initial investment, typically ranging from $50 million to $3 billion. Depending on the real-estate markets, the cost of the land value itself could be very high. Theme parks required over 50 acres of land for a full scale development, with some of the theme parks utilizing 10,000 to 30,000 acres. Since accessibility of the park location was a key success factor in the industry, theme park developers chose land sites in a central area which was relatively expensive. Alternatively, they could choose a remote area at a low cost and develop the transportation network. In either case, the land development costs constituted nearly 50 per cent of the overall investment. The amusement machinery constituted 20 to 30 per cent of the total investment, and the working capital requirements took up the remaining 20 to 30 per cent of the investment. The amusement equipment required for the park was also expensive, most of it going from $1 million to $50 million. Businesses which had an in-house land development expertise or equipment technology had better control of these costs.

Many parks periodically added new attractions or renovated existing ones to draw repeat customers. The parks typically reinvested much of their revenue for expansion or upgrading purposes. The economies of scale and scope were significant in the industry. Increasingly, parks got larger and larger to generate more operating revenues. Also, companies had multiple parks to take advantage of the learning curve effects in the management of theme parks and the increased economies of scope. Most of the operating expenses for theme parks (about 75 per cent) were for personnel.

Admission fees[1] constituted over 60 per cent of the total revenues of a theme park, while the rest came primarily from food, beverage, and merchandise sales. To handle the admissions revenue a centralized ticket system was generally preferred. An all-inclusive admission price entitled customers to as many rides and shows as they desired. This approach led to longer stays at parks resulting in increased food and beverage sales. Another centralized admission method was to sell ride/show tickets in sets or coupon books (i.e., five coupons for $5, but 12 coupons for $10). Both approaches to centralized ticket sales minimized the number of employees handling money throughout the park resulting in improved efficiency and control.

Walt Disney Company's financial profile was generally used to assess the return on investment within the industry. The revenues for the theme parks segment of the Walt Disney Company were at US$2.042 billion in 1988 and grew to US$3.4 billion in 1993. Operating income was pegged at US$565 million in 1988 and US$747 million in 1993. The return on equity for the Walt Disney Company was pegged at 17 to 25 per cent. One of the analysts remarked on the theme parks segment of Walt Disney:

> Theme parks are going to become increasingly stable and annuity-like, with the ability to generate $700 to $750 million in cash flow a year.

There were signs of declining profitability in the U.S. operations, since the market was maturing and the competition was getting more intense. Tokyo Disneyland, the Japanese operation, was growing and profitable. However, EuroDisney, the European theme park, was a disaster for the company with huge losses since operations began in 1992. The company was expecting a break-even in 1995.

MARKETING AND SOCIAL ISSUES

The traditional appeal of theme/amusement parks was to preteens, teens, and young adults. Changing demographics were causing most parks to think in terms of a broader market, particularly families, corporate groups, and even senior citizens. There were five major market segments for theme parks:

- Local Families—people within a day's drive who visited mostly on weekends. Most parks focused exclusively on this segment, which generally constituted 60 to 75 per cent of the attendance.
- Children's Groups—schools, churches, recreation agencies, scouts, and other groups who traveled in buses on summer weekdays.
- The Evening Market—teens and young adults who came for entertainment, concerts, and romancing at night.
- Corporate Groups—included consignment sales and group parties.
- Tourists—a substantial market for large theme parks in destination areas such as Florida.

Customer satisfaction was a critical issue in theme parks management. Successful park managers used extensive marketing research to understand their customers and also spent a lot of effort in promoting the park. To reach the diverse groups, parks emphasized increased beautification and the range of entertainment and food services offered. Theme park managers were working with tour operators and government tourist promotion boards to draw the tourist crowds to their parks. Theme parks spent about 10 per cent of their annual revenues for advertising. Radio, newspaper, yellow page (telephone book) advertisements, family and group discounts, and direct mail were the most common promotional methods. Among large theme parks, television advertising was an excellent visual medium to capture the excitement. Some parks expended a major portion of their advertising budget for television promotion.

An issue for the theme parks industry was the seasonal and intermittent nature of the business. Theme parks' attendance peaked in the spring/summer and in the school holidays. Even in the holiday season, bad weather could adversely affect the attendance. The seasonal fluctuations put a lot of strain on the theme parks' management. During the peak season, the requirement for employees shot up; quite often the management had to find employees beyond the domestic territory and provide housing for out-of-town employees. The sudden surge in demand often choked the service systems such as transportation, building management, etc.

It was the availability of leisure time and a high discretionary income that drove the commercial recreation industry. Economic downturns had a severe impact on industry revenues. Also, consumers could substitute a visit to theme parks with other modes of entertainment. Consumers substituted products/services in order to try something new, different, cheaper, safer, better, or more convenient. Free admission parks and beaches, camping trips, or even video-movies at home were competing options for leisure time.

REGULATORY ISSUES

Government regulations were quite strict because of the extensive land use, and the potential for serious accidents. Licensing requirements and methods of ascertaining operational expertise to ensure visitors' safety varied from country to country. In some countries, where land was scarce, governments limited the area of the land that the developers could take up for theme parks. Park administration was dependent on the government for utilities such as power, gas and water. A typical period required for arranging government approval for a theme park could be as high as two to five years, depending on the country.

A related issue was insurance premiums. Given the likelihood of accidents in the amusement parks and the possibility of serious injury, 100 per cent insurance coverage was a must in the industry. Although safety records in the industry were very good, the insurance premiums were extremely high in some parts of the world, particularly in the United States. However, the large premiums often drove the small players in the industry out of business. Countries in Asia did not have this handicap.

TECHNOLOGY ISSUES

The theme park industry had three classes of inputs: the building and construction services that provided landscaping and architectural support; the hardware providers that supplied amusement machinery; and the software providers that supplied management know-how.

The amusement machinery industry had grown over the years. Most of the large drives, such as the Hurricane or the Giant Wheel, were manufactured in Japan, Europe or the United States. There were fewer than 10 suppliers who were capable of developing quality machinery, such as DOGO of Japan, HUSS of Germany, and ARROW of the United States. Most of these suppliers worked globally, and the machinery were custom designed and made to order to fit the particular market and environment conditions. There were a large number of suppliers for the smaller machines, and quite often, they could be manufactured domestically. Special simulators for amusement purposes using proprietary technology were being developed by technology-intensive companies such as Sega Japan and Simex Canada.

The park management expertise commonly referred to as the "software" in the industry was not easily available. Leading theme park companies, such as Walt Disney Company, charged huge licensing fees which were over 10 per cent of the revenues. Also, they were very selective in choosing joint ventures in other countries. Disney went through an extensive market analysis and partner profile analysis for over three years in Europe before finalizing the venue in France with the joint venture partner. Mr. Yu, director-in-charge of the Farmland project, commented:

> We wanted to go for a joint venture with Walt Disney Corporation. But they somehow were not interested in Korea. So we had to go it alone. It takes a long time for theme park managers to develop service delivery of world class quality.

Although Walt Disney offered a number of educational programs to train other managers in the "Disney Management" style, the know-how seemed to be too sophisticated for the competitors to emulate.

Virtual reality (VR) was increasingly becoming a highly lucrative mass-market entertainment phenomenon. A new entry that was due to open in July 1994 was Joypolis, a $70 million interactive theme park owned by Sega Enterprises, with projected revenues of $37 million per annum. Sega had plans to open 50 such parks in Japan, and was negotiating with Universal Studios, California, for its first U.S. installation of a VR theme park.

YONGIN FARMLAND

Yongin Farmland (Farmland), opened in 1976, was the first amusement park in Korea. It was managed by Joong-Ang Development Company, one of the wholly owned subsidiaries of Samsung with a mission to provide a better quality of life through healthy open-air leisure activities. In addition to the Farmland management, Joong-Ang was responsible for the building maintenance at all Samsung's offices, as well as maintaining two golf courses. Farmland was located about an hour south of Seoul, and was

The late Chairman Lee Byung-Chul founded the Samsung Group in 1938. Though started as a trading firm to supply rice and agricultural commodities to neighboring countries, Samsung moved quickly into import substitution manufacturing activities such as sugar refining and textiles. In the 1960s Samsung moved into electronics by establishing Samsung Electronics that developed VCRs, integrated circuits for televisions and telephone exchanges, electron guns for cathode ray tubes (CRTs), and cameras. The 1980s marked a major expansion for Samsung with its evolution into high-tech industry, such as semi-conductors, telecommunications, computers, factory automation systems, and aerospace. Samsung had accomplished remarkable growth (see Table 7, p. 15). The 1994 revenues were expected to be about US$70 billion.

Samsung, with 206,000 employees operating in 65 countries, had recently reorganized the group into four core business subgroups, Electronics, Machinery, Chemicals, and Finance & Insurance, and one subgroup of independent affiliates. While the core groups represented specific technological areas, the independent affiliates subgroup represented a diverse mosaic that included the trading activities of the company, Korea's highest-rated hotel, Korea's leading newspaper publisher, state-of-the-art medical and research institutes, and cultural and welfare foundations. The Joong-Ang Development Co. Ltd., the developer of the Yongin Farmland came under this subgroup.

In 1987, Lee Kun-Hee, son of the late Lee Byung-Chul, was appointed the chairman of the Samsung group. Lee accelerated the pace of growth at Samsung by pursuing aggressively high-technology areas and pushed the group to change from a quantity-oriented company to a quality-oriented company. Samsung's goal was to become one of the world's top ten corporations by the year 2000 by achieving annual sales of US$200 billion, and by producing products and services of the highest quality. Service quality and customer satisfaction became key phrases in all Samsung's activities and all the companies in the group were taking active part in the "quality revolution" initiated by Lee.

Exhibit 1   Samsung Group

owned by the Korean conglomerate, the Samsung Group (see Exhibit 1). The 3,700-acre attraction began as an agricultural center to demonstrate how mountainous land could be used productively for growing food products. Mr. Lee of Joong-Ang said,

> At that time, we had trouble raising enough food for our country. We created a model farm of how to work with an abandoned mountain by building a pig farm and planting fruit orchards. We changed the land use gradually through the years as we added entertainment elements.

The Wild Safari was opened in 1980, and the Rose Festival, an impressive rose garden filled with 6,000 rose bushes of 160 different varieties arranged according to various themes, opened in 1985. To provide for winter entertainment, the Sled Slope was opened in 1988. A drastic departure from the traditional theme parks was taken when Yongin Farmland opened a Motor-Park in late 1993. The motor park operations incurred a

loss in the first year of operations (see Table 2 for the profit and loss statement).

In November 1993, Her took over as the President and Chief Executive Officer of the Joong-Ang Development Company. Prior to his assignment to Joong-Ang, Her was the CEO of Cheju Shilla, a luxury hotel on Cheju Island in Korea. Her was credited with developing a world-class sea resort at Cheju Shilla which surpassed in customer service established hotel chains such as Hotel Hilton. Since taking over the reins of the company, Her had focused on improving the customer satisfaction level at Farmland, and had also been developing the plans for Farmland's expansion. One of the major challenges was to see how the expansion plans for Farmland would match with the corporate strengths of the Samsung group. Her was aware that earlier attempts by previous management to expand Farmland had not met with the approval of the group's Chairman. There were concerns in many quarters that the theme park industry did not fit well with the "high-tech" and

	1991	1992	1993
Revenue			
Net Sales			
Admissions	24,829	30,885	35,004
Merchandise	3,255	3,684	5,378
Restaurants	10,309	12,604	14,835
Total	38,393	47,173	55,217
Expenses			
Park Operations	26,209	33,487	40,409
Sales and Administration	8,524	8,980	10,145
Others	1,215	1,350	1,433
Total	35,948	43,817	51,987
Operating Profit	2,445	3,356	3,230
Less Interest Expense	(1,724)	(1,100)	(3,417)
Profit/(Loss) After Interest	**721**	**2,834**	**(18)**

Table 2   Profit and Loss Statement for Yongin Farmland (millions Korean Won)

the "global" image of the Samsung Group, and also that the profitability might be very low.

The theme park industry was still in its early stages in Korea, and had a history of less than two decades. However, indications were that the industry was growing globally, with more players entering. Nevertheless, some of the managers did not see profitable growth opportunity in the theme park industry. One of the managers in Joong-Ang said:

Theme parks may be a growing industry worldwide. That does not mean that it should be so in Korea. In Korea, we work five and a half days a week and we have annual vacation of only four to five days a year. Where do Korean people have time for theme parks?

FARMLAND CUSTOMERS

Traditionally, Farmland focused on the local customers. Most of its customers came from surrounding areas within two hours' drive (see Table 3). The economic growth in Korea had been a major driving force in industry growth (see Exhibit 2).

Despite the early stage of growth in the Korean leisure industry, there were six theme parks in the Seoul area including Farmland. Most notable among these were Lotte World and Seoul Land. Lotte World, started in 1989, prided itself on having the world's largest indoor theme park with adjoining hotel, department store, shopping mall, folk village and sports centre. Commenting on Lotte's strategy, one of the managers at Lotte World said:

We focus on a segment different from Farmland. Since we are located downtown, we cater to a clientele who want to drop by for a shorter period. Typically, we get office people who want to relax after a hard day's work or couples who would like to spend some time in a romantic environment.

Seoul Land, located near Seoul at Kyungkido, was also a key competitor to Farmland. With attendance at 3.37 million, Seoul Land ranked 23rd in the "Top 50 theme parks worldwide." Mr. Woon, one of the managers at Seoul Land, remarked:

The park has a good reputation for quality special events and the people enjoy coming to the park because of its fresh air, beautiful scenery, and easy access.

Market Type	Per Cent of Total Attendance From the Market Type (%)	Population From the Market Type (in millions)	Estimated Current Capture Rate (%)	Projected Population in 2000 AD (in millions)
Primary resident market	73	19.2	19.30	20.2
Secondary resident market	20	13.8	7.30	14.7
Tertiary resident market	8	12.5	4.10	12.3
Total	**100**	**43.5**	**11.30**	**47.2**

Table 3   Target Segments—Attendance and Population Data

Notes:

1. The primary resident market is within one hour drive from Farmland, typically in a radius of up to 60 miles. The secondary market is within one to two hours, and the tertiary market is outside the two hour drive limit but within driving distance.
2. Percentage of total attendance is based on three repeat surveys of visitors to Farmland in early 1994.
3. The estimated capture rate is based on statistical projections from the survey respondents.
4. The analysis does not include overseas visitors, which constituted 25 per cent of the total attendance in 1993. Visitors were mostly from other Asian countries, such as Japan and Singapore.

Korea, with its population of 44 million people, had seen tremendous economic growth over the 1980s and 1990s, despite the political difficulties. Over 10 million Koreans lived in Seoul, and along with the other five metropolitan cities, the urbanization rate was at 74.4 per cent. Korean economic growth has often been dubbed as an "economic miracle." The per capita GNP had risen from US$4,210 in 1989 to US$7,513 in 1993. The growth rate for the second half of the 1990s was expected to be eight to nine per cent. The growth of the Korean economy was accompanied by an increasing prominence of large business groups, commonly known as "chaebol"—privately held industrial conglomerates involved in a wide range of businesses. Samsung, Hyundai, Sunkyong, Daewoo, Lucky-Goldstar, and Ssangyong were some of the better known chaebols.

Korean weather was a temperate climate since it was in the transitional zone between continental climate and subtropical maritime climate. The winter time stretched from December to mid-March when intense, cold dry spells alternated with spells of milder weather. Temperatures dropped to –20 degrees Celsius in some places. Heavy snow was expected in the mountains. Summer, stretching from June to early September, was hot and humid with temperatures rising to 35 degrees Celsius with heavy showers in June and July. Mid-July to mid-August was the peak of Korean vacation season. Many festivals came together in October. Despite the pressing political problems, the country was successful in attracting international events to the country—the most prominent being the Olympic games in Seoul in 1988. Tourist growth had been steady and approximately one third of the tourists in Seoul used a travel package from some travel agencies.

Exhibit 2   Korea in the 1990s

Despite the competition from other parks, Farmland had the highest growth rate within the Korean industry (Table 4). The seasonal nature of the theme park industry affected all the competitors, not necessarily in the same pattern (Table 5).

PRICING

Farmland was also going through a major change in its pricing structure. The pricing strategy in place (Table 6) was a combination of "pay-as-you-go" and "pay-one-price" system. Users had

	1990	*1991*	*1992*	*1993*
Yongin Farmland	3,786	4,300	4,810	5,113
Lotte World	4,578	4,529	4,605	4,476
Seoul Land	2,198	2,819	2,834	2,648
Dream Land	971	1,319	1,236	1,325
Children's Grand Park	2,107	2,334	2,263	2,159
Seoul Grand Park	1,356	1,431	1,590	1,772

Table 4   Comparative Attendance in Seoul Area Amusement Parks (figures in thousands)

Month	*Farmland*	*Lotte World*	*Seoul Land*
January	641	618	220
February	158	390	93
March	190	290	115
April	844	380	378
May	952	363	460
June	801	241	171
July	220	406	182
August	392	646	413
September	193	226	184
October	351	323	302
November	99	214	54
December	270	381	75
Total	**5,111**	**4,478**	**2,647**

Table 5   Comparable Monthly Attendance: Seoul Area Theme Parks (1993) (figures in thousands)

the option of paying the admission fees and buying separate tickets for rides (pay-as-you-go), that were available as coupons (Big 5 for five rides). Membership in the park was available for a price, which provided free admission for a year. The other option was to buy a "passport" (termed as "pay-one-price") that provided admission as well as unlimited rides for one full day. The passport users were estimated at 17.4 per cent of the attendance in 1993, and the membership holders were estimated at 75 per cent. Farmland wanted to switch gradually to the pay-one-price scheme, which was the most common pricing scheme in the leading markets.

The prices across the major competitors were comparable. In 1993, average admissions and ride fee per person was 6,667 Won in Farmland, 7,279 Won in Lotte World, and 6,494 Won in Seoul Land. Theme parks also monitored the amount a visitor spent on food, beverages, and souvenirs. In 1993, average per-capita expenditure on food and beverage in the three parks was 2,874 Won in Farmland, 2,017 Won in Lotte World and 1,804 Won in Seoul Land and merchandise sales per capita were 996, 1,319, and 722 Won, respectively.

OPERATIONAL ISSUES

While there was some indication that the Samsung Group would be willing to consider a

	Adult	Teen	Child
Admission			
Individual	3,200	2,250	500
Group	2,550	1,150	500
Big 5	12,000	10,000	7,000
Passport	17,000	14,000	10,000
Membership Public			
Individual	39,000	31,000	29,000
Family 3		85,000	
Family 4		95,000	
Group 3		75,000	
Group 4		85,000	
Ski Sled Passport	13,000	13,000	10,000
Snow Sled Common		7,000	
Grass Sled		3,000	
Swimming Pool			
Admission	1,850	1,350	1,000
Rides			
Suspended Coaster	3,200	2,700	2,200
Major Rides (7)	3,000	2,500	2,000
Medium Rides (6)	2,500	2,000	1,700
Secondary Rides (5)	2,000	1,700	1,400
Tertiary Rides (5)		1,400	
Kiddy Rides (3)		800	
Pony Rides		1,700	
Time Machine	2,000	5,000	8,000
Lift	550	450	350

Table 6   Yongin Farmland Pricing Policy (figures in Korean Won)

	1992	1993	1994 (projected)
Domestic Sales	23,680	24,609	27,736
Export Sales	14,531	16,755	23,578
Total Assets	38,016	40,964	50,491
Stockholder's Equity	5,089	5,900	8,440
Return on Equity	6%	7%	16%
Employees (thousands)	189	191	206

Table 7   Samsung Group Financial Highlights (in billions Korean Won)

Exchange Rates: Korean Won/US$: 1992: 773   1993: 808   1994: 806

proposal for expansion of the Farmland, Her had to contend with a number of operational issues at Farmland. Based on discussions with a number of managers and customers, Her had some idea of the various issues involved in the operation of Farmland.

Transportation

One major issue was accessibility to the park. Yongin was 60 kilometres south of Seoul, and during peak hours, it took as long as two hours to drive from Seoul to Farmland due to traffic jams. One resident who lived very close to the Yongin area said:

> Actually, it should take only 15 minutes to drive from my home to Farmland. But the traffic jam is so intense that if I go to Farmland, it may take almost an hour of crawling in the traffic. That's one main reason why I have not visited it so far.

One of the managers in the marketing group commented on the critical nature of this problem:

> In Korea, we work five and a half days a week. Most of the time on the working days the travel time is long. All the house chores have to be done only on the weekends. Given this fact, it is only to be expected that Korean customers would not be so keen to travel on a Sunday or on a holiday if the traffic is heavy.

However, many managers in Joong-Ang believed that the accessibility problem was only a temporary issue. Mr. Yu, Director of Personnel at Joong-Ang, commented:

> Travel difficulties are part of our life in Korea, given the small land and the large number of people. The government has plans to bring the subway up to Yongin, in which case Farmland would have a subway terminal, which will provide a lot of convenience to our people.

This was echoed by one of the visitors to Farmland, who commented:

> I hate sitting inside my house all day. I have to get out somewhere. Seoul is too crowded and I would like to go to some place to breathe some clean air. Beaches are closed most of the season, and if I want to go for some mountains or Pusan, it is too far away. So, I don't mind driving down to Yongin to spend a relaxed day. I will skip the rush hour by leaving early from the park.

Parking

Another related issue was parking. Farmland had ample parking space for about 8,000 cars at one time around the four sides of the park. One of the managers who conducted an extensive analysis of the parking space said:

> What we have now is more or less enough for the time being. We have enough space for about 8,000 cars and at four people per car we can accommodate about 32,000 people. If we assume the lot turning over at 1.7 times a day (at an average stay of six to eight hours), we can handle a peak attendance of 52,000. But the real problem is the seasonality. On peak days, we may get more visitors and quite often people may spend more time. If we are going to expand, this will be a major bottleneck.

Part of the expansion plan included augmenting the parking spaces and also providing a "Park and Ride" scheme for visitors so that they could travel comfortably from the various car parks to the entrance.

Environmental Issues

Expanding Farmland meant taking over more of the land mass available in the Yongin valley. A farmer living in the Yongin valley, who was vehemently opposed to the expansion ideas, said:

> They (Samsung) just want to expand their business. But they don't realize that one of the problems with cutting down the trees and leveling the ground will cause potential flooding in the surrounding region. This will damage all our crops. How will they compensate us?

Organizational Inertia

It was also a challenge to introduce a dynamic environment within the Farmland organization. In order to succeed in the industry, Farmland had to go through a major reorientation in its organizational style. Farmland had initiated customer satisfaction surveys recently and it was brought to the attention of the management that the customer satisfaction levels were lagging behind the key competitor, Lotte World. As one of the marketing managers noted:

> Repeat business is very important to our survival. If we don't satisfy our customers, they won't come back and we won't have any business left. But, it is not in our Korean nature to smile at strangers. We are very serious people. So it becomes all the more difficult to get the type of service you can see at Disneyland.

Mr. Yu, who had pioneered a number of changes within the organization, recalled one event which demonstrated the type of organizational inertia the management had to deal with:

> Previously we had the head office at Seoul and we were managing the Farmland by "remote control." We were faxing information and directives up and down. But I somehow did not see that this would be the best way to work. I insisted that the head office had to be located where our products are and only after much persuasion could we move to this place.

Among other things, management was also considering a change in the recruitment process. Traditionally, Farmland had gone after the "academically best" graduates and students, which was the standard practice at Samsung. The management felt that they needed more service oriented people. The management wanted to recruit more female workers, the level of which at that time was below 25 per cent, but anticipated problems since most Korean women stopped working after marriage. Mr. Yu said:

> I think times are changing. For that matter, even if we have a high turnover, it may be good for us since fresh blood always brings in fresh ideas and we would be able to preserve some dynamism in our organization.

THE MASTER PLAN

Based on a detailed survey (Table 8) and tentative analysis, the management had put together a master plan to invest about $300 million in revamping Farmland. There were also suggestions of changing the name to provide a better image of the company. A master plan, for a phased investment of about $300 million over the next two years, was being developed. Everland, Green Country, and Nature Land were some of the names proposed for the new "mountain resort." Included in the master plan were:

- A waterpark to be built adjacent to the existing theme park, at an estimated cost of US$140 million, with a Caribbean theme.
- A Global Fair, a fun-fair indicative of the major countries in the world, at an estimated cost of $85 million.
- Expansion of existing zoo, and parks including a night time laser show and a fable fantasy garden at an estimated cost of $50 million.

The funding would come mainly from the parent, Samsung Group, and also through corporate sponsorship of the other companies within the Samsung Group. The master plan also indicated that if the first phase was successful, a second phase of developing a resort town in Yongin, with luxury hotels, golf courses, and resort accommodations would occur. (Exact budget for the second phase was not available at that stage.) A number of managers within the company who were closely involved in developing the master plan felt strongly that the theme park expansion was not only a priority but also would be a profitable venture. The General Manager of the planning group commented:

> What we want to create is a destination resort town and a residential community where people can come, relax and enjoy themselves in a low-stress

Question: Which is your most favoured spot for a one day holiday trip?

Selected Choice		Theme	Nature	Resort/Spa	Fishing	Historic Place	Other
Total Response:	10,043	22.2%	22.0%	9.9%	7.0%	22.6%	6.3%
Sex:							
Male	5,354	19.7	22.2	8.4	9.8	22.1	17.8
Female	4,690	25.0	21.8	11.6	3.8	23.3	14.5
Age:							
10–20	1,359	41.5	15.1	2.1	3.7	22.1	15.5
21–30	2,634	23.2	26.5	4.3	6.5	22.7	16.8
31–40	2,799	24.8	22.5	7.9	9.4	20.3	15.1
41–50	1,586	12.0	23.0	13.7	8.1	26.5	16.7
Over 50	1,665	10.3	18.7	24.8	5.2	22.9	18.1
Education:							
Elementary	719	11.5	22.7	25.5	3.6	18.5	18.2
Middle school	678	46.2	11.0	2.6	3.9	20.2	16.1
Junior high	840	12.2	21.9	18.4	7.1	24.5	15.9
Senior high	491	37.4	19.6	1.6	2.1	26.0	13.3
School graduate	4,286	20.8	23.3	9.9	8.5	21.7	15.8
University	3,030	21.8	22.9	6.7	7.1	24.3	17.2
Occupation:							
Professional	264	14.7	19.0	6.9	12.4	28.4	18.6
White collar	1,597	20.4	23.5	6.0	6.9	23.8	19.4
Sales and marketing	1,794	16.5	24.4	10.3	10.0	22.8	16.0
Service industry	772	20.6	21.2	10.6	9.2	21.8	16.6
Farming	281	12.8	31.5	19.3	6.9	15.5	14.0
Manufacturing	577	18.5	25.4	8.4	10.9	21.0	15.8
Housewife	2,582	22.1	21.9	14.8	4.1	22.6	14.5
Student	1,656	38.3	16.3	2.3	4.5	22.2	16.4
Unemployed	520	12.2	21.9	17.4	8.7	23.5	16.3

Question: Normally, when you go to theme parks, how many others accompany you?

Selected choice	0	2–3	4–5	6–10	11–20	over 21
	2%	33%	38%	13%	4%	11%

Question: How many hours do you spend in a theme park?

Selected choice	0–5 hours	6–7	8–9	10–11	12–13	14–15	over 16
	22%	19%	18%	18%	12%	6%	5%

Question: How much do you spend at the park in one day excluding admission (in thousands of won)?

Selected choice	0–5	5–10	10–15	15–20	20–25	25–30	30–35	35–50	over 50
	2%	8%	19%	10%	21%	5%	16%	6%	15%

Question: How do you normally come to the theme park?

Selected choice	Car	Tour bus	Bus	Train/subway	Other
	68%	9%	13%	6%	4%

Table 8   Leisure Patterns of South Korean Customers (1994)

Source: Korea Research Institute.

environment. Samsung employs more than 180,000 people here in Korea. This will give them a place to come and be proud of. There will be plenty here for all members of the family as they grow.

We feel it is time to change from a farm-oriented name to a name which represents our new mission, which is to create a zeal for long-lasting life that is combined with the harmony of nature. If this plan is approved, we will become the prototype destination resort town in the entire world. We have visited them all, and when we're finished, there won't be any better!

Her wanted a comprehensive analysis of the theme park industry to ascertain the profitability of the industry. He wanted to present to the chairman of the Samsung Group a clear rationale why Samsung should invest in this industry.

NOTE

1. Admission fees varied from $5 to $25 depending on the location and reputation of the park.

PHARMAPLUS IN HUNGARY[1]

Prepared by Trevor Hunter under the supervision of Professors David W. Conklin and Jeffrey Gandz

Copyright © 1998, Ivey Management Services   Version: (A) 1998-01-29

Always the optimist, Bernard "Boomer" Borschke was reviewing yet another setback in his plans to build a chain of North American-style drugstores in Hungary. As the recently appointed president of PharmaPlus Co. he had targeted 20 store openings in the first twelve months of operations but had fallen far short of his goal. Indeed, only one store had been opened in a small city 200 km from Budapest, while one roadblock after another seemed to be preventing further progress. As he prepared for a meeting with his senior management team, Borschke felt that it was time to review their experiences to date and decide whether the initial concept, which would revolutionize the pharmacy business in Hungary, was truly viable

HISTORY OF PHARMAPLUS

PharmaPlus was a division of The PharmaLand Share Holding Co. (PharmaLand), a privately owned Hungarian company. Initially, PharmaLand was a small producer of synthetic drugs, natural and healthcare products, cosmetics and food additives. Due to the phenomenal success of its main product, "Swedish Bitter," a herbal health tonic, the company was in the fortunate position of having excess resources at a time when the Hungarian government was privatizing its pharmacy industry.

Naturland acquired Pharmafontana in April 1996, and in August 1997, restructured itself into a new company called PharmaLand Holding Co. under the ownership of three entrepreneurs; Emil Szanto as President, Jozsef Szabo as Chief Executive Officer and Jozsef Medgyesi as Deputy General Manager.

Since the pharmacy industry had recently been privatized and was now fully open to competition, the company decided to complete its vertical integration and purchase a number of pharmacies. The goal was to create a chain which focused on the customer by providing good service, product selection and fair pricing. In short, the goal was to create a North American-style "drugstore" chain which would be named PharmaPlus.

To do this the three owners knew they would need someone with experience in this process to assist them. Through contacts in Canada, they learned that the pharmacy industry in Hungary was not that different from the Canadian situation 25 years ago. They decided it would be useful to look for guidance from someone who had helped develop the Canadian pharmacy industry. Their search led them to Boomer Borschke.

Borschke was a veteran of the pharmacy industry, and as CFO of a major Canadian "drugstore" chain was well positioned to give advice. He was initially made aware of the Hungarian group while on a ski trip in Vail, Colorado in 1997. The group met in Toronto, and it was agreed that Borschke would visit the Hungarian operations in October to give them his opinion about the viability of the concept.

> In October 1996, I came over after our meeting in September. So I took a week, did some consulting, and wrote a report on my findings—about where they were and what they should be doing in the future.

People were hired to run operations based on the report that Borschke provided, but it was clear after just a few months that they were not leading the organization the way the owners had envisioned. They realized that if they wanted to set up a Canadian-style "drugstore," they needed senior management with experience running a Canadian-style "drugstore."

> We had all these meetings, and we discussed the same things again and again. Nothing was happening when I wasn't here even though the two individuals we had hired had been to Canada and understood what we were trying to accomplish.

> Jozsef Szabo asked me if I would consider taking on the presidency. I said, "I'll give you a week a month." They said "We want three weeks a month." We settled on three weeks a month, with a week off, but it's really been more like full-time.

THE HUNGARIAN BUSINESS ENVIRONMENT IN 1997

Hungary, which celebrated its 1001th anniversary in 1997, had a population of 10.2 million, of which 20 per cent lived in the capital city, Budapest. Although Hungary had long rebelled against the Soviets, it was a country caught between Western ideas and reforming Soviet communism, since it was bordered by Austria in the West and Ukraine in the East. The influence these countries had on Hungarian reform created an invisible division of the country into two regions.

The Western part of the country was the recipient of the majority of the recent foreign investment surge, while the East had been virtually ignored as the Soviet's support vanished. The Hungarian government encouraged the development of industries in the West, since there was interest there, but provided no incentives for investment in the East. Companies like General Motors, Suzuki Motor Corp., Ford, IBM, Matsushita, Nokia, Audi, and Philips-Grundig had collectively invested over $3.4 billion in Western areas since 1990. The Eastern regions had received a fraction of this amount. Alone, Gyor and Szekesfehervar, both in the West, had new investments totalling $1.5 billion and $1.3 billion in 1995.

Toward the end of 1997, the government decided to make the East a priority and attempted to attract investment, with limited success in Miskolc and Nyiregyhaza. These efforts could be best described as suggestions rather than concrete incentives. No tax breaks, grants or monetary offerings were proposed.

Areas around Lake Balaton in the West were popular vacation areas for tourists from Germany and Austria due to the natural beauty and the favorable Hungarian exchange rate.

There was also a great deal of cross-border consumerism from the West into Hungary. The East did not have affluent neighbors to come and spend time and money. The Ukraine was a politically unstable and poor area of the former Soviet Union.

In the middle of the country sat the heart of Hungarian business, Budapest, a thriving city with a long history and good infrastructure. The Budapest Stock Exchange's BUX index was formed in 1991. In a country that was in the final phase of privatization, that by all accounts was one of the most successful in Eastern Europe, having a concentrated source for investment capital (both domestic and foreign) was crucial. After an initial difficult period, the BUX reached a market capitalization of $8 billion in 1997. The strongest year for growth was 1996, when the BUX increased 133 per cent. However, 1997 promised to top that mark since the index officially doubled in August. Despite the high returns, international analysts were somewhat concerned about future growth due to the fact that the number of traded companies had fallen below 50 by mid-1997. Still, the prosperity of the city and the relative homogeneity of the market made Budapest a most lucrative opportunity.

The Hungarian government had privatized most of its industries, and had done so by a unique method. The State Privatization and Holding Company (APV Rt) acted as an agent between the owner (the State) and the purchaser. At times the APV Rt purchased the company outright or in a joint venture with the eventual full owner, maintaining ownership for some time, and receiving a high return on investment. Sometimes it just facilitated the sale. In any case, the State had strong powers to determine how the companies were operated after they were sold, by virtue of its control over the APV Rt.

The APV Rt was a type of venture capitalist for the government which was highly successful. The privatization of state assets had raised approximately $17 billion USD since it began in 1990,[2] giving Hungary the highest per capita rate of foreign direct investment in Eastern Europe at $1475 per year, and reducing the country's

consolidated state debt from 86 per cent of GDP to 66 per cent.[3]

The rationale for privatization was twofold. First, Hungary was trying for fast-track admittance to the European Union (EU). Secondly, as a lightly populated, land-locked, former Soviet Bloc country that was rich in natural resources, it had little choice but to reform its economy. Hungary had few other sources of hard currency to support its economy with the support of the Soviets now gone. Hungary had progressed so far socially and economically, that by 1997 it was invited to become a member of NATO in 1999.

Although industries were being reformed, the amount of government intervention was still high and the level of competition was intense and strong. Easy foreign access to the Hungarian market was a certainty with Hungary's impending acceptance to the EU. Closer associations with the West through contact via the EU and NATO would lead to higher expectations among Hungarian consumers.

THE HUNGARIAN PHARMACY INDUSTRY

Hungary's pharmacies were similar in fashion to those found in North America in the 1960s. The industry was highly regulated and traditional, with most of the regulations dating back to the days of the communist system. The traditions, however, were based on over 500 years of Hungarian pharmacy culture.

There were clear distinctions between what was considered a "pharmacy" and a "druggery."

Pharmacy

A pharmacy dispensed solely drugs and other over-the-counter (OTC) products related to health needs. The number of stock keeping units (SKUs) a pharmacy could carry was strictly limited, as was the size, location and method of advertising they could use. Pharmacies had a common look and layout to them. They were very formal, and all the products were behind glass where the customers could not handle them. Approximately three per cent of the products sold in a Hungarian pharmacy were mixed on site compared with less than one per cent in Canada. Based on this fact, there were strict regulations concerning the design, layout and characteristics of the laboratory, and the storage and control of raw materials. Pharmacies were strictly regulated as to where they could be located. (See Exhibit 1.) In a city with a population of more than 100, 000, there needed to be a minimum distance of 250 metres between stores; in larger cities there needed to be a 300-metre distance. Pharmacies could only serve areas which had a minimum of 5,000 people close by; hence they had to be in densely populated areas.

The Hungarian social security system covered many prescription drugs, referred to as "listed" products. Many of these drugs were on a "negative" margin meaning the more expensive the drug, the lower the margin for the pharmacist. The Health Ministry had recently "de-listed" several drugs from the "prescription only" list, but because they were no longer covered by the social security, sales dropped radically, seriously affecting the already slim profits of pharmacies.

Products which were sold in a pharmacy were generally purchased from a wholesaler who, in turn, dealt with the producer. By law, wholesalers could only add a 10 per cent mark-up to the retailer; however, they often offered certain forms of unregulated rebates. Retailers usually took a gross margin of 12–30 per cent, with the lower amount mainly on medicines, and the higher margin on health care products which were limited in number. There was also a value added tax (VAT) on other health care, non-medicinal products, which ranged from 12 to 25 per cent, that was passed directly to the end consumer. The consumer ended up paying nearly twice the price of the wholesaler. The result was that pharmacy products were very expensive for the average Hungarian whose monthly gross pay was FT 38,000 ($211 USD).

Druggery

A "druggery" was more like the notion of a North American "drugstore," except no pharmaceutical products were sold. The selection of products was wide. There were large chains such as the Hungarian AZUR, and the German Rossmans that had most of the best locations. Druggeries could sell the same higher margin products and services found in North America such as film processing, hosiery, cards, toys etc., which were often "impulse" buys. Druggeries were bright and had popular music playing in the background, although the staff wore white coats to look more official.

The owners of the druggeries could buy in bulk directly from the producer, thus making larger margins ranging between 25 to 35 per cent. They could advertise and have sales and had no location restrictions. In fact, it was very common to walk down a street and see several stores from the same chain only one or two blocks apart.

There were over 2,000 pharmacies in Hungary, and roughly twice as many druggeries, ranging from large chains to small corner stores. Of these pharmacies, only 200 were located in Budapest. Since many Hungarians lived in rural settings, they were dependent on the smaller druggeries and pharmacies which were not owned by large chains. Industry insiders predicted there would be a rationalization of these businesses as competition intensified.

REGULATION

The pharmacy industry was regulated by three levels of bureaucracy, the top level being the Ministry of Health headed by the Minister of Health who was an elected government representative and appointed to the position by the Prime Minister. The Health Minister was responsible for all matters concerning the health of Hungarian citizens.

Specific to the pharmacy industry, there was a board under the portfolio of the Ministry of

1. *Act LIV of 1994* provides for certain rules related to the establishment and operation of pharmacies. The Act stipulates that a pharmacy is a **health care institution** which carries out health care service activities aimed at the supply of medicines.

Pharmacies may operate as public pharmacies, subsidiary pharmacies, institutional dispensaries, or medicine cases.

Public pharmacies provide for the direct and complete supply of medicine to the ill.

A **subsidiary pharmacy** operates as a part of the public pharmacy, however, its premises are not the same, and its principal responsibility is to supply medicine directly to the ill.

An **institutional dispensary** is an institution, established as part of a bed-patient medical institution, which provides a complete supply of medicine required for the operation of the latter.

A **medicine case** provides a specific range of medicines required for the remedial work of general practitioners.

According to the Act, public pharmacies may be established in settlements where the population numbers at least 5,000 or, in cities of a population exceeding 100,000, there is a distance of at least *250 metres*—in other settlements at least 300 metres—between the existing public pharmacy and the one to be established.

The address and operating area of new public pharmacies must be specified in the license issued for its establishment. The Minister of Public Welfare makes the decision on establishing public pharmacies after being informed of the Chamber. The Act regulates in detail the contents of the application for establishing public pharmacies and its appendices by pharmacy type.

The establishment of public pharmacies may be requested by pharmacists, subject to individual rights and entitled to manage pharmacies, or the representative body of the given settlement's local government.

It is only possible to operate public pharmacies subject to personal rights. Personal rights mean a personal right to operate a pharmacy, which is only permitted for pharmacists with suitable professional training. The legal rule prescribes at least five years of on-the-job training at a pharmacy. It is furthermore a requirement that the individual in question be authorized to manage the pharmacy (holder of a Hungarian or adopted pharmacist's degree trained, a member of a Chamber on the National pharmacists' registry, etc.) and agree to ANTSZ (the State Public Health and Medical Officer Service) assigning an official manager in cases specified by the legal rule.

Personal rights, as a main rule, may only be authorized on the basis of a national-scale tender and after the opinion of the Chamber is obtained. Within the pharmacy privatization process, the favored bidder in the process may receive personal rights without an invitation of the tender.

Except where provided otherwise by the Act, public pharmacies must be managed by the party entitled to personal rights.

A manager in charge must be appointed if the party entitled to personal rights is unable to discharge his personal management obligation. If the manager in charge must prospectively be employed for a duration not exceeding sixty days, this must simply be reported to ANTSZ, however, if a longer period is necessary, an ANTSZ license is required. If the party entitled to personal rights reaches pensionable age, it may enter a lease contract with the authorized pharmacist concerning the management on the public pharmacy, of course with the approval of ANTSZ and considering the Chamber's opinion.

Supervision of the pharmacies is a government task. Professional supervision is carried out by the Minister via ANTSZ. ANTSZ notifies the Chamber of any measures taken in the course of professional supervision. The Chamber is entitled to hold a professional inspection at the pharmacy if it is necessitated by any procedure carried out by a body of the Chamber.

ANTSZ may appoint an official manager in cases specified by the legal rule. The appointed official manager is obliged to report monthly to the party entitled to personal rights, or in his absence, to ANTSZ.

Exhibit 1   The Legal Aspects of the Operation of Pharmacies   *(Continued)*

2. Pharmacies may be operated in an individual enterprise or a limited partnership company.

A limited partnership company is an unincorporated association established by contract. Those members carry out common economic activities. Company registration is a requirement of operation. At least two members are required for founding, one of whom is the acting member whose liability is unlimited. The acting members of a limited partnership company established for operating a pharmacy may only be pharmacists, with one of them being the pharmacist who has obtained personal rights. Individuals subject to personal rights may not be unlimited members of another limited partnership company established to operate a public pharmacy. The share ownership of the acting members within a limited partnership company must exceed 25 per cent.

The liability of non-acting members is limited to the proportion of their invested assets. Non-acting members are not entitled to manage the business.

Limited partnership companies may be established by a deed of association. The deed of association must be signed by all members. The following must be specified in the deed of association:

- the firm name and premises of the company,
- the names and addresses of the members,
- the activities of the company, and
- the amount of the company assets and the manner and time it is made available.

The deed of association must be countersigned by an attorney.

Non-acting members of limited partnership companies may only take part in the activities of the company if so authorized by the deed of association.

Non-acting members are not entitled to represent the company.

A limited partnership company is terminated if all acting members leave the company.

Exhibit 1   The Legal Aspects of the Operation of Pharmacies

Health called the Chamber of Pharmacists. This Chamber was *the* seat of influence in this industry because it was made up of actual pharmacists. The Chamber was given its authority by the Ministry. Members of the Chamber were appointed by the Association of Pharmacists which was comprised of elected pharmacists from around the country, on a basis of one member for every 20 pharmacists. Management at PharmaPlus was not sure exactly how a pharmacist became an appointee, because its power and the process of creating the Chamber came from two separate groups.

The Chamber held the real power within this industry because it could grant and revoke a pharmacist's license without which she or he could not practise. A pharmacist needed two things to operate a pharmacy, a license and a "right." A "right" was assigned to a certain geographic area, in which there could be a pharmacy. Aside from being a qualified pharmacist (i.e., having a license), a pharmacist needed the "right" to practise in any area. Like the licenses, these "rights" were granted and revoked by the Chamber.

Each of the nineteen counties or provinces of Hungary, and Budapest itself, had a Head Pharmacist who was appointed by the Chamber. The Head Pharmacist's role was that of a watchdog and regulator of the pharmacies in her/his area. She/he inspected the pharmacies to ensure they were following the laws, and reported any infractions to the Chamber. The Head Pharmacist also acted upon complaints of infractions against pharmacy laws.

Finally, there were the individual pharmacists. These people were responsible for the operation of their pharmacy, but had an even more important responsibility to their patients. Since this industry was health care-based, the relationship between the business and customer was more personal; hence the expectations of ethical operations were higher. Pharmacists were expected to adhere to a "Code of Ethics," which was external to the regulations of the Ministry of Health and Chamber of Pharmacists, yet run and enforced by the Chamber. This code extended beyond the dispensing of drugs into advertising, store appearance and the general operations of the business. Violations of the Code of Ethics could lead to a loss of the pharmacist's license.

By 1997, all the pharmacists "owned" their pharmacies thanks to the privatization effort of the Hungarian government. In actuality, however, the pharmacists usually had to find alternative sources of financing. Often the large wholesaling companies would provide loans to a pharmacist for her/him to "buy" the store and then would retain the pharmacist under salary allowing the pharmacist to "own" the minimum 25 per cent required by law. In most cases the financing arrangements required the pharmacists to assign their "right" to the wholesaler, giving the wholesalers the ability to install any pharmacist they chose within their assigned area. The arrangement was beneficial to the pharmacists because by becoming part of a chain, their costs were somewhat lowered, and the salaries they were paid were generous by Hungarian standards. But being part of a chain meant that they were subject to the wishes of the wholesaler who now controlled their "right." Thus by controlling the pharmacists' "right," the wholesalers had a strong influence over the pharmacists and to some extent could influence the Chamber.

There was a group of pharmacists, most of whom were in Budapest, who were fortunate enough to be in good locations and had been in business prior to the privatization of the market, and who were able to buy their stores and others outright. These pharmacists were very influential in the Chamber and very resistant to change since they had historically been successful. They were part of Hungary's newly rich. This group continued to do well after the privatization as a result of various factors: connections, location, customer loyalty etc.

Exhibit 1 shows some of the regulations pharmacies faced.

PHARMAPLUS

By November 1997, PharmaPlus was a group of 25 operating pharmacies (which were owned by PharmaPlus) and one "drugstore." "Drugstore" was the term PharmaPlus used to distinguish its proposed stores from the existing pharmacies or druggeries. To PharmaPlus, a "drugstore" was the combination of the two stores, which combined the best of each into a customer-focused retail chain similar to those found in Canada. The company had licenses for nine more pharmacists as well. The current location of the head office was in downtown Budapest in an office building owned by PharmaLand. (See Exhibit 2 for the PharmaLand information package.) There were plans to move the offices to the brand new office building on the grounds of the Pharmafontana production facilities on the edge of the city.

In an empty corner of one of Pharmafontana's warehouses, PharmaPlus built a complete, fully stocked prototype of the dream "drugstore" it called its "phantom" store. The purpose was to give visitors a realistic view of what the company eventually hoped to accomplish. The company took government officials, suppliers, pharmacists whose stores the company wished to buy, and even some competitors on the tour, usually to rave reviews. This phantom store was stocked with all the products and services PharmaPlus wished it could sell in the market, and was an important tool in the process of influencing those in power.

The one "drugstore" was located in a small town called Miskolc (pronounced Mish-coltz) 200 km north-east of Budapest. Miskolc had a population around 200,000 and was very economically depressed. Unemployment levels reached about 25 per cent, and the average monthly income was well below the national average. The store carried approximately 80 per cent of the

(Text continues on page 33)

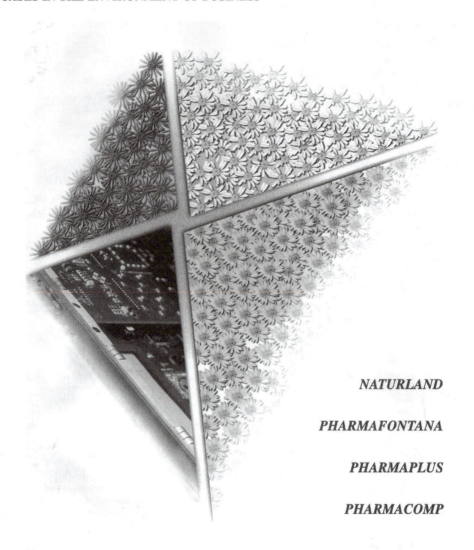

NATURLAND

PHARMAFONTANA

PHARMAPLUS

PHARMACOMP

PHARMALAND

Exhibit 2   *(Continued)*

PharmaLand Holding Co.

PHARMALAND

MISSION STATEMENT

IT IS OUR GOAL AT PHARMA-LAND TO ENSURE THAT ALL OF OUR VALUED BUSINESS PART-NERS ARE COMPLETELY SATIS-FIED WITH OUR DIVERSE RANGE OF SERVICES, THUS ENABALING THEM TO ACHIEVE SUCCESS IN ALL OF THEIR BUSINESS ENDEAVORS.

IT IS OUR AIM THAT THE USE OF OUR PRODUCTS WILL HELP OUR CUSTOMERS TO ENJOY HEALTHY AND HAPPY LIVES.

Emil Szántó *completed his secondary school studies in 1982 and then attended the University of Agriculture in Mosonmagyaróvár where he achieved an agricultural degree in 1988. After completing his undergraduate degree he obtained a foreign trade education at the Faculty of Foreign Trade of István Széchenyi School of Polytechnics in Győr. He is a co-founder of M-Land Ltd., the predecessor of Naturland Co.. Emil has been the President of Naturland Co. since its inception in 1993. At present, he is the also the President of PharmaLand Holding Co.*

After completing his secondary school studies in Győr in 1977, **József Szabó** *then obtained his degree in agricultural engineering in 1983 at the University of Agriculture in Mosonmagyaróvár. Following his studies at the university, he became a member of the College for Post Graduate Studies set up by the Committee for Qualification of the Hungarian Academy of Sciences. He also lectured at the Chair of Plant Cultivation of the University of Agriculture between 1986 and 1988. During this period he was published both locally and internationally. He is a co-founder of M-Land Ltd. the predecessor of Naturland Co. and its Managing Director. Currently, József is the Chief Executive Officer of PharmaLand Holding Co.*

In 1979, **József Medgyesi** *graduated from the Horticultural College in Kecskemét a division of the University of Gardinery and Food Industry in Budapest following completion of his secondary school studies. In 1980, he began cultivating medicinal herbs in the Mátraalja countryside where he set up an oil distillery and introduced the cultivation of plants containing volatile oils. He also took part in the cultivation, processing and commercialization of spices and naturally available medicinal herbs. From 1987, he was head of a branch of the MatraMed Economical Association for the Production of Paramedicines, eventually becoming the Director of the Association. After the acquisition of MatraMed Paramedicine Producing Ltd. by Naturland Co. in 1991, József became an executive of Naturland Co. and is presently the Deputy General Manager of PharmaLand Holding Co.*

Exhibit 2   *(Continued)*

PharmaLand Holding Co.

The story of the Pharmaland Holding Co.

Social precedents

The economic and political system of Hungary has fundamentally changed over the past few years. The return of free elections in 1990 presented opportunities for a multi-party society and also for development of a market economy based on private companies.

The Naturland Share Holding Co.

In the first years of this change, hundreds of thousands of private enterprises were founded in Hungary. Some of these companies such Naturland Co. have shown outstanding progress. Naturland Co. was founded by its current owners in 1993, through restructuring their earlier companies.

The main profile of Naturland Co. was developing, manufacturing and distributing products of "natural origin". Within a relatively short period of time, the company reached outstanding professional and economic goals, resulting in rapid growth.

The Pharmafontana Share Holding Co.

By winning the privatization tender of Pharmafontana Co., the profile of Naturland Co. was dramatically changed. Pharmafontana Co. was the second largest state-owned wholesaler company for drugs in Hungary. Due to this new profile the structure of the company had to undergo a total reorganization.

The PharmaLand Share Holding Co.

PharmaLand Share Holding Co. was created to manage the diverse lines of business now controlled by this group. It has a capitalization of HUF 5.2 billion, employing over 750 people. During 1996, the firms encompassed by Pharma-Land Holding Co. reached yearly sales of more than HUF 25 billion. The structure of the Holding Co. was formed by organizing each activity field into separate companies, thus ensuring a logical and clearly arranged organization for its work of word class standards.

PHARMALAND

The PharmaLand Share Holding Co.

Naturland Co.	Pharmafontana Co.	PharmaPlus Co.	PharmaComp. Co.
research & development consumer product manufacturing	drug and paramedicinal product wholesaler	retail pharmacy chain·	computer support services for pharmacy related activities

---

Exhibit 2

(Continued)

Naturland Co. (Manufacture)

Naturland Co. was established in 1993 through restructuring of the owner's earlier companies. The main profile of Naturland Co. was the developing, manufacturing and marketing of "natural products". Of these products, the biggest success was "Swedish Bitter", which became one of the company's largest exported products.

The development and the financial and professional achievements of Naturland Co. called for international expansion, during which it participated in 6 international joint ventures.

1996 was a turning point in the life of the company. During the privatization process it acquired the Pharmafontana pharmaceutical manufacturing and wholesale company. The size of the company formed as a result prompted the creation of a new structure. Within the resulting PharmaLand Holdings, all production capacities, as well as the Research and Development are concentrated in Naturland Co.

The main activities of Naturland Co.

Manufacture of:

· synthetic drugs

· natural and healthcare products

· cosmetics and food additives

Research & Development of:

· cosmeceuticals

· plant extracts

· analytical research

· medicine production technology

The manufacturing process

The production takes place in a modern plant in an area of 2,500 square meters in the following Gaelic forms:

· aqueous and alcoholic solutions

· extracts of medicinal herbs

· ointments, gels, emulsions

· powders, granulates, tablets

· tea blends of medicinal herbs

Manufacturing agreements have been formed with numerous multi-national companies such as Procter & Gamble, Glaxo Wellcome, Ciba Geigy and Bayer AG.

Exhibit 2

(Continued)

Naturland Co. (Manufacture)

NATURLAND®

Quality assurance

The quality and content uniformity are guided by the principles and regulations of the GMP and GLP. The in-process control, as well as the professional skill of the employees in all fields of the manufacturing process fulfill the expected standards of quality. The manufacturing process is controlled and documented by a state of the art computer system.

The Research and Development at Naturland Co.

At Naturland Co., a great emphasis is placed on Research and Development. During this activity, the results of the traditional healing are matched with the new scientific trends and methods.

The level of the R&D and the therapeutic safety of the products are provided by cooperation with "Semmelweis" Medical University, "Loránd Eötvös" University of Sciences and Naturland Co.

In meeting with the expectations of contemporary life styles, the strategic aims of Naturland Co. are focused on helping the prevention of disease, and the formation of a healthy way of life. Naturland Co. provides products in accordance with modern medicine and the expectations of society.

PRODUCTION	SALES
1995	550 M HUF
1996	660 M HUF
1997	expected 920 M HUF

Exhibit 2

(Continued)

PharmaPlus Co.

PharmaPlus stores represent a totally new concept in marketing for Hungarian Pharmacies. These stores are the first in Hungary to combine professional pharmacy services and a full selection drug store all under one roof.

The PharmaPlus chain of stores is very proudly 100% Hungarian owned and operated. We are also extremely proud to be the marketing leaders in this exciting new era of drug store retailing.

value and service

PharmaPlus endeavours to embody the North American concepts of good value, combined with fast, friendly customer service.

Fulfilling the customers' medication needs is always our top priority at PharmaPlus. We constantly strive to maintain the highest levels of professionalism in pharmacy while at the same time offering the customer a full selection of name brand health and beauty aid products at very competitive prices.

This innovative approach to pharmacy and drug store retailing will help us to realize the long term growth goals of PharmaPlus which is to have a retail presence in every major centre in Hungary.

Exhibit 2   *(Continued)*

Exhibit 2

services and products the "phantom" store held, and was in fact pushing the envelope of legality with some products.

Borschke explained the rationale for opening their first store in this harsh environment:

> Miskolc just appealed to me in that it was a great centre of a lot of high-rise apartments on the main road in the city. There was a lot of pedestrian traffic by the store with a grocery store and doctors' offices right next door. It was poorer there, and we knew that going in, but if it worked there, it would surely work in Budapest.

The store was opened in July 1997 to a tremendous turnout due in part to a give-away promotion. PharmaPlus gave out "grab-bags" of health and beauty aids made up of free samples provided by suppliers. The give-aways were a part of the strategy devised for Miskolc. The whole concept of PharmaPlus was to provide fair prices with occasional advertised sales in a store that combined a pharmacy and a druggery, a friendly shopping environment based on service, and promotions. These elements were intended to differentiate PharmaPlus from the druggeries. Over 1000 people lined up outside for hours, and sales were brisk.

> I was driving from Budapest and every 15 minutes I would get a phone call: "It's close to a riot." "There are 300 people here." "Now there are 400." "They have been lined up since 4:00 in the morning." By the time we opened there were 1,000 people there, and they just kept coming out of the woodwork. The doctors next door phoned the police. We had a riot.

In the weeks that followed the opening, PharmaPlus gave out 1000 cloth bags with the PharmaPlus name and logo on the outside. Borschke called these "walking billboards." Products which were seen as necessities, such as toilet paper, diapers etc., were targeted for price promotions and continued to attract crowds of customers. Other products were often bundled together such as cosmetics and a free cosmetic bag, or two of the same product for a lower price. Promotions like this were new to the customers and were meant to attract them from the local druggeries. After its opening sales continued to increase by over 10 per cent monthly, the store appeared to be a success.

The retail outlet was divided into two sales areas: pharmacy and front-shop. The front-shop area consisted of the higher margin, non-pharmaceutical products found in druggeries. It was planned that sales between the two areas would be roughly 50–50 as time went on. In the first months, sales were roughly 80–20 per cent in favor of the pharmacy.

Borschke had nearly complete autonomy to operate the company as he saw fit. (See Exhibit 3 for the organizational structure of PharmaPlus.) His management team was a young, entrepreneurial combination of Canadians and Hungarians. The owners were supportive of Borschke, but they were very busy. Since there was so much opportunity in the country at this time, they were constantly looking for new business investments that might or might not have been synergistic with current operations.

For example, since the production facilities of Pharmafontana were operating at 30 per cent of their capacity, the upper management was looking for ways to increase productivity. Emil Szanto travelled to the US to a private label drug manufacturers' convention to communicate the advantages of contracting with Pharmafontana to North American chains and distributors.

Borschke felt it was important to make the owners aware of what he felt was required monetarily and operationally. If the owner's goal was a chain of PharmaPlus stores, he felt an investment of at least FT 800 million ($4.3 million USD) in renovations, staff training, etc., was needed.

> We have turned down opportunities. We don't want to invest money if we can't do anything with it. The dream is to expand, but the money isn't there.

34

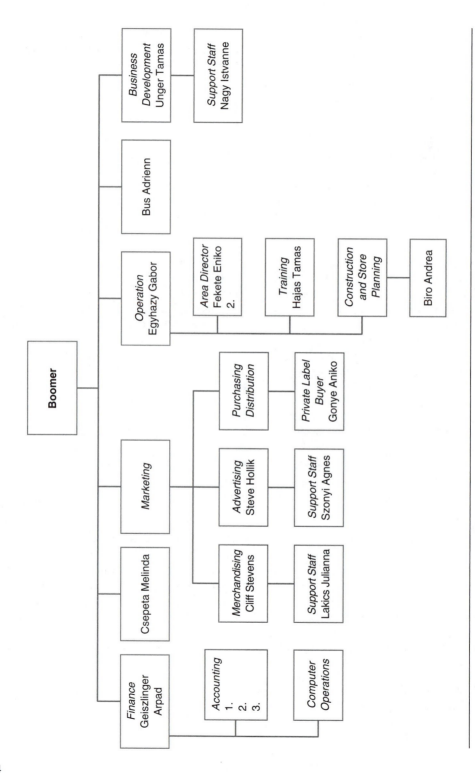

Exhibit 3   Organization Chart "Franchise Group"

In this organization, because it's a very large group, the pay-roll was one pay-roll. There were no cost centres, so finding out whether a location was making any money was impossible. I demanded to have monthly statements. I could demand all I wanted, but it never did anything because those kinds of control systems didn't exist.

Years of operating under communism led to inefficiencies which still permeated the company Boomer Borschke now ran. Internally and externally, there was a lack of control, and little information about the activities of the business.

CHALLENGES

Laws

Borschke did not go into this venture naively; he expected some difficulty with the regulatory nature of a former communist country. However, he encountered strong resistance to change. It was a reflection of a society which had developed under a socialist mentality where there was no incentive to question or change the regulations.

It wasn't a rude awakening. It was a slow awakening. Each day there was a new law which we didn't know before, and each law created more constraints and consumed more time.

It's one of those things where people took a law and started to interpret it in their own way. That was the way the old system worked—there was no push to get anything done. There was no advantage to helping us. They could say, "You can't do that. There is a law against it." Then they wouldn't have to do it. The attitude was to not do anything because it was a lot easier than to try to do something for which there was no reward. I would say "Show me the law," and had many translated into English. Every time it turned out that the law allowed what we wanted to be done. It was the interpretation of the law that allowed them to not do something, which stopped the project.

There were times when the law was clear, but following it to the letter would be a detriment to business.

We were developing our software in-house, but they had a law for using software as well. If you were using software, it had to be approved by the government. So the software was approved, but only for use on Hewlett Packard equipment. This equipment was prohibitively expensive. They wouldn't approve anything else. So we couldn't afford it. It would cost roughly two per cent of sales for the hardware and two per cent of sales for the software. That's sales! I'm sorry, I couldn't afford that. We couldn't throw that kind of money around.

This online accounting system would have allowed the operations manager to monitor inventory levels, sales, margins, etc. from his office in Budapest, rather than travelling to each store. This plan was shelved.

Traditions

While there were no direct competitors in the "drugstore" industry (since this industry did not exist), there were definitely strong substitutes to the new idea of a "drugstore." As noted, pharmacies were firmly entrenched in the social fabric of Hungary, and there was a strong resistance to change within the industry. Druggeries were a lot more abundant, well known and successful. PharmaPlus wanted to take high margin business from the druggeries by attracting the customers to their "one-stop-shopping" retail outlets.

Borschke spoke about the steps they planned to follow to create a change in the industry by trying to work with their competitors and the government.

With the products listed today, it's difficult to have excitement in ads because you are going to have the same products featured all the time. The plan was to work with the Minister of Health and expand the number of products we carried. The next step was to get approval for a druggery and pharmacy together in one form or another. We had to get a license to run both of them together. What we have to do now is convince the pharmacists that are in the Chamber of Pharmacists that they need to change.

Borschke felt that it was a fundamental misunderstanding of what PharmaPlus was trying to accomplish for the whole industry, rather than just for themselves, which led to the resistance by other pharmacists. Pharmacies tended to be less profitable than druggeries due to the limitations on the products that could be offered. Margins on a pharmacy's products were slim, and the number of products they could sell exclusively was decreasing. Also, of the remaining products they could sell exclusively, thousands were being de-listed from the group of drugs covered by the social security. Borschke's experience had shown him that this would mean a rapid drop in sales of these products. The pharmacists tried to lobby the Ministry to "re-list" more drugs to increase their sales. In fact, the majority of these products were "negative margin" drugs with high costs and low margins. Thus, by having more listed products which could only be sold in pharmacies, the pharmacies would have reduced profitability.

PharmaPlus wanted to change the laws to make the market more profitable for everyone and could not make its competitors see this, and in fact, the competitors fought to keep things the way they were.

> Their reasoning was this: if they sold more products in their stores, this would be seen as another way of making money, so the government would not give them more exclusive products to sell. That's short-term thinking if I've ever heard it before.

Jozsef (Szabo, CEO of PharmaLand) was dealing with the Minister talking about the need for change, and the Minister was on our side. He agreed to allow us to sell more products in our "drugstore," giving us a wider selection so that we could earn money another way and still maintain a pharmacy. So he's on our side. But you have these bureaucrats sitting here in between the Minister and us, and they're listening to the short-term

thinking groups and calling for more products to be re-listed.

Some of the pharmacists that are running the stores are coming to us saying "We like your plan," but there is a group in the Chamber that got in real early in the game, and they are driving Mercedes. They don't want change. They don't have to work. They've got the best locations and those things are pumping cash into their pocket. So they won't change. But this is only a short-term situation we and they are in. When the market changes, and it is changing, they won't be able to adjust and will be out of business.

The Miskolc store was proof to PharmaPlus that the concept of combining the druggery and pharmacy could be popular to the market. It also showed its competitors that PharmaPlus could be a threat to their comfortable way of life. Other pharmacists within the city were contacting the Chamber of Pharmacists in Budapest claiming that the PharmaPlus pharmacists were violating numerous codes, including the Code of Ethics.

> We were under total scrutiny. Everybody was watching. Last week the Minister gave us a license for our Dunahas store and the Chamber of Pharmacists and the Pharmacists Association took the Minister to court, not us, the Minister to court, for granting us a license. So it will be three months before we find out whether they have the right to challenge the Minister and a year for the court to make a decision.

> Since we fought them on other legal battles and won, they threw the Code of Ethics at us which is a tough one because if you go to court on the Code of Ethics, they are going to bring in the pharmacists that represent the Code, which are those people in the middle, who are not responsible to anybody. That's why we said earlier that our challenge was to get the pharmacists who were running the stores to realize what is going to happen by re-listing products. We need them to go to the Chamber and say, "You're offside; we're going to replace you." We have 25 operating pharmacies from which we can most likely gather a good 10 strong pharmacists and then go out and get some of their friends.

My position since last October has been that you have to develop a base. You have to have a picture so people can see that a "drugstore" works. That's what Miskolc is. There is a certain group that don't want us to do it. We'll get the Minister of Health into the store and he'll say, "Yeah, there's no reason why you shouldn't be able to do that."

The Non-Service Mindset

The strategy for PharmaPlus' competitive advantage lay in offering products at a fair price with the opportunity for sales in a friendly, helpful atmosphere. Thus, it was crucial to the company's success that its employees embrace a mentality of strong customer focus. This concept was familiar to Borschke as a Canadian, but to a society which was reforming from communist rule, it was truly foreign.

> The service mentality does not exist here. The whole area of service has never been addressed here from my point of view. I think we can distinguish our stores from our competition by having a friendly place, easy, and quick.

Before Borschke was permanently hired as president, PharmaPlus had a Hungarian training its staff in customer service. The trainer was selected because of his experience in the West, but Borschke was not impressed with his efforts, and he was replaced. Borschke realized he first had to "train the trainer."

> That aspect, that training, we had to change the mentality so that they were servicing people and that the reason for our being is the customer. I went to one of our competitors on the opening day of our Miskolc store and they had 80 people in the store. We stood in line. We stood in line. We stood in line. They didn't care about us as customers. We were an interruption.

> Ensuring that our people don't operate like that is going to be one of the biggest challenges that we will deal with. We can meet all the prices on the market, but we want to be a neighbourhood "drugstore" that gives fast convenient service. That requires the right attitude from everyone, from the pharmacist to the cleaners.

THE PRESENT AND FUTURE OF PHARMAPLUS

The law stated that a druggery could advertise as much as it liked, but a pharmacy could only advertise once a year. As a "drugstore," the only retail outlet of PharmaPlus did not fit either classification. PharmaPlus was said to be in violation of the Code of Ethics by trying to advertise; thus it was forced to stop, despite the fact that there was no law directly forbidding advertising. Borschke's goals were clear:

> I want to develop 20 North American-style "drugstores" in key locations and prove that they work. Then the idea would be to franchise.

> Once we get this operational, we'll go to the stock market; get the money to do the franchise; and, that is Joszef's dream, then we'll do Bulgaria, Romania, Slovakia, Slovenia, Croatia—all of the Eastern bloc. That's how we'll do it. I've been there to those countries and everything is the same. There is just a ton of potential.

> But, you know, that is what's frustrating. You know what you are doing is correct. You know that if you do it, it will work.

PharmaPlus could have advertised and lobbied the government further, but they risked losing the license of their only store and best source of revenue. They could also give in and ensure the safety of the license but risk the customer awareness they needed to be successful. Borschke and his management team needed to make some difficult decisions about the future strategy of the company.

NOTES

1. PharmaPlus is of no affiliation to the Canadian Company Pharma Plus Drugmart Ltd.

2. Gabor Jelinek, "After Sell-off: New Bait Needed for Foreign Funds," *Budapest Business Journal* (November 17–23, 1997): 3-A.

3. Gabor Jelinek, "Privatization to Slash Debt Ft 100bln," *Budapest Business Journal* (November 17–23, 1997): 10.

SINGAPORE INTERNATIONAL AIRLINES: PREPARING FOR TURBULENCE AHEAD

Prepared by Professor Kannan Ramaswamy

It was July in 2003. Mr. Chew Choon Seng, the CEO of Singapore International Airlines (SIA), put away the analyst reports that he had been poring over. Mr. Chew had just taken over the job of CEO from Mr. Cheong, who had retired after a long and spectacularly successful tenure at the helm of one the world's most admired airlines. Mr. Chew's initial tenure was, however, fraught with challenges.

Reeling from the fallout of the SARS (Severe Acute Respiratory Syndrome) outbreak in Singapore, Hong Kong, China, and neighboring regions which decimated passenger traffic, SIA had laid off over 400 employees in June to bring down its operating costs. An additional 156 cabin crew staff were laid off in late July. Senior management salary cuts averaging 22% had been announced, and negotiations were on with cabin and ground staff for further wage cuts. SARS, unfortunately, accompanied the outbreak of hostilities in Iraq, which itself dampened traffic through the prime Middle East markets. Faced with rising breakeven load factors,[1] the company appeared to have no choice but to trim its operating costs. However, these moves were viewed with widespread skepticism since SIA had the full backing of its majority shareholder, the Government of Singapore, a stance that the unions deemed unfriendly. Some believed that the company was using SARS and the Iraq war

as convenient excuses to downsize. Analysts feared that these moves could have a negative impact on employee morale and, consequently, on passenger service, the hallmark of SIA's business strategy.

SIA had built its enviable track record around its superior strategy of differentiation. While this approach had worked for a long time, there were some chinks in the armor that were becoming evident. Competitors had been quick to copy many of the remarkable service innovations pioneered by SIA. The avenues for tangible differentiation that SIA had used in the past had become the norm. Every major air carrier now offered a choice of meals in economy class, innovative entertainment options in the cabins, and all the trappings of luxury that used to be the sole domain of SIA. Of particular concern was the increasing competition from international carriers headquartered in neighboring countries, such as Thai Airways, Cathay Pacific, Malaysian, and Qantas. These carriers had learned to duplicate some of the key features of SIA's competitive strategy, from recruitment to in-flight service and fleet management. This placed growing pressure on the firm to refine its differentiation strategy.

Low-cost carriers were beginning to make their presence felt in Asia for the first time. Some local firms such as Air Asia and Virgin Blue were ramping up to offer regional low-cost services along sectors that SIA had dominated for a long time. The Government of Singapore had recently authorized a new low-cost start-up to be based in Changi, the heart of SIA's empire. The government had also suggested that it might sell its 57% stake in SIA. This, some believed, would force SIA to compete on an even keel with other airlines. All along, they had felt that the unfair partnership between the government and SIA gave the company access to deep pockets—a charge that SIA had consistently denied.

The company had begun to spread its wings into major international markets a few years earlier with the acquisition of ownership interests in Air New Zealand and Virgin Atlantic. The Air New Zealand deal turned sour and SIA lost $157 million. Market watchers believed that the 49% ownership stake in Virgin that had cost SIA $1.6 billion in 1999 had already lost over 60% of its value. It was rumored that there were formidable obstacles in architecting a smooth partnership between the disparate, albeit service-oriented, cultures of Virgin and SIA.

Mr. Chew, it appeared, had his work cut out for him. He faced the challenging task of redefining the competitive strategy of SIA in turbulent times.

THE INTERNATIONAL AIRLINE INDUSTRY

The airline industry, traditionally, has been fragmented, primarily due to the limiting effects of national and international regulations. Constrained by landing rights and local ownership requirements, even large airline companies have only been able to develop dominance over their own regional markets at best. With the exception of the United States, dominant national flag carriers, typically owned by the national governments, have remained the only locally owned international carriers in their countries. However, the competitive dynamics in this industry started to change dramatically during the late 1990s. Deregulation, privatization, and the advent of new technologies started to reshape the industry on a global level.

The United States deregulated its airlines in 1978 and has since witnessed heightened competition and aggressive jockeying for market position. Europe entered the throes of a similar escalation of competition following the creation of the European Union and the disbanding of country-specific barriers to free-market competition among air carriers. In Asia, deregulation occurred in fits and starts, with some major regions allowing greater access to foreign carriers. For example, Japan made major strides in deregulation after selling off its shares in the then state-owned Japan Airlines, and permitted All Nippon Airways to serve international markets. In Latin America, many of the smaller national flag carriers were privatized. Countries such as Mexico and Argentina infused significant levels of market competition in their airline industries by removing anticompetitive barriers and privatizing their national airlines.

The trend seemed certain to gain further momentum. The major European nations were already in discussions with the United States to implement an open transatlantic market area where landing rights would be determined by free-market forces rather than regulatory policy. Open-skies agreements are bilateral agreements between countries that agree to provide landing and take-off facilities for air carriers originating in any of the partner countries. Such an agreement does not have the typical restrictions related to landing rights that are determined on a city-pair basis. For example, Singapore and the U.S. had signed an open-skies agreement under which a Singapore carrier could travel to any destination city in the U.S. and vice versa.

The twin trends of privatization and deregulation resulted in an increasingly global approach to strategic positioning in this industry. Although most large carriers still retained their regional dominance, many forged alliances with other leading carriers to offer seamless services across wider geographic areas. These alliances made most of the larger airline companies into de facto global organizations. With increasing geographic reach and decreasing regulatory barriers, many of the regions were witnessing acute competition, often in the form of fare wars. Consumers, in general, became much more price-sensitive than ever before. In attempting to keep up with the competition, many carriers upgraded their service offerings, contributing to declining yields in a price-conscious market. Chronic excess capacity worldwide only exacerbated this situation. Not surprisingly, there was a decline in passenger revenue yield in all geographic regions, and the airlines were fighting an uphill battle to extract higher levels of efficiencies from their operating structures.

The Rise of Alliances

By the late 1990s, alliances between air carriers in different parts of the world had become the norm rather than the exception. By 2004, most of the leading carriers around the world were part of mega-alliances which had evolved to include several carriers under a single alliance brand. The Star Alliance, for example, included ten carriers representing Asia-Pacific, North America, Latin America, and Europe. Oneworld, a similar network of partnerships, encompassed eight carriers spanning a similar geographical territory to Star. Alliances such as these were expected to redirect traffic, increase profitability, help leverage scale economies in operations, and differentiate services in the minds of consumers who wanted to buy travel services through a single carrier.

While they did seem like a wonderful strategic option even to established carriers, alliances brought their own set of thorny issues. There were invariably questions relating to level of service across carriers, safety records of the partners, and willingness to cede control to an alliance. The key issue seemed to be the difficulty in developing a consensus about how the partners would establish common safety, service, and performance standards. Further, in the European markets there was a potential for cross-shareholdings between carriers as privatization accelerated. It was feared that this could create a parallel network that might undercut alliances. Since individual airlines were typically allowed to negotiate side deals with other carriers on their own irrespective of their alliance membership, the likelihood of inter-network rivalry was also high.

SINGAPORE INTERNATIONAL AIRLINES

History and Culture of Singapore

Singapore witnessed bountiful growth and had become the envy of many neighboring countries by the late 1990s. Its per capita GNP increased by a phenomenal 32% in the 1990s, and currently stood at $37,401.[2] Much of the growth in modern Singapore could be traced back to the policies and priorities established by Mr. Lee Kuan Yew, the most powerful Prime Minister in the country's history. He was able to tap the patriotic spirit of his people when he announced his intent to develop Singapore to rival Switzerland in terms of standard of living. His emphasis on superior education standards, a controlled labor environment, and significant outlays for training and development all helped to enhance the quality of human capital. At the end of 2002, Singapore boasted a literacy rate of 93.7%, among the highest in the region. Singapore's Confucian work ethic dovetailed very well with Kuan's ambitions. It emphasized responsibilities over rights and placed enormous value on attributes such as hospitality, caring, and service. As a result of these efforts, Singapore in 2004 ranked among the best countries in terms of human capital and was often rated among the world's friendliest places to do business. Rising standards of living meant higher wages. Coupled with the small size of the local population and a very low unemployment rate, the availability of labor was seen as a potential stumbling block in the drive toward further growth. Many of the larger companies already depended on a sizable number of expatriates from neighboring countries, as well as the West, to staff positions.

A staunch believer in free trade and internally driven growth, Mr. Lee made it clear from the start that the "world does not owe Singapore a living." For example, in the air transportation sector, Mr. Yew's government declared that SIA, although the national carrier, would not receive any subsidies or protection from the government. It would have to sink or swim based on its own

Exhibit 1 — Key Financial and Operating Statistics for Global Air Passenger Carriers

	Cathay Pacific				Malaysia Airlines				QANTAS				Singapore				Thai			
	2000	2001	2002	2003E	2000	2001	2002	2003E	2000	2001	2002	2003E	2000	2001	2002	2003E	2000	2001	2002	2003E
Capacity																				
Fleet Strength (Ns.)	64	75	79	80	93	97	100	100	147	178	193	196	92	93	92	96	79	81	81	81
Available ATK	11630	11827	12820	13576	7531	8055	7824	7978	11117	12187	12317	12506	16917	18034	18305	19774	7752	8490	8752	9022
Passenger ASK	61909	62790	63050	57249	48906	51238	52595	54266	85033	92943	95944	99509	87728	92648	94559	99566	55517	60459	63198	66061
Actual Traffic																				
Overall RTK	8650	8201	9522	8284.14	4853	5379	5150	5497	1718	1859	1598	1530	12038	12985	12735	14060	5469	5818	6027	6244
Passenger RPK	47153	44792	49041	35309.52	34930	38313	34709	37653	64149	70540	75134	77225	65718	71118	69995	74183	41347	45167	46571	50874
Load Factors																				
Overall (OLF)	75%	70%	76%	64%	65%	67%	66%	69%					71%	72%	70%	71%	71%	69%	69%	70%
Passenger (PLF)	76%	71%	78%	64%	71%	75%	66%	69%	75%	76%	78%	78%	75%	77%	74%	75%	75%	75%	74%	75%
Break-Even Load	63%	70%	65%	71%									66%	67%	71%	71%	65%	66%	67%	66%
Yield																				
Overall (¢/RTK)	44.8	42.5	42.2	39.8					10.9	11.3	11.3	11.2	66.0	68.0	64.9	64.5	19.4	21.0	20.4	20.3
Passenger (¢/RPK)	6.1	5.8	5.7	5.4									9.1	9.4	9.0	9.1	2.1	2.2	2.2	2.2
Cargo (¢/RTK)	24.8	22.2	21.6	20.3									33.7	34.2	32.2	34.2	11.6	12.1	11.3	11.7
Operating Costs																				
Staff (¢/ATK)	7.6	7.7	9.5	9.9	4.7	5.2	6.0	6.4	12.9	14.3	10.0	11.2	4.6	5.2	5.5	6.5	6.0	6.0	6.0	6.5
Fuel ($/ATK)	6.5	6.0	5.5	6.0	3.5	5.2	6.0	6.1	4.9	7.5	7.0	6.9	4.6	6.7	5.5	6.6	5.5	5.5	5.5	6.0
Maintenance (¢/ATK)	2.8	3.1	3.2	2.6	11.6	11.6	13.0	13.6	17.9	20.9	22.0	23.1	3.1	2.4	4.1	4.6	2.7	2	2.3	2.3
Tot.Oper.Costs/ATK	28.7	29.2	28.2	26.6									43.7	45.4	44.9	45.5	45.2	32.1	32.6	36.6
Financials																				
Sales (local curr. - m)	34523	30,436	33090	28219	8288.3	9261	8695	8894	9107	10188	10868	11375	8899	9951	9448	10515	123352	129173	129015	127180
Oper. Income	5289	832	4750	-2850.119	-255.7	-1330	-836	339.1	874	696	680	567	1140	1347	482.3	717	14932	12227	18688	15282
Oper. Margin %	15.32%	2.73%	14.35%	-10.10%	-3.09%	-14.36%	-9.61%	3.81%	9.60%	6.83%	6.26%	4.98%	12.81%	13.54%	5.10%	6.82%	12.11%	9.47%	14.49%	12.02%

	British Airways				Lufthansa				KLM				AIR FRANCE				SWISS		
	2000	2001	2002	2003E	2000	2001	2002	2003E	2000	2001	2002	2003E	2000	2001	2002	2003E	2000	2001	2002
Indicator																			
Available ATK (bn)	25.84	25.58	22.85	21.33	23.56	23.94	22.76	22.57	13.12	13.18	12.69	12.95	102.30	110.28	116.46	119.60	0.91	0.85	5.15
Passenger ASK (bn)	168.36	166.68	151.05	139.17	122	128	120	120	76.05	75.22	72.29	74.82					6.5	6.25	31.52
Passenger Load Factor	69.8%	71.2%	70.4%	71.9%	71.3%	71.0%	74.0%	72.0%	77.0%	80.0%	79.0%	79.4%	76.0%	78.0%	76.0%	76.0%	71.8%	52.8%	71.0%
1Yield (¢/RTK)	47.01	49.21	51.28	49.33	1.39	1.31	1.40	1.26	47.1	51.7	51.4	51.5					0.22	0.16	0.22
Operating Costs																			
Staff	2481	2491	2409	2107	3625	4481	4660	4588	3693	1675	1747	1907	20295				1107	313	983
Fuel	804	984	1028	842	2437	1621	1300	1316	1431	1038	983	886	6668				355	174	551
Maintenance	661	640	673	592					1533	757	686	697	2925				541	17	117
Tot. Operating Costs	8856	9227	8450	7393	15404	18505	17500	17800	6201	6683	6626	6618	38642				5905	1684	5304

Exhibit 1 Key Financial and Operating Statistics for Global Air Passenger Carriers (Continued)

41

Exhibit 1 Key Financial and Operating Statistics for Global Air Passenger Carriers

European carriers

	British Airways				Lufthansa				KLM				AIR FRANCE				SWISS		
	2000	2001	2002	2003E	2000	2001	2002	2003E	2000	2001	2002	2003E	2000	2001	2002	2003E	2000	2001	2002
Financials																			
Sales (local curr. - m)	8092	8556	8340	7688	16886	16690	16971	15144	13875	6960	6532	6485	67729	12280	12528	12687	6414	1282	4278
Opr. Income (m)	922	1087	−110	295	1482	−316	1592	−238	209	277	−94	−133	2355	443	235	192	108	−909	−299
Opr. Margin %	11.4%	12.7%	−1.3%	3.8%	8.8%	−1.9%	9.4%	−1.6%	1.5%	4.0%	−1.4%	−2.1%	3.5%	3.6%	1.9%	1.5%	1.7%	−70.9%	−7.0%

USA

	United				American		Delta			Northwest			US Airways		
	2000	2001	2002	2003E	2001	2002	2000	2001	2002	2000	2001	2002	2000	2001	2002
Indicator															
Capacity															
Passenger ASM (bn)	175.49	164.85	148.83	161.03	174.69	172.2	154.97	147.84	141.72	103.36	98.36	93.42	66.57	66.74	56.36
Actual Traffic															
Passenger RPM (bn)	126.93	116.64	109.46	116.59	120.61	121.75	113	101.72	102.03	79.13	73.13	72.03	45.98		40.04
Passenger Load Factor	72.30%	70.80%	73.50%	72.40%	69.40%	70.70%	72.90%	68.80%	72.00%	76.60%	74.30%	77.10%	68.90%		71.0%
Passenger Yield (¢/RPM)	13.25	11.7	10.8	14.06	13.08	11.86	13.86	12.74	12.08	12.04	11.24	10.76	16.13	14.32	13.05
Operating Costs (m)															
Staff	6730	7080	7029	6783	8032	8392	5971	6124	6165	3610	3963	3878	3637	3726	3255
Fuel	2511	2476	1921	2495	2888	2562	1969	1817	1683	1872	1727	1439	1284	1103	782
Maintenance	698	701	560	1095	1165	1108	723	801	711	640	669	576	504	532	405
Tot. Operating Costs	18698	19909	17123	18322	21433	20629	15104	14996	14614	10846	10773	10335	9322	9971	8294
Financials															
Sales (local curr. - m)	19352	16138	14286	19703	18963	17299	16741	13879	13305	11415	9905	9489		8288	6977
Opr. Income (m)	654	−3771	−2837	1381	−2470	−3330	1637	−1602	−1309	569	−868	−846		−1683	−1317
Opr. Margin %	3.4%	−23.4%	−19.9%	7.0%	−13.0%	−19.2%	9.8%	−11.5%	−9.8%	5.0%	−8.8%	−8.9%		−20.3%	−18.9%

Source: Annual Reports, S.G. Securities Research, ABN Amro.

Note: Definition of terms in Appendix.

resources and ingenuity. Singapore literally adopted a free-skies approach whereby foreign flag carriers from other countries were welcome to serve the city-state without any restrictions. This meant heightened competition for SIA right from the start. However, the free-market philosophy also resulted in sharper rates of market growth. For example, roughly 35% of the equity base of Singapore was foreign in origin, and foreign investors owned 17% of all companies in the country, both testaments to the successful programs that attracted foreign capital and commerce to the island nation.

Tourism played a very significant role in the overall development of the country. Handicapped by small size and the lack of natural resources, Singapore had to rely on service industries such as tourism and finance to generate growth. It had always enjoyed an enviable status as an important geographic hub dating back to the pre-British colonization era. During its history as a British colony, Singapore provided an important stop-off point for travelers from Europe and Britain to the outlying colonies of Australia and New Zealand. Building on this historical reputation, Singapore evolved into an important Asian tourist hub.

Singapore International Airlines: The Company

SIA traced its roots to an organization called Malayan Airways that offered its first commercial passenger service in May 1947. The modern incarnation of SIA was born in 1972 when the Malaysia Singapore Airlines was officially split into two new airline companies, SIA and Malaysian Airlines System (later called Malaysia Airways). The long association with the Malaysian counterpart had proved to be quite beneficial to the fledgling company. The crews gained significant flight experience operating over rough geographical terrain in Southeast Asia. Their safety records were impeccable. This association also provided SIA personnel with crucial operating experience ranging from flight operations to matters of administrative importance. As part of

the split, SIA got half the combined assets, most of the overseas offices, its headquarters building in Singapore, and a fairly new computer reservation system. By early 2003, SIA reached over 90 destinations in more than 40 countries in Asia, Europe, North America, the Middle East, the Southwest Pacific, and Africa. Its subsidiary, Silk Air, served feeder routes and reached 24 destinations in the South/Southeast Asian region. It was promoted as the choice for vacation travelers looking to travel short distances between various points of tourist interest in the region, such as Penang, Siam Reap, and Yangon.

SIA had established an enviable record both in terms of its operational performance and its profitability history. It was one of the few Asian airlines that had continuously posted profits even during lean years such as the 1990s economic downturn in Asia. Its short-term performance record had, however, begun to flag as a result of SARS, the war in Iraq, and the general economic malaise that had taken hold of most of its critical markets. It was against this backdrop that the company had to debate alternative courses of action.

On the Ground

SIA's legendary commitment to superior service began on the ground. It built a network of wholly owned subsidiaries and joint ventures to provide operational support in areas such as catering, terminal management, and aircraft maintenance. These subsidiaries were largely managed as autonomous entities that had to bid for orders from the parent and were rated number one in many of their core areas. The Singapore Airlines Terminal Services (SATS) subsidiary was one of the largest in the group. It offered a variety of terminal management services including catering, passenger and baggage handling, and ramp operations. SATS operated one of the largest flight kitchens in the world at Changi International Airport, producing an average of 45,000 meals a day. It had an impressive client list that included British Airways, Quantas, Lufthansa, and Japan Airlines and served more than 70% of all airlines flying into Singapore. SATS had also gone global through joint ventures in Beijing, Hong Kong, Ho Chi Minh City, Macau, Chennai, Male, Manila, Osaka and Taipei.

The Changi International Airport was indeed a crown jewel for SIA. Given its status as a national flag carrier, SIA occupied a pride of place at Changi, an airport that it also managed. The airport itself was rated among the best in the world by several global organizations. It often got top honors for its people-handling efficiency and cleanliness. For example, SIA made a promise to deliver a passenger's baggage within ten minutes after arrival in Changi and consistently delivered on that promise. Such a high standard would have been difficult but for the excellence of its subsidiary network, especially SATS. Changi was also the headquarters of SIA Engineering Company, a subsidiary that provided aircraft maintenance and engine overhaul services. As a testament to its engineering prowess, many global carriers engaged SIA Engineering to service their fleets. SIA Engineering also had a global presence through joint ventures with reputable companies such as Rolls-Royce and Pratt & Whitney.

The obsessive attention to detail began the moment the passenger decided to travel on SIA. The company was at the forefront of introducing electronic ticketing through its Web site. Online ticketing was being rolled out across all destinations in its network. To make it easy on the passengers, the company introduced automated check-in systems on certain flights that tended to attract a large number of travelers. It embraced technology in a variety of forms, allowing check-in via e-mail, telephone, and fax. The Silver Kris Lounge that SIA offered its first-class and raffles-class (business-class) passengers could be best described as "an oasis of peace and quiet"[3] amidst the hustle and bustle of the airport. It featured an environment with plush armchairs, deep-pile carpeting, aquariums, tropical gardens, and a décor that included original paintings by Singapore artists. Top-of-the-line business equipment such as computers, fax services, and a stock ticker were standard amenities. It was one of the largest and most luxurious airport lounges in the world.

Fleet Acquisition and Management

Singapore Airlines came a very long way from its origins as a company that had a fleet of just ten aircraft serving a network of 22 cities. By 2003, it operated a fleet of 97 aircraft, almost all of them capable of long-haul, large-capacity flights. It had 28 more on order and was in line to be among the first companies to buy the 500-plus passenger, double-decker megaliner that Airbus would unveil shortly. It had planned its fleet acquisitions judiciously such that its fleet average was a little over five years old.[4] It was the world's largest operator of the Boeing 747-400 Megatops, a roomy aircraft capable of long-distance flights. Among the largest air carriers in the world, Delta Airlines came closest to SIA in terms of fleet age, with an average of roughly eight years. Most of the other carriers had large segments of their fleets in the 14+ years range.[5] Maintaining youth in its flight operations was no small achievement. It was a facet of competition that SIA took very seriously. It maintained an office in Seattle, Washington just to interface with Boeing designers and oversee the development of new additions to the SIA fleet. Newer aircraft were typically more fuel efficient and less maintenance intensive than older generations. SIA used a mix of leasing and outright purchase, primarily during economic lulls, to feed its appetite for new fleets, thus extracting maximum value for its investment.

SIA emphasized fleet selection because of strong signaling value. Newness implicitly signaled the potential customer that s/he could expect top-of-the-line technology, comfortable seating, and a safe trip, all of which were critical aspects around which differentiation could be built. SIA designed aircraft interiors that encompassed the latest amenities. For example, it was among the first to offer a personal video screen in every seat, even in its economy class. Its in-flight entertainment system, KrisWorld, delivered 22 video channels, 12 audio stereo channels, and ten Nintendo game channels at every seat, with a Dolby surround-sound system that was specially designed for SIA. Its first-class cabins became the gold standard in the industry. They were outfitted with armchair-type seats that converted into comfortable beds at the push of a button. Clad in Connolly leather (the company that supplies leather products to Rolls Royce, Ferrari, and Jaguar) and trimmed in burl wood, the seats included built-in communication devices and an inflatable air mattress. The cabin crew provided a turn-down service where the bed linen was replaced on long trips. The famous French fashion house, Givenchy, designed all the serviceware. SIA tried to convey this air of exclusivity in its other cabins as well. Even in coach class, the seats were wider than average, with spacious leg room, leg rests, video screens, and ergonomic headrests. As part of its drive to be a top-notch air carrier, SIA gathered several firsts along the way. In 1991, it was the first transcontinental carrier to introduce in-flight telephones using advanced communications technology. It was the first with the Dolby surround-sound and personal video screens in coach. It was the first to offer fax services in the air. The list goes on. Plans were under way to upgrade the communications package to allow Internet access while in the air. It premiered an on-demand entertainment system called WISE-MEN in its first-class and raffles-class cabins as early as 1990. This system was designed to function just like a personal home theater, featuring a range of movies and entertainment options that each passenger could individually choose and control.

The Softer Side of SIA

The company firmly believed that its employees were the primary drivers of the success that it enjoyed in the marketplace. Through a deft mixture of organizational culture, indoctrination, and ritual, SIA was able to meld the human assets into a formidable source of competitive advantage. A large number of its employees came from Singapore and Malaysia. As of 2003,

it employed 14,000 people worldwide, and was the largest private sector employer in the country. The company established an extensive SIA Training Center in Singapore that served as the focal point for training programs targeted at cabin crew, commercial staff, flight crew, and flight operations personnel.

SIA executed a finely tuned recruitment and training strategy to keep its ranks stocked with exceptional talent. Most of the employees arrived at the company either through a cadetship (similar to an internship) program that attracted generalists, or a specialist program geared to functional experts in areas such as computer services and finance. The cadetship was an intensive on-the-job training program that cycled employees through a variety of functions as they moved up the hierarchy. SIA's commitment to employee training and development was reflected in the fact that it spent roughly 14 times as much per employee as the average Singaporean company. The company instituted a system of proven controls and mentoring guidelines that helped the employees develop their potential to contribute to the success of the organization. Over time, this built an enormous sense of camaraderie among the team, a very strong sense of identity and belonging, where the employees truly took pride in their organization. Although the employees had been quite accommodating in negotiating wage cuts during periods of economic crises, the cuts in 2002–2003 left a bad taste. The normally friendly unions had publicly expressed concern over the layoffs and salary reductions that followed in the wake of SARS and the Iraq war. Many among the rank and file viewed these actions as self-serving and suspect since the company had achieved close to normal passenger loads after the specter of SARS had faded. This distrust was indeed disturbing and seemed to spread across all ranks of employees from pilots to ground crew. It was the first time in recent memory that the company had to lay off employees in significant numbers.

The pool of talent with respect to pilots was indeed global. SIA had pilots from over fifty countries flying its fleet. Many of these pilots were expatriates drawn by the allure of flying the latest equipment under professional working conditions at very generous levels of compensation. The company operated its own flying college with facilities in Jandakot, Australia, that focused on improving training efficiency and producing qualified pilots. The college served as an incubator for developing Singaporean pilots to meet SIA's growing demands. The company had a state-of-the-art flight training facility in Singapore which housed eight flight simulators where pilots were trained. All flight personnel were required to go through mandatory biennial proficiency checks. It was generally believed that the training programs, in this regard, were quite well administered, as reflected in the very high levels of safety that the company was able to achieve. It was the long-term intent to induct more Singapore nationals into the cockpit, a daunting proposition, especially since the number of local pilots available was quite low. This was augmented by graduates of the Singapore Armed Forces (SAF) which trained pilots for defense purposes. After completion of the mandatory employment with SAF, some of the trained personnel took jobs with SIA. Roughly half of SIA's pilots were expatriates. Normally, the expatriates were more expensive since the company had to bear a variety of expenses such as housing, schooling for children, travel, etc., in addition to base pay.

The complement of cabin crew was chosen through a very rigorous selection process. SIA considered them to be the brand ambassadors who should reflect the high standards of service excellence that its passengers expected. Although they were drawn from many ethnicities within the South/Southeast Asian region (mainly Malaysia, India, Japan, Korea, Taiwan, and Indonesia), they were mostly Singaporean. This recruitment strategy posed a stumbling block since the pool of available talent within Singapore was insufficient to draw from for long. Given the fact that SIA had some of the lowest labor costs among leading carriers, this home-based cost advantage had proven to be a critical ingredient in the success of the company. Any fall-off in the

availability of local talent could adversely impact operating costs, especially if it necessitated the increased recruitment of expatriate personnel. Such a move would also raise questions about how globalizing its workforce would fit in with its historic branding approach, "The Singapore Girl." When SIA was formed, it had to compete against other airlines that had much more sophisticated fleets and passenger options. In combating this handicap and to distinguish itself in the marketplace, SIA launched the Singapore Girl as the embodiment of caring, comfortable, hospitable service. It also played well to the Oriental mystique that was then prevalent in the Western world where the company sought to establish a footing.

The image of the Singapore Girl was carefully nurtured. It began with a rigorous selection process and extensive training soon thereafter. The training program emphasized aspects such as passenger handling, social etiquette, and grooming. While no different on the surface from other competitors, the SIA program was far more intense and demanding. For starters, it lasted much longer than competitors' training programs and embraced some nontraditional aspects. For example, many of its cabin crew spent extensive periods of their training program in homes for the aged to gain a better appreciation of the special needs of this fast-growing passenger segment. The company's approach to molding attitudes and service-oriented behaviors transcended mere internalization of a set of physical practices and dos and don'ts by the cabin crew. The arduous training process was to be repeated periodically through preplanned refresher courses so that the crew could get acquainted with new cabin management technologies and service standards. Once in the fold of the organization, there was a marked effort on the part of management and staff to help each employee perform at his/her best potential. Various practices, such as detailed performance reviews and feedback at all levels, career counseling, and performance-based reward systems, were designed toward this end.

SIA was able to take advantage of local labor laws and practices in staffing cabin positions.

About 60% of the cabin staff was female, and it was expected that most of them would only fly for five to ten years. While male cabin crew members were employed as regular employees, female crew had to work through a system of five-year renewable contracts. Only five such contract renewals were permitted.[6]

SIA's in-cabin service became legendary; the standard that other airlines aspired to reach. In a recent survey by *Condé Nast Traveler*, a well-respected travel magazine, SIA was ranked overall as the "Best International Airline." This was the tenth time that SIA was chosen for the prestigious honor in the eleven years that the award had been given. The respondents rated SIA's cabin service as the best in the world, a testament to the company's emphasis on excellence in this arena. Such awards were nothing new for SIA, which had garnered over a hundred from august organizations such as Zagat, Condé Nast, OAG Worldwide, ASEAN (Association of South East Asian Nations) Tourism Association, and magazines such as *Asia Money* and *Business Traveller*.

COMPETING IN THE NEW MILLENNIUM

By the late 1990s, competition in the airline business had become decidedly global, although very few carriers could legitimately claim to be global carriers. Carriers in the Asia-Pacific region had taken a page from the SIA playbook in offering premium services at consistently low fares. Those in Europe and North America had strengthened their positions through alliances. SIA had already taken some important steps to fortify its position globally. It had joined the Star Alliance, a powerful network of carriers that included Lufthansa, United, Ansett, Air New Zealand, All Nippon Airways, South Africa Airways, Air Canada, Thai, Varig, and SAS. It was believed that this would allow the members to offer code-sharing services, fine-tune traffic flows to increase revenues and efficiency, and combine their buying power to negotiate favorable terms for securing

inputs such as food and allied services. Translated from an SIA perspective, this opened several destinations that SIA did not yet serve. It could take advantage of code sharing to carry a greater number of passengers to destinations within Europe and the United States. For example, it served only four major cities in the U.S., Los Angeles, San Francisco, Las Vegas, and New York. Hence, the relationship with United could extend that limited set of destinations to encompass a considerably larger number of primary and secondary cities. A similar argument could be made with respect to leveraging the new relationship with Varig to fly to more destinations in South America, a region that was not well represented in SIA's route structure. However, despite the obvious advantages, the alliance network did bring with it some concerns.

It remained to be seen whether the other network carriers would be able to rise to the levels of SIA's hallmark service standards. Should there be shortfalls, it was quite likely that the brand image that SIA had so carefully nourished could be tarnished, especially among its loyal first-class and business-class passengers. Joining a network amounted to delegating some aspects of brand management to the collective group of companies such that the identity of the network would transcend the individual identities of the members. The loss of control over some key decisions, such as scheduling and flight frequency, could also pose challenges in the future. It also raised critical questions about the imitability of core competences. Would the partner firms be able to learn more about the critical aspects of SIA's recipe for sustainable competitive advantage?

Equity Partnerships

In balancing growth potential against the ability to control the alliance, SIA acquired an 8.3% equity stake in Air New Zealand to cement a long partnership with the New Zealand carrier. Since Air New Zealand already owned 50% of Ansett Airways, SIA would have the benefit of the additional alliance with Ansett as well. It was expected that these moves would strengthen SIA's position in the Australasian market that was growing significantly. However, this grand design crumbled when Air New Zealand's fortunes started turning sour. The government of New Zealand injected capital to shore up the company, but this had the negative effect of diluting SIA's ownership position. In very short order, SIA was left with a sizable loss and had to beat a hasty retreat from this initial foray to establish control of the key Australia-Asia routes.

In late 1999, the company had made a bold move to acquire 49% of the equity of U.K.-based Virgin Atlantic Airways for $1.6 billion. This was considered a fairly steep price to pay for a deal that offered little operating control in the near term for SIA. However, the company felt that the partnership would cement SIA's ability to leverage Virgin's transatlantic routes, among the most lucrative worldwide. Virgin was also well-known for its exacting service standards, and consistently turned up in the number two spot behind SIA in most surveys of customer satisfaction. The partnership, however, did come with its own baggage. Virgin had clearly stated that it would not consider joining the Star Alliance, thus placing SIA in a delicate position. This meant that SIA would invoke the ire of other alliance partners should it favor Virgin over United and others for channeling some of its transatlantic passengers.

Sir Richard Branson, the founder and CEO of Virgin, had imbued his company with an aggressive style of management. The company was a trendsetter and known for breaking traditional barriers in its march toward recognition. Mr. Branson himself was a bit of a publicity seeker and seemed to revel in periodically taking controversial public positions. For example, when British Airways decided to retire its fleet of the supersonic Concorde jetliners, Mr. Branson offered to pay £1 in exchange for the fleet, believing it was a fair price for BA, which had been virtually given the fleet for free by the British government. Some believed that the swashbuckling management style of Virgin contrasted sharply with the button-down conservative style of SIA. Soon after the partial purchase of Virgin

was completed, Branson announced plans to move into the Australasia market with low-cost services through a new company named Virgin Blue. He offered SIA the opportunity to participate in the venture, but SIA passed on the deal since it felt that it had already established significant market presence with its partial ownership of Air New Zealand. This proved to be a costly decision. When the Air New Zealand deal failed to bear fruit for SIA, the company was left with no viable alternative to capitalize on growth in the region. It was rather ironic to see that Virgin Blue was posting very good returns in that region.

As the company was itself reeling from the misfortunes of the post-9/11 era, its alliance partner, Virgin, was going through a similar trough that required fresh injection of capital. The partners had to plough in more funds at a particularly difficult time. It remained to be seen how well the partnership would be able to weather the sequential shocks that plagued global aviation.

Low-Cost Carriers in Asia

Unlike the U.S. and Europe, Asia had been slow in responding to the phenomenon of low-cost carriers. Propelled by the success of companies such as easyJet and Ryanair in Europe and Southwest and Jet Blue in the U.S., many new competitors were setting their sights on the Asian market. Historically, the Asian market seemed immune to the low-cost approach, given the traditional barriers to entry such as the longer flight distances, fewer alternative airport options, and lower passenger densities. However, in recent times many of these barriers had begun to fall, and some legitimate low-cost carriers were jockeying for position. There were at least six main contenders in the market as of early 2003, and an additional player was gearing up for entry using Singapore as a base. Based on the experience of large network carriers in Europe after the advent of easyJet and Ryanair, the large players in Asia, such as SIA, were bound to face incredible pricing pressures. Many of the new players were focusing on South Pacific and East Asian routes, prime SIA territory.

Air Asia and Virgin Blue were credible threats. Air Asia was based in Malaysia and offered services at highly discounted rates to domestic destinations within the country. Its operations model used Kuala Lumpur as its central hub, but plans were on the anvil for expanding into Johor, a location that was within driving distance from Singapore. Although it had a very small fleet of only seven Boeing 737s, it planned to carry close to two million passengers by 2004. Its attractive fares would certainly drive traffic its way. For example, it was offering a round-trip ticket from Kuala Lumpur to the resort island of Penang for US$10, while its closest competitor, Malaysia Air, charged US$101 for the same trip. Network carriers were suddenly at a disadvantage. Air Asia also boasted that it had the lowest cost base of any passenger airline in the world at US2.5¢ per available seat kilometer compared to US5.1¢ for SIA. Air Asia was set to bring the competition to SIA in the near future. It had recently scouted Changi International and Seletar Airport in Singapore to explore the possibility of setting up operations there. The company suggested that it would offer a one-way fare of US$28 from Changi to Kuala Lumpur, a sector where SIA was currently charging US$109.

A group of investors in Singapore had marshaled a substantial amount of money to mount a low-cost carrier to be named ValuAir that would operate from Singapore. The company, the brainchild of former SIA Deputy Chairman Mr. Lim Chin Beng, promised to be a formidable competitor in the near future.

Virgin Blue, an offshoot of Virgin Airways, had captured 30% of the domestic Australian market within three years. In its aggressive rise to market dominance, Virgin Blue acquired control over blocks of gates and terminal space in key airports such as Sydney. This all but eliminated the possibility of another carrier besides Virgin Blue and Qantas, the national flag carrier, from building rival air service networks in that country. Virgin Blue was also contemplating service offerings from Australia to New Zealand and Fiji. In the very short period of time that Virgin Blue was active in Australia, it had demonstrated

how vulnerable network competitors were to low-cost competition. Qantas was at the receiving end of this onslaught in Australia and wound up losing a significant chunk of its market share. It was clear that SIA could not wish away the impending threat.

THE FUTURE OF SIA

Mr. Chew Choon Seng had a host of challenging competitive issues ahead of him. How should SIA continue to differentiate itself from the copycats who seemed to be doing a very creditable job at imitating SIA in terms of cabin service and amenities? What new signaling devices could SIA harness to set itself apart from the competition? The very people who had been instrumental in helping the company become the best in its class were now disgruntled after the staff cuts and salary givebacks. They would somehow have to be motivated once again to help SIA ride the successive waves of crisis. It was of paramount importance to stem the threat of low-cost competition before it became a larger phenomenon. How should the emergence of low-cost carriers be addressed? SIA was at a crossroads in its history. The next few strategic moves would determine whether it would rise from its status as the best Asian airline to become a global player commanding the respect of the world's largest carriers.

NOTES

1. Breakeven load factor is an industry measure of capacity that must be carried for the flight to break even.

2. Government of Singapore, Department of Statistics, www.singstat.gov.

3. BBC program.

4. Fleet data and age obtained from www.singaporeair.com.

5. *Asian Airline Analyzer*, UBS Investment Research, June 2003.

6. J. Clark. "They Enjoy Being a 'Girl,'" *USA Today,* November 19, 2002.

APPENDIX

Available Seat Kilometers (ASK) A measure of seat capacity available defined by the number of seats multiplied by kilometers flown

Available Seat Mile (ASM)

Available Ton Kilometer (ATK) A measure of capacity expressed in terms of aircraft payload multiplied by kilometers flown

Break-Even Load Factor Unit cost per ATK divided by overall yield—provides an indication of the load factor needed for the airline to break even at the operating profit level

Cargo Load Factor (CLF) Cargo load in RTKs expressed as a percentage of ATKs which indicates utilization of total capacity

Overall Load Factor (OLF) Total passenger and cargo load expressed as a percentage of total passenger and cargo capacity (ATKs) which indicates utilization of total capacity

Passenger Load Factor (PLF) Passenger Load Factor in RPKs is expressed as a percentage of ASKs which indicates utilization of seat capacity (RPK/ASK)

Revenue Passenger Kilometers (RPK) A passenger traffic measure expressed as the total number of passengers carried multiplied by kilometers flown

Revenue per Available Seat Mile (RASM) Also referred to as unit revenue. Represents how much a carrier made spread across all seats that were available

Revenue Ton Kilometers (RTK) The total traffic carriage measured by the revenue-generating weight (in tons) of load carried multiplied by kilometers flown

Unit Cost Expenditure required to produce a unit of capacity expressed in cents per ATK for cargo or cents per ASK for passengers

Yield Amount of revenue generated by each unit of load expressed in cents per RTK for cargo or cents per RPK for passengers

SWATCH AND THE GLOBAL WATCH INDUSTRY[1]

*Prepared by Cyril Bouquet under the
supervision of Associate Professor Allen Morrison*

Version: (A) 1999-09-23

In early June 1999, the management of the Swatch Group could be satisfied with the company's accomplishments over the last 15 years. Thanks to its 14 brands and unusual approach to marketing, and with 116 million finished watches and movements produced in 1997, the Swatch Group had helped resuscitate the Swiss watch industry and become, in value terms, the world's largest watch manufacturer. Despite an enviable track record, there was a growing sense of anxiety over the future of the company in an industry that seemed to be in a perpetual state of change.

EARLY HISTORY

Until 1957, all watches were mechanical. The aesthetics of the exterior visible elements (dials, hands and case) as well as the reliability and accuracy of a traditional timepiece depended on the meticulous care and precision that had been dedicated to its manufacturing and assembling processes. Mechanical watches consisted of between 100 and 130 components that were to be fitted together in the ébauche (winding stem, gear train) and regulating parts (mainspring, escapement, balance wheel). Most expensive watches contained at least 15 jewels (very hard stones such as synthetic sapphires or rubies that had been drilled, chamfered and polished), which were inserted in places that were most subject to metal wear. The tiny dimensions of a watch case did not leave much room for approximation, and watchmakers were required to have a great deal of micro-mechanical engineering expertise, craftsmanship spirit, patience, experience and ingenuity.

By most accounts, the first reliable pocket watch was invented in 1510 by Peter Henlein, a locksmith from Nuremburg, but the promising art of watchmaking in Germany was rapidly killed by the Thirty Years War (1618 to 1648). Starting in the late 1500s, the development of the watchmaking industry in Europe traced its roots to the flight of protestant Huguenots who were driven out of France by a series of religious persecutions. The Huguenots found refuge in Geneva, bringing with them skills in numerous handicrafts. For centuries, Geneva had been a centre of ornate jewelry making, but it was left with little industry after John Calvin's famous *Sittenmandate* edicts against luxury and pleasure had progressively put an end to the goldsmiths' activities in the city. Looking for a new source of income, and with their knowledge of metals, skills in jewelry making and artistic flair, many Genevan goldsmiths embraced the watchmakers' profession.

As they were becoming more and more numerous, watchmakers decided to regulate their activities, and incorporated into a guild in 1601. The development of the industry in Geneva and the surrounding Jura mountains was rapid. By 1686, there were 100 masters in Geneva; 165 in 1716; and 800 in 1766 employing some 3,000 people. By 1790, Geneva exported more than 60,000 watches throughout Europe. Many of the Genevese moved north along the French frontier in the Vallée de Joux, Neuchatel and La Chaux-de-Fonds (see Exhibit 1).

The emergence of the watch industry in Switzerland was a blessing for the local farmers who could extract only modest agricultural revenues from their mountainous terrain. In fact, many families—who had been educated through a close-knit system of community schools—were looking for an additional source of income, particularly during the long and snow-filled winters. Thanks to advances in new machine powered watchmaking tools, individual Swiss families began to specialize, some in the production of single components, others in assembly. The small size of watches and watch components allowed for relatively easy transportation from mountain farms and villages to commercial centres.

Swiss watches were sold exclusively through jewelry and up-scale department stores, which were also fully responsible for repair and after-sales services. Watches were purchased as lifetime investments and were often handed down from generation to generation. Swiss watches found ready acceptance throughout Europe and later in the U.S., in part because of their promotion by jewellers who saw them as a source of ongoing revenues through their repair services.

In the 18th and 19th centuries, English competitors were a constant challenge for the Swiss who undertook serious efforts to overcome early British supremacy. First, the Swiss invested in education and training, establishing several watchmaking academies at home and watch-repair schools in major foreign markets. Second, and to strengthen their image internationally, they created a "Swiss made" label, which would become by 1920, an important symbol of quality, style and prestige. Third, the Swiss significantly improved process technology, setting up the world's first mechanized watch factory in 1839. British watchmakers made no attempt to mass manufacture watches until much later. Seeing mass production techniques as a threat to their craft, they persuaded Parliament to pass a law barring the use of specialty production tools in the British watch industry, and devoted

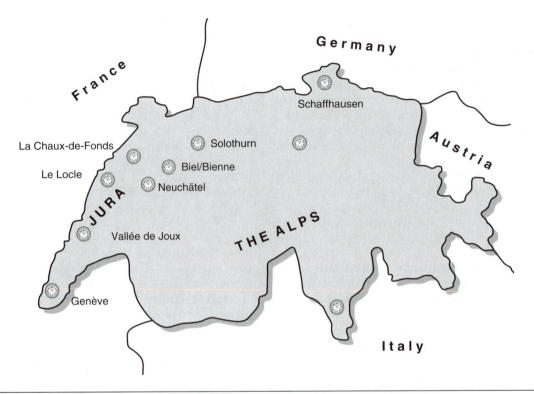

Exhibit 1   Watch Production in Switzerland

Source: FH, Federation of the Swiss Watch Industry.

themselves to the production of very expensive marine chronometers. As a result, the British watch industry steadily declined during the 19th century, while the Swiss industry was on its way to achieving world dominance, thanks to significant advances in design, features, standardization, interchangeability of parts and productivity. In 1842, Adrien Philippe introduced complicated watches featuring perpetual calendars, fly-back hands and/or chronographs. Other early Swiss names included Beaume & Mercier (1830), Longines (1832), Piaget (1874), Omega (1848), Movado (1881) and Rolex (1908).

The U.S. watch industry appeared in the middle of the 19th century. Local production consisted of high-volume, standardized products manufactured in machine-driven factories. U.S. watches—such as the US$1 *Turnip* pocket watch

introduced under the Ingersoll brand name by the Waterbury Clock Company—were cheap but also of very poor quality. Anyone who wanted a "real" watch bought Swiss.

In the early 20th century, the hard economic times (collapsing sales and soaring unemployment) following the First World War, led to a profound reorganization of the Swiss watch industry. Almost 2,500 distinct watchmaking firms grouped together into three associations, namely the Federation of the Swiss Watch Industry (FH) in 1924, the Ebauches SA in 1926, and the group Union des Branches Annexes de l'Horlogerie (UBAH) in 1926. The associations agreed to co-ordinate activities (for example, watch components had to be bought from members of the associations only) and maintain high prices. The Swiss Laboratory for Watchmaking Research

(CEH) was also founded in 1924, with the objective of strengthening the country's technological advantage. Finally, and in response to the world depression at the time, the Swiss government pushed several important watch assembly firms to form a holding company, ASUAG, in 1931.

POSTWAR COMPETITIVE CHANGES (1945 TO 1970)

By 1945, the Swiss accounted for 80 per cent of the world's total watch production, and 99 per cent of all U.S. watch imports. Swiss watch production was divided among nearly 2,500 distinct companies, 90 per cent of which employed fewer than 50 people. Despite the 200-year dominance of Swiss watchmaking companies, much would change in a short period of time.

U.S. Competitors

The main source of competition for the Swiss arose from two American watchmakers, Timex and Bulova. Using a combination of automation, precision tooling and simpler design than that of higher-priced Swiss watches, U.S. Time Corporation introduced in 1951 a line of inexpensive (US$6.95 to US$7.95), disposable, yet stylized and highly durable Timex watches, whose movements had new hard alloy bearings instead of traditional and more expensive jewels. Hard alloy metals allowed for the creation of durable watches at lower costs than jewelled lever timepieces. They also allowed U.S. Time to more effectively automate its production lines, further lowering costs.

Traditional jewellers were very reluctant to carry the brand for a variety of reasons. Its prices and margins were slim compared to those offered by the Swiss, while the watches' riveted cases could not be opened, thereby eliminating the possibility for jewellers to generate aftersales repair revenues. Locked out of jewelry stores, Timex had no choice but to innovate in its

marketing and distribution strategy. Their first extensive worldwide advertising campaign on television, "Took a licking and kept on ticking," was to become a legend in marketing history. Consumer demand soared after John Cameron Swazey, a famous U.S. news commentator, was featured in live "torture tests" commercials emphasizing the watch's low cost and incredible durability. The disposable aspect of Timex watches (no local repair involved) pushed the company to develop new distribution channels, including drugstores, discount houses, department stores, catalogue showrooms, military bases and sporting goods outlets. By 1970, Timex (having changed its name from U.S. Time) had established a manufacturing and/or marketing presence in over 30 countries and become the world's largest watch manufacturer in terms of units sold.

Bulova was the leading U.S. manufacturer of quality, jewelled-lever watches. Integrating the highly accurate tuning fork technology bought from a Swiss engineer in 1959, after the main Swiss companies had turned down the technology, Bulova introduced *Accutron* in 1962. Five years later, *Accutron* was the best selling watch over $100 in the U.S. Bulova also formed a partnership with Japan's Citizen Watch Company to produce the movements for the *Caravelle* line, designed to meet the low-cost/high quality challenge imposed by Timex. By 1970, Bulova had expanded its international presence all around the world, and become the largest seller of watches, in revenue terms, in both the United States and the world overall.

Japanese Competitors

Like the U.S. industry, the Japanese watch industry was highly concentrated. In 1950, three main competitors, K. Hattori (which marketed the Seiko brand), Citizen and Orient accounted for 50 per cent, 30 per cent, and 20 per cent of the Japanese market respectively. Their positions were protected by the 70 per cent tariff and sales tax imposed on all imported watches by the Japanese government.

As the Japanese market became saturated in the 1960s, Hattori and Citizen moved aggressively into other Asia Pacific countries. After first exporting from Japan, Hattori and Citizen established component and assembly operations in low cost Hong Kong, Singapore and Malaysia. With hundreds of millions of unserved consumers, the region was also a highly attractive market. From a position of strength in Asia, the Japanese watch companies began in earnest to push into Europe and North America.

The Swiss response to the growing power of U.S. and Japanese competitors was limited. In 1962, the Swiss FH and ASUAG created a research organization, the Centre Electronique Horloger (CEH) to develop a competitive alternative to the tuning fork technology patented by Bulova. These efforts were unsuccessful, in part because of only lukewarm support from member companies. A rising worldwide demand for watches did little to slow the steady decline in the Swiss share of the world market (from 80 per cent in 1946 to 42 per cent in 1970).

Changing Technologies (1970 to 1990)

The advent of light-emitting diodes (LED) and liquid crystal display (LCD) watches constituted a true revolution in the world of watchmaking, as they allowed the digital display of time. In 1970, Hattori Seiko became the first to develop and commercialize a quartz watch named *Astron*, based on LED technology.

Despite their novelty, LED watches had many flaws. A button had to be pushed to activate the display of LED watches, a process that consumed a lot of electrical energy and wore out batteries quickly. Additionally, most people felt that LEDs were distracting and inconvenient to use. In 1973, Seiko introduced the world's first LCD quartz watch with six-digit display and by the late 1970s, LCDs dominated the digital segment. However, digital watches remained largely plagued by quality problems, and consumers never fully embraced the style. Quartz analogue watches, which involved a more delicate

manufacturing, and conserved—with their hands and gear train—the traditional appearance of mechanical timepieces, increasingly gained consumers' acceptance. By 1984, over 75 per cent of all watches sold around the world were based on quartz technology, versus only three per cent in 1975. The large majority of quartz watches were analogue.

Quartz watches used an integrated circuit, made up of numerous electronic components grouped together on the basis of a few square millimetres. Extremely accurate, thanks to their high frequency of vibrations (32 kHz), they were accurate to less than one second per day. Generally more sophisticated—in terms of functions—than their mechanical counterparts, they were also far less expensive to manufacture. The average production cost of a standard quartz watch fell from US$200 in 1972 to about US$0.50 in 1984, the cost of components being constantly driven down by the main U.S. chipmakers such as National Semiconductor and Texas Instruments.

Faced with soaring international competition, the Swiss abolished all internal regulations in 1981, and the industry began to consolidate. Many firms merged in an attempt to leverage their marketing and/or manufacturing capabilities. The largest operation resulted in the creation of the Société Suisse pour L'Industrie Horlogère (SSIH), which controlled brands such as Omega and Tissot, among others.

The Japanese Industry

Convinced that technologically sophisticated watches could allow Swiss prices at Timex costs, Hattori Seiko and Citizen made important efforts to promote the new quartz technology. Large investments were made in plant and equipment for fully automated high-volume production of integrated circuits, batteries and LCD panels. Hattori's production lines were designed to produce up to 1,000,000 watches per year per product line. Manufacturing/assembly facilities were set up all around the world (Japan, the

United States, western Europe, Australia, Brazil, Hong Kong, Korea, Mexico). To ease the transition, employees were retrained, relations with distributors were reinforced, and advertising budgets were increased.

By 1979, Hattori produced about 22 million watches annually and became the world's largest watch company in terms of revenues, with sales approaching US$1.2 billion, versus only US$503 million for the Swiss ASUAG. Citizen launched the world's first wristwatch movement with a thickness of less than one millimetre in 1978, and became the global leader in both movement and finished wristwatch production volumes in 1986.

Casio entered the watch market in 1974 with a digital model priced at US$39.95. Its subsequent low-cost, multifunction digital plastic watches were rapidly fitted with gadgetry such as timers and calculators. By 1980, the company had captured 10 per cent of the Japanese digital watch market, and became the world's second most important player in the under US$50 world watch market, behind Timex.

Hattori, Casio and Citizen were largely integrated companies. Most operations, from the production of movements and components to the assembly and distribution of finished watches, were carried out through wholly owned subsidiaries and/or majority joint ventures. In 1980, Japan produced about 67.5 million watches, up from 12.2 million in 1970.

THE U.S. INDUSTRY

U.S. competitors were relatively slow to get on the electronic bandwagon. Neither Bulova nor Timex's facilities easily allowed the production of quartz crystal or integrated circuits. In fact, they were rapidly becoming obsolete in light of those new technologies sweeping the industry. In addition, Timex was struggling with management problems as Mr. Lehmkuhl—who had run the business for almost 30 years with no clear successor—fell ill and could no longer work. Nevertheless, both companies finally entered the quartz watch market in the mid-1970s, sourcing their quartz components from a variety of suppliers and backing their product lines with full-scale advertising and promotion campaigns. The Timex model was priced at US$125, which was 60 per cent below Seiko's least expensive watch on the market at that time.

About 100 semiconductor firms such as National Semiconductor, Texas Instruments (TI), and Litronix, were also attracted to the promising market for digital watches and circuits for electronic movements in the mid-1970s. Most started as suppliers of quartz movements and components, then invested in high-volume, fully automated watch-manufacturing plants. The belief was that their huge existing distribution channels for consumer electronics products would give them a strong competitive advantage. Watches were introduced at very aggressive prices (TI's retailed at $19.95 in 1976 and $9.99 in 1977). In 1978, TI's digital watch sales reached $100 million, for a pretax profit of US$28 million. However, stagnant demand coupled with continuous price wars and numerous distribution problems led all semiconductor firms to exit the market one by one. In the end, most customers felt uncomfortable buying watches in electronic stores where the semiconductor firms had a distribution advantage.

The price wars following the arrival of these semiconductor firms were also largely detrimental to the main U.S. watchmaking companies. Although it was constantly underpriced by Texas Instruments, Timex turned down a number of propositions to form manufacturing partnerships with several chipmakers. Some observers argued that Timex was probably too proud to accept the idea of co-operation. Timex lost US$10 million in 1980, being surpassed by Seiko as the world's largest watch manufacturer company (both in units and total sales), while its share of the U.S. market fell to under 33 per cent. The two other U.S. players remaining in the industry were not in a much better situation. Bulova experienced three years of significant losses before being purchased by Loews Corporation; Hamilton lost $15 million in 1970 and went bankrupt in 1978: the

Pulsar rights were bought by Seiko and the remaining assets purchased by SSIH.

WATCHMAKING ACTIVITIES IN HONG KONG AND KOREA

By the end of the 1970s, Hong Kong had become the highest volume producer of timepieces in the world. Japanese, American and European watchmakers had all established assembly plants (mechanical, digital and quartz analogue watches) in the city to take advantage of highly skilled, cheap labor and favorable tax conditions. Numerous local semiconductor firms had also engaged in the production of low-cost digital quartz watches that were then distributed through local retail chains and department stores, or exported, mainly towards mainland China.

The timepiece industry in Korea also experienced considerable growth in the 1970s. By 1988, the country's total watch exports amounted to US$39 million, along with a rising reputation in the eyes of the world for quality assembling capabilities.

The Hong Kong and Korean watch industries benefited from their flexible manufacturing systems, capable of handling small quantity orders in different styles. However, downward pressures on prices and low profit margins discouraged local watch producers from investing in technology and branding.

THE SWISS INDUSTRY RESPONDS SLOWLY

Although the Swiss pioneered quartz technology, they were particularly reluctant to adopt the new technology. Contrary to the Japanese, their industry structure was very fragmented and, therefore, not adapted to high-volume mass production procedures. Besides, electronic watches were regarded as being unreliable, unsophisticated, and not up to Swiss quality standards. Consequently, digital and analogue quartz watches were regarded as just a passing fad, and in 1974, accounted for only 1.7 per cent of the 84.4 million watches exported from Switzerland. Instead, the Swiss focused on the high-end, mechanical segment of the industry, where traditional craftsmanship remained the deciding factor.

As SSIH and ASUAG regularly increased prices to maintain profitability, foreign competition rapidly established a strong foothold in the low and middle price ranges where the Swiss were forced to abandon their leadership, virtually without a fight. Compounding the problems faced by the Swiss, the U.S. dollar more than halved its value against the Swiss franc during the 1970s. The appreciating Swiss franc effectively raised the export prices of Swiss watches (see Exhibit 2).

The Swiss industry experienced a severe crisis in the late 1970s and early 1980s. Its exports of watches and movements decreased from 94 million in 1974 to 43 million in 1983, while its world market share slid from 43 per cent to less than 15 per cent during that same period. Employment fell from 90,000 (1970) to 47,000 (1980) to 34,000 (1984) and bankruptcies reduced the number of firms from 1,618 to 860 to 630 respectively. These competitive changes resulted mainly from the seeming inability of the Swiss to adapt to the rapid emergence of new watch technologies.

	1950–1970	1971	1972	1974	1976	1978	1980
Swiss Franc	4.37	4.15	4.15	3.58	2.89	2.24	2.18

Exhibit 2 Exchange Rate to the U.S. Dollar (annual average)

Source: International Monetary Fund Yearbook of Statistics.

Near Death Experience

In the early 1980s, Swiss watch production hit an all time low. SSIH and ASUAG faced liquidation and a profound restructuring of the Swiss industry became necessary. The Swiss government provided financial assistance and initiated the "electronic watch" program in 1978 to promote new technologies as well as the production of electronic watch components in Switzerland. But this initiative was not sufficient, and in 1981 SSIH reported a loss of SFr142 million, giving the company a negative net worth of SFr27.4 million. The Swiss creditor banks—which had just taken over the country's two largest watchmaking groups—were getting ready to sell prestigious brand names, such as Omega, Tissot or Longines to the Japanese. But Nicolas Hayek, the already well-known founder and CEO of Hayek Engineering, a consulting firm based in Zurich, was convinced he could revive the Swiss industry and regain lost market share, primarily in the lower-end segment. He invested $102 million—mostly his own money—and led a group of 16 investors in buying back the two groups, before orchestrating their merger in 1983.

SMH and Swatch

Hayek teamed with Dr. Ernst Thomke to head the new group, Société Micromécanique et Horlogère (SMH). After the merger, SMH owned many of the country's famous watchmaking names, such as Omega, Tissot, Longines and Rado. Five years later, the group had become the world's largest watchmaking company. Its first product initiative, Swatch, was to become an enormous commercial success, as well as the main instrument behind the revitalization of the entire Swiss industry.

The Swatch mania marked the 1980s for the Swiss industry. The Swatch (contraction of "Swiss" and "watch") was conceived as an inexpensive, SFr50 (US$40), yet good quality watch, with quartz accuracy, water and shock resistance, as well as a one-year guarantee. The concept was challenging. Particular efforts were needed to reduce production costs down to Asian levels. Watch engineers slashed the number of individual parts required in the production of a watch from 91 to 51, and housed them in a standardized plastic case that could be produced on a fully automated assembly line. For the first time ever, it became possible to produce cheap watches in high cost Switzerland. By 1985, production costs were decreased to under SFr10 per unit, and only 130 people were needed to assemble the first eight million Swatch models. By comparison, 350 people were still required to assemble 700,000 Omega watches.

Swatch was an immediate success. Within two years of its 1983 launch, sales were averaging 100,000 units a months, for a cumulative total of 13 million sold. In 1985, Swatch accounted for over 80 per cent of SMH's total unit sales, and by 1989, just six years after its debut, the company had placed 70 million Swatches on customers' wrists.

Marketing was key to the watch's success. Franz Sprecher, an independent consultant, and Max Imgrüth, a graduate of New York's Fashion Institute of Technology, helped SMH position the watch as a lifestyle symbol and fashion accessory, not as a traditional timekeeping instrument. With their trendy and colorful designs, models were created for every occasion.

Initially, the media appeared to be mesmerized by Hayek's charismatic style and unusual approach to marketing. This resulted in lots of free media coverage and publicity. The company also spent liberally on special events and public relation activities. SMH budgeted about SFr5 million per Swatch product line per year in promotional money, and used celebrity endorsements extensively. Swatches were sold through nonconventional channels of distribution such as discount houses and department stores, where variety and low prices constituted the main selling points. Swatch made a few attempts to diversify, but its line of accessories (casual clothing and footwear, umbrellas, sunglasses, and cigarette lighters) experienced mixed success and was discontinued in 1988.

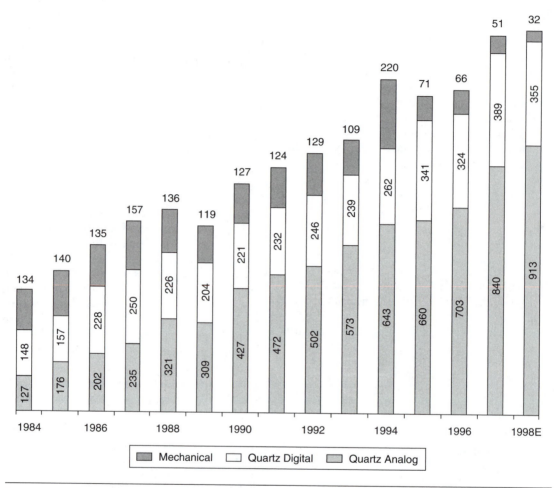

Exhibit 3   Global Watch Production; 1984 to 1998

Source: FH, Federation of the Swiss Watch Industry, and Japan Clock and Watch Association.

COMPETING IN REAL TIME (1990s)

Global watch production grew steadily in the 1990s, at a rate of about four per cent per annum, and reached 1.3 billion watches in 1998, equivalent to 22 per cent of the world's population (see Exhibit 3). The production of mechanical watches (and to a lesser extent, that of digital watches) gradually decreased over the years, while that of analogue quartz watches rose 11 per cent per year on average. In 1998, quartz watches—digital and analogue—accounted for about 97 per cent of the worldwide industry's production in volume. On average, annual watch purchases were about one unit per person in North America, and 0.6 unit per person in Europe and Japan. Together these three regions—which accounted for 14 per cent of the world's population—generated about 56 per cent of global watch demand (see Exhibit 4).

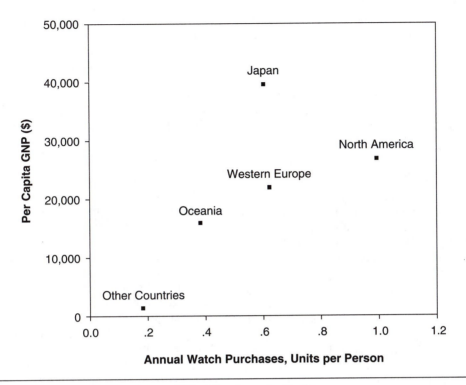

Exhibit 4   Per Capita GNP and Annual Watch Purchases, by Region

Source: Japan Clock and Watch Association, United Nations Demographic Yearbook, The World Bank.

Industry Restructuring

The global watch industry experienced downward profit pressures in the 1990s, as many watchmakers incessantly cut prices—driven in part by a push for economies of scale. Overcapacity and tough head-to-head competition led prices of basic watch movements to be slashed by over 30 per cent in 1998 alone. By the end of the decade, consolidation had reduced the number of watch movement manufacturers from 30 to just three (the Swatch Group—having changed its name from SMH—as well as Seiko and Citizen). The achievement of a critical mass was becoming a necessity to compete globally in all segments of the industry.

Several types of internal reorganizations allowed companies to realize economies of scale and/or maintain profitability. These included:

Restructuring Initiatives

Many watchmaking companies reacted to declining prices in their core business by increasing productivity and shifting manufacturing overseas. With the exception of the Swatch Group, most watch companies manufactured in Southeast Asia exclusively.

Pursuing Acquisitions

In tune with its strategy to reinforce its position in the luxury or prestige brands, the Swatch Group acquired Blancpain in 1992, thereby also taking control of Frederic Piguet, a company admired for its complex, high-quality mechanical movements. In January 1999, the Swatch Group purchased the total shares of Favre and Perret, the highly reputed producer of quality

Swiss watchcases. As another example, Gucci, the luxury Italian company, acquired Severin Montres, its 23-year Swiss watch manufacturer, for $150 million in November 1997. The following year, Gucci's watch sales increased by 160 per cent to $60.1 million. "There is no question that Gucci is destined to become more than a shoe and bag business," said De Boisgelin, an equity analyst with Merrill Lynch in London.[2]

Accessing New Distribution Channels

Watchmakers traditionally used independent agents to sell products around the world. However, increasing difficulties controlling the merchandising and pricing policies used by local retailers led many of them to alter their strategies. In 1997, the Swatch Group opened 61 new free-standing Swatch stores (mostly operated as franchisees), bringing the total to 120 (including five megastores) in more than 20 countries. Despite the risks involved, the strategy was promising: sales at New York's Swatch Time Shop boutiques approached 100,000 units in 1998, up 32 per cent over 1997. By taking over 85 per cent of its distribution network, Tag Heuer increased its gross margins from 45 per cent to 65 per cent, which more than offset the cost of running local subsidiaries. According to CEO Christian Viros, the move allowed "greater control of our destiny, better control of the implementation of our marketing programs, better understanding of local issues, and greater reactiveness to new developments."[3]

Creating New Niche Products

Despite ongoing consolidation, there was a viable place for niche companies with clearly defined brands and images. By the late 1990s, Switzerland had about 600 watchmaking companies, employing 34,000 employees, in addition to the big four (The Swatch Group, The Vendôme Luxury Group, Rolex and Tag Heuer), which together accounted for 75 per cent to 80 per cent of Swiss industry turnover. As examples of niche players, St. John Timepieces entered the industry in 1997 with a collection of Swiss watches specifically designed for sophisticated women, retailing from $450 to $18,000. Breitling scarcely deviated from the aerial image it established in 1884. In 1999, it equipped Breitling Orbiter 3's pilots, Bertrand Piccard and Brian Jones, with wristwatches for their successful, first nonstop 26,602-mile balloon flight around the world.

Increasing Advertising

The overabundance of supply in the industry implied that watchmakers had to find ways to distinguish their offerings from those of their competitors. Advertising expenditures reached unprecedented levels. In the 1990s, 40 per cent of the value of all Swiss advertisements in international media promoted wristwatches, not banking institutions. Seiko's 1998 *Electricity* campaign was backed with a 60 per cent increase in media spending, while Timex allocated about US$8 million in 1999 to market its *Turn 'n' Pull Alarm* watches.

Huge advertising budgets were not, per se, a guarantee of success. The campaigns also needed to be creative in order to get consumers' attention. Companies turned down conservative ads in favor of eye-popping, humorous, and thought-provoking messages that obtained an emotional reaction from viewers. For example, Bulgari formed a one-year partnership with Alitalia, Italy's national airline, to have a personalized Boeing 747 fly around the world with a three-dimensional image of its latest cutting-edge aluminum timepiece painted on the fuselage. Audemars Piguet's ad crusade, "Who is behind an Audemars Piguet Watch?" featured mysterious men and women showing off their watch faces while their own faces remain obscured. Other watchmakers tried to get exposure in action-packed movies such as *Men in Black* and *Lethal Weapon 4* (Hamilton), James Bond (Omega), or *Armageddon* (Tag Heuer). Strong marketing muscle was also put behind sports partnerships. For example, Tag Heuer and Hugo Boss had long been associated with Formula One auto racing, and Spanish-based Festina with cycling events such as the Tour de France.

Emphasizing Quality

Faced with strong competition from independent, low cost Asian producers, many European and U.S. watchmakers chose to gradually reposition their brands in the upper market, and proposed increasingly expensive and sophisticated watches. According to the Federation of the Swiss Watch Industry, the average price of a Swiss wristwatch, taking account of all materials, rose from US$132 in 1996 to US$157 in 1997. A growing number of customers were becoming aware of quality and increasingly wanted a watch with lasting value.

Emphasizing Technology

The end of the 1990s looked promising in terms of technological breakthroughs. Bulova's *Vibra Alarm* watch featured dual sound and vibrating alarms. In Seiko's *Kinetic*, an oscillating weight was set in motion by the slightest movements of the wearer's arm ("If you're going to create electricity, use it!"). Timex's *DataLink* pioneered the utilization of wristwatches as wearable information devices. Following Timex's lead, various watch manufacturers introduced multifunctional watches that could be interfaced with personal computers. Other manufacturers designed watches with built-in global positioning systems (Casio, Timex), or offered fast, customized and reliable access to Internet services.

Accentuating Fashion

Another noticeable trend was the entry of fashion house designers. By 1999, and partly thanks to the Swatch revolution, people increasingly believed that they were judged by what they wore on their wrists. Fashion designers strove to create new watch brands to meet every one of their possible fashion needs. Some decided to put their signatures on stylized watches produced in co-operation with major specialist manufacturers. Examples included Emporio Armani (Fossil), Calvin Klein (The Swatch Group), Guess (Timex) and Yves St Laurent (Citizen). Others, such as Bulgari, Hermes, and Dior set up their own in-house manufacturing operations. "We have very high expectations for this side of the business," said Guillaume de Seynes, director of Hermes Montres. "Watches are already our fourth biggest product in sales terms after leather, silk, and ready-to-wear. We've made a significant investment in the new factory because we expect even faster growth in the future."[4]

DEVELOPMENTS IN THE HONG KONG AND JAPANESE INDUSTRIES

In the late 1990s, Hong Kong was the world's dominant centre for watch assembly. In 1998, about 80 per cent of all watches produced worldwide were assembled in the city (see Exhibit 5).

Japanese watch manufacturers saw their combined domestic and overseas watch production rise about 14 per cent per year in the 1990s. Particularly strong in the sports watch segment, the Japanese offered an impressive range of multifunction chronographs for virtually any type of outdoor activity, including diving, mountain climbing and flying. However, sales and profitability deteriorated between 1993 and 1996 due to a rapid appreciation of the yen. In addition, the average unit price of analogue quartz movements fell by nearly 50 per cent to ¥234 in the first half of the decade, and by over 30 per cent in 1998, as major companies boosted production. This collapse severely shook the industry, and many manufacturers, such as Orient Watch, had to exit the market. Throughout the last half of the 1990s, Seiko and Citizen began cutting production in order to hold prices firm.

Citizen maintained its world's volume leadership with 2,500 new models released every year and 311 million timepieces produced in 1997 (about 25 per cent of the world's total and 36 per cent of the global market for analogue quartz watches). Sales were mainly dependent upon Japan (38 per cent), Asia (32 per cent), America (15 per cent) and Europe (14 per cent). Two new collections—the light-powered *Eco-Drive* watches and the affordable luxury *Elegance Signature* dress watches—marked the company's desire to

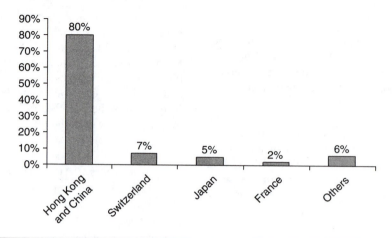

Exhibit 5   World Production of Finished Watches: 500 Million Pieces (1997)
Source: Federation of the Swiss Watch Industry.

move from traditional sports watches towards more sophisticated or expensive timepieces.

Seiko introduced a few technological marvels in the early 1990s, such as the *Perpetual Calendar* watch, with the first built-in millennium plus (1,100 years) calendar, the *Scubamaster*, with the first integrated computerized dive table, and the *Receptor MessageWatch*, with paging functions and built-in antenna that allowed access to specialized information services and incoming alphanumeric messages. In 1995, Seiko introduced the *Kinetic* series, backed with a $20 million advertising campaign. The futuristic line became the driving force behind the company's growth in the late 1990s, accounting for 25 per cent of Seiko's $3 billion global sales. Great hopes were also placed on *Kinetic*'s lower-cost cousin, the $200 *Pulsar* solar-powered quartz watch, which was launched at the end of 1996.

Casio enjoyed a significant expansion of its wristwatch division, thanks to the successful launches of the *G-shock* and *Baby-G* product lines. The company was particularly strong in the U.S. (second largest market share after Timex), but also heavily dependent on domestic Japanese sales, which made up two-thirds of total *G-shock* and *Baby-G* sales. A depressed Japanese economy in the late 1990s had a profound negative effect on the company's profits, which were

estimated to drop from ¥38 billion in 1998 to ¥19 billion in 1999.[5]

THE U.S. INDUSTRY

The biggest single watch market in the world was also the one with the largest trade deficit. In 1991, exports amounted to $73.4 million compared to an import total of $1.84 billion. Thanks to a factory in Little Rock, Arkansas, Timex was the only U.S. watch company with any domestic production in the late 1990s.

Timex

From sports watches and classic styles to watches featuring *Star Trek* and Walt Disney characters, Timex offerings strove to address a variety of consumer trends in the 1990s. The production of watches for Guess, Timberland, Nautica, and Reebok further emphasized Timex's willingness to reach a mass audience. Two innovations distinguished the company. The first was the durable, multi-function *Ironman Triathlon* watch, named after the gruelling annual Hawaiian sports event. Initially positioned as an instrument for serious athletes, the watch rapidly appealed to a wider audience of pedestrian

Timex	30.6%	Gitano	2.0%
Casio	7.8%	Gucci	1.9%
Seiko	7.4%	Swatch	1.6%
Guess (Timex)	5.0%	Rolex	1.1%
Armitron (Gluck)	4.5%	Movado	1.0%
Citizen	4.0%	Tag Heuer	0.8%
Fossil	3.5%	Hamilton (Swatch)	0.7%
Pulsar (Seiko)	3.1%	Tissot (Swatch)	0.7%
Lorus (Seiko)	2.5%	Omega (Swatch)	0.5%
Bulova	2.2%	Rado (Swatch)	0.2%

Exhibit 6   Share of Purchasers by Brand in the U.S. Market—1999

Source: Euromonitor.

customers. By the late 1990s, it was the word's best selling sports watch with more than 25 million units sold since its 1986 introduction. The second was *Indiglo*, a patented luminescent dial technology launched in 1992, and credited with more than doubling the company's sales by 1994. *Indiglo* received considerable attention in 1993 after a group of people trapped in the World Trade Center bombing had been led to safety by an *Indiglo* owner, who guided them down 34 flights of pitch-black stairs through the glow of his Timex watch. Other technological innovations rapidly followed, with Timex *DataLink*, a $139 wristwatch allowing wireless transfer to and from a desktop PC, and *Beepwear*, a $160 alphanumeric pager wristwatch developed and commercialized in partnership with Motorola.

Timex's annual sales exceeded $600 million in the late 1990s, one-quarter of which came from the U.S. market where the company remained the top selling watch company, far ahead of its main competitors. By 1999, with a 30 per cent market share in its hands, Timex had sold more watches in the U.S. than the next five competitors combined (see Exhibit 6). However, the huge majority of these watches were manufactured in Asia.

NEW ENTRANTS IN THE 1990s

By the early 1990s, mainland China and India had emerged among the fastest growing watch markets in the world. With a combined population of 2.1 billion people, these markets could not be ignored, especially after a series of government decisions to liberalize trade and investment in those countries. A number of reputable watch-making companies had established a presence in India and mainland China, despite the threat of counterfeiting (about 50 per cent of wristwatches sold in those markets were either counterfeited or smuggled in). Most came in via the trading route, appointing local distributors such as Dream Time Watches in India. This strategy was ideal for the Swiss, who could capitalize on the well-appreciated label "Swiss made." Others such as Timex, Seiko and Citizen established their own production facilities, often in co-operation with key local partners.

Titan Industries was probably one of the most remarkable industry success stories of the 1990s. The group was established in 1987, with a greenfield investment of $130 million from giant Indian conglomerate Tata Group and the government of Tamil Nadu state, where Titan built one of the world's biggest integrated watch factories, near India's technological centre Bangalore. Constantly scanning the world for best practices, Titan sourced designs and technology from France, Switzerland and Germany, watchstraps from Austria, and cases from Japan. This world-class strategy created a remarkably successful company. During its first year of operation, 750,000 high-quality finished timepieces were produced and, in 1997, the company enjoyed a dominant 60 per cent share of the organized Indian watch market, with pretax profits amounting to US$7.5 million on turnover of US$96 million. Titan's management believed the company had little choice but to internationalize, partly to defend its own domestic position. Mr. Desai, Titan's vice-chairman and managing director commented on the need to globalize: "India is being globalized and the whole world is now turning up in India. So the kind of protection we've enjoyed will go. It's going to get very crowded."[6] By 1997, the company exported over 600,000 watches annually and had established offices in Dubai, London, New York and Singapore. However, by the end of the 1990s and despite the company's recent $20 million advertising campaign, it was difficult to predict international success. Seducing consumers into buying $120 to $700 Indian-made wristwatches was challenging given the country's poor reputation for the quality of its exports.

THE SWISS INDUSTRY IN THE LATE 1990S

In the late 1990s, watch production in Switzerland was the country's third most important industry behind the chemical-pharmaceutical and electronic industries. In 1998, 34 million timepieces were produced in Switzerland for a total value of SFr8.2 billion.[7] Of those, 90 per cent were exported, positioning the country as the world's leading exporter—in value—of finished watches (see Exhibit 7).

The Swiss industry had the ability to provide consumers with a comprehensive choice of products in all market segments. Whatever their needs and preferences (mechanical versus quartz technologies; diamond set watch of precious metals versus stainless steel, plastic or ceramic; classic appearance versus trendy design), consumers could always find a "Swiss made" solution when shopping for their wristwatches. Of course, the Swiss industry stood apart in the upper market range where its watches had gained an unequalled reputation for quality, styling, reliability and accuracy. In 1998, the average price

of watches exported by Switzerland was SFr235, four times higher than the average of the world industry (see Exhibits 8 and 9). The "Swiss made" label remained one the oldest examples of a registered and fiercely protected national branding name, which could be used only on watches and clocks containing at least 50 per cent Swiss-manufactured components by value.

The Vendôme Luxury Group accounted for about 20 per cent of Swiss industry turnover, privately-held Rolex for 15 per cent, and Tag Heuer—which sold over 673,000 units in 1997, for seven per cent. The Swatch Group was the main player with a third of industry turnover. Thanks to its 14 brands (Blancpain, Omega, Rado, Longines, Tissot, Calvin Klein, Certina, Mido, Hamilton, Pierre Balmain, Swatch, Flick Flack, Lanco, and Endura), the group had gained a presence in all price and market categories.

Swiss watches were sold all around the world. Exports to the United States increased by more than 10 per cent in 1998 for the third consecutive year. Sales in Europe were also on the rise, especially in Spain (+41.3 per cent), Italy (+18 per cent) and France (+16 per cent). In Asia, the ongoing economic crisis depressed demand and put downward pressures on prices (the demand in Hong Kong, Singapore, Thailand and Taiwan dropped by 23 per cent or SFr500 million in 1998). In 1997, Tag Heuer saw Asian sales drop by 21.4 per cent from SFr130 million to SFr102.9 million, accounting for the brand's overall 5.4 per cent decrease.

The Swatch Group

In value terms, the Swatch Group was the world's leading manufacturer of watches (14 per cent share of the world market). In 1998, the Swatch Group increased its gross sales and net profits by 7.1 per cent and 7.5 per cent respectively. With a growth averaging 15 per cent to 25 per cent per year, Omega had been a major profit driver for the group (see Exhibit 12, p. 68), thanks to a successful repositioning strategy initiated in the early 1990s. To rejuvenate the brand, cheaper, silver-plated gold was used to replace

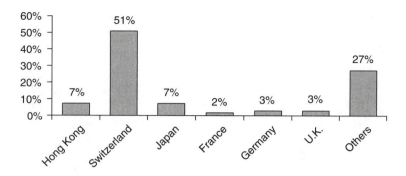

Exhibit 7   World Production of Finished Watches in Value Terms: 16 Billion Swiss Francs (1997)
Source: Federation of the Swiss Watch Industry.

	Turnover in SFr. Million	Market Share
Rolex	2,200	28%
Vendôme*	1,540	20%
Swatch Group**	1,000–1,100	14%
Gucci	620	8%
Tag Heuer	470	6%
Patek Philippe	250	3%
Bulgari	215	3%
Chopard	195	3%
Jaeger LeCoultre	180	2%
Audemars Piguet	120	2%
Other (Ebel, IWC, Breguet, . . .)	910	12%
Total	**7,750**	**100%**

Exhibit 8   Luxury, Prestige and Top Range: Global Market Players (1998)
Source: Bank Leu estimates, Vendôme Group Data.

*(Cartier, Piaget, Vacheron and Constantin, Beaume & Mercier)
**(Blancpain, Omega, Rado, Longines)

more expensive metals (platinum, titanium, solid gold and special steel alloys). The company also streamlined its models from 2,500 to 130 representing four distinct product lines. Other major initiatives consisted of integrating distribution and launching a new advertising campaign (with Cindy Crawford, Michael Schumacher, Martina Hingins and Pierce Brosman as high-profile

"ambassadors"). The strategy was quite successful and with an average price point 50 per cent lower than its main competitor, Rolex, Omega seemed to have plenty of room to grow.

Despite the success of the Omega brand, the Swatch Group was facing several issues. Management problems were plaguing the organization. Key figures such as Klaus Schwab, a

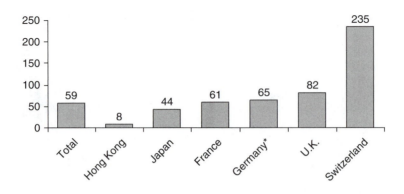

Exhibit 9   Average Price of Watches in 1998 (in Swiss Francs)

Source: Federation of the Swiss Watch Industry.

	Units	%	Value	%	Swatch Market Share
Mass (under $50)	124,653	78%	2,056	34%	9%
Middle Market ($50–299)	31,840	20%	2,219	37%	4%
Upper/Luxury ($300)	2,705	2%	1,771	29%	21%
Total	**159,198**	**100%**	**6,046**	**100%**	**11%**

Exhibit 10   U.S. Market and Swatch Group's Market Share—1999

Source: Dresdner Kleinwort Benson estimates.

professor at the University of Geneva and founder of the World Economic Forum in Davos, Drs. Stephan Schmidheiny, Pierre Arnold and Walter Frehner all stepped down from the board of directors in the mid-1990s. Several managing directors also left the group in the last two years. Hayek's management style was resulting in growing criticism in the company. Dr. Ernst Thomke, a former partner, had less-than-flattering comments about Hayek: "He has to be the big boss alone, and can never share opinions. He was a consultant all his life and he wanted to become a marketer and product developer. But he never learned that job."[8]

The Swatch Group was also experiencing persistent difficulties in establishing a strong foothold in the U.S. market, where it faced stiff competition from Timex, Casio, Seiko and Citizen. Even the Swatch Group's role as the official timekeeper of the 1996 Summer Olympic Games in Atlanta failed to significantly boost interest in the company's offerings. Although the group generated about 19 per cent of its sales in the U.S., its market share in the basic and middle-priced segments was particularly weak (see Exhibits 6 and 10). Finally, its highly successful and emblematic Swatch brand appeared to be at a crucial crossroads.

The brand had sold a total of 200 million watches since its introduction in 1983. A Collectors' Club (100,000 members worldwide) was founded in 1990 to create an international link between fans around the world. Limited edition watches, special events, and the quarterly *Swatch World* journal also contributed to reinforce the value of the brand. Demand rapidly exceeded supply for a number of special launches and collectors started to compare the rarity of their collections, to trade and to speculate around Swatches during auction sales. In the early 1990s, it looked as if Swatch's expansion had no limit. So great was management's confidence that the group even decided to actively contribute to the development and market introduction of the small ecological smart car.

Despite the growing interest of many, Swatch sales had plateaued at 18 million to 20 million units a year. In 1998, sales and profit margins were well below the levels achieved in the early 1990s as Swatch was facing increased competition from the likes of Fossil and Guess. One concern was whether there were too many Swatch products on the market. Another concern centred on the product mix. Many young Swatch fans of the past wanted more expensive and sophisticated watches as their incomes increased. A proliferation of products also led to a growing problem with Swatch distributors. Many retailers were dropping Swatch from their shelves. The number of stores selling the trendy watch decreased from 3,000 in the early 1990s to 1,200 in 1998. Steven Rosdal, co-owner of Hyde Park Jewelers, expressed the views of some retailers: "Swatch came out with more products than the market could bear, and the consumers seemed to back off. I guess if you use the word 'fad' for anything, it could be used for Swatch."[9]

The group was undertaking several steps to revamp and differentiate the brand. First, Swatch was trying to reposition itself from a low-margin, high-volume business involved in day-to-day fashion watches to a high-margin, high-volume enterprise focusing on watches fitted with state-of-the-art electronic gadgetry. As an example of its repositioning efforts, it launched the *Access* watch in 1995, which could be programmed to function as a pass to access ski lifts, hotel chains, public transport and numerous other applications. Although the watch had yet to achieve its commercial potential, there were promising signals: Swatch equipped the Lisbon universal exhibition with one million units and about 200 ski resorts in some 17 countries. Also, with assistance from German Electronics giant

Siemens, Swatch developed *Swatch Talk*, a Dick Tracy type wristwatch with an integrated mobile telephone. Finally, Swatch created the *Swatch Beat,* as a completely new global concept of time, as well as a whole new area of market potential. With *Swatch Beat*, time was the same all over the world—"No Time Zones, No Geographical Borders." People using the same clock could agree to a phone call at "500," without time zone arithmetic required. The day was divided into 1,000 units (each one being the equivalent of one minute and 26.4 seconds) with a new BMT meridian created in Bienne, home of the Swatch Group.

As a second initiative, Swatch launched a new advertising campaign ("Time is what you make of it") designed to reinforce the brand's primary message ("Innovation, provocation, fun. Forever."). Sponsorship was primarily focused on new and youth-oriented sports or events with an offbeat lifestyle, such as snowboarding, mountain biking, bungee jumping, and rock climbing.

However, in October 1998, Swatch sold its minority 19 per cent shareholding of Micro Compact Car, the vehicle producer, to manufacturing partner Daimler-Benz. Although the group was still looking for key partners to develop the hybrid electric *Swatchmobile,* management made it clear that its core business remained the watch industry and microelectronics.

STRATEGIC DECISIONS

In early June 1999, Hayek was under growing pressure to clarify the company's strategy. Many observers and shareholders were wondering whether the original management philosophy that shaped the company's success remained viable.

Conventional wisdom suggested that all watch companies should locate manufacturing activities in countries that offered low-cost production solutions. The Swatch Group had always remained committed to its Swiss home base, leaving the bulk of its technology, people and manufacturing in the isolated villages

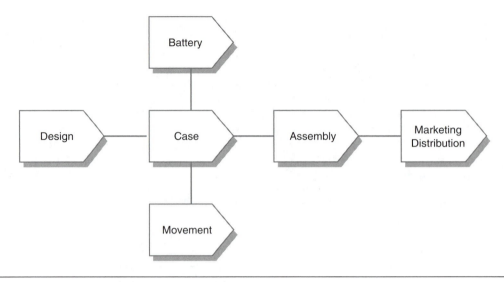

Exhibit 11   Watch Production and Value Added Chain

	Units in thou.	Average Price in SFr*	Turnover in SFr. million	% of Total	EBIT in SFr. million	% Total	Margin in %
Omega	550	1,200	670	28%	147	47%	22%
Swatch	26,000	36	925	38%	79	25%	9%
Tissot	1,600	100–150	210	9%	20	6%	10%
Rado	300	570	170	7%	31	10%	18%
Longines	550	270	150	6%	23	7%	15%
Calvin Klein	600	130	75	3%	4	1%	5%
Blancpain	10	6,500	65	3%	6	2%	9%
Other	1,500	80	145	6%	3	1%	2%
Total	**31,110**	**80**	**2,410**	**100%**	**312**	**100%**	**13.0%**

Exhibit 12   The Swatch Group's Turnover and Margin Estimates for 1998

Source: Bank Leu estimates.

*Factory gate price.

surrounding the Jura Mountains. Those places possessed hundreds of years of experience in the art of watchmaking. Employees had spent generations in the factories controlled by the Swatch Group, where they developed a special feel and touch for this business along with a true sense of organizational commitment. However, the company's junior secretaries in Switzerland earned more than senior engineers at competitors in Thailand, Malaysia, China or India. Maybe it was time to move on and stop building watches in one of the most expensive countries in the world. But which, if any, of the value-added chain activities should be moved (see Exhibit 11)?

With its huge domestic demand and low-cost labor, India offered interesting sourcing opportunities. Many industry analysts believed that Titan Industries was looking for key foreign partners, after the demise of an early alliance with Timex. Would a partnership with a company like Titan make sense, or if and when the company were to move, should it go it alone?

Another trend management had to address was the movement of many watch companies into ever-more narrow or differentiated market niches. The Swatch Group was present in all market segments and price categories, but its performance depended mainly on four brand names, Omega, Swatch, Tissot and Rado, which together accounted for 82 per cent of total sales and 88 per cent of operating profit in 1998 (see Exhibit 12). Perhaps it was time to reorganize the company's portfolio. Advertising budgets had already been reallocated towards the luxury and high-tech markets, where the company was also constantly looking for key partners and acquisition targets. However, for many industry observers, this product market strategy (luxury-high tech and/or

globalization) was becoming too complex for the company's internal capabilities, as indicated in the failure of the smart car project.

Notes

1. This case has been written on the basis of published sources only. Consequently, the interpretation and perspectives presented in this case are not necessarily those of the Swatch Group or any of its employees.

2. *Women's Wear Daily,* March 20, 1998.

3. *Chief Executive,* 1998.

4. *Financial Times,* April 24/25 1999.

5. In June 1999 US$1 = ¥119.

6. Financial Times London Edition. *Financial Times.* September 10, 1997; 43.

7. In June 1999, SFr 1 = US$0.66.

8. *Time,* March 28, 1994.

9. *Jewellers' Circular-Keystone,* December 1998.

THUNDERBIRD
THE GARVIN SCHOOL OF INTERNATIONAL MANAGEMENT

WHIRLPOOL CORPORATION'S GLOBAL STRATEGY

Prepared by Meredith Martin, Simon Algar and Vipon Kumar under the supervision of Professor Andrew C. Inkpen

We want to be able to take the best capabilities we have and leverage them in all our companies worldwide.

—David Whitwam,
Whirlpool CEO, 1994, Quoted in
the *Harvard Business Review*

In 1989, Whirlpool Corporation (Whirlpool) embarked on an ambitious global expansion with the objective of becoming the world market leader in home appliances. Beginning with the purchase of a majority stake in an appliance company owned by Philips, the Dutch electronics firm, Whirlpool purchased a majority stake in an Indian firm, established four joint ventures in China, and made significant new investments in its Latin America operations.

However, by the mid-1990s, serious problems had emerged in the company's international operations. In 1995, Whirlpool's European profit fell by 50% and in 1996, the company reported a $13 million loss in Europe. In Asia, the situation was even worse. Although the region accounted for only 6% of corporate sales, Whirlpool lost $70 million in Asia in 1996 and $62 million in 1997. In Brazil, Whirlpool found itself a victim in 1997, and again in 1998, of spiraling interest rates. Despite the company's investments of hundreds of millions of dollars throughout the 1990s to modernize operations there, appliance sales in Brazil plummeted by 25% in 1998. Whirlpool expected that 1999 would be the third straight year of declining sales for the Brazilian subsidiary.

In response to these problems, Whirlpool began a global restructuring effort. In September 1997, the company announced that it would cut 10% of its global workforce over the next two years and pull out of two joint ventures in China. In announcing the cuts, Whirlpool's CEO David Whitwam said, "We are taking steps to align the organization with the marketplace realities of our industry."[1] In Latin America, 3,500 jobs were abolished, and significant investments were made to upgrade plants and product lines.

After the optimism of the early 1990s, what went wrong with Whirlpool's global strategy? Was the company overly ambitious? Was there a lack of understanding about how to create an integrated global strategy? Or, were the problems the result of changes in the competitive and economic environments in Europe, Asia, and Latin America? Should Whirlpool have foreseen the problems and reacted earlier?

THE APPLIANCE INDUSTRY IN THE LATE 20TH CENTURY

Approximately 120 million home appliances are sold in developed countries each year.[2] The appliance industry is generally classified into four categories: laundry, refrigeration, cooking, and other appliances. Appliances are constructed in capital intensive plants, and design usually varies among countries and regions.

The North American Industry

Although it was estimated that 46 million appliances were sold in North America annually, the market was expected to grow little in the late 1990s. Saturation levels were high, with virtually 100% of households owning refrigerators and cookers and over 70% owning washers. Because of the limited growth opportunities, competition was fierce. In the United States, the industry had consolidated in the 1980s, leaving four major competitors: Whirlpool, General Electric, Electrolux, and Maytag (see Exhibit 1 for more detail). These four firms controlled about 80% of the market.[3] Each firm offered a variety of products and brands segmented along price lines. Distribution of these appliances was generally through sales to builders for new houses or to retailers, such as department stores and specialty resellers.

In a *Harvard Business Review* article in 1994 called "The Right Way to Go Global," David Whitwam, Whirlpool's CEO, described the competitive situation that existed in the early 1990s:

> Even though we had dramatically lowered costs and improved product quality, our profit margins in North America had been declining because everyone in the industry was pursuing the same course and the local market was mature. The four main players—Whirlpool, General Electric, Maytag, and White Consolidated, which had been acquired by Electrolux—were beating one another up everyday.[4]

With limited growth opportunities and a handful of major players in the United States, it was critical that firms focus on cost reduction, productive efficiency, and product quality. Product innovation was also critical, although few major innovations had occurred in recent years. The appliance firms segmented their

GE Appliance

General Electric Appliance was the second-largest manufacturer of household appliances in the U.S. (behind Whirlpool). Other brand names produced by the company included Monogram, Profile, Profile Performance, Hotpoint, and some private brands for retailers. GE Appliance comprised approximately 6% of the parent company's sales and had the top market share position in India and Mexico. In addition, the company had a 50–50 joint venture with General Electric Co., the leading appliance firm in the United Kingdom.

Maytag

Maytag's products were generally aimed at the mid-to-high end of the market and commanded a premium price based on product quality and reliability. Other brand names produced by Maytag included Jenn-Air, Magic Chef, Performa, and Hoover. Maytag entered the European market in 1989, but after a decline in profits, pulled out of Europe in 1995. Maytag had a limited international presence in China.

AB Electrolux

AB Electrolux was the world's largest producer of household appliances. Other Electrolux brand names included Frigidaire, Tappan, and Kelvinator. The Swedish company had the number one market share in Europe and number four market share in North America. Electrolux entered the United States when it bought White Consolidated Industries in 1986. The firm was actively expanding overseas into Eastern Europe, China, India, South East Asia, and Latin America.

Exhibit 1   Major Competitors in the United States

Sources:

Hoovers Online. Accessed 2/9/00.

Remich, Norman C. "A Kentucky Thoroughbred That Is Running Strong," *Appliance Manufacturer*, July 1995: GEA-3.

Steinmetz, Greg and Carl Quintanilla. "Tough Target: Whirlpool Expected Easy Going in Europe, and It Got a Big Shock," *Wall Street Journal*, 10 April 1998: Sec. A:1.

products according to different consumers' needs, and each strived to achieve greater economies of scale. Still, by the end of the 1990s, the competitive landscape remained unattractive. Profit margins continued to decline for most firms. Many analysts believed that the market for appliances was saturated and that there would be little increase in growth rates. This saturation had left the distributors focusing primarily on replacement purchases and purchases for new housing developments.

The European Industry

In the early 1980s, there were approximately 350 producers of household appliances in Europe. With consolidation in the industry, by the late 1980s the number had shrunk to about one hundred.[5] By early 1995, it was estimated that five of the companies, including Electrolux (with a 25% market share), Philips Bauknecht,

and Bosche-Siemens, controlled over 70% of the market.[6] The industry was highly regionalized, with many of the companies producing a limited number of products for a specific geographic area.

The European market consisted of more than 320 million consumers whose preferences varied by country and by region. For example, Swedes preferred galvanized washing machines to withstand the damp salty air.[7] The British washed their clothes more often than the Italians did, and wanted quieter machines. The French liked to cook on gas at high temperatures, splattering grease on cooking surfaces, and so preferred self-cleaning ovens, while the Germans liked to cook on electric stoves at lower temperatures and did not need such features.[8]

Distribution of the appliances in Europe was different than in the United States. Most appliances were sold through independent retailers, who had become organized in buying groups or as multiple store chains.[9] A smaller channel was through independent kitchen specialists who sold complete kitchen packages, including appliances.[10]

The Asian Industry

Asia, the world's second-largest home appliance market, was also the fastest growing market of the 1980s. By the mid-1990s, it was growing at a rate of between 8% and 12% annually, a rate that was expected to continue well past the year 2000.[11] The industry was highly fragmented, consisting of manufacturers primarily from Japan, Korea, and Taiwan. Matsushita, the market leader, held less than 10% market share outside Japan.

Asian consumer preferences were different from those in Europe or North America. Kitchen appliances needed to be smaller to fit in Asian kitchens. Lack of space sometimes required the consumer to store the appliance in an outside hallway and transport it into the kitchen for use.[12] Therefore, high value was placed on appliances that were portable, usually lightweight and on wheels, and easily hooked up to electrical and water supplies. Refrigerators also tended to be smaller and more colorful. Indeed, when Asian countries first began to experience significant economic growth, some East Asians viewed their refrigerators as status symbols and liked to display them prominently, perhaps even in the sitting room. Clothes dryers and dishwashers were uncommon in most Asian countries, but most homes had microwaves.

Appliances in Asia were traditionally sold through small retail shops. However, the industry was beginning to witness a shift away from these small shops and towards distribution through national, power retailer organizations, especially in China and parts of Southeast Asia.

The Latin American Industry

The economic stability in Latin America in the 1990s made the region an attractive growth proposition. The appliance makers hoped that the days of hyperinflation and economic mismanagement were over, and they were pleased to see that governments were reducing tariffs. Distributors in Latin America were generally responsible for marketing a company's appliances to small independent retailers in the region.[13] In 1994, there were over 65 competitors in the Latin American market, many of them subsidiaries of U.S. parents.

WHIRLPOOL CORPORATION

Whirlpool was founded in 1911 as The Upton Machine Co. in St Joseph, Michigan, to produce an electric motor-driven wringer washer. The company merged with The Nineteen Hundred Washer Company in 1929 and began to sell their first automatic washing machine through Sears, Roebuck & Co. in 1947. The Whirlpool brand was introduced in 1948 and steadily built a strong retail relationship with Sears. Through a series of acquisitions and mergers, the company emerged as a leading force in the U.S. appliance industry with annual revenue reaching $2 billion in 1978 (see Exhibit 2 for more detail on Whirlpool's history). Whirlpool's headquarters was in Benton Harbor, Michigan.

As of 1998, Whirlpool Corporation claimed to be the world's leading manufacturer of major home appliances. The company manufactured in thirteen countries and marketed its products under eleven major brand names (including Kenmore, Sears, KitchenAid, Roper, Inglis, and Speed Queen) to over 140 countries. Whirlpool's sales were $8.2 billion in fiscal year 1997.

THE GLOBALIZATION OF WHIRLPOOL

Whirlpool's first international investment was in 1957 when the firm acquired an equity interest in Multibras S.A., a Brazilian manufacturer of white goods. In 1969, the company entered the Canadian market by purchasing an equity interest in Inglis Ltd. and acquired sole ownership in 1990.

By the mid-1980s, Whirlpool saw that, despite increasing efficiencies and product quality, its profit margins were rapidly decreasing in North

1911	Upton Machine Co. is founded in St. Joseph, Michigan, to produce electric motor-driven wringer washers.
1916	First order for washers is sold to Sears, Roebuck and Co.
1929	Upton Machine merges with Nineteen Hundred Washer Company of Binghamton, New York. The new firm, Nineteen Hundred Corp., operates plants in Michigan and New York until Binghamton is closed in 1939.
1942	All facilities are converted to wartime production until end of World War II in 1945.
1947	The company's first automatic washer is introduced to the market by Sears.
1948	A Whirlpool brand automatic washer is introduced, thus establishing dual distribution—one line of products for Sears, another for Nineteen Hundred.
1950	Nineteen Hundred Corporation is renamed Whirlpool Corporation. Automatic dryers are added to the product line.
1951	LaPorte, Indiana, plant is acquired. It will become the company's parts distribution center. Whirlpool merges with Clyde (Ohio) Porcelain Steel and converts the plant to washer production. All washers eventually will be produced here.
1955	Manufacturing facilities are purchased in Marion, Ohio, from Motor Products Corp., and dryer production is transferred there. Whirlpool merges with Seeger Refrigerator Co. of St. Paul, Minnesota, and the Estate range and air conditioning divisions of R.C.A. RCA Whirlpool is established as the brand name; Whirlpool-Seeger Corporation, as the company name. A refrigeration plant is acquired in Evansville, Indiana, from International Harvester.
1956	First full line of RCA Whirlpool home appliances is introduced. RCA will be used with the Whirlpool brand name until 1967. New administrative center is completed on 100-acre site in Benton Harbor.
1957	Company name is changed back to Whirlpool Corporation. Appliance Buyers Credit Corporation is established as a wholly owned finance subsidiary. It will be renamed Whirlpool Financial Corporation in 1989.
1957	Whirlpool invests in Brazilian appliance market through purchase of equity interest in Multibrás S.A. It is renamed Brastemp S.A. in 1972.
1966	The Norge plant in Fort Smith, Arkansas, is acquired, adding more than one million sq. ft. of refrigeration manufacturing space.
1967	Toll-free Cool-Line® Telephone Service begins. Renamed the Consumer Assistance Center in 1990, it gives customers direct, 24-hour access to Whirlpool. The company's first totally new manufacturing facility is completed in Findlay, Ohio. Dishwashers and, later, ranges will be manufactured there.
1968	The Elisha Gray II Research & Engineering Center is completed in Benton Harbor. For the first time, annual revenues reach $1 billion.
1969	The company enters the Canadian appliance market through purchase of an equity interest in Inglis Ltd. Sole ownership is established in 1990.
1970	Construction is completed on a new plant in Danville, Kentucky. Production of trash compactors and, later, vacuum cleaners is transferred there.
1976	Whirlpool increases its investment in the Brazilian market through purchase of equity interests in Consul S.A., an appliance manufacturer, and Embraco S.A., a maker of compressors.
1978	Annual revenues reach $2 billion.
1983	The company announces a phaseout of washer assembly at St. Joseph. All washers will be made at Clyde.
1984	The St. Paul Division is closed. Production of freezers and ice makers moves to Evansville.
1986	Whirlpool purchases the KitchenAid division of Hobart Corporation. A majority interest is purchased in Aspera s.r.l., an Italian compressor manufacturer. Whirlpool will become sole owner before the business is sold to Embraco of Brazil in 1994. Whirlpool closes most of its St. Joseph Division. The remaining machining operation is renamed the Benton Harbor Division.
1987	Whirlpool and Sundaram-Clayton Limited of India form TVS Whirlpool Limited to make compact washers for the Indian market. Whirlpool will acquire majority ownership in 1994.
1988	A joint venture company, Vitromatic S.A. de C.V., is formed with Vitro, S.A. of Monterrey, to manufacture and market major home appliances for Mexican and export markets. Whirlpool acquires the Roper brand name, which it will use to market a full line of value-oriented home appliances.

Exhibit 2   Whirlpool History   *(Continued)*

1989	Whirlpool and N.V. Philips of the Netherlands form a joint venture company, Whirlpool Europe B.V., from Philips major domestic appliance division, to manufacture and market appliances in Europe. Whirlpool will become sole owner in 1991. Appliance operations in the United States, Canada, and Mexico are brought together to form the North American Appliance Group (NAAG). Annual revenues catapult over the $6 billion mark.
1990	A program is launched to market appliances in Europe under the dual brands Philips and Whirlpool. Whirlpool Overseas Corporation is formed as a subsidiary to conduct marketing and industrial activities outside North America and Western Europe. An Estate brand of appliances targeted to national accounts is introduced.
1991	The company commits globally to its Worldwide Excellence System, a total quality management program dedicated to exceeding customer expectations. NAAG repositions its refrigeration business. The Port Credit, Ontario, plant is closed. Top- and bottom-mount refrigerators are consolidated at Evansville, side-by-side refrigerators at Fort Smith.
1992	Whirlpool assumes control of SAGAD S.A., of Argentina. Whirlpool Hungarian Trading Ltd. is formed to sell and service appliances in Hungary. Whirlpool Tatramat is formed to make and sell washing machines and market other major home appliances in Slovakia. Whirlpool will take controlling interest in 1994. A Small Appliance Business Unit is formed to operate on a global basis. Revenues top $7 billion. The South American Sales Co. (SASCo), a joint venture with Whirlpool's Brazilian affiliates, begins directing export sales to 35 Latin American countries.
1993	Whirlpool Overseas Corporation is replaced by two separate regional organizations: Whirlpool Asia and Whirlpool Latin America. Whirlpool Asia sets up headquarters in Tokyo with regional offices in Singapore, Hong Kong, and Tokyo. Sales subsidiaries are opened in Poland and the Czech Republic, adding to Whirlpool Europe's growing presence in Eastern Europe. Whirlpool wins the $30 million Super Efficient Refrigerator Program sponsored by 24 U.S. utilities. Inglis Ltd. becomes Canada's leading home appliance manufacturer.
1994	Whirlpool Asia and Teco Electric & Machinery Co. Ltd. form Great Teco Whirlpool Co. Ltd. to market and distribute home appliances in Taiwan. Whirlpool becomes a stand-alone brand in Europe. Brazilian affiliates Consul and Brastemp merge to form Multibrás S.A. Electrodomésticos. Whirlpool breaks ground in Tulsa, Oklahoma, for a new plant to make freestanding gas and electric ranges. Whirlpool's Asian headquarters is moved to Singapore, and the number of operating regions is increased from three to four. Whirlpool exits vacuum cleaner business. To strengthen competitiveness, a major restructuring is announced in North America and Europe. One U.S. and one Canadian plant close. Total revenues top $8 billion.
1995	An executive office is formed in Whirlpool Asia to lead the company's rapid growth and manage strategic deployment in the region. Whirlpool acquires controlling interest in Kelvinator of India Ltd., one of India's largest manufacturers and marketers of refrigerators. TVS Whirlpool Ltd. changes name to Whirlpool Washing Machines Ltd. (WWML). Construction is completed on a new plant in Greenville, Ohio. KitchenAid small appliances will be manufactured there. Whirlpool begins to sell appliances to Montgomery Ward. Whirlpool Europe opens representative office in Russia. Whirlpool Financial Corporation (WFC) is established in India. Whirlpool assumes control of Beijing Whirlpool Snowflake Electric Appliance Group Co. Ltd., a refrigerator and freezer manufacturing joint venture. Beijing Embraco Snowflake Compressor Co. Ltd., a compressor manufacturing joint venture, is formed between Embraco and Beijing Snowflake. Whirlpool has a minority position in the joint venture. Whirlpool acquires controlling interest in Whirlpool Narcissus (Shanghai) Co. Ltd., a washing machine manufacturing joint venture. Whirlpool acquires majority ownership of SMC Microwave Products Co. Ltd., a microwave oven manufacturing joint venture. Shenzhen Whirlpool Raybo Air-Conditioner Industrial Co. Ltd., an air conditioner manufacturing joint venture, is formed with Whirlpool having a majority stake. Whirlpool investments in Asia increase to over US$350 million, and employees total more than 9,300.
1996	Whirlpool Europe opens sales subsidiaries in Romania and Bulgaria. Production of electric and gas ranges officially begins in Whirlpool's new plant in Tulsa, Oklahoma. The company's new Greenville, Ohio, plant, which manufactures KitchenAid small appliances, begins production. The Ft. Smith Division in Arkansas begins production of trash compactors. Whirlpool Asia employees total more than 12,000. Whirlpool Europe acquires the white goods business of Gentrade of South Africa. The acquisition provides Whirlpool a sales and manufacturing base in this country.

Exhibit 2   Whirlpool History

Source: http://www.whirlpool.com.

America. Top management believed that if the company continued to follow its current path, the future would be "neither pleasant nor profitable."[14] They considered restructuring the company financially or diversifying into related businesses but eventually settled on further global expansion for two main reasons: the company wished to take advantage of less mature markets around the world and it did not want to be left behind by its competitors, which had already begun to globalize.

Whitwam's Vision and Platform Technology

David Whitwam joined Whirlpool in 1968 as a marketing management trainee and rose through the sales and marketing ranks to succeed Jack Sparks as CEO in 1987. Although Whitwam admitted that he had never actually run a multinational company until Whirlpool bought Philips in 1989, he believed that:

> The only way to gain lasting competitive advantage is to leverage your capabilities around the world, so that the company as a whole is greater than the sum of its parts. Being an international company—selling globally, having global brands or operations in different countries—isn't enough.[15]

Whitwam was convinced that most companies with international divisions were not truly global at all, as their various regional and national divisions still operated as autonomous entities rather than working together as a single company. He believed that the only way to achieve his vision of an integrated international company, or one company worldwide, was through intensive efforts to understand and respond to genuine customer needs and through products and services that earn long-term customer loyalty.

Whitwam talked about his vision of integrating Whirlpool's geographical businesses so that the company's expertise would not be confined to one location or product. He forecast appliances such as a World Washer, a single machine that could be sold anywhere, and he wanted to standardize the company's manufacturing processes. According to Whitwam,

> Today products are being designed to ensure that a wide variety of models can be built on the same basic platform . . . Varying consumer preferences require us to have regional manufacturing centers. But even though the features . . . vary from market to market, much of the technology and manufacturing processes involved are similar.[16]

Given this view that standardization should be the focus, Whirlpool planned to base all its products, wherever they were built or assembled, on common platforms. These platforms would produce the technological heart of the product, the portion of the product which varied little across markets. The products could then be diversified to suit individual and regional preferences. In this way, the parts that the customer sees—the dimensions of the appliance, the metal case, and the controls—could be varied by segment or market to fulfill consumers' needs. The products would also have to meet rigorous quality and environmental standards to ensure that they could be used in different countries around the world.

Whitwam believed that the platform technology would bring a $200 million annual savings in design and component costs by the time it was fully implemented in the year 2000.[17] In addition, management was convinced that the platform strategy would put the company two to three years ahead of its competitors.

Platform technology, however, represented only the beginning of Whirlpool's globalization strategy. According to Whitwam in the 1994 interview, Whirlpool could not truly achieve its goal of globalization until:

> . . . we have cross-border business teams . . . running all of our operations throughout the world . . . There will also come a day when we'll identify a location where the best skills in a certain product area should be concentrated, and that place will become the development center for that type of product . . . [but] while we may have only one major design center for a given product, not everyone associated with that product will have to be located there.[18]

DEVELOPING AND IMPLEMENTING THE GLOBAL STRATEGY

By 1987 Whirlpool had adopted a five-year plan to develop a new international strategy. The company's 1987 Annual Report included the following statement:

> The U.S. appliance industry has limited growth opportunities, a high concentration of domestic competitors, and increasing foreign competition. Further, the United States represents only about 25% of the worldwide potential for major appliance sales. Most importantly, our vision can no longer be limited to our national borders because national borders no longer define market boundaries. The marketplace for products and services is more global than ever before and growing more so every day.

Recent industry forecasts indicated that approximately three-quarters of the growth in domestic appliance sales between 1995 and 2000 would be in East Asia (including Australia), Eastern Europe, and South and Central America. According to the forecasts, by 2000 these three regions (excluding Japan) would account for about 34% of sales.

European Expansion

In 1989, Whirlpool bought a major stake in N.V. Philips, a struggling Dutch appliance operation, and then purchased the remaining equity in 1991 for a total of $1.1 billion.[19] Whitwam believed that the U.S. and European markets were very similar and hoped that Whirlpool would be able to replicate their successes in the United States in the new market through implementation of a pan-European strategy. Whirlpool management also believed that the European market was becoming more "American." Research performed by the company indicated that European integration was making it more difficult for smaller companies to survive and that the industry was ripe for consolidation. Whirlpool's plan was to be one of the big players following

this consolidation, and Whitwam was expecting a 20% share of the $20 billion market by the year 2000.[20] Whirlpool's strategy was to focus on brand segmentation and operational efficiency. It was believed that the company that produced the most innovative products while reducing costs would capture the market.

The European subsidiary, Whirlpool Europe BV (WEBV), created a brand portfolio segmented by price. Bauknecht (Philips' German brand) served as the company's high-end product while Ignis served as the lower-end, value brand. The Philips/Whirlpool brand filled the middle range.[21] However, the company decided to heavily market the Whirlpool brand name at the expense of managing its other European brands. Managers at Bauknecht in Germany saw their marketing budgets slashed and Bauknecht's market share fell from 7% to 5%.[22] By 1995, however, consumer research showed Whirlpool to be the most recognized appliance brand name in Europe, despite the fact that many Germans, Italians, and French had a problem pronouncing the name.

To better manage sales and service throughout the region, Whirlpool set up two centralized distribution centers: one in Cassinetta, Italy, and one in Schorndorf, Germany. Operations were streamlined in order to achieve reduced costs through economies of scale, and considerable efforts were put toward product innovation and increasing operational efficiency. This strategic focus was overlaid with a global outlook, and managers were regularly rotated between Europe and the United States. The rotation generated a crossover of ideas but annoyed retail clients who felt that they had no continuity when dealing with senior managers.

The early years of European expansion were successful. Sales and profits increased steadily, and Whirlpool made a profit of $129 million in Europe in 1993. The company was able to cut costs by reducing the number of suppliers it dealt with and by using common parts in its appliances.

However, Whirlpool was not the only company aggressively attacking the market, and competition subsequent to Whirlpool's entry grew fierce. Electrolux and Bosch-Siemens both greatly improved their efficiency, along with many of the smaller European companies. The European companies laid off large numbers of workers, built up their core businesses, and concentrated on generating profits. Bosch-Siemens expanded its overseas operations while keeping production local and the company managed to raise its non-German revenue by more than 30% in five years. Electrolux shed all of its non-appliance businesses and cut its workforce by 15,000, closing 25 factories. Electrolux invested in new factories and achieved higher efficiency. Both Electrolux and Bosch-Siemens increased their profitability.

Across the industry, European plants doubled their output from 1990 to 1998 and cut the time needed to build a washing machine from five days to eight hours. Companies embraced computer-aided design techniques to speed the development of products. In 1997, it was reported that a new washing machine could move from the ideas stage to the shops in just 2-1/2 years, twice as fast as only a few years before. The "value gap" which existed between appliances in the United States and Europe also closed by an estimated 15% to 20% for all appliances.[23]

The state of the retail sector also changed. Traditionally, the producers had determined price in the European appliance industry. These producers had been able to reduce their costs through greater operational efficiencies and had allowed the retailers to keep their margins constant. However, by the 1990s, the number of retail outlets across Europe had fallen significantly, giving the larger surviving retailers more power when dealing with manufacturers. Recession in Europe also caused consumers to become more cost-conscious, and brands such as the low-price firm Indesit won considerable market share.

With all companies becoming more efficient as producers, there was a shift towards product innovation as the basis for competition. For example, Whirlpool increased the size of the

entrance of its front-loading washing machines, thus allowing clothes to be pushed into the machine more easily and contributing to increased sales. Companies also attempted to improve customer service and to create appliances that were more friendly to the environment. Such changes were not going unnoticed, but the industry appeared to be extremely mature. Not only were new entrants, such as Whirlpool, GE, Daewoo of South Korea, and Malaysia's Sime Darby, trying to build up sales from a small base, but the traditional European producers had become more aggressive. More than that, few were making tactical or strategic errors. Seeing the increased costs of competition and the growing intensity of rivalry, Maytag left the European market in 1995, selling its Hoover unit at a $130 million loss. Leonard Hadley, Maytag's chairman, commented, "Europe isn't an attractive place to try to go in and dislodge the established players."[24]

Eastern Europe was seen as the next great battleground and Whirlpool expanded its operations in 1996 to newly developing countries in Eastern and Central Europe. In 1997, Whirlpool opened new offices in Romania, Bulgaria, Turkey, Morocco, and South Africa from its European headquarters. Sales in the initial years were disappointing.

PROBLEMS FOR WHIRLPOOL

Whirlpool's sales leveled off in the mid-1990s and profits began to fall. Sales only increased 13% from 1990 to 1996, which was far from the levels management had expected. The company initiated a major restructuring in 1995 and laid off 2,000 employees. The restructuring did not solve the problems and in 1996, the company's European operations recorded a loss of $13 million. Between 1995 and 1997, the company also witnessed a rise in materials and labor costs. Exhibit 3 shows Whirlpool's stock prices versus the S&P 500. Exhibits 4 and 5 show Whirlpool corporate and business unit financial information.

Exhibit 3 Whirlpool Share Price*

*The Whirlpool share price is on the bottom.

Whirlpool announced a second restructuring in 1997. The company planned to cut a further 4,700 jobs worldwide, or about 15% of its workforce, mostly in Europe. In 1998, WEBV had a 12% market share and held the number three market position. However, in 1998, the profit margin had reduced further to 2.3%, compared to 10% in the U.S.

Whirlpool's managers blamed a number of causes—reduced consumer demand, poor economic growth, the rising Italian lira, intense competition, and even the European Monetary Union—for its poor performance in Europe but shareholders were unimpressed. Indeed, Scott Graham, analyst at CIBC Oppenheimer, commented in 1998, "The strategy has been a failure. Whirlpool went in big [into overseas markets] and investors have paid for it."

In 1998, Whirlpool's goals remained the same, but the timeframes for delivery grew. Whitwam attributed the performance to temporary problems in the newer regions of activity and believed that Whirlpool was now "coming through the challenges." He and the rest of his management team remained resolute:

> We were convinced when we first bought [the Philips operation] and we're convinced now. The benefits from Europe have begun to flow. But they have yet to be recognized.[25]

ASIAN EXPANSION

Whirlpool's strategy in Asia consisted of five main points: partnering to build win-win relationships; attracting, retaining, and developing the best people; ensuring quality in all aspects of the business; exceeding customer needs and expectations; and offering four key products (refrigerators, washers, microwaves, and air conditioners). Although Whirlpool announced in 1987 a full-scale cooperation with Daiichi, a department store retailer in Japan, the company decided to focus its efforts in Asia primarily on India and China. There were two main reasons

Balance Sheet	Dec-98 US$MM	Dec-97 US$MM	Dec-96 US$MM	Dec-95 US$MM
Cash	636	578	129	149
Securities	0	0	0	0
Receivables	1,711	1,565	2,366	2,117
Allowances	116	156	58	81
Inventory	1,100	1,170	1,034	1,029
Current Assets	3,882	4,281	3,812	3,541
Property and Equipment, Net	5,511	5,262	3,839	3,662
Depreciation	3,093	2,887	2,041	1,883
Total Assets	7,935	8,270	8,015	7,800
Current Liabilities	3,267	3,676	4,022	3,829
Bonds	1,087	1,074	955	983
Preferred Mandatory	0	0	0	0
Preferred Stock	0	0	0	0
Common Stock	83	82	81	81
Other Stockholders' Equity	1,918	1,689	1,845	1,796
Total Liabilities and Equity	7,935	8,270	8,015	7,800

Income Statement	Dec-98 US$MM	Dec-97 US$MM	Dec-96 US$MM	Dec-95 US$MM
Total Revenues	10,323	8,617	8,696	8,347
Cost of Sales	9,596	8,229	8,331	6,311
Other Expenses	39	377	65	31
Loss Provision	45	160	63	50
Interest Expense	260	168	165	141
Income Pre Tax	564	−171	130	242
Income Tax	209	−9	81	100
Income Continuing	310	−46	156	209
Discontinued	15	31	0	0
Extraordinary	0	0	0	0
Changes	0	0	0	0
Net Income	325	−15	156	209
EPS Primary	$4.09	($0.20)	$2.08	$2.80
EPS Diluted	$4.06	($0.20)	$2.07	$2.76

Exhibit 4   Whirlpool Financial Statements

Source: Whirlpool Annual Reports.

for this decision. First, recent changes in government regulations in both countries made it possible for foreign corporations to own a controlling interest in a manufacturing company. Second, the large populations of India and China reduced the risk of establishing large-scale operations there.

Whirlpool decided that the best way to enter the Asian market was through joint ventures, as they would allow the company to quickly establish a manufacturing presence in Asia. Once it had accomplished this goal, Whirlpool planned to build its own manufacturing facilities in the region. In 1987, Whirlpool announced an agreement with Sundram Clyton of India to manufacture compact washers for the Indian market, a joint venture which later became known as Whirlpool Washing Machines Limited. In 1993,

| | Dec-97 | Sales (in millions of US dollars) | | |
		Dec-96	Dec-95	Dec-94
North America	5263	5310	5093	5048
Europe	2343	2494	2428	2373
Asia	400	461	376	205
Latin America	624	268	271	329
Other	−13	−10	−5	−6
Total	**8617**	**8523**	**8163**	**7949**

| | Dec-97 | Operating Profit (in millions of US dollars) | | |
		Dec-96	Dec-95	Dec-94
North America	546	537	445	522
Europe	54	−13	92	163
Asia	−62	−70	−50	−22
Latin America	28	12	26	49
Restructuring charge	−343	−30		−248
Business dispositions	−53			60
Other	−159	−158	−147	−154
Total	**11**	**278**	**366**	**370**

Exhibit 5   Whirlpool Business Unit Sales and Operating Profit

Source: Whirlpool Annual Reports.

the Asian group established regional headquarters in Tokyo and a pan-Asian marketing, product development, and technology center in Singapore.

Whirlpool intensified its Asian acquisition strategy in 1995 with various acquisitions and joint ventures in both India and China. The company bought controlling interest in Kelvinator in India, combined it with Whirlpool Washing Machines Limited, and renamed the new entity Whirlpool of India (WOI). In addition to giving Whirlpool a 56% interest in WOI, the Kelvinator purchase gave the company direct access to more than 3,000 trade dealers in India. Between 1994 and 1995, the company also set up four joint ventures in China, as it believed that China's market for appliances was likely to equal or surpass that of North America within ten years. By 1996, Whirlpool's investment in Asia had reached $350 million and they employed over 12,000 people. In 1997, the Asian businesses generated over $400 million in sales.

Despite its investments, however, the company suffered operating losses in Asia of $70 million in 1996 and $62 million in 1997. In 1997, Whirlpool decided to restructure its Chinese operations when overcapacity in the refrigerator and air-conditioning markets drove prices down significantly. In 1997, Whirlpool decided to find strategic alternatives for the two money-losing joint ventures which catered to these two markets.

Smaller Chinese companies were also seizing considerable market share away from the multinational foreign competition. Haier, a Chinese producer of air conditioners, microwave ovens, refrigerators, and dishwashers publicly announced plans to become a global brand by 2002 and had already expanded into Indonesia and the Philippines. In addition, the Chinese government was strongly encouraging consumers to "buy Chinese."[26] Too many producers were making similar goods, and production soon outpaced demand. For example, although Whirlpool believed it would take approximately five to six years for the market to become saturated, the refrigerator and air conditioning markets were deemed saturated just two years after Whirlpool established its joint ventures in China. In addition, the company's Asian operations produced products of poorer quality than its Japanese rivals.[27]

Competition and overcapacity were not the only problems for Whirlpool. The company had overestimated the size of the market. The Chinese middle class that could afford new home appliances numbered only about 120 million and there was no tradition in China of changing appliances that worked properly.

Once in China, Whirlpool also realized that it had not properly understood the distribution system. The company discovered that there were huge geographical distances between Chinese cities and that the country lacked strong distribution channels. The company had not expected to face major problems with telecommunications and, despite the country's huge labor supply, Whirlpool had difficulties finding qualified people for its factories.

The situation in India was similar. Despite having invested heavily in advertising and promotions, Whirlpool blamed overcapacity and difficult trading conditions in the refrigerator sector for its losses. Nevertheless, Whitwam remained confident:

> Our lower cost structure and focus on the remaining majority-owned joint ventures in China, combined with our strong market position in India and Asia-Pacific sales subsidiaries, leave Whirlpool well positioned for future growth and profitability in this region . . . Our growing knowledge of Asia and ability to draw on the other global resources of Whirlpool will lead to continued improvement in our operating performance in 1998 and beyond, especially as we manage through a difficult market and economic environment.[28]

Whirlpool continued to invest money in India and committed over $100 million to build a new plant near Pune to produce chlorofluoro-carbon-free and frost-free refrigerators for the Indian market. The company began construction of the new facility in 1997 and the factory began commercial production in the first quarter of 1998.

LATIN AMERICAN EXPANSION

Throughout most of the 1990s, Brazil was Whirlpool's most profitable foreign operation.[29] The company first bought into the Brazilian market in 1957 and held equity positions in three companies: Brasmotor S.A., Multibras, and Embraco. These companies held a 60% market share and after 40 years of operating in Brazil, had extremely high brand recognition and brand loyalty. Whirlpool took over Philips' Argentine subsidiary, SAGAD, in 1992. In the mid-90s, sales and profit figures were good, with sales up 28% in 1994–1995, and 15% in 1996. In 1997, Brazilian operations recorded approximately $78 million in earnings.

Because Latin America had lower appliance penetration rates than Europe and the United States (e.g., only 15% of Brazilian homes owned microwaves, compared with 91% in the United States), the region appeared to be a good target for expansion. By the mid-1990s, Latin America was beginning to achieve economic stability, and growth was sure to follow. Consumers felt the same way. Many consumers were now able to replace old and worn-out appliances using budget plans and credit arrangements.

In 1997 in Brazil, Whirlpool spent $217 million to increase its equity share in Brasmotor from 33% to 66%. Whirlpool then invested another $280 million in 1997 and 1998 to renew plants and product lines. The company introduced data transfer systems, flexible production lines, and launched new products. Shortly after Whirlpool made these large investments in Brazil, however, interest rates in the country began to climb. The Brazilian government doubled interest rates in October 1997 and again in 1998. As a result, the currency depreciated and the economy suffered. In real terms, the *real* fell more than 50% in the six months prior to January 1999. Total foreign investment in Brazil slumped, and the country was eventually forced to request a $41.5 billion credit line from the International Monetary Fund in order to help rescue the economy.

Worse yet, Whirlpool's market research told them that consumers had reacted quickly to the economic problems. Many were afraid of job cuts in the worsening economy and were wondering whether Brazil would resort to the traditional solution of printing money to solve the economic problems. Consumers foresaw inflation and realized that they would not be able to afford to purchase Whirlpool's appliances, especially on credit. As Antonio da Silva, a 37-year-old maintenance worker said, "I'm afraid to pay over many months because you don't know if interest rates or inflation will rise again."[30]

In 1998, Whirlpool's Brazilian sales fell by 25%, or $1 billion.[31] Equally important, Whirlpool's *real* reserves had shrunk in value against the dollar, and the company was expecting inflationary pressures. As a result, in late 1998 the company announced more restructuring to its Latin American operations. Whirlpool immediately cut 3,200 jobs (about 25% of the workforce) to improve efficiency, and the company planned to cut out levels in the production chain in its seven factories in Brazil, Argentina, and Chile. At the same time, the company increased its marketing efforts in the region.

As of 1998, Whirlpool was still confident of a return to profitability in Latin America. The company believed that industry shipments to Brazil in 1999 would equal those in 1997. *Business Week* characterized the company as bullish:

> The experience of surviving Brazil's many debt crises, bouts of hyperinflation, and military governments has given Whirlpool a been-there, done-that aura of confidence.[32]

But, given Whirlpool's poor showing in the earlier phases of its globalization plan, it still had far to go in convincing the many skeptics and disappointed shareholders that globalization was the best strategy. Many analysts were unsure whether Whirlpool's self-confidence was actually deserved or if it was little more than self-delusion.

NOTES

1. C. Quintanilla and J. Carlton, "Whirlpool Announces Global Restructuring Effort," *Wall Street Journal*, 19 Sept. 1997: A3, A6.

2. Weiss, David D. and Andrew C. Gross, "Industry Corner: Major Household Appliances in Western Europe," *Business Economics*, Vol. 30, Issue 3, July 1995: 67.

3. Echikson, William, "The Trick to Selling in Europe," *Fortune*, 20 Sept. 1993: 82.

4. Maruca, Regina Fazio, "The Right Way to Go Global: An Interview with Whirlpool CEO David Whitwam," *Harvard Business Review*, March-April 1994: 137.

5. Weiss and Gross.

6. Jancsurak, Joe, "Holistic Strategy Pays Off," *Appliance Manufacturer*, Feb. 1995: W-3, W-4.

7. Steinmetz, Greg and Carl Quintanilla, "Tough Target: Whirlpool Expected Easy Going in Europe, and It Got a Big Shock," *Wall Street Journal*, 10 April 1998: Sec. A:1.

8. Schiller, Zachary, et al., "Whirlpool Plots the Invasion of Europe," *BusinessWeek*, 5 Sept. 1988: 70.

9. Jancsurak, Joe, "Group Sales: Channel Focused," *Appliance Manufacturer*, Feb. 1995: W-14.

10. "Group Sales," W-14.

11. Babyak, Richard J., "Strategic Imperative," *Appliance Manufacturer*, Feb. 1995: W-21.

12. Babyak, Richard J., "Demystifying the Asian Consumer," *Appliance Manufacturer*, Feb. 1995: W-26.

13. Jancsurak, Joe, "South American Sales Co.: Linking the Americas, Europe," *Appliance Manufacturer*, Feb. 1995: W-39.

14. Maruca, p. 136.

15. Maruca, p. 137.

16. Maruca, p. 136.

17. Whirlpool Corporation, Annual Report, 1997.

18. Maruca, p. 145.

19. Steinmetz and Quintanilla, A:6.

20. Steinmetz and Quintanilla, A:1, A:6.

21. "Holistic Strategy," W-3.

22. Steinmetz and Quintanilla, A:6.

23. Jancsurak, Joe, "Marketing: Phase 2," *Appliance Manufacturer*, Feb. 1995: W-10.

24. Steinmetz and Quintanilla, A:6.

25. Steinmetz and Quintanilla, A:6.

26. Shuchman, Lisa, "Reality Check," *Wall Street Journal*, 1998 April 30: Global Investing Section: 1.

27. Vlasic, Bill and Zachary Schiller, "Did Whirlpool Spin Too Far Too Fast?" *BusinessWeek*, 24 June 1996: 136.

28. Whirlpool Corporation. Annual Report, 1997.

29. Katz, Ian, "Whirlpool: In the Wringer," *BusinessWeek*, 14 Dec. 1998: 83.

30. Katz, 83.

31. Katz, 83.

32. Katz, 83.

THUNDERBIRD
THE GARVIN SCHOOL OF INTERNATIONAL MANAGEMENT

WAL-MART STORES INC.: DOMINATING GLOBAL RETAILING

Prepared by Professor Kannan Ramaswamy

Mr. Lee Scott could afford the look of confidence. He had just spoken to investment analysts about the phenomenal results from the second quarter of 2003. Despite the general weakness in the world economy and the uncertain environment that prevailed, Wal-Mart had reported sales growth of 11%, amounting to $6.4 billion. The company's associates were indeed doing the Wal-Mart cheer in faraway places like Germany, South Korea, China, and the United Kingdom. In three decades, it had grown from its rural Arkansas roots to become the world's largest company, and quite possibly the most powerful retailer.

The meteoric growth did bring with it a fair share of problems. At a macro level, there had always been questions about the ability of Wal-Mart to sustain the pace of growth it had demonstrated in recent years. Once the company vaulted over the $200 billion level in annual sales, it was clear that incremental growth would be challenging. There was a nationwide backlash against big-box retailers, and Wal-Mart was front and center in that controversy. Some of the upstart chains such as Dollar General were gearing up to nip at the heels of Wal-Mart. They claimed that customers felt lost inside the cavernous stores of Wal-Mart and that they would gladly shop at Dollar General stores, which, although much smaller, offered comparable low prices.

The emerging markets that held a lot of promise were being bitterly contested by other major players such as Carrefour, Metro, Auchan, Ahold, and Tesco. Since many of these competitors had moved into the international marketplace long before Wal-Mart, there was an experience curve handicap that Wal-Mart had to contend with.

From an operational viewpoint, the suppliers were in for a rocky ride, since the nature of their relationship with Wal-Mart had begun to change radically. Given its huge base of power, the company was able to extract significant price concessions from its suppliers. It had recently intensified promotion of its own labels and store brands that competed directly against the likes of Procter & Gamble (P&G) and Kraft. The suppliers felt that their long years of belt-tightening were not being rewarded by Wal-Mart and that they were increasingly asked to do more for less. Some had been reduced to contract manufacturers, churning products that would be sold under one of Wal-Mart's many labels.

All was not well within the Wal-Mart family either. Some employees had filed suit against Wal-Mart, alleging that the company forced them to work overtime without any pay. This suit, some believed, had the makings of a large class-action suit, probably amongst the biggest in the realm of employment law in recent years. A similar case in Oregon was decided in favor of the employees. There was yet another pending lawsuit that charged that the company routinely discriminated against women in job promotions, especially at the supervisory and managerial levels. It was reported that although roughly 90% of Wal-Mart associates were women, they represented only 15% of the positions in top management, a disparity that was at the heart of the gender discrimination suit. To complicate matters further, in late October 2003, Wal-Mart was the target of raids by the Immigration and Naturalization Service of the U.S. Government. The agency reported that it was examining whether Wal-Mart was hiring illegal immigrants in contravention of the law.

The challenges were indeed formidable, despite the legendary strengths that the company had built upon in the past. Even Mr. Lee Scott acknowledged the uphill climb when he observed, "We'd be silly to sit here and tell you it's not a challenge."[1] Although Wal-Mart had systematically decimated the negative projections of analysts in the past, it was once again the subject of doubt and naysaying. Mr. Scott had to prove himself all over again.

THE WORLD OF DISCOUNT RETAILING

Discount retailing had evolved into a global industry within a fairly short span of time. Pushed in large part by Wal-Mart in the U.S. and counterparts such as Carrefour, Ahold, Metro, Tesco, and others worldwide, global discount chains had cornered a significant chunk of the global retail business. The fundamentals of the business models that had evolved in various parts of the world seemed to coalesce around the principles that had been perfected by Wal-Mart. All the chains leveraged global economies of scale in purchasing, and negotiated favorable volume-based contracts with manufacturers, many of whom were themselves global. Coupled with sophisticated information systems that optimized supply chain planning and execution, the retailers were able to cut a lot of excess cost from the system and pass on some of the savings to the end customer. The competitive battle was, therefore, fought largely in terms of their ability to lure shoppers on the basis of their merchandise mix, price offers, and convenience. International expansion outside their own regions of familiarity became the norm rather than the exception. Carrefour, for example, operated in 32 countries; many of them, such as Taiwan and Brazil, were distinctly different from France, the company's home base. The global expansion was based on the simple premise that customers everywhere, irrespective of nationality, would be attracted to the value of the offer that the global retail chains

Rank	Retailer	Sales ($bn)	Earnings ($ mil)	Stores (#)	Nationality
1	Wal-Mart	244.5	8039	4688	USA
2	Carrrefour	86.3	1440	9725	French
3	Ahold	81.7	n/a	8800	Dutch
4	Metro	57.9	464	2310	German
5	Tesco	45.8	1178	2291	British

Exhibit 1   The World's Five Leading Global Retailers*

Source: DSN Retailing Today, July 7, 2003, and MMR, May 26, 2003.

*Data for 2002.

Country	Global Retailers (#)
France	14
Poland	13
Spain	12
Germany	11
USA	11
Belgium	11
UK	10
Thailand	10
Taiwan	10
China	10
Portugal	10
Czech Republic	10
Denmark	8
Netherlands	7
Italy	7

Exhibit 2 Global Market Penetration by International Retailers*

*Data from www.planetretail.net 2004.

made—a selection of merchandise that was unrivalled at prices that were unequalled.

The evolution of the discount concept had come full circle, and the major players were locked in competitive battles that transcended mere national boundaries. They catered to a global customer base that was very much multi-cultural. They carefully orchestrated strategies in each country setting so that they could dominate both at the local and global levels, often using mergers and acquisitions to gain market share quickly. As a result of this growth trajectory, many of the large markets were contested by more than one global retailer. Competitive advantage in this elite group seemed to turn on deep pockets, innovative strategic thinking, and faultless execution. Contemporaneous with the jockeying for position in the developed country markets, the major chains were locked in battles for supremacy in the emerging markets as well. Many of the emerging markets had begun a wave of deregulation and allowed even *de novo* entry of established global players. Markets such as Argentina, Brazil, Hungary, Turkey, and India

were within sight of the global discount retailing revolution. Given the significantly higher growth rates that these markets promised, the early entrants were sure to profit.

CREATING THE WAL-MART EMPIRE

Mr. Sam Walton founded the first Wal-Mart in 1962, originally christened as Wal-Mart Discount City. The store was located in Rogers, Arkansas, a rural town of budget-conscious shoppers. The Wal-Mart concept had evolved from a chain of Ben Franklin stores that Mr. Walton and his brother operated in Arkansas and Missouri as franchisees. When Sam took his discount retailing concept to Ben Franklin's management, they did not seem interested in it. He decided to set off on his own—and the rest, as they say, is history.

Mr. Walton was an astute entrepreneur beyond compare. He quickly realized that volume and inventory-turn velocity were the defining elements of competitive advantage in the discount retail business. He was convinced that the concept would work in small towns with populations of 5,000 to 25,000 people, locations that often lacked viable retail alternatives. Armed with the conviction of a true entrepreneur, Mr. Walton and his brother had opened 18 Wal-Mart stores by 1969 when the company was incorporated formally. In a little over the three decades that followed, the company had 4,750 stores in a variety of formats across the globe, and sales had grown to roughly $245 billion. The company was widely seen as the beacon of shareholder value, the darling of investors, and the customer's champion.

Wal-Mart capitalized on its rural locations to establish important competitive advantages during its infancy. Many rural markets were characterized by populations that were scratching a subsistence level of living with very few employment alternatives. Mr. Walton saw this as a captive market that was tailor-made for a successful rollout of the discount retail model.

It also proved to be a recruiter's paradise where a steady job at a decent wage was all that was needed to attract employees to staff its stores. Retail competition was minimal, and this allowed some flexibility in pricing merchandise, since price wars were unlikely. Local labor and real estate costs were also much lower compared to competitors who were focused on the larger cities. The stores were decidedly austere in appearance. They were essentially big boxes illuminated brightly with fluorescent lighting, stocked with shelves that carried a wide range of merchandise. All of these advantages translated into a superior operating cost structure and a veritable fortress of profitability for Wal-Mart that its city rivals found impossible to duplicate.

The company was able to quickly expand its range of merchandise in becoming a convenient one-stop shop for a large rural base. However, the rural market strategy did come with its own challenges. Wal-Mart initially found it difficult to persuade its suppliers to serve the remote stores that formed its network. This meant that inventories were replenished more slowly, leaving empty shelves and lost sales. Since inventory velocity was such an important part of Mr. Walton's original concept, the company was forced into building large warehouses to fill its own needs. This subsequently led to establishing its own logistics operations, complete with a fleet of trucks, and a private satellite system as well. All of this saved money and helped the company deliver on its promise to offer some of the lowest prices to its customers.

In becoming the largest company in the world, Wal-Mart spawned a wide range of best practices across all managerial functions. The wheel had turned full circle from the days when Mr. Walton would scour discount chain competitors for best practices, to a time when Wal-Mart was being constantly studied for new wisdom on management and strategy. Contemporary thinking on retail operations, location, and supply chain management was being shaped by Wal-Mart's success.

THE WAY THINGS WORKED

By 2003, Wal-Mart stores were located very close to major cities, mostly along the outer edges in the suburbs. The rural network was still intact and the company had stores in all 50 states in the United States. All stores were quite uniform, both in their external and internal appearance. A substantial part of the real estate was leased and custom-built by the property owners. Given the fact that many of the smaller communities had been blanketed with stores, the company started driving into suburbs. It was, however, not met with quite the same enthusiasm that it received in the rural settings. Local community activists in various parts of the country were banding together to use zoning laws to keep the big-box retailer out of their backyard. It was against this backdrop that Wal-Mart started conceptualizing new store formats that would have a small enough footprint to remain unobtrusive.

Irrespective of the store format, some of the fundamentals remained the same. Every prospective Wal-Mart shopper was greeted at the door by a cheerful greeter. Most of the greeters were senior citizens from the local communities. The company found that the greeters had the desirable effect of reducing pilferage as well, and the cheerful welcome did help the courteous image. The shelves were fully stocked with a wide range of products—over 120,000 in standardized layouts. The stores did not carry any backroom inventory, and this helped maximize retail selling space. Each store was broken down into smaller departments such as housewares, pharmaceuticals, and horticulture—each with a department manager in control. A substantial portion of employee bonuses was linked to departmental level performance, thus motivating employees to do their best within their assigned departments. Although centrally orchestrated, managers did have some leeway in adjusting prices to factor in local realities. Wal-Mart did not necessarily price its products below the lowest competitor price; instead, it aimed to set prices as low as possible. This meant that the prices did vary from store to store to reflect the level of competition that prevailed. The company did very little direct advertising. In contrast to competitors such as Target, who regularly featured glossy advertisements, Wal-Mart limited its advertising to 12 or 13 circulars a year. The circulars reflected the same bare-bones approach that the stores had adopted. There were no expensive models or glossy spreads. The company used its own associates as models for the circulars, and even used it as a motivational tool by choosing associates based on their performance.

Selling to Wal-Mart

The second worst thing a manufacturer can do is sign a contract with Wal-Mart. The worst? Not sign one.

—Anonymous Consultant[2]

Wal-Mart managed all its purchasing functions from its offices in Bentonville, Arkansas. It deployed a fairly small group of buyers who were charged with managing the entire buying function for the giant retailer. Manufacturers were not permitted to use middlemen or agents to mediate the relationship with the buyers. All negotiations were carried out in small, windowless offices with a décor that could be described as Spartan at best—"one fluorescent light, one table, one photo of Mr. Sam."[3] The buyers were tough negotiators and demanded a wide array of price and service concessions. For example, Mr. Katzenberg, CEO of DreamWorks, one of the world's leading movie companies, was requested by Wal-Mart to produce a customized video of *Shrek,* a mega-hit cartoon character, doing the Wal-Mart cheer, as a motivating tool for Wal-Mart associates. DreamWorks produced a suitable video in keeping with Wal-Mart's wishes. Despite the bare-knuckles negotiating environment, Mr. Katzenberg observed, "I've been there three times in the last 45 days. I cannot tell you how much I respect and love the bare-essentials efficiency . . . I'm flattered by the opportunity

they've offered."[4] Indeed, Wal-Mart was the largest single revenue generator for Hollywood. The same was true of several other industries as well. For example, Wal-Mart in the U.S. was individually responsible for selling 35% of all pet food, 24% of all toothpaste,[5] the largest volume of jewelry, groceries, DVDs, CDs, toys, guns, diapers, sporting goods, bedding, and much, much more. Needless to say, this retail channel power was instrumental in helping establish a very favorable negotiating position for the company. Its purchasing volumes were gargantuan and the company had the power to bestow its riches on any supplier it chose. It was clear that the legion of over 30,000 suppliers needed Wal-Mart much more than Wal-Mart needed them, and they would do all they could to make sure that the retail giant was appeased and happy.

Right from its inception, the company had employed a "national brand" strategy in its merchandising. By carrying all the well-known brands at relatively lower prices, it was able to demonstrate the superior value it brought to its customers. The national brands were also important from an advertising point of view. Since the manufacturers either ran large campaigns themselves or shared campaign expenses with retailers, Wal-Mart was able to proportionately reduce its advertising budgets. The national brand approach was also central to Wal-Mart's approach of capturing market share from its competitors. For example, in September 2003, well ahead of the peak of the toy season, Wal-Mart began discounting the price of a dancing toy, a sure winner from Fisher Price, a unit of Mattel, the leader in toys. It was priced at an amazing 22% below what Toys 'R' Us was charging. Wal-Mart believed that its discounting approach would help customers clearly see where the bargains were and help pull market share from its toy store rivals. After all, national brands were quite visible and sought after. Mattel, however, was quite concerned that its brand might be tarnished as a result of such discounting practices.

Supplier Company	Main Products	% of Sales From Wal-Mart
Dial Corporation	Toilet soaps	28
Clorox Corporation	Liquid bleach	23
Mattel Corporation	Toys	23
Revlon	Perfumes/cosmetics	22.5
Procter & Gamble Co.	Toilet soaps, detergents	17
Energizer Holdings Inc.	Batteries	16.3
Kraft Foods	Packaged foods	12.2
Gillette Co.	Shavers, batteries	12
Kellogg Co.	Breakfast cereals	12

Exhibit 3   Wal-Mart's Influence Over Its Suppliers*

Source: Company annual reports.

Once the stores had gained some recognition of their own, Mr. Walton launched the idea for in-store brands, starting with a dog food named Ol' Roy after his pet golden retriever. Since then, the company leveraged its scale and shelf space to pit its own brands against those that are nationally established. The bad news for its suppliers was that Wal-Mart was winning big with its in-store brands. Ol' Roy, for example, was the world's largest selling dog food, outstripping such established giants as Ralston Purina and Nestle. Nationally, the trend toward store brands was gathering momentum. According to a study by A. C. Nielsen, national brands grew by 1.5% in 2001 and 2002, but store brands grew by 8.6%. The loss of share for the national manufacturers had been so steep that many of them had shifted their manufacturing capacity to produce store brands for the leading retailers such as Wal-Mart.[6] One analyst estimated that about 40% of Wal-Mart revenues were attributable to its in-store brands, which ran the gamut from batteries to ibuprofen, from tuna to dog food, and most other items in between.[7]

Getting Wal-Mart supplier credentials was a laborious and taxing process. The company articulated very stringent requirements ranging from product quality, shipping, stocking, and in-store displays. It required all its suppliers to transact business using Retail Link, a proprietary electronic data interchange (EDI), an information processing system that allowed the electronic tracking of purchase orders, invoices, payments, and inventories. The company had moved to require some of its suppliers to incorporate RFID (Remote Frequency Identification Devices) technology in all their packaging. These RFID chips were small, unobtrusive chips that would form part of individual packages of goods that the suppliers sold through Wal-Mart. This technology would offer the company significantly enhanced capabilities in tracking sales of individual items within the stores, a potential gold mine of inventory and customer preference data. Although many suppliers had to scale a steep learning curve and make significant resource commitments to make their operations compatible with Wal-Mart's automated technology demands, there were tangible payoffs. Given the close linkage with Wal-Mart, the system allowed suppliers to monitor inventory levels and stock movements in each store. This was valuable in understanding customer preferences and also in predictive modeling to plan for inventory several months ahead of time. The company was a willing teacher, often educating its suppliers on the finer points of cost control and efficiency. It routinely dispensed advice to its suppliers on how they could redesign their product, packaging, or process to reduce costs. When Wal-Mart taught, the suppliers were willing pupils. Jack Welch, the former CEO of General Electric, once observed that he learned more about the customers who bought GE light bulbs from Wal-Mart's supplier reports than he did from his own marketing department. After all, the relationship between the manufacturer and the end user was no longer a direct one. It increasingly went through Wal-Mart.

Raising prices was unheard of. Suppliers who sent in invoices at higher prices compared to the past continued to be compensated at old rates. Wal-Mart simply ignored price increases. As a matter of management practice, it had even begun billing its suppliers for missed or delayed deliveries. It was experimenting with a new system called *Scan 'n Pay* under which suppliers would be paid for an item after it had been scanned out upon sale to a customer. Thus, the supplier was actually going to bear much of the risk associated with the goods that it had offered for sale at Wal-Mart. Suppliers had to participate in *Roll Back* campaigns which were essentially funded by selling at extremely low margins, often much lower than the already low margins that Wal-Mart negotiated. The roll-back price offerings were meant to attract store traffic.

Rubbermaid's brush with Wal-Mart was a textbook example of the company's approach to supplier management. When resin prices rose by 80%, Rubbermaid was forced to increase its prices for plastics products that were bestsellers at Wal-Mart stores. Wal-Mart believed that Rubbermaid ought to absorb much of the price increases instead of passing it along to buyers. When Rubbermaid seemed disinclined to listen, Wal-Mart cut the shelf space it had allocated for Rubbermaid products and promoted competitors who were more willing to listen. Rubbermaid was soon forced into a merger with Newell as a consequence.

On-time delivery was not just a goal that suppliers aspired to reach—it was demanded as a prerequisite for a continued working relationship with Wal-Mart. On-time delivery meant that the products were expected to show up just as they were needed—not earlier, and certainly not later. There was an opportunity cost associated with empty shelf space, and the supplier who caused the stockout was held responsible for compensating

the company. These penalties were typically deducted before Wal-Mart settled its payments with the supplier in question. The company used a supplier scorecard to keep track of the performance metrics of each of its suppliers. Much of this data was also accessible to the suppliers in the spirit of full transparency. In addition to superior supply-chain performance, suppliers were required to uphold quite stringent standards of employment and fair labor practices at all their manufacturing facilities worldwide. Wal-Mart deputed audit teams to ensure compliance at manufacturer locations. The range of standards included issues such as compensation and overtime pay, working conditions and environment, and discrimination. All suppliers were required to prominently display the Wal-Mart code of standards at their facilities. Although this had the desirable effect of emphasizing an image of honesty and fairness, critics often viewed these measures with suspicion, seeing them as public relations ploys.

In building its *Modular Category Assortment Planning System* (MCAP), Wal-Mart designated *category captains* in each product category. The category captain had to pull together a variety of such packages integrating its own products with those of other competitors. These packages had to take into account local demand patterns and preferences, store traffic flows, and mix of price points to fit with market needs. Some of the category captains designed over a thousand such integrated packages each year for Wal-Mart.

Suppliers employed a wide variety of strategies to sell to Wal-Mart. These options ranged from passive submission to the dictates of the giant retailer, to active engagement in maximizing their own piece of the Wal-Mart pie. Newell-Rubbermaid exemplified a creeping shelf-capture approach. It offered a wide range of largely nonseasonal, low-technology, high-volume essentials that were relatively low priced. It positioned itself as a single source for a large range of products that included a diverse portfolio spanning paint brushes, blinds, storage containers, plastic furniture, writing instruments, household tools, and cookware. Although seemingly diverse, the company used its portfolio to acquire more and more shelf space at the mass-market retailers. Wal-Mart accounted for 16% of Newell's sales in 2003. The company had positioned itself as a very responsive, highly flexible supplier, often taking the lead in proposing new ways to improve retailer efficiency. Newell was the originator of the legendary supplier scorecard that Wal-Mart used to rate all its suppliers. Its inventory management skills were admired at Wal-Mart to such an extent that Wal-Mart began using Newell as the benchmark for supplier performance. Newell had even invested a sizable sum in building a scaled version of a Wal-Mart store at its Bentonville office. It experimented with various in-store displays and storage optimization techniques, using its scale model of the store, before recommending alternatives to the giant retailer. It adopted a good, better, best approach to managing its product lines. Each line had options across the three price points. This provided the important benefit of capturing shelf space because the mass market retailer did not have to shop with multiple suppliers to fill out its offerings across a range of price points. Newell had multiple sales teams that specialized in each product line. Initially, this had the additional advantage of having different personnel negotiate with Wal-Mart buyers for distinct pieces for Newell's business. However, all its dealings with Wal-Mart were internally coordinated through a separate office dedicated to Wal-Mart and managed by a presidential level executive. It continuously sought to acquire new product lines by taking over poorly managed manufacturing operations. Every single acquisition had to meet the basic requirement of using the mass retailer as its primary sales channel. These acquisitions benefited from the pre-existing relationship with retailers such as Wal-Mart who were willing to give the new lines a shot in the marketplace. The company was very forthcoming in sharing its insights about its customers and product ideas with Newell, all in the name of making Wal-Mart a more comprehensive shopping experience. After all, distribution channel access was half the battle.

Rayovac, the battery manufacturer, chose a different path in entrenching itself at Wal-Mart. To begin with, it offered prices that were about 20% lower than Duracell and Energizer, the competing battery brands. In some cases, it was able to offer 50% more product at the same price points as its competitors. This was an important encouragement to Wal-Mart, which proceeded to designate more shelf space for Rayovac products. Seeing the rise of Rayovac's market share, Wal-Mart declared that it would enter the battery business with its own private label. Although Rayovac shares dropped dramatically in response to the announcement, the company was able to work out a private label manufacturing arrangement with Wal-Mart, restricting the entry to alkaline batteries. The belief was that Rayovac's superior branding and dominant market share (> 80%) in its high margin products, batteries for hearing aids, would be protected from the Wal-Mart juggernaut. This strategy had the twin benefits of giving Wal-Mart what it wanted and at the same time ensuring that Duracell and Energizer were held at bay. Rayovac had, in essence, used Wal-Mart to outrun its competitors. By 2003, Wal-Mart accounted for 26% of Rayovac revenues in a relationship that was very much similar to that between a vassal and the king. Rayovac even acquired Varta, a large battery manufacturer in Germany, to keep pace with Wal-Mart's globalization effort.

Leveraging Technology and Logistics

Wal-Mart was a leader in the use of technology to maximize operational efficiency. Very early on, the company realized the value of proactive investments in technology and deployed a private satellite network. The satellite network worked in conjunction with the EDI system and a point-of-sales system to capture store sales data in real time. Every time a customer made a purchase, the point-of-sales system transmitted the details of the transaction through the satellite network to the warehouses which were the staging grounds for inventory management.

Wal-Mart had progressively moved from simple inventory management to data mining, an approach that offered the company rich insights into customer buying patterns. This allowed the company to better customize some of its offerings on a regional basis along with its usual traiting approaches which factored in local consumer tastes and preferences. These insights helped manufacturers understand regional differences much better and design their products accordingly.

The company managed much of its own logistics through a central hub-and-spoke system of warehouses and distribution centers. It was estimated that the corporate logistics department handled over a million loads each year. These central hubs were located in such a way as to cater to Wal-Mart stores within a 250-mile radius. All of them had easy access from interstates and were conveniently located in less-populated rural areas that were within driving distance from store concentrations. The warehouses were quite massive structures with loading and unloading bays on either side of the building. There was very little inventory storage in these centers. Instead, the company designed them to use cross-docking, a practice that allowed the transshipment of inventory from an inbound truck to an outbound truck that was loading to carry merchandise to the stores. The whole process was orchestrated through a system of conveyors within the warehouse to route the correct merchandise to each truck. Much of the seasonal merchandise was unloaded from trucks coming in from manufacturers to trucks that were outbound to stores in a matter of ten minutes. Distribution orders were generated based on previous-day sales, with allowances for weather patterns and seasonality. This resulted in a replenishment cycle that was only 48 hours long at most.

During the return leg of the trip to deliver merchandise, the trucks stopped off at manufacturer locations to haul inventory to the warehouses. This process, known as backhauling, minimized the need for contracted shipping services, and saved shipping costs. Instead, the suppliers had to pay a fee for using the Wal-Mart system for distribution. It was believed that most of the suppliers willingly did so because they were unable to match the efficiency levels that Wal-Mart's distribution setup offered. All suppliers were required to use the Retail Link system to keep the logistics planners in Bentonville informed about the availability of cargo for shipping to warehouses, thus enabling backhauling. It was a veritable logistics company with a level of efficiency that rivaled even dedicated trucking fleets. Appendix 1 provides indicators of comparative efficiency for major U.S. retailers.

Different Stores for Different Folks

By early 2004, Wal-Mart had come a long way from its big-box rural beginnings. It now operated four different store formats: Wal-Mart discount stores, Supercenters, Neighborhood Markets, and Sam's Clubs, in addition to its walmart.com online store. Within the U.S., the first three formats were referred to as *Domestic One* formats.

Appendix 2 provides comparative financial and operating statistics for major U.S.-based retailers that compete against Wal-Mart.

Culture, People, and Processes

By 2004, Wal-Mart was the largest employer in private industry worldwide. It counted over 1.3 million associates amongst its ranks. Mr. Walton had imparted a very strong sense of identity among his employees, which was largely rural at the time. The company employed a flat organizational structure with the store managers playing pivotal roles in linking management personnel in Bentonville with field operations.

Frugality was a central tenet at the company, and every associate was expected to fully adopt this value in all its manifestations. This meant that, as a matter of policy, all company travel was limited to economy class, although Wal-Mart had a fleet of 20 aircraft that ferried executives to various parts of its empire. Associates who traveled on buying trips to manufacturer locations were expected to stay in a budget motel. Even executives stayed two to a room and

Format	Size	Unique Features
Discount Stores	40,000–120,000 sq. ft. 80,000 SKUs 1,600 in operation	• The original format for Wal-Mart in rural locations • Brightly lit atmosphere • Wide product selection ranging from apparel to lawn and garden items • Offered the initial learning for the firm in inventory management
Supercenters	110,000–220,000 sq. ft. 100,000 SKUs, of which 30,000 are grocery items 1,300 in operation	• Combines fresh vegetables, dairy products, and other groceries with nonfood items • Open 24 hours a day • Includes additional features such as a tire and lube outlet, restaurant, portrait studio, film processing, hair salon, bank, and gas station • Ideal vehicle to leverage the frequency of grocery purchase to increase spillover nonfood revenues
Neighborhood Markets	42,000–55,000 sq. ft. 24,000 SKUs	• Targeted toward the urbane city markets • Styled as a more modern retail format with contemporary fittings and fixtures • Carries an extensive range of fresh vegetables, fruits, dairy products, and other groceries • More accessible in-city locations • Offers a drive-through pharmacy, bakery, and an in-store coffee bar • Typically located in markets where Supercenters are located so that distribution synergies can be leveraged while reaching a distinctly different market audience
Sam's Clubs	110,000–130,000 sq. ft. 4,000 SKUs	• Geared toward the small businesses that buy in bulk and large families that might be attracted to buying in larger quantities to take advantage of price discounts • Warehouse format with little customer service • Requires an annual membership ($35 for individuals and $30 for small businesses) to shop at these stores

Exhibit 4   Store Formats, Target Markets, and Unique Features

eschewed taxis to the extent possible. Wal-Mart's buyers sometimes called suppliers collect. New supplier proposals that lacked detail were returned at the expense of the suppliers. The company's headquarters were also reflective of the tightfistedness. They were housed in warehouse style buildings with a minimalist décor. Visitors had to pay for a cup of coffee or a soda even at headquarters.

The customer centric dictum permeated everything that Wal-Mart did. Mr. Walton had set out the basic tenets of the company upon its founding. These tenets included a "10-foot rule," which required every employee to greet a customer who came within ten feet of the employee. Mr. Walton exhorted all his associates to practice "aggressive hospitality," to exude caring, warmth, and hospitality towards every single customer who walked into the store. Given the rural roots of the company, these basic values of customer service became an integral part of the way in which Wal-Mart did business.

The company prided itself on the deep connections that it had with its associates. It offered a range of development opportunities spanning scholarships to college-bound associates, business skill acquisition programs, and a systematic mentoring program that paired successful managers with junior associates, to name a few. Almost all senior positions within the company were filled through promotions from within. Many amongst the upper echelon had started on the shop floor or in the warehouses and had moved their way up the ladder. Roughly 65% of Wal-Mart's management associates started out as hourly associates.

It hired locally for most of its foreign operations, supplementing the local workforce with a handpicked team of managers who had to go through a grueling program in the U.S. before they took charge of overseas operations. Employees who worked at the foreign stores had an equal chance at being promoted into management ranks and moved to headquarters. The company launched a new *Accelerated International Management Program* for a select group of associates who were identified for assuming leadership roles in international operations. This premier program was run collectively by the senior leadership of the company and focused on cross-border learning, knowledge management, and international best practices. The company was quite receptive to the idea of job enrichment and job rotation as a means of developing its human resources. Many of these lateral and vertical moves resulted from an elaborate performance appraisal system that the company had developed. The appraisal included elements of the 360° feedback approach under which the associates were evaluated by their peers, superiors, and subordinates.

Harnessing a veritable army of associates did indeed pose important challenges. The company was accused of paying very low wages—about $8.23 an hour in the case of sales clerks, according to *Business Week*.[8] This amounted to $13,861 per year, below the federal poverty line of $14,630 for a family of three. Its record in terms of employee diversity also came under increasing fire. Some critics noted that although women comprised 90% of the customer service managers, they accounted for only 15% of store manager positions. This alleged unfair labor practice was the subject of a lawsuit in California. This lawsuit had the potential of ballooning into a major issue for the company since the judge was considering class action status so that a large number of plaintiffs might join the class action against the company. Wal-Mart associates nationwide filed 40 cases against the company, alleging that it sought to keep labor costs low by leveraging its clout to force employees to work overtime without offering overtime pay.[9] These transgressions were closely watched by the unions who had always wanted to bring Wal-Mart employees under their fold. The nonunion moniker was being chipped away. The first salvo had been launched by the meat-cutters in a store in Jacksonville, Texas, who won the right to unionize in early 2003. They would have been the first group in 41 years to bargain collectively with Wal-Mart but for an operational change that was instituted by the company. Wal-Mart announced that it would sell only pre-cut meat in its stores, with immediate effect.

IT'S A SMALL WORLD AFTER ALL

Wal-Mart first set foot outside the U.S. in 1991 when it acquired a minority interest in a joint venture with a Mexican company, Cifra, a retailer of repute. In a short span of time, the company set up operations in nine countries with over 1,300 stores system-wide. By 2003, international operations accounted for close to 17% of total revenues. It had started in textbook fashion, sticking close to home with forays into countries of geographic proximity such as Mexico, Puerto Rico, and Canada. After penetrating promising regions of South America, the company had ventured into Europe.

Wal-Mart evaluated market potential based on economic and political risk, growth potential, and availability of real estate for development. In countries where the market had become saturated, Wal-Mart used acquisitions to gain a toe-hold. In markets where land was easily available, it pursued organic growth. The acquisition strategy paid off in locations such as Puerto Rico and the U.K. where the target firms were already adopting many of the core Wal-Mart practices, but in countries like Germany, there were big questions that remained.

The Americas

Wal-Mart launched it globalization efforts with an initial foray into Mexico with a local partner, Cifra. Boosted by the tremendous success of the Mexican operations, Wal-Mart increased its ownership position over time, and controlled 62% of Walmex, the joint venture, by 2004. The Mexican strategy was a blend of elements culled from the successful approach that the company had adopted in the U.S., along with significant local twists. The partner, Cifra, brought along a range of store formats and retail outlets including restaurants, apparel stores, a chain of Bodega Aurrera stores targeted at the lowest income strata, and Superama stores which were geared to middle- and high-income customers. The company managed to rationalize these different store formats, focusing on the Bodega stores as the primary vehicle for expansion along with Sam's Club and Supercenter concepts imported from the U.S. After some initial hiccups, the Mexican operations became an important shot in the arm for Wal-Mart, contributing 26% of all international revenues. The company leveraged important location specific advantages in Mexico to grow a supplier base at

relatively low cost and augment needs in other parts of the world. It held major buyer-seller meets and was able to groom close to 300 reliable suppliers with enough muscle to export to the U.S., and also pursue additional opportunities in other markets in the Wal-Mart empire. The Mexican retail experience served as a good template for stores in Brazil and Puerto Rico as well. In Brazil, for example, Wal-Mart duplicated many of the defining features of its Bodega stores from Mexico in its Todo Dia stores that were geared toward the low income customer segment. The company also pursued opportunistic product expansion in Mexico to enter segments that were outside the scope of traditional retail operations. For example, it offered a money transfer service between the U.S. and Mexico that targeted the immigrant community. This service was so popular that the industry leader, Western Union, witnessed steep declines in its market share.

The company's fortunes outside Mexico were quite mixed. Brazil and Argentina had been quite unstable given the fluctuating fortunes of their respective economies. In Brazil, the company was a victim of intense price wars and strategic maneuvering by its rival, Carrefour, which adopted aggressive tactics. Wal-Mart accused its rivals of leaning on suppliers to choke its supply lines. Carrefour demonstrated a new variation of the "Everyday Low Price" strategy when its employees began distributing fliers in Wal-Mart parking lots showing price comparisons between the two stores on an almost real-time basis. Wal-Mart had also taken longer to climb the experience curve in these markets since its merchandising approach had to be rethought several times before it captured the attention of the local customers. Rivals such as Carrefour were much ahead in the merchandising game and were able to leverage their longer experience in South America to their advantage.

Europe

Breaking into Europe was quite difficult and expensive. Wal-Mart first set foot in Europe

Country	Mode of Entry	Store Population	Associates
Argentina	Greenfield	11 Supercenters, 1 Distribution Center	4,000
Brazil	Greenfield	13 Supercenters, 9 Sam's Clubs, and 2 Todo Dia stores	6,000
Canada	Acquisition	213 Discount Stores	52,000
China	Joint venture	21 Supercenters, 5 Sam's Clubs, and 2 Neighborhood Stores	15,000
Germany	Acquisition	92 Supercenters	15,500
Japan	Joint venture	400 Supermarkets	30,500
Korea	Acquisition	15 Supercenters	3,000
Mexico	Joint venture	124 Bodega Stores, 51 Sam's Clubs, 78 Supercenters, and 457 other stores	96,000
Puerto Rico	Greenfield Acquired local chains after entry	9 Discount Stores, 9 Sam's Clubs, 2 Supercenters, and 33 other stores	11,000
United Kingdom	Acquisition	247 Discount Stores, 21 Distribution Centers	125,000
United States		1,494 Discount Stores, 1,386 Supercenters, 56 Neighborhood Markets, and 532 Sam's Clubs	Over 1 Million

Exhibit 5   Wal-Mart's Global Empire

when it acquired Wertkauf, a German retailer that had fallen on bad times in 1997. It subsequently bought another chain, Interspar, to gain more reach and size in the country. It proceeded to import its own management team from the U.S. to convert these chains into Wal-Mart stores. Wal-Mart's rural culture did not blend well with German sensibilities, and integration soon became a flashpoint. The peculiarities of German law that prohibited some of the staple discounting approaches of the company, combined with the language differences and distinctive market preferences, further accentuated the problems. Local competition was quite strong, and the reigning leader, Metro, A.G., proved to be a formidable competitor. The home-grown management talent was surprisingly unable to implement the Wal-Mart way at the new acquisitions. As one analyst observed, "One of the surprises about Wal-Mart is how weak in conventional managers they are. They are very good at what they do in the Wal-Mart way. But you wouldn't put them in the same roles in other groups."[10]

Beleaguered by troubles in Germany, Wal-Mart decided to search for a better foothold in Europe and was attracted to Asda, a Wal-Mart look-alike that had a sizable footprint in the U.K. Asda had imbibed some of the very same practices in inventory control, merchandising, and pricing that Wal-Mart had pioneered, right down to its own morning cheer. The acquisition proved to be phenomenally successful even at the steep price of £6.7 billion in 1999. Since Asda was a successful venture even at the time of the acquisition, and perhaps reeling from the bad experience at *Wal-Martization* in Germany, the company did not send in the troops of managers from Bentonville to oversee the Asda integration. Local managers were given much more leeway in decision-making. Asda managers actually helped Wal-Mart resuscitate its failing German business. They also developed new techniques in merchandising. John Menzer, the chief of Wal-Mart's International division, observed, "What we learnt from Asda is now incorporated in our systems in Korea, the U.S., South America, and everywhere."[11] One example was the adoption of the *George* line of fashion clothing that was developed by Asda. This line had proven to be such a powerful draw among the fashion-conscious buyers that Wal-Mart decided to bring the line to its operations in the U.S. as well. It was part of Wal-Mart's desire to expand its appeal to the up-market clientele that was the exclusive domain of Target, its competitor in the U.S. "As we grow around the world, it is important to our success that we exchange best practices among all the countries where we operate," observed Mr. Craig Herkert, Executive Vice President and COO of Wal-Mart International.

Although Asda had proven to be a remarkable success, the rivalry for supremacy in Europe was far from settled. Carrefour, Tesco, Ahold, and Metro were all fighting for the crown. Carrefour had a much wider reach and a portfolio of different store formats that seemed to give it an advantage in the marketplace where property was expensive. Tesco also proved to be a worthy rival since it, too, had originated with a "pile 'em high and sell 'em cheap" philosophy. It had expanded rapidly from its fresh-food origins as a grocer into nonfoods and hard goods. It had also built a network of stores across significant markets in Europe, especially in developing countries and emerging markets of the old Communist world. These were regions where price was a key competitive weapon and being first counted a lot.

Asia

Wal-Mart's Asia strategy began to unfold in 1996 with the opening of a Supercenter and a Sam's Club in the economically rich region of Shenzhen in China. The company later established operations in Korea through an acquisition of four stores from Makro. Given the relatively high real estate costs in Seoul, Wal-Mart adopted a multistory format, with stores often encompassing six to eight stories. Japan was the third component of the Asia strategy. Wal-Mart built on its Mexican experience with joint ventures and initially entered Japan through a minority joint venture with Seiyu, a well-established local retail chain. In two years, the company was quite happy with the results of the joint venture, and hence exercised its option to increase its holdings and become a majority partner. While China and Japan proved to be relatively successful entries, the performance in Korea was disappointing. Chains owned by the Korean *chaebols* had forged better supplier links than Wal-Mart could, and in a tradition-bound society, those ties were vital. These chains also had better access to real estate and, consequently, proved to be tenacious competitors.

China was especially promising since the company had been able to roll out many of its core strategies successfully. It bought 95% of its products locally, and even leveraged its Chinese supply network to export products worth $12 billion[12] to its U.S. operations and close to $20 billion by mid-2003. The company was China's eighth largest trading partner, ahead of Russia and the U.K. After entering Shenzhen, the company moved into Beijing through a separate joint-venture arrangement and also expanded to the rural heartland of the country. Asia was indeed a very promising market, but one fraught with challenges like the Korean experience had shown. It was clear that the company had a long way to go before it dominated these regional markets.

The value of the global network that Wal-Mart was building could be gleaned from a comment made by Mr. John Menzer, the Chief of International Operations at Wal-Mart. In describing the key elements of Wal-Mart's strategy for its apparel lines, Mr. Menzer observed, "Fashion starts in Europe. Next stop is now South America, because they are half a season behind. We're able to forecast U.S. buying patterns by what happens in South America. That is globalization."[13]

Being Big Isn't So Easy

As Wal-Mart moved forward to assert its dominance as the world's largest retailer, the road was not very clear. The company was increasingly coming under fire on a variety of fronts, ranging from employee compensation to supplier control and de facto censorship. On the competitive front, although there was no obvious threat that was readily visible, it was believed that the emergence of Dollar General and similar firms in the U.S. was serious enough to warrant a close watch. The mixed results of international expansion were yet another aspect that required long-term thinking.

Given the large size and reach that the company had built, many feared that it had grown to become too powerful. For example, some recording artists contended that Wal-Mart filtered the music that it sold in its stores, thus acting as a self-appointed censor. Music that was believed to carry a message that did not blend with Wal-Mart's values was not sold in its stores. This, some said, had a chilling effect on creativity and was working toward homogenizing the marketplace by letting smaller towns dictate popular culture. The same filtering effect was noticed in magazines and books. Publications such as *Maxim's* and *Stuff* were summarily banned from stores. The covers of magazines such as *Cosmopolitan, Glamour, Redbook,* and *Marie Claire* were routinely obscured with opaque binders. The enforcement appeared selective in the eyes of some. Wal-Mart claimed that it was just responding to the concerns expressed by the local community. The censorship even spread to drugs and medications. Wal-Mart was the only large pharmacy chain to refuse to stock *Preven,* a morning-after contraceptive manufactured by Gynetics that was legally approved for sale in the U.S. by the Food and Drug Administration. Gynetics' salespeople were apparently told that Wal-Mart did not want its pharmacists grappling with the moral dilemma of abortion. The drug, however, prevented pregnancies and did not cause abortions, according to the manufacturer. Mr. Roderick McKenzie, the founder of Gynetics, observed, "When you speak to God in Bentonville, you speak in hushed tones,"[14] although it did not seem to help Gynetics. Was Wal-Mart deciding what was good for the world?

Dollar Stores was a phenomenon that had the makings of a niche-based challenger. This company was catering to the low-income strata, "the salt of the earth" as it characterized it. The market was indeed sizable since 37% of all U.S. households earned less than $25,000 per year. Interestingly, this was also one of the fastest growing segments of the population. The Dollar General store was about 6,800 square feet—roughly $\frac{1}{6}$ the size of the smallest Wal-Mart store. It kept its inventory low by trimming the variety of products it offered. It carried about 3,500 items on average, leaning more heavily on hard goods and nonperishables. It used an innovative pricing approach that comprised only 20 price points, ranging from $1 to $35. The simplicity of this system was an important factor in attracting a customer's attention to potential bargains. The stores did not offer special sales, nor did they use advertising to attract customers. They relied on word-of-mouth instead. Although it was a tough negotiator when it came to suppliers, the suppliers were indeed happy to do business with Dollar General. After all, they were assured that they would not be competing against the top brand in their category. Dollar General largely relied on a #2 brand approach, stocking a selection of five or six brands at most, a mix that typically excluded the top industry brand. The company had over 6,000 stores in the U.S., most of them in communities of less than 25,000 or in low-income urban neighborhoods. The company relished its locations that were close to the big-box retailers. Mr. Cal Turner, Jr., remarked, "We love to be next to them. We are in a different niche. We're a convenience bargain store, and our prices are excellent, relative to theirs. They run their promotions . . . we inherit the traffic."[15] The company had almost doubled its sales revenue in the five-year period from 1999 to 2003. Although with over $6 billion in sales (it was still not anywhere comparable in size to Wal-Mart), it did seem to have the ingredients of a disruptive innovator in the retailing world.

NOTES

1. Neil Buckley, "As annual sales reach $240bn, can Wal-Mart conquer markets outside the U.S.?" *Financial Times*, January 8, 2003.

2. "Is Wal-Mart too powerful?" *Business Week*, October 6, 2003.

3. J. Useem, "One Nation under Wal-Mart," *Fortune*, March 3, 2003.

4. Ibid.

5. O. Thomas, "Lord of Things," *Business 2.0*, March 2002.

6. M. Boyle, "Brand killers," *Fortune*, August 11, 2003.

7. Ibid.

8. A. Bianco and W. Zellner, "Is Wal-Mart too powerful?" *Business Week*, October 6, 2003.

9. M. Freedman, "Wal-Mart's Women Trouble," www.forbes.com, July 22, 2003.

10. N. Buckley, "As annual sales reach $240 bn, can Wal-Mart conquer markets outside the U.S.?" *Financial Times*, January 8, 2003.

11. Ibid.

12. For the year 2002.

13. N. Buckley, "As annual sales reach $240 bn, can Wal-Mart conquer markets outside the U.S.?" *Financial Times*, January 8, 2003.

14. A. Bianco and W. Zellner, "Is Wal-Mart too powerful?" *Business Week*, October 6, 2003.

15. W. Joyce, N. Nohria, and B. Roberson, *What Really Works*. New York: HarperCollins. 2003.

APPENDIX 1: COMPARATIVE EFFICIENCIES (SALES PER FOOT: SPF) OF LEADING U.S. RETAILERS

Merchandiser	SPF 2000	SPF 2001	SPF 2002	Sq. ft. Basis	Avg. sq. ft. per Store	Sales per Store	Total Stores	Total Sales ($000)
Costco	$763	$757	$771	gross	137,000	105,683,152	374	37,993,093
Sam's Club	$469	$491	$497	gross	124,462	61,857,561	525	31,702,000
Wal-Mart	$387	$406	$422	gross	135,195	55,924,898	2,875	244,524,000
Target	$268	$274	$278	selling	122,280	32,942,045	1,147	36,236,250
Kmart	$236	$235	$212	selling	73,601	15,603,348	1,829	30,762,000
Dollar Tree Stores	$238	$217	$199	selling	5,442	1,083,000	2,263	2,329,188
Dollar General		$142	$148	gross	6,739		6,113	
Home Depot	$415	$388	$370	gross	108,000	40,144,000	1,532	58,247,000

Source: www.bizstats.com/spf1.htm.

APPENDIX 2: COMPARATIVE STATISTICS FOR LARGE U.S.-BASED DISCOUNT RETAILERS

Indicator	Wal-Mart			Costco			Dollar General			Target		
	2001	2002	2003	2000	2001	2002	2001	2002	2003	2001	2002	2003
Sales	193116	219672	244524	31621	34137	37993	4550	5322	6100	36851	39826	43917
Cost of sales	150255	171562	191838	28322	30598	33983	3300	3813	4376	25214	27143	29260
Operating expenses	31550	36173	41043	2805	3207	3648	935	1136	1297	8218	8924	10181
Advertising expenses	574	618	676							824	924	962
Operating profit	11311	11937	13644	1037	992	1131	1250	1509	1724	3419	3759	4476
Net income	6295	6671	8039	631	602	700	71	208	265	1264	1368	1654
Net income per share	1.4	1.49	1.81	1.35	1.29	1.48	0.21	0.62	0.79	1.4	1.52	1.82
Inventories	21644	22614	24891	2490	2739	3127	896	1131	1123	4248	4760	4449
Long-term debt	12501	15687	16607	790	859	1211	720	339	330	5634	8088	10186
Shareholders equity	31343	35102	39337	4240	4883	5694	862	1041	1288	6519	7860	9443
Total stores	4188	4414	4688	313	345	374	5000	5540	6113	1307	1381	1475
Total assets		83527	94685	8634	10090	11620		2552	2333		24154	28603
International sales												
International assets												
Operating profit (Intl)												
ROS (Intl)												
ROA (Intl)												
Cost of sales/sales	0.78	0.78	0.78	0.90	0.90	0.89	0.73	0.72	0.72	0.68	0.68	0.67
Operating margin	5.86%	5.43%	5.58%	3.28%	2.91%	2.98%	27.47%	28.35%	28.26%	9.28%	9.44%	10.19%
Net margin	3.26%	3.04%	3.29%	2.00%	1.76%	1.84%	1.56%	3.91%	4.34%	3.43%	3.43%	3.77%
Inventory/sales	0.11	0.10	0.10	0.08	0.08	0.08	0.20	0.21	0.18	0.12	0.12	0.10
Inventory turns	6.94	7.75	8.08	11.37	11.70	11.59	3.68	3.76	3.88	5.94	6.03	6.35
Operating exp./sales	0.16	0.16	0.17	0.09	0.09	0.10	0.21	0.21	0.21	0.22	0.22	0.23
Adv. exp/sales	0.30%	0.28%	0.28%							2.24%	2.32%	2.19%
Sales/assets		2.63	2.58	3.66	3.38	3.27		2.09	2.61		1.65	1.54
Return on assets		7.99%	8.49%	7.31%	5.97%	6.02%	8.24%	8.15%	11.36%		5.66%	5.78%
Return on equity		19.00%	20.44%	14.88%	12.33%	12.29%	19.98%	19.98%	20.57%	19.39%	17.40%	17.52%
Return on sales	3.26%	3.04%	3.29%	2.00%	1.76%	1.84%	1.56%	3.91%	4.34%	3.43%	3.43%	3.77%

THE GLOBAL BRANDING OF STELLA ARTOIS

*Prepared by Professors Paul W. Beamish
and Anthony Goerzen*

　　　　Version: (A) 2002-11-22

In April 2000, Paul Cooke, chief marketing officer of Interbrew, the world's fourth largest brewer, contemplated the further development of their premium product, Stella Artois, as the company's flagship brand in key markets around the world. Although the long-range plan for 2000–2002 had been approved, there still remained some important strategic issues to resolve.

A BRIEF HISTORY OF INTERBREW

Interbrew traced its origins back to 1366 to a brewery called Den Hoorn, located in Leuven, a town just outside of Brussels. In 1717, when it was purchased by its master brewer, Sebastiaan Artois, the brewery changed its name to Artois.

The firm's expansion began when Artois acquired a major interest in the Leffe Brewery in Belgium in 1954, the Dommelsch Brewery in the Netherlands in 1968, and the Brassiere du Nord in France in 1970. In 1987, when Artois and another Belgian brewery called Piedboeuf came together, the merged company was named Interbrew. The new company soon acquired other Belgian specialty beer brewers, building up the Interbrew brand portfolio with the purchase of the Hoegaarden brewery in 1989 and the Belle-Vue Brewery in 1990.

Interbrew then entered into a phase of rapid growth. The company acquired breweries in Hungary in 1991, in Croatia and Romania in 1994, and in three plants in Bulgaria in 1995. Again in 1995, Interbrew completed an unexpected major acquisition by purchasing Labatt, a large Canadian brewer also with international

interests. Labatt had operations in the United States, for example, with the Latrobe brewery, home of the Rolling Rock brand. Labatt also held a substantial minority stake in the second largest Mexican brewer, Femsa Cervesa, which produced Dos Equis, Sol, and Tecate brands. Following this major acquisition, Interbrew went on, in 1996, to buy a brewery in the Ukraine and engaged in a joint venture in the Dominican Republic. Subsequently, breweries were added in China in 1997, Montenegro and Russia in 1998, and another brewery in Bulgaria and one in Korea in 1999.

Thus, through acquisition expenditures of US$2.5 billion in the previous four years, Interbrew had transformed itself from a simple Belgian brewery into one of the largest beer companies in the world. By 1999, the company had become a brewer on a truly global scale that now derived more that 90 per cent of its volume from markets outside Belgium. It remained a privately held company, headquartered in Belgium, with subsidiaries and joint ventures in 23 countries across four continents.

THE INTERNATIONAL MARKET FOR BEER

In the 1990s, the world beer market was growing at an annual rate of one to two per cent. In 1998, beer consumption reached a total of 1.3 billion hectolitres (hls). There were, however, great regional differences in both market size and growth rates. Most industry analysts split the world market for beer between growth and mature markets. The mature markets were generally

Region	% of Global Consumption	Growth Index ('98 Vs '92)	Per Capita Consumption
Americas	35.1%	112.6	57
Europe	32.8%	97.7	54
Asia Pacific	27.2%	146.2	11
Africa	4.6%	107.7	8
Middle East/Central Asia	0.4%	116.0	2

Exhibit 1   The World Beer Market in 1998

Source: Canadean Ltd.

considered to be North America, Western Europe and Australasia. The growth markets included Latin America, Asia, Central and Eastern Europe including Russia. Although some felt that Africa had considerable potential, despite its low per capita beer consumption, the continent was not considered a viable market by many brewers because of its political and economic instability (see Exhibit 1).

Mature Markets

The North American beer market was virtually stagnant, although annual beer consumption per person was already at a sizeable 83 litres per capita (lpc). The Western European market had also reached maturity with consumption of 79 lpc. Some analysts believed that this consumption level was under considerable pressure, forecasting a decline to near 75 lpc over the medium term. Australia and New Zealand were also considered mature markets, with consumption at 93 lpc and 84 lpc, respectively. In fact, volumes in both markets, New Zealand in particular, had declined through the 1990s following tight social policies on alcohol consumption and the emergence of a wine culture.

Growth Markets

Given that average consumption in Eastern Europe was only 29 lpc, the region appeared to offer great potential. This consumption figure,

however, was heavily influenced by Russia's very low level, and the future for the large Russian market was unclear. Further, some markets, such as the Czech Republic that consumed the most beer per person in the world at 163 lpc, appeared to have already reached maturity. Central and South America, on the other hand, were showing healthy growth and, with consumption at an average of 43 lpc, there was believed to be considerable upside. The most exciting growth rates, however, were in Asia. Despite the fact that the market in this region had grown by more than 30 per cent since 1995, consumption levels were still comparatively low. In China, the region's largest market, consumption was only 16 lpc and 20 to 25 lpc in Hong Kong and Taiwan. Although the 1997 Asian financial crisis did not immediately affect beer consumption (although company profits from the region were hit by currency translation), demand in some key markets, such as Indonesia, was reduced and in others growth slowed. The situation, however, was expected to improve upon economic recovery in the medium term.

BEER INDUSTRY STRUCTURE

The world beer industry was relatively fragmented with the top four players accounting for only 22 per cent of global volume—a relatively low figure as compared to 78 per cent in the soft drinks industry, 60 per cent in tobacco and

44 per cent in spirits. This suggested great opportunities for consolidation, a process that had already begun two decades prior. Many analysts, including those at Interbrew, expected that this process would probably accelerate in the future. The driver behind industry rationalization was the need to achieve economies of scale in production, advertising and distribution. It was widely recognized that the best profit margins were attained either by those with a commanding position in the market or those with a niche position. However, there were several factors that mitigated the trend towards rapid concentration of the brewing industry.

One factor that slowed the process of consolidation was that the ratio of fixed versus variable costs of beer production was relatively high. Essentially, this meant that there was a limited cost savings potential that could be achieved by bringing more operations under a common administration. Real cost savings could be generated by purchasing and then rationalizing operations through shifting production to more efficient (usually more modern) facilities. This approach, however, required large initial capital outlays. As a result, in some markets with "unstable" economies, it was desirable to spread out capital expenditures over a longer period of time to ensure appropriate profitability in the early stages. A second factor that may have had a dampening effect on the trend towards industry consolidation was that local tastes differed. In some cases, beer brands had hundreds of years of heritage behind them and had become such an integral part of everyday life that consumers were often fiercely loyal to their local brew. This appeared to be a fact in many markets around the world.

INTERBREW'S GLOBAL POSITION

Through Interbrew's acquisitions in the 1990s, the company had expanded rapidly. During this period, the company's total volumes had increased more than fourfold. These figures translated to total beer production of 57.5 million hls in 1998 (when including the volume of all affiliates), as compared to just 14.7 million hls in 1992. Volume growth had propelled the company into the number four position among the world's brewers.

Faced with a mature and dominant position in the declining Belgian domestic market, the company decided to focus on consolidating and developing key markets, namely Belgium, the Netherlands, France and North America, and expansion through acquisition in Central Europe, Asia and South America. Subsequently, Interbrew reduced its dependence on the Belgian market from 44 per cent in 1992 to less that 10 per cent by 1998 (total volumes including Mexico). Concurrently, a significant milestone for the company was achieved by 1999 when more than 50 per cent of its total volume was produced in growth markets (including Mexico). Interbrew had shifted its volume so that the Americas accounted for 61 per cent of its total volume, Europe added 35 per cent, and Asia Pacific the remaining four per cent.

Taken together, the top 10 markets for beer accounted for 86 per cent of Interbrew's total volume in 1998 (see Exhibit 2). The Mexican beer market alone accounted for 37 per cent of total volume in 1998. Canada, Belgium, the United States and the United Kingdom were the next most important markets. However, smaller, growing markets such as Hungary, Croatia, Bulgaria, and Romania had begun to increase in importance.

Adding to its existing breweries in Belgium, France and the Netherlands, Interbrew's expansion strategy in the 1990s had resulted in acquisitions in Bosnia-Herzegovina, Bulgaria, Canada, China, Croatia, Hungary, Korea, Montenegro, Romania, Russia, the Ukraine, the United States, in a joint venture in South Korea, and in minority equity positions in Mexico and Luxembourg. Through these breweries, in addition to those that were covered by licensing agreements in Australia, Italy, Sweden and the United Kingdom, Interbrew sold its beers in over 80 countries.

Rank	Country	Volume (000 hl)	Market Share
1	USA	3,768	1.6%
2	China	526	0.3%
3	Germany	—	—
4	Brazil	—	—
5	Japan	—	—
6	UK	3,335	5.5%
7	Mexico	21,269	45.0%
8	Spain	—	—
9	South Africa	—	—
10	France	1,915	8.4%
Total		**30,813**	**3.6%**

Exhibit 2   Interbrew's 1998 Share of the World's Top 10 Markets

Source: Canadean Ltd.

INTERBREW'S CORPORATE STRUCTURE

Following the acquisition of Labatt in 1995, Interbrew's corporate structure was divided into two geographic zones: the Americas and Europe/Asia/Africa. This structure was in place until September 1999 when Interbrew shifted to a fully integrated structure to consolidate its holdings in the face of industry globalization. Hugo Powell, formerly head of the Americas division, was appointed to the position of chief executive officer (CEO). The former head of the Europe/Africa/Asia division assumed the role of chief operating officer, but subsequently resigned and was not replaced, leaving Interbrew with a more conventional structure, with the five regional heads and the various corporate functional managers reporting directly to the CEO.

RECENT PERFORMANCE

1998 had been a good year for Interbrew in terms of volume in both mature and growth markets. Overall, sales volumes increased by 11.1 per cent as most of the company's international and local brands maintained or gained market share. In

terms of the compounded annual growth rate, Interbrew outperformed all of its major competitors by a wide margin. While Interbrew's 1998 net sales were up 29 per cent, the best performing competitor achieved an increase of only 16 per cent. Of Interbrew's increased sales, 67 per cent was related to the new affiliates in China, Montenegro and Korea. The balance was the result of organic growth. Considerable volume increases were achieved also in Romania (72 per cent), Bulgaria (28 per cent), Croatia (13 per cent), and the United States (14 per cent). While volumes in Western Europe were flat, duty-free sales grew strongly. In the U.S. market, strong progress was made by Interbrew's Canadian and Mexican brands, and Latrobe's Rolling Rock was successfully relaunched. In Canada, performance was strong, fuelled by a two per cent increase in domestic consumption. Labatt's sales of Budweiser (produced under license from Anheuser Busch) also continued to grow rapidly.

Given that the premium and specialty beer markets were growing quickly, particularly those within the large, mature markets, Interbrew began to shift its product mix to take advantage of this trend and the superior margins it offered. A notable brand success was Stella Artois, for which total global sales volumes were up by

19.7 per cent. That growth came from sales generated by Whitbread in the United Kingdom, from exports, and from sales in Central Europe where Stella Artois volumes took off. The strong growth of Stella Artois was also notable in that it was sold in the premium lager segment. In Europe, Asia Pacific and Africa, Interbrew's premium and specialty beers, which generated a bigger margin, increased as a proportion of total sales from 31 per cent in 1997 to 33 per cent in 1998. This product mix shift was particularly important since intense competition in most markets inhibited real price increases.

Success was also achieved in the United States specialty beer segment where total volume had been growing at nine per cent annually in the 1990s. In 1998, Interbrew's share of this growing market segment had risen even faster as Labatt USA realized increased sales of 16 per cent. The other continuing development was the growth of the light beer segment, which had become over 40 per cent of the total sales. Sales of Labatt's Blue Light, for example, had increased and Labatt Blue had become the number three imported beer in the United States, with volumes up 18 per cent. Latrobe's Rolling Rock brand grew by four per cent, the first increase in four years. Interbrew's Mexican brands, Dos Equis, Tecate and Sol, were also up by 19 per cent.

Following solid volume growth in profitable market segments, good global results were realized in key financial areas. Net profit, having grown for each of the previous six consecutive years, was 7.7 billion Belgian francs (BEF) in 1998, up 43.7 per cent from the previous year. Operating profit also rose 7.9 per cent over 1997, from 14.3 to 15.4 BEF; in both the Europe/Asia/Africa region and the Americas, operating profit was up by 8.5 per cent and 4.9 per cent respectively. Further, Interbrew's EBIT margin was up 58.1 per cent as compared to the best performing competitor's figure of 17.0 per cent. However, having made several large investments in Korea and Russia, and exercising an option to increase its share of Femsa Cerveza in Mexico from 22 per cent to 30 per cent, Interbrew's debt-equity ratio increased from 1.04 to 1.35. As a result, interest payments rose accordingly.

Interbrew also enjoyed good results in volume sales in many of its markets in 1999. Although Canadian sales remained largely unchanged over 1998, Labatt USA experienced strong growth in 1999, with volumes up by 10 per cent. There was a positive evolution in Western European volumes as well, as overall sales were up by 6.5 per cent overall in Belgium, France and the Netherlands. Central European markets also grew with Hungary showing an increase of 9.6 per cent, Croatia up by 5.5 per cent, Romania by 18.9 per cent, Montenegro by 29 per cent, and Bulgaria with a rise of 3.6 per cent in terms of volume. Sales positions were also satisfactory in the Russian and Ukrainian markets. Further, while South Korean sales volume remained unchanged, volumes in China were 10 per cent higher, although this figure was still short of expectations.

INTERBREW CORPORATE STRATEGY

The three facets of Interbrew's corporate strategy, i.e., brands, markets and operations, were considered the "sides of the Interbrew triangle." Each of these aspects of corporate strategy was considered to be equally important in order to achieve the fundamental objective of increasing shareholder value. With a corporate focus entirely on beer, the underlying objectives of the company were to consolidate its positions in mature markets and improve margins through higher volumes of premium and specialty brands. Further, the company's emphasis on growth was driven by the belief that beer industry rationalization still had some way to go and that the majority of the world's major markets would each end up with just two or three major players.

Operations Strategy

Cross fertilization of best practices between sites was a central component of Interbrew's operations strategy. In the company's two main markets, Belgium and Canada, each brewery monitored its performance on 10 different dimensions against its peers. As a result, the gap between the best and the worst of Interbrew's operations had narrowed decisively since 1995. Employees continuously put forward propositions to improve processes. The program had resulted in significantly lower production costs, suggesting to Interbrew management that most improvements had more to do with employee motivation than with pure technical performance. In addition, capacity utilization and strategic sourcing had been identified as two areas of major opportunity.

Capacity Utilization

Given that brewing was a capital-intensive business, capacity utilization had a major influence on profitability. Since declining consumption in mature markets had generated excess capacity, several of Interbrew's old breweries and processing facilities were scheduled to be shut down. In contrast, in several growth markets such as Romania, Bulgaria, Croatia and Montenegro, the opposite problem existed, so facilities in other locations were used more fully until local capacities were increased.

Strategic Sourcing

Interbrew had begun to rationalize its supply base as well. By selecting a smaller number of its best suppliers and working more closely with them, Interbrew believed that innovative changes resulted, saving both parties considerable sums every year. For most of the major commodities, the company had gone to single suppliers and was planning to extend this approach to all operations worldwide.

Market Strategy

The underlying objectives of Interbrew's market strategy were to increase volume and to lessen its dependence on Belgium and Canada, its two traditional markets. Interbrew dichotomized its market strategy into the mature and growth market segments, although investments were considered wherever opportunities to generate sustainable profits existed. One of the key elements of Interbrew's market strategy was to establish and manage strong market platforms. It was believed that a brand strength was directly related to a competitive and dedicated market platform (i.e., sales and distribution, wholesaler networks, etc.) to support the brand. Further, Interbrew allowed individual country teams to manage their own affairs and many felt that the speed of success in many markets was related to this decentralized approach.

Mature Markets

Interbrew's goals in its mature markets were to continue to build market share and to improve margins through greater efficiencies in production, distribution and marketing. At the same time, the company intended to exploit the growing trend in these markets towards premium and specialty products of which Interbrew already possessed an unrivalled portfolio. The key markets in which this strategy was being actively pursued were the United States, Canada, the United Kingdom, France, the Netherlands and Belgium.

Growth Markets

Based on the belief that the world's beer markets would undergo further consolidation, Interbrew's market strategy was to build significant positions in markets that had long-term volume growth potential. This goal led to a clear focus on Central and Eastern Europe and Asia, South Korea and China in particular. In China, for example, Interbrew had just completed an acquisition of a second brewery in Nanjing. The Yali brand was thereby added to the corporate portfolio and, together with its Jingling brand, Interbrew became the market leader in Nanjing, a city of six million people.

In Korea, Interbrew entered into a 50:50 joint venture with the Doosan Chaebol to operate the Oriental Brewery, producing the OB Lager and Cafri pilsener brands. With this move, Interbrew took the number two position in the Korean beer market with a 36 per cent share and sales of 5.1 million hls. The venture with Doosan was followed in December 1999 by the purchase of the Jinro Coors brewery. This added 2.5 million hls and increased Interbrew's market share to 50 per cent of total Korean volume. Thus, the Interbrew portfolio in Korea consisted of two mainstream pilsener brands, OB Lager and Cass, the two local premium brands, Cafri and Red Rock, and Budweiser, an international premium brand.

In Russia, Interbrew expanded its presence by taking a majority stake in the Rosar Brewery in Omsk, adding the BAG Bier and Sibirskaya Korona brands. Rosar was the leading brewer in Siberia with a 25 per cent regional market share, and held the number four position in Russia. New initiatives were also undertaken in Central Europe with acquisitions of a brewery in Montenegro and the Pleven brewery in Bulgaria, as well as the introduction of Interbrew products into the Yugoslavian market. Finally, although Interbrew had just increased its already significant investment in Mexico's second largest brewer from 22 per cent to 30 per cent, Latin America remained a region of great interest.

Brand Strategy

A central piece of Interbrew's traditional brand strategy had been to add to its portfolio of brands through acquisition of existing brewers, principally in growth markets. Since its goal was to have the number one or two brand in every market segment in which it operated, Interbrew concentrated on purchasing and developing strong local brands. As it moved into new territories, the company's first priority was to upgrade product quality and to improve the positioning of the acquired local core lager brands. In mature markets, it drew on the strength of the established brands such as Jupiler, Belgium's leading lager brand, Labatt Blue, the famous Canadian brand, and Dommelsch, an important brand in the Netherlands. In growth markets, Interbrew supported brands like Borsodi Sor in Hungary, Kamenitza in Bulgaria, Ozujsko in Croatia, Bergenbier in Romania, Jingling in

China, and OB Lager in Korea. In addition, new products were launched such as Taller, a premium brand in the Ukraine, and Boomerang, an alternative malt-based drink in Canada.

A second facet of the company's brand strategy was to identify certain brands, typically specialty products, and to develop them on a regional basis across a group of markets. At the forefront of this strategy were the Abbaye de Leffe and Hoegaarden brands and, to a lesser extent, Belle-Vue. In fact, both Hoegaarden and Leffe achieved a leading position as the number one white beer and abbey beer in France and Holland. The Loburg premium pilsener brand also strengthened its position when it was relaunched in France. Further, in Canada, Interbrew created a dedicated organization for specialty beers called the Oland Specialty Beer Company. In its first year of operation, the brands marketed by Oland increased its volumes by over 40 per cent. More specifically, sales of the Alexander Keith's brand doubled and the negative volume trend of the John Labatt Classic brand was reversed. The underlying message promoted by Oland was the richness, mystique and heritage of beer.

To support the regional growth of specialty beers, Interbrew established a new type of café. The Belgian Beer Café, owned and run by independent operators, created an authentic Belgian atmosphere where customers sampled Interbrew's Belgian specialty beers. By 1999, Belgian Beer Cafés were open in the many of Interbrew's key markets, including top selling outlets in New York, Auckland, Zagreb and Budapest, to name a few. The business concept was that these cafés were to serve as an ambassador of the Belgian beer culture in foreign countries. They were intended to serve as vehicles to showcase Interbrew's specialty brands, benefiting from the international appeal of European styles and fashions. Although these cafés represented strong marketing tools for brand positioning, the key factors that led to the success of this concept were tied very closely to the individual establishments and the personnel running them. The bar staff, for example, had to be trained to serve the beer in the right branded glass, at the right temperature, and with a nice foamy head. It was anticipated that the concept of the specialty café would be used to support the brand development efforts of Interbrew's Belgian beers in all of its important markets.

The third facet of Interbrew's brand strategy was to identify a key corporate brand and to develop it as a global product. While the market segment for a global brand was currently relatively small, with the bulk of the beer demand still in local brands, the demand for international brands was expected to grow, as many consumers became increasingly attracted to the sophistication of premium and super-premium beers.

THE EVOLUTION OF INTERBREW'S GLOBAL BRAND STRATEGY

Until 1997, Interbrew's brand development strategy for international markets was largely *laissez faire*. Brands were introduced to new markets through licensing, export and local production when opportunities were uncovered. Stella Artois, Interbrew's most broadly available and oldest brand, received an important new thrust when it was launched through local production in three of the company's subsidiaries in Central Europe in 1997. This approach was consistent with the company's overall goals of building a complete portfolio in high growth potential markets.

By 1998, however, the executive management committee perceived the need to identify a brand from its wide portfolio to systematically develop into the company's global brand. Although the market for global brands was still small, there were some growing successes (e.g., Heineken, Corona, Fosters and Budweiser) and Interbrew believed that there were several basic global trends that would improve the viability of this class of product over the next couple of decades. First, while many consumers were seeking more variety, others were seeking lower prices. It appeared that the number of affluent and poor

consumer segments would increase at the expense of the middle income segments. The upshot of this socioeconomic trend was that eventually all markets would likely evolve in such a way that demand for both premium and economy-priced beers would increase, squeezing the mainstream beers in the middle. A second trend was the internationalization of the beer business. As consumers travelled around the world, consuming global media (e.g., CNN, Eurosport, MTV, international magazines, etc.), global media were expected to become more effective for building brands. A global strategy could, therefore, lead to synergies in global advertising and sponsoring. In addition, the needs of consumers in many markets were expected to converge. As a result of these various factors, Interbrew believed that there would be an increasing interest in authentic, international brands in a growing number of countries. Interbrew had a wide portfolio of national brands that it could set on the international stage. The two most obvious candidates were Labatt Blue and Stella Artois.

The Labatt range of brands included Labatt Blue, Labatt Blue Light and Labatt Ice. To date, however, the exposure of these brands outside of North America had been extremely limited and they were not yet budding global brands. Of the total Labatt Blue volume in 1998, 85 per cent was derived from the Canadian domestic and U.S. markets, with the balance sold in the United Kingdom. The Labatt brands had been introduced to both France and Belgium, and production had been licensed in Italy, but these volumes were minimal. The only real export growth market for Labatt Blue appeared to be the United States, where the brand's volume in 1998 was some 23 per cent higher than in 1995, behind only Corona and Heineken in the imported brand segment. The Labatt Ice brand was also sold in a limited number of markets and, after the appeal of this Labatt innovation had peaked, its total volume had declined by more than 25 per cent since 1996. Total Labatt Ice volume worldwide was just 450,000 hls in 1998, of which 43 per cent was sold in Canada, 33 per cent in the

	1995	1996	1997	1998
Budweiser (incl. Bud Light until '98)	69.48	71.10	72.43	40.00
Bud Light	n/a	n/a	n/a	30.00
Heineken	3.87	3.78	3.85	3.78
Beck's	1.68	1.71	1.72	1.78
Carlsberg	1.47	1.39	1.31	1.22
Stella Artois	1.08	1.00	0.96	0.92
Foster's	1.48	1.11	1.40	1.43
Kronenbourg	5.65	5.53	5.35	5.60
Amstel	2.30	2.23	2.21	2.18
Corona	12.89	14.09	14.80	15.18

Exhibit 3   Domestic Sales History of Major International Brands (million hectolitre)

United States, and 21 per cent in the United Kingdom.

STELLA ARTOIS AS INTERBREW'S INTERNATIONAL FLAGSHIP BRAND

The other potential brand that Interbrew could develop on a global scale was Stella Artois, a brand that could trace its roots back to 1366. The modern version of Stella Artois was launched in 1920 as a Christmas beer and had become a strong market leader in its home market of Belgium through the 1970s. By the 1990s, however, Stella's market position began to suffer from an image as a somewhat old-fashioned beer, and the brand began to experience persistent volume decline. Problems in the domestic market, however, appeared to be shared by a number of other prominent international brands. In fact, seven of the top 10 international brands had experienced declining sales in their home markets between 1995 and 1999 (see Exhibit 3).

Stella Artois had achieved great success in the United Kingdom through its licensee, Whitbread, where Stella Artois became the leading premium lager beer. Indeed, the United Kingdom was the largest market for Stella Artois, accounting for 49 per cent of total brand volume in 1998. Stella Artois volume in the U.K.

market reached 2.8 million hls in 1998, a 7.6 per cent share of the lager market, and came close to 3.5 million hls in 1999, a 25 per cent increase over the previous year. By this time, over 32,000 outlets sold Stella Artois on draught.

Apart from the United Kingdom, the key markets for Stella Artois were France and Belgium, which together accounted for a further 31 per cent of total brand volume (see Exhibit 4). With these three markets accounting for 81 per cent of total Stella Artois volume in 1999, few other areas represented a significant volume base (see Exhibit 5). Beyond the top three markets, the largest market for Stella Artois was Italy, where the brand was produced under license by Heineken. Stella Artois volume in Italy had, however, declined slightly to 166,000 hls in 1998. Licensing agreements were also in place in Sweden and Australia, but volume was small.

Stella Artois was also produced in Interbrew's own breweries in Hungary, Croatia and Romania, with very pleasing 1998 volumes of 84,000 hls, 120,000 hls, and 60,000 hls, respectively. After only three years, the market share of Stella Artois in Croatia, for example, had reached four per cent—a significant result, given that the brand was a premium-priced product. In all Central European markets, Stella Artois was priced at a premium; in Hungary, however, that premium was lower than in Croatia and Romania where, on an index comparing Stella's price to

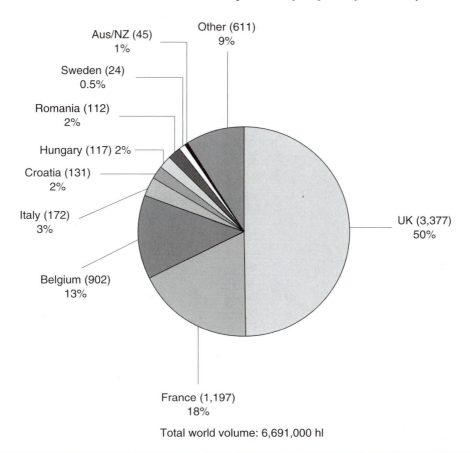

Aus/NZ (45)
1%

Sweden (24)
0.5%

Romania (112)
2%

Hungary (117) 2%

Croatia (131)
2%

Italy (172)
3%

Belgium (902)
13%

Other (611)
9%

UK (3,377)
50%

France (1,197)
18%

Total world volume: 6,691,000 hl

Exhibit 4 1999 World Sales Profile of Stella Artois

that of core lagers, the indices by country were 140, 260 and 175 respectively.

Promising first results were also attained in Australia and New Zealand. Particularly in New Zealand, through a "seeding" approach, Interbrew and their local partner, Lion Nathan, had realized great success in the Belgian Beer Café in Auckland where the brands were showcased. After only two years of support, Stella Artois volume was up to 20,000 hls, and growing at 70 per cent annually, out of a total premium segment of 400,000 hls. Interbrew's market development plan limited distribution to top outlets in key metropolitan centres and priced

Stella Artois significantly above competitors (e.g., 10 per cent over Heineken and 20 per cent over Steinlager, the leading domestic premium lager brand).

The evolution of the brand looked very positive as world volumes for Stella Artois continued to grow. In fact, Stella Artois volume had increased from 3.4 million hls in 1992 to a total of 6.7 million hls in 1999, a rise of 97 per cent. Ironically, the only market where the brand continued its steady decline was in its home base of Belgium. Analysts suggested a variety of reasons to explain this anomaly, including inconsistent sales and marketing support, particularly as the

	1997	1998	1999
Production:			
Belgium	965	921	902
France	1,028	1,110	1,074
Hungary	59	84	117
Croatia	54	120	133
Romania	17	60	112
Bulgaria	—	—	3
Bosnia-Herzegovina	—	—	2
Montenegro	—	—	0
Total Production	**2,123**	**2,295**	**2,343**
License Brewing:			
Italy	162	166	172
Australia	6	11	22
New Zealand	7	11	22
Sweden	29	27	24
Greece	7	7	10
UK	2,139	2,815	3,377
Total Licensed	**2,350**	**3,037**	**3,627**
Export:			
USA	—	—	7
Canada	—	—	5
Other Countries	92	49	202
Duty Free	245	389	507
Total Export	**337**	**438**	**721**
Overall Total	**4,810**	**5,770**	**6,691**

Exhibit 5   Stella Artois Sales Volume Summary (000 hectolitre)

organization began to favor the rising Jupiler brand.

Overall, given Interbrew's large number of local brands, especially those in Mexico with very high volumes, total Stella Artois volume accounted for only 10 per cent of total Interbrew volume in 1999 (14 per cent if Femsa volumes are excluded). Interbrew's strategy of nurturing a wide portfolio of strong brands was very different as compared to some of its major competitors. For example, Anheuser-Busch, the world's largest brewer, focused its international strategy almost exclusively on the development of the Budweiser brand. Similarly, Heineken sought to centre its international business on the Heineken brand and, to a lesser extent, on Amstel. While the strategies of Anheuser-Busch and Heineken focused primarily on one brand, there were also great differences in the way these two brands were being managed. For example, Budweiser, the world's largest brand by volume, had the overwhelming bulk of its volume in its home U.S. market (see Exhibit 6). Sales of the Heineken brand, on the other hand, were widely distributed across markets around the world (see Exhibit 7). In this sense, Heineken's strategy was much more comparable to that of Interbrew's plans for Stella Artois. Other brands that were directly comparable to Stella Artois, in terms of total volume and importance of the brand to the overall sales of the company, were Carlsberg and Foster's with annual sales volumes in 1998 of

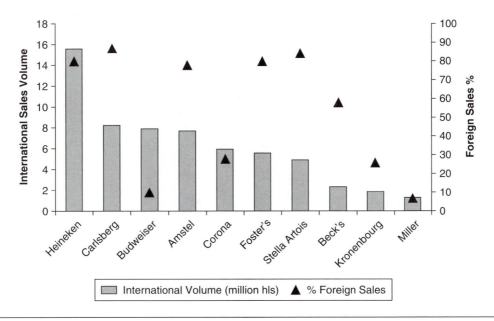

Exhibit 6   Top 10 Brewers by International Sales

9.4 million hls and 7.1 million hls, respectively. While Foster's was successful in many international markets, there was a heavy focus on sales in the United Kingdom and the United States (see Exhibit 8). Carlsberg sales volume profile was different in that sales were more widely distributed across international markets (see Exhibit 9).

STELLA'S GLOBAL LAUNCH

In 1998, Interbrew's executive management committee settled on Stella Artois, positioned as the premium European lager, as the company's global flagship brand. In fact, the Interbrew management felt that stock analysts would be favorably disposed to Interbrew having an acknowledged global brand with the potential for a higher corporate valuation and price earnings (P/E) multiple.

As the global campaign got under way, it became clear that the organization needed time to adapt to centralized co-ordination and control of Stella Artois brand marketing. This was, perhaps, not unexpected given that Interbrew had until recently operated on a regional basis; the new centralized Stella brand management approach had been in place only since September 1998. In addition, there were often difficulties in convincing all parties to become part of a new global approach, particularly the international advertising campaign that was the backbone of the global plan for Stella Artois. Belgium, for example, continued with a specific local advertising program that positioned Stella as a mainstream lager in its home market, and in the United Kingdom, Whitbread maintained its "reassuringly expensive" advertising slogan that had already proved to be so successful. For other less-established markets, a global advertising framework was created that included a television concept and a series of print and outdoor executions. This base advertising plan was rolled out in 1999 in 15 markets, including the United

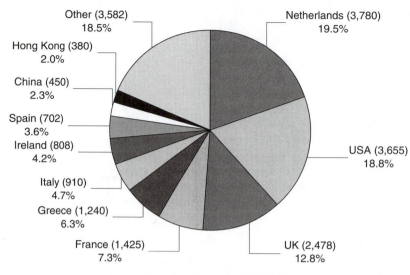

Total world volume: 19,400,000 hl

Exhibit 7 1998 Heineken World Sales Profile

States, Canada, Italy, Hungary, Croatia, Bulgaria, Romania, New Zealand and France (with a slightly changed format) after research suggested that the campaign had the ability to cross borders. The objective of this campaign was to position Stella Artois as a sophisticated European lager. It was intended that Stella Artois should be perceived as a beer with an important brewing tradition and heritage but, at the same time, also as a contemporary beer (see Exhibit 10).

In 1998, an accelerated plan was devised to introduce Stella Artois to two key markets within the United States, utilizing both local and corporate funding. The U.S. market was believed to be key for the future development of the brand since it was the most developed specialty market in the world (12 per cent specialty market share, growing 10 per cent plus annually through the 1990s), and because of the strong influence on international trends. Thus, Stella Artois was launched in New York City and Boston and was well received by the demanding U.S. consumer

and pub owner. Within 1999, over 200 pubs in Manhattan and 80 bars in Boston had begun to sell Stella Artois on tap. To support the heightened efforts to establish Stella Artois in these competitive urban markets, Interbrew's corporate marketing department added several million dollars to Labatt USA's budget for Stella Artois in 2000, with commitments to continue this additional funding in subsequent years.

CURRENT THINKING

Good progress had been made since 1998 when Stella Artois was established as Interbrew's global brand. However, management had revised its expectations for P/E leverage from having a global brand. The reality was that Interbrew would be rewarded only through cash benefits from operational leverage of a global brand. There would be no "free lunch" simply for being perceived as having a global brand. In addition, in an

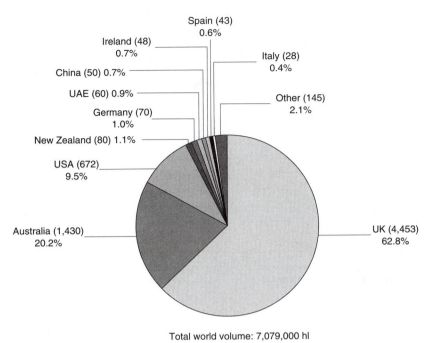

Total world volume: 7,079,000 hl

Exhibit 8 1998 Foster's World Sales Profile

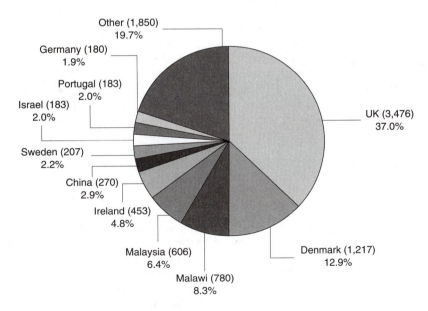

Total world volume: 9,405,000 hl

Exhibit 9 1998 Carlsberg World Sales Profile

Brand Positioning

To males, between 21 to 45 years of age, that are premium lager drinkers, Stella Artois is a European premium lager beer, differentially positioned towards the product.

Stella Artois offers a modern, sophisticated, yet accessible drinking experience with an emphasis on the very high quality of the beer supported by the noble tradition of European brewing.

The accent is on the emotional consequence of benefit: a positive feeling of self esteem and sophistication.

Character, Tone of Voice

Sophistication
Authenticity, tradition, yet touch of modernity
Timelessness
Premium quality
Special, yet accessible
Mysticism
European

Exhibit 10   Global Positioning Statement

---

era of tight fiscal management, it was an ongoing challenge to maintain the funding levels required by the ambitious development plans for Stella Artois. As a result, in early 2000 the prevailing view at Interbrew began to shift, converging on a different long-range approach towards global branding. The emerging perspective emphasized a more balanced brand development program, focusing on the highest leverage opportunities.

The experience of other brewers that had established global brands offered an opportunity for Interbrew to learn from their successes and failures. Carlsberg and Heineken, for example, were two comparable global brands that were valued quite differently by the stock market. Both sold over 80 per cent of their total volumes outside their domestic market, and yet Heineken stock achieved a P/E ratio of 32.4 in 1999 versus Carlsberg's figure of only 17.1. According to industry analysts, the driving force behind this difference was that Heineken maintained a superior market distribution in terms of growth and margin (see Exhibit 11). The key lesson from examining these global brands appeared to be that great discipline must be applied to focus resources in the right places.

In line with this thinking, a long range marketing plan began to take shape that made use of

a series of strategic filters to yield a focused set of attractive opportunities. The first filter that any potential market had to pass through was its long-term volume potential for Stella Artois. This volume had to trace back to a large and/or growing market, the current or potential sizeable premium lager segment (at least five per cent of the total market), and the possibility for Stella Artois to penetrate the top three brands. The second screen was the potential to achieve attractive margins after an initial starting period of approximately three years. The third filter was whether or not a committed local partner was available to provide the right quality of distribution and to co-invest in the brand. The final screen was the determination that success in the chosen focus markets should increase leverage in other local and regional markets. For example, the size and stature of Stella Artois in the United Kingdom was a significant factor in the easy sell-in of Stella Artois into New York in 1999.

Once filtered through these strategic market development screens, the global branding plans for Stella Artois began to take a different shape. Rather than focus on national markets, plans emerged with an emphasis on about 20 cities, some of which Interbrew was already present in (e.g., London, Brussels, New York, etc.). This

Profit Exposure by Market Type

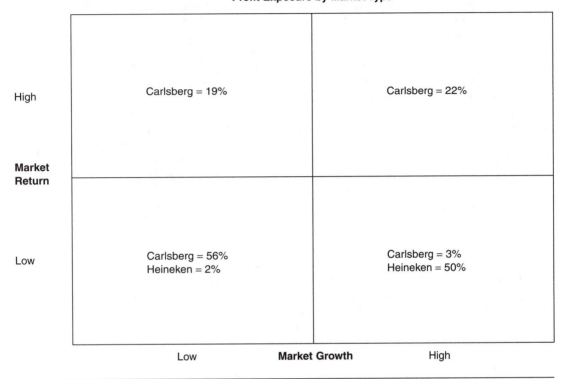

Exhibit 11   A Comparison of Carlsberg and Heineken

approach suggested that the next moves should be in such potential markets as Moscow, Los Angeles and Hong Kong. Some existing cities would receive focused efforts only when distribution partner issues had been successfully resolved to solidify the bases for sustained long term growth. The major cities that fit these criteria provided the right concentration of affluent consumers, who would be attracted to Stella's positioning, thus providing scale for marketing and sales, investment leverage, as well as getting the attention and support of motivated wholesalers and initial retail customers. These venues would thereby become highly visible success stories that would be leveragable in the company's ongoing market development plans.

Thus, the evolving global branding development plan required careful planning on a city-by-city basis. Among the demands of this new

approach were that marketing efforts and the funding to support them would have to be both centrally stewarded and locally tailored to reflect the unique local environments. A corporate marketing group was, therefore, established and was charged with the responsibility to identify top priority markets, develop core positioning and guidelines for local execution, assemble broadly based marketing programs (e.g., TV, print advertising, global sponsorships, beer.com content, etc.), and allocate resources to achieve the accelerated growth objectives in these targeted cities. To ensure an integrated development effort the company brought all pivotal resources together, under the leadership of a global brand development director. In addition to the brand management team, the group included regional sales managers who were responsible for licensed partner management, a customer services group, a Belgian beer café manager, and cruise business management group. Another significant challenge that faced the corporate marketing group was to ensure that all necessary groups were supportive of the new approach. This was a simpler undertaking among those business units that were wholly owned subsidiaries; it was a more delicate issue in the case of licensees and joint ventures. A key element of managing brands through a global organizational structure was that the head office team had to effectively build partnerships with local managers to ensure their commitment.

Fortunately, much of the initial effort to establish Stella Artois as a global brand had been done on a city-by-city basis and, as such, there was ample opportunity for Interbrew to learn from these experiences as the new global plan evolved. In the late 1990s, for example, Stella Artois was introduced to various Central European cities (e.g., Budapest, Zagreb, Bucharest and Sofia). In each of these cities, Interbrew's marketing efforts were launched when the targeted premium market was at an early stage of development. Further, distribution and promotion was strictly controlled (e.g., product quality, glassware, etc.) and the development initiatives were delivered in a concentrated manner (e.g., a media "blitz" in Budapest). In addition, results indicated that the presence of a Belgian Beer Café accelerated Interbrew's market development plans in these new areas. These early successes suggested that brand success could be derived from the careful and concentrated targeting of young adults living in urban centres, with subsequent pull from outlying areas following key city success.

The key lessons of these efforts in Central Europe proved to be very valuable in guiding the market development plan in New York City. In this key North American city, the rollout of Stella Artois was perceived by the analysts as "one of the most promising introductions in New York over the last 20 years" and had generated great wholesaler support and excitement. Among the tactics used to achieve this early success was selective distribution with targeted point of sale

materials support. In addition, a selective media campaign was undertaken that included only prestigious outdoor advertising (e.g., a Times Square poster run through the Millennium celebrations). Similarly, the sponsoring strategy focused only on high-end celebrity events, Belgian food events, exclusive parties, fashion shows, etc. Finally, the price of Stella Artois was targeted at levels above Heineken, to reinforce its gold standard positioning. This concerted and consistent market push created an impact that resulted in the "easiest new brand sell" in years, according to wholesalers. The success of this launch also built brand and corporate credibility, paving the way to introductions in other U.S. cities as well as "opening the eyes" of other customers and distribution partners around the world.

To pursue this new global development plan over the next three years, a revised marketing budget was required. Given that the corporate marketing department was responsible for both the development of core programs as well as the selective support of local markets, the budget had to cover both of these key elements. To achieve these ends, total spending was expected to more than double over the next three years.

While great progress had been made on the global branding of Stella Artois, Cooke still ruminated on a variety of important interrelated issues. Among these issues was the situation of Stella Artois in Belgium—would it be possible to win in the "global game" without renewed growth in the home market? What specific aspirations should Interbrew set for Belgium over the next three years? Further, what expectations should Interbrew have of its global brand market development (e.g., volumes, profit levels, number of markets and cities, etc.)? How should global success be measured? With respect to Interbrew's promotional efforts, how likely would it be that a single global ad campaign could be successful for Stella Artois? Was there a particular sponsorship or promotion idea that could be singled out for global leverage? And what role should the Internet play in developing Stella Artois as a true global brand?

2

UNDERSTANDING AND MANAGING MACROECONOMIC RISKS

E̲ffective decision making requires the ability to understand and forecast broad macroeconomic forces and to incorporate this information within the decision-making process. Topics covered in these cases include inflation, exchange rates, unemployment, business cycles, and the impacts of monetary and fiscal policies. A macro-economics text may be essential, depending on the level of student knowledge of the subject (Kennedy, 2000). Additional references include the competitiveness ranking (www.imd.ch/wcy), opacity index (www.opacityindex.com), index of economic freedom (www.fraserinstitute.com), and the corruption perception index (www.transparency.org).

Traditionally, the economics literature draws on the experiences of Western Europe and North America. The inclusion of other countries' economic experiences demonstrates limitations to some economic theories, highlighting the assumptions on which they are based and questioning their universal applicability. For example, the potential limitations of expansionary monetary and fiscal policies in a depression can be clearly understood in a discussion of Japan's post-1990 difficulties, in which fiscal deficits and low interest rates failed to achieve economic recovery. The need for a strong and stable banking system to implement monetary policy successfully has become most evident in the rapid inflation and frequent foreign exchange crises of less developed countries such as Argentina and Mexico. The applicability of the International Monetary Fund (IMF) formula for dealing with foreign exchange crises might not be appropriate for less developed countries where the sudden imposition of tight monetary policy and fiscal constraints could cause political disarray, economic dislocation, and severe deprivation for low-income groups (Stiglitz, 2002).

Some countries present an economic paradigm of repeated inflation-devaluation cycles. This set of relationships offers a particularly important insight into macroeconomic relationships, such as "purchasing power parity." The general populace in these countries seems not to appreciate the benefits of sound macroeconomic policies, and so governments are reluctant to raise taxes or reduce expenditures, operating with ongoing fiscal deficits. The fiscal deficits are funded largely by money supply expansion, which in turn causes inflation rates to be high and volatile. Governments also finance their deficits through borrowing abroad, and these capital inflows create a vulnerability for the foreign exchange rate because capital inflows can quickly change direction. Large foreign debt service payments create an ongoing drain in the current account. Domestic investors have extended their horizons so that they, as well as foreign investors, may shift their savings abroad in response to any threat of devaluation, creating frequent crises. The primary products that these nations export often experience price volatility, which results in volatility in export earnings, with implications for the foreign exchange rates. Foreign exchange crises can lead to temporarily high interest rates, which in turn can cause bank crises and corporate crises. Argentina's experiences clearly illustrate the nature of this cycle. Although Argentine President Carlos Menem was able to halt inflation and devaluation by instituting tough IMF-type policies in the early 1990s, the cycle reappeared by 2000.

"Domino devaluations" often occur as investors' fears about one nation spread to other nations. A devaluation in the exchange rate of one country automatically creates pressure for devaluation in other countries' exchange rates. For example, the 1999 Brazilian devaluation increased the Brazilian prices of imports from Argentina and decreased the Argentinean prices of imports from Brazil, with the result that the Argentine currency encountered severe downward pressure as the Argentinean balance of trade deteriorated.

To stop this inflation-devaluation cycle, some countries have eliminated their own currency, using only U.S. dollars. However, these economies must then accept U.S. monetary policy—which at times may not be appropriate for them. Furthermore, ongoing fiscal deficits can still lead to the risk of debt default, with a need to borrow from the IMF to support the domestic financial sector.

Foreign exchange crises and devaluations have often become more general economic crises. Countries that have been hurt most are those with a banking system that lacks adequate regulatory supervision and that lends to corporations and individuals without due diligence. As banks become insolvent, the foreign exchange crisis becomes a financial crisis. When some banks close and others call in their loans to maintain solvency, businesses are hurt and economies are dragged into recession. Many businesses and governments have borrowed in foreign currencies, and devaluation sharply increases their debts in terms of domestic currencies. Consequently, managers must focus on relationships between domestic inflation, the balance of payments, and the level of exchange rates.

Of central concern are students' recommendations for the IMF and other international assistance programs. The traditional "IMF formula" for dealing with a foreign exchange crisis is now being criticized (Stiglitz, 2002), and this debate forms an interesting focus for analyses. The IMF has offered most countries rescue packages consisting of foreign currency loans to support each country's international exchange rate but also required a tightening of fiscal and monetary policies. Although these efforts have often been successful in developed countries, the impacts of the crises and rescue packages on less developed economies have been different. In fact, some argue that such economies have been hurt by the IMF's efforts. The IMF rescue packages have stabilized foreign exchange rates in the short term, but they have severely damaged domestic businesses that suddenly confronted high interest rates and the demand for loan repayments. Hence, the effects of these measures may have worsened the financial crises and deepened economic recession.

Furthermore, this process has inflicted major harm on low-income families, especially those experiencing unemployment.

Although macroeconomic texts discuss the theoretical limitations of fiscal and monetary policies, classroom analyses of Japan's economy add important practical insights in regard to these limitations. Large ongoing fiscal deficits failed to cause a recovery, and the fiscal deficits resulted in a cumulative national debt so huge that it became an added burden on recovery prospects. This situation illustrates the warnings of "rational expectations" economists that a fiscal deficit may be offset by increased savings because taxpayers know that taxes will have to be raised in the future to cover the increasing national debt. Meanwhile, loose monetary policy with interest rates below 1% also failed to stimulate aggregate demand. Both consumers and businesses in Japan chose not to increase their expenditures in response to fiscal deficits and low interest rates—at least not enough to lead to a rapid recovery. "Stuck in a depression," the Japanese experience points dramatically to the possibility of both a low fiscal "multiplier" and a low "money multiplier," as well as the dependence of macroeconomic policies on underlying microeconomic features: the inability of the banking system to adjust in the face of mounting bad debts, the lack of consumer and business confidence, and the downward inflexibility of wages and prices. These forces combined to create deflation. An important learning experience for students is to consider the impacts of falling prices on macroeconomic theories and policies. Some analysts have expressed serious concerns about these impacts of deflation, and some have feared that Japan's experience may threaten other modern economies, particularly Germany.

The "ING and Global Financial Integration" case sheds light on additional themes in the macroeconomics literature. Western European countries have expensive social welfare programs, high tax rates to pay for these programs, legislation to protect the rights of workers, and extensive government ownership and regulation of industry. Many analysts blame this set of policies for having created "Eurosclerosis": high unemployment rates, slow productivity growth, and declining international competitiveness (Eltis, 2000; Modigliani et al., 1998). Western Europe has appeared to be relatively unsuccessful compared with America in terms of macroeconomic indicators. Some academics remain pessimistic about future growth in Europe, suggesting that these traditional forces will continue to place a burden on all European countries, constricting investment opportunities (Smith, 1999). However, many Europeans believe that high unemployment levels can best be reduced through schemes to share work, for example, by shortening the workweek and by encouraging early retirement.

Western Europe also provides insights into "the optimal currency area" (Hughes Hallett & Piscitelli, 2002). The gradual integration of Europe—with the establishment of common standards throughout Europe and the adoption of a single currency—may have enhanced its attractiveness for investment and may have increased growth prospects. Students will debate the relative importance of various aspects of integration. Currency risk will be eliminated, and previous restrictions on cross-border investments and mergers will be lifted. Beyond these obvious changes, a series of questions remains. Will heightened competition among European-wide financial institutions improve the functioning of capital markets? Will "disintermediation" enable entrepreneurs to raise capital directly from households and institutional investors rather than relying on traditional bank loans that require physical assets as security? Will this transformation of financial practices stimulate innovation and productivity? Many observers believe the creation of the European Monetary

Union (EMU) with a single currency will indeed be a major stimulus for economic growth. The EMU is the result of a gradual intensification of the integration process over a 50-year period. Students will evaluate whether a similar lengthy time horizon is required for the social and political integration that would be needed to create a single currency area elsewhere, say in Asia or the Americas.

The theory of purchasing power parity is demonstrated much more dramatically in countries that have experienced very rapid inflation, rather than in the economically advanced nations with their restrained inflation rates. The linkages between micro- and macroeconomic theories are also most apparent in countries where industry structures retard productivity growth and where, consequently, successful macro-policies depend on successful micro-policies. For example, countries struggling with the transition from communism to free enterprise have demonstrated these micro-macro linkages to a significant degree. Corruption might be ignored in traditional texts, but the relationships between corruption and economic growth are important in countries where bureaucrats have the power to deny or impede business plans on a case-by-case basis.

With the "Bank Vozrozhdeniye" and "Proctor & Gamble in Eastern Europe" cases, students can compare the macroeconomic policies of the free enterprise model and the macroeconomics of the central planning paradigm (Rosser, 1996). Central planning promised a greater certainty concerning macroeconomic outcomes. By determining production levels for each enterprise, central planning hoped to avoid the accumulation of excessive inventory and consequent business cycles; full employment for each citizen could be guaranteed. In practice, however, macroeconomic success depended on the transfer of complete and accurate information from each enterprise to the central planners, and this process encountered frequent errors. Several trends gradually complicated the macroeconomic achievements of the central planning paradigm. Products became more complex and required a wider variety of inputs, so enterprises became increasingly interrelated. Both industrial and consumption goods were produced in a growing number of versions with a wide array of modifications. From the central planners' viewpoint, the number of items to be considered increased. There was a modern emphasis on quality or appropriateness, and many such aspects of a commodity could not be quantified easily, as the planning process required. When a nation neared the forefront of international technology, it had to foster domestic innovation, and the need to obtain and evaluate information concerning potential innovations presented central planners with an additional complication.

With the "Proctor & Gamble in Eastern Europe" case, students can evaluate the transition challenges experienced by these nations and can debate the "preconditions" necessary for free-enterprise macroeconomic policies (Greenspan, 1993). Of particular concern are the skill sets necessary for the successful operation of independent enterprises and also for the determination and implementation of macroeconomic policies. Governments often set prices below a market equilibrium, and so the transition brought with it a sudden inflation. This inflation, in turn, led to downward pressure on foreign exchange rates, with the risk of periodic foreign exchange crises. Under central planning, monopolies were created in many sectors to achieve economies of scale. With the shift to free markets, these monopolies were able to increase prices above competitive equilibrium levels, raising concerns about the need for antitrust policies. The process of privatization and deregulation has involved a multitude of additional challenges. In this context, students can question the optimal time profile for transition and the advisability of "a leap to the market" (Stiglitz, 2002). The very lengthy Chinese transition contrasts sharply with the position of Jeffrey

Sachs, who emphasized that all reforms should be implemented together (Sachs, 1991). Finally, students can question the validity of the estimates of aggregate economic activity. An extensive "underground economy" may explain part of the decline in measured gross domestic product (GDP) and the increase in unemployment. Rapid price changes may cast doubt on the particular set of prices used to calculate GDP and inflation rates.

The United States has come to play an ever greater role in many economies. It appears that U.S. fiscal and monetary policies now have an increasing impact on other countries, placing constraints on policy options each country faces. In Canada and Mexico, for example, the North American Free Trade Agreement (NAFTA) has completely altered most corporate strategies, leading to significant structural adjustments in the national economy of each country (Keating & Loughlin, 1997; Rugman, 1994). Latin American economies offer relatively low wage rates, and the likelihood exists of a major shift of certain kinds of jobs from Canada and the United States to low-wage countries, particularly with prospective extension of free trade agreements. Yet Latin American countries rank low in indices of international competitiveness and are vulnerable to inflation-devaluation cycles, and these characteristics may affect the extent and nature of foreign investment (International Institute for Management Development, 2002).

A GLOBAL MANAGER'S GUIDE TO CURRENCY RISK MANAGEMENT

Since the advent of the floating exchange rates, any time that a transaction—whether that transaction is in goods, services, people, capital, or technology—has crossed borders, it has been subject to the influence of changes in exchanges rates. The basic problem posed by exchange rates on the cross-border firm is that money across borders has no fixed value. Consequently, neither does the transaction undertaken across borders. The purpose of this note is to understand, categorize, and define the specific types of exchange rate risks that firms face across borders and to address how managers can plan for, manage, and hedge these risks. Specifically, this note provides an overview of the risks posed by exchange rates to the cross-border firm, as well as the major strategies and solutions managers can employ to deal with them.

CHAUVCO RESOURCES LTD.: THE ARGENTINA DECISIONS

A focus of this case is a comparison between Canada, where Chauvco began, and Argentina, where technologies that were common in Canada offered a unique competitive advantage. Argentina's traditional hyperinflation and devaluations seemed to have been eliminated by President Menem's reforms of the early 1990s, but students must determine whether these macroeconomic risks remained and the degree to which they posed a threat to Chauvco's profitability.

CRISIS IN JAPAN

This case is presented as a dialogue among four friends, who examined the economic crisis that affected Japan since the beginning of the 1990s and who focused on the situation of recession and deflation. Extensive macroeconomic data are provided, as well as information on the policies implemented by the government since 1992. How did Japan get into the crisis, and why was it so slow in achieving a recovery?

Procter & Gamble in Eastern Europe (A)

In 1990, the management team of Procter & Gamble (P&G) confronted a series of tough issues in deciding how and where to enter the newly liberated economies of Eastern Europe. If P&G were to enter joint ventures, it and its domestic partners would be motivated by different values and objectives, and these differences could become increasingly important. Although many of the Communist governments were allowing foreign companies to increase their business activities in their once restricted markets, many remaining government regulations would constrain P&G's expansion.

Bank Vozrozhdeniye (V.Bank)

"V.Bank" struggled to survive the difficulties that accompanied Russia's liberalization reforms. The environment of business included poor regulation, unfair and intense competition, inflation, currency devaluation, political risk, and civil unrest. A "twinning arrangement" with a Western bank promised technological advances and improved banking practices, but the August 1998 devaluation and default interrupted V.Bank's progress.

ING and Global Financial Integration

European integration, particularly the adoption of a single currency, would affect many European businesses, as a single set of standards and regulations would replace those imposed by individual governments. Consequently, ING had to consider the creation of a new European strategy in place of previous country strategies. ING also had to evaluate its unsatisfactory performance in emerging markets. Meanwhile, the rapid growth of electronic banking could also change many traditional banking practices.

THUNDERBIRD
THE GARVIN SCHOOL OF
INTERNATIONAL MANAGEMENT

A GLOBAL MANAGER'S GUIDE TO CURRENCY RISK MANAGEMENT

Prepared by Professors Michael H. Moffett and Anant K. Sundaram

INTRODUCTION

Since the advent of the floating exchange rates, any time that a transaction—whether that transaction is in goods, services, people, capital, or technology—has crossed borders, it has been subject to the influence of changes in exchange rates. The basic problem posed by exchange rates on the cross-border firm is that money across borders has no fixed value. Consequently, neither does a transaction undertaken across borders. In this Note, our purpose is to understand, categorize, and define the specific types of exchange rate risks that firms face across borders, and to address how managers can plan for, manage, and hedge these risks. Specifically, this Note provides an overview of the risks posed by exchange rates to the cross-border firm and the major strategies and solutions managers can employ to deal with them.

WHY SHOULD COMPANIES HEDGE?

Peter Drucker once noted that, "Not to hedge is to speculate. Exchange rates are a cost of production that financial executives must manage."[1] But what constitutes hedging and what constitutes speculation? What is the purpose of hedging? How, if at all, does hedging create value for shareholders?

An exchange rate hedge is an asset or position whose value changes (ΔH) in the opposite direction to that of an exposure (ΔX) as a result of a change in the exchange rate. A perfect hedge would be one whose value changes in an equal and opposite direction, resulting in a net change of zero in the value of the combined position:[2]

$$\Delta V = \Delta X + \Delta H$$

Hedging therefore protects the owner of the existing asset from loss. It is, however, important to note that while a hedge protects the firm against an exchange rate loss (relative to being unhedged), it can also eliminate any gains from an exchange rate change that is favorable.

But this does not really answer the question as to what is to be gained from hedging. The value of a firm is simply the net present value of all expected future cash flows discounted at an appropriate risk-adjusted discount rate. Hedging reduces the *variance* in expected cash flows, but does not necessarily affect the expected cash flows themselves. Reducing the variance—or what is referred to as "total risk" in the theory of finance—is not necessarily the same as reducing "risk," and therefore not necessarily the same as reducing the discount rate from the standpoint of the investor. From the investors' standpoint, the risk that matters is that portion of the total risk that cannot be diversified away, often called the "systematic risk." If currency risk is defined as "unsystematic risk" or "noise" in expected future cash flows arising from exchange rate changes, it has no impact on firm value. According to this argument, all that a manager does is waste the shareholder's money by such hedging.

That said, proponents cite a number of reasons for why hedging can be valuable to the firm. The argument most often made is that reduction of variance in future cash flows improves the planning capability of the firm. If the firm can more accurately predict future cash flows, it may have a greater incentive to undertake specific investments or activities which it might otherwise not consider. In a related (and somewhat more subtle) vein, hedging can put a floor on the internally generated cash flows of the firm, and, by doing so, can obviate the need to source externally generated capital in meeting its investment and growth needs. This can be valuable if external capital is more expensive than internally generated capital—and, for a number of reasons such as transactions costs and signaling costs, it turns out that external capital is, indeed, more expensive than internal capital.[3]

Reduction of risk in future cash flows reduces the likelihood that the firm's cash flows will fall below the minimum required to make debt-service payments. Hedging can therefore reduce the likelihood of financial distress. Yet another reason that is advocated is that management has a comparative advantage over the investor in knowing the actual currency risk of the firm.[4] Regardless of the level of disclosure provided by the firm to the public, management may possess an advantage in knowing the depth and breadth of the real risks and returns inherent in the firm's business. Thus, they may be aware of the benefits to a hedge that an investor does not see. Markets can be in disequilibrium because of structural and institutional imperfections, as well as external shocks (such as an oil crisis or war).

Management is in a better position than stockholders to recognize disequilibrium conditions and to take advantage of one-time opportunities to enhance firm value through selective hedging.[5] Finally, there are those who argue that by reducing the variance in cash flows, hedging can smooth the reported net income, and this may be valuable in a financial market that pays undue attention to quarterly earnings fluctuations rather than focus of the long-term free cash flows.

Opponents of currency hedging make a number of equally persuasive arguments:[6] Stockholders are much more capable of diversifying currency risk than management of the firm. If stockholders do not wish to accept the currency risk of any specific firm, they can diversify their own portfolios or directly hedge against such risks. As noted above, reducing currency risk is not necessarily the same as adding value to the firm. In fact, since they are not free, hedging instruments use up precious resources of the firm which can lead to a net reduction in value. It is also possible that management conducts hedging activity because it benefits them, even if it is at the expense of the stockholder. Deriving from the idea of separation of control and ownership, agency theory argues that management (control) is generally more risk-averse than stockholders (ownership) because their undiversifiable human capital is tied up in the firm. If they bear firm-specific risks that are nondiversifiable, they will have the incentive to worry about, i.e., want to lower, total risk rather than just systematic risk.

Similarly, many argue that managers cannot outguess the market. If foreign exchange markets are in equilibrium with respect to parity conditions, the expected net present value of hedging is zero—in other words, all hedges will be fairly priced by the market. How would managers know when the market is not in equilibrium? Indeed, if they did have such special skills and know that, would they not be able to create more value for both themselves and their stockholders by speculating in currencies, rather than producing and selling goods and services? It is also possible that management's motivation to reduce variance is sometimes driven by accounting reasons, rather than market value reasons. Management may believe it will be criticized more severely for incurring foreign exchange losses in its financial statements than for incurring similar or even higher cash costs in avoiding the foreign exchange loss by undertaking hedging. However, efficient market theorists believe that investors can see through the "accounting veil" and therefore have already factored the foreign exchange effect into a firm's market valuation.

As is the case with any such debate, the conclusion will vary with the individuals—both stockholders and managements—involved. If there is any indication of who is winning the "why hedge?" debate, the reality is that more and more firms globally are practicing currency risk management every day. Hence what follows.

MANAGEMENT OF FOREIGN EXCHANGE RISK

The Management Process

Successful management of foreign exchange risk requires a well-designed and well-implemented risk management program. This requires a five-step process of understanding the motivation, the perception, the identification, the construction, and the implementation of a comprehensive risk management program.

a. **Motivation**. Management strives to combine maximum sustainable growth in earnings with adequate yet prudently minimized commitments of capital. Some combination of these financial dimensions—the income statement and the balance sheet—give rise to the cash flows which are the true sources of value. And value is found by growth of stockholder wealth. If the assumption is then made that value arises from the business line(s) of the firm, i.e., the real activities that it undertakes, financial risks such as those posed by exchange rates, interest rates, and commodity prices can be seen for what they are—risks to the successful pursuit of the business's value. It is therefore management's responsibility to organize, structure, and

operate the business and its variety of financial functions to capture as many of the positive characteristics of exchange rate changes as possible, while minimizing the downsides associated with them. The premise is that stockholders invest in a firm's ability to profit from its line of business, not from its ability to speculate or maneuver in the world's currency markets.

b. **Perception**. Risks are managed on the basis of how they are perceived. For example, risks may be interpreted as continuous or discrete. A risk which is continuous can be accepted as inevitable, and gains and losses to the business arising from this risk can be accepted passively. A risk which is perceived as discrete, as foreign exchange risk often is, may be considered as one which occurs only periodically and will perhaps be more actively managed.

c. **Identification**. If a risk cannot be measured accurately, it cannot be managed. The most common error made by managers with regard to currency risks is to rush into the selection of a financial fix or a derivative which will eliminate a risk which has been only barely identified. Mistakes are commonly made because inadequate time and effort have been spent in trying to understand the complexity of the problem. A comprehensive exposure analysis must include all traditional functional dimensions of the business including pricing, marketing, operations, accounting, finance and even compensation.

d. **Construction**. Although the subject of most of the literature (particularly sales literature by financial services providers), this is in many respects the easiest part of the problem. Once an exposure has been properly identified and the firm's risk management motivations and needs acknowledged, the construction of the hedge can be undertaken. This is in many ways one of the simpler aspects of the entire decision process.

e. **Implementation**. The highly publicized derivative debacles of the 1990s have raised the consciousness that risk management programs may *themselves* constitute a risk to the firm when not identified, constructed, or implemented properly. Lack of front office/back office separation (the organizational separation of the traders or dealers taking the positions and the legal and

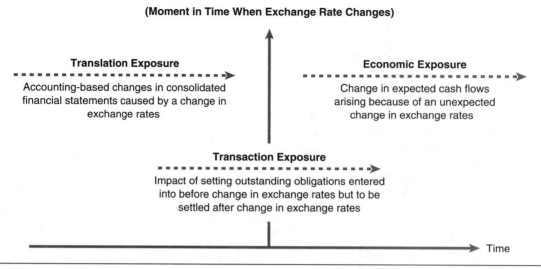

Figure 1   Conceptual Comparison of Difference Between Economic, Transaction, and Translation
Foreign Exchange Exposure

Source: Based on D. K. Eiteman, A. I. Stonehill, and M. H. Moffett, *Multinational Business Finance,* 10th edition, Addison-Wesley Longman, 2004.

documentary staff recording and monitoring the positions taken) led to many of the major fiascos, including the currency losses of Allied Lyons of the United Kingdom, Procter & Gamble in the United States, and Shell Showa in Japan. Questions such as the following need to be thought through. Who should manage and oversee the risk management process? Should it be centralized or decentralized? What are the performance evaluation issues raised by the risk management process for divisions and subsidiaries? What are the information technology and reporting needs to manage such values at risk in real time?

Types of Exchange Rate Exposure

The cross-border firm is affected by exchange rate changes three different ways. These three types of exposure (see Figure 1) are: transaction exposure, translation exposure, and economic exposure.

a. **Transaction exposure**. A transaction exposure arises whenever the firm commits (or is contractually obligated) to make or receive a payment at a future date denominated in a foreign currency. Transaction exposures can therefore arise from operating and free cash flows, e.g., accounts receivable and payable arising from the conduct of business; commitments to buy or lease capital equipment or financing cash flows, e.g., debt or equity service obligations arising from the funding of the firm's business.

b. **Translation exposure**. A cross-border firm must periodically remeasure all of its global operations into a single currency for reporting purposes. This requires that the balance sheets and income statements of all affiliate operations worldwide be translated and consolidated into the currency of the parent company. Imbalances resulting from translation represent a potential change in the firm's reported consolidated income, reported capital base, or both.

c. **Economic exposure**. Aside from existing obligations of the firm which will be settled in foreign currencies at future dates (transaction exposure) and the imbalances resulting from consolidation practices (translation exposure), the firm's present value—firm value—will change as the value of expected future cash flows (and costs of capital) change as a result of unexpected exchange rate changes. More precisely, a firm is said to have economic exposure to exchange rates when unanticipated *real* (as opposed to nominal, a distinction we will clarify later in the Note) exchange rate changes have a nonzero effect on its expected future cash flows. People also sometimes use the terms operating exposure, real exposure, and competitive exposure as synonyms for such economic exposure.

TRANSACTION EXPOSURE MANAGEMENT

A transaction exposure of the firm is a singular event, an individual foreign currency-denominated cash flow commitment which exposes the firm to a loss or gain upon settlement of the outstanding obligation. The individual transaction exposure can be measured in a number of different ways. Consider, for example, a U.S.-based manufacturer of heavy machine tools who accepts an order from a British buyer and agrees to invoice the sale in British pounds. He is exposed to the movement of the U.S. dollar/ British pound exchange rate. If the sale is made for £100,000, payment due in 90 days from receipt of invoice, the U.S. firm will not know the exact amount in U.S. dollars until actual cash settlement.

When the British buyer first asked for a price quote from the American firm, a transaction exposure was implicitly created. Although far from certain at this point—many price quotes are made by sellers without receiving orders—the American firm has committed itself for some specified period of time to making the sale at the stated foreign currency price. The price is quoted

as £100,000, and suppose the spot exchange rate on that date is $1.6000/£. Seven days later, when the spot rate is $1.6300/£, the order is made. Now this quotation becomes a contractual obligation of the firm, a true transaction exposure. But even at this stage, it is an obligation which is largely invisible. This is because although the firm has committed itself to the production and shipment of the machine tool, the contract itself is essentially work-in-process and not individually identified among the assets of the firm as a foreign currency-denominated asset. For this reason many firms do not identify the transaction as a transaction exposure at this point in time. It may take an additional few weeks to fill the order and ready for shipment.

Upon shipment, however, things change. When the firm ships the product, losing physical control over the goods, an accounts receivable is issued and the sale is now entered into the books of the firm as a foreign currency denominated receivable. Settlement is due in 90 days. The value of the receivable is then booked in current sales at the spot exchange rate in effect on the posting date. If the spot rate was $1.6200/£ on the shipping date, the sale would be booked as £100,000 × $1.6200/£, or $162,000. At the end of the 90-day period upon settlement of the receivable, the final settlement is recorded at the spot rate of exchange on that date, $1.6100/£, and any difference between booking and settlement is categorized as a currency gain or loss.

How are these gains and losses accounted for? In this case, a foreign currency loss of $1,000 is recorded on the American firm's books, settlement of $161,000 less a booked amount of $162,000. The somewhat counter-intuitive result of accounting practices is seen here, as a loss is recognized on the company's income statement although the transaction's value is higher at all dates, including settlement, than it was upon the initial quotation! As illustrated it is obvious that although generally accepted accounting practices record the transaction and exchange rate at the booking date, internally, the firm itself should be expecting a home currency value at settlement closer to that at which it initially quoted the potential sale.

Management Alternatives in Transaction Exposure

Transaction exposures can be managed, or hedged, using either contractual solutions or operational solutions. Contractual solutions include forward contracts, foreign currency options, and foreign currency futures. These are financial derivatives, with their values changing over time as the asset underlying their value—in this case, a currency—changes. Contractual solutions enter the firm into derivative-based positions which manage the individual transaction exposure, at the end of which they are either liquidated or simply expire. Their cost ranges from zero out-of-pocket expense (forward contracts, although the bid-ask spreads represent an implicit transaction cost) to up-front payment (currency options).

Operational solutions include risk-sharing agreements and currency matching. Risk-sharing agreements are pricing agreements whereby the buyer and seller of goods or services agree on a formula-based "sharing" of exchange rate changes. Currency matching is the ongoing process of matching cash inflows and outflows by currency per period of time. Although operational solutions are inherently multi-period, many firms will, as a result of the structure of their continuing business, incur the same basic transaction exposure over and over again. Although many firms do not view operational solutions as relevant to the individual transaction exposure, they are as relevant a choice for transaction exposure management as are forwards, futures, and options.

Directional Views, Forwards and Options. The selection of the proper hedge is as much about the firm's philosophy towards exchange rate risks as it is about the financial theories underlying derivative instruments. There are two determinants in the hedge instrument selection process:

(1) the willingness of the firm to take a directional view on the movement of exchange rates over the period of the exposure and (2) the willingness to accept downside risk upon getting the directional view wrong.

A firm which wishes to hedge an individual transaction exposure, such as the £100,000 receivable described previously, could enter into a forward contract with one of its banks to sell pounds at a specific exchange rate upon receipt in 90 days. This forward contract eliminates the currency risk and the firm gains the knowledge now of what the foreign currency denominated cash flow's value will be in domestic currency terms upon settlement. Risk—both downside and upside—has been eliminated. The firm will now know with certainty the dollar revenues to be received and the currency gain or loss to be incurred.[7] While the use of the forward contract does not require management to explicitly predict the movement of exchange rates, it is important to recognize that the firm incurs an opportunity loss associated with the gain foregone if the foreign currency had moved in the firm's favor by the end of the life of the exposure. (In our example, this would be the case if the British pound appreciated instead of depreciating.)

The use of currency options, however, requires the firm to form a directional view on the movement of the exchange rate over the period in question. If management predicts that the exchange rate will move against it—in the case of the British pound denominated receivable, this would be for the pound to depreciate from $1.6000/£ toward, say, $1.5500/£—the firm could purchase a put option on British pounds. The put option will give it the right, not the obligation, to sell the British pounds at a future date (maturity) for an agreed-upon exchange rate (the exercise price). The option would be purchased as insurance against a depreciation of the British pound relative to the exercise price.[8] If the British pound appreciates, i.e., ends up greater than $1.6000/£, the put option would be allowed to expire worthless, since the firm can now bring back home more dollars than initially anticipated. If, however, the British pound depreciates to below $1.6000/£, the put option would be exercised to guarantee that the firm receives an exchange rate that is the originally agreed upon exercise price at settlement. In other words *by using a put option to protect its U.S. dollar receivable against the depreciation of the foreign currency, the firm has put a floor on the home currency value of its expected receipts.*

In a similar vein, when the firm wishes to hedge a foreign currency payable—or more generally expected future payments in the foreign currency—and it has formed the directional view that the foreign currency would appreciate, it will buy a call option on the foreign currency. The call option will give it the right, not the obligation, to buy the foreign currency at maturity for a certain exercise price. If the foreign currency depreciates, the call option would be allowed to expire worthless, since the firm can now put out fewer dollars than initially anticipated to meet its foreign currency payment obligation. If, however, the foreign currency appreciates, the call would be exercised to guarantee that the firm pays no more than the exercise price for the exchange rate originally agreed upon. In other words, *by using a call option to protect its U.S. dollar payable against the appreciation of the foreign currency, the firm has put a ceiling on the home currency value of its expected payments.*

There are, however, complexities. Given the increasing sophistication of derivative securities like currency options, it is easy for management to lose sight of the significance of the individual transaction within the context of management's general financial responsibilities. A firm which only occasionally incurs foreign currency denominated transactions may be comfortable using only the simplest in financial derivatives, for example, forward contracts, whereas firms which denominate large proportions of their cash flows in foreign currencies may develop a more aggressive approach. Often the resources employed by firms to monitor markets and form directional views do not justify the resulting occasional gains and losses arising from a directional view-based hedging program. In most

firms, currency gains above some benchmark such as the forward rate do not justify the losses incurred when directional viewpoints prove off the mark.

A second complexity is that of derivative accounting and hedge accounting. Hedge accounting practices, as outlined by the Financial Accounting Standards Board (FASB),[9] allow that gains and losses on hedging instruments be recognized in earnings at the same time as the effects of changes in the value of the items being hedged are recognized, assuming certain criteria are met. If a forward contract was purchased as a hedge of the British pound receivable noted previously, changes in the value of the forward contract would only be recognized in firm income when the changes in the value of the receivable were recognized, typically on settlement.

This would seem obvious except for the possibility that the 90-day receivable was created during one year, but would be settled in the following year, e.g., after December 31, the firm's end-of-year balance sheet date. Under traditional accounting practices, the firm would have to value the forward contract and the receivable on December 31 at the spot exchange rate on that date, and recognize those valuation impacts in current income.[10] This alters reported current income even though no cash flows have occurred. Many firms legitimately feel that such a practice defeats the purpose of hedging. The criteria set forth by FASB for hedge accounting sometimes create a difficulty. According to FAS 52, paragraph 21:

> A foreign currency transaction shall be considered a hedge of an identifiable foreign currency commitment provided both of the following are met:
>
> 1. the foreign currency transaction is designated as, and is effective as, a hedge of a foreign currency commitment.
>
> 2. the foreign currency commitment is firm.

The first condition focuses on the ability of the forward contract to act effectively as a hedge, its value moving in the opposite direction to that of the exposure given a spot exchange rate change. This condition is typically met. The second condition is controversial. For a commitment to be considered "firm," the exposure must have some type of financial certainty of occurring. For example, if a company has sold merchandise to a foreign buyer, a contract exists and the buyer can be expected to actually pay as agreed. If, however, the receivable resulted from the sale of merchandise to an affiliate of the same firm, there must be some basis for expecting the payment to occur in the amount and on the date designated. This is a difficult requirement for most multinational firms to meet since most intra-firm sales and transactions do not have explicit contracts or penalties for nonperformance.

TRANSLATION EXPOSURE MANAGEMENT

Translation exposure arises because financial statements of foreign affiliates must be restated in the parent's currency in order to consolidate financial statements. Foreign affiliates of U.S. companies must restate local currency statements into U.S. dollars so the foreign values can be added to the parent's balance sheet and income statement. Although the main purpose of translation is to prepare consolidated statements, they are also often used by management to assess the performance of foreign affiliates. Such restatement of all affiliate statements into the single common denominator of one currency facilitates management comparison. Translation or accounting exposure results from change in the parent's net worth, assets, liabilities, and reported net income caused by a change in exchange rates since the last translation.

According to FAS Statement No. 52, the motivation for consolidation procedures is the following:

> Financial statements are intended to present information in financial terms about the performance, financial position, and cash flows of an enterprise. For this purpose, the financial statements of separate entities within an enterprise, which may exist and operate in different economic and currency environments, are consolidated and presented as

though they were the financial statements of a single enterprise. Because it is not possible to combine, add, or subtract measurements expressed in different currencies, it is necessary to translate into a single reporting currency those assets, liabilities, revenues, expenses, gains and losses that are measured or denominated in a foreign currency.[11]

The objectives of translation according to FAS No. 52 are: (1) to provide information that is generally compatible with the expected economic effects of a rate change on an enterprise's cash flows and equity and (2) to reflect in consolidated statements the financial results and relationships of the individual consolidated entities as measured in their functional currencies in conformity with U.S. generally accepted accounting principles.

Functional Versus Reporting Currency. FAS Statement No. 52 uses what is termed the "functional" currency approach. According to the FASB: "An entity's functional currency is the currency of the primary economic environment in which the entity operates; normally, that is the currency of the environment in which an entity primarily generates and expends cash."[12] The selection of the functional currency for the remeasurement of the financial statements of a foreign operation has two primary effects: (1) it determines the procedures to be used in the measurement—in home currency terms—of its financial position and operational results, and (2) whether the exchange gains and losses resulting from remeasurement are to be included in the consolidated net income of the firm or reported as a separate component of the consolidated stockholders' equity.

The problem is that a foreign affiliate's functional currency can differ from its reporting currency. A reporting currency is the currency used by the parent to present its own financial statements and thus normally its home currency. The determination of functional currency is left up to management. Management must evaluate the nature and purpose of its foreign operations to decide on the appropriate functional currency for each. The core principle behind functional currency determination is the identification of which currency cash flow is the driving force of the affiliate's business. The choice of functional currency, in turn, determines the method—the "current rate" method or the "temporal" method—that is used to restate the financial statements of the foreign affiliate. A proper understanding of the differences between these restatement procedures depends on a number of very specific definitions of how certain assets, liabilities, and cash flows do or do not change with exchange rate movements.

Methods Used to Restate Financial Statements. When the foreign affiliate's functional currency is the same as the currency of its books, the appropriate procedure is referred to as "translation" by FAS No. 52. Translation requires that all elements of the affiliate's balance sheet be restated into U.S. dollars using the exchange rate that prevails on the translation date and income statement items be translated at the actual exchange rate at which transactions occurred, or some weighted average exchange rate. Any resulting gains or losses resulting from the translation of the foreign affiliate's financial statements are reported as adjustments to stockholder's equity and are termed translation adjustments or cumulative translation adjustments (CTAs). Income statement items are translated as the actual exchange rates prevailing on the date of transaction (or some weighted average). This method is often referred to as the "current rate" method.

When the foreign affiliate's functional currency is the U.S. dollar then the appropriate procedure is referred to as "remeasurement." Remeasurement, as described by FAS No. 52, requires that both historical and current exchange rates be used in the restatement of the foreign affiliate's financial statements into U.S. dollars. All monetary assets and liabilities are restated at current exchange rates, while all nonmonetary assets and liabilities are restated at the historical exchange rates. Monetary assets and liabilities are those balance sheet items whose amounts are fixed in currency units. For example, the accounts receivable of the German subsidiary

which are denominated in euro are fixed in the quantity of euro which are to be received on a specific future date. Because the exchange rate on that future date is not now known, the receivable is valued at the spot exchange rate on the date of restatement. Nonmonetary assets and liabilities are those balance sheet items whose amounts change with market prices. Any gains or losses resulting from the remeasurement of the foreign affiliate's financial statements are included in consolidated income. This method is often referred to as the "temporal" method.

Figure 2 demonstrates the current rate method and the temporal method for the translation of the balance sheet of a Mexican subsidiary of a U.S.-based company. Note that the current rate method results in translation adjustment loss (which would go to consolidated equity), whereas the temporal method results in a translation gain (which would go to consolidated income). The primary issue from management's viewpoint is where the translation gains (losses) are reflected. Since the temporal method views the currency of economic consequence of the subsidiary to be the same as the parent's, any gains (losses) arising from remeasurement are reflected in consolidated income. For a subsidiary whose functional currency is that of the local market, however, gains (losses) resulting from its translation will be reflected in consolidated equity, not in current income.

Management of translation exposure continues to be a topic of substantial debate. On the one hand, the accounting method itself produces no underlying cash flow changes. On the other hand, under the "remeasurement" procedures of the temporal method, consolidated income could be affected dramatically.

Management Alternatives in Translation Exposure

There are a number of motivations for active management of translation exposure and not all of them are justifiable. The first is in the event of subsidiary liquidation. If a subsidiary has created CTAs, these gains and losses will be realized in

Panel A: Current Rate Method (Mexican peso is functional currency)					
Assets	Mexican Pesos	Ps/$	U.S. Dollars	Ps/$	U.S. Dollars
Cash	1,000,000	3.20	312,500	5.50	181,818
Accounts receivable	7,500,000	3.20	2,343,750	5.50	1,363,636
Inventory	13,000,000	3.20	4,062,500	5.50	2,363,636
Net plant and equipment	18,500,000	3.20	5,781,250	5.50	3,363,636
Total assets	**40,000,000**		**12,500,000**		**7,272,727**
Liabilities & net worth					
Accounts payable	2,500,000	3.20	781,250	5.50	454,545
Short-term bank debt	3,000,000	3.20	937,500	5.50	545,455
Long-term debt	15,000,000	3.20	4,687,500	5.50	2,727,273
Equity capital[a]	15,000,000	3.00	5,000,000	3.00	5,000,000
Retained earnings	4,500,000	3.10	1,451,613	3.10	1,451,613
Total liabilities & net worth	**40,000,000**		**12,857,863**		**10,178,886**
Cumulative translation adjustment (CTA)[b]			**(357,863)**		**(2,906,158)**

Panel B: Temporal Method (U.S. dollar is functional currency)					
Assets	Mexican Pesos	Ps/$	U.S. Dollars	Ps/$	U.S. Dollars
Cash	1,000,000	3.20	312,500	5.50	181,818
Accounts receivable	7,500,000	3.20	2,343,750	5.50	1,363,636
Inventory	13,000,000	3.10	4,193,548	3.10	4,193,548
Net plant and equipment	18,500,000	3.00	6,166,667	3.00	6,166,667
Total assets	**40,000,000**		**13,016,465**		**11,905,670**
Liabilities & net worth					
Accounts payable	2,500,000	3.20	781,250	5.50	454,545
Short-term bank debt	3,000,000	3.20	937,500	5.50	545,455
Long-term debt	15,000,000	3.20	4,687,500	5.50	2,727,273
Equity capital[a]	15,000,000	3.00	5,000,000	3.00	5,000,000
Retained earnings	4,500,000	3.10	1,451,613	3.10	1,451,613
Total liabilities & net worth	**40,000,000**		**12,857,863**		**10,178,886**
Translation gain (loss)[b]			**158,602**		**1,726,784**

Figure 2   Balance Sheet Translation of a Mexican Subsidiary of a U.S.-Based Company: A Comparison of the Current Rate Method and Temporal Method

a. Equity capital was injected when the exchange rate was Ps3.00/$, and retained earnings reflect a vintage of exchange rates and earnings as retained.

b. Translation adjustments and gains (losses) are in essence a plug value which maintains the balance of the entire translated balance sheet.

	3Q/2000 Operating Income ($ m)	Reduction Because of Euro Depreciation
Goodyear	$68	30.0%
Caterpillar	$294	12.0%
McDonald's	$910	5.0%
Kimberly-Clark	$667	2.5%

Figure 3   The Impact of the Depreciating Euro on Selected U.S. Multinationals

Source: "Business Won't Hedge the Euro Away," *Business Week*, December 4, 2000.

current income upon liquidation. A firm planning such a liquidation could hedge against those in the period prior to liquidation.

A second motivation is to preserve the integrity of balance sheet ratios, particularly in light of covenants or other restrictions by creditors. A firm experiencing continual translation losses which are accumulating in its equity accounts may see deteriorating ratios. To the extent that this leads to an increase in the firm's cost of debt financing and, hence, its cost of capital, it could have an impact on the value of the firm.

A third motivation for the management of translation is managerial compensation. Management compensation is frequently based on post-translation financials. During periods of appreciation of the consolidation currency, management of subsidiary operations may feel that they are being unfairly held to account for the movement of currencies, rather than for their ability to manage and grow the subsidiary.

The fourth situation in which translation exposure may deserve active management is when a subsidiary is operating in an economic environment in which the currency is rapidly depreciating. Although accounting standards refer to this as "hyper-inflation," the problem is currency depreciation, not necessarily inflation. (The linkage between prices and exchange rates is explored in the following section in detail.) For example, according to FAS No. 52, a subsidiary operating in an economic environment with a cumulative inflation rate of 100% or more over a three-year period must use the temporal method and pass all remeasurement losses

through current income. This could obviously result in a substantial impact on consolidated income, something that the parent may wish to manage.

The final instance in which management or hedging of translation exposure has become significant is in the protection of consolidated reporting earnings. In recent years a number of major multinational firms have discovered that they can protect the reported U.S. dollar value of foreign earnings by hedging them. For example, in the third and fourth quarters of 2000, a number of major U.S. multinationals grew increasingly concerned over the depreciation of the euro (see Figure 3). Given the significant contribution of profits earned in euros to total profits, the depreciation of the euro resulted in deterioration of reported earnings per share. Some, like the Coca Cola Company which hedged the dollar value of its projected euro earnings, showed little material declines in consolidated earnings. Others, like Goodyear and Caterpillar, saw double-digit percentage reductions in consolidated earnings as a result of their unhedged euro earnings.

Actual management of translation exposure is difficult and potentially costly. Currency gains (losses) associated with liquidation may be covered with something as simple as a forward contract. CTA losses which are accumulating over time in the parent's consolidated equity, however, are much more difficult to deal with. The basic balance sheet of the subsidiary must be altered by currency of denomination in order to reduce "exposed assets" without simultaneously reducing "exposed liabilities." For example, if the Mexican subsidiary were to acquire additional debt and hold the proceeds in non-peso denominated assets of some kind—say, U.S. dollars—it could effectively reduce its exposure to losses arising from translation. This can, however, have a real cash flow impact in terms of differences in interest rates either paid or received when altering assets and liabilities purely for translation purposes.

MANAGEMENT OF ECONOMIC EXPOSURE

On June 21, 1994, John F. Welch, then-Chairman and CEO of General Electric, wrote an op-ed article in the *Wall Street Journal* arguing that "Global competitors [of U.S. firms] are taking actions that could push U.S. manufacturers from the deceptive tranquility of the eye back into the turbulence of a hurricane, a hurricane that this time will come with a ferocity that could be intensified should the currency go the wrong way." He went on to say, "If the Japanese are preparing to compete at 90 yen [to the U.S. dollar], the U.S. must be ready to compete at 130. Until we are, we delude ourselves if we think we are in control of our own fate."

What was Mr. Welch talking about?

As it turns out, he was addressing an important issue concerning the impact of exchange rates on the competitive position of U.S. multinationals, or a type of exchange rate exposure referred to as "economic exposure to exchange rates." It is an issue that many CFOs—let alone General Managers and CEOs—do not actively think about for a number of reasons. One, it deals with the effects of exchange rates that have not happened yet, but could happen. Unfortunately it is inherent in the nature of many incentive systems that managers get rewarded for their ability to deal with problems that have arisen in the past rather than their ability to avoid problems of the future by careful anticipation. Two, it deals with the effects of exchange rates that are sometimes difficult to pin down and measure; since information systems have a bias toward focusing attention on

those things that can be measured, this issue often gets overlooked. Three, understanding economic exposures requires us to understand a subtle distinction between *nominal* and *real* exchange rates, a distinction that managers often do not worry about.

Economic exposure to exchange rates says that the only exchange rate change that matters for the value of cross-border cash flows is an *unexpected real change* in the value of a firm's home currency against the currencies in which a firm is conducting its business; a purely nominal change in the exchange rate does not matter. Unlike the cases of translation and transaction exposures which can be managed using appropriate tools of risk management, economic exposure often requires resolution through longer-term operational and strategic decisions made by the firm. Financial risk management tools may not only be ineffective in managing economic exposure to exchange rates, but they may actually be counterproductive.

The Intuition Behind Real and Nominal Changes in Currency Values

Analogous to concerns with the effects of inflation in the domestic setting on nominal versus real price levels, the effects of relative inflation rates between the home economy and the foreign economy matter for the exchange rate between the two countries.

Taking the purely domestic case, when inflation rates are higher, goods and services cost more in an economy. But does that mean that purchasing power has eroded in that economy? Not necessarily. Whether or not purchasing power has eroded depends on what happens to incomes in the domestic economy. If incomes go up by exactly the same percentage as the rate of inflation in prices, nothing happens to the real value of purchasing power in the economy. More precisely, there has been a nominal increase in price levels, but real purchasing power has remained the same.

An analogous idea holds in the international setting. When the foreign inflation rate is higher—and the domestic inflation rate does not change—the foreign country currency would be expected to depreciate against the domestic currency. In other words, the foreign currency costs less to buy using domestic currency. But that does not necessarily mean that the real value of our purchases of goods and services across borders has become cheaper. Why? Since inflation rates are higher abroad than at home, if the increase in foreign prices for goods and services has exactly offset the decline in the value of the foreign currency, then purchasing power would remain the same. Just as in the domestic case, while the foreign currency has undergone a nominal depreciation, it has not undergone a real depreciation.[13]

Thus, what matters for purchasing power across any two countries is the change in the nominal value of a currency after adjustment for the changes in the relative inflation rates between the two countries. This change, i.e., the change in nominal currency value between two countries over and above that which would be predicted by the relative inflation rates between the two countries, is called the real exchange rate change. When a currency appreciates in real terms, its purchasing power abroad has increased; when it depreciates in real terms, its purchasing power abroad has eroded.

Currencies and Purchasing Power Parity

Assume the United States (U.S.) is the home country and the dollar ($) the home currency, and the European Union (EU), with its currency the euro (€), is the foreign country. Define the $/€ exchange rate—that is, the number of U.S. dollars it takes to buy each euro—as e.[14] Suppose the $/€ exchange rate one month ago was $0.80/€, but the exchange rate is now $0.90/€—in other words, e has gone up by ¢10. But since it costs ¢10 more to buy the euro than it did one month ago, the dollar has depreciated by ¢10 against the euro (or equivalently, the euro has appreciated by ¢10 against the dollar). Suppose we denote the percentage change in the value of the dollar

against the euro as Δe. Then during the past month, $\Delta e = (0.90-0.80)/(0.80) = 12.50\%$ or, the euro has appreciated by 12.50% against the U.S. dollar. Note that this is a positive number, that is, $\Delta e > 0$. What if e had moved down to $0.70/€? In this case, the euro has become ¢10 cheaper during the past month, and $\Delta e = (0.70-0.80)/(0.80) = -12.50\%$ or the euro has depreciated nominally by 12.50% against the U.S. dollar. Note that this is a negative number, that is, $\Delta e < 0$.

The theory of PPP, perhaps one of the most influential ideas in all of economics, establishes a link between prices in any two countries and their exchange rate. Suppose the domestic price level is P, the foreign price level is P*, and the exchange rate (direct quote from the standpoint of the domestic country) is e. Then a version of PPP theory called Absolute PPP (APPP for short) would argue that the domestic price level must equal the exchange rate-adjusted foreign price level, or:

$$(1)\ P = eP*$$

Consider a simple example. Suppose a BMW automobile costs €60,000 in France and the $/€ exchange rate is $1/€. Then APPP (using the formula above) says that a similar BMW should cost $60,000 in the U.S. If not, the argument goes, there would be an arbitrage opportunity to buy in the country where the exchange rate-adjusted price is cheaper and sell in the country where it is more expensive. The very process of a free goods market undertaking such transactions would eliminate such an arbitrage opportunity, with the result that APPP will become true in equilibrium.

Suppose, for instance, the BMW costs only $50,000 in the U.S. At the current $/€ exchange rate, this works out to €50,000. French traders would have the incentive to start buying their BMWs in the U.S. by paying $50,000 and selling in France for €60,000, thereby making an arbitrage profit of €10,000. However, this happy situation will not last long. The demand for BMWs in the U.S. would go up, and thereby start to increase the U.S. price; likewise, the excess supply of BMWs in France would start to lower the euro price. Moreover, in the process of paying for their BMWs in the U.S., the French traders would be supplying euros and demanding dollars in the foreign exchange markets; this would, in turn, depreciate the value of the euro and appreciate the value of the dollar (in other words e, defined from the dollar viewpoint, will start to decrease). More generally, going back to our APPP definition, P would start to rise and both e and P* would start to fall, until such time that the prices for BMWs would be the same in the two countries. In other words P (the U.S. dollar price) would be equal to eP∗ (the euro price adjusted for the exchange rate).

This insight can then be used across a wide range of traded goods and services between any two countries (or even a country and all of its trading partners). The result is the idea of PPP holding at the national level (with respect to some aggregate measure of prices such as the producer or consumer price index) and with respect to the exchange rate between the two countries.

But note something important from the example above. Since prices were higher in France, the ultimate result of this disequilibrium was to depreciate the euro against the U.S. dollar, so as to bring things back into equilibrium. More generally, we might say that when inflation rates are higher in France relative to the U.S., we would expect the euro to undergo a nominal depreciation against the U.S. dollar. This idea can be made more precise, and it provides us with the most commonly used and understood version of PPP (it is, sometimes, also called Relative PPP). If we call ΔP the expected domestic inflation rate, $\Delta P*$ the expected foreign inflation rate, and Δe is the expected change in the value of the U.S. dollar against the €, then the precise definition of relative PPP, or RPPP, says that:

$$1 + \Delta P = (1 + \Delta e)(1 + \Delta P*)$$

This can be rearranged to form a simple expression for predicting the expected exchange rate change given expected inflation rates between the two countries:

$$\Delta e = \frac{(1 + \Delta P)}{(1 + \Delta P*)} - 1$$

Note that when the domestic inflation rate is higher than the foreign inflation rate (that is, ΔP is greater than $\Delta P*$), Δe will be a positive number, and hence, the foreign currency would be expected to appreciate. When the reverse is true, Δe would be a negative number and the foreign currency would be expected to depreciate.

For example, if the expected inflation rate in France is 10% and the expected inflation rate in the U.S. is 5%, then PPP would predict that $\Delta e = [(1.05)/(1.10)] - 1 = -4.55\%$ meaning the euro would be expected to depreciate by 4.55% against the U.S. dollar. Given the initial exchange rate of \$1/€, the new predicted exchange rate (e_{New}) would be:

$$e_{New} = 1 \times (1 - .0455) = \$0.9545/€$$

Now we are ready to tackle the idea of changes in the real exchange rate. Once we have done so, it becomes possible to precisely define economic exposure to exchange rates and to explore the managerial implications. In the example above, we saw that if PPP held, then given our inflation assumptions, we would expect the euro to depreciate by 4.55% against the U.S. dollar. Suppose, however, that the actual depreciation—or the *nominal* depreciation—turned out to be, say, only 2.5%. In other words, as events actually turned out, the euro depreciated by less than was predicted by PPP (by 2.05% less).

This difference of 2.05% is the real exchange rate change. In this particular case, although the euro has undergone a nominal depreciation of 2.5%, the French franc has undergone a *real appreciation* of 2.05%! Why? Inflation differentials, i.e., RPPP, would have predicted a 4.55% depreciation; instead, the actual (or nominal) depreciation was only 2.5%. The euro ended up depreciating by less than predicted, and hence in real terms, this is tantamount to an appreciation.

More generally, if we define the real exchange rate as *s,* and the change in the real exchange rate as $\Delta s,$ then the real exchange rate change is defined as:

(4) Δs = {Actual exchange rate change} *minus* {PPP-predicted exchange rate change}

$$= \{\Delta e_{Actual}\} - \left\{ \frac{(1 + \Delta P)}{(1 + \Delta P^*)} - 1 \right\}$$

In the example above, the PPP-predicted change was –4.55%, and the actual (or nominal) change was –2.5% (recalling that appreciation will have a negative sign when using direct quotes). The value of the actual minus the PPP-predicted change is $-2.5\% - (-4.55\%) = +2.05\%$, and since we are using direct quotes and the change is a positive number, it is a real appreciation of the euro.

Definition and Sources of Economic Exposure

A firm is said to have economic exposure to exchange rates when unanticipated changes in real exchange rates have a non-zero effect on its expected future cash flows.[15] (People also sometimes use the terms operating exposure, real exposure, and competitive exposure as rough synonyms for such economic exposure.) In the previous section we argued that what matters for economic exposure is real, and not nominal, exchange rate changes.

Let us now see why through a simple example. Suppose a U.S. firm is competing against a Japanese firm (in Japan) by exporting its products from the U.S. Its products are priced in yen (¥), but its costs are incurred in US$. Assume that the initial exchange rate is ¥100/US$ (the direct quote from the Japanese standpoint). Assume further that: (1) Initially, price per unit and average costs are the same for the U.S. and the Japanese firm (they both are equally competitive); (2) They both sell the same number of units, in fact, just one each of the product; and (3) The price per unit is, say, ¥100 (= $1 at the current exchange rate) and cost per unit is, say, ¥80 (= $0.80 at the current exchange rate). All of these are simplifying assumptions. The initial profit margin for both firms is, therefore, 20%.

Panel A of Figure 4 summarizes the initial competitive situation for the two firms.

Panel A: Initial Situation		
Exchange rate = ¥100/$	U.S. Exporter	Japanese Competitor
Revenue	$1.00	¥100
Costs	$0.80	¥ 80
Profits	$0.20	¥ 20
Profit Margin	20%	20%
Panel B: PPP Holds (10% U.S. inflation; 0% Japanese inflation)		
Exchange rate = ¥90.9/$*	U.S. Exporter	Japanese Competitor
Revenue	$1.10	¥100
Costs	$0.88	¥ 80
Profits	$0.22	¥ 20
Profit Margin	20%	20%

Figure 4   Real Currency Changes and Economic Exposure: Initial Situation (Panel A) and PPP Holds (Panel B)

*The new exchange rate is derived by applying PPP formula to obtain Δe, and then multiplying $(1 + \Delta e)$ by the initial exchange rate of ¥100/$.

Suppose the U.S. inflation rate goes up to 10%, while there is no price inflation in Japan (that is, the Japanese inflation rate is 0%). Using the RPPP formula (and treating Japan as the home country), we can calculate what would be expected to happen to the ¥/$ exchange rate:

$$\Delta e = \frac{(1 + \Delta P)}{(1 + \Delta P^*)} - 1 = (1/1.1) - 1 = -9.1\%$$

Thus, RPPP would predict that, given the 10% higher inflation rate in the U.S. compared to Japan, the U.S. dollar will depreciate by 9.1% against the Japanese yen. Therefore the new predicted exchange rate would be:

$$e_{New} = (¥100/\$) \times (1 - 0.091) = ¥90.9/\$.$$

Suppose the exchange rate moves exactly as predicted by PPP—in other words, all of the exchange rate change is purely nominal. What would happen to the competitive position of the U.S. firm against the Japanese firm? Panel B of Figure 4 examines this. First, note that nothing happens to the Japanese firm (since there is no inflation in Japan): it still sells its product for ¥100, incurs a cost per unit of ¥80, and makes a profit of ¥20 for a profit margin of 20%. What about the U.S. firm? Given the 10% inflation in the U.S., its costs have gone up by 10%, to 88 cents for each unit produced and sold. However, its revenues have also gone up by 10%. This is because, at the new exchange rate of ¥90.9/$, its Japanese sales of ¥100 are translated to $1.10 back in the U.S. Its profit is now 22 cents and its

profit margin is the same 20% as before. In other words, because PPP held, all the change in the exchange rate was purely nominal, and nothing happens to the competitive position of either firm.[16]

Now let us see what happens if PPP fails to hold. Despite the 10% inflation rate in the U.S., suppose the ¥/$ exchange rate stayed the same as before, at ¥100/$. This would imply that, instead of depreciating by the expected 9.1% as predicted by PPP, the US$ stayed put, and therefore, it actually appreciated in real terms by 9.1%. Figure 5 addresses what happens to the competitive positions of the two firms.

Again, we see that nothing happens to the Japanese firm: its domestic revenues stay at ¥100, its cost at ¥80, profit at ¥20, and its profit margin is the same 20% as before. But the U.S. firm is now in trouble—since there is 10% inflation in the U.S., its costs have still gone up, 88 cents. However, its yen revenue of ¥100, when translated into US$, brings in only $1.00 at the still prevailing exchange rate of ¥100/$. The U.S. firm's profit shrinks to 12 cents, and its profit margin to 12%. (And the manager of this firm might be asking, "What is going on here?" given that the exchange rate hasn't even changed.)

In fact, this is a relatively benign scenario. A worse competitive situation would be one where the Japanese competitor, knowing this, was to start lowering his yen prices and thereby start to take away market share. This would put pressure on the U.S. firm to either reduce its profit margins further (by matching the competitor's pricing move in order to keep market share) or lose share and lower total profits.

Exchange rate = ¥100/$*	U.S. Exporter	Japanese Competitor
Revenue	$1.00	¥100
Costs	$0.80	¥80
Profits	$0.12	¥20
Profit Margin	12%	20%

Figure 5   Real Currency Changes and Economic Exposure: PPP Does Not Hold

*Assumes 10% U.S. inflation rate, 0% Japanese inflation rate, but exchange rate does not change from the initial level of ¥100/$ as shown in Panel A of Figure 4.

We can take away a number of important insights from this seemingly simple example:

- Purely nominal changes in currency values are irrelevant for economic exposure to exchange rates. What matters is a real appreciation or a real depreciation.
- A real appreciation of the home currency is bad news for those whose costs are incurred in the home currency and revenues are incurred in the foreign currency. This is typically the case with export-intensive firms, or firms that have sales subsidiaries abroad that are financed in the home currency, or firms that rely on income sources such as royalty payments from abroad. A real depreciation, on the other hand, is good news for such firms.
- A real depreciation of the home currency is bad news for those whose revenues are incurred in the home currency and costs are incurred in the foreign currency. This is typically the case with import-intensive firms, or firms that have subsidiaries abroad that supply to the parent company, or firms that have to make royalty payments in the foreign currency. A real appreciation, on the other hand, is good news for such firms.
- If your costs are denominated in the home currency and your competitor's costs in the foreign currency, then a real appreciation will make you less competitive. The reverse is true with a real depreciation.

Management Alternatives for Economic Exposure

The simple example above suggests that there are three categories of exchange rates that matter in order to figure out whether (and how much) a firm or division has economic exposure: (1) The currency of denomination of the firm's revenues; (2) The currency of denomination of the firm's costs; and (3) The currency of denomination of the firm's competitors' revenues and costs. A firm is likely to have economic exposure to exchange rates whenever the currency of denomination of its revenues is different from the currency of denomination of its costs, i.e., when (1) and (2) are in different currencies, or when

the currency of denomination of its revenues and costs are different from that of its competitors, i.e., even if (1) and (2) are in the same currency, when they are different from (3).

Thus, the first set of questions that a manager needs to ask concerning the possible existence of economic exposure are the following:

- What is the currency of denomination of my costs versus that of my revenues? Are they different?
- What is the currency of denomination of my costs and revenues versus those of my competitor? Are they different?

If the answer to either question is "yes," then a firm (or a division) is likely to have economic exposure to exchange rates.

An Example: The Case of Jaguar plc. Towards the end of 1984, Jaguar plc, a U.K.-based manufacturer of luxury high-priced automobiles, was assessing its economic exposure to exchange rates. In their London offices, CFO John Edwards was getting advice from his economic advisors and he himself was convinced that the sustained real appreciation of the U.S. dollar had begun to run out of steam, and the currency value was about to reverse course. To the extent that price changes took place in this market, one firm usually played the role of price leader—in the U.S. market, Daimler Benz plays this role.

Jaguar sold over 50% of its cars in the U.S., and its production costs and factories are U.K.-based; further, labor accounts for a significant portion of the cost base for luxury cars. In the recent past, Jaguar has performed extremely well in the U.S. market, thanks in large part to the substantial real appreciation of the U.S. dollar against all European currencies. While the strong dollar gave Jaguar the opportunity to cut its prices, it had not done so (nor had its competition). Mr. Edwards knew that the projected depreciation of the U.S. dollar would seriously cut into his profitability, and some upward revision of prices would be required if the depreciation did happen. For starters he had to make a broad assessment of the nature of Jaguar's economic exposure to exchange rates.

The first question confronting Mr. Edwards was, which are the main currencies that he should worry about vis-à-vis his economic exposure to exchange rates? The U.S. dollar only, the U.K. pound only, or the Deutsche mark only, or all three? The answer is all three.

His exposure to the US$ and UK£ is fairly obvious. First, since a substantial part of his revenues are denominated in the US$, he should worry about the US$ as the currency of denomination of his revenues. Second, since most of his costs are U.K.-based, the currency of denomination of costs is the UK£. Given the mismatch between the two, the $/£ exchange rate is a crucial (and direct) determinant of his economic exposure. Any real appreciation of the UK£ (and thus a real depreciation of the US$) will have the immediate effect of lowering his revenues in UK£ terms (or increasing his costs in US$ terms). If he were to increase his US$ prices of cars to keep his profit margins constant at the pre-U.S. dollar depreciation level, demand would drop and he would sell fewer cars. If he kept his US$ price the same, his profit margins would be squeezed, and hence possibly the company's share price as well.

On top of these considerations, he also must worry about the indirect, competitive exposure to the DM, since that is the currency of denomination of the costs of his major competitor, Daimler Benz. Daimler Benz's ability to price its products in the U.S. (and hence create competitive pressure for Jaguar sales in the U.S.) will depend on what happens to the $/DM exchange rate, and since that, in turn, will automatically imply an exchange rate between the UK£ and the DM, Mr. Edwards must closely monitor developments in the UK£/DM exchange rate as well.

Assuming that a real depreciation of the U.S. dollar is a very strong likelihood, what would be the ideal scenario of exchange rate changes that Jaguar could hope for, in order to at least mitigate the impact of the dollar depreciation? His only hope from a competitive standpoint is that the US$ depreciates by a greater percentage

against the DM than it does against the UK£. That would squeeze his competitor's margins worse than his own, and perhaps force Daimler Benz to raise its US$ prices, thereby providing Jaguar the cover for a price increase of its own.

Sources of Economic Exposure. Any time that a firm undertakes a transaction across borders—whether that transaction is in goods, services, capital, people, or technology—it puts itself into a situation where there is the likelihood of direct economic exposure to exchange rates. In addition, as we have seen, even a firm (or division) that considers itself purely domestic (in other words it both sources and sells locally) is not necessarily immune to economic exposure: If the source of its competition is from abroad, it faces competitive exposure to exchange rates. Thus, economic exposures arise from the operational and strategic decisions that a firm makes. Any time that a market is chosen, a sale is made, a product or raw material is purchased, financing is taken on, royalty payments received, or a new plant is located in a foreign country, the firm faces the likelihood of economic exposure to exchange rates. In addition, any time that a foreign competitor enters the competitive picture, there is possibly competitive exposure as well.

Thus, it is important to recognize that exposures are created continuously, at the frontlines of corporate activity. More often than not, economic exposures are actually created by the marketing manager, the production manager, and the purchasing manager. While this may seem obvious after the fact, it is nonetheless an important point to make—nonfinancial managers often simply assume that exchange rates are something to "just let the Treasury worry about." Indeed, the office of the CFO has a relatively limited role in creating economic exposure. It does so only if it makes financing decisions in currencies that are different from the currency of denomination of its assets. Given the fact that the source of economic exposure is the operational and strategic decisions made by a firm, the solutions also largely lie in the operational and strategic arena. Unlike the case of the other two types of exposure, the

CFO's role is more limited (although, as we will see, the CFO's office can also perform a role in limiting economic exposures)—management of economic exposures is the task of a General Manager more than it is a task of the CFO.

Managing Economic Exposure on the Revenues' Side. In managing economic exposure on the revenues' side, the fundamental issue comes down to that of finding the appropriate mix between the price at which the product is sold abroad and the volume sold. In turn, there are at least eight factors to consider:

    i. the demand elasticity;

    ii. the nature of returns to scale;

    iii. whether the currency change is expected to be temporary or permanent;

    iv. whether the firm can create entry barriers;

    v. whether the product is differentiated;

    vi. how distribution channels and consumers will react to price cuts;

    vii. the currency invoicing strategies used;

    viii. and finally, whether competitors will react passively or aggressively to any pricing moves.

Suppose, for specificity, that we are considering a U.S. exporter selling a product in Japan, incurring most of its costs in the U.S., competing against Japanese firms. Also, suppose the Japanese yen has undergone a real appreciation against the dollar. The firm is now faced with an interesting choice: (1) maintain the yen price at the pre-depreciation level, let the dollar price rise thereby yielding extra dollar profits on each unit sold and maintain market share; or (2) lower the yen price, maintain the dollar price at the previous level, maintain per-unit profitability at least at previous levels, thereby gaining extra market share from the increased Japanese demand resulting from lowered yen prices. How should the exporter respond to this situation?

The price elasticity of demand for its product would determine the extent of increase in demand—the higher the elasticity, the better off the firm in terms of increasing its market share in Japan from a price cut. It is possible that the firm may have scale economies resulting from the increased volume, e.g., because it may have excess capacity, or it might be able to take advantage of the learning curve by producing extra units, or there may be cost savings through access to fixed distribution and transportation costs, etc. Such scale economies would actually increase the dollar per-unit profit margin (compared to previous levels).

Next, the firm has to form a judgment on whether the depreciation is expected to be a temporary phenomenon. For example, what if, a few months later, the yen depreciated back to its original level? If this happened the exporter might have to raise its yen prices in order to return to its original level of profitability. Whether or not it can do so will depend on a number of factors, including its ability to create entry barriers (e.g., is the product differentiated and does the firm have blocking access to distribution channels?); whether and how consumers will react to price fluctuations (e.g., are consumers likely to be alienated by the uncertainty at the point of purchase resulting from price changes that occur every time exchange rates fluctuate?); the competitive structure of the product-market (e.g., does the firm compete in a market with "aggressive" competitors or "passive" competitors?).

Moreover, the firm has to consider whether the distribution channels in Japan would simply soak up the yen price cut, so that the consumer does not see any significant price reduction at the point of purchase. If this happened, then the firm would see no benefits from cutting yen prices. Invoicing strategies also matter. If the exporting firm invoices in its home country currency (in this case, the dollar), then the appreciation automatically translates, by default, to the market share-increasing decision, i.e., maintain the dollar price, thereby lower the yen price by the full extent of the depreciation. If, on the other hand, the exporting firm invoices in the foreign currency (in this case, the yen), its decision, by default, is to maintain the yen price, thereby automatically increasing the dollar price and maintaining market share.

The main thing to note from the discussion above—we are in the realm of operational and strategic decisions that would have to be made by a marketing manager or a general manager, rather than financial risk management decisions by a CFO!

Managing Economic Exposure on the Cost Side. Most import-based firms, particularly those that rely on natural resources such as petroleum and minerals (e.g., firms in oil, steel, and commodities) and firms in food processing and textiles as well as firms that tend to outsource their component and parts supplies from abroad (e.g., firms in computers, commercial aircraft, and automobiles), are often equally affected by real currency movements on the cost side as they are on the revenues side.

In many ways, cost management strategies in the face of a real currency movement are the reverse of those related to revenue strategies, in that a similar underlying set of variables affect strategic choices. First, note that currency movements matter for the firm's costs only in situations where the firm sources some or all of its inputs, e.g., raw material, intermediate products, labor, technology, from abroad. If the firm buys its inputs solely in the domestic markets, any direct currency effects are unlikely. If the firm's home currency appreciates against the supplier's currency, cost management is less of a problem, and indeed, becomes more of an opportunity for managing additional profits arising from cost reduction. The reason is that, under an appreciation, the firm has to pay fewer units of its home currency to buy the same amount of inputs in the foreign currency. There is, however, the issue of whether the firm should pass on any of the currency-related savings to its input suppliers.

The difficult cost management issue arises from a depreciation of the home currency against supplier currencies and is as follows: given that most firms have input sourced from abroad, how much of the home currency depreciation can be (i) passed-through to the suppliers of these inputs; (ii) in the event that pass-through of costs to suppliers is difficult, how

much can be passed-through to consumers through price increases; (iii) in the event that both (i) and (ii) are difficult to accomplish, what are the options available to diversify into new sourcing alternatives from more favorable currency areas? The answers to these questions depend on (a) the buyer power that the firm exercises over its suppliers; (b) the nature of the contracting relationship between the supplier and the firm; (c) the currency invoicing strategies used; (d) the availability of alternate suppliers of inputs and (e) the permanence of currency movements.

Clearly, the firm's ability to pass-through the impact of a depreciation to suppliers will depend on the power it has over its suppliers, as well as the nature of contracting with its suppliers. The higher the buyer power of the firm, the greater its ability to insulate its costs from the impact of currency movements. However, the more formal and long-term the contracting between the firm and its suppliers, the lower its ability to insulate its costs from the impact of currency movements. Similarly, if the firm invoices its supplies in its home currency, it obviates the problem and lowers the impact of currency movements. On the other hand, if it invoices its supplies in the seller's currency, any currency movement impacts are passed-through directly to the firm's costs.

What if a firm has little power over its suppliers, or is unable to undertake spot contracting with its suppliers, or operates in a supplier market in which the invoicing is done in the seller's currency? The first option is to examine whether the impact of the cost increase resulting from the currency depreciation can be passed-through to customers. Decision variables in this case revert to those we discussed under pricing and revenue strategies in the previous section. A more stable—and longer term—option is for the firm to diversify its supplier base across at least two or three major currency areas, e.g., the U.S. dollar, euro, and Japanese yen currency blocs. This sourcing flexibility is particularly crucial if the currency movement can be expected to be more than temporary—say, expected to last two or three years, not an unusual scenario if the events of the past decade are any guide. Again note, the appropriate responses to economic exposure require operational and strategic, rather than financial, decisions. That said, it turns out that the CFO's office can help.

Managing Economic Exposure Through Financial Decisions. Financing decisions can play a role, too, in hedging economic exposures. However, these opportunities present themselves primarily in the management of revenue-based economic exposure rather than cost-based or competition-based economic exposure. When the firm has revenues denominated in a currency other than its home currency, what it has, in essence, is an asset denominated in the foreign currency. This can be managed by creating an appropriate liability (that is, financing) in the foreign currency. If the foreign asset is long-lived, that is, the firm foresees the possibility that such foreign currency revenues will be an integral part of its long-term global strategy, then it would be appropriate to take on long-term financing in that currency.

There are two broad choices: issue foreign currency debt, or issue equity by listing its stock in the foreign country. It is beyond the scope of this Note to go into the ramifications of the debt versus equity decision, except to point out that if debt is chosen as the source of long-term foreign currency financing, the firm may wish to consider whether there are opportunities to undertake foreign currency swaps. In many instances, the markets for foreign currency swaps are more liquid (and go out to longer maturities) than the markets for straight debt issues. Moreover, it may be possible for the firm to profitably swap some of its existing home currency long-term liabilities rather than issue new debt.

Consider the case of Walt Disney Company in the 1980s. In the mid-1980s, Disney set up Tokyo Disneyland as a franchise from which it was expecting substantial (and fast-growing) yen revenues well into the foreseeable future—thus it had a substantial yen asset on its books. Soon thereafter Disney undertook a number of foreign currency swaps worldwide. It issued debt in many different currencies, e.g., Swiss francs, French francs, and so forth, and swapped them

back to yen to create a yen liability, with a counterparty that was interested in getting rid of its yen liability and taking on the liability in the currency in which Disney was issuing its debt. Disney, however, refrained from issuing equity in Japan, perhaps because a royalty stream is a relatively steady, senior, and nonresidual cash flow to Disney, and hence there was no need to back it with an equity-type financial instrument. As a result of such financing decisions, by the early 1990s, Disney was able to hedge away a major portion of its economic exposure to yen.

An Example of Economic Exposure Management by Japanese Firms. The period 1994 to early 1995 was a rough one for many Japanese exporters. During this period the yen appreciated by 33% in real terms against the dollar (from about ¥120/$ to ¥80/$). The earnings of many well-known firms in Japan were quite substantially hurt and many of them reported record losses because of this sudden and severe appreciation of the yen against the dollar. How did Japanese firms cope with this appreciation?

Japanese firms undertook aggressive cost-cutting. Specifically: (1) they focused on continuous cost improvement, by cutting production costs and by laying off later entrants into the workforce; (2) they altered sourcing strategies, by moving production abroad, especially to low-to-middle income Asian countries such as the Philippines and Thailand and by aggressively squeezing their second-tier and third-tier suppliers; (3) they altered their pricing strategies, by cutting profit margins rather than increasing the dollar price of their exports.

As a result, by mid-1995, many Japanese firms were leaner and more cost-competitive (measured purely in the domestic currency) than they were prior to the yen appreciation. The results of this cost-cutting were strikingly evident in an annual survey conducted by the Economic Planning Agency of Japan on the breakeven yen per dollar exchange rate at which major Japanese exporters would cease to be profitable. The survey results, for the years 1994–96 are shown in Figure 6.

	1994	1995	1996
Less than ¥100/$	Neg	13.7%	22.9%
¥100/$ to ¥110/$	14.1%	37.3%	41.4%
¥110/$ to ¥120/$	36.9%	30.1%	25.4%
¥120/$ to ¥130/$	37.7%	14.2%	8.5%
More than ¥130/$	10.8%	4.7%	1.8%

Figure 6 Breakeven Exchange Rates: Percentage of Japanese Firms Placing Own Breakeven Rates in the Range Indicated

Source: Economic Planning Agency of Japan.

In 1994 about 50% of Japanese firms said that they would remain profitable if the yen appreciated to less than ¥120/$—in other words, it would require a yen-dollar exchange rate of ¥120/$ and above for nearly half the Japanese firms to continue to make a profit. Indeed, fewer than 1% of firms surveyed indicated that they would be profitable if the yen were to appreciate to less than ¥100/$.

By 1996, after two years of cost-cutting, things had changed quite a bit. Over 90% of Japanese firms indicated that they would be profitable if the yen were to stay at a level of ¥120/$ or above. Most striking of all, compared to less than 1% of all firms in 1994, nearly one-quarter of the surveyed Japanese firms indicated that they would remain profitable even if the yen were to appreciate to less than ¥100/$. No wonder Mr. Welch was worried![17]

OVERALL GUIDELINES ON CURRENCY EXPOSURE MANAGEMENT

It should be obvious by now that active management of economic exposure requires a firm-wide response and one that should be the concern of a General Manager rather than just the CFO. One, the first step is to ask the two key questions raised earlier regarding the currency of denomination of a firm's revenues and costs and the currency of its competitors' revenues and costs. In making this assessment, it is not necessary for the firm to expend its resources to track every exposure by every single currency; rather, it makes sense to use an 80/20 approach, i.e., 80% of what is relevant is often to be found in just 20% of the detail. Usually, two or three currencies tend to account for a large portion of direct economic exposures, just as competitors from just one or two major currency areas often account for a major portion of competitive exposures. It is imperative that General Managers of multinational firms know what these currencies are.

Two, the firm must set up a currency reporting system to track exposures as they develop. Such a system should encompass exposures by currency, by maturity, and by operating unit. It is necessary to make operating divisions responsible for reporting their exposures at least monthly, so that the firm can keep track of developments before real currency values stray too far.

Three, it is necessary to involve Treasury at early stages of major sales or purchase decisions that involve a currency other than the firm's home currency. This does not mean that the Treasury must have a say in the choice of currency (let alone the structure of the deal), but it does mean that line managers must take on the responsibility of alerting Treasurers at an early enough stage so that any potential problems that might arise further down the road can be anticipated and managed better. Moreover Treasury is often the source of information concerning natural currency offsets or operational hedges that may be available elsewhere in the firm and may

Currency Exposure	Percentage of Firms Surveyed Who:				
	Identify	*Hedge*	*Do Not Hedge*	*Fully Hedge*	*Partially Hedge*
Translation	80%	30%	70%	15%	15%
Transaction	60%	80%	20%	30%	55%
Anticipated	70%	57%	43%	2%	55%
Contingent	52%	15%	85%	4%	11%
Economic	54%	5%	95%	5%	Neg
Balance Sheet	30%	22%	78%	6%	15%
Income Statement	44%	39%	61%	6%	33%

Figure 7   Bank of America Corporate FX Risk Management Survey Results, 1996

Source: "Corporate America: FX Risk Management 1996," Global Capital Markets Group, Bank of America, Monograph 78, Winter 1996/97, pp. 1–3.

also be able to mitigate exposures by making smarter financing choices early on.

Four—and perhaps most important—it is necessary to inculcate a clear sense among line managers that they are the ones that actually create the exposures and they are also the ones that can be most effective in managing the risks. Too many line managers in too many organizations have the tendency to dismiss currency-related issues with the view that "it's Treasury's problem."

Finally, all of these suggestions presume that incentive systems in organizations are, at least to some reasonable degree, geared toward rewarding managers for their skills of anticipation (i.e., dealing before-the-fact with major problems that could have arisen, but didn't), rather than solving problems (i.e., dealing after-the-fact with problems that do arise).

Setting Up a Risk Management Program

Evidence of foreign exchange risk management provides some insight into how firms today are addressing and managing their currency exposures.

Figure 7 provides some results from a recent survey conducted by Bank of America. Whereas only 54% of surveyed firms actually identify their economic exposures, 70% identified transaction exposure and a full 80% identified translation exposure. As might be predicted, firms continue

to be quite active in the hedging of transaction exposures (80% hedge them), but few are hedging their translation exposure at this time (30% hedge translation). Due to the inherent complexity of identification and management, only 5% of the firms surveyed are actively hedging their economic exposure.

The continuing challenges lie within the realm of economic exposure management.

There are a number of additional practical concerns which will need to be addressed before the firm can operationalize a truly effective risk management program and although they are beyond the scope of this Note, they are worth mentioning:

a. Should risk management be centralized or decentralized?

b. What are the managerial compensation issues, and multinational control issues raised by the firm's risk management policies?

c. Are there operational and control issues related to conflicts between currency exposures and interest rate exposures?

d. What is the process of confirmation and settlement of contractual commitments involving financial derivatives?

e. What are the information technology needs for real-time value-at-risk analysis of the multitude of exposures and positions which the firm deals with in a cross-border setting?

Many of the well-known currency-related losses suffered by nonfinancial firms in the past decade have arisen either from lack of exposure planning and identification, or from inadequate controls imposed over commitments of the firm, or from inadequate real-time monitoring of derivative values associated with positions outstanding. These losses are the failures of management, not failures inherent to the financial derivatives utilized. A risk management program is no better or worse than the skills of those who construct, operate, and monitor it. Perhaps most importantly, unless the motivations behind such risk management are clearly thought out and well-articulated, the risk management tools themselves can take the firm only so far.

Suggested Readings

Bodnar, G. M., S. H. Gregory, and R. C. Marston, "1998 Wharton Survey of Financial Risk Management by U.S. Non-financial Firms," *Financial Management,* Vol. 27, No. 4, 1998.

Dornbusch, R., "Exchange Rates and Prices," *American Economic Review,* 77, 1987.

Dufey, G., "Corporate Finance and Exchange Rate Variations," *Financial Management,* Summer 1972, pp. 51–57.

Eiteman, D. K., A. I. Stonehill, and M. H. Moffett, *Multinational Business Finance,* 9th edition, Addison-Wesley Longman, 2001.

Fisher, E., "A Model of Exchange Rate Pass-Through," *Journal of International Economics,* 26, 1989.

Froot, K., and P. D. Klemperer, "Exchange Rate Pass Through When Market Share Matters," *American Economic Review,* 80, 1990.

Froot, K., D. Scharfstein, and J. Stein, "A Framework for Risk Management," *Harvard Business Review,* 72, September-October 1994, 59–71.

Froot, K., J. Stein, and D. Scharfstein, "Risk Management: Coordinating Corporate Investment and Financing Policies," *NBER Working Paper No. 4084,* 1992.

Jorion, P., "The Exchange Rate Exposure of U.S. Multinationals," *The Journal of Business,* 63, 1990.

Knetter, M., "Goods Prices and Exchange Rates: What Have We Learned?" *Journal of Economic Literature,* September 1997.

Krugman, P., "Pricing to Market When the Exchange Rate Changes," *NBER Working Paper No. 1926,* 1986.

Lessard, D., and E. Flood, "On the Measurement of Operating Exposure to Exchange Rates: A Conceptual Approach," *Financial Management,* Spring 1986.

Lessard, D., and J. B. Lightstone, "Volatile Exchange Rates Can Put International Operations at Risk," *Harvard Business Review,* July-August, 1986.

Levi, M. D., and P. Sercu, "Erroneous and Valid Reasons for Hedging Foreign Exchange Rate Exposure," *Journal of Multinational Financial Management,* Vol. 1, No. 2, 1991, pp. 19–28.

Luehrman, T., "The Exchange Rate Exposure of a Global Competitor," *Journal of International Business Studies,* 21, 1990.

Meulbroek, L., "Integrated Risk Management for the Firm: A Senior Manager's Guide," *Harvard Business School Working Paper No. 02-046,* 2002.

Moffett, M. H., and D. J. Skinner, "Issues in Foreign Exchange Hedge Accounting," *Journal of Applied Corporate Finance,* 8, No. 3, Fall 1995.

Moffett, M. H., and J. K. Karlsen, "Managing Foreign Exchange Rate Economic Exposure," *Journal of International Financial Management and Accounting,* 5, No. 2, June 1994.

Smith, C. W., and R. M. Stulz, "The Determinants of Firms' Hedging Policies," *Journal of Financial and Quantitative Analysis,* Vol. 20, No. 4, December 1985, pp. 390–405.

Smith, C. W., C. W. Smithson, and D. S. Wilford, "Why Hedge?" *Intermarket,* July 1989, pp. 12–16.

Smith, C. W., "Corporate Risk Management: Theory and Practice," *Journal of Derivatives,* Vol. 2, No. 4, 1998.

Stulz, R. M., "Optimal Hedging Policies," *Journal of Financial and Quantitative Analysis,* Vol. 19, No. 2, June 1984, pp. 127–140.

Stulz, R. M., "Rethinking Risk Management," *Journal of Applied Corporate Finance,* 9, Fall 1996.

Sundaram, A., and J. S. Black, "The Environment and Internal Organization of Multinational Enterprises," *Academy of Management Review,* October 1992.

Sundaram, A., and J. S. Black, *The International Business Environment: Text and Cases,* Prentice-Hall: NJ, 1995 (see Chapters 3 to 5).

Sundaram, A., and V. Mishra, "Currency Movements and Corporate Pricing Strategies," *Recent Developments in International Banking and*

Finance, S. Khoury (ed.), Volume IV–V, Elsevier, 1991.

Sundaram, A., and V. Mishra, "Economic Exposure to Exchange Rates: A Review," *Tuck School Working Paper,* March 1990.

NOTES

1. Keynote Address, Peter Drucker, Business International's Chief Financial Officers Conference, San Francisco, 1990.

2. Of course, as we will see, perfect hedges are nearly impossible to come by. To quote a professional colleague, Gunter Dufey (Professor Emeritus at the University of Michigan Business School), "A perfect hedge is only found in a Japanese garden."

3. See K. Froot, D. Scharfstein, and J. Stein, "A Framework for Risk Management," *Harvard Business Review,* 72, September-October 1994, 59–71. The set of ideas surrounding the costs of externally generated versus internally generated capital and its implications for financial decisions is sometimes referred to as the "pecking order theory of capital structure."

4. See Rene M. Stulz, "Optimal Hedging Policies," *Journal of Financial and Quantitative Analysis,* Vol. 19, No. 2, June 1984, p. 127.

5. Selective hedging usually refers to the hedging of large, one-time, exceptional exposures, or the occasional use of hedging when management has a definitive expectation on the direction of exchange rates.

6. Good overviews of the "why hedge?" debate include Stulz (1984), Smith and Stulz (1985), Levi and Sercu (1991), Froot, Scharfstein, and Stein (1992), Smith (1998), and Muelbroek (2002).

7. Because the forward rate is calculated from the current spot rate and the differential in the two currencies' euro-currency deposit interest rates using a model known as the Covered Interest Parity model, the forward rate will normally differ from the spot rate. This will result in the firm realizing a currency gain or loss on settlement; the gain or loss will, however, be known on the date on which the position is taken. For more details on Covered Interest Parity and the basics of how currency markets work, see the Thunderbird Case Series Note "Currency Markets and Parity Conditions."

8. The option would require an up-front payment for purchase, the premium, which may vary between 1% and 8%, depending on market conditions.

9. The Financial Accounting Standards Board (FASB) is the authority in the U.S. that determines accounting policy for U.S. firms and certified public accountants. FAS Statement No. 52, applying to fiscal years beginning on or after December 15, 1982, contains the primary provisions and practices to be used in the financial reporting related to foreign currency. FAS Statement No. 133, applying to fiscal years beginning on or after June 15, 2000, altered some of the primary terminology related to the use of financial derivatives used in foreign currency accounting and reporting, but largely left the reporting treatments for foreign currency established under Statement No. 52 unchanged (and as amended by FAS No. 138).

10. Accounting practices would simply require the firm to value the forward contract and the receivable independently and at current market value (marked-to-market). This is the procedure followed for all financial contracts or speculative instruments which any or all firms may enter into.

11. FAS No. 52, paragraph 4.

12. Statement of FAS No. 52, Foreign Currency Translation, FASB, December 1981, paragraph 5.

13. The idea that currencies will be expected to depreciate in nominal terms when their inflation rates are expected to be relatively higher is one of the most basic ideas in the theory of international finance, and is called the *theory of purchasing power parity (PPP).* The theory is developed more precisely in the next section. For a more substantial development of the ideas in this section, see the Thunderbird Case Series Note, "Currency Markets and Parity Conditions."

14. Such a definition of exchange rates—the number of units of domestic currency it takes to buy each unit of the foreign currency—is called the *direct* (or American) quote. The reverse quotation—the number of units of the foreign currency its takes to buy one unit of the domestic currency—is called the *indirect* (or European) quote. All of the following discussion will use direct quotes.

15. As an aside, economists would define it as follows: A firm is said to have economic exposure to exchange rates when $\partial\pi\partial s$ is greater than or less than zero (where π is the firm's cash flows, s is the real exchange rate, ∂ can be interpreted as the "change in." Thus, $\partial\pi\partial s$ captures the idea of the "change in the firm's cash flows with respect to a change in the real exchange rate."

16. But, you may be asking, "Isn't the U.S. firm making 22 cents now compared to 20 cents before?" The answer is, "Of course!" but the 22 cents today is

worth only yesterday's 20 cents in terms of purchasing power, since there is a 10% inflation rate in the U.S.!

17. The survey also found that if the exchange rate stabilized to around ¥110/$, Japanese car manufacturers would, on average, more than double their profits (relative to ¥80/$). As of the time of writing, the exchange rate had stabilized around ¥118/$.

CHAUVCO RESOURCES LTD.: THE ARGENTINA DECISIONS[1]

Prepared by David W. Conklin and John Knowles

Copyright © 1995, Ivey Management Services

Version: (A) 2002-05-22

INVESTMENT DECISIONS: THE 1995 CROSSROADS

At 29 years of age, Guy Turcotte, an MBA graduate, founded Chauvco Resources Ltd. In its first decade, Chauvco focused on acquisitions of Alberta oil fields that already had operating wells. By the early 1990s, Chauvco was ranked as one of the top 30 oil companies in Canada. However, the projected profits in Alberta were losing their attractiveness: shrinking oil supplies in Western Canada caused land prices to escalate; world oil prices remained low; royalties and taxes were higher than in many other countries; and operating costs were rising. Faced with these realities, Chauvco began to consider other countries, and in 1992, it invested in Argentina by purchasing an interest in an oil and gas block that was being privatized. However, Argentina had a history of extreme economic and political instability, with hyperinflation that could reappear at any time, and actual costs of doing business were higher than Chauvco expected. Shortly after the Argentine property purchase, Chauvco incorporated into its growth strategy the plan to extend its activities to other countries. In 1994, net earnings exceeded $29 million, annual cash flow reached nearly $100 million, and the shareholders' equity exceeded $280 million. In what proportions should Chauvco divide its future investments between Canada, Argentina, and other countries? What criteria should it use in evaluating investment opportunities?[2]

THE 1981 START-UP

During the late 1970s, political events in the Middle East drove up world oil prices, and rates of return in the oil business escalated. The number of oil companies in Calgary, Alberta, grew from 300 in 1975 to 700 in 1980. In January 1981, Guy Turcotte invested his life savings of $80,000 and personally called 500 acquaintances over a three-week period to get his startup capital of $2 million, sold in units of $5,000 each. The company's first office was the kitchen table of Turcotte's townhouse. By the fall of 1981, however, the picture was changing rapidly as the Canadian economy fell into recession, interest rates climbed to over 20 per cent, and governments were vying to claim windfall revenues from high oil prices.

In 1981, Alberta was embroiled in a political dispute over Canada's National Energy Program (NEP). The federal Conservative government of Joe Clark[3] declared in 1980 that rising oil prices should not accrue solely to the benefit of foreign-owned oil companies. This position was entrenched in the NEP, implemented in October 1980 by the Liberal government under Pierre Trudeau, who defeated Clark in the elections that year. The goals of the NEP were to make Canada self-sufficient in oil, to expand Canadian ownership of the industry, to increase government ownership, and to capture resource "rents" or "excess profits" for Canadians as a whole.

A new Petroleum Incentives Program (PIP) offered subsidies for exploration and development in proportion to the degree of Canadian ownership of a company, and this provided Canadian companies with incentives to buy subsidiaries of U.S. firms. To equalize oil prices in Western Canada which consumed Alberta oil, and Eastern Canada which imported oil from abroad at the world price, a "petroleum compensation charge" (PCC) was levied on the wellhead price. The level of the charge was set so that when the proceeds of the tax were used to subsidize the price of imported oil, the refineries in Eastern Canada would face an effective oil price equal to the after-tax Alberta price.

In Chauvco's first annual report, Turcotte declared that Chauvco would do well under the NEP, and he estimated that Chauvco would be eligible for the maximum grant levels under PIP. Canadian tax incentives reduced the cost to investors of the $5,000 investment units to $2,000. "All of these developments favor small Canadian-owned and controlled companies," Turcotte said in Chauvco's first annual report. "Overall we expect 1982 to be another difficult year for the oil industry. However we believe our current financial status leaves us in a favorable position." Unfortunately, soon after Chauvco's start-up, industry analysts were projecting a surprising and unwelcome event: the arrival of a world oil glut, with a negative impact on oil and gas prices.

THE DETERMINATION OF OIL AND GAS PRICES

Companies often had to choose between investing in properties that were "oil-prone" and investing in those that were "gas-prone," relying on the geophysical data and production history of neighboring areas to distinguish between

them. Prices for natural gas were much more localized than those of oil because gas required pipelines for transportation. Alberta gas was sold in Western and Central Canada and the neighboring United States, making prices extremely responsive to winter weather in North America.

Crude oil could be bought and sold as a commodity with very little information about the product. Although prices differed across densities and origins, these price differentials were relatively constant; prices of different kinds of crude all moved together. Thus, profitability of Alberta oil companies depended heavily on the "world price" of oil, which referred to a particular grade of oil, for instance Saudi Light Crude, or West Texas Intermediate (WTI) density crude. The world price fluctuated enormously, from US$3 per barrel in 1973 to US$35 per barrel in 1980 and back down to $12 in 1985. With the Iraqi invasion of Kuwait in 1990, it rose to $40, but fell at the end of this conflict to the $15 to $22 range, where it remained in 1995. This extreme volatility was a major factor in the oil business, given the long-range planning and large sunk costs. Canadian oil companies relied increasingly on energy futures contracts to hedge prices. Crude oil options, propane futures and natural gas futures were all introduced on NYMEX in the late 1980s.

The Organization of Petroleum Exporting Countries (OPEC) attempted to sustain high world prices by requiring member countries to keep oil exports below assigned quotas, agreed upon at periodic meetings of OPEC governments. When the cartel declared an oil embargo in response to the 1973 Arab-Israeli war (oil would not be shipped to countries aligned with Israel or the United States), the price of Saudi Light Crude catapulted from $3 to $5 per barrel to $10 to $12 in 1974. As a result of the success of the OPEC system, oil prices remained high throughout the 1970s, creating stable and lucrative market conditions for oil producers based in Alberta. However, one unintended result of the high prices was the development of relatively higher-cost oil reserves throughout the world. The higher prices were leading inexorably to the 1980s world surplus of oil that persisted into the 1990s. To maintain their own revenues in the face of falling prices, poorer OPEC member countries, such as Venezuela and Nigeria, were increasingly likely to cheat by producing more than their quotas allowed, leading to a further depression in prices. To some extent, Saudi Arabia was able to keep the cartel together by reducing its own output to accommodate the surplus of other countries, but after 1985 Saudi Arabia decided to relinquish its costly role of "swing producer."

CHAUVCO IN THE 1980s: GROWTH THROUGH ACQUISITIONS

Oil and gas industry analysts usually divide the industry into "upstream" and "downstream" sectors, referring respectively to exploration and development on the one hand, and refinement and petrochemicals on the other. One feature of the upstream sector was the co-existence of very small and very large companies. The small companies, known as "independents," operated wells to which the business systems of the large companies were not geared—wells that were isolated from major fields or that had low production levels. Some of the large companies, known as "integrated oil companies," operated downstream as well as upstream, possessing a network of refineries and retail operations. The integrated firms included the Canadian subsidiaries of multinational firms such as Imperial and Chevron, as well as wholly Canadian-owned firms such as Dome and Petro-Canada. Whereas the large companies financed exploration and other projects from internal funds, small independent companies often put together financing specific to a project. In addition to privately raised capital, independents relied on consortia and other joint-venture arrangements to finance exploration projects. Chauvco's initial investments occurred as a member of these consortia.[4]

By the end of 1983, Chauvco was operating 26 oil-producing wells and two wells that produced gas. The emphasis on oil was justified by the "uncertainty of natural gas markets."[5] The company estimated the value of its reserves after two years of operation at nearly $10 million.

Chauvco was doing well, achieving a profit of $170,000 in 1983 and raising funds through the Canadian equity market. Its strategy included: conservative balance sheet, safe investments, oil preferred to gas, producing fields preferred to exploration, and geographical concentration.

Although times were hard for many companies in the oil sector, Chauvco's strong balance sheet and concentration on producing properties were paying off. "There were lots of opportunities available for anyone who had cash flow," Turcotte said of those early days. "It was very easy to get deals."[6] When oil prices crashed in the late 1980s, Chauvco was in good shape to take on some of the less fortunate victims in the oil patch. "We are virtually debt-free," Turcotte announced in 1987, when Chauvco acquired a much larger independent, Tripet Resources, financing the merger with a share exchange rather than resort to debt. By 1988, Chauvco had 30 employees and held 600,000 acres, 85 per cent of which were in Alberta and 15 per cent in Saskatchewan. The Calgary trade magazine *Oilweek* picked Chauvco as one of five companies that were "drilling to success."

Bolstered by this success, Chauvco embarked on a period of rapid growth through acquisition. Chauvco's production doubled in 1990, and the *Oilweek's* Top 100 Canadian Oil Firms[7] raised Chauvco from 53 to 32 in ranking. At this time, Turcotte's financial objectives were to keep debt below 1.5 times cash flow, and earn a 15 per cent return on equity.

The Chauvco Way: Financial Strategies

- Keep debt below 1.5 times cash flow.
- Obtain 15 per cent return on Canadian investments, 20 per cent on international.
- Increase production and reserves by 15 per cent annually per share.
- Use interest-rate and commodity-price hedging.
- Maintain a low cost structure.

In January 1990 alone, Chauvco bought the Canadian assets of Ultramar and select assets of Carlyle Energy, for a total of $85 million. The Financial Times of Canada called Chauvco "the premier junior oil and gas acquisitor of the 1980s."[8] Also that year, the company spent $55 million on Esso properties, breaking its debt guidelines to do so. Turcotte argued that it was worth borrowing to make the acquisitions, because he believed that oil prices were "in a trough at the bottom of the range," and unlikely to fall in the near future. The debt target would be restored by the end of 1991, simply by devoting one-third of cash flow to debt reduction. Turcotte considered over 40 different acquisitions before deciding that these were the best properties for Chauvco. Low world oil prices resulted in acquisitions at bargain-basement prices.[9] The stock market agreed, as Chauvco stock, which sold for $5 in 1988, soared from $13 in 1990 to a high of $22 in 1991. The company had done well by its investors, who now found that their initial $5,000 investment units, which actually cost $2,000 after taxes, were worth $95,000 each.

According to management, what Chauvco had going for it was low drilling costs (a dry hole cost the company only $150,000 in the 1980s, reducing exploration risk) and specialized geophysical expertise. Furthermore, Chauvco was still small enough that it could rely for its growth on the relatively small undiscovered pools of oil remaining in Alberta. "I'm sure there are not a lot more Leducs to be found," said Turcotte, referring to the 1947 discovery that launched the Alberta oil industry, "but that's not what we're looking for. We're looking for pools that are more like one million barrels in size."[10]

WHY INVEST INTERNATIONALLY?

By the summer of 1991, Chauvco was thinking about a new growth strategy. For the Alberta oil patch, 1991 was disastrous, with revenues falling by $3 billion. Analysts disagreed on prospects for the future. Were the "Awful Eighties" turning into the "Nasty Nineties," as one Calgary Herald headline put it? Others saw golden opportunity. The major acknowledged problems were:

- The international oil price might stay below $20 per barrel; 1991 saw prices stabilize at US$21.50, then drop at year end to US$19 per barrel WTI. Some industry experts predicted that the price would stabilize below $20 for the foreseeable future.
- Reserves in the Western Canada Sedimentary Basin were being depleted. Both land costs and drilling costs rose due to an increasingly frantic search for new reserves in Alberta. Production in Alberta had grown in the last few years mainly from improvements in extractive technology, rather than from discovery of new oil. New techniques such as under-balanced drilling and horizontal drilling allowed companies to lift more oil out of the same holes, but as reservoir levels fell, more expensive "secondary" methods were required to maintain production.
- The drilling sector was also driving finding costs upwards. Pipe became a scarce commodity, and there was a shortage of drill rigs.
- As volume per oil well fell, the cost per barrel rose, with production costs divided over a smaller volume of oil from each well.

For a growth-oriented company like Chauvco, the Alberta prospects were starting to look slim and over-priced. Profitable development in Alberta required oil prices of at least $20 per barrel, because operating costs were high, and Chauvco's growth target of 15 per cent would soon translate into a very high annual addition to reserves. Expansion abroad began to be discussed seriously at Chauvco, and the company hired a senior geologist with experience in third-world oil and gas to help review South American opportunities. There were many countries with under-developed prospects: Argentina, to be sure, but also Russia, Australia, Malaysia, and Venezuela. The United States and Canada were the two most densely drilled countries in the world; other countries offered the prospect of larger unexplored reservoirs of oil and gas, lower land costs, and lower taxes and royalty payments. In October 1991, after attending a meeting on Argentine oil and gas sponsored by the Calgary Chamber of Commerce, Chauvco was approached by a major Canadian oil and gas company looking for a partner on an exploration bid in Santa Cruz, Argentina. Chauvco declined to participate, but its interest in Argentina had been kindled.

ARGENTINA: A NATION OF EXTREME ECONOMIC AND POLITICAL INSTABILITY

Similar in population and resources to Canada, Argentina was a prosperous nation at the end of the Second World War, with significant food exports and a well-developed, albeit tariff-protected, local industry. However, this changed with the 1945 election of Juan Peron. Peron rapidly increased the size of the civil service, nationalised many businesses, and imposed detailed regulations throughout the economy. The economic policies pursued by him and his successors led to inefficiency, low growth, budget deficits, trade deficits, hyper inflation, and currency devaluation. The political system became increasingly chaotic, climaxing in a 1976 military coup. In the 1976 to 1983 period, the military killed 15,000 to 20,000 civilians, ruthlessly eradicating all forms of opposition. During this "dirty war" as it was known in Argentina, the foreign debt tripled, and economic growth was virtually zero.

It had been clear to the military government that the solution to Argentina's problems was to shift towards a market economy. The economic reforms announced by Economy Minister Martinez de Hoz in 1976 were strikingly similar to those that succeeding governments would implement. Arguing that the economy had been strangled by state interference and by Argentina's isolation from international trade, the minister announced that the role of the state would be reduced and that the Argentine economy would be completely opened to trade and capital movements. However, to avoid imposing further distress on an already comatose economy, the reforms would be introduced gradually. Politically, the government felt that the hardships of sudden reform would increase public support

for guerilla groups, as well as trade unions and opposition political parties.

This gradual approach to reform resulted in partial implementation, with dismal results. By liberalizing trade in 1976, but failing to devalue the peso, imports increased 75 per cent versus a 22 per cent increase in exports in the first year alone; consequently, the trade deficit increased tremendously. Financial reforms sparked vigorous development of the banking sector, but then the banking sector crashed in 1980 under expectations of a major currency devaluation and a reduction in government deposit insurance. Capital quickly fled the country. As a result of the current account deficit, the capital outflows and the bailout of the banks, foreign debt doubled from $12 billion in 1978 to $24 billion by the end of 1980. Embarrassed by its economic failure, the military then sought to deflect discontent by re-asserting Argentina's claim to the Falkland Islands, a colony of distant Britain, who seemed unlikely to risk war over such a desolate possession. The economic strain of the ensuing war, added to the cost of the failed reform, proved to be an overwhelming burden.

By 1983, when the military regime ended, no civilian government had completed its term of office in 30 years. Argentina had seen six military coups in 60 years, had lost the Falklands war with Britain, and was ravaged by hyper inflation at an annual three-digit level. Business practices in Argentina were reputedly extremely corrupt, and wealth and power were concentrated in a few families. More than 50 per cent of the economy was owned by the government. Foreign investment was stifled by taxation, corruption, and government regulation. Imports of equipment and materials required government permits, and these permits were subject to refusal if local substitutes were available. Import tariffs were as high as 210 per cent. In addition to punitive discrimination in taxation, foreign businesses were prohibited from operating in certain sectors, and they were subject to detailed regulation.

Raoul Alfonsin, leader of the Radical Party, was elected president in 1983. Under this new civilian government, the Austral Plan was initiated in 1985, named for the new currency that it introduced to replace the peso. Based on a wage and price freeze and the maintenance of a fixed exchange rate, the goal of the program was to stop inflation, which had surpassed 1,000 per cent on an annual basis.[11] The government deficit would be reduced by increased taxes, higher utility rates, and cuts in government expenditures. The initial results were encouraging; inflation fell immediately and stayed low for the rest of 1985, as did domestic interest rates. Additional reforms were announced at year's end, including privatisation of state-owned steel and petrochemical companies, tax credits for exports, agricultural incentives, and subsidies for domestic capital goods. But the inflation rate did not subside completely, falling to a monthly 2.7 per cent average. As a result, the pressure for wage increases forced the government to allow a limited, closely regulated movement in wages and prices, and inflation regained some momentum. Plans to reduce the role of the state were blocked in Congress by members of both the opposition and the government parties.

A key element in attacking inflation was to demonstrate the government's ability to draw on international loans to cover its deficit; otherwise, people would rationally anticipate further inflation. But the problem was that by the time the generals had finished with their own economic experiments and the expensive war in the Falklands, Argentina's foreign debt was already so high that the government's ability to service the existing debt, let alone take on servicing of more future debt, was highly doubtful. At first, Alfonsin had considered repudiating the foreign debt, but this possibility made investors so nervous that the crisis only worsened as investors converted their holdings into U.S. dollars, driving down the austral and increasing prices at a hyper inflationary rate. Eventually, the IMF agreed to support further loans to Argentina under the condition of deficit-reduction targets and resumption of debt payments, making reform possible.

A patchwork succession of reform measures kept the inflation rate under control, but still very high, until late 1988 when it became apparent that the international financial community had lost faith once more. There was "no miracle in sight" declared the 1988 report of the Economist Intelligence Unit, predicting that annual inflation would continue at 100 per cent through the early 1990s, and the external debt would grow to $75 billion. Alfonsin could no longer count on the foreign loans necessary to finance the recurrent budget deficits in a non-inflationary way. Once again, Argentina was on the brink of a debt crisis. In the aftermath of the reform's initial failure, the Alfonsin government survived two military revolts. Elections were due in May 1989, and investors were alarmed that, in the atmosphere of impending economic crisis, the Peronist party was regaining popularity, and, worse yet, under the new populist leader, Carlos Saul Menem. By March 1989, inflation was a monthly 17 per cent. As investors converted their holdings into U.S. dollars, the inflationary spiral accelerated; by election day, inflation had reached 5,000 per cent in annual terms.

Alfonsin's failure showed that stopping hyper inflation was not sufficient in itself. Durable success required some fundamental structural changes in the Argentine economy. A central problem was that Alfonsin had to deal with democratic institutions in a society where special-interest groups had developed enormous political clout. From the labor syndicates to the business elites, these groups had strong incentives to block or reverse particular reforms, even if their general interest was in seeing the reforms succeed as a whole. Furthermore, ideological opposition to privatization was still strong. Although privatization was a key to deficit reduction, nevertheless, privatization faced insurmountable political opposition. Economic reform required a government with the kind of political strength and commitment that seemed impossible under both dictatorship and democracy.

CARLOS MENEM: SUCCESSFUL REFORMS?

Few investors or analysts would have predicted that Carlos Menem would bring successful economic reform to Argentina. As governor of the poverty-stricken La Rioja province, Menem had fought unemployment by simply increasing the size of the civil service, shrewdly bargaining with Alfonsin for more subsidies to meet the payroll. While the Radical party platform in the 1989 election called for economic liberalization, Menem's election campaign was run on the theme of social justice, with Menem claiming to be the new Peron. His economic pronouncements were limited to calling for a suspension of foreign debt payments, while denouncing the international conspiracy against Argentina. Menem's rhetoric won strong working class support, sufficient to get him the presidency of Argentina without much support among more affluent voters or the powerful families that ran Argentina's economy. To the extent that the hyper inflationary spiral was fuelled by jittery investors, it is clear that Menem as a presidential candidate contributed significantly to the destabilization that preceded the election.

As president, however, Menem immediately changed direction, and many felt he betrayed his party and his supporters. Before taking office, the newly elected Menem conferred closely with economists from the one major Argentine corporation that was not reliant on the complex system of government contracts and protectionist measures: Bunge y Born (B&B), a multinational conglomerate based in agricultural and related industries. Menem heeded the lessons from Argentina's economic disaster, as drawn by the company's economists, and he appointed several of the company's economists and executives to the ministry of economics, including the first two Economy Ministers. Furthermore, he excluded all other leading Peronists from the cabinet, cutting himself off from pressure by the special interest groups. The leader of the conservative party, a well-known advocate of liberalisation, was appointed chief negotiator of foreign debt. Thus, Menem successfully signalled from the beginning of his administration that his policy would not be beholden to the traditional Peronist interests and party factions, including the labor unions, and the businesses that thrived on government support. Instead, the government allied itself with the international business community, and signalled to this community that it had both the will and the power to institute change.

Menem's 1989 reform package, known as Plan BB, was similar to the 1985 Alfonsin Plan. Stabilization of the economy would be combined with fundamental restructuring of the public sector. However, the key difference was that restructuring would be imposed immediately. The government announced it was prepared to sacrifice short-term economic stability for the sake of genuine reform. Menem capitalized on his support immediately, passing reform laws in the congress that gave the cabinet the power to privatize state-owned businesses, to reorganize the financial sector and to conduct economic reforms—all without recourse to the legislature. By stipulating plan BB in law, Menem not only centralized the power to take economic stabilization measures, but also implicated the other political parties in a democratic reform process. The 1985 Austral program had merely been decreed over radio and television, Alfonsin having taken for granted that the populace would be opposed to the plan in the short term. Nevertheless, the concentration of powers under Menem's strong leadership did weaken the constitutional checks and balances, making the government more vulnerable to future arbitrary rule.

An immediate goal of the reform was to eliminate the government deficit. In addition to privatizing major state-owned companies, the government increased taxes and the prices charged by public utilities, some by as much as 1,000 per cent, overnight. The currency was stabilized at 650 australs to the dollar, and an informal price "agreement" was made with leading industries.[12] Structurally, the reform had already gone further than any previous attempt, but the plan did not immediately stop inflation. The central bank allowed the money supply to increase in the fall of 1989, and inflation led once again to currency flight into U.S. dollars. The spectre of hyper inflation returned, and rumblings were heard about the possibility of a military coup.

In November 1989, monthly inflation was six per cent, and in December hyper inflation returned.

The second reform phase began on December 15, 1989. Instead of retreating in the face of hyper inflation, the government accelerated the pace of reform. Foreign exchange controls were abolished and the exchange rate was freed. However, since it was cut off from international loans, the government had to refinance its huge debt in Argentina at double-digit interest rates, and this contributed directly to the inflationary spiral. On January 1, 1990, the government immediately transformed all of its debt with Argentine banks, in the form of one-day certificates of deposit, into 10-year bonds denominated in U.S. dollars with interest paid every six months. This cut the money supply (M2) by 60 per cent overnight. Aggregate demand was reduced by this loss of personal savings, and by a 43 per cent reduction in the federal budget. However, it was clear that by doing this the government would not be able to rely on domestic borrowing again for a very long time; this meant it had to eliminate the deficit.

The result of this new stabilization was unprecedented success. In 1990, monthly inflation fell from 95 per cent in March to 12 per cent in April; by November it was eight per cent. The austral climbed steadily and dramatically in value throughout the year. Tariffs were removed, exposing local industry to foreign competition.

All branches of government but one were reduced drastically in size. The exception was not, as one might have expected from past experience, the military, which saw its budget cut 50 per cent, but the tax collection agency. With a large part of the economy underground, tax evasion became a major threat to deficit control. Companies that were scheduled to be privatized were required to fire employees immediately and to sell off assets in preparation. The biggest state enterprise in Argentina, the petroleum company YPF, was required to auction off many of its oil and gas properties, as well as drastically reduce its work force of 50,000 employees. To counter charges that the reforms were amateurish and the privatization process corrupt, the

respected Harvard-trained economist, Domingo Cavallo, was appointed Economics Minister in January 1991.

June 1991 seemed to be the turning point in the reform. The success of the stabilisation plan was certified by the lowering of interest rates and by the return of foreign investment to Argentina, with a surge in private capital inflows. As inflation fell and the economy recovered, deficit reduction was made easier by a resurgence in tax revenue. By September 1991, Menem's economic success was entrenched by success in congressional elections. However, veteran observers of the Argentine economy were quick to point out that even with the help of the international agencies, Menem had only bought a little time. Further debt reduction, particularly in the provinces, would still be urgent. It was also possible that other problems, especially labor unrest, could undermine the reforms.

By 1992, the reforms were generally accepted and highly successful, both financially and in terms of increased efficiency. To consolidate this economic success, the austral was replaced in 1992 with a new peso which the government pledged to maintain at parity with the dollar. This policy was a powerful commitment by the government, since henceforth it would not have the option of printing money to finance its deficits. No restrictions were placed on privatization bids by foreigners, except in the case of the sale of the national airline. Furthermore, in most cases, the companies were sold for foreign debt bonds and foreign currency, reducing the national debt as well as that portion of the debt held by foreigners. Hopeful of Argentina's determination to reform, international agencies returned to the country's aid.

Coping With Hyper Inflation

In the 1980s, the initial success of major reforms repeatedly ended in failure, with increasingly severe crises. When Chauvco considered investing in Argentina in January 1992, Menem's reform effort had met with initial success, though the outcome was far from certain. For Chauvco, an important question was whether the company would be able to cope successfully if hyper inflation returned. Oil and gas exports would be priced in U.S. dollars. Consequently, an escalation in Argentine costs might reduce profits. Fortunately, by borrowing in Canada and the United States, Chauvco would be isolated from interest rate volatility. On the other hand, a period of hyper inflation might be accompanied by an equivalent devaluation of the Argentine peso, and this could result in a constant level of costs in terms of U.S. dollars. However, if hyper inflation led to the re-imposition of price controls on domestic sales of oil and gas, then Chauvco might be caught in a serious price-cost squeeze for at least part of its production. While hedging might reduce foreign exchange risks, nevertheless, hedging could not prevent such a profit squeeze. Furthermore, a financial crisis could disrupt established business practices, as suppliers and customers struggled to survive. Economic forecasts rested upon the assumption that political stability would continue, but social forces might lead to a recurrence of the previous political turmoil. Given the wide range of possible outcomes, the impact of hyper inflation could not be predicted with much certainty.

CHAUVCO'S 1992 DECISION

One of Chauvco's board members, John M. Browning, had been employed by Tenneco (Tennessee Oil and Gas) in Argentina many years earlier, and still retained contacts in Argentina's oil and gas sector. Browning was "the reason this company was perhaps more aware than others of the changes taking place [in South America]."[13] In Argentina, the state-owned oil monopoly, YPF, was scheduled to be privatized by 1992, and to achieve this, the two-year-old reform government of Carlos Menem had appointed a new CEO, with orders to trim YPF to a saleable size. By 1990, YPF had begun selling off marginal producing properties and had ceded

its privilege as exclusive buyer of Argentine crude, thereby deregulating prices. Foreign companies from the United States, the United Kingdom and Spain had spent $252 million for marginal producing areas by year-end 1990, the first foreign companies to operate state-owned fields for over 80 years. Except for Texaco and Shell, the foreign companies bought in with Argentine partners.

For Chauvco, the geological similarity between Argentina's sedimentary basins and those of Western Canada was a key feature of Argentina's appeal.[14] The fields were likely to be too small to interest the majors, who prefer billion-barrel fields; but for independents, the hundred-million barrel potential was just right. The number of existing wells, 25,000, was minuscule compared to the size of the oilfields, where most of the basins averaged one test per 8,700 miles. By North American standards, the property was under-explored. Furthermore, Chauvco had developed an expertise in the analysis of geological formations for the purpose of utilizing sophisticated techniques in extracting "secondary reserves," and for the purpose of determining where additional wells should be drilled within a field. This competitive advantage was ideally suited to the small deposits and the widely varying geological structures within each Argentine field. Being among the first with this expertise to enter Argentina, Chauvco could acquire its choice of fields at relatively low cost. Furthermore, it was expected that rapid economic growth would raise domestic consumption of gas, and a new pipeline to Chile would also increase the market for gas. These forces would enable Chauvco to earn larger profits than previous operators of the Argentine fields.

Browning was able to use his personal relationships in Argentina to arrange a meeting in January 1992 with Jose Estensorro, the CEO of YPF. At the meeting, Chauvco learned that a 35-year production concession in Tierra del Fuego, the southern tip of Argentina, was being sold that month. Chauvco's senior management immediately visited the properties and formally qualified the company to obtain technical data and to bid. The reserves consisted largely of natural gas and associated natural gas liquids, but the property also included some high-quality oil production. Chauvco formed a consortium with Bridas, a major Argentine oil company, and the U.S.-integrated company, Coastal, to submit a $150 million bid. Under the agreement, Bridas would be the operator of the property. On January 21, 1992, the consortium learned its bid had won by a very narrow margin. With a 23.34 per cent interest in five Tierra del Fuego fields, Chauvco was now an international oil and gas company.

With this production and cash flow base, Chauvco was able to set up an office in Argentina and evaluate further prospects. As it did in Canada, Chauvco had once again grown through the acquisition of producing properties. With further privatizations expected in the months leading to YPF's eventual sale, cash flow could turn out to be as critical in Argentina as it had been in Alberta in the oil bust of the 1980s.

Some industry analysts were not keen on Chauvco's foreign adventure, figuring Turcotte had got in too deep, too fast for a small independent with no previous international exposure. But at least one broker, Midland-Walwyn, favored Chauvco's decision, and in the *Financial Post,* analyst Pentti Karkkainen, while deprecating the foreign strategies of other Calgary oil firms, praised Chauvco's geographical specialization: "They have established a strong foothold in Argentina . . . you don't see them all over the place."

Two numbers stood out when considering Argentine oil: a royalty rate of just 12 per cent, and a corporate income tax rate of 30 per cent or less, in contrast with Alberta's 20 per cent and 45 per cent, respectively. In order to stimulate development in the remote region of Tierra del Fuego, and to solidify its territorial claims vis-à-vis Chile, Argentina offered income tax-free status for investments there. Furthermore, there were no foreign exchange controls on profits being taken out of the country. "The differences between local companies and foreign companies have disappeared," according to Guimar Vaca Coca, president of Chauvco's Argentine subsidiary.[15]

DIFFICULTIES OF DOING BUSINESS IN ARGENTINA

The difficulties of doing business in Argentina became quickly apparent. "It's 30 to 50 per cent more expensive to do business here than in Canada," said Vaca Coca.[16] Higher costs were the result of many elements of Argentina's business environment.

Transition Difficulties in Moving to a Free-Market Economy

Prior to Menem's reforms, the government owned and regulated most of Argentina's economic activities. Rather suddenly, Menem began privatizing government-owned activities and changing regulations to permit a greater role for private sector decision-making. For businesses, this meant uncertainty about the current and prospective scope for decisions. As Chauvco's senior management outlined:

> We have broken ground as that change has taken place, dealing with new regulations as they pertain to oil and gas development; new regulations as they pertain to pipeline construction, drilling, and expansion; and new regulations as they relate to the MNEs (multinational enterprises). As a result of the transition, much of the business framework has not been in place. This has meant that business–government relations have had a high priority.

Furthermore, "Argentina had been isolated for a very long period of time." The shift towards an open international economy had also created transition uncertainties.

The Legacy of Bureaucratic Planning

Guy Turcotte emphasized that "it takes a long time to get any type of documentation." Paperwork and time-consuming approval systems were slow to change. The legal system also was slow to adapt. This delayed the transfer of title to property, and it impeded many business activities, such as opening a bank account. Extensive reporting requirements still existed, and these could be subject to frequent change, most notably with regard to payroll issues. Often, as Chauvco's management suggested, "the long way is the normal way. But we cannot bulldoze culture; we have to work within it."

Renegotiation of Agreements

Turcotte pointed out that:

If somebody sends you an invoice, you know it is negotiable. Everything is up for negotiation—a $100 invoice or a $1 million invoice. This is very much a part of the Argentine culture, and it creates inefficiencies.

Inadequate Communication Systems

Since Chauvco had field operations as well as a head office in Buenos Aires and senior management in Calgary, there was a need for inexpensive and efficient communication systems. Chauvco's reaction was to establish its own satellite linkages, so that all Chauvco locations could easily talk with each other or send electronic information.

The Need for International Financing

Since Argentina's banking system and stock market were poorly developed, foreign-owned businesses generally relied on financing from outside of the country. Conversely, financing abroad could give foreign companies a competitive advantage over domestic firms.

Head Office Costs

The cost of operating a head office in Buenos Aires, which was the seventh most expensive city in the world, was considerably higher than in Calgary.

Human Resources

The lack of technicians trained to Canadian standards, combined with a shortage of state-of-the-art technology, meant a larger number of employees were required to accomplish a task. Machinery breakdowns in the field were frequent, causing increases in operating costs. For managerial staff, a special difficulty was the lack of training and experience in cost accounting and decentralized decision-making. Chauvco's senior management observed:

People take their instructions from the individual they work for, with a traditional hierarchal approach to the organization. This contrasts with Canada where you expect employees to be much more self-driven, and to operate within a framework of company policy, not waiting to be told what to do.

For Chauvco, this cultural difference required special training sessions and ongoing encouragement to take initiatives. Related to this was the traditional lack of financial incentives. In Canada, Chauvco relied upon stock options for employees, but the nascent state of the Argentine stock market and the distance from Canadian markets prevented this. Consequently, Chauvco had to develop new bonus schemes, linked, for example, with cost reduction goals.

Wages and Salaries

Chauvco found the work force to be highly educated. However, salaries for middle-management levels were higher than in Canada. Furthermore, the annual cost of placing a Canadian in Argentina was several times the salary paid in Canada. As a result of introducing new management systems, Chauvco was able to reduce the number of employees in one of its field operations from the previous high level of 62 under the former owner, to a level of only 23. However, Bill Ibbitson, the Operations Manager, indicated that the Canadian equivalent might be as low as 10.

The Difficulties of Expatriate Adjustment

While expatriates found many of these differences to be disconcerting, the major adjustment problems lay within the area of language and personal life. For families, children could have difficulties adjusting to school and the community. Housing could cost three or four times the level of that in Calgary. Break-ins and theft could be an ever-present threat.

Outsourcing

Prior to Menem's reforms, government ownership meant that there were relatively few privately owned service companies. As a result, service companies, such as drilling operators, were often not available and were less efficient than in Alberta; therefore, outsourcing costs were higher.

Lack of Access to Data

According to Ray Baird, Chauvco's Exploration Manager, finding needed technical data from among the unorganized records of YPF was like "looking for a contact lens in a lake." Data processing was done in Calgary instead of Buenos Aires. "Its not worth cutting corners for that," Baird said. "It's easier to send it to Calgary where there is a corporate infrastructure already in place to do what we need done."

Outdated Technology

The oilfields Chauvco bought were already in operation, with their own technology, "in the 1950s models of things," as Baird put it. "But the equipment is expensive, so unless it's broken, it stays." "There is less technology, so you require more manpower here," Guimar Vaca Coca said. "There is less automation, and not the high degree of communications as in Canada, so more infrastructure is needed to work efficiently. That's something we had to realize."[17]

Materials and Contractors

Much of the local economy was still run by monopolies, raising input costs. For example, a *Globe and Mail* article pointed out that nitrogen, which is essential for the oil business, was supplied by only one company, and cost five times more than in Canada.

Personal Relationships

As in many other countries, Argentine business was conducted on the basis of personal relationships. In the context of the business uncertainties discussed above, it was important to feel that there were elements of trust on which one could rely, apart from the content of documents. This emphasis on personal relationships posed difficulties for a foreign-based company in its initial investments.

Bribery and Kickbacks

While Chauvco did not participate in any such practices, nevertheless, many refer to these as being normal in Argentine business. In August 1995, Domingo Cavallo, Argentina's Economy Minister, created a significant public uproar when he accused business people and politicians of corruption and illegal influence peddling.

THE POSITIVE SIDE

On the positive side, Chauvco encountered several significant benefits during its learning process.

Relying Upon a Joint Venture Partner

For Chauvco, many of these difficulties were alleviated through the initial decision to invest as a joint venture partner with a domestic company. This arrangement enabled Chauvco to learn about the environment of business in Argentina, and it facilitated relations with government agencies. After a year as a joint venture partner, Chauvco felt comfortable enough to create its own independent operations, while also continuing its original alliance. As a crucial part of this second step, Chauvco hired a U.S. oil executive to head its Argentine operations. Guimar Vaca Coca had been born in Latin America and had previously worked in Argentina. In retrospect, Turcotte felt that the success of this pattern would lead Chauvco to consider a joint venture arrangement as a first step into other countries as well.

Argentine Preferences to Deal With Canadians

Many Argentines preferred to deal with Canadian rather than U.S. businesses. Both Canada and Argentina have large immigrant populations which have maintained their cultural identities. The countries have similar climates; Canadians are perceived as being more open than Americans; and Canadians tend to speak more slowly, so that language difficulties are not as severe. From an Argentine perspective, Canadians also seem more willing to compromise and to adjust to local practices. Both countries share a history of anti-American sentiment. This pro-Canadian attitude helped Chauvco to become established.

Lessons for Investing in Other Countries

Chauvco's management felt that their experiences in learning how to do business in Argentina had given them a range of skills that would help them with investments in other countries as well. This learning created an understanding of how to operate in a different culture than Canada's.

Chauvco's initial investment was highly profitable and, by September 1992, was generating a net cash flow of $1 million per month. However, crude oil production was lower than expected, and operating costs were much higher than the expected $3.75 per barrel. Investment analysts at Wood-Gundy firmly laid the blame on the doorstep of Chauvco's operator. "While Bridas has been capable on a project-specific basis, it has been disappointing in terms of overall management."[18] Chauvco decided to develop its own independent activities in Argentina, headed by Vaca Coca, and to transfer management personnel from Calgary.

In general, Vaca Coca said:

I think you just have to realize that it takes longer to do things here and the job is a little more difficult to finish. Be flexible. Once you realize that, it's a great place to do business.

Between 1992 and 1994, Chauvco acquired interests in 11 other properties in Argentina, operating all but one of the new properties, and maintaining a high working interest in all. By 1995, about 40 per cent of Chauvco's total capital was invested in Argentina. Chauvco bought into both gas, with a strictly local market, and oil, with a world-wide market. Chauvco also bought a larger share of the original Tierra del Fuego operation, and it invested heavily in the central province of Neuquen. In November 1994 alone, the company spent $29 million on 500,000 acres in Neuquen, and planned a development program that was projected to double oil production in 1995/1996.

THE 1995 DECISIONS

The financial terms and conditions under which a company could develop oil and gas fields varied significantly among countries. In some, like Venezuela, the government maintained its ownership of mineral rights, and it contracted to pay the operator a certain amount per barrel of oil extracted. In Argentina, the government privatization created a system of 25 year leases, often renewable for a further five or 10 years. This system offered much greater opportunity for a business to increase its profits per barrel. In many countries, governments imposed special taxes and royalties on this sector. Consequently, the decision to invest in a particular country was influenced by predictions concerning future financial levies of this kind. For the oil and gas business, social and political stability involved the continuation of existing government policies, not just the maintenance of a certain political system, or a particular regime.

The Alberta oil patch had a very good year in 1994, its best since 1985, due largely to the effect

Year Ended December 31 (thousands)	1994	1993	1992
Revenue			
Petroleum and natural gas sales (Note 9)	$189,061	159,034	142,723
Royalties, net	(29,961)	(23,811)	(22,474)
Overhead recoveries and other income	1,650	1,412	1,537
Foreign exchange gain (loss) and investment income	3,631	543	(131)
	164,381	137,178	121,655
Expenses			
Operations	42,481	35,020	29,771
Interest on long term debt	10,226	4,559	5,160
Administration	8,295	7,206	5,782
Depletion, depreciation and amortization	62,762	56,591	49,188
	123,764	103,376	89,901
Earnings before taxes	40,617	33,802	31,754
Provision for taxes			
Capital taxes	466	490	387
Income taxes (Note 7)	11,099	5,092	8,641
	11,565	5,582	9,028
	29,052	28,220	22,726
Net earnings for the year	29,052	28,220	22,614
Retained earnings at end of year	$122,512	93,460	65,240
Net earnings per common share	$0.65	$0.64	$0.53
Weighted average common shares outstanding	44,441	44,032	42,435

Exhibit 1   Consolidated Statement of Earnings and Retained Earnings[1]

1. 1994 Annual Report, Chauvco Resources Ltd., 45.

on oil demand of a recovering North American economy.[19] Gas prices were high, oil prices were stable, equity markets were friendly, and the fall of the Canadian dollar helped oil exports and profits as expressed in Canadian dollars. Chauvco announced it was shifting from its traditional Alberta exploration focus on oil to an increased emphasis on natural gas.

By February 1995, however, gas prices had fallen to a two-year low, as a result of a relatively mild winter, and new pipelines that increased supply. Predictions of a recovery in gas prices by year end, combined with evidence of slowly increasing demand, kept gas exploration going without a slump in the early part of the year, but a major slump was predicted for the spring and summer of 1995.[20] Alberta's reserve life of gas had fallen, making exploration more important and more difficult. New and expensive drilling techniques were necessary to keep marginal oil pools in production.

The world oil price peaked at US$19.82 in April 1995, but began to fall thereafter. By the end of June 1995, Wood-Gundy lowered its

Year Ended December 31 (thousands)	1994	1993	1992
Operating activities			
Net earnings for the year	$29,052	28,220	22,614
Add: Depletion, depreciation and amortization	62,762	56,591	49,188
Deferred income taxes	5,911	(1,552)	6,339
Minority interest and other	(363)	—	112
Cash flow from operations before changes in working capital	97,362	83,259	78,253
Changes in non-cash working capital (Note 8)	(14,993)	15,252	(6,024)
	82,369	98,511	72,229
Financing activities			
Share capital	2,113	2,099	47,268
Bank loan	48,730	1,102	(3,124)
Senior notes payable	80,580	—	—
Other	(1,047)	(891)	(351)
	130,376	2,310	43,793
Total cash resources provided	212,745	100,821	116,022
Investing activities			
Major acquisitions (Note 2)	85,174	35,709	84,446
Petroleum and natural gas	129,145	55,879	32,104
Corporate	3,029	5,054	902
Investments	(733)	1,430	—
	216,615	98,072	117,452
Increase (decrease) in cash	(3,870)	2,749	(1,430)
Cash at beginning of year	1,768	(981)	449
Cash at end of year	$(2,102)	1,768	(981)
Cash consists of:			
Cash	1,180	2,040	471
Bank indebtedness	(3,282)	(272)	(1,452)
	(2,102)	1,768	(981)
Working capital (deficiency) at end of year	$ (749)	(11,872)	631
Cash flow from operations before changes in working capital per common share			
– Basic	$2.19	$1.89	$1.84
– Fully diluted	$2.17	$1.86	$1.81

Exhibit 2   Consolidated Statement of Changes in Cash Position[1]

1. 1994 Annual Report, Chauvco Resources Ltd., 47.

December 31 (thousands)	1994	1993
Assets		
Current assets		
Cash	$1,180	2,040
Accounts receivable	36,031	13,554
Other	2,681	748
	39,892	16,342
Capital assets, at cost		
Petroleum and natural gas	768,565	554,552
Corporate	12,990	9,199
	781,555	563,751
Accumulated depletion and depreciation	(258,273)	(197,035)
	523,282	366,716
Investments and deferred charges	1,478	1,545
	$564,652	384,603
Liabilities		
Current liabilities		
Bank indebtedness	$3,282	272
Accounts payable	35,956	21,542
Taxes payable	—	4,742
Notes payable (Note 2[iii])	1,403	1,658
	40,461	28,214
Bank debt (Notes 2 and 4)	100,135	51,405
Senior notes payable (Note 5)	80,580	—
Deferred credits (Note 6)	4,286	3,506
Deferred income taxes (Note 7)	57,568	51,201
	283,210	134,326
Shareholders' equity		
Share capital (Note 3)	158,930	156,817
Retained earnings	122,512	93,460
	281,442	250,277
	$564,652	384,603

Exhibit 3   Consolidated Statement of Financial Position[1]

1. 1994 Annual Report, Chauvco Resources Ltd., 49.

prediction of 1996 oil prices from US$18.50 to US$17.50 per barrel, and warned that unless OPEC brought its members back to quota, overproduction would drive prices below the $15 mark. Overproduction by OPEC was expected to add 1.6 million barrels per day to world inventories during the third quarter for 1995. Due to the weak U.S. dollar, oil prices had fallen, in terms

Year Ended December 31	1994	1993	1992
Argentina			
Neuquen Province (i) (iii)	$38,368	14,942	—
Tierra del Fuego (ii) (v)	46,806	—	56,536
Canada			
Lookout Butte (iv)	—	20,767	—
Tripet minority interest (vi)	—	—	16,279
Woods Petroleum (vii)	—	—	11,631
Total acquisitions	**$85,174**	**35,709**	**84,446**

i.   During 1994, the Company acquired two properties in the Neuquen Basin of Argentina for $38,368,000 (US$28,265,000) cash.

ii. Effective April 1, 1994, the Company acquired for $46,806,000 (US$33,781,000) cash plus a contingent note payable of US$1.0 million (based on future production levels and oil prices) an additional 11.66 per cent working interest in the Tierra del Fuego properties. The purchase brings the total working interest in the properties to 35 per cent.

iii. During 1993, the Company acquired two properties in the Neuquen Basin of Argentina for $14,942,000 (US$11,664,000), which includes notes payable due in 1994 for $1,658,000 (US$1,250,000) and in 1995 for $1,326,000 (US$1,000,000). In addition, one of the acquired properties carries a contingent note which calls for additional payments of up to US$3,500,000 to be made after the Company has accumulated production of one billion cubic metres of natural gas.

iv. On September 29, 1993, the Company purchased the interests of Solex Energy Corporation at Lookout Butte, Alberta for $20,767,000. The acquisition carries a contingent note payable over the next four years, in the amount of $2.0 million, should the contract natural gas price exceed $2.25 per MmBtu in 1995, $2.50 per MmBtu in 1996, and $2.65 per MmBtu in 1997.

v.   Effective February 3, 1992, the Company acquired for $56,536,000 (US$48,172,000) cash a 23.34 per cent working interest in certain properties located in the Austral Basin in Tierra del Fuego, Argentina under the terms of a 35 year production concession agreement.

vi. Effective May 1, 1992, the Company acquired the 11 per cent minority interest in Tripet Resources Limited for $13,670,000 cash and the issue of 115,101 common shares valued at $2,609,000.

vii. Effective August 1, 1992, the Company purchased the shares of the wholly owned Canadian oil and gas subsidiary of Woods Petroleum of Canada Ltd. for $11,631,000 cash.

Exhibit 4   Major Acquisitions, 1992–1994[1]

1. 1994 Annual Report, Chauvco Resources Ltd., 52–53.

---

of Yen or Deutschemarks, to levels not seen since the 1970s.

For Chauvco's Canadian expansion, 1994 to 1995 was less than satisfying. Chauvco spent $41.2 million on exploration and acquisitions in 1994, including $19 million on land, $7 million on seismic, and $15 million on drilling for a company record of 43 exploratory wells. Twenty of those wells came up dry, 17 resulted in natural gas and six in oil, for a low success rate of 53 per cent and high finding costs of $28.40 per barrel.[21] The company's land purchases shifted towards undeveloped, more prospective land in a new focus region, northeastern British Columbia, and the neighboring area in Alberta.

Although Chauvco's 1994 annual report declared that the company was satisfied with the political and economic climate in Argentina, it was clear to most observers that prospects for the Argentine economy were shaky. The continuation of reforms, including the sale of YPF in the summer of 1993, and deregulation of foreign trade had resulted in an extremely vigorous economy by 1994, with the third highest growth rate in the world, and inflation at a mere 3.3 per cent annually. But a mounting current account deficit, the reappearance of a major government budget deficit, and signs of an incipient recession had investors worried by the end of 1994. Then on December 20, 1994, Mexico devalued its peso. Ripples of investor panic soon spread to Argentina's own currency, causing a run on bank deposits, and effectively cutting the country off from international capital markets. Unable to borrow to finance the deficit, the government was forced to impose drastic spending cuts and tax increases, and it announced a new round of privatizations. Furthermore, the crisis destabilized the financial system. Although the IMF was prepared to offer a credit facility of $2.4 billion, the financial targets required seemed unattainable as of mid-1995. Nevertheless, with the re-election of Menem for a four-year term in May 1995, private capital began to return, with a 1.3 billion peso increase in bank deposits in the week following the elections. In combination with the external aid package the government had assembled, it appeared that this return of private capital would help Argentina surmount the financial crisis. However, the economy appeared headed for a major recession, with 15 to 20 per cent unemployment and negative growth predicted to continue throughout the year.[22]

Faced with constraints in the environment of business in both Alberta and Argentina, Chauvco's 1994 annual report stated:

> Chauvco is dedicating additional resources to looking at opportunities in other parts of the world.

Over the next five to 10 years, the company would like to find another one to three countries, besides Canada, that provide a good opportunity for profits and growth.

The company had already investigated, and rejected, an opportunity in Russia.[23] In 1995, Chauvco announced it would participate in a small joint venture with another Calgary company in Turkey. For Chauvco, 1995 had become another crossroads.

NOTES

1. The authors would like to express their appreciation for the information and assistance provided by management and staff at Chauvco, both in Argentina and in Calgary. The authors would also like to thank the Canadian Energy Research Institute, Calgary, for providing its research studies of the "Petroleum Industry in Latin America."

2. See Exhibit 4, Major Acquisitions, 1992–1994.

3. On December 7, 1980, Clark announced in the House of Commons: "We are now actively discussing the mechanism that will ensure that virtually 100 per cent of the revenues that would go to the [oil] companies as a result of the increase in energy prices will, in fact, be regained by the Government of Canada for the specific application by the Government of Canada for national energy purposes." Peter McKenzie-Brown, Gordon Jaremko, and David Finch, *The Great Oil Age* (Calgary, AB: Detselig Enterprises, 1993), 128.

4. Appendix 1 discusses various technical aspects of exploration and production.

5. 1983 Annual Report, Chauvco Resources Ltd., 2.

6. Drew Fagan, "Burgeoning Chauvco Helped by Hard Times," *Globe and Mail,* 13 June 1988.

7. Bob Curran, "Five That Thrived," *Oilweek,* June 17, 1991.

8. Barry Nelson, "The Uplifting View at Contrarian Chauvco," *Financial Times of Canada,* 25 December 1989.

9. Edward Clifford, "Chauvco May Become the Next Oil Patch Darling," *Globe and Mail,* 21 June 1991.

10. Bob Curran, "Five That Thrived," *Oilweek,* June 17, 1991.

11. Appendix 2 discusses this hyper inflation in more detail.

12. David G. Erro, *Resolving the Argentine Paradox* (Boulder, CO: Lynne Rienner Publishers, 1993), 204.

13. Jeffrey Jones, "Southern Exposure," *Oilweek,* March 21, 1994.

14. 1994 Annual Report, Chauvco Resources Ltd., 19.

15. Natasha Bacigalupo, "Oil Companies Look to Argentina," *Globe and Mail,* 25 October 1993.

16. "Oil Companies Look to Argentina," *Globe and Mail,* 25 October 1994.

17. "Chauvco Taps Argentine Oil Patch," *Globe and Mail,* 26 October 1994.

18. David Stenason, "Chauvco Resources Limited," Wood Gundy Investment Research: The Drill Bit, September 11, 1992.

19. Projections and analysis based largely on Robert Curran, "Life at the Crossroads," *Oilweek,* February 20, 1995.

20. Robert Curran, "Life at the Crossroads," *Oilweek,* February 20, 1995.

21. 1994 Annual Report, Chauvco Resources Ltd., 18–19.

22. EIU Country Report, 2nd quarter 1995.

23. David Stenason, "Chauvco Resources Limited," Wood Gundy Investment Research: The Drill Bit, January 25, 1993.

APPENDIX 1: OIL AND GAS EXPLORATION

Wells produce the liquids "crude oil" and "condensate" as well as natural gas, a mixture that includes methane. Condensate is a hydrocarbon product associated with natural gas production. Natural gas liquids of propane and butane may also be recovered from gas production. Crude oil is graded according to its density, or specific gravity, measured in degrees API. The higher the API index, the lighter and more valuable the oil. Generally "the price of a barrel of oil," as in the news media, is for intermediate oil, 34 degrees API or light oil, 40 degrees API. Gas production is often associated with oil wells, but natural gas is also found in "gas wells" that have little petroleum; then it is known as "non-associated" gas.

Exploration is conducted by specialists in petroleum geology and geophysics, including geochemists, who analyse subsurface water and soil, and seismologists, who conduct geophysical surveys in the field and interpret the results. A seismic survey is conducted by detonating explosives at various locations beneath the surface of the area to be surveyed, and recording the response on a grid of digital "geophones" at the surface as shock waves are bounced back by rock formations deep under the ground. The data can be used to construct two-dimensional profiles of underground formations. These can be integrated into a "seismic cube," a three-dimensional computer-synthesized picture of the subsurface. These techniques can also be applied offshore by special research vessels equipped for geophysical surveys.

Exploration companies generally share the costs for these expensive surveys, using the data individually to prepare bids for auctions of the mineral rights. Globally, seismic is still a minor part of the exploration budget, accounting for $3 billion in 1992, against $30 billion for the traditional technique of drilling "wildcat" wells to look for oil. In modern exploration, due to the great cost of drilling, "wildcatting" is only done after extensive seismic tests and geological analysis indicate a particularly promising area. Until the hole is drilled, the geophysical data, no matter how precise, are at best suggestive of oil-bearing formations or "traps." Offshore exploration and development involve much higher costs, often 20 times as high as required on land.

The high-risk moment in the exploration phase is the decision to drill a "wildcat" well, in a field where there is no proof that oil is to be found. This decision typically is only made after huge amounts of geophysical data have been processed, either at company headquarters or by specialised consultants. Because drilling is very expensive and risky, small firms often diversify their risk by "participating" with other companies in several different "drilling programs." Drilling costs depend on the accessibility of the site, the depth of the well, and the material to be drilled through. One of the risks in drilling is losing equipment in a partially-completed hole, in which case a tedious and expensive "fishing expedition" is required to recover the equipment. As drilling proceeds, more information is accumulated; a high speed of penetration of the drill, for example, suggests the presence of porous rock which could contain oil or gas. Data from producing wells, such as core samples which reveal the type of underlying rocks and their porosity, are also used, to determine the likelihood of a known oilfield extending into an unexploited area.

Once oil has been found and reserves estimated, a great deal of investment is required to "develop" the oil field. This includes a development drilling program: a spatial pattern of wells designed to maximize the extraction of oil from the underlying pool. In the 1990s, most drilling in North America was developmental. As costly as drilling itself is the "completion" of each successful drill hole. The hole must be sheathed with "casing" and pumps installed to raise the oil.

Production of the well will be highest at the beginning; after the most accessible reserves are depleted, techniques of "secondary recovery" are required. These include:

- Precise 3-D seismic studies are undertaken in each oil field.
- Each well's unique geological structure is analysed intensively, and a unique plan is created for developing each well.
- Water and sand may be pumped into various levels of the geological structure to create new subterranean channels through which oil and gas can flow to the well.
- For certain geological formations, new types of pumps can be lowered down the pipe to the bottom of the well, and pumping may stimulate the flow into the well.
- The formation around the well may also be stimulated by chemical means, as another process for increasing the flow of hydro carbons. Acids may be injected under pressure into a rock formation at specific levels where it is

believed that dissolving limestone or dolomite may increase oil flow.
- Various ways of injecting water, natural gas, or gas liquids may be used as flooding techniques to force oil and gas up a neighboring well.
- The casing of the well consists of tubular steel pipe, and this prevents oil or gas from entering the well. Consequently, holes have to be made through the casing and into the earth and rock surrounding it. This process involves studying the formation in which the well is located in order to know at what levels these holes should be made. An explosive device is lowered into the well to the required depths. Explosive charges perforate the casing and create channels through which oil and gas may enter the pipe.

The Petroleum Communication Foundation, in its book "Our Petroleum Challenge," has suggested that "even with all these techniques, the average recovery in light oil fields is only about 30 per cent of the original oil."[1]

Improvement in these techniques has extended well-life to the point that by 1995 it could now be economical for oil producers to re-start a well that was considered marginal only a few years earlier. YPF was unable to drill enough wells on its producing fields to maintain production, and was not especially good at secondary recovery. Consequently, properties that were marginal for YPF were potentially productive for North American companies with better drilling and recovery techniques. However, the lack of consultants or contractors experienced in these techniques in Argentina was a problem for Canadian independents like Chauvco. Because of limited resources or specialization of firms, the owner of the mineral rights will often contract with another firm to explore or operate the site, as YPF did in Argentina, or Petropro did with Chauvco in Alberta.

NOTE

1. Robert Bott, *Our Petroleum Challenge: Into the 21st Century,* 5th ed. (Calgary: Petroleum Communication Foundation, 1993), 37.

APPENDIX 2:
THE ARGENTINE HYPER INFLATION

The annual rate of inflation is the rate of growth of prices over a year. HYPER INFLATION refers to rates of inflation that are so high that money becomes virtually useless. Prices change daily.

Inflation in Argentina was caused by the inability of the government to finance its spending. By the 1970s, the budget deficit had grown to 10 per cent of total output. A major portion of the deficit was due to losses in the state-owned enterprises, which through their inefficiency were also seriously impeding competitiveness in the private sector. The two standard options for financing a deficit are to borrow from the public (issue government bonds or get loans from international banks), or to borrow from the Central Bank which prints money and increases the government's accounts with the Bank.

The problem with printing money is that although there is more money in the economy, there is no change in the amount of real resources that money represents; hence the value of money is diluted in the same way that a stock issue by a private company dilutes the value of outstanding shares. Anticipating that their money will be worth less in the future, investors are less likely to lend at a given rate of interest, producers of goods and services less willing to sell at a given price, and workers less willing to work for a given money wage.

Assuming that markets for investment, goods and services, and labor were in equilibrium before the money supply was increased, then borrowers should be willing to pay a higher rate of interest, buyers pay higher prices, and employers pay higher wages to stay at the same levels of activity where they were originally. Thus, when inflation is high and persistent, expectations of further inflation get built into the system through higher interest rates and continually increasing wages and prices. Even if inflation is difficult to anticipate because it varies wildly, as was the case in Argentina before Menem, contracts can be "indexed" to the rate of inflation, so that wages, prices, and interest rates all automatically can vary according to the inflation rate.

While it is easy to see how printing money leads to inflation, it is not so easy to explain why inflation should matter to a business. If all prices are adjusting continuously, the economy is always in equilibrium. However, prices do not all adjust continuously. It is no easy task to figure out the inflation rate on a daily basis; even monthly estimates are only available with some delay, and are subject to correction as more data become available. Furthermore, for a business that imports or exports, the domestic prices are not the only issue at stake. Also of concern are the level of domestic prices vis-à-vis foreign prices. Here the exchange rate plays a key role, and so the linkages between HYPER INFLATION and the exchange rate can become crucial.

The option of borrowing from the public to cover a budget deficit is less inflationary because it does not increase the money supply. In the case of Argentina, however, the long tradition of volatile inflation had eroded faith in the currency and in financial markets. People bought durable goods with their money rather than deposit it in banks or invest it in other financial instruments. The government could not borrow from domestic financial markets and had to look abroad for loans. Since foreign loans were denominated in U.S. dollars, the government would be committed to a given rate of payment of interest, principal and fees that would rise in terms of Argentina's costs if the Argentine currency lost value.

The hyper inflationary periods occurred when people lost faith in the ability of the government to maintain a non-inflationary policy. Investors, for instance, could easily convert their holdings into U.S. dollars if they thought their returns in Argentine funds were going to fall below those of U.S. dollar holdings. This capital flight put pressure on the currency as investors sold australs for U.S. dollars, forcing the government to sell U.S. dollars for australs to maintain the exchange rate. Were the value of the austral to fall, the price of imports would rise, driving up the cost of living, and causing further inflation as wages and prices adjusted to compensate. This would lower the return to investments in australs yet further, provoking further capital flight. Fears of future Argentine inflation and devaluation encouraged everyone to buy U.S. dollars, accelerating the inflation-devaluation spiral.

In addition, the ability of the government to keep purchasing australs was limited by its reserves of U.S. dollars; even with IMF support, reserves were finite, so unless reform was immediately successful in stopping inflation, an eventual devaluation was certain. This prospect provoked further capital flight, increasing the downward pressure on the value of the austral in terms of foreign currencies, and accelerating inflation. Another aspect of the inflationary spiral was that when prices were rising rapidly, government tax receipts lost value between the time they were levied and the time they were collected. This aggravated the deficit, and the government had to increase taxation rates to compensate for this loss.

Thus, the hyper inflationary spiral rested on two structural elements: large and recurrent budget deficits, and an overwhelming burden of foreign debt. The key planks of Alfonsin's reform addressed the wage indexation and currency instability, but ongoing budget deficits and increases in foreign debt would inevitably cause a return of the crisis.

The first phase of Menem's reforms, in 1989, restrained inflation through a relatively informal system of price controls. The system failed in part because from the outset people found ways to increase their own prices or wages to reflect their own anticipations of inflation. When it became quickly apparent that the structural reforms were not going to be deep enough to eliminate the deficit, then people began to anticipate the return of HYPER INFLATION, and raised their prices at an increasing rate, while moving their savings and investments into U.S. dollars, thereby weakening the value of the austral.

Menem's response, to immediately sell off large subsidized state corporations and to cut the government budget by 43 per cent, showed that the government was indeed going to the heart of the structural problems, so that in the long term, under normal conditions, HYPER INFLATION would not return. The forced conversion of deposit certificates into long-term U.S. bonds achieved both price and currency stability. Inflation was reduced directly because the monetary base fell 60 per cent; banks needed deposit certificates as reserves to make loans, so that when their reserves vanished, credit became very tight. As a result, aggregate demand fell immediately, taking a lot of pressure out of the urge to raise prices. To consume, people needed to liquidate their savings, now denominated in U.S. dollars; essentially they were selling U.S. dollars against the austral, driving up the price of the austral, and as a result stabilizing the currency. Furthermore, the government took advantage of this time to increase its reserves of U.S. dollars which could be used to support the austral in the event of another crisis, further increasing confidence in the austral.

APPENDIX 3: FISCAL PERFORMANCE AND TARGETS, 1995–1996 (Ps[1] MILLIONS)

	IMF Target, 1995	Actual Outturn, 1995
Primary balance	6,086	1,539
Interest payments	4,080	4,084
Overall deficit (excl. privatizations)	2,006	−2,544
Privatizations	2,400	1,171
Overall balance	4,406	−1,131

Balance of Payments (in millions of dollars)

	1994
Exports (fob)	15,839
Imports (fob)	−20,077
Trade balance	−4,238
Services balance	−5,349
Current-account balance	−9,272
Capital-account balance	9,841
Change in international reserves	569

1. Ps = Peso.

CRISIS IN JAPAN

*Prepared by William Aldridge under the
supervision of Professor Jean-Philippe Bonardi*

Version: (A) 2002-08-01

On February 13, 2002, Prime Minister Koizumi announced emergency countermeasures against deflation with the primary goal of solving the immediate problems of the financial system. Will it be enough to get the country out of trouble?

Every Sunday morning, Masa, Shogo, Toshio and Haru got together to play a round of golf at the Tokyo Continental Country Club. Masa, Toshio and Haru were childhood friends, all the same age. Shogo had been their high school teacher and was a golf instructor for the high school golf club where the three classmates first learned the game. Golf for the foursome was competitive but the Sunday game gave the old friends a chance to catch up on the week's events. Inevitably, each week the conversation turned to the Japanese economy and the impact of Japanese government policy on each of their lives.

Masa: Looks like our prayers for good weather didn't get answered fellas! Good for me though—I always play better when it's drizzling. Shogo, looks like you're up first. Let's have some fun.

Shogo was 67 years old and had been retired for two years. He mainly spent his time at his small suburban Tokyo home, gardening with his wife or catching up on reading. Shogo had four children: three daughters and a son. They were married and all of them worked in Tokyo, commuting each day from the suburbs. He had no grandchildren yet but was hopeful.

Shogo: Just what I needed! A good clean start to my round. Looks like I got 200 yards out of that drive. Should set me up for a par on this hole.

Toshio: Great shot, Shogo. Let's hope I can do the same.

Toshio was 47 years old and a senior vice-president at Mizuho Financial Group, one of Japan's largest banks, and the result of the merger of three large Japanese banks. Toshio had recently been appointed to a task force charged with focusing on Mizuho's increasing non-performing loan portfolio. It was widely expected by Toshio that Mizuho would register the largest bad debt write-down of any Japanese bank in the year 2002.

Masa: Great shot, Toshio. That ought to put you in a good position for your next shot. Am I up next?

Masa was a committed entrepreneur and had created significant wealth for his family during the 1980s, as a developer of golf courses and highrise apartment buildings. The 1990s, unfortunately, had been less kind and Masa had seen much of his wealth disappear as prices in the Tokyo real estate market continued to deteriorate. As an entrepreneur, opportunities to "make a quick buck," as Masa liked to say, had been infrequent. Masa had grown frustrated with the impact that government policies were having on his endeavors. He often wondered whether the good times would return. And he also just shanked his opening drive.

Haru: Not a great start, Masa! Looks like you may be able to tap that one out of the woods though. I don't think it went in too far. I'll help you hunt for your ball.

Haru had obtained employment with the Bank of Japan (BOJ) immediately following his education at the prestigious Nippon University in Tokyo. During his university days, he became fascinated with the impact of macroeconomic policy on the lives of the everyday Japanese. His strong beliefs in the power of monetary policy had been put to the test in the 1990s, however, as BOJ policies had been ineffective in the effort to rescue Japan from the perils of recurring recession.

The foursome played out the first hole with three pars and a bogey for Masa after he was unable to find his ball in the woods. As they marked the scores on the second tee, the conversation turned to the Japanese economy.

Masa: Has anyone else renewed his annual membership dues yet? I paid my fees before you guys arrived and was pleasantly surprised to find that the annual fee has come down in price compared to last year! I really needed that. Things haven't been too good in my business lately.

Shogo: I don't know what to make of these falling prices. I'd rather not spend anything and wait to see what happens. Too much uncertainty for a man my age. Remember gentlemen, I'm in my retirement years now. I know lots of my friends think the same thing. . . .

Haru: Of course, Shogo. Consumer prices have now fallen every month for more than two years. And falling prices have led to poor retail sales.

Masa: Why spend now when things will be cheaper later?

Haru: Not everyone benefits from this thinking, Masa. Falling prices lead to decreased profits to companies, as they are unable to recoup costs. Falling profitability leads to deterioration in company balance sheets and the inability to service debts. Companies then attempt to stem the weakened financials by laying off workers. This impairs public confidence and leads to decreased spending, which further impacts the prices firms are able to charge for their products and services. Even the healthiest firms are impacted in this continual vicious cycle.

Shogo: I remember a time when a Japanese worker never considered the possibility of being laid off. Things were good. The economy hummed along. When I was a child, Japan was an agricultural society. But what a transformation!

Haru: Did you know, Shogo, that in 1938, Japan's GNP[1] equaled five per cent that of the United States. By 1990, it reached 80 per cent. Moreover, its GDP[2] per capita exceeded that of the U.S. by the mid-1980s at market based exchange rates.

Masa: Ah, the early 1980s. Now *that* was a great time.

Haru: Perhaps for an entrepreneur, Masa. Starting in 1986, prices of assets, ranging from equity prices to golf club memberships, appreciated dramatically. For example, the Nikkei[3] rose from around 13,000 in December 1985 to a peak of almost 39,000 four years later. Similarly, the price index for commercial land in six metropolitan cities tripled from March 1986 to 1990. This period was characterized by increased monetary growth, a declining real interest rate, and optimistic expectations about future returns of stock and land assets.

Masa: I remember how easy it was to grow a business. My first love was development. Golf courses, apartment buildings, condominiums. . . . You know what they say, "Build it and they will come." Sure, land prices were going through the roof. But the banks were lending money to anyone, making it easy to secure loans for my development projects. I really thought I was set for life. Build a few condominiums, a few golf courses. . . . Sit back and let the money flow in. So I built, but no one bought! Sometimes I still wonder what happened. Demand just vanished. And so did my wealth. . . .

Haru: The world gazed at Japan in amazement and envy during those four years. But the market peaked on the last trading day in 1989. Stock prices declined 60 per cent between 1990 and August 1992, falling to 15,000 by summer 1992. Land prices also declined, by about half, from 1991 to 1995. Concern about asset inflation had led the BOJ to increase the discount rate by 350 bps[4] by August 1990, as the BOJ focused on general price inflation as the primary policy objective. As well, the Ministry of Finance had introduced measures to slow land-price appreciation, including controls over banks' real estate lending practices and increases in various real estate taxes. Asset price deflation led to a period of unprecedented low growth in real GDP in postwar Japan of less than one per cent from 1992 to 1995. The BOJ interest rate cuts of 550 bps to 0.5 per cent in 1995 failed to stimulate the economy. In addition to monetary stimulus, the government implemented a series of fiscal packages to stimulate the economy. Excess capacity, accumulated during the asset-inflation period, however, and slow sales led to reluctance by firms to borrow, despite low interest rates. As a result of strong yen appreciation, firms were encouraged to invest less domestically and to shift production facilities and investments abroad. Consumption fell as households saw the real value of their equity and real estate holdings decline.

Shogo: Haru, I always knew you were smart. Sure, you seem to know *what* happened. The thing is, I can't figure out why you guys at the BOJ can't do something to get this country back on track. I mean, if you can't do it, who will?

Haru: Thanks for the compliment, Shogo. And I wish I had the answers. I'm as frustrated as you are. Hey, I read the papers every day. All those analysts at Moody's and Goldman Sachs, over in New York.... They write their research reports like they know how to fix our problems. Telling us to spend more, to increase the money supply, to target inflation at 3.2 per cent.... Damn it! Who do they think they are? If it was that easy, don't you think we would have figured it out? You guys don't know the pressure I face every day. I've got my doorman telling me to lower interest rates! Hell, sometimes I even want to listen to him.

Shogo: The way I see it, if the banks hadn't been so forthcoming with loans for all those silly projects, things never would have gotten out of hand and we wouldn't have found ourselves in this state today.

Toshio: Remember, Shogo, banks are businesses too. There were a number of features of the Japanese financial system in the mid-1980s that created a fertile ground for asset inflation. Financial deregulation and liberalization increased the flexibility of banks to lend to more speculative debtors, such as speculative real estate ventures and developers. And as bank lending was based on collateral, as opposed to cash flow analysis, rising real estate prices led to loose credit standards. Also, price competition began to place downward pressure on the banks' risk adjusted interest rate margins. So banks sought out new markets, as corporations found the capital markets an increasingly attractive place to raise funds. Here, the cost of capital was virtually free. These new markets, of which the banks had little previous experience, carried higher risks than the banks were used to. Banks increased lending to consumers and small- and medium-sized enterprises.

Shogo: Sounds like a recipe for disaster.

Toshio: Indeed it was, Shogo. Plunging share prices were wiping out bank capital. And as Japan crept into recession in the early 1990s, the deteriorating economy led to the inability of firms, especially the small- and medium-sized enterprises that operated at the fringe of an expanding economy, to service their loans. So bank balance sheets deteriorated. Declines in real estate values were particularly troublesome for institutions with large loan exposure to that sector. The collateral on which the lending was based lost much of its value in the early 1990s. All that remained of the developers' visions were half-finished hotels that nobody wanted, defunct golf courses that added to an already saturated market and dilapidated rental properties.

Haru: But the banks were reluctant to allow their borrowers to default on their loans for various reasons. For one, it would reflect poorly on their reputation in the loan market because they had failed to monitor their loan portfolio adequately. So, the banks began to exercise forbearance, or tolerance, even though the long-term viability of the borrower was in question. The banks were simply restructuring nonviable loans by reducing interest rates, extending the loan maturity, capitalizing unpaid interest and opening new credit lines so that borrowers could repay overdue loans.

Masa: But how does this help a guy like me? Listen. If the banks are propping up all these poor companies in poor industries, what does that do for competition in the marketplace? They are like the walking dead. Non-performing companies that just won't die. God knows they aren't doing anything *good* for this country! They are perpetuating the deflationary cycle. And successful entrepreneurs can't even get new loans! It's so frustrating.

Haru: I think we're all feeling frustrated, Masa.

Masa: I almost forgot to tell you guys—I thought I finally had a buyer for that land where I had planned the golf course, years ago. But every time, it's the same story—the banks simply won't lend to developers anymore. They have made it impossible for anyone to build and here I am, stuck with all this half-developed land with little use! I can't turn it into another golf course. And nobody is buying housing land anymore with all these half-developed lots around. I really don't know what I am going to do. Times used to be so good.

Toshio: Masa, can you blame the banks for not wanting to lend? The last thing Japan needs is another development project. Nobody needed all those condos then and they certainly don't need them now. Let's face it. The banks are worried. They aren't making any money. And now the government knows it must do something about the deteriorating loan portfolios.

Shogo: The banks aren't the only ones who are worried. Look, if these banks are in such trouble, what does that say about my retirement funds? Right now I am making no interest on my savings, due to the interest rate cuts that have taken rates down to zero per cent! What happens to my money if these banks go under? Starting next year there won't be any depositor insurance on my savings. They want us to spend to get the economy moving again. Let me ask you—why would I spend when goods are getting cheaper and the future of this country is so uncertain? Hell, I'm too scared to spend. Listen, can we focus on our game here! All this talk about our deteriorating country is making me lose my concentration. Who's up next?

They were on the sixth hole and Haru had crept into the lead for the day and was two under par. Both Shogo and Toshio were at even par while Masa was clearly not having a good day and had fallen to four over par.

Haru: I won the last hole so I guess it's my honor to tee off first.

Masa: I agree, Shogo. Things have been going downhill for years now. Our government keeps trying to spur on the economy but nothing changes. And now that we have Koizumi as prime minister, everyone is hoping that he can change things. But let's face it. The LDP[5] has been in power every year since 1955, when the party was formed, except for a brief period in 1993 to 1994. So how many prime ministers have we seen? And all of them from the same party? Something tells me we'll need more than the "Koizumi Revolution" to really shake things up.

Haru: I couldn't agree more, Masa. With the government running deficits in an attempt to spur on an economy that is bordering on its third recession in the past decade, our public debt has risen to over 130 per cent of GDP. Moody's[6] has downgraded Japan's credit rating and threatened to give us the same rating as Poland and South Africa. Remember, my friends, that in a deflationary environment, the burden of debt increases.

Shogo: To think we were once the envy of the world! Haru, as an employee of the Bank of Japan, tell me again. Why are you not able to lift us out of this mess?

Haru: I am afraid that our power is limited, Shogo. As you have made plain, to the everyday Japanese citizen, deflation means cheaper jeans at Uniqlo.[7] And that doesn't sound so bad. Expectations of falling prices have served to bring spending to a standstill. And with interest rates at zero, the BOJ is purchasing government bonds to make more funds available to the banks. But as Masa has pointed out, banks are simply not willing to lend. Their primary concern is maintaining adequate capital requirements.

Shogo: Don't you have any other weapons in your arsenal? Look what Greenspan[8] has done in America!

Haru: Greenspan. . . . Look Shogo, you know how low interest rates are. That's why you haven't received any income on your bank account in years! We've lowered the discount rate in an attempt to increase the supply of funds. It's just not working. . . .

Masa: So what do they pay you the big bucks for anyways, Haru?

Haru: Look guys, how do you think *I* feel? I grew up *knowing* that monetary policy was the salve for any economic wound. And now here I am, 47 years old, questioning everything I have ever believed and learned.

The foursome finished their putts at the ninth hole and decided to grab a beer in the clubhouse. They tallied up the scores after the front nine to find Toshio ahead at two under par, Haru and Shogo at even par and Masa at two over par. As they sat down for refreshments, the conversation continued. . . .

Toshio: I think we all agree that *something* has to change. I mean, we have been in a downward spiral for more than a decade now. And just when you think things are looking up, it gets worse. Or at least that's what they tell us in the papers!

Haru: It's almost like there are two worlds here. On the one hand, prices are falling, goods are getting cheaper, and here we are, golfing every week. . . .

Masa: And on the other hand, unemployment is increasing, our government debt is piling up and the stock markets last saw these levels almost 20 years ago! My son was laid off last week from Hitachi.[9] He had only been with the company for a year, but still, it hurt.

Shogo: Your son is not alone, Masa. The last time unemployment reached five per cent of the labor force, it was World War II. Everyone is worried about his job nowadays.

Haru: I feel awful for your son, Masa. But these job cuts could turn out to be just what Japan needs to get back on track. At least these huge companies are starting to recognize that they are becoming increasingly uncompetitive. The American companies have better technology and the Asian companies can do things more cheaply. Where does that leave Japanese companies?

Toshio: Well, that is what Koizumi has promised us, right? Gain without pain is no gain at all. But is it just more political rhetoric? Do you think the Japanese people are ready to hunker down?

Shogo: We shouldn't have to hunker down! If we could only go back to how things were before, things would be better. . . .

Toshio: Hitachi banks with us. Of course, we have been concerned. Their profits have taken a real beating. And they aren't getting any help from the global economy. But I have noticed a change in the company, if only slight. I think they are starting to recognize that they aren't infallible anymore. And competition *can* affect their bottom line. They are worried. Which is why we are seeing the layoffs. By restructuring, these companies are able to pass on a lower cost structure to the end user. Which is why we are seeing lower prices. Our Japanese companies are becoming more competitive. They are unshackling some of the cultural chains that have led to deterioration in their competitiveness. Remember, these conglomerates were known for the concept of lifetime employment.

Shogo: Exactly! What could be better than knowing that once you had a job, you could never lose it! This is what made Japan such a great country.

Toshio: Well, I am just suggesting it's one of the reasons why Japanese companies found themselves uncompetitive on the world stage.

After they had finished their beers, the foursome trotted down to the 10th tee to start the back nine. The rain had stopped and the sun was starting to break through the clouds. Haru lagged the others, as he had to buy some golf balls at the clubhouse after losing his last golf ball in a water hazard on the ninth hole. He placed his billfold back in his pocket and commented. . . .

Haru: My concern is that the sliding yen gives our government a free pass to reform by increasing the attractiveness of our country's exports.

Toshio: Let's face it, Haru, depreciation in the yen can serve to increase Japanese profitability and give our economy a shot in the arm.

Haru: Remember, Toshio, economic stability is often viewed as synonymous with exchange rate stability. Some of the most volatile periods in recent Japanese economic history have come at times of extreme yen volatility.

Toshio: Of course. Fluctuations in exchange rates directly impact our trade relations with our major trading partners. And our economy is export driven. . . .

Shogo: Sure, Japan doesn't operate in a vacuum. But messing around with the yen . . . ?

Haru: Take, for example, the Plaza Accord of 1985. The finance ministers of the G5 countries met at the Plaza Hotel in New York in September and agreed to encourage depreciation in the American dollar, and so, appreciation of the yen against the dollar. They felt that shifts in the underlying countries' economic conditions had not been fully reflected in the currency exchange markets. Well, the policy worked and the dollar depreciated significantly against the yen. But this forced the BOJ to reverse policy. It began to sell yen and buy dollars. The result was an increase in the money supply and expansionary monetary policy by the BOJ.

Masa: Which takes us to the economic boom of the late 1980s, right?

Haru: Remember, the idea was to create a strong yen-trading region in Southeast Asia, a yen bloc, similar to the Euro region today.

Toshio: But with the collapse of asset prices in the early 1990s, and the onset of the banking problems, the yen lost some credibility.

Shogo: The world lacks confidence in our country, gentlemen. Whereas we were once envied, we are now seen as a liability. Can we not arise from such ignominy . . . ?

The foursome had just finished the 15th hole. The sun that had shone brightly during the past five holes now began to drift behind gray clouds that had gathered in the late morning sky. The gentle breeze had picked up and was making the golfers' shots difficult to predict.

Shogo: My friends, what is the answer to this country's problems? Will we ever retain our glory?

Toshio: I believe we are seeing inklings, Shogo. But much to your dismay, we cannot simply go back to the way things were before. In fact, many of the policy decisions that were made historically laid the foundation for today's state.

Shogo: Maybe they shouldn't do *anything*. All those policy decisions don't seem to be getting us anywhere. Maybe intervention is what has driven this country into the ground. Interest rates, inflation targeting, yen exchange rates . . . ? Damn it! Flip a coin, I say. Or just leave it to the markets to figure out. . . .

Masa: I believe Koizumi is on the right track with reform. We all know it has to happen. As an entrepreneur, nothing is more frustrating than not having a level playing field on which to compete. By removing the protection that these huge firms have enjoyed for years, I believe innovation will flourish. Of course, the banks need to lend and supply capital to budding firms.

Toshio: I agree, Masa. Once the banks are cleaned up and the full impact of nonperforming loans is taken into account, banks will get back to the business of lending. And while unemployment may rise further, jobs created by new firms will lay the foundation for future growth in Japan.

Shogo: Clean up the banks? You guys tell me how. . . .

Haru: I think we all agree that our country needs structural reform. Overcapacity, ridiculous debt levels, miniscule returns on equity. . . . Our government has to recognize the positive impact competition can have on productivity.

Toshio: You're right, Haru. But my main concern is with debt levels. Deflation makes these liabilities more burdensome over time. Unless we can figure out a way to reflate this economy, our government will continue to muddle along, trying this and that, but with no clear direction.

Shogo: So what *is* the right direction? OK, so we know prices have to start increasing. But what happens if they increase too much? I remember the 1970s. Inflation was 24 per cent in 1974!

Masa: Maybe we'll be able to export this deflation to China or South Korea, which will help us to solve our problems. . . . Oh, well. . . .

Masa tapped in the last putt on the 18th green. The friends shook hands and began to wander back to the clubhouse to tally the final scores. Each player hung his head as he walked, staring at the ground deep in thought. As always, the weekly golf game had given the friends an opportunity to discuss the most pressing issues of the Japanese economy. They would return next week for another round. And their conversation would continue. . . .

Notes

1. Gross national product
2. Gross domestic product
3. The Nikkei 225 stock index, a benchmark for the Japanese stock market.
4. Bps = basis points. 1 basis point is equivalent to 0.01 per cent.
5. Liberal Democratic Party
6. A credit rating agency.
7. A popular Japanese retail clothing chain.
8. Alan Greenspan, the chairman of the Federal Reserve, the U.S. central bank.
9. Hitachi was one of the largest Japanese conglomerates. It consisted of 1,069 subsidiary companies.

Appendix 1: Overview of Economic Policies in Japan (1977 to 2002)

Date	Content
1977	• Bank of Japan (BOJ) lowers the discount rate to 4.25%. 1978 BOJ lowers the discount rate to 3.5%
1980	• BOJ doubles the discount rate to 7.25%
1985	• Plaza Accord with the United States and the main European countries to support a stronger yen and weaker dollar
1986–1990	• BOJ increases the money supply at 10.5% a year from 1986–1990 • The Export-Import Bank of Japan makes loan guarantees for investment and trade in Asia (Japan becomes the world's largest creditor nation). The BOJ discount rate is 2.5% in 1988
1990–1992	• The increase of money supply decreases from 12.1% in 1990 to 4.1% in 1991, and 1.2% in 1992 • BOJ raises the discount rate to 6.5% in 1990
1990s	• Nine stimulus packages, totaling US$888 billion introduced, each resulting in: – Government spending and debt – Bailouts – Reflation • In 1995, the government extracts 30% of the GDP, compared to 18% in 1965 • Progressive cut of the discount rate: from 6% in 1991 to 0.5% in 1997 • 10.5% increase in the supply of money from mid-1997 to mid-1998

Date	Content
1998	• Tax cuts introduced • Creation of a bailout fund (to buy shares of stock in troubled banks and to nationalize and restructure, or liquidate failed banks). Banks, in exchange, must cut payrolls, slash overseas ventures and write off bad loans • Very loose monetary policy
1999	• Bailouts are extended to corporations. Example: Nissan Motors received a US$833 million loan from the government-run Japan Development Bank • Japan issues 90% of all industrial countries net new bond issues (US$352 billion), the total of its bond issue being US$517 billion • Ultra-loose monetary policy
2001	*Koizumi comes to power on an explicitly reformist platform. His strategy is fourfold:* • to cap annual Japan government bond issuance • to privatize several institutions, such as the Post Office (including the vast pool of Post Office savings) • to force private banks to write off all bad debt within three years • to accelerate structural economic reforms, even at the price of a period of slow economic growth
2002	• Bank of Japan decides to maintain its ultra-loose monetary policy • The government announces emergency countermeasures to deflation in order to prevent a financial crisis

APPENDIX 2: GROSS DOMESTIC PRODUCT

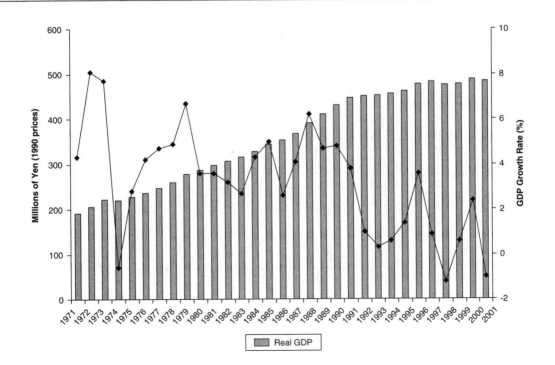

Real GDP

APPENDIX 3: BALANCE OF PAYMENTS (US$ BILLION)

	1986	1987	1988	1989	1990	1991	1992	1993	1994	1995	1996	1997	1998	1999	2000	2001
Current account	85.8	87.0	79.6	57.0	35.9	68.2	112.6	131.6	130.3	111.0	65.9	92.6	120.7	115.0	116.9	74.3
Export	205.0	224.0	259.0	269.0	280.0	308.0	332.0	352.0	386.0	428.0	400.0	401.0	374.0	399.0	460.0	386.0
Import	(112.0)	(128.0)	(164.0)	(192.0)	(216.0)	(121.0)	(207.0)	(213.0)	(241.0)	(297.0)	(317.0)	(301.0)	(252.0)	(272.0)	(343.0)	(319.0)
Trade balance	93.0	96.0	95.0	77.0	64.0	187.0	125.0	139.0	145.0	131.0	83.0	100.0	122.0	127.0	117.0	67.0
Net services	(14.2)	(22.1)	(31.9)	(38.6)	(44.7)	(41.8)	(44.0)	(43.1)	(48.1)	(57.4)	(62.2)	(52.8)	(49.4)	(54.9)	(47.6)	(53.6)
Net income	9.3	16.4	20.6	23.0	22.5	26.0	35.6	40.4	40.2	44.3	53.6	54.3	56.6	52.6	57.6	69.1
Net transfers	(2.3)	(3.3)	(4.1)	(4.4)	(5.9)	(103.0)	(4.0)	(4.7)	(6.8)	(6.9)	(8.5)	(8.9)	(8.8)	(10.1)	(9.8)	(8.5)
Financial account	(73.5)	(45.4)	(66.2)	(47.9)	(21.5)	(67.7)	(100.3)	(102.2)	(85.1)	(64.0)	(28.1)	(124.8)	(145.4)	(30.6)	(75.4)	(55.1)
Direct investment	(14.3)	(18.4)	(34.7)	(45.2)	(46.3)	(30.3)	(14.6)	(13.7)	(17.2)	(22.5)	(23.2)	(22.2)	(25.9)	(10.0)	(23.2)	(33.6)
Portfolio investment	8.7	26.0	(9.8)	(24.9)	(14.4)	(50.3)	(5.9)	(35.1)	(63.0)	(50.5)	(57.6)	29.6	(56.2)	(21.5)	(37.6)	(47.1)
Errors and omissions	2.5	(3.7)	3.1	(21.8)	(20.9)	(7.7)	(10.4)	(0.5)	(18.0)	13.8	0.6	41.3	5.2	17.7	16.8	7.4
Reserve assets	(14.8)	(37.9)	(16.5)	12.8	6.6	8.4	(0.6)	(27.5)	(25.3)	(58.6)	(35.1)	(6.2)	9.4	(77.2)	(48.8)	(40.8)

APPENDIX 4: MONEY SUPPLY GROWTH (%)

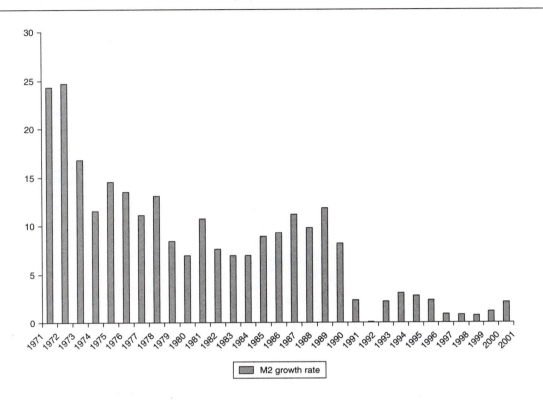

M2 growth rate

APPENDIX 5: OFFICIAL DISCOUNT RATE (%)

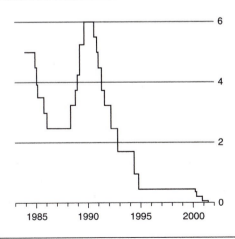

Source: The Economist, April 20, 2002.

APPENDIX 6: CONSUMER SPENDING AND INFLATION

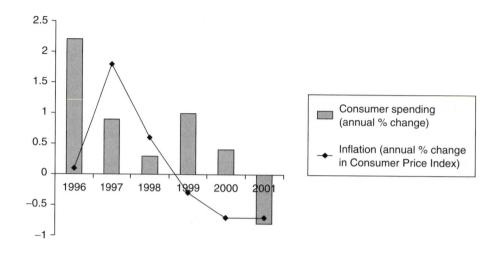

APPENDIX 7: LONG-TERM DEFLATION

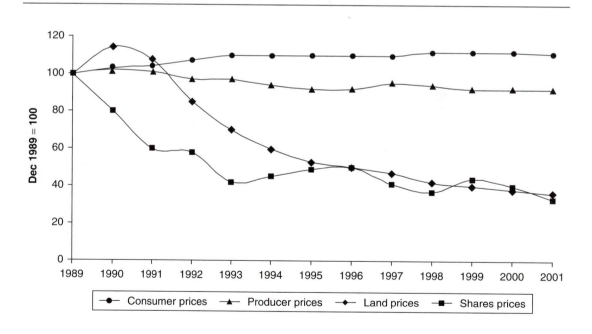

APPENDIX 8: SAVINGS AS PERCENTAGE OF PERSONAL INCOME

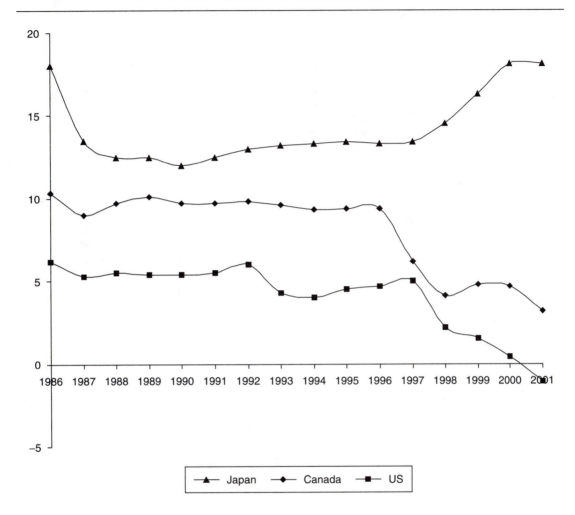

APPENDIX 9: WAGES AND SALARY—PER CENT
CHANGE OVER FOUR QUARTERS (ENTERPRISES MORE THAN FIVE EMPLOYEES)

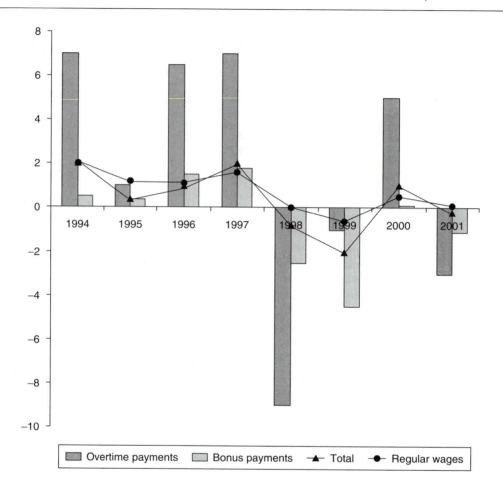

APPENDIX 10: UNEMPLOYMENT

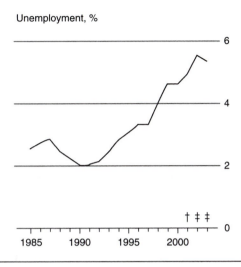

Source: The Economist, April 20, 2002.

Note: † Estimate ‡ Forecast

APPENDIX 11: STOCK MARKET EVOLUTION

From trough to trough

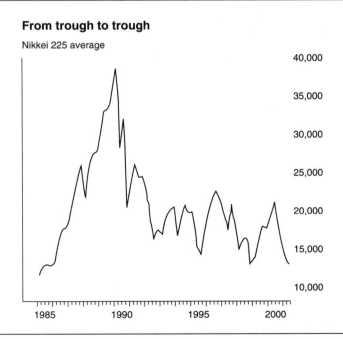

Source: The Economist, March 1, 2001.

APPENDIX 12: JAPAN AGAINST U.S. DOLLAR

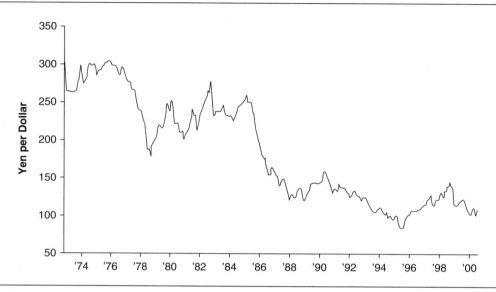

Source: David F. DeRosa, *In Defense of Free Capital Markets: The Case Against a New International Financial Architecture, 2001.* Reprinted by permission of Bloomberg Press. Source for charts is Bloomberg L.P.

APPENDIX 13: GOVERNMENT DEBT

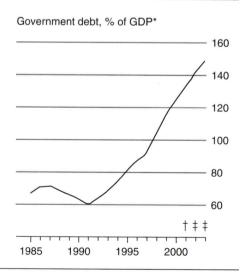

Government debt, % of GDP*

Source: The Economist, April 20, 2002.

Note: † Estimate ‡ Forecast

APPENDIX 14: BANKS: NON-PERFORMING LOANS (TRILLIONS OF YENS)

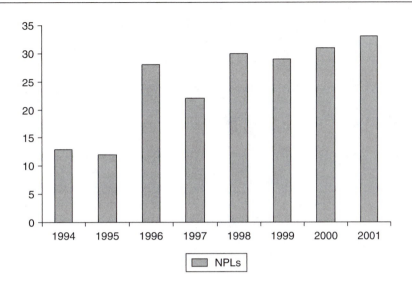

APPENDIX 15: BANKS: BAD DEBT PROVISION (2001 TO 2002) (TRILLIONS OF YENS)

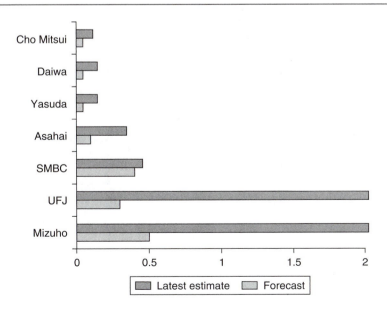

Appendix 16: The Formation of Japanese Megabanks

New Bank	Banks Included	Date of Merger/Set-Up of a Joint Holding Company
Mitsubishi Tokyo Financial Group	• Bank of Tokyo-Mitsubishi • Mitsubishi Trust and Banking • Nippon Trust Bank	April 2001
Mizuho Financial Group	• Dai-Ichi Kangyo Bank • Fuji Bank • Industrial Bank of Japan	September 2001
Sumitomo Mitsui Banking Corporation	• Sakura Bank • Sumitomo Bank	April 2001
United Financial of Japan Holdings	• Sanwa Bank • Tokai Bank • Toyo Trust and Banking	April 2001

APPENDIX 17: BANK LENDING PER CENT CHANGE YEAR ON YEAR

1999	Jan	Feb	Mar	Apr	May	Jun	Jul	Aug	Sep	Oct	Nov	Dec
Total	(4.0)	(4.2)	(3.9)	(5.3)	(5.4)	(5.7)	(6.1)	(6.5)	(5.6)	(5.7)	(5.7)	(5.9)
City banks	(6.0)	(6.5)	(6.2)	(7.8)	(7.8)	(8.3)	(8.6)	(8.7)	(7.0)	(7.0)	(6.0)	(5.2)
Long-term credit banks	(7.8)	(7.8)	(6.2)	(7.3)	(7.8)	(7.9)	(8.7)	(11.7)	(12.5)	(12.9)	(15.3)	(19.7)
Trust banks	(8.4)	(8.4)	(7.6)	(11.3)	(11.5)	(11.0)	(11.4)	(11.2)	(7.9)	(7.9)	(8.0)	(8.1)
Regional banks (Tier 1)	0.1	0.1	0.2	(0.2)	(0.4)	(0.7)	(1.1)	(1.4)	(2.0)	(2.0)	(2.5)	(2.6)
Regional banks (Tier 2)	2.0	2.0	1.7	0.1	0.1	(0.3)	(0.5)	(0.7)	(0.6)	(0.6)	(2.8)	(4.9)

2000	Jan	Feb	Mar	Apr	May	Jun	Jul	Aug	Sep	Oct	Nov	Dec
Total	(6.1)	(6.3)	(6.0)	(4.2)	(4.7)	(4.7)	(4.6)	(4.3)	(4.0)	(4.0)	(4.0)	(3.8)
City banks	(5.3)	(5.6)	(4.6)	(1.9)	(3.1)	(3.3)	(3.4)	(3.3)	(3.2)	(3.1)	(3.4)	(3.7)
Long-term credit banks	(19.8)	(20.3)	(22.7)	(21.2)	(21.7)	(21.9)	(22.1)	(19.6)	(18.1)	(18.2)	(16.1)	(11.6)
Trust banks	(8.1)	(8.3)	(8.4)	(4.1)	(4.8)	(5.0)	(5.3)	(5.2)	(5.2)	(5.5)	(5.9)	(6.1)
Regional banks (Tier 1)	(2.9)	(2.9)	(2.8)	(1.8)	(1.5)	(0.9)	(0.5)	(0.3)	(0.1)	(0.4)	(0.4)	(0.4)
Regional banks (Tier 2)	(5.4)	(5.6)	(5.3)	(7.3)	(7.3)	(7.3)	(7.0)	(7.0)	(6.9)	(6.8)	(6.4)	(6.0)

2001	Jan	Feb	Mar	Apr	May	Jun	Jul	Aug	Sep	Oct	Nov	Dec
Total	(3.7)	(3.6)	(3.6)	(3.4)	(3.8)	(3.8)	(4.0)	(4.2)	(4.2)	(4.1)	(4.3)	(4.3)
City banks	(3.5)	(3.2)	(3.2)	(3.1)	(3.7)	(3.6)	(3.9)	(4.2)	(4.4)	(4.7)	(4.8)	(4.8)
Long-term credit banks	(11.6)	(11.1)	(11.1)	(8.8)	(8.8)	(8.8)	(9.6)	(9.6)	(8.5)	(7.9)	(9.4)	(10.4)
Trust banks	(5.8)	(5.9)	(5.9)	(6.2)	(6.2)	(6.4)	(6.5)	(6.6)	(6.2)	(6.2)	(6.1)	(6.2)
Regional banks (Tier 1)	(0.6)	(0.5)	(0.5)	(1.2)	(1.3)	(0.8)	(1.0)	(1.1)	(1.2)	(0.8)	(0.8)	(0.7)
Regional banks (Tier 2)	(5.7)	(7.1)	(7.1)	(5.2)	(6.0)	(7.4)	(7.4)	(7.5)	(7.2)	(6.9)	(7.0)	(7.1)

2002	Jan	Feb	Mar	Apr	May	Jun	Jul	Aug	Sep	Oct	Nov	Dec
Total	(4.6)	(4.7)	(4.6)	(5.0)								
City banks	(5.3)	(5.8)	(5.8)	(7.1)								
Long-term credit banks	(11.0)	(11.5)	(11.9)									
Trust banks	(6.7)	(6.1)	(5.5)									
Regional banks (Tier 1)	(0.6)	(0.6)	(0.7)	(0.7)								
Regional banks (Tier 2)	(7.4)	(5.9)	(4.2)	(4.4)								

APPENDIX 18: NUMBER OF COMPANY BANKRUPTCIES (IN THOUSANDS OF DOLLARS)

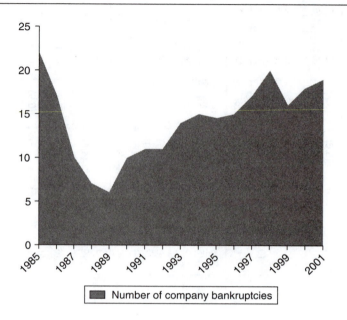

APPENDIX 19: EXPORTS AND IMPORTS

Main Destinations of Exports (% of total)				
	2001	*1999*	*1997*	*1995*
United States	30.1	30.7	27.8	27.3
Taiwan	6.0	6.9	6.5	6.5
Hong Kong	5.8	5.3	6.5	6.3
South Korea	6.3	5.5	6.2	7.0
China	7.7	5.6	5.2	5.0
Main Destinations of Imports (% of total)				
	2001	*1999*	*1997*	*1995*
United States	18.1	21.7	22.4	22.4
China	16.6	13.8	12.4	10.7
South Korea	4.9	5.2	4.3	5.1
Indonesia	4.3	4.1	4.3	4.3
Australia	4.1	4.1	4.3	4.3

PROCTER & GAMBLE IN EASTERN EUROPE (A)

*Prepared by Maurice Smith
under the supervision of Jeffrey Gandz and
David Conklin and with the assistance of Asad Wali*

Version: (A) 2002-10-21

In December 1990, John Pepper, President of The Procter and Gamble Company (P&G), was discussing the successes of the company's globalization efforts with Herbert Schmitz, a senior executive with P&G's European operations. Early in 1988, Wolfgang Berndt, then Group Vice President for Latin America and Canada, had correctly predicted that business opportunities would soon emerge within the countries of the Soviet block and had led an investigation which resulted in the establishment of an export business into East Germany and the U.S.S.R. With the fall of the Berlin Wall in the autumn of 1989, political change of unprecedented speed had been transforming the former Iron Curtain countries of East Germany, Albania, Bulgaria, Romania, Hungary, Poland, Yugoslavia, and Czechoslovakia. The U.S.S.R. itself was undergoing profound economic, political, and social changes under President Mikhail Gorbachev's "glasnost" and "perestroika" programs.

Pepper and other senior executives of the company had recently completed a tour of some of these former Eastern block countries and had concluded that they offered substantial opportunities for P&G. Pepper explained:

> We believe that now is the time to make a push into Eastern Europe, and I want you to lead the show. We want you to develop an overall strategy for Eastern Europe that will move us into a leading position. You should try to achieve a break-even in the third year of operations and be in a positive cumulative cash-flow position by 1998.

Schmitz believed that opportunities for Procter & Gamble to achieve a leadership position in the countries of the former Soviet block were clearly there. But how fast should P&G proceed to develop these different markets and in what priority should they be attacked? As well, what ought to be the priority product categories with which to enter and what kind of organization should be developed to carry out the eventual strategy? As Herbert Schmitz pondered these strategic questions, he knew he needed a clear set of criteria to guide P&G's approach to these markets.

PROCTER & GAMBLE: A WORLD-CLASS MARKETER

Procter & Gamble was founded in Cincinnati, Ohio, in 1837, as a partnership between James Gamble, an Irish soap maker, and William Procter, a British candle maker.[1] The Procter & Gamble Company which emerged from this agreement quickly gained a reputation for honesty that won the trust and respect of its suppliers and customers, and became known for its innovative products, which offered superior benefits at competitive prices. In every decade following its incorporation in 1905, sales more than doubled, propelled by new product introductions, continual product improvements, and diversification into related businesses.[2]

By the 1980s, P&G was, by most accounts, the world's pre-eminent marketer as well as a leading U.S. advertiser and a major supporter of basic research and development.[3] The company manufactured and marketed over 300 brands within 39 categories that were organized into four product groups: i) Laundry and Cleaning products; ii) Personal Care products; iii) Food and Beverage products; and iv) Pulp and Chemical products. (Exhibit 1 describes further each product group.) P&G brands were highly valued by consumers: they held first place in terms of market share within 22 product categories in 1990, up from 17 in 1985,[4] and in the other categories, P&G brands ranked a close second or third.[5] The overall success of P&G's products within the marketplace was revealed in an early 1980s' study which showed that 95 per cent of bathrooms, laundry rooms, and kitchens in American homes contained at least one P&G

A. PRODUCTS

Procter & Gamble manufactured and marketed over 300 brands within 39 product categories divided into the following four product groups:

1. Laundry and Cleaning products included detergents, hard surface cleaners and fabric conditioners. Well known product names included: Bounce, Bounty, Cascade, Charmin, Cheer, Comet, Downy, Mr. Clean, Spic and Span, and Tide.

2. Personal Care products included personal cleansing products, deodorants, hair care products, skin care products, oral care products, paper tissue products, disposable diapers, digestive health products, cough and cold remedies, and other pharmaceuticals. Well known product names in North America included: Always, Bain de Soleil, Chloraseptic, Clearasil, Cover Girl, Crest, Head & Shoulders, Ivory, Camay, Luvs, Metamucil, Oil of Olay, Pampers, Pepto-Bismol, Pert, Scope, Secret, Vicks, Vidal Sassoon, and Zest.

3. Food and Beverage products included shortening and oil, snacks, prepared baking mixes, peanut butter, coffee, soft drink and citrus products. Well known North American products included: Citrus Hill, Crisco, Duncan Hines, Folgers, Jif, Pringle's, and Sunny Delight.

4. Pulp and Chemical products: approximately one-third was sold to other P&G product groups.

B. FINANCIAL RESULTS AND ASSETS BY PRODUCT GROUPS (millions of U.S. dollars)

1. **Laundry and Cleaning products:**

	1990	1989	1988	1987	1986	1985	1984	1983
Net sales:	7,942	7,138	6,668	5,784	5,348	4,884	4,715	4,756
EBT:[1]	781	754	699	510	667	691	740	725
Assets:	3,296	2,964	2,852	2,690	2,369	2,038	1,845	1,670
Capital Expenditures:	383	273	285	245	233	216	228	199
Depreciation/Amortization:	170	151	149	120	99	79	75	76

2. **Personal Care products:**

	1990	1989	1988	1987	1986	1985	1984	1983
Net sales:	11,767	10,032	8,676	7,512	6,451	5,107	4,930	4,780
EBT:	1,314	1,031	888	498	625	332	689	694
Assets:	8,786	7,511	7,114	6,679	6,446	3,776	3,242	2,918

Exhibit 1   Segment Information, the Procter & Gamble Company and Subsidiaries   *(Continued)*

	1990	1989	1988	1987	1986	1985	1984	1983
Capital Expenditures:	586	510	483	473	539	594	321	204
Depreciation/Amortization:	464	428	375	332	243	165	142	133

3. Food and Beverage products:

	1990	1989	1988	1987	1986	1985	1984	1983
Net sales:	3,318	3,029	2,963	2,976	2,923	2,815	2,461	2,249
EBT:	304	(14)	32	(282)	(64)	(110)	(91)	117
Assets:	2,726	2,023	1,721	1,690	1,761	1,717	1,556	1,219
Capital Expenditures:	131	101	120	142	157	165	234	116
Depreciation/Amortization:	117	90	88	95	72	64	48	41

4. Pulp and Chemical products/Other products:

	1990	1989	1988	1987	1986	1985	1984	1983
Net sales:	1,666	1,778	1,532	1,186	1,161	1,237	1,309	1,079
EBT:	307	362	248	148	74	104	96	29
Assets:	1,450	1,431	1,410	1,273	1,279	1,244	1,169	1,151
Capital Expenditures:	197	138	117	52	108	110	113	81
Depreciation/Amortization:	101	90	79	77	74	69	64	59

C. FINANCIAL RESULTS AND ASSETS BY GEOGRAPHY (millions of U.S. dollars)

1. United States:

	1990	1989	1988	1987	1986	1985	1984	1983
Net sales:	14,962	13,312	12,423	11,805	11,210	10,243	9,554	9,074
Net earnings:	1,304	927	864	354	634	521	707	758
Assets:	9,742	8,669	8,346	8,483	8,394	6,829	6,072	5,344

2. International:

	1990	1989	1988	1987	1986	1985	1984	1983
Net sales:	9,618	8,529	7,294	5,524	4,490	3,625	3,737	3,685
Net earnings:	467	417	305	95	143	96	125	105
Assets:	6,516	5,260	4,751	3,849	3,461	1,946	1,740	1,614

3. Total:[2]

	1990	1989	1988	1987	1986	1985	1984	1983
Net sales:	24,081	21,398	19,336	17,000	15,439	13,552	12,946	12,452
Net earnings:	1,602	1,206	1,020	635	709	635	890	866
Assets:	18,487	16,351	14,820	9,683	13,055	9,683	8,898	8,135

Exhibit 1   Segment Information, the Procter & Gamble Company and Subsidiaries

Sources: 1990, 1987, 1985, 1983 Annual Reports, The Procter & Gamble Company; Form 10-K, The Procter & Gamble Company, Securities and Exchange Commission, Washington, DC, 1990.

Notes:

1. EBT: Earnings Before Taxes.
2. The differences between "Total" and the sum of "1. United States" and "2. International" are due to allocations to "Corporate."

brand. No other company had ever before achieved this level of mass-market penetration in the United States.[6]

During the 1980s, growth in revenues was fuelled to a large extent by the expansion of P&G's International Division. The number of countries in which the company had on-the-ground operations more than doubled from 22 to 46, and the number of countries served only by export sales grew to over 90.[7] By 1990, approximately 40 per cent of P&G's worldwide sales were generated outside the United States as opposed to 25 per cent 10 years earlier. Exhibit 1 presents P&G's financial results by business segment and geography.

Acquisitions also played an important role in fostering P&G's growth. The 1989 purchase of Noxell Corporation (brands: Cover Girl, Clarion, and Noxzema) in a 22-million common-share stock swap instantly moved the company to the number one ranking in the US$3-billion mass market cosmetics business.[8] Many other acquisitions during the 1980s resulted in "a medicine chest full of health-care products"[9] and elevated P&G to the number one producer of over-the-counter pharmaceuticals. Companies purchased included: Norwich-Eaton (brands: Pepto-Bismol, Chloraseptic), and Richardson-Vicks (brands: Clearasil, Nyquil, and other cold remedies), the latter being acquired after numerous rejected offers of a friendly takeover. Interestingly, P&G had been asked to intervene as a white knight when this formerly elusive acquisition target became the subject of a hostile takeover launched by Anglo-Dutch Unilever PLC, P&G's arch rival. P&G's total acquisitions from 1988 to 1990—excluding the Noxell deal—amounted to nearly $1.4 billion.

In fiscal 1990, P&G earnings and sales attained record highs, continuing the trend of the past two years. Sales, up by 13 percentage points, reached $24 billion and net earnings came in at $1.6 billion, a jump of 33 percentage points over the previous year. The company also recorded its largest year-to-year percentage increase in worldwide unit volume in 32 years, and it achieved a return on equity of over 20 per cent for the first time since 1950.[10] Wall Street's opinion of this new-found darling was summed up in a newspaper headline appearing in late 1990: "Lone critic runs counter to P&G's horde of admirers by questioning pace of growth."[11] Exhibit 2 presents P&G's financial statements, 1988–1990.

DOING WHAT'S RIGHT FOR THE LONG TERM

To many insiders, P&G's success was fundamentally due to its willingness to operate every aspect of its business in a manner consistent with the values of "integrity, doing what's right for the long term, respect for the individual, and being the best at what we do." These tenets were inculcated early on within the organization by the founders who had both been raised in religious families and were known to be frugal and scrupulously honest.[12] James Gamble was once quoted as saying: "If you cannot make pure goods and full weight, go to something else that is honest, even if it is breaking stone."[13]

Over the years, P&G's set of values molded its practices and management policies which, in turn, helped to maintain and perpetuate these through the successive generations of managers.[14] In 1930, the advice given by a Procter to the first president of P&G who was neither a Procter nor a Gamble was: "Always try to do about what's right. If you do that, nobody can really find fault."[15] Edward G. Harness, Chairman of P&G from 1974 to 1981, stated:

> Our predecessors were wise enough to know that profitability and growth go hand-in-hand with fair treatment of employees, of customers, of consumers, and of the communities in which we operate.

The company's "Statement of Purpose and Strategy" (Exhibit 3) which was formally adopted in 1986 enshrined these values and principles and, combined with 150 years of industry experience, dictated the company's success through its commitment to them.

CONSOLIDATED STATEMENT OF EARNINGS
THE PROCTER & GAMBLE COMPANY AND SUBSIDIARIES
(millions of U.S. dollars except per share amounts)

Years Ended June 30	1990	1989	1988
Income			
Net sales	$24,081	$21,398	$19,336
Interest and other income	561	291	155
	24,642	21,689	19,491
Costs and Expenses			
Cost of products sold	14,658	13,371	11,880
Marketing, administrative, and other expenses	7,121	5,988	5,660
Interest expense	442	392	321
	22,221	19,750	17,861
Earnings before income taxes	2,421	1,939	1,630
Income taxes	819	733	610
Net earnings	1,602	1,206	1,020
Net earnings per common share*	$4.49	$3.56	$2.98
Net earnings per common share assuming full dilution*	$4.27	$3.47	$2.96
Dividends per common share*	$1.75	$1.50	$1.38
Average shares outstanding (in millions)*	346.1	334.4	338.6

Adjusted for two-for-one stock split effective October 20, 1989

CONSOLIDATED STATEMENT OF RETAINED EARNINGS,
THE PROCTER & GAMBLE COMPANY AND SUBSIDIARIES
(millions of U.S. dollars)

Years Ended June 30	1990	1989	1988
Balance at beginning of year	$5,587	$5,688	$5,170
Net earnings	1,602	1,206	1,020
Dividends to shareholders			
– Common	(592)	(504)	(466)
– Preferred	(47)	(16)	(11)
Excess of cost over the stated value of common shares purchased for treasury	(177)	(787)	(25)
Noxell retained earnings at July 1, 1989	208	n/a	n/a
Balance at end of year	$6,581	$5,587	$5,688

n/a: not applicable

Exhibit 2 Procter & Gamble's Financial Statements, 1988–1990 *(Continued)*

CONSOLIDATED BALANCE SHEET,
THE PROCTER & GAMBLE COMPANY AND SUBSIDIARIES
(millions of U.S. dollars)

June 30	1990	1989	1988
Assets			
Current Assets			
Cash and cash equivalents	$1,407	$1,587	$1,065
Accounts receivable, less allowance for doubtful accounts of $29 in 1990, $24 in 1989, and $21 in 1988	2,647	2,090	1,759
Inventories	2,865	2,337	2,292
Prepaid expenses and other current assets	725	564	477
	7,644	6,578	5,593
Property, plant, and equipment	7,436	6,793	6,778
Goodwill and other intangible assets	2,594	2,305	1,944
Other assets	813	675	505
Total	$18,487	$16,351	$14,820
Liabilities and Shareholders' Equity			
Current Liabilities			
Accounts payable—trade	$2,035	$1,669	$1,494
Accounts payable—other	350	466	341
Accrued liabilities	1,690	1,365	1,116
Taxes payable	445	523	371
Debt due within one year	897	633	902
	5,417	4,656	4,224
Long-term debt	3,588	3,698	2,462
Other liabilities	706	447	475
Deferred income taxes	1,258	1,335	1,322
Shareholders' equity			
– Convertible class A preferred stock	1,000	1,000	—
– Common stock—shares outstanding(*): 1990 - 346,294,159; 1989 - 323,980,816; 1988 - 169,365,668	346	162	169
Additional paid-in capital	510	529	463
Currency translation adjustments	44	(63)	17
Reserve for employee stock ownership plan debt retirement	(963)	(1,000)	—
Retained earnings	6,581	5,587	5,688
	7,518	6,215	6,337
Total	$18,487	$16,351	$14,820

(*) Adjusted for two-for-one stock split effective October 20, 1989

Exhibit 2   Proctor & Gamble's Financial Statements, 1988–1990 *(Continued)*

CONSOLIDATED STATEMENT OF CASH FLOWS,
THE PROCTER AND GAMBLE COMPANY AND SUBSIDIARIES
(millions of U.S. dollars)

Years Ended June 30	*1990*	*1989*	*1988*
Operating Activities			
Net earnings	$1,602	$1,206	$1,020
Depreciation, depletion, and amortization	859	767	697
Deferred income taxes	(129)	(16)	176
Increase in accounts receivable	(387)	(331)	(154)
Increase in inventories	(312)	(103)	(97)
Increase in payables and accrued liabilities	236	779	318
Other	137	193	97
	2,006	2,495	2,057
Investing Activities			
Capital expenditures	(1,300)	(1,029)	(1,018)
Proceeds from asset sales and retirements	263	98	81
Acquisitions	(484)	(506)	(399)
	(1,521)	(1,437)	(1,336)
Financing Activities			
Dividends to shareholders	(639)	(520)	(477)
Change in short-term debt	205	(385)	369
Additions to long-term debt	734	532	47
Reductions of long-term debt	(786)	(369)	(60)
Issuance (redemption) of preferred stock issues	—	1,000	(250)
Purchase of treasury shares	(179)	(794)	(26)
	(665)	(536)	(397)
Increase (Decrease) in Cash and Cash Equivalents	$(180)	$522	$324

Exhibit 2   Proctor & Gamble's Financial Statements, 1988–1990

Sources: 1990, 1989 Annual Reports, The Procter & Gamble Company.

Valued Employees

Central to P&G's management practices was the high value it placed upon its individual workers. The company's long-time belief was that its interests were inseparable from those of its employees, its "greatest asset." According to John Smale, Chairman and CEO of P&G from 1981 to 1989:

The essential strength of this company is its people, and the values that the company has, and the values that the employees in the company embrace. Those values haven't changed.[16]

This principle dictated human resource management policies over the years and yielded distinctive P&G practices such as: i) recruiting of high-quality people and promotion from within

A STATEMENT OF PURPOSE AND STRATEGY

We will provide products of superior quality and value that best fill the need of customers.

We will achieve that purpose through an organization and a working environment which attracts the finest people; fully develops people and challenges our individual talents; encourages our free and spirited collaboration to drive the business ahead; and maintains the Company's historic principles of integrity, and doing the right thing.

We will build a profitable business in Canada. We will apply P&G worldwide learning and resources on the most profitable categories and on unique, important Canadian market opportunities. We will also contribute to the development of outstanding people and innovative business ideas for worldwide company use.

We will reach our business goals and achieve optimum cost efficiencies through continuing innovation, strategic planning and the continuous pursuit of excellence in everything we do.

We will continuously stay ahead of our competition while aggressively defending our established profitable businesses against major competitive challenges despite short-term profit consequences.

Through the successful pursuit of our commitment, we expect our brands to achieve leadership share and profit positions and that, as a result, our business, our people, our shareholders, and the communities in which we live and work, will prosper.

These are the principles that guide our actions as a Company and our attitudes about our employees:

- We will employ throughout the company, the best people we can find without regard to race or gender or any other differences unrelated to performance. We will promote on the same basis.
- We recognize the vital importance of continuing employment because of its ultimate tie with the strength and success of our business.
- We will build our organization from within. Those persons with ability and performance records will be given the opportunity to move ahead in the Company.
- We will pay our employees fairly, with careful attention to the compensation of each individual. Our benefit programs will be designed to provide our employees with adequate protection in time of need.
- We will encourage and reward individual innovation, personal initiative and leadership, and willingness to manage risk.
- We will encourage teamwork across disciplines, divisions and geography to get the most effective integration of the ideas and efforts of our people.
- We will maximize the development of individuals through training and coaching on what they are doing well and how they can do better. We will evaluate Procter & Gamble managers on their record in developing their subordinates.
- We will maintain and build our corporate tradition which is rooted in the principles of personal integrity; doing what's right for the long-term; respect for the individual; and being the best in what we do.

These are the things that will enable us to achieve the category leadership that is our goal in every business in which we compete:

- We will develop a superior understanding of consumers and their needs. This is the foundation and impetus for generating the superior benefits and value consumers seek in our brands.
- We will develop strategies and plans capable of giving us the competitive advantage needed to meet our business objectives.
- We will create and deliver product and packaging on all our brands which provide a compelling advantage versus competition in bringing consumers superior benefits that best satisfy their needs. To do this we will be the world leader in the relevant science and technology.
- We will seek significant and sustainable competitive advantages in quality, cost and service in our total supply and delivery systems so as to meet our business objectives.
- We will have superior, creative marketing on all our brands. We will have enduring superior copy, and promotion programs distinguished by their creativity, effectiveness, and efficiency.

Exhibit 3   P&G's Statement of Purpose and Strategy   *(Continued)*

> - We will develop close, mutually productive relationships with our trade customers and our suppliers. We will work with these partners in ways that are good for both of our businesses.
> - We will promote a sense of urgency, and a willingness to try new things. This will enable us to get better ideas working in the market ahead of competition.
> - We will follow the principles of Total Quality to achieve continual improvement in everything we do. Whatever level performance we have achieved today, we know that we can and must improve upon it tomorrow.

Exhibit 3   P&G's Statement of Purpose and Strategy

based solely on merit; ii) developing individuals through training and coaching; and, iii) encouraging and rewarding individual initiative, innovation, and leadership as well as teamwork across disciplines, divisions and geography, in order to achieve the most effective integration of ideas and people's efforts. By 1990, worldwide employment at P&G was approximately 89,000 people.[17]

The Famed Brand-Management System

Teamwork and strong internal competition characterized Procter & Gamble's well-honed organizational practices and management processes. The company's famed brand-management system, which had been devised in the early 1930s, was subsequently copied on a grand scale in corporate America and the world. Essentially, this system provided each brand with a management focus and drive at a low level of the organization and identified a group of people responsible for its performance in the marketplace. Each of these brand groups was led by a brand manager and included a number of assistants. Together, they planned volume objectives, and developed and implemented the total marketing effort, including marketing support, strategy and tactics. The group worked closely with line departments such as sales, product development, manufacturing, and finance.

In 1987, a new level of supervisors named category managers was created. Each of these new managers was given profit and loss responsibility for an entire product line such as

detergents.[18] Prior to this major change, brand managers working within the same product category had reported to different associate managers who were responsible for a variety of P&G brands from different categories. They, in turn, promoted the interests of their many brands to a divisional manager who co-ordinated the use of divisional resources, since he/she was ultimately responsible for the total marketing effort of the division's brands. Changes in the business environment in the early 1980s and sagging financial results revealed the weaknesses in this decades-old system as intense internal competition engendered conflicts, inefficiencies, and a lack of focus on how brands could work together and on what the competition was doing. In a bid to correct these problems, category managers were, therefore, introduced. They were given spending power and decision-making authority and made responsible for an entire product line's marketing plans, volume objectives, and advertising plans.[19] Divisional services such as advertising, distribution, and purchasing, along with sales, manufacturing, R&D, engineering, and, of course, brand groups, now all reported to category managers.[20]

P&G's well-established organizational processes and internal operations had been described by some as thorough, creative and aggressive; and by others as slow, risk averse and rigid.[21] Prior to the changes in 1987, every proposal generated at lower levels had been reviewed three stages up before receiving final approval. Although slow and, at times, bureaucratic, this system was designed to minimize the risks inherent in the very risky consumer-marketing business. As one observer noted: "The company

[P&G] is painstakingly thorough in the development of everything from a cookie to a disposable diaper."[22] By pushing authority down to category managers, P&G was also seeking to get much closer to the customer and speed up the decision-making process without sacrificing its thorough and cautious approach to doing business.[23]

Answering Consumer Needs

Procter & Gamble's corporate values were also at the basis of its marketing policy of providing products of "superior value that answer the needs of the consumer." Indeed, as John Pepper, President of P&G, explained, "You are not doing right . . . by the consumer" when a problem brand is not achieving the desired degree of share and profit.[24] According to him, the fundamentals of P&G's marketing strategy were: "Know the consumer better, what they want; deliver that better than the competition, in our products; communicate that . . . in our advertising . . . [and] have a competitive price."[25] Attaining brand leadership share and profit in each of its product categories was P&G's goal.

The key to P&G's marketing strategy was superior product performance developed through intensive research and development. In 1988, it spent twice as much on R&D as Unilever, and almost 10 times more than long-time competitor, Colgate-Palmolive.[26] The company invested nearly $700 million or three per cent of sales in 1990 on its efforts to create better products.[27] Each product it developed went through extensive testing that could last up to three years. Before receiving a major brand-launch decision, a new product needed to demonstrate a clear advantage within the marketplace.[28] Once it was launched, however, P&G was 100 per cent committed to pursuing the new product's long-term potential.[29] An integral part of P&G's research and development program was the continuous and detailed market research it conducted in order to spot trends early, and then lead them. P&G interviewed over 10,000 consumers each day: to gain a better understanding of their needs and wants; to track attitudes towards P&G and competitor brands; to evaluate packaging, advertising, promotion and pricing; and to assess new product ideas.[30]

Other key features of P&G's product strategy included the use of innovative breakthrough technologies to reinvent product categories, and the continuous adaptation of brands to evolving consumer needs. The company's R&D efforts yielded Tide, the detergent that replaced soap, and invented the first disposable diaper that worked.[31] Since the latter was introduced in the early 1960s, however, the company's R&D had scored few megahits, although Olestra, the first zero-calorie fat substitute awaiting Food & Drug Administration approval, was expected to be a major win.[32] Building brand and consumer loyalty often involved putting a familiar brand name on a new product; for example, "Crest Tartar Control" used the well-known name of a toothpaste introduced in 1987.[33] As a result of this practice, and in defiance of conventional product-life-cycle theory, P&G brands often remained healthy and profitable over long periods of time. For example, Ivory Soap was over 100 years old and Tide more than 35. This strategy often drove P&G's acquisitions as well. New brands were bought in part to take advantage of P&G's distribution strength, and in part to apply P&G's technological advantages to the acquired products in order to enhance their performance within the marketplace.[34]

Having developed superior product technology, P&G then applied massive advertising to communicate the benefits of its products. In 1989 alone, more than $2 billion was spent on this activity, over five times as much as Colgate-Palmolive's advertising budget. As one observer commented, "If a product can't be advertised, it doesn't belong in P&G's stable."[35]

Finally, maintaining competitive pricing required a continual striving for economies of scale within the company's worldwide operations. Interrelated raw materials and manufacturing facilities, centralized R&D and administrative staff functions, and sharing of advertisements between markets, sometimes with translated or dubbed soundtracks, were some of the ways P&G used to continually drive costs down.

THE CHANGING BUSINESS ENVIRONMENT

Beginning in the early 1970s and carrying on into the 1980s, the competitive dynamics within P&G's markets underwent significant change. This, combined with the increased globalization of the industry and P&G's slowness to respond to this new environment, caused margins, earnings and brand leadership to slowly erode. By the mid-1980s, however, a major restructuring program within the company was launched in order to reverse this slide in performance.

One of the most important impacts on P&G's traditional way of doing business was the consolidation of the retail trade. The arrival of large supermarkets and warehouse retailers such as Wal-Mart, together with new point-of-sale technology, shifted the balance of power within the marketplace away from manufacturers of consumer products. For example, over 80 per cent of Procter & Gamble's U.S. grocery business was now conducted with 100 retail chains versus 15 per cent 20 years ago. As a result of this change in market power, retailers benefitted by exploiting rivalries between manufacturers to extract concessions and dictate terms of trade.[36]

Competition within the consumer packaged goods industry was intensifying, and many of P&G's competitors, who had reacted more quickly to change, were benefitting from restructured operations better suited to the new competitive environment.[37] P&G faced much stronger competition in every product category, much of it emanating from foreign-based competitors such as France's L'Oreal, Germany's Henkel, Japan's Kao and the giant Unilever, who was waging a fierce battle in category after category. American producers, including longtime competitors Colgate-Palmolive and Kimberly-Clark, were also stealing significant share in the dentifrice and diapers markets. According to one analyst, more than 1,000 new products a month were popping up on supermarket shelves.[38] Exhibit 4 gives a brief summary of some of P&G's main competitors.

Within developed economies, the changing market dynamics were accompanied by maturing and splintering markets. Detergent unit sales, for example, increased by 17 percentage points over a 10-year period ending in 1989, while the number of brands competing within this category almost doubled to 46 from 27.[39] Brand extensions in various niches proliferated while total sales growth slowed to a crawl; in the United States, supermarket sales volume grew a meagre one percentage point from 1988 to 1989.[40] Further, breakthrough and clearly superior products that revolutionize categories were becoming harder to find. Changing demographics compounded this fragmentation, as the increasing number of women in the workforce, plus the proliferation of media outlets, made it more difficult and expensive to reach the growing number of segments.[41]

P&G was slow to respond to this changing and more competitive global industry. The feeling among many observers was that, through its decades of successes, the company had become "a corporate Kremlin: bureaucratic, risk averse, and arrogant."[42] As a result, financial performance suffered as flagship products such as Crest and Pampers lost substantial market share: in the United States, Crest fell to a 30.5 per cent share in 1985 from 40 per cent in 1977, with each point worth $10 million in revenues; and Pampers dived nearly 40 points to a 33 per cent share in roughly the same time period. Profitability at P&G's European operations was experiencing severe pressure, and its Japanese operation had accumulated losses in the order of $250 million since the subsidiary's opening in 1972. P&G's post-tax profits saw little growth during this time period and return on equity slid from over 10 per cent to below five per cent. In 1985, P&G posted its first annual decline in earnings since 1952.[43]

"Perestroika in Soapland"

Procter & Gamble's deteriorating results had not gone unnoticed and, by 1987, the company was well underway in implementing a wide range of internal changes, from marketing and sales to manufacturing and distribution. Modifications to its management structure and the creation of category managers were key

Unilever: Unilever had two parent companies, Unilever PLC and Unilever NV, located in the United Kingdom and the Netherlands, respectively. With 1989 sales of over US$33 billion, the company offered a wide range of products and services in over 75 countries, and was one of the two top packaged goods companies in the world. It had 10 per cent of the world personal-care products market, and one per cent of the world food market and was the largest detergent manufacturer in the world. Through careful planning it was seeking to expand to every corner of the globe, especially India, South America and Asia. Over 60 per cent of sales were realized in Europe. Brands included Imperial Margarine, Lipton Tea, Ragu Foods, Dove (handsoap) and Sunlight (dishwashing soap).

Colgate-Palmolive: A U.S.-based company, Colgate-Palmolive's primary growth strategy had been one of acquisition. With 1990 sales of US$5.04 billion, the company was the second largest soap, detergent and toothpaste company in the United States. It enjoyed, however, world leadership in oral care with over 40 per cent share of the world toothpaste market. With operations in over 100 countries, Colgate's overseas sales accounted for over 60 per cent of revenues, 30 per cent emanating from Europe. Its core businesses were personal-care and household products lines, with brands that included Colgate toothpaste, Irish Spring soap, and Palmolive dishwashing liquid.

Gillette: Gillette was a personal-care products company that through a series of acquisitions had expanded into the pen, stationery supplies and small appliance business. Sales in 1990 totalled US$3.82 billion, with shaving equipment accounting for 70 per cent of the business. Over 63 per cent of its sales were generated outside the United States. It manufactured in 27 countries, had operations in another 23 countries and sold in a further 200 countries.

Henkel Kgaa: A German-based manufacturer of chemical products, Henkel had 1990 sales of US$6.89 billion. Two-thirds of Henkel's sales were made outside of Germany, despite being Germany's largest chemical manufacturer. Product ranges were broken down as follows: detergents and household cleaners—31 per cent of sales, chemicals—31 per cent of sales, institutional hygiene and industrial cleaning products—15 per cent of sales, adhesives and related products—15 per cent of sales, cosmetics and toiletries—seven per cent of sales.

Johnson & Johnson: Johnson & Johnson provided a wide range of consumer and professional-care products. It was the world's largest manufacturer of health-care products. With sales of US$9.76 billion, brands included Tylenol (OTC pain reliever), Band-Aid, and Stayfree (a feminine hygiene product).

Kao Corporation: A highly diversified Japanese manufacturer of household and personal-care products, KAO had been referred to as the P&G of Japan. Kao revolutionized the business of selling personal-care products in Japan by using a technical approach to advertising, rather than one based on image. Brands included Attack detergent and the Sophia line of cosmetics. Sales in 1990 were US$4.32 billion.

Kimberly-Clark: Based in the United States, this company had products ranging from tobacco paper to transportation equipment. The company's operations were broken down into three principal divisions: consumer products (including disposable diapers), newsprint and paper products, and aircraft services and air transportation. Sales in 1990 were US$5.73 billion.

L'Oreal: This France-based company had sales of US$4.23 billion in 1990. L'Oreal was the largest manufacturer in the world of high-quality cosmetics and boasted the highest research and development budget in the industry. Brands included Lancome, Ambre and Solaire, and Cacharel.

Exhibit 4   Main P&G Competitors

Source: L. Mirabile (ed.), *International Directory of Company Histories*, volumes II and III, St. James Press, Chicago, 1991.

applications. P&G became more customer-focused as well; to work with its large retail customers, it created customer teams that were led by product supply managers and staffed by representatives from manufacturing, engineering, distribution, purchasing, and finance. Other changes included restaffing top-management with managers experienced in international markets, increasing capital spending for modernization, and overhauling advertising strategy.

According to one consultant close to P&G: "Smale revitalized the company without losing the basic values of P&G or getting into the short-term thinking that dominates American industry."[44] That year, a one-time write-off of $500 million for restructuring was recorded.

GLOBALIZATION

Market changes driven by globalization were also pressuring P&G to turn outward for growth. Said Jurgen Hintz, Executive Vice President at P&G:

> In the past a company could succeed in its home market and not worry about the rest of the world, . . . but those days are gone. Yet in the end, we are only as good as our ability to compete in every local market.[45]

Globalization had become the key to P&G's future growth and competitiveness, and its International Division was being tuned to meet the needs of diverse and growing foreign markets.

A Tough International Marketplace

International markets were tough ones in which to compete. The number of competitors in places such as Europe was higher than in the United States, P&G's home market. Powerful non-U.S. competitors such as Unilever and Henkel which were entrenched in many countries tended to accept lower shareholder returns than P&G found acceptable. Profit margins were generally lower as excess capacity held prices down in most developed markets. According to Edwin Artzt, Chairman and CEO of P&G as well as the former President of the International Division:

> International markets have tended to be rapid growth markets; therefore, you get an enormous amount of price competition and people willing to sacrifice in order to build share.[46]

Established in the early 1950s, P&G's International Division was developed by replicating the company's U.S. business strategy within each international market entered. The division's first vice president stated at the time:

> We must tailor products to meet consumer demands in each nation. We cannot simply sell products with a U.S.A. formula. They won't work. We believe [however] that exactly the same policies and procedures which have given our company success in the United States will be equally successful overseas.[47]

In 1953, an export operation was set up in Geneva to market P&G's core products—soap, toothpaste, diapers, and shampoos—to the rest of the world. The strategy was to build local demand first and then establish country-specific operations that were closer to the business and its customers. Over time, this method led to the development of a network of highly successful and profitable foreign ventures, each operating independently.

P&G's international strategy worked well until the mid-1970s, when increased competition caused growth to slow, prices to weaken, and profits to slide. In many instances, P&G was being beaten to new markets, sometimes with newer technology, or its own product innovations were being copied faster than it could introduce them within international markets. Partly to blame was the structure of P&G's international operations, which hampered effectiveness and slowed the global introduction of new products. The company was also not comfortable in undeveloped markets or in those where the local culture differed from American culture. Indeed, P&G once believed that its marketing prowess could ignore such differences when developing marketing strategy.[48]

Through its share of international marketing stumbles, missteps, and struggles within this environment, P&G eventually succeeded in building formidable worldwide operations by 1990. The International Division's share of company profits rose to 30 per cent, a substantial increase from its 20 per cent share four years earlier. Much of P&G's foreign expansion was achieved through acquisitions and joint ventures. During the 1980s, it spent $3 billion in 16 countries around the world, making more than twice the number of acquisitions that it had made in the 1960s and 1970s combined.[49] Acquired companies gave P&G strong international distribution channels, which were further leveraged with P&G brands already sold in the United States. The Richardson-Vicks acquisition, for one, gave the company strong organizations in Australia, India, Indonesia, Thailand, and the countries of Latin America. According to one estimate, only one-third of P&G's products was distributed overseas in 1989,[50] and two-thirds of the company's international sales were coming from 24 brands including Crest, Head & Shoulders, and Pampers.[51] Tapping this growth potential led to strong earnings growth: international profits were up by 12 percentage points in 1990 after two consecutive years of increases of more than 37 percentage points.

Asia

After operating in Japan since 1973, P&G finally attained profitability in 1987 and was challenging national competitors Kao, Lion, and Unicharm who had almost driven P&G out of the market a few years earlier. P&G had initially enjoyed huge successes with its detergent and diaper brands, the latter gaining up to 90 per cent market share at one point. But by mistakenly assuming that what worked at home would also work halfway around the world, P&G made a number of tactical errors. Improperly managing the multi-tiered distribution system, of critical importance to consumer-product companies operating in Japan, proved to be a major one. The company was also overtaken by quickly improved local brands better suited to the market, while a number of advertisement faux-pas caused further deterioration in the company's market position and public image. Finally, the few brands marketed in Japan made it difficult to cover the high costs of maintaining the operation.

By 1990, however, P&G had gained the number one market position with seven of the over 20 brands it was offering in Japan which, with $1 billion in sales, was poised to replace Germany as P&G's second largest market outside the United States.[52] Elsewhere in Asia, P&G was playing catch-up with Unilever in Indonesia and India, two rapidly developing markets in which P&G and its competitors, including Kao, Johnson & Johnson, Lion Corp., and Colgate-Palmolive, were waging fierce brand warfare to establish dominance. P&G had also recently entered Korea and China through joint ventures, the latter in 1988 with the shampoo "Head & Shoulders" in what was seen as an aggressive early move into this market.

Europe

First entered in the 1930s via the United Kingdom (U.K.), Europe was traditionally P&G's largest international business. It accounted for 60 per cent of non-U.S. sales in 1990 or over $5.7 billion.[53] The United Kingdom and Germany were the most important European markets, the latter generating more than $1.2 billion in sales.[54] Fierce competition in Europe led to thin profit margins: less than four per cent versus almost nine per cent in the U.S. business and over six per cent in the other combined P&G businesses in Canada, Asia and Latin America.

P&G made important changes in its European organizational structure to counter heightening economic and competitive pressures. During the 1960s, subsidiaries were opened in almost every West European country, each being a miniature P&G with complete development and marketing capabilities. To boost profitability, this structure was replaced by a "Euro-market" organization in the late 1970s. By treating Europe as one market conceptually and organizationally, P&G developed a common strategy among country organizations for product research, development, manufacturing and advertisement, while allowing for local execution at the marketing and day-to-day management levels. A matrix organization was implemented that required each country's brand manager to report to both his/her country manager and to a Euro-brand manager (usually a brand manager from a selected lead country). The benefits derived from this restructuring included a reduction in operating costs, higher consistency in product quality, and greater speed in Europe-wide expansion of new or improved products. P&G's other international operations were eventually re-organized along these lines.

Latin America

The Latin America division, which began in Mexico in the 1950s, had subsidiaries in nine countries and exported to 10 others. It was a star performer within P&G, with sales reaching $1 billion or 15 per cent of international revenues in 1990, and a profit margin exceeding the average for the entire international division.[55] In many regions of Latin America economic and political turmoil that included hyper-inflation, governments as competitors, kidnappings of business people, leftist insurgencies, and strict price controls presented obstacles. However, P&G remained committed to these markets. When violence escalated in Chile in 1963, the company sold its operations to Unilever, the only time it ever voluntarily pulled out of a country, and later came to regret this move as it tried to catch up to Unilever after re-entry in 1983. Latin America—with its richness in raw materials, large numbers of young consumers eager for North American products, and greater political and economic stability projected for the future—was now central to P&G's global strategy.

Global Expansion to the Year 2000

For the decade leading to the year 2000, P&G's main marketing focus was further global expansion. It projected that foreign operations would contribute 50 per cent of revenues by 1995 through application of the following strategy:

> We will plan the growth of our investments on a worldwide basis to achieve maximum competitive advantage. We will take advantage of our strongest technologies and ideas by reapplying and tailoring them to meet consumer needs everywhere. We will market world brands that share global technology and common positioning, but with appropriate regional testing of product

aesthetics and form, packaging materials, and market execution to best satisfy local customer demands for quality and value.[56]

Examples of this strategy included the reapplication of Crest's tartar-control ingredients to non-Crest toothpastes sold in foreign markets, and changes to core products to suit local tastes such as the smell of Camay, the taste of Crest or the formula of Head & Shoulders. Added John Pepper:

> We are finding that our superior technologies are gaining great consumer acceptance. That is true whether those consumers are in undeveloped economies, or in the most advanced.[57]

THE FALL OF COMMUNISM IN EUROPE[58]

The fall of the Berlin Wall on November 9, 1989, became the dramatic symbol and starting point of a new era in Europe. Budding democracies and extraordinary new market opportunities for Western goods were rapidly opening up in countries that had been under the tight control of the Union of Soviet Socialist Republics (U.S.S.R. or Soviet Union) since the Second World War. As one journalist reported:

> With its thirst to rejoin the western world, its intellectual people and willing work force, its opportunities for investment and clear slate for nation building, Central Europe [Poland, Czechoslovakia, Hungary, Yugoslavia, Albania, Bulgaria, and Romania][59] has more potential for future prosperity than any region on earth.[60]

At the base of this new era in Central Europe were the deep and broad economic and political reforms underway in the U.S.S.R. since the mid-1980s.

Gorbachev, Glasnost and Perestroika

In 1985, when Mikhail Gorbachev became the Soviet Communist Party's General Secretary—the de facto head of state of the U.S.S.R.—Soviet society was at a bursting point. Decades of economic mismanagement, failed attempts at reforming the economic system, and tight controls over intellectual, cultural and personal freedoms had generated widespread disenchantment and cynicism with the country's leadership and political system. Deep dissatisfaction, which had been secretly germinating since the 1960s, prevailed at every level of Soviet society: consumers were weary of lengthening queues for goods typically of poor quality; ordinary people were outraged by the arrogant, pervasive, Mafia-like corruption of ministries, high party officials, underground millionaires, and black marketers; farmers were demoralized by rural decay, and scientists and engineers by industrial stagnation and growing technological inferiority with the West; army officials were alarmed by the inability of the U.S.S.R. to compete on world markets and by the prospects of becoming a fourth-rate power. The decaying Soviet-style system of socialism, the increasingly pompous and arrogant propaganda, and the widening gap between communist ideals, people's expectations and reality solidified the belief that only wide-ranging reforms could reset the union on a course to prosperity.

To revive the U.S.S.R.'s stagnating economy, Gorbachev initially focused on: reducing rigidity inherent to the central planning economic system; increasing discipline and efficiency within factories; and ending corruption among state officials. To set his plans in motion, he had first to give people a voice, free up ideas and information, and remove the dead hand of dogma which had stifled initiative and suppressed creativity for decades. "Glasnost"—or openness— therefore, called for the reduction of state control over cultural, intellectual and religious activities, and encouraged more realistic scrutiny of state institutions by the people and the media.

By late 1986, plans for the restructuring—or "perestroika"—of the Soviet economy, the most dramatic in the history of the U.S.S.R. since Stalin, were initiated. Implicit to them was the realization by Gorbachev and his supporters that the market mechanism was useful and desirable in the resource allocation process. The main thrust of the reforms was, therefore, the freedom given to state enterprises to manage their operations and finances, decoupling them to a certain extent from an overbearing Communist Party bureaucracy. Managers, however, were still subject to state price controls, minimum deliveries to other state firms, restrictive labour laws, etc. In May 1988, private enterprise in the form of cooperatives was sanctioned in most areas of economic activity outside wholesale trade, but this reform excluded the possibility of owning property. By early 1990, over 244,000 co-operatives were contributing approximately one per cent to national income. Stronger trade and commercial links with the West were also sought. In 1988, all Soviet enterprises were granted the right to deal independently with foreign trade. As well, majority foreign ownership of joint ventures was legalized and allowed to operate outside the control of central planners.

Gorbachev also undertook major reforms to the U.S.S.R.'s power structure. He ended the Communist Party's constitutional monopoly over political power; although it still retained its leading role in Soviet society, it would now have to struggle for its privileged position. Within the party, two important groups were emerging: the radicals who were wanting speedy reforms, and the conservatives who were fighting for the status quo. In 1989, multi-candidate, but not multiparty, elections for the country's new parliament, the Congress of National Deputies, occurred. Many high-ranking party officials were defeated by radicals who included the long-time and well-known dissident, Andrei Sakharov, and the outspoken reformer, Boris Yeltsin. In 1990, Gorbachev created a new U.S./French-style presidency for himself with sweeping executive powers moderated by a new Presidential Council, which replaced the Politburo as policy maker. Within four years, adult universal suffrage would choose the U.S.S.R.'s next head of state. Through all of these changes, Gorbachev replaced many Old Guard politicians associated with previous General Secretaries.

In Soviet foreign policy, a whole new attitude was propelling Central European countries to assert their independence from Moscow's long-time hegemony. In 1988, Gorbachev sanctioned the unification of East and West Germany and encouraged national governments of Central Europe to proceed with their own brands of political and economic "glasnost" and "perestroika." At the same time, Gorbachev was negotiating arms limitation treaties with the United States and the removal of medium-range nuclear missiles from Europe. By the end of 1989, Soviet troop and military withdrawal from Central Europe had passed the critical level beyond which surprise attack on Western Europe was feasible. Gorbachev's objective was to convert a major portion of the U.S.S.R.'s military production complex, which consumed annually 12 to 14 per cent of the country's national income, to the production of civilian goods. In July 1990, the world was offered proof that the Brezhnev doctrine— that no socialist state should be allowed to destroy socialism within its own country—had indeed been laid to rest. At the 20th Congress of the Soviet Communist Party, Gorbachev defended the lack of intervention in Central Europe as Soviet-style socialism was being massively rejected in favour of capitalistic ideals: "There is no way of bringing yesterday back. No dictatorship, if someone has this crazy idea in his head, can resolve anything."

Mounting Chaos in the U.S.S.R.

The plan to achieve a market socialist system in the U.S.S.R. by the early to mid-1990s had produced more problems than solutions. A combination of breakdown in the traditional, centralized distribution system, production bottlenecks due to the faltering rigid and taut planning system, growing consumption, and an increasing tendency to hoard had emptied most of the shops in Moscow and other large cities by late 1990. Leningrad was facing food shortages reminiscent of the wartime siege by the Nazis. Black market prices, rising quickly, were several times higher than official state prices. The government's budget deficit, now at 17 per cent of state expenditures or 10 per cent of national income, was rising rapidly, and the country's external economic situation was deteriorating quickly. Its negative trade balance with the West grew to over $6 billion and its hard currency net debt in 1989 surpassed $30 billion, over twice its value in 1985 and more than the country's total hard currency earnings in 1989. Several Soviet trading partners were delaying hard currency payments for exports already delivered. In 1990, economic activity within the Soviet Union declined by four percentage points.

Gorbachev's reforms had done little to reverse the economic stagnation in his country. Reformers blamed bureaucrats for sabotage, while conservatives blamed the break-down in central planning, "profiteering," and a faltering distribution system. To many, it had become clear that Gorbachev's original concept of a synthesis of central planning and the invisible hand of the market was simply a chimera. Although the adoption of various new reforms at different levels of government spelled the official acceptance that the U.S.S.R. should make the transition to a full fledged market economy, albeit a "regulated" one, little progress had yet been made on the manner and conditions for this transition.

Amid the political and economic confusion that raged in the U.S.S.R., many of its 15 republics intensified demands for autonomy. Azerbaijan and Armenia were increasingly out of control and independence movements in the Baltics were gaining momentum and strength as Lithuania declared its independence in March 1990, and Estonia and Latvia threatened to follow suit. Ethnic and nationalist unrest in the southern republics was creating further instability. In response to these forces, Gorbachev proposed in June 1990, a new union treaty that would allow greater autonomy within a loose federal or confederal structure. On the same day of this announcement, the Russian Republic's parliament, led by its newly elected President Boris Yeltsin, voted overwhelmingly to assert the sovereignty of its laws over those of the U.S.S.R. The spectre of military rule loomed larger in the U.S.S.R.

By late 1990, Mikhail Gorbachev had lost his personal popularity, assaulted by political developments quickly running beyond his control. The Union of Soviet Socialist Republics was close to the precipice, its imminent fall, leading to either its complete breakdown or reconstitution into a voluntary federal state.

REFORMS IN CENTRAL EUROPE[61]

By mid-1990, every country in Central Europe was embarking upon an uncertain journey of deep structural reforms to its political and economic systems. According to one reporter:

> The desired destination in each case is some nebulous mix of democratic institutions, the alluring but confusing benefits of capitalism [excluding its negative costs such as unemployment and inflation], and the social safety net to which they've all become accustomed during more than 40 years of Marxist stagnation.[62]

Most were in the process of establishing Christian democratic forms of government; each was starting from a different historical background, level of development, type of reforms, and speed of implementation. But due to their common heritage, all the countries of Central Europe were suffering, to varying degrees, from the following conditions:

- Uncompetitive and inefficient economies (compared to those of the developed OECD countries) due to the economic heritage of Soviet-style communism, which created the following conditions: general economic disequilibrium due to the absence of free functioning markets (budgetary imbalances in industry and government, chronic mismatch between supply and demand in most markets, external imbalance, etc.); actual or suppressed inflationary pressure due to price controls and a high overhang of money; continued reliance on central directives, and the lack of private enterprise; and a structural heritage of inefficient industrial plants, excessive consumption of energy and materials, technological obsolescence, and

the lack of competitiveness of exports. (The Appendix further describes the competitiveness of these economies and the nature of their foreign trade.)

- Economies teetering on the brink of collapse: the restructuring process of their command-based economies, cutbacks in government subsidies to industry and consumers, falling demand throughout Eastern and Central Europe, and rising prices to market levels were conspiring with the breakdown of trade among themselves to create serious recession, even depression, exacerbated by hyper-inflation.
- Disputes among themselves due to rising unfulfilled trade agreements where a rising proportion of payments was being demanded in scarce hard currency.
- Serious tensions with the U.S.S.R. who was resisting their push to scrap the Warsaw Pact—the mutual defence alliance created in the 1950s—while there remained a very high dependency on Soviet raw materials.

The following is a summary of the political and economic situations in the countries of Central Europe as of late 1990 (Exhibit 5 presents various market and economic data series):

Albania

A strategy of cautious reform had crumbled in December: the year was ending amid violent demonstrations, top leadership purges, the legalization of the opposition Democratic Party and the promise of free elections on March 31, 1991. Planned economic reforms included decentralizing economic decision-making, deregulating prices, and lifting the constitutional ban on foreign credits. It was hoped that this last measure would open the way to foreign investment. Albania was desperately seeking capital goods but was being held back by its limited ability to earn hard currency. Although more individual freedoms had been granted, there was a danger of protracted and bloody conflict as the conservatives and the secret police fought a rearguard battle. Clashes with the neighbouring Yugoslav province of Kosova with its 1.8 million ethnic Albanians was possible.

(Text continues on page 211)

Table 1: Market Indicators

1990	Albania	Bulgaria	Czech.	Hungary	Poland	Romania	U.S.S.R.	Yugoslavia	Greece	FRG[a]
Population (millions):[1]	3.27	8.95	15.6	10.2	38.0	23.3	290.8	23.8	10.1	61.7
Average annual % change 1986–1990	2.1	0.2	0.1	−0.08	0.3	0.5	0.8	0.6	0.2	0.3
Two largest cities (population, millions)	Tirane (0.2) Durres (0.1)	Sofia (1.1) Plovdiv (0.4)	Prague (1.2) Bratislava (0.4)	Budapest (2.0) Debreen (0.2)	Warsaw (1.7) Lodz (0.9)	Bucharest (2.0) Brasov (0.3)	Moscow (9.0) Leningrad (5.0)	Belgrade (1.5) Zagreb (0.8)	Athens (3.0) Salonkia (0.9)	W. Berlin (2.0) Hamburg (1.6)
Number of cities population > 500,000	0	1	1	1	5	1	24[2]	NA	2	11
NMP in billions of local currency[1,3]	NA Lek	26.4 Lek	605.0 Crowns	2,200.0[4] Forints	587,514 Zloties	640.0[5] Lei	665.0 Roubles	442.5[6] Dinars	10,670[4] Drachmas	2,410.0[4] DM
% Volume growth (1991 forecast)	1.0 (1.0)	−12.0 (−5.0)	−3.5 (−7.0)	−2.5 (−3.0)	−15.0 (5.3)	−15.0 (−10.0)	−3.0 (4.0)	−6.0 (−1.0)	1.3 (2.0)	4.0 (3.5)
Average annual % change 1986–1990	3.0	0.9	1.2	0.5	−0.7	−7.2[7]	−0.9	−0.9	1.6	3.1
Per capita income (US$) PPP[8]	NA	$7,510	$10,140	$8,660	$7,270	$4,490	$8,850	NA	NA	NA

Exhibit 5   Central and Eastern Europe

(Continued)

1990	Albania	Bulgaria	Czech.	Hungary	Poland	Romania	U.S.S.R.	Yugoslavia	Greece	FRG[a]
Avg. commercial exchange rate per US$	6.00	2.313	18.8	62.82	9,500	23.9	0.58	11.58	158.4	1.69
(1989 avg. value)	(6.48)	(0.828)	(15.07)	(59.07)	(1,439)	(14.9)	(0.64)	(2.88)	(162.4)	(1.88)
Per capita income (US$)[9]	$688	$2,505	$3,050	$3,132	$1,631	$1,648	$5,306	$3,849	$6,587	$24,477

a. Federal Republic of Germany (West Germany).

1. Estimates.
2. Number of cities with a population over one million.
3. Net Material Product (NMP): the value added output of goods and services relating to physical production, transportation, and distribution. Banking, health, education, public administration, and defence are all excluded. NMP is therefore smaller than GNP or GDP. But, in some cases, it tends to be more variable. In Hungary, for example, NMP growth for 1990 was estimated at −4.5 per cent and GNP at −2.5 per cent.
4. For Hungary, Greece and West Germany, GNP figures are reported.
5. 1989 value.
6. Gross Social Product (GSP) figures, marginally less than GNP or GDP, are used.
7. Average annual over 1988 to 1990 only. Government statistics for prior years are of doubtful accuracy.
8. Source (excluding Albania, Yugoslavia, Greece and FRG): USA Central Intelligence Agency, *Handbook of Economic Statistics*, 1989, at purchasing power parities (PPP).
9. Per capita GDP at current 1990 prices (US$); source, *Statistical Yearbook*, 40th issue, United Nations, New York, New York, 1995.

Exhibit 5   Central and Eastern Europe   *(Continued)*

Table 2: Economic Structures

1990	Albania	Bulgaria	Czech.	Hungary	Poland	Romania	U.S.S.R.	Yugoslavia	Greece	FRG
Origins of Output (%)[1]										
Agriculture & Forestry & Fishing	34	12	7	20	13	15	12	15	13	2
Industry	43	60	60	—	—	59	—	—	—	39
Manufacturing, Mining, Utilities	—	—	—	36	48	—	43	42	25	—
Construction	8	9	11	7	12	7	13	7	5	—
Production Services	15	18	22	20	—	—	—	—	—	28
Transport & Communications	—	—	—	—	—	8	6	7	11	15
Trade	—	—	—	—	—	7	15	7	16	—
Non-Productive Services	NA	NA	NA	NA	NA	NA	NA	—	—	—
State & Private Households	—	—	—	16	—	—	—	—	—	13
Others	—	—	—	—	27	4	—	30	30	4
Output by Use (%)[1]										
Consumption	NA	75	—	—	—	—	75	—	—	—
Private Consumption	NA	—	58	61	67	56	—	48	72	54
Government Consumption	NA	—	25	11	12	6	—	8	17	18
Gross Fixed Investment	NA	—	—	21	12	27	25	19	16	20
Stockbuilding and Est. Error	NA	—	—	4	8	3	—	23	3	1
Net Exports	NA	—	—	3	NA	4	NA	2	-7	6
Accumulations	NA	25	18	—	—	—	—	—	—	—
Main Destination of Exports (%)[2]										
Socialist States	NA	86	61	42	35	46	64	22	NA	4
Developed Countries	NA	7	31	31	24	19	22	65	64	96
Main Origins of Exports (%)[2]										
Socialist States	NA	76	62	40	28	57	67	14	NA	4
Developed Countries	NA	17	31	38	27	9	25	67	63[2]	96
% of Output Exported	NA	34	33	23	23	26	2	20	27	35
Largest Western Trading Partner	NA	FRG	FRG	FRG	FRG	FRG	FRG	FRG	EC[3]	EC

1. Figures reported are based on GNP, NMP, or GSP, and are the latest available.
2. Case writer's estimate based on national account figures as given by *Economist Intelligence Unit*. Figures for each country are from the latter part of the 1980s, and exclude trade activity in 1990.
3. EC: European Community.

Exhibit 5   Central and Eastern Europe

(Continued)

Table 3: Foreign Trade and Money

1990	Albania	Bulgaria	Czech.	Hungary	Poland	Romania	U.S.S.R.	Yugoslavia	Greece	FRG
Consumer Price Inflation (%) Annual	NA	30	10	30	580	40	8	120	20	3
Average Annual Inflation	NA	9	2	15	186	8	4	354	17	1
1991 Forecast	NA	50	50	40	45	NA	12	50	20	4
Hard Currency										
Exports US$ billions	0.3	1.5	5.0	6.5	9.4	1.5	29.0	11.6	6.3	402.0
Imports US$ billions	0.3	2.0	5.5	5.9	5.9	2.9	35.0	15.1	17.7	337.0
Current Account US$ billions	NA	-2.0	-0.1	-0.1	0.9	-2.5	-2.0	-0.2	-3.5	49.4
Current Account US$ billions 1989	NA	1.3	-1.4	-1.4	-1.6	2.6	-4.5	12.0	-2.6	55.4
Reserves excluding gold US$ billions (Dec)	NA	NA	NA	1.0	5.2	NA	NA	8.2	4.0	66.0
Gross External Debt US$ billions (Dec)	NA	10.4	7.5	21.0	44.7	1.0	62.0	NA	20.7	97

Exhibit 5   Central and Eastern Europe

Sources: "World Outlook 1991," *Economist Intelligence Unit*, January 1991; "Country Reports, No. 4, 1991: Albania, Bulgaria, Czechoslovakia, Hungary, Poland, Romania, U.S.S.R., Yugoslavia, Greece, and West Germany," *Economist Intelligence Unit*, 1990–1991; and "Country Profiles, 1990–1991: Albania, Bulgaria, Czechoslovakia, Hungary, Poland, Romania, U.S.S.R., Yugoslavia, Greece, and West Germany," *Economist Intelligence Unit*, 1990.

Although the country's living standards were the lowest in Europe, the perception of poverty was mitigated because everybody had a job of some sort, little was known of life in foreign countries, and there prevailed a widespread sense of national achievement and progress. Total labour force was about 1.5 million, and, although interest on savings was two to three per cent, Albania claimed to be the world's most saving society. Prices were very stable.

Bulgaria

Lack of strong political leadership and direction had continued unabated since the country had embarked on the road to democracy and market-based reforms. The transition was likely to be more protracted and torturous than that experienced by Poland, Hungary and Czechoslovakia, because Bulgaria had failed to make a clean break with communism; the party was returned to power in the country's first freely contested elections. In March, the government unilaterally suspended payments on its external debt and froze interest payments in response to a rapidly deteriorating economic situation. A package of reforms consisting of sweeping privatization, price liberalizations, and abolition of subsidies was likely to be implemented but would probably lack vigour in their application due to political deadlock.

Bulgarians had a higher living standard than Romanians and Albanians, but a lower level of employment due to a long term decline in the country's birth rate. Employment was shifting away from agriculture towards communications, trade, and services. Inflation was expected to be as high as 30 per cent as reforms progressed, but price and wage data were difficult to obtain from the communist government. As with most centrally planned economies, prices changed infrequently but sharply.

Czechoslovakia

Following the "Velvet Revolution" of November 1989, democratic politics had been quickly restored and the first freely contested elections since 1946 were held in June 1990. With an elected right-of-centre government, the country's Communist Party was headed toward further isolation. Slovakia's demands for devolution of power in favour of the country's two states was being met to counter a nationalist, and possibly separatist, revival within. The government was pressing ahead with radical market reforms. Liberalization of domestic prices, the elimination of subsidies, and the introduction of "internal currency convertibility" were set for January 1, 1991. Other reforms included the elimination of subsidies to industries and consumers, the distribution of shares in nationalized enterprises to the population, and the implementation of restrictive monetary and fiscal policies to keep a check on inflationary pressures. Opponents to these reforms were warning of extreme disruptions. They were exerting strong pressures to delay them, and were suggesting more state involvement in managing the economic transition. The process of reform was proving far more complex than expected, and the privatization programme was yet to be finalized. The Czechs were searching for a slow route to risk-free capitalism; as well, they had more to start with given their rich prewar industrial base.

Although 56.6 per cent of the population was of working age, the country suffered from a shortage of skilled workers due to practices such as overmanning in enterprises and the use of labour intensive technology. As firms were being cut off from government subsidization, this problem was expected to revert to one of unemployment. In 1988, average real wages, disregarding additional hidden inflation, were only 34 per cent higher than those in 1978.

Hungary

In the autumn of 1989, opposition political forces including the country's Communist Party agreed to a peaceful transition to democracy and free elections, the first since the Second World War. These were held in March 1990, and the majority of seats were won by well-organized and dynamic democratic parties. Communist and socialist parties were further marginalized. The government appeared to be the most well-balanced in Eastern Europe. Trade was quickly shifting to OECD countries from those of Eastern Europe; the country had managed over the last decade to move more significantly toward a mix of Marxism and market economics than any other East and central European country. In agreement with the International Monetary Fund (IMF), Hungary operated an active exchange rate policy: the rate was adjusted several times a year to reflect domestic and foreign rates of inflation. The process of privatization was gaining momentum, and large U.S. and Japanese multinationals were beginning to make long-term commitments to the country. The government's three-year economic renewal programme stressed gradualism versus shock, and it hoped to reduce state ownership within the economy by 50 percentage points within five years. Critics accused the government of being seriously unfocused in its economic reforms, suggesting that gradualism was a naive attempt at avoiding the necessary pain of reform. Sharp debate over foreign ownership, privatization, and land reform was bogging down the process. Hungary was never a highly industrialized nation, and it never was willing or able genuinely to privatize its economy.

Consumption levels were relatively higher than in other countries of Eastern and Central Europe. About 90 per cent of the population possessed televisions, washing machines and refrigerators. However, Hungarians worked more hours per day than citizens in other countries of Europe; in general, purchasing simple consumer goods required this, and many held two, even three, jobs as a result. As restructuring continued, unemployment was expected to rise. Inflation over the last five years, although significant, was controlled, mostly due to the government's gradual approach of eliminating subsidies.

Poland

At the start of 1990, Poland's new Solidarity government launched an ambitious IMF-backed program it called its "leap to the market": reductions of government subsidies with the aim of generating a balanced budget, backed by a highly restrictive tax-based incomes policy, and anchored to a sharply devalued exchange rate and decontrolled prices. The impact was dramatic and the Polish authorities were taken aback by the extent of the recession that was induced. However, export growth which was higher than anticipated led to an unexpected hard currency surplus, and the zloty was now convertible. Social support (or acquiescence) for this programme was remarkable throughout most of 1990. External worries and evolving internal political situations could blow the country off course and delay economic recovery. Poland benefitted from a degree of political unity unknown in the rest of Central Europe: genuine political revolution ran deeper through the bureaucratic hierarchy of government. Parliamentary elections were to be held in spring or summer 1991. It was widely accepted that Poland would be unable to carry much longer the burden of its US$45-billion external debt. A debt-reducing gesture of some generosity was likely to be announced.

At the end of August 1990, unemployment, a new phenomenon in Poland, stood at 4.5 per cent of the work force (roughly 50 per cent of the population). In the past, labour tended to be in short supply. Recent hyper-inflation was also a new phenomenon being experienced, although wages tended to inflate at the same rate.

Romania

Romania's first freely contested elections were held in May 1990. The transition to democracy was marred by unrest and violence, including the beating of demonstrators in Bucharest in June and ethnic violence in Transylvania which left many dead and injured. Action against former secret police was also limited. Because of skepticism on the part of the West about the new leadership's commitment to the applications of genuine democratic principles, economic assistance was being withheld. A pro-Western government was nominated by the prime minister and key economic portfolios were taken over by two economists with strong free market leanings. A blueprint for reforms over 1990–1992 was published and included immediate price increases, measures for widespread privatization, and the gradual introduction of convertibility. Living standards were deteriorating and political considerations would continue constraining the progress of economic reform.

During the 1980s, the country suffered from a slowdown in employment growth due to a lack of capital given the external debt-repayment program. The labour force in 1987 was about 11 million. Each age cohort under the age of 22 contained approximately 400,000 people, which was approximately 150,000 larger than the age cohort leaving the working population each year. While actual wage rates were unavailable, the trend since the early 1980s had been toward large wage increases followed by correspondingly large increases in commodity prices. The labour force situation was compounded by the anti-abortion policy instituted in 1968.

Yugoslavia

The emergence of democracy in 1990 coincided with the unleashing of age-old ethnic antagonisms and with the most serious and fundamental economic reform yet undertaken. The country had the opportunity of becoming the leading emerging democracy of East and Central Europe in terms of economic adaptation to the markets of Western Europe. Centrifugal forces of nationalism were creating doubts about the future existence of Yugoslavia in the minds of Western governments and business. Some observers considered it possible that the high tide of destructive nationalism had been reached and that Yugoslavs—above all, the two nationalities which were the two key pillars of the federation, Croatia and Serbia—would come to recognize that they both had to live together. A program to reform the ownership structure of enterprises was in place with employees and ex-employees given much more favourable offers than elsewhere in East and Central Europe. The Federal Executive

Council led by the prime minister would try to obtain democratic legitimacy through national elections in 1991. The danger of a total collapse of central authority leading to prolonged economic and financial chaos was very real.

Yugoslavia's domestic labour force was estimated to be 10.4 million people including 2.5 million employed within the private sector, which was primarily agriculture. During the 1980s, the gradual freeing of prices created substantial inflation: on average, prices rose by 1,256 per cent in 1989, 199 per cent in 1988, and 118 per cent in 1987. By June 1990, the monthly inflation rate was wrestled down to zero due to wage freezes, a tight monetary policy, a fixed exchange rate against the deutschmark and internal convertibility against the country's currency. During this time, real wages fell sharply.

OPPORTUNITY IN EASTERN AND CENTRAL EUROPE

In February 1990, John Pepper, Wolfgang Berndt, just-retired Chairman John Smale, and several of P&G's European managers set off to investigate first-hand the political upheavals sweeping through Eastern and Central Europe, and size up the business opportunities that might result for P&G. After listening to government officials, they realized that political, economic, and social transformations would proceed very quickly in many of these countries. Hungary seemed to be following a more pragmatic transformation program than Poland and Czechoslovakia, but the latter two countries were more desirous of wanting change and were active in planning for it. The U.S.S.R. was a country completely perplexed by the very notion of privatizing businesses. When they visited the Kremlin, a high official suggested that P&G take over the Soviet Union's entire detergent and pulp industries without delay. "That perception of how a free market business works gave us a pretty clear signal that things weren't going to change there overnight."[63]

Of significance to P&G was the fact that communist countries had created a very large middle class. Incomes tended to be much more evenly distributed among the population than in most western countries, although income differences with the West could be as high as seven to one. The entire region, including the U.S.S.R., had a population of over 430 million people, almost twice as much as that of the United States, and its combined 1989 GNP was $3.5 trillion or 90 per cent of West Europe's. For certain countries, per capita income was as high as in Greece. Consumer habits differed, however, and appliances such as washing machines were much less advanced. Effective TV and radio infrastructures seemed to be in place to reach these markets.

Consumers in Eastern and Central Europe had long prized the occasional Western goods, and were now eager to have these on a regular basis. At a U.S.-sponsored trade show in Moscow in 1989, hundreds of people lined up every day at the Colgate-Palmolive Co. stand to receive a free tube of toothpaste, a product in constant short supply.[64] The large population had been deprived of abundant and quality consumer goods for years. When P&G explored various detergent manufacturing facilities, it discovered that the employees within one of the best factories of the region were often haphazardly substituting ingredients irrespective of the impact this had on the detergent's cleaning ability. This practice occurred because of chronic shortages in raw materials and the need to achieve output targets dictated by the state plan. Most of these plants, built 20 years earlier by foreigners, had not been well-maintained or upgraded with newer technology, and were, therefore, in poor shape.

Despite the pervasive low levels of productivity, work forces in these countries tended to be highly skilled and educated. Most of these countries had industrial and commercial traditions that only seemed stunted and not uprooted by communism. Rich cultures, ancient universities, devotion to learning, vivid inventiveness, and powerful ambitions, especially among the younger generations, appeared to be abundant. Education levels were considerably higher than in most developed countries, especially in the applied sciences and related technical fields. Labour wage rates,

extremely low by Western standards, made investment in labour-intensive businesses attractive. As well, most land and equipment were undervalued. These factors, together with the special trading relations that were being developed with the European Community, suggested that investing in these economies could be achieved at low levels of capital with the added benefit of access to the rich markets of Western Europe. Tax holidays and duty-free zones that enabled manufacturers to import raw materials and export finished products were some of the incentives being offered to foreign investors.

There were, of course, significant risks to investing in any of the countries of Eastern and Central Europe: most currencies were not yet convertible, and the high levels of external debt in many of these countries meant that hard currency would be extremely scarce; the economies were in recession, compounded by the breakdown in trade among themselves, and reforms among these countries were progressing at widely different speeds; laws were unclear, governments were still shaky, and the political outlook in many of them was unclear as socialist parties still held sway with sizeable portions of the populations. As well, the distribution infrastructure, especially in Russia, was very inefficient, and people were unaccustomed to advertising and mass marketing on the scale done in the West. North American marketers knew little of the tastes and needs of these citizens who were still somewhat secretive and indirect in their responses, a behaviour born out of decades of totalitarianism. Further, the vast majority of companies were state-owned. With the sweeping transformations, one could also sense an undercurrent of social and ethnic tension that stretched back decades, if not centuries, with little indication of its depth or magnitude.

Many Western companies had already made plans to enter Eastern and Central Europe. Ford Motor Co. had decided to build an $80-million automotive components plant in Hungary, and other firms such as General Electric and Levi Strauss & Co. were pursuing serious ventures of their own. The number of Western joint ventures in some of these countries had increased dramatically since 1988: in the U.S.S.R., 1,000 were signed compared to 162 in 1988; in Hungary, this number had increased from 150 to 600, and in Poland, from 20 to 400.[65]

Of P&G's competitors, Colgate-Palmolive, which had exported many products into Eastern Europe for a number of years, was reported to be planning operations in Hungary, the U.S.S.R., and Poland, either by acquisition or start-up. Its Colgate dental products had recently received the prestigious seal of approval from the Soviet Ministry of Health's Central Scientific Research Institute. The company was pursuing an aggressive expansion program in all areas of the oral care business throughout the world. Unilever had recently announced that it was planning to move back into Eastern and Central Europe through buy-backs and joint ventures with former off-shoots seized by communists after the Second World War. In 1990, it already had sales of over $200 million in East Germany and was soon likely to establish joint ventures in Poland and Hungary for detergents and edible oils. It was less interested in the countries of Romania, Yugoslavia and Bulgaria because of perceived political instability. Gillette Co., which had been exporting to these countries for over 10 years, had recently signed a joint venture in the U.S.S.R. where its trademarks had long been registered to protect them from piracy. Estee Lauder Inc. and Revlon had shops in these markets and were hoping to expand further. Henkel had recently entered into four joint ventures to produce laundry detergents: one in the U.S.S.R., one in East Germany, and two in Yugoslavia at a cost of DM40 million. Henkel was planning to modernize the JV sites and apply its management expertise to supporting the local brands before launching its own in 1991. Establishing a venture in Czechoslovakia would take longer. The company was already operating in Hungary and Poland in other chemical-related products. Kao of Japan had recently entered Europe via its purchase of the German hair care company, Goldwell. It was also engaged in the modernization of laundry detergent plants in the U.S.S.R.

THE DECISIONS

Herbert Schmitz faced a number of critical decisions concerning P&G's foray into the uncharted waters of Eastern and Central Europe:

1. Which of the countries should P&G enter first? How fast should it proceed?

2. Should P&G introduce a wide array of brands or hit hard with one or two key products? From which category should these come? What kind of advertising and promotion should be used?

3. A regional source of supply would likely be needed if the company was to manufacture the products locally in order to match costs with revenues. How should this production capacity be allocated throughout the region? Should P&G import product instead in order to minimize risks?

4. What type of people and organizations would be required to manage this new business?

5. What other unusual problems, given the communist history within these countries, should be anticipated?

Although P&G's globalization experiences offered many insights and success models to work with, Schmitz knew he needed a set of criteria to help make the appropriate decisions given his mandate and the unusual nature of the business environment he was entering.

NOTES

1. "Everybody's Business: A Field Guide to the 400 Leading Companies in America," *Doubleday Currency*, 1990.

2. Descriptions of P&G's management systems and practices found throughout this case are based, in part, on i) A. MacDonald Court, "Procter & Gamble Company (A)," Harvard Business School (HBS) Case # 9-584-047, 1983 and ii) C. A. Bartlette, "Procter & Gamble Vizir Launch," HBS Case # 9-384-139, 1983.

3. "The House that Ivory Built," *Advertising Age*, August 20, 1987.

4. "P&G Rewrites the Marketing Rules," *Fortune*, November 6, 1989.

5. "Everybody's Business."

6. "Everybody's Business."

7. 1990 Annual Report, The Procter & Gamble Company.

8. "P&G Tops in Cosmetics: Purchase of Noxell Stings Lintas," *Advertising Age,* September 25, 1989.

9. "Everybody's Business."

10. 1990 Annual Report, The Procter & Gamble Company.

11. *Wall Street Journal,* October 23, 1990.

12. "Everybody's Business."

13. A. MacDonald Court, "Procter & Gamble Company (A)," HBS Case # 9-584-047, 1983.

14. "Patience and Perspective," *Advertising Age,* August 20, 1987.

15. "Everybody's Business."

16. "Patience and Perspective."

17. Form 10-K, The Procter & Gamble Company, Securities and Exchange Commission, Washington, DC, 1990.

18. "The Marketing Revolution at Procter & Gamble," *Business Week,* July 25, 1988.

19. "Marketing Rules."

20. "Marketing Revolution."

21. A. MacDonald Court, "Procter & Gamble Company (A)," HBS Case # 9-584-047, 1983.

22. "Through Eyes of Wall Street," *Advertising Age,* August 20, 1987.

23. "Marketing Rules."

24. "Back to Basics," *Advertising Age,* August 20, 1987.

25. Ibid.

26. "Marketing Rules."

27. Form 10-K, The Procter & Gamble Company, Securities and Exchange Commission, Washington, DC, 1990.

28. "Perestroika in Soapland," *The Economist,* June 10, 1989.

29. Ibid.

30. 1990 Annual Report, The Procter & Gamble Company.

31. "Everybody's Business."

32. "Marketing Rules."

33. "P&G Sends Crest Rinse After Colgate," Advertising Age, September 2, 1987.

34. "P&G Company Report, Donaldson, Lufkin & Jenrette Securities, November 30, 1990.

35. "Everybody's Business."

36. "Perestroika in Soapland."

37. "Marketing Rules."

38. "Perestroika in Soapland."

39. "Marketing Revolution."

40. "Perestroika in Soapland," *The Economist,* June 10, 1989.

41. "Washday Miracle," *Financial World,* November 3, 1987.

42. "Marketing Revolution."

43. "Washday Miracle."

44. "Slow and Steady."

45. 1990 Annual Report, The Procter & Gamble Company.

46. "A Global Comeback," *Advertising Age,* August 20, 1987.

47. "Procter & Gamble Europe: Vizir Launch," HBS Case #9-384-139, 1983.

48. "Marketing Rules."

49. "Slow and Steady."

50. "Procter & Gamble Company Report," Merrill Lynch Capital Markets, July 27, 1989.

51. "Marketing: After Early Stumbles, P&G Is Making Inroads Overseas," *Wall Street Journal,* February 6, 1989.

52. "Japan Rises to P&G's No. 3 Market," *Advertising Age,* December 10, 1990.

53. 1992 Annual Report, The Procter & Gamble Company.

54. "Japan Rises."

55. "Foreign Formula: Procter & Gamble Fixes Aim on Tough Market—The Latin Americans," *Wall Street Journal,* June 15, 1990.

56. 1990 Annual Report, The Procter & Gamble Company.

57. Ibid.

58. This section is based on: M. Smith, D. Conklin, and J. Gandz, "The U.S.S.R.: A note on the rise and fall of communism in Europe, 1917–1990," Western Business School, 1996.

59. Eastern Europe refers to Central Europe plus the western republics of the U.S.S.R. including the Baltic republics, Russia, the Ukraine, Moldavia, and Byelorussia.

60. Longworth, R., "Central Europe: Potential for Prosperity," *European Affairs,* July/August, 1990.

61. Sources: Excerpts from "World Outlook 1991," *Economist Intelligence Unit,* January 1991; "Country Reports, No. 4, 1991: Albania, Bulgaria, Czechoslovakia, Hungary, Poland, Romania, U.S.S.R., Yugoslavia, Greece, and West Germany," *Economist Intelligence Unit,* 1990; and "Country Profiles 1990–1991: Albania, Bulgaria, Czechoslovakia, Hungary, Poland, Romania, U.S.S.R., Yugoslavia, Greece, and West Germany," *Economist Intelligence*

Unit, 1990. "In East Europe, only Poland makes hard decisions," *Wall Street Journal,* June 5, 1990.

62. "In East Europe, only Poland makes hard decisions," *Wall Street Journal,* June 5, 1990.

63. Pioneering Pays Off in Eastern Europe," *P&G World,* January–March 1995, 20–22.

64. "Corporate America Flocking to Moscow; Lure of Untapped Market Overrides Perestroika's Complexities," *Wall Street Journal,* October 24, 1989.

65. *The American Banker,* July 26, 1990.

APPENDIX: FOREIGN TRADE AND COMPETITIVENESS OF EAST AND CENTRAL EUROPEAN ECONOMIES (1990)

The fall of communism in Eastern Europe, as well as the democratising process in the Soviet Union, led to profound shifts at the Soviet bloc-wide level, especially within the Council for Mutual Economic Assistance (CMEA) or Comecon. Founded in 1949 by Bulgaria, Czechoslovakia, East Germany, Poland, Romania, Mongolia, Cuba, the U.S.S.R., and Viet Nam (since 1978), Comecon, it was often argued, was set up by Stalin as a Soviet response to the Marshall Plan for the reconstruction of Europe. Its purpose was to provide a means to encourage specialization and co-operation among member states, but its achievements were modest. By 1990, there remained little rationale or interest in the continued existence of this organization and its demise in the era of market-oriented, post-communism transition became inevitable.

The "socialist economic integration" under the CMEA's aegis never functioned as a tool for increased trade and efficient specialization. Many observers identified it as a "trade-destroying union"; that is, without it, there would have been more intra-regional, as well as East-West, trade. The CMEA was, nonetheless, successful in assuring member countries stable supplies of (chiefly Soviet) energy and raw materials on advantageous terms; "hard" goods (energy) would be obtained for "soft" East European manufactured goods, which could be sold for hard currency (outside the CMEA) only at substantial discounts. As one youthful Hungarian reformer quipped: "We trade our stray dog for their blind cat." This implicit subsidization had, over the years, shielded East European industries from competition, thereby contributing to the region's economic decline and wasteful use of resources.

There was a strong drive in the East European capitals to do away with Comecon as soon as possible and to forge links with Western countries. All European CMEA countries (except Romania) had concluded trade agreements with the European Community by late 1990, and some were aspiring to full membership by the year 2000. East European policy makers tended to dismiss proposals for a separate East European payments union, regarding it as a Western ploy to delay East European accession to the EC, even though this would be a tool for stimulating their mutual trade and, hence, improving their position in their approach to the EC.

As of January 1991, trade between these countries was to be cleared in U.S. dollars and at the going world market prices. As a result, either the quality of East European exports would have to be substantially improved, or their prices deeply discounted.

The transition to this new system would entail dramatic change in intra-CMEA terms of trade in the U.S.S.R.'s favour (for the short term, at least), and a further contraction in East European-Soviet trade (in certain cases, up to 50 per cent in 1990). The U.S.S.R. was reducing its shipments of energy and other raw materials, forcing Comecon countries to buy on world markets. Pressure on world oil prices due to the Persian Gulf conflict was exacerbating this negative shock to their economies. In view of this, it was believed that each country would try to negotiate cushioning mechanisms with the U.S.S.R. for the period of transition.

Sources: Selected excerpts from "Hungary: Country Profile, 1990–1991," *The Economist Intelligence Unit* (October 1990): 36–39; and "In East Europe, only Poland makes hard decisions," *Wall Street Journal,* June 5, 1990.

BANK VOZROZHDENIYE (V.BANK)

*Prepared by Trevor Hunter under the
supervision of Professor David W. Conklin*

Russia faces a daunting task in transforming the wreckage of its banks into a banking system which will prevent a similar systemic meltdown occurring in the future.[1]

—Anthony Robinson,
The Banker

In 1988, the single Soviet State Bank for domestic banking, Gosbank, lost its monopoly. Initially, about 3,000 banking licences were issued to companies formed by existing companies. Various segments of the State Bank were set up as independent banks and ownership was transferred to employees and to new investors. Through acquisitions and innovative management, Moscow Joint Stock Commercial Bank "Vozrozhdeniye" (V.Bank) had grown to become one of the 25 largest banks in the new Russia. However, in October 1998, as the Russian economy grew worse, management of V.Bank wondered if it would be able to survive the crisis, let alone continue towards its goal of transforming its operations into those which would be competitive with the Western banks.

THE RUSSIAN BANKING MARKET

With the fall of Communism in Russia, a new free market economy emerged. A lack of understanding of the mechanics of capitalism and unrealistically high expectations severely threatened successful growth as the economy struggled to free itself from old, inefficient, yet comfortable, ways.

Since there were no formal instruments for the issuing of credit, companies began setting up banks to finance themselves. Their banks were able to get credits from the state budget which were then passed on to themselves as clients of their own bank. As formerly state-owned industries were privatized, the Russian government sold them in a "shares-for-loans" scheme which gave many banks ownership of huge companies for low-interest loans to the state. These assets were then to be sold to third parties in public share offerings, but more often than not, they were simply purchased in whole by the banks. The Russian government ultimately lost control of many of its assets at dramatically undervalued prices and did not achieve its goal of placing the state assets in the ownership of the people. Financial-Industrial Groups (FIGs) were created, initially centering on those who were in control of these large companies. They assumed a position of great power and influence in the economy and to some extent, over the government. The people who controlled the FIGs and their component banks were made very wealthy.

High inflation and a devalued currency made arbitraging and hard currency exchanges extremely profitable. To compensate for capital flight, the Russian government began issuing billions of dollars worth of short-term treasury bills, known as GKO bonds, which had high interest rates. GKO bonds were purchased by the banks by issuing long-term debt at a lower rate, and the spread on the difference was "profit" to the banks. Two problems arose. First, the "profit" was generally overstated due to inflation. Secondly, and more importantly, when interest rates fell as the currency stabilized in 1997, the interest rates of the short-term GKO bonds became significantly lower than the long-term debt some banks had issued and many became insolvent. The Central Bank was forced to step in and buy the bonds back at the high interest rate in order to keep smaller banks solvent. This action further burdened the government.

Many small banks were initially set up to "cash in" on these types of opportunities. Russian banking licences were easy to obtain and there were few regulations to follow once a bank was established. The authority of the few regulators that did exist was limited. By 1994 the number of Russian banks exceeded 2,500. No bank dominated the commercial banking business. Some were fly-by-night or operated by organized crime syndicates. Many were more like currency speculators than banks, offering no deposits or lending services. Corruption and fraud were commonplace. Because there were few experienced managers, many banks could not control their operations and bankrupted themselves. Some financial companies became more like pyramid schemes and many investors lost what little savings they had. Confidence in the independent banks plummeted. Most of the depositors who were willing to keep money in a bank turned to Sberbank, which, as the portion of the Gosbank that handled personal savings, was the most stable by virtue of its large asset base. By 1998, Sberbank still held more than 80 per cent of the total personal savings of Russian citizens. However, much more of the country's actual savings was not held in banks but, in general, kept at home in the form of U.S. 100 dollar bills. In other words, the public followed a banking pattern similar to the one followed under Communism.

Most foreign transactions were concentrated among a few relatively sophisticated institutions. Moscow banks dominated the economic landscape with about 70 per cent of the market, measured by customer loans and other assets. Banking profitability was based on access to state credits that were "on-lent" without risk according to budget requirements. In 1992, banks were granted powers to provide foreign exchange services that provided the majority of profits for several years. In August 1995, the Central Bank introduced the "ruble corridor" providing for a controlled devaluation of the ruble against the U.S. dollar. At the same time, stringent control of the money supply expansion created an inter-bank liquidity crisis causing failure of several significant banks. Many smaller banks also ceased activities.

Since early 1996, inflation had been declining, reaching 15 per cent per annum by 1997. Banking profitability was dominated by investment activity, particularly in short-term government bonds. With the reduction in inflation, short-term interest rates declined from 160 per cent to about 40 per cent and were expected to fall significantly lower prior to the predicted crisis in 1998.

Commercial lending was seen as the source of future profitability. The regulatory and legal framework was evolving rapidly, but there was still little practical experience with credit decision making, effective security for bank lending and bankruptcy. Cheques were not used and there was no domestic cheque-clearing system. All payments were made through labor-intensive payment orders cleared through the Central Bank. Payrolls were beginning to be made by direct deposit in Moscow and some major cities, but throughout the rest of the country people were paid by cash; in many instances, particularly in declining state-owned industries, people were paid with a significant delay. Cash-cards existed, but credit cards were rare. Most individual transactions were carried out with cash, or when shortages of cash existed, through bartering.

Russian Accounting standards were rigorously applied, but their major purpose was to enable taxes and government regulations to be enforced, not to provide management information. Western or International Accounting Standards (IAS) were virtually non-existent and financial statements did not accurately reflect the performance or financial position of the banks. Competition was intense, and since there was little regulation for credit requirements or reserve levels, or an understanding of how a bank should operate, fees were often charged at "below cost" in order to gain a competitive advantage. Other banks were thus forced to follow suit, and they would literally price each other out of business. As bank after bank failed, confidence continued to fall. Any hint of insolvency created a panic that led to a mass withdrawal of funds, which, in turn, created an insolvent bank where one initially did not exist.

It was felt that around fifty of the top Russian banks would develop significant stature over the long term. The World Bank and the European Bank for Reconstruction and Development's Financial Institutions Development Project (FIDP) were major factors working to create "international banking standards." By 1997, 31 Russian banks had been accredited to the FIDP.

Eventually, due in part to external pressure, the Central Bank played a more important role in bank regulation. Some, but not enough, regulation was introduced, such as the institution of a bank start-up capital requirement of US$2.3 million; increased reserve levels; the revoking of licences. There was a real attitude of Darwinism as large, better organized banks took over smaller, less efficient banks. Standards for accounting were introduced to raise the Russian banks to a comparable level with Western banks and investors. During the period between 1992 and 1998, nearly 1,000 of the over 2,500 Russian banks were either forced to close or merge.

V.Bank

V.Bank was created in 1990 from most of the operations of the then newly privatized Moscow Region operations of Agroprom Bank. Agroprom was the specialized Soviet State Bank for agriculture and the food industry. The first shareholders of the bank were clients, and they gradually formed a corporation (known as a joint stock company in Russia), which named itself Moscow Joint Stock Commercial Bank "*Vozrozhdeniye,*" or V.Bank. *Vozrozhdeniye* translates into Renaissance, and for the first few years of its existence, V.Bank was a successful renewal from its old Agroprom roots.

Initially, the agriculture industry formed 75 per cent of its client base, but by the end of 1998, it only comprised between three and four per cent. By 1997, V.Bank's retail banking operations served over 170,000 individuals and over 30,000 commercial clients. When the bank was privatized it owned 30 branches around the *Oblast,* the Moscow Region, which was a rough doughnut with a radius of 240 kilometres around, but separate from, the City of Moscow. By 1995, it had added over 30 branches, including six in Moscow City and 18 in other more distant regions, through new development and acquisitions. Another 60 sub-branches were formed reporting to the main branches in Oblast cities. An average branch would have 60 to 80 people on staff, but some of the larger ones had over 100 staff.

International analysts agreed that V.Bank was one of the better managed Russian banks. In the first five years of its existence, V.Bank increased its assets 450 times to nearly RR4.5 trillion in 1997[2] and six consecutive years of profitable operations. (See Exhibit 1 for V.Bank's financial statements.) While the majority of large Russian banks were involved in Financial Industrial Groups with other large businesses through ownership relationships, V.Bank's ownership was broadly based, having no shareholder with more than five per cent voting capital. This meant the bank was free from undue political or shareholder influence. In an environment where banks were mainly tools set up to cash in on arbitraging, V.Bank appeared to be committed to banking.

In all its policies, the goal of V.Bank's management was the evolution towards operations that were at the same level of Western banks. Controlled expansion through acquisition was V.Bank's strategy for growth. Evidence of this commitment could be seen in the products and services it offered as well as the programs it instituted or with which it was involved. Alexander Dolgopolov, Deputy Chairman of V.Bank, described management's rationale for wanting to be more "Western" and how they tried to accomplish this:

When *Vozrozhdeniye* was first founded, there were few competitors; now there are thousands. There

BALANCE SHEET OF "VOZROZHDENIYE" BANK AS OF JANUARY 1, 1997 (RR millions)

Assets

Balances on accounts in the Central Bank, cash and correlative funds	512,494.50
Incl. deposited compulsive reserves	246,711.20
Deposits with credit institutions	69,704.90
Government securities	277,892.00
Securities in trading	30,877.30
Lendings extended to institutions, enterprises, private clients, credit institutions, and leasing to clients	2,409,111.70
Provisions for losses on loans	9,387.50
Lendings, incl. leasing to clients (line 8 = line 6 − line 7)	2,399,724.20
Fixed assets and intangible assets	594,734.70
Long-term investments in securities	52,508.90
Other assets	204,034.70
Assets, total	**4,141,971.20**

Liabilities

Own Funds

Authorized stock capital	102,160.00
Other funds and other own resources	608,545.10
Profit (+) / losses (−) of the year under review	157,217.80
Profit utilized in the year under review	134,947.10
Retained profit (loss) of year under review	22,270.70
Own sources, total	732,975.80

Borrowings

Loans from the Central Bank	0
Loans of credit institutions	794,073.70
Customer's funds, savings included	1,968,956.40
Debt receipts, notes, bills issued	531,223.10
Other	95,194.70
Borrowings, total	3,389,447.90
Other assets	19547.50
Liabilities, total	**4,141,971.20**

Off-balance sheet items

Executive documents to credit institutions	0
Irrevocable liabilities of credit organizations	2,627,893.80
Guarantees, sureties issued	11,925.40

PROFIT AND LOSS ACCOUNT OF 1996 (RR millions)

Earnings

Interest returns on loans	1,345,608.00
Returns from securities operations	216,920.10
Returns on foreign currency operations	83,743.20
Other returns	111,021.40
Earnings, total	**1,757,292.70**

Exhibit 1   Balance Sheet of "Vozrozhdeniye" Bank as of January 1, 1997 (RR millions)   *(Continued)*

Expenses	
Interest paid on received loans and for deposits	971,676.70
Operational expenses for securities operations	285,328.00
Operational expenses for foreign currency operations	61,843.60
Other expenses	284,298.80
Expenses, total	**1,603,147.10**
Funds directly added to the financial results of credit institution	3,072.20
Profit / Loss +/–	157,217.80

Exhibit 1   Balance Sheet of "Vozrozhdeniye" Bank as of January 1, 1997 (RR millions)

was little regulation and many of these banks were run very poorly and would soon fail. They were tied to too few customers and made bad loans to them and themselves as they speculated on currency and interest rates. As the Central Bank started implementing stronger regulations and interest and inflation rates fell, these banks closed. We saw the opportunity to be the Russian bank that would be a safe place for investors and at the same time be profitable while operating a sound business.

In 1996, we totally reorganized our branch management structure to orient them more towards sales and service. We wanted them to be market-focused. We gave them more autonomy and used the central office for support. To help them we developed products and marketing which would attract clients. At first we had few computers, but now we have a good network and thousands of computers. We have a network of bank machines. We also began projects to increase non-interest revenue, such as fees and service charges. To ensure our managers found *good* business we began to provide incentives to them based on the quality, not the quantity, of business.

We began to provide cash transactions and small business loans, which were uncommon, along with the services we provide to our larger clients. We have strong relationships with government structures like the Ministry of Finance, the Moscow Region Administration and the Ministry of Food Supplies for the City of Moscow, for whom we provide promissory notes and lending. These are clients with good strong assets. We also look for the same from clients who are small to

medium-sized within the Moscow Region and this provided us with a diversified client base.

V.Bank was one of the first banks to take savings deposits from private individuals, ranging from saving accounts to flexible investments of up to one year with floating rates. Although lending to individuals existed in Russia, it was uncommon, and V.Bank did not offer this service. It did, however, provide loans to businesses and many state industries.

V.Bank and FIDP: Changing From a Domestic to a Global Bank

Accreditation to The World Bank-EBRD FIDP required an audit by a western firm according to IAS and the implementation of accounting and reporting processes which met the international standards developed by the World Bank, as well as an audit to ensure operations were well managed. This audit investigated the assets, lending practices, investments, ownership and structure to ensure the bank was stable. V.Bank received its accreditation in July 1996.

The Program itself had two components. The first component of the FIDP was the Twinning Project—Technical Services for Bank Development. The second allowed the Russian bank to borrow at concessionary rates, US$10 million to US$15 million for investments in technology infrastructure. (See Exhibit 2 for a copy of the World Bank-EBRD outline of FIDP.)

THE FINANCIAL INSTITUTIONS DEVELOPMENT PROJECT (FIDP)

Objectives

The ultimate objectives of the FIDP are to improve the quality and range of banking services provided by the participating banks (PBs), to promote banking stability, and to contribute to the more efficient mobilization of financial resources and utilization of bank credit. This will be achieved through the creation of a core group of banks which will be developed to western operating standards, thereby enabling them to act as models for the financial system as a whole and achieve enhanced access to international finance.

Selection of Participating Banks

Work on the selection of banks for participation in the Project was initiated during the summer of 1993. With assistance from the Russian authorities, significant resources were deployed to identify throughout the Russian Federation banks that would be suitable for participation in the project. An initial selection process was completed for a first batch of banks that involved the screening of more than 2,000 institutions, selection of those which should be diagnosed more intensively, detailed reviews of 43 banks, and selection of an initial group of 22 candidates.

The main selection criteria for inclusion in the program are capital adequacy, diversification of ownership, profitability, liquidity, credit policies and procedures, lending activity, internal controls, management capability and autonomy, degree of self-development, and focus on the private sector. Detailed diagnostic audits were conducted on each of the 22 banks for the purposes of their formal accreditation to the FIDP and to assist the drafting of the individual development programmes. Of these 22 banks, six have been accredited, and the remainder will be presented for accreditation in due course, together with a further five banks, which were identified during a later review of potential participating banks that will be considered for inclusion in early 1996. However, the total number will be limited to between 30 and 40 in order that the project can remain manageable. Annex I summarizes the accreditation criteria used.

The banks selected so far have their headquarters in nine cities, all important economic centres, spanning the Russian Federation: Moscow (12), St. Petersburg (4), Togliatti, Tver, Ekaterinburg (2), Tyumen, Omsk, Kemerovo (2), Khabarovsk and Vladivostok (2). Among the banks is a mixture of "zero" (new) banks and "spin-offs" from the former state specialised banks. The 27 banks also range widely in size, from the largest commercial banks to the relatively small banks.

Project Financing

The total loan financing to be provided by the World Bank and European Bank will be US$300 million with additional grant funds totalling US$70 million from the European Union, Japan and bilateral country funds. An average amount around US$3 million will be required for the financing of each twinning contract and 50 per cent of this amount will be provided from grant resources. The balance of the available funds under the FIDP will be provided for the financing of the IT programs.

The World Bank and European Bank loans will be provided through the Ministry of Finance, who will onlend to each of the PBs under terms and conditions agreed with the two International Institutions.

Project Management and Organization

The policy oversight body for the Project will be a Government Task Force comprised of senior representatives from Ministry of Finance and Central Bank of Russia. A Deputy Minister of Finance will act as chairman. The Task Force will work in close consultation with the European and World Banks and will have the final say on all decisions related to accreditation of PBs. A group of senior bankers with extensive experience within western banks will comprise a full-time advisory group called the Bank Review Unit. This unit will monitor key elements of the

---

Exhibit 2   World Bank-EBRD Description of the FIDP for the Russian Federation   *(Continued)*

Project's implementation and the ongoing financial and operational status of the PBs, in addition to providing advice to the Task Force and having a problem-solving role for the Project's implementation.

All administrative arrangements for the FIDP and related credit line projects will be undertaken by a Project Implementation Unit (PIU), which will be staffed and operated under a contract between the Ministry of Finance and a foreign consulting firm.

The World Bank and European Bank each have senior and administrative staff assigned on a full-time basis to the FIDP. These staff will continue to play a key role in the implementation and ongoing supervision of the Project.

TWINNING

What is Twinning?

Twinning is an approach to the strengthening of commercial banks that was first used during the early 1990s in Poland, for the restructuring of former state banks.

Under this approach, a number of western banking institutions are identified that would be willing to form contractual "consultancy" arrangements with local banks.

Each contract will require the provision of specific personnel and other resources over a two- to three-year time frame to help build, strengthen and develop the local banks in accordance with carefully drafted and agreed terms of reference. These terms of reference will cover most major components of the local banks' operations.

Such an arrangement was found to be relatively successful in Poland, and in all cases, close and effective working relationships were developed between the local banks and their contractors, although some problems were initially encountered in some cases. Given this relative success, it has been decided to follow a similar approach in Russia, although different characteristics of the Russian banks, being on average smaller and more advanced in the transition process, will be borne in mind.

Obligations

The obligation of the foreign bank is restricted to the successful completion of the twinning contract. There is no obligation to provide more than the institution building work defined in the contract, and no requirement to provide loans or equity investments, enter joint ventures or undertake any kind of financial engagement with the partner. Neither is there any requirement to participate in correspondent banking arrangements with a Russian bank although this would be a logical progression. The risk is restricted to performance of the contractual arrangement. (See Risks below.)

Any longer-term results of building a business relationship between the two banks under a twinning contract are achieved voluntarily. This is not a prerequisite for providing the specified technical assistance services but may evolve out of working together, learning about each other's capabilities, achieving mutual trust and finding mutually beneficial business interests.

Fees

The western bank will be compensated for the twinning work at international consultant fee rates. The western banks bidding for twinning contracts will quote their fee structures as part of the tendering procedure.

Benefits and Rewards

For the Russian Bank

There are three special advantages of twinning for the Russian bank: (i) bankers can work with bankers and draw on each other's experiences, learning from past successes and failures; (ii) the foreign bank has the full range

---

Exhibit 2   World Bank-EBRD Description of the FIDP for the Russian Federation   *(Continued)*

of skills, policies, procedures, systems and practical experience of a working bank to draw on, from which to provide the required technical expertise; and (iii) the short-term technical relationship could evolve into a mutually beneficial long-term business relationship, which would also help continue the Russian bank's development.

For the Foreign Bank

- Risk-free entry into the largest developing market in the FSU,
- Development of an in-depth relationship with a leading Russian bank,
- Obtaining a detailed understanding of Russia and its banking system,
- Significant staff development opportunities,
- Providing assistance where it is crucially needed,
- Assisting in the largest privatisation process the world has ever seen, and
- Being paid for the consultancy services from which a profit should be earned.

The Twinning Contract

The contract will be signed between the western and Russian banks following submission of a proposal, its acceptance by the Russian bank (see Contracting Procedures below) and intensive negotiations between the two parties. Although the contract may be fully comprehensive, there will always be disputes, differences of opinion and disappointments relating to the twinning deliverables. This can be mitigated through open and honest discussions between the two parties at the outset, on an on-going basis and at an appropriate seniority level. The Bank Review Unit, World Bank staff and European Bank staff will be available to assist in resolving any contractual difficulties that may arise.

Negotiations should include the following:

- Definition of what needs to be done in each segment, by whom, when, and what the results should be,
- What deliverables will be produced at each stage and in each segment,
- Specifying the implementation controls that should be put in place,
- Who decides that the correct actions are being taken and that individuals are achieving their commitments,
- The process for agreeing that the goals have been achieved,
- A process for resolving disputes and disagreements,
- Availability of qualified Russian staff,
- Availability of good translators,
- Availability of western standard of living accommodation, and
- A reporting and control system to monitor the project progress and success.

It is important that both parties nominate "project managers" at a senior (Vice President) level so that both trainers and trainees receive the right messages and support from their organizations on an on-going basis. If senior management in both organisations are not fully committed to the implementation of the twinning contracts, chances for success may be significantly reduced.

Approach and Planning

It may be advantageous for the western bank to use a qualified consulting firm to assist with establishing and implementing the twinning contract as consultants normally have well-developed skills in analysis, project management, and the implementation of practical solutions in diversified environments. Where individual twinning banks do not have the full spectrum of expertise to conduct the required work, or do not have cost-effective resources to do so, the best approach for providing technical assistance may be a combination of a twinning bank and a consulting firm. In this case, the twinning bank would be expected to take full responsibility for the work, including the work of sub-contractors.

Exhibit 2   World Bank-EBRD Description of the FIDP for the Russian Federation   *(Continued)*

Risks

As mentioned above, the risks which the foreign bank must face will relate specifically to its ability to meet its contractual obligations. Some of these risks are as follows:

- Difficult interpersonal relations among twin partners,
- Disappointments and disputes,
- Constantly changing staff,
- Language and cultural differences,
- Poor interpreting skills,
- Lack of high level support and management committed to achieving results,
- Failure of foreign staff to cope with difficult living conditions in Russia, and
- Understanding the difficulties of the project and resource requirements.

Resource Requirements

The Polish experience indicates that between 265 and 450 work weeks will be required for each twinning contract with these inputs being provided over a two- to three-year period. Based on an average of 360 work weeks for a contract covering nine business segments over a three-year period, around 12 work weeks would be required for each segment each year. It is clear, therefore, that a team of up to 15 people will be required by the western bank, prepared to spend eight or more weeks a year in Russia, perhaps in three separate trips. Some of the training can be done in the twinner's home country but most must be done in Russia.

As mentioned previously, it is essential to nominate a project manager with overall responsibility for the twinning. Experience has shown that this individual might best be located at the home office, making regular visits to the Russian bank for high level discussions as well as detailed supervision and control. In this way the person can have a better overview and perspective of the project and is removed from day-to-day issues.

Building personal relationships is clearly crucial to success and individuals should aim at building firm relations with their Russian peers. Only by working together can success be achieved.

Do not underestimate the importance of providing sufficient, experienced, hands-on trainers with good communication skills and patience, individuals who get a real kick out of training, working closely with people in difficult circumstances and building the right environment for effective skills transfer.

Exhibit 2   World Bank-EBRD Description of the FIDP for the Russian Federation

---

In a press release announcing V.Bank's involvement with FIDP, Mr. Dolgopolov described the Twinning program as one which was designed to help "improve our bank's planning, daily operations, financial structure and staff capability. This would be accomplished via consulting activities, training and direct work with our management and operations staff." (See Exhibit 3 for the cover page of the invitation for a proposal from V.Bank.) V.Bank received funds through the World Bank-EBRD program which were administered through the Russian Ministry of Finance to solicit potential "twins" to assist it in becoming recognized as an international bank. In the statement to the Moscow press, Mr. Dolgopolov explained why the twinning component of the FIDP was of interest to V.Bank:

> More important is the twinning or partnership. Twinning opens wide access to a western bank's experience and gives opportunities for mastering it. Foreign experts consult our specialists, offer verified methods and schemes of work in various fields, and provide an opportunity for short periods of work for our staff in the foreign bank. Our banking system is very young. We should study western banking experience because our foreign partners are ahead of us in banking equipment, in the

MOSCOW JOINT STOCK COMMERCIAL BANK "VOZROZHDENIYE"

V.BANK

7/4 Luchnikov Lane, 103696, Moscow, Russia
Telephone   (095) 929-18-88
Telefax   (095) 929-19-99
Telex   414680 vbnk ru
S.W.I.F.T.   VBNKRUMM

Your ref:

Our ref: *24c1/5463*

19 *12* 19 *96*

TO: Mr. D. Robbie
         Vice-President
         Trade Finance Division
         CIBC
         Commerce Court West, 9th floor,
         Toronto, ON
         Canada M5L 1A2

RE: Financial Institutions Development Project (FIDP)
         "Twinning - Technical Services for Bank Development"

DATE: December 19, 1996

Dear Mr. D. Robbie

1. You are hereby invited to submit a proposal for consulting services required for the institutional development of Moscow Joint Stock Commercial Bank "Vozrozhdeniye" in Moscow, Russia which could form the basis for future negotiation and, ultimately, a contract between your firm and our bank (hereinafter called "the Client") to perform the indicated work.

GENERAL INFORMATION.

2. The assignment will consist of the provision of professional services as detailed in Terms of Reference, Attachment 1 to help us improve our bank's planning, daily operations, financial structure and staff capability. This would be accomplished via consulting activities, training and direct work with our management and operations staff.

3. The contract services being solicited are part of a larger program (Financial Institutions Development Project) wherein the World Bank and the European Bank for Reconstruction and Development are assisting the Government of the Russian Federation to improve commercial banking operations and supervision of the banking system throughout the country. The Ministry of Finance has received loans from the World Bank and the EBRD in various currencies toward the cost of this project. Diagnostic reviews have been conducted for our bank to support our candidacy within this proposed development program. On July 2, 1996 our bank was accredited to participate in the Financial Institutions Development Project by the Task Force of the Russian Government, comprising of representatives of the Ministry of Finance, the Central Bank and other government institutions. After that, a Subsidiary Loan Agreement was signed between our bank and the Ministry of Finance of the Russian Federation wherein parts of the available loans are to be on–lent to our bank. We intend to apply the proceeds of this

---

Exhibit 3   V.Bank Invitation for Twinning Proposal

number of banking products they offer, and in arranging work processes.

V.Bank sent invitations to five banks:

1. Canadian Imperial Bank of Commerce (CIBC)

2. Berliner Bank AG

3. Allied Irish Bank

4. Bank Austria AG

5. Core States Bank

Eventually, the CIBC submission was accepted. Neil Withers, General Manager of CIBC's Trade Finance Division, moved to Moscow to head up a team of 18 consultants for a planned 400 person-weeks of consulting spread over two years. Team members would visit Moscow several times per year for trips averaging three weeks each.

The team from CIBC consulted on the following areas:

- Strategy
- Financial Management
- Asset/Liability Management
- Credit Management
- Marketing
- Branch Management
- Human Resources
- Information Technology
- Project Management

Each area was called a "module" and each module was organized into work-packages focusing on the practical application of each area. The consultants discussed what the areas meant to western banks and helped Russians decide how they could and should be applied to V.Bank. The team from CIBC encouraged V.Bank to focus on the areas of business in which it was most successful. It suggested market surveys to understand its clients, their needs, the competition and the market in general. Committees and teams were set up to work on instilling a service mentality within the branches.

Although there were definite cultural differences, management and staff at V.Bank followed the suggestions of the CIBC team and generally felt that the suggestions were positive. A real cultural and operational shift was in process by the summer of 1998, nearly one year into the twinning project. Mr. Dolgopolov commented on the progress of the twinning:

> On the whole, the Program is a type of "higher school" of banking activity. By the end of the Program the "graduates" become banks of international standards. This is very important because of tough competition. Our working together has shown complete mutual understanding and friendly terms and we have already got the first results of our cooperation.

V.Bank was one of the first three Russian banks to implement an ADR program. American Depository Receipts, or ADRs, were instruments through which foreigners could own shares of a Russian bank. Each ADR was denominated in U.S. dollars and equalled one common share in the bank. The ADRs were underwritten by a U.S. bank with approval of the Russian Central Bank. By law, Russian banking shares were only traded on the Moscow Stock Exchange and ownership to non-Russians was forbidden. By issuing ADRs through an American bank, the Russian banks were able to gain some much needed access to foreign capital, although this was initially limited to three per cent of the total capitalization of the bank.

The three per cent for V.Bank representing 306,480 common shares with a par value of RR10 was underwritten by the Bank of New York, and sold to CS First Boston in March 1997.[3] The deal was priced at RR20 or US$3.50 per share.[4] Management later wanted to expand its ADR issue, which would have equalled 15 per cent of the market capitalization of the company, but the Central Bank would only allow them to increase to five per cent in October 1997. Mr. Dolgopolov explained his company's interest in ADRs:

> We had a lot of contact with analysts. We wanted to increase our capital through the creation of a secondary market for our shares. Liquidity in the Russian stock market was low even during the growth periods, so we decided that the best way

to raise capital was through foreign investors who were eager to invest in Russia anyway.

In order to be internationally accredited as a good risk for ADRs, V.Bank had to be audited to ensure that its financial information conformed to international standards of accounting. Mr. Dolgopolov recalls the process:

> We first met with representatives from the EBRD in 1994. At that time they offered a program whereby accredited banks could receive loans at a low rate of interest. Since we were expanding at that time, we had good use for the funds to upgrade our technical systems, but also, we were happy to be part of FIDP since it would help us to bring our operations up to Western standards.

Mr. Dolgopolov was not exaggerating when he suggested the association was producing the results that V.Bank management wanted. In January 1997, V.Bank received its first international credit rating by the international banking analyst Thompson BankWatch. In February, they upgraded their initial rating from a B to a B+. A quote in the upgrade bulletin said everything that V.Bank management wanted to hear: "Opportunities: FIDP accreditation substantially raises V.Bank's international profile."[5] V.Bank ADRs were trading well in the United States, and had been listed in Germany as well. V.Bank began to expand internationally with the Czech Republic bank *Investioni a Postovni Banka* to form First Czech-Russian bank, based in Moscow, of which V.Bank was a 49 per cent owner. The goal was to facilitate Czech-Russian trade and currency exchange. V.Bank was also able to establish correspondence links with banks in 42 countries for services ranging from payments to foreign exchange.

Modest GDP growth in 1997 soon turned to recession in 1998 as budget deficits increased due to falling revenues. Many strange actions on the part of Boris Yeltsin reduced investor confidence and foreign direct investment started to wane or leave. In March 1998, Yeltsin fired his prime minister, Viktor Chernomyrdin, and installed a young, inexperienced Sergei Kiriyenko

who was not supported by the state duma. As the value of the ruble slid, the Central Bank raised its interest rates to 150 per cent.

In July 1998, the IMF announced it would provide a bail-out package worth US$22.6 billion provided the Russian government instituted strong reforms such as revenue collection. The duma then amended the government's reforms and reduced the planned revenues by two-thirds. On August 14, 1998, Yeltsin boldly announced that there would be no devaluation of the ruble, as many economists suggested should happen. Three days later, the government announced that it would allow the ruble to devalue, and it would be forced to default on and restructure its government debt. In addition, it imposed a 90-day ban on the payment of external debt. Analysts predicted that the currency would devalue by as much as 50 per cent by the end of 1998, inflation would average 45 per cent and the economy would contract by three per cent for the year. Millions of rubles were printed to meet short-term commitments. Finally, Yeltsin replaced Kiriyenko, after five months in office, with former prime minister Chernomyrdin.

Unfortunately for the Russian people, Chernomyrdin too was not accepted by the duma, and for weeks there was no government in place while the Communist-controlled parliament squared off against Yeltsin. Finally, Yeltsin gave in to the duma and selected his Foreign Minister, Yevgeni Primakov, the former head of the Foreign Intelligence Service, the renamed KGB, as his new candidate.

Although Primakov was supported by reformers like Grigori Yavlinsky, head of one of the opposition parties *Yabloko,* he was also considered an ally of the communists based on his past. Primakov was not considered anti-U.S., but was, as *Time Magazine* described him, "a proponent of a strong centralized Russian state in foreign and domestic affairs," whose "opposition to American policies stems from this world view."[6] Observers felt that Primakov had no plans to reform the economy which had suffered greatly in the struggle to name a prime minister. If anything, it was believed that he would adopt a more Soviet style of government. In a statement he

	1994	1995	1996	1997	1998
GDP growth %	(12.7)	(4.2)	(3.5)	0.8	(4.6)
GDP per capita (US$)	1,884	2,120	2,661	2,748	1,845
Inflation, annual avg. %	307.4	197.4	47.6	14.6	27.8
Unemployment, annual avg. %	7.4	8.3	9.3	10.8	11.9
Current account balance (US$ bn)	9.3	7.9	12.1	4.1	2.5
Lending interest rate	n/a	320.3	146.8	32.0	41.8
Foreign exchange rate (US$)	2.19	4.56	5.12	5.79	9.71
Fiscal deficit/surplus as % of GDP	(9.8)	(5.4)	(7.9)	(7.1)	(5.0)
Public debt as % of GDP	n/a	55.1	55.9	55.6	n/a
Real private consumption (RR billions)	3,807	3,359	3,199	3,353	3,245
Real gross fixed investment (RR billions)	1,822	1,544	1,217	1,120	981

Exhibit 4   Annual Indicators—Russia

"denied any plans to return to the Soviet past but said flatly, 'The government should intervene in economic affairs and regulate them.'"[7] His first two cabinet appointments were the former head of Soviet State Planning under Gorbachev, Yuri Maslyukov as Minister of Finance, and the re-appointment of Viktor Gerashchenko as head of the central bank. Gerashchenko was widely criticized for printing billions of rubles and extending credit to unproductive state enterprises in his previous tenure in the early 1990s. These appointments were initially regarded as inappropriate by western governments, international aid agencies, and many businesses.

The repercussions of the crisis in Russia's economy were described by the Economist Intelligence Unit's third quarter report on Russia:

> In abandoning its defence of the ruble and the preservation of price stability, Russia has reversed its main economic achievement since the transition process began. The devaluation and accompanying default on domestic government and certain external obligations will have a profound adverse effect not only on the Russian economy and the standard

of living of the Russian population, but will also have wide-reaching political ramifications for the government, the presidency and the wider polity.[8]

In all the turmoil one thing remained clear: Boris Yeltsin, increasingly sidelined by illness, would or could do nothing to help the economy. Grigori Yavlinsky commented that "we cannot even dream of an economic recovery until Yeltsin leaves the Kremlin."[9]

Effects of the Crisis Internally and Externally

As the political squabbling continued, Russia's economy continued to deteriorate. In August 1998, monthly inflation was 15 per cent. Imports of goods decreased by 45 per cent, and distribution of goods ceased due to strikes by unpaid railway workers. Stores that were full of all manner of goods mere months ago were now empty. Foreign imported goods were being replaced with domestic goods that in some cases were over-priced and still of poor quality.

Consumers had no access to their own funds because their savings were frozen and inaccessible in many banks. Bartering was the only reliable way to do business, and observers estimated that nearly three quarters of all transactions between firms no longer used the banking system.

Over all, what little investor confidence there was in the country was fading fast. Many western companies, particularly banks, had large exposures to Russia and were anxious to leave and cut their losses. For example, Credit Suisse was estimated to have lost US$250 million between August and September 1998, and had exposure in excess of US$2 billion. Barclays had provisions for US$420 million and George Soros' Quantum Fund stated losses of US$2 billion. Other reports suggested that all together, British, German, Japanese and U.S. banks would lose around US$9 billion on loans and a staggering US$40 billion to US$50 billion in forward contracts.[10]

Although Russia was not a serious contributor to the global GDP (accounting for only two per cent), there were many global investors who would lose large amounts of money due to the country's economic collapse. These losses had serious repercussions for other developing markets. Due to the worldwide tightening of credit policies as a result of the Asian crisis which had begun in late 1997, credit was already difficult to come by in emerging regions. These losses would only make banks more cautious. Also, many of the European banks would need to raise interest rates to compensate for higher risk on what credit they did issue.

Perhaps just as frightening to potential foreign investors was the impending regionalization of the once-assumed homogeneous marketplace of Russia. As Moscow's authority diminished, regional governments began to ignore the Kremlin's demands for taxation revenue and many began to set up their own "economic zones" with regulations that were different from other regions. Shortages of goods led to the imposition of restrictions on the movement of goods out of certain regions.

In its October 24 issue, *The Economist* had the following outlook on doing business in Russia:

> Doing business in Russia looks more forbidding than ever: bad infrastructure, corrupt officials, idiosyncratic staff, weak institutions (the courts, for example, are powerless to enforce the payment of debts); and the ever-present curse of organized crime. All these were overlooked amid the greed and optimism of past years. But not anymore.

> Meanwhile the government of Yevgeny Primakov is doing none of the things needed to help the economy recover. Mostly, it is simply doing nothing. The result is a slow strangling of the firms that had started to think rationally about costs, customers and competitors. The rest of Russian business, still wedded to the bad habits of the past, has even less reason to change than before.[11]

While there were problems to be sure, some observers believed that there were still opportunities to enter the Russian market. The costs of expatriate salaries and real estate in Russia (among the highest cost rental market in the world in the early months of 1998) were all falling. Russian businesses were forming to fill the gaps left by the absence of foreign goods and services. A consultant at A. T. Kearney said, "multinational companies know the demand is still out there. This is the time to snap up good staff, reduce costs, and expand outside of Moscow. Russia remains a large market in which western companies have made billions."[12]

THE RUSSIAN CRISIS OF 1998

The summer of 1998 began on a promising note as the twinning partnership continued to produce excellent results. With the help of the CIBC team, V.Bank had completed some comprehensive marketing surveys and was working on new projects in human resources. However, the business environment of Russia was volatile to say the least and as summer turned into autumn, it was clear that V.Bank would have to put its plans on hold.

As the ruble devalued and inflation and interest rates jumped, the Russian banks, V.Bank included, were not prepared for the liquidity crisis which ensued. The domestic market for equities disappeared and so too did interest from the rest of the world. The phenomenal growth in the Russian stock market of the last two years was replaced by weekly losses of double-digit proportions. Investor confidence which was weak at best was completely gone. The only way to raise funds was through debt which was made more expensive by risk premiums for Russia and high inflation. The poor business environment caused clients to begin defaulting on loans despite the relatively strict credit policies V.Bank had instituted. Other clients began to withdraw their funds as inflation destroyed the value of their savings. The inability of major banks to allow depositors to retrieve their savings threatened to create civil unrest. Another round of mass bank failures began. Russians' emerging fragile faith in banks was once more disappointed.

To cut costs, V.Bank laid off over 30 per cent of its staff. The CIBC team left Moscow for Canada. Neil Withers described the state of affairs of the Twinning relationship at that time:

> CIBC felt strongly that we had made a commitment to V.Bank and that we should not abandon them immediately, especially as in the current situation, they might need help even more than before. I went back to Canada in late September, partly to give V.Bank some breathing space—and partly to ensure that my "team" held together and kept up its interest. I returned after three weeks. Most other twinning partnerships closed down and all their western staff left Moscow. With only a week's official notice, we were told that no work could be done (and invoiced through the World Bank) past mid-November. David Robbie, vice-president of CIBC's Trade Finance Division, said that as I had intended to come back in mid-December for Christmas anyway, why didn't I stay and see if there was anything I could continue to do for V.Bank?

As soon as V.Bank had official notification of the project's suspension, they approached me to see if they could make some arrangement for me to stay. They were willing to pay CIBC for its out-of-pocket expenses for my time and I was able to convince my boss to let me stay and work on getting V.Bank through the re-accreditation process.

In the month after I returned, we continued to work on several things: restructuring of external debt, investor relations, and strategic tasks, as well as the re-accreditation process. V.Bank was funding this from their own current resources (with only a possible hope of reclaiming the cost from the World Bank program when and if it gets resurrected).

It appeared that I was the only "Project Director" still in Moscow of the 15 western banks in the twinning program and CIBC-V.Bank was the only one where the Russian bank thought enough of twinning to fund it with their own resources.

By the end of 1998, five of the 10 largest non-state-owned banks had failed. As V.Bank's management faced this terrible situation, they wondered how this could have happened. Of all the Russian banks, it had seemed as though they had prepared themselves the best. They sincerely wanted to be a legitimate bank. How could they maintain the course they had started in 1994? They needed an infusion of capital badly, but how could they get it in this environment of investor pessimism and lender fear? Could V.Bank somehow take advantage of the weakness of its competition? What opportunities were there? What would V.Bank look like at the end of the crisis?

NOTES

1. Robinson, Anthony, "Wipeout in Moscow," *The Banker,* October 1998.

2. In Spring 1997, the exchange rate from Russian ruble (RR) to U.S. dollar was 5,800:1.

3. On January 1, 1998, Russia dropped three zeros from the end of its currency in an attempt to make prices and currency more manageable since inflation was relatively under control at the time. The ruble was not revalued, so 10 new rubles were the same value as 10,000 old rubles. By mid-1998, the old rubles were still in circulation and the population used

prices that reflected the old and new bills (i.e., bread would carry a price of 2,000 old rubles and two new rubles, which was about Cdn$0.50).

4. ADR Market Watch website, http://spca.ru/adrwatch/profiles/profile010.html, Oct. 26, 1998

5. Moscow Joint Stock Commercial Bank "VOZROZHDENIYE," *Thompson BankWatch,* January 1997.

6. Nelan, Bruce, "Better than nothing," *Time,* Sept. 21, 1998.

7. Ibid.

8. Russia, Country Report, *EIU,* 1998.

9. Nelan, Bruce, "Better than nothing," *Time,* Sept. 21, 1998.

10. Pryce, Vicky, "Russian bear faces the market test," *Accountancy,* Oct. 1998.

11. Anonymous, "Business: As winter draws in," *The Economist,* Oct. 24, 1998.

12. Ibid.

ING AND GLOBAL FINANCIAL INTEGRATION[1]

Prepared by David Conklin and Yury Boshyk with the assistance of Greg Kudar and Marc Trudeau

THE CHALLENGES AND OPPORTUNITIES OF THE TWENTY-FIRST CENTURY

Centred in the Netherlands, the ING Group's strategy had developed on the basis of European insurance and retail banking. Yet, by 1999, ING operated in 55 countries, had more than 50,000 employees and US$350 billion in assets. Over many decades, ING had built a global insurance business with holdings in more than 40 insurance operations, and it had recently sought to create a global banking business. The global banking vehicle, ING Barings, was created by the 1997 merger of three organizations that had offered different products and operated independently: Barings Securities, ING Bank International and ING Capital. Barings Securities was a global brokering business; ING Bank International focused on bond trading, trade finance and payment services; ING Capital traded emerging market debt. Approximately 75 per cent of ING's profits originated in its insurance activities, while 25 per cent originated in its banking activities. Global financial integration was bringing with it both threats and challenges, and as it entered the twenty-first century, ING faced a series of difficult issues.

The creation of a single currency in Europe was posing new challenges for all of Europe's banks. In recent decades, the role of banks within the financial system had developed very differently in Europe compared with the U.S. Many observers felt that European unification would compel European banks to shift to the U.S. model. This could require major changes in ING's European strategy. At the same time, European integration would inevitably create new opportunities for ING, as it could participate in mergers and acquisitions, as well as the shift from traditional banking to other forms of financial services, particularly investment banking.

ING made newspaper headlines throughout the world when it took over Barings in 1995. Singapore-based rogue trader Nick Leeson's foray into derivatives had destroyed Barings, and ING stepped in to create, it was hoped, a turnaround in Barings' fortunes. Barings had extensive operations with over 8,000 jobs in emerging markets and an active investment banking business. However, the first three years following the takeover presented a series of financial setbacks, and in the third quarter of 1998, ING Barings lost US$168.5 million, much of it as a result of losses in emerging markets. As one observer summarized the situation in February 1999, "The question remained whether ING's takeover of Barings, which it rescued from bankruptcy after Nick Leeson ran up huge derivatives losses, was a whim that went wrong."[2] Some observers concluded that "the market would like to see ING quit investment banking altogether."[3]

The Asian financial crisis had been followed by crises in Russia and Brazil, and many other emerging markets seemed vulnerable, raising serious concerns about banking in emerging markets. Yet the international financial crisis was creating new opportunities, with the elimination in many countries of foreign ownership restrictions in banking, and with many governments hoping that foreign banks would be able to bring new efficiency and competitiveness to financial systems that were a major cause of their country's economic difficulties.

Over the past few years, some countries had seen a dramatic increase in electronic banking. Financial institutions that operated through an extensive network of retail branches experienced high operating costs that were vulnerable to the inexpensive transactions that could now be conducted electronically. In many countries, the use of home computers had become commonplace, enabling the average person to participate easily in electronic banking. ING had pioneered expansion into new markets on the basis of low-cost electronic banking. As it entered the twenty-first century, ING faced the question whether its strategy should place even more emphasis on expansion through electronic banking.

EUROPEAN INTEGRATION

Impacts on the Financial Sector

Many predicted that the European Monetary Union (EMU) would dramatically alter the banking industry. Banks derived their profits largely from interest income, as opposed to U.S. banks, which gained a larger percentage of their profits from trading income, such as dealing in swaps and derivatives. The shift to a single currency would expose the banks to far more competition, both from banks in other countries, and also from other types of financial institutions. It was expected that free capital movements would inevitably squeeze the interest rate spreads that banks enjoyed, and, hence, their profits. Nout Wellink told Reuters in an interview:

> EMU is likely to act as a catalyst to reinforce already prevailing trends in the banking industry. It will put more pressure on profits, it will reinforce pressure on reducing excessive capacity, it will lead to increased internationalisation as well as increasing consolidation and mergers and acquisitions.[4]

Many observers warned that the European financial systems were fragile, being dominated by banks, over half of which were government-owned and subsidized, and that seemed to have built up substantial bad loan portfolios. Furthermore, this environment had not only fostered inefficiency but had also created unfair advantages for certain banks. In particular, subsidies to the German state-owned Landesbanks were seen as inappropriate and unfair in the new competitive environment. As an *Economist* review stated:

> As markets become more competitive, banks have much to lose from even the slightest disadvantage. Accusations fly that, like the Japanese in the 1980s, the Germans hope to use regulatory tricks to support their banks and to strengthen Frankfurt's pretensions to become Europe's leading financial centre.

> The Landesbanks attract criticism on two main grounds: that the state has provided them with capital on subsidised terms, and that they benefit unfairly from an implicit public guarantee that allows them to raise capital cheaply. All of which, say commercial bankers, distorts markets and stymies much-needed consolidation among Germany's 3,400 banks. These privileges caused little fuss so long as the Landesbanks kept off commercial rivals' turf and stuck to their job as bankers

to Germany's state-owned savings banks and to its 16 states. But in recent years several have started to compete aggressively with private-sector banks for corporate clients both at home and abroad. Olivier Szwarcberg of Barclays Capital reckons that, at the most pushy Landesbanks, commercial assets now outweigh those linked to traditional business.

The benefits of a state guarantee are obvious. The Landesbanks generally carry the same credit rating (usually, the top one, AAA) as the state that backs them, despite operating on wafer-thin margins and making an average return on equity of only five per cent. Credit-rating agencies, such as Moody's, usually give them a lower financial-strength rating, which strips out external support and reflects banks' intrinsic creditworthiness. . . . By one estimate, it costs the biggest Landesbanks 15 basis points (hundredths of a percentage point) less than their healthier private competitors to raise money. An internal study by the European Commission says the advantage is even bigger, at DM250m–500m for every DM100 billion ($55 billion) borrowed. As private banks' ratings have fallen (Deutsche Bank was downgraded by two notches earlier this month) they have become more agitated—and, as the Landesbanks have spread their wings overseas, so have foreign competitors.[5]

European financial systems had grown up in a protected environment. European integration would dramatically change this. For example, "The vast majority of European savings remain trapped within their domestic financial systems, re-tracing patterns from the days of exchange controls. These have remained in place thanks to oligopolistic banking systems, underdeveloped private pensions, and protectionist taxes and regulations."[6]

Observers pointed to the effects that EMU would have on capital markets. These included:

- A transfer of capital market services from domestic providers to global investment banks.
- A shift in focus from markets to products.
- A broadening of their investor base.
- Greater market efficiency due to elimination of tax and regulatory barriers to drive diversification of European investment portfolios.
- The disappearance of price and information advantages for domestic banks.

- The loss of foreign exchange business, and so the search for credit and/or restructuring risk to compensate.[7]

However, a number of obstacles remained before complete European financial integration:

Different national regulations will continue to hamper the complete integration of financial markets in Europe and that the low stock market capitalization of European firms is likely to guarantee the predominance of the U.S. stock market—at least over the medium term.[8]

Changes in European Financial Regulations

Throughout Europe, each country had given birth to a number of banks that concentrated their activities within that particular country, and where these activities were regulated by the government of that particular country. Integration of all these financial markets would require changes in the regulatory structure. If a Spanish bank were to be regulated solely by the government of Spain, would this not place individuals and corporations in other countries at risk? Anyone in the U.K. doing business with a Spanish bank could have no assurance that this bank was subject to the same regulations as a U.K. bank. Yet the creation of a single regulatory structure for the banks would be such a huge change that many opposed the concept. As the following quotation indicates, this dilemma had perplexed Europe for two decades:

The European Union has spent a good part of the past two decades trying to reconcile the claims of national regulators and global financial markets. It has tried two different approaches. The first is dear to EU bureaucrats' hearts: harmonisation. If national regulators harmonise their rules and standards, banks and exchanges can expect the same regulatory treatment wherever they offer their services in Europe. That keeps regulators happy too: their standards apply everywhere. One product of this approach, for instance, is Europe's capital-adequacy directive, which applies common European standards to the amount of capital banks and brokers must have.

The second tack the EU tried was mutual recognition of each other's regulatory regimes (and differences). Thus, the EU's second banking directive granted banks a "single passport" so that they can offer their services throughout the EU without incurring regulations from lots of different jurisdictions. That led to the development of distinctions between a "home" regulator, who keeps an eye on the soundness of the bank, and a "host" regulator, who is concerned only with the bank's business practices. Host regulators must recognise the competence of home regulators.

With the benefit of hindsight, it seems clear that hamonisation, although quite useful in some areas—such as aligning accounting and disclosure standards—holds limited appeal. European countries have found it difficult to agree on common standards. Sometimes there is no single "correct" standard on which to agree. Some of the common rules on which the EU did reach agreement quickly went stale. For instance, at precisely the time when the capital-adequacy directive came into force in 1996, regulators were busy amending an international accord on bank capital to allow banks more freedom to judge their own risks (and hence capital requirements). The EU directive had to go straight back to the drawing board.[9]

By 1998, the issue of creating an appropriate regulatory structure had become a major focus for the European Commission, as EU leaders at their June meeting in Cardiff asked the commission to submit a proposal for action. In response to this mandate, the European Commission developed an agenda for consultation that focused on several key questions:

- What can be done to make the financial services market function more effectively in Europe?
- How can the interests of consumer protection be best reconciled with the functioning of an internal market?
- How can the capital and financial markets in Europe be operated most efficiently in the wake of EMU?
- How can the current gap be filled on EU-level regulation for pensions?
- What changes are most needed to adapt financial reporting?[10]

Changing the Basle Accord

At the same time, international negotiations were being held in regard to capital requirements for financial institutions. The Basle Accord of 1988 had specified a target of eight per cent as a level of capital that must be set aside against their loans in order to ensure a minimum level of safety for depositors and that would, it was hoped, prevent financial catastrophes. By 1999, many felt that this target should be raised and that it should be differentiated in accordance with the nature of each bank's assets. International differences of opinion had developed in this regard. In particular, German banks felt that the eight per cent capital-adequacy ratio was unduly high for their property loans, which had traditionally been a very safe portfolio. Banks in other nations were reluctant to accept the German position in view of the traditional volatility of real estate prices, and in view of the competitive advantage this would give the German banks. How these negotiations might affect market opportunities and competitiveness within Europe was unclear. As a 1999 *Economist* article noted:

As the years have passed since the accord was agreed in 1988, its terms have come to seem ever more arbitrary and capricious. The amount of capital it demands often conflicts with banks' own assessment of asset riskiness. Securitisation has made it easy to shed assets that seem to require too much capital, which has contributed to a general deterioration in the quality of banks' balance-sheets. Bill McDonough, president of the Federal Reserve Bank of New York, who became chairman of the Basle committee last year, has therefore been trying hard to get it to revise the accord to reflect more closely bank assets' true riskiness. . . .

Yet the revised accord is being held up by Germany. The Germans are insisting that their banks should be allowed to put aside against commercial mortgages an amount of capital that most other regulators, and America's in particular, think inappropriately meagre. On the liability side, they also insist that banks which buy *Pfandbriefe,* bonds issued by German mortgage banks, should continue to set aside only a minimal amount of capital, meaning that the mortgage banks get much cheaper funding than do their rivals. A third, simmering, problem, is the complaint that German regulators allow the country's banks to issue a form of subordinated debt to bolster core capital that other regulators last year agreed not to countenance.

The Germans are not entirely without a case. Commercial-property lending, for example, has indeed been less risky historically in Germany than it has been in other countries. But regulators in any country can always point to specific, less risky elements in their banking systems. Simple rules demand compromise and consistency. And a level playing-field demands an end to special subsidies.[11]

The basic concepts involved in calculating risk were also being challenged as the Basle Accord modification was debated. A key question was how many categories should be established for risk and the degree to which these different categories should have different reserve ratios. Related to this was the question of whose corporate risk ratings should be used for corporate loans. For example, U.S. banks might have an advantage since a higher percentage of

companies in the U.S. had credit ratings than was true in Europe.

The following chart shows how the eight per cent reserve ratio could be modified in accordance with various risk categories. The chart presents percentages of the standard eight per cent ratio. For example, a 20 per cent rating means a 1.6 per cent capital requirement.

Economic Prospects for Europe

Many observers believed the creation of EMU would be a major stimulus for economic growth and, hence, would create exciting new opportunities for banks operating in Europe:

> EMU will create an area whose economic potential will be comparable to that of the United States. Structural changes will occur primarily in financial markets. The present segmentation will be overcome in many respects and the European financial market will become truly integrated. The implied greater competition between banks and financial systems in general will lead to efficiency gains in terms of resource allocation and ultimately stimulate investment and job creation.[12]

Basle Balance[1] Proposed Weightings, %						
Claim	*AAA to AA–*	*A+ to A–*	*BBB+ to BBB–*	*BB+ to B–*	*Below B–*	*Unrated*
Sovereigns	0	20	50	100	150	100
Banks: Option 1*	20	50	100	100	150	100
Banks: Option 2+	20	50++	50++	100++	150	50++
Corporates	20	100	100	100	150	100

Exhibit 1

Source: Basle Committee on Banking Supervision.

1. "Banking Regulation: Growing Basle," *The Economist*, June 5, 1999, 70.

*Based on risk weighting of sovereign in which the bank is incorporated.

+ Based on the assessment of the individual bank.

++ Claims on banks of a short original maturity, e.g., less than six months, would receive a weighting that is one category more favorable.

ING shared this optimistic view:

They see corporate finance in Europe booming as companies become more acquisitive and raise money through the capital markets rather than through house banks. They want to target their efforts on growth sectors such as telecommunications and media . . .

The bank is placing much of its hope on what it argues is the comparatively virgin territory of the European corporate sector. Explains Robins: "We believe that the cake is going to be growing very rapidly in Europe in the coming years because of the likely explosion of activity in cross-border mergers and acquisitions and the development of an equity culture with the consequent explosion of business in equity markets." Tilmant believes a boom in corporate finance, as opposed to lending, is imminent. "The market worldwide is moving in the direction of more and more disintermediation. U.S. companies fund themselves through the markets—bond or equity—rather than only through bank loans, and we believe this will accelerate in Europe because of the impact of the euro."[13]

In 1997, the report of the executive board of ING clearly stated this optimism:

Because of the substantially enlarged market that will be created, EMU will provide opportunities for expansion on a European scale. The advent of the euro will also create many openings for new products and markets. The NN Euro Fund, the Euro Plus Fund and the Euro Single-Premium Policy are examples of new products for personal customers in the euro market. Customer information is provided via the ING Eurodesk and other channels.[14]

Some academics remained pessimistic about the future growth in Europe, suggesting that the traditional forces of government regulation and ownership, expensive social security systems and high taxes would place a growing burden on all European countries, thereby constricting financial opportunities. David Smith, for example, pointed to this possibility:

What if, as Walter Eltis suggests, Europe, particularly those parts of it participating in the single

currency, are condemned to a future in which cyclical upturns have little effect on high unemployment levels but each downturn produces a further rise in the jobless total? In my book *Eurofutures* I sketched out a scenario, "the dark ages," in which this would happen, with an initial rise in emu unemployment to an average of 15 per cent, disguising rates in the most depressed regions of 30 to 40 per cent. Looking further ahead, it was possible to see the average unemployment rate climbing to 20 to 30 per cent, with rates in the worst-hit regions reaching 50 to 60 per cent. Inevitably, if such a scenario came about there would be a dangerous rise in social tensions. But there would also be other responses. Peter Jay, in his Darlington economics lecture, envisaged a situation in which, in such circumstances, there would be a forced increase in geographical mobility, not of the kind where workers would seek opportunities elsewhere to better their living standards, but, instead, something like a mass migration of economic refugees.[15]

The EMU would create one of the largest government bond markets in the world, since all new issues of government bonds would be in euro. Nevertheless, each member state would issue its own bonds, and so the market would assess the risk of default for each member state. Consequently, yield differences would remain, and investors would have to study carefully each country's fiscal policies. Of course, the European Stability Pact pledged each member to constrain its fiscal policy within specified targets, namely deficits equal to three per cent of GDP and debt equal to 60 per cent of GDP. A crucial question was whether these targets could be met by all member states on an ongoing basis.

Some commentators suggested that the default risk for any member would have an impact on the strength of the euro:

Sharing a single currency means that all countries issue their debt denominated in it and consequently when one country threatens to default the others may be called upon to "bail it out." Why? There is a common concern for the reputation of the currency—in other words lenders may require a higher interest rate from all if one debt-issuer defaults, because lenders have inadequate information to distinguish between borrowers in fine detail.[16]

Coping With the Threat of U.S. Banks

It was not clear whether a European bank would be capable of taking advantage of the new opportunities. Instead, it might be U.S. banks that would come to dominate the European financial landscape. The European banks had been protected by national barriers and these would disappear with EMU, exposing them to a degree of competition far greater than they had previously experienced. For many banks, EMU could bring dire threats rather than opportunities. A study by Andersen Consulting analysed this situation:

It finds that the performance gap in financial services is widening. A minority of organizations are generating high returns to their shareholders, and fewer still are combining shareholder return with high revenue growth. A worrying fact for institutions that have been protected by national entry barriers is that firms in more competitive, deregulated markets perform far better for their shareholders, in general, than the firms in the more tightly regulated markets. . . . If those institutions are performing badly already, they could really suffer when they have to start competing in an open market—a case of competition acting as a kill-or-cure remedy.[17]

The Andersen study suggested three alternative paths to success. First, what it referred to as "optimizers" would dispose of low-margin businesses, eliminating certain products and customers, and focusing on cost reduction. A second group of "consolidators" would achieve cost savings through mergers and acquisitions. Third, "innovators" would identify new trends in customer preferences and market conditions, creating new products to fit these changing circumstances:

To carve a niche in the new European financial services industry, companies will have to decide quickly what their route to value is going to be. The removal of market barriers with the arrival of the euro will create unprecedented opportunities for companies that have the strategic vision to respond. Those that want to stand still may not have any future at all.[18]

The May 1999 issue of *Euromoney* presented ING's decisions in regard to selecting a market niche:

ING is initially setting its sights on selling corporate advice to the 2,000 borrowing customers of the parent bank, where it already has a foot in the door. ING Baring's corporate and investment finance department is analysing these clients according to size and activities. They tend to have a market cap of $300 million to $3 billion and Le May believes that "middle-size" companies are a more natural hunting round for us. The top 200 European companies are over-banked and have good relationships with top banks. They are also very sophisticated and do a lot of the business themselves, so we can add less value than for smaller companies. The sort of companies we want to service would be off the radar screen for the big American firms.

ING Barings is unlikely to aim for a role in major privatizations, saying it would be a "waste of energy," and Robins rules out completely any claim to want to compete with the global bulge bracket. "We are not setting ourselves up, nor do we have any ambition, to compete with Goldman Sachs, Merrill Lynch or Morgan Stanley."

Market observers argue, however, that the industry is increasingly excluding those outside the bulge-bracket on the basis of the cost of capital. The flow of deals through the largest firms means they have to wait much less time to offload positions than do smaller firms such as ING.

One banker who used to worked [sic] for Barings has doubts about the new style. "I wish Robins well," he says. "They may make a success of a small-companies strategy but the economics of that business are pretty unattractive."[19]

Emerging Markets

Many believed that globalization of trade and investment depended upon the globalization of financial markets and perhaps even of financial institutions themselves. This set of relationships was seen as crucial for successful economic growth in the less-developed countries:

The financial markets are something like the flywheels of globalisation. Free capital movements and efficient financial markets greatly facilitate direct investment. They provide the basis for transactions and for the safety of payment flows, which are the financial equivalent of real integration.

The global financial markets promote and strengthen market structures. They also make it possible for investment in emerging economies to be funded privately, rather than officially, today on a much greater scale than previously. Capital is allocated today, more than it used to be, in accordance with economic, rather than political, criteria. Conversely, the integration of the emerging economies into the global financial markets provides new investment outlets for savings. This must also be seen against the backdrop of the ageing [sic] populations in most industrialised countries. They in particular must accumulate and invest capital today so as to be able to maintain their relative standard of living in the future, too.

And the global capital markets have assumed a role which is bearing fruit in the disciplining of national policies. They offer opportunities, but also pose a risk, to countries which fail to follow the economic constraints. Nowadays they are an effective part of the checks and balances.[20]

Faced with these apparent realities, ING, in 1997, was determined to expand in emerging markets far beyond the Barings structure that it had acquired in 1995. The report of the executive board emphasized that it intended to maintain a leading position in emerging markets:

ING is internationally recognised as a specialist in corporate and investment banking, life insurance and asset management in emerging markets. ING Barings intends to selectively expand its corporate and investment banking activities in countries with sufficient growth potential. New greenfields were set up in 1997 in Romania, the Philippines and, in cooperation with a local partner, in Indonesia. In Mexico, ING has formed a joint venture with Bital, a local bank, to address the privatised pension market. Furthermore, commercial banking activities (banking products for personal customers and small and medium-sized enterprises) were launched and existing operations were expanded in several countries. Adding banking products to the range offered by insurance greenfields can provide a useful stimulus for these young businesses. In addition, asset management activities were initiated in several emerging markets.[21]

In 1997, *The Economist* issued an article entitled "A Survey of Banking in Emerging Markets" in which it presented a very cautious analysis of such opportunities, giving its survey the title, "Fragile, Handle with Care":

Since 1980 more than 100 developing countries have suffered some kind of serious banking-sector crisis. . . . Many bank-watchers worry that, on the evidence of the past few years, things are getting worse. In Africa, banking systems have been going down the tubes at the rate of two a year. . . . In Eastern Europe, banks in almost every country have run into trouble as they swapped communism for capitalism. . . . Banks in Latin America have been just as accident-prone. . . . Japan's banks have become mired in bad loans. Once-invincible bankers in other Asian countries have been caught out by falling markets, and are starting to pay the price for a long lending binge. Decades of protectionism, corruption and lax regulation are taking their toll.[22]

This survey emphasized that banks played an even more important role in emerging markets than they did in the advanced countries, since they remained the main source of finance. Alternative financial institutions had not yet been developed. Yet their deposits as a percentage of GDP, often below 50 per cent, were far less than the percentages in advanced countries where this ratio might approach 100 per cent. From this perspective, emerging market banks had been inept at mobilizing savings and at being an efficient conduit for financial transactions. *The Economist* article suggested that "they [knew] little about their borrowers, and [had] poor credit-assessment skills, emerging-market banks typically [needed] wide spreads to maintain quite low profitability." [23]

The Economist Survey pointed to four potential dangers for banks in emerging markets:

1. Macroeconomic volatility seemed to be inevitable, and this would continue to present banks with the difficulty of evaluating loan proposals and the recurrence of serious corporate bad debt problems.

2. The political and business culture in emerging markets would continue to create pressures for "connected" lending to the employees or owners of banks, to political figures and to companies with which they were linked.

3. The political environment would be subject to ongoing changes that would impact the fortunes of the banks.

4. Financial liberalization would create significant changes as new institutions entered the marketplace.

In regard to regulatory solutions to these dangers, *The Economist* argued that three major gaps would continue to exist:

1. The problems of regulating large financial industrial groups.

2. The increasing use of derivatives.

3. The possibility of evading domestic restrictions through offshore operations, particularly using customized derivative contracts in offshore markets and hiding bad loans offshore.

Shortly after this survey was published, Asia, Latin America and Russia experienced a new round of financial crises. The Asian foreign exchange crisis dramatically altered the country risks and competitive advantage in Asia. Although strengthening the export sectors, the currency devaluations severely damaged both the import sectors and businesses serving the domestic market.

Some argued that the Asian economy had been hurt by the IMF's efforts. Since the IMF insisted upon a considerable tightening of monetary and fiscal policy as a condition for its loans, the effects of these measures worsened the financial crisis and heightened economic recession. The IMF rescue packages may have stabilized foreign exchange rates in the short term, but they severely damaged domestic businesses that suddenly confronted a tight monetary policy and high interest rates. Furthermore, this process inflicted major harm on low-income families experiencing unemployment.

While foreign exchange volatility was reduced, the country risk for potential investors might actually have increased. The Indonesian currency board debate illustrated this dilemma. Some argued that the Indonesian rupiah should be pegged at a certain fixed exchange rate to the U.S. dollar. An independent currency board would supervise the money supply with the sole objective of maintaining this fixed rate. The money supply would be backed by reserves of dollars and expanded only in accordance with the rate of foreign currency inflows. Such a commitment might, at times, require extremely high interest rates to attract the capital inflows that would support the fixed rate. Even the IMF had argued that a currency board approach could create economic devastation in a future exchange crisis and that some future exchange rate flexibility would be necessary.

Further, the Asian crisis had created a new risk of heightened foreign exchange volatility for some countries. Exchange rates were maintained at unrealistically high levels as a result of considerable inflows of foreign capital. Now, the optimism of the foreign investor had been replaced by caution. In the future, capital flows would be much more sensitive to changes in each country's financial system and general economic conditions than they had been in the past. Future surges in capital flows activity might translate into increased volatility of foreign exchange rates for some countries.

For financial institutions everywhere, an ongoing challenge was that the time profile of liabilities was not the same as that of assets. Banks borrowed short-term from depositors and lent long-term. This exposed the banks to the risks that fixed assets might fall quickly in price and that depositors might make sudden withdrawals. Further to the non-performing loan problem, Asian banks had been confronted with dramatic reductions in land and stock prices. Bank loans made on the security of real estate and stocks suddenly were at a major risk of default, further exacerbating the effects of the financial crisis overall.

The insurance sector also faced problems caused by the difference in time profile of assets and liabilities. In Japan, insurance companies had based their premium schedules on expectations that they would be able to earn reasonable rates of return. However, over the past decade, Japanese interest rates and returns on equity had been far below the levels necessary to earn the expected returns. Consequently, the Japanese insurance sector faced new solvency risks—a problem that might add a new dimension to the Asian financial crisis.

In Latin America as well, the risk of foreign exchange rate movements had become a paramount consideration, as had the risk that the government might simply lack the economic capacity to repay loans. The devaluation cycle remained a key economic risk in Latin America. Many Latin American countries had been experiencing ongoing fiscal deficits and money supply growth that exceeded that of each of the United States, Canada and Western Europe. Consequently, inflation rates remained high. And the realities of exchange rates meant that devaluation crises would appear from time to time. A devaluation in the exchange rate of one country automatically created pressure for devaluation in other countries' exchange rates. The 1999 Brazilian devaluation increased the Brazilian prices of imports from Argentina, and decreased the Argentinean prices of imports from Brazil with the result that the Argentine currency encountered severe downward pressure as the Argentinean balance of trade deteriorated. Competitive domino devaluation pressures were intensified because of the reliance of Latin American countries on primary product exports with their price volatility.

With the fall of communism in Russia, a new free market economy emerged. A lack of understanding of the mechanics of capitalism and unrealistically high expectations severely threatened successful growth as the economy struggled to free itself from old, inefficient, yet comfortable ways.

Modest GDP growth in 1997 soon turned to recession in 1998 as budget deficits increased due to falling revenues. Many strange actions on the part of Boris Yeltsin reduced investor confidence and foreign direct investment started to wane or leave. In March 1998, Yeltsin fired his prime minister, Viktor Chernomyrdin, and installed a young, inexperienced Sergei Kiriyenko who was not supported by the state duma. As the value of the ruble slid, the Central Bank raised its interest rates to 150 per cent.

In July 1998, the IMF announced it would provide a bail-out package worth US$22.6 billion provided the Russian government instituted strong reforms such as revenue collection. The duma then amended the government's reforms and reduced the planned revenues by two-thirds. On August 14, 1998, Yeltsin boldly announced that there would be no devaluation of the ruble, as many economists suggested should happen. Three days later, the government announced that it would allow the ruble to devalue, and it would be forced to default on and restructure its government debt. In addition, it imposed a 90-day ban on the payment of external debt. Analysts predicted that the currency would devalue by as much as 50 per cent by the end of 1998, inflation would average 45 per cent, and the economy would contract by three per cent for the year. Millions of rubles were printed to meet short-term commitments. Finally, Yeltsin replaced Kiriyenko, after five months in office, with former prime minister Chernomyrdin.

The repercussions of the crisis in Russia's economy were described by *The Economist Intelligence Unit*'s third quarter, 1998 report on Russia:

> In abandoning its defence of the ruble and the preservation of price stability, Russia has reversed its main economic achievement since the transition process began. The devaluation and accompanying default on domestic government and certain external obligations will have a profound adverse effect not only on the Russian economy and the standard of living of the Russian population, but will also have wide-reaching political ramifications for the government, the presidency and the wider polity.[24]

Faced with its disastrous losses in the context of the Asian financial crisis and the consequent Latin American devaluations and recessions, and faced with the Russian default on government bonds, ING now had to decide whether emerging markets really did offer opportunities in the twenty-first century.

Euromoney was extremely negative in its evaluation: "If one institution best demonstrates the effects of the Asian and Russian crises on a bank, ING Barings is it. It's a salutary tale of billion dollar losses, of individuals left to go their own way at the expense of group strategy, of management failures."[25]

ING was not alone in this dilemma. Barclays Bank PLC had also announced a US$400 million write off in Russian ruble bonds in 1998. Perhaps these losses were simply "business as usual" in the global financial markets. If so, how should global financial institutions cope with these emerging market risks?

ELECTRONIC BANKING

The Internet was playing an increasingly important role in the financial and insurance services landscape—ING faced the problem of how to incorporate Internet banking into its global financial strategy. Perhaps this was the ideal vehicle to create a global retail banking business. Perhaps the Internet could form an important component of future insurance sales and also banking for small and medium-sized companies. Canada was a new market that could be viewed as an experiment in this regard.

There was extensive debate about the impact of technology, especially the Internet, on banking and the financial services sector. The WTO suggested that technology would allow banks to lower costs and increase revenues while delivering higher levels of service, resulting in higher profits:

> Potential cost savings in the financial services sector are enormous: while the administrative (marginal) cost of clearing average US$1.20, and for a

debit or credit card payment US$0.40–US$0.60, the transaction costs for an Internet payment can be as low as one cent. . . . The full cost of an Internet transaction (US$0.13) is only half the cost of PC-based banking and one-eighth the cost of a transaction made over a bank counter.[26]

Yet despite the higher revenues and lower costs, the WTO warned that lower barriers to entry and increased competition could commoditize parts of the financial services sector.

> For established providers, technology is a double-edged sword. While it offers new opportunities to serve consumers better, it can give advantage to new competitors and threaten existing franchises. This is especially true for institutions with legacy technology and distribution systems requiring complex and costly re-engineering or replacement.[27]

Others agreed with Bill Gates, who declared that banks were dinosaurs destined to suffer from lower margins, greater competition, commoditization and eventual replacement by other technological solutions such as e-money and financial management software.[28]

According to a study by Ernst & Young, there were five leading-edge technologies that would alter the finance sector: Internet, PC banking, smart cards, data warehousing and document imaging.[29] The common link between these technologies was that they relied on efficient, low cost telecommunication infrastructure and the willingness of consumers to adopt new technologies.

Given that Canadian consumers had shown an eagerness to adopt new financial technologies, such as debit cards, the question facing Canadian finance firms was whether the regulatory environment would allow them to invest in new technologies. There was evidence that Canadian banks were spending less than U.S. banks on new technology, which suggested that there were policy or regulatory barriers to technological investments in Canada.[30]

The Canadian finance sector was small by world standards, both in terms of the size of its overall market and the relative size of its financial institutions.[31] Moreover, Canadian banks and other financial services companies were less efficient and less profitable by world standards.

> Compared to the best operating companies, Canada's banks lack a true performance ethic. Their cost efficiency, while collectively competitive, lags the leading performers in the United States and the United Kingdom. . . . Moreover, though their risk management skills are conventional and sound, the banks' legacy technology inhibits both rapid product innovation and more efficient processes overall.[32]

In Canada, the result was a tremendous concentration of banking services into the Schedule I banks, which commanded 86 per cent of total domestic bank sector assets (and most of this 86 per cent is under the control of the Big 5 banks).[33] This concentration had resulted in limited competition, which made banks less efficient and raised prices for users of banking services, making the Canadian finance sector, and all companies that used it, less competitive relative to the rest of the world.

In most industries, underperforming firms were threatened by new, more innovative and efficient competitors. However, in 1997, the record of new entry in the Canadian banking sector was very poor—there had only been two new Schedule I banks since 1987, compared with 207 new banks in the U.S.[34] In many smaller countries, foreign competition was used to maintain competition and innovation in sectors that were underdeveloped. However, regulations in Canada had prevented foreign competitors from entering the market as full-fledged equals of the Canadian banks.

Canadian Regulatory Perspectives

Until 1980, foreign competitors were strictly forbidden from entering Canada. After 1980, foreign banks were allowed in, provided they met certain criteria. The number of foreign banks in Canada peaked in 1987 at 59, but had declined to only 42 in 1999.[35] These foreign competitors, while not a threat to the big banks in terms of deposit-taking or wealth management, were extremely important for business customers as these competitors tended to target specific clients (Wells Fargo) or communities (Hongkong Bank of Canada).[36]

New legislation advanced by the Department of Finance, passed in June 1999, allowed foreign banks to operate branches in Canada without incorporation. However, there was still no allowance for providing banking services without a branch network. The laws in this regard were developed at a time when it was not possible to conduct banking without a physical presence. As a result, the regulations were not only confusing, but penalized foreign banks. A prominent example was Wells Fargo bank, which sought to use its marketing expertise to extend credit to Canadian small businesses, an underserviced market according to many critics of the Canadian big banks. The bank required no physical presence in Canada, and, therefore, was not entitled to incorporate in Canada.

In order to meet Canadian regulations where possible, Wells Fargo held discussions with the Canadian banking regulator, Office of the Superintendent of Financial Institutions (OSFI). The outcome of these discussions was that technically the Wells Fargo direct mail campaign did not qualify as "banking business," despite the fact that it would in fact be lending to small Canadian companies. As a result, Wells Fargo agreed to meet certain requirements recommended by OSFI. Wells Fargo would have to mail its materials from the U.S., locate its call centre outside Canada and arrange for cheques drawn on its correspondent Canadian bank to be mailed to the U.S. and trucked back to the Canadian bank. The end result was that Wells Fargo incurred extra costs and Canadians lost jobs from the mailing and call centre activities.

The dearth of new entrants into the banking sector was also the result of the dominance of the Canadian banks in terms of their extensive branch network (over 8,000 branches across Canada). In addition, Canadians were reluctant to try new competitors, especially unknown foreign banks.

While foreign competition had received attention from policymakers, branch closures had received significant attention from the general public. Combined with the need to cut costs in order to be more competitive internationally, pursuing customers by alternative channels such as electronic banking had created a redundancy in the 8,000 branches currently operating in Canada. Many of these branches were in rural areas with declining populations, which could be equally well-served with appropriate technologies. Unfortunately, the affected constituents were most often seniors or individuals with lower incomes—two cohorts that were unlikely to use the Internet and related e-banking technologies. The result had been well-publicized outcries over branch closures, which had reached the ears of politicians. Criticism of banks over branch closures had been exacerbated by concerns regarding bank service to Canadians with below-average incomes (a high-cost, low-margin clientele).

With respect to foreign entry, the McKay Report and Department of Finance report recommended that the criteria for foreign entry be made less stringent, particularly in regard to capital requirements. The implications of technology were far-reaching for regulators, for two primary reasons.

First, regulators had no way to prohibit foreign banks from accessing domestic customers when solicitation and transactions were conducted by electronic means such as the Internet. This, in turn, had important implications, especially for Canadians who put their savings in potentially unhealthy foreign banks, as they might not have legal recourse in Canadian courts to retrieve their money in case of a bank closure. Electronic financial transactions could also facilitate money laundering and tax evasion, making it almost impossible for governments to trace profits flowing across the Internet.

Second, the fact that Canadian customers could deal with U.S. or other foreign financial firms meant that the Bank of Canada might lose some control over monetary policy.[37] For example, though it could restrict credit in the

domestic marketplace (either through interest rate hikes or moral suasion with the big banks who conducted most of the lending), if Canadian borrowers could easily and cheaply access credit abroad, how could the Bank of Canada control money supply or interest rates domestically?

A final concern with respect to electronic banking, insurance and investment services was how to regulate the workers in those sectors. Currently, all levels of Canadian government had rules governing investment dealers, mutual fund sales staff and insurance brokers/sellers.[38] The laws governing these individuals were not designed with e-commerce in mind such that selling these items over the Internet had created a policy vacuum. While all laws applied to e-commerce, they were likely unenforceable.

In this context, ING decided to enter the Canadian banking business on the basis of electronic banking as opposed to the expense of setting up a physical branch network. It decided to offer simple financial products, such as no-fee savings accounts, guaranteed investment certificates and registered retirement savings plans that offered a higher interest rate than rival banks, and to offer personal loans of up to $50,000 at lower interest rates than rival banks.

ING Groep NV, one of the largest financial services organization in the world, is aggressively positioning its Canadian business to take advantage of consumers' willingness to make bank deposits and buy insurance over toll-free telephone lines. The company has built the second-largest property and casualty insurance group in Canada with $1.3 billion in annul premiums. ING's assets in Canada total $4 billion. With the deep financial pockets of its Dutch parent available, the Canadian operations have staying power, marketing muscle and ambition. To date, ING has acquired six companies, established an electronic bank, become a major seller of life insurance, bought a mutual fund dealer and developed a network of about 7,500 brokers to sell the company's products. "We are diversifying beyond core insurance and developing a number of different distribution systems to deliver an array of financial services and products to the consumer," said Yves Brouillette, president of ING Canada Inc., a Montreal-based holding company for the insurance operations. "The goal is to be a major integrated financial services player," he said. [39]

The very difficult Canadian regulatory environment posed a variety of obstacles for ING's electronic banking experiment. Furthermore, the relatively very large Canadian banks quickly responded with their own electronic banking programs, creating intense competition. ING faced the problem of how to evaluate this experiment and whether to extend the concept globally. At the same time, ING faced the question of how best to integrate its various financial services, particularly the insurance business, into the electronic banking structure.

CHALLENGES IN THE TWENTY-FIRST CENTURY ENVIRONMENT OF BUSINESS

For the financial services industry, the twenty-first century would be very different from the twentieth century. Several basic forces were already seriously impacting this sector in the 1990s. For ING, an analysis of these forces would be a crucial step in developing an appropriate strategy.

NOTES

1. This case has been written on the basis of published sources only. Consequently, the interpretation and perspectives presented in this case are not necessarily those of The ING Group or any of its employees.

2. Karen Iley, *Reuters,* Amsterdam, February 11, 1999.

3. Karen Iley, *Reuters,* Amsterdam, February 9, 1999.

4. *Reuters,* Amsterdam, January 11, 1999.

5. "Germany's Protective Wings," *The Economist,* May 22, 1999, 81.

6. "The Euro: Remaking Europe's Financial Markets," *Mondaq Business Reading,* Credit Suisse First Boston, July 1, 1998.

7. Ibid.

8. British Management Data Foundation, "The International Role of the Euro," Helmut Schieber Deutsche Bundesbank, Frankfurt, September 21, 1998: http://www.euro-know.org/speeches/Paperschieber1.html

9. "Border Control (Survey 11 of 12)," *The Economist,* U.S. ed., May 9, 1998.

10. "Financial Services: First Hearing on the Future 'Framework for Action,'" *European Report,* September 16, 1998.

11. "German Banks under Fire," *The Economist,* May 22, 1999, 20.

12. http://europa.eu.int/euro/html/page-dossier5.html?dossier=100&lang=5&page=2&nav=5, May 13, 1999.

13. "One Last Push from the Trenches," *Euromoney,* May 1999, 36, 41.

14. ING DIRECT Corporate Profile, August 1998, 27.

15. David Smith, *Will Europe Work?* http://www.euro.euro-know.org/articles/wew.html, July 18, 1999.

16. Patrick Minford, *Editor's Guide,* 1999: http://www.euro-know.org/biblio.html (annual guide)

17. "UK: EMU, Bank Strategy, Find Your Niche and Stick to It," *Reuters,* 10/08/98.

18. Ibid.

19. "One Last Push from the Trenches," *Euromoney,* May 1999, 41.

20. Professor Dr Dr h.c. Hans Tietmeyer, president of the Deutsche Bundesbank, "Financial and Monetary Integration: Benefits, Opportunities and Pitfalls," the 1998 Mais Lecture delivered at the City University Business School in London on May 18, 1998: http://www.euro-know.org/speeches/text1.html

21. ING DIRECT Corporate Profile, August 1998, 24.

22. "A Survey of Banking in Emerging Markets," *The Economist,* April 12, 1997, pp. 5, 26.

23. Ibid., p. 7.

24. Country Report, Russia, *EIU,* 1998.

25. "One Last Push from the Trenches," *Euromoney,* May 1999, 41.

26. "Electronic Commerce and the Role of the WTO," *World Trade Organization,* 1999, 29–30.

27. "Change, Challenge Opportunity: Report of the Task Force on the Future of the Canadian Financial Services Sector," September 1998, 27. Hereafter referred to as the McKay Report

28. "Survey of International Banking," *The Economist,* April 17, 1999, 32.

29. "Canadian Financial Institutions and Their Adoption of New Technologies," Ernst & Young, research paper prepared for the *Task Force on the Future of the Canadian Financial Services Sector,* 1998, 5.

30. See McKay Report, 28.

31. "The Changing Landscape for Canadian Financial Services: New Forces, New Competitors, New Choices," *McKinsey & Co.,* 1998, pp. 11–12.

32. Ibid., p. 54.

33. Ibid., p. 13.

34. "Reforming Canada's Financial Services Sector: A Framework for the Future," *Department of Finance,* 1999, chap. 3, p. 1.

35. "Reforming Canada's Financial Services Sector: A Framework for the Future," *Department of Finance,* 1999, chap. 3, p. 12.

36. "The Changing Landscape for Canadian Financial Services: New Forces, New Competitors, New Choices," *McKinsey & Co.,* 1998, 13.

37. See "Electronic Commerce and the Role of the WTO," *World Trade Organization,* 1998, 42.

38. See *McKay Report,* chap. 7, and "Canadian Financial Institutions and Their Adoption of New Technologies," Ernst & Young, research paper prepared for the Task Force on the Future of the Canadian Financial Services Sector, 1998, 28–30 for a discussion regarding financial intermediaries and licensing.

39. Dennis Slocum, "Canada: Aggressive ING Rings Up Growing Sales in Canada—Phone Is Key to Dutch Financial Giant's Strategy," *Globe and Mail,* 02/12/97.

3

MANAGING WITHIN ALTERNATIVE GOVERNMENT STRUCTURES

The political environment of business is shaped by government structures—from parliamentary and presidential systems to dictatorships—and with differing allocations of responsibility between national and provincial/state governments. For each government structure, the lobbying process may be unique, and so may the role and importance of business-government relations. The paradigm on which much of the public choice literature is based is the U.S. system, with the opportunity for individuals in Congress to initiate legislation and to vote independently, yet most of the world does not share this political paradigm (Chrystal & Pennant-Rea, 2000; McNutt, 2002; Pardo & Schneider, 1996; Peacock, 1992). Consequently, international businesses have to adjust their management structure and procedures to deal most effectively with whatever government structure exists in each country. Furthermore, the concept of political risk becomes more complex when opposing parties advocate very different policy positions and where significant policy changes will accompany a change in leadership—as opposed to systems such as those in the United States and Western Europe where centrist parties may not threaten such abrupt changes (Ougaard, 2004).

Throughout the world, governments attempt to alter private-sector decisions in the interests of what they perceive to be the public good. Such intervention may rest on a belief that "market failures" prevent an optimal set of outcomes (Acocella, 1998; Mitchell, 1994; Weimer, 1999). However, in recent years, countries throughout the world have implemented liberalization reforms that reduce the degree of government intervention to stimulate economic growth. China and India illustrate the challenges in liberalization reforms. China's state-owned enterprises (SOEs) have been poorly managed (O'Leary, 1998), the pension system is largely unfunded, and corruption is widespread. Chinese banks have accumulated huge political loans to state-owned enterprises (Kynge, 1999, 2002; Loong, 2000), and the development of foreign-owned banks and alternative financial instruments could result in a reduction in deposits at Chinese banks. Hence, the liberalization of the Chinese financial sector, combined with the growth of the stock exchange and the expansion of foreign banks, may be creating new risks for the country's domestic financial sector. Furthermore, World Trade Organization (WTO) membership may exacerbate the financial difficulties of the SOEs as they will face better quality imports and competition from the foreign-owned corporations that are investing in China. China's leaders have expressed the view that unprofitable SOEs should be allowed to go bankrupt if their debts exceed assets. However, the process for bankruptcy is not clear. Furthermore, the threat of massive unemployment brings with it the risk of social unrest, as well as the prospect of authoritarian crackdowns as a political response. Some commentators have expressed the view that a successful economic transition will require political reform with a shift toward democracy, free speech and investigative journalism, and modern commercial laws with an independent judiciary (Kynge, 2002). China's economic liberalization began in 1978 with the creation of "special economic zones" in coastal cities where foreign corporations could operate separate from the administrative structure of central planning. The success of this experiment meant that this economic progress contrasted starkly with the ongoing rural stagnation of the rest of the country, presenting serious problems in regard to the economic development of the nation as a whole and demonstrating the limitations of national macroeconomic policies.

In India, liberalization began in 1991 in reaction to a foreign exchange crisis, when the IMF urged the government of India to privatize and deregulate to stimulate economic growth. The IMF expected that the removal of foreign ownership restrictions would bring new technologies as well as managerial expertise, whereas a reduction of import barriers would increase domestic competition, stimulating efficiency and innovation. However, the path of the "New Industrial Policy" of 1991 has not been smooth, and some doubt whether substantial progress will be made anytime soon (Conklin & Lecraw, 1997). State governments still exert considerable regulatory power, quite apart from the national government, and the pervasive bureaucracy carries with it the possibility of corruption in attaining regulatory approvals. With this discussion, students will compare China and India, evaluating liberalization reforms as a prerequisite for macroeconomic success.

Government policies that traditionally were regarded as "domestic" have now become of international relevance, as they distort price ratios and hence trade patterns, or even act as trade barriers. Consequently, in recent years, trade negotiations to reduce tariffs have been broadened to include a wide variety of government programs and policies that act as nontariff barriers and that have restricted foreign investment (Adamantopoulos, 1997; Hufbauer & Schott, 1993; Krueger, 1998). As a result, business decisions that once could be made on the basis of a domestic industry structure are increasingly rare. Even businesses that focus solely on the local market are forced to deal with competitive threats against which tariff and nontariff barriers once protected them. Trade agreements lead some governments to alter traditional strategies for supporting "strategic" industries and to consider an array of alternative policies and programs they can use to favor their domestic firms. A major cause of trade disputes has to do with these domestic preferences, such as subsidies, and the "unfair competition" that results.

Many elements in a nation's political environment of business deserve consideration in light of these new international realities. International trade in services may be hampered by travel and immigration restrictions and the need to establish local offices. With the growth of high-tech businesses and brand-name merchandise, the protection of intellectual property has become increasingly important for international business. Other issues include dumping and competition policy, environmental and labor standards, harmonization of taxation, and differing technical standards. For many countries, the preservation of culture justifies barriers to the inflow of foreign-produced entertainment and media content. International agreements are signed by national governments, and so provincial, state, and local governments may not be bound by these agreements. At the same time, regional agreements have been able to pursue trade and investment liberalization to a greater degree than the WTO—in the case of the European Union (EU), even so far as a single currency.

For businesses, the changing content of trade and investment agreements creates opportunities as well as challenges. Although international negotiations are aimed at creating a level playing field, businesses do not necessarily want "a level playing field"—indeed, individual firms are constantly seeking ways to obtain an advantage out of the legislative and regulatory frameworks that governments create. These cases seek to enhance understanding of what government does and how it does it, so that participants can be informed players in this complex arena.

MEKONG CORPORATION AND THE VIET NAM MOTOR VEHICLE INDUSTRY

Viet Nam became a focus of business attention in Southeast Asia as the government began to reduce some of its restrictions with respect to trade and foreign investment. However, the government was reluctant to open its markets completely to free trade. This case examines issues of doing business in newly emerging markets and the liberalization challenges that must be managed by business and government.

THAI TELECOMS IN THE NEW ECONOMY: PRIVATIZATION & LIBERALIZATION

The economic crisis that had ravaged Thailand in 1997 was an impetus that started the country down the difficult road of liberalization, under an agreement with the IMF. The major issues involved in the transformation of the telecom industry from a state-run duopoly to a free market–based sector were daunting: the process for corporatization and the subsequent privatization of the state-owned telecom operators, the conversion of revenue-sharing agreements between private operators and the two state-run telecom agencies, the process of establishing a regulatory body to oversee privately owned firms, and the full liberalization of the sector by 2006, with the reduction—perhaps even elimination—of foreign ownership restrictions.

LUCENT IN INDIA

The government of India promised to institute economic reforms that would privatize government-owned telecom systems and that would give telecom firms much greater freedom from traditional government regulations. However, it was not clear whether—or to what degree—India's economic reforms would actually materialize, nor was it clear whether India would achieve macroeconomic stability.

CITIGROUP IN POST-WTO CHINA

China's entry into the WTO, at the end of 2001, brought promises that foreign financial institutions would be permitted to operate throughout China. In 1998, Citicorp and Travelers Group, Inc. had merged to create the new entity Citigroup, Inc. Travelers brought a vast array of financial services that added to Citibank's existing portfolio of consumer and commercial lending. Citigroup now had to determine the business prospects for each of its activities in the growing China market. Fears of social and economic dislocation might lead China to impose regulatory restrictions limiting the pace of foreign expansion. Economic growth might be impeded by the existing political structure, and reforms might not occur in the near term. A myriad of other challenges included human resource difficulties, e-commerce limitations, and regional disparities. The pace of privatization of state-owned enterprises and the societal preferences in regard to alternative insurance and investment products added to uncertainties.

POINT LISAS INDUSTRIAL ESTATE: TRINIDAD

Challenges included the uncertainty about government policies, particularly future pricing policies for oil and natural gas, and the possibility of obtaining financial concessions from the government. Environmental and societal issues loomed, and local citizen groups could react negatively toward the growth of the Point Lisas Industrial Estate (PLIE), with its implications for land prices and the nature of the economy. The focus of petrochemical businesses in Trinidad would inevitably be export, and various trade agreements determined the terms and conditions under which a Trinidad company could export to various potential customers. Also of importance would be projected changes in Trinidad's foreign exchange rate. Trinidad's natural gas reserves were relatively small compared with many other countries. Venezuela offered an attractive alternative location in regard to the availability and cost of oil and natural gas, and so the case compares the environment of business in Trinidad with that in Venezuela.

DELL'S DILEMMA IN BRAZIL: NEGOTIATING AT THE STATE LEVEL

Dell had concluded a site selection process in Brazil to determine where it would locate its manufacturing plant in that country, which would be its first manufacturing plant in Latin America. After a lengthy site selection process in the first half of 1998 involving five states in Brazil—São Paulo, Rio de Janeiro, Paraná, Minas Gerais, and Rio Grande do Sul—Dell decided to locate the plant in the state of Rio Grande do Sul, Brazil. Although a number of factors influenced Dell's decision, one of them was the generous incentives that Governor Antonio Britto of the relatively centrist Partido do Movimento Democratico Brasileiro (PMDB) had offered Dell. However, after Dell made the decision, a new governor, Olivio Dutra of the Partido dos Trabalhadores (PT, or Workers' Party), was elected in October 1998 and took office in January 1999. The PT was a socialist party. Having made an issue of what he considered to be overly generous incentives offered to transnational corporations during his campaign, Governor Dutra seemed likely to rescind the incentives that the Britto government had offered. Given the situation, Keith Maxwell, Dell's Senior Vice President for Worldwide Operations, had to make a recommendation to Michael Dell. The case presents three possible options for Dell: (a) leave Brazil entirely, (b) move the plant to another state within Brazil, or (c) try to renegotiate with Governor Dutra.

ENRON AND THE DABHOL POWER COMPANY

In September 2001, Houston-based Enron Corporation (Enron) was embroiled in a long-running dispute with various levels of government in India. In April 1995, Enron began construction of a $2.8 billion power plant in the state of Maharashtra. In August 1995, the Maharashtrian government announced that the project was canceled based on the recommendations of a committee set up by the government to review the project. After the contract was renegotiated, construction resumed, and Phase I was completed in 1999. In 2001, with Phase II of the project 95% complete, Enron announced that it would sell its Dabhol Power Company (DPC) stake because of payment disputes with its sole buyer, the Maharashtra State Electricity Board (MSEB), and the failure of the Indian central government to honor its counterguarantee. The case illustrates the difficulty of predicting and understanding local political conditions and coping with the threat of project cancellation or forced renegotiation. It also raises issues dealing with the appropriate rate of return for a large capital-intensive project in an uncertain political environment, corruption, and transfer payment equity. This is a rich case that can be the basis for discussion on various other issues, such as the usefulness of a local partner in dealing with political issues, how to establish a positive corporate reputation through public relations, the dangers of being accused of bribery, the visibility of infrastructure projects developed by foreign companies, and the nature of development projects and project finance.

BOMBARDIER VERSUS EMBRAER: CHARGES OF UNFAIR COMPETITION

In both Brazil and Canada, governments sought to stimulate high-tech industries to create high-paying jobs, but the mechanisms for this assistance differed. Government assistance could take a variety of forms, and it was difficult to quantify the extent of assistance. The WTO imposed limitations on subsidies, but the ultimate outcome in this trade dispute was uncertain.

MEKONG CORPORATION AND THE
VIET NAM MOTOR VEHICLE INDUSTRY

*Prepared by Huan Ngo under the
supervision of Professor David Conklin*

Version: (A) 2002-12-05

THE CHALLENGES OF 1996

Mekong was incorporated in 1991 as the first automobile and truck assembly company in Viet Nam. Mekong's manufacturing process involved the assembly of imported "Complete-Knock-Down" (CKD-2) units. Imports of automobiles and trucks in either knock-down or assembled units required a government license that stipulated the permitted number to be imported, and imports of assembled units also had to pay high import duties. Because of these protectionist policies, Mekong expected in 1991 that it would face only limited competition over the life of its 30-year license. Other manufacturers would have to obtain a license prior to building a plant, and Mekong believed that only a few additional production licenses would be issued. As a joint venture of Saeilo Machinery Japan Inc. (51 per cent), SeaYoung International Inc. of Korea (19 per cent), Viet Nam Engine and Agricultural Machinery of the Ministry of Industry (18 per cent), and Sakyno Co. of the People's Committee of Ho Chi Minh City (12 per cent), Mekong was well-positioned to play a prosperous leadership role in Viet Nam's motor vehicle industry.

However, with the liberalizing reforms of succeeding years and the 1993 elimination of the U.S. trade embargo, Mekong soon found itself in a completely new environment. Viet Nam was shifting from a "closed economy" to an increasingly "open economy." By 1996, many foreign-owned automobile companies were announcing plans to build plants in Viet Nam, and their proposed large-scale facilities might produce at lower cost than Mekong's low-volume assembly operations. The government's import quotas for "Semi-Knocked-Down" (SKD) and CKD units, as well as import quotas and tariffs for completely assembled units, would place a limit on Mekong's future production and sales volumes. Meanwhile, a huge expansion was predicted for motorbike production, which might turn out to be the preferred motor vehicle for the coming decade. Optimistic forecasts for sales of automobiles and trucks might not materialize. Mekong and its new competitors might find themselves in a position of oversupply, with continual downward pressure on prices.

By 1996, the government had decided that it could increase jobs in the motor vehicle industry by compelling the assembly corporations to source at least some of their components domestically. While this "localization program" might increase costs, the post-1994 tariffs of 200 per cent would protect assemblers from foreign competitors. The high tariffs did create a protected market place, but Mekong had little experience in the production of the parts and components that would be required to meet these new domestic content requirements. Meanwhile, many elements of the localization program were not clear, including the definition of what processes would qualify as local content. Furthermore, Viet Nam's 1995 entry into the ASEAN trade agreement raised the possibility that tariffs might be reduced in the future, on motor vehicle imports from other ASEAN countries, thereby exposing Mekong to new low-cost competition. Faced with these changes in its business environment, how was Mekong to reevaluate its corporate strategy?

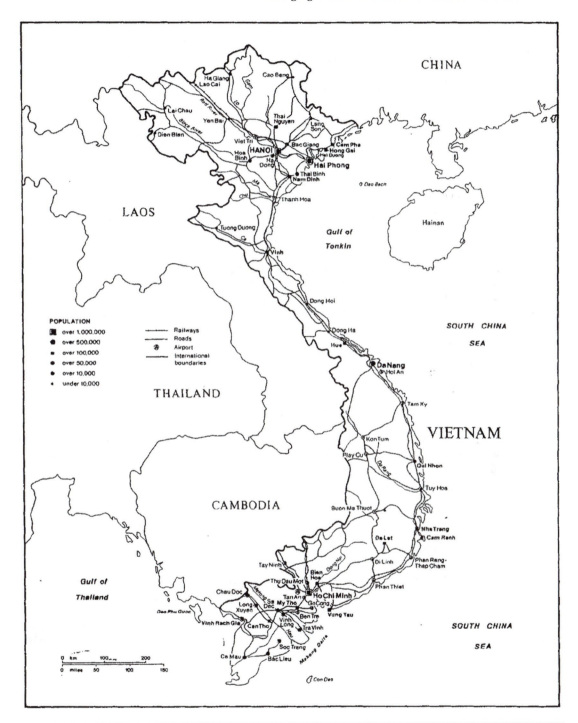

Figure 1   Map of Viet Nam

The Vietnamese Economy

Following their 1954 military victory over the French at Dien Bien Phu, and with the subsequent Geneva Accord, the Communist Party in Viet Nam assumed control of North Viet Nam's economy. Private ownership of business activities was prohibited, except for the small-scale retail and service sectors. Government ownership and operation involved central planning, with detailed directives sent from government offices to each enterprise. Each government department was given a set of related businesses to supervise. At the end of the war of liberation, and with the reunification of Viet Nam in 1975, this economic system was also imposed on the economy of South Viet Nam. The nation became a closed economy to a major degree, with relatively little international trade or investment. International economic relations were limited to other Communist nations.

However, this centrally planned economic system failed to produce the growth rates that were being achieved in other Asian countries that had freer markets. The persistence of low per capita incomes in contrast to rapid economic progress elsewhere led in the late 1980s to a reevaluation of Viet Nam's economic system. Extensive liberalization reforms throughout the Communist world provided a direct stimulus to this reevaluation. In 1986, the initial Vietnamese reforms began to be implemented, under the phrase "Doi Moi."

Compared with other Communist nations, however, Viet Nam's reforms occurred later in time, and they were more limited in nature. By 1996, privatization had not yet been implemented. Rather, the focus of debate had been the concept of "equitisation," under which certain enterprises would have the right to make their business decisions independently of the government officials. While still owned entirely by the government, these enterprises would have to survive without government financial assistance. It was hoped that this new management structure would reduce the financial losses being experienced by Viet Nam's businesses. It is true that by 1996 public discussion revolved around the possibility of sales of shares to the public, and particularly to the employees of each enterprise. However, the absence of a stock market and the non-convertibility of the "dong" meant that privatization would not be implemented quickly.

As part of the "Doi Moi" program, foreign investment was to be encouraged in those sectors where modern technology was essential to achieve low-cost production. From this perspective, the motor vehicle industry became a prime target in the government's attempts to modernize the economy. While Mekong was surprised by the sudden government approval of many investment proposals from its foreign competitors, nevertheless, the opening of the Vietnamese economy meant that multinational automobile corporations would inevitably study Viet Nam's market potential. The desire to be among the first to establish a market presence was a major motivating force, as the multinational corporations looked towards the future.

Viet Nam's congested cities offered little room for modern manufacturing plants, and so Mekong and others created their own industrial sites on vacant land near villages outside of the cities. The mid-1990s saw a proliferation of industrial parks built to facilitate the construction of new plants.[1] In June 1996, Viet Nam News reported that 17 industrial and export-processing zones had been created since 1991.

> More than 190 investors, including 160 from foreign countries, have invested in infrastructure construction in the industrial and export-processing zones. Total capital includes US$1.8 billion, accounting for more than eight per cent of Viet Nam's total foreign investment.[2]

By 1996, the government of Singapore had created an industrial park 20 kilometers north of Ho Chi Minh City, in Song Be province, and it was planning another near Ha Noi. Japanese investors were planning to create a similar zone next to Singapore's Song Be industrial zone. A Korean project, led by Daewoo, was also being planned for the Gia Lam District. Three infrastructure projects offered great promise for an influx of foreign manufacturers.

By 1996, a great deal of uncertainty existed about the path of future market liberalization reforms. Not all Vietnamese were satisfied with the rapid inflow of foreign investment. It seemed that existing businesses that remained outside the joint venture system would experience a sharp loss of sales and, accompanying this, severe financial difficulties. Local products were losing their popularity. It was not clear how the government would react to these impacts of market liberalization.

Apart from possible changes in the regulations governing ongoing operations, there were also other issues of concern. For foreign investors, the tax system involved special concessions for specific industries and even for individual corporations. Some tax rates might be reduced as a reward for achieving certain government objectives, and some government officials suggested that this approach might be used to support the auto parts localization program. In general, taxation involved an eight per cent tax on total revenue, as well as a tax of five per cent to 20 per cent on the repatriation of capital. Appendix 4 presents a summary of Viet Nam's tax system as of 1996. Political leaders were advocating extensive changes to this tax system. In an address to the National Assembly, Prime Minister Vo Van Kiet emphasized: "First of all, it should be affirmed that the need to reform the tax system has become more and more urgent."[3] The journal, Business Viet Nam, indicated that "as the overseas remittance involves not only profit but also tax-exempted bank interest, management fees, royalties . . . , law makers are considering either abolishing this tax or finding a more effective measure to collect it."[4] Meanwhile, it was generally reported that "value-added taxes [would] replace the current income tax."[5]

Because the Vietnamese currency, the dong, was not yet freely convertible, foreign investors could not be sure that they would be able to transfer future earnings out of Viet Nam. Since the foreign exchange rate itself was the result of complex government import regulations, the exchange rate was somewhat artificial. It would not be easy to predict its future movements. The complex system of import licenses and of production licenses could lead to great difficulties in purchasing necessary inputs and components. For the foreign investor, the Vietnamese economy remained a very challenging enigma.

From a political perspective, the whole country was governed by one political party, the Vietnamese Communist Party (VCP). All legislative matters originated from the VCP. Law enforcement was handled by government agencies whose top-ranked officers were also members of the VCP and other legislative bodies. Similarly, judges of all courthouses were VCP members who interpreted the laws according to the interests of the VCP. Prime Minister (Mr. Vo Van Kiet), the Party's Secretary General (Mr. Do Muoi), Head of State (Mr. Le Duc Anh), and top officials were elected from within the party. Regional representatives of the Party Congress were selected from key organizations and locales around the country. After many years of governing the country with tight control measures, severe punishments, and just-in-time flexibility, the political scene was stable with very little threat of civil unrest.

VIET NAM'S MOTOR VEHICLE MARKET

By the mid-1990s, many forecasts anticipated a huge increase in the number of passenger cars and commercial vehicles that would be sold in the Vietnamese market. These forecasts rested largely on an extrapolation of the phenomenal growth in sales over the 1989 to 1994 period. As Table 1 indicates, total sales grew from 300 vehicles in 1989 to more than 10,000 vehicles in 1994. Of the 1994 total, approximately half were imported, while half were assembled in Viet Nam.

A 1995 Economist Intelligence Unit Report presented extremely optimistic forecasts, largely based upon predictions by Mitsubishi. By the year 2000, it was expected that demand would rise to about 60,000 vehicles a year, and by the

	1989	1990	1991	1992	1993	1994
Sales (000 units)						
Passenger cars	0.3	0.3	0.3	1.0	1.3	2.3
Commercial vehicles	0.0	1.5	0.5	5.0	6.2	8.0
Total	0.3	1.8	0.8	6.0	7.5	10.3
Per cent change	n/a	500.0	−55.6	650.0	25.0	37.3
Assembly						
Passenger cars	0	0	0	0.1	0.5	0.9
Commercial vehicles	0	0	0	0.9	1.8	4.4
Total	0	0	0	1.0	2.3	5.3
Per cent change	0	0	0	100.0	130.0	130.0

Table 1[1] The Automobile Industry's Market and Output

1. International Motor Business 2nd quarter, 1995, 53.

year 2005, over 80,000 vehicles. Based upon these forecasts, the stock of registered vehicles would reach 652,000 in the year 2005. The Economist Intelligence Unit Report pointed out that even with these huge increases in demand, Viet Nam's stock of motor vehicles would be far below the level found in other comparable countries. By 1991, for example, there were about 2.5 million registered vehicles in the city of Bangkok, Thailand.[6]

In the early 1990s, the Vietnamese economy enjoyed a rapid growth rate, and many observers predicted that Viet Nam would become the next country to experience the "Asian miracle." Many expected that Viet Nam would be able to follow the successful footsteps of Asia's "four tigers"— Hong Kong, Singapore, South Korea, and Taiwan. With rising per capita incomes, the relatively large Vietnamese population of 74 million people should create a huge new market for cars and trucks.

A major part of the Vietnamese economy remained underground and not reported through income taxes or other economic measures. This part of the economy, however, was the major source of income for many Vietnamese families. With such "irregular" incomes as well as an average income of US$50 per month, their "Honda Dream" (a motorbike) became a reality with total monthly income adding up to US$150–US$200 or even higher for some. Given the 1996s' price of a "Honda Dream" at US$2,500, it was becoming possible for the emerging upper middle class Vietnamese to buy a car at US$10,000–US$30,000 instead of buying four or more "Honda Dreams" for the family.

On the other hand, some observers were more pessimistic. The level of Viet Nam's GDP was still extremely low, less than $16 billion in 1995. A 1995 article in International Motor Business pointed to several factors that could restrain demand.

The enthusiasm that has been generated over the possibilities in Viet Nam has to be tempered, however. Viet Nam's GDP is only a fraction of that of Bangladesh, and its GDP per head, at only $181 in 1993, is less than half that of Pakistan and a tiny fraction of the level in bankrupt North Korea. The rate of inflation, although under better control now, was nearly 70 per cent in 1991. External debt is

	1989	*1990*	*1991*	*1992*	*1993*	*1994*	*1995*
GDP (VND at current price, trn)	28.1	41.7	76.7	110.5	136.6	170.3*	210.2#
GDP ($ billion)	7.0	8.0	8.2	9.9	12.8	13.5	19.1
GDP real growth (%)	7.5	5.1	6.0	8.7	8.1	8.8*	9.5#
GDP per head ($)	109	121	120	143	181	187	257
Population (million)	64.4	66.2	67.8	69.3	70.9	72.1	74#
Population growth	n/a	2.80	2.42	2.21	2.31	1.69	2.08
Inflation (%)	34.7	67.5	67.6	17.5	5.2	14.4*	12.7#
Exchange rate (VND:$1)	4,000	5,200	9,390	11,181	10,641	10,900#	11,000#
Deficit (per cent of GDP)*		5.8	1.5	1.7	4.8	1.7	
Employed labor force (000)*		28,941	30,294	30,974	31,819	32,716	
Net domestic assets (D billions)*		9,701	13,595	16,549	26,678	31,880	
Liabilities (D billions)*		13,787	22,525	31,935	37,002	44,230	
Trade balance ($ millions)*		−41	−63	−60	−665	−900	
Current-account balance ($ millions)*		−259	−132	−8	−869	−1,510#	−1,930#
Capital-account balance ($ millions)*		122	−60	271	−146	300	
Total external debt ($ millions)*		19,373	22,111	22,280	23,688	24,224	
Official development assistance ($ millions)*		120.0	189.8	238.6	579.6	258.7	

Table 2[1]   Viet Nam: Key Economic Statistics 1989–1995

1. International Motor Business, 2nd quarter, 1995, 51.

*EIU Country Profile, 1995–1996, Reference Tables.
#EIU Country Report, 2nd quarter 1996, p. 3.

more than $120 per head and rising. The memories of the civil and U.S. wars are still fresh, and fresher still, next door, in Cambodia. Even China seems more liberal and certainly more advanced economically. Skilled labor is in short supply, the government faces serious long-term financing problems and the infrastructure is woefully inadequate.[7]

Smuggling seemed to be common given the high import duties, and this could limit the demand for locally produced vehicles. Important

factors in predicting the demand for motor vehicles were the extent and quality of the road system. Even in 1996, it was not possible to drive easily between Ha Noi and Ho Chi Minh City. At the edges of the cities, most paved roads became traditional earth pathways. Even within the city, the roads were generally in extremely poor condition. Without massive investment in the road systems, prospective vehicle owners would be limited in where they could drive. Furthermore,

	Viet Nam	Indonesia	Philippines	Thailand	China	Japan
GDP ($ billions)	15.6	174.6	64.7	141.1	548.3	4,591.0
GDP per head ($)	215	904	964	2,373	459	36,722
Consumer price inflation (%)	14.4	9.6	7.2	5.4	21.7	0.7
Current account balance ($ billions)	−1.0	−2.8	−3.0	−8.5	6.5	129.1
Exports of goods ($ billions)	3.6	40.2	13.4	43.9	102.6	384.2
Imports of goods ($ billions)	4.5	32.3	21.2	48.3	95.3	238.2
Foreign trade (per cent of GDP)	51.9	41.5	53.5	65.3	36.1	13.6

Table 3   Comparative Economic Indicators 1994

Sources: National sources, EIU.

	1991	1992	1993	1994	1995
Viet Nam's CPI (%) @	67.5	17.5	5.2	14.4	12.7
Japan's CPI (%) #	3.3	1.6	1.3	0.7	−0.1
France's CPI (%)*	3.2	2.4	2.1	1.7	1.7
Viet Nam's FX (D:$) @	9,390	11,181	10,641	10,900	11,000
Japan's FX (Y:$) #	134.7	126.7	111.2	102.2	94.1
France's FX (FFr:$)*	5.64	5.29	5.66	5.55	4.99

Table 4   Consumer Price Inflation and Exchange Rate for Viet Nam's Major Trading Partners

@ EIU Country Report, Vietnam, 2nd quarter 1996.
# EIU Country Report, Japan, 2nd quarter 1996.
*EIU Country Report, France, 2nd quarter 1996.

the cities had been built without considering motor vehicles, and consequently, there were few places to park. The narrow city streets and the very small space devoted to each building meant that vehicle owners might not be able to park at their residences. Few downtown parking lots had been built. A 1996 article on the parking shortage estimated that Ha Noi had 60,000 square metres of acreage devoted to parking lots while the city already needed 1.4 million square metres.[8] Projected increases in motor vehicle sales would add to this congestion.

Another factor that might limit demand was that many Vietnamese were concerned about the threat to personal safety if a huge increase in automobile ownership were permitted, given the poor condition of the narrow city streets, and the hundreds of thousands of bicycles and motorbikes that clogged the roadways. Many were also concerned about the air pollution that would accompany the greater use of motor vehicles. These social pressures might force the government to maintain a low limit on the number of vehicles that could be imported or assembled. All these factors cast doubt on the optimistic forecasts for motor vehicle demand.

Also of importance could be the growth of motorbike sales as a substitute for automobiles and trucks. The motorbike seemed to be much more appropriate in the context of Viet Nam's narrow streets, shortage of parking, low income, and poor road quality. Some forecasts suggested that the demand for new motorbikes would rise to 600,000 annually by the year 2000. In response to these forecasts, several foreign companies were planning to build huge new plants. In 1994, the Ching Fong Group began construction of two motorcycle assembly plants with a total capacity of 500,000 units per year. In 1995, Honda signed a joint venture contract to build and sell motorbikes, with production to begin in 1997. Honda expected to produce 200,000 motorcycles in 1997, with production climbing to 450,000 a year by 2005. For many Vietnamese, a personal dream was someday to buy a "Honda Dream." To some degree, the growth in motorcycle sales might reduce the forecasted demand for automobiles and trucks. However, Mekong's management regarded these as two distinct markets, with the future demand for automobiles and trucks being independent of the demand for motorcycles.

THE THREAT OF NEW ENTRANTS

Prior to 1995, the only automobile and truck assemblers in Viet Nam were Mekong Corporation and Viet Nam Motors Corporation. In 1995, both Mitsubishi and Daewoo also began domestic assembly of CKD units. These two new entrants brought large-scale production, modern technology, and brand recognition. Furthermore,

1995 saw a flood of other foreign corporations seeking to gain approval for the construction of manufacturing capacity in Viet Nam. Some of these investment plans were reported in the July 17, 1995 issue of Automotive News:

> Lured by the promise of robust economic growth following the normalization of relations between Viet Nam and the United States, the world's biggest automakers are racing to set up shop here. Ford Motor Co., Chrysler Corp., Toyota Motor Corp. and France's PSA/Peugeot-Citroen SA are among the companies investing or applying to invest a total of more than $650 million in assembly plants here. Mercedes-Benz AG, Daihatsu Motor Co. Ltd., and Suzuki Motor Co. Ltd. received project licenses in April. Four additional joint ventures are assembling Mazda's, BMW's and other vehicles from imported kits. If all the proposed projects are built, 11 joint ventures will be assembling more than 120,000 cars, trucks and buses each year by 2007.[9]

By 1996, additional investment proposals had been approved, bringing the potential total number of assembly firms to 12, with the threat of a substantial oversupply of motor vehicles, especially if production were geared solely towards the Viet Nam market. A June 1996 International Herald Tribune article pointed to the difficulties that this kind of situation had created in many Asian countries:

> Most Asian countries are trying to build up their own automobile industries and many are requiring local manufacturing by foreign car makers. As a result, the factories in Asia are often small, economies of scale tend to be limited and profits are usually low—and the possibility of oversupply is high. . . . Chrysler is shying away from an earlier plan to assemble vehicles in Viet Nam, because a dozen companies will be getting permission to serve a market of only 10,000 to 30,000 vehicles a year. "How do you go and produce 500 or 1,000 or 1,500 units?" asked Denis Root, General Manager of Asia-Pacific operations for Chrysler.

Faced with this problem of many small country markets, several of the major international automobile firms were studying the possibility of designing a unique "Asia car." Such a model would be geared to the special needs of people in Asia. A group of components could be built in each country throughout the region. This would offer employment opportunities in each Asian country. Each production site would achieve low-cost economies of scale since each plant would be manufacturing a small number of components for the entire Asian market. Each multinational assembly firm could plan its integrated Asian production on the basis of free trade among ASEAN members. The International Herald Tribune article explained:

> So far, most companies sell existing models to Asia. But some, like Honda, are trying to gain an edge by designing a car tailored to the region's social habits and geographic traits—a car cheap enough for $3000-a-year salaries, roomy enough for families with several kids, sturdy enough for rocky mountain roads, practical enough to eliminate such unnecessary features as heaters and sleek enough to look as if it belongs in a suburban American driveway. . . . "With the Asia cars, you have first-time buyers, and you know what that means" about building brand loyalty, said Michael Dunne, President of Automotive Resources Asia, a Bangkok-based consulting and market-research firm.[10]

GOVERNMENT MOTOR VEHICLE POLICIES IN TRANSITION

For many years, all Vietnamese businesses with more than a few employees were owned and operated by the government. While liberalization reforms had been implemented by 1996, nevertheless, even foreign-controlled corporations were still subject to many regulations that limited their investment and production decisions. The license decisions discussed above were perhaps the most important of these restrictions. Import licenses were not allocated on an annual basis. Rather, each corporation received a license for a certain number of imports, often 500 units, and then it had to reapply for more when this quota had been achieved. Consequently, continual dialogue with government officials was

necessary. Furthermore, only the Central Bank was permitted to exchange the dong for hard currencies. As a result, corporations had to obtain both an import quota license and also gain Central Bank approval for the currency exchange. This dual set of restrictions greatly complicated the production planning. What was particularly significant was the way that government policies had been changing dramatically in this regard. In a June 1996 interview, Mr. Huynh Ngoc An, Vice Chairman of Mekong, emphasized the difficulties that this situation had created for his company:

> When we got our assembly license, the government promised that they would keep the number of licenses to a total of four. All of the sudden, there are 12 licenses to assemble automobiles in Viet Nam. What can I say? Changes in the investing environment in addition to changes in bilateral diplomatic relationships cause significant shifts in government policies regarding the auto industry. When Viet Nam had few diplomatic relationships, four assembly licenses were an absolute. As soon as freer trade policies were implemented and the U.S. trade embargo lifted, the big corporations created tremendous pressures on the government to issue licenses. For example, Toyota got its license so easily that our first mover advantage in Viet Nam was useless. Then Ford and Chrysler proposed to come in. Then Chancellor Helmut Kohl visited Viet Nam, then Prime Minister Do Muoi visited Korea and met Hyundai. Who could refuse those big guys? This involves political and national policies at the top level. The government may be exchanging a license for something else that we don't know about. It's all situational. We had no ability to influence those decisions.

In order to obtain a license, a foreign corporation had to present an investment proposal to the government. Traditionally, the government claimed ownership of all land in Viet Nam, which it held on behalf of the people of Viet Nam. Generally, the government provided land to the foreign corporation on a leasehold basis in return for a percentage ownership in a joint venture company. For the 12 automobile assembly licenses, government ownership was about 30 per cent of each joint venture company. During the first few years of the reform period, the government remained a "silent partner," leaving the day-to-day decisions in the hands of management, who were generally appointed by the foreign owners. However, this corporate structure left considerable uncertainties about the rights of foreign owners to make future strategic decisions. In particular, some government officials expressed the view that government ownership in joint ventures should be increased towards 50 per cent in order for Viet Nam to play a greater role within each joint venture.

Beginning in 1995, the government adopted new policies to stimulate job creation within the Vietnamese motor vehicle industry. It prohibited the import of SKDs and allowed only CKDs to be imported, thereby compelling the domestic assemblers to do more work locally. It required that paint applications be done domestically, a procedure that involved a great deal of investment in paint facilities as well as the hiring of more local labor. It also introduced specific domestic content requirements, referred to as the "localization program." In an analysis of this program, the Viet Nam Economic Times emphasized that these requirements posed great difficulties for Viet Nam's motor vehicle industry:

Localization is the issue that will make or break auto manufacture in Viet Nam. Companies licensed to assemble and eventually manufacture here must localize five per cent of their components within five years, and increase that figure by five per cent per year until it reaches 30 per cent localized components after 10 years of assembly. Vice Minister Chuan says the government hopes its policies will induce components manufacturers to follow automakers to Viet Nam.

"Localization goals are realistic, in theory," says Ha Noi-based consultant James Rockwell, who has advised on the industry for American automakers. "But you are only going to get localization when the market makes localization possible." VMC, for instance, has entered its fifth year of production. "We are working on it," says Chongbian about meeting the localization deadline, but he's not sure it's going to be possible. "Localization is the toughest question to be faced in this industry," he says.

"Unfortunately, localization doesn't happen that quickly," says Rockwell. "You won't be able to force the auto industry to use local parts just by enforcing a law."

While automakers can use their pull, it's going to take more than the clout of a Mercedes or Toyota to lure components manufacturers to Viet Nam: tax holidays, land grants, infrastructure development. With such incentives in 40 other industry-hungry countries around the world, Rockwell explains, Viet Nam will remain low on the priority list for years.[11]

In June 1996, the vice minister of Industry, Le Huy Con, was asked about these changes in government policies. He indicated uncertainty about how the localization would be achieved, but he emphasized its importance:

We do not encourage foreign automobile factories currently to carry out business or investment in our country to assemble automobiles in CKD form. . . . The question is how to implement the program of localization. This depends very much on the foreign partners in auto assembly joint ventures.[12]

Faced with these rapid and significant changes in government policies, Mekong's Vice Chairman expressed his concerns in 1996 about the uncertain political environment:

Until this minute, nobody can be sure of anything about the race in the Vietnamese automobile industry, including global investors such as Toyota or Chrysler. We can't tell what will happen in 10 or 20 years from now. There is not enough information to do so. This is partly due to constant changes in the law, taxes, import/export regulations. There is no clear government policy. Even as local Vietnamese, we do not know what is going on with government policies. We can guess, of course, about what the government will do and can even get forecasts as well as long-term plans from the ministries, but nobody knows for sure.

THE POLICIES OF OTHER ASEAN NATIONS

Viet Nam was not alone in its attempt to create more jobs in the automobile sector. In 1985,

Malaysia instituted tax and tariff policies that enabled Mitsubishi to build a low-cost automobile plant that used parts manufactured in Malaysia. In 1995, this joint venture produced 180,000 cars and was able to export 30,000 of these. In 1996, Indonesia announced a similar package of tariffs and tax policies to encourage domestic production of automobile components. A joint venture between Korea's KIA Motors and a son of President Suharto was expected to take advantage of these provisions. Special tax concessions depended upon the joint venture achieving the goal of 60 per cent local content by the year 2000. Indonesia's Minister for Investment, Sanyoto Sastrowardoyo, was quoted as saying, "We would like to build our own auto industry in the real sense, not just turn screwdrivers for someone else."[13]

In May 1996, General Motors announced that it had chosen Thailand as the site of its first Southeast Asian plant. Donald Sullivan, President of GM's Asian and Pacific Operations, explained the preference for Thailand: "In the final analysis, Thailand was our preferred location because of the strength of the domestic vehicle market, proven infrastructure, and well-established supplier base."[14]

In analyzing GM's decision, the Far Eastern Economic Review emphasized that "more than 570,000 cars and trucks were sold in Thailand in 1995. By 2000, that figure is expected to surpass 900,000. The large sales volumes, combined with government regulations requiring assemblers to buy components locally, has also helped to create a strong base of local auto parts suppliers."[15]

In order to assist GM in the integration of its components production in the various countries throughout Southeast Asia, the government of Thailand agreed with GM's request to drop Thailand's local-content requirement for cars sold in the country. GM's plant was scheduled to produce 100,000 to 150,000 cars annually, with 80 per cent of these to be exported, largely to other Asian countries. Meanwhile, GM responded to Indonesia's May 1996 imposition of a 60 per cent local content requirement by publicly stating that it would not invest further in Indonesia under these conditions.

Viet Nam's localization program was motivated by the same concerns and objectives that had been prevalent in other countries like Malaysia, Indonesia, and Thailand. Whether this localization program could succeed in Viet Nam—with its extremely low income, poor road infrastructure, and other adverse factors—remained to be seen. Furthermore, the experience of Thailand with GM's 1996 plant location decision raised an interesting question about different stages of economic growth. Might a domestic-content requirement be necessary in a country's initial attempts to create an auto parts sector, but perhaps not be necessary at a later stage, when many components suppliers had been created? If so, was it realistic to assume that all ASEAN countries, with their varying stages of development, could implement complete free trade within the foreseeable future? Should Viet Nam and its trade partners accept the reality that Viet Nam's localization program had to be an exception in any free trade agreement? Viet Nam's government officials indicated that this subject was an issue of current debate within ASEAN, where Thailand was advocating complete free trade, while others like Viet Nam felt the need to maintain localization programs.

For Mekong and its Vietnamese competitors, a major issue then was the future of trade relationships among the ASEAN group. If complete free trade were permitted, then Viet Nam's automobile industry would face an enormous new threat from the established manufacturers of the other ASEAN countries. Perhaps the localization program might become a strong non-tariff barrier that would protect Mekong from this threat.

MEKONG'S STRATEGY

In its initial 1991 corporate strategy, Mekong's vehicles were destined for the Vietnamese market only. However, by 1996, the company was also considering possibilities for exporting some of its assembled vehicles to other countries in the region, on the basis of cost advantages in Viet Nam and its proximity to large foreign populations. In 1995, Mekong assembled 1,210 vehicles, of which 1,100 were sold locally and the rest were exported to Japan, China, and Austria for market testing purposes. These figures were far below the estimated plant capacity of 15,000 in Ho Chi Minh City and 20,000 in Ha Noi. Although Mekong experienced losses in its first three years, Mr. Naoki Tatebe, Mekong's General Director, was optimistic about hoping for a profit in 1996.

Mekong's total number of employees, including both production and distribution, had reached 600 by 1996. The average monthly wage was $100. Mr. Tatebe, Mekong's General Director, emphasized the importance of skills training and management education throughout the organization. Employees were often sent to Korea, Japan, and Italy for training and education.

Mekong offered four different types of vehicles including passenger cars, vans, trucks, and large buses. Each type of vehicle had two or three models and two to four options. For all vehicles, the advertising brochures were in both English and Vietnamese in order to appeal to both foreigners and local Vietnamese. For its 4WD Mekong Star Sport Utilities, the company emphasized its Mercedes-Benz-designed engine, reliability, room, comfort, and fitness for all land surfaces. For Fiat's vehicles, Mekong emphasized Fiat's leadership in Europe and the company's worldwide operations as assurance of quality and reliability. Mekong located its two distribution centres in Ha Noi and Ho Chi Minh City, the heart and brain of Viet Nam's economy, with several showrooms in the various areas of these cities. In addition to its own showrooms, various sales agencies displayed Mekong's vehicles in their own showrooms and received an agent's fee for sales.

The first assembly line was established at Cuu Long plant just outside Ho Chi Minh City. It was initially used for the Mekong Star 4WD sport utilities. By 1996, the Cuu Long plant's single assembly line alternated between Mekong Star and Fiat Tempra. The company also established a second assembly plant at Co Loa, a small town outside of Ha Noi. This assembly line was used to assemble large buses, trucks, and vans, with different vehicle models going through the same production line.

From the date of incorporation in June 1991, Mekong's license to assemble and manufacture automobiles in Viet Nam was due to expire in the year 2021.

THE FUTURE OF MEKONG

For Mekong, production in Viet Nam began in May 1992 as an assembly operation based on imported CKDs. By 1996, Mekong's business had become a far more complex and challenging operation. The threat of new competition had suddenly increased. It was possible, of course, that the flood of new foreign competitors might not actually materialize. GM had given up its investment plans for Viet Nam, and Chrysler seemed hesitant to proceed. Some of the other foreign corporations were suggesting they would reduce the scale of their planned investments. It was also possible that the government's localization program might be modified. Perhaps Mekong, in cooperation with its competitors, might be able to convince the government to adopt a favorable definition of "local content."

In its May–June corporate newsletter, Fiat presented its plans for its new "world car," the "Palio." Mekong's management believed that someday it was possible that Mekong could be a member of Fiat's future integrated Asian production for the Palio. Fiat's worldwide success was a strong basis for optimism about Mekong's future. Confronted with the many new foreign car manufacturers, Mr. Tatebe, General Director of Mekong, pointed to Mekong's many competitive advantages: operating factories, skilled workers, a strong dealer network, and good relationships with Fiat, its suppliers, and the government, which still played such a major role in directing economic activities. From Mr. Tatebe as perspective, "We have no choice; we are here; we have to compete."

For Mekong, enormous uncertainty remained. This situation led Mr. Huynh Ngoc An to suggest that "this is a war zone where guerilla warfare is feasible. We can use our lessons from the Viet Nam war in our economic conduct. We can't fight a bigger enemy face-to-face. The big guys have not brought in their full forces yet. They are only sending in their part-time power from Indonesia, Thailand, and Malaysia to keep a foot in the door and for water-testing purposes. The deciding factors are yet to show up in Viet Nam." By 1996 it seemed that the time had come to reevaluate Mekong's corporate strategy.

NOTES

1. *Business Viet Nam,* May–June 1996, 20.
2. *Viet Nam News,* June, 1996.
3. *Viet Nam Law and Legal Forum,* April 1996, 6.
4. *Business Viet Nam,* May–June 1996, 17.
5. *Viet Nam News,* June 8, 1996, 9.
6. *EIU Country Report,* 1st quarter, 1995, 22.
7. *International Motor Business,* 2nd quarter, 1995, 49.
8. *Viet Nam News,* May 30, 1996, 4.
9. *Automotive News,* July 17, 1995.
10. *International Herald Tribune,* Friday, June 7, 1996, 10.
11. "Downshifting," *Viet Nam Economic Times,* May 1996, 30.
12. "Eyes on Industrialisation," *Viet Nam Economic Times,* June 1996, 16.
13. "Like Father, like Son," *Time International,* June 10, 1996, 40.
14. *Viet Nam News,* May 31, 1996, 9.
15. *Far Eastern Economic Review,* June 13, 1996, 60.

APPENDIX 1: NOTE ON THE ASSOCIATION OF SOUTH EAST ASIAN NATIONS (ASEAN)

Established in August 1967 in Bangkok by the "ASEAN Declaration," ASEAN originally had five members including Indonesia, Malaysia, the Philippines, Singapore, and Thailand. The formation of ASEAN was to resolve immediate conflicts among Malaysia, Indonesia, and the Philippines. ASEAN also addressed common concerns of the founding states "including a commitment to anti-communism and anxiety about the long-term prospects for the U.S. intervention in Indochina and the regional intentions of China, at that stage enmeshed in the Cultural Revolution."[1]

However, leaders of the founding nations expected ASEAN's role to encompass several other dimensions including political, economic, cultural, and social goals. To Prime Minister Prem of Thailand, "ASEAN . . . stands for peace and prosperity for Southeast Asia."[2] With the peace objective in mind and the fear of interference from outside powers such as the Soviet Union, China, and United States, the founding members of ASEAN signed the Kuala Lumpur Declaration (ZOPFAN Declaration, 1971) recognizing Southeast Asia as a Zone of Peace, Freedom, and Neutrality. After the victory of communist Powers in Indochina (Vietnam, Laos, and Cambodia) in 1975, the spread of communism throughout Southeast Asia, or the Domino Effect, was real and threatening. To consolidate ASEAN's collective strength and intentions against external Powers, the "Treaty of Amity and Co-operation in Southeast Asia" and the "Declaration of ASEAN Concord" were signed by the five founding countries in 1976. One year later, the "Agreement on ASEAN Preferential Trading Arrangements" (PTA, 1977) was established to promote economic activities within the block. In 1985, Brunei was admitted as the sixth member of the ASEAN group.

Over the years, "ASEAN's Treaty of Amity and Friendship is still open to all in Southeast Asia, including war-weary, indebted Vietnam—a prime candidate to realize that competition is futile, foolish, and costly."[3] Nevertheless, members of the ASEAN group have different perceptions of Vietnam:

Indonesia and Malaysia have dutifully stood by their partners to maintain the image of solidarity vis-à-vis Viet Nam despite their own policy preferences. But they see themselves as natural allies of Viet Nam against China and share Viet Nam's anxiety about China's entry into the region via the Cambodian war. On the other hand, Thailand and Singapore perceive a common cause with China against Vietnam. In effect, the ASEAN process cuts across two alliance camps. Not enough time has passed for all ASEAN states to judge the effects or sincerity of Viet Nam's new policies. Its "renovation" approach to development, allowing for more enterprise and foreign investment, signals better chances for accommodation to the pro-Vietnam in ASEAN. But those suspicious of Ha Noi fear that economic success will make Viet Nam a more formidable foe; this parallels the interpretation that the anti-China camp puts on Chinese modernization. Even what might be a clearer sign of good will, the Vietnamese withdrawal from Cambodia, was greeted with skepticism by hard-liners.[4]

As of 1996, ASEAN was composed of seven countries including Brunei, Indonesia, Malaysia, the Philippines, Singapore, Thailand, and Vietnam. The whole region was populated by approximately 400 million people. Potentially, ASEAN's membership could grow to ten nation states with a total population of 500 million people. One year after admission to the ASEAN block, Viet Nam had made significant progress and showed initiative in the integration process. "As a full member of ASEAN, Viet Nam undertakes to fulfill all the obligations and responsibilities of a member country according to the targets, objectives, principles, and regulations that have been clearly specified in the ASEAN charter, including its joining of AFTA," said Foreign Minister Nguyen Manh Cam at the admission ceremony on the 27th of August, 1995.[5] Other ASEAN diplomats were also positive about Viet Nam's progress one year after joining the organization:

"Within a year Viet Nam has made tremendous progress in integrating itself into the organization . . . I am especially impressed that Viet Nam's national committee coordinating its activities in ASEAN is directly under the Office of the Government. . . . Special mention should be made of the efforts made by Viet Nam to create a large corps of English-speaking officials trained in ASEAN diplomacy. One such group of Vietnamese officials received training at the Foreign Service Institute in Manila. . . . Because of its achievements in such a short time, Viet Nam has been given the opportunity to host the sixth ASEAN Summit in 1998. This signifies the belief of other ASEAN countries in the abilities and potential of Vietnam," said Ms. Rosalinda V. Tirona, Ambassador of the Philippines to Vietnam.[6]

Nevertheless, both Ms. Tirona and Mr. Djafar H. Assegaff, Indonesian Ambassador to Vietnam, shared some concerns about Viet Nam's legal and taxation systems. When asked about Viet Nam being a competitor against other ASEAN countries, attracting investment dollars and promising low cost production to international investors, Mr. Assegaff said:

We should realize that it is not cheap labor but investment security and transparent legal framework which are the main factors that attract foreign investment. Viet Nam will not emerge as a challenging competitor until the legislative investment framework is improved . . . AFTA will introduce a healthy spirit of competition into Viet Nam's market which will help increase the efficiency of labor in the country. A protected industry is always inefficient . . . Viet Nam must reform its taxation system. And in order to develop, Viet Nam should maintain two requirements: consistency in economic reforms and political stability. We believe the forthcoming eighth Congress of Viet Nam's Communist Party will ensure these conditions.[7]

Similarly, Mr. Chalermpon Ake-uru, Ambassador of the Kingdom of Thailand to Viet Nam, was both optimistic and concerned about Viet Nam's progress:

In my opinion, Viet Nam has followed this path of [promoting FDI and] liberalising investment regulations. This transformation can be seen in Viet Nam's new legislation, which has opened up more economic sectors for foreign investors. However, there are some difficulties that Thai investors encounter when entering Vietnam. Most complaints concern the inconsistency of regulations and policies, the different interpretation of laws, the unavailability of information concerning business opportunities, and the lack of clarity of the procedures via which investment licences are obtained. I believe that these complaints are similar to those of other foreign investors and it is a good sign that the Vietnamese government is now tackling those issues seriously.[8]

Furthermore, Viet Nam's membership in ASEAN is of strategic importance to all member states of the organization. It may induce future membership of neighboring countries including Laos, Cambodia, and Myanmar. Such expansion will further secure regional peace, economic development, international recognition, and global influence. Yet, local experts were divided regarding this issue. A Thai economic analyst described it in 1992, "Making the Indochinese states members of ASEAN now will be like trying to marry a duck with a hen—they won't be able to produce a duckling nor a chick—you might get a 'chickling' but that is not functional, to say the least."[9]

In his article, "Impact of Joining AFTA on Viet Nam's Economy," Dr. Vu Tuan Anh, Research Fellow at the Institute of Economics in Viet Nam, clarified the process of integration for Viet Nam into the ASEAN Free Trade Area (AFTA) as well as the Common Effective Preferential Tariff (CEPT):

Theoretically speaking, the international economic integration consists of different stages and levels. The first step of this process is the setting up of a free trade area (FTA) in which the participating countries willingly abolish their respective customs barriers, but still maintain their particular tariff policy toward the countries locating outside the FTA. The next level of economic integration is creation of a taxation alliance in which the member countries conduct a common tax policy toward the non-member countries. Afterwards, the economic integration is raised to a higher level with the shaping of a common market in which countries members would allow mutual circulation of all goods. The final level of economic integration is the formation of an economic alliance in which countries-members would apply common financial and monetary policies, and even use a common currency. . . . The main and most important component of the setting up of the AFTA consists in the implementation of the CEPT. It is the program which will gradually reduce the import tariff of goods among ASEAN countries to the level zero to five per cent [by the year 2007]. . . . In January 1996, Viet Nam has committed itself to begin implementing the CEPT and has proposed to complete this program within ten years, so far the year 2006.[10]

According to Dr. Vu, 16 per cent of all foreign direct investments in Viet Nam by the end of 1995, totalling US$2.7 billion, were from ASEAN countries. At this time, 53 per cent of all Viet Nam's tariff items (3,211 in total) were subjected to a zero per cent to five per cent rate, which fit well with CEPT requirements. In its 1996 CEPT package, Viet Nam proposed to reduce another 857 tariff items from above to below five per cent tax rate. Nevertheless, motor cars and all less-than-16-seat motor vehicles belong to Viet Nam's general exclusion list and not in the CEPT package. Those vehicles, therefore, would be taxed as seen fit by Viet Nam, "with the aim of avoiding traffic jams," noted Dr. Vu.

NOTES

1. Frank Frost, "Introduction: ASEAN since 1967," ASEAN into the 1990s, Alison Broinowski, 1990, 4–5.

2. Prem Tinsulanond, "Opening Address," 16th ASEAN Ministerial Meeting, 10.

3. Michael Antolik, "ASEAN and the Diplomacy of Accommodation," 1990, 158.

4. Michael Antolik, "ASEAN and the Diplomacy of Accommodation," 1990, 163.

5. "Moving towards the Highest Form of Integration," *Viet Nam Economic Times,* June 1996, 32.

6. *Viet Nam Economic Times,* June 1996, 32.

7. *Viet Nam Economic Times,* June 1996, 33.

8. *Viet Nam Economic Times,* Thai Section, June 1996, 7.

9. Michael Vatikiotis, "Action at Last," *Far Eastern Economic Review,* February 6, 1992, 11.

10. Institute of Economics, Viet Nam's Socio-Economic Development, no. 5 (Spring 1996): 56.

APPENDIX 2: NOTE ON VIET NAM'S BUSINESS ENVIRONMENT

Viet Nam is a country of 74 million people, residing in a geographical area about one-third the size of Ontario. Ha Noi is Viet Nam's capital city, located in the North, having most government offices located in this city. It is a city of three to four million people and the second largest economic centre of the country. The largest economic centre of the country is Ho Chi Minh City, formerly called Saigon, located in the southern part of the country. It is a city of approximately five to seven million people, packed in a geographical area about the size of London, Ontario.

Viet Nam has three ports located along the shoreline of the country. Hai Phong is located in northern Viet Nam, about 80 kilometres from Ha Noi, providing ocean access to the capital of the country and neighboring towns. Another important port is Da Nang, located in the central area of Viet Nam, giving access to this part of the country. The third and most developed port of the three is at the edge of Ho Chi Minh City. In the past, those three ports were the main facilities for most import and export activities of Viet Nam.

The whole country is connected by Highway Number 1, running North-South and along the shore line between Ha Noi and Saigon. Connecting to Highway 1 is a system of small highways giving access to small towns all over the country. The speed limit on Highway 1 is about 70 kilometres per hour with sections where no vehicle can go faster than 40 kilometres per hour due to road conditions and traffic load. Traffic on the Highway includes all types of vehicles including trucks, buses, cars, motorbikes, and motor-powered tricycles. Bicycles and animal-pulled carriages are often seen on smaller highways connecting towns and rural areas.

City streets are packed with motorbikes, locally termed "Hondas," bicycles, and pedicabs. Passenger cars and vans have been seen more and more often in the last few years; however, they are very few compared to the number of motorbikes and bicycles and pedicabs on the roads. In fact, it is faster to travel on motorbikes than by car or bus due to the traffic load on city streets. In Ha Noi, city streets are narrow and crowded, with inconspicuous and confusing traffic signs. Traffic lights only exist on intersections of main streets in the downtown area (the area with major hotels and offices where foreigners reside and work the most). In Ho Chi Minh City, the streets are much wider and in better condition; however, the streets are still overcrowded due to a much larger population and the level of economic activities in the region. Given such road conditions and the traffic level, owning large vehicles is a definite inconvenience in terms of parking and mobility. However, it is much safer to sit in a car than to ride a motorbike through the streets of Ha Noi or Ho Chi Minh City. For many areas in Ho Chi Minh City and Ha Noi, the sewage system has not worked well for many years. As a result, flooding is normal during the rainy season and passenger cars, stuck in the middle of the road surrounded by water, are not strange sights to local people.

In rural areas, farmers use bicycles and carriages for transportation. Roads surrounding the farms are earth-paved pathways that are wide enough for only one car or a small truck. More often, those roads are used for animal-pulled—sometimes man-powered—carriages, transporting product from farms to villages or vice versa. With an average income of about US$10 per month per capita, buying a pick-up truck to do the transportation job is out of the question. Indeed, using the cows to pull the plows in the field and to pull the carriages on the road, then selling the beef in the end is a very effective way of leveraging live stock. Due to such low level of income, there is a recent flow of migration from rural areas to the city's suburbs in the hope of finding a job that pays better than farming.

In Ha Noi and Ho Chi Minh City, waitresses and maids are paid an average of US$20 per month plus meals and housing. High school and primary school teachers bring home an official monthly salary of US$30. With overtime or after hours tutoring in the afternoon plus private tutoring in the evening, one can net an extra US$40 of honest earnings. Working for a foreign company is much better. As a laborer, one can expect to earn from US$100 to US$150 per month plus benefits. As an office worker, one can earn up to US$200 per month plus benefits. A local Vietnamese director, working for a foreign company, would expect to earn US$500 per month plus benefits. At this level of earnings, one can expect a very comfortable living standard, in Vietnamese terms, of course, except for imports of durable goods. In the public sector, a government employee's official salary averages US$50 per month plus benefits. A "well-connected" government officer working at the management level of an "economically well-to-do" organization would net another US$150 or even much more on "irregular income."

With such levels of income, it is very desirable for local Vietnamese to work for foreign companies. As a result, foreign companies usually get the cream of the crop when they do search for employees in any field. For example, almost all line workers in auto assembly plants are engineers graduated from Vietnamese universities. Waiters and waitresses in hotels usually have a degree in English or Tourism and can speak two languages other than Vietnamese. One receptionist at a hotel in Ha Noi is a doctor and medical researcher who took on a second job in order to continue his language training in English. Most university students plan to take a second degree in another discipline, usually economics or languages, if they had not one previously. Overall, Vietnamese youths are very keen, ambitious, hardworking, and intelligent. It is, therefore, a common practice for foreign companies to hire young, energetic, and intelligent local employees, then develop them from the start into productive workers, specifically trained for the business. In fact, with 40 per cent of the population under the age of 20, the supply of low-cost labor will remain abundant and a competitive advantage for Viet Nam over the next two decades.

On the other hand, the lack of Vietnamese managers has been a problem for many foreign companies. According to Dr. Gottschang,

Dr. McCornac, and Dr. Westbrook, who were Visiting Lecturers at the National Economics University in Ha Noi, their students "have had very little exposure to the most basic aspects of market economics." The basic aspects of market economics referred to by the professors include supply and demand, marginal cost, externality, GDP, multiplier, discount rate, and exchange rate. To make matters worse, about 70 of those surveyed claim that they have the highest degree in economics and 50 to 60 per cent of them have taught in Economics or related fields. Nevertheless, in an article "Economic Training for Sustainable Development in Vietnam," the professors were very positive about their students' calibre:

> The participants in the training program have been bright, motivated and highly sophisticated in their understanding of economic problems and issues, but their lack of exposure to the fundamental vocabulary and analytical tools of market economics is a serious impediment to their ability to teach market economics and to contribute to policy analysis.

> In order to achieve a strategy of sustainable growth with equity, Viet Nam must train analysts and policy makers capable of addressing the problems generated by a market economy. The effects of economic reform on all elements of society are profound. Analyzing these effects and guiding policy require sophisticated analysis by scholars who are highly trained and who are Vietnamese.[1]

The requirements of economic reform not only include training but also political and economic policies. In the "Draft Political Report of the Central Committee on the VIII National Congress of the Communist Party of Vietnam,"[2] the Communist Party of Viet Nam (CPV) were determined to "firmly grasp the two *strategic tasks of building socialism* and defending the Homeland [which were] stepping up industrialization and modernization." Through industrialization and modernization, the CPV would "develop the multi-sector economy and apply the market mechanism to successfully build socialism, *not allowing the country to stray onto the capitalist path.*" Such a plan of action was derived from the CPV's stated perception of the world:

> The collapse of the socialist regime in the Soviet Union and East European countries has driven socialism into a *temporary regression.* However, that has not changed the nature of the times; Mankind is still in the era of *transition from capitalism to socialism.* The basic contradictions in the world still exist and continue to develop, growing more acute in some respects and assuming many new types of manifestation. National struggle and class struggle continue to unfold in diverse forms.

When asked to explain the CPV's perception of socialism, Secretary General Do Muoi stated:

> The Party Platform identifies six characteristics of the socialist society that we are pursuing. They include a society:
>
> - which is owned by working people;
> - which has a highly developed economy based on modern productive forces and the public ownership of major means of production;
> - which has an advanced culture with a high degree of national identity;
> - in which people are free from repression, exploitation and inequity; people work according to their ability and enjoy according to their work efforts; people have affluence, freedom and happy lives; and have the environment for multidimensional development of their individuals;
> - in which all nationalities are equal and consolidate and help one another for betterment;
> - which has amicable and cooperative relations with people in all other countries of the world.[3]

With such a political agenda and the Economic Administrative Reform program implemented over the last 10 years, Viet Nam has grown rapidly in economic terms. GDP real growth has been over eight per cent annually since 1992. (See Table 2, page 259.) Living standards in cities have improved significantly over the last five years. New houses were built, sewage systems were improved, and power outages were less frequent. New jobs were created in the private sector while government jobs were disappearing. Goods were transported more easily within the country. Small business people found a freer trading environment than a few years ago. People felt free to criticize the government; however, such freedom is limited to the neighborhood and to friends only, not on public media.

Given the trade deficit, current account deficit, double digit inflation, and constant nominal exchange rate,

> . . . there is likely to be an excess demand for foreign exchange, and the government will have to make some hard choices. It may try to borrow more foreign exchange, perhaps through an international bond issue . . . [or] . . . the government may be tempted to restrict imports. . . . Another alternative is to devalue the dong. Although domestic prices have doubled since 1991, the nominal exchange rate (relative to the U.S. dollar) has hardly changed, making Vietnamese goods increasingly expensive on world markets. Large inflows of aid, restrictions of imports, foreign investment and remittance, coupled with the lack of serious effort to service foreign debt, explain the strength of the dong, but this situation is not sustainable beyond another year or so. By the end of the year, and after the Party Congress, decision-makers will begin to recognise this and prepare to guide the dong down gradually.[4]

NOTES

1. Viet Nam Socio-Economic Development, no. 6 (Summer 1996): 70–80.

2. Viet Nam Socio-Economic Development, no. 6 (Summer 1996): 3–24.

3. "A Rich People, a Powerful Nation & an Equitable, Civilised Society," *Viet Nam Economic Times,* May 1996, 15.

4. *EIU Country Report,* 1st quarter, 1996, 5–6.

APPENDIX 3: NOTE ON THE AUTOMOBILE ASSEMBLY PROCESS

Throughout the world, there has been a shift by the major automobile producers towards outsourcing of auto parts and components. To an increasing degree, the large automobile corporations have become assembly operations. Nevertheless, there is an enormous technological range with regard to the assembly process.

In the United States, Japan, and Western Europe, the automobile assemblers use highly automated assembly lines with robots performing many of the welding and assembly tasks.

In small volume, low-income countries, automobile assemblers utilize low-wage labor instead of the capital-intensive microelectronics technology. In corporations like Mekong, parts may be brought to the plant in containers that have 30 to 100 units. Each automobile body may be assembled individually using hand-welding, with the parts temporarily held together with jigs. The assembled unit, if it is made of unpainted body parts, is then taken through a cleaning and painting process. The painting process involves heavy capital investment and sophisticated technology in order to ensure a durable, long-lasting automobile. Finally, the engine, transmission, seats, and other interior parts are placed by hand in the automobile body.

The government of Viet Nam has imposed a schedule of tariff rates that will encourage the automobile assemblers to import fewer finished components, so that further finishing is completed in Viet Nam, in order to increase employment and domestic value added. The following table indicates the tariff rates in June 1996. The category SKD consists of semi-knocked down components; CKD-1 consists of completely knocked down units that are finished and painted; and CKD-2 consists of completely knocked down units that are unpainted.

Tax for Passenger Cars (%), Effective From 1996

Seats Assembly Type	Under 5 Seats			Under 15 Seats			Under 24 Seats			Over 24 Seats		
	A	B	D	A	B	D	A	B	D	A	B	D
CBU	55	0	100	55	0	60	55	0	30	50	6	0
SKD	50	0	100	45	0	60	40	0	30	40	6	0
CKD-1	50	4	0	40	4	0	25	4	0	12	1	0
CKD-2	30	4	0	20	4	0	10	4	0	6	1	0
IKD	5	4	0	5	4	0	7	4	0	3	1	0
Spare Parts	60	4	0	60	4	0	45	4	0	30	2	0

Note: Import Duty = A* C.I.F.
Sales Tax = B* Selling Price.
Special Consumption Tax = D* (C.I.F. + Import Duty).

APPENDIX 4: FACTS ON VIET NAM'S TAXES

1. *Licence taxes:* Licence taxes are applied to all businesses operating in Viet Nam. They are collected every year at different rates. Independent and dependent economic units have to pay VND 650,000 and VND 420,000 each year. The six license tax rates for

individuals range from VND 20,000 to VND 650,000, in accordance with monthly income levels.

2. *Income tax:* Income tax is evaluated at 11 rates ranging from zero to 30 per cent. The zero per cent rate is applied to businesses which pay agricultural tax, special consumption tax, export tax, or have credit activities at commercial banks and financial companies.

3. *Special consumption tax:* Special consumption taxes range from 15 per cent to 100 per cent and are applied to businesses involved in tobacco, wine, beer, four-wheeled vehicles (excepting domestically made vehicles), petroleum and fireworks. The tax calculation is based on the turn-over tax paid by the producers or the importers.

4. *Export and import taxes:* Export and import taxes are collected at border checkpoints. There are 11 rates, ranging from zero to 45 per cent, calculated on the Free on Board (FOB) rate export tax. The import tax has 34 rates, from zero to 80 per cent, calculated on Cost Insurance Freight (CIF).

5. *Profit tax:* Profit tax is applied to all profitable business units, excluding agricultural tax payers and businesses subject to the Viet Nam Foreign Investment Law. Profit tax is applied at a rate of 25 per cent for heavy industry, 35 per cent for light industry, and 45 per cent for trade services.

6. *Agricultural tax:* Agricultural tax payers are organisations and individuals using the land for agricultural production aims, i.e., farming, aqua products, forestry, etc. Tax exemptions are given to agricultural business activities subject to Foreign Investment Law because these business units pay for their land lease. The tax rate is defined by the location, terrain, climate, water irrigation system and fertility of the land for lease.

7. *Land transfer tax:* Land transfer tax must be paid in all transferred land-use-right cases. It is calculated on the value of the transferred land and collected at the time the transfer takes place. Agricultural land attracts a rate of 10 per cent, while 20 per cent is paid for residences and construction land. For land-use paid for before the allocation, the rate of tax is five per cent. Tax exemption cases cover government-confiscated land, the transfer of land-use rights to inheritor, divorces, family divisions, private estate businesses and private land used for leasing.

8. *Estate tax:* Estate tax is applied to all individuals and private organisations with the right to use houses, residential land and construction land. All businesses subject to the Foreign Investment Law are exempted from this tax. The estate tax is based on the land classification and is determined in part by the grade of the agricultural land.

9. *Natural resource tax:* The natural resource tax is calculated in accordance with eight natural resources. Each resource is taxed from one to 10 per cent or from 20 to 40 per cent. The rate of tax charged is based on the value of the exploited resource.

10. *Personal income tax:* Personal income tax for Vietnamese people has seven rates ranging from zero to 60 per cent. The lowest tax rate starts from salaries at VND 1.2 million. For foreigners who have resided in Viet Nam from 183 days to 12 months, or for Vietnamese working abroad, the lowest tax rate starts at VND 5 million per month.

Tax policies for foreign investors are covered by the Foreign Investment law and include profit taxes, profit transfers abroad, import taxes and land lease taxes. Foreign investors are also subject to the general tax revenue system. Slaughter taxes and various registration taxes also exist.

THAI TELECOMS IN THE NEW ECONOMY: PRIVATIZATION & LIBERALIZATION

Prepared by Brock Judiesch under the supervision of Professor David Conklin

Version: (A) 2002-06-03

PROSPECTS FOR PRIVATIZATION AND LIBERALIZATION

Direk Charoenphol had been Thailand's Deputy Minister of Transport and Communications and a former senior advisor to the Deputy Minister of Finance. In August 2000, he had quit the latter of the two posts to avoid any perceived conflict of interest as he vied for one of seven seats on the new National Telecommunications Commission—the entity that would assume the authority, among other things, to issue telecom licences in the soon-to-be-liberalized Thai telecommunications sector. As Khun Direk (in Thai it is the custom to formally refer to someone by attaching the title "khun" to the first name) strolled the grand old halls of the Ministry of Transport and Communications in Bangkok, he pondered the liberalization of the telecom industry and the business opportunities that might be created. Thailand's entry into e-commerce and the new economy would depend upon the new technologies and enhanced efficiencies that privatization and liberalization of the telecom sector might bring.

The economic crisis that had ravaged the country in 1997 was an impetus that started Thailand down the difficult road of liberalization. The major issues involved in the transformation of the telecom industry from a state-run duopoly to a free market-based sector were daunting: the process for corporatization and the subsequent privatization of the state-owned telecom operators; the conversion of revenue-sharing agreements between private operators and the two state-run telecom agencies; the process of establishing a regulatory body to oversee privately owned corporations; and finally the full liberalization of the sector by 2006, with the reduction—perhaps even elimination—of foreign ownership restrictions, under an agreement with the World Trade Organization. The stakes involved in the liberalization of the industry were high. Political careers, personal fortunes and the social and economic welfare of the citizens in Khun Direk's beloved Thailand hung in the balance.

Nonetheless, despite the many obstacles—including chronic bureaucratic delays, political posturing and allegations of corruption and accommodation of special interests—some observers believed that the goal of liberalization seemed attainable. "The challenges ahead are huge, but top level commitment is there," noted Stuart Macpherson, consultant to the Royal Thai Government on matters of telecom privatization and former executive director of telecommunications at the Canadian Radio-television & Telecommunications Commission (CRTC), whose job it had been to bring local competition to the Canadian telecom industry. Others expressed concern that, at this stage in Thailand's economic development, liberalization was inappropriate.

The terms "liberalization" and "privatization" are often used as synonyms. However, a distinction should be made in analysing the reform process. "Liberalization" refers to the opening up of a market to more competition by allowing easier entry of domestic and foreign entities, and it refers to freer competition through the removal of government regulations. "Privatization" refers to the sale or transfer of state-owned assets to the private sector. Privatization is usually viewed as a necessary component of liberalization. However, privatization can be put in place without liberalization. Furthermore, the privatization process may require new government regulatory agencies—contradiction of liberalization, in some sense—at least during a transition period.

THAILAND AT THE DAWN OF THE NEW MILLENNIUM

The Economic Crisis

In 1997, after decades of virtually uninterrupted growth, Thailand plunged into a severe economic crisis that shook investor confidence and raised fundamental questions about the country's competitiveness. Attacks from large foreign hedge funds led to the devaluation of the Thai currency—the Baht—which exposed and exacerbated glaring flaws in the financial system, including massive unhedged private-sector foreign debt, that had not always been productively invested. A critical economic issue faced by Thailand was the banking system's non-performing loan (NPL) problem. In the economic crisis and its aftermath, banks tended to reschedule rather than restructure their loans. This bad debt was a deterrent for banks to issue new loans, and it also discouraged foreign investment in the banks. Consequently, the capital many businesses needed to get back on solid ground was unavailable, as the Thai stock market was also down 37 per cent in value in 1999. Unless the NPL problem was reduced, the financial system would not strengthen and Thailand's recovery would be very much in jeopardy. Beginning in August 1997, the International Monetary Fund (IMF) devised a rescue package that was designed to

rebuild foreign exchange reserves, restructure the financial sector, and improve transparency in both business and government. As described by the *Economist Intelligence Unit:*

> . . . economic policy has been governed by the performance criteria set out in the quarterly letters of intent prepared by the Ministry of Finance and the Bank of Thailand (BOT, the central bank) in collaboration with the IMF. These were initially aimed at stabilizing markets and restoring investor confidence by restrictive demand management policies.
>
> The IMF agreement of August 1997 initially insisted that the government achieve a budgetary surplus of one per cent of GDP for the 1997/98 fiscal year (October to September) by trimming expenditure by Bt100 billion (US$2.5 billion) and increasing the value-added tax (VAT) rate from seven per cent to 10 per cent. The IMF also called for a substantial rise in interest rates to limit further exchange-rate depreciation, and a tight money policy to ensure that inflation was maintained at moderate levels.[1]

With the return of some macroeconomic stability in 1999, the IMF and Thailand agreed to move to a more expansionary fiscal policy, including tax cuts and increased government spending. The economy, as measured by gross domestic product, grew by 4.2 per cent in 1999 after a huge 10.2 per cent contraction in 1998. In 2000, the government estimated a 4.5 per cent growth, with inflation a benign 2.5 per cent to three per cent. Due to stimulus measures to attain this growth, government debt remained at a high level—about 60 per cent of GDP. Reducing this debt, restructuring the huge corporate sector debt, and implementing effective bankruptcy foreclosure laws were major problems facing Thailand.

The Political Framework

Thailand was a constitutional monarchy ruled by King Bhumipol Adulyadei (Rama IX), a much-revered monarch who had reigned since 1946. The King played no part in day-to-day government operations, but served as a powerful symbol of Thai national identity and commanded enormous love and moral authority, which he used on occasion to resolve national crises or to draw the government's attention to pressing social problems. On many occasions he initiated and implemented pilot projects to resolve such issues.

Real power, however, lay in the hands of a democratically elected government led by a prime minister. Since World War II, Thailand had alternated between periods of democratically elected civilian government and authoritarian rule, brought about by coups d'etat. The military last seized power in 1991, but after middle class protest and royal intervention, civilian rule was restored in 1992. Since then, the military had taken pains to avoid interfering in the operation of the civilian government.

Because Thailand had so many political parties, each civilian government had been a multiparty coalition and inherently unstable. No elected government had yet completed a four-year term. Chuan Leekpai of the Democratic Party headed the current government, which came to power in November 1997. Prime Minister Chuan's cabinet included several noted economic experts; the cabinet was generally praised for the quality of its members.

Foreign investors were concerned that the financial reforms carried out by Prime Minister Chuan's government might be stalled by elections, which had to be called by November 2000 at the latest. A general election for members of the House of Representatives, in accordance with the new constitution, would be held on January 6, 2001. While the military retained a major influence in Thai society, strong public opinion against coups d'etat—and a vocal press—appeared to be limiting its role in politics.

External Political and Economic Relations

Thailand's external political relations were increasingly centred on the development of strong international economic and security forums. Thailand was a major force in the Association of Southeast Asian Nations (ASEAN), of which it held the presidency in 2000: Thailand also played an active role in economic organizations such as the Asia-Pacific Economic Cooperation forum (APEC) and world forums such as the World Trade Organization (WTO). Commerce Minister Supachai Panitchpakdi was currently Deputy Head and was scheduled to become Head in 2002. In 1996, Thailand hosted the first Asia-Europe Summit (AEM), which brought together heads of government from 25 countries in the European Union (EU) and East Asia. With little immediate military threat to its sovereignty, Thailand had focused its international policy on trade development and investment, while addressing security concerns both bilaterally and in a formal regional dialogue known as the ASEAN Regional Forum (ARF).

Thailand's trade relations had traditionally been oriented toward distant markets, particularly those in North America and Europe, though more recently also in Japan. Implementation of an ASEAN Free Trade Area (AFTA) was contributing to a growing trade between Thailand and its ASEAN partners. This trend would likely continue, as AFTA was to be fully implemented by 2003. Thailand had already implemented the first round of duty cuts on very high-tariff goods imported from other ASEAN countries. On the trade front, the United States was Thailand's most important export market, accounting for US$12.2 billion of Thailand's US$52.9 billion in exports in 1998. In the same year, Thailand imported a total of US$40.7 billion, a sharp fall from US$61.4 billion in 1997, before the economic crisis.

In 1998, the trade surplus was US$12.2 billion as imports slumped amidst recession. In 1999, the trade surplus was about US$8.9 billion and it was expected to narrow further in 2000. In 1999, Thai exports grew moderately by 7.4 per cent (year-on-year). Imports grew 17.7 per cent. Imports continued to grow faster than exports in 2000 and threatened to turn Thailand's trade surplus into a deficit by 2001. Increasing capital inflows of equity and direct investment were expected to mitigate the effects of a shrinking trade surplus on the balance of payments. Privatization, with sales to foreigners, could contribute substantially to these capital inflows (see Exhibit 1).

The History of Privatization/ Liberalization in Thailand

Privatization and liberalization had been on the policy agendas of successive Thai governments since the 1980s. However, and perhaps understandably, less progress was made in the previous nearly two decades of strong economic growth. The government and public mindset was that as long as the government's coffers continued to grow year on year, there was little need to be concerned about the inefficiency of government spending. This mindset changed abruptly in the summer of 1997 when the Thai government, after obtaining a US$17-billion loan from the IMF, finally committed to liberalize several key industries including telecommunications. Realizing that the monopoly state-owned enterprises (SOEs) were hugely bureaucratic and inefficient and therefore unable to compete in a liberalized market, the Thai government chose to privatize several of them. As a result, a Privatization Master Plan was accepted by the State Enterprise Policy Commission in January 1998.

The Master Plan was then approved by the Cabinet on September 1, 1998.

The government looked upon liberalization as a vehicle to:

- Increase competition and thereby improve the quality of service;
- Jump-start the economy;
- Lay the foundation for the re-establishment of sustainable growth;
- Decrease government involvement and increase private participation in the economy.

Through privatization, the government aimed to:

- Free up public resources;
- Promote productivity and higher labor welfare;
- Reduce the public debt and increase private investment;
- Intensify preparation for the globalization of trade and industry.

Certain SOEs were selected for "fast track" privatization, thereby shortening the time required. These SOEs included the Telephone Organization of Thailand (TOT)[2] and the Communications Authority of Thailand (CAT);[3] the Petroleum Authority of Thailand Exploration and Production; Thai Airways; and the Electricity Generating Authority of Thailand (EGAT).

	1998	1999	2000*
GDP growth %	(10.2)	4.2	4.9
GDP per capita	$1,823	$2,002	$1,916
Inflation, annual avg. %	8.9	0.3	2.1
Unemployment, annual avg. %	4.4	4.2	3.7
Current account balance (millions of dollars)	$14,239	$11,290	$8,100
Current account balance as % of GDP	12.7	9.0	6.7
Interest rates—Short-term (90 day T-bills)	6.0	3.75	N/A
Interest rates—Long-term (10 years)	(–)	(–)	(–)
Foreign exchange rate (US$)	41.37	37.84	40.39
Fiscal deficit/surplus as % of GDP	(2.5)	(3.0)	(2.8)
Fiscal debt as % of GDP	76.5	59.6	N/A

Exhibit 1   Thailand Key Economic Indicators

Source: EIU.

*EIU estimates.

Use of Proceeds From Privatization

The Government of Thailand stated that privatization proceeds would be used for reinvestment in the economy and for social, health and welfare benefits of the Thai people. Where proceeds were received directly by the government, they would be used in accordance with the cabinet resolution of May 19, 1998, which stipulated that 50 per cent would be used to fund needed social services such as education, public health, labor welfare and agriculture, and the other 50 per cent would be allocated to the Financial Institutions Development Fund (FIDF).[4]

Social, Labor and Environmental Concerns

The government publicly recognized that privatization proposals must include commitments regarding the treatment of labor and other social obligations after privatization and decisions concerning the employment impacts. The government also pledged to evaluate the pricing policies in the new private sector, and it committed to seeking appropriate resolution of these issues. Programs that benefited state employees in the transition to privatization would be encouraged. These included share distribution schemes, early retirement packages and retraining efforts. The government intended to pursue plans that minimized any negative impacts on social, labor and environmental issues while still meeting the reform objectives of the program. The privatization program would address these concerns in the following manner:

New privatization plans—all enterprise privatization plans would be required to include measures of their social (tariff rates), labor (employment) and environmental (pollution) impacts.

Enforcement of existing measures—programs already existed to provide employees with specific benefits if they were terminated due to privatization. The government intended to ensure that such benefits were paid and received by employees.

Public Information and Education

The privatization program was to be accompanied by a dedicated public awareness campaign that addressed key audiences and stakeholders in the process and responded to their particular concerns. Key audiences included the SOE employees, investors, the media and the public at large. Immediate efforts to be pursued included the establishment of an interactive State Enterprise Reform Committee (SERC) Web site,[5] the publishing of a bi-monthly newsletter and the holding of public seminars and forums. These channels would seek to disseminate both general information on privatization and sector-specific details to identified audiences.

In telecommunication, the proposed market structure was based on a three-tier model comprising a primary market, a resale market and a retail market. It was hoped that this market structure would allow industry participants a broad range of market entry strategies and business opportunities based on free market competition. The end result was to be an industry that offered greater consumer choice, quality and level of service—with competitive pricing.

New Regulations

The creation of an independent regulator in the communications sector seemed to be critical to the promotion of competition and consumer benefit. The proposed independent regulatory body, coupled with a new Telecommunications Act, was meant to provide the necessary framework on which competition, consumer, technical and legal safeguards would be based. Similar individual subsector regulators or agencies were envisaged for both the postal service and broadcasting.

While new independent regulatory structures and practices seemed necessary, it was understood by some that this might simply create a new type of bureaucracy and government intervention that could cause new inefficiencies and distortions. The difficult task of proving the skeptics wrong lay in the hands of the new regulatory authority. Both optimists and skeptics agreed that the goal of liberalization would not be easily attained.

THE WORLD BANK'S "THREE PRINCIPLES OF PRIVATIZATION"

Excerpts taken from a transcript of the speech by Dr. Stefan Koeberle, Country Economist, World Bank, at The Thailand Infrastructure Privatization Forum, July 17, 1998:

> Based on international experience, there are really three principles that stand out as absolutely necessary for ensuring that privatization and private participation in infrastructure is successful. The first and most critical is the need for political commitment. Without government support we are all wasting our time. The second key to success is to have a business-oriented privatization process from start to finish. This doesn't only mean that you should maximize competition wherever possible. You also do it all in a very professional manner. You need to have a very clear agenda, which you should proceed with without delay, all the while sending very clear, unambiguous signals to investors and speaking with one voice.

> This brings us to the third key ingredient for successful privatization, namely, transparency. Privatization is usually subject to all kinds of suspicions about the role of insiders and corruption, and a government is probably bound to face frequent complaints. However, the government is called to task to avoid any situation where key decisions are overturned at the last minute, where it sets out a strategy that it doesn't follow, where it doesn't speak in a coherent way and where foreign and domestic investors are confused about what it really wants to do.

> A final necessity for the success of the privatization and liberalization program is to have an effective communications strategy. Although there has been much talk about privatization in the popular media over the past five to 10 years, there is still considerable confusion about it, especially among employees of state enterprises. All too often the term privatization is simply associated with selling assets to foreigners, insider deals, nepotism, high tariffs and redundancies.

The Primary Methods of Privatization

Private participation in business can come in many forms:

- Asset Liquidation (Stripping)—whereby a corporation or investor makes a profit by acquiring and then selling many or all of a state-owned enterprise's assets rather than continuing to operate the business.
- Build, Own, Operate, Transfer (BOOT)—a private entity constructs an asset (e.g., a telecom infrastructure) and operates it in the hope of making a profit, but then transfers ownership back to the state at the end of the contract.
- Build, Own, Operate (BOO)—same as BOOT without the requirement to sell the asset back to the state at the end of the contract.
- Build, Transfer, Operate (BTO)—a private entity constructs an asset and then transfers ownership to the state in exchange for the right to operate. (For reasons described below, this is the method of private participation that the Royal Thai Government had preferred in the past.)
- Concession Contracts—agreements between a state and individual companies whereby a company is given a monopoly or protected market in return for undertaking duties traditionally assumed by the government.
- Convertible Bond Offerings—bonds that can be converted into a stated number of common shares in an SOE.
- Debt for Equity Swaps—equity is given to a private company in exchange for assuming responsibility for all or part of an SOEs debt or, if equity is issued to the creditor, for easing of debt covenants.
- Derivative Mechanisms—a contract where the final purchase price a private concern pays for government assets depends on the future profit generated from those assets.
- Management Buy Outs (MBOs)—sale in part or in full to incumbent management with the advantages of job retention, independence and a share in the equity.

- Management Contracts—professional managers from private industry are brought in to manage SOEs.
- Options—a contract in which an SOE agrees to sell an asset to a private party for a specified price during a specified period of time. Exercising the option is at the discretion of the private party.
- Private Placements/Joint Ventures with Strategic Partners—sale in part or in full to preselected private interests.
- Public Offerings—offer of shares to the general public.
- Regulation, Deregulation—creating rules that either directly (by regulation) or indirectly (by deregulation) promote private participation in a sector.

STRUCTURE OF THE TELECOMMUNICATIONS SECTOR

The Royal Thai Government was committed to privatizing and liberalizing the Telecom sector. However, few were optimistic that the process would go smoothly or quickly. "The path to an affordable, efficient and world-class telecommunications network in Thailand is jammed by a conspiracy of politics, corruption, crippling regulations and archaic legislation."[6]

An unwieldy web of laws and regulations were at the root of the problem. According to decades old legislation, it was illegal for private telecom operators to own telecom infrastructure assets in Thailand. However, in the late 1980s, it had become evident that Thailand required an expanded and more efficient telecom network than could be provided by the two state-run telecom agencies, the Telephone Organization of Thailand (TOT) and the Communications Authority of Thailand (CAT). In response, the state allowed a select few private companies to set up their networks on the basis of a fixed-period, BTO (build, transfer, operate) contract through either one of the state-run agencies. In return for allowing the private company the right to operate for the contract period, ownership of the assets would be passed to the TOT or CAT. These state agencies would also receive a portion

of the firm's revenue that ranged from an oppressive 43 per cent in the case of Thai Telephone & Telegraph (TT&T) to a low of 22 per cent for most other operators. A lack of real ownership had traditionally given little incentive to private firms to improve the networks as new technologies became available.

Telephone Organization of Thailand

The Telephone Organization of Thailand (TOT) was formed in 1954 as the exclusive operator of the country's domestic telephone network. The TOT, similar to other state enterprises, had to seek Cabinet approval for certain activities such as borrowing from financial institutions, issuance of bonds and commercial papers, joint investments with the private sector, disposal of assets, termination of a telephone exchange, increasing capital, investment budgets and the setting of service charges. Apart from operating the domestic telephone network, the TOT had also embarked on the provision of other telecommunications services such as cellular telephone, data communication and paging services, through a total of 15 BTO contracts awarded to private sector companies.

Communications Authority of Thailand

The Communications Authority of Thailand (CAT) was established in 1976 to operate the country's postal, money order and international telecommunications services. The CAT used the TOT's domestic telephone network for its international telephone services and paid a percentage of its revenues to the latter for every service that utilized domestic telephone lines. The CAT had awarded BTO contracts to 10 private companies who offered mobile telephone, satellite, data communication and/or paging. All private companies operated under the standard BTO arrangement. The CAT was also an investor in several Internet Service Providers (ISP).

The relationship between the TOT and CAT had often been somewhat acrimonious.

Telecom Asia Corp PLC

In 1991, Telecom Asia (TA) was awarded a 25-year BTO contract from the TOT to build and operate 2.6 million fixed lines in Bangkok in return for a 16 per cent share of its revenues. The company claimed that 1.43 million of these lines had been sold as of August 2000. Bell Atlantic of the United States held 18.2 per cent of the publicly traded company. TA had a total debt of Bt58 billion or US$1.38 billion as of September 2000. A large portion of this debt (US$843 million and Yen 45.5 billion) was borrowed offshore when the Baht traded at Bt25: US$1. In September 2000,

the exchange rate was approximately Bt42: US$1. As shown in Exhibits 2 and 3, the devaluation of the Baht severely damaged TA's bottom line.

Thai Telephone & Telecommunications PLC

Also in 1991, Thai Telephone & Telecommunications (TT&T) was granted a 25-year BTO contract from the TOT to construct and operate 1.5 million lines in the provinces in return for a crippling 43.1% share of its revenues. TT&T claimed to have sold 1.3 million lines by May

TA Earnings Estimate Sensitivity to Bt/US$ Forex Rate		
Bt/US$ Forex Rate	*2000E Net Income (Bt mn)*	*% Chg. From Base Case**
Base Case (Bt30/US$)	(760)	—
40	(2,076)	(173)
41	(3,391)	(346)
42	(4,707)	(519)
43	(6,022)	(692)
44	(7,338)	(866)
45	(8,654)	(1,039)

Exhibit 2   Telecom Asia (TA)

Source: Merrill Lynch estimates.

*Base case is Bt39/US$.

TA Earnings Estimate Sensitivity to Foreign-Debt Interest Rates		
Increase in Interest Rate (Bps)	*2000E Net Income (Bt mn)*	*% Chg. From Base Case**
Base Case (8.0%)	(760)	—
0.5	(924)	(22)
1.0	(1,089)	(43)
1.5	(1,253)	(65)
2.0	(1,418)	(87)
2.5	(1,582)	(108)
3.0	(1,746)	(130)

Exhibit 3   Telecom Asia (TA)

Source: Merrill Lynch estimates.

*Base case refers to TA's average interest rate of 8.0 per cent.

TT&T Earnings Estimate Sensitivity to Bt/US$ Forex Rate		
Bt/US$ Forex Rate	2000E Net Income (Bt mn)	% Chg. From Base Case*
Base Case (Bt 39/US$)	(1,559)	—
40	(2,039)	(31)
41	(2,519)	(62)
42	(2,998)	(92)
43	(3,477)	(123)
44	(3,957)	(154)
45	(4,437)	(185)

Exhibit 4   Thai Telephone & Telecommunications (TT&T)

Source: Merrill Lynch estimates.

*Base case is US$ at Bt39.

TT&T Earnings Estimate Sensitivity to Foreign-Debt Interest Rates		
Increase in Interest Rate (Bps)	2000E Net Income (Bt mn)	% Chg. From Base Case*
Base Case (8.0%)	(1,559)	—
0.5	(1,644)	(5)
1.0	(1,729)	(11)
1.5	(1,813)	(16)
2.0	(1,898)	(22)
2.5	(1,983)	(27)
3.0	(2,068)	(33)

Exhibit 5   Thai Telephone & Telecommunications (TT&T)

Source: Merrill Lynch estimates.

*Base case refers to TT&T's average interest rate of 8.0 per cent.

2000. At the same time, TT&T had an estimated Bt44 billion in debt (US$480 million of foreign currency debt) and had hovered on the brink of collapse since the Asian financial crisis of 1997. An attempt to revive the company and restructure the debt had been ongoing for over two years (see Exhibits 4 and 5).

FOUR STEPS ALONG THE ROAD TO LIBERALIZATION

The Telecommunications Master Plan, which was first made public in 1997, was a subset of the Royal Thai Government's Privatization Master Plan. Its major goals were to liberalize the Thai Telecommunications business in Thailand, to privatize the TOT and the CAT, and to establish an independent regulatory body called the National Telecommunications Commission (NTC). By the summer of 2000, three years, two governments and one economic crisis later, nothing had yet changed. Nonetheless, change was still promised. "It is inevitable,"[7] stated a leading Thai telecom expert.

There were four key steps that had to be completed for Thailand to achieve its goals of privatization and liberalization. Many believed there was an optimal order to the steps: establishment of a regulatory body (NTC); compensating the TOT and CAT for the loss of revenue from the premature termination of the BTO contracts that they had granted; privatization of the TOT and CAT; and liberalization of the sector to allow new domestic and foreign entrants.

It was generally agreed that this order made the most sense. For example, it seemed prudent to first establish an independent regulatory body for the industry. This body, due to its "independent" nature would then be the most suitable institution to charge with solving the BTO contract conversion issue. It also seemed to make sense from a valuation standpoint to wait until the outstanding contracts (worth several billion baht) were settled before the TOT and CAT embarked on privatization. Finally, for the sake of the incumbents (both the two SOEs and the current private BTO contract holders), liberalization and the entry of new competitors should wait until they had adapted to the new operating environment.

National Telecommunications Commission

In 2000, the TOT and CAT acted as both industry regulators (issuing concessions, allowing private participation in the industry and ensuring "fair" competition) and as telecom network operators themselves. The newly forming National Telecommunications Commission (NTC) would take the job of regulating the industry and issuing new licences away from the TOT and CAT and also advise on concession conversion.

After much delay and political posturing, the law allowing the establishment of the NTC was passed in March 2000 (seven months after the original deadline for the institution to be up and running). However, appointments to the seven seats on the NTC had to pass the Thai legislature. Since the last parliamentary session of the year closed on October 22, 2000, it was highly unlikely that the NTC would be formed that year. Estimates were that the body would be formed in

February 2001 and become fully functional four to five months later.

This delay was seen as a major victory for Taksin Shinawatra, majority owner of the telecommunications conglomerate Shin Corporation (cellular telephone, television and satellite), which was the leading bidder to purchase struggling TT&T, because Khun Taksin was also the leader of the largest new political party as Thais prepared to head to the poles in January 2001 for a general election.[8] *The Economist Intelligence Unit* reported "Thaksin's empire could suffer greatly under regulations that opened the market, but he stands to benefit even more if he gets to power in time to steer the liberalization of the industry."[9]

Not surprisingly, there was a serious concern among industry watchers that the NTC would not be truly independent or transparent. Echoing these concerns, an editorial in *The Nation* (26/08/2000) entitled "New Watchdog, Same Old Bark" stated, "All the old names are back, and judging from the list of contenders, the country's first telecom regulatory body seems likely to turn out to be just another bureaucratic superpower." Indeed, few expected the NTC to be truly independent in a country with such close ties between government and business. The formation of the NTC offered a prime patronage opportunity; its seven members would be elected for six-year terms, during which they could not be dismissed except under rare circumstances, as stipulated in the law creating the NTC.

BTO Contract Conversion

Private ownership of telecom assets was still illegal in Thailand. Therefore, as previously mentioned, private sector telecom firms operated through build-transfer-operate (BTO) concessions granted by the government (through state enterprises like the TOT and CAT). Private operators constructed the assets and then transferred them to the relevant licensor. The private operators then had exclusive right to use the assets while at the same time (in most cases) sharing the revenue with the licensors (either the TOT or CAT) under terms agreed to in the contracts.

In the past couple of years, paying royalties had become a severe burden for telecom operators such as Thai Telephone and Telecommunication (TT&T) and Telecom Asia (TA) who were struggling to survive under mountains of debt spurred by currency devaluation and the economic slump. To add to their troubles, once the market was liberalized, TA and TT&T's outstanding contracts would fall in value, due to the entrance of new competitors.

In order to address the contract conversion issue, a government commission was scheduled to issue non-binding guidelines by December 2000. In lieu of binding guidelines for settlement of the outstanding revenue-sharing agreements, some industry insiders felt that "If no conversion is accomplished by December 2000, both the SOEs and contract holders should be forced to wait five years until they are given the chance to settle again. This will deter the parties from dragging their feet until their favorite political party takes power."[10] Echoing these concerns about political influence in the conversion process, Khun Direk Charoenphol, who had applied for selection as one of the directors of the new NTC, stated, "The NTC should not be allowed to assist players (such as TA and TT&T) with the resolution of onerous concessions. The NTC must be impartial."[11]

The difficult challenge was how to terminate the contracts to the satisfaction of both the SOEs and the contract holders. The sticking points were:

- Whether or not to sell the networks back to TA, TT&T etc. Some proposed leaving the TOT and CAT as owners, with contract holders leasing the networks. The TOT and CAT had publicly stated that they did not want to sell back the networks.
- Calculating the present value of all revenues the contract holders would have earned over the life of their contracts, and therefore how much money (or equity) to remit to the TOT and CAT

in return for cancelling those contracts. The difficulty was that several mutually agreeable assumptions had to be made. For example:

- What market share the new entrants would wrest from the incumbents.
- What the future revenue streams of the former contract holders would be, in light of greater competition through liberalization.
- The overall prosperity of the country and its effect on the demand for telecommunications.

The TOT Held All the Cards

It was commonly agreed that the SOEs held the power positions in the ongoing contract conversions. As an example, the TOT wielded four primary levers over TA and TT&T.

- More than 90 per cent of the network assets of both companies had been turned over to the TOT, which retained legal ownership of the networks.
- While TA and TT&T billed customers, the cheques were made out to the TOT, which then passed on revenues (less its share) to TA and TT&T.
- Under the existing scheme, the TOT retained 16 per cent of TA's revenues and 43 per cent of TT&T's revenues.
- All domestic long distance had to be sent down the TOT's trunks.

Officials of the TOT, CAT and the Ministry of Transport and Communications (MOTC) had expressed a desire to complete the conversion of telecom BTO contracts before the privatization of TOT and CAT, but they had also publicly espoused a belief that the privatization could proceed even with the BTOs still in place. Others were not so sure. Though theoretically feasible, potential strategic investors would be very hesitant to invest in the new entity with the uncertainty of conversion still outstanding. At the very least, they would almost certainly pay significantly less to compensate for the uncertainty.

The government had stated that it did not intend to take over the private operators (i.e., own more than a 50 per cent stake), even though the value of its future revenue share could conceivably be worth more than half of some private companies. Hence, in order to complete the contract conversion, it appeared the government would have to "leave value on the exhibit," regardless of the ultimate form of conversion. It therefore seemed that no agreement would be reached if the government insisted on retaining the theoretical full value of its revenue share streams under the BTOs.

Alternatives to Equity

To date, the most commonly discussed form of BTO conversion had been to issue new equity to the TOT/CAT, which was in fact, a kind of reverse privatization. If this happened, all telephone companies in Thailand would have cross holding shares, which would undermine competition.

Receipt of equity in lieu of royalty payments was clearly not the only viable solution. Assuming a present value of future revenue share payments could be agreed upon, that present value could be securitized in several ways, including:

- Cash—Unfortunately, Advanced Information Service (AIS) was probably the only private carrier potentially able to make such a payment quickly, though payments could theoretically be made on an installment basis.
- Subordinated Debt—Issuing sub-debt to the TOT/CAT would be similar to an installment payment scheme. However, commercial lender approval to violate existing loan covenants (most of which had already been breached) would not likely happen.
- Non-voting Preferred Equity—This was more likely to be acceptable to commercial lenders and would also maintain existing shareholders' management control.

Since the early 1990s, Thailand had been undergoing limited privatization in the telecommunications sector through BTO arrangements. The private sector was now the driving force behind the development of the industry, providing a significant portion of the manpower, financing and technology.

The Telecommunications Master Plan originally stipulated that the TOT and CAT would be privatized by October 1999, with their regulatory roles taken over by a new agency. This deadline was missed. The government then stated that privatization would occur by mid-2000. This target too had come and gone with little progress. In December 2000, the law allowing the corporatization of the TOT and CAT became effective. This allowed for the TOT to be incorporated as TOT Co. Ltd. (TOTC) and for the CAT to be split into CAT Telecommunications Co. Ltd. (CATT) and CAT Postal Services Co. Ltd. (CATS). The Ministry of Finance (MOF) and MOTC would jointly establish a holding company, which would initially hold 100 per cent in TOTC, CATT and CATS.

Overcoming this hurdle had paved the way for eventual privatization under which the government (through the MOTC and MOF) would own less than 50 per cent of the TOT and CAT, which would no longer possess regulatory power. Private strategic partners would be invited to hold 25 per cent each in TOTC and CATT while 22 per cent of each company would be sold to private institutional investors, each of whom would hold no more than five per cent. The TOT and CAT employees would hold three per cent in TOTC and CATT, respectively. The government estimated that it would have private investors in place by December 2001.

By 2005, the TOT planned to list on the Stock Exchange of Thailand and make an initial public offering of shares.

The CAT Wanted a Share Deal Before the TOT

The government had planned to privatize the TOT and CAT at the same time. Nonetheless, it had been noted in the local press that the CAT was determined to sell its 25 per cent stake to a foreign partner ahead of the TOT.

The CAT was now in the process of drawing up a set of criteria to screen candidates. "We are smaller than the TOT. Selling the stake at the same time as TOT will not be good for both for us," stated Kravud Kusuvarn, Senior Executive VP, CAT.[12]

A source close to the MOTC, Minister Suthep Thuagsuban, said the evaluation of the CAT's equity had been finished. In 1999, the CAT's value was put at Baht 71.9 billion, as recommended by a Goldman Sachs-led consulting group, and at Baht 74.9 billion as suggested by another consortium led by JP Morgan Securities (The TOT's value was approximately Baht 200 billion).[13] The source noted that the two figures were estimated on the basis of the agency's telecom businesses. Its postal businesses would be spun off as a separate entity.

Many Questions Yet to Be Resolved

Before privatization could be implemented, a few bold decisions had to be made. For example, how would the TOT and CAT be privatized? Would they be privatized so that the private sector would actively participate in the TOT/CAT's management? If such was the case, how much participation would the private sector have in the TOT/CAT's management? Or would they be privatized in a manner to get the equity from the private sector and not the private sector's expertise? In such a case, how could the private sector investing in the state-run enterprises be assured that the state employees would resist the possible political pressure to operate the enterprise as a non-profit public service at a cost to the shareholders?

Privatization also led to the need to resolve personnel issues. The salary levels of employees of the TOT and CAT were considerably lower than their counterparts in the private sector, but on the other hand, most staff had been enjoying a more relaxed work environment and state-provided welfare. In addition, if the private sector invested in the corporatized TOT or CAT, it would likely be concerned by the size of the workforce. Efforts and creativity would be required to resolve the personnel issue to the mutual satisfaction of both the employees and the investors.

TOT/CAT Must Compete on an Equal Footing Basis

In order to promote development in telecommunications activities, the TOT/CAT should be structured so as to compete with other operators on an equal footing basis. Namely, the TOT/CAT should not be allowed:

- To be exempted from any costs that other operators would have to pay. For example, if other operators were required to pay the state any royalty or fees, the TOT/CAT should be required to do the same;
- To prescribe or approve specifications for telecommunications equipment;
- To have authority to approve or disapprove new types of telecommunications services;
- To regulate service charges; or
- To force others to use its services rather than the services that might be provided by new entrants.

The Optimal Reform Process

Due to pressure from the World Trade Organization and particularly the United States—which had been campaigning aggressively for the liberalization of the world telecommunications industry—the Thai government would most likely have had to open up Thailand's telecommunications industry to more foreign participation eventually. However, it was Thailand's obligations to the WTO and IMF, under which Thailand agreed to liberalize many sectors of the economy including telecommunications, that brought a real sense of urgency to the push towards liberalization.

According to the Telecommunications Master Plan, a series of telecom services were to be opened up for full domestic competition (with foreign stakes capped at 20 per cent) by

January 1, 2000: content/information service (e.g., directory, operator-assisted service); value-added services (video conference, non-voice Internet); and infrastructure service (transmission lines). However, this assumed that the establishment of the NTC, concession conversion and privatization would have taken place as scheduled. As none of the goals had yet been attained, the deadline for liberalization was missed.

The subsequent liberalization milestones were: January 2003, network service (mobile phones, overseas calls, fixed-line service) was to be liberalized (foreign ownership still subject to the 20 per cent limit); and January 2006, by which time Thailand was obliged under the WTO General Agreement on Trade and Services (GATS) to increase the maximum level of foreign ownership to 49 per cent.

With the 2006 deadline looming on the horizon, there had been calls from many quarters including the press, foreign owners and even Mr. Sombat Uthaisang, board chairman of the TOT, that the sequence of events as outlined in the Master Plan be ignored. Instead, it was argued that liberalization should occur as soon as the NTC was up and running and able to undertake its regulatory and licence issuing roles in the summer of 2001, regardless of the state of progress in BTO contract conversion or privatization. The reasoning was that the longer reform was delayed, the less time that the domestic operators would have to prepare themselves for the inevitable increase in foreign participation beginning in 2006. Besides, it was argued, the entry of more efficient competitors into the sector would force the contract holders and the TOT/CAT to come to an agreement as soon as possible to rid themselves of their revenue-sharing agreements. Once these BTOs were converted, valuation of the newly privatized TOT and CAT would also be made much easier.

The most appropriate sequence of events continued to be hotly contested (see Exhibit 6).

INVESTOR SENTIMENT

Not surprisingly, foreign investors were less than enthusiastic about getting involved in an industry with so many unresolved issues. The missed deadlines and lack of consistency in government policy only increased the distaste foreign investors were showing for this sector. "They will not invest until the dust settles," said Amarit Sukhavanij, senior research analyst—Telecoms, Merrill Lynch (Thailand).[14] As illustrated in Exhibit 7—which chronicles the frustrations of six foreign companies who had their winning bids to build an SDH (Synchronous Digital Hierarchy) high-speed fibre-optic network scrapped six times in the past four years—investing in Thailand was not for the faint of heart (see Exhibit 7).

Foreign investors' reluctance to enter the Thai telecom market was perhaps understandable: "Investors are wary, and besides, there are better telecom opportunities elsewhere, like in China and India."[15] However it was unfortunate, not only for the telecom sector, which could have

Ideal Scenario	Original Deadline	Possible Scenario	Possible Time Frame
Establishment of NTC	Jul-99	Establishment of NTC	Mar-01
BTO Contract Conversion	Sep-99	Liberalization (partial)	Jul-01
Privatization	Oct-99	Privatization	Dec-01
Liberalization (partial)	Jan-00	BTO Contract Conversion	??

Exhibit 6   Several Ways to Order the Steps

Source: Dataconsult Ltd./The Nation.

	1993	TOT initiates SDH (Synchronous Digital Hierarchy) project to develop high-speed fibre-optic network
12-Dec	1995	SDH project, budgeted at Bt9 billion, wins cabinet approval
22-Apr	1996	TOT board divides project into six zones to prevent price collusion
7-Oct	1996	14 suppliers enter bids
2-Jan	1997	Nine bidders short-listed
4-Jan	1997	TOT names winners: Ericsson, Tomen, Siemens, Jasmine, Mitsui and Loxely. Total price: Bt10.7 billion
11-Jan	1997	TOT board scraps first bid, alleging price collusion among suppliers
27-Jan	1997	New bid called and original six winners chosen again. New price: Bt9.92 billion
6-Aug	1997	TOT board scraps bid results again
23-Aug	1997	Third bid called and same six groups win. New price: Bt12.29 billion*
15-Sep	1997	Six winning suppliers agree to lower price to Bt12.28 billion. TOT board scraps bid.
25-Sep	1997	Forth bid called with same six winners. New Price: Bt12.17 billion
18-Nov	1997	TOT board approves bid results but bargains price down to Bt11.52 billion after excluding some items
28-Feb	1998	Cabinet approves project
25-May	1998	Transport and Communications Minister Suthep Thaugsuban gives TOT go-ahead to sign the contracts with the winners
	1999	TOT board voids bid results and scraps six zone plan. New proposal calls for two components: SDH network equipment and fibre-optic cable
8-Sep	2000	Fifth bid called. Alcatel wins SDH portion with a price of Bt1.79 billion. Fujikura/Tomen offers lowest cable price at Bt6.48 billion. TOT board scraps bid.
23-Sep	2000	Sixth bid called. Fujikura/Tomen agrees to cut price to Bt6.19 billion. TOT board scraps bid.
4-Oct	2000	Seventh bid called

Exhibit 7   SDH Chronicles

Source: "New allegations surround bidding," *Bangkok Post,* October 4, 2000.

*Post large Baht devaluation.

sorely used more foreign investment to improve infrastructure and foster efficiencies that the two SOEs were not capable of, but also for the future economic well-being of the country, which would require a world-class telecommunications infrastructure.

MOBILE VERSUS FIXED LINE PLAYERS

In August 2000, while Thai mobile phone companies were recovering as Thailand pulled out of three years of recession, fixed-line operators remained deep in debt. Adding to the woes of

fixed line operators TA and TT&T, demand for their fixed lines had not increased significantly since the economic collapse of 1997 because their average customer was poorer than a mobile customer and had yet to benefit from the economic rebound.

Thailand's two large cellular companies, Advanced Info Services (AIS) and Total Access Communication (TAC) had both benefited from a revival in consumer demand. AIS was considered by industry analysts to be the most dynamic of the two companies, and it had gained at least 20,000 new subscribers per month since September 1999.[16] As the economy continued to recover, mobile companies were likely to benefit more quickly, as their customers were in higher income groups.

Looking forward, a key issue facing the telecom industry worldwide as a result of the rapid pace of technological change was that of "stranded costs" when new technology suddenly made existing technology obsolete. In telecommunications the issue was if, or when, wireless made traditional fixed lines obsolete, how would one value existing fixed line telecom networks?

However, in Thailand at least, the consensus of opinion was that the issue of stranded costs was in fact a "non-issue."

> The reason is that mobile phones are now, and for the foreseeable future, too costly in a country with a GDP per head of only US$3,000 . . . there is also the fact that there is an excess of fixed-line capacity which keeps price down in an effort to sell more lines and the reality that fibre-optic cable enjoys much greater bandwidth over wireless.[17]

Spectrum Allocation

Throughout the world, a major political issue concerned the question of how best to allocate spectrum for wireless operators. In the past, the Thai government had used an auction process. However, recent experiments with auctions in other countries had encountered serious problems. *The Economist* had emphasized:

> The auction process was designed almost entirely by experts in game theory, one of the economics profession's most esoteric fields . . .
>
> . . . Poorly designed auctions can make governments look foolish. For example, in 1990, New Zealand conducted a so-called second-price sealed-bid auction. Under this scheme, the highest bidder wins, but instead of paying its own bid price, the winner pays the next-highest bid price. In New Zealand many bidders got spectrum rights for prices far below what they had offered. In one case, the top bid was NZ$100,000 (US$60,000) but the winner paid only NZ$6.

A large number of auction questions remained. Should winners be required to pay immediately, or should payments be spread over a certain time period? Would "the winner's curse" frequently mean that the winning bidder would have paid too much? Would licence interdependencies be impeded by the bidding process that allocated each regional spectrum individually? Would some bidders simply not have the capability or qualifications to implement their plans? Should forfeiture penalties be incurred by bidders who failed to comply with certain commitments? Should there be reserved prices and minimum opening bids? Should there be a series of rounds in the bidding process in order for each bidder to arrive over time at an optimal bid?

As an alternative process for spectrum allocation, some governments used a comparative selection process in which public servants examined a wide variety of aspects of each applicant's proposal. Of particular importance to some governments was the concept of universal service, and each proposal could be evaluated on the degree to which it promised to serve high-cost as well as low-cost areas. With the anticipated growth in wireless, the Thai government had to come to some resolution of these issues, as well.

PROSPECTS FOR E-COMMERCE

The e-commerce revolution in Thailand was still in its embryonic stage, compared to the regional hi-tech vanguards, Hong Kong and Singapore. A January 2000 report by Thammasat University stated that the e-business sector was worth about US$2 million in 1999 and projected to reach a meagre US$30 million by 2001.

Nevertheless, demographics favored a rapidly expanding Internet industry in Thailand and, hence, more robust e-commerce predictions over the longer term. Although there were only about 200,000 ISP subscribers and about 800,000 Internet users in the country as of March 2000,[18] estimates were that the number of users was growing at 50 per cent per annum with most of the growth coming from the Kingdom's relatively young population (28 per cent or 17 million of Thailand's 60 million people are under the age of 15).[19] It was this potential for growth in the user base that led others to speculate that the value of business-to-business e-commerce transactions alone (excluding business-to-consumer) in Thailand could reach $11 billion by 2005.[20]

Nonetheless, even the optimists recognized that in order to meet such lofty expectations, Thailand had to grapple with certain unresolved issues including the formation of a unified e-commerce governmental action plan and the fostering of co-operation between local banks with regard to payment transaction settlement.

Thailand currently lacked a coherent approach to the new economy. Some speculated that this lack was because different ministries were responsible for different components of what should have been an integrated policy. For example, the Science and Technology Ministry oversaw information technology policy, and the Transport and Communications Ministry was responsible for telephone and other basic telecom infrastructure. Meanwhile, the Commerce Ministry was charged with trying to promote e-commerce. As a result, the existing policies for guiding Thailand into the new economy were "fractured and ineffective" according to Deputy Commerce Minister Goanpot Asvinvichit. He felt strongly that the next government should therefore consolidate these policies and assign a capable cabinet member as e-minister. He pointed to several countries that had already done this, such as Singapore.

Singapore: An E-Commerce Model

Among ASEAN countries, many cited Singapore as an example of a nation that had successfully promoted the Internet and e-commerce. As of January 2001, ebusinessforum.com, a division of the Economist Intelligence Unit, listed Singapore an impressive eighth out of 60 countries in its e-business readiness rankings. The credit for developing the city-state into a "regional e-commerce leader"[21] largely belonged to the government. As early as 1996, the Singaporean government understood that online businesses needed a particular type of operating environment that included network services, trust systems and payment services in order to implement their online business processes. Therefore, the government incentivized Singapore's information technology (IT) industry and financial institutions to work in partnership with the government to develop these infrastructure services such as online payment systems, trust and security systems, directory services and other intermediary e-business services. Primary responsibility for the growth of the Internet and e-commerce was given to the Info-Communications Development Authority of Singapore (IDA)[22] which implemented various support schemes, including consulting and funding, that were made available to small and medium-size businesses wishing to participate in e-business.

In addition, many other government agencies had the promotion of e-commerce incorporated into their mandate. These agencies included The Economic Development Board, The Monetary Authority of Singapore, The Tourism Board, The Trade Development Board, The Productivity & Standards Board and The National Science & Technology Board.

Several laws were also enacted or amended to promote the growth of e-commerce including:

- The Evidence Act was amended (1997) to allow the use of electronic records as evidence in courts;
- The Electronic Transactions Act (July 1998) was enacted to provide a legal foundation for electronic signatures, and gave predictability and certainty to contracts formed electronically.

As a consequence of its government's proactive stance, Singapore boasted "one of the most advanced Internet economies in the world"[23] and was preparing to take even further strides. In January 2001, the Singaporean government's future plans included:

- A three-year, $11.7-million plan to prod the city's growing logistics industry into doing more with the Internet.
- Setting up a help desk at the IDA for businesses seeking guidance on e-commerce policy. The aim would be to provide one-stop assistance for companies that were planning to set up online businesses.
- Singapore's Ministry of Communication and Information Technology was to fully liberalize the telecoms sector on April 1, 2001.

Some felt Thailand should emulate Singapore's approach and support the development of e-commerce in specific ways. For example, the government could share the risk of new ventures by setting up incubators and venture capital funds to provide seed money to start-ups. These emerging e-businesses could also benefit from several years of tax exemption. The government could also create equal opportunity for access to the Internet nationwide. In addition, the government could support the private sector by providing tax incentives for educating the public about e-commerce and other aspects of the new economy. Some, like Mr. Goanpot, also felt the government should set up IT centres nationwide. Such an integrated approach however, taking place within the slow moving bureaucracies of three separate Thai ministries, would indeed be a challenge.

A major difficulty stunting the growth of e-commerce in Thailand was that the country's financial institutions could not agree on developing a co-operative, Internet-based invoicing and payment platform. So far, the banks preferred to ignore recent evidence of the benefits of co-operation and go their own way. However, judging from experiences in the United States, Europe and recently Hong Kong, organizations were fighting a losing battle when they chose to develop their own proprietary trading platforms and systems in the hopes of beating their competitors to the punch.

The General Motors and Daimler-Chrysler-led auto exchange was a good example of competitors establishing business exchanges that could dramatically reduce procurement costs and boost bottom line profits. In Hong Kong, an Internet application service provider (ASP), iMerchant.com, grouped more than 51 banks, which handled more than 80 per cent of all bank transactions, into an ASP known as Jetco Online. Jetco Online was to be launched in late 2000.

On the brighter side, unlike the situation in banking, a select few Thai business organizations did seem to be heading in the right direction with co-operative efforts. Thai Union Foods, a diversified food processor with both domestic and export operations established a food exchange with more than 20 other competitors in the spring of 2000.

Nonetheless, it was the banks that had to learn the benefits of co-operation, hopefully sooner than later. "Having the ability to close the loop on payments is what's going to distinguish those market places that succeed from those that fall by the wayside," stated Peter Hohenstein, Bank of America.[24]

TELECOMS AND THE NEW ECONOMY: THE ROAD AHEAD

Most observers felt that the reasons to privatize and liberalize the telecommunications industry were sound. Besides meeting Thailand's commitment to the international community, privatization of SOEs and liberalization would likely bring increased private participation and competition and thereby improve the quality of service and reduce consumer prices in several key sectors of the economy including telecommunications. It would also free up public resources and likely allow for a reduction in the public debt.

However, some thought that these gains would be realized only if the liberalization and privatization process was accomplished correctly. This led to the obvious question: What was the correct way to restructure the industry? Was the correct order, as many had suggested, to first establish the NTC, then to convert the BTO contracts, then to privatize the TOT and CAT and then finally to liberalize? What if, due to bureaucratic delays, political posturing, nepotism and accommodation of special interests, this "optimal" order wasn't followed? What were the consequences for the telecommunications industry, and therefore Thailand's participation in the new economy, if privatization happened before contact conversion or liberalization happened before privatization?

Furthermore, would foreign investors be interested in Thai telecoms despite a perception of corruption and a seeming lack of transparency regarding the whole privatization/liberalization process? Was opening up the telecom sector to foreigners the right thing to do? Or was that a moot question in light of Thailand's commitments to the international community and its desire to one day become a "first world" nation?

As it entered the 21st century, Thailand would have to ensure that its telecom sector would provide the advanced technologies and enhanced efficiencies necessary for Thailand to enter the New Economy and e-commerce. The "Conclusions from an UNCTAD Conference on E-Commerce and LDC's" presented a set of guidelines that Thailand's leaders would have to analyse, and perhaps implement (see Appendix).

NOTES

1. EIU Country Profile 2000. Thailand.
2. See the TOT Web site at: www.tot.or.th/.
3. See the CAT Web site at: www.cat.or.th/.
4. Draft Telecommunications Master Plan, MOTC, August 1997.
5. As of December 2000, an SERC Web site did not appear to exist.
6. "Mobile Mess," EIU Country Briefing (Thailand), as reproduced in *Thailand Corporate Alert,* July 7, 2000.
7. From an interview with Dr. Sumeth Vongpanitlerd, Senior Research Specialist, Thai Development Research Institute, August 29, 2000.
8. As of January 6, 2001, Taksin Shinawatra and his Thai Rak Thai party appeared to have won the general election. However, estimates were that it would take a month or more for the election results to be made official because of the need to investigate allegations of illegal activities, including vote buying by many of the political parties.

9. "Mobile Mess," EIU Country Briefing (Thailand), as reproduced in *Thailand Corporate Alert,* July 7, 2000.
10. From an interview with Dr. Sumeth Vongpanitlerd, Senior Research Specialist, Thai Development Research Institute, August 29, 2000.
11. From an interview September 1, 2000.
12. From an interview August 24, 2000.
13. From an interview with Peter Raymond, Partner, Arthur Andersen (Thailand), August 28, 2000.
14. From an interview August 30, 2000.
15. From an interview with Dr. Sumeth Vongpanitlerd, Senior Research Specialist, Thai Development Research Institute, August 29, 2000.
16. "Thai Lines 2Q00," *Merrill Lynch,* June 13, 2000.
17. From an interview with Stuart Macpherson, Telecommunications Consultant to The Royal Thai Government, August 30, 2000.
18. "Lack of leadership hinders online drive," *Bangkok Post,* March 20, 2000.
19. Country Data, Thailand, August 2000, *www.eiu.com.*
20. "E-Commerce: Settling Accounts," *Far Eastern Economic Review,* August 24, 2000.
21. ebusinessforum.com.
22. See the IDA Web site at: www.ec.gov.sg.
23. ebusinessforum.com.
24. "E-Commerce: Settling Accounts," *Far Eastern Economic Review,* August 24, 2000.

APPENDIX

Following are the "Conclusions" from the Roundexhibit on "E-Commerce and less developed countries (LDCs)," Kathmandu (Nepal), 21–30 May 2000, sponsored in part by the United Nations Conference on Trade and Development (UNCTAD).

Conclusion No 1

Electronic commerce is not a dream or a distant reality. It has started to affect in a fundamental and qualitative fashion the ways in which enterprises and countries produce, trade and compete. Even in countries with poor infrastructure and access to information technology, evidence exists that dynamic enterprises and governments have started to take advantage of the possibilities offered by e-commerce.

Conclusion No 2

LDCs can derive benefits by participating actively in e-commerce. By contributing to lowering transaction costs and to reducing geographical disadvantages, e-commerce is of direct importance to all LDCs; in the absence of appropriate domestic and international action, however, the "trillion dollar economy" could bypass LDCs, which would then run a distinct risk of being on the wrong side of a growing Digital Divide.

Conclusion No 3

Specific and co-ordinated action is necessary to allow LDCs to integrate profitably into the emerging global information/knowledge economy; in this context, e-commerce should be considered as a priority. Because e-commerce has the potential to yield visible benefits in a relatively short period, because it stimulates mutually beneficial relations between governments and enterprises, and because it has multiplier effects on other key areas of the development of LDCs (including education, infrastructure and better governance), its development in LDCs should receive priority attention and support from the governments and enterprises of LDCs themselves, but also from relevant international organizations and donors, bilateral and multilateral.

Priority Areas for Action

1. Develop an autonomous vision. The governments and enterprises of LDCs interested in developing e-commerce policies and strategies should design such policies and strategies without being excessively fascinated with current "success stories" or "models" of e-commerce. For example, LDCs should grant priority attention to developments in the area of business-to-business transactions (B2B) and business-to-government transactions (B2G) rather than to business-to-consumer (B2C),

which remains the dominant activity of most dot-com companies in developed countries. Both enterprises and governments should also focus on the commerce part of electronic commerce, rather than on its electronic component: success in e-commerce starts with a good understanding of what e-commerce will help buying or selling.

2. Ensure proper linkage between the old and the new economy. Through disintermediation and reintermediation, as well as through the emergence of new ways of creating and distributing value, e-commerce has started to change radically our modes of production and trade. The successful introduction of e-commerce in LDCs will hence require a complete review of the value chain and supply chain in the sectors most likely to benefit from/be affected by e-commerce. At the same time, the "new economy" should not be seen as a world of "pure bits"; eventually, atoms will also have to cross borders in the form of goods and materials. Infrastructure and trade-supporting services (transport, banking, insurance, telecommunications, customs i.a.) will remain key to the success of LDCs in e-commerce. Efficiency in such sectors is a prerequisite to the development of any e-commerce strategy. Moreover, macro-economic considerations relating to trade, finance (including debt) and investment must also be taken by governments into account in making decisions in the area of e-commerce. From an enterprise point of view, the basic principles of good management (including accounting practices) fully apply in the area of e-commerce. Priority attention needs to be granted to the ways in which old industries and practices can be adapted to modern ways of doing business and trade.

3. Responsibilities of enterprises. In many instances, private enterprises will have to take the lead in creating an "e-commerce culture" in LDCs, because they are generally closer to the relevant sources of knowledge and good practice. However, it must be kept in mind that, in many LDCs, the private sector is still embryonic: in such cases, appropriate governmental action remains necessary, and should aim at stimulating the growth of healthy and private enterprises ready to compete in the new economy. Foreign enterprises and international business alliances

can greatly help such efforts by maintaining contacts with the enterprises (especially SMEs) of LDCs, and sharing with them knowledge and experiences in the area of e-commerce.

4. Responsibilities of governments. In LDCs, governments willing to stimulate e-commerce should focus on six main areas of action, namely:

- *Develop an explicit long-term vision* of the role of information, information technology and knowledge in their social and economic strategy; designing and communicating (to all parts of civil society) a clear IT policy appears as of particular importance in this context;
- *Implement appropriate fiscal, legal and regulatory policies;* such policies should aim inter alia at stimulating the development of appropriate infrastructure (e.g., in telecommunications) and reducing the cost of access to relevant equipment and networks (in particular the Internet);
- *Grant central priority* to the development of adequate human resources: vocational training and basic education in fields such as informatics and telecommunications are critically important;
- *Provide guidance and incentives* for the rapid and balanced development of information infrastructure, especially in rural and remote areas;
- *Stimulate the involvement* of all groups of population in the knowledge revolution, inter alia by encouraging the participation of women in relevant sectors and activities;
- *Encourage the production of local content on the Internet;* information in local languages, and multilingual content reflecting local cultures and ways of living will contribute not only to promoting LDC products abroad, but also to the diversity (and hence the sustainability) of the Internet.

5. Responsibilities of the international community. Relevant international organizations and external donors can contribute to making the efforts of LDCs more successful by focusing on the following six areas:

- *Provide the analytical, conceptual and statistical elements* likely to help local players to design and implement an efficient e-commerce vision;
- *Stimulate exchanges of experiences* among the governments and enterprises of LDCs on one hand, and the governments and enterprises of other countries on the other hand;
- *Bring support to the LDC authorities* responsible for institution building, as they relate to telecommunications, regulation or other areas relevant to e-commerce such as certification;
- *Offer relevant tools* to increase the level of information available in LDCs about e-commerce, and help LDCs to participate more actively in relevant international fora, whether inter-governmental (such as WTO) or not (such as ICANN);
- *Pursue inter-organizational efforts* in order to simplify the task of LDCs in obtaining relevant information and support in the area of e-commerce; joint Web sites (such as the ITU-UNCTAD-WIPO site on e-commerce) and publications (such as the ITC-UNCTAD-WTO leaflet on e-commerce) are examples of such co-operation and need to be expanded; co-operative efforts such as those displayed through the Kathmandu Roundexhibit on "LDCs and e-commerce" should be considered as an example to be followed;
- The international community has the central responsibility in bringing the theme of "LDCs and e-commerce" to the attention of global fora, and to use such fora as a way to generate the support of donors for efforts in this area. In that context, *priority attention should be granted to the upcoming Third United Nations Conference* on the LDCs (Brussels, June 2001).

LUCENT IN INDIA

*Prepared by Harnek Minhas under the
supervision of Professor David Conklin*

Version: (A) 2002-01-10

THE LUCENT DOWNTURN
AND THE INDIA OPPORTUNITY

India appeared to be a nation of enormous investment opportunity, with its population of one billion people and its relatively high growth rate. India's telecom sector, in particular, appeared to offer first-mover advantages, as the government of India promised to institute economic reforms that would privatize government-owned telecom systems and that would give telecom corporations much greater freedom from traditional government regulations. However, the year 2000 brought a substantial downturn to the global telecom sector, and Lucent was hurt severely. Analysts debated whether this was a temporary global downturn or whether the global telecom industry faced long-term structural challenges. Perhaps the hopes for e-business had been naively optimistic. Analysts also debated whether the less-developed nations would be able to leap into the Internet age or whether there would be an increase in polarization between rich and poor nations with regard to telecom opportunities. Meanwhile, it was not clear whether—or to what degree—India's economic reforms would actually materialize, nor was it clear whether India would achieve macroeconomic stability.

In Lucent's 1999 annual report, Richard McGinn, chairman and chief executive officer of Lucent Technologies Inc., expressed enthusiastic optimism regarding the company's future:

> I am pleased to report that this year Lucent was recognized as the global leader in the communications networking market and in more than a dozen high-growth market areas. We achieved that leadership by growing faster than the market and by taking market share. Lucent leads in our ability to design, build and service networks for the next generation. Demand for our communications semiconductors and optoelectronic devices also continues to grow as communications becomes the new driver for the industry. Today, Lucent is the worldwide leader in chips and devices specifically built for communications products such as cell phones, modems and personal computers. In addition, we are a leader in the hottest semiconductor trend since the microprocessor-systems-on-a-chip solutions. This new technology, which places the electronics for an entire system like a cell phone on a single fingernail-sized slice of silicon, offers our customers benefits such as lower cost, reduced power consumption and easier integration into their products.

Within 12 months of this self-congratulatory optimism, Lucent came crashing down to earth. As the company's stock melted from a high of $82 in December 1999 to a low of $12 in November 2000, Lucent lost close to $200 billion in market value. In October 2000, the company dismissed Richard McGinn as its CEO. As the U.S. economy slowed, Lucent struggled to survive in a rapidly declining telecom equipment market. A number of prominent Wall Street analysts downgraded the stock, and the company announced a series of restructuring efforts in order to stem the flow. As part of the restructuring announcements, Lucent sold its power systems division and spun-off two of its own business units into new companies.

Nevertheless, Lucent reported consolidated revenues of approximately $33.8 billion for the year 2000 and a net income of $1.2 billion. More than 33 per cent of these revenues came from outside North America, due largely to rapidly growing sales in Asia.

Amidst these tough times, Vijay K. Gupta rejoined Lucent in India as president and CEO. In early 2000, Lucent decided to take a more positive position in the Indian market. As Gupta contemplated the past 10 years of Lucent's existence in the Indian market, he recognized the slow process of privatization of the telecom services sector and the consequent difficulties for an equipment supplier like Lucent. Times of optimism had repeatedly given way to disappointment, and the corporate difficulties Lucent now faced would not give the company much scope for misjudgment.

Gupta had been involved with AT&T—and then with Lucent in one way or another—ever since AT&T had set up operations in India in the late 1980s. Both Lucent and AT&T had a checkered past in the Indian market. Lucent had entered the Indian market in the hope of emerging as a dominant player in the local telecom industry. While the company had enjoyed some modest success in the recent past, the very slow pace of reforms in the Indian telecom sector had frustrated the growth efforts of the business.

Nevertheless, in 2000 Lucent had emerged as one of the most successful telecom equipment manufacturers in India and had signed a string of contracts with Indian service providers to supply and build modern telecom networks all over India. As the pace of reforms in the Indian telecom sector increased, the market appeared to be on the verge of a dramatic expansion.

REGULATORY STRUCTURE

In 1994, the government announced the National Telecom Policy (NTP), which defined the objectives for growth of the telecom infrastructure in India. NTP 1994 also recognized that the required resources for achieving these targets would not be available from government funding and concluded that private investment and involvement was required to bridge the resource gap. The NTP paved the way for the entry of the private sector into telecom services and the introduction of cellular and value-added services. As is the case with most countries, separate licences were issued for basic, cellular, ISP, satellite and cable-TV operators, each with a separate industry structure, terms of entry and varying requirements to create infrastructure.

The 1994 telecom policy reforms had certain shortfalls, and the liberalization process failed to get off the ground. First, allocations of licences for basic and cellular services were based on the highest bid, which led to companies quoting unrealistic amounts in their attempt to be awarded the circle (the telecom policy defines a circle as a region for which licences are granted). Also, the government had set a minimum reserve price for the licensee fee. Bids for basic services were therefore not received for eight circles because prospective bidders found the licence fee too high. This led to aggressive and unrealistic licence fee bids and made financial closure difficult to achieve. It also resulted in the entry of operators who had not been evaluated rigorously in terms of their cost-revenue projections, their ability to manage the capacity build-up and operations, or their motive for participating in the bidding process (for instance, to sell the licence later if permitted). Finally, only six licenses were awarded for basic services for the 21 existing circles for cellular services.

By 1999, the targets as envisaged in the objectives of the NTP 1994 had remained unfulfilled. The private sector entry was slower than was envisaged in the NTP 1994. The cabinet approved its "New Telecom Policy" in March 1999, and the policy was implemented in April 1999.

- The new policy envisaged a telephone density of seven per cent by 2005 (approximately 75 million lines) and 15 per cent by 2010 (approximately 160 million lines).
- A significant shift from the fixed licence fee regime to a licence fee based on a revenue-sharing mechanism. Licensed telecom service providers were required to pay a one-time entry fee and a licence fee based on revenue sharing.

The share of revenue to be paid was set at a maximum 15 per cent.

- Licences for access services (basic, cellular, radio paging, radio trunking) were issued for an initial period of 20 years, extendable by 10 years.
- Licences for basic and cellular services were granted on a non-exclusive basis.
- Sharing of telecom infrastructure by all service providers was permitted. Interconnectivity among various service providers within the same area of operations was also permitted.
- Lastly, the national long-distance services sector was opened to competition from January 1, 2000.

While there had been a rapid rollout of cellular mobile networks in the metros and states with over two million subscribers, most of the projects were facing problems. The main reason, according to the cellular and basic operators, was that the actual revenues realized by these projects fell far short of the projections, and the operators were unable to arrange financing for their projects and therefore could not complete their projects on time. Basic telecom services by private operators had commenced in a limited way in only two of the six circles where licences were awarded.

The licensing, policy-making and service provision functions were under a single authority. The government decided to separate the policy and licensing functions from the service provision functions. The Department of Telecom (DoT) and Department of Telecom Services (DTS) became Government of India Departments under the Ministry of Communications. DoT had its role in policy-making, licensing and co-ordination matters relating to telegraphs, telephones, wireless, data, facsimile and telematic services and other like forms of communications. In addition, DoT was responsible for frequency management in the field of radio communication in close co-ordination with international bodies. It also enforced wireless regulatory measures for wireless transmission by users in the country. DTS was the premier telecom service provider in India. The main functions of DTS included

planning, engineering, installation, maintenance, management and operation of voice and non-voice telecommunications services all over the country.

A History of Lucent

AT&T and the Justice Department settled an antitrust suit in 1974 when AT&T agreed to divest its local telephone companies, effective January 1, 1984, into Regional Bell Operating Companies, or Baby Bells, as they were popularly known. As part of divestiture, the new unit, AT&T Technologies, received market-focused business units to manufacture and sell consumer products, network systems, technology systems and information systems. AT&T was allowed to retain its domestic and international long distance business only.

During the 1990s, several business units, including AT&T Network Systems, AT&T Global Business Communications Systems, AT&T Microelectronics, AT&T Consumer Products and Bell Labs, combined to become Lucent Technologies. An initial public offering of stock was issued in April 1996, and the spin-off was completed in September 1996, when AT&T distributed its shares of Lucent to AT&T shareholders.

Since its launch, Lucent had become a major player in optical, data and wireless networking; Web-based enterprise solutions that link public and private networks; communications software; professional network design and consulting services; and communications semiconductors and optoelectronics.

Lucent's research and development arm, Bell Laboratories, remained one of the most prolific invention factories, with more than 40,000 inventions since 1925. Bell Labs played a pivotal role in inventing key communications technologies for most of the 20th century, including transistors, digital computers, digital networking and signal processing, lasers and fiber-optic communications systems, communications satellites, cellular telephony, electronic switching of calls, the Unix operating system, fault-tolerant software, software-based communication services, speech synthesis and voice recognition, stereo sound, the fax machine, touch-tone dialing, and modems.

Bell Labs provided Lucent with leading-edge technology in network switching, communications software, optical networking, networking services and support, communications integrated circuits, optoelectronic components for communications, wireless network equipment, and many other areas. While the majority of Bell Labs operations were originally located in Whipanny, New Jersey, since then they had opened research and development (R&D) centres in a number of countries. By 2000, Bell Labs had become a global R&D community comprising more than 30,000 engineers and scientists located across 25 countries. Their research had produced 11 Nobel laureates.

LUCENT IN INDIA

After operating as a liaison office in New Delhi, India, since the late 1980s, AT&T, which was offering its long distance services to India, decided to establish a direct presence in the country. Back in the early 1990s, the combined AT&T operated as a giant telecom conglomerate with businesses ranging from long distance services to telecom equipment manufacturing. As part of its push to expand business outside of the United States, the company decided to target emerging economies like India and China. In 1992, AT&T announced its first joint venture in India, called the Trans-India Network Systems Pvt. Ltd. with Tata Telecom Ltd., a subsidiary of Tata Group. Their purpose was to manufacture, market and distribute telecom network access systems, optical multiplexers, digital line systems, multiple access radio systems and any other telecommunication transmission products that were uniquely suited to the needs of the Indian market. The Tata group was one of India's largest business groups, with annual revenues of US$8 billion and 290,000 employees in 80 principal companies. The Group had interests in

steel, chemicals, automobiles, finance, information technology, communications and power, among others.

Another agreement followed between AT&T and the Tata group when the two companies formed the joint venture AT&T Switching Systems (India) Pvt. Ltd. to produce AT&T's flagship central office switching equipment called the 5ESS switch for use in India's telecommunications network. This allowed AT&T to hold a 51 per cent majority in the equity partnership, and Tata held the remaining 49 per cent in the agreement valued at approximately $35 million. The agreement called for setting up a manufacturing facility located in the city of Bangalore in the southern state of Karnataka, India's high-tech region for research, development and manufacturing of electronic products. India was one of the first developing countries where AT&T had decided to manufacture its flagship switching product 5ESS, the heart of the core telecom networks.

After its separation from AT&T in 1996, Lucent consolidated its businesses in India into the following:

- **Tata Lucent Technologies Ltd.**—a joint venture between Tata Industries (50 per cent) and Lucent Technologies (50 per cent) that focused on systems for network operators such as central office switches, network access systems, transmission systems, network management systems and network wireless products such as global systems for mobile communications (GSM) and personal communications services, wireless systems, InterNetworking Systems, wireless local loop solutions and power systems.
- **Lucent Technologies Finolex Ltd.**—a joint venture between Lucent Technologies (51 per cent) and Indian partner Finolex Cables Ltd. (49 per cent) that manufactured fibre-optic cables in India.
- **Tata Telecom Lucent Technologies**—a joint venture between Tata (25.5 per cent), Lucent Technologies (25.5 per cent), and public and financial institutions (49 per cent) to provide top-end communications technology, products and customer service to enterprises.

Before AT&T separated its services and manufacturing business, the company had also announced a series of agreements with Indian partners to operate as a telecom services provider in India. The company had formed an alliance in January 1994 with the Birla Group, one of India's leading industrial conglomerates. This joint venture was part of the AT&T effort to push into the Indian telecom services business. The alliance was formed to bid on licences auctioned by the Indian government to operate and provide both basic and cellular services to business and residential customers in India. The joint venture operated three cellular mobile service licences in Western India. Through these and other activities, Gupta saw AT&T and Lucent as having played a key role in telecom development in India:

> I would say that we have contributed enormously to the development of the telecom sector in India. During the past decade, we have established manufacturing facilities in India that now produce the very latest telecom networking equipment. We manufacture the entire range of telecom equipment products in India, from network elements to switches to fibre-optic cables.

Tata Lucent Technologies Ltd., the 50-50 joint venture of Lucent and Tata Industries, was created after merging the three different joint ventures Lucent had in India with the Tata group. Vijay Gupta was named the chief executive officer and managing director and led the new joint venture, Tata-Lucent Technologies Ltd. However, Gupta resigned after the joint venture had been in operation for about a year.

With the "New Telecom Policy" of 1999 and the government's decision to jump-start the telecom sector reform announced many years earlier, Lucent Technologies decided to take a majority stake in its flagship venture, Tata-Lucent Technologies, by buying out the stake of its Indian partner, Tata Industries. The Tata-Lucent joint venture company was renamed Lucent Technologies Hindustan Ltd., and Lucent assumed full control of the businesses in India.

Gupta, who had left the joint venture, once again joined Lucent Hindustan as its CEO and president.

In 2000, Lucent's operations in India were grouped under several divisions. Its systems group, the largest, looked after the sales of its switching and transmission equipment to various telco and ISP customers. The software group handled the network management systems and billing software products, which Lucent sold through its own systems team as well as through distributors. Lucent also had a services group, which had not won any substantial business in India.

One of Lucent's main points of focus was to win the big telco rollout orders for its switching and transmission products. Of the five private basic telecom service providers to start operations in India, four became Lucent customers. Lucent also supplied its switching equipment to the Department of Telecom, the government-controlled monopoly services provider.

Another focus was that of structured cabling. Lucent Technologies continued to be the dominant player in this space. In spite of an increased number of competitors, Lucent was able to hold its market share of around 35 per cent in India. The cellular market offered additional opportunities.

By 2000, Lucent's facility in Pune designed and developed multimedia messaging platforms, while the Bangalore facility concentrated on software development related to wireless, switching, data networking, Internet and multimedia technologies. Lucent's scientists conducted software development for the company's global third-generation mobile networks platform. Third-generation wireless networks offered high-speed mobile Internet capabilities and two-way multimedia communications from mobile devices. With the expansion, Lucent planned to employ more than 200 engineering professionals by the end of 2001 in Hyderabad. Bell Labs was also firming agreements with leading academic institutions, such as Indian Institutes of Technology.

Bangalore was a favored destination to setup software ventures in India. It was a city of close to four million and was a high-tech hotspot in India. The city boasted more than 60,000 software jobs, a plethora of multinational software corporations and accounted for almost one quarter of India's $4 billion in software exports. Bill Clinton, past president of the United States, praised the success of Bangalore:

> You embraced IT and now when Americans and other big software companies call for consumer and customer support, they are just as likely to find themselves talking to an expert in Bangalore as one in Seattle.[1]

During the past decade, India emerged as a desired region for sourcing cheap software. Indian engineers had been hired in droves by a number of North American companies, and the current Internet-fuelled boom was partly ascribed to the Indian software writers who had made the Silicon Valley their favorite destination. Yet a still-larger number of Indian software engineers were employed in India. Gupta commented on the scenerio in India for Lucent:

> India is now one of our main destinations for research and development. We at Lucent firmly believe that India has a very huge comparative advantage in terms of supplying fully trained engineers.

Over the past decade, India experienced rapid GDP growth, which averaged six per cent annually. However, the government fiscal deficit had consistently been substantial, leading to relatively high inflation rates and high real interest rates. Inflation had averaged five per cent to six per cent annually and was expected to rise to perhaps eight per cent in 2001, due to increases in energy prices and accelerating growth. The need for government to borrow to cover its fiscal deficit had tended to squeeze out corporate borrowers and keep real interest rates high. India was a relatively closed economy, and external debt was a manageable 20 per cent of GDP.

Consistently high inflation had caused the rupee to devalue on an ongoing basis. Capital inflows were not adequate to sustain the value of the rupee, as the balance of trade deteriorated due to inflation and the rise in prices of imported oil.

Many of the government's reform programs had repeatedly encountered obstacles that stalled them. Privatization plans faced continual negative political reaction. India's trade unions were a powerful force in blocking many reforms, and they were joined by various nationalist groups who also opposed foreign investment and reductions in government subsidies to particular sectors.

Serious doubts existed about the strength of India's financial sector. Non-performing loans formed a large percentage of many banks' portfolios. Meanwhile, the stock market seemed subject to speculative swings that impeded corporate attempts to raise capital.

The IMF urged the government of India to follow traditional macroeconomic prescriptions. Reducing the fiscal deficit and tightening money supply growth would hopefully reduce inflation and put a break on the devaluation cycle. Privatization and deregulation would stimulate economic growth. Removal of foreign ownership restrictions would bring new technologies as well as managerial expertise. A reduction of import barriers would increase domestic competition, stimulating efficiency and innovation. However, the path of these various reforms was not smooth, and some doubted whether substantial progress would be made over the coming few years.

Telecom sector reforms appeared to be caught in a tangled loop of legislative amendments, regulatory restructuring, contrary pulls within the government, and incumbents (both in the public and private sector) crying wolf once too often. However, with the year 2001, things were finally moving in terms of resolving the outstanding issues, and a consensus was emerging among incumbents, potential competitors and, most importantly, among the bureaucracy and political parties. The pace of activity in the telecom sector had picked up considerably with significant new investments.

A world class telecom infrastructure was seen as a key enabler to growth in information

	1996	*1998*	*2000*
GDP at market prices (Rs billion)	13.6	17.6	21.3
GDP (US$ billion)	384.0	419.5	490.5
Real GDP growth (%)	7.4	6.8	6.2
Consumer price inflation (average; %)	9.0	13.2	5.4
Population (millions)	939.5	970.9	1,002.8
Exports of goods fob (US$ million)	33,737.0	34,076.0	43,084.6
Imports of goods fob (US$ million)	43,789.0	44,828.0	60,803.9
Current-account balance (US$ million)	−5,957.0	−6,903.0	−12,801.8
Foreign-exchange reserves excluding gold (US$ million)	20,170.0	27,341.0	31,500.0
Total external debt (US$ billion)	93.5	98.2	99.6
Debt-service ratio, paid (%)	23.2	21.2	18.3
Exchange rate (average) Rs:US$	35.43	41.26	44.82

Exhibit 1   Annual Indicators: Economic Trends in India

Source: EIU Country Report November 2000 (November 13, 2000 Rs 46.73:US$1).

technology (IT). According to the McKinsey and Indian National Association of Software and Service Companies (NASSCOM) joint study, India should aspire to achieve global parity in all three elements of telecom infrastructure: local loops, national backbone and international gateways. India fell short of current global standards in the quality of its communications infrastructure owing to its poor reliability, bandwidth, costs and range of services.

As India entered the 21st century, reliability was well below global standards on domestic circuits. The downtime varied from three per cent to 15 per cent against the global benchmark of less than 0.1 per cent. On international circuits, the downtime varied from 0.9 per cent to two per cent against the global benchmark of less than 0.3 per cent.

Bottlenecks in local loops hampered bandwidth availability. The lack of high-speed national data backbone also forced companies to locate outside the main metros. International gateway capacity was also bottlenecked. The high cost of telecom services and limitations in telecom service acted as a major block for IT-enabled services in the country.

To achieve the McKinsey forecast of $87 billion of IT exports by 2008, India had to develop over 2.2 million high-quality knowledgeable workers. It had to ensure that its workforce had the right mix of technical, business and functional skills to meet the needs of the individual business segments and customers in different markets of the world. Even the regulatory environment had to be tuned so that e-commerce could operate effectively in the country and so that better investment opportunities would exist for venture capitalists who were planning to fund startups in the country. New laws had to be developed in fields such as cyber laws, telecom regulations, investment policies, capital market regulations, procedures, labor laws and taxation.

THE PROSPECTS FOR INFORMATION TECHNOLOGY IN INDIA

"India is on the threshold of a second tryst with destiny." These were the words of Rajat Gupta, the chief executive officer of McKinsey & Co, when he described India's opportunity to be a leading player in the knowledge-driven global economy of the new millennium. Gupta was commenting on a joint study by the NASSCOM and McKinsey on the Indian IT industry in 1999. The study predicted that India had the potential to become a global player in IT and could achieve export revenues of $87 billion by 2008. The study also estimated that the domestic market for software and services within India would be

at $18 billion by 2008. Of this, domestic IT services would be $6.5 billion; domestic products, $1.9 billion; services to e-businesses, $2 billion; and resale of products would be $7.8 billion.

To gauge the dimensions of the IT industry in India, it would be pertinent to look at the achievements, indicators and growth prospects of the Indian IT industry, as indicated in Exhibit 2.

- In the year 1998–99, the Indian IT industry earned revenues of US$6.1 billion, a growth of 32.79 per cent over the revenue in year 1997–98. This high growth rate was achieved in spite of otherwise slow growth in the Indian economy, the uncertain political situation and the not-so-healthy GDP growth.
- In India, IT spending as a percentage to GDP was currently less than one per cent. In the United States however, IT spending as a percentage to GDP was more than 3.5 per cent. The government of India resolved to increase IT spending and it predicted that by 2003, India's IT spending could be 2.5 per cent of its GDP.
- More than 203 of Fortune 1000 companies outsourced their software requirements to Indian software houses in 1998–99.

	Estimated 2000	Target 2008
Total Number of PCs	4.3 million	20 million
Internet Subscribers	0.77 million	35 million
Internet Users	3.2 million	100 million
Cable TV Subscribers	37 million	70 million
Fixed Phones	26 million	125 million
Television Sets	75 million	225 million
Software Industry in India	5.7 billion	87 billion
Software Exports From India	3.9 billion	50 billion
IT Industry in India	US$8.6 billion	US$140 billion

Exhibit 2 India's IT Sector Projections

Source: NASSCOM.

Date	Internet Connections (in millions)	Users (in millions)
August 15, 1995	0.002	0.01
March 31, 1996	0.05	0.25
March 31, 1997	0.09	0.45
March 31, 1998	0.14	0.7
March 31, 1999	0.28	1.4
March 31, 2000	0.9	2.8
August 31, 2000	1.6	4.8
December 31, 2003 (projected)	15.0	50.0

Exhibit 3   Growth of Internet in India

- During 1998–99, more than 820,000 PCs were sold in India. This took the PC penetration in India to 3.2 PCs per 1,000 people by the end of 1998–99 (31 March 1999).

India's telecommunications sector contributed 1.25 per cent (about US$5.75 billion) to the country's GDP in the fiscal year ended March 31, 2000.

Despite a growth in direct exchange lines (DELs) to 26.7 million by 2000, fixed-line penetration in India was one of the lowest in the world at 2.69 per cent. Activity in the basic services segment of the Indian telecom sector picked up with the country's first private telecom service provider—Hughes Tele.com.

To attain the NTP 1999 objective of seven per cent teledensity by 2005, 54 million additional DELs had to be installed. Of this, the government planned to install 24 million, with the remainder expected to be rolled out by private operators. Total investment from private operators was projected at US$16.4 billion compared with US$985 million invested previously. The presence of a huge waiting list, combined with the expected GDP growth of 7.5 per cent p.a. in the long term, augured for a strong growth in the demand for fixed lines in the future. However,

this distribution of penetration levels was skewed toward the metro cities like Delhi and Mumbai, where the penetration levels were far higher at 12.5 per cent and 12.3 per cent respectively. The waiting list in the metros was lower than that in other cities, which gives a further thrust to the argument that fixed-line business in the metros might not grow at the same rates as it did in the past.

Wireless Services Market

Wireless penetration in India was extremely low at 0.22 per cent, so there was plenty of scope left for the wireless technologies to catch up. The cellular subscriber base in India continued to grow at about six per cent per month, and the total subscriber base stood at over 2.32 million cellular as of March 2000. As is the case with fixed-line penetration, cellular penetration was skewed toward the metropolitan areas in India.

Internet

The Internet market in India had only 750,000 subscribers by 2000, but was likely to witness high growth. ISP and telecom industry deregulation was propelling Internet user growth. IDC, an international market research firm expected 6.8 million Indian ISP subscribers by 2003. Historically, as in other markets, reality exceeded Internet expectations for India by a large margin. India's tryst with the Internet began in 1996 when VSNL, a government agency, was granted a monopoly status as an ISP. Subsequently, in late 1998, private ISPs were granted permission. Since then the market had exploded with connections nearly tripling to an estimated 750,000 as of 31 March 2000. But nearly three-quarters of the Internet subscribers were located in the seven major metros of Delhi, Mumbai, Chennai, Calcutta, Bangalore, Hyderabad and Pune. Simultaneously, there had also been a surge in the number of India-oriented portals with over 20,000 Indian Web sites in cyberspace.

THE FUTURE ACCORDING TO LUCENT

Lucent's 2000 annual report was still optimistic about its investments in developing countries:

> Our business outside the United States is growing stronger every year. Revenues from outside the United States increased 47 per cent in the fiscal year, accounting for 32 per cent of total revenues— up from about 23 per cent when Lucent was created four years ago. One-third of our current business and two-thirds of our total opportunity lie outside the United States. To address this opportunity, we are focusing on countries that will yield the most profitable returns, including key customers in the Asia/Pacific region, Latin America and Europe. In Latin America we experienced phenomenal growth. We signed more than 20 major contracts, valued at more than $2 billion, and grew 100 per cent over 1998. In Europe, the Middle East and Asia, where we signed contracts with over 100 new service providers, we're growing twice as fast as the market. Throughout these regions, we have forged strategic relationships with service providers like Telefonica in Spain and Portugal Telecom.

Lucent's 2000 annual report also pointed to a long list of innovations that would enable it to achieve outstanding success:

> Bell Labs researchers announce production of a device with features as small as 80 nanometers; it's the smallest working electronic device ever made with optical lithography, the technology now used to make silicon chips.

> Lucent unveils portfolio of products, called R/Evolutionary Networking, that will allow network operators worldwide to deliver over packet networks virtually every service and feature available on today's public network.

> Lucent announces world's first single-chip Internet telephony solution, which allows us to design a solution that reduces the electronics costs of current Internet telephones.

> Lucent's flagship 5ESS switch sets new record, becoming the only switch in history to achieve 99.9999 per cent up-time and continues to lead the industry in reliability, according to an analysis of a Federal Communications Commission report.

> One key was packet switching—a technology that shunts bits of digitized voice, data or video across a network. Now, the true power of broadband networking is emerging as Lucent integrates it with optical technology, which will deliver almost unlimited bandwidth. It will open the door to the applications of tomorrow and let people communicate without limit. Software is another key. Software confers network intelligence to support communications services over the different networks that will be part of tomorrow's broadband communications. Software will unify optical networks, packet networks like the Internet, and networks using a super-fast switching technology, called Asynchronous Transfer Mode, into a single network of networks.

As he pondered India's telecom future and that of Lucent, Vijay Gupta was extremely optimistic:

> No company is better able than Lucent to integrate these technologies. During 1999, we solidified our leadership in broadband networking. We acquired new businesses. We added 7,000 people from those acquisitions to our broadband thrust. We rolled out dozens of broadband products, including PacketStar™ and Stinger™ DSL Access

Concentrators. Lucent entered a new market in 1999—the cable television market—with a product portfolio that includes our breakthrough PathStar™ Access Server Comcast, a leading cable company that views services based on Internet protocol technology as a key to its broadband future, is trialing the PathStar system. Part of Lucent's CableConnect™ Solutions portfolio, PathStar helps transform a cable operator from a video supplier to a full-service supplier of video, high-speed data and telephony.

The Indian Telecom market is experiencing rapid growth. Teledensity (telephones per capita) in India is likely to triple from a current low of around 2.5 per cent to more than seven per cent in the next five years. This translates to a growth from about 26 million telephone lines to over 70 million lines by year 2005. This represents an enormous opportunity for Lucent. My aim is to take a leadership position in India and emerge as a dominant supplier of switching capacity. Coming to your question about comparing India with other Asian countries and especially China, I would say that we compare quite favorably. Our Indian operations are much smaller than what we have in China, but given the potential in India, I would say that India is one of the top priority markets for Lucent.

Additional Concerns of Analysts

The Bharatiya Janata Party, which came to power in 1998, had advocated a strong military position vis-à-vis Pakistan, and recent years had witnessed a heightened bitterness between the two countries. In May 1998, India detonated five nuclear devices, and Pakistan reacted with its own nuclear tests. In response, the United States led other nations in imposing trade sanctions. In November 2000, the *Financial Times* commented:

Washington's motives for devoting unprecedented attention to New Delhi are clear enough. After the Kargil mountain war between India and Pakistan in the summer of 1999 dashed earlier hopes of détente, there was genuine fear of a nuclear war between the two adversaries, triggered by their dispute over Kashmir.[2]

Bill Clinton described South Asia as the most dangerous place on earth when he came to India for five days in March, the first U.S. president to do so since 1978.[3]

In its December 16, 2000, issue, *The Economist* included an article titled "Telecoms In Trouble." The article began with the words "The grand dreams of some of the world's biggest telecom giants lie in ruins." The article pointed to three main drivers of the previous rapid telecom growth:

First was the kick to competition given by liberalizing and market-opening in both America and Europe. Next came the arrival of the Internet as a serious platform for business and as a consumer phenomenon, resulting in an explosion in data traffic and new services. And third was the accelerating growth of mobile telephony . . .[4]

This *Economist* article pointed to at least three factors that had halted the telecom success. First, the very rapid investments in long-haul fibre-optic networks had created intense competition "driving prices inexorably towards zero." Second, a new tightness in capital markets was creating problems for many telecom companies that had borrowed heavily. Third, the bottleneck in the "last mile" to the individual home and business, also referred to as the local loop, was limiting access to the new broadband miracle. Nevertheless, *The Economist* emphasized that "the fundamentals have not changed. The Internet-driven demand for capacity is still doubling roughly every three months. . . ."

There were concerns that even if the very rapid growth in telecom companies were to reappear, nevertheless, this growth might be concentrated in the developed nations. In a September 23, 2000, article, the *Economist* noted that:

. . . Many people worry that developing economies, which have far fewer computers and Internet connections than the rich world, will get left behind. The income gap between rich and poor countries will widen further. . . . Much of the developing world is too poor to buy computers or telephones.[5]

A central concern had to do with the extent and pace of economic reforms. Liberalization had begun in 1991, at the urging of the World Bank and IMF, and in reaction to a foreign exchange crisis. However, this "New Industrial Policy" had retained foreign ownership limits of 51 per cent in many sectors, including telecoms, with the need to obtain specific government approval if a foreign owner wished to exceed these 51 per cent limits. State governments still exerted considerable regulatory power, quite apart from the national government, and the pervasive bureaucracy carried with it the possibility of corruption in attaining regulatory approvals. Furthermore, labor legislation and strong unions could also present challenges, and contracts were often subject to further negotiations. On November 17, 2000, the *Financial Times* reported on an optimistic interview with a key figure in India's reform movement:

> India's reforms are reaching "critical mass" which could lead to a significant improvement in the country's economic performance and help reduce poverty, its foreign minister said yesterday.
>
> Jaswant Singh who has played a central role in developing the government's infrastructure, IT and telecommunications policies, said the reform drive was now moving from the realm of decision-making into that of implementation . . .
>
> . . . in an interview with the FT in London, Singh argued that this conviction had now taken root among India's population, leading to a greater consensus for change.
>
> "The constituency for economic reform has expanded," Singh said.[6]

The Role of India in Lucent's Future

January 2001 brought news of more cut-backs at Lucent, with the *Wall Street Journal* predicting in a headline, "Lucent expected to cut as many as 10,000 jobs."[7] This reduction of 10 per cent in the work force was expected to be accompanied by restructuring charges. "Most analysts said they are expecting the charge, which could include write-offs for inventory, discontinued products, real estate, plant closings, defaults on debts by customers, to be between $1-billion and $2-billion."[8]

As the global economy entered the year 2001, it appeared that the miracle of "dot.coms" had crashed. Lucent's customers depended on the growth of e-business, so Lucent's new technologies might not find a market. On the other hand, perhaps this downturn was simply temporary. Even if the downturn represented a long-term trend, perhaps India was a market where Lucent would achieve the revenue increases it would need. To repeat the previous retreats in India might be a waste of precious resources.

Notes

1. Department of Information Technology, Government of Karnataka, *Financial Times,* November 6, 2000, India vii.

2. David Gardner, "Closing the cold war book," *Financial Times,* November 6, 2000, India 3.

3. Ibid.

4. "Telecoms in trouble," *The Economist,* December 16, 2000, pp. 77–79.

5. "Falling through the net?" *The Economist,* September 23, 2000, pp. 34–39.

6. John Thornhill et al., "Indian reforms close to critical mass," *Financial Times,* November 17, 2000, 8.

7. Shawn Young, "Lucent expected to cut as many as 10,000 jobs," *The Wall Street Journal,* January 24, 2001, 13.

8. Ibid.

CITIGROUP IN POST-WTO CHINA[1]

Prepared by Professor David W. Conklin

Version: (A) 2003-02-12

When China entered the World Trade Organization (WTO), at the end of 2001, Citigroup was still at an early stage in its China strategy. In 1998, Citicorp and Travelers Group Inc. (Travelers) had merged to create the new entity Citigroup Inc. Travelers brought a vast array of financial services that added to Citigroup's existing portfolio of consumer and commercial lending. Travelers had developed a very extensive business in investment banking, asset management, life insurance and property casualty insurance, as well as consumer lending. Travelers' operating companies included: Salomon Smith Barney, Salomon Smith Barney Asset Management, Travelers Life & Annuity, Primerica Financial Services, Travelers Property Casualty Corp and Commercial Credit.

Following the merger, John Reed and Sanford Weill became co-chairmen of the new Citigroup. After a brief period of turmoil, Sanford Weill became sole chairman and chief executive officer of the merged entity. Citigroup's 2001 Annual Report indicated remarkable success in the integration of Citigroup's many divisions. In his letter to shareholders, Weill emphasized that:

> In 2001, Citigroup solidified its position as one of the most successful financial services companies in the world, outperforming and leading the field in the most profitable and attractive growth areas. We registered double-digit increases across many lines of business, and a 20 per cent return on equity. . . . Our achievements received important recognition when Citigroup, for the first time, was named one of America's 10 Most Admired Companies by *Fortune* magazine and ranked number one in our industry category.[2]

In March 2002, Travelers' Property Casualty unit was spun off in the expectation that its activities would not be central to the financial services package being offered by Citigroup, and its rate of profit would likely be less than that of the other financial services.

Citibank, part of Citigroup, was one of the first foreign firms that had obtained licences to conduct a limited range of commercial activities in China. By 2002, Citibank had become one of the strongest foreign banks operating in the People's Republic of China (PRC), but as a foreign bank it had only limited market access, even for its limited array of services. At headquarters, Citigroup wanted to determine the growth prospects for each of its divisions, and which of its vast array of financial services should be the focus for expansion in China. Could Citibank be a "model" for the other Citigroup divisions? One possibility, of course, would be to continue with Citibank's existing China services, and for Citigroup to "wait and see" the results of WTO membership.

THE LIBERALIZATION DILEMMA

> *Optimism about the economic benefits of China's WTO membership may be premature. Realising them will require wrenching structural change that will produce losers as well as winners. The shocks could strain international trade relations for years to come.*
>
> —Guy de Jonquières,
> "Enter the dragon,"
> *Financial Times,*
> December 10, 2001, 14.

Can the WTO's rules be implemented? If they are not, does the global trading club have sufficient regulatory clout to provide adequate redress for foreign interests? A cornerstone principle of the WTO is that member nations apply trade and investment rules in a transparent manner evenly across the country, and accord national treatment to foreign companies. In China's case, experience and discernable economic pressures suggest that the equal application of transparent laws enforced by an impartial legal system may remain a mere concept for many years to come.

—James Kynge,
"Can Beijing make trade rules
stick?" *Financial Times,*
November 17, 1999, 6.

Prior to China's WTO membership, Citibank had been licensed only to provide corporate banking services, and only to foreign-invested enterprises. Furthermore, Citibank had been licensed to operate branches in only a few of the Chinese cities open to foreign banks. In order to grow beyond these cities and to expand from foreign corporate banking to the large and potentially lucrative domestic retail and corporate financial business, Citibank needed licences from the central bank.

The terms and conditions for WTO membership required China to open its financial system to foreign corporations. However, the pace for liberalization of regulatory restrictions was uncertain. Meanwhile, prior to WTO entry, overall results for foreign financial corporations had been poor:

The Asian financial crisis has taken its toll on foreign banks' gains in China. Figures collated from government documents indicate that foreign banks and financial institutions made an aggregate net profit of US$256 million in 1997 and US$215 million in 1998—and a loss of US$150 million in 1999. Most foreign banks do not break out their China operations in their annual reports and country CEOs decline to disclose how much their businesses are making—or losing. But *Asiamoney*

believes that, apart from the 32 banks allowed to do renminbi business and those with capital market skills, many foreign institutions are still chasing the pot of gold at the end of the rainbow.[3]

On the one hand, the People's Bank of China (PBOC), China's regulatory agency, was under pressure in regard to China's WTO commitments. On the other hand, China's state banks were in appalling shape. Generally, they were run by bureaucrats, up to their knees in bad debts, still required to provide cheap funding to nearly bankrupt state enterprises and unable to set their own deposit and interest rate levels. It might take them years to become properly competitive. Meantime, it was up to the PBOC to see that strong foreign competitors like Citigroup had no chance to bulldoze them out of the market. Commentators presented frequent warnings about this dilemma:

China's accession to the World Trade Organization could cause a banking crisis unless radical reforms to its debt-ridden state banks are pushed through, the country's top government think-tank warned yesterday.[4]

Says a high-ranking central banker in Beijing: "We are happy for foreign banks to come in. But at the same time we are very concerned about the impact of WTO. Our banks lag behind the foreigners on almost every front: capitalization, overseas networks, services and modern management expertise."[5]

In a 2002 *Financial Times* article, James Kynge attempted to estimate the extent of non-performing loans in China's banking system:

Nowhere is the cost of China's politically driven economy clearer than in the financial system. Lending directed by the state is largely responsible for the burden of non-performing loans in the big four state banks. Official estimates put bad loans at about 30 per cent of assets, but most analysts believe the figure to be nearer 50 per cent. Bad loans elsewhere—such as at city commercial banks and rural credit co-operatives—take the total to more than 50 per cent of the country's GDP in 2000, say several academics in state think-tanks.[6]

The terms and conditions for WTO membership stipulated that all non-geographic restrictions with respect to type of customer were to be removed immediately for foreign currency business. This would permit foreign banks to conduct foreign currency business with Chinese-owned enterprises and Chinese persons, but only in specific cities provided for in a licence. Over the five-year period from 2002 to 2007, restrictions on renminbi business and remaining geographic restrictions were also to be removed.

However, China's initial regulatory reforms in response to WTO membership included several provisions that would retard the promised expansion of foreign banks. In particular, to be eligible to participate in renminbi business, a foreign bank had to have been engaged in business operations in China for three years, and these operations had to have been profitable for two consecutive years prior to an application for a licence. Furthermore, each foreign bank branch would have to put in place very onerous funding requirements.

Commentators believed that the PBOC would likely be imposing a wide range of additional restrictions, for example, in regard to: deposits, interest rates on loans, fees, reserve requirements, capital adequacy ratios, limits on the size of a single borrower's credit line, equity/asset ratios, ratios of renminbi capital to renminbi assets, and reserves against bad and doubtful loans. As of 2002, domestic foreign currency deposits could not exceed 70 per cent of a bank's total foreign currency assets within China. Renminbi lending was limited to 50 per cent of a foreign bank's total lending.

As a result of mandatory waiting periods and high funding requirements for additional branches, banks were likely to find their expansion impeded. A 2002 Business Week article summarized these restrictions in a rather pessimistic commentary:

> There are new banking regulations, which foreign lenders say are aimed at protecting China's debt-laden banks. As of early February (2002), new branches are required to have a minimum of $72 million in operating capital, up from $15.7 million, in order to do local retail business. The requirement will likely make it too expensive for any but the largest foreign banks to set up mainland

networks. Particularly galling to foreign bankers is the fact that the regulation was announced as part of a package intended to fulfill China's WTO commitments. Joachim Fuchs, general manager of the Shanghai branch of Commerzbank, says the requirement's real purpose "is to give the local banks breathing time."[7]

As early as 1997, Chris Tibbs, the vice-president and head of corporate finance of Citibank's China operations, had been optimistic about regulatory change.

> The banking system in China is evolving faster than most other countries. Generally speaking, the bureaucrats who are responsible for the financial market reforms are quite intelligent people. They know very much where they want to go. They are more efficient than most of the countries I have worked in (Japan, North and South America, and Hong Kong). I am optimistic that things will work out. PBOC operates in a very cautious but intelligent manner. The PBOC will not hold off our expansion. Actually, it is encouraging us to expand: it wants to use Citibank as a tool to force Chinese banks to become more competitive as soon as possible.[8]

Though Citibank's senior China executives had worked hard to develop a good relationship with the PBOC and were clearly positive about that relationship, they may also have had reason to be concerned. Citibank was one of the most powerful foreign banks in China, and given Citigroup's deep pockets and obvious interest in emerging markets, Citigroup was the one that posed the most obvious competitive threat to China's struggling domestic banks. Should the PBOC feel that Citigroup was too large, too ambitious or too successful in China, it might respond by putting the brakes on Citigroup's China expansion plans and giving early licences to smaller, less threatening foreign financial institutions instead.

Early in 2002, Citibank became the first foreign bank to be given approval for foreign currency dealings with Chinese customers. While Chinese held 90 billion dollars in foreign denominations in mainland banks, the Citibank licence would give access only to Chinese in the city of Shanghai. Citibank hoped that other cities would soon be opened for this business. Meanwhile, other divisions of Citigroup would need to develop China strategies as well.

IMPEDIMENTS TO ECONOMIC DEVELOPMENT

The Need for Political Reforms

While the economy of China had experienced rapid growth, commentators pointed to a series of substantial challenges that confronted ongoing economic development. China's state-owned enterprises (SOEs) were poorly managed. SOEs still controlled more than 70 per cent of all fixed assets and 80 per cent of all working capital in manufacturing. The Chinese banks were unable to collect a major portion of the loans that they had made to the state-owned enterprises. The pension system was largely unfunded. Corruption was widespread.

WTO membership would exacerbate the financial difficulties of the SOEs, as they would now face better-quality imports and competition from the foreign-owned corporations that were now investing in China. China's leaders expressed the view that unprofitable SOEs should be allowed to go bankrupt if their debts exceeded assets. However, the process for bankruptcy was not clear. Furthermore, bankruptcies would throw tens of millions of Chinese workers out of their jobs. The threat of massive unemployment brought with it the risk of social unrest, and the prospect of authoritarian crackdowns as a political response.

Some commentators expressed the view that a successful economic transition would require political reform with a shift towards democracy, free speech and investigative journalism, and modern commercial laws with an independent judiciary:

> All of these problems are structural in nature. They are all, to varying degrees, the products of an unreformed political system that has become a drag on development and a serious barrier to China's ambitions to become a global superpower.

Nowhere in the WTO agreement, which took 15 years to negotiate, is it specified that Beijing must undertake political reform. But many Chinese academics and other experts believe that, without changes to government, China may be unable to deliver on its WTO promises.

It is still dangerous in China to advocate an end to the Communist party's monopoly on power. But an increasing number of academics, officials and ordinary people say in private that there is no alternative. Without checks and balances on Communist influence, China may be unable to provide the type of detached, impartial government that its increasingly sophisticated economy requires.[9]

Human Resource Challenges

The qualifications necessary for successful corporate management in a free enterprise market economy are quite different from the qualifications required for management of SOEs under central planning. Somehow, the Chinese managers would have to learn a new set of skills and develop a new set of business procedures. Among the many business practices that would have to be developed were those related to accounting, cost control, finance and advertising. The concept of marketing and a concern for customer satisfaction had to be ingrained in managerial decision-making. Throughout the corporation, the necessary concern for quality and innovation might be slow to develop. A key issue was how quickly China's educational system could create business administration courses for university students and for part-time executive education.

Beyond the issue of skills and capability many observers pointed to traditional cultural impediments to income differentials, an essential aspect of motivation and reward in free enterprise economies. Government ownership focused on interpersonal harmony, and this fostered a distrust of performance appraisals. The hierarchical structure of SOEs meant that employees were not socialized to develop initiative. The absence of "consumerism" meant that there was little emphasis on the Western "work ethic."

One might look to expatriate managers to bridge the gap while the Chinese human resource portfolio was broadened and attitudes changed, but foreigners found it difficult to adapt culturally to life in China. For a corporation seeking to hire from the Chinese labor market, there was a difficulty in getting employees to leave the SOEs. A fluid labor market has not yet developed.

A separate but related set of human resource challenges had to do with the government bureaucrats, whose skill sets and practices also would have to be transformed if they were to regulate private sector corporations effectively and if they were to conduct macroeconomic policies appropriately. China faced the prospect of developing new systems for taxation, expenditure control, monetary policy and a host of sector-specific supervisory and regulatory programs, together with new commercial laws and procedures for their enforcement. For many decades, "Western" universities had offered programs in economics and public administration that could prepare students for careers in the civil service. In China, a revolution would be needed in traditional university curricula, which could require a very long time.

E-Commerce Limitations

In Western nations, the growth of e-commerce and the "new economy" had dramatically altered business practices and had brought ongoing productivity improvements. For China, participation in the new economy seemed a long distance away. The basic telecom infrastructure lacked broadband capacity except for a few cities, and so was limited in its ability to convey the files necessary for e-commerce. There was a possibility that foreign corporations could enter China and revolutionize the telecom infrastructure. WTO membership did require that foreign operators be permitted to enter China, but in 2002, they were restricted to ownership of less than 50 per cent of each Chinese company. These ownership restrictions were likely to restrain the shift of necessary technologies and new plant and equipment investment from the advanced nations to China.

Apart from the weaknesses of the telecom infrastructure, there was an ongoing supervision on the part of the Chinese government in regard to Internet content. In recent years, for example, the rapid expansion of the Falun Gong movement had rested on Internet communications, and the government regarded Falun Gong as a political protest that should be quelled. Consequently, the government had imposed supervisory controls that could impede corporate Internet transactions. Various agencies played an active role in supervising the Internet, and the Ministry of Information Industry (MII) controlled the international Internet gateway.

Regional Disparities

China's economic liberalization began in 1978 with the creation of "special economic zones" where foreign corporations could operate separate from the administrative structure of central planning. The success of this experiment meant that the coastal cities where these zones were located experienced economic progress that contrasted starkly with the ongoing rural stagnation of the rest of the country. In regard to prospects for e-commerce, Exhibit 1 indicates that over 75 per cent of information technology investment in China was concentrated in just three cities: Guangzhou, Beijing and Shanghai. The enormous gap between the coastal cities on the one hand and the rest of the country on the other presented serious problems in regard to the economic development of the nation as a whole. Of course, the government of China clearly understood the difficulties that it faced in this regard, and was attempting to redress the balance, but it would likely take decades before the rest of China could become a part of the rapid growth paradigm.

OPPORTUNITIES FOR FINANCING FOREIGN-OWNED CORPORATIONS

The prospect of China joining the WTO stimulated a huge increase in foreign direct investment (FDI), as Exhibit 2 indicates. China's current

	Households (millions)	Annual Discretionary Income per Household (RMB)
Guangzhou (16% of IT investment)	2.0	12,018
Beijing (37% of IT investment)	3.9	9,183
Shanghai (25% of IT investment)	4.7	8,773
Wuhan	2.1	6,262
Xi'an	1.8	5,999
Chongqing	9.2	5,896
Shenyang	2.1	5,364

Exhibit 1   China—Major Markets

	1998	1999	2000	2001*
GDP growth (%)	7.8	7.1	8.0	7.3
GDP per capita (US$)	758	784	853	937
Inflation, annual average (%)	−0.8	−1.4	0.4	0.7
Current account balance % of GDP	+3	+2	+1.9	+1.8
Foreign exchange rate (US$)	8.3	8.3	8.3	8.3
Debt as % of GDP	16	16	13	12
FDI inflows (US$ billion)	45	40	40	45
Internet users (millions)		16.9	26.5	

Exhibit 2   China's Economy

Source: EIU Report—China 2002.

*Estimates.

stock of FDI was already enormous in global terms. In 2001, it stood at $350 billion, with an annual increase of $40 billion to $45 billion. This placed China as No. 3 in the world in terms of the stock of FDI, behind the United States at $1.1 trillion and Britain at $400 billion.

The mainland now accounts for about one-third of emerging markets' total stock of FDI, according to Nicholas Lardy of the Brookings Institution in Washington. Nearly four-fifths of all FDI going to Southeast and East Asia, not counting Japan, is sucked up by China—and to its neighbors' growing alarm.[10]

Citigroup could focus on providing foreign-owned corporations with certain of its services—but which services and how to organize them remained a question. Several economic realties would be important as Citigroup contemplated the future in China for its additional financial activities. Competition from other foreign banks had become intense. Japanese banks, in particular, seemed not so concerned with profit margins as with obtaining market share. Furthermore, it was not clear whether foreign capital inflows would be maintained at these levels.

While China's population—more than one billion, 200 million—and the economy's high growth rate were attractive to investors, nevertheless, the average per capita income for the nation as a whole was so low that decades of growth would be necessary before mass marketing of consumer goods and services could be effective. In fact, some pointed to the high growth rate of the economy as simply due to the very low level of production and consumption, and warned that growth was low in absolute dollar terms and would inevitably slow down as higher levels were reached. Perhaps investment would be focused principally on manufacturing for export, based on industrial wages as low as 20 to 30 cents per hour.

OPPORTUNITIES FOR INVESTMENT BANKING SERVICES

With the privatization of SOEs, a huge opportunity would develop for Citigroup to participate actively in investment banking. Initial public offerings (IPOs) might include the sale of shares on either foreign or Chinese stock exchanges.

SOEs would need a great deal of advice in the IPO process, and the valuation of shares would be particularly difficult. Assets had been acquired at prices that had no relationship with free market prices. Future profit streams were perhaps impossible to predict. How to deal with debts to the state banks remained a common problem. Consequently, it was expected that the IPO process would generally involve a "bought deal" in which the investment bank would underwrite the entire issue, financing the deal with its own

capital and then reselling to the public at a slightly higher price.

However, as of 2002, China's stock markets were fragmented, with restrictions on ownership of various types of shares, and they were at a very early stage of development. Foreigners tended to invest only in Chinese companies that had listed shares in the Hong Kong market, referred to as "H shares" or "red-chips." The legal system and regulatory standards in Hong Kong provided assurances that were not yet available in mainland China.

From a positive perspective, the privatization of SOEs would create an array of shareholders that would hopefully improve corporate governance and transparency and would provide an ongoing spur to competitiveness.

Perhaps investment banking, and provision of various services to privatized SOEs, might be a new and profitable strategy. Citigroup's 2001 annual report was extremely optimistic about the strength of its investment banking activities:

> By combining world-class investment banking services through SSB and world-class commercial banking through Citibank, we provide unique value propositions to our clients. . . . We became the leading global underwriter in combined equity and debt for the first time. . . . We became the leading global investment firm as measured by revenue. . . . We became the No. 1 global fixed-income underwriter with record new-issue volume, earning *International Financing Review's* Global Bond House of the Year award.

> . . . In 2001, CitiCapital, the commercial finance business of Citigroup, continued integrating acquisitions into its operations, most notably Associates Commercial Finance and the leasing businesses of the European American Bank. As the second-largest U.S.-based leasing company, CitiCapital serves equipment manufacturers, as well as dealers and buyers of transportation equipment, material handling and construction equipment, and business technology and medical equipment. It is also a leading provider of master leasing programs to large corporations.[11]

Citigroup Global Investments (CGI) undertook direct investments in the complete range of financial and real assets, utilizing the deposits and premiums of Citigroup's related divisions. These investments included fixed-income, equities, real estate, private equity, hedge funds and various structured investments. Through CitiStreet, Citigroup offered administrative and investment management services for pension, health and welfare plans. Should these activities be pursued in China?

OPPORTUNITIES FOR INSURANCE, PENSIONS AND ANNUITY PRODUCTS

China's insurance sector was expected to be one of the most lucrative and highly competitive over the next few decades. Insurance industry premiums in the Peoples Republic of China (PRC) had experienced a 20 per cent increase year-over-year for the past several years. Despite such rapid growth, gross insurance receipts accounted for less than one per cent of China's GDP, much below that of other developing countries and significantly below the worldwide premium average of five per cent.

Lured by such staggering opportunity, over 90 foreign insurance companies had set up over 100 rep offices in China even prior to WTO entry. As these offices were restricted from signing legally binding contracts, they could not conduct business. However, they were in place to develop crucial relationships with key Chinese officials and industry contacts, as well as to conduct regional market research.

China's acceptance into the World Trade Organization (WTO) was contingent upon foreign access to its insurance markets. However, China's terms and conditions for WTO membership permitted China to restrict foreign ownership to 50 per cent or less. This requirement to accept a joint venture partner—in practice, some government agency or SOE—could prove to be a major stumbling block for foreign insurance corporations. Despite the presence of so many rep offices and pressure from the United States, European Union (EU) and others to allow greater foreign access to its insurance market, the general consensus was that China would be slow in the gradual opening of its insurance market.

Beijing had awarded the first licence for a foreign company to operate in China on a trial basis in 1992, when the American International Group (AIG) received a licence to operate in Shanghai. By 1995, AIG was a successful operation, generating annual premiums of US$50 million, accounting for 88 per cent of the market share for life insurance in Shanghai (800,000 individual policies). The success of AIG's operations in Shanghai had taken even their own executives by surprise, who consequently suspended their projections in light of performance that was "way beyond" their expectations. AIG's commanding market leadership position in the Shanghai market, gained at the expense of China's national insurers, and the speed at which they took over the market frightened many Chinese insurance firms, who were devastated by AIG and fearful that if Beijing did not respond quickly, China would be handing over their market to foreign insurers "on a silver platter."

In response, to protect China's infant domestic insurers, the People's Bank of China (PBOC) acted on several fronts. First, it applied pressure to domestic insurers to improve their marketing, products and service. It also increased licensing quotas to domestic insurers. Most seriously, however, was the PBOC's decree in 1995 that joint ventures (JVs) would be the only mode of entry available to foreign insurance firms. In 1996, Manulife launched the first Sino-foreign joint venture insurance company. However, many foreign corporations such as Citigroup might refuse to enter a joint venture, and even if they did, their rate of expansion could be limited by the financial strength of the joint venture partner.

Citigroup, through its Travelers Life and Annuity division (TL&A), achieved record operating earnings in 2001, placing it in the top three U.S. companies that provided individual life and annuity products. Over the period 1998 to 2002, TL&A moved from No. 38 to No. 18 in life insurance sales. It focused on high-net-worth customers, and it had record annuity sales in the pension close-out and structured settlement segments. With China's shift away from the government and SOE "safety net" to individual responsibility for personal financial planning, Citigroup faced perhaps unlimited growth potential for TL&A's services.

OPPORTUNITIES FOR PERSONAL BANKING, CREDIT CARDS, E-BANKING, MORTGAGES AND WEALTH MANAGEMENT

The domestic savings rate in China had been exceptionally high at about 40 per cent of GDP. Liberalization of the financial services market could allow foreign banks to tap into these savings, which had previously been deposited in the state banking system.

While credit cards were an important and lucrative part of the Citibank consumer banking lineup elsewhere in Asia, many were pessimistic about the credit card business in China in the near term. Why? The Chinese government and the PBOC had great sensitivity toward inflation. The government believed, analysts said, that along with corruption, one of the contributing factors to the 1989 Tiananmen problem was out-of-control inflation. Thus, from the point of view of the government, inflation constraint was a very important goal. The prevailing view, furthermore, was that if China was to maintain its exemplary rate of economic expansion, the national savings rate would have to be maintained. Encouraging borrowing—via credit cards, for example—would increase inflation and discourage saving. Thus, analysts suggested, it would not be in the best long-term interest of either the country or its financial institutions to encourage hasty development of a retail credit card market. In any case, there were important economies of scale at the industry level, dependent on the overall development of credit agencies, automatic banking machines and merchant enrolment. In determining its strategy, Citibank would have to project the growth rate of the credit card industry as a whole.

Citigroup was making rapid advances in offering its wide range of products on the Internet. It had established alliances with AOL Time Warner and Microsoft, and its online consumer accounts reached 15 million in 2001. In addition to providing Internet services to its customers, Citigroup achieved ongoing efficiencies within its organization as a result of Internet usage.

The shift from communism to free enterprise would bring with it the practice of personal home ownership. Conceivably, even rental apartment buildings might be privatized through the sale to corporations or through a transfer to the condominium concept. All of these actions would require mortgage financing of some type. One of Citigroup's divisions was the Citigroup Private Bank which acted as a gateway for the wealthy to the full resources of Citigroup, offering affluent families the complete range of portfolio management and investment advisory services. This gave clients of the Citigroup Private Bank multiple touch points with the various other divisions globally. Another division, Citigroup Asset Management (CAM) had over $400 billion in assets under management as it entered the year 2002, offering institutional, high-net-worth and retail clients a broad array of products and services. CAM was a market leader in U.S.-managed retail accounts, with a variety of mid-size mutual funds. CAM included a global research organization which contributed to Citigroup's institutional and retail asset management business. How long would it be before China might have a substantial number of high-net-worth families that could support these divisions?

CITIGROUP WORLDWIDE

Citigroup was significantly more international in scope than its international competitors: it operated in more than 100 countries, had 268,000 employees, and in 2001, it derived more than $2.8 billion in core income from emerging markets (see Exhibit 3). Within Citigroup, Citibank had a particularly long history of emerging market expertise.

	2001
Adjusted Revenue	$83,625
	Segment Income
Global Consumer	
Banking/Lending	4,217
Insurance	720
Western Europe	483
Japan	928
Emerging markets	1,166
e-Consumer/Consumer Other	−148
Total Global Consumer	7,366
Global Corporate	
Corporate & Investment Bank	3,509
Emerging Markets Corporate Banking and Global Transaction Services	1,644
Commerical Lines Insurance	691
Total Global Corporate	5,844
Global Investment Management & Private Banking	
Travelers Life & Annuity	821
The Citigroup Private Bank	378
Citigroup Asset Management	336
Total Global Investment Management & Private Banking	1,535
Investment Activities (A)	530
Corporate/Other	−706
Core Income	14,569
Restructuring and Merger-Related Items—After Tax	−285
Income Before Cumulative Effect of Accounting Changes	$14,284
Cumulative Effect of Accounting Changes (B)	−158
Net Income	$14,126
Return on Common Equity (Core Income)	20.4%

Exhibit 3 Citigroup Financial Highlights (in millions of dollars)

Source: Citigroup Annual Report 2001.

Citibank had not always been a world-class success story, however. The bank suffered through a very difficult period in the late 1980s and early 1990s as a result of its decentralized decision-making structure and what *Euromoney* called a "near fatal brush with commercial real estate lending"[12] in the United States. Thus, chairman and chief executive officer (CEO) John Reed spent much of the early 1990s engineering the bank's recovery—a brutal but apparently successful process. One of his most well-known re-engineering efforts was the G-15. In 1993, at the height of the bank's real-estate lending crisis, he created a committee of the bank's top 15 business managers, who all reported directly to him. He required them all to fly to New York once a month for meetings that lasted an entire day and sometimes two, and were frequently highly confrontational, punishing all the managers involved, but analysts said it worked. By centralizing the decision-making in New York and forcing his managers to fight him on every major strategic decision, Reed managed to repair the bank's balance sheet, rebuild its tier-one capital and restore its credit ratings by 1996.[13] Although the G-15 structure was modified later, decision-making was still much more centralized at the time of the 1998 merger that it had been in the 1980s. For Citigroup, this issue of centralization and decentralization of decision-making would continue to be important, particularly in the unique market of China.

Reed had believed that Citibank's strategic advantage was in its international operations: global reach, local ties. Again, for Citigroup, whether to strive for a global presence would be an important issue in regard to each of its divisions and activities, as would the question of whether a major presence in China was necessary as a component of a global presence.

CITIBANK'S COMPETITIVE ADVANTAGES

Citibank had created a unique and enormously successful set of competitive advantages in emerging market banking, and these competitive advantages would greatly help its China expansion. Whether these attributes could be extended to create synergies with Citigroup's other divisions remained a key question.

The Global Network

> When a multinational company wants to enter an emerging market it calls its lawyers, its accountants, the embassy and Citibank.—Shaukat Aziz, head of Asia/Pacific global finance operations.[14]

Citibank executives, as well as most banking analysts, would probably agree that Citibank's only true and sustainable advantage was its sprawling global network which was important in serving its powerful list of corporate banking clients but crucial too in developing its consumer franchise in lucrative offshore markets.

This network, moreover, was extraordinarily strong in the emerging markets which were most attractive to Citibank's key corporate banking clients and to its own consumer finance division. How had Citibank developed its emerging markets advantage?

Time and Experience

Citibank had been in some of these markets for nearly 100 years. In the case of China, Citibank had originally entered the market in 1902 and so the year 2002 marked its centenary. By the 1930s, Citibank was one of the country's major foreign banks, operating 14 branches in nine cities. However, with the communist takeover, all of Citibank's branches were closed. In 1984, Citibank at last opened a new office in China in the city of Shenzhen and began the slow process of applying for licences to expand its operations.

Reed had clearly believed in the value of first-mover advantage and had worked to ensure that Citibank was usually among the first foreign banks to get its foot in any emerging market door. The bank's relative experience in these volatile markets created a level of operational expertise that, in times of turbulence, other banks found difficult to match. This was a particularly valuable asset in attracting and keeping important multinational accounts. Could other Citigroup divisions build on this Citibank expertise and reputation?

Localization and Commitment

Citibank worked hard to develop close ties with the community and with the local central bank. Over 95 per cent of Citibank's jobs held outside the United States were held by locally hired staff. The bank had a well-established reputation for commitment too, which made Citibank popular with governments: Unlike some other banks which moved into countries on the expectation of brisk profits and then moved out again when they were slow to materialize, Citibank moved in early with intent to stay.

Executives routinely emphasized the bank's ability and eagerness to help the local financial services industry grow. Employees were seconded to central banks. Technology was transferred. Locals were trained.

Citibank was not above currying political favor either. In Taiwan, for example, the bank "wowed Taipei" by bringing former U.S. President George Bush and former British Prime Minister Margaret Thatcher to visit in the 1990s. This seemed to have worked particularly well. Rival bankers said, after that, Citibank got "just about anything they wanted from the central bank."[15] Someone, somewhere inside Citigroup was almost certainly wondering how this model could be made to work for the other divisions if they adopted a China expansion strategy.

Technological Superiority

According to a Lehman analyst, Citibank was "ahead of the curve" with respect to technology and financial innovation.[16] Judging from the number of awards the bank won, this was not an uncommon view. Citibank was broadly perceived to be very strong in corporate banking services ranging from foreign exchange to cash management, debt capital markets to derivatives. And if this was the case in the United States, it was even more obvious in emerging market nations where competition was less well developed, financial systems less evolved. This was also the reason Citibank won numerous awards as best bank overall: best emerging markets bank, best Asian bank, best foreign bank in China, best foreign bank in a number of other emerging markets.[17] In other words, Citibank could usually provide better corporate banking service than local banks in many of its markets, and competitive service in more markets than any of its "foreign bank" competitors.

Human Resources Practices

According to Chris Tibbs, human resources development had been one of the bank's most pressing issues in China in the 1990s. "The most challenging thing for us today is the human resource side of our business. Normally, a person needs to have about seven years of experience before becoming a capable manager. We started branch banking activity in China in the 1990s, and so we have trained local people to be successful managers for less than a decade." Despite this, the bank's human resources practices were broadly perceived as a powerful competitive advantage, in China and throughout Asia. Analysts in China said that Citibank people were frequently poached by other banks. Tibbs confirmed this, noting that the bank's counterstrategy (salary, environment and opportunity) was helpful in holding staff and even in bringing them back. "As a matter of fact," said Tibbs, "our people who went to work for ABN-Amro want to return to Citibank. We are the college of banking and the best bank in the world."

Accounting Practices

The bank also had an advantage in Asia in its audit and accounting practice. This was particularly true in China, where Citibank was the bank the PBOC chose to work with to improve internal auditing within the domestic banking system. As of 1997, the PBOC was actually using Citibank's internal auditing standards as a guide for its own, and extending that standard to other Chinese banks. According to Tibbs, in fact, the PBOC was so pleased with Citibank's recommended internal control system that they used it to audit the bank's new Beijing branch only six months after opening.

After our branch in Beijing had been open for about six months, we received a message from PBOC that it was going to audit us, it seemed strange that we had just been working for six months and it wanted to audit us. It turned out that it was because PBOC wanted to test its team of auditors, who were trained by us. This was the first time that Citibank was tested by its own students. After the team of auditors went through the auditing, Citibank suggested to them where they could possibly improve.

Analysts wondered if, in China, this advantage was a sustainable one.

In 1995, Reed had defined a clear strategy: Build on what the bank was already good at and on what was already profitable. Under the Citigroup umbrella, this focus on excellence continued in Citibank. As the 2001 Annual Report noted:

> Importantly, every business within the Consumer Group is either the leader or near the top of its class. In the primary areas of cards, consumer finance and banking, the businesses maintain distinct competitive advantages:
>
> - Low-cost producers with superior credit management,
> - Exportable business models with superior acquisition capabilities, and
> - A strong brand.[18]

Global Relationship Banking (GRB)

In focusing on the top multinationals—most of them pursuing aggressive overseas growth strategies—Citibank was "serving global companies globally,"[19] an area where it had a distinct competitive advantage over both domestic and "foreign" banks in virtually all of the most attractive emerging markets.

In China prior to the WTO entry, Citibank also had a strategy for targeting strong SOEs.

> Our strategy is to identify 10 industries which would develop the fastest in a country, and target profitable companies within those industries. We are different from other banks in that we choose companies not only based on their numbers on the financial statements, but also the industrial sectors they are in and the qualities of the management team.[20]

In order to serve these customers seamlessly, each major Citibank GRB client had a "team" of its own. Bankers were encouraged to think of themselves as, for example, "on the Motorola team" instead of "in foreign exchange" or "from the Hong Kong office."

In the "Asian model" that Citibank executives would apply in thinking about their China

strategy, the GRB franchise usually represented an important platform, allowing Citibank to embed itself in new economies, hiring locally, developing a relationship with domestic regulators and (this was an emerging idea at Citibank) beginning to serve ambitious local companies as well as Western multinationals. With licences and regulatory relationships in place, the consumer bankers could then move in,[21] offering whatever range of financial products was appropriate, marketing *Citibanking*® as the country's new premium banking product.

Global Consumer Finance

What Citibank aimed to provide worldwide was a one-stop shop for consumer financial services. This would mean uniform service wherever consumers chose to bank, and with the convenience and reliability that emerging markets clients probably associated more closely with their local McDonald's than with the kind of banking services they were receiving from their domestic banks. Citibank charged a premium price for these services but expected that, usually, the internationally minded and newly wealthy business elite in these nations would be willing to pay more for first-rate banking services.[22] Income statement figures suggest that they were.

Marketing the Experience: Citibanking®

In emerging market countries like China, Citibank had the capacity to develop what marketers like to call "strong brand equity." It had cachet as an overseas bank. It had or could develop a reputation as a bank that provided superior service to those with money. And those who had money (who were increasing in number in these countries) were generally pleased to pay a premium for the level of reliable service and convenience—and the level of prestige—that they could get only from banking with Citibank. Citibank marketed its package of consumer banking services as an experience: "*Citibanking*®." This branding strategy was not yet an advantage in China as Citibank was not allowed to provide retail banking services there. Brand equity was perceived to be a great asset elsewhere in Asia, where Citibank's consumer banking business was growing at a very healthy clip. The importance of brand image to Citibank's financial franchise should not be underrated, therefore, and would certainly be a factor in any discussion of joint ventures or strategic acquisitions.

Citibank's Joint Venture Strategy

Citibank had been strongly averse to joint venture relationships, entering into such agreements only when forced by central bank authorities.[23] Citibank operated in China, as in most countries, as branches of the parent, not subsidiaries. In August 1997, Tibbs agreed with this negative attitude towards joint ventures (JVs).

> We recognize that most JVs do not last very long, JVs give an institution a short-term advantage, but not long-term benefit. A JV in China would be an expensive practice. We do not think that we need to do a JV in China. Up to three years ago, many institutions favored JVs. Now they realize that the environment in China is such that it is unnecessary for them to do JVs in order to get business. Today, foreign institutions are looking for majority shares of the partnership, or even 100-per-cent ownership. The expansion of Citibank in China may be possibly through merger and acquisitions instead of joint ventures.

The door had not, however, been closed to the concept of growth through acquisition. In 1996, John Reed had suggested[24] that he was more comfortable with the concept of strategic acquisition than he had been in the past, as long as such an acquisition would build up one of the bank's key lines of business. The idea of an acquisition in China offered, at the very least, an opportunity to make another positive impression on China's central bank, the People's Bank of China. It might also reinforce Citibank's image as a committed foreign presence, deserving of access to the retail market. It would certainly, however, create branding issues. Thus, if Citibank's China staff were to propose an acquisition, they would do so with the expectation of significant concern from the Citigroup board.

For Tibbs in the late 1990s, the acquisition of an existing Chinese financial institution was not a likely scenario, or even a desirable one:

> Acquiring a financial institution in China is not only not on our "radar screen," it is not something which I could see the government allowing anytime soon. Further, the time, resources and market momentum lost in repairing someone else's wrecked bank (portfolio) is so significant that this is not one's rational dream of how to get ahead quickly.[25]

A UNIQUE STRATEGY FOR CHINA?

> *We want to be totally global and totally local.*
>
> —John Reed, Chairman
> and CEO, Citicorp (1993)[26]

As Citigroup entered the 21st century, adaptation to local realities remained a central principle. The 2001 Annual Report emphasized what it referred to as its "embedded bank" strategy.

> Our goal is to grow our market share over the next five years through our embedded bank strategy. By "embedded bank" we mean a bank that has roots in the country as deep as any local indigenous bank, building a broad customer base, offering diverse products, actively participating in the community and recruiting staff and senior management from the local population. Our long history in these regions positions us as a genuinely local bank.[27]

> Citigroup participates in a broad range of community building initiatives that foster healthy economies: microlending, affordable housing and special-needs facilities, small-business development and savings incentive programs. Our involvement includes offering customized products and services and access to technical assistance, along with the volunteer efforts of our employees.[28]

As China entered the WTO, Citigroup faced many strategic issues, including:

- How could executives ensure that Citibank would maintain its first-mover advantage in

China? How could China executives ensure that Citibank would be among the first foreign banks to capture the domestic retail market? Was the most obvious option a PBOC-sanctioned joint venture with a local bank?

- What additional financial activities should be the focus of Citigroup's China strategy? Could credit cards and e-banking play a significant role? Should substantial amounts of capital be put at risk in investment banking and "bought deals"? If not, would Citigroup be missing a chance of a lifetime to capture an exploding market of SOE privatizations? Would SOE privatizations and the new emphasis on individual responsibility bring with them a mushrooming demand for insurance and pension products?
- To what degree, and in what ways, could the other Citigroup divisions benefit from Citibank's experience in China in order to build a market there?

Citigroup's senior management recognized the need to be proactive in a wide range of strategic issues. Could the China strategy be a model and learning platform for Citigroup as it extended its umbrella of activities in other emerging markets? As emphasized by Robert Rubin, member, board of directors and office of the chairman:

In the years ahead, globalization, the spread of market-based economics and new technologies will continue to present great opportunities in the developed and emerging markets. But the challenges will also be great, both to policymakers and to each of us as participants in the global economy.[29]

Notes

1. This case has been written on the basis of published sources only. Consequently, the interpretation and perspectives presented in this case are not necessarily those of Citigroup or any of its employees. This case is an update on Richard Ivey School of Business #9A97G016, "Citibank N.A. In China."

2. Citigroup Annual Report 2001, 2–3.

3. "What WTO means for Chinese banking," *Asiamoney,* July/August 2000, 23.

4. James Kynge, "Fears for banks over China entry into WTO," *Financial Times,* November 17, 1999, 1.

5. "What WTO means for Chinese banking," *Asiamoney,* July/August 2000, 20.

6. James Kynge, "China's burden," *Financial Times,* January 3, 2002, 10.

7. "The wait for free trade with China just got a little longer: Beijing's new trade rules are slowing down imports," *Business Week Online,* March 11, 2002.

8. L. Li, A. Young, D. Conklin, *Citibank N.A. in China,* Richard Ivey School of Business, Case# 9A97G016, 1997.

9. James Kynge, "China's burden," *Financial Times,* January 3, 2002, 10.

10. "China's economic power," *The Economist,* March 10, 2001, 23.

11. Citigroup Annual Report, 2001.

12. Peter Lee, "Reed Reshuffles the Pack," *Euromoney,* April 1996, 34–39.

13. Peter Lee, "Reed Reshuffles the Pack," *Euromoney,* April 1996, 34–39.

14. Lehman Brothers Inc., Citicorp Company Report, December 12, 1996.

15. James Peng, "U.S. Giant Shakes up Taiwan Banking, Eyes China," *BC Cycle,* July 17, 1996.

16. Lehman Brothers Inc., Citicorp—Company Report, December 12, 1996.

17. Titles awarded by Euromoney, Corporate Finance, Institutional Investor.

18. Citigroup Annual Report, 2001.

19. Lehman Brothers Inc., Citicorp Company Report, December 12, 1996.

20. L. Li, A. Young, D. Conklin, *Citibank N.A. in China,* Richard Ivey School of Business, Case# 9A97G016, 1997.

21. Kenneth Klee, "Brand Builders," *Institutional Investor,* March 1997, 89.

22. Ibid.

23. The only joint venture banking relationships Citibank had been involved in during recent times was a joint venture branch with the Bank of Hungary (Citibank reacquired the last of the central bank's shares in 1995 and presently owned 100 per cent of the branch) and the Saudi American Bank, a joint venture bank with the Saudi central bank.

24. At his December 1996 meeting with equity analysts, quoted in many analyst reports on Citicorp, including the Merrill Lynch report of January 24, 1997.

25. L. Li, A. Young, D. Conklin, "Citibank N.A. in China," Richard Ivey School of Business, Case# 9A97G016, 1997.

26. Bryan Batson, "Thinking Globally, Acting Locally," *China Business Review,* 20, no. 3. (May/June 1993): 23–25.

27. Citigroup Annual Report 2001, 18.
28. Citigroup Annual Report 2001, 26.
29. Citigroup Annual Report 2001, 7.

POINT LISAS INDUSTRIAL ESTATE: TRINIDAD

*Prepared by Jeffrey Chung
and Trevor Hunter under the supervision of
Professors Jeffrey Gandz and David Conklin*

                    Version: (A) 1999-10-27

INTRODUCTION

On a sliver of coastal land, in the tiny Caribbean island of Trinidad, stood the Point Lisas Industrial Estate (PLIE), an integrated large-scale maritime industrial estate with world-class port facilities. Huge export-oriented, gas-based petrochemical industries supported a wide range of downstream activities on PLIE (see Appendix 1), which was the largest project of its kind in the Caribbean and one of the largest in Latin America. It was anticipated that before the start of the new millennium, PLIE would position the country as the world's leading exporter of both methanol and ammonia, displacing Russia and Canada respectively. To reach this position, however, PLIE had to face a number of competitive challenges from both within and outside Trinidad's borders.

THE HISTORY OF POINT LISAS INDUSTRIAL ESTATE

PLIE began in 1956 when a group of business-men, led by Robert Montano, formed the South Trinidad Chamber of Industry and Commerce (STCIC). Montano championed the idea of developing a deepwater harbor in San Fernando, a small town in the southern part of the island. The rationale for this was based on the belief that the economic depression in the south, at the time, was mainly attributable to the development of the deepwater harbor in the north, Port of Spain. In the past, ships anchored in the sheltered Gulf of Paria and smaller boats unloaded cargo on the south and north wharves on a fairly equal basis. However, with the development of Port of Spain, ships were now able to dock and unload their cargo directly. With all the cargo being handled in the north, commerce in the south was significantly hampered.

As the south's economic situation worsened, the group of entrepreneurs from STCIC put forward a strong case to the government for the development of a port in the south. Instead of focusing on the benefits accruing to commerce in the south, STCIC sketched out the concept of an industrial port that would be a magnet for new industry and benefit the entire country. This strategy was necessary because of the government's lukewarm attitude and Port of Spain's skepticism towards the development of another general cargo port on the island given the relatively small volume of cargo handled.

The government allotted TT$88,000, (TT$6.29 = US$1), for a feasibility study to determine the viability of a port in the south. The study concluded that Point Lisas, a piece of coastal land midway between San Fernando and Port of Spain, was economically viable and technically feasible for port development. The report also recommended the inclusion of an industrial estate, a free trade zone and a container terminal to service the southern Caribbean. However, the report warned that a great deal of capital expenditure and promotion would be required to persuade investors that the estate could be a profitable manufacturing location.

In 1966, STCIC registered the Point Lisas Industrial and Port Development Company (PLIPDECO) (see Appendix 2) as a private sector company in the business of estate and port management. A few years after PLIPDECO was registered, management realized that STCIC did not have the financial and marketing resources needed to develop the infrastructure of the estate and to attract any substantial investments. Five years later, the government took controlling interest of the company and PLIPDECO became a state enterprise.

It was believed that only with government involvement could the capital be mobilized to begin operations. Legally and politically, it was not possible for the government to provide substantial public funds to a privately controlled company, and any involvement by international institutions such as the International Monetary Fund (IMF) or the World Bank would require government guarantees. The massive infrastructural inputs, the complex international negotiations and the long payback periods demanded government intervention.

The Trinidadian oil industry was experiencing consistent growth at this time. Several huge multinational companies controlled the entire industry and paid royalties and taxes to the government in return for the crude oil that was refined and exported. With significant reserves of oil on the east coast of the island, the oil industry was slated as the nation's economic driver for years to come. As a result, the sugarcane, cocoa and coffee estates, which were the backbone of the economy in the colonial days, slowly withered away.

An oil crisis was created in 1973 when the Organization of Petroleum Exporting Countries (OPEC) refused to sell oil to countries that supported Israel in the Middle East conflict. Trinidad was not a member of OPEC, and benefited greatly from sharply rising oil prices. As oil production increased dramatically to meet the huge demand, the government received unexpected windfalls of foreign exchange revenue from the corporate taxes and royalties collected. The dream of transforming the nation into a modern industrial society was becoming a reality due to the sudden inflow of capital.

With its newfound financial strength, the government engaged in a massive spending spree. In 1974, the government formed the Industrial Development Corporation (IDC), headed by Professor Ken Julien, dean of the Engineering School at The University of the West Indies. IDC was given the mandate to shape and develop a strategy for industrialization that would utilize the country's precious natural resources. It had to determine what industries would provide the most value and stability for the country in the long term.

Around this time, the oil producers discovered substantial reserves of natural gas. The dilemma for IDC was how to best use them. It was decided that the natural gas resources should be used to fuel a major industrialization thrust geared towards international markets. The IDC determined that the best use of the gas and the most promising gas-dependent industries were methanol, ammonia, urea, aluminum and iron and steel. The site selected to support these ventures was PLIE.

DEVELOPMENT AT PLIE

World demand for ammonia was growing steadily and the trend was expected to continue. Carbon dioxide, the byproduct of ammonia production, could be used to manufacture urea. Urea enjoyed the largest slice of the world's nitrogenous fertilizer market and was in demand for adhesives and plastics. Methanol, used largely for formaldehyde production, was also in demand, though there were more serious freight and tariff concerns involved. The expectation was that PLIE would require an investment of TT$9 billion[1] but would create 10,000 primary jobs and become the economic driver of the future for the island.

The government formed the Co-ordinating Task Force (CTF) in 1975, as recommended by the IDC. CTF's mandate was to undertake the planning and design that would make the estate a reality and get it ready to support new heavy industry with the required infrastructure. CTF operated outside the government bureaucracy with the flexibility to pull together all the inputs necessary to allow the project to take shape. The priorities for PLIE were the construction of three ammonia plants, a steel mill, and the expansion of a cement plant. PLIPDECO worked closely with CTF on the plans for power generation, road construction, water supply and drainage systems. That same year, the National Gas Company of Trinidad & Tobago (NGC) (see Appendix 3) was created to engage in the purchase, transport and sale of all the natural gas on the island.

CTF worked under the umbrella of the IDC and was loosely and informally structured with only five core members. But Julien assembled a team who he felt could overcome all the obstacles and difficulties and get the job done. Professor Julien recalls:

> We all worked together. The reality was that we had a group of people spread through all relevant companies, working their tails off, all sharing the same enthusiasm and working smoothly without fighting or bickering.

> It had a lot to do with the political mood and the will of the time. There was a strong, almost obsessive desire to get the energy sector moving. You had to perform and do your studies to make sure all the options had been properly examined, but once you had your act together and knocked on the door, you got decisions quickly.

After the main goals and objectives of CTF were completed in 1979, the National Energy Corporation (NEC) was formed and took over the project and development work. Conceived as a holding company for several state enterprises, it became instead a project development and management company. The mandate for NEC was to: evaluate investment proposals and develop natural gas-based projects into the implementation phase; advise the government on an appropriate regime of incentives to stimulate the development of downstream industries based upon steel, ammonia, urea, methanol and other natural gas-based products; promote Trinidad & Tobago as a prime location for investment in gas-based industries; and function as a project research and development company for the government.

It was only in 1979, more than two decades after the estate was deemed economically viable, that heavy construction activities really got going on the estate. That year the marine port was finally completed at a cost of TT$24 million and made the transportation of machinery and equipment to PLIE much easier. Since then, PLIE developed at a phenomenal rate.

TRINIDAD

Trinidad was the most southerly island in the Caribbean, located less than 10 miles from Venezuela. Together with Tobago to the northeast, the two islands made up a unitary state. Trinidad & Tobago had the most diversified and industrialized economy in the English-speaking Caribbean. The energy sector, based on the country's reserves of oil and gas, was the mainstay of the economy.

Although agriculture contributed only about two per cent to the country's Gross Domestic Product (GDP), it employed 12 per cent of its labor force, or 46,000 people. Under British rule in the 1950s, sugarcane, cocoa, coffee and other agricultural products contributed up to 19 per cent of GDP. In 1996, the petrochemical industry made history when it outperformed the oil industry for the first time in terms of foreign exchange revenues earned.

During the 1970s, unusually high world oil prices and the subsequent increase in domestic oil production created a rapid expansion of the local economy, with real GDP growing by 72.5 per cent between 1970 and 1977. However, depressed oil prices coupled with high levels of public expenditure led to a prolonged period of economic contraction that began in 1988 and finally ended in 1993. Radical economic adjustments by the government, under strict IMF and World Bank supervision, were required to control the situation. This resulted in a period of political upheaval and widespread social discontent.

The government implemented a number of specific reforms aimed at increasing private sector investment in 1985. The main adjustments were tax reforms that reduced personal and corporate income tax levels and implemented a value-added tax; restructuring, divesting and liquidating a number of state-owned enterprises in telecommunication and petrochemical industries; and changing the system of fixed exchange rates to a managed float of the dollar by the central bank in April 1993. As time passed much emphasis was placed onto diversifying the economy into tourism, marine services, Information Technology (IT) services, agriculture and manufacturing to lessen the country's dependence on oil and gas.

GOVERNMENT'S ENERGY POLICY

In the early 1990s, the country underwent a profound economic crisis brought about in part by plummeting oil prices. The major macroeconomic indicators clearly revealed the magnitude of the crisis. Inflation, swelling fiscal deficits and climbing unemployment levels bore witness to the depth and breadth of the situation. External factors such as rising interest rates and worsening terms of trade were compounded by internal developments. Exhibit 1 presents some key economic information.

In 1996, the Minister of Energy, Finbar Gangar, released the government's energy policy discussion paper. In his presentation he noted that:

> The resuscitation of Trinidad & Tobago's energy sector, which has for years been slipping further into decline and stagnation and was threatening to take with it the nation's chances for economic recovery and development, is complete. It is breathing again and the prognosis for a complete recovery to perfect health is excellent.

With the increasing inflow of direct foreign investments through the developments at PLIE, several major initiatives were being pursued by the government to revitalize the energy sector:

1. Effective utilization of available oil refining capacity currently running at 40 per cent. This entailed upgrading the petroleum refinery in order to improve the yield and value of its products with a view of promoting it as the main refining centre in the Caribbean.

2. Strengthening the administration of the energy sector. This included the development of an efficient, administrative, regulatory, legal and fiscal framework with the capability to adapt to change and promote sustainable development. The government was of the view that it was time for such a body given the transmission and distribution challenges that would arise from the large-scale production and use of natural gas.

3. Securing the country's energy reserves by implementing efficient reserve depletion policies, new exploration programs and supply/demand side management.

4. "Monetization" of natural gas resources as demand would likely double by the year 2000.

5. Promotion of clean energy options that are both user and environmentally friendly.

6. Protection and preservation of the environment.

7. Training, research and development—prerequisites to ensure that the country remained competitive in the industry. Despite the country's small size, budgetary constraints and limited resources, the government was committed to being on the frontiers of technology.

Principal Exports of Trinidad & Tobago (US$m)

Mineral Fuels	1170
Chemicals	611
Manufactured Goods	322
Food and Live Animals	138

Principal Imports 1995 of Trinidad & Tobago (US$m)

Machinery and Equipment	630
Food and Live Animals	226
Manufactured Goods	224
Mineral Fuels	124

Source: EIU Reports.

Macroeconomic Indicators of Trinidad & Tobago

Economic Indicators	1992	1993	1994	1995	1996
GDP at current prices TT$ billion	23.1	24.5	28.6	30.7	32.8
Real GDP Growth %	−1.1	−2.6	5.0	3.2	2.8
Consumer Price Inflation %	6.5	10.8	8.8	5.3	3.3
Exports US$ millions	1,691	1,500	1,778	2,456	2,505
Imports US$ millions	996	1,953	1,037	1,869	2,153
Current-account balance US$ millions	138.9	113.1	217.8	293.8	70.6
Total external debt US$ millions	2,375	2,131	2,221	2,555	2,595
Debt service ratio, paid %[1]	26.4	32.5	24.8	14.8	15.5

Source: TIDCO Info Pak.

1. Debt service ratio, paid per cent measures the ratio of external debt as a percentage of exports on an annual basis.

Average Exchange Rates (1 US$ = ___ TT$)

Year	Avg. Rate	Year	Avg. Rate	Year	Avg. Rate
1986	3.60	1990	4.25	1994	5.87
1987	3.60	1991	4.25	1995	5.89
1988	3.84	1992	4.25	1996	6.15
1989	4.25	1993	5.34	1997	6.30

Exhibit 1   Main Macroeconomic Indicators of Trinidad & Tobago

Source: Central Bank of Trinidad & Tabago.

The Foreign Investment Climate

In the 1970s and early 1980s, the trend was to nationalize foreign-owned companies, and to engage in inward-looking, import-substituting policies. When oil prices dropped and global competition increased, the country had to give in to the structural reformation of the economy outlined by the IMF and World Bank. In 1998, the economy could be characterized as a free-enterprise system, with a trend toward divestment of state enterprises, currency and trade liberalization, and emphasis on diversifying the non-energy sector.

In 1995, past protectionist legislation was replaced by the Investment Promotion Act, which made the industrial climate in Trinidad & Tobago more favorable for overseas investors.

With a domestic market of only 1.3 million people, Trinidad & Tobago had to look outside its borders to achieve sustainable growth. A key element in the government's investment promotion strategy was positioning the country as a regional export hub and strengthening its relationships with South America. Limited transport links to South America, underdeveloped capital markets and high levels of bureaucracy and inefficiency were some of the deterrents to investment that potential foreign investors cited as reasons for failing to invest.

Trade Blocs and Market Access

Trinidad & Tobago was a signatory to the treaty establishing the Caribbean Community[2] (Caricom), which provided for economic, social, cultural and educational co-operation between 14 former British colonial territories. It had long been recognized that the Caribbean islands needed each other to survive in the global marketplace.

In 1995, a wider trade grouping comprised of 25 Caribbean and Latin American countries called the Association of Caribbean States (ACS) was established. It ranked fourth among economic groupings behind the North American Free Trade Agreement (NAFTA), Association of South East Asian Nations (ASEAN), and the European Union (EU), with population of 200 million and total Gross National Product (GNP) of US$500 billion. However, with the implementation of NAFTA, Trinidad & Tobago and other ACS members focused their attention on acquiring membership to this market as a predecessor to the Free Trade Agreement of the Americas (FTAA) that, it was thought, would create free trade throughout the Western Hemisphere by 2005.

The main trade agreements between Trinidad & Tobago and North America were the Caribbean Basin Initiative (CBI), where a number of manufactured goods were entitled to exemptions or reductions of import duties upon entry to the U.S. market, and Caribcan, the Canadian version of CBI. CBI and Caribcan had several products that were subject to regular trade tariffs; among them were petroleum products.

Trinidad & Tobago was also a signatory of the Lome Convention, signed in Lome, Togo, through which certain developing African, Caribbean and Pacific countries were offered access to the EU market completely exempt from duties. The connection with the Lome Convention allowed Trinidad to export its products to the EU and other African countries. However, in 1996, the EU banana arrangement with the Caribbean was under threat from the U.S. which lodged complaints to the World Trade Organization. If the EU was forced to discontinue its preferential treatment of the Caribbean banana industry, many of these small island economies would be devastated. The power that the larger trade groups, in which Trinidad was a member, possessed was clear rationale for the need of such Caribbean trade alliances to both protect regional interests as well as to assert them on the world market with some force.

NATURAL GAS: THE LIFEBLOOD OF PLIE

Natural gas in Trinidad was considered "sweet gas" because of the negligible amounts of hydrogen sulfide, a chemical that was harmful to the environment and equipment, contained therein. Based on the Ministry of Energy's estimates and

Country	Proven Reserves (tcf)
Commonwealth of Independent States	1942.3
Qatar	227.0
Saudi Arabia	182.6
U.S.	167.1
Venezuela	126.5
Nigeria	120.0
Canada	95.7
U.K.	19.1
Trinidad	10.1

Table 1 Proven Gas Reserves by Country 1994

an evaluation by an independent and international petroleum consulting firm, Trinidad & Tobago's proved natural gas reserves were about 10.1 trillion cubic feet (tcf). This represented about 0.2 per cent of the world's reserves. Table 1 illustrates the world's major natural gas producers.

Approximately 70 per cent of the reserves occurred in the east coast marine area that were under development by the main supplier of natural gas, Amoco. The government negotiated long-term supply contracts with the natural gas producers in the country. All the gas produced was purchased by the state-owned National Gas Company of Trinidad & Tobago (NGC) at competitive prices. In 1997, the government renegotiated its contract with Amoco and doubled the quantity to be supplied from 350 million standard cubic feet per day (mmscfd) to 700 mmscfd over the following 20 years.

After NGC purchased the gas from the producers, most of it was transported via pipeline directly to PLIE. NGC owned the 480 km pipeline network that ran through the island. Most of NGC's income came from the sale of gas to the tenants of PLIE, as well as a growing number of commercial businesses around the country. There was practically no domestic demand for natural gas in Trinidad & Tobago other than a small amount of compressed natural gas (CNG), which was used as an alternative fuel for automobiles.

When the gas arrived at PLIE, it was processed by Phoenix Park Gas Processors Ltd. (PPGPL) (see Appendix 4) before it was distributed to the companies on the estate. Propane, butane and natural gasolines, valuable liquids found in natural gas, were removed from the gas stream and sold to regional and international markets. With gas demand expected to reach 1,400 mmscfd by the year 2000, PPGPL was evaluating the feasibility of an ethylene production plant, expanded storage facilities, as well as expanded processing capacity so the plant could handle up to one billion cubic feet of gas per day.

After the gas was processed by PPGPL, it was distributed by NGC to the various plants via pipeline. Most of the gas was used as a source of energy in the generation of electricity for both heavy and light manufacturing operations, and as a feedstock in the petrochemical industry, namely methanol and ammonia production. New applications for natural gas were being developed and its popularity as the preferred fuel over other fossil fuels was increasing.

Natural Gas Pricing

The price of natural gas was one of the most critical factors in attracting foreign investors to PLIE. The pricing system used by NGC was based on a framework that allowed a great deal of flexibility through negotiations. In fact, NGC used this to encourage the growth and development of certain industries that the government found attractive. Before negotiation started, companies were categorized based on their intended use of the gas and the quantities required. For example, if the gas was to be used as the main raw material in the manufacturing process of some product, then the price of gas was related to the market price of that product.[3] The pricing mechanism employed by NGC sometimes led to differences in gas pricing among companies in the same industry, and this had been a source of concern to some companies.

One of the benefits of instituting a natural gas regulatory body called for by the government was the implementation of more structure to the natural gas pricing mechanism employed by NGC, which resolved conflicts between companies. It was believed that the government's increased control over the gas industry would accrue greater benefit to the country by maximizing the returns to the island's natural resources.

THE SITUATION AT PLIE

Over 75 local and foreign-owned companies, covering a range of activities using natural gas as either feedstock or an energy source, occupied the estate. The availability of natural gas had attracted a number of major foreign investors to PLIE. Examples of these companies included Ferrostaal of Germany, which had interests in four methanol plants; PCS Nitrogen of the U.S.,

with ammonia/urea production in three plants; Nucor, the iron carbide pioneer; Norsk Hydro of Norway, which also produced urea and ammonia; and Mittal Group of India, one of the largest steel manufacturers in the world.

Gas demand stood at about 820 mmscfd and was used mainly for power generation, and the methanol or ammonia plants at PLIE. Several world-scale projects were scheduled for completion by the year 2000, and the demand for gas was expected to double as a result. There were to be six ammonia plants capable of producing over three million tonnes per annum, and five methanol plants producing three million tonnes per annum. Most of these new projects to produce liquid ammonia were foreign investments made by international companies such as:

1. A 620,000 tonnes per annum (tpa) ammonia plant by a joint venture between U.S.-based Farmland Industries and Mississippi Chemicals requiring 52 mmscfd of gas (1998).

2. A 600,000 tpa ammonia plant by U.S.-based PCS Nitrogen (1998).

3. A 500,000 tpa iron reduction plant by U.S.-based Cleveland Cliffs (1998).

4. A 450 mmscfd liquid natural gas (LNG) plant by Atlantic LNG, and joint venture between U.S.-based Amoco, Spain's Respol and Trinidad's NGC (1999).

5. A 630,000 tpa ammonia project by DSM (1999).

6. A 830,000 tpa Titan methanol project by Amoco (15%), Saturn Methanol (10%), and Beacon Energy Fund (75%) (1999).

7. A 550,000 tpa Methanol IV project (1999).

Feasibility studies were also in progress for a number of other projects. Two of the most promising projects were the construction of an ethylene plant and an aluminum smelter. The projects had the potential to create a multitude of down-stream business when they came on line. In the past, the large petrochemical industries had provided the base for downstream companies that manufactured plastics, cereal, animal feed and industrial gases. In particular, methanol and ammonia were the building blocks for hundreds of diverse applications, and there was enormous potential for growth in the petrochemical sector.

NGC performed most of the planning activities needed to attract huge petrochemical plants to PLIE. Potential projects were evaluated on criteria such as the capital cost of plants, the amount of jobs that could be created, the formation of strategic linkages with other countries, the export potential of the products, the foreign exchange earnings that could be generated, the formation of downstream industries leading to the diversification of the economy, and the associated environmental risks. If the projects were approved and the foreign investors accepted the preliminary terms and conditions of the agreement, PLIPDECO then became involved in siting the project to ensure adequate infrastructure was provided.

With the projects currently underway and those proposed, dramatic growth and expansion in the petrochemical and energy sectors was expected throughout the next five years. Barring unforeseen circumstances, Trinidad & Tobago would be positioned as the number one exporter of both methanol and ammonia in the world.

Social Concerns at PLIE

PLIE was located on 1,125 hectares of coastal land that were once rolling fields of sugarcane. The original estate was initially located on 800 hectares, and there was little expectation that it would be used up so quickly. PLIE had a 95 per cent occupancy rate until the additional 325 hectares of land to the north was acquired. Still more land was aggressively sought by PLIPDECO. The acquisition of suitable land for the expansion of the estate was a major challenge for PLIPDECO.

The Gulf of Paria, which separates Trinidad and Venezuela, limited the expansion of PLIE to the west. Although a significant amount of land was reclaimed through dredging in the 1980s, there were questions about the stability of the reclaimed land for heavy industrial development. The gulf was an important source of fish, shrimp and shellfish for domestic consumption, and hundreds of fishermen relied on this body of water to make a living. With the fish stock depleting through industrial pollution and overfishing, the local fishermen were forced to trawl further offshore. This resulted in regular conflicts between local fishermen and the Venezuelan coast guard. Serious diplomatic tensions threatened the cordial relationship between the two countries built up over the years.

California Village prevented eastward expansion of the estate. The village established itself along a main road with about 10,000 residents and a variety of commercial businesses. Beyond the village, were wide expanses of sugarcane fields and a sugar refinery owned by Caroni (1975) Ltd.[4] Couva, a larger town of 25,000 inhabitants was located about one kilometre away from PLIE to the northeast. The mostly East Indian population had traditionally been dependent on agriculture as the main source of employment. They were on the verge of experiencing huge development of the area as a result of the growth at PLIE. Plans had reached an advanced stage for the construction of a hospital, a market, a stadium, schools, upgraded library facilities, picnic areas, a theme park, an expanded heliport, a hotel, and shrimp/fish processing facilities. Interestingly, the parliamentary representative for Couva was the prime minister of Trinidad & Tobago, Mr. Basdeo Panday.

Additional land that had been reclaimed in the past could be found to the south of PLIE, but expansion beyond this was limited by the establishment of a nearby cement plant. Adjacent to the cement plant was Claxton Bay, a small fishing village of about 5,000 people. The experiences of this rural village illustrate the impact of industrialization on a community.

With the startup of Trinidad Cement Ltd. in 1980, many jobs were provided and the economic status of the village improved significantly. However, the nearby environment and community suffered in the following years. Fine red dust generated by the manufacturing process coated surrounding trees, gaseous emissions polluted the air and several lawsuits by nearby residents brought the company to court after the dust started to affect their respiratory systems.

One of the more pressing issues facing PLIPDECO concerned the development of several residential areas and housing projects organized by the National Housing Authority (NHA) and Town & Country Planning, two state-controlled bodies responsible for providing shelter and making land-usage plans throughout the island. These low-value residential areas were located dangerously close to PLIE, on the opposite bank of the Caroni River, and any industrial development on the newly acquired lands to the north would sandwich the residents between chemical producing plants.

With the rapid industrialization of the area, there was huge demand for residential housing and commercial buildings, but all the available land around PLIE had already been allocated. Even within PLIE, there were desolate pockets of land where dozens of squatters lived in wooden shacks, oblivious to the massive developments taking place a stone's throw away. PLIPDECO had provided some relocation incentives for some residents, but did not have the financial and political strength to properly address this very sensitive and delicate situation.

The Environmental Impact of PLIE

Responsible management of the environment was a critical issue facing the future development of PLIE. The potential damage that could be done on an industrial estate with the size and scope of PLIE would be devastating. A concoction of deadly, highly flammable gases and liquids were manufactured by the tonnes every day. (See Appendix 5 for a list of hazardous by-products of PLIE.) One human error or even an uncommonly strong hurricane or earthquake could wreak horrifying damage to PLIE and the nearby communities. Although this scenario was highly improbable, it was not impossible.

Dr. John Agard, lecturer in Environmental Management at The University of the West Indies implored PLIPDECO:

Before any additional plants are constructed at PLIE, an environmental impact study of the area should be taken. Currently it is very close, if not beyond its environmental capacity, and the recent upsurge of accidents indicates that we have to be very careful about extending the estate.

In the past, there had been a noticeable lack of adequate standards and legislation to protect the environment. This factor had played a part in foreign investors choosing to build their plants on the island. In developed countries, the high cost of implementing emission and loss control technology needed to satisfy stringent regulatory boards like the U.S.-based Environmental Protection Agency (EPA), was a huge barrier that deemed many projects unprofitable. Although this was not the primary reason why PLIE had developed with such rapidity, the lack of a coherent environmental policy had given the industry substantial flexibility in setting its own targets in terms of environmental performance.

It was only in 1995 that the long-awaited Environmental Management Act was passed. The act provided a framework that facilitated the formulation of future legislation for environmental management, the development and enforcement of standards, the control of activities in areas designated under the act as being environmentally sensitive, and the handling of hazardous wastes. The act required companies to record their operations every day and to conduct self-imposed environmental audits and included incentive programs for rewarding good environmental performance in waste reduction and recycling. It also facilitated private parties to institute civil action against persons violating the rules and deliberately endangering human life through the release or handling of pollutants.

With the passing of the act, the petrochemical industry was expected to:

1. Obtain licences to conduct all business activities related to oil and gas

2. Obtain permits for the discharge of atmospheric pollutants and waste water

3. Obtain certificates of environmental clearance and conduct environmental impact assessment studies (EIAS) before the construction of new plants and projects

4. Document the results of routine audits and submit them to the Environmental Management Agency (EMA)

5. Implement waste reduction and recycling programs

Despite the intentions of the act, implementing it remained a huge challenge. Before the various companies at PLIE could do any EIAS, a baseline study of the environment had to be made. This involved a comprehensive analysis of the geology, water, air, fauna, flora and the community in the area. Such a detailed study was expected to be completed in 1998, the results of which would be made available to current and potential petrochemical plants at PLIE.

PLIPDECO had been mandated by the minister of planning and development to come up with an environmental report for PLIE, in collaboration with EMA. The environmental engineer at PLIPDECO, Raouf Ali, was responsible for leading the environmental challenge facing the estate. He felt the environmental committee had to be strengthened and hinted at the importance of the task when he stated:

> We needed to be more aggressive. We needed to increase the profile of what we were doing and what was expected for the community and from the companies on the estate in case of any accident in the area. A public awareness program was crucial for the residents, and we needed to act urgently on this. There was a lot of serious work to be done.

COMPETITIVE CHALLENGES TO PLIE: VENEZUELA[5]

One of the key external variables that could determine the sustainability of the development at PLIE was competition from neighboring Venezuela. This Spanish-speaking country was about 200 times the size of Trinidad, 10 times as populated, and one of the wealthiest countries on the South American continent. It was the world's leading exporter of oil and third-largest oil producer. The oil and gas sector accounted for over 90 per cent of Venezuela's foreign exchange earnings and 25 per cent of GDP.

Venezuela's proven gas reserves were over 10 times those of Trinidad, and the cost of natural gas for industrial use was the lowest in the Western Hemisphere. Over 95 per cent of the natural gas produced in Venezuela was associated gas, and it had traditionally been viewed as a secondary product derived from oil production. To maximize the returns from the huge gas reserves, the Venezuelan government had fixed unnaturally low gas prices to woo foreign investment in the petrochemical sector and to provide a cheap supply of electrical power throughout the country.

Like Trinidad, Venezuela benefited from the oil crisis in the 1970s. Being the only OPEC member in the Western Hemisphere gave it substantial power in controlling the oil market. With a resulting increase of foreign exchange earnings, Venezuela also embarked on a strategy of nationalizing foreign companies and instant industrialization that many developing oil-producing nations quickly employed. The problems that Trinidad underwent when oil prices dropped to less than US$10 per barrel in 1986 were much more acute in Venezuela, and the country struggled to recover from that dismal period.

Despite the attractiveness of the gas prices in Venezuela, the political, social and economic instability of the country remained the main deterrent to foreign investment. In 1989, radical economic liberalization programs led to a spate of violent protests and two unsuccessful coups under President Carlos Perez. He was later impeached for the misappropriation of public funds in 1993. One year later, the banking sector collapsed and several large banks were nationalized to steady the financial sector. This series of events led to the local currency, the bolivar (Bs), being devalued from Bs 170 to the U.S. dollar, to Bs 290 in 1995, and to Bs 417 in 1996.

However, a two-phase adjustment program for the economy that started in 1996 under the IMF and the World Bank was addressing the problems. Most price and foreign exchange controls were abolished, and the country was slowly opening up its markets and privatizing some of its inefficient state-owned companies. This resulted in violent labor protests and the government was under tremendous pressure while executing the rest of the adjustment program.

The chief executive officer of PLIPDECO, Neil Rolingson, summarized the situation when he said:

> The future of PLIE was at issue. This country needed to decide whether it wanted to be involved in the industrial estate business along with PLIPDECO. It was an urgent question because Trinidad had to take advantage of Venezuela's difficulties. We could not compete for international investors once Venezuela regained its economic footing. They were our only competitor in the region for international investors interested in setting up an industrial estate. We could not compete with them as far as the price of natural gas, but we could compete on political stability.

THE PROBLEM

PLIE was Trinidad's most ambitious industrialization attempt ever. What had started as a need for a deep water harbor to boost commerce had grown into the establishment of a huge gas-based industrial complex attracting multinational companies from around the globe. PLIE developed at a phenomenal rate and the economic benefits accruing to the country directly attributable to PLIE were unmistakable.

There seemed to be a growing imbalance between the economic and the social and environmental benefits. The industrialization of the estate had a significant economic impact on the area; however, calls for consolidation of the estate were intensifying. Critical environmental variables were close to, if not past their maximum capacity levels, with escalating fears that these levels could cause serious problems to the environment and nearby communities.

These communities were also a threat and at the same time threatened. PLIE needed to expand, but there was no room to move. The creation of jobs had brought workers in numbers for which the surrounding communities were not prepared. There was a lack of proper housing, and other community services.

The difficulty in reaching an equilibrium point where economic gains were balanced by social and environmental stability in a small developing country such as Trinidad & Tobago were made even harder by external factors such as trade liberalization and increasing global competition. In particular, NAFTA and the emergence of Venezuela as a potential player in gas-based industries were two challenges facing continued economic development of the country and the competitive advantage PLIE had over other similar industrial estates worldwide.

NOTES

1. In 1975, US$1 = TT$2.40
2. Caricom was established by the Treaty of Chaguaramas on July 4, 1973.
3. Average market prices in 1996 for methyl tertiary butyl ether (MTBE), ammonia and methanol were US$310, US$120, and US$130 per tonne respectively.
4. Caroni (1975) Ltd. was a state-owned company that was the largest owner of land in the country and was involved in agricultural activities mainly for export.
5. See Appendix 6 for more background on the political/economic history of Venezuela.

APPENDIX 1: THE NATURAL GAS
DYNAMICS AT THE POINT LISAS INDUSTRIAL ESTATE

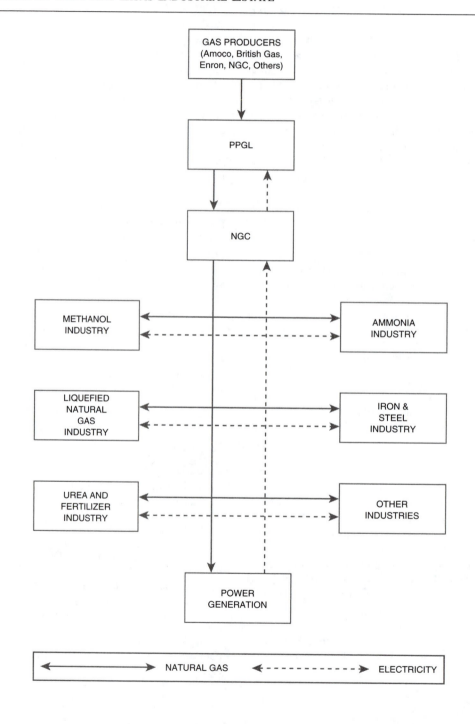

APPENDIX 2: POINT LISAS INDUSTRIAL PORT DEVELOPMENT CORPORATION LIMITED (PLIPDECO)

Mission Statement

To be recognized as the dominant regional leader and a global leader in the development and administration of profitable, customer-oriented ports and industrial estates. In support of this process, to forge strategic alliances and act in a spirit of entrepreneurship in our principal activities.

General

PLIPDECO is a public company with Government owning 43%, Caroni (1975) Ltd. 8% and private shareholders 49%. Its core business activities are marine activities, industrial real estate management and cargo holding activities.

APPENDIX 3: THE NATIONAL GAS COMPANY OF TRINIDAD & TOBAGO (NGC)

Mission Statement

To be a dynamic, efficient, technology-based, profitable and integrated natural gas company that:

a. provides leadership in the development of gas-based and related industries;

b. provides rewarding, challenging opportunities and environments for employees;

c. fulfills the needs of its customers and shareholders.

Created by the government in 1975 to buy, transport and sell natural gas, NGC has presided over the phenomenal growth of the gas industry that has grown at 8.7 per cent per annum over the last two decades. NGC's primary growth objective over the next five years is to increase the sales of natural gas to beyond the level of 1,000 mmscfd by the year 2000. In the pursuit of this overriding objective, NGC's business strategies will:

1. Pursue the development of new energy intensive projects in the petrochemical and metals sector, while seeking to maximize value added from natural gas by placing greater emphasis on new downstream developments.

2. Secure adequate and competitively priced supplies of natural gas to sustain the international competitiveness of its customers, present and future.

3. Promote Trinidad & Tobago as a strategic location for gas-based industrial development.

Consolidated Income Statement Year Ended 31 December ('000)		
	1996	*1995*
Turnover	50,280	67,335
Profit Before Tax	9,819	15,033
Taxation	503	4,588
Net Income	9,316	10,445
EPS	.32	.37

Source: Company documents.

4. Extend the transmission and distribution network to provide a safe and reliable supply of natural gas to existing and new customers.

5. Pursue strategic alliances with industry leaders and innovative enterprises that support the strategic intent of NGC.

Five-Year Financial Review 1991–1995

Income Statement $000	1995	1994	1993	1992	1991
Sales	2,078,262	1,920,036	1,064,898	789,422	780,856
Cost of Sales	−1,247,574	−713,373	−567,032	−567,031	−504,358
Gross Profit	830,688	901,353	351,525	222,391	276,498
Net Operating Costs	−95,221	−90,277	−84,261	−83,021	−74,589
Operating Profit	735,467	811,076	267,264	139,370	201,909
Interest & Investment Income	112,169	28,313	26,550	18,795	26,649
Interest Expense	−24,496	−22,811	−15,911	−20,387	−21,649
Other	−44,300	1,498	33,446	−24,488	—
Profit Before Tax	778,840	818,076	311,349	113,290	201,109
Taxation	−433,682	−450,979	−149,938	−80,376	−80,433
Net Profit	345,158	367,097	161,411	32,914	126,666

Source: Company reports.

NGC's Balance Sheet $000	1995	1994	1993	1992	1991
Net Current Assets	553,696	369,555	304,195	258,348	322,097
Joint Venture Facility	20,905	29,212	19,585	14,285	14,185
Long-Term Loans & Investments	353,602	280,975	260,830	325,683	207,125
Fixed Assets	487,594	477,225	260,816	246,708	156,284
	1,415,797	1,156,967	845,426	845,024	699,791
Long-Term Debt	127,837	109,805	289,317	377,848	146,551
Deferred Items	97,972	21,632	17,474	19,952	28,083
Shareholders' Equity					
Share Capital	240,766	140,766	50,339	50,339	37,339
Capital Reserves	260,134	258,890	—	—	—
Retained Earnings	689,088	625,874	488,296	396,885	487,818
	1,415,797	1,156,967	845,426	845,024	699,791

Source: Company reports.

Major Customers of NGC

	Core Business	Capital Invested ($TTm)	Production (tonnes/yr.) 1995	Export (tonnes/yr.) 1995	Avg. Gas Demand (mmscfd)
Caribbean Methanol (CMC)	To produce and market chemical grade methanol locally and internationally	$1,300	1,164,400	897,600	150
Caribbean ISPAT Ltd.	Production of steel wire coils and rods	$1,200	600,000	N/A	40
PCS Nitrogen (Arcadian)	Production of urea and anhydrous ammonia	$750	1,003,300	793,500	135
PowerGen	Generation of electricity	$290	N/A	N/A	160
HydroAgri	Production of fertilizers, urea and ammonia	$840	1,036,300	981,200	140
Others	Amoco, PPGPL, Petrotrin, Nucor, TCL, Light industry	N/A	N/A	N/A	195
Total					820

Source: PLIE reports.

APPENDIX 4: PHOENIX PARK GAS PROCESSORS LIMITED (PPGPL)

Mission Statement

To be a dynamic company that adds value to our shareholders through the operation of a safe and efficient gas-processing plant, pursuit of value-added growth opportunities in related businesses and through superior service to our customers.

General

Phoenix Park Gas Processors Ltd. (PPGPL) is a joint venture among the National Gas Company of Trinidad & Tobago (NGC), Cononco Inc. of Houston, Texas (U.S.) and Pan West Engineers and Constructors Inc. of Houston, Texas (U.S.). PPGPL was created to construct and operate a natural gas liquids recovery plant to remove natural gas liquids contained in the natural gas stream of NGC and to convert those liquids into valuable products for export into international markets. Construction began in 1989 on a 30-hectare site in PLIE and was opened in May 1991.

Market Distribution

The propane and butane produced by the PPGPL facility are exported and sold as liquefied petroleum gas (LPG) to be used for domestic purposes in Latin America and the Caribbean such as Dominican Republic (17%), Chile (13%), the Eastern Caribbean (15%), and Panama (8%). Natural gasoline, a heavy hydrogen component in the gas stream, is exported to North America and Europe, where it is used in the manufacture of motor gasoline or as a petrochemical feedstock.

APPENDIX 5: DEADLY GASES AT PLIE

Elements of Products	% Release	Effect on Life and Safety
Carbon Dioxide	10.0	Swelling of lungs. Death within several minutes
Carbon Monoxide	1.3	Poisons by asphyxiation. Death after several breaths
Hydrogen Sulphide	4.0 to 7.0	Dizziness and pain in respiratory system
Sulphur Dioxide	.05	Irritation to eyes
Ammonia	.25 to .65	Irritation to eyes, throat and lungs. Lethal
Hydrogen Cyanide	.03	Rapid fatality
Nitrogen Dioxide	.02 to .07	Rapid fatality
Methanol	5.0	Fatal
Acetylene	2.5	Explosive
Hydrogen	4.0	Suffocation if in confined areas
Natural Gas	n/a	Highly flammable
Urea Formaldehyde	n/a	Combustible
Chlorine	n/a	Irritating to respiratory system and highly corrosive

APPENDIX 6: VENEZUELA: A NATION OF EXTREME VOLATILITY

Before 1958, Venezuela experienced long periods of dictatorial rule, with brief periods of elections and with many civil conflicts. In 1958, the military shifted the nation towards democratic rule. Rafael Caldera was president from 1969 to 1973, during which time he pursued active government ownership and regulation, with barriers to foreign ownership and imports. In order to appeal to voters, the government instituted extensive social welfare programs, and it imposed price controls on basic commodities, particularly gasoline, as a way of ensuring that the general public could afford to purchase them.

Andres Perez was president from 1974 to 1978, and he continued with a government-led development program and social welfare programs. High oil prices supported government investments.

Corruption was commonplace. Little industrial diversification occurred. In 1989, Andres Perez became president again, and he was followed by Mr. Caldera once more. Powerful vested interests seemed to have controlled government decisions. Many have been critical of the judicial process as well as the electoral process.

In 1992, a military leader, Hugo Chavez, led an armed military uprising; however, this attempted coup failed. In 1998, Chavez was elected president on a social democratic platform, with many extremist positions. By 1999, it was still not clear what Chavez's policies would be.

The banking sector has never been strong. At times, political leaders have nationalized the banks, and, at other times, they have privatized them. In 1994, the government provided substantial financial assistance to the privately-owned banks.

Venezuela's inflation rate has generally been very high, and this has led to repeated foreign exchange rate crises and devaluations.

Venezuela has enormous oil and gas reserves, ranking among the top few nations in the world in regard to oil and gas potential. The entire economy depends upon oil. This includes government revenues and civilian employment. The constitution required government ownership of the oilfields. Many have been critical of the government in its operation of the oilfields, pointing to inefficiencies and lack of investment. However, in recent years, special arrangements have been made to allow private sector development.

For foreign investors, the advantage of low oil and gas prices is offset by the risk of new government policies that might restrict their activities and tax their profits. The oil industry has maintained relatively high wages, and the workers' movements are strong. Furthermore, the risk of social unrest and even civil war limits investment in Venezuela.

THUNDERBIRD
THE GARVIN SCHOOL OF INTERNATIONAL MANAGEMENT

DELL'S DILEMMA IN BRAZIL: NEGOTIATING AT THE STATE LEVEL

Prepared by Professor Roy Nelson,
based on his interviews and field research in Brazil

In mid-March 1999, Keith Maxwell, Senior Vice President for Worldwide Operations, Dell Computer Corporation, looked out the window of his office at Dell's headquarters in Round Rock, Texas, and pondered the frustrating situation he faced in Brazil, where Dell had decided to locate its first manufacturing plant in Latin America.

In early 1998, Maxwell had led the site selection team that visited five different states in Brazil in order to decide where Dell should locate its manufacturing plant.[1] In June 1998, after the team had confirmed its initial findings and concluded its negotiations, Maxwell had made the final recommendation to Michael Dell: the plant should be built in Brazil's southernmost state, Rio Grande do Sul. By mid-March 1999, Dell had already signed agreements with the local state government on the terms of the investment, the process of hiring local personnel to manage the plant had begun, and construction on the plant itself was scheduled to start soon.

Suddenly, however, the political climate in Rio Grande do Sul had changed. A new governor, Olivio Dutra of the Partido dos Trabalhadores (Workers' Party),[2] had taken office in Rio Grande do Sul on January 1, 1999 and appeared likely to rescind the entire agreement. This was a setback, and Maxwell would have to decide on a course of action to recommend: (1) leave Brazil entirely; (2) move the plant to another state; or (3) try to renegotiate with Governor Dutra.

DELL AND THE BRAZILIAN COMPUTER MARKET

As Maxwell considered the options, he reflected on the events that had led to this situation.

Dell had begun the process of selecting a site for its manufacturing plant in Brazil in 1998, after the company had experienced a long period of astonishing growth. Founded in 1984 by Michael Dell in his University of Texas dorm room, by 1999 Dell Computer Corporation had annual revenue of over $23 billion and a market capitalization of $98 billion. In just 15 years, the revenues Dell generated were the second largest in the world for personal computer manufacturers, just behind Compaq, and the company was still one of the fastest growing PC makers in the industry.

Most of Dell's success could be attributed to its revolutionary business approach, which had become known as the Direct Model. Following the Direct Model, Dell shipped its products to its customers directly from the factory, without any intermediary retailers. Dell also set up its supply chain of parts and components using the latest just-in-time (JIT) methods, which allowed the company to maintain minimal inventory. These highly efficient practices enabled Dell not only to get its products to customers faster than its competitors could, but also to reduce its costs substantially. The resulting ability to pass on these savings directly to customers created a tremendous competitive edge that enabled the company to control 25% of the U.S. market for personal computers, and 11% of the market worldwide.[3]

In order to maintain its rapid growth, Dell adopted a strategy of emphasizing international expansion. From its headquarters in Round Rock, Texas, the company expanded its operations to the point that by the late 1990s, it had offices in 34 countries around the world, sales in over 170 countries and territories, and manufacturing facilities in five countries, including Ireland and China. Although the company outsourced some of its manufacturing to contract manufacturers in Mexico, it did not have any manufacturing facilities of its own in Latin America when, in early 1998, it began evaluating possible sites for the construction of its own manufacturing plant in Brazil.

Brazil was a logical place for a manufacturing plant. In the late 1990s, sales of personal computers were growing faster in Latin America than anywhere else in the world and Brazil, the largest Latin American country with a population of over 170 million, was a very attractive market for the company. Despite the maxi-devaluation of the Brazilian currency, the *real,* in January 1999, Dell had decided to continue with its plans to invest in Brazil as part of its long-term strategy. Dell executives realized that having a plant in Brazil would be essential if the company were to enter the Brazilian market successfully. Although in 1992 the Brazilian government had abandoned its market reserve policy of allowing only domestic manufacturers to make computers in the country, Brazil's protectionist barriers for imports were still high. Moreover, Brazil was a member of Mercado Comun do Sul (Mercosul), the South American customs union that included Argentina, Uruguay, and Paraguay, with Chile and Bolivia as associate members. The benefit of Mercosul was that any company that produced at least 60% of a given product in any of the Mercosul countries would, with some exceptions, be able to export the product to any of the other Mercosul countries at zero tariffs. Clearly, Brazil's Mercosul membership was another plus for putting the plant in Brazil.

Once Dell had selected Brazil, however, the question remained as to exactly where the manufacturing plant would be located. Brazil had a federal system, with 26 separate states—each with its own governor and state legislature, as well as a federal district—and many of these states eagerly sought Dell's investment. Having chosen Brazil as the site for the new manufacturing plant in Latin America, Dell's executives would have still another decision to make.

Maxwell and the others on Dell's site selection team visited five different states in Brazil: São Paulo, Minas Gerais, Rio de Janeiro, Paraná, and Rio Grande do Sul. All of these states essentially met the requirements for levels of education and sufficient numbers of qualified personnel, adequate supply of electrical energy, and quality of telecommunications and transportation infrastructure. The main differences of interest to the Dell team were the special financial incentives each state offered, and the nature of the agency with which the company interacted when making the investment decision.

COMPETITION BETWEEN THE STATES

The Guerra Fiscal

In their exuberance during Brazil's transition to democracy, politicians elected to Brazil's Constituent Assembly approved a constitution in 1988 that gave states considerably more power than before. Among other things, states were authorized to collect state sales taxes, or Impostos sobre a Circulação de Mercadorias e Serviços (ICMS). Although the current average for these taxes was 12%, states had some leeway to reduce these taxes in order to attract investment.

In theory, individual states could not change their ICMS tax rates unless all states agreed to do so within the Conselho Nacional de Política Fazendária (CONFAZ), the representative body for the states on finance and taxation policy. Nevertheless, from the beginning, states made such changes without CONFAZ approval. Since the early 1990s, the competition between the states to lower their taxes and attract investment had become so fierce that journalists called it the "guerra fiscal," or taxation war.

Taxation rates mattered to large transnational corporations trying to decide where to invest. Competition among these companies was fierce, and a difference in sales tax meant that companies could offer their products at reduced costs without passing on the tax burden to consumers. Such incentives also compensated for extra costs associated with investing outside of the more industrialized and heavily populated locations of Brazil, especially the state of São Paulo, which traditionally received, by far, the greatest proportion of Brazil's foreign investment. Significantly, São Paulo itself did not offer this particular incentive—it did not need to do so.

But many in Brazil saw this policy as detrimental to the country's overall interests. Critics of the *guerra fiscal* argued that transnational corporations (TNCs) could use it to play one state against another for their own benefit, without concern for the welfare of the country as a whole. Poor Brazilian states, these critics maintained, were in no position to be giving tax concessions to large, wealthy transnational corporations.[4] Supporters of the policy, on the other hand, argued that without such incentives, the TNCs would not invest at all in states far from the more industrialized regions.[5] And as one supporter of the policy put it, "12% [the full taxation rate] of nothing is still nothing."[6]

The incentives Brazil's states could offer to attract foreign investment went beyond reductions in the ICMS. State governments could (and did, in many cases) also offer to provide free land on which to build infrastructure (usually roads or port facilities), and to provide government loans on highly concessional terms, including lengthy grace periods and low interest rates. As with the ICMS tax reductions, these incentives also came under harsh attack from critics. This was the environment that Maxwell and the Dell team had entered when they began their site selection process in Brazil.

Financial Incentives and Contrasting Approaches to Investment Promotion

During the site selection process, one of the team's chief concerns had been to investigate the prospects for obtaining financial incentives in each state. Upon actually visiting each state, however, the site selection team's initial and most important contacts were with the agency responsible for investment promotion. The nature of the working relationships Maxwell and the rest of the team established with these agencies also turned out to play a major role in the decision-making process.

Each state in Brazil that the Dell executives visited had a unique approach to promoting foreign investment; and in every state, the investment promotion organization responsible for meeting with the Dell team had a slightly different organizational structure and style. With the sole exception of Pólo-RS, Agência de Desenvolvimento (Pólo), the independent, private, nonprofit investment promotion agency that collaborated with the state government of Rio Grande do Sul, all of the state agencies the Dell executives encountered were government agencies.

This made a difference in how these agencies interacted with Dell. While other states such as Minas Gerais offered Dell similar financial incentives, only in Rio Grande do Sul did the Dell executives, working with Pólo as an intermediary, encounter an investment promotion agency that they felt had made a concerted effort to understand Dell's specific needs. In other states, in contrast, Dell executives perceived that the government officials they were dealing with either did not sufficiently understand Dell's unique requirements, or were not sufficiently committed to attracting high-technology investment.

São Paulo, for example, was a state that initially attracted Dell. It had a large pool of skilled labor and, because of its large, relatively prosperous population, it was the principal market for computers in Brazil. São Paulo's sheer market size was the main reason that in the final selection process, two possible sites in the state, one in the city of São Jose dos Campos and the other in Campinas, were ranked high on the list, although still below Rio Grande do Sul.[7] But the Dell site selection team formed a negative impression of São Paulo when harried state government officials appeared to be somewhat indifferent to Dell's specific concerns.[8] Moreover, the state, which already had significant investment, had a policy of not offering special financial incentives.[9]

In Rio de Janeiro, the team encountered a different situation. The head of the Companhia de Desenvolvimento Industrial do Estado do Rio de Janeiro (CODIN), Rio de Janeiro's investment promotion agency, was accustomed to long drawn-out negotiations with automobile firms that sometimes lasted for a year or more. Consequently, he made a very low initial offer for financial incentives to Dell, expecting the company to come back with a counter offer. He was stunned when the Dell executives, accustomed to making decisions on a much speedier basis, never returned.[10]

In Paraná, the state government was not able to offer Dell the same financial incentives that Rio Grande do Sul offered.[11] In addition to that, Maxwell and others on the Dell team also perceived that the state was giving the same sort of presentation to them that it gave to all companies, regardless of the specific sector the company represented.[12]

Other than São Paulo, which was ranked high principally because of the size of its market rather than its investment promotion efforts, only Minas Gerais came close to winning the competition with Rio Grande do Sul for Dell's investment. In Minas, the Dell executives met with state government officials from various agencies, as well as with *técnicos* from the Instituto de Desenvolvimento Industrial de Minas Gerais (INDI).

Created in 1968, INDI had a unique structure. It was financed partly by the Companhia Energética de Minas Gerais (CEMIG), the state energy company—a mixed enterprise, 70% state-owned, 30% private—and partly by the Banco de Desenvolvimento de Minas Gerais (BDMG), the state-owned Minas Gerais Development Bank. While INDI was a government institution, then, the partially private ownership of one of INDI's supporting institutions, CEMIG, gave INDI more flexibility in hiring personnel than it would have had if it were purely a state-owned institution.[13] As a result, at least some of INDI's staff also received salaries that were considerably higher than those working in regular government agencies.[14] In this way, INDI was able to recruit highly qualified staff that specialized in at least six broadly diversified industrial sectors—mining and metallurgy; chemicals and nonchemical materials; industry and tourism; agroindustries; textiles, garments, leather, footwear, furniture, and publishing; and mechanics, electroelectronics and computers—who might otherwise have taken jobs in the private sector.[15]

It is a testament to INDI's effectiveness that members of Dell's site selection team made three separate visits to Minas Gerais to meet with state government officials. The final proposal that INDI prepared was only slightly less favorable than that of Rio Grande do Sul—the state that ultimately won Dell's investment. Minas Gerais was able to offer Dell a 70% reduction in the ICMS tax for 10 years; a loan for R\$20 million (20 million *reais*), with a four-year grace period and a four-year repayment period; and free land for the plant site.[16] But in the end, Dell chose Rio Grande do Sul.

INDI was in some ways a victim of its own success. The agency's past achievements in attracting companies from the mining, steel, and automobile sectors had made such an impact on the state that when the Dell site selection team arrived, they had the impression that this was the primary focus of the government's activities. Historically, of course, Minas Gerais had always had a strong mining sector. (Minas Gerais itself means "General Mines" in Portuguese.) INDI's later success in attracting foreign investment from companies in the heavy capital equipment and automobile sectors further contributed to the state's industrial development. Observing the results of this prior industrialization, however, the Dell executives came away with the impression that Minas Gerais, especially in the vicinity of the Fiat plant and the greater metropolitan region of Belo Horizonte, was a heavy-industry, rust-belt region. This reinforced their sense that the government officials they were dealing with in Minas had grown accustomed to working with the large, capital-intensive, heavy-industry firms that were common in the mining and automobile industries, and would not fully be able to appreciate Dell's specific needs as a fast-paced, just-in-time-oriented, knowledge-intensive company.[17] Fair impression or not, the INDI staff were unable to change this view during the Dell executives' time in Minas Gerais, and it had a strong influence on the company's decision not to invest there.

RIO GRANDE DO SUL, THE ULTIMATE CHOICE

Rio Grande do Sul had not even been on Dell's short list when representatives from Pólo and the state government visited the company in early 1998 and convinced Dell's senior executives that

the state deserved a closer look. But by June 1998—less than six months after that initial visit—Maxwell and the team had made the recommendation that Dell should establish a plant in Rio Grande do Sul.

Certainly, Rio Grande do Sul had a lot to offer. It had a well-developed, modern infrastructure; and as the first state to privatize its telecommunications company, its telecommunications infrastructure was among the more efficient in the country. In fact, a quick analysis indicated that, even before factoring in any incentives the state government might offer, lower costs in Rio Grande do Sul for the plant's overall facilities would already compensate for the additional expense associated with shipping computers to customers elsewhere in Brazil.[18] And although customers in São Paulo, for example, would have to wait a day longer to receive their computers from a plant in Rio Grande do Sul than they would if the plant were located in São Paulo itself, previous studies had indicated that this would not be a serious problem.[19]

Security was another factor. In terms of security from hijackings and robbery, the main road from Rio Grande do Sul to São Paulo, Dell's principal market, appeared to be considerably safer than many of the roads within the state of São Paulo itself. In addition, the Dell executives felt personally safe in and around the vicinity of Porto Alegre, Rio Grande do Sul's capital, where the plant would be located. Expatriate executives and suppliers from out of town might not know which areas to avoid in a large, unfamiliar city, but this was not really a serious problem in the greater metropolitan region of Porto Alegre, where the crime rate was relatively low.

Home to a number of well-regarded universities, Rio Grande do Sul had a well-educated population. It was one of the most prosperous of Brazil's states, with a standard of living that some rated as the highest in Brazil. In the end, too, the Rio Grande do Sul state government was able to offer very generous terms: a 75% reduction in the ICMS tax for 12 years, plus a R\$20 million loan (over USD \$16 million at the prevailing exchange rate), with a five-year grace period, to be paid back over a 10-year period.[20]

While offering generous incentives, the state government made sure that Dell would be providing benefits to Rio Grande do Sul as well. In the contract that the government signed with the company, Dell promised to develop joint research and development projects with local universities, such as the Universidade Federal de Rio Grande do Sul (UFRGS) and the Pontifícia Universidade Católica (PUC).[21] In addition to the company's R$128 million investment in its plant (USD $108.5 million), which alone would create beneficial linkage effects in the local economy in its construction and continued operation, Dell also promised to hire 260 direct employees in the first year and 700 employees within five years. If it did not, the contract would be nullified.[22]

These potential benefits help to explain why so many states in Brazil considered Dell's investment to be such a prize, and why Rio Grande do Sul was willing to offer such attractive incentives. Nevertheless, without Pólo's intervention Dell would not even have considered the state. Because Pólo played such an instrumental role in this outcome, further background on the agency itself is in order.

The Creation of Pólo

Pólo originated in the early 1990s within the Federação das Associacoes do Rio Grande do Sul (FEDERASUL), which represented commercial enterprises in the state, and the Federação das Industrias do Rio Grande do Sul (FIERGS), which represented industries. Leaders within these two organizations proposed creating an independent, private agency to promote foreign investment that would be more flexible and nimble than a government entity. Funding for the agency would come from the private sector, but Pólo would work in conjunction with the state government to promote economic development in Rio Grande do Sul by attracting direct foreign investment in the state. Representatives from FEDERASUL and FIERGS presented it to the

two candidates for governor in the 1994 election: Olivio Dutra, a socialist from the Partido dos Trabalhadores (PT), and Antonio Britto, a pro-business moderate from the relatively centrist Partido do Movimento Democrático Brasileiro (PMDB). Although holding widely divergent political views, both candidates endorsed the idea, and thus Pólo was formally created in December 1995.

Pólo's founders sought to maintain a connection with the government by allowing the governor a key role in selecting the agency's president. This was done to ensure that the governor would maintain a close working relationship with the agency.[23] Ideally, both the government and the agency would work in concert to attract foreign investment that would contribute to the development of the state. However, this rule was changed in 1999, and the Board of Directors became solely responsible for selecting Pólo's president.[24]

The New High-Technology Emphasis

Antonio Britto, the pro-business moderate, won the 1994 gubernatorial campaign and took office in January 1995. Having campaigned on a promise to promote foreign investment in areas that would bring jobs and economic development to Rio Grande do Sul, Britto was, for the most part, able to follow through with his plans. Using tax and other incentives aggressively, he was able to land large investments.[25] In order to convince General Motors (GM) to establish a plant in the state, for example, Britto had offered substantial reductions in the ICMS state sales tax and generous loans at low interest rates, totalling hundreds of millions of dollars.[26]

José Cesar Martins, who became president of Pólo midway through Britto's administration in 1997, collaborated closely with the state government in an aggressive effort to attract more foreign investment like the GM plant. The agency maintained close contacts with several of what it called its "virtual" representatives: expatriate business people from Rio Grande do Sul working in New York City and San Francisco, who helped the agency by keeping tabs on investment trends and providing advice about how to deal with foreign investors. Martins also made sure that Pólo's staff participated in frequent investment forums and road shows around the world, in order to make contacts with potential investors and persuade them of the merits of investing in Rio Grande do Sul.

On one of these visits, Martins and other representatives from Pólo accompanied Governor Britto himself, as well as Nelson Proença, head of the Secretaria do Desenvolvimento e dos Assuntos Internacionais (SEDAI)—the state agency charged with attracting foreign investment to Rio Grande do Sul—to New York City for a series of meetings with potential investors. Marcelo Cabral, U.S. Managing Director for Banco Fator (a Brazilian investment bank) in New York City and one of Pólo's virtual agents in the U.S., had a substantial role in arranging this event.

A former equity analyst for Morgan Stanley, Cabral had extensive experience dealing with U.S. institutional investors who invested in Latin America, such as Scudder and Alliance Capital, and knew something about what made them tick. As an informal (virtual) advisor to Pólo, he explained to Martins that such investors would want to hear only briefly from the Governor and from Proença before speaking directly with managers of local companies looking for investment capital. To Cabral's surprise, Martins, a businessman himself, understood immediately and followed his suggestion.[27]

At the meeting, one of the investors that Cabral had invited argued that Rio Grande do Sul should seek to attract high-technology companies. Although Governor Britto was at first resistant to this idea, Nelson Proença, who had been an executive for IBM in Brazil for 10 years before working in the Britto government, was intrigued by this possibility. He reasoned that focusing on high-technology investment made a lot of sense given Rio Grande do Sul's unique characteristics: the large number of universities in the state already offering degrees in Computer Science and Electrical Engineering, and the overall high levels of education in the state's population as a whole.[28]

José Cesar Martins also thought the idea was worth pursuing. After discussing it further with Proença, Martins asked Cabral to help Pólo find a consultant in the area of high technology. From his extensive contacts in the financial community, Cabral knew the person to call was Duane Kirkpatrick, head of international operations for Robertson Stephens in San Francisco, one of the leading investment banks in the world in financing for high-technology businesses. Kirkpatrick agreed to serve as an outside consultant to Pólo to assess Rio Grande do Sul's prospects for attracting investment from high-technology companies.

After an extended visit to Rio Grande do Sul, Kirkpatrick came to the conclusion that high-technology investment would provide the state with high-wage jobs, in addition to linkages to the local economy. He also provided a number of suggestions about how Pólo and the state government of Rio Grande do Sul could attract such firms. Impressed, Pólo—in collaboration with Nelson Proença and Governor Britto—decided to focus future investment promotion efforts in this area.[29]

Rio Grande do Sul Makes the Short List: An Exchange of Visits

As part of the new strategy, in February 1998, José Cesar Martins and a number of representatives from Pólo flew to San Francisco to attend a symposium for high-technology industries sponsored by Robertson Stephens bank. By this time, Pólo, with the help of Kirkpatrick and its virtual agents at Banco Fator (Marcelo Cabral and Dennis Rodriques), had already identified a list of high-technology companies that it would like to attract to Rio Grande do Sul. One of these was Dell Computer Corporation.

During the conference, Marcelo Cabral came upon an article in *América Económica* magazine about Dell's interest in building a manufacturing plant in Brazil, and he showed it to Martins. Demonstrating just how quick and flexible Pólo could be, Martins and his staff immediately left the conference, went back to their hotel and put in a call to Dell. When they got through to Tom Armstrong, Dell's Vice President of Tax and Administration, Armstrong told him that the company's preliminary site selection team, reporting to Keith Maxwell, had already been to Brazil three times and was closing its short list of potential sites in Brazil. "You are going to lose a big opportunity," Armstrong said. Martins protested, "But we are fast!" Martins told Armstrong that he, his staff, and Nelson Proença (who was in New York at the time) could be at Dell's headquarters the next day. They packed up, left the hotel, and were on a plane to Texas that night.

At Dell headquarters, the group was to be received by some of Dell's senior executives, including Daryl Robertson, Vice President of Dell Latin America, Tom Armstrong, and Keith Maxwell. But before the meeting at which Proença and Martins would make their pitch to Dell, they were given a tour of Dell's facilities and manufacturing plant in Round Rock. During this tour, something fortuitous happened. One of the workers in the plant, a skilled technician, happened to be Brazilian. The group stopped briefly to speak with him in Portuguese.

"I'll tell you how to win the hearts of Dell management," he told José Cesar Martins. "Tell them that Pólo is like the Irish Development Authority."[30] He explained that Dell's executives had had an excellent experience working with that organization. The Irish Development Authority (IDA) was Ireland's investment promotion agency. Dell executives had returned from a site selection trip to Ireland raving about how professional and helpful the IDA had been. Dell's experience with the IDA was an important factor in its decision to build a plant in Ireland.

Significantly, although Pólo had not consciously modelled itself after the IDA, it had many of the same characteristics. Pólo was entirely private, but worked in close collaboration with the government. It also had a targeted investment promotion strategy: it selected specific industries, and then focused on attracting investment from specific companies in those industries. Similarly, IDA's targeted investment promotion strategy allowed it to research an industry and specific companies thoroughly to anticipate any questions that site selection teams might have and address questions, concerns, or potential problems in advance, before the team even raised them. This is what made the organization so effective.

In its effort to focus on high-technology companies, Pólo clearly was pursuing a strategy similar to IDA's. In the meeting with Dell's senior management, then, José Cesar Martins did emphasize that Pólo was like the IDA. He noticed that this comment definitely caught their attention. The Dell executives listened attentively to presentations from Proença and Martins, and asked a number of penetrating questions about Rio Grande do Sul's level of education, rules regarding unions, and infrastructure. The Dell executives told the visitors that members of the site selection team had already visited São Paulo, Paraná, and Minas Gerais, but would like to return to Brazil to visit Rio Grande do Sul.

The site selection team came to Rio Grande do Sul sooner than expected, only about a week after that first meeting. Nevertheless, with only a short advance notice of the visit, Pólo called upon all its speed and agility. Notified over the weekend that the Dell executives were arriving Monday, Martins immediately called his staff and explained that they would have to make some urgent preparations for the meeting: charts would have to be prepared, statistics ready; in short, everything that would be relevant to Dell's concerns. Martins also called Proença, who convinced the governor to cancel meetings that Monday in order to give a presentation to the visiting Dell team. Thinking ahead, Martins made sure to hold the Monday meeting with Dell in a hotel, rather than in Pólo's offices, in order to avoid unwanted press attention at this delicate stage of the negotiations process.

It helped Pólo's case considerably that Martins was able to use his contacts in the business community to arrange private interviews for the Dell team with important business leaders in the state. These included high-level executives from three local companies: Gerdau, a steel conglomerate; Ipiranga, a gasoline distribution firm; and Rede Brasil Sul de Comunicações (RBS), a media company. Also present was one U.S. multinational, Coca-Cola, with which everyone on Dell's team would be familiar. A businessman himself, Martins was sensitive to the concerns of business executives. He knew that the Dell team would want to talk privately with local business executives in order to gain a perspective that was independent of Pólo and the state government officials.

The Pólo officials also made sure, on the first night the Dell executives were in town, to take them to visit a very popular local microbrewery called Dado Bier. They knew that the ambience of this popular local restaurant and bar would make a favorable impression on the Dell executives, and it did. To the visitors from Dell, the obviously well-educated, high-energy young clientele at Dado Bier seemed very similar to the kind of crowd that frequented such places in Austin, Texas.[31] This seemed to be just another indication that Dell would be able to find the kinds of employees it needed in Rio Grande do Sul. In addition to executives, engineers, and technicians, Dell's new plant in Brazil (which would also become its headquarters there) would need a large staff of personable, articulate, and technically proficient employees to take orders and handle technical questions over the telephone.

All of Pólo's quick, highly focused preparations worked. After listening to the presentations, speaking privately with business executives already in the state, and touring greater Porto Alegre for possible manufacturing sites, the Dell team said that they were interested.[32] They would send more teams later to examine potential sites more carefully, to ask additional questions, and to negotiate financial incentives. The Dell executives made clear that they would continue to negotiate with other states, but that they had decided that Rio Grande do Sul was definitely one of the leading candidates. To that extent,

then, Pólo had been successful. Rio Grande do Sul would now just have to win against the other competing states.

In the end, of course, this was what happened. Tom Armstrong and Charlene Coor, as well as others at Dell whose job it was to confirm the site selection team's initial findings, made more visits and continued negotiations. Ultimately, determined to win high-technology investment for the state, the Britto government offered Dell the best terms for its investment. Less than six months after beginning negotiations with Pólo and the state government, Maxwell recommended to Michael Dell that the company should build its manufacturing plant in Rio Grande do Sul.

THE CHANGE IN GOVERNMENT

Michael Dell agreed with this recommendation, and the company's plans to build its plant finally appeared to be set. But then the time came for another round of gubernatorial elections in 1998. Unfortunately, Britto's challenger—Olivio Dutra, once again—did not approve of the deal that Britto had negotiated with Dell. A member of Brazil's socialist Partido dos Trabalhadores, the Workers' Party, Dutra was against the government's granting of benefits to foreign transnational corporations. One of the main charges he had raised against Britto in his last campaign for governor was that "excessive" concessions granted to foreign transnational corporations would have to stop.

Dutra had served as mayor of Porto Alegre, where both he and the PT had a reputation for honest and effective government. Moreover, the Workers' Party was popular in 1998 as Brazil's financial crisis deepened and the federal government attempted to solve it with higher interest rates and other austerity measures. Perhaps not too surprisingly, then, Dutra won the 1998 election.

Since during his campaign Dutra had talked so much about the excessive benefits given to TNCs, once he was in office he had to take action. During the first several weeks, he argued that the tax incentives granted to Dell, and also to Ford, which planned to build a multi-million dollar plant in the state and had been offered millions in incentives, would have to be renegotiated.[33]

Ford's attempts to negotiate with Dutra were futile. The new governor held fast to his position regarding the incentives by suspending the payment of loans the Britto government had promised the company.[34] Realizing that other states would offer the same incentives, and with minimal capital sunk into the project, Ford investigated its opportunities elsewhere. The state government of Bahia was quick to offer incentives identical to those the Britto administration had offered. Additionally, by locating its plant in Bahia, Ford would receive special incentives from the federal government for automobile manufacturers investing in the poorer northeastern states of Brazil.[35]

It helped Bahia's case considerably, of course, that the federal government was more than willing to intervene to make Bahia an attractive alternative to Rio Grande do Sul. Antonio Carlos Magalhães (ACM), President of the Brazilian Senate at the time, was an enormously influential politician from Bahia who was a key member of President Cardoso's governing coalition. It was ACM who pushed through the Congress a modification of the legislation on incentives for manufacturing automobiles in the northeast, so that Ford could still take advantage of it—even though the deadline for additional companies to do this had passed.[36] The federal government even approved additional incentives in order to make up for the extra costs Ford would face by putting its plant in Bahia rather than the more conveniently located Rio Grande do Sul. It was also significant that Brazil's national development bank, Banco Nacional de Desenvolvimento Económico e Social (BNDES), provided a low interest loan of over US$300 million to Ford, more than it had planned to give for Ford's investment in Rio Grande do Sul. Again, the justification was that the additional amount was needed to make up for the extra costs associated with locating the plant in Bahia.[37] Realizing that

Ford was now likely to withdraw from its plan to invest in Rio Grande do Sul, Dutra tried to negotiate with the company. But he was too late. Ford had already made its decision, and soon signed a contract with the Bahian state government.

The loss of Ford's investment was politically disastrous for Dutra. Residents of the town where the plant was to have been located protested.[38] The press lambasted the governor. And, of course, the political opposition had a field day lamenting the jobs that had been lost.

Nevertheless, Dutra had made his views very clear. It was at this point, by mid-March 1999, that Maxwell realized something had to be done.

DELL'S OPTIONS

Maxwell considered his options again:

1. Dell could simply leave Brazil altogether. After all, the country had just experienced a massive devaluation in January 1999. Dell had continued with its plans in the immediate aftermath of the devaluation, demonstrating its faith in Brazil's long-terms prospects. But the country clearly had a significant degree of economic volatility, and even a fair amount of political volatility, or at least policy uncertainty, as Governor Dutra's recent actions indicated.

2. Dell could stay in Brazil but go to another state, such as Ford had done in Bahia. Certainly, the other states on the list that the site selection team had considered offered some interesting possibilities. Bahia would not be an option for Dell, but Minas Gerais might be. Minas met Dell's basic selection criteria and had offered an incentives package that was very similar to what Dell had received in Rio Grande do Sul.

Minas Gerais had other benefits also. It did not have the same level of partisan differences, at least with regard to attracting foreign direct investment, that Rio Grande do Sul seemed currently to be experiencing. INDI, the state government's investment promotion agency, had seemed interested in working with Dell and knowledgeable about Dell's needs, if not quite to the same extent that Pólo had been. Perhaps the impression that members of the site selection team had—that Minas Gerais was too oriented toward the mining and automobile industries—had been misleading. After all, that did not mean that the state could not also develop a niche in high-technology investment as well.

Dell had not yet begun construction on the plant in Rio Grande do Sul. As of yet, it really had no sunk costs that would make it difficult to leave the state and go elsewhere. Going to Minas was definitely still a possibility.

3. Dell could stay put and try to negotiate with the new governor. Fernando Loureiro was a talented Brazilian executive whom Dell had already hired to serve as its new Corporate Affairs Director in Brazil. He proposed that Dell could attempt to negotiate with the governor by showing how keeping Dell in the state could help him, or at least would not be inconsistent with his own goals and agenda.

Loureiro's idea was that Dell executives could reason with the new governor by pointing out the harmony between the governor's objectives and Dell's. After all, Loureiro's argument went, Dell was a very different company from Ford. Unlike an automobile company, Dell did not manufacture something that damaged the environment; it manufactured computers. Computers provided people with access to the Internet. The Internet provided even people in poor slum areas access to information. This had a democratizing effect on society. Giving people everywhere access to information in this way could potentially create the conditions for a more just and egalitarian social order. Thus, Dell's goal to provide people with computers was in harmony with the governor's goal of working to create a more just and egalitarian society!

This last option seemed somewhat dubious to Maxwell. But, it was true that the governor had suffered a major political blow when Ford left. It would be very bad for him indeed if

another major U.S. company decided to move to another state.

With such logic, perhaps the governor could be persuaded to let Dell keep all of its incentives. Loureiro had suggested this might be possible, provided that Dell offered to donate some computers to poor areas as a gesture of goodwill.

Should Dell take a chance on this last option or follow one of the others? Maxwell realized that there were risks either way. But he would be the one making the final recommendation to Michael Dell, and the decision would have to be made quickly.

NOTES

1. The principal members of the initial team, in addition to Maxwell, included Daryl Robertson, Vice President, Dell Latin America; Tom Armstrong, Vice President, Tax and Administration; Kip Thompson, Vice President, Worldwide Facilities Management and Corporate Real Estate; and Charlene Coor, Director of International Tax.

2. Brazil's Partido dos Trabalhadores (PT), the Workers' Party, is a leftist political party with a socialist ideology.

3. "IDC Results Show Compaq Finished 1999 as Number One in Worldwide PC Market, but Dell Heads into Millennium Leading in the US," *PR Newswire,* January 24, 2000.

4. Talita Moreira, "Business Leaders Praise Responses to Incentives Dispute," *Gazeta Mercantil Invest News,* <http://lexis-nexis.com/universe>, January 11, 2000; Denise Neumann et al., "Guerra Fiscal Abala Finanças dos Estados," *Estado do São Paulo,* July 13, 1997, p. 31; and Maria Quadros, "Governors Fail to Find Consensus on Fiscal War," *Gazeta Mercantil Invest News,* <http://lexis-nexis.com/universe>, January 28, 2000.

5. Ricardo Caldeira, "Os Incentivos Fiscal Gera Desenvolvimento," *Gazeta Mercantil,* March 23, 1999, p. 2.

6. Interview with Ricardo Hinkelman, Former Technical Adviser, SEDAI, Porto Alegre, November 10, 1999.

7. Interview with Keith Maxwell, Senior Vice President, Dell Computer Corporation, Round Rock, Texas, March 20, 2000.

8. Ibid.

9. Interview with Jorge Funaro, Chief of Staff, Secretariat of Science, Technology and Economic Development, São Paulo, November 15, 1999.

10. Interview with Enrique Weber, President of CODIN, Rio de Janeiro, March 13, 2000.

11. Interviews with Fernando Sicuro, Technical Adviser of State Government of Paraná, and Clemente Simião, Coordinator, Secretariat of Industry, Commerce and Economic Development, State Government of Paraná, Curitiba, Parana, November 23, 1999.

12. Maxwell, March 20, 2000.

13. In fact, strictly speaking INDI did not have its own staff because all of INDI's personnel worked either for CEMIG, BDMG, or were outsourced from other agencies, and were technically on loan from these other institutions, Khoury Rolim Dias 2001, 2002.

14. Interview with Romulo Ronan Fontes, Manager of Technical and Economic Studies Department, INDI, Belo Horizonte, November 26, 1999.

15. INDI, <http://www.indi.mg.gov 2001>, January 23, 2002. Clearly, INDI, an older, larger, more established institution with a wider range of investment promotion activities, did not have what Pólo was able to develop in a very short time: a specific focus on attracting high-technology industries.

16. Governo de Minas Gerais, Dell Proposal, Belo Horizonte, 1998.

17. Maxwell, March 20, 2000.

18. All computers were to be shipped by truck. This service was to be outsourced to local shipping companies.

19. Telephone interview with Keith Maxwell, August 4, 2003.

20. Guilherme Diefenthaeler, "O Dedo da Dell," Amanha, November, 1999, p. 39.

21. Of course, in order to qualify for a tax incentive, the federal government gave to the computer industry known as the Proceso Produtivo Básico (PPB), which included a reduction of up to 50% of corporate income tax, companies such as Dell had to invest 5% of their total revenue in Brazil on research and development (R&D) within the country. At the time, at least 2% of this had to be invested in universities or other government-approved institutions; the rest could be invested inside the company. (Renato Bastos, "Computer Hardware and Peripherals," US Department of Commerce Industry Sector Analysis for Brazil, São Paulo, Brazil, 1998, p. 15.) As a result of these provisions, Dell would have to spend some money in Brazil on R&D in any case. The federal law, however, did not specify where in Brazil this expenditure on R&D would have to be made.

22. "Alvorada Instala Pólo Tecnológico Com A Dell," Jornal do Comércio, August 21, 1998, p. 8; and Paulo Ricardo Fontoura, "Empresa Receberá Mais de 25 Anos de Incentivos Fiscais," Gazeta Mercantil August 26, 1998, p. 4.

23. Interview with Telmo Magadan, former President of Pólo, Porto Alegre, December 17, 1999.

24. Pólo-RS, Agência de Desenvolvimento, <http://www.polors.com.br>, January 11, 2000.

25. "Portas Abertas Para Novos Investimentos," Zero Hora, December 30, 1998, p. 11.

26. Darcy Oliveira, "A Qualquer Custo," Istoé, April 14, 1997, pp. 34–6.

27. Interviews with Marcelo Cabral, Former Managing Director of Banco Fator, Porto Alegre, December 17, 1999, and José Cesar Martins, former president of Polo, Porto Alegre, November 11, 1999, and December 15, 1999.

28. Interview with Nelson Proença, Congressman, Chamber of Deputies, National Congress of Brazil, Brasília, December 5, 1999.

29. Interviews with José Cesar Martins, November 11, 1999 and December 15, 1999; and Nelson Proença, December 5, 1999.

30. Martins, November 11, 1999, and December 15, 1999.

31. Telephone Interview with Keith Maxwell, August 4, 2003.

32. Interviews with Miguelangelo Azário, Former Investment Analyst, Pólo, November 19, 1999, and November 1, 2001; Alex Martins, Former Director of Investments, Pólo, December 16, 1999, and Maxwell, March 20, 2000.

33. Rosane de Oliveira, "A Opção e Seu Risco," Zero Hora, March 22, 1999, p. 10.

34. Peter Fritsch, "Ford and GM Clash with Brazilian State—Dispute Over Incentives, Tax Breaks May Hurt Investment," Wall Street Journal, April 9, 1999, p. A11.

35. Nelson Silveira, "Ford Promove Festa Política na Bahia," Jornal do Brasil, June 29, 1999, p. 16.

36. Denise Madueño, "Governo Muda Lei Para Beneficiar Ford," Folha de São Paulo," June 30, 1999, p. 1.

37. Denise Chrispim Marin, "Receita e Ford Já Negociam Incentivos à Fábrica da BA," Folha de São Paulo, July 14, 1999, p. 1.

38. "Guiaba, De Luto, Grita 'Fica, Fica'; Prefeito Chora," Folha de São Paulo, April 30, 1999, p. 5.

APPENDIX 1: BRAZILIAN STATES

APPENDIX 2: PRINCIPAL SITE OPTIONS

	Rio Grande do Sul	Minas Gerais	São Paulo
General			
Population	10.2 Million	17.8 Million	37 Million
Area	281,749 sq. km	586,528 sq. km	1,522,000 sq. km
Demographic density	36.1 inhabitants/ sq. km	30.5 inhabitants/ sq. km	149.2 inhabitants/ sq. km
Capital (population)	Porto Alegre (1.3 M)	Belo Horizonte (2.2M)	São Paulo (10.4M)
Economic active population	53.5%	49.7%	47.6%
Life expectancy	71.7 years	70.4 years	70 years
Population annual growth	1.2%	1.4%	1.8%
Population distribution	Urban: 81.6%; Rural: 18.4%	Urban: 82%; Rural: 18%	Urban: 93.4%; Rural: 6.6%
Economic Indicators			
Total GDP	US$41.7 Billion	US$51.9 Billion	US$188.3 Billion
GDP per capita	US$4130	US$2928	US$5148
Commercial balance	+ US$2.8 M	+ US$3.8 M	+ US$253 M
Principal industries	Tobacco, Chemicals, Automobiles, Steel, Engineering, Footwear, Foodstuffs	Metallurgy, General Engineering, Agribusiness, Minerals, Automobiles	Metallurgy, Automobiles, Foodstuffs, Electronics
Infrastructure			
Homes with fixed telephone lines	67.9%	57.5%	77.9%
Paved roads	10,332 km	19,234 km	26,377 km
Incentives			
ICMS	75% reduction for 12 years	70% reduction for 10 years	N/A
Free land	no	Free land for plant site	N/A
Loan Agreements			
Amount	R$ 20 Million	R$ 20 Million	N/A
Grace period	5 years	4 years	N/A
Repayment period	10-year program	4-year program	N/A
Nature of Investment Agency			
	Pólo	INDI	Secretaria da Ciência e Tecnologia (SCT)
	Private, nonprofit agency	70% state-owned; 30% private	State institution

Source: Instituto Brasileiro de Geografia e Estatistica (IBGE).

ENRON AND THE DABHOL POWER COMPANY

*Prepared by Professor Andrew Inkpen with research
assistance from Chee Wee Tan and Katherine Johnston
and assistance from Professor Arvind Phatak, Temple University*

In September 2001, Enron Corporation (Enron) was embroiled in a long-running dispute with various levels of government in India. The dispute involved the Dabhol Power Company (DPC), a 2184-megawatt (MW) power project in the Indian state of Maharashtra. With Phase II of the multi-billion dollar project 95% complete, Enron announced that it would sell its DPC stake because of payment disputes with its sole buyer, the Maharashtra State Electricity Board (MSEB), and the failure of the Indian central government to honor its counter-guarantee.

In response to the ongoing dispute, Enron CEO Kenneth Lay sent a strongly worded letter to India's Prime Minister Atal Behari Vajpayee questioning the government's willingness to honor its contracts and its future ability to attract foreign investment. Lay wrote:

> Our experience would indicate that contracts with governmental authorities in India really do not seem to represent anything more than a starting point for a later renegotiation and are broken by Indian governmental authorities whenever and as often as they prove inconvenient or burdensome.

ENRON CORPORATION

Houston-based Enron, formed in 1985 in a merger between InterNorth, Inc. and Houston

Natural Gas Corp., was involved in various worldwide energy industries. In the 1990s, Enron coined the slogan "Creating Energy Solutions Worldwide" and its stated vision was to become "The World's Leading Energy Company—creating innovative and efficient energy solutions for growing economies and a better environment worldwide." Enron was the largest natural gas company in the United States and operated the largest gas pipeline system in the world outside of Gazprom in Russia.

In 2001, Enron had five main businesses:[1]

- Enron Wholesale Services delivered natural gas and power and was Enron's largest and fastest-growing business. In 2000, income before interest, minority interests, and taxes (IBIT) rose 72% to $2.3 billion, with record physical energy volumes of 51.7 trillion British thermal units equivalent per day (TBtue/d)—a 59% increase over 1999.
- Enron Energy Services was the retail arm of Enron, serving business users of energy in commercial and industrial sectors. The value of its contracts in 2000 totaled more than $16 billion, increasing its cumulative contract value to more than $30 billion since late 1997.
- Enron Broadband Services was a new market for bandwidth intermediation. In 2000, Enron completed 321 transactions with 45 counterparties.

- Enron Transportation Services was responsible for U.S. interstate natural gas pipelines and provided innovative solutions to its customers.
- EnronOnline, created in 1999, was Enron's Web-based eCommerce system used to trade more than 1200 products and streamlined Enron's back-office processes. EnronOnline allowed customers to view Enron's real-time pricing.

Enron's International Projects. Prior to 1985, Enron generated virtually all of its revenue in the United States. By 2001, Enron was involved in energy infrastructure projects across the globe. See Exhibit 1 for a summary of international projects, most of which involved natural gas (note that these projects were at varying stages of completion). The firm had a reputation as a reliable provider of turnkey natural gas projects on a timely basis, virtually all of which were project-financed and had long-term contracts with pricing agreements reached in advance. Revenues were tied to the US dollar and the host government or an outside agency held responsibility for currency conversions. The development of Enron projects involved multi-functional teams that were compensated, in part, based on incentive payments tied to the Net Present Value (NPV) of the project itself. After projects were completed, operating responsibility shifted from the development team to an Enron operating group (for projects that Enron built and operated).

With reference to Enron's international business, an Enron executive stated:

> We have created a new model based on an at-risk, entrepreneurial culture; we look for opportunity in chaos . . . we make our own rules; most people look at the world and think too small; when we went to India, the majors said we were crazy.

MARKET REFORM IN INDIA

India's population of more than one billion inhabited the seventh largest country in the world. Issues of language and religion played a major role in Indian culture, politics, and business. Fifteen national languages were recognized by the Indian constitution and these were spoken in over 1600 dialects. India's official language, Hindi, was spoken by about 30% of the population. English was the official working language and, for many educated Indians, English was virtually their first language. Hinduism was the dominant religion, practiced by over 80% of the population. Besides Hindus, Muslims were the most prominent religious group, making up 14% of the population.

On a purchasing power parity basis, the Indian economy was the fifth largest in the world. GDP per capita was $2101 in 2001.[2] After India gained its independence from Great Britain in 1947, and until the mid-1980s, the government pursued an economic policy of self-sufficiency. This policy was often referred to as *swadeshi,* a Hindi word meaning indigenous products or made in India. The term was first used by Mahatma Gandhi during the independence movement to encourage people to buy native goods and break the British economic stranglehold on India. To many Indians, *swadeshi* evoked images of patriotism and Indian sovereignty.

After decades of socialist-oriented/statist industrial policy focused on achieving self-sufficiency, India was financially strapped and bureaucratically bloated. High tariffs kept out imports, and official government policy discouraged foreign investment. In the 1970s, Coca-Cola and IBM were among the multinational firms that left India. Efforts to reform the Indian economy began after the 1991 federal elections. The Indian government was on the verge of bankruptcy, and foreign exchange reserves were sufficient for only three months of imports. After considerable prodding by the IMF, then Prime Minister Rao introduced free market reforms in July 1991. India's economic liberalization plan moved the economy away from its traditionally protectionist policies toward actively encouraging foreign participation in the economy. As part of the plan, the Prime Minister's office set up a special "fast-track" Foreign Investment Promotion Board to provide speedy approval for foreign investment proposals. In October 1991, the Government of India opened the power industry to private sector foreign direct investment.

Africa

Benin	Benin Integrated Gas and Power Project
Mozambique	Maputo Iron and Steel Project, Pande Gas Project
Nigeria	Lagos State Power Project

Middle East

Gaza Strip	Gaza Power Project
Gulf	Dolphin: Gas Supply, Distribution, and Marketing Project

Asia Pacific

Australia	Power Trading
People's Republic of China	Hainan Island Power Project, Chuanzhong Block, Chengdu Cogen Project, Gasification Utility Island for BASF/YPC Integrated, Petrochemical Project (BASF), Sichuan-Wuhan Pipeline & Power Projects & Wuhan Loop
Guam	Enron Piti Power Project
India	Dabhol Power Project, LNG Terminal at Dabhol, MetGas Pipeline Project, LNG Vessel Construction Joint Venture, Gas Authority of India (GAIL)
Japan	Industrial Power Sales and Services
Philippines	Batangas Power Project, Subic Bay Power Project, First Gas Power Corporation Fuel Supply
South Korea	Gas Distribution and Liquefied Petroleum Gas

Central America/Carribean

Dominican Republic	Puerto Plata Power Project
Guatemala	Puerto Quetzal Power Project, PQPLLC
Jamaica	Industrial Gases Limited
Mexico	Desarollos Hidraulicos de Cancun, Industrias del Agua
Nicaragua	Corinto Power Plant
Panamá	Empresa de Generacion Electrica Bahía Las Minas
Puerto Rico	Ecoelectrica, San Juan Gas, ProCaribe, Progasco

Europe

Croatia	Natural gas combined cycle power plant at Jertovec
Italy	Sarlux Power Project
Poland	Elektrocieplownia Nowa Sarzyna Project
Spain	Arcos de la Frontera, Mora la Nova
Turkey	Trakya Power Project
United Kingdom	Teesside Power Project, TPS Black Start Project, Wilton Power Station, Wessex Water

South America

Argentina	Transportadora de Gas del Sur Pipeline, Gas Marketing, Power Marketing
Bolivia	The Bolivia-to-Brazil Pipeline, Transredes S.A.
Brazil	CEG/Cegrio, Cuiaba Integrated Energy Project, Elektro Electricidade e Serviços S.A., Gaspart
Colombia	Centragas Pipeline, Promigas E.S.P.
Venezuela	Accro III & IV Project, Venatane, Bachaquero III, CALIFE, Citadel Venezolana

Exhibit 1   Enron International Energy Infrastructure Projects

The economic reform program had a powerful effect. From 1994 to 1998, GDP grew at an average of almost 7% annually, and inflation remained under 10%. Foreign direct investments (FDI) reached a record high of US$2.4 billion in 1998, 20 times higher than in 1991. In January 2001, the country had a record level of $41.1 billion in foreign reserves, up from $13.5 billion in 1994 and only $1 billion 1991. Tariffs, while still high and ranging from 30–65%, were one-fifth the level before liberalization. By some estimates, the government's policies had produced up to $100 billion in new entrepreneurial projects in India since 1992.

Despite these efforts to encourage market reform and economic development, many hurdles remained. China attracted ten times as much FDI. About 40% of the industrial economy remained government-owned. Perhaps the greatest impediment to both rapid growth and attracting foreign investment was the lack of infrastructure that met international standards. In particular, India suffered from a substantial electricity shortage.

Demand for Electricity

The Indian population was starved for electricity. It was estimated that many of India's industries were able to operate at only half their capacity because of a lack of electric power. Though India had the capacity to produce 100,000 MW, power cuts were an almost daily occurrence and parts of the country were regularly blacked out for days at a time. Analysts estimated that India urgently needed to double its capacity to maintain growth and ease poverty. The government targeted capacity increases of 111,500 MW by 2007.[3]

Virtually all of India's power was generated and managed by state-owned electricity boards (SEBs). It was widely acknowledged that these boards suffered from chronic managerial, financial, and operational problems.[4] Government-run power plants typically operated at about 50% capacity. In comparison, the private power plants run by Tata Steel, an Indian company, operated at around 85% capacity. Across India, an estimated 30% of power was stolen, much of it by factory owners who found that it was cheaper to pay off the SEB than to pay for electricity.

Indian power rates were among the lowest in the world. Most Indian farmers had free, or virtually free, power. Although the SEBs had been trying to raise rates, this had proved to be very difficult. In 1994 in the state of Gujarat, the opposition government encouraged farmers to blockade roads and burn government property after rural power rates were increased. The government was forced to back down and lower the amount of the increase.

Because of these problems and because all levels of government were so short of funds, the Central Government decided to turn to the private sector. The Electricity Act was amended in October 1991 to make this possible. However, the response from the private sector was poor. The act was amended again in March 1992 to provide further incentives, including a 16% rate of return to investors. Still, potential investors remained skeptical of the Central Government's commitment to reform and were doubtful of the SEBs' ability to pay for privately generated power. The Government took one more step. In May 1992, a delegation of Indian Central Government officials visited the United States and the United Kingdom to make a pitch for foreign investment in the power sector. The delegation included then Power Secretary S. Rajagopal, Finance Secretary K. Geethakrishan, and Cabinet Secretary Naresh Chandra. The visits were a major success. Many independent power producers (IPPs) immediately sent executives to India. By July 1995, more than 130 Memorandums of Understanding (MOUs) had been signed by the Government of India with IPPs. Twenty-three of the 41 pending electricity projects bid on by non-Indian companies were led by American firms.

The Dabhol Project

In turning to the private sector for power plant development, the Indian Government decided to give the first few private sector projects the status of pioneer projects; later these projects became known as "fast-track" projects (of which eight such projects were eventually signed). For the fast-track projects, the Central Government decided not to follow the standard public tendering process. Instead, it would negotiate with IPPs for individual projects. The rationale was that the Government was not in a strong negotiating position and, therefore, the financial risk to the IPPs had to be reduced to entice them to invest in India. At a press conference, Power Secretary S. Rajagopal said the first few projects "would not be allowed to fail."

Enron's Rebecca Mark met with the Indian delegation when it visited Houston. In June 1992, Mark and several other Enron employees, at the Indian Government's invitation, visited India to investigate power plant development opportunities. Within days, Enron had identified a potential site for a gas-fired power plant on the western coast of India in the port town of Dabhol, 180 miles south of Bombay in the state of Maharashtra. Maharashtra was India's richest state and the center of Indian industrialization. The huge port city of Bombay was the capital and the headquarters of most of India's major companies, including Air India and Tata Enterprises, the largest Indian industrial conglomerate.

Enron, acting on the Government's assurances that there would not be any tendering on the first few fast-track projects, submitted a proposal to build a 2,015 MW gas-fired power plant. The proposed project would be the largest plant Enron had ever built, the largest of its kind in the world, and, at $2.8 billion, the largest foreign investment in India. The liquefied natural gas (LNG) needed to fuel the Indian power plant would be imported from a plant Enron planned to build in Qatar. The proposal was very favorably received by both the Central Government and officials in the Maharashtra State Government. The Maharashtra State Electricity Board (MSEB) had long wanted to build a gas-fired plant to reduce its dependence on coal and oil.

Enron was the first IPP to formally submit a proposal. Later, in June 1992, Enron signed an MOU with the MSEB. A new company called Dabhol Power Company (DPC) was formed. Enron held 80% of the equity in DPC, and its two partners, General Electric and International Generation Co., each held 10%. International Generation was a joint venture between Bechtel Enterprises Inc. (Bechtel) and San Francisco-based Pacific Gas & Electric formed in early 1995 to build and operate power plants outside the United States. General Electric was contracted to supply the gas turbines, and Bechtel would be the general contractor. Exhibit 2 lists the various individuals involved with DPC, and Exhibit 3 shows the timing of the various events.

After the MOU was signed, the Maharashtra state requested that the World Bank review the project. A World Bank team also found many irregularities in the agreement and noted the government had not set up an overarching framework within which to privatize power in India. The World Bank's analysis concluded that the government had not provided an overall economic justification of the project and that the agreement was one-sided in favor of Enron and encouraged the government to "verify Enron's experience" as an electricity generating company before proceeding with the project. The government of India's Central Electricity Authority experts also conducted their own analysis and concluded that the MOU was one-sided in favor of Enron and its partners. Nevertheless, the project went forward.

Following the signing of the MOU, Enron began a complex negotiation process for proposal approval, followed by more negotiations on the actual financial details. Officially, no power project could be developed without technical and economic clearance from the Central Electricity Authority. Typically, this process could take many months, or possibly years. The Foreign Investment Promotion Board (FIPB) was the Central Government's vehicle for a speedy approval process. The FIPB asked the Central Electricity Authority to give initial clearance to the Dabhol project without the detailed

Name	Title and/or Role
Lal Krishna Advani	President of the Federal BJP Party in 1996
Vinay Bansal	Chairman of MSEB
Manohar Joshi	Chief Minister of Maharashtra, deputy leader of Shiv Sena
Kenneth Lay	CEO of Enron Corporation
Rebecca Mark	Chairman and CEO of Enron
Neil McGregor	Dabhol's President
Gopinath Munde	Deputy Chief Minister of Maharashtra with direct responsibility for the state energy ministry, BJP party member
Ajit Nimbalkar	Chairman and Managing Director of Maharashtra State Electricity Board
Sharad Pawar	Former Chief Minister of Maharashtra, voted out of office March, 1995; known as the Maratha strongman
Suresh Prabhu	Federal Power Minister in 2001
P. V. Narasimha Rao	Former Prime Minister of India (prior to 1996), and then party leader for Congress (I) Party
N. K. P. Salve	Former Federal Power Minister
Joseph Sutton	Enron Managing Director
Balashaheb "Bal" Thacker	Leader of Shiv Sena
Atal Behari Vajpayee	Prime Minister of India in 2001 and party leader for BJP

Exhibit 2   Individuals Involved in the Dabhol Project

information normally required. However, final clearance would still be necessary at a later date.

In November 1992, Enron made a detailed presentation at a meeting chaired by the Central Government Finance Secretary and attended by various other senior government officials, including the chairman of the MSEB. (Note: The Finance Secretary was the senior civil servant in the finance department and reported directly to the Finance Minister.) From this meeting came a recommendation to the FIPB to approve the project. In turn, the Central Power Ministry, acting on the advice of the FIPB, asked the Central Electricity Authority to expedite the approval process. The Central Electricity Authority gave an in-principle (not final) clearance to proceed with the project since the Ministry of Finance had found the project satisfactory.

In March 1993, with the necessary government approvals largely in place, Enron was in a position to negotiate the financial structure of the deal. The most critical element was a Power Purchasing Agreement (PPA) with the MSEB. The PPA was the contract under which Enron, as the owner of the power plant, would supply power to the MSEB electric grid. Over the next year or so, Rebecca Mark visited India 36 times. Ajit Nimbalkar, chairman and managing director of MSEB, described the negotiations:

This is the first project of this kind that we are doing. MSEB did not have any experience in dealing with international power developers. It was a complicated exercise, for the money involved is large, and so the negotiations took a long time.[5]

October 1991	Government of India invites private sector participation in the power sector
May 1992	Indian delegation visits UK and US; Enron invited to India by government of India
June 1992	Maharashtra State Electricity Board signs MOU with Enron
February 1993	Foreign Investment Promotion Board (FIPB) grants approval
March 1993	Power Purchase Agreement negotiations start
November 1993	Central Electricity Authority clears Dabhol project
February 1994	Government of Maharashtra signs guarantee
September 1994	Government of India signs guarantee
March 1995	Dabhol financing completed
March 1995	Maharashtra State election results announced
April 1995	Construction begins; Government of Maharashtra orders a review; Munde Committee set up to investigate Dabhol Project
August 1995	Project canceled by Government of Maharashtra
January 1996	New Deal announced
December 1996	Indian High Court dismisses last of 25 lawsuits filed by workers unions and environmental groups; construction resumes
December 1996	London tribunal agrees to terminate arbitration proceedings against State Government of Maharashtra
February 1997	Police detain 1400 trade union protesters at the construction site
May 1999	Phase 1 begins operation; Financing for Phase II secured for $1.87 billion
September 1999	Congress (I) Party wins Maharashtra state elections
August 2000	Rebecca Mark leaves Enron
December 2000	Maharashtra government official announces that the Dabhol contract should be renegotiated because the power cost is too high
January 2001	Enron no longer interested in building power plants in India; Enron assisting Indian government in redrafting Electricity Act
February 2001	Dabhol invokes Indian government guarantee to collect $17 million in overdue bills
April 2001	Enron issued a notice of arbitration to India's government to recover, at the Court of Arbitration in London, $21.9 million
April 2001	MSEB agrees to pay $28.6 million and says there are no more outstanding bills
May 2001	State government sets up a panel, the Godbole Committee, to study the contract between Dabhol and the electricity board; MSEB said it is rescinding its contract to buy electricity from Dabhol; Enron rejects payment of $29.1 million because it came with a note saying it was submitted "under protest."
September 20	Letter to India PM from Ken Lay

Exhibit 3   Timing of Events Associated With Dabhol Power Company

MSEB turned to the World Bank for advice in the negotiations. The World Bank offered to fund a team of international consultants. The MSEB chose Freshfields, a British law firm, and the British office of the German Westdeutsche Landesbank Girozentrale as consultants in the PPA negotiations. The World Bank concluded that the project was "not economically viable," citing that the type of plant proposed would produce too much power at too high a price for the state.[6] Again, the World Bank's advice was not heeded and negotiations continued. In addition to negotiating the project financial structure and gaining state and central government approvals, Enron had to obtain dozens of other government approvals, some of which were based on regulations dating back to British colonial times. For example, to get permission to use explosives on the construction site, Enron had to visit the western Indian town of Nagpur, where British Imperial forces once stored munitions.[7]

In November 1993, the Central Electricity Authority officially cleared the Dabhol project. In December 1993, the MSEB signed the Dabhol PPA. The state government of Maharashtra signed a financial guarantee in February 1994 and the Central Government signed a guarantee in September 1994. These guarantees provided financial protection for Enron in the event that the MSEB was unable make its payments. The Central Government's guarantee, which was to become very controversial, was signed with Enron before the government's guarantee policy was announced publicly.

Structure of the Dabhol Project

Although the original plans were for a 2015-MW project, the Maharashtra government decided to break the project into two phases. Phase I would be a 695-MW plant using distillate fuel instead of natural gas, and Phase II would be a 1320-MW gas-fired plant. The capital cost for Phase I would be $920 million, with an estimated turnkey construction cost of $527 million.[8] The second phase would cost about $1.9 billion.

Dabhol was broken into two phases because Enron had been unable to finalize its gas contracts and because the government had become concerned about the mounting criticism of the project. The shift from gas to distillate was done because distillate could be sourced from local refineries, helping deflect the criticism that gas imports would be a persistent drain on India's foreign exchange. Furthermore, using distillate instead of gas eliminated the need to build a port facility for Phase I.

The capital cost for Phase I included some costs for infrastructure items that would normally have been provided by the state, such as a pipeline. If these costs were deducted from the total capital cost, the cost per MW was comparable with the other fast-track power plant projects. However, Dabhol was the only project that had been finalized. The other projects were still going through planning and approval stages.

The Indian Government generally followed what was known as a fixed rate of return model. Investors were assured a 16% rate of return on net worth for a plant load factor of up to 68.5%. Beyond 68.5%, the rate of return on equity would increase by a maximum of 0.70% for each 1% rise in the plant load factor. Net worth was based on the total costs of building the power plant. The main objection against this model was that it provided no incentive to minimize the capital costs of investment.

The Dabhol project used a different model. An estimated tariff of Rs2.40 ($1 equaled about 36 rupees) per unit (kilowatt/hour) of electricity was established. The tariff consisted of two components: (1) a capacity charge of Rs1.20 based on the capital cost of the plant and operating and maintenance costs, and (2) an energy charge of Rs1.20 for the price of fuel. It was estimated that the plant would run at 90% capacity. MSEB had to make capacity payments on the established baseload capacity irrespective of the actual power purchased (a so-called take-or-pay contract). The energy charge was based on estimated fuel costs and could rise or fall. Both the capacity and energy charges had a mix of rupee and dollar components. The MSEB was required to bear the exchange risk.

With this type of tariff, the problems of a cost-plus system were eliminated and consumers would not be affected by increases in the capital cost of the project. However, the tariff was not fixed and, in particular, changes in fuel costs and exchange rates would impact the power price. For Enron and its partners, there was an incentive to become more efficient to improve shareholder returns. Based on the capital costs per MW, Dabhol was comparable to other proposed projects in India. As to the tariff of Rs2.40, other fast-track power projects had similar tariffs, as did several recently approved public sector projects. Several existing public sector plants were selling power in the Rs2.15 range (although the average tariff for state electricity boards in India was Rs1.20). Enron's projected internal rate of return on the project was 26.5% before tax. Dabhol was granted a five-year tax holiday and the initial purchase agreement was for 20 years. Failure to achieve electricity targets would result in substantial penalty payments by the DPC to the MSEB. In the event that MSEB and DPC could not settle disagreements, international arbitration proceedings in London would be possible as specified in the PPA.

Nevertheless, because there was no competitive bidding on the Dabhol project, critics argued that the Rs2.40 per unit was too high and that the company would be making huge profits. Kirit Parekh, director of the Indira Gandhi Institute of Development and Research, was an ardent critic:

> In the United States, power generated from gas-based plants is sold to utilities at 3–4 cents while Enron is charging 7 cents. It is a rip-off. The China Power Company, which is setting up a 2000-MW power plant in Hong Kong, and which will go on stream in 1996, is doing so at 15 per cent less capital than Enron.[9]

Further criticism was directed at the company's lack of competitive bidding for its principal equipment supplier, General Electric, and its construction partner, Bechtel. Although General Electric and Enron had worked closely in the past, some critics suggested that foreign equipment suppliers were favored over Indian suppliers. Enron countered with the argument that it had awarded more than 60 contracts worth more than $100 million (Rs3.6 billion) to Indian companies.

Enron was also subject to criticism because of its plan to import gas for Phase II from its gas processing plant in Qatar. When completed, this plant would be owned by a joint venture between Enron Oil & Gas and the Qatar government. Although Enron vigorously denied it, critics suggested that Enron would make excessive profits through transfer pricing and charging arbitrary prices for the fuel. From Enron's perspective, taking responsibility for fuel supply was a means of reducing its risk, since the contract specified penalties when the plant was not able to generate electricity. Fuel supply failure would not constitute sufficient grounds for being unable to generate electricity.

The federal guarantee also came in for criticism. A World Bank report questioned the guarantee arrangement because, in its opinion, it was nothing more than a loan made by the federal government on behalf of the MSEB if it could not cover its payments to Enron. Enron's Sutton countered:

> It is only after the government of India decided as a policy to give guarantees that we also decided to ask. It would have been impossible to raise money from international bankers at competitive rates without the guarantee when others are approaching the same bankers with guarantees in their pockets.[10]

INDIAN POLITICS AT THE CENTRAL LEVEL

India's political process was based on a parliamentary system. From 1947 to 1989, some form of the Congress Party ruled India at the national, or central, level in an unbroken string of governments. Indira Gandhi, who had been Prime Minister since 1964, founded the Congress (I) Party after her defeat in the 1977 election. In

1980, Indira Gandhi and the Congress (I) Party regained power. After Indira Gandhi was assassinated in 1984, her son Rajiv became Prime Minister. In the 1989 election, Congress (I) lost and turned power over to a minority government. During the 1991 election campaign, Rajiv Gandhi was assassinated and P.V. Narasimha Rao became Congress (I) Party leader. Congress (I) regained power in a minority government and Rao became Prime Minister. Rao resigned as party president in September 1996 after being charged with bribery.

In 1998, the Bharatiya Janata Party (BJP) led a 13-party coalition that defeated the Congress (I) Party. The BJP's leader, Atal Behari Vajpayee, became the Prime Minister. In English, BJP translated to the Indian People's Party. The BJP platform emphasized support for traditional Hindu goals and values, making the party less secular than the Congress (I) Party. Many of its members belonged to the urban lower middle class and distrusted free-market reforms and modern cultural values. The BJP believed it could build support among the business community that sought decentralization and deregulation but resented intervention on the part of foreign multinationals.

In the early 1990s, the BJP was openly affiliated with the Hindu fundamentalist movement known as Rashtriya Swayamsevak Sangh (RSS), which translated as National Volunteers Core. In 1990, the RSS formed the Swadeshi Jagaran Manch, or National Awakening Forum, to promote economic nationalism. The Forum deemed the marketing of Western consumer goods frivolous and wasteful ("India needs computer chips, not potato chips"). According to the Forum's Bombay representative, "Soft drinks and instant cereals do not serve the mass of Indian people. We are not pleased with the way [Coke and Pepsi] are demolishing their rivals."[11] After elections in 1996, the BJP realized that it had been crippled by its identification as an extremist party. The central BJP government elected in 1998 took a more moderate stance, and its economic policy included free-market liberalization, except in sensitive areas where it still maintained economic nationalism.[12]

STATE POLITICS AND THE 1995 MAHARASHTRA ELECTION

The political parties of the 25 Indian states level mirrored those at the central level, although the Congress (I) historically had been less dominant. The BJP was particularly strong in the industrial, heavily populated, and largely Hindu northern states. Decision-making was decentralized in India, and many of the states had a substantial amount of power and autonomy.

On February 12, 1995, a state election was held in Maharashtra. Results were to be announced about four weeks later because the chief election commissioner in Maharashtra had a policy of delinking voting from the counting of votes. The incumbent Congress (I) Party and an alliance between the BJP and Shiv Sena parties were the primary contestants. State elections were normally held every five years. In the previous election in 1990, the Congress (I) Party had formed a majority government under Chief Minister Sharad Pawar. Pawar was confident of retaining power in the 1995 election.

The Shiv Sena was a Maharashtra-based party with the stated objective of protecting the economic interests and identity of Maharashtrians and safeguarding the interests of all Hindus. The official leader of Shiv Sena was Manohar Joshi, but he had limited power and openly admitted that the real authority was Bal Thackeray (sometimes referred to as Mr. Remote Control for his ability to control the party from an unofficial capacity). Thackeray was a newspaper cartoonist before he became a right-wing activist. A talented organizer and rousing orator, he set up the Shiv Sena Party in the mid 1960s to appeal to poor Hindus who resented the influence of foreigners and non-Maharashtrians, particularly those from South India. Thackeray was prone to provocative and somewhat threatening statements. He proposed changing the name of India to Hindustan and, during the Maharashtra election, talked about chasing non-Maharashtrians out of the state.

The Dabhol power project was a major campaign issue leading up to the 1995 election.

Election Commission norms in India prohibited a state government from making decisions on vital matters in the run-up to an election. However, the BJP and Shiv Sena did not make this an issue in February. Had they done so, the Election Commission might have ordered the state government to defer the decision on Dabhol.

The BJP/Shiv Sena election campaign rhetoric left little doubt as to their sentiments—one of their slogans was "Throw Enron into the Arabian Sea." The BJP platform promoted economic nationalism and sovereignty and denounced the Dabhol project. The BJP attempted to isolate Chief Minister Pawar as the only defender of Enron. The Dabhol project was described as a typical case of bad government: the failure of the ruling party to stand up to pressure from multinationals, corruption, and compromises on economic sovereignty. The BJP had always been opposed to the project for various reasons: the social and environmental aspects, alleged bribes, the project's cost, and the lack of competitive bidding. The BJP/Shiv Sena campaign strategy painted the Congress (I) Party as anti-poor, corrupt, and partial to foreign firms. This platform evidently appealed to Maharashtrians. On March 13, the election results were announced. The BJP/Shiv Sena coalition won 138 of 288 seats in the election and, with the help of several independent members, formed the new government. The Shiv Sena's Manohar Joshi became the new Chief Minister.

Not long after the election, Enron CEO Kenneth Lay noted, "If something happens now to slow down or damage our power project, it would send extremely negative signals to other foreign investors."[13]

CONSTRUCTION BEGINS

On March 2, 1995, Enron completed the financing for Phase I of the Dabhol project. Phase I financing would come from the following sources:

- A 12-bank syndication led by the Bank of America and ABN-Amro (loans of $150 million)
- U.S. Export-Import Bank ($300 million; arranged by GE and Bechtel)
- The U.S.-based Overseas Private Investment Corp. ($298 million)
- Industrial Development Bank of India ($98 million)

Construction was soon under way. But, almost simultaneously, the new state government in Maharashtra, in keeping with its campaign promises, decided to put the project under review.

THE MUNDE COMMITTEE

One week after coming to power, Deputy Chief Minister and state BJP president Gopinath Munde ordered a review of the Dabhol project. The committee formed to carry out the review had two members from the BJP and two from the Shiv Sena. Munde, a known critic of Dabhol, was the Chairman. An open invitation to individuals to appear before the committee was followed up by letters to the MSEB and Dabhol Power Company. The committee was scheduled to submit its report by July 1.

Over the next few months, the committee held more than a dozen meetings and visited the site of the power plant. The committee was assisted by five state government departments: energy, finance, industries, planning, and law. All requests for appearances before the committee were granted. Among those making depositions were: environmental groups, energy economists, a former managing director of the Bombay Suburban Electric Supply Company, representatives of other IPPs, and representatives of the IPP Association. The Industrial Development Bank of India, a prime lender to the project, representatives from the former state government, and the Congress (I) Party did not appear before the committee.

During the committee hearings, the BJP continued its public opposition to Dabhol. The issue of irregularities—a euphemism for bribes—was raised. According to a senior BJP official:

> Though it is impossible to ascertain if kickbacks were paid to [former Maharashtra Chief Minister] Pawar, even if we can obtain circumstantial evidence, it is enough. The project has been padded up and if the review committee can establish that, it is sufficient to cancel the project.[14]

Allegations of bribery were vigorously denied by Enron. Joseph Sutton, Enron's managing director in India, had told delegates at India Power '95, a conference on the power sector held in New Delhi in March, "during the three years we have been here, we have never been asked for, nor have we paid, any bribes."[15]

On June 11, the RSS (the Hindu fundamentalist group) issued a directive to the BJP that it would like the party to honor its commitment to the *swadeshi* movement. The economic advisor to the Central BJP Party, Jay Dubashi, said:

> We think canceling this project will send the right signals. It will demonstrate that we are not chumps who can be taken for a ride. Enron probably never imagined that Sharad Pawar [former Maharashtra Chief Minister] would go out of power. They thought he would see the deal through.[16]

Pramod Mahajan, the BJP's All-India Secretary, was also fervently against Dabhol, stating that "we will go to court if necessary and decide in the long-term interest of the country."[17] Mahajan also ruled out paying penalties to Enron if the project were scrapped.

Meanwhile, Enron officials were shuttling back and forth between New Delhi and Bombay, trying to convince the press and the government of the viability of the Dabhol project. At one point, the US ambassador to India, Frank Wisner, met with the BJP president, L. K. Advani. Advani refused to meet Enron officials (in 1996, Advani was indicted on corruption charges). The issue was even discussed during U.S. Treasury Secretary Robert Rubin's visit to India in April. According to the Assistant Secretary of the Treasury, "we pushed for resolution of the issue."[18] In May 1995, the U.S. Department of Energy warned that failure to honor the contract would jeopardize most, if not all, other private projects proposed for international financing in India. Maharashtra had attracted more than $1 billion of U.S. investment, and more than half of all FDI projects in India were in this state. Furthermore, more than 25% of all FDI in India was from the United States.

In the meantime, Bechtel had not stopped construction. A spokesman for Bechtel said the company could not afford to have its 1300 workers idled during a month-long review. "We have to meet a schedule; we have to provide power according to the power purchase agreement."[19]

CANCELLATION OF THE DABHOL PROJECT

The Munde Committee report was submitted to the Maharashtra government on July 15, 1995. Prior to the release of the report, N.K.P. Salve, India's Power Minister, stressed that the "Enron contract can be canceled only if there is a legal basis for doing so, not for any arbitrary or political reason."[20] On August 2, the Indian Supreme Court dismissed a petition by a former Maharashtra legislator challenging the Dabhol project on the grounds of secrecy.

On August 3, Chief Minister Joshi (who had visited the United States in the previous month to attract investment to India) announced to the Maharashtra legislature that the cabinet unanimously agreed to suspend Phase I of the project and scrap Phase II. The following are excerpts from Chief Minister Joshi's lengthy statement in the Assembly:

> The Enron project in the form conceived and contracted for is not in the best interests of the state. . . . The sub-committee whole-heartedly recommends that the Enron-MSEB contract should be canceled forthwith. . . . Considering the grave issues involved in the matter and the disturbing facts and circumstances that have emerged pointing to extra-commercial considerations and probable corruption and illegal motives at work in the

whole affair, immediate action must be initiated under the penal and anti-corruption laws by police.

The wrong choice of LNG as fuel and huge inflation in capital costs, along with unprecedented favours shown to Enron in different ways, including in the fuel procurement [had all resulted in an] unreasonable fuel cost to the consumers. . . . The documentary evidence obtained by the committee shows beyond any reasonable doubt that the capital cost of Enron Plant was inflated and jacked up by a huge margin. The committee believes that the extent of the inflation may be as high as $700 million. . . . Being gas-based, this project should have been cheaper than coal-based ones but, in reality, it turns out to be the other way about.

The Government should have sought some part of this for itself. . . . This contract is anti-Maharashtra. It is devoid of any self-respect; it is one that mortgages the brains of the State which, if accepted, would be a betrayal of the people. This contract is no contract at all and if, by repudiating it, there is some financial burden, the State will accept it to preserve the wellbeing of Maharashtra.[21]

Other grounds were given for cancellation: there had been no competitive bidding; Enron held secret negotiations and used unfair means to win its contract; there was potential environmental damage to a region that was relatively unpolluted; the guaranteed return was well above the norm; and concerns about the $20 million earmarked by Enron for education and project development. The BJP government charged that concessions granted to Enron would cause the state of Maharashtra to lose more than $3.3 billion in the future. The committee was also outraged that loose ends in the Dabhol project were being tied up by the Maharashtra government as late as February 25, almost two weeks after the state election. In effect, the contract had been made effective by an administration that had already been rejected by voters.

When the decision was announced, then Prime Minister Rao was on a trade and investment promotion trip to Malaysia. He indicated that the economic liberalization policies initiated by his government would not be affected by this decision. Sharad Pawar, the Chief Minister of Maharashtra at the time the original agreement was signed with Enron, criticized the BJP's decision to cancel the Dabhol power project:

If the government of Maharashtra was serious about the industrialization of Maharashtra, and its power requirements for industrialization and agriculture, they definitely would have appointed an expert group who understands the requirement of power, about overall projection, about investment which is coming in the fields of industry and agriculture, legal sides, but this particular angle is totally missing here and that is why I am not so surprised for this type of decision which has been taken by the government of Maharashtra.[22]

On the day after the government's cancellation announcement, the *Saamna* newspaper, known as the voice of the nationalist Shiv Sena Party, published a headline that read, "Enron Finally Dumped into the Arabian Sea." Later that week, *The Economic Times* in Bombay reported that local villagers celebrated the fall of Enron.

About 2600 people were working on the Dabhol power project, and it was nearly one-third complete. More than $300 million had been invested in the project, and estimated costs per day if the project were shut down would be $200,000 to $250,000. Cancellation of Phase II was less critical because Enron had not yet secured financing commitments for this portion of the project.

A few days before the Munde Committee report was made public and anticipating a cancellation recommendation, Rebecca Mark had offered publicly to renegotiate the deal. She told the media that the company would try to meet the concerns of the MSEB. On August 3, Enron announced that while it was aware of the reported announcement in the Maharashtra Assembly on the suspension of Dabhol, the company had received no official notice to that effect. The statement issued in Houston said:

[Enron] remains available for discussions with the government on any concerns it may have. . . . [Enron] has very strong legal defenses available to it under the project contracts and fully intends to pursue these if necessary. The DPC and the project sponsors would like to reiterate that they have acted in full compliance with Indian and U.S. laws.[23]

RENEGOTIATION

Shortly after receiving a single sentence note from the Maharashtra state government canceling the project, Enron filed for arbitration (in London), claiming $300 million in damages. The arbitration date was set for November 17, 1995. Meanwhile, DPC and its sponsors signed a standstill agreement with all international lenders that froze current loan agreements for DPC and extended protection to its creditors.

In September, Enron opened the doors to a negotiated settlement by publicly offering to lower the tariff to a rate similar to other Indian power projects. In January 1996, Enron announced that DPC had received a formal offer from the government of Maharashtra state in India to revive the project. The Maharashtra government said that it would go ahead with the project if the American partners reduced the cost of the power to be sold to the state. Enron then offered to reduce the capital cost of the project and lower the price of that power. As well, the MSEB was

given the option to acquire a 30% equity stake in DPC. Although press reports indicated that DPC's expected rate of return dropped because of the new deal, a senior executive at Enron described the power tariff reduction as a "price reduction that was not really a price reduction. . . . Why? Because of technological advances, falling hardware costs, weakening rupee." According to Rebecca Mark:

> It's [the renegotiated deal] resulted in a good project for India and a structure that will allow us to recover our costs, including our suspension costs, and provide a very fair return to our shareholders. . . . We now have a better idea of the LNG costs, now that Enron has a more solid agreement with the government of Qatar. That's allowed us to reduce the cost of the power plant to $2 billion. Regasification will add $400 million-plus to the project. But that will be recovered through a separate gas charge.[24]

By April 1996, the new contract had been approved by the Maharashtra state cabinet, and final approval was given in July 1996. See Exhibit 4 for details on the new deal. In December 1996, 16 months after the project was suspended, construction resumed. Despite the problems with DPC, Enron continued to pursue and bid on other projects in India.

---

1. Tariff for Phase I reduced from Rs 2.4/MW to Rs 2.03/MW. Tariff for Phase II reduced from Rs 2.4/MW to Rs 1.86/MW.

2. Phase I increased in capacity from 695MW to 740MW. The overall project increased from 2015MW to 2184MW.

3. Cost savings from capital cost reductions in Phase II of the project and price reductions from GE and Bechtel.

4. Regasification project taken out of the project. Phase II to use LNG from an Enron project in Qatar. This helped reduced the overall capital costs by US$300 million.

5. MSEB given an option to purchase 30% of the equity in DPC.

6. Switching from distillate to naphtha for Phase I.

Exhibit 4   Renegotiated Terms for the Dabhol Power Project

COMPLETION OF PHASE ONE

In May 1999, Phase I was completed and became operational. Also in May, Enron secured financing for the $1.87 billion Phase II and by the end of the year had signed long-term gas supply agreements with Oman LNG and Abu Dhabi Gas. The second-phase financing used basically the same lenders as Phase I, with the exception of two Export-Import Banks from Japan and Belgium, which replaced the U.S. Export-Import Bank. U.S. sanctions resulting from India's nuclear testing had suspended lending by the U.S. Export-Import Bank. The financing included five loans totaling $1.414 billion, plus an equity investment of $452 million from Enron, GE, and Bechtel, based on their ownership percentage. Phase II did not have a central government counter-guarantee.

At around the same time, Enron pulled out of a $500 million LNG project in Kerala, blaming regulatory delays that had put construction two years behind. Enron was actively pursuing other non-power projects in India. In November 1999, Enron signed an MOU with an undersea-cable operator and was in negotiations for a venture to build a fiber-optic telecommunications network in India.

NEW PROBLEMS

In a Maharashtra state election campaign in September 1999, Congress (I) Party leadership promised, if elected, to halt DPC's second phase and renegotiate the power tariff. However, Congress (I) Party leaders in New Delhi quickly distanced themselves from the anti-Enron rhetoric. A Congress official dismissed the statement as an expression of frustration by local politicians who were struggling to regain control of Maharashtra. The Congress (I) Party eventually formed a coalition government that included the Janata Dal and the Peasants and Workers Party. The Maharashtra State Electricity Board Workers' Federation also demanded renegotiation of the PPA and scrapping of the second stage of the venture.

In December 1999, Maharashtra again found itself with a power deficit. MSEB announced that certain rural areas would have uninterrupted power for only five days a week. Once Phase II of the DPC project was completed, it was expected that Maharashtra would be a power-surplus state. Also in December, Maharashtra deputy Chief Minister and Home Minister Chagan Bhujbal said at a press conference:

> We do not want to repeat the previous government's mistake of attempting to stop the [Dabhol] project. The government wants to examine how the previous government sanctioned Phase II of the project without examining the result of the first phase. Secondly, it will also review the tariff. Thirdly, it will examine whether the project was essential for a state like Maharashtra.[25]

Facing huge financial losses, the MSEB agreed in November 2000 to sell half of its 30% stake in DPC (acquired after the renegotiations in 1996) to Enron. This reduced the MSEB's overall stake in DPC to 15% and increased Enron's equity to 65%.

Also in November 2000, new problems arose. The MSEB's take-or-pay PPA was based on 90% capacity utilization. The greater the capacity utilized, the lower the per unit cost of power to MSEB. At this time, the MSEB was purchasing between 33% and 60% of the output of DPC. The government's explanation for reducing the off-take from DPC was that demand for power in the state had not grown as estimated earlier. In any event, it looked increasingly unlikely that the MSEB would be able to pay for electricity from DPC over the next few months. A declining rupee and a dollar-denominated price and increased naphtha costs were contributing to higher charges for DPC power.

On February 6, 2001, Enron invoked the central government's counter-guarantee to recover $17 million that was owed by the MSEB for November 2000 power. Dabhol's president, Neil McGregor, said the government must "recognize the serious domestic and international implications of contractual agreements not being honored."[26] India's federal Power Minister, Suresh

Prabhu, said that the government was "obliged to pay and [will] definitely make the payment." Enron was the first foreign company to invoke the central government's counter-guarantee.

In March 2001, MSEB imposed a claim of about $86 million on DPC for taking five hours to restart the plant after a brief shutdown, two hours longer than the contract specified. Enron disputed the claim and said that the timing suggested the MSEB was looking for ways to absolve themselves from payments that were contractually due. DPC then threatened to cut off electricity, in an effort to protect the project lenders, who had expressed concerns about difficulties getting payments. MSEB had failed to make payments since December.

On April 27, 2001, MSEB paid its March bill after Enron said it might stop selling power to the utility. In an unusual twist, DPC rejected the $29.1 million check to make a legal point (the check was then direct-deposited in a DPC bank account). DPC also delivered a sharply worded four-page letter to MSEB responding to the utility's decision to rescind its power-purchasing contract based on a claim that Dabhol misrepresented its "ramp-up" speed—the time the plant takes to go from a cold start to full power.

In May 2001, DPC turned up the heat by taking a formal step toward ending its contract with MSEB. DPC issued a preliminary termination notice, the first of several prescribed steps toward ending the contract, and said it was owed $48 million. This triggered a six-month cooling-off period. Vinay Bansal, chairman of MSEB, said it would respond to the notice. Prior to this incident, the state government had set up a panel, the Godbole Committee, to study the contract between Dabhol and MSEB. In July 2001, the MSEB was no longer buying power from DPC. In August, the Godbole Committee concluded that "the venture was always too big and too expensive for the state of Maharashtra to handle." One passage in the report described how "numerous infirmities" in the approvals process "bring into question the propriety" of such decisions.

ENRON'S RESPONSE

Enron announced that it was open to ideas, but rejected the Godbole report as a basis for discussions. Construction on Phase II, which was 95% completed, was stopped and thousands of workers were laid off. In the meantime, Cogentrix of the United States, National Power of the UK, Daewoo of Korea, and Electricite de France had withdrawn from the Indian power sector over the previous two years.

In the September letter from Enron CEO Ken Lay to the Indian Prime Minister, Lay proposed selling the DPC equity for approximately $1.2 billion and the purchase of offshore lender's debt for $1.1 billion, for a total cost of $2.3 billion. He also said that "this amount strikes me as exceptionally reasonable when compared to the size of our legal claim," which Enron estimated to be between $4–5 billion. Lay concluded that if Enron were to get anything less than its full investment, it would consider this to be "an act of expropriation" by the Indian government.

NOTES

1. Enron Annual Report, 2000.
2. Country Watch, http://www.countrywatch.com/includes/grank/gdpnumericppp.asp.
3. India Country Forecast, *The PRS Group, Inc.,* November 20, 2001, p. 53.
4. Michael Schuman, India Has a Voracious Need for Electricity: U.S. Companies Have a Clear Inside Track, *Forbes,* April 24, 1995.
5. Bodhisatva Ganguli & Tushar Pania, The Anatomy of a Controversial Deal, *Business India,* April 24–May 7, 1995, p. 57.
6. *The New York Times,* March 20, 2001, C1.
7. Marcus W. Brauchli, A Gandhi Legacy: Clash Over Power Plant Reflects Fight in India for Its Economic Soul, *Wall Street Journal,* April 27, 1995, A6.
8. Ganguli & Pania, p. 59.
9. Ganguli & Pania, p. 58.
10. Ganguli & Pania, p. 56.
11. India Power Down: A Major Blow to Rao's Reform Drive, *AsiaWeek,* August 18, 1995.

12. India Country Forecast, *The PRS Group, Inc.*, December 1, 2001, p. 28.

13. Emily MacFarquhar, A Volatile Democracy, *U.S. News and World Report,* March 27, 1995, p. 37.

14. Ganguli & Pania, p. 56.

15. Ganguli & Pania, p. 55.

16. Ibid.

17. Ibid.

18. Ibid.

19. *San Francisco Business Times,* May 5, 1995, Sec. 1, p. 1.

20. Foreign Investment in India: The Enron Disease, *The Economist,* July 29, 1995, p. 48.

21. Indian State Axes $2.8 BN Dabhol Power Project, in International Gas Report, *The Financial Times,* August 4; Mahesh Vijapurkar, Enron Deal Scrapped, Ongoing Work Halted, *The Hindu,* August 4, p. 1.

22. All-India Doordarshan Television, 3 August 1995.

23. Vijapurkar, p. 1.

24. Gottschalk, Arthur, "Cabinet's OK Brings Enron Closer to Completing India Power Deal," *Journal of Commerce,* January 9, 1996.

25. State Govt Will Review Enron Project, Says Bhujbal, *The Economic Times of India,* December 7, 1999.

26. *Wall Street Journal,* July 2, 2001, A21.

Bombardier Versus Embraer: Charges of Unfair Competition

Prepared by Trevor Hunter under the supervision of Professor David W. Conklin

Version: (A) 1999-07-12

It's not PROEX the program we object to, rather it is the way Embraer uses PROEX that is an abuse of the program.

—Michael Lord, vice-president communications, Bombardier[1]

By 1998, Canadian aircraft manufacturer Bombardier felt it had no choice but to take its fight with Embraer Empresa Brasileira de Aeronautica S.A. (Embraer) to the World Trade Organization (WTO) to force Brazil to cease what Bombardier felt were unfair subsidies. In its own defense, Embraer stated that since Brazil was a developing country, it had the right to subsidize industries and, in addition, charged the Canadian government with unfair subsidization of Bombardier. In the competitive market of commercial aircraft manufacturing, the stakes were high and any advantage was hotly contested.

On November 23, 1998, the WTO dispute panel began its long process of determining if any of the programs run by either government constituted unfair trade practices.

The Commercial Aircraft Manufacturing Industry[2]

Entering and competing in the world aircraft industry demanded skills, technology and resources beyond the requirements of most other industries. Aircraft manufacturing was among the most complex functions performed in 20th century manufacturing: hundreds of suppliers co-ordinated and contributed their input to the manufacture, assembly, integration and certification of thousands of individual components.

The primary customers for this industry—the world's airlines and armed forces—were sophisticated and demanding, with rigorous quality, safety and performance requirements. As these customers were relatively few in number, they exerted considerable buyer power in a highly competitive marketplace where there were few uncontested niches. Major airlines demanded price and financing concessions, whereas military purchasers traditionally focused on superior performance.

The industry relied on substantive scale and scope economies, and faced high barriers to entry. The up-front development costs for a new aircraft or aeroengine were daunting, and could typically be recouped only over a successful 20-year product life cycle in highly volatile and uncertain global markets. With such formidable financial and market risks, the industry was regarded as a "bet the company" business.

Aircraft manufacturing generally was a labour-intensive, low-volume business with few opportunities for large-scale automation. Rarely, for example, did complete aircraft production exceed one unit per week.

The international aircraft manufacturing industry operated within a three-tiered capability hierarchy. An important aspect of the pyramid structure was the upward flow of parts and components within the industry. At the peak of the hierarchy, were the relatively few "prime manufacturers" with the capability to design, integrate, gain certification for and market complete aircraft.

Primes, in turn, relied on a far-reaching international network of second-tier suppliers of proprietary aircraft subsystems (for example, aeroengines) and major structural components (for example, wings). Competition among second-tier suppliers was particularly "global"; it was commonplace for an airframe to contain major structural components designed and manufactured in several different nations.

Serving both first- and second-tier companies were numerous third-tier suppliers of smaller parts, components and services. Production equipment and techniques for these build-to-print operations were readily available to all competitors.

Prime and second-tier activities in the international industry were dominated by large U.S. and European aerospace and defence conglomerates closely aligned with their home countries' national security and military procurement needs. Bombardier, the only Canadian-based, large multinational in the industry, with aircraft manufacturing plants in Canada, the U.S. and Northern Ireland, was small in comparison with the U.S. and European aerospace and defence giants.

Canada, with a much smaller economy, had a four per cent share, and led the second tier of exporting nations, ahead of such larger economies as Italy and Japan. The range of design and manufacturing expertise that had been developed in the Canadian aircraft industry was comparable with that of the German industry, and was broader than that of nations such as Japan, Italy, the Netherlands and Sweden.

Worldwide deliveries of new aircraft (i.e., excluding sales of subsystems, subcomponents and parts, and repair and overhaul services) were expected to total US$70 billion in 1996. Sales of commercial jet transports accounted for approximately one-half of this amount.

Markets for aircraft were extremely volatile, experiencing turbulence from economic cycles as well as from government policy and regulatory decisions. As a result of this market volatility, the aircraft industry suffered through periods of low capacity utilization and widespread workforce reductions during each business cycle.

The swings in aircraft markets were much more pronounced than are those in overall economic activity. This resulted in part from the relatively long lead times required for an aircraft order. Because changes to the level of production (either up or down) were quite expensive, manufacturers tried to schedule an orderly transition through the business cycle.

Governments around the world coveted an indigenous aircraft industry because of its strong links to national defence and sovereignty, its prestige value, and its economic benefits such as export revenues, technology spillovers to other industrial sectors and its high-paying jobs. As a result, the hand of government was pervasive in the development of the international aircraft manufacturing industry—through tariff and non-tariff barriers, direct subsidies such as Research and Development (R&D) support, financing assistance for export sales, government procurement practices that favoured domestic industries, and requirements for industrial offsets. The enthusiasm of governments was instrumental in maintaining the chronic excess capacity that plagued many segments of both civil and military aircraft markets.

Furthermore, the aircraft purchase decision was influenced as much by the nature and cost of financing as it was by the price of the aircraft. Given the cyclical nature of the airline industry and the availability of sophisticated financing instruments, airlines were increasingly leasing rather than purchasing (an estimated 10 to 30 per cent of new aircraft were leased to airlines). In this regard, they became extremely sensitive to the terms under which these leases were structured and to the level of credit support that manufacturers or their supporting government (through export credit agencies) could offer.

Aircraft financing was a particularly important issue in the commuter/regional aircraft market, where a significant number of customers did not have a strong financial position, and there was an oversupply of competing regional aircraft products. This situation brought downward pressures on prices, and led to aggressive manufacturer financing and related incentives such as buy-backs, offsets and very low interest rates. In this market, government support in the form of loan guarantees in the event of lessee default or return of the aircraft to the lessor before expiry of the lease was usual. This was especially the case with new aircraft models that had not yet gained widespread market acceptance and for which stable residual values had not yet been established.

BOMBARDIER INC.

Although it was headquartered in Montreal, Canada, Bombardier Inc. (Bombardier) was truly a global company. Over the years, it had evolved from a small, one-man operation into a diversified conglomerate with interests in transportation, aerospace, defense, and motorized consumer products. By the mid-1990s, nearly 90 per cent of its revenues came from sales from outside of Canada, and the company had production facilities in several locations throughout North America and Europe.

Bombardier was founded by Joseph-Armand Bombardier as L'Auto-Neige Bombardier Limiteé in 1942. Conceived as a mode of transportation for the people of Quebec during harsh winter weather, Bombardier snowmobile products gained recognition during World War II. For many years after the war, sales resulted from the development of a wider variety of snowmobiles, and this line sustained the growth of the company. When Bombardier died in 1966, his son-in-law Laurent Beaudoin, was named president and ran the company until late 1998.

Through well-timed acquisitions, Beaudoin transformed Bombardier into a leader in some of the most competitive industries in the world. Acquisitions in the early 1970s brought Bombardier into the rail transit industry. Then, later that decade, through the purchase of a company that produced landing gear, Bombardier had its first taste of the aerospace market. Successful contracts in the rail industry coming from Canada, America and Mexico provided the funds for expansion and allowed the company to acquire competitors during downturns in the industry. In the early 1980s, Bombardier gained the rights to market a highly successful military truck, which again was a "cash cow."

The excess cash gave Bombardier the freedom to push further into aerospace with its purchase of the Canadian company Canadair. Canadair had been receiving financial assistance from the Canadian government and had produced a technically superior corporate jet known as the Challenger. However, the company was losing money, and Bombardier was able to buy it for what was considered an undervalued price from a government eager to cut its loses, and turn it into a profitable business in a short period of time. This positive experience led to further acquisitions, such as Learjet Corporation, de Havilland and Short Brothers PLC, until the aerospace division accounted for around 50 per cent of Bombardier's revenue. By the late 1990s, Bombardier was structured into six business units: Bombardier Transportation, Bombardier Recreational Products, Bombardier Aerospace, Bombardier Services, Bombardier Capital and Bombardier International. (See Exhibit 1 for consolidated financial statements for Bombardier.)

Bombardier Aerospace

Bombardier Aerospace focused on three sectors of the commercial aircraft market: business aircraft, regional aircraft and amphibious aircraft. According to the company Web site, 75 per cent of division revenue came from the first two sectors. The fastest growing sector was regional aircraft. Many smaller airlines were emerging to meet the needs of travellers taking connecting flights within the regional hub network. Global carriers had deemed these routes uneconomical.

Carriers in this segment of the airline market were looking for economical, reliable, safe aircraft to shuttle their passengers. Bombardier's 50-seat Canadair Regional Jet (CRJ) 100 set the standard for medium-range transportation. Due to the success of the Canadair jet, and the growth in demand for medium-range aircraft, by late 1997, there were 307[3] CRJ-100s sold (priced at US$20 million), with firm orders for 86 more, and options for an additional 198.[4] Bombardier had designed a new series of jets, the Canadair 700 series. These planes, which ranged from 70 to 78 seats, were based on the 50-seat design and could be operated at nearly the same cost, but had a greater capacity and efficiency. Demand for the CRJ-700 plane was expected to be 600 over the next 20 years. Industry analysts expected this market to be worth about US$9 billion by the year 2003, and new players like the recently formed U.S.-German partnership

Fairchild Dornier were targeting Bombardier's position.[5] However, Bombardier was the market leader in this segment and had no real competitive challenge to its position until the emergence of Embraer.

EMBRAER

Founded in 1969, Empresa Brasileira de Aeronautica S.A. (Embraer) was a state-owned company until it was privatized in 1994, and was located in Sao Jose dos Campos, Brazil. Although it was a publicly held company, the majority of the shares were owned by the following consortium of institutional investors:

- **Bozano Simonsen Group**: among the largest financial conglomerates in Brazil, also in mining, real estate, industry and agriculture. Pool of 41 companies, directly or indirectly controlled.
- **Previ—Banco do Brazil Pension Fund**: first pension fund in Brazil, 145,000 associates with reserves of US$12 billion (25 per cent of Brazilian pension fund system). Portfolio of around 90 companies.
- **Sistel—Telebras Social Security Foundation**: second largest pension fund in Brazil, serving all employees of all government-owned telecommunication companies. Capital of over US$2.7 billion.[6]

Since 1969, Embraer had produced and sold over 5,100 aircraft for civilian and military customers worldwide. Embraer's product line, which was comprised of six different aircraft, included turboprops, jets, attack and training aircraft. The company was one of the major consumers of imported aerospace equipment and parts in its assembly process. Exhibit 2 presents financial statements for Embraer.

The bulk of Embraer's non-military sales came from the ERJ-145, a 50-seat regional jet, of which Embraer sold 120 in 1997,[7] and the newer ERJ-135, a 37-seat jet. These planes were comparable to Bombardier's jets and had been quite successful in stealing market share from them. An example of this market share gain, which was particularly upsetting to Bombardier,

BOMBARDIER INC. CONSOLIDATED STATEMENT OF INCOME FOR THE YEARS ENDING JANUARY 31, 1998 AND 1997 (millions of Canadian dollars)

	1998	1997
Revenues	$8,508.9	$7,975.7
Expenses		
Cost of sales and operating expenses	7,614.9	7,137.3
Depreciation and amortization	180.1	106.8
Interest expense	86.7	66.3
Income from BC	—	—
	7,881.7	7369.4
Income before income taxes	627.2	606.3
Income taxes	207	200.1
Net income	**420.2**	**406.2**
Earnings per share		
Basic	$1.18	$1.18
Fully diluted	$1.17	$1.16
Average number of shares outstanding during the year	338,270,503	336,082,947

BOMBARDIER INC., CONSOLIDATED BALANCE SHEET AS AT JANUARY 31, 1998 AND 1997 (millions of Canadian dollars)

	1998	1997
Assets		
Cash and term deposits	$1,227.7	$895.7
Accounts receivable	693.2	358.4
Finance receivables and other	2,969.4	1,811.4
Inventories	3,790.9	3,455.2
Investment in BC	—	—
Other assets	227.3	229.6
	$10,575.2	**$7,950.3**
Liabilities		
Short-term borrowings	$2,265.5	$1,402.4
Accounts payable and accrued liabilities	2,663.0	2,124.6
Advances and progress billings in excess of related costs	851.6	691.4
Long-term debt	1,548.7	1,354.9
Other liabilities	357	264.4
	7,685.9	5,737.7
Shareholders' equity (investment in BC)	2,889.3	2,212.6
	$10,575.2	**$7,950.3**

Exhibit 1   Bombardier Inc. Consolidated Statement of Income for the Years Ending January 31, 1998 and 1997 (millions of Canadian dollars)

Source: Bombardier Web site, http://www.bombardier.com/rapport98/htmen/9_1.htm, and http://www.bombardier.com/rapport98/htmen/9_3.htm, December 1998.

**CONSOLIDATED STATEMENTS OF INCOME FOR THE NINE MONTHS
ENDED SEPTEMBER 30, 1998 AND 1997 (stated in thousands of Brazilian reals)[1]**

	1998	1997
Net sales	1,099,817	824,070
Cost of sales	(791,345)	(603,789)
Gross profit	**308,472**	**220,281**
Operating expenses		
Administrative	(36,307)	(40,007)
Selling	(75,963)	(64,648)
Other (net)	(49,322)	(84,176)
Income (loss) from operations before financial expenses	**146,880**	**31,450**
Financial expenses	(51,454)	(90,942)
Financial income	25,478	5,926
Income (loss) from operations after financial expense	120,904	(53,566)
Non-operating expense	(5,914)	(7,471)
Income (loss) before tax	114,990	(61,037)
Provision for tax	(30,700)	(186)
Employee profit sharing	(6,395)	—
Extraordinary items		
Amortization of deferred charges		(84,000)
Income and social contribution tax benefits on tax loss carry forwards		112,183
Net income (loss)	**77,895**	**(33,040)**

**CONSOLIDATED BALANCE SHEETS—SEPTEMBER 30, 1998, 1997
(stated in thousands of Brazilian reals)**

	1998	1997
ASSETS		
Current assets		
Case and case equivalents	190,309	104,442
Trade receivables	142,507	74,479
Inventories	560,947	367,367
Prepaid expenses	10,471	8,293
Other receivables	35,957	25,935
	940,191	**580,525**

Exhibit 2   Embraer-Empresa Brasileira de Aeronautica S.A. and Subsidiaries   *(Continued)*

Non-current assets		
Trade receivables	9,052	21,514
Compulsory loans	7,555	7,173
Other receivables	36,851	12,113
Tax loss carry forward credits	87,605	112,183
	141,063	152,983
Permanent assets		
Investments	248	148
Property, plant and equipment	293,845	300,901
Deferred charges	388,883	389,959
	682,976	691,008
Total assets	**1,764,230**	**1,424,516**
LIABILITIES AND SHAREHOLDERS' EQUITY		
Current liabilities		
Suppliers	243,848	251,818
Loans	408,079	190,063
Taxes and social charges payable	22,355	30,661
Dealers and sales agents	4,201	3,867
Customers' advances	157,567	173,701
Accrued liabilities	47,271	29,544
Accounts payable	48,359	22,191
Dividends	21,316	—
	952,996	701,845
Non-current liabilities		
Loans	151,099	130,745
Financed taxes and social charges	54,841	78,399
Customers' advances	119,560	76,408
Accrued liabilities	61,580	72,842
Accounts payable	48,359	14,206
Other	11,868	8,077
	412,905	380,677
Deferred income	669	914
Shareholders' equity		
Capital	354,619	1,925,081
Capital reserves	—	29,782
Accumulated deficit	—	(1,613,783)
Retained earnings	43,041	—
Total liabilities and shareholders equity	**1,764,230**	**1,424,516**

Exhibit 2   Embraer-Empresa Brasileira de Aeronautica S.A. and Subsidiaries

Source: Embraer Web site, http://www.embraer.com, December 1998.

1. From the EIU Report for Brazil, 4th Quarter: Exchange rate as of November 25, 1998 R1.20 = US$1. All figures are before the devaluation of the real in late 1998.

was the 1997 decision by the American regional airline, American Eagle, to split its 67 plane order between the two companies.

American Eagle initially ordered 25 CRJ-700s from Bombardier for Cdn$900 million, and wanted to purchase 42 additional CRJ-100s providing Bombardier would reduce the price by $3 million each in view of Embraer's low-cost financing. Bombardier refused and as a result the order went to Embraer.[8]

A CANCELLED BUSINESS TRANSACTION LEADS TO A TRADE DISPUTE

From early 1997, Embraer and Bombardier had been trading threats to bring a petition to the WTO about unfair subsidies from each other's government. However, neither had lodged a complaint with the WTO. The situation closely mirrored the dispute between The Boeing Company and Airbus Industrie, in the late 1980s and early 1990s, with a major difference being that the ownership group of Airbus Industrie included the French government.

In November 1997, Bombardier was awarded a $2.85-billion NATO training contract, which was awarded to Canada. The contract required Canada to train pilots for combat, and to do this state-of-the-art training aircraft were needed. It was the biggest military services contract in Canadian history, and it went, untendered, to Bombardier. Bombardier was then in charge of all the subcontracting for the project.

An amount of US$90 million was set aside for the purchase of 24 units of a specific type of training aircraft, the kind of which Embraer was one of the world leaders in production. According to a report by the BBC:

> Embraer was one of the companies preselected for the program. Bombardier hinted to the Brazilian company that it would win the bidding. Bombardier even encouraged Embraer to make some changes to the project. Thus, the Brazilian government and diplomats were surprised when the Canadian firm announced that it would purchase the planes from Raytheon (an American company) for "technical reasons."[9]

The Brazilian government and Embraer were not impressed, and the foreign ministry issued a statement in which it announced that the government was set to "review all Canadian aeronautics industry projects in Brazil and to carry out consultations with its Mercosur (Common Market of the South) to suspend the negotiations for a Canada-Mercosur trade agreement."[10]

The Canadian response was one of concern since Prime Minister Jean Chrétien and a team of Canadian business people were to visit Brazil in January 1998. Brazil suggested the creation of a task force, which would analyse the situation and make recommendations. Headed by former Canadian cabinet minister, Marc Lalonde, and Brazilian Luis Olavio Baptista, a report was presented in May 1998.

The report called for negotiations "aimed at setting a benchmark for judging government funding of aircraft manufacturing and export sales based on the final price of the aircraft"[11] rather than using the current complex system of non-transparent subsidies. Brazil was to agree to not use the PROEX program in an "abusive manner," and Canada was to refrain from starting any new programs that would not be in the spirit of the proposed new agreement. Both countries would be closely audited by an independent monitor.[12]

Both countries rejected the recommendations of the report and later that autumn, official trade disputes were filed with the WTO by both Canada and Brazil.

TRADE REGULATIONS AND GOVERNMENT INTERVENTION

Since a commercial aircraft industry was of such a value to a nation's economy, governments were eager to protect the industry, but proponents of free trade were eager to ensure fair competition globally. International agreements created some limited disciplines on government intervention. For example, the 1979 Civil Aircraft Agreement on Tariffs and Trade under the General Agreement on Tariffs and Trade (GATT), and later the WTO, eliminated tariff barriers between signatories on civil aircraft product. (Exhibit 3 presents the text of the first three amendments to the WTO, which describe some of the restricted practices.) Many aspiring aerospace nations, including Brazil, were not signatories to the 1979 agreement. Signatories to the agreements used national security exceptions to impose domestic content requirements on (primarily military) government procurements and to provide direct financial assistance to the industry. Yet, financial assistance for producing military aircraft would give Embraer a competitive advantage in its pricing of civilian aircraft. Furthermore, domestic content regulations would deprive Canadian first- and second-tier suppliers of potential sales, thereby weakening Canada's "cluster" of aircraft corporations.

What Was the WTO?

Beginning January 1, 1995, the WTO officially replaced the GATT as the world's largest and most comprehensive multilateral trading system. The WTO was formed from the Uruguay Round of trade negotiations, which lasted from 1986 to 1994.

The WTO was the only international body that dealt with the rules of trade between countries for not only goods, but also services, traded inventions, creations and designs. The agreements defined by the WTO were negotiated and ratified by nearly all the world's trading nations. They were "essentially contracts, binding governments to keep their trade policies within agreed limits."[13]

There were three main purposes of the WTO:

1. Facilitate trade flow: The agreements tried to make trade flow as freely as possible, so long as there were no undesirable side effects. This involved the removal of obstacles and the education of governments and individuals about trade rules. The establishment of defined practices gave companies confidence that the rules would not be arbitrarily changed.

2. Serve as a forum for trade negotiations: New trade agreements that were not global in scope, but between two or more nations, could be negotiated within a known and accepted framework.

3. Dispute settlement: Conflicting interests could be worked out in a specified manner within a process written into the WTO agreement and, thus, based on an agreed legal framework.

CANADA AND BRAZIL: TRADING ACCUSATIONS

Bombardier's Attack

At the centre of the Canadian government's complaint to the WTO was Brazil's *Programma de Financiamento as Exportações* (PROEX), which was implemented in 1986 to foster Brazil's export market. As a developing economy, under WTO regulations, Brazil was allowed to compensate for its "country risk," the risk its relatively unstable economy presented investors. This risk effectively raised the cost of financing in Brazil since interest rates had to be higher to attract investors. PROEX was designed to "pay back" a portion of the risk premium added to financing costs through a government fund administered by the Government Unit of Banco do Brazil. By equalizing the interest rates, firms that were buying goods from Brazil were encouraged to obtain financing for their purchases within Brazil rather than looking outside the country.

The Brazilian newspaper *Gazeta Mercantil Invest News* described PROEX by saying that:

> Exporters have the right to use the two options: the financing, in up to 85 per cent of the funds originating from the Treasury, and also the equalization of interest rates in which the Treasury pays a part of the interest rates on loans taken out by exporters with commercial banks, at a rate varying between two and 3.8 per cent per year, depending on the merchandise and the length of time for the financing. The possibility of using equalization of interest rates over external funding brings the added benefit of reducing the cost of money to the exporter.[14]

Bombardier and the Canadian government felt that this was an unfair subsidy, which ran counter to the regulations of the WTO and the

(Text continues on page 382)

Members hereby *agree* as follows:

PART I: GENERAL PROVISIONS
Article 1
Definition of a Subsidy

1.1   For the purpose of this Agreement, a subsidy shall be deemed to exist if:

(a)   (1)   there is a financial contribution by a government or any public body within the territory of a Member (referred to in this Agreement as "government"), i.e. where:

   (i)   a government practice involves a direct transfer of funds (e.g. grants, loans, and equity infusion), potential direct transfers of funds or liabilities (e.g. loan guarantees);

   (ii)   government revenue that is otherwise due is foregone or not collected (e.g. fiscal incentives such as tax credits);[2]

   (iii)   a government provides goods or services other than general infrastructure, or purchases goods;

   (iv)   a government makes payments to a funding mechanism, or entrusts or directs a private body to carry out one or more of the type of functions illustrated in (i) to (iii) above which would normally be vested in the government and the practice, in no real sense, differs from practices normally followed by governments;

or

(2)   there is any form of income or price support in the sense of Article XVI of GATT 1994;

and

(b)   a benefit is thereby conferred.

1.2   A subsidy as defined in paragraph 1 shall be subject to the provisions of Part II or shall be subject to the provisions of Part III or V only if such a subsidy is specific in accordance with the provisions of Article 2.

Article 2
Specificity

2.1   In order to determine whether a subsidy, as defined in paragraph 1 of Article 1, is specific to an enterprise or industry or group of enterprises or industries (referred to in this Agreement as "certain enterprises") within the jurisdiction of the granting authority, the following principles shall apply:

(a)   Where the granting authority, or the legislation pursuant to which the granting authority operates, explicitly limits access to a subsidy to certain enterprises, such subsidy shall be specific.

(b)   Where the granting authority, or the legislation pursuant to which the granting authority operates, establishes objective criteria or conditions[3] governing the eligibility for, and the amount of, a subsidy, specificity shall not exist, provided that the eligibility is automatic and that such criteria and conditions are strictly adhered to. The criteria or conditions must be clearly spelled out in law, regulation, or other official document, so as to be capable of verification.

(c)   If, notwithstanding any appearance of non-specificity resulting from the application of the principles laid down in subparagraphs (a) and (b), there are reasons to believe that the subsidy may in fact be specific, other factors may be considered. Such factors are: use of a subsidy

---

Exhibit 3   Agreement on Subsidies and Countervailing Measures[1]   *(Continued)*

(c) programme by a limited number of certain enterprises, predominant use by certain enterprises, the granting of disproportionately large amounts of subsidy to certain enterprises, and the manner in which discretion has been exercised by the granting authority in the decision to grant a subsidy.[4] In applying this subparagraph, account shall be taken of the extent of diversification of economic activities within the jurisdiction of the granting authority, as well as of the length of time during which the subsidy programme has been in operation.

2.2 A subsidy which is limited to certain enterprises located within a designated geographical region within the jurisdiction of the granting authority shall be specific. It is understood that the setting or change of generally applicable tax rates by all levels of government entitled to do so shall not be deemed to be a specific subsidy for the purposes of this Agreement.

2.3 Any subsidy falling under the provisions of Article 3 shall be deemed to be specific.

2.4 Any determination of specificity under the provisions of this Article shall be clearly substantiated on the basis of positive evidence.

PART II: PROHIBITED SUBSIDIES
Article 3
Prohibition

3.1 Except as provided in the Agreement on Agriculture, the following subsidies, within the meaning of Article 1, shall be prohibited:

(a) subsidies contingent, in law or in fact,[5] whether solely or as one of several other conditions, upon export performance, including those illustrated in Annex I,[6]

(b) subsidies contingent, whether solely or as one of several other conditions, upon the use of domestic over imported goods.

3.2 A Member shall neither grant nor maintain subsidies referred to in paragraph 1.

ANNEX I

ILLUSTRATIVE LIST OF EXPORT SUBSIDIES

(a) The provision by governments of direct subsidies to a firm or an industry contingent upon export performance.

(b) Currency retention schemes or any similar practices which involve a bonus on exports.

(c) Internal transport and freight charges on export shipments, provided or mandated by governments, on terms more favourable than for domestic shipments.

(d) The provision by governments or their agencies either directly or indirectly through government-mandated schemes, of imported or domestic products or services for use in the production of exported goods, on terms or conditions more favourable than for provision of like or directly competitive products or services for use in the production of goods for domestic consumption, if (in the case of products) such terms or conditions are more favourable than those commercially available[7] on world markets to their exporters.

Exhibit 3   Agreement on Subsidies and Countervailing Measures[1]   *(Continued)*

(e)   The full or partial exemption remission, or deferral specifically related to exports, of direct taxes. The term "direct taxes" shall mean taxes on wages, profits, interests, rents, royalties, and all other forms of income, and taxes on the ownership of real property; The term "import charges" shall mean tariffs, duties, and other fiscal charges not elsewhere enumerated in this note that are levied on imports; The term "indirect taxes" shall mean sales, excise, turnover, value added, franchise, stamp, transfer, inventory and equipment taxes, border taxes and all taxes other than direct taxes and import charges; "Prior-stage" indirect taxes are those levied on goods or services used directly or indirectly in making the product; "Cumulative" indirect taxes are multi-staged taxes levied where there is no mechanism for subsequent crediting of the tax if the goods or services subject to tax at one stage of production are used in a succeeding stage of production; "Remission" of taxes includes the refund or rebate of taxes "Remission or drawback" includes the full or partial exemption or deferral of import charges or social welfare charges paid or payable by industrial or commercial enterprises.[8] Paragraph (e) is not intended to limit a Member from taking measures to avoid the double taxation of foreign-source income earned by its enterprises or the enterprises of another Member.

(f)   The allowance of special deductions directly related to exports or export performance, over and above those granted in respect to production for domestic consumption, in the calculation of the base on which direct taxes are charged.

(g)   The exemption or remission, in respect of the production and distribution of exported products, of indirect taxes in excess of those levied in respect of the production and distribution of like products when sold for domestic consumption.

(h)   The exemption, remission or deferral of prior-stage cumulative indirect taxes on goods or services used in the production of exported products in excess of the exemption, remission or deferral of like prior-stage cumulative indirect taxes on goods or services used in the production of like products when sold for domestic consumption; provided, however, that prior-stage cumulative indirect taxes may be exempted, remitted or deferred on exported products even when not exempted, remitted or deferred on like products when sold for domestic consumption, if the prior-stage cumulative indirect taxes are levied on inputs that are consumed in the production of the exported product (making normal allowance for waste).[9] This item shall be interpreted in accordance with the guidelines on consumption of inputs in the production process contained in Annex II.

(i)   The remission or drawback of import charges in excess of those levied on imported inputs that are consumed in the production of the exported product (making normal allowance for waste); provided, however, that in particular cases a firm may use a quantity of home market inputs equal to, and having the same quality and characteristics as, the imported inputs as a substitute for them in order to benefit from this provision if the import and the corresponding export operations both occur within a reasonable time period, not to exceed two years. This item shall be interpreted in accordance with the guidelines on consumption of inputs in the production process contained in Annex II and the guidelines in the determination of substitution drawback systems as export subsidies contained in Annex III.

(j)   The provision by governments (or special institutions controlled by governments) of export credit guarantee or insurance programmes, of insurance or guarantee programmes against increases in the cost of exported products or of exchange risk programmes, at premium rates which are inadequate to cover the long-term operating costs and losses of the programmes.

Exhibit 3   Agreement on Subsidies and Countervailing Measures[1]   *(Continued)*

(k) The grant by governments (or special institutions controlled by and/or acting under the authority of governments) of export credits at rates below those which they actually have to pay for the funds so employed (or would have to pay if they borrowed on international capital markets in order to obtain funds of the same maturity and other credit terms and denominated in the same currency as the export credit), or the payment by them of all or part of the costs incurred by exporters or financial institutions in obtaining credits, in so far as they are used to secure a material advantage in the field of export credit terms.

Provided, however, that if a Member is a party to an international undertaking on official export credits to which at least twelve original Members to this Agreement are parties as of 1 January 1979 (or a successor undertaking which has been adopted by those original Members), or if in practice a Member applies the interest rates provisions of the relevant undertaking, an export credit practice which is in conformity with those provisions shall not be considered an export subsidy prohibited by this Agreement.

(l) Any other charge on the public account constituting an export subsidy in the sense of Article XVI of GATT 1994.

Exhibit 3   Agreement on Subsidies and Countervailing Measures[1]

Notes:

1. *Source:* http://www.wto.org/wto/legal/finalact.htm#subsidies, 25/01/99.
2. In accordance with the provisions of Article XVI of GATT 1994 (Note to Article XVI) and the provisions of Annexes I through III of this Agreement, the exemption of an exported product from duties or taxes borne by the like product when destined for domestic consumption, or the remission of such duties or taxes in amounts not in excess of those which have accrued, shall not be deemed to be a subsidy.
3. Objective criteria or conditions, as used herein, mean criteria or conditions which are neutral, which do not favour certain enterprises over others, and which are economic in nature and horizontal in application, such as number of employees or size of enterprise.
4. In this regard, in particular, information on the frequency with which applications for a subsidy are refused or approved and the reasons for such decisions shall be considered.
5. This standard is met when the facts demonstrate that the granting of a subsidy, without having been made legally contingent upon export performance, is in fact tied to actual or anticipated exportation or export earnings. The mere fact that a subsidy is granted to enterprises which export shall not for that reason alone be considered to be an export subsidy within the meaning of this provision.
6. Measures referred to in Annex I as not constituting export subsidies shall not be prohibited under this or any other provision of this Agreement.
7. The term "commercially available" means that the choice between domestic and imported products is unrestricted and depends only on commercial considerations.
8. The Members recognize that deferral need not amount to an export subsidy where, for example, appropriate interest charges are collected. The Members reaffirm the principle that prices for goods in transactions between exporting enterprises and foreign buyers under their or under the same control should for tax purposes be the prices which would be charged between independent enterprises acting at arm's length. Any Member may draw the attention of another Member to administrative or other practices which may contravene this principle and which result in a significant saving of direct taxes in export transactions. In such circumstances the Members shall normally attempt to resolve their differences using the facilities of existing bilateral tax treaties or other specific international mechanisms, without prejudice to the rights and obligations of Members under GATT 1994, including the right of consultation created in the preceding sentence.
9. Paragraph (h) does not apply to value-added tax systems and border-tax adjustment in lieu thereof; the problem of the excessive remission of value-added taxes is exclusively covered by paragraph (g).

Organization for Economic Co-operation and Development (to which Brazil was not a signatory). Exhibit 4 presents a summary of the Canadian case to the WTO.

The PROEX program was not singularly applied to the commercial aircraft industry, it covered thousands of products, however, Bombardier claimed that PROEX had created subsidies to that industry of nearly US$2.5 billion in the last two years alone. Bombardier claimed that the PROEX interest equalization was being applied to firms that were obtaining financing *outside* of Brazil and, thus, amounted to a subsidy of roughly US$4.3 million over the standard 15-year financing period,[15] or US$2 million off the purchase price.[16] Considering that the Embraer jets were priced at nearly US$4 million lower than Bombardier's CRJ-100 series, this was a major advantage. Bombardier believed that the PROEX subsidy was worth about US$100 million to American Eagle and cost Bombardier millions in lost revenue.[17]

Embraer's Defence and Retaliation

"It is a way of levelling interest rates, to decrease the Brazil risk," explained Embraer vice-president Frederico Curado. Mr. Curado stated that the PROEX program allowed Embraer to provide financing at rates ranging from two to 3.8 per cent per year lower than the normal financing rates through Brazilian banks. He further contended that although the PROEX program did lower interest rates, they were still higher than the average cost of financing in Canada, which he claimed was 2.7 per cent at the same point in time.[18]

It was the contention of both Embraer and the Brazilian government that since the economy was classified as "developing," the interest rate equalization was within WTO regulations. In an interview with a trade magazine, Embraer CEO Mauricio Botelho explained further:

Brazil is an emerging country, a country on which financial institutions and the international markets place risk perceptions. This risk perception represents the establishment of a spread on any finance involved with Brazil or with Brazilian companies. And this spread represents a burden on us in anything we do with respect to financing our exports, or guaranteeing a refusal value, or a remarketing agreement. It is defined by subjective perceptions of risk imposed by developed countries on emerging countries. So, there is unfair competition in the international markets where we have to face this threat.[19]

Botelho was very direct in his rebuttal to Bombardier's accusations in a press release from Embraer:

The Government of Canada has poured billions of dollars into Bombardier in the last five years. We can compete with Bombardier and its aircraft, but it isn't fair to expect us to compete with the Treasury of the Canadian government. Canada's exporting finance subsidies and several other direct and indirect development and production subsidies worth several billion dollars contribute to reduce Bombardier's production costs.[20]

The company went on to describe five distinct "operations and mechanisms," which they felt were direct and indirect subsidies:

a. Use of the so-called Canada Account, a fund not subject to public debate, used to support export transactions, where the Canadian government, acting on behalf of its national interest, operates where the Export Development Corporation cannot do it, either by the size or risk of the operation;

b. Unrefundable financing and zero-cost loan guarantee provided by the Export Development Corporation;

c. Current and previous programs of TPC—Technology Partnerships Canada—which is the major source of subsidies to the Canadian aerospace industry, through the creation of funds for aircraft design and manufacture;

d. Benefits provided by the Quebec government;

e. Financing to Research and Development through the Defense Productivity Program, which has been replaced by interest-free loans and not refundable TPC, for unspecific times.[21]

On July 10, 1998, Canada requested that a WTO Panel be established to examine Brazil's PROEX program. PROEX reduces the interest rate on financing for Brazilian aircraft by 3.8 percentage points. Canada has argued that PROEX is an export subsidy.

In response to Canada's challenge of PROEX, Brazil has challenged a range of Canadian programs, including export financing by the Export Development Corporation, and Industry Canada support for research and development. Brazil also requested that a WTO Panel be established to examine the Canadian measures.

The two panels were named on October 22, 1998 and will run on parallel timetables, with both panel reports due in early March 1999. The Panel members are as follows:

Brazil—Export Financing Programme for Aircraft:

Dariusz Rosati (Poland)—Chair
Akio Shimizu (Japan) and Kajit Sukhum (Thailand)

Canada—Measures Affecting the Export of Civilian Aircraft:

David de Pury (Switzerland)—Chair
Maamoun Abdel Fattah (Egypt) and Dencho Georgiev (Bulgaria)

Panel Schedules for the cases are as follows:

1998	*Brazilian Programme*	*Canadian Programmes*
Nov. 3	First Submission of Canada	First Submission of Brazil
Nov. 16	First Submission of Brazil	First Submission of Canada
Nov. 23–24	Hearing	
Nov. 25–26		Hearing
Dec. 4	Written Rebuttals	Written Rebuttals
Dec. 12		Hearing
Dec. 14	Hearing	
1999		
March 5	Final Report	Final Report
		Canada's submissions
		to these two Panels were
		developed in consultation with
		the provinces and private
		sector stakeholders.

A Summary of Canada's Submission in the Case Against the Brazilian PROEX Programme

At issue in this dispute is whether the Programa de Financiamento às Exportações (PROEX), the export financing support programme of Brazil, confers export subsidies on sales of Brazilian regional aircraft that are prohibited under Article 3 of the *the Agreement on Subsidies and Countervailing Measures* (SCM Agreement).

Canada will show that payments made by the Government of Brazil under the "Interest Equalisation" component of PROEX on export sales of Brazilian regional aircraft constitute subsidies within the meaning of Article 1. Canada will further prove that such subsidies are contingent on export performance and are therefore prohibited by Article 3.

PROEX payments are financial contributions by the Government of Brazil that, in the case of exported Brazilian aircraft, reduce the cost of such aircraft to the purchaser. The purchaser (for example, an airline) may receive these payments in one of two ways. First, PROEX payments may be used to lower the rate of interest paid by a purchaser by up to 3.8 percentage points per year. The net benefit conferred on a purchaser as a result of such an interest rate reduction can amount to as much as half of the total interest that would be payable by a purchaser in the absence of the payments. Second, a purchaser may, instead, receive these payments in the form of a lump-sum payment that reduces the cost of the aircraft by at least 13 to 15 percent.

Exhibit 4   Canada/Brazil WTO Panels—Aircraft[1]   *(Continued)*

The payments are made even where the financing is done by a non-Brazilian entity. The payments are made even in circumstances where the purchaser borrows funds, at commercial rates based on its own credit-worthiness, from non-Brazilian creditors in financial markets outside of Brazil. The payments are made even where elements of the financing are guaranteed by non-Brazilian multinational corporations. The payments are not made in return for any goods or services. The payments are never repaid and are not required to be repaid. The payments operate directly to increase the exports of Brazilian regional aircraft.

In short, in the regional aircraft market, PROEX payments are grants tied to the purchase of Brazilian regional aircraft exports. Such grants are subsidies within the meaning of Article 1. As they are contingent on export performance, these grants constitute prohibited subsidies within the meaning of Article 3. PROEX subsidies to Brazilian regional aircraft have resulted in serious distortions in the regional aircraft market—the market for jet and turboprop aircraft that have between 20 and 90 seats. The significant reduction in the cost of Brazilian regional jet aircraft in a highly competitive market has resulted in a five-fold increase in the market share of exported Brazilian regional aircraft over the past two years and the displacement of not only other regional jet aircraft, but also turboprop aircraft in the market.

In view of the damage caused by PROEX subsidies, Canada brought this matter to the attention of Brazil two years ago and attempted to resolve it through negotiation, both within and outside the framework of the WTO dispute settlement mechanism. Despite expressions of concern by Canada and other members of the WTO, Brazil has, contrary to Article 3.2, continued to grant and maintain such prohibited subsidies.

Further, Brazil has done nothing to phase out these export subsidies. Indeed, it has expanded the scope and availability of PROEX subsidies. It has progressively increased expenditures under PROEX, both generally and more specifically with respect to regional aircraft. It has increased the value of the financing to which PROEX subsidies apply from 85 percent to 100 percent of the purchase amount. It has, in practice, waived Brazilian content requirements and increased the period in which PROEX subsidies are available from ten to fifteen years. It has increased the term for which PROEX subsidies are available for spare parts and engines for regional aircraft. Finally, it has made PROEX subsidies available as lump-sum grants and therefore more attractive to purchasers.

Canada seeks a resolution of this matter before the WTO that will put an end to the serious market distortions caused by PROEX subsidies. Canada seeks a finding that payments made under PROEX on export sales of Brazilian regional aircraft constitute export subsidies prohibited by Article 3. Canada requests that the panel recommend, in accordance with Article 4.7, that Brazil withdraw without delay PROEX subsidies granted under the "Interest Equalization" component of PROEX.

A Summary of Canada's Submission in Defense of Canadian Programmes

In this dispute, Brazil alleges that Canada grants or maintains an extensive array of subsidies for the Canadian industry producing civil aircraft which are inconsistent with Canada's obligations under Article 3.1(a) and Article 3.2 of the Subsidies Agreement. Canada submits that this allegation is false.

Brazil proceeds under the expedited process of Article 4 of the *Agreement on Subsidies and Countervailing Measures* (SCM Agreement) and seeks a remedy for one kind of violation only: the alleged inconsistency of certain Canadian programmes, activities and transactions with the prohibition on export subsidies in Article 3.

Brazil has challenged a large number of disparate programmes, activities and transactions. Brazil's interpretations of the legal provisions in question are not based on the principles of treaty interpretation in customary international law. Brazil's case rests on inaccurate facts and unsupported assumptions. Canada notes that Brazil, as the complainant, has the responsibility of establishing its claims. To do so in this case with respect to each of the impugned Canadian programmes, activities, and transactions, Brazil must demonstrate two distinct and necessary elements:

i)   that as a result of that programme, transaction or activity, a subsidy exists (SCM Agreement Article 1); and

ii) that the subsidy is contingent, in law or in fact, upon export performance (SCM Agreement Article 3).

Exhibit 4   Canada/Brazil WTO Panels—Aircraft[1]   *(Continued)*

If Brazil fails to demonstrate either one of the two necessary elements, its allegations must be dismissed. Canada submits, therefore, that it is enough for Canada to show, in respect of each impugned programme, activity or transaction, that Brazil has failed to demonstrate inconsistency with either one or the other condition. Similarly, in accordance with the principle of judicial economy, if the Panel finds that Brazil has not demonstrated its claim with respect to either prong of the test, it is not necessary to enter upon an enquiry in respect of the other element of the test; that is, it is not necessary for the Panel to determine whether the impugned programmes, activities or transactions are subsidies, if it finds that they are not contingent upon export performance.

Indeed, given the accelerated time-frame of the Article 4 process, the Panel should address only those claims that must be addressed in order to resolve the matters at issue.

Canada will demonstrate that Brazil's interpretation of Article 3 of the SCM Agreement is not consistent with the ordinary meaning of its terms, read in the light of its context and the object and purpose of the SCM Agreement. Moreover, without admitting that the following programmes, activities or transactions challenged by Brazil constitute subsidies within the meaning of Article 1, Canada requests that this Panel find that the following programmes, activities or transactions are not contingent upon export performance, and therefore the requirements of the second element of Brazil's case are not met: Technology Partnerships Canada (TPC), the sale of de Havilland by the Government of Ontario, benefits under the Canada-Québec Subsidiary Agreement on Industrial Development (the Subsidiary Agreement) and benefits under the *Société de Développement Industriel du Québec* (SDI). Canada will show that Brazil has failed to demonstrate the inconsistency of these programmes, activities or transactions with Article 3 of the SCM Agreement. More specifically, Canada will demonstrate that:

1. TPC contributions by the Canadian Department of Industry are made for research and development projects with respect to enabling technologies (technological developments cutting across manufacturing sectors to increase productivity), environmental technologies (technologies developed, in any industrial or agricultural sector, for the protection of the environment), and aerospace and defence. TPC contributions are not, in law or in fact, contingent upon export performance: contributions are not made on condition that exports take place, there are no penalties if no exports take place and repayment is not reduced if exports are made.

2. On January 28, 1997, the Government of Ontario exercised its option, agreed to by Ontario and Bombardier Inc., a Canadian aircraft manufacturer, to sell its 50 percent interest in de Havilland, a manufacturer of turboprops and aircraft parts, for C$49 million. Bombardier agreed, in return, to maintain de Havilland operating as a manufacturer of aircraft and aircraft parts in accordance with commercial considerations. The sale price was paid in the form of a promissory note from Bombardier to Ontario; Bombardier has already made its first interest payments on the note. The sale was in no way contingent upon export performance: the sale price will not increase if there are no exports and will not be reduced if exports are increased.

3. The Subsidiary Agreement was entered into on March 31, 1992 by the Governments of Canada and Québec for a period of five years, subject to a one-year extension. It expired on March 31, 1998. Contributions under the Subsidiary Agreement were intended to increase the competitiveness of Quebec's economy and were available for domestic as well as export projects. These contributions were in no way contingent upon export performance.

4. The SDI is a generally available programme of the Government of Québec aimed at improving the competitiveness of Québec's economy. Loans, loan guarantees and repayable contributions are available for domestic projects as well as projects related to exportation out of the province of Québec (to the other provinces of Canada as well as to other countries). These contributions are in no way contingent upon export performance.

Exhibit 4   Canada/Brazil WTO Panels—Aircraft[1]   *(Continued)*

Canada further requests that this Panel find that Canada Account and Export Development Corporation (EDC) financing in the civil aircraft sector are not inconsistent with Article 3. More specifically, Canada will demonstrate that:

1. Brazil's portrayal of EDC activities is both inaccurate and incomplete. The EDC operates on commercial principles. The financial transactions it enters into are based on commercial pricing practices. Such activities, conducted on the corporate account of the EDC, are not subsidies and are therefore not inconsistent with Article 3. (EDC corporate account financing or other activity is referred to in this Submission as EDC financing or other activity.)

2. As an official export credit agency and agent in all respects for the Government of Canada, the EDC has a public policy function that it carries out while applying commercial disciplines and principles. It may also conduct financial activities that the Government may deem to be in the national interest; any obligations under such activities would be funded by the Government of Canada. (This is called the Canada Account; any activity conducted by the EDC under the Canada Account is referred to in this Submission as Canada Account activity.) The EDC conducts Canada Account activities in accordance with its broad mandate, prudent risk management and international export credit disciplines. Canada Account loans and loan guarantees on exports committed following the entry into force of the WTO Agreement are consistent with the interest rate provisions of the OECD Consensus and are therefore not inconsistent with Article 3.

3. Brazil's factual allegations with respect to loan guarantees, residual value guarantees and equity infusions by the EDC are not accurate. The EDC does not provide loan guarantees to supplement its financing activities. The EDC does not provide residual value guarantees in support of civil aircraft. The EDC does not make equity infusions into special purpose corporations that purchase and lease civil aircraft.

As the complaining Party, Brazil has the onus of establishing its claims. As it has not done so, its claims must fail.

Exhibit 4   Canada/Brazil WTO Panels—Aircraft[1]

1. *Source:* http://wwwdfait-maeci.gc.ca/english/trade/wto/wto_aircraft-e.htm 12/14/98, Department of Foreign Affairs and International Trade.

There was no denying that Bombardier had received significant assistance (both financial and otherwise) from the Canadian government. The question was: did this help constitute unfair trade practices.

- When Bombardier entered the aerospace industry, it did so by taking over Canadair for around $100 million after the federal government absorbed over US$1 billion in debt.
- In 1992, Bombardier paid less than US$40 million for de Havilland, saving thousands of jobs. The Ontario and federal governments agreed to provide over $400 million in subsidies.
- In 1994, Bombardier received an $18-million interest-free loan to expand its Canadair plant through the Canada-Quebec Agreement on Industrial Development.

- In October 1997, Ottawa agreed to lend Bombardier $87 million under the Technology Partnerships to help improve the fuel efficiency of the CRJ-700, and $57 million for the de Havilland DHC-8-400 in 1996.[22] The funds are repayable once a program becomes financially viable.
- Bombardier used the Export Development Corporation (EDC) to finance its sales with alleged low-interest loans, guarantees and equity infusions, which were sometimes significantly lower than market expectations. In 1995, then president of the EDC, Paul Labbe, said that the "EDC is happy if it earned inflation-level return on its assets and admitted that 'in the real world' it should be seeking a return between 13 and 20 per cent."[23] He later stated that "The Canada Account is for someone who is looking for financing below market prices."[24]

Awaiting the Decision

In November 1998, two official panels were set up to examine the protests of Canada and Brazil. The implications of their decisions would have important repercussions to the companies and countries involved but also to other countries around the world.

The company against whom the decision was made would likely have to increase the prices of its aircraft since it would be unable to rely on the government funding to which it was accustomed. An increase in price would affect the many options and backlogged orders both Bombardier and Embraer had on their books. Their costs, and, thus, selling prices, would increase by US$1 to $2 million, instantly giving the other party a double competitive advantage. This WTO decision would determine the structure of one of the most lucrative industries in the world. With few other competitors, the victor would gain nearly insurmountable market dominance.

Canada was struggling to diversify its economy from one which was mainly resource oriented, and Brazil was struggling to achieve stability in its economy. How should an extra-governmental organization weigh the scales? Since the aerospace industry was so vital for national competitiveness, other countries like Germany and the U.S. were concerned with the outcome.

NOTES

1. Dwyer, Rob, "Bombardier goes into battle," *Airfinance Journal,* October 1998.

2. This information comes from the Strategis Web site, http://strategis.ic.gc.ca/SSG/ad03051e.html, Sector Competitiveness Framework Series, Aircraft and aircraft parts. 12/23/98

3. Morton, Peter, "Bombardier dogfight could buffet Canada-Brazil talks," *The Financial Post,* December 6, 1997.

4. Came, Barry, "Sky King," *Maclean's,* August 11, 1997.

5. Leger, Kathryn, "Tough Guy on the Tarmac," *The Financial Post,* August 1, 1998.

6. "Embraer Update," Embraer Web site, http://www.embraer.com/ing/embhoje.htm, December 1998.

7. Morton, Peter, "Bombardier dogfight could buffet Canada-Brazil talks," *The Financial Post,* December 6, 1997.

8. Came, Barry, "Sky King," *Maclean's,* August 11, 1997.

9. "BBC Summary of World Broadcasts," December 30, 1997.

10. Ibid.

11. Morton, Peter, "No new subsidies, Brazil report says," *The Financial Post,* May 28, 1998.

12. Ibid.

13. WTO Web site: http://www.wto.org/wto/about/facts1.htm, December 1998.

14. Gazeta Mercantil Inc., May 4, 1998.

15. Morton, Peter, "Canada, Brazil make their cases to Geneva panel," *National Post,* November 4, 1998.

16. Shifrin, Carole A., "Canada-Brazil Dispute Returns to WTO," *Aviation Week & Space Technology,* July 20, 1998.

17. Morton, Peter, "Bombardier dogfight could buffet Canada-Brazil talks," *The Financial Post,* December 6, 1997.

18. Gazeta Mercantil Inc., July 23, 1998.

19. Lennane, Alexandra, "Champagne remains on ice," *Airfinance Journal,* September 1988.

20. Embraer Press Release, Sao Jose dos Campos, July 10, 1998.

21. Embraer Press Release, Sao Paulo, July 23, 1998.

22. Dwyer, Rob, "Bombardier goes into battle," *Airfinance Journal,* October 1998.

23. Ibid.

24. Ibid.

4

RESPONDING TO
SOCIETAL FORCES

The subject of ethics forms a central element in managerial responses to societal forces. In many situations, an individual must reach a personal decision in regard to what is the right thing to do. This component of the course encourages students to focus on principles that may help them when confronted by ethical dilemmas. In this process, the individual may look to philosophy or religious beliefs concerning what is right and wrong or may turn to history and laws for guidance. Some situations may require the student to consider resigning from the corporation or becoming a "whistle-blower" by going to law enforcement authorities. Alternatively, the student may decide that it would be best to attempt to change corporate decisions over time by working from within the organization.

The case of "John McCulloch—United Beef Packers" introduces this subject with a clear personal challenge in which McCulloch believes strongly that many corporate policies are wrong in an ethical or societal sense. The objective of profit maximization has led to exploitation of particularly vulnerable immigrant workers, whereas lax enforcement of product safety regulations has put consumers' health at risk. "NES China: Business Ethics" extends this discussion of ethics to national differences in generally accepted norms and values—in this case, concerning bribery. In the "Textron" case, management recognizes that to shift manufacturing facilities to China would reduce costs substantially, but that cost reduction would involve working conditions and labor standards grossly inferior to those in the United States. In considering these issues, students will find many helpful articles in the *Journal of Business Ethics* and the *Business Ethics Quarterly*. Thomas Donaldson (1996), in a *Harvard Business Review* article, has focused on culture relativism and the search for guiding principles when making decisions in countries whose norms and values differ from those in one's home country.

Recent years have seen a proliferation of academic articles and media commentary concerning "corporate social responsibility," with the search for consistent corporate positions on these issues. Many firms have sought to develop guidelines and formal statements that can assist employees when they confront ethical dilemmas. Management may look to such pronouncements rather than having to focus solely on personal evaluations of each issue. However, it is not easy for an organization to develop clear and useful pronouncements. Values, cultural behaviors, and even ethical standards differ significantly among countries. For some issues, such as those relating to social interaction, there may be a general acceptance of local norms. For certain issues, such as prohibitions against bribery of government officials, some firms attempt to enforce their home-country code of conduct globally while realizing that this could handicap their financial success; other firms adapt to local practices. In each country, managers need to understand such cross-cultural differences and consider what adjustments in corporate practices would be appropriate.

Recent years have also witnessed a proliferation of stakeholder groups who believe that their views should be incorporated into the decision-making process of the firm. Stakeholders may use a variety of mechanisms to influence corporate decisions. Laws and regulations, lobbying, media relationships, and boycotts all differ substantially among countries, and so the nature and power of stakeholders also differ. Confronted with this reality, students may find it helpful to develop a decision-making framework in which they delineate the stakeholders in a particular decision, seeking to understand their interests and power in the context of social norms. Students may discuss appropriate mechanisms for consultation with relevant stakeholders, in which they can better understand the objectives of each. Such an approach can be used to generate alternative courses of action that students can then compare, recognizing that they must differentiate between the short term and the long term in reaching their decisions. Short-term gains may well lead to expensive long-term costs. With many issues, stakeholder interests and strength will vary over time, requiring continual revisitation of corporate decisions.

Several subject areas have become particularly important as the focus for corporate social responsibility and stakeholder actions. Concerns about environmental pollution now cover a host of corporate activities. Investments in new technologies to reduce pollution may be expensive, and so investment decisions can also be affected by differences in environmental regulations and labor standards, as firms locate in countries with lower standards and/or lax enforcement. Alternatively, a firm's subsidiary in a country with low standards could decide to adhere to the higher levels required in economically advanced nations. Here the subject of ethics again enters the cross-country analysis of comparative costs. Examining such societal differences and their impacts on business draws students into ethical perspectives that might not be raised in a traditional course with a domestic focus. There is a concern that corporations may tend to invest in less developed countries because they have lower environmental standards. At the same time, air and water cross national boundaries, and so corporate pollution has increasingly become an international concern, with new international agreements creating new environmental regulations. From this perspective, corporate decisions may have to be based on expectations concerning future stakeholder and government actions rather than solely the current situation.

Government programs and policies are affected by societal pressures, and societal pressures may also affect a firm directly. Societal forces differ significantly among countries, and they change significantly over time. Corruption and human rights violations have become international concerns rather than just domestic issues and have led to new international agreements that seek to create common standards. For businesses, trade sanctions in response to human rights violations pose a recurring dilemma. The repressive violation of human rights has led people throughout the world to urge their governments to place embargoes on certain countries, placing a halt to trade and investment with them.

The current "antiglobalization debate" deserves consideration because many express the view that poverty and inequality have been exacerbated by the reduction of trade and investment barriers (Held & McGrew, 2002; Oestreich, 2002). Antiglobalization protestors blame corporations for exploiting less developed countries in their trade and investment decisions, and the "Planet Starbucks" case provides the context for a discussion concerning the validity and implications of this movement. This debate extends to the obligations that rich nations should accept in assisting poor nations in the development process, including criteria for foreign aid and debt forgiveness (Dragsbaek Schmidt & Hersh, 2000; Torres, 2001). This debate also extends to the appropriate role for international institutions, especially the International Monetary Fund (IMF) and World Bank (Stiglitz, 2002). Students have to make specific managerial decisions in the context of these societal forces.

Both shareholders and stakeholders look to boards of directors for leadership and corporate decision making in many of these societal issues. Consequently, the role and responsibilities of boards of directors have tended to increase in many countries. Meanwhile, with the extension of business activities internationally, board members face an increasingly complex array of information that they must understand and evaluate.

The recent proliferation of literature on corporate social responsibility and the role of boards of directors attracts considerable interest in the context of recent corporate scandals, as well as debates about appropriate corporate reporting (Bulik, 2002; Hartman, 2002; Hatcher, 2002; "Special Report," 2002). In examining the implications of these societal forces for management decisions, a key question is, "Whose decision is it?" For firms with branches in many countries, this question raises the allocation of responsibilities between local management and the head office. In many countries, governance practices have been changing significantly in recent years. For some societal issues, employees may have the right to participate in the decision process. The board of directors may feel that it should be the final decision maker with regard to certain societal issues, and the law may in fact require the board to bear responsibility (Grundfest, 1997; "Special Report," 2003; Stiles, 2001).

JOHN MCCULLOCH—UNITED BEEF PACKERS

John McCulloch took a job as assistant general manager at a meatpacking plant with a large number of immigrant workers. After a short time in the job, he discovered it was nothing like he expected; worker safety was constantly compromised, the safety of the public from consuming tainted food was compromised, and everything was subordinated to the production line's constant movement. He had to decide whether he would stay with the company.

NES CHINA: BUSINESS ETHICS (A) & (B)

NES was one of Germany's largest industrial manufacturing groups. The company wanted to set up a holding company to facilitate its manufacturing activities in China. It authorized representatives in its Beijing office to draw up the holding company application and to negotiate with the Chinese government for terms of this agreement. To maximize their chances of having their application accepted, the NES team in Beijing hired a government affairs coordinator who was a native Chinese and whose professional background had familiarized her with Chinese ways of doing business. NES's government affairs coordinator found herself in a difficult position when she proposed that gifts should be given to government officials to establish a working relationship that would improve NES's chance of having its application approved. This method of doing business was quite common in China. The other members of the NES team were shocked at what would be considered bribery and a criminal offence in their country. The complementary (B) case (9B01C030) gives a brief summary of the eventual solution to this problem.

TEXTRON LTD.

Textron Ltd. was a family-owned manufacturer of cotton and sponge fabricated items. The company wanted to expand its business with an offshore manufacturing enterprise that would fit with the company's policy of caring for its employees and providing quality products. The company was looking at two options: a guaranteed outsourcing purchase agreement or a joint venture. After several meetings with offshore alliance candidates, the vice president of the company had to analyze the cross-cultural differences to established corporate guidelines of global ethics and social responsibility that the company could use in its negotiations with a foreign manufacturing firm.

NOTE ON THE POLLUTION PROBLEM IN THE MEXICO-U.S. BORDER REGION

Many argue that the global expansion of capitalism threatens to create an environmental nightmare as countries compete to attract investment and generate growth, even at the cost of acting as "pollution havens" for foreign multinationals. Others point to the rising tide of environmental consciousness, along with more stringent regulations at the national and international levels, as heralding a new era of "sustainable development." Managers need to understand the various aspects of the issue to formulate and implement effective environmental strategies.

PLANET STARBUCKS (A)

The case details the history and development of the company, highlighting the evolution of the corporate concept of a "third place," and the key individuals in the organization in this development. The second part of the case details the international expansion activities of the firm, highlighting the potential cultural and economic challenges that it may increasingly face as it expands to more traditional coffee-drinking markets and low-income emerging markets. The third and final section of the case details the increasing pressure placed on Starbucks by the anti-globalization movement. Although Starbucks has actively pursued a number of socially responsible operating policies, such as the purchase of Fair-Trade coffee, the subsidization of health care facilities in Central America, and the introduction of a number of socially responsible coffee products in its stores, it continued to be the target of antiglobalization activities. Ultimately, the case is useful for debating whether a firm can be successful internationally employing a different strategy and structure than it employed in the construction of its already successful domestic business.

SIAM CANADIAN FOODS CO., LTD.

Although relatively undeveloped compared with the rest of Southeast Asia, Myanmar (Burma) had been experiencing increasing levels of foreign investment activity in recent years. Siam Canadian Foods, which had considered entering Myanmar (Burma) in the past but declined, needed to determine if the time was now appropriate to enter the market. This case introduces the issue of human rights violations and the imposition of trade sanctions in response to these.

ROYAL TRUSTCO

This case examines the role of the board of directors with regard to decisions that might jeopardize the future of the company. How should the board ensure that it is made aware of all necessary information, how should it analyze this information, how should it focus this analysis on the concrete issues facing the company, and how should it relate with management, shareholders, and other stakeholders? These questions were complicated by the firm's expansion to other countries.

JOHN MCCULLOCH—UNITED BEEF PACKERS

*Prepared by Eric Dolansky under the
supervision of Professor James A. Erskine*

Version: (A) 2003-06-12

In August 2003, three months after John McCulloch had started working as assistant general manager at the United Beef Packers Blue River processing plant in Nebraska, he already felt trapped. He reread the latest memo from his boss ordering him to terminate the employment of a line worker. McCulloch was not sure he could go through with it. McCulloch began wondering why he had taken this job in the first place and how he was going to get out of this mess.

THE MEAT PACKING INDUSTRY[1]

By the turn of the 21st century, the American meat packing industry had gone through many changes since the early 1900s. First dominated by independent ranchers, corporations took control and created the Beef Trust, a council whereby the major beef packers could control prices, wages and supplies and therefore maximize profits. Inspired by Upton Sinclair's book

The Jungle, an exposé of the industry from the point of view of a laborer, President Teddy Roosevelt ordered the Beef Trust dismantled and anti-competitive actions ended.

Regional competition and small players kept competition in the industry active until the 1970s, when large food processors began consolidating the industry again. In 1980, the top four meat packers processed 20 per cent of the beef in the United States; by the year 2000, the top four companies processed 82 per cent of the beef available for sale in the United States.

A trade association, the American Meat Institute (AMI), represented meat packing companies. According to the AMI, major meat packing companies were at the cutting edge on technology, worker safety, hygiene, and environmental responsibility. Recent attacks on the industry were explained by jealousy of the success of these companies. The AMI pointed to advances in ergonomic tool design (to reduce repetitive stress disorders) as an example of the companies putting the well-being of the employees first. Furthermore, complaints of tainted meat and food poisoning (by salmonella, E. coli, or other pathogens) were deemed frivolous and inappropriate by AMI. According to the AMI, the highest standards of cleanliness were being observed and if there were cases of food poisoning, they were the fault of improper preparation of the meat (by the restaurant or the chef) and not the meat itself.

UNITED BEEF PACKERS

United Beef Packers (UBP) was one of the "big four" meat producers in the United States, and was owned by Wholly Pure Foods, Inc. UBP operated several plants across the Great Plains, primarily in states such as Nebraska, Texas, Iowa, Colorado and Kansas. Founded in the late 1960s, UBP represented the pinnacle of what could be achieved when management and employees worked together with common goals and ideals. The founder of the company, Ken Hill, was a great believer in communication and teamwork,

and he treated his employees well. The workers at Hill's Blue River plant enjoyed high wages, a clean work environment, and a general sense that the company was looking out for them. The relationship between the union and the company was amicable, and each tried to help the other out when necessary.

Then towards the end of the 1970s and in the early 1980s, the recession hit, and it hit the meat packing industry hard. Consolidation of the industry began. Hill found he could no longer enjoy profits and still treat his employees well, so he opted for the former and cut wages. Conditions in the various plants deteriorated. Hill bought a new slaughterhouse a few miles down the highway and fired the unionized workers there upon purchase of the plant. He reopened it shortly thereafter without a union, staffing it primarily with recent immigrants and poorly educated locals. The union at the Blue River plant decided to hold a strike in protest. Hill hired "scabs" as retaliation, and soon received numerous death threats. Unionized workers who were let back into the plant posing as scabs committed acts of sabotage. In frustration, Hill closed the Blue River plant and fired the entire unionized workforce. After six months, he reopened the plant with immigrants and new employees. The days of cordial relationships were gone.

In the mid-80s, amidst the consolidation boom, Wholly Pure Foods, Inc. (WPF) bought UBP in a friendly takeover. Hill retired from active duty and accepted a seat on WPF's board. Consultants, industry experts and top managers from other divisions of WPF were brought in to study and direct UBP. By 1994, no upper management from the early days of the company remained.

PLANT OPERATIONS

Despite technological advances, cattle slaughter and processing in 2000 was done in much the same way it had been done 100 years before. Because cows were not grown to uniform size (unlike chickens), automation of meat processing was not possible. It was still a very labor-intensive process. Cattle were led into the plant and struck on the head with a mallet, rendering them unconscious. After this "knocking," a worker wrapped a chain around the hind legs of the cow and the live cow was hoisted far up into the air. There the cow encounters the "sticker," an employee whose job it was to kill the cow with one lance of a long, thin blade, severing the animal's carotid artery and causing death as quickly as possible. From there the carcass had its hide removed, was decapitated, disemboweled and the body split in two by a worker with a large chainsaw. After this, workers began their individual tasks of removing meat and organs from the cattle, grinding the bones (for fertilizer and animal feed), and disposing of the useless and possibly infectious parts of the animal, such as the brain, spine and lower intestines.

In the 20 years leading up to 2000, line speeds in cattle plants increased from approximately 175 cattle an hour to 400 cattle per hour. Because of this, safety and sanitation in the plants had declined. For example, there was a team of workers whose job it was to remove the bowel of the carcass. This was a job that must be done carefully, because if the intestine or bowel was pierced, manure would spray the area and raise the chance of infecting the meat. Even the most competent people on this job still pierced the intestines of one out of every 200 cattle. This meant that, at best, pathogens were released into the plant twice an hour. There were cleaning techniques for the meat, but these were typically reserved for whole cuts of meat (steaks, roasts, etc.). For ground beef, there was no way to ensure that meat sold was clean. Because some plants could produce 400,000 pounds of ground beef per eight-hour shift, one or two accidents could have serious health consequences.

Per-capita beef consumption in the United States had remained flat with little growth in the 12 years leading up to 2000 (see Exhibit 1). The high line speeds, according to the AMI, were necessary to meet demand for beef. New techniques of ensuring safety were under review,

such as irradiation of meat (or, as the meat producers prefer to call it, "cold pasteurization"). The concern of the United States Department of Agriculture (USDA), which regulates beef, was that better end-of-line safety mechanisms would cause health standards throughout the line to decline because of the fail-safe at the end. As one journalist, commenting on irradiation, put it, "Irradiation is fine; I just don't want irradiated [manure] with my meat."

PLANT EMPLOYEES

By 2000, most meat processing plant employees were immigrants, legal and otherwise. The big four companies used Mexican radio to advertise job openings. Many workers who had earned $7 a day in Mexico jumped at the chance to earn more than that per hour at the U.S. meat plants. The migrant immigrant worker had changed from going from farm to farm to pick seasonal fruits and vegetables into an individual who went from meat plant to meat plant to work until they were injured, fired or otherwise forced off the job. Annual industry turnover was extremely high. On average, an employee remained at a meat packing plant for six months.

Until the industry consolidated, meat processing plant employees were some of the most highly paid workers in the country. In 1983, however, the national average hourly wage for someone working in industry passed the average meat packer's wage. Since then, the industry average wage was typically 25 per cent to 40 per cent higher than the meat industry's average wage (see Exhibit 2), which was due to a number of factors, not least of which was the lack of unions in the sector. Today, less than one-third of all meat packers are unionized. Because of high industry turnover, it was difficult to maintain a union; twice a year, a whole new group of employees must be sold on the idea.

The area where the meat companies had really taken power was in the field of employee safety. All the major meat companies were self-insured, which meant that every dime paid out in

Year	Turkey Pounds	Beef Pounds	Pork Pounds	Chicken Pounds	Total Red Meat & Poultry
1990	13.9	64.1	46.7	42.7	169.3
1991	14.2	63.3	47.3	44.4	171.2
1992	14.2	63.0	49.9	46.4	175.3
1993	14.1	61.6	49.2	46.6	174.5
1994	14.1	63.7	49.8	47.1	177.5
1995	14.1	64.2	49.2	46.7	177.1
1996	14.6	64.4	46.1	48.1	175.5
1997	13.9	63.6	45.7	49.2	174.4
1998	14.0	64.8	51.0	51.2	182.7
1999	14.1	65.8	51.1	53.2	186.0
2000	14.1	66.1	50.5	55.8	188.0
2001	14.1	63.4	50.8	57.1	187.8

Exhibit 1   U.S. per Capita Meat Consumption

Source: Research Education Advocacy People (REAP) 2001 Annual Report.

worker's compensation claims came from the company's bottom line. As a result, the meat producers did everything they could to avoid paying for employees' medical costs. The powerful AMI lobby had rendered the U.S. government's regulatory body, the Occupational Safety and Health Administration (OSHA), virtually powerless. OSHA had to announce all plant visits at least 48 hours prior to the inspection. It was even legal for plant managers to keep two sets of worker accident records; one log for OSHA, and one that listed all the accidents.

Worker injuries remained very common in this industry. On-the-job injuries such as lacerations, repetitive stress disorder, infections, amputations and chemical burns occur frequently (see Exhibit 3). The level of repetitive stress disorders in meat packing plants was 75 times the national average. Despite all this, the AMI and the meat producing companies claimed they met all necessary standards for worker safety.

JOHN MCCULLOCH

John McCulloch was born in Chicago, Illinois, in 1972. Because both of his parents were Canadian (his father was studying at university), McCulloch was given dual citizenship so, when the time came, he could decide where he wished to live and work. With his undergraduate degree in engineering, McCulloch found a job in an auto parts plant in Albuquerque, New Mexico. He truly enjoyed working there; the people were friendly, the management/union relations were cordial and he enjoyed living in a culture and community so different from his Welland, Ontario, upbringing. McCulloch even learned Spanish from some of the employees he supervised. He married a local Albuquerque girl, Selena, and they had a son, Theodore.

A reduction in the workload at the plant gave McCulloch the opportunity to continue his education. Using his "golden parachute" from the

Year	Meat Packing Processing	Meat Packing Slaughter	U.S. Manufacturing
1975	$5.36	$5.67	$4.83
1976	$5.87	$6.06	$5.22
1977	$6.28	$6.57	$5.68
1978	$6.73	$7.09	$6.17
1979	$7.40	$7.73	$6.70
1980	$8.06	$8.49	$7.27
1981	$8.73	$8.97	$7.99
1982	$9.08	$9.00	$8.49
1983	$8.83	$8.58	$8.83
1984	$8.89	$8.17	$9.19
1985	$8.74	$8.10	$9.54
1986	$8.76	$8.24	$9.73
1987	$8.85	$8.41	$9.91
1988	$9.04	$8.48	$10.19
1989	$9.22	$8.64	$10.48
1990	$9.37	$8.74	$10.83
1991	$9.43	$8.92	$11.18
1992	$9.62	$9.16	$11.46
1993	$9.89	$9.26	$11.74
1994	$10.06	$9.44	$12.07
1995	$10.41	$9.61	$12.37
1996	$10.47	$9.82	$12.77
1997	$10.74	$10.03	$13.17
1998	$11.03	$10.34	$13.49
1999	$11.17	$10.81	$13.91
2000	$11.80	$10.94	$14.38
2001	$12.27	$11.38	$14.84

Exhibit 2   Average Hourly Wage Comparison: Meat Packing Compared to U.S. Manufacturing According to the U.S. Bureau of Labor Statistics

Source: REAP 2001 Annual Report.

Year	Poultry	Slaughter	Processing	All Private Industry
1996	17.8	30.3	16.3	7.4
1997	16.6	32.1	16.7	7.1
1998	16.8	29.3	13.4	6.7
1999	14.3	26.7	13.5	6.3
2000	14.2	24.7	14.7	6.1

Exhibit 3   Occupational Injuries and Illness per 100 Full-Time Workers, U.S. Bureau of Labor Statistics

Source: REAP 2001 Annual Report.

plant as funding, he enrolled in an MBA program. Though it was nice to be close to his family again, McCulloch was anxious to get out into the workforce. He loved working in operations, and he made that the focus of his studies and job search. McCulloch found UBP through an independent job search on the Web. The pictures on the site and the description of the job sounded great: he would supervise a large number of employees, work for a large multinational with lots of room for advancement, receive good pay (especially relative to the cost of living where the plants were located), and there were many process/control challenges to tackle.

Through e-mail, McCulloch applied for the position of assistant general plant manager and he followed up with a phone call. He met with a contingent from UBP's human resource department following a successful phone interview, and he had the opportunity to ask about the plants, the employees and the day-to-day mechanics of the job. A few weeks later, McCulloch was flown to UBP headquarters in Omaha, Nebraska, where he met with the vice-president of plant operations. Following a short conversation, McCulloch was presented with an offer sheet. After discussing the matter with Selena, he accepted the position.

THE FIRST DAY

When McCulloch reported to the plant for his first day of work and orientation, he did not know how he would possibly be able to work there. The place stank of blood and meat. It was hot and humid. There were hundreds of workers, mostly Mexican, walking around in bloody aprons that looked like chain-mail armor, and carrying knives, lots of knives; long, short, thin, it seemed like everyone had at least one. The plant general manager, Greg Kramer, was waiting for him. Kramer was the only one dressed normally. He had been with UBP for four years, having taken the job after earning his business degree.

The two retired to Kramer's office to discuss McCulloch's role at the plant. Even in Kramer's

clean office, McCulloch could still smell the plant and hear the shouting, the grinding of the machinery and general sounds of a slaughterhouse. According to Kramer, the Blue River plant was the best-functioning beef plant in the state. The processing line moved at an average of 350 cattle per hour, and that average was maintained no matter what. Any shutdowns would be made up for by speeding up the line later. The line, however, was Kramer's responsibility; as he put it, he got paid to ensure that the right amount of meat came out of the plant every day.

McCulloch's responsibility was to be much more operational. He was to work closely with the floor supervisors to make sure that all worker issues were taken care of quickly. He would report directly to Kramer. The message was received loud and clear: no problems that could shut down the line would be allowed. Kramer then showed McCulloch to his office and suggested they tour the plant.

Both men suited up in what looked like space-suits. They ventured out into the plant. The floor was covered in blood, inches deep in some places. The line, or chain as it was called, moved above, carrying beef carcasses in various stages of dismemberment. And everywhere, the workers cut and hacked at the pieces of meat in front of them, in a constant, repetitive motion. McCulloch noticed that he and Kramer were the only people wearing protective garb. Other than the aprons, the workers had only metal gloves and chest-plates to protect them from the many knives in motion.

THE FIRST THREE MONTHS

Over the next four weeks, McCulloch met with the floor supervisors and tried to learn from them. These meetings, unfortunately, made him depressed. It seemed that his direct reports would feel more at home as slave drivers than as plant supervisors. They had no respect for the workers and were trained to care only about keeping the line moving and keeping workers working. McCulloch decided to try to get a different view by talking to others in the plant.

Concerned with the high incidence of workplace accidents, McCulloch went to see the plant nurse. She was a friendly woman who responded to McCulloch's naïveté by letting him know that this was just how the industry worked. They were interrupted by a pair of workers coming in with deep lacerations. The nurse said, "I guess they're making up for lost time today. I can always tell how fast the chain is moving by how many injuries there are."

Just then, one of the supervisors came in. He shoved a piece of paper in front of one of the injured workers and ordered him, in Spanish, to sign it. When McCulloch asked what it was, the supervisor explained in English that all injured workers had to sign a waiver that allowed UBP to administer medical treatment and disallowed the worker from getting an outside medical opinion, seeing a non-company doctor, or suing the company. Signing waivers was standard operating procedure, according to the supervisor. The supervisor then demanded that the other worker sign a copy of the waiver. Because this worker's lacerations were to his hands, he had to sign it by writing with a pen in his mouth.

McCulloch then went to see Kramer and asked about the waiver procedure. Kramer told him that because the company was self-insured, it had a right to insist that all medical treatment come from company personnel. When McCulloch asked what happened when a worker did not sign the waiver, he was told that the worker was then fired. Because an employee could not collect benefits if fired, almost everyone signed the waiver. Kramer assured McCulloch that everything was legal and that he had better get on board with the policy if he was going to last at the plant. Although McCulloch had tried to talk to individual workers on the line, no one would give him the kind of low-down, nitty-gritty information he wanted. McCulloch felt it was all well and good to know how the plant was supposed to operate and how it was supposed to look to the outside world, but if he was going to be an effective manager, he had to know what really went on.

On his way into his office one day, McCulloch saw a large, muscular man in a wheelchair sorting files. He had never seen this man before. After introducing himself, McCulloch asked this man (Bobby Vasquez) if he would be willing to tell McCulloch what went on in the plant. Vasquez seemed more than happy to oblige.

Vasquez started working at the plant in the late 1970s at the age of 24. In 1994, he heard someone yell "watch out!" and, looking up from his work, saw a 100-pound box of meat falling towards him. He reached out and caught it with one arm, but the force of the box caused him to fall backwards hitting his back on a metal table. The company doctor told him it was a pulled muscle, but after months of excruciating pain he got a second opinion and found out he had two herniated discs. A month after surgery, Vasquez was back doing heavy labor in the plant. Taking on an extra shift, one night he was ordered to clean the gigantic blood tanks with liquid chlorine. Because no protection was given to him, he ended up in the hospital with severe chemical burns to his lungs. He still returned to work. Subsequent accidents included a shattered ankle and a broken leg, the reason for his being in a wheelchair and restricted to "light duty" work.

McCulloch could not believe the litany of horrors that had befallen Vasquez. But what the man said next chilled McCulloch even more:

John, you should get out as soon as you can. You really don't want to know what goes on in the plant. Your supervisors are loyal only to the company, because they know they'd never get a job managing others anywhere else. They sell drugs to the workers so that they can work faster and longer. They harass and abuse female employees in exchange for easier work. They let tainted meat go out for sale. Trust me, the less you know the better.

A few days later, Vasquez was back on the line, cutting meat.

THE MEAT RECALL AND THE LOADING DOCK

Around two months after McCulloch had begun working at UBP, head office sent a task force to

Date: August 12, 2003

To: John McCulloch, Assistant General Manager

From: Greg Kramer, General Manager

Re: Bobby Vasquez

John:

If you haven't already heard from the floor supervisors, plant employee Bobby Vasquez is seriously incapacitated and unable to work at the plant for the next several months due to a heart attack.

Vasquez has never been that valuable an employee and is quite accident-prone. He was recently confined to a wheelchair because of a broken leg, and he has had problems with his back in the past as well. He has also displayed contempt for the company and is not considered loyal.

Head office and I agree that we would benefit from no longer having this individual on our payroll and enrolled in our benefits plan. Please ensure his employment is terminated as soon as possible. Do not wait until Vasquez contacts the plant; track him down and serve him with his termination papers. I understand he is recuperating at Blue River General Hospital, room 1115.

Greg

Exhibit 4   Memorandum

the Blue River plant. UBP had gotten some bad press after several E. coli infections were traced back to some ground beef produced at Blue River. UBP upper management wanted to hold a press conference at the plant to announce a recall and show that they had nothing to hide. The company was recalling 250,000 pounds of ground beef, though by now, McCulloch knew that there was no way the company could be certain of how much meat had been infected. It mattered little; the USDA could only ask for a recall of tainted meat; it did not have the power to force the company to pull the meat from the shelves.

Greg Kramer was furious because this episode meant that the line had to be shut down for extensive cleaning. Shifts were added for the sanitation effort, and others were cancelled so the line did not look as frenetic when the reporters arrived. "We'll be running at 400 an hour for a month to make up for this," Kramer complained.

The task force assigned McCulloch the duty of inspecting the non-core areas of the plant, such as the offices and loading dock, for anything that would look out of the ordinary. Upon arrival at the loading dock, McCulloch saw several boxes of beef sitting on the dock with no truck to pick them up. The time stamp on the box was six hours old, and the meat was sitting in 30-degree Celsius temperatures. When he asked the dock foreman why this meat was there, the man looked at McCulloch quizzically. McCulloch repeated his question, and the foreman explained that this meat was "seconds," not of high quality, and would be sold under a brand name other than UBP's, so it was okay that it sat outside for a while until the truck came to get it.

BREAKING POINT

After three months of lost sleep, no appetite, depression and the stench of cattle constantly around him, McCulloch wondered how much more he could take. He was in constant fear: of public exposure, of legal liability, of his wife and son's health and of the loss of his own sanity. He knew he had made a mistake coming to work for

UBP, but there seemed to be little he could do about it now, short of uprooting his life and those of his family.

Looking through his in-box tray, McCulloch found a memo from Kramer (see Exhibit 4). It seemed that Vasquez suffered a heart attack the previous week and was in the hospital. The doctors said he would no longer be able to work in the plant, and his recovery would be long and expensive. Kramer was ordering McCulloch to fire Vasquez, as the company did not want to pay for his medical bills any longer. McCulloch sat down, put his head in his hands and wished he were someplace else.

NOTE

1. Based on information from *Fast Food Nation,* by Eric Schlosser. Published by the Houghton Mifflin Company, 2001.

NES CHINA: BUSINESS ETHICS (A)

Prepared by Xin Zhang under the supervision of Professor Joerg Dietz

Version: (A) 2002-08-30

By April 1998, it had been almost a year since the Germany-headquartered multinational company NES AG had first submitted its application to the Chinese government for establishing a holding company in Beijing to co-ordinate its investments in China. The application documentation had already been revised three times, but the approval by the government was still outstanding. Lin Chen, government affairs co-ordinator at NES AG Beijing Representative Office, came under pressure from the German headquarters and had to find a way to obtain approval within a month.

During the past year, Chen had almost exclusively worked on the holding company application. In order to facilitate the approval process, she had suggested giving gifts to government officials. But her European colleagues, Steinmann and Dr. Perrin, disagreed because they thought such conduct would be bribery and would violate business ethics. Confronted with the cross-cultural ethical conflict, Chen had to consider possible strategies that would satisfy everybody.

COMPANY BACKGROUND

NES and NES AG

NES was founded in Germany in 1881. Over the following 100 years, by pursuing diversification strategies, NES had grown from a pure tube manufacturer into one of the largest industrial groups in Germany, with sales of US$14 billion in 1997. NES built plants and heavy machinery, made automotive systems and components, manufactured hydraulic, pneumatic and electrical drives and controls, offered telecommunications services and produced steel tubes and pipes.

NES was managed by a holding company—NES AG—that implemented value-oriented portfolio management and directed its financial resources to the areas with the greatest profit potentials. In 1997, NES AG owned NES's 11 companies in four business segments: engineering, automotive, telecommunications and tubes. These companies generally operated independently and largely at their own discretion, as

NES AG was interested in their profitability and not their day-to-day operations.

NES had always been committed to move along the road of globalization and internationalization. Headquartered in Germany, NES had businesses in more than 100 countries with over 120,000 employees. In the process of globalization and internationalization, NES established a business principle that demonstrated its responsibilities not only to shareholders, employees and customers, but also to society and to the countries where it operated. As an essential part of the company's corporate culture, this principle pervaded the decentralized subsidiaries worldwide and guided the decision-making and conduct of both the company and its employees.

NES China Operations

NES's business in China dated back to 1889, when it built the flood barrages for the Canton River. In 1908, NES supplied seamless steel tubes for the construction of a waterworks in Beijing. Through the century, NES continued to broaden its presence. From the mid-1950s to 1997, NES supplied China with an enormous 5.2 million metric tons of steel tube and 1.6 million tons of rolled steel.

Since China opened up to foreign trade and investment in the late 1970s, NES's presence had grown dramatically. From 1977 to 1997, NES had completed more than 40 technology transfer and infrastructure projects. It had also set up 20 representative offices, six equity joint ventures and three wholly owned enterprises.

In developing business links with China, NES adhered to its business principle. Most NES enterprises in China had highlighted this principle in their codes of conduct in employment handbooks (see Exhibit 1). These codes required employees to pursue the highest standards of business and personal ethics in dealing with government officials and business customers, and to avoid any activities that would lead to the involvement of the company in unlawful practices. Instead of tendering immediate favors or rewards to individual Chinese officials and

customers, NES relied on advanced technology, management know-how and top quality products and service as a source of its competitive advantage. NES emphasized long-term mutual benefits and corporate social responsibility. Since 1979, NES had trained more than 2,000 Chinese engineers, master craftsmen, technicians and skilled workers in Germany. It had also offered extensive training programs in China. Moreover, NES was the first German company to adopt the suggestion of the German federal government to initiate a scholarship program for young Chinese academics to study in Germany. As a result, NES had built a strong reputation in China for being a fair business partner and a good guest company.

NES Beijing Representative Office

In 1977, NES was the first German company to open its representative office in Beijing. Along with NES's business growth, the Beijing Representative Office continued to expand. In 1997, it had 10 German expatriates and more than 40 local staff in nine business units. One unit represented NES AG. This unit was responsible for administrative co-ordination and office expense allocation. The other eight units worked for the German head offices of their respective NES companies in the engineering, automotive and tube segments.

Chinese legal restrictions severely limited the activities of the Beijing Representative Office. It was allowed only to engage in administrative activities, such as conducting marketing research for the German head offices, passing on price and technical information to Chinese customers, and arranging for meetings and trade visits. Moreover, it could not directly enter into employment contracts with its Chinese employees. Instead, it had to go through a local labor service agency designated by the Chinese government and consult with the agency on almost all personnel issues including recruitment, compensation and dismissal. As a result, the German managers of the Beijing Representative Office found it difficult to effectively manage their Chinese employees. In the absence of direct

Article 3 Employment and Duties

3.1 The Company employs the Employee and the Employee accepts such employment in accordance with the terms and conditions of the Employment Contract and this Employment Handbook.

3.6 The Company expects each Employee to observe the highest standards of business and personal ethics, and to be honest and sincere in his/her dealings with government officials, the public, firms, or other corporations, entities, or organizations with whom the Company transacts, or is likely to transact.

3.7 The Company does business without favoritism. Purchases of materials or services will be competitively priced whenever possible. An Employee's personal interest or relationship is not to influence any transaction with a business organization that furnishes property, rights or services to the Company.

3.8 Employees are not to solicit, accept, or agree to accept, at any time of the year, any gift of value which directly or indirectly benefits them from a supplier or prospective supplier or his employees or agents, or any person with whom the Company does business in any aspect.

3.9 The Company observes and complies with all laws, rules, and regulations of the People's Republic of China which affect the Company and its Employees. Employees are required to avoid any activities which involve or would lead to the involvement of the Company in any unlawful practices and to disclose to the proper Company authorities any conduct that comes to their attention which violates these rules and principles. Accordingly, each Employee should understand the legal standards and restrictions that apply to his/her duties.

3.10 All Employees are the Company's representatives. This is true whether the Employee is on duty or off duty. All Employees are encouraged to observe the highest standards of professional and personal conduct at all times.

Article 13 Discipline

13.1 The Company insists on utmost discipline. The Employee's misconduct or unsatisfactory performance will be brought to the attention of the responsible Head of Department or Member of the Management when it occurs and will be documented in the Employee's file.

13.2 Some offences are grounds for immediate dismissal and disciplinary procedures will apply to other offences.

13.3 Offences which are grounds for immediate dismissal include:
   (i) Breach of the Company's rules of conduct.
   (j) Neglect of duties, favoritisms or other irregularities.

Exhibit 1   Excerpt From the Employment Handbook of One of the NES's Enterprises in China

Source: Company files.

---

employment contracts, the managers had to rely on an internal reporting and control system.

CURRENT SITUATION

Establishing China Holding Company

In early 1997, NES AG had decided to establish a holding company in Beijing as soon as possible after carefully weighing the advantages and disadvantages of this decision. Establishing a China holding company was advantageous because, unlike a representative office, a holding company had its own business licence and could therefore engage in direct business activities. In addition to holding shares, a holding company could co-ordinate many important functions for its enterprises, such as marketing, managing government relations, and providing financial support. As a "country headquarters," a holding company could also unite the NES profile in China and strengthen the good name of NES as a reliable business partner in the world's most populous country. Moreover, it could hire staff directly and thus retain full control over its own workforce. In light of these advantages, NES AG expected substantial time and cost efficiencies from the China holding company.

Several disadvantages, however, potentially outweighed the advantages of a China holding company. First, Chinese legal regulations still constrained some business activities. For example, a Chinese holding company could not balance foreign exchange accounts freely and consolidate the taxation of NES's Chinese enterprises, although this might be permitted in the future. Second, the setup efforts and costs were high. To establish a holding company, NES had to submit a project proposal, a feasibility study, articles of association and other application documents to the local (the Local Department) and then to the central trade and economic co-operation departments (the Central Department) for examination and approval. Third, there was only a limited window of opportunity for NES AG. Once the China holding company had received its business licence, within two years, NES AG would have to contribute a minimum of US$30 million fresh capital to it. The Chinese regulations prescribed that this capital could be invested only in new projects, but otherwise would have to remain unused in a bank account. NES currently was in a position to invest the capital in its new projects, but the company was not certain how much longer it would be in this position.

Working Team

NES AG authorized the following three individuals in the Beijing Representative Office to take up the China holding company application issue:

Kai Mueller, 58 years old, had worked for NES in its China operations since the 1970s and had experience in several big co-operative projects in

the steel and metallurgical industries. He would be the president of the holding company.

Jochen Steinmann, 30 years old, was assigned to Beijing from Germany in 1996. He would be the financial controller of the holding company.

Dr. Jean Perrin was a 37-year-old lawyer from France who had an in-depth understanding of Chinese business laws. He would work as the legal counsel. His previous working experience included a professorship at the Beijing International Business and Economics University in the 1980s.

The trio had advocated the idea of a China holding company to NES AG for quite some time and were most happy about NES AG's decision, because the future holding company would give them considerably more responsibilities and authority than did the Beijing Representative Office.

Considering the complexity and difficulty in coping with the Chinese bureaucratic hurdles, Mueller decided in March 1997 to hire Lin Chen as a government affairs co-ordinator for the working team. Chen, a native Chinese, was a 28-year-old politics and public administration graduate who had worked four years for a Chinese state-owned company and was familiar with the Chinese way of doing business. Mueller expected that Chen would play an instrumental role in obtaining the holding company approval from the Chinese government. He also promised that Chen would be responsible for the public affairs function at the holding company once it was set up.

Chen's View of Doing Business in China

Chen officially joined the Beijing Representative Office in June 1997. She commented on doing business in China:

China's economy is far from rules-based; basically, it is still an economy based on relationships. In the absence of an explicit and transparent legal framework, directives and policies are open to interpretation by government officials who occupy positions of authority and power. In such circumstances, businesspeople cultivate personal *guanxi* (interpersonal connections based implicitly on mutual interest and benefit) with officials to substitute for an established code of law that businesspeople in the Western society take for granted.

In building and nurturing *guanxi* with officials, gifts and personal favors have a special place, not only because they are associated with respect and friendship, but also because in today's China, people place so much emphasis on utilitarian gains. In return for accepting gifts, officials provide businesspeople with access to information about policy thinking and the potentially advantageous interpretation of the policy, and facilitate administrative procedures. Co-operation leads to mutual benefits.

Although an existing regulation forbids government officials to accept gifts of any kind,[1] it remains pervasive for businesspeople to provide officials with major household appliances, electric equipment, "red envelopes" stuffed with cash, and overseas trips. There is a common saying: "The bureaucrats would never punish a gift giver." Forbidding what the West calls bribery in a *guanxi*-based society where gift giving is the expected behavior can only drive such under-the-table transactions further behind the curtain.

While sharing benefits with officials is normal business conduct in China, it is interpreted as unethical and abnormal in the West. Faced with their home country's ethical values and business rules, Western companies in China cannot handle government relationships as their Asian counterparts do. They often find themselves at a disadvantage. This dilemma raises a question for a multinational company: Should it impose the home country's moral principles wherever it operates or should it do what the Chinese do when in China, and, if so, to what extent?

Different Opinions on Bribery

When Chen started working in June 1997, Mueller was sick and had returned to Germany for treatment. Steinmann and Dr. Perrin told Chen that NES had submitted the holding company application to the Local Department in April 1997 and that the Local Department had transferred the documents to the Central Department at the end of that month. But nothing had happened since then. Chen felt that she had to fall back to her former colleague, Mr. Zhu, who had close personal *guanxi* with the Central Department, to find out first who had the authority in the Central Department to push the processing and what their general attitudes towards the application were.

In July, Chen reported her findings to Steinmann and Dr. Perrin:

> The approval process at the Central Department is difficult. Because holding companies are a relatively new form of foreign investment in China, the officials are unsure whether they are a good idea for China. They have been very prudent to grant approval. Hence, we don't have much negotiating leverage, although we are a big company and have products and technologies that China needs. The officials say that they will consider a holding company's application within 90 days of its submission. They issue approval however, only when the application is deemed "complete and perfect" (in that all issues have been resolved to the Central Department's satisfaction). The Central Department is under no real obligation to approve any holding company application. They can always find some minor issues. So the approval procedure may be lengthy. The legal basis for establishing holding companies is provided by the Holding Company Tentative Provisions, Supplementary Rules and some unpublished internal policies. This provisional and vague status allows the officials to be flexible in authorizing a holding company. In such circumstances, maintaining close connections with the responsible officials is absolutely critical.

Chen suggested:

> The quickest and most effective way to build such connections is to invite the responsible officials to dinner and give gifts. It won't cost the company too much. But what the company will gain in return—efficiency in obtaining approval and flexibility in the interpretation of the wording within the scope permitted by law—is worth much more.

Upon hearing Chen's report and suggestion, Steinmann was shocked:

That would be bribery. In Germany bribing an official is a criminal offence for which both the briber and the bribed are punished. NES is a publicly traded company with a board of directors that reports to shareholders and monitoring authorities in Germany.

We have met the criteria for setting up the holding company. What we should do now is organize a formal meeting with the officials and negotiate with them. This is the way we have done it in the past, and it has always worked. I am not aware that we ever had to use bribery. NES does not have a history of wrongdoing.

Knowing how critical it was to follow China's customary business practices in tackling such issues, Chen argued:

Yes, it is correct. NES did not have to give gifts of this kind in the past. But don't forget: virtually all of NES's projects or joint ventures in the past were approved by agencies responsible for specific industries or local governments that were very keen on having access to NES's technology. As a result, NES always has had considerable bargaining power. It is different this time: we need to found a holding company, and we have to deal with the Central Department that we have never contacted before. Even Mueller does not have relations in this department. Moreover, our contacts at the industrial and local levels won't help much because they have very limited influence on the Central Department and, hence, the holding company application issue.

Moreover, you can't equate gifts with bribes. The approval letter doesn't have predetermined "prices" and no one forces us to pay. We give gifts just to establish relationships with officials. We develop good relationships, and favorable consideration of these officials comes naturally. According to Chinese law,[2] to give gifts to government officials and expect them to take advantage of their position and power to conduct *illegal* actions is bribery. Our intent is to motivate officials to handle our application legally but without delay. I see no serious ethical problem.

In some ways it's also hard to blame officials for feathering their nest because they are poorly paid. Whether they process our application quickly or slowly has absolutely no impact on their US$200 monthly income. Then, how can we expect them to give our case the green light? They are not morally wrong if they accept our gifts and don't create obstacles for us in return.

Negotiation doesn't help much. Unless we have close relationships with them, they will always find some minor flaws in our documents. After all, they have the authority for interpreting the regulations. Therefore, we have to be open-minded and get accustomed to the Chinese way of doing business.

Chen hoped that Dr. Perrin would support her, as she had a feeling that the French were more flexible and less ethically sensitive than the Germans. Dr. Perrin, however, shared Steinmann's view. Perrin said:

We should not give officials anything that has some value, with the exception of very small objects (pens, key holders, calendars and the like) given mainly for marketing and advertisement purposes. I also think that these officials should not accept any gifts. It's unethical and illegal. If we think it is unethical, we should combat it and refrain from it.

Nonetheless, Dr. Perrin understood the importance of *guanxi* as an informal solution to Chinese bureaucracies. So he agreed that Chen could invite one of the two responsible officials to dinner through Mr. Zhu and present a CD player to this official as an expression of respect and goodwill, although he thought it went too far and was approaching bribery.

On a Saturday evening in July, Chen met the official at one of the most expensive restaurants in Beijing. At the dinner, the official promised to work overtime the next day on NES's documents and give feedback as soon as possible.

The following Monday, Chen got the government's official preliminary opinion demanding a revision of 16 clauses of the application documents. Steinmann and Dr. Perrin found it difficult to understand this. NES had drafted the documents with reference to those of another company, whose application had been approved by the Central Department a few months ago. Why didn't the Central Department accept the similar wording this time? Chen again contacted her former colleague Zhu, who told her:

> You should never expect to get things done so quickly and easily. It takes time to strengthen your relationships. I can ask them to speed up the procedure without changing too much of the wording. But you'd better offer them something generous to express your gratitude since they would consider it a great favor. RMB3,000 (US$360) for each of the two will be OK. Don't make me lose face anyway.

Steinmann and Dr. Perrin thought it was straightforward bribery even if gifts were given through a third party. If they agreed to do so, they would run high personal risks by violating the corporate business principle and professional ethics. As controller and lawyer, they were expected to play an important role in implementing strict control mechanisms in the company and keeping the corporate conscience. Moreover, they were worried that the potential wrongdoing might damage the strong ethical culture of the Beijing Representative Office and the good corporate image among the Chinese employees of the office, although it likely would not affect the whole company because NES was so decentralized.

However, Chen thought that *renqing* (social or humanized obligation) and *mianzi* (the notion of face) were more important and that NES's business ethics and social responsibility could be somewhat compromised. In Chen's eyes, Steinmann and Dr. Perrin were inflexible and lacked knowledge of the Chinese business culture. Steinmann and Dr. Perrin told Chen that she needed to learn Western business rules and values in order to survive in a multinational company.

Recent Developments

In August 1997, the vice-president of NES AG led a delegation to visit China. Chen arranged a meeting for the delegation with a senior official of the Central Department. It turned out just to be a courtesy meeting and did not touch upon the details of the holding company approval issue.

In November, Steinmann and Dr. Perrin met the two responsible officials in hopes of negotiating with them such that the officials would allow NES to leave some clauses unchanged. But the officials insisted on their original opinion without giving a detailed explanation of the relevant legal basis. The negotiation lasted only half an hour, and Steinmann and Dr. Perrin felt that it accomplished nothing.

Because of the limited window of opportunity (that is, new investment projects required an immediate capital injection), they felt that they had no choice but to modify the documents according to the officials' requirements. Modifying the documents was an administrative struggle with NES AG, because due to company-internal policies, the German headquarters had to approve these modifications. The application was resubmitted at the end of November. When Chen inquired about the application's status in December, the officials, however, said that the case needed more consideration and then raised some new questions that they said they failed to mention last time. This happened once again three months later in February 1998.

What Next?

In April 1998, Steinmann, Dr. Perrin and Chen submitted the newest revision of the application. As NES AG could not defer funding the new projects, it demanded that the Beijing working team obtained approval within a month so that NES AG could use the China holding company's registered capital of US$30 million. Otherwise, NES AG would have to re-evaluate the China holding company and might abandon it all together. In that case, Mueller, Steinmann and Dr. Perrin would miss opportunities for career advancement. As for Chen, she was concerned about her job because the Beijing Representative Office would no longer need her position.

Being very anxious about the current situation, Mueller decided to come back to Beijing immediately. Chen wanted to be able to suggest a practical approach that would gain the co-operation of the bureaucrats while conforming to the German moral standards. Chen also contemplated some challenging questions. For example, what constituted bribery? When ethical values conflicted, which values should people follow? How could these differences be resolved? To what extent should a multinational company like NES adapt to local business practices? Should the future China holding company develop special ethical codes to recognize the Chinese business culture? The answers to these questions were very important to Chen, because she expected to face similar ethically sensitive issues in the future.

NOTES

1. The China State Council Order No. 20 promulgated on 1988.12.01. Article 2 Any State administrative organization and its functionary shall not give and accept gifts in activities of domestic public service. The China State Council Order No. 133 promulgated on 1993.12.05. Article 7 Gifts accepted in activities of foreign public service shall be handled properly. Gifts above the equivalent of RMB200 (about US$24) according to the Chinese market price shall be . . . handed over to the gift administrative department or acceptor's work unit. Gifts of less than RMB200 belong to the acceptor or to the acceptor's work unit. P. R. China Criminal Law (revised edition) promulgated on 1997.03.14. Article 394 Any State functionary who, in his activities of domestic public service or in his contacts with foreigners, accepts gifts and does not hand them over to the State as is required by State regulations, if the amount involved is relatively large, shall be convicted and punished in accordance with the provisions of Article 382 and 383 of this law. (Article 382 and 383 regulate the crime of embezzlement.)

2. The China State Council Order No. 20 promulgated on 1988.12.01. Article 8 Any State administrative organization and its functionary who give, accept or extort gifts for the purpose of securing illegitimate benefits shall be punished in accordance with relevant state law and regulations on suppression of bribery. The P. R. China Criminal Law (revised edition) promulgated on 1997.03.14. Article 385 Any State functionary who, by taking advantage of his position, extorts money or property from another person, or illegally accepts another person's money or property in return for securing benefits for the person shall be guilty of acceptance of bribes. Article 389 Whoever, for the purpose of securing illegitimate benefits, gives money or property to a State functionary shall be guilty of offering bribes.

NES CHINA: BUSINESS ETHICS (B)

Prepared by Xin Zhang under the supervision of Professor Joerg Dietz

                    Version: (A) 2002-08-30

Mueller was coming back to the office the next day. His secretary was sorting out the mail and faxes on his desk, when Chen came in and accidentally found a letter sent from a Chinese law firm a few months earlier. The firm had learned from the Central Department that NES was applying for a holding company and would like to provide consulting service. Chen thought that using this firm would be a solution to the ethical conflict that her working team was facing.

The next day, Chen talked to Mueller about the letter. Mueller liked the idea because it could solve the problem in a legal way. That same afternoon, Mueller met a partner of the firm who promised to help NES get approval within a month. The partner also said that his firm had good relationships with the Central Department and was experienced in handling holding company applications. Mueller decided to have this law firm involved.

Ten days later, the Central Department issued approval for NES China holding company and the NES Beijing Representative Office paid the law firm US$10,000.

TEXTRON LTD.

Prepared by Lawrence A. Beer

Copyright © 2001, Ivey Management Services   Version: (A) 2002-01-24

INTRODUCTION

Gary Case, executive vice-president of Textron Ltd., sat at his desk and slowly drew a circle around the words *ethics* and *social responsibility*. Above the circle he wrote in bold letters the phrase "public opinion," and sat back to ponder his symbolic illustration of a potential problem that only he seemed to envision.

Case was thinking ahead and letting his mind focus on an issue that seemed out of the realm of the tenets of basic managerial principles that his undergraduate and MBA studies had prepared him for during his scholastic years. While he well appreciated the strategic decision-making concepts of running a transnational business, he felt himself personally wondering how to approach the complex subject of applying global ethics and social responsibility to an international venture that was being pushed on his company.

BACKGROUND

Textron Ltd. was a 65-year-old, family-held business based in Youngstown, Ohio. As a producer of cotton and sponge fabricated items for the beauty trade, selling to intermediate users as components in their make-up compact cases as well as direct to the retail trade for onward sale

to consumers, the company was under constant attack from Far Eastern manufacturers. The need to enter into some type of offshore manufacturing enterprise was now evident in order to maintain a cost competitive position for the firm to continue to prosper and grow.

As a maker of cotton puffs for the application of make-up cosmetics, the company had grown from a loft in Brooklyn, New York, back in the mid-1930s to a medium-sized enterprise with sales of $25 million and pre-tax earnings of $1 million plus. In the category of cosmetic applicators, Textron's fine reputation had been built on years of excellent service to the trade with attention to detail. Using, at first, the hand sewing abilities of seamstresses from the garment centres of lower Manhattan, the company had been a pioneer in developing customized machinery to produce quality cotton puffs to the precise custom requirements of modern cosmetic manufacturers. Today, 100 per cent virgin cotton rolls would enter Textron's factory at one end and exit as soft velour pads in numerous shapes, contoured sizes and colors at the other end of the process.

These puffs would be either sewn or glued with ribbon bands and satin coverings bearing the well-known brand names of the major franchised cosmetics companies of the world from Revlon, Estee Lauder, Maybelline and Max Factor as well as numerous others. They might also contain the names of retail store house brands or the internationally recognized trademarks of their own company. Currently, a new collection had been created through a licensing arrangement bearing the name of a highly respected fashion beauty magazine, whose instant recognition with the teenage trade was propelling the company to new sales levels. While historically Textron Ltd. primarily had produced components, supplying cosmetic companies with custom applicators tailored to their cosmetic ingredient requirements, the growth of its retail business in this sub-category was developing at a rapid pace. Major drug store chains, supermarkets and specialty shops featured Textron brands and their lines were becoming synonymous with the best in cosmetic applicators and assorted beauty accessories. With the launch of an additional range under the guise of a high fashion authority, featuring highly stylized "cool shapes" and "hot colors" designed to entice younger adolescent buyers, their reputation was achieving enhanced public notice. Such products using uniquely descriptive trendy phrases evoked an image of "hip to use applicators" and a whole new generation of teenage users was being developed.

The firm also was a key purveyor to the entertainment industry directly servicing the Hollywood movie and TV production companies, Broadway and the theatrical community, along with indirect sales to professional make-up artists and modeling studios thanks to the quickly developing beauty store trade. All in all, the future for Textron Ltd. was most promising.

Gary Case, a college friend of the company's president and principal owner, was brought into the business because of his experience at the retail sales and marketing level. The chief executive officer, who possessed an engineering background, was more than capable of overseeing the manufacturing side of the business; however, the strong movement of the organization into direct consumer goods, coupled with the overall expansion of the company, necessitated Case's hiring.

As the company began to prosper in the early 1970s, other stateside competitors emerged, but none could match the quality and inherent reputation of Textron Ltd. Their attention to detail and expertise of their original equipment manufacturer (OEM) sales staff servicing the franchise cosmetic companies gave Textron a competitive edge. They were called upon to work closely with their industrial customers to develop cotton puffs that matched the trends in new cosmetic ingredients and application methods at the research and development (R&D) stage of such developments. Such progressive fashion-oriented but facially skin-sensitive cosmetic formulas required applicators that matched the demanding specifications of these new advances in the cosmetic field. Cotton materials were needed to sustain the look on the skin and provide the user with the same result that the cosmetic cream, lotion or powder promised. While women, the prime purchasers of such products, wanted to obtain the dramatic results the franchise cosmetic companies advertised, professional make-up artists had long known that the choice of applicators to transfer the pressed powder in the compact, the lotion in the bottle or the cream in the jar, was the key to the process. The right puff was therefore needed to complement the make-up process.

In the late 1980s, Far Eastern manufactures of cosmetic applicators began to emerge, offering cheaper versions of such items. While the detailed processing of the raw cotton material used in such production was inferior to the quality and exacting details of those manufactured by Textron Ltd., the cost considerations necessitated a strong consideration of their offerings by the company's clients. As textile manufacturing began to develop in the Indochina region and more and more American firms brought their expertise to the area, the overall quality of goods as well as the base materials used began to improve. As an outgrowth of improvements in the generic textile business emerged, better methods of production, selection of raw materials and attention to quality filtered down into the cosmetic cotton applicator category.

Case, along with the president of the company, David Grange, and the head of product development group, Nancy Adams, had made periodic trips to the Hong Kong Beauty Exhibition to constantly gauge Far Eastern competitors. For many years, they observed a display of poor offerings and found themselves returning from such visits confident that the threat of offshore competition was not yet emerging as a viable alternative for their clients. Their regular customers, both beauty companies and retailing organizations, were rarely evident at such conventions and hence their positive feelings were continuously strengthened.

Current Issues

Over the last few years, however, it became evident that startup companies, beginning as derivative plants of the large textile manufacturers throughout China, Taiwan, Korea and Thailand, could become a real danger to their ever-growing global business. While many of these enterprises still produced inferior merchandise, Textron noticed that a number of their American competitors were now forming alliances with such organizations. These associations brought with them the knowledge of how to deal with the beauty industry both in America and Europe, instilling in them a deep appreciation for quality and endurance of raw materials to work with the new cosmetic preparations. Once such considerations took a foothold and a reputation for delivering such competitively detailed quality merchandise with vastly lower costs was discovered by Textron's clients, the company could be in for some rough times ahead. During the last visit to the Hong Kong show, Grange had bumped into a number of his key franchise cosmetic component buyers as well as a few of his retail chain merchandise managers. They had all acknowledged the quality advances made by these emerging new players. It was felt however that the distance of such suppliers from their own factories and key decision-making staffs and the fact that the shapes and designs were still not up to the innovative expertise of the Textron company created a hesitation among clients wanting to

deal with them. Grange knew full well however that with advanced global communication technology and the alliances with American-based representative organizations, the gap would be closed shortly. If such alterations were made and a fully competitive quality product could be offered with the inherent deep labor and overhead cost advantages that Far Eastern firms possessed, Textron was due for some major sales competition in the future.

After their last trip to the Asian convention in September of 1999, Grange and Case spent the hours on the return trip discussing strategic alternatives for the company in the years ahead. This wasn't the first time such matters were approached and, in fact, two years earlier, the company entered into an alliance with a United Kingdom manufacturer for the production on a joint basis of cosmetic sponges. Grange had always been reluctant to place his production facilities out of his geographical everyday domain. He was a "hands on" entrepreneur who felt strongly that all facets of one's business should be at arm's reach. Grange was deeply committed to his people and his door was always open to everyone in his organization. He was involved in every area of the business and it was not until Case joined Textron that Grange began to relinquish control over selective daily operations. This desire to closely preside over and monitor his people was born out of a heritage of family involvement as exemplified by his father. His dad had instilled in Grange a great empathy for workers and staff, and even today the company's culture still carried such roots of benevolent carrying.

When the firm had moved from the greater New York area to Youngstown, key personnel were given liberal incentives to move to the new location, and great care was given to those who could not make the journey. Still today, the company showed great pride in its relationship with employees. Textron's human resources department was not merely a conduit for processing applications for employment and overseeing payroll but a large fully functional multitalented group that ran off-site improvement seminars and cross training exercises. Besides offering a full array of benefit packages, the company had a well-supervised child-care facility on the premises at no charge to employees. The human resources director attended all managerial meetings, thereby maintaining a strong presence in all company decision-making and the position was considered on par with senior management executives. The commitment to maintaining hands-on control of his organization and the strong, caring relationship with his people made for a close-knit family and a kind of patriarchal role for Grange. He prided himself on the fact that union attempts to organize his factory labor force never got off the ground, as his employees felt that they were best represented by Grange himself.

Years ago, a satellite retail packaging assembly plant and distribution facility in San Antonio, Texas, which had been part of the purchase of a small professional beauty applicator business, was dissolved in favor of consolidating all operations in Youngstown. All personnel at this redundant factory were given an opportunity to relocate in Youngstown or they received good termination benefits.

The United Kingdom alliance was finalized due to Grange's long and valued friendship with the principal of that company. The two also shared similar feelings about managing people and a common cultural background. Both parties had spent many years working together and enjoyed a special relationship, which had been fostered by the fact that the U.K. managing director's family resided in Ohio, thereby bringing the two executives together on a monthly basis as the Englishman came home often. Grange also visited the British facility every two months and the two executives spoke weekly on the phone. Both men viewed the alliance as more of a partnership than an arm's length sourcing arrangement.

Grange always felt that one of his prime differentiated product marketing characteristics was that up until the U.K. association for sponge material applicators, all his products were made in the United States. He believed that such designation symbolized quality of material and manufacturing excellence as well as innovative styling and technologically advanced, state-of-the-art compliance. Even with the English sponge production unit, all the cotton puff applicators were still made in the States. To drive home this important selling issue, all packages of retail cotton finished goods bore the American flag proudly stamped on them next to the words "Made in the U.S.A." Grange had recently seen consumer products bearing the slogan "Designed in America" as well as "Product Imported From China and Packaged in the U.S.A." but felt that the global customer still valued the U.S.A. slogan indicating the country of origin on his retail line. But in Grange's recent discussions with component buyers in the cosmetic and fragrance industry, such designation did not seem so important, given the fact that both the sponges and cotton puffs were slightly undistinguishable or hidden parts in the total presentation of the makeup compact, the accent being on the brand name, ingredients and plastic case; imported items could be utilized if quality was maintained. The recent acceptance of the sponges made in England by Textron's clients gave credence to the fact that quality, price and service were the prime criteria for the industry, rather than the country of origin.

DECISION-MAKING TIME

Following the conference on the plane ride home from the Orient, Grange and Case had assembled their managerial staff and charged them with putting together a preliminary plan to form an association with a Far Eastern manufacturer of cotton puffs. At the initial briefing meeting, samples of cotton puff merchandise collected from a variety of Far Eastern producers were evaluated by the manufacturing quality control people as well as by representatives of the marketing and sales groups from the retail and OEM divisions. The immediate consensus was that with a little direction in fashion styling composition and adjustment in fixative dyes to sustain color in the cotton velour, a quality comparative range to supplement their domestic manufacturing output could be produced abroad. When Case presented the factory cost quotations for the samples being reviewed, the vice-president of finance exclaimed, "Such values were way below our own manufacturing standard costs before administrative overhead." He further added that "even with anticipated duty and freight via containerized shipments, the projected landed price at our door would eclipse our costs by a good 20 per cent or more reduction." When Case noted that "these foreign price quotations were based on minimum quantities and could be subject to economies of scale discounting," all participants quickly realized that their projected stock keeping unit (SKU) sales for 2000 would easily allow for even greater margins.

When the meeting broke up, Chris Jenkins, the vice-president of finance, cornered Grange and Case in the hallway.

> Guys, if these numbers can be confirmed, and if future production of these Chinese puffs can be modified to accommodate our quality stability color standards and slightly altered for design modification, we need to jump on this as soon as possible. Better still, if we can manufacture over there ourselves via our own factory or through a joint venture, our profit potential would be magnified at least three times.

ALTERNATIVE PROPOSALS

It was now six months since that initial meeting. In the interim, Case had been back and forth a number of times, holding substantial discussions with what was now a short list of two potential alliance candidates, both of which were co-operative ventures, with local Chinese governmental bodies holding a share in them. While these companies' abilities to alter their production to accommodate changes in the color additive process and make design modifications were verified, and the exchange of cost quotations were proceeding well, Case had not yet proposed the final type of alliance he wanted.

In the back of his mind, Case wanted to form his own subsidiary but felt that such initial market entry strategy was both costly and risky,

given the large investment required. Besides Case and Grange, the company did not have any other executives familiar with managing abroad. Given such considerations, Case's discussions to date with his Chinese associates had produced only two feasible alternatives to begin the relationship:

1. An initial three-year guaranteed outsourcing purchase agreement wherein, following the detailed specifications of Textron Ltd., supplies of cotton powder puffs would be produced at base prices. Such quotations would be subject to preset quantity discounting but offset slightly by an inflationary yearly adjustment. The right to pre-approve the samples of each and every shipment before departure would also be included in the arrangement. In essence a simplistic arm's-length purchasing association was contemplated.

2. The creation of a joint venture wherein Textron Ltd. would own 48 per cent of the company and the alliance partner would own the rest. Textron would be primarily responsible for sales and marketing worldwide along with periodic on-site technical assistance as to product design, quality assurances and engineering considerations by their technical staff. The plant facility, the manufacturing process itself and everyday operations would be under the direct control of the Chinese partner. Textron Ltd. would contribute a yet-to-be-finalized small dollar investment to help upgrade machinery and in general modernize the physical facilities. The partners would share the revenue generated by the sales efforts of Textron for the items produced in the plant.

Although exacting details of either proposed strategy needed to be worked out, with the former option requiring more legal and regulatory considerations, Case was confident that both situations could be accomplished. With the additional help of some local Chinese alliance specialists whom Case had utilized during the days when he had actually lived and worked in Hong Kong for a former employer, all seemed to be progressing nicely. Case knew he had to give additional thought to many other operational and administrative issues, and he wanted to obtain some sound advice from his internal teams before deciding which alternative to pursue. Questions as to the capital investment and how such funds would be utilized would require more discussions with the potential partners if the joint-venture route was chosen, but such issues would be addressed during Case's next trip to the Far East.

CHINA AS THE PRIME CHOICE OF SUPPLY

The focus on China was due mainly to Case's familiarity with the people and business environment. He felt very comfortable, given his prior experiences in the region and his knowledgeable appreciation of the culture and the way relationships were constructed. Beyond Case's personal considerations, the Chinese manufacturers he had encountered already had the necessary machinery and were well versed in the production of cotton puffs. Many already supplied the worldwide beauty trade but did not possess the sophisticated marketing and sales competencies practised by Textron, nor had they gained the reputation Textron historically enjoyed with the franchise cosmetic industry. An alliance with Textron would enhance the Chinese manufacturers' technical abilities and provide them with a wider entrée to the trade. The annual beauty show in Hong Kong attracted a global following, which would allow Textron to even create an offshore sales office and showroom close to the prime production facility to entertain prospective clients. Besides the Chinese connection, Case had opened initial discussion with makers of sponge applicators and other beauty accessories in Japan and Korea so that his trips to the China could be combined with other business opportunities he wanted to pursue in the Far East.

Case had entertained pursuing a Mexican manufacturer, as he had had prior dealings with companies producing a variety of cotton products in Mexico. Given the background of many of them in the cotton and aligned textile trade, this seemed a natural consideration, especially given the NAFTA accords and geographical proximity to Textron's major market, the United States. All potential companies Case visited, however, were located in the central part of the country, none near the border where the *Maquiladoras* were available. Case's Mexican contacts were not familiar with the specific production of cotton puff applicators as their cotton experience was in the manufacturing of surgical dressings, bandages, feminine hygiene pads and simple cotton balls. They would need to buy machinery and train a staff in such manufacturing operations. If Textron would fund such investment and provide technical assistance, a number of them agreed to manage such a facility on the U.S.-Mexican border through a joint venture. Case was hesitant to provide the funding, and he was worried that starting up a new plant would not let Textron achieve the inherent historical benefits that the more mature existing production in China would instantly allow.

Besides the economic considerations, Case found the Mexican manager's attitude a bit troublesome. Textron had once used a Mexican plant to supply, in final packaged form, cotton pads for the removal of facial cosmetic make-up. While his dealings with the principles of this family owned and operated business were most cordial and personally gratifying, Case had found that their attention to manufacturing details left much to be desired. The quality inspection of the raw cotton coming into their plants had given Case cause for concern. Many openly told him they mixed first quality fibres with "seconds" and remnants from the textile manufacturers in their local areas to achieve cost efficient production. As Textron always claimed its materials for cotton puff applicators were of "100 per cent virgin cotton," such an assertion might be difficult to enforce and supervise, given the pronouncements by his prior supplier. When discussions as to the importance of schedules to insure timely supply arose, the Mexican sources seemed to give the impression that they would do their best to comply. This slight hesitation bothered Case, as his component buyers demanded on-time delivery and were always changing specifications at the last minute.

Case had deep reservations on the business competencies exhibited by such Mexican firms, as his communications with them in the past, wherein days would go by before he heard from them, had left a poor impression on him. Many times, when he had repetitively inquired by e-mail, fax and telephone as to shipping dates for packaged finished products, he was eventually told that third-party suppliers of the packaging materials for the cotton pads caused the assembly delay. Inquiring further, during a visit with his Mexican supplier, Case learned that when local Mexican firms contract with each other, time promises are flexible and it seemed that an attitude of "when they are available, we get them" took precedence over definite schedules. During the year the company utilized the Mexican supplier, not one shipment was dispatched within the required period, and Case had given up contacting them, even paraphrasing the Mexican explanation when queried by his own inventory/warehouse manager.

The decision to go with a Chinese partner in some format seemed to be the best solution.

CASE'S PERSONAL REFLECTIONS

As Case pondered what other matters needed to be resolved, his mind began to focus on his three-year posting, back in the early 1990s in Hong Kong, with an electronics manufacturer to oversee their Chinese network of suppliers. When Case and his family had first arrived in the then-British colony, the excitement of this new foreign land and it's unique culture had made a lasting impression on him. He had marveled at the sights, sounds, smells and overall ambience of the city state that mixed East and West. Coming from a middle class American lifestyle, the treatment the family received was like being transformed into a rich conclave of the elite. His children went to a specialized English-type boarding school and rarely mixed with local natives of their own age. In fact, such young

Chinese children were lucky to get a basic elementary school education before being forced out into the real world and into the working community. The outskirts of the city, and even sections within, contained deep pockets that were below some extreme poverty levels Case had seen in other depressed regions of the world. Within a severely overpopulated area that was strained every day with new immigrants from the mainland, the concept of work, any job, took on a new meaning. People would work for what seemed like slave wages to Case, and he wondered how they survived, just attaining a mere sustenance level. His wife could afford household maids and cooks that were more like indentured servants than domestic employees. They worked long hours at meagre wages and never complained.

During Case's visits to plants in mainland China, both during his expatriate posting years and subsequent trips back in the mid-1990s, the conditions at such facilities had initially deeply disturbed him. The environments he witnessed were nothing like he had ever seen in the United States. Factories were like prison compounds. The laborers seemed to toil at their job stations never looking up, never smiling and always looked like they were staring out with blank facial expressions. Rarely had Case seen them take a break, with many workers eating lunch at their desks and at their worktables or machinery. He seldom witnessed the laborers even taking bathroom breaks. The air in the facilities was always stale with no ventilation except for a few fans, and it was always very hot or very cold, depending on the outside temperature. He witnessed children, younger it seemed that his two adolescent kids, toiling in the plants alongside the elderly. He watched infants placed alongside their mothers on the floor of the factories being rocked by feet as the mothers' hands moved on the table above them. As these visits became more frequent, Case's disdain for such initially horrific working conditions began to lessen and he began to accept what he saw.

Many times, in social conversations with other executives and managers, Case had voiced his concerns about the treatment of the workers. He listened as they tried to get him to understand and appreciate that while the conditions were terrible, the alternative might be even worse. With the expanded population, growing at a massive rate, the supply of people outstripped employment opportunities. In order to survive, people would take any job and children as well as the elderly all had to work. Public governmental assistance was not only inadequate but almost impossible to administer, even if the resources could be found. The old communist philosophy of all society working for the good of the common proletariat, and hence the state, had been indoctrinated with the birth of the Mao regime; people saw it as their duty and obligation to endure hard times.

Case's Chinese friends had often remarked that if China were to catch up to the Western capitalistic nations and be a participant in the world's expanded trading economies, its people were its greatest competitive asset. In order to be a member in the world community and to provide enrichment for future generations, sacrifices had to be made. Capital for the improvement of factory environmental conditions was secondary to the need to update basic machinery and gain technology. The government had to build a sound internal infrastructure of roadways, rail and port facilities to ship its goods before the physical welfare of its people could be considered. With power still a scarce commodity, any electricity flowing into a factory needed to be first used to run the machinery and not for hot or cool air to be produced. The only way to achieve the goal of making mainland China competitive with the rest of the world was through the exportation route which was founded in the country's ability to produce cheaper goods than the rest of the globe. This simple fact necessitated low labor and overhead operating costs that contributed to poor working conditions in the factories.

Obviously, Case understood this economic argument was the main reason his company—and therefore he himself—had come to the region. In order for his own organization to remain competitive in the cotton puff business both at home and abroad, it would have no choice but to locate a portion of its operations in China or some other emerging nation.

Case had seen the TV footage of the protesters at the 2000 WTO conference in Seattle who had destroyed that meeting and in later months had done the same in Washington, D.C., and Ottawa, Canada. He heard them voicing and physically demonstrating their deep concerns against governments and transnational companies as to worker rights and environmental conditions in emerging and developing nations. Case was well aware of the attention the press gave to large multinational companies like Levi Strauss, Reebok and others over their treatment of employees, accusing them of almost slavelike practices in their foreign factories. Even personalities who lent their names to the labels of garments, like Kathy Lee Gifford, had come under strong pressure for allowing their third party licensees in the United States to operate sweat shops and mistreat workers. Companies that did not even have a direct relationship wherein they exercised straight control over employee conditions were still questioned about the suppliers they used abroad as the social conscience of the world seem to be focused on these issues.

Although Case himself deplored the hiring of adolescent children, he understood the economic and social context that existed in China for their use. China wasn't America. Young kids grew up much faster and much more was expected of them as contributors to the family unit. Even the government mandate, made within the framework of the message of a collective good of the nation for families to have only one child, did not alleviate the problem. In fact, in many families it just made the burden deeper. Most Chinese families were made up of extended relatives who grouped together to pool their resources for their common survival. In these family units, all members had to work. The simple luxury of going to a public school, playing games and watching TV, as American children enjoyed, was not part of their world. In numerous families, children, mostly young girls, were sent away from their rural villages to emerging urban industrial centres to look for work. After paying large portions of their meagre weekly salaries back to their employers for dormitory housing and food within the confines of the factory compound, any amount left over was sent to the family.

Even the elderly felt such pressure to work, as retirement after years of service and a reasonable pension was almost a non-existent consideration. No true governmental program like social security existed, and the family had to care for the elderly in their homes, putting a great burden on the whole extended unit. Political dissidents and even criminals were conscripted into the labor force to help offset the cost of the State having to provide for them. Plant conditions, treatment of workers and even caring about the environment were not primary issues for an emerging country trying to first find work for its population during the transformation process into a competitive world economic nation.

Case pondered if it was time for the company to prepare a written corporate moral compass. Should it publish a code of ethics, as many transnational firms had been doing? What should it consist of, what specific criteria defining norms of behavior should be stated? and should it be incorporated as an obligation in the arm's length purchasing agreement being considered with the Chinese supplier? If the announced provisions were violated, should this be viewed as an automatic right for Textron to terminate the agreement, or should there be a time frame in which to cure such conditions? Case also wondered how his firm could monitor such matters to ensure compliance. If the alternative joint venture were chosen, how should such values be incorporated into the partnership agreement and how should Case process such matters during the negotiation?

Case was comfortable with discussions on costs, quality and delivery specifications as they had a finite measurable logic to them. Social responsibility and ethics touched upon many emotional areas that were harder to define. He had seen firsthand how different cultures approached them from divergent viewpoints, and

he had gained a respect for the saying "when in Rome do as the Romans do." He also, however, maintained the feeling that there were core human values that at times transcended such local traditions and social context.

MORAL DILEMMAS— UNANSWERED QUESTIONS

What worried Case was even if the business decision was the right one, could the company be entering a relationship that might some day backfire? If a factory that Textron bought merchandise from or, because of the joint venture, was more deeply involved in was alleged to be mistreating employees, would public opinion injure the company's reputation? Was the focus of the world now on China and its historic practices of human rights abuse? Would someone be watching companies more closely that associated themselves with Chinese partners in any form?

What if Textron's buyers of components, the franchised cosmetic houses, were themselves chastised for using slave-type labor in the supplies used in their own manufacturing of their brand named products? Would they in turn cease to buy from Textron Ltd.? What if consumers of the retail packaged lines decided to boycott the products for similar reasons? What if the licensor of the new collection felt that such foreign sourcing of items bearing their trademark was injurious to their image and reputation, and they objected?

Given his company's strong traditional organizational culture of placing employees first, Case also wondered what effect any such ethical and social responsibility issues stemming from a Chinese association could have on his own domestic operational employees.

He wondered about such matters again as he thought to himself that going global was more than just an exercise in financial, legal and operational logistical decision making; it involved taking a moral position in Textron's commercial relationships with overseas entities.

NOTE ON THE POLLUTION PROBLEM IN THE MEXICO-U.S. BORDER REGION

Prepared by Dan Campbell, David Eaton and Tony Frost

    Version: (A) 1999-02-18

History has shown that pollution increases in the first part of the country's major growth and this is certainly where Mexico is right now.

—Adolfo Gonzalez Calvillo, Director of Baja California's Department of Ecology

You don't solve problems in underdeveloped areas just by passing out money; 90 per cent of the problem is human attitude.

—Victor Miramontes, Managing Director of the North American Development Bank

The Chilpancinco settlement in Tijuana sits in the shadow of Otay Mesa, on top of which sprawl dozens of the city's maquiladora factories, on the California-Mexico border. Many of them are owned by U.S. corporations, including a now closed battery recycling plant. A white chemical crust rims the clods of dirt in the field outside the plant, and pools of strange, yellow water dot the barren landscape. Lead and heavy metal deposits have been measured in the soil on the mesa at concentrations 40,000 times over safe levels. In this unincorporated settlement, or colonia, six babies were reported born without brains in 1993, and 13 in 1994, just one of several clusters of this rare birth defect, called anencephaly, on the border.[1]

In the wake of the passage of the North American Free Trade Agreement (NAFTA) in 1994, numerous national and binational organizations were created to study and attempt to alleviate the environmental crisis in the Mexican-U.S. border region. This crisis, precipitated by 30 years of exponential growth in manufacturing activity along the Mexican side of the border, had a direct impact on the 11 million people that inhabited the region and the natural environment that struggled to sustain them.

Contrary to what was often portrayed in the public press, solutions to the pollution problem in the border region were neither obvious nor easy to implement. Many economists argued that it was misplaced for a developing country like Mexico to implement U.S. and Canadian-level environment standards. In fact, the chief economist for the World Bank, Lawrence Summers, had written an internal memo (subsequently leaked to the press) stating that "the economic logic behind dumping a load of toxic waste in the lowest wage country is impeccable." According to this view, environmental consciousness, along with greater enforcement of environment laws should—and surely would—follow Mexico's long march out of poverty toward economic prosperity. To environmental groups, such arguments were misconceived, and ignored both the very real costs of the pollution hazards for those living in the region, as well as the long-term costs of a badly degraded natural environment.

In the political sphere, the environmental problems in the border region were just one more in a litany of economic, social and political problems that had plagued the U.S.-Mexico relationship in the post-NAFTA era. Between the 1994 peso crisis, Mexico's growing political instability, the drug problem, the continued influx of illegal immigrants into the U.S. and the rapidly escalating trade deficit with Mexico, the voice of free trade in U.S. politics had grown increasingly dim. Although in 1997, President Clinton was again asking the U.S. Congress for "fast track" authority to further the free trade agenda, stories of massive environmental degradation and lax and/or corrupt enforcement of pollution regulations did little to further that agenda.

One thing was clear: stakeholders, activists and policymakers were operating in an "information vacuum" with respect to the environmental situation in the border region. Arguments on both sides of the issue were plagued by the paucity of data and scientific evidence. Had the environmental situation along the border improved under NAFTA, as some claimed? Had it gotten worse? Who exactly was responsible for the "white chemical crust" and "pools of strange, yellow water"? And, most importantly, what should be done?

THE MEXICO-U.S. BORDER REGION

In 1965, new Mexican legislation permitted the creation of a new form of manufacturing operation in the Northern border region, called a *maquiladora*. Under a set of rules outlined in the Mexican Border Industrialization Program (BIP), a maquiladora factory could temporarily import supplies into Mexico duty-free. After the manufacturing process, the goods could be returned to the U.S., again duty-free. Only the value added in Mexico was taxed by the Mexican government as the goods left the country.

With few exceptions, the next 30 years in the border region were characterized by rapid and sustained industrial growth. In the early years, development was limited to low capital factories that relied heavily on cheap manual labor. Without the commitment of fixed capital,

investors were quick to move or close facilities if they became dissatisfied with local conditions. As a result, the Mexican government offered exceptions from its stringent labor laws to continue to attract U.S. investment. Under a program called EL PACTO, the Mexican government, working with co-opted union officials, guaranteed preferential wage rates in order to attract direct foreign investment and curb inflation.[2] In later years, under pressure from external sources such as the International Monetary Fund (IMF) to encourage more permanent industry, Mexico began to support capital intensive activities that, although requiring fewer laborers, were hoped to provide a more stable economic base.

By 1997, the border region, 3,200 kilometres long and just 200 kilometres wide, was one of North America's fastest growing regions.[3] It was also the only geographical boundary in the world in which a free trade zone existed between an advanced industrial country and a developing country neighbor.

With output estimated at US$150 billion, the economy of the border region was larger than Poland's and nearly the size of Thailand's. Growth was not projected to slow in the years ahead, despite the fact that NAFTA would eliminate most of the tariff advantages accruing to maquila operations. Proximity to the U.S. market and the further decline of real wage rates in Mexico following the peso crisis ensured that foreign companies—and not just U.S. companies— would continue to invest heavily in the border region. Indeed, the rapid influx into the region of major Asian companies such as Sony, Samsung and Daewoo had led the mayor of Tijuana to declare: "This is going to be the Hong Kong of North America's Pacific coast."[4]

THE BORDER ENVIRONMENT

The rapid growth rates of the past 30 years had not come without cost. Infrastructure development was largely unable to keep up with the expansion. Standards of living were extremely low: maquiladora workers earned between US$5 and US$7 per day. The daily struggle for survival left precious little for "luxuries" such as running water and proper sewage disposal that might contribute to a cleaner environment. Economists estimated that the entire border region required additional infrastructure investment of $8 billion to bring drinking water, sewage treatment and garbage collection to all residents. Others put the price tag at closer to $20 billion.

INFRASTRUCTURE AND TAX BASE

Environmental activists argued that low wages were not all that foreign multinationals were taking advantage of in the maquiladoras. Andrea Durbin, policy analyst with Friends of the Earth made the following comments before the House Ways and Means Subcommittee on Trade:

> Annex III of the La Paz Agreement and the 1988 Mexico Law of General Equilibrium require maquiladora industries to export their hazardous waste to the country of origin for treatment and disposal. The thinking behind the agreement is that Mexico lacks facilities to treat these wastes in a manner equivalent to the treatment they would receive in the U.S.

> The U.S.-owned maquiladoras widely flaunt this law. The Environmental Protection Agency estimates that only about one-third of the hazardous waste generated in the maquiladoras is returned to the U.S., leaving somewhere around 20,000 tons in Mexico.

> This situation is not in the Mexican or the U.S. interest. The improperly dumped toxic wastes can lead to public health problems and huge long-term clean-up costs for Mexico. Industries may relocate to Mexico to take advantage of the situation and avoid the costs of proper disposal in the U.S. The problem is not isolated to Mexico, since the toxics

[sic] can cross back into the U.S. through the air, water, or groundwater.[5]

Although Durbin was not alone in predicting that NAFTA would precipitate the migration of dirty industries from Canada and the U.S. to Mexico, others disagreed. The U.S. Environmental Protection Agency (EPA), for one, dismissed this prediction as unlikely:

> NAFTA will not encourage U.S. firms to relocate to Mexico for environmental reasons because pollution abatement costs represent a small share of total production costs in most industries.

MEXICAN ENVIRONMENTAL LAWS AND ENFORCEMENT

Based on U.S. legislation, Mexican environmental laws and regulations were relatively strict. Where Mexico and the U.S. diverged in terms of environmental legislation was mostly in areas that were only secondarily related to the environment, such as so-called "right to know laws" and provisions for civil liability. For example, companies in Mexico were not required to make public the nature of their manufacturing activities to interest groups or the general public. Even when individuals or groups were able to collect evidence of damages caused to them by a polluting company, the Mexican legal system did not provide an adequate opportunity to seek restitution. Multi-million dollar class-action settlements were non-existent in Mexico.

Most of the criticism surrounding Mexico's environmental record was aimed at the country's ability to enforce the legislation already in place. Fears of lax enforcement were, in fact, central to the so-called "pollution haven hypothesis"— the notion that free trade would precipitate a race to the bottom in environmental standards as countries competed for foreign investment. Carlos De Orduna, former president of the National Council of Maquiladoras, commented that:

On the environment, Mexico has more difficult rules to comply with than the United States. Now, how well they can enforce the law is another story.

Under Mexican law, authorities had four enforcement mechanisms at their disposal:

Plant Closings: Ordered by an inspector while visiting a facility, plant closings were reserved for situations in which there is an imminent risk of "ecological disequilibrium" or if contamination exists that has "dangerous repercussions" for the environment.

Fines: Fines could be imposed on companies found to be violating environmental regulations ranging from 20 to 20,000 times the daily minimum wage.[6] A fine could only be issued after an administrative resolution, not at the time of the inspection.

Criminal Penalties: Depending on the severity of the crime, penalties could be issued against officers of offending companies ranging from one month to six years in prison, as well as fines of up to 20,000 times the daily minimum wage. If the environmental crime was carried out in a populated area, an additional three years of imprisonment could be imposed.[7]

Administrative Arrest: In extreme cases, corporate officers could be held for up to 36 hours by Profepa, Mexico's attorney general for the protection of the environment.

Until 1991, Mexico had only 109 environmental inspectors for the entire country. Many lacked basic training and tools, such as laboratories to test soil, water and waste. Moreover, the environmental bureaucracy in Mexico was widely viewed as an inept, if not openly corrupt, agency. As a result, orders were often routinely ignored. Inspections were thought to be rare and were targeted mainly at highly visible companies. One Mexican manager of a major multinational firm commented:

Unless a small company is being visible about its environmental contamination, environmental authorities don't bother them. They go to the big companies. That's where the money is.

Not surprisingly perhaps, the level of enforcement of environmental regulations appeared to improve as talks about the NAFTA intensified. In the two years leading up to the signing of the NAFTA, the number of inspectors tripled, while inspections and enforcement actions increased dramatically. However, in 1994, a presidential election year, inspections dropped off substantially. Many argued that the ruling party did not want to risk potential backlash from plant closures and lost jobs. The severe economic crisis in 1995 made enforcement initiatives that could lead to job losses even less politically appealing.

NAFTA and the Environment

The controversey over the environmental impact of NAFTA led the Clinton administration to negotiate a parallel side agreement pertaining to the environment. The agreement established several bodies designed to deal with environmental issues and to investigate "persistent patterns of failure to effectively enforce (a country's) environmental law."[8]

Under NAFTA, the United States, Mexico and Canada were also expressly forbidden to lower environmental standards to attract investment. The agreement also supported harmonizing environmental standards and allowed the three nations, as well as states and cities to adopt more rigorous standards. Under NAFTA, the United States and Canada maintained the right to block the importation of goods that failed to comply with its health or environmental standards.

Despite claims that NAFTA was the "greenest trade agreement in history," its environmental provisions had been criticized on several accounts. First, environmentalists complained that the dispute resolution process was secretive, exclusive and lacked provisions for enforcement. No apparent means existed for public comment on environmental matters presented before NAFTA panels. A second complaint was with the burden of proof provisions, which required the challenging party to establish that the sanitary (health) or phytosanitary (plant health) measure in question is inconsistent with or in violation of NAFTA. In addition, no specific trade sanctions were provided as a means to combat noncompliance with the provisions of either NAFTA or the side agreement on the environment. Moreover, the sanctions specified under NAFTA were considered to be unenforceable and too complex to be of much use.

The signing of NAFTA had also established the Border Environmental Co-operation Commission (BECC) and the North American Development Bank (NADBank), which were created to complement existing funding to improve the border region's environmental infrastructure and to strengthen co-operation on addressing the region's environmental problems. The BECC's purpose was to certify environmental infrastructure projects—primarily for drinking water, wastewater treatment and municipal solid waste—for subsequent financing by the NADBank in the form of loans and loan guarantees at market interest rates with flexible repayment terms. The agreement was intended to encourage private sector investment in projects funded through user fees paid by polluters and the border communities benefiting from these projects.

The remainder of this note describes two companies operating in the border region: Sanyo North America Corporation, a subsidiary of the Japanese electronics giant Sanyo Electric; and Guillermo Jiron y Asociados, a Mexican company, which provided hazardous waste disposal services to Sanyo and other maquiladoras in the border region.

SANYO NORTH AMERICA CORPORATION

The border operations of Sanyo North America Corporation (Sanyo) consisted of nine plants in Tijuana, Mexico, which bordered San Diego in the U.S. Although Sanyo had a long history of sales and manufacturing operations in the U.S., it had decided in 1996 to relocate its North American headquarters from New York to San Diego—closer to its manufacturing operations in Tijuana.

The Tijuana plants consisted mainly of low-cost assembly operations that manufactured products for the U.S., Canadian and other export markets: two refrigerator plants, two video cassette recorder plants, two plants manufacturing rechargeable batteries, and three others making televisions, appliances and laptop computers respectively. Most of the raw materials for these factories arrived as goods in process from factories in Japan. Materials entered the United States at the port of Long Beach in Southern California.

Sanyo's environmental policies were established by headquarters in Japan. In 1995, the company had launched a worldwide initiative to establish an environmental management system based around ISO 14000, an international standard of environmental management similar to the well known ISO 9000 quality standard. Sanyo had set the ambitious target of having each of its domestic and overseas factory sites as well as business headquarters, regional management centres, and research and development laboratories receive ISO 14000 certification by the end of the 1997 fiscal year.[9]

In part, to show its commitment to the border region, Sanyo had presented its corporate environmental policies to the North American organization at a conference in July at the company's North America headquarters in Tijuana. The conference brought together company management, environmental consultants, academics, and representatives from the EPA. Speaking at the conference, Mr. Yasuo Ohira, managing director of Sanyo Electric outlined the fundamental premise behind the company's environmental philosophy:

Sanyo cannot overcome competitors without superior, environmentally-conscious products.

Mr. Ohira went on to explain what this meant for Sanyo in terms of its corporate environmental policies. He stated that Sanyo needed to:

- Define the environment as one of our major management issues.
- Strictly observe environmental laws, regulations and international accords.
- Achieve compatibility between sustainable development and environmental preservation, and promote business activities that harmonize the environment.
- Determine voluntary regulations and standards, and implement ongoing programs for continuously improving the environment.
- Develop products that harmonize with the environment, including: introduction of life cycle assessment (LCA); improved recycling and energy-conserving qualities of products; and reduced use of environmentally hazardous chemical substances.

As part of its environmental management effort, the company had laid out a broad set of internal environmental targets to be reached by the year 2000. These targets were known as the "Second Voluntary Plan" and are summarized in Exhibit 1.

Sanyo Energy Corporation—Battery Division

Sanyo's North American battery division was created in 1986 with the construction of a cell assembly plant.[10] In 1990, the division was expanded with the addition of a battery assembly plant that linked multiple cells together to form rechargeable power packs for a variety of applications. The most common were wireless hand tools such as drills and radio controlled model vehicles.

Assembly

The cell assembly plant, using goods-in-process from Japan, manufactured single nickel-cadmium (NICAD) rechargeable cells. Manufacturing involved the winding together of nickel and cadmium plates into a cylinder approximately four centimetres long and two centimetres in diameter. The windings were then placed in a metal cylinder casing and filled with a chemical electrolyte before being sealed at either end with another metal plate.

During the winding of the plates, nickel and cadmium dust were created. Although the nickel dust was relatively harmless, the cadmium particles, while invisible to the naked eye, were extremely hazardous if ingested. To protect Mexican employees working within the plant, a ventilation system had been installed, with vacuum openings at each work station. Employees also wore masks and followed other procedures as dictated by the Materials Safety Data Sheet (MSDS) for cadmium dust that was published under the Workplace Hazardous Materials Information System (WHMIS).

Ultimately, the air from the ventilation system was vented into the external atmosphere, but not before being cleaned thoroughly. Plant management frequently tested the air leaving the ventilation system. Plant management admitted that they were unaware of any Mexican standard for these types of emissions, but levels were held below guidelines set out by the parent company for similar plants in Japan. As one plant manager noted:

> There is no way that a company like Sanyo is polluting. We are checking, watching everything. We test water going out into sewage, even though all we use it for is our restrooms. Our factories are practically brand new, newer than what we have in the United States.

In fact, the majority of the production process had been designed and implemented in Japan. Sanyo had several almost identical factories in other parts of the world, and the Tijuana operation was a copy of the Japanese factory. Most of the equipment came to the Tijuana plant second-hand as it was replaced in a Japanese manufacturing operation. This included a waste water treatment facility. Philipe Rujana, the Mexican plant manager, recalled the installation of the facility:

Action Objectives of the Second Voluntary Plan

SANYO Electric Co., Ltd.

Items		Target for 2000
Measures against global warming	Development of energy-saving products	Power usage levels compared with level in 1990 Air conditioner (main models) — 35% (Cooling mode) reduction / 20% (Heating mode) reduction Refrigerator (main models) Compared with level in 1995 — 30% reduction TV (main models) — 5–20% reduction
	Reduction of energy consumption per unit sales value	Compared with level in 1990 25% or more
Product assessment	Increase of recyclability Reduction of disassembling time Reduction of packaging use foam styrene	70% or more (main products) 55% or more (main products, compared to 1992) 50% or more (main products, compared to 1990)
Measures against industrial waste	Improvement in total volume of waste per unit sales value	70% or more (compared to 1990)
Promotion of environmental management system	Reduction of global environmental load	Fulfillment in accordance with guideline
Environmentally relevant substances (ERS)	Reduction of ERS use	(1) Selection of ERS concerned, establishment of investigation system for content in products until end of 1997 (2) Completion of content investigation, construction of data base, adoption of risk assessment guidelines and reduction targets until end of 1998 (3) Establishment of ERS management system in production stage covering whole SANYO company until end of the year 2000
Promotion of LCA	Reduction of global environmental load caused by products	Beginning of trial in 1996 for main products

Exhibit 1   Sanyo Electric Co., Ltd. Action Objectives

I wasn't even consulted about the installation of the water treatment facility. Management in Japan decided it was necessary for the operations in Japan, so they installed it here too. Where Sanyo and the environment are concerned, money has not been an issue. Even without local pressures, we would still have the same high level of environmental protections. They are willing to do "whatever it takes."

GUILLERMO JIRON Y ASOCIADOS

Located in Tijuana, Guillermo Jiron y Asociados (GJyA) was a waste management company that offered a complete range of services required to dispose of hazardous wastes generated in maquiladora manufacturing operations. Sanyo was the company's largest client and provided it with 15 per cent to 20 per cent of total revenues.

Maquiladoras contracted companies like GJyA to classify and remove hazardous wastes directly from their manufacturing operations and to ensure that they were properly transported back into the U.S. To legally transport and dispose of hazardous waste materials was a multistep process that included waste characterization, brokering and transportation.

Waste Characterization

Before waste materials could leave the manufacturing facility where they were created, the nature of the waste had to be determined and classified under a complicated set of guidelines outlined by the Mexican and U.S. governments. Because classifications were so narrow, a single manufacturing operation could generate waste materials that fell under numerous categories, each with their own handling and documentation requirements. The situation was further complicated by poorly defined requirements that were modified so frequently that even government and custom officials had a limited understanding of regulations and jurisdictions. The problem was exacerbated by confusion as to jurisdictional responsibilities in Mexico. For example, the management and movement of hazardous waste was considered federal jurisdiction whereas waste water treatment fell under state and local jurisdictions.[11]

Brokering

Due to the complexity of regulation, the services of a broker were required to work together with customs and other regulatory officials. The capacity and condition of customs facilities, as well as the training and staffing of officials at points-of-entry into the U.S. were insufficient to handle the large volume of traffic in the border region. The broker also negotiated with hazardous waste storage and disposal facilities in the U.S. to place or destroy the numerous categories of hazardous materials.

Transportation

GJyA had almost no transportation equipment of its own. Instead, the company contracted the transportation of the materials to several independent transport companies. Two different companies needed to be contracted to return goods to the U.S. because Mexican trucks were not permitted to cross the U.S. border. GJyA included the use of transportation contractors in their overall service package to end users. Often, clients of GJyA did not know which carrier was actually transporting their waste products.

Industry Conduct

Because maquiladoras were legally required to return their wastes to the U.S., Mexico had never developed a large hazardous waste storage or disposal capacity in the border region. The transportation industry, however, had developed rapidly and competition to provide hazardous waste trucking and disposal services was intense.

Guillermo Jiron, president of GJyA, explained:

This is a cost driven business. You'd be amazed at some of the operations we compete with. It doesn't take much to get into the industry . . . just a truck really.

Less stringent safety requirements for trucks and low levels of enforcement reduced barriers to entry, allowing numerous carriers with substandard capital equipment to offer hazardous waste transportation services to the region's manufacturers. Another factor affecting competition in the industry was the nature of the liability affecting producers and handlers of hazardous waste. Jiron explained:

> In the U.S. and Canada, manufacturers are still liable for hazardous wastes produced in their facilities when the wastes are being transported by a third-party contractor. This is not the case in Mexico. Liability for hazardous waste infractions by transportation companies can only be placed on the carrier itself. As a result, manufacturing operations are generally less concerned with the level of safety in the transportation companies they contract with . . . price is one of the few means of differentiation . . . carriers are forced to reduce costs whenever possible.

Costs were often reduced by cutting corners on measures taken to comply with regulations. Such activities included: not purchasing emergency response equipment, failing to train drivers to deal with emergencies and carrying noncompatible wastes in one trailer or container, which laws state should be kept separate. Perhaps the easiest way to cut costs was simply to dump the waste in one of the many illegal sites in the country's northern deserts, where thousands of barrels of toxic waste dotted the countryside.

The incentive to cut corners was intensified by several other factors:

Minimal Enforcement: Generally, transporters of hazardous waste did not fear a punitive reaction from government officials.

Lack of a Civil Liability: The absence of civil liability mechanisms, similar to those in

the U.S., eliminated the risk of civil suits in the event of damage to individuals or the natural environment.

Limited Use of Insurance: Because the risk of civil liability was not present, few companies felt the need to carry insurance. In the U.S. and Canada, where insurance companies were responsible for damages, they either demanded that responsible risk management procedures be followed, or charge higher premiums. Mexican companies, lacking the need for insurance, also lacked the incentive toward responsible behavior that was imposed on their U.S. and Canadian counterparts.

Jiron also pointed to upcoming provisions, stipulated under NAFTA, as providing a potentially important change in the structures and incentives governing the handling of hazardous waste in Mexico:

> In the year 2001, goods entering Mexico from the U.S. will no longer require a temporary importation permit to cross the border duty free. Instead, they'll fall under the NAFTA and move freely from one country to another.

> Basically, what that means is that hazardous wastes produced in Mexico will be able to remain in Mexico. My guess is that many companies will start to look for domestic options for hazardous waste storage and disposal. Hey, I would, too: why expose myself to U.S. civil law by bringing waste back into the U.S.? Trucking waste across borders is also a real administrative headache: not only are Mexican regulations different than U.S. regulations, but California's are different than Arizona's, which are different than Texas's.

In 1997, some estimates suggested that only one-sixth of Mexico's domestic demand for disposal facilities was being met. Attempts to create new facilities had met with strong opposition from interest groups such as Greenpeace Mexico. David W. Eaton of the Center for Interamerican Trade and Commerce at the Monterrey Institute of Technological and Superior Studies commented:

We don't know exactly what is going to happen to the hazardous wastes generated in the maquilas after the year 2001. The whole hazardous waste relationship that exists currently must be changed.

THE POST-NAFTA EXPERIENCE

In the two plus years following NAFTA's passage, numerous claims had been advanced about the environmental impact of the agreement. Several assumptions that had underpinned the green aspects of the agreement appeared not to have been correct.

The first was that NAFTA would fuel investment into Mexico's interior, thus relieving the pressure on the border ecosystem. However, the number of maquiladora workers had increased by more than 25 per cent from 546,000 in 1993, to 689,000 in September 1996. Nearly 400 new factories had opened along the frontier in 1996 alone. If anything, foreign investment in Mexico had become even more concentrated in the border region following NAFTA.

A second assumption was that rising income in the region—an outcome of greater trade and investment—would allow for greater investment in infrastructure to clean up the environment. However, the collapse of the peso in 1994, which reduced Mexican incomes by about half, caused federal and local governments in Mexico to cut environmental spending dramatically. According to some estimates, over 50 million gallons of untreated waste were still being dumped daily into the Rio Grande River in the town of Juarez, which lacked a waste treatment facility, threatening exposure to cholera, hepatitis and dysentery. Hepatitis rates on the border were two to five times the U.S. national average. In 1997, 40 per cent of the population on the Mexican side of the border were still thought to lack sewers, potable water or both.

A third assumption was that NAFTA institutions such as the BECC and NADBank would create a pool of funds for environmental projects. However, by mid-1997 BECC had certified only 16 projects for financing. Moreover, the

NADBank, which was to fund these projects, was not expected to be fully capitalized until 1998. To date, it had only approved funding for four projects.

Supporters of the agreement, including the Clinton administration, countered with arguments and evidence of their own. A report issued by the U.S. government noted that while environmental problems along the U.S.-Mexico border "were decades in the making and cannot realistically be corrected overnight . . . progress is evident." Since NAFTA's passage, enforcement of Mexican environmental law appeared to have improved. The number of Mexican environmental inspectors had increased, and an environmental crimes unit had been created. From 1993 to 1996, Mexico reported a 72 per cent reduction in serious violations from maquiladora facilities. This view was echoed by Jeanette Moorhouse of the Border Environmental Technology Resource Center:

> With (Mexican President) Zedillo and his predecessor, there has been a lot less corruption, and that means better enforcement of environmental laws. Today, businesses in Mexico can't just pay off a fine and keep continuing to illegally pollute like they could a few years ago.

In this atmosphere of uncertainty and incomplete information, the environmental situation on the U.S.-Mexican border was unlikely to disappear either from the public conscience or from the impending debates on the expansion of trade in the Americas.

EPILOGUE

More than 3,200 kilometres to the east of Tijuana, in Brownsville, Texas, a rash of birth defects, similar to those that occurred in Chilpancinco, saw 25 children born with spina bifida and another 30 babies born with anencephaly. Families of the dead and deformed babies subsequently filed a suit, claiming that contamination from factories, located across the

Rio Grande, but owned by U.S. corporations, caused the defects.

In 1995, the defendants, comprised of multiple U.S. corporations including General Motors, agreed to an out-of-court settlement of US$17 million. General Motors, in a letter to the Cable News Network (CNN), commented that "the primary cause of these types of birth defects is lack of sufficient folic acid in the diet" of the expectant mother. In 1997, *Time Magazine* reported that "many companies cleaned up their worst environmental excesses after the outbreak of fetal deformities, [and the outbreak] ended as suddenly as it began."[12]

NOTES

1. *Environmental Action Magazine,* "After NAFTA," September 22, 1995.

2. Maquiladora development history taken from Kopinak, Desert Capitalism: Maquiladoras in North America's Western Industrial Corridor, 1996.

3. The width of the border region was defined by the La Paz Agreement in 1983. The La Paz Agreement was signed by Mexico and the United States for the Protection and Improvement of the Environment in the Border Area.

4. Ibid.

5. Testimony of Andrea Durbin, policy analyst, Friends of the Earth before the House Ways and Means Subcommittee on Trade, September 21, 1993.

6. In 1997, the daily minimum wage was roughly US$3.25.

7. *Economist Intelligence Unit,* Managing Mexico's Environmental Challenge.

8. *Business and Society Review,* September 22, 1994.

9. Similar to ISO 9000 quality certification, ISO 14000 required that the environmental policies and practices be evaluated by recognized ISO 14000 auditors. Unlike ISO 9000 where objectives were measured by an absolute set of quality standards, ISO 14000 was based on the identification of, and progression toward, goals determined by each company on an individual basis. Within Sanyo, there were 34 sites in Japan and 48 overseas applying for certification.

10. Single units, often referred to as a battery by the general public, are actually a single cell. A battery is created when multiple cells are linked together.

11. The majority of wastes which were dumped illegally were liquid poured into the municipal drainage system.

12. Information about the Brownsville birth defects and ensuing legal action taken from, "The Border Babies; Did Toxic Waste from U.S. Factories Across the Border Damage the Environment of a Texas Town?," *Time Magazine,* May 26, 1997.

THUNDERBIRD
THE GARVIN SCHOOL OF
INTERNATIONAL MANAGEMENT

PLANET STARBUCKS (A)

Prepared by Professors Michael H. Moffett and Kannan Ramaswamy

You get more than the finest coffee when you visit Starbucks. You get great people, first-rate music, a comfortable and upbeat meeting place, and sound advice on brewing excellent coffee at home. At home you're part of a family. At work you're part of a company. And somewhere in between there's a place where you can sit back and be yourself. That's what a Starbucks store is to many of its customers—a kind of "third place" where they can escape, reflect, read, chat or listen.

—1995 Annual Report,
Starbucks Corporation

During the World Trade Organization talks in November 1999, protesters flooded Seattle's streets; and among their targets was Starbucks, a symbol, to them, of free-market capitalism run amok, another multinational out to blanket the earth. Amid the crowds of protesters and riot police were black-masked anarchists who trashed the store, leaving its windows smashed and its tasteful green-and-white decor smelling of tear gas instead of espresso. Says an angry Schultz: "It's hurtful. I think people are ill-informed. It's very difficult to protest against a can of Coke, a bottle of Pepsi, or a can of Folgers. Starbucks is both this ubiquitous brand and a place where you can go and break a window.

—"Planet Starbucks,"
BusinessWeek,
September 9, 2002, p. 100.

Ubiquitous—that was the term often applied to Starbucks. It had indeed become omnipresent within the United States and Canada throughout the 1990s. Now the company—and its founder, Howard Shultz—had set its sights on the global marketplace. Howard Schultz had stepped down as Chief Executive Officer and President in 2000 and taken on the title with associated duties of Chief Global Strategist (he remained Chairman of the Board). Between 1999 and 2002, the company averaged sales growth of over 25% per annum, and despite the recession wracking the global economy, 2003 was expected to show the same rapid growth. But the North American coffee markets were quickly reaching saturation. Howard Schultz and Starbucks knew that if Starbucks was to continue to meet the market's expectations for growth, the global marketplace would have to support it. By 2003, Starbucks had become the growing target of the anti-globalist movement, and many questioned its ability to successfully expand the U.S.-based business model to the global marketplace.

STARBUCKS HISTORY AND ORIGINS

Starbucks was founded in Seattle by Gerald Baldwin, Gordon Bowker, and Ziev Siegl in 1971 as a gourmet coffee bean roaster and distributor. The Starbucks name was a combination of Seattle's past, the *Starbo* mining camp of the nineteenth century and the first mate's name in *Moby Dick,* the classic American novel of whaling on the open seas. In 1982, Howard Schultz joined the company as a member of their marketing team. After a visit to Italy, Schultz urged the partners to consider opening Espresso bars in conjunction with their coffee sales. In 1984, Starbucks opened its first Espresso bar, a small corner of the company's downtown Seattle Starbucks store, to rave reviews. Although Schultz urged the company to expand the Espresso bar line, the controlling partners, now Baldwin and Bowker, were unwilling to enter what they considered the fast-food business, wishing to focus on the coffee-roasting niche market. The company had recently purchased Peet's Coffee and Tea, a Berkeley, California, coffee roaster and distributor, straining the company's management and financial capabilities. The partners wished to focus on these two main businesses.

Howard Schultz then left Starbucks and, actually with the financial backing of his former partners, opened *Il Giornale* in 1985, an espresso bar that sold coffee and assorted coffee beverages made exclusively with Starbucks' beans. Two years later, Schultz bought the former Seattle Starbucks company, six stores and roasting plant, for $3.8 million from Baldwin (who wished to focus on managing Peet's) and Bowker (who wished to cash out of the business). Schultz now was in control of Starbucks and with new investors, began building a global business which reached sales of $3.3 billion in 2002 and was acclaimed one of the top 100 growing global brands.

The Starbucks Concept

Howard Schultz's dream was to take the concept of the Italian—specifically Milan—espresso bar to every corner of every city block in the world. By the fall of 2002, the Starbucks business was a complex three-legged stool for global development: (1) retail coffee and assorted specialty items; (2) specialty sales; and (3) Frappuccino coffee drinks and specialty coffee ice creams sold through other retailers globally.

What We Are About. Starbucks purchases and roasts high-quality whole bean coffees and sells them along with fresh, rich-brewed, Italian-style espresso beverages, a variety of pastries and confections, and coffee-related accessories and equipment—primarily through its company-operated retail stores. In addition to sales through its company-operated retail stores, Starbucks sells primarily whole bean coffees through a specialty sales group, a direct response business, supermarkets, and online at Starbucks.com. Additionally, Starbucks produces and sells bottled Frappuccino® coffee drink and a line of premium ice creams through its joint venture partnerships and offers a line of innovative premium teas produced by its wholly owned subsidiary, Tazo Tea Company. The Company's objective is to establish Starbucks as the most recognized and respected brand in the world.

To achieve this goal, the Company plans to continue to rapidly expand its retail operations, grow its specialty sales and other operations, and selectively pursue opportunities to leverage the Starbucks brand through the introduction of new products and the development of new distribution channels. (starbucks.com)

Starbucks' initial public offering was in 1992 (NASDAQ: SBUX). The company had, however, broken new ground the previous year when it became the first privately held company in the United States to offer its employees a stock ownership plan. The plan, termed *Bean Stock,* offered shares to both full-time and part-time employees.

The company had seemingly re-energized the entire coffee industry. Although Starbucks itself made up a relatively minuscule percentage of the entire North American coffee industry, it had sparked the expansion of coffee cafes like itself, rejuvenated the traditional mass market coffee sellers, and expanded all facets of the industry as distributed through the traditional supermarket distribution system. This *Starbucks Effect* as it was termed, was based on the *perceived* premium product's cachet extending to all of the collateral products, both complements and substitutes. In the case of Starbucks itself, the perceived premium was both in the product's quality and in the method of its delivery.

> First, every company must stand for something. Starbucks stood not only for good coffee, but specifically for the dark-roasted flavor profile that the founders were passionate about. That's what differentiated it and made it authentic.

> Second, you don't just give the customers what they ask for. If you offer them something they're not accustomed to, something so far superior that it takes a while to develop their palates, you can create a sense of discovery and excitement and loyalty that will bond them to you. (Howard Schultz, *Pour Your Heart Into It,* Hyperion Press, 1997, p. 35.)

THE STARBUCKS EXPERIENCE

The concept of Starbucks went far beyond being a coffeehouse or coffee brand. Emerging from Howard Schultz's original idea of an Italian Espresso coffee bar, it had evolved into its own Americanized version of a specialty coffee provider of coffee shop services. As described in the introductory quote from Howard Schultz, Starbucks based its customer's retail experience on high quality coffee, *arabica* bean-based coffee, but then surrounded the delivery of the coffee with specialty services and atmosphere.[1] Special pastries and selected music provided an atmosphere of both warmth and comfort.[2] Employees were trained to not only provide a wide array of advice on coffee selection and appropriateness to potential customer needs, but to engage the customer. The customer was to feel they were not at home, not at work, but at "a third place."

The People

The maintenance and development of this quality experience required a strong organizational commitment. The decade of the 1990s saw Starbucks expand its talent pool on the most influential senior levels, with key additions contributing greatly to the evolution of the company's business lines. Howard Schultz began assembling an experienced team of professionals to drive Starbucks' growth.

In 1989, Howard Behar, with more than 20 years in retail, joined the company as the director of store operations. Behar refocused much of the Starbucks development away from the pure product itself—coffee, to the consumer's experience in a Starbucks. Behar believed the core component of the experience was in quality of service. Starbucks' employees (termed *partners* by Starbucks) needed to be highly motivated to pay continuing attention to repeat customer needs. The company invested in extensive employee training, but this investment was lost if the company could not retain its people. One of the biggest barriers to retention was, in turn, compensation and benefits, in which the service industry was notoriously deficient.

Starbucks' solution was to offer health care benefits to all employees who worked more than 20 hours per week. Although an expensive benefit to provide by industry standards, Behar argued that if employee retention was improved and quality of service preserved, it would more than pay for itself. The company followed this first instrumental move with the introduction of the employee stock ownership plan in 1991 (Bean Stock), which was intended to increase the ownership culture of store management. Howard Behar would eventually become President of North American operations.[3]

In 1990, Orin Smith joined the company as Chief Financial Officer and quickly filled the role of the company's right-brain to Howard Behar's left-brain. Smith had extensive experience in a number of organizations and consulting, and was a strong believer in process development. Where Behar had focused on the people, Smith focused his development efforts within Starbucks on the organizational processes which would support effective execution of strategies. Smith believed in strict organizational discipline, including careful use of the Starbucks brand and insisted for many years on company-owned and operated stores, rather than the franchising common among most American retailers. Behar became the unofficial defender of the quality of the Starbucks brand. Orin Smith would eventually become President and Chief Executive Officer of Starbucks. As illustrated by Exhibit 1, the Starbucks experience was based on people.

The Supply Chain

The pursuit of premium quality also drove Starbucks back up the coffee supply chain. Coffee, although second only to petroleum in volume of global trading, was highly fragmented. It was estimated that a full one-third of the world's coffee farms were three acres or less in size. This typically resulted in a consolidation process which handed off coffee from farmer to collector, collector to miller, miller to exporter or broker, and finally to importer. In the past, the importer and brokers then sold coffee to the large mass-market coffee roasters and producers.

Starbucks wished to improve the quality and integrity of its coffee by working back up the supply chain to the actual growers. As a result, Starbucks refined its coffee quality while effectively bypassing much of the middle market. As Starbucks developed expertise and relationships with the coffee growers themselves, the company worked tirelessly to increase the quality of the *green coffee* (unroasted beans) purchased while taking cost out of its supply chain. This would eventually prove a point of exposure for Starbucks politically, but also position the firm for opportunities in sustainable economic initiatives with these growers.

Howard Schultz continued to add key leaders in the business in the early 1990s—people who would continue to fill out the gaps in the organization and solidify a corporate culture which was a difficult balance between entrepreneurship and disciplined growth. These decisions proved critical, as Starbucks embarked upon a massive

---

Establish Starbucks as the premier purveyor of the finest coffee in the world while maintaining our uncompromising principles as we grow.

The following six principles will help us measure the appropriateness of our decisions:

1. Provide a great work environment and treat each other with respect and dignity.
2. Embrace diversity as an essential component in the way we do business.
3. Apply the highest standards of excellence to the purchasing, roasting, and fresh delivery of our coffee.
4. Develop enthusiastically satisfied customers all the time.
5. Contribute positively to our communities and our environment.
6. Recognize that profitability is essential to our future success.

Exhibit 1   Starbucks Mission Statement

Source: starbucks.com.

expansion which would test the organization's capabilities.

Expansion

At McClintock Drive and Ray Road, you can walk out of a Starbucks, built into a grocery store lobby, and gaze across the parking lot—at a brand new Starbucks. With the retailer's rapid expansion, it isn't unusual to find multiple sites within a mile or two of each other. And although having two in the same parking lot certainly isn't the norm, it's something that does happen on occasion. ("2 Starbucks, 1 Lot," *Arizona Republic,* October 21, 2002, p. B5.)

As Starbucks moved into a market, it focused on location. Providing ready access to consumer foot traffic, such as commuting routes, allowed Starbucks to place its third place directly between the other two places. Stores were located in pivotal positions for consumer recognition and access. Corner locations, the hallmark of the early store growth, provided high visibility and maximum exposure. As stores expanded in North America to more and more of the automobile-based cities, plentiful parking became critical to any store's accessibility.

The company was also admired and criticized for its market-swarming expansion techniques. As stores proliferated, Starbucks broke with many retail distribution traditions by infilling, introducing stores which could not help but cannibalize existing store sales. This also led to the characterization of Starbucks as *ubiquitous.* With stores appearing across the street from existing stores, the firm did often actually appear to be everywhere you looked. The strategy, although not acknowledged officially, prevented competitor entry in established Starbucks markets through store proliferation. It had, however, led to a disquieting downward trend in sales per store. Between 1995 and 1998, Starbucks had averaged $0.69 million per store per year. Beginning in 1999, this revenue per store value had continuously declined, falling to $0.559 million per store in 2002.

The company was widely considered ruthless in its real estate practices. Practices included paying premiums over existing rental prices to push square footage prices up, retaining closed properties to prevent competitor entry, and generally aggressive property negotiations. The refusal to franchise allowed the firm to pursue real estate and store proliferation strategies which did not conflict with corporate goals; all stores were Starbucks-owned and operated, and therefore "turf" was not an issue.

Through the later 1980s and early 1990s, Starbucks focused expansion in the Pacific Northwest and California markets. Howard Schultz's expansion strategy revolved around establishing regional beachheads which the company needed to provide logistical support for stores while maintaining quality. In 1993, the company entered the Washington D.C. market, followed soon after in 1994 by Boston.[4] The Boston entry was through acquisition, buying out the Coffee Connection chain in the region. Beginning in late 1994, the company expanded rapidly to the major metropolitan areas of Minneapolis, New York, Atlanta, Dallas, and Houston. By the mid-1990s, Starbucks had stores in more than 40 states and was starting to look to the limitations of market saturation.

There were no hard and fast rules for store growth or saturation. Starbucks itself believed that only Seattle, with one store per 9,400 people, was actually at the saturation point. The island of Manhattan, with one store per 12,000 people, was still considerably below that point.

INTERNATIONAL EXPANSION

"We remain highly respectful of the culture and traditions of the countries in which we do business," says Howard Schultz, chairman and chief global strategist. "We recognize that our success is not an entitlement, and we must continue to earn the trust and respect of customers every day."

Although the first Starbucks store outside the United States was opened in Vancouver, British

Columbia in 1988, this was essentially a regional expansion—from Seattle outwards and north-ward in the Pacific Northwest—rather than an intended international expansion. Beginning in the mid-1990s, the company aggressively pursued true international expansion. Starbucks used two basic structures for international expansion—company-owned and licensing agreements—to move first across Asia (1996), the Middle East (1998), and finally Europe (2001) and Latin America (Mexico, 2002).[5]

The company had defied many of its critics with the growth and success of its international stores. Market analysts and critics had argued that Starbucks' premium prices, paper cups, and smoke-free cafes would not fit within traditional cultural practices in places like Tokyo and Vienna. Once again the chain proved the naysayers wrong by seemingly creating their own market and their own third place experience in some of the largest coffee-consuming cultures in the world.[6]

Japan

Starbucks' true international expansion had begun in Japan in October 1995 with the formation of a joint venture (JV) with Sazaby, a Japanese retailer and distributor with its own chain of Afternoon Tea stores. Sazaby proved to be an excellent partner, with expertise in both retail beverages and real estate.

The JV had opened its first store in Ginza in 1996 and had flourished. By 2002, it had more than 250 stores nationwide, and projected more than 500 stores by 2003. Although average Japanese store sizes were half that of the United States, they averaged nearly twice the sales. The JV had proven so successful that it undertook an initial public offering in October 2001, the only unit within Starbucks' international network to be listed independently of the parent.

Sazaby was also the prototype of the qualities Starbucks looked for in potential business partners. Starbucks officially listed the following characteristics as desired in its international partners:[7]

- Shared values and corporate culture
- Strong multi-unit retail/restaurant experience
- Dedicated human resources
- Commitment to customer service
- Quality image
- Creative ability, local knowledge, and brand-building skills
- Strong financial resources

China

With the opening of its first store in January 1999 in the World Trade Centre in Beijing, Starbucks added the People's Republic of China to its growing list. In the next three-and-a-half years, its footprint had been expanded to 35 shops, focused in and about Beijing and Shanghai. The reception to Starbucks in a culture grounded in tea was remarkably successful. Although Starbucks was heavily criticized for opening an outlet in a souvenir shop in Beijing's Forbidden City in 2001, the shop flourished.

Europe

The company's entry into Continental Europe had been anticipated for years, but with much trepidation. Europe's longstanding traditions of coffee consumption and independently owned and operated coffeehouses constituted an established market which was not considered open to American entry. Starting in Switzerland and Austria in 2001, the company then expanded into Spain, Germany, and Greece in 2002. Although many critics argued—as they had in Japan before—that local customers would not be attracted to smoke-free, paper-cup coffee consumption, the lines had been long.

Each country of entry was evaluated in detail, including focus groups, quantitative market assessment, and detailed identification of appropriate business partners. As part of the expansion process, Starbucks brought all foreign managers to its Seattle offices for a rigorous 13-week training course in the Starbucks experience. By the end of 2002 Starbucks had 1,312 of its total 5,886 stores outside of the United States. The current plan was to open two international stores for every one new domestic store.

CORPORATE SOCIAL RESPONSIBILITY

Starbucks defines corporate social responsibility as conducting our business in ways that produce social, environmental, and economic benefits to the communities in which we operate. In the end, it means being responsible to our stakeholders.

There is growing recognition of the need for corporate accountability. Consumers are demanding more than "product" from their favorite brands. Employees are choosing to work for companies with strong values. Shareholders are more inclined to invest in businesses with outstanding corporate reputations. Quite simply, being socially responsible is not only the right thing to do, it can distinguish a company from its industry peers. (Corporate Social Responsibility Annual Report Starbucks Coffee, Fiscal 2001, p. 3.)

Starbucks had found itself, somewhat to its surprise, an early target of the anti-globalist movement. Like McDonald's before it, it appeared to be yet another American cultural imperialist, bringing a chain-store sameness to all countries everywhere. Like McDonald's, Starbucks found that its uniquely defined brand and experience did not have to conform to local cultural norms, but could exist alongside traditional practices, creating its own market and successfully altering some consumer behaviors.

Unlike McDonald's, however, Starbucks was the purveyor of a commodity, coffee, which was priced and sold on global markets. Coffee was sourced from hundreds of thousands of small growers in Central and South America, many of which were severely impoverished by all global income and purchasing power standards. As coffee prices plummeted in the late 1990s, companies like Starbucks were criticized for both benefiting from lower-cost sourcing and for their unwillingness to help improve the economic conditions of the coffee growers themselves.

By 2001, Starbucks had implemented a multitude of programs to pursue its program for corporate social responsibility (CSR) and pursue sustainable economic development for the people in its supply chain. Although not wishing to own the supply chain, Starbucks' strategy was a complex combination of altered business practices in procurement, direct support to the coffee growers, and the formation of brands which would provide conduits for consumers wishing to support CSR initiatives. Exhibit 2 provides a brief overview of some of these programs.

Procurement

Coffee was traditionally bought and sold using *market pricing,* buying from wholesalers at a global market price—the so-called New York "C." Since Starbucks purchased only arabica bean premium grade green coffee, it always paid a premium above New York "C." Both New York "C" prices and the premium, however, moved up and down with global market conditions. Traditional robusta bean purchases by mass-market labels were made on the wholesale markets through brokers and buyers.

Starbucks, however, preferred to purchase using *outright pricing,* in which the price was negotiated directly with small and medium-sized farmers, cutting out the segment of the supply chain which the wholesalers usually occupied. In principle, a greater proportion of the price went directly to the producers, assuring a higher return to the small farmer. In addition to the pricing structure, Starbucks was also attempting to break from traditional market practices of always buying in the cash market. As illustrated in Exhibit 3, the company was moving aggressively to purchase more and more of its coffee under long-term contract (3 to 5 years, on average), guaranteeing prices to growers over multiple crop years.

A long-term dilemma of coffee farmers was the lack of access to affordable credit. Farmers without adequate working capital financing were often forced to accept low prices for coffee from buyers—so-called *coyotes* in Central and South

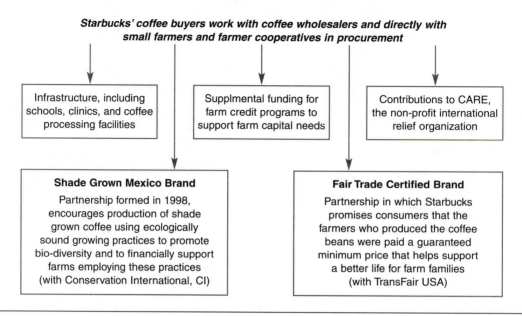

Starbucks' coffee buyers work with coffee wholesalers and directly with small farmers and farmer cooperatives in procurement

| Infrastructure, including schools, clinics, and coffee processing facilities | Supplmental funding for farm credit programs to support farm capital needs | Contributions to CARE, the non-profit international relief organization |

Shade Grown Mexico Brand

Partnership formed in 1998, encourages production of shade grown coffee using ecologically sound growing practices to promote bio-diversity and to financially support farms employing these practices (with Conservation International, CI)

Fair Trade Certified Brand

Partnership in which Starbucks promises consumers that the farmers who produced the coffee beans were paid a guaranteed minimum price that helps support a better life for farm families (with TransFair USA)

Exhibit 2   Starbucks' CSR Programs Focusing on Coffee Growers

	Percentage of Total Coffee Purchased	
	Fiscal 2001	Fiscal 2002
Price Basis		
Market pricing (New York C-basis)	88%	26%
Outright pricing (negotiated)	12%	74%
Relationships		
Direct relationships (from farms and co-ops)	9%	32%
Indirect relationships (through wholesalers)	91%	68%
Purchase Terms		
Purchased under long-term contract	3%	36%
Purchased in cash market	97%	64%

Exhibit 3   Starbucks Coffee Sourcing Practices, 2001–2002

Source: Corporate Social Responsibility Annual Report, Starbucks Coffee, Fiscal 2002, p. 6.

Note: Amounts by category are not mutually exclusive.

America—in relative desperation. In an effort to stop this financial exploitation, Starbucks had initiated a number of loan guarantee programs in 2002 to provide pre-harvest and post-harvest financing for coffee farmers. As a result, Starbucks provided financing for more than 1.2 million pounds of coffee in 2002 (205 farmers received pre-harvest financing, 691 post-harvest financing).[8]

Direct Support

Starbucks was a regular and growing giver, supporting relief organizations such as CARE,

| | Pounds of Coffee Purchased | | |
	2000	2001	2002
Conduit Brand			
Fair Trade Certified Coffee	190,000	653,000	1,100,000
Certified Organic Coffee	570,000	874,000	1,700,000
Conservation (Shade Grown) Coffee	304,000	684,000	1,800,000

Exhibit 4   Conduit Brand Coffee Purchases by Starbucks, 2000–2002

Source: Corporate Social Responsibility Annual Report, Starbucks Coffee, Fiscal 2002, p. 8.

Note: Volumes are by fiscal year. Certified Organic includes Organic Fair Trade and Organic Conservation (Shade Grown) coffee. Amounts by category are not mutually exclusive.

the nonprofit international relief organization, as well as providing direct support to farmers and farm communities around the world.[9] For example, Starbucks had contributed $43,000 in 2001 to the construction of a health clinic and school in Guatemala and a health clinic in East Timor. The company was also providing aid in a variety of ways to the improvement of coffee processing facilities in a number of the countries of origin.

Conduit Brand Development

Much of the growing pressure on all multinational companies for sustainable development and social responsibility arose directly from consumer segments. In an effort to provide a direct conduit for these consumer demands, Starbucks had initiated a company program called *Commitment to Origins,* "dedicated to creating a sustainable growing environment in coffee originating countries." Under the program, Starbucks had introduced *Shade Grown Mexico* coffee, *Fair Trade Certified* coffee, and *Serena Organic Blend* coffee.

Shade Grown Mexico coffee was introduced in 1998 in partnership with Conservation International (CI), a nonprofit environmental organization. Coffee purchased by Starbucks from CI's Conservation Coffee Program was cultivated under the canopy of shade trees in origin countries. This practice was considered ecologically sound and helped support bio-diversity. Shade

Grown Mexico coffee purchases had grown from 304,000 pounds in 2000 to 1.8 million pounds in 2002 (see Exhibit 4).[10] The Shade Grown Mexico coffee had been selectively introduced in Starbucks stores in North America and through online sales at starbucks.com.

Beginning in 2000, Starbucks began working with TransFair USA, a non-profit organization which provided independent certification for all *Fair Trade* coffee in the United States.[11]

The concept of Fair Trade addressed the question of the just distribution of the burdens and benefits of trade. The Fair Trade movement argues that when most of the customers' purchasing dollar goes to the retailer, the marketer, the wholesaler, and the speculator and very little goes to the laborer or the farmer, something is wrong with the mutual benefits of the exchanges, particularly when those who provide the product have earnings that do not even cover subsistence costs.[12]

Although Starbucks had introduced *Fair Trade* coffee in North American stores, and promoted it through various brochures and promotions ("Coffee of the Day" monthly), it continued to be heavily criticized for not expanding the program faster. Fair Trade coffee purchases also expanded rapidly, rising from 190,000 pounds in 2002 to more than 1.1 million pounds in 2002.

The third category of conduit brand development was Serena Organic Blend coffee. Organic coffee was grown without the use of synthetic pesticides, herbicides, or chemical fertilizers. Like Shade Grown coffee, Organic Blend was an environmental-sustainable development conduit. As illustrated in Exhibit 4, Starbucks' purchases of organic coffee had more than tripled between 2000 and 2002.

These product brand programs allowed consumers wishing to support these sustainable development initiatives to express their interest through purchasing—at a price.[13] All three coffees were roughly 20–25% more expensive compared to Starbucks' traditional blends (whole bean coffee sales).

GROWING PRESSURES

By the spring of 2003, Starbucks was at what many thought the pinnacle of its prospects.

- It was operating nearly 5,700 stores in 28 countries.
- It had made more than $215 million in profit on $3.29 billion in sales in 2002, and sales and profits were both expected to grow 25% in 2003.
- It was named by *Interbrand* one of the most recognizable global brands, although the company still spent less than $20 million per year in advertising.
- The New York "C" coffee prices remained at near-record lows, decreasing sourcing costs and increasing gross operating margins.

Starbucks was one of the few companies to continue rapid sales and earnings growth through the 2001–2002 period and the company was continuing to expand international operations at a breakneck pace. But all was not aromatic in the Starbucks marketplace.

Service quality and employee motivation and retention were continuing issues. Although *barrista* (the coffee brewers in Starbucks lingo) pay was still superior to other low-end wage jobs, rapid expansion was confronting the firm with employee fatigue. Store managers and employees were overworked and underpaid. Required overtime for store managers had only been eliminated in 2000 as a result of the settlement of a class action suit brought in California by disgruntled store managers.[14]

The limits to remaining expansion opportunities in North America were now in sight. Seattle, with a Starbucks store for every 9,400 people, was considered by the company the limit.[15]

Participate in the Organic Consumers Association "Global Week of Action Against Starbucks," September 21–28.

In October 2001, Starbucks made a commitment to buy 1 million more pounds of Fair Trade coffee and brew Fair Trade coffee once a month. Don't let Starbucks stop there—Send a Free Fax to demand that Starbucks brew Fair Trade Coffee of the Day EVERY WEEK!

The coffee industry is in crisis. Coffee prices are at an all time low, remaining below $.50 since August with no increase in sight. This means that farmers are becoming even more impoverished, going further into debt and losing their land. Meanwhile, coffee companies such as Starbucks have not lowered consumer prices but are pocketing the difference, even taking into account the quality premiums in the specialty industry.

The Fair Trade Labeling Organizations International recently released figures that show a total production by groups on the Fair Trade Coffee Register of 165,000,000 pounds in year 2000, whereas total sales were only 30,000,000 pounds. This leaves an additional 135,000,000 pounds of Fair Trade coffee produced by cooperatives that are not receiving a Fair Trade price.

Exhibit 5   The "Starbucks Campaign"

Source: Global Exchange, Global Economy, www.globalexchange.org/economy/coffee/starbucks accessed 10/6/02.

Manhattan, with 124 stores or one store per 12,000 people, was considered still open to further development. But same store sales in the United States, Canada, and even Japan were now beginning to show declines which persisted; in the past, in-filling store entry had caused only temporary same-store sales declines for the most part.

Although very aggressive in the eyes of many, the anti-globalization movement continued to focus much of its efforts on Starbucks. Plummeting coffee prices on world markets in 2001 and 2002 had led to more and more pressure on Starbucks to increase the prices it paid to growers. Howard Shultz himself increasingly became the target of mail, fax, and e-mail campaigns to pressure Starbucks into more proactive policies for grower income support (see Exhibit 5). Although Starbucks had actively pursued a number of corporate social responsibility initiatives, it was accused of polishing its image more than truly working to improve the lives of those its existence depended upon: the coffee growers.

Rapid international expansion seemed to only magnify the growing pressures. As Starbucks moved into more and more countries, labor and real estate practices came under increasing scrutiny, as did its image as global imperialist. Wall Street looked on with a critical eye as the firm entered the global marketplace through joint ventures which assured the firm of less profits per store than in the domestic past. Earnings growth was sure to slow. The question grew as to how far and how fast the company could still go.

NOTES

1. The traditional coffee sold by U.S. mass market brands like Folgers and Maxwell House was the lower grade and cheaper robusta bean.

2. The experience itself had evolved. In his early attempts to reproduce the Italian coffee bar, Schultz had provided little seating with opera music. The seating was expanded and the music replaced, as American customers complained.

3. Behar had retired in 1999, but returned to the company on a full-time basis in 2001.

4. The choice of Washington, D.C. was a surprising choice to everyone but Starbucks' management team. The company had tracked closely the catalogue sales of Starbucks products in the early 1990s, identifying the Washington, D.C. area as an extremely strong market for Starbucks mail order products, and therefore a logical first step on the East Coast.

5. A third structure, company ownership, had been confined to the United Kingdom, Thailand, and Australia.

6. According to the Coffee Research Institute, the 10 largest coffee importing countries for the decade of the 1990s were the United States (25.6% of global imports), Germany (14.2%), Japan (7.7%), France (7.5%), Italy (6.3%), Spain (3.8%), Holland (3.4%), the United Kingdom (3.4%), Canada (2.8%), and Sweden (2.2%). Note that these are importation statistics, and not consumption. Source: www.coffee research.org/market/importations, accessed 10/6/02.

7. www.starbucks.com/aboutus/international.asp, accessed on 9/28/02.

8. Corporate Social Responsibility Annual Report, Starbucks Coffee, Fiscal 2002, p. 8.

9. Starbucks was one of CARE's largest North American corporate donors. Cumulative contributions to CARE by Starbucks over time totaled more than $2 million. Starbucks work with CARE had begun in 1991.

10. Starbucks also noted that growers of Shade Grown Mexico coffee received price premiums of 60% over local coffee prices in fiscal 2001.

11. TransFair USA is associated with Equal Exchange, a Fair Trade organization promoting socially responsible business practices with coffee growers in Central and Latin America.

12. John Kohls and Sandra L. Christensen, "The Business Responsibility for Wealth Distribution in a Globalized Political-Economy: Merging Moral Economics and Catholic Social Teaching," *Journal of Business Ethics,* February 2002, p. 12.

13. Starbucks reported that buyers paid $1.26/lb. for non-organic green and $1.41/lb. for organic green in 2001, when New York "C" prices were hovering at roughly $0.50/pound. Although production costs varied significantly across countries and regions, coffee growers associations estimated average production costs to be $0.80/pound.

14. In a highly publicized settlement, Starbucks had settled a class action suit in 2001 brought by store managers in California who complained the company refused to pay legally mandated overtime. Prior to the

case, managers were required to sign affidavits upon hiring that they agreed to work 20 hours per week overtime without additional compensation.

15. "Planet Starbucks," *BusinessWeek,* September 9, 2002, p. 101.

APPENDIX 1: STARBUCKS CONSOLIDATED STATEMENT OF EARNINGS, 1998–2002 (MILLIONS OF US$)

Income Items	1998	1999	2000	2001	2002
Net revenues	$1,308.7	$1,686.8	$2,177.6	$2,649.0	$3,288.9
Retail	1,102.6	1,423.4	1,823.6	2,229.6	2,792.9
Specialty	206.1	263.4	354.0	419.4	496.0
Less cost of sales & occupancy costs	(578.5)	(747.6)	(961.9)	(1,112.8)	(1,350.0)
Gross operating income	730.2	939.2	1,215.7	1,536.2	1,938.9
Less store operating expenses	(418.5)	(543.6)	(704.9)	(875.5)	(1,121.1)
Less general & admin expenses	(77.6)	(89.7)	(110.2)	(151.4)	(202.2)
Less other operating expenses	(52.4)	(54.6)	(78.4)	(93.3)	(127.2)
Income from equity investees	—	3.2	20.3	28.6	35.8
EBITDA	181.8	254.5	342.5	444.6	524.3
EBITDA margin (%)	13.9%	15.1%	15.7%	16.8%	15.9%
Less depreciation & amortization	(72.5)	(97.8)	(130.2)	(163.5)	(205.6)
Operating income	109.2	156.7	212.3	281.1	318.7
Net interest income (expense)	7.1	7.3	7.1	10.8	9.3
Internet investment losses & other	—	—	(58.8)	(2.9)	13.4
Earnings before tax (EBT)	116.4	164.0	160.6	288.9	341.4
Less corporate income tax	(48.0)	(62.3)	(66.0)	(107.7)	(126.3)
Net income or earnings	68.4	101.7	94.6	181.2	215.1
Return on sales (%)	5.2%	6.0%	4.3%	6.8%	6.5%
Effective tax rate (%)	41.2%	38.0%	41.1%	37.3%	37.0%
Shares outstanding	358.5	363.7	376.3	380.0	385.6
Earnings per share (EPS)	$0.19	$0.28	$0.25	$0.48	$0.56
EPS growth rate	11.4%	46.6%	−10.1%	89.8%	17.0%

Source: Starbucks Coffee Company, Annual Report, 1999, 2000, 2001, 2002. EBITDA = Earnings before interest, taxes, depreciation and amortization.

APPENDIX 2: STARBUCKS CONSOLIDATED
BALANCE SHEET, 1998–2002 (MILLIONS OF US$)

	1998	1999	2000	2001	2002
Assets					
Cash & cash equivalents	$123.5	$117.8	$132.2	$220.6	$402.2
Accounts receivable	51.0	47.6	76.4	90.4	97.6
Inventories	143.1	180.9	201.7	221.3	263.2
Prepaid expenses & other	19.7	40.2	48.0	61.7	84.6
Total current assets	$337.3	$386.5	$458.2	$593.9	$847.5
Investments in unconsolidated subsidiaries	38.9	68.1	55.8	63.1	106.0
Property, plant & equipment, net	600.8	760.3	930.8	1,135.8	1,265.8
Other assets	15.8	37.7	46.7	58.2	73.5
Total fixed assets	$655.5	$866.0	$1,033.3	$1,257.1	$1,445.2
Total Assets	$992.8	$1,252.5	$1,491.6	$1,851.0	$2,292.7
Liabilities & Equity					
Short-term debt	$33.6	$63.8	$56.3	$62.0	$74.9
Accounts payable	49.9	56.1	73.7	127.9	136.0
Accrued payroll	35.9	43.9	69.7	81.5	105.9
Accrued occupancy costs	17.5	23.0	29.1	35.8	51.2
Income taxes payable	18.3	30.8	35.8	70.3	54.2
Other current liabilities	24.2	33.6	47.0	67.7	115.3
Total current liabilities	$179.5	$251.2	$311.7	$445.3	$537.5
Long-term debt	—	7.0	6.5	5.8	6.1
Deferred taxes & other long-term liabilities	19.0	33.3	21.4	19.1	22.5
Common equity	794.3	961.0	1,152.0	1,380.9	1,726.6
Total liabilities & equity	$992.8	$1,252.5	$1,491.6	$1,851.0	$2,292.7

Source: Starbucks Coffee Company, Annual Report, 1999, 2000, 2001, 2002.

APPENDIX 3: STARBUCKS STATEMENTS OF CASH FLOW, 1998–2002 (MILLIONS OF US$)

	1998	1999	2000	2001	2002
Operating Activities					
Net earnings	$68.4	$101.7	$94.6	$181.2	$215.1
Adjustments to reconcile to net cash:					
Depreciation and amortization	80.9	107.5	142.2	177.1	221.1
Gain on sale of investment	—	—	—	—	(13.4)
Internet-related investment losses	—	—	58.8	2.9	—
Provision for impairment and asset disposals	7.2	2.5	5.8	11.0	26.6
Deferred income taxes, net	2.1	0.8	(18.3)	(6.1)	(6.1)
Equity in income of investees	0.0	(2.3)	(15.1)	(15.7)	(22.0)
Tax benefit from exercise of stock options	10.5	18.6	31.1	30.9	44.1
Cash provided/used by changes in working capital:					
Net purchases of trading securities	—	—	(1.4)	(4.0)	(5.7)
Accounts receivable	(19.8)	3.8	(25.0)	(20.4)	(6.7)
Inventories	(23.5)	(36.4)	(19.5)	(19.7)	(41.4)
Prepaid expenses and other current assets	(2.5)	(7.6)	0.9	(10.9)	(12.5)
Accounts payable	4.6	4.7	15.6	54.1	5.5
Accrued compensation and related costs	9.9	7.6	25.4	12.1	24.1
Accrued occupancy costs	5.3	5.5	6.0	6.8	15.3
Accrued taxes	7.2	12.4	5.0	34.5	(16.2)
Deferred revenue	—	—	6.8	19.6	15.3
Other accured expenses	1.8	10.3	5.7	2.8	34.0
Net cash provided by operating activities	**$152.2**	**$229.2**	**$318.6**	**$456.3**	**$477.3**
Investing Activities					
Purchase of available for sale securities	$(51.4)	$(122.8)	$(118.5)	$(184.2)	$(340.0)
Maturity of available for sale securities	5.1	3.6	58.8	93.5	78.3
Sale of available for sale securities	112.1	85.1	49.2	46.9	144.8
Purchase of businesses, net of cash acquired	—	(15.7)	(13.5)	—	—
Additions to equity and other investments	(12.4)	(30.9)	(43.9)	(12.9)	(6.1)
Proceeds from sale of equity investment	—	—	—	—	14.8
Distributions from equity investees	2.8	9.0	14.3	16.9	22.8
Additions to property, plant and equipment	(201.9)	(257.9)	(316.5)	(384.2)	(375.5)
Additions to other assets	(3.2)	(6.9)	(3.1)	(4.6)	(24.5)
Net cash provided (used) by investing activities	**$(148.8)**	**$(336.4)**	**$(373.2)**	**$(428.5)**	**$(485.3)**
Financing Activities					
Increase (decrease) in short-term debt	$4.8	$29.9	$(7.5)	$5.7	$12.9
Proceeds from sale of common stock under esop*	4.6	9.4	10.3	13.0	16.2
Proceeds from exercise of stock options	20.8	33.8	58.5	46.7	91.3
Principal payments on long-term debt	(2.0)	(1.2)	(1.9)	(0.7)	(0.7)
Repurchase of common stock	—	—	—	(49.8)	(52.2)
Net cash provided by financing activities	**$28.3**	**$71.9**	**$59.4**	**$14.8**	**$67.4**

Source: Starbucks Coffee Company, Annual Report, 1999, 2000, 2001, 2002.

*esop = employee stock ownership plan.

APPENDIX 4: STARBUCKS CORPORATION STORE, REVENUE AND PROFIT GROWTH, 1992–2002 AVERAGE

	1992	1993	1994	1995	1996	1997	1998	1999	2000	2001	2002	Average Annual Growth Rate
United States & Canada												
Company-Owned	162	261	399	627	929	1,270	1,622	2,038	2,446	2,971	3,496	36%
Licensed	3	11	26	49	75	94	133	179	530	809	1,078	80%
International												
Company-Owned	—	—	—	1	9	31	66	104	173	295	384	
Licensed	—	—	—	—	2	17	65	177	352	634	928	
Total Stores												
Company-Owned	162	261	399	628	938	1,301	1,688	2,142	2,619	3,266	3,880	37%
Licensed	3	11	26	49	77	111	198	356	882	1,443	2,006	92%
Total Stores	165	272	425	677	1,015	1,412	1,886	2,498	3,501	4,709	5,886	43%
Percent of Total Licensed	2%	4%	6%	7%	8%	8%	10%	14%	25%	31%	34%	
Revenues & Profits												
Revenues (millions)	$93	$164	$284.9	$465	$698	$975	$1,309	$1,680	$2,169	$2,649	$3,289	43%
Change (%)		76%	74%	63%	50%	40%	34%	28%	29%	22%	24%	
Net Profit (millions)	$4	$9	$10.2	$26	$42	$55	$68	$102	$95	$181	$215	49%
Change (%)		107%	20%	155%	62%	31%	24%	50%	-7%	92%	19%	
Revenue/Store	$0.564	$0.601	$0.670	$0.687	$0.688	$0.691	$0.694	$0.673	$0.620	$0.563	$0.559	0%
Change (%)		7%	12%	2%	0%	0%	1%	-3%	-8%	-9%	-1%	
Net Profit/Store	$0.025	$0.031	$0.024	$0.038	$0.041	$0.039	$0.036	$0.041	$0.027	$0.038	$0.037	4%
Change (%)		26%	-23%	60%	8%	-6%	-7%	13%	-34%	42%	-5%	
Earnings per Share (EPS)	$0.03	$0.04	$0.05	$0.09	$0.14	$0.17	$0.19	$0.27	$0.25	$0.46	$0.56	34%
Change (%)		33%	25%	80%	56%	21%	12%	42%	-7%	84%	22%	
Share Price (eoy)	$1.89	$0.42	$2.88	$4.73	$8.25	$10.45	$9.05	$12.39	$20.03	$14.84	$14.84	23%
Change (%)		81%	-16%	64%	74%	27%	-13%	37%	62%	-26%	0%	

Source: Company reports and Thomas Weisel Partners LLC, "Starbucks Corporation," February 6, 2002, pp. 14–17.

APPENDIX 5: STARBUCKS' INTERNATIONAL OPERATIONS

Asia-Pacific	Middle East	Europe
Australia	Bahrai	Austria
Guam	Israel	Germany
Hong Kong	Kuwait	Greece
Indonesia	Lebanon	Portugal
Japan	Oman	Spain
Malaysia	Qatar	Switzerland
New Zealand	Saudi Arabia	United Kingdom
P.R. of China	United Arab Emirates	
Philippines		
Singapore	North America	
South Korea	Canada	
Taiwan	Mexico	
Thailand	United States	

Source: starbucks.com, 10/07/02.

APPENDIX 6: STARBUCKS CORPORATION, CLOSING SHARE PRICE (WEEKLY, ADJUSTED FOR SHARE SPLITS)

SIAM CANADIAN FOODS CO., LTD.

Prepared by Tom Gleave under the
supervision of Professors John Kennedy and Tony Frost

                    Version: (A) 2002-10-17

In July 1996, Jim Gulkin, Managing Director and founder of Bangkok-based Siam Canadian Foods Co., Ltd., was considering the emerging business opportunities in neighbouring Burma (also known as Myanmar). Although relatively undeveloped compared to the rest of Southeast Asia, Burma had been experiencing increasing levels of foreign investment activity in recent years. Gulkin, who had considered entering Burma in the past but declined, needed to determine if the time was now appropriate for him to enter the market.

COMPANY PROFILE

Siam Canadian Foods Co., Ltd. (SC) was a brokerage business based in Bangkok, Thailand. It was started in April 1987 after Canadian Jim Gulkin quit his job in the oil industry and invested his life savings of Cdn$130,000 in the business. Gulkin was raised in Montreal where he remained until he graduated from grade 11 "with a stratospheric 51 per cent average." With school out of the way, he began travelling and working in various parts of the world and became enamoured with Thailand after holidaying there in 1979. SC's role as a food broker was to identify overseas customers, usually food importers, and negotiate sales with them on behalf of food processors in Thailand. SC's initial activity was limited to brokering canned pineapple and tuna; however, it gradually expanded its offerings to include a wide range of products such as frozen seafood, frozen poultry, canned and frozen fruit and vegetables as well as dehydrated fruit and juice concentrates. Over time, SC also began to source various products from both Burma and India on an ad hoc basis.

When first starting out, Gulkin was admittedly very inexperienced in the food brokering business. He commented:

> I didn't have a clue what I was doing . . . I didn't know what a letter of credit, invoice or cross-check was. I didn't even have a business plan or a marketing plan.

Adding to this inexperience, Gulkin found that local processors were reluctant to deal with him, despite the fact that he spoke fluent Thai. As a newcomer to an industry tightly controlled by Thailand's highly assimilated Overseas Chinese community, Gulkin struggled to develop comfortable levels of trust and confidence with the processors.

The food brokerage business generally operated on low margins, thus necessitating movements of large volumes of goods in order to achieve profitability. As the business evolved, SC began to focus mainly on brokering frozen seafood because the commissions were the most attractive. The company earned an average commission revenue of 1.25 per cent on sales contracts, usually denominated in U.S. dollars, that it negotiated on behalf of the food processors. During the late 1980s and early 1990s, the frozen seafood business was in a state of expansion in North America and Europe. At the same time, Thailand was quickly becoming a globally recognized source of frozen seafood, largely on the strength of overseas market acceptance of Black Tiger Shrimp. Gulkin estimated that

Thailand harvested about 200,000 tons of Black Tiger shrimp in 1995, 90 per cent of which came from aquaculture facilities.

The following is an estimate of Thailand's recent fresh and frozen shrimp exports:

Year	1990	1992	1994
Baht (Billions)	20.5	31.7	49.2

25 Baht = US$1.00

In 1991, Gulkin opened up a representative office in Vietnam with the help of Philippe Vo. Vo was born in France to a French mother and Vietnamese father and, prior to moving to Vietnam, managed a seafood exporting business in California. The purpose of the representative office was to procure frozen seafood products for sale to overseas importers. Several months later, Gulkin, Vo and another local partner started a separate importing and distribution business, SC Food Services, in Ho Chi Minh City.

In 1992, Gulkin began to investigate the possibility of setting up a representative office in Burma but decided against it because he felt "very uncomfortable" with the local players in the seafood industry. This investigation made him realize that, apart from the necessary start-up capital which would be required, he also needed "connections" to people favoured by the ruling military junta, SLORC. He returned to Burma in 1994 when he discovered that new activity in the seafood industry was being generated by independent, non-politically connected businesspeople. Discussions with the new players gave him a much higher level of comfort that business could be done in Burma without the need for buying favours. However, Gulkin also found that these new players were "sincere but incompetent" given that his attempt to export US$100,000 of frozen seafood collapsed due to insufficient raw material supplies of acceptable quality, resulting in a net loss to SC of about US$30,000. He later recalled that "it was a cheap lesson for the market knowledge we gained."

In 1994, SC secured one of the most significant contracts in the company's history on the strength of the relationship it had established with one of its key German importers. The contract called for SC to procure 600 tons of breaded shrimp to be shipped for ultimate sale to McDonald's Restaurants in Germany. A second contract for 450 tons was awarded to SC in 1995, with shipments this time going to McDonald's in Germany and Austria. The trading value of the 1995 shipment was US$7 million to US$8 million. Under the terms of the contracts, SC received a commission from the processor as well as a supervision fee paid by the importer. The latter was paid because SC dispatched quality control personnel to the processor's site to oversee the production and packaging of the breaded shrimp.

SC first achieved profitability in 1991 and had remained in the black ever since. In 1995, SC's trading volume was valued at about US$85 million, 90 per cent of which was attributable to frozen seafood. By 1996, SC employed 15 staff who were involved in sales, quality control and administration. The main destinations for the company's shipments were importers from the following countries, in descending order of sales value: United States, France, Germany and Canada.

The combination of increasing success in the food brokering business and the growing affluence in Bangkok in recent years led Gulkin to form a separate sister company, Siam Canadian Gourmet Ltd., in early 1996. This importing and distribution business was initially focused on importing wines and coffees for sale to hotels, restaurants and specialty food retailers. It was later expected to expand its product range to include imported cheeses, sauces and other gourmet cuisine items. Initial results were considered "very promising."

SC's Vietnamese Experience

Gulkin's motivation for entering Vietnam in 1991 was largely based upon his assessment that, as an undeveloped country with a large, intelligent and hard-working population, many opportunities were becoming available to small firms with limited resources such as SC. As well, entering Vietnam was also consistent with Gulkin's view that in order to succeed in the food brokering business, firms had to adopt a diversification strategy in terms of both supply sources and product line offerings. Furthermore, the amount of foreign investment in Vietnam had been escalating, due largely to the implementation of the Vietnamese government's so-called "doi moi" or "renewal" policy, which was designed to attract foreign investment. This meant that there would be a limited window of opportunity for SC to enter the market before being shut out permanently by bigger players. Therefore, with the help of Vo, Gulkin opened up Siam Canadian Foods (Vietnam) in order to gain access to frozen seafood for shipment overseas. Apart from Vo, SC (Vietnam) employed four quality control staff and an administrative assistant. Gulkin held 100 per cent ownership of SC (Vietnam) while maintaining a 50 per cent profit-sharing arrangement with Vo. Later, Gulkin, Vo and a local Vietnamese partner opened up SC Food Services, a separate distributorship that imported meats and dairy products, and sourced local fruits and vegetables, for sale to hotels and restaurants in the Ho Chi Minh City area.

Gulkin's view on the performance of SC Foods (Vietnam) was mixed. The business had experienced modest profitability since its inception, something that he felt was "very good, all things considered." On the other hand, daily operations were frustrating, particularly with respect to the honoring of contracts by food processors. Gulkin offered the following as a simple, typical example of a Vietnamese contract gone bad:

> We enter into a contract with a Vietnamese processor to supply us with 30 metric tonnes (mt) of frozen cuttlefish tentacles per month for 12 months. We, in turn, contract to sell this quantity of product to a European buyer. One month into the contract the Japanese, all of a sudden, become interested in this particular commodity. The raw material price, therefore, goes up and out of 360 mt contracted, we might get to ship 15 or 30 mt. The

Vietnamese processor has absolutely no intention of honouring our contract if it means that he loses money or even makes less than he originally hoped. The contract is meaningless to him. It is nothing more than a piece of paper. His word or his reputation are not tangible concepts to him. My company, however, has to find a way to pacify our buyers who are none too happy. Sometimes it costs some money but fortunately our relationships with our buyers are strong. We do tend to make it very clear to our buyers beforehand that a contract in Vietnam is basically worthless and we, therefore, give ourselves a very wide notwithstanding clause in any contract we involve ourselves in.

These frequent experiences left Gulkin with the impression that local processors only considered the short-term implications of their business, often leading him to ponder the question "why bother?"

BURMA

Burma, also known as The Union of Myanmar, was the largest mainland country in Southeast Asia and had a population of about 47 million. The country bordered on Bangladesh and India in the northwest, China in the northeast, Laos in the east and Thailand in the southeast. It was a diverse nation with over 135 distinct cultural groups, the predominant one being the Bamars, representing about 69 per cent of the population. The country was considered by the World Bank to be among the poorest in the world, with a per capita income of US$676, based on purchasing-power parity. The capital city of Rangoon (also known as Yangon) had a population of approximately six million and was the nation's main port through which over 90 per cent of all ocean-going trade passed. The physical geography of the country was a mixture of tropical mountains, plains and delta lowlands. Burma had a coastline that totalled over 2,830 kilometres bordering along the Andaman Sea and the Bay of Bengal. The country was thought to have abundant natural resources, particularly in teak wood, oil and seafood. (See Exhibit 1 for a Regional Map of

Cambodia, Myanmar, Laos

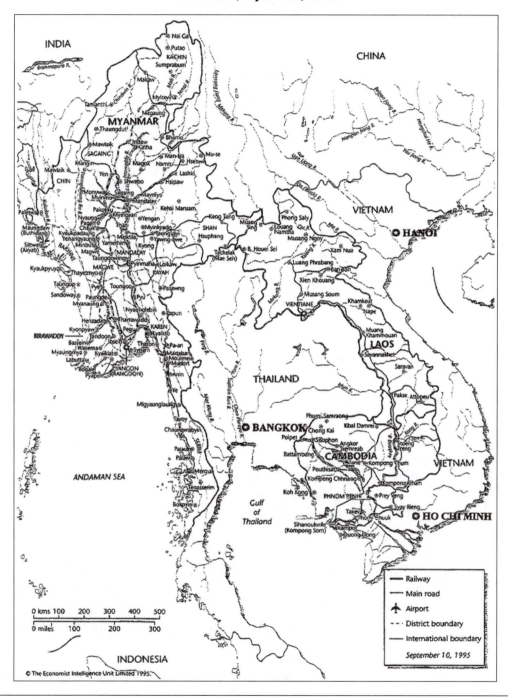

Exhibit 1   Map of Southeast Asia

	1991/1992	1992/1993	1993/1994
Nominal GDP (kyat—billions)	187	248	339
Real GDP* (kyat—billions)	50	55	58
Real per Capita GDP (kyat—millions)	1,202	1,289	1,341
Real GDP Growth Rate (%)	−0.6	+9.3	+6.0
Consumer Price Index (1986 = 100)	349.30	460.49	541.51
Total Exports (kyat—millions)	2,932	3,655	4,071
Total Imports (kyat—millions)	5,337	5,365	7,218
GDP Area of Economic Activity (%)			
Agriculture	37.5	38.5	38.3
Trade	22.1	22.1	22.1
Processing/Manufacturing	8.9	8.8	9.2
Livestock/Fishing	7.6	7.3	7.2
Social Administration	7.2	6.7	6.7
Rental and Other Services	4.8	4.5	4.4
Transportation	4.0	4.0	3.9
Construction	2.9	3.0	3.0
Other	5.0	5.1	4.2

Exhibit 2   Recent Economic Indicators—Burma

Source: Investing in Myanmar, Union of Myanmar Investment Commission, 1995.

*Real GDP figures given use 1985/1986 fiscal year as benchmark.

1994 exchange rates: US$1.00 = 5.08 kyat; Cdn$1.00 = 3.78 kyat

Southeast Asia and Exhibit 2 for Recent Economic Indicators on Burma.)

Burma's seafood resources were plentiful given its exclusive economic fishing zone of 486,000 square kilometres along its coastline. Prior to 1994, the Myanmar Fisheries Enterprise, a state-run company controlling the nation's seafood harvesting and processing, was the dominant player in the Burmese fishing industry. This company was dissolved in 1994 in an effort to improve the industry through attracting private investment. The total marine harvest for Burma was estimated to be as follows:

Year	1990	1992	1994
Tonnes (Thousands)	645.7	650.7	689.0

Gulkin estimated that the total current annual harvest of all shrimp species in Burmese waters was about 20,000 tons. Given that the state of

Firm	Activity	Origin of Foreign Investor
1. Myanmar Bangladesh Fisheries Ltd.	Shrimp farm management	Bangladesh
2. Myanmar American Fisheries Co., Ltd.	Fish and marine products	United States
3. General Fisheries Co., Ltd.	Fishing, breeding, processing of fresh and saltwater products	Thailand
4. Myanmar Niino Joint Venture Co., Ltd.	Culturing and marketing of high quality pearls	Japan
5. Hanswaddy Fisheries Co., Ltd.	Fishing, prawn farming, processing and marketing of fresh and saltwater products	Thailand
6. Myanmar P.L. International Ltd.	Prawn farming, processing and marketing	Singapore
7. Myanmar Garming Fisheries Ltd.	Shrimp cultivation, fish processing and marketing	Hong Kong
8. Myanmar Seafoods Ltd.	Procurement, processing, handling and marketing of fresh and saltwater products	Singapore

Exhibit 3   Recent Joint Venture Investments in the Burmese Fisheries Sector

development within the seafood industry was relatively low, he felt that the placement of modern fishing fleets and aquaculture facilities, spurred on by recent measures to liberalize the industry, would increase Burma's seafood output considerably over the next several years, but not to the extent that it would match Thailand's output.

In 1988, Burma passed the Foreign Investment Law which, much like Vietnam's "doi moi" policy, was designed to attract foreign capital to industries which would promote exports and provide for the acquisition of new technologies. This Law was seen by the Burmese government as a market oriented measure because it allowed 100 per cent foreign ownership of firms, repatriation of capital and an "unequivocal guarantee" against the nationalization or expropriation of businesses. Firms operating under the guidelines of the Law paid a flat tax of 30 per cent; however, there existed numerous provisions which could

be used to lessen a firm's tax burden, including the following:

- a tax holiday period of three consecutive years inclusive of the year of start-up with a possible extension if the Myanmar Investment Commission deemed it appropriate
- exemption or relief of tax paid on profits which were held in reserve and re-invested into the firm within one year
- accelerated depreciation of capital assets
- exemption or relief from customs duties paid on various equipment and instruments imported during the start-up phase of the firm

By 1994, 113 enterprises involving foreign ownership were engaged in a variety of agricultural, seafood processing, manufacturing, mining, energy and transportation activities in accordance with the provisions of the Law, eight of which were directly related to the seafood industry. (See Exhibit 3.)

Recent Political History

In April 1947, Burma took a significant step towards gaining independence from British colonization by having its first free elections after WWII. The winner of the election was Aung San, the leader of the Anti-Fascist People's Freedom League (AFPFL). On July 19, 1947, Aung San, along with six of his senior cabinet colleagues, was assassinated. This became known as Martyr's Day. U Nu, the ranking AFPFL politician remaining, took over the leadership of the country and gained Burma's independence from Britain in early 1948. During these early years, U Nu attempted to establish his party's concept of Buddhist-based socialism. However, in March 1962, General Ne Win led a left-wing military takeover of Burma in support of the Burmese Socialist Programme Party (BSPP) and subsequently imprisoned U Nu and his supporters. In July 1962, several students who protested this takeover were shot to death at Rangoon University. These killings were followed by the complete destruction of the student union building on the campus. In the ensuing years, Ne Win began to direct the country towards the "Burmese way to socialism" in accordance with the doctrine of the BSPP. As a consequence, virtually all businesses were nationalized and there was a gradual closure of trade with most of the outside world. This eventually led to the collapse of the Burmese economy.

In 1987 and 1988, many Burmese organized mass demonstrations protesting the legacy of incompetence of the Government and calling for the removal of Ne Win. In July 1988, Ne Win stepped down following six weeks of bloody confrontations between pro-democracy demonstrators and the military, in which an estimated 3,000 people were killed. The BSPP did not relinquish power, however. In September 1988, a BSPP-backed military coup was staged resulting in the establishment of the new State Law and Order Restoration Council (SLORC), under the leadership of General Saw Maung, Commander-in-Chief of the armed forces. Saw Maung immediately imposed a state of martial law while promising to hold a democratic election in the near future. This quickly led to the forming of the National League for Democracy (NLD), a coalition of parties opposed to the BSPP, under the leadership of Aung San's daughter, Aung San Suu Kyi. The NLD went on to win the election which was held in May 1989, despite allegations that SLORC had attempted to manipulate the outcome. After the election, SLORC refused to allow the NLD to assume the role of government and arrested the party's leadership and soon after placed Suu Kyi under house arrest.

On July 10, 1995, Suu Kyi was released from house arrest after six years of detainment, and four years after she had won the Nobel Peace Prize, in absentia, for her dedication to democratic reform in Burma. Despite SLORC's warning that Suu Kyi should abstain from political activism, she continued to hold press conferences and political rallies outside of her housing compound on University Avenue in Rangoon. Furthermore, she repeatedly called upon the United States and the European Community to impose economic sanctions against Burma as a means to force democratic reform in the country and was successful to some degree. During 1995, the four U.S. cities of Santa Monica and Berkeley, California, Ann Arbor, Michigan and Madison, Wisconsin passed "selective purchasing" legislation which barred these cities from buying goods and services from companies doing business in Burma. Similar legislation had also been tabled and was awaiting ratification by the cities of Oakland, San Francisco, New York and Colorado Springs.

By July 1996, several recent events had caused the issue of human and democratic rights in Burma to gain political attention and press coverage worldwide. Two months previously, in May, the Burmese government arrested 262 NLD members, thus preventing them from holding their first national congress since the 1990 election. This incident was followed by the mysterious death of James Nichols, a Burmese resident and former honorary consul in Burma for Denmark, Finland, Norway and Switzerland, who died in jail under vague circumstances. The 69-year-old Nichols, a close friend of Suu Kyi, had served two months of a three-year prison sentence for possessing an unlicensed fax machine.

These events led Suu Kyi to escalate her call to the Western powers for sanctions against Burma. At one point, she was able to have a video-taped speech smuggled out of the country. The message, which was played to members of the European Parliament, prompted the European Union to support Suu Kyi's position that economic sanctions were needed in Burma in order to move the democratic reform process forward. The culmination of these events led Heineken to announce on July 1 that it would divest itself of its interest in its Burmese joint venture. Soon after, Carlsberg announced that it had cancelled its plans to develop a brewery in the country. These announcements occurred about four months after Pepsi sold off its 40 per cent stake in a Burmese joint venture.

That same July (1996), leaders from the Association of Southeast Asian Nations (ASEAN), whose members included Thailand, Vietnam, Malaysia, the Philippines, Brunei, Singapore and Indonesia, met in Jakarta for their annual conference. ASEAN was a forum used to discuss issues that were of mutual interest to its members, including political, economic, security and environmental concerns. Burma had been invited to the conference as an observer for the first time, a move that was seen by many as the first step towards eventually granting it full membership status. Interestingly, by the time the conference concluded in late July, the United States Senate had passed a bill approving the use of sanctions against Burma if SLORC engaged in any acts which suppressed the pro-democracy movement of the NLD. The only hurdle which remained for full passage of the bill was the signature of President Clinton who, only several months previously, approved the Helms-Burton Bill, a measure designed to penalize firms and firm managers who continued to conduct business with Cuba.

The issue of democratic and human rights abuses in Burma was very prominent at the conference. However, while the United States and the European Union considered applying economic sanctions on Burma, ASEAN's policy position called for "constructive engagement" with SLORC. ASEAN's view was that the region's economic and security interests would be better served if Burma was not isolated. To this end, many ASEAN firms were encouraged by their governments to invest in Burma. In fact, Singapore-based Fraser and Neave immediately offered to take over Heineken's ownership stake in its Burmese joint venture. Similarly, discussions about building a new brewery between the Golden Star Group, Carlsberg's former Burmese partner, and Malaysia's Asia-Euro Brewery were already underway, less than three weeks after Carlsberg announced its pull-out.

GULKIN'S PERSPECTIVE ON BURMA'S POLITICS

In considering his position on the question of democratic and human rights in Burma, Gulkin offered the following:

> Aung San Suu Kyi is a decent, intelligent, well-intended, brave and selfless person. I realize that the politically correct trend is to call for sanctions against Burma, but economic isolation simply does not work. Take a look a Cuba, Chile, North Korea and Iraq. All of those countries have experienced economic sanctions of varying degrees, but their leaders still remained. People will often use South Africa as an example that sanctions work, but their case was unusual. The new South Africans were an island of Europeans isolated both within their own country and from the rest of the world.

> Economic empowerment raises hope for democracy. Just take a look at Taiwan, South Korea and even here in Thailand. All of these countries went from dictatorships to democracies as their level of wealth increased. In 1992, when the Thai military tried to take over the government, the people said "No!" and what happened? Democracy prevailed. Many Thais had started to enjoy the benefits of increased economic power and were not going to give them up. It is the economically deprived that

lack money and education. These people are easy to keep in place.

On the question of human rights, Burma is no worse than Indonesia or China. The Indonesian government has brutally occupied East Timor for over 20 years. As for China, there are tens of thousands of executions happening there each year, some even for economic crimes. Amnesty International is constantly citing China as a major human rights offender but I don't see Pepsi or Carlsberg pulling out of there.

RECONSIDERING BURMA IN 1996

Gulkin recognized that time was of the essence if he was going to finally commit to Burma. On the positive side, Rangoon had seen the development of at least five new seafood processing plants in past two years financed by independent firms. Having had preliminary discussions with some of the independents, Gulkin's instincts led him to believe that corruption would not be a problem and that he would be able to quickly develop relationships of trust and confidence with them. As well, the lack of economic development within the country meant that smaller firms such as his own might be able to gain a sustainable foothold before many larger, well-financed firms entered the market. It was Gulkin's view that bigger multinational corporations could afford to be "politically correct," while smaller firms needed to take advantage of the windows of opportunity while they existed. A further incentive for establishing operations in Burma was his belief that, given the underdeveloped state of the Burmese seafood industry, he would be able to realize significantly larger commission margins than he was currently receiving in Thailand or Vietnam.

Investment in Burma was also consistent with Gulkin's business philosophy of developing and managing diverse supply sources and product ranges. This was particularly important when he considered that the Thai seafood market was simultaneously experiencing increased levels of competition as well as dwindling supplies of raw materials. He estimated that the seafood industry in Thailand had reached the saturation point in terms of the number of processors operating and that raw material supply levels would gradually deplete to the point where the industry would be in definite decline within ten years. At the same time, relations between Thailand and Burma had moved in a decidedly favourable direction in recent months. In March 1996, Banharn Silpa-archa became the first Thai Prime Minister in 16 years to visit Burma. The primary objectives of the trip were twofold: first, to re-establish border trade between the two countries, given that cease-fires between insurgent ethnic groups along the border had been sustained, and second, to give Thai business interests a chance at gaining a stronger foothold in the country given the recognition of increased interest that other nations in the region were showing in Burma.

Gulkin's view was that most of the other nations in the region did not offer the same potential for developing his seafood exporting business further. For instance, although neighbouring Cambodia had a sizeable coastline along the Gulf of Siam and thus strong potential as a seafood exporter, the country was still experiencing the devastating effects that years of brutal war and governance under the Khmer Rouge had brought to the country. A strong consensus among many business people living in Thailand was that Cambodia was not a secure place to travel, let alone conduct business. Evidence of this insecurity was shown by the recent kidnapping of a British landmine disposal expert, along with 20 Cambodian colleagues who were working on behalf of the Mines Advisory Group. Additionally, in a highly publicized incident in 1994, three foreign backpackers were kidnapped and subsequently murdered by the Khmer Rouge.

Gulkin had also dismissed the possibility of entering Malaysia because it had experienced very strong economic growth in recent years which, in turn, allowed the seafood exporting industry to become well developed. Gulkin viewed Indonesia as having potential, given that it was a large, resource-rich archipelago; however, he dismissed this option because of its considerable distance from Thailand. Furthermore, Indonesia was currently experiencing political turmoil of its own, brought on by the arrest of Megawati Sukarno, daughter of Indonesia's founding President Sukarno and the principal political foe of the current President, General Suharto.

Several factors existed which were working to dissuade Gulkin from making the leap to Burma, however. First, Gulkin was concerned about competing against PL Corporation, a local seafood exporting company controlled by General Ne Win's son-in-law, particularly since local companies were often shown preferential treatment by local suppliers and producers. Additionally, there was increased interest in the region from two of SC's key competitors, the Hong Kong-based Sun Wah Trading Company and a sourcing division for the Japanese trading giant, Mitsui. Sun Wah was a well-financed firm which maintained its own fleet of transport ships and had a well-established reputation in the seafood trading business. Its solid financial position allowed the firm to extend million dollar financing arrangements to processors, thus enabling them to remain open in times when cash flow was squeezed, something SC was not able to do for its customers. Mitsui's sourcing division was interested in Burma's raw material supply so that other members of the Mitsui keiretsu would be assured of having inputs for their value-added food processing operations. Gulkin viewed Mitsui, as well as the increasing interest of Japan's other big trading companies, as his largest threat in Burma. This was because the Japanese giants would be able to outbid many of the smaller players, and in turn, limit their ability to secure reliable supply sources. Additionally, the recent trend of the Japanese Yen was also cause for some concern because its rising value gave the Japanese greater purchasing power throughout the world.

The recent political attention given to Burma also worried Gulkin. While Gulkin viewed economic isolation as harmful, he also needed to consider the view of his overseas customers. He remained cautiously optimistic that his customers would not view his possible foray into Burma as unduly harmful. At the same time, however, he realized that if the economic sanctions movement gained momentum, some of SC's customers might "black list" Burma. Adding further confusion to this situation was the recognition that an increasing number of Asian firms were making inroads into Burma, despite the calls for sanctions elsewhere in the world. It was quite clear that Asia's view of Burma was considerably different from that of the Western powers.

The level of development of Burma's infrastructure was also cause for some concern. It would clearly be difficult to conduct business in a country which lacked an adequate system of roads or communication linkages. The port facility in Rangoon was especially problematic and was considered to be the biggest bottleneck in the country. It was not uncommon for vessels to wait for several days or even weeks before they could be loaded or unloaded. The matter was so grave that it prompted several foreign investors from Singapore and Hong Kong to begin the development of a new port across the river from Rangoon; however, it was expected to be about a year before the port became operational.

Decision

In considering his Burmese investment decision, Gulkin had to consider several trade-offs. Could he afford to take a "wait and see" approach to Burma while other Asian firms started to tap into the market? Similarly, could he afford to allow this opportunity to pass him by given that other seafood exporting opportunities in the region were quite limited? Alternatively, if Gulkin entered Burma, could he be assured that his investment was secure given the state of political governance in the country? At the same time, would he run the risk of losing some key clients who would discontinue doing business with him because of his involvement in Burma?

ROYAL TRUSTCO[1]

Prepared by Alan W. Andron under the
supervision of Professor David Conklin

Version: (A) 1999-11-29

You have a board of directors that has worked diligently, assiduously, in your interests. I never in my life have known a better group of people and I think you should recognize that they have saved this company.

—Hartland MacDougall,
Royal Trustco Chairman,
comments to a shareholders'
meeting as quoted in "A question
of governance," *Globe & Mail,*
July 19, 1993, Pg B1.

You know, it's like in my game. Second guessing after something happened is much easier than when you have to make the decision.

—Jean Beliveau, Royal Trustco
Director, as quoted in "A question
of governance," *Globe & Mail,*
July 19, 1993, Pg B1.

COMPANY BACKGROUND

Royal Trust[2] opened for business in Montreal on November 24, 1899. The company started with one employee and a desk located in the Bank of Montreal on Place D'Armes. The company's first president and board of directors were the same as the Bank's, although the Bank did not own Royal Trust.[3]

By the early 1980s, Royal Trustco had grown to have corporate assets of $11.1 billion, and assets under administration of $37.6 billion.[4] The company had diversified to include intermediary and real estate brokerage businesses. Royal Trustco classified business into three broad groups: 1) intermediary services, which consisted of deposit accounts, chequing accounts, personal loans and mortgages; 2) trustee services for both corporations and individuals, which included managing stock transfers and administering estates; and 3) managed assets, where Royal Trustco would manage a person's assets (not estates), provide financial advice, and other investment management services such as mutual funds on a fee for service basis.[5] Exhibit 1 provides a five-year income statement and balance sheet for Royal Trustco.

1980: THE CAMPEAU CORPORATION TAKEOVER BID

On August 28, 1980, Ottawa-based Campeau Corporation, a property developer headed by Robert Campeau, announced a take-over bid for Royal Trustco. Originally an Ottawa home builder, Campeau had moved into land development and built several large office complexes in downtown Ottawa and Hull. In recent years, Campeau had expanded into several major Canadian and United States markets. Campeau's bid for Royal Trustco surprised many investment analysts.[6]

Royal Trustco's management recommended to the board that the offer be opposed.[7] To help fight the take-over bid, Royal Trustco filed suit in both Canadian and U.S. courts,[8] as well as complaints with the Ontario Securities Commission

CONSOLIDATED INCOME STATEMENT 1988 TO 1992
($ millions)

	1992	1991	1990	1989	1988
Net Investment Income	352	484	453	542	479
Provision for Loan Losses	(421)	(155)	(209)	(22)	(18)
Fees and Other Income	351	337	291	278	229
Net Revenues	282	666	535	798	690
Operating Expenses					
Salaries and Benefits	296	281	282	252	223
Premises, Computer & Equipment	160	154	149	131	115
Other Operating Expenses	179	167	186	186	150
Write-Off of Good Will	93	—	—	—	—
Income Taxes	213	19	(85)	(35)	(10)
Income From Operations	(659)	45	3	264	212
Sale of Stock Transfer Business	—	21	—	—	—
International Restructuring	—	—	(30)	—	—
Write-Down of Investments	—	—	(84)	—	—
Income—Discount'd Operations	(193)	41	46	1	—
Net Income	(852)	107	(65)	265	212

CONSOLIDATED BALANCE SHEET 1988 TO 1992
($ millions)

	1992	1991	1990	1989	1988
Cash and Short Term Investments	3,131	3,227	4,810	5,265	5,310
Securities	2,905	4,581	4,526	4,605	3,920
Loans and Investments	17,790	20,320	22,649	21,457	18,803
Other Assets	417	698	688	510	444
Net Discontinued U.S. Assets	817	998	582	444	—
Total Assets	25,114	29,824	33,255	32,281	28,477
Demand Deposits	4,120	4,026	3,828	3,906	4,451
Term Deposits	16,928	20,038	23,572	22,516	19,361
Bonds, Debentures, Borrowings	1,436	2,253	2,510	2,789	2,243
Other Liabilities	234	209	179	203	235
Total Liabilities	22,718	26,526	30,089	29,414	26,290
Minority Interest	9	8	7	26	42
Subord. Notes; Capital Debent.	1,419	1,334	1,335	766	661
Shareholders' Equity	968	1,956	1,824	2,075	1,484
Total Equity	2,396	3,298	3,166	2,867	2,187
Total Liabilities and Equity	25,114	29,824	33,255	32,281	28,477

Exhibit 1

Source: Royal Trustco Annual Report 1992.

Note: All values are quoted in Canadian funds.

(OSC). Both the courts[9] and the OSC[10] ruled that the Campeau bid was valid.

During the take-over bid, a group of Canada's top corporations, including Toronto Dominion Bank (TD), Noranda, and Olympia & York Developments (O&Y), actively purchased Royal Trustco stock.[11] Campeau eventually withdrew the offer because the desired number of shares were not tendered.

1982/83: The Brascan Revolution

Brascan, which was a part of the Edper Group (Exhibit 2 outlines the member companies of the Edper Group; Exhibit 3 lists directors of key Edper companies) controlled by Edward and Peter Bronfman, purchased its original interest (14.9 per cent) in Royal Trustco in early 1981.[12] In 1983, Trilon, a member of the Brascan family, purchased the Brascan interest in Royal Trust, as well as the large interest held by O&Y. Trilon indicated that it was interested in purchasing more shares in the future.[13] By 1983, Trilon had gained control of Royal Trustco[14] through a series of share purchases from other shareholders. Michael Cornelissen was appointed to the position of President and Chief Executive Officer of Royal Trustco and its operating subsidiaries.

1983–1992: The Cornelissen Era of Entrepreneurship

Michael Cornelissen was a chartered accountant by training. He had worked for Touche Ross in his native South Africa, and in Montreal, where he met Jack Cockwell, who in 1975 would hire Cornelissen to work for the Hees-Edper group. Following his time in Montreal, Cornelissen returned to South Africa to return to school, and later worked for a large public company in Johannesburg. In 1975, Cornelissen became one of the original group of employees to work on the building of the Hees-Edper businesses (Hees was one of the subsidiaries of Edper, and Jack Cockwell, Cornelissen's new boss, was one of the key personnel in the organization). Cornelissen rose to prominence in the early 1980s after managing a turnaround at the Edper-controlled Trizec Corp, a Calgary-based real estate developer.[15]

At the time Cornelissen was appointed president and CEO of Royal Trustco, the company was described with such terms as "ossified," "hierarchical," "inwardly oriented," and "unexceptional."[16] His assignment was to develop an entrepreneurial culture within Royal Trustco. The goal was to give the organization a sales and marketing orientation, and transform its culture from one that was risk averse.[17] Under Cornelissen, Royal Trustco set a target of annual growth in earnings per share of 15 per cent,[18] and formulated a strategic plan which outlined how the earnings growth would be achieved.[19]

To achieve these goals, Cornelissen followed the Hees philosophy[20] of how to run a firm. He reduced the levels of management and bureaucracy within Royal Trustco. Senior managers were required to start at 7 a.m., traditional long lunches were eliminated, and everyone was required to work flat-out; those who couldn't work in the new environment were replaced.[21] An extensive internal communications plan was implemented to deliver the customer service message to the employees in the branches.[22]

In order to motivate senior and middle level managers, Royal Trustco required enrolment in its stock purchase plan.[23] Royal Trustco provided 100 per cent financing of the stock purchases; stocks were kept in a trust account for a five-year period, managers repaid 20 per cent of the principal each year and took possession of the stock, or could wait five years, pay off the loan in one payment, and take possession of the stock.[24] Loan interest payments were set to equal the dividends available on the stock.[25] The assumptions behind the plan were that: a) an ownership position would ensure that managers acted in the best interests of the stockholders, and b) stock price was the best indicator of the performance of the company.[26] Management salaries were significantly lower (an estimated 30 to 50 per cent)

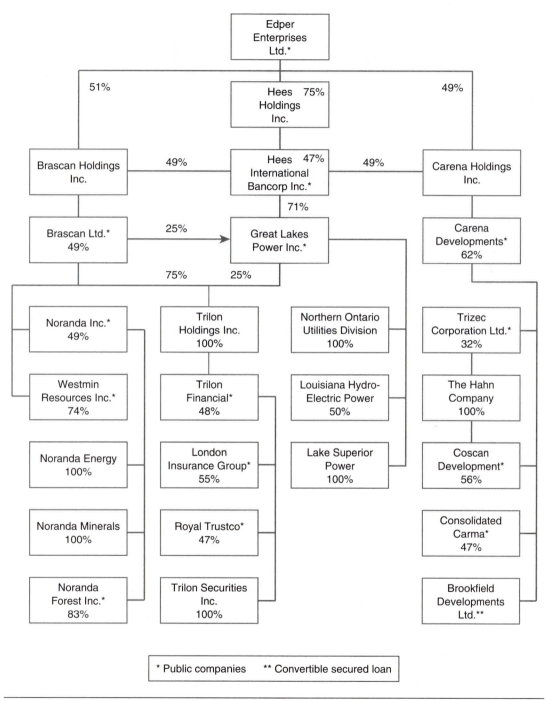

Exhibit 2   Edper Enterprises Ltd Corporate Organization

Source: Edper Enterprises Ltd. Annual Report 1992.

ROYAL TRUSTCO BOARD OF DIRECTORS

Hartland MacDougall C.V.O.; James Miller; Hon. James Balfour Q.C.; Jean Beliveau O.C.; Thomas R. Bell; Brian Canfield; Kenneth R. Clarke; Adrienne Clarkson O.C.; Jack L. Cockwell; Gordon R. Cunningham; David L. Donne; Hon. J. Trevor Eyton Q.C.; Fraser Fell Q.C.; Paul Gobeil; Melvin Hawkrigg; Dr. Warren McFarlan; Neil McKelvey O.C., Q.C.; Earl Orser; Roger Phillips; Richard Pound O.C., Q.C.; Hon. Maurice Riel P.C., Q.C.; Margaret Southern C.M., L.V.O.; James M. Tory Q.C.; Marshall Williams

Source: Royal Trustco annual report 1992.

TRILON FINANCIAL BOARD OF DIRECTORS

Hugh Aird; Peter F. Bronfman; Kenneth R. Clarke; Jack L. Cockwell; George Cormack; Gordon R. Cunningham; William Dimma; Gary Goodman; Melvin Hawkrigg; Alan Hockin; Joseph Jeffery OBE, CD, LLD; Allen Lambert O.C.; Frank Lochan; Donald Lowe; Hon. Edward Lumley; Hartland MacDougall; David McCamus; Ross McKenzie; George Myhal; Earl Orser

Source: Trilon Financial annual report 1992.

BRASCAN LTD BOARD OF DIRECTORS

Roberto P. Cezar De Andrade; Hon. Conrad M. Black P.C., O.C.; Bruce A. Bronfman; Edward M. Bronfman; Peter F. Bronfman; Jack L. Cockwell; Robert A. Dunford; Hon. J. Trevor Eyton O.C., Q.C.; Rhys T. Eyton; Hon. Edwin A. Goodman P.C., O.C., Q.C.; Lewis B. Harder; Patrick J. Keenan; David W. Kerr; Allen T. Lambert O.C.; Hon. E. Peter Lougheed P.C., C.C., Q.C.; Paul M. Marshall; Harold P. Milavsky; Alfred Powis O.C.; John A. Scrymeour; Peter N.T. Widdrington

Source: Brascan Ltd annual report 1992.

EDPER ENTERPRISES LTD BOARD OF DIRECTORS

Bruce A. Bronfman; Edward M. Bronfman; Linda E. Bronfman; Peter F. Bronfman; Donald Carr Q.C.; Jack L. Cockwell; Hon. J. Trevor Eyton O.C., Q.C.; Jack Rabinovitch; Manfred J. Walt; Sheila Zittrer

Source: Edper Enterprises annual report 1992.

Exhibit 3 Royal Trustco Board of Directors

than those paid by competitors; this difference was to be compensated by increases in the value of the manager's stock.

Royal Trustco's accounting system was revamped so that management could track its products on a client-centred basis, thereby easing the process of cross-selling related financial services.[27] Account managers at the branch level were placed on a compensation system that rewarded results, including a commission component based upon the amount of loan business (and other fee-based services) written.[28] The company also set out to increase the size of its branch network from 111 to 190 branches, in order to improve its access to depositors as a source of stable and inexpensive funds.[29]

Royal Trustco survived the recession of the early 1980s, and enjoyed profitability for the remainder of the decade. The Canadian economy had climbed out of recession, and by the end of the decade was "running full steam ahead." Royal Trustco met its target of 15 per cent earnings growth every year until 1990; from 1985 to 1989, earnings had doubled. At the 1989 shareholders' meeting, Cornelissen spoke of profits doubling again in the next five years.[30]

During the 1980s, Royal Trustco introduced several innovative products to the Canadian market. One popular product was the "Double Up" Mortgage, which allowed customers to make an additional mortgage payment without penalty.[31] Through its affiliation with Royal LePage Real Estate, Royal Trustco created the concept of the "pre-approved mortgage" for the residential market. The mortgage applications and paperwork were handled through the realtor, while the mortgage itself was issued by Royal Trustco. In addition to these innovative mortgage products, loans officers in Royal Trustco branches were given generous lending limits within which to write loans.[32]

In addition to its innovations in the residential mortgage market, Royal Trustco placed heavy emphasis on the commercial loans sector, particularly commercial real estate. In 1990, Royal Trustco's Canadian portfolio included $5 billion in commercial loans. The U.S. and U.K. subsidiaries were also aggressively lending into the commercial real estate market.

EXPANDING INTERNATIONALLY

In 1988, Royal Trustco moved into the European and U.K. markets, primarily through its U.K. subsidiary, Royal Trust Bank. The stated goal was to serve the same type of clientele as in Canada (older and affluent customers dealing with branches specifically located in neighbourhoods with high populations of wealthy and high income citizens), based upon a "relationship banking" theme. However, growth in the U.K. was fuelled by moving downscale and lending to the mid-market of small-business loans and commercial mortgages.[33]

In 1989, Royal Trustco made further moves into the United States market,[34] purchasing Seattle-based Pacific First Financial Corporation, considered to be a financially solid thrift.[35] Within twelve months, Royal Trustco purchased two savings and loan firms from Resolution Trust, the U.S. Government's liquidator of failed

thrifts. Cornelissen's goal was to merge the three U.S. institutions, realize operating economies, and in the process, create a super regional bank in the U.S. Pacific Northwest.[36]

Royal Trustco's international expansion was driven by several factors. The federal government was actively reviewing the Bank Act and other financial legislation. It was expected that trust companies, banks, and insurance companies would be able to enter into each other's traditional lines of business, thus increasing competition. Canada's market was seen by management as being too small to enable Royal Trustco to maintain its earnings growth at the expected levels.[37] Royal Trustco (and the Edper group in general) had frequently been the target of comments by politicians, academics, and media commentators about the concentration of commercial and financial companies. Cornelissen was noted to have said that the protests were driving Royal Trustco into other markets, such as the United States.[38] Finally, the U.S. market was seen as being fragmented, providing room to develop a large financial institution with scale efficiencies.[39]

1990: THE RECESSION HITS

The U.K. economy went into a severe recession early in 1990. The Canadian and U.S. economies started to slow down in late 1990, and went into full recession in 1991. In all three cases, the recession resulted in a decline in values in the real estate market, into which Royal Trustco had lent funds.[40] Further, the housing market in southern Ontario, where Royal Trustco had a large residential mortgage portfolio, declined along with the commercial markets.[41,42]

Royal Trustco's fourth quarter loss in 1990 was $251 million, the total loss for the year was $65 million. Loan loss provisions for the year increased from $23 million in 1989 to $220 million; the largest portion of the increase was for European loans.[43] This loss only affected shareholders in part. While the value of the stock dropped, the firm maintained its common share dividends at previous levels.[44]

1991: HAPPY DAYS ARE HERE AGAIN

The U.S. operations had been affected because of declines in the value of the California real estate market. First Pacific had been hit by non-performing loans, especially in California where it had a large loan portfolio in the commercial real estate market. While the recession had weakened the market, it was predicted that eventually the continuing growth in California's population would pick up the slack.[45]

In spite of the apparent gloom coming from the U.S. operations, 1991 turned out to be a good year for Royal Trustco. The company reported a net income for the year of $107 million. Shareholders were told that the worst of Royal Trustco's loan problems were behind it, with appropriate provisions having been made for potential loan losses.[46]

1992: THE LOAN-LOSS STEAMROLLER

In 1992, Royal Trustco sold its United States operations. First Pacific was draining cash out of its Canadian parent, and U.S. regulators had started to watch the company.[47] In their efforts to clean-up First Pacific, regulators and managers discovered even more problems in the lending department.[48] Furthermore, a wave of mergers in the U.S. had created several large regional competitors to the Royal Trustco operations.[49] In order to complete the sale of its U.S. subsidiary, Royal Trustco had to keep $900 million in non-performing loans; with the sale of First Pacific, Royal Trustco took a charge of $193 million against earnings.[50]

The publicity surrounding Royal Trustco's problems led to further revenue problems for the company. Depositors started taking their money out of Royal Trustco and placing it elsewhere. The result was that earnings from operations declined for the 1992 fiscal year.[51]

In 1992 came the announcement that Michael Cornelissen would be stepping down as president and CEO of Royal Trustco, and serving as vice-chairman in a non-executive role.[52] Following a search for a successor, James Miller, an accountant formerly with Touche Ross (now Deloitte Touche) in Vancouver, was appointed president and CEO.

DIVIDENDS

Even though Royal Trustco had lost money in 1990, it maintained its policy of holding dividends constant. In 1991, the company paid out $73 million in preferred dividends, and $108 million in common dividends; earnings in 1991 were $107 million. In 1992, despite losing $852 million for the year, the company declared and paid out $55 million in preferred dividends (meeting the full obligations on preferred shares), and $80 million in common dividends. Common dividends had been changed for 1992: for the second quarter onward, common dividends had been reduced from 18.5 cents per share to 10 cents per share; for the third quarter onward, they were reduced to five cents per share.[53]

MILLER AND THE END OF THE DREAM

Upon taking over in December 1992, Miller brought in independent consultants to review the loan portfolio. The conclusion of the review was that provisions for loan losses were inadequate.[54] Miller's action had been prompted, in part, by a visit from Michael Mackenzie, the federal government's top bank and trust company regulator. Mackenzie had visited Miller to issue a warning to watch out for Toronto real estate, as prices were in what he called a "free fall."[55]

Miller's conclusion was that in order to save the trust company, especially its depositors and assets, the only option was to sell the company outright.[56] Earlier in 1992, Royal Trustco had started looking for a partner willing to inject equity into the firm—in Miller's view, that was no longer an option. The response to Miller's analysis by the Royal Trustco board was disbelief; members did not believe things were as bad as Miller claimed.[57]

NOTES

1. This case has been written on the basis of published sources only. Consequently, the interpretation and perspectives presented in this case are not necessarily those of Royal Trustco or any of its employees.

2. The name "Royal Trustco" is used in the balance of the case. Although founded as Royal Trust, the parent company eventually came to be known as Royal Trustco, with Royal Trust as one of its operating divisions.

3. Ivey Business School Case #9A86B044 "Royal Trust (A)."

4. Ibid.

5. "Royal Bust," *Canadian Business,* November 1992, p. 46.

6. "Campeau makes bid for Royal Trust," *Globe & Mail,* August 28, 1980, pp. B1, 4.

7. "Royal Trustco management to fight Campeau takeover," *Globe & Mail,* August 29, 1980, p. B1.

8. "Battle heats up for Royal Trustco," *Globe & Mail,* September 9, 1980, p. B1.

9. "Royal Trustco to appeal ruling," *Globe & Mail,* September 17, 1980, p. B1.

10. "OSC allows Campeau to take up Royal Trustco shares," *Globe & Mail,* September 19, 1980, p. B1.

11. "TD buys interest in Royal Trustco," *Globe & Mail,* October 7, 1980, p. B1.

12. "Brascan buys 14.9 per cent of Royal Trustco," *Globe & Mail,* March 26, 1983, p. B1.

13. "Trilon purchases 42 per cent of Royal Trustco," *Globe & Mail,* July 29, 1983, p. B1.

14. "Royal Bust," *Canadian Business,* November 1992, p. 36.

15. Ibid, p. 38.

16. Ibid, p. 37.

17. Ibid, p. 38.

18. "Blue chip turns red, investors go white," *Globe & Mail,* March 30, 1993, p. B1.

19. Royal Trustco Annual Report 1984.

20. The philosophy, as described in "Royal Bust," included such aspects as managers becoming shareholders to unlock their entrepreneurial flair, a culture of hard work and dedication.

21. "Royal Bust," *Canadian Business,* November 1992, p. 39.

22. Ibid, p. 40.

23. Ibid.

24. "How the loan plan went wrong," *Globe & Mail,* March 29, 1993, p. B1.

25. "The Hollow Men," *Report on Business Magazine,* August 1993, p. 13.

26. "Royal Bust," *Canadian Business,* November 1992, p. 40.

27. Ibid.

28. Ibid.

29. Ibid, p. 42.

30. "A question of governance," *Globe & Mail,* July 19, 1993, pp. B1, 6.

31. Royal Trustco Annual Report 1984.

32. "Royal Bust," *Canadian Business,* November 1992, p. 42.

33. "Royal Bust," *Canadian Business,* November 1992, p. 44.

34. In 1987, Royal Trustco had purchased 9.9 per cent of a California savings and loan called GlenFed Inc.

35. "Royal Trustco," Canadian Research Flash, Prudential–Bache Securities, February 9, 1989.

36. "Royal Bust," *Canadian Business,* November 1992, p. 44.

37. "The Hollow Men," *Report on Business Magazine,* August 1993, p. 12.

38. "Royal Trustco to buy U.S. financial firm," *Globe & Mail,* February 7, 1989, pp. B1, 6.

39. Ibid.

40. "Blue chip turns red, investors go white," *Globe & Mail,* March 30, 1993, pp. B1, 8.

41. Royal Trustco Annual Report 1990.

42. According to the 1992 Royal Trustco Annual Report, as of December 31, 1992, Royal Trustco's net Ontario residential mortgage portfolio stood at $4,604 billion, or 51.4 per cent of its total Canadian residential mortgage portfolio. Net commercial real estate loans in the Ontario market totaled $2,463 billion, or 52.8 per cent of the company's Canadian commercial real estate loan portfolio.

43. Royal Trustco Annual Report 1990.

44. "Blue Chip turns red, investors go white," *Globe & Mail,* March 30, 1993, pp. B1, 8.

45. Royal Trustco Annual Statutory Report 1991, p. 17.

46. Ibid, pp. 28, 29.

47. "Royal Bust," *Canadian Business,* November 1992, p. 44.

48. Ibid.

49. Ibid.

50. "Royal Trust sells prize assets," *Globe & Mail,* March 19, 1993, pp. B1, 6.

51. Royal Trustco Annual Report 1992. "Net investment income" dropped by $132 million in 1992 over 1991. During this same period, "Fees and other income" increased by $14 million, for a net decrease in operating income before allowances for loan losses of $118 million.

52. "Royal Bust," *Canadian Business,* November 1992, p. 37.

53. Royal Trustco Annual Report 1992.

54. "A question of governance," *Globe & Mail,* July 19, 1993, p. B3.

55. Ibid.

56. Ibid.

57. Ibid.

5

INVESTMENT DECISIONS IN THE CONTEXT OF TECHNOLOGICAL CHANGES

I n many of the cases discussed in earlier chapters of this book, technological forces have played an important role in managerial decisions. In "Thai Telecoms in the New Economy: Privatization & Liberalization," students have dealt with the opportunities and challenges created by technological advances in the telecom structure and the Internet. A central issue concerns the degree to which the telecom infrastructure can provide new value-added activities that may enhance revenue far above what a firm could obtain from traditional telephone service. The "ING and Global Financial Integration" case includes a section on new e-banking opportunities and the degree to which these differ among countries. In all of these cases, societal attitudes play an important part in determining the degree to which technological innovations can create profitable opportunities.

For countries outside North America and Western Europe, several business features tend to support the expansion of e-business activities. The value chain consists of very many stages, each of which involves additional costs and may be eliminated through e-business. In many industries, competition is limited, and so corporations have been able to charge relatively high profit margins, creating opportunities for new e-business entrants. With e-business activities, much of the necessary capital may be located physically outside of less developed countries, thereby minimizing business risks.

On the other hand, many less developed countries have a traditional culture that prefers a face-to-face shopping experience and a culture that is reluctant to use credit cards. Personal relationships may not be severed easily between customers and their traditional business suppliers. Government regulations may be entrenched in ways that impede certain types of e-business activities. These realities may require a careful segmentation of the market, with new technologies focused on only a limited portion of the population.

Business models may have to be modified for technologies that have been successful in advanced nations to achieve similar success in less developed countries.

Throughout much of the world, technological gaps can be severe and long lasting, with important impacts on how a firm organizes its activities. Infrastructure deficiencies can require private ownership of power facilities, satellite transmission, or transport facilities. Most significant in recent years, the gap in e-commerce may necessitate corporate strategies that differ among countries. Resulting from differences in broadband telecom capacity, shopping habits, and banking systems, this e-commerce gap may persist for decades, with perhaps more serious business implications in the future. The telecommunications infrastructure has become increasingly important for each nation, not just as a stand-alone industry but because of the role it now plays in increasing the efficiency of existing business and in creating new start-up enterprises throughout the economy. The text by Rayport and Jaworski (2001) provides helpful insights in regard to this technological revolution. The competitiveness of a nation depends at least in part on the ability of the telecom infrastructure to support this array of new enhanced services, and so governments are participating actively in this technological revolution.

Students have discussed a variety of other technologies in previous cases. Of special interest in this chapter are the previous cases that have dealt with government attempts to subsidize research and innovation in certain industry sectors. The "Bombardier Versus Embraer" case included a discussion of the role of new technologies in determining international competitiveness in aircraft manufacturing. In this chapter, "Malaysia's Multimedia Development Corporation" carries this perspective to a broader level, with the attempt to transform a national economy through the creation of a new cluster of high-tech corporations. Of particular importance, this case encourages students to consider the location determinants for cutting-edge technologies as they contemplate the relative attractiveness of Malaysia's new high-tech corridor, compared with other countries throughout the world.

The "Global Warming and the Kyoto Protocol: Implications for Business" case presents the attempt by governments to change the technologies used by firms in such a way as to reduce the emissions that cause global warming. Students will debate the likelihood that new technologies will in fact be able to achieve this objective, and they will discuss the cost implications for businesses of this enormously significant international commitment. The fact that less developed countries have not signed the Kyoto Protocol raises the possibility that technologies may become increasingly differentiated between the rich and poor nations (Organization for Economic Cooperation and Development [OECD], 1999). A substantial component of "greenhouse gas emissions" is caused by businesses that generate electricity, and so the "Enron Wind Corporation" case has been written to explore the business opportunities that may be created by new technologies in electricity generation (Chambers, 2001).

Shifts in technology can dramatically alter an industry structure and can reduce or eliminate a firm's competitive advantage. Incumbent firms often confront new competitors that possess very different strategies and capabilities and may have to make major, sometimes "bet-the-company," investments to survive. The "Eurograin (Philippines) and Hybrid Corn" case illustrates this situation and encourages students to think about the relationship between technological innovations and business opportunities. Several issues affect this relationship, including the degree of competition with alternative innovations, the protection of intellectual property, and intercorporate relationships. The "Shire Pharmaceuticals Group's Acquisition of BioChem Pharma" case introduces the subject of biotechnology and emphasizes the dependence of pharmaceutical profitability on continual innovation. Economies of scale occur at many levels, from basic research through the drug approval process to marketing. These forces push corporations toward globalization and lead to cross-border mergers and acquisitions. Here again governments play a role, as they seek to create an industry structure that will ensure an adequate degree of competition.

PRIVATIZING POLAND'S TELECOM INDUSTRY: OPPORTUNITIES AND CHALLENGES IN THE NEW ECONOMY AND E-BUSINESS

Affordability, quality, and breadth of telecom service had become critical components in determining the value of the telecom system to other businesses. Hence, it was important for Poland to turn to privatization and a set of regulatory policies that would place a greater emphasis on enhancing innovation through greater competition. As the marginal cost of carriage tended toward zero, and as competition fostered huge investments in fiber-optic cable, DSL technologies, and wireless networks, telecom carriers were entering an era of commoditization of basic service provision. Future profits would rest on the ability of telecom companies to provide value-added services to their customers.

MALAYSIA'S MULTIMEDIA DEVELOPMENT CORPORATION

In 1996, the Malaysian government announced its plan to achieve "developed nation" status by the year 2020. To facilitate this transformation, the nation decided to create a "cybercity" that would be a new cluster for multimedia development—a multimedia super-corridor to attract foreign direct investment and encourage technology transfer. This area would be governed by new laws, would be connected globally by the latest telecommunications technology, and would be a prototype for other cybercities around the country. The government began recruiting high-tech leaders. Observers speculated about the success of a planned, government-stimulated cluster and debated the viability of such a venture.

GLOBAL WARMING AND THE KYOTO PROTOCOL: IMPLICATIONS FOR BUSINESS

Through the Kyoto Protocol, many nations collaborated to restrain global warming by restricting greenhouse gas emissions. These new restrictions would place a heavy financial burden on firms—and their shareholders and customers. With the threat of global warming, businesses confronted a two-sided challenge: Without political interventions, such as the Kyoto Protocol, an increase in the number and intensity of natural disasters would create new business risks and costs, yet compliance with new regulations to limit this damage would also increase their costs substantially. New technologies might assist in this industrial transformation.

Enron Wind Corporation: Challenges and Opportunities in the 21st Century

Enron Wind Firm (EWC) was considering building a wind farm in Fortaleza, Brazil. This region on Brazil's northeastern coast had experienced strong industrial growth, and the increase of power consumption in the region had exceeded all expectations. This project could provide Enron Wind with an attractive opportunity to enter the Brazilian wind energy market. Brazil had a vast and untapped wind energy resource, as well as a rapidly growing demand for new electrical capacity. However, Brazil also had a history of political and economic instability.

Eurograin (Philippines) and Hybrid Corn

Eurograin had a 35% share of the hybrid seed market in the Philippines, up from 4% just 4 years ago, but less than the 60% share of Pioneer, a key competitor. At the time, Eurograin focused its resources on product development, contracting sales and distribution to Ayala Agribusiness. The hybrid seed industry was very competitive, and there was a race to develop a one-way cross-hybrid seed that would increase yields by 20%. Competing for this new product were Eurograin, Pioneer, Ayala Agribusiness, and the government. Eurograin planned to enter the market with its version of the cross-hybrid seed, with a goal of 50% market share. However, given the complexities and uncertainties of the external environment, such as (a) the current development of laws around plant variety protection, (b) deregulation of the corn market, (c) political unrest in one of the two major corn-growing areas in the Philippines, and (d) the conflict of interest posed by Ayala Agribusiness, Eurograin was questioning if and when it should implement the product introduction. Related to this question was whether it should invest substantial funds to undertake its own production, sales, and distribution operations rather than rely on Ayala.

Shire Pharmaceuticals Group's Acquisition of BioChem Pharma: Broadening Product Portfolio and Achieving Economies of Scale in Pharmaceuticals

Throughout the world, pharmaceutical companies were merging to achieve economies of scale in all of their activities, from research and product development to distribution and marketing. Although BioChem had several successful products and a track record of rapid expansion, nevertheless, in this new global environment, it was now necessary for Bio-Chem to achieve economies of scale through a consolidation of some type. The U.K. firm Shire was approximately the same size as BioChem and faced the same dilemma. In a sense, Shire's acquisition of BioChem was a merger rather than a takeover, and both corporations could achieve a unified global strategy that was beyond the means of each individually.

PRIVATIZING POLAND'S TELECOM INDUSTRY: OPPORTUNITIES AND CHALLENGES IN THE NEW ECONOMY AND E-BUSINESS

Prepared by Marius Siwak under the supervision of Professor David Conklin

Version: (A) 2001-01-31

As it entered the 21st century, the Polish government faced the dilemma of how to develop an optimal telecom structure and related services. For decades, a government owned and operated telecom, TPSA, had held a monopoly, but in the late 1990s the Polish government gradually allowed the entry of some competitors, many of whom brought new technologies.[1] The government had undertaken a major privatization program throughout the economy, and it faced the question of whether and how it should privatize TPSA. Yet privatization would have to be accompanied by ongoing regulation in order to ensure that managerial decisions were made in the interests of the nation, as a whole. A number of comments by Izabela Moziek, a representative of TPSA, served to emphasize the concerns of the government.

> The government will never release its grip on the company because we are strategically such an important part of the nation . . .

> . . . We have several new development plans in place now to secure a leadership position in the future. Most of all, the Polish government has several military and other contracts with the company and it will always have an interest in preserving TPSA's well-being . . .

> There is still a strong government presence in the day to day operations of the company.

This challenge of continual government intervention could reduce the attractiveness of acquiring TPSA, in spite of its market dominance. For potential foreign investors, a host of additional difficulties appeared to be so severe that perhaps the privatization bidding process should be ignored. Existing infrastructure was largely obsolete, and employees lacked the skills and motivation to transform TPSA into a modern, competitive entity. Meanwhile, alternative modes of entry into the telecom sector might be pursued, and some, like wireless and the Internet could threaten TPSA's future.

In the new era of e-business, would Poland be able to retain the economic momentum that its 1990s market reforms had created? A new investor could be very discouraged about the prospects for the "new economy" and e-business. The future success of the Polish economy as a whole would depend very much upon a transformation in Poland's telecom industry, but would this transformation occur soon? A special report on Poland in "Computer World Top 2000" emphasized:

> Another threat is looming on the horizon—the new model of the economy. The development of electronic business, which will most likely become an economic standard in the developed parts of the world, puts Poland in the dramatic pursuit after escaping leaders. Every Polish enterprise must take a long and hard look at itself once again and answer the question: "to which part of the chain of value creation does it want to belong?" How well Poland adopts e-business solutions will dictate whether it will belong to the part of the world that engages in costly production or the part that carries out lucrative distribution.

Poland's leaders had been shifting the nation successfully from communism to free enterprise, and analysts expected that they would continue along the path of transferring decision-making to the private sector. Many potential investors recognized the key role to be played by the telecom structure and e-business. Perhaps now was the time to achieve a "first mover advantage." The very low level of Poland's involvement in the new economy and e-business might be seen as an ideal business environment for developing market share and attaining extraordinary profits.

THE DEAL2

> *The government wanted to ease TPSA into a competitive environment. The logic behind our decision was that the company had never operated in a competitive environment before and we were afraid that opening up the lucrative long distance segment of the market too quickly might bring the company down. First of all, TPSA is, strategically, an important part of our development policy. Second, the Ministry of Treasury planned to sell off part of the company to a strategic investor. If TPSA's earnings degenerated dramatically, simply no one would buy it. Besides those reasons, we wanted to create a much needed local infrastructure, given the low telephone penetration ratio in the country.*

> —Andrzej Plachecki, Director of Strategic Development—Ministry of Telecommunications

In 1999, the Ministry of Communication issued an invitation to foreign telecom providers to participate in the sale of a 35 per cent stake in the national telecom carrier—TPSA. From a dozen companies that expressed their interest, two bidders emerged: France Telecom and SBC Communication. In November, 1999, SBC withdrew from the negotiation process citing ambiguity of the Polish telecom market regulation as a main reason for its exit from negotiations. France Telecom remained the only interested party and in December, 1999, the Ministry of Treasury rejected the French offer giving two main reasons for the rejection: too low a price (about US$2.5 billion), and planned employment cuts that were too drastic.

After this failed effort, the government considered selling its stake in TPSA through capital markets, but the potential price that the Ministry could attain would be lower than that from selling off a package to a strategic investor. Furthermore, the government rightly perceived the importance of the much needed business expertise which a strategic investor would bring to the organization. TPSA lacked experience in customer service and was far behind the cutting edge of the new economy and e-business. Therefore, for TPSA to survive in the long run, a strategic investor's influence seemed necessary.

Early in 2000 the Ministry of Treasury issued another invitation to telecoms around the world. This time two bidders emerged and remained till the end: France Telecom once again and Telecom Italia. On May 22, 2000, the government of Poland named France Telecom as a winner of the bidding process. Analysts estimated that France Telecom paid approximately US$5 billion for a 35 per cent stake in TPSA. France Telecom had an option to buy additional 16 per cent of the company, thus eventually achieving a controlling stake in the Polish national carrier.

Five billion dollars is not the only expenditure, however, that France Telecom would face in the near future. The next stage of negotiations would involve a so-called "Social Package." TPSA employees were represented by several labor unions. In order to restructure properly and to revive the company, the new investor would likely have to release a large number of people. Izabela Moziek was clear in regard to the employee profile: "Until recently, the hiring process has been based more on family and friends than on necessary skills."

A new collective agreement had to be negotiated with the unions prior to any major layoffs. In particular, the severance pay might turn out to be very expensive. It was estimated that in order to avoid problems with the unions, France Telecom would have to pay two full years of pay to each laid off employee. An average salary within TPSA was about US$500 per month, thus, if the company decided to lay off, say, 15 per cent of its workforce, it would cost at least an additional US$200 million to complete the restructure. Even such a generous package did not fully protect the company from a conflict with the unions, nor did it guarantee its acceptance. Bickering among unions could stall the process for months. Furthermore, France Telecom would have to invest additional billions of dollars if it wanted to transform TPSA into a modern telecom provider with broadband capacity.

The company generated over US$200 million a year in net profit.[3] But so far TPSA operated uncontested and no company other than TPSA even had a permit to build a true alternative infrastructure. In the years 2002/03 this situation would change. The entire Polish market would open up to competition without restrictions. Given that alternative networks existed, such as cable TV, or were in the planning stage, could the company sustain its profitability in the long run?

After 2003, what would stop an American telecom company or any major European telecom provider from entering the market, with superior financial resources and technical expertise, to establish modern broadband telecom services? Was the high price paid for the stake in TPSA well justified in light of technological changes reshaping the telecom industry? Was TPSA well positioned to become a modern telecom provider by the world standards?

From Communism to Capitalism![4, 5]

With the legalization of Solidarity in 1989 and the ensuing democratization of the government, Poland emerged from the communist rule that had endured from the end of the World War II. From the ashes of a centrally planned economy, a decade after embarking on aggressive restructuring, Poland, by 2000, had become one of the most successful economies in Eastern Europe. Initially, investment may have appeared risky

and uncertain. However, history demonstrates that the often-oppressed Poles are a resilient and adaptable people; perhaps an ideal site for economic reform and a platform into eastern European countries. Starting with no banking laws and no property rights, there were now more than two million entrepreneurs in such sectors as retail trade, construction, and light manufacturing. Private business now accounted for about 60 per cent of the GDP.

Except for a very minor increase in 1999, inflation and unemployment had steadily trended down. The economy had made consistent progress with annual real growth between five and seven per cent. In the 1990s, the Monetary Policy Council (MPC) enhanced its credibility with swift and decisive policies to manage economic crises. In 1997/98, when the economy appeared to be overheating, the MPC responded with a tightening of monetary policy. Poland did not escape the late 1990s financial crises of less developed countries entirely, as growth slowed to 1.5 per cent in 1Q99 but it rebounded to 4.9 per cent by 3Q99. Economic reform had become an ongoing process with the Polish government. In 1997 large scale privatization was initiated, resulting in restructuring of entire sectors of the economy. Privatized businesses typically demonstrated improved efficiencies very quickly. Despite these efforts, in 2000 the state still owned some 3,000 enterprises (125 with more than 500 employees) and still dominated many sectors. Government plans anticipated privatization of 70 per cent of the remaining businesses by 2001. All this progress had been achieved despite having nine different governments in ten years.

The foremost economic objective of Poland was ascension into the EU. As two-thirds of Poland's trade was with the EU a large degree of integration had already been achieved by 2000. The MPC was attempting to maintain the budget deficit at 2.5 per cent of GDP. With the minor crisis in 1999 it reached 3.5 per cent, but a budget law required a maximum of 2.75 per cent by 2000. The concern with these statistics was that many of the state owned enterprises were accumulating accounts payable by not remitting taxes and social security contributions. The EU inflation target of zero to two per cent was beyond reach for Poland in the near term. The MPC preferred to set a realistic target: four per cent by 2003. This was a very practical approach as inflation declined from 800 per cent in 1989 to a rate of 7.7 per cent in 2000. Poland managed foreign currency exchange with a "crawling peg regime." The zloty was allowed to trade within a 15 per cent band either side of a centrally fixed rate that was depreciated at 0.3 per cent per month against a euro/dollar basket. This policy was changed in 1999, and the currency was allowed to flow freely in the market, without initially losing any value.

Poland's imports had recently substantially exceeded exports. Imports peaked in 1998 at 146 per cent of exports and were anticipated to decline gradually. Encouragingly, the bulk of the imports were in the category of investment goods. Despite the fiscal budget deficit and the current account deficit, Poland had increased its international reserves as a result of capital inflows. Foreign debt declined on a real basis and as a percentage of GDP. Poland's success in funding its expansionary policy was due to the high level of foreign direct investment (FDI). For the ten years ending 1998 FDI was US$30.7 billion, and it was forecast to be US$10.5 billion in 2000. Privatization was a significant element of these FDI inflows.

Poland recently embarked on a major restructuring of its social safety net, employment and tax laws. These latter reforms were essential to improve the effectiveness of public spending and to remove the ambiguity of hidden subsidies. The government had recognized the need to modernize infrastructure; specifically roads, airports, and seaports. Despite the fact that unemployment had steadily trended down, it remained the highest in eastern Europe with the natural rate of unemployment (NRU) estimated at 10 per cent. Poland reputedly had the most profligate welfare system in eastern Europe. Furthermore, the discouraged worker phenomenon was supplemented by hidden unemployment in rural areas, second wave baby boomers and the potential for nearly half of the work

force to be women. Planned tax reforms were significant and positive; corporate tax reduction from 34 per cent to 22 per cent by 2004, personal tax reduction from a 20 per cent, 32 per cent, and 44 per cent three-tier structure to a two-tier structure of 18 per cent and 28 per cent by 2001. Increases in VAT and consumption taxes plus economic growth were expected to offset these reductions in tax revenue. Tax reform was a significant prerequisite of EU compliance. It was hoped that educational initiatives to eliminate the gap with the EU would help address the high NRU. These reforms would hopefully counteract rising tensions in the labor force.

However, many observers saw serious difficulties for the Polish economy. In a general survey in May 1999, the following comments suggested that all was not well.[6]

> Most of the people who lived in Poland during the intervening years think about how much more change is needed, how unfair the transition from communism has been, how their safe, secure lives have been irretrievably upset, how much uncertainty lies ahead.

> By most accounts, about a third of Poles felt better off than they did a decade before, a third thought they were in roughly the same position and a third believed themselves to be worse off.

> Polish Finance Minister Leszek Balcerowicz was equally clear in his own mind about what should be done: "Our financial and economic strategy for the next 10 years focuses on the crucial issues of tax reform, public finance and privatization . . . Key to the economic strategy must be privatization of the state sector, which still controls some 40 per cent of the Polish economy."

Joining the EU would not be easy. Many Poles argued for special entry concessions, and negotiations over the terms and conditions for EU membership would involve internal conflicts. Unemployment among rural youth was very high, and threatened social instability. Polish farmers struggled to survive with low agricultural prices, in the context of cheap food imports. Lurking in the background, was a widespread set of concerns

	1994	1998	2000E
Real GDP growth, %	5.30	4.80	5.50
GDP per capita, US$	2,407.00	3,872.00	4,190.00
Inflation, annual average %	33.30	11.70	7.70
Unemployment, annual average %	15.00	10.60	10.50
Current account balance, US$ million	(944.00)	(6,858.00)	(10,500.00)
Current account balance as % of GDP	(1.00)	(4.60)	(6.50)
Interest rate, short term, %		24.50	15.50
Foreign exchange rate, US$	2.27	3.48	4.15
Fiscal deficit/surplus as % of GDP		(2.50)	(2.50)

Exhibit 1   Polish Economic Statistics

about the rapidly increasing foreign ownership of Polish land and industry.

THE TECHNOLOGICAL REVOLUTION IN THE GLOBAL TELECOM INDUSTRY

In recent years, especially in the North American market, traditional plain telephone service had become a commodity. One of the loudest buzzwords in the new era of telecommunication in the 21st century was a "residential gateway" that promised to deliver an integrated set of telephony, Internet connectivity, data transmission, home networking, and entertainment features through one box that connected to virtually everything. Such a prediction pointed to broadband as necessary for the telecommunications future. The pipes leading from the Internet to the living rooms of consumers, capable of carrying digital bits in torrents would enable households to download music and video from vast entertainment libraries, shop in real time, or make a video call to a distant relative.

The most substantial bottleneck in this telecom revolution was in the local loop, the last mile of infrastructure linking the system to each household or business. Hence the issue of capacity enhancement in the local loop became truly significant for each nation's twenty-first century competitiveness.

At this point in time, it was not clear how the constriction in the local loop could best be overcome. The cable industry covered only a portion of the population, and required huge capital outlays in order to provide optimal "broadband" access. For traditional telecoms, digital subscriber lines (DSL) offered more carrying capacity on existing copper wires, but deteriorated with distance, and signals interfered with each other if more than a limited number of customers were covered in each neighborhood. Wireless and satellite technologies were still in the early stages of development, and some technologies encountered weather difficulties and needed "line-of-sight" with customers. Likely, there would be a variety of solutions, each geared to certain market niches: urban versus rural, large business versus small- and medium-sized businesses, and an array of differing preferences among residential consumers. It was quite possible that the technologies that would be most successful had not yet been developed.

In the twenty-first century, telecommunications would become increasingly important for each nation, not just as a stand alone industry, but because of the role it played in increasing the efficiency of existing business and in creating new start-up enterprises throughout the economy. Poland's competitiveness as a nation would depend on the ability of the telecom infrastructure to support this array of new enhanced services, and Poland's productivity improvements, with increases in living standards, would depend on ongoing innovations in these enhanced telecom services. Affordability, quality and breadth of service had become critical components in determining the value of the telecom system to other businesses. Hence it was important for Poland to turn to a new set of policy and regulatory issues that would place an even greater emphasis on enhancing competition.

As the marginal cost of carriage tended towards zero, and as competition fostered huge investments in fibre optic cable, the DSL technologies, wireless networks, and telecom carriers in many countries were entering an era of commoditization of basic service provision. Future profits would rest on the ability of telecom companies to provide value-added services to their customers in the face of heightened Polish and global competition. These realities would change the structure of Poland's telecom industry.

In many countries, the Internet and all its associated technologies were creating a new economy and new industry structures. Its effects were well documented. But what was not as well known—except among technology visionaries, such as Bill Gates, Steve Case, and John Chambers—was the extent to which the convergence revolution would change the way all businesses and governments operated, thus enabling enormous productivity improvements. For this reason, the term e-enhanced services (electronically-enhanced) came to represent the various services and products that could be delivered over the telecommunications infrastructure. By no means an exhaustive list, the following were important sectors that would present profound regulatory challenges over the coming years:

1. E-Retail

2. E-Advertising

3. E-Banking and E-Financial Services

4. E-Entertainment

5. E-Pornography

6. E-Gambling

7. E-Medicine

In the context of major global telecom changes, the enhancement of domestic culture would become increasingly difficult. Many enhanced services dealt with the provision of content, and this relationship raised a series of issues in regard to how to enhance domestic involvement in this content. For instance, vertical integration in the telecommunications field was stretching into traditional content arenas that were previously the sole domain of broadcasters. Whether and how a government should regulate the Internet and its content had become a major issue for most countries. How could the government effectively promote domestic content on the Internet, particularly in light of international trade agreements that required increasingly open international competition?

Furthermore, throughout the world, the challenge for regulators was to entrench competition and innovation in an industry characterized by economies of scale and scope in service delivery, while protecting consumers and investors from fraud, misleading advertising, and certain other socially unacceptable behaviors. For example, if an entrepreneur set up a website to sell mutual funds, should the entrepreneur be subject to the same regulations as a broker at an investment firm? If so, were these regulations enforceable?

Many countries were finding that the traditional regulatory environment in each business sector had to be re-examined to determine its appropriateness in the new telecom era. However, the government's ability to regulate each of the sectors that used the telecom infrastructure would be severely constrained. In countries with radio and TV broadcasts sent over the telecommunications infrastructure and Internet commerce growing by leaps and bounds, a key question was whether over arching regulation of telecoms must be combined in some way with the separate regulation of each service provider that was using the telecom infrastructure. Telecom policy would then be seen as much broader in scope than it had been in the past, for it would include social policy and commercial regulation. Conversely, telecom policy, per se, could in turn become limited in scope, as social policy and commercial regulation determined the optimal telecom framework.

The number of people who had taken advantage of broadband services was still quite small in most countries, including Poland. The take-up rate was low because of high hardware prices and the lack of compelling new reason for consumers to step up their services. When traffic increased, images decayed. The problem was expected to ease as long distance telecom companies and Internet providers improved their networks and electronics. As the technical problems with broadband effectiveness disappeared, the new battle for a "residential gateway" could become intense.

The recent merger between AOL and Time Warner and its European equivalent between United Pan European Communications and SBS Broadcasting reflected the perception that those who controlled content and direct access to homes would be best poised to be the future leaders in the new era of telecommunication and e-business. However, which of the many existing technologies or transmission media were best positioned to become a standard for the future telecommunication services? In 2000 there were no clear leaders. The experts were widely divided over which technology was best suited to accommodate the rapid evolution of electronic business. Some pointed to DSL as a future standard of broadband, others name DTH (Direct To Home), cable, or wireless as the potential leader of broadband telecommunication services. Meanwhile, satellites might also come to play a role. Unfortunately, it seemed too early to tell which technology was likely to live on, and which was likely to fail.

POLAND'S REGULATORY ENVIRONMENT

The main regulatory body of telecom services was the Ministry of Communication. However, the Ministry of National Defense and Internal Affairs had a limited influence, as well as contracts with the TPSA regarding national security. Telecom services were considered to be of national strategic importance. A separate board—KKRiTV—was a regulatory body appointed by the government of Poland to regulate and control radio and television content. Although there was a trend toward creation of multimedia telecommunications

including TV programming and radio transmission, there was no plan to merge the two regulatory organs. Furthermore, because of an extreme political segregation within Polish government such fusion seemed to be impossible, at least for the time being.

On November 23, 1990, the Polish government decided to de-monopolize its telecommunication market.[7] The government started selling off licenses for various services (these licenses were not subject to an automatic renewal). Separate licenses were sold for data transmission, telephony, Internet services, mobile telephony, and cable TV services. For example attaining a license for telephone services did not mean that the operator was free to provide a full range service offering. Additionally, cable providers were not allowed to provide voice services, and only one license was awarded for telephone services per small region in order not to create too intense competition for TPSA. Moreover, the telecom providers were not allowed to provide their services or build infrastructure across the regions, thus TPSA still held its monopoly in the highly lucrative long distance segment. There was no maximum connection or transfer price established by the Ministry, which left TPSA free to dictate any price for connection to its long-distance system.

The law was amended several times since 1990 to accommodate change in the telecom industry as well as to solve problems and disputes as they arose. For instance, Era GSM, a subsidiary of Elektrim, started providing long distance telephone calls via the Internet, at about one-third the price compared with TPSA. However, TPSA claimed to be cross subsidizing high cost rural telephony from its long distance profits, and so lobbied the government to prohibit Internet telephony. The Ministry of Telecommunication agreed with the TPSA position and threatened to pull out the license from Era. However, confronted with the company's appeals to other European governments, the Ministry backed off and eventually allowed Era's Internet telephony. Nevertheless, as Andrzej Plachecki emphasized, "Internet telephony has not really taken off despite all the savings that it has promised."

As of 2000 there was a new telecom law in the makings. The new act included sweeping changes. In 2003, when the new law would take effect, the market would open up to any firm that wanted to provide any telecom services upon getting an appropriate license. The licenses would be renewable, not subject to being reviewed, as before. A license would be sold based on the carrier's capability to provide a service. The Ministry of Communication would cease to exist and a small telecom regulatory entity would be formed under the Ministry of Transportation. However, the telecom services were still perceived to be of a strategic national importance. This fact combined with the government's desire to develop much needed telephone infrastructure in less developed regions of the country presented an opportunity for TPSA to influence the authorities in the future.

THE STATE OF THE TELECOMMUNICATIONS MARKET IN POLAND[8]

Telekomunikacja Polska S.A. (TPSA) was established in December, 1991, when the Polish Post, Telegraph, and Telephone Office, founded in 1928, was broken into separate entities. However, Telekomunikacja Polska S.A. remained wholly owned and operated by the government of Poland. From the very beginning of its existence, TPSA operated profitably and by 2000 was the most profitable organization in the country.[9] Until 1995, TPSA operated as a single telecommunication service provider without any competition. Only in 1995 did the Ministry of Communication decide to deregulate the telecom market slightly in order to prepare Poland for the integration with the European Union and to prepare TPSA to operate in a competitive environment. Thus at the end of 1995, TPSA for the first time faced so called competition. However, TPSA still held an exclusive right to provide intercity as well as international phone services until 2002 and 2003, consecutively, and competed locally only with one company for innercity telephone services, with the exception of the Warsaw region where two competitors were allowed.

In the Polish market, broadband services were mainly geared towards data transmission. TPSA, and a few other companies, banks in particular, provided fast DSL services. Their networks, however, were still underdeveloped and their services extremely expensive.

The Telecom market in Poland could be characterized as extremely underdeveloped, with under 30 fixed lines per 100 inhabitants.[10] In comparison, developed European countries had about a 60/100 ratio. This low penetration indicator was even lower outside the major cities in Poland. For example, in more remote and less developed regions,[11] which represented about 40 per cent of the country, this percentage was 10 to 12 per cent or less. These regions had a much poorer and more dispersed population, which made the development process more expensive and unprofitable. TPSA held about 96 per cent of the fixed line telecom service market in Poland (nine million subscribers).[12]

Netia SA

The second largest telecom provider was Netia S.A. The company was established in 1990 to exploit anticipated deregulation of the telecom market in the country. In 1998, Netia launched its IPO on NASDAQ. About 30 per cent of the company was held by Telia AB, a Swedish national carrier. Telia was also dynamically involved in the telecom market in the majority of the Baltic States. Telia had three mobile telephone systems and one cable TV subsidiary in Sweden. An additional 40 per cent of Netia S.A. was held by GE Capital, Motav (a cable system media company from Israel), Danker (a diversified telecom provider also from Israel), Goldman Sachs Capital Partners, and Shamrock Holdings Inc. (a private investment firm owned by R.E. Disney). Netia Telekom S.A. had serviced 458,251 lines and had 260,388 subscribers.[13] The corporation had a permit to provide fixed line telephone services in five major Polish cities and covered a territory inhabited by 33 per cent of the country's population. Aside from fixed telephony, Netia had three permits to provide Internet services and one permit to provide data transmission using ISDN protocol.

	Company Name	Services Provided	Number of Subscribers of Fixed Telephone Service	Number of Cellular Subscribers	Market Share in Mobile and Fixed Service Provision	Net Profit in US$—Last Reported
1	TPSA	Fixed telephone Mobile Satellite Radio broadcasting Internet Data transmission	9 million	400 thousand	96% 17%	200 million
2	Netia SA	Fixed telephony Internet Data transmission	250 thousand	N/A	2%	(100.1 million)
3	Elektrim SA	Fixed telephony Internet Cable TV Mobile Data transmission	120 thousand	1.5 million	1% 51%	25 million
4	Polkomtel	Mobile Data transmission Internet		1.1 million	32%	40 million
5	UPC (WIZJA TV)	Cable TV DTH				N/A

Exhibit 2   Polish Telecommunications Providers—Overview

Netia's infrastructure was based on modern fiber optic technology. Although no telephone operator other than TPSA had a license to provide inter-city and international services, or even build inter-city infrastructure, Netia already started to lay down fibre optic cables to connect its five local area networks in anticipation of further market deregulation. Once completed, such a network would finally create a truly alternative telecom service, free of dependency on TPSA's infrastructure. Also, given that Telia AB was a modern telephone company with extensive infrastructure in Northern, Central, and Eastern Europe, in 2003 when the Polish market would become fully opened to competition, the company would be able to provide international call services.

Elektrim S.A

Elektrim S.A., with its subsidiary "Era," was the third largest telecom provider in Poland. Vivendi Corporation was the majority shareholder with a 49 per cent stake in Elektrim. Vivendi also had a large stake in the two largest European pay TV companies: BskyB and Canal Plus. In addition to fixed line telephone services, Elektrim held a majority stake in Era GSM, a leading cellular telephone provider, as well as in Aster City, which was a cable TV operator with 240,000 subscribers[14] mainly in the Warsaw region. Through Aster City, Elektrim planned to provide full multimedia telecom services in the near future. This was the only company other than TPSA that could provide a full range of multimedia telecom services.

There were about 70 other local telecom service providers in Poland.[15] The great majority of them were small and undercapitalized, however, by 2000, one could observe a slow but steady consolidation trend among them.[16] It was safe to assume that once the full scale market deregulation became a reality, these small operators would either merge or be taken over, creating yet another full range telecom alternative to that of TPSA.

The Wireless Market

Mobile telephony appeared in Poland in 1991 with the establishment of PTK Centertel (owned by TPSA), although the network only began operating several years later. At the beginning, Centertel based its services on the analogue network. The analogue market was now saturated with 260,000 subscribers.[17] Digital networks began to dominate in 1997. At the end of 1996 two competitors were awarded licenses by the Ministry of Communication to provide cellular telephone services using the digital system GSM 900. Era GSM (owned by Elektrim) and GSM Plus (owned by Polkomtel) dominated the market.

The Ministry of Communication did not initially issue the same permit to use GSM 900 technology to Centertel to prevent TPSA from establishing yet another monopolistic position in the mobile telephone market. However, Centertel was given such a license in 1999, perhaps because its two competitors were firmly entrenched and perhaps to increase the value of the firm in light of the planned sale of a 35 per cent stake in TPSA to a strategic investor. At the end of 1999 the size of the mobile telephone market in Poland was estimated to be over three million subscribers, and it was growing at the rate of 25 per cent per annum.

Spectrum Allocation

Throughout the world, a major political issue concerned the question, how best to allocate spectrum for wireless operators. In the past, the Polish government had used an auction process. However, recent experiments with auctions in other countries had encountered serious problems. *The Economist* emphasized:

> The auction process was designed almost entirely by experts in game theory, one of the economics profession's most esoteric fields. . . .

> . . . Poorly designed auctions can make governments look foolish. For example, in 1990, New Zealand conducted a so-called second-price sealed-bid auction. Under this scheme, the highest bidder wins, but instead of paying its own bid price the winner pays the next-highest bid price. In New Zealand many bidders got spectrum rights for prices far below what they had offered. In one case, the top bid was NZ$100,000 (US$60,000) but the winner paid only NZ$6.

A large number of auction questions remained. Should winners be required to pay immediately, or should payments be spread over a certain time period? Would "the winner's curse" frequently mean that the winning bidder would have paid too much? Would license interdependencies be impeded by the bidding process that allocated each regional spectrum individually? Would some bidders simply not have the capability or qualifications to implement their plans? Should forfeiture penalties be incurred by bidders who failed to comply with certain commitments? Should there be reserve prices and minimum opening bids? Should there be a series of rounds in the bidding process in order for each bidder to arrive over time at an optimal bid?

As an alternative process for spectrum allocation, some governments used a comparative selection process in which public servants examined a wide variety of aspects of each applicant's proposal. Of particular importance to some governments was the concept of universal service, and each proposal could be evaluated on the degree to which it promised to serve high cost as well as low cost areas.

Alternative Telecom Infrastructures

There were other alternative potential telecom infrastructures. For instance, the Polish Railway Company ran its trains almost exclusively on electricity, and so the company had a very extensive electric cable network throughout Poland. Polish Hydro possessed similar infrastructure. There were several studies underway to adopt electric wire for data transmission. Although the necessary hardware and software were still very expensive and underdeveloped, the possibility existed that in the future this alternative medium could create effective competition for traditional telecom providers.

It was important to note the presence of a major broadband communication provider—United

Pan-European Communication Company—in the Polish Market. UPC, headquartered in Amsterdam, was one of the most innovative broadband communication providers in Europe and owned and operated the largest broadband communication network on the continent. UPC provided cable TV, satellite services, telephony, high-speed Internet access, and programming services in 18 countries across Europe and Israel. As of March 31, 2000, on an aggregate basis, UPC's systems passed approximately 11.5 million homes (over one million in Poland).

UPC was a consolidated subsidiary of Denver based United Global Com Inc. (NASDAQ: "UCOMA"), and Microsoft had an interest of approximately seven per cent in UPC.[18] The company had some of the most technologically advanced cable systems available anywhere in the world today. UPC owned a unique cable infrastructure backbone called AORTA (Always On Ready Time Architecture) which would eventually interconnect each of the UPC's local country operations. Long-term leasing arrangements for two dedicated high capacity fiber optic routes provided a transatlantic link for this AORTA backbone with the dynamic North American market. At this time in Poland, UPC owned and operated a cable TV provider—Wizja TV—satellite services, and Internet access. In 2003, there would be no obstacles for the company to provide a full range of telecom services of the highest quality, thus weakening the dominant role of TPSA in the Polish telecom industry.

TPSA Position in the Polish Market

On November 18, 1998, TPSA floated its shares on the Warsaw and London Stock Exchanges, and the company ceased to be wholly owned by Poland's State Treasury. Fifteen per cent of its shares were now in private hands. Additionally, 15 per cent of the company shares were distributed among its employees, leaving the State with a 70 per cent stake. Although the company had a new management structure composed mainly of professional managers, the president of TPSA, Pawel Rzepka, had been appointed by the government and represented "Unia Wolnosci," one of Poland's ruling political parties.

TPSA employed 72,800 people (12.7 per cent with a university degree)[19] and could be characterized as overstaffed. Work on the company's restructure was initiated in 1998, to prepare the organization for real competition in 2003, when the Polish telecom market would completely lose most restrictions. However, several strong labor unions existed within the company, making it extremely difficult to reduce multiple duplications within TPSA. Furthermore, many employees had been working for the company for a long time and their attitudes towards change remained questionable, making it difficult, despite management's effort, to create a modern, lean and flexible telecom provider out of TPSA.

Since 1991 the company had diversified its services into a multitude of different areas of telecommunication, but each had a very small number of customers concentrated in certain geographical areas. These included:[20]

Polpak

This was a public tele-info network commissioned in 1992 and used for data transmission. Polpak, in 1998, comprised 53 nodes covering the entire country and connected to 140 states worldwide. The network was particularly useful to small- and mid-size enterprises. Polpak also allowed for simultaneous data transmission between subscribers working with various protocols and speeds. The system was fully compatible with several international standards. The maximum speed at a subscriber's port was up to two Mbits/sec.

Polpak-T

This was a new, more modern network based on frame relay and ATM protocols. It was the only European network based fully on the ATM technology operating with a speed of up to 150 Mbits, allowing connections to networks in 220 countries. Polpak-T permitted the creation of virtual channels. In the next two years, the network was supposed to connect all major cities in Poland.

VSAT

VSAT was a satellite data transmission and telephone connection system, which used Eutelest. There was very limited information about the system.

Polkom 400

Available since 1996, Polkom was a modern, public electronic mail system based on the X.400 international standard.

ISDN

TPSA offered fast data transmission based on DSL-like technology. It was also involved in radio and television broadcasting, and land and marine radio communication. Also, TPSA was the largest Internet provider in Poland. It allowed free of charge access to the net through its countrywide telephone number, however, the company charged on per minute basis for staying connected to phone lines. The charge varied depending on the day and the time of use, but a person extensively using the Internet (four to five hours per day) could expect to pay approximately US$150 per month, which in terms of an average Polish salary equaled roughly 25 per cent of monthly pay.

Centertel, a mobile telephone company, was another TPSA subsidiary, in which the company held a majority stake, however, Centertel did not have a monopoly in the mobile telephone market (currently the firm held only 19 per cent of the entire market)[21] and it competed with two dynamic enterprises—Era GSM, owned by Polska Telefonia Cyfrowa, and GSM PLUS, owned by Polkomtel. The number of cell telephone subscribers at the end of 1999 exceeded three million people. As the numbers suggest, mobile services were emerging as a strong substitute for fixed telephony, especially because the cost of using cellular telephones was often comparable to or even lower than that of stationary phone service.

Nonetheless, the great majority of TPSA revenue came from the fixed line telephone market. The company held 96 per cent of this segment, which amounted to about nine million subscribers. Due mainly to limited competition and lack of price regulation from the government, the cost of any telephone call was extremely high for the average Pole. For instance, an international phone call was 81 per cent more expensive than that made from Canada, taking into account purchasing power parity. In real terms, an overseas call cost, on average, US$1.50 per minute.

In 1998, the company earned a profit of approximately US$200 million on $2.5 billion revenue.[22]

TPSA's plans for future developments included, among others, investment in Data Transmission systems, developing its cellular subsidiary, upgrading its obsolete infrastructure, and heavy investment in Internet services.

Although there were many question marks surrounding the company, TPSA held a leading position in every segment of the Polish telecom market. The company was strongly involved in Internet commerce, broadband, and wireless services, which had been named as a strategic objective in TPSA's several consecutive annual reports.

The Threat of Call-Back Service

In recent years, a new industry had been developing to take advantage of differentials in long distance telephone rates among countries. Customers throughout the world were provided with the U.S. telephone number of a call-back service. The user would telephone this number and then hang up after one or two rings and the call-back's computer would immediately call back the customer using a U.S. line. With this connection, the customer would be able to dial any number in any country using U.S. lines and being billed at U.S. rates. This process threatened to reduce the long distance business of carriers that were charging rates above the U.S. levels. By 2000, this process was being used largely by U.S. residents travelling abroad and by U.S. corporations with branches located in foreign countries. However, call-back corporations were looking eagerly to markets such as those of Poland where long distance rates were much higher than U.S. rates. Call-back corporations could hire local agents who would actively solicit the international telephone business of local residents and corporations.

WAS THERE A FUTURE FOR THE INTERNET AND E-BUSINESS IN POLAND?

The Internet market in Poland was still in its infancy. The size of the market was estimated to be between US$50 million and US$55 million annually. Approximately 350 licensed ISPs serviced the industry. However, there were only a few companies with their own networks. TPSA and NASK (Science and Academic Computer Network) together controlled more than half of the Internet market. TPSA currently operated international links to the United States and Canada and NASK operated a link to Sweden.

At this time, TPSA offered a country wide telephone number to access the Internet at the cost of a local telephone connection, which was approximately 10 cents per three minutes or five cents per three minutes after ten o'clock at night. TPSA modems and access numbers were always overloaded and the quality of an access was poor. For instance, the file transfer rate throughout the day equaled approximately 0.5 to 1.5 kbs. After ten at night, it was nearly impossible to gain an Internet access, as almost every Internet user went on line to take advantage of low night rates. Flat fee, unlimited Internet access existed; however, it cost about US$50 per month and there was a one time connection fee which equaled US$250. In general, relatively problem free Internet access existed between midnight and six o'clock in the morning.

There seemed to be an urgent need for more ISPs as well as better infrastructure. Unfortunately, TPSA was not forthcoming to offer special arrangements for ISPs using TPSA's infrastructure,

and it was often being accused of monopolistic practices by blocking the possibility for other Internet providers.[23]

NASK, with its Internet partner Netia S.A., provided similar services. Their service was slightly cheaper and more easily accessible. However, Netia, with fewer than 300,000 phone subscribers, offered its services to a rather limited number.

Internet was also becoming available through cable TV providers such as Wizja (owned by UPC) and Aster City (owned by Elektrim). Although the quality of service was quite good and the price significantly lower when compared to that offered by TPSA, cable modems were still very expensive (US$300 which represents approximately 80 per cent of a good monthly salary in Poland). Overall, without more providers with their own bone infrastructure, Internet services in Poland would lag behind those of Western European and North American countries.

E-business was almost non-existent in Poland. Even though there were more than 300 web sites offering products and services, their average turnover amounted to only US$12,500 per year. Most users quoted lack of trust in an online payment security system as a reason for not shopping on the Internet. Fraud seemed to be quite widespread in everyday life and the lack of an efficient legal system to deal with the problem would likely remain a major stumbling block to e-business evolution in Poland.

The attitude towards shopping in general was quite different from that in North America. It was strongly embedded in the Polish culture to shop in person with the possibility to touch and see the products. Catalogue sales did not exist in the past, and so there was no tradition to shop this way either.[24] Furthermore, for e-business to develop properly, an efficient payment system had to exist. Only six per cent of Poland's population had a credit card. The great majority of cardholders did not use them because of the interest charges and widespread fraud involving credit cards.

In addition, only 35 per cent of the country's population had a bank account and almost everyone preferred to pay cash for products and services.[25] Moreover, the banking system in Poland was insufficient to support online transactions. Previously the Polish government planned to sell off a majority of its banking holdings. However, the government decided not to proceed with bank privatization because it was perceived that allowing foreign capital into the Polish banking system would somehow threaten national interest and security. The logic behind the decision was not very clear, especially because the major stakeholders in the largest Polish banks were insurance companies which were being sold to foreign investors. Instead, the government decided to sell its stake in the banks to Polish investors through the Warsaw Stock Exchange in order to preserve national ownership.

Another obstacle to a wider acceptance of e-business, especially business-to-business (B2B) was, of course, poor access to the Internet. First of all, an average Pole had to spend his or her two monthly salaries to buy a non brand computer. Only about six per cent of Poles had a computer at home. Second, Internet access was extremely expensive. Only 14 per cent of Poland's population was online, and of these, 80 per cent accessed the Internet from work. The average age of an Internet user in Poland was about 25 years of age.

Interest in Internet banking was limited to the young and wealthy generation. A recent survey showed that two-thirds of Poles never heard of home banking and 80 per cent of them did not want it.

B2B accounted for more than half of e-business transactions in Poland.[26] Multinational companies were the main users. Mid-size and smaller businesses simply could not afford the necessary hardware or usage fee to participate in this sector. As of 2000, about 70 per cent of Polish companies did not have any plans to participate in any form of electronic business. The entire European e-business market lagged behind that of North America. Perhaps the difference stemmed from the social attitude towards shopping, perhaps it was tied to the economic performance of the region, or perhaps the obstacle was the poor telecom infrastructure when compared to that of North America.

However, the current situation could change in the European's favor. The third generation of cellular technology, UMTS, which was well developed, could overcome the problem with an inadequate fixed infrastructure.[27] The UMTS protocol, which would be fully introduced in 2003, was capable of transferring data at speeds of up to 2 Mbps. With such a transfer rate, full multimedia content could be easily handled by service providers. Furthermore, unlike in North America where wireless companies used different standards, this protocol was likely to become widely accepted across the European continent. Also, the introduction of the Euro, which was going to eliminate the need for currency exchange, was likely to increase e-business volume. Even by 2000 the majority of credit cards allowed charges expressed in Euro. And, upon joining the EU, which still remained questionable, any border tariffs would cease, thereby boosting Internet shopping on the continent.

In Eastern Europe, Poland included, cellular telephony seemed to be the most dynamic segment of the telecom market. The prices of wireless services were almost identical to those of fixed telecom providers. International phone calls made from the cellular phone were slightly cheaper than those made through TPSA. The service was quite reliable and the handsets were often given away in exchange for signing a one year lease. Moreover, the volume of purchased computers was growing at approximately 25 per cent a year despite the low average personal income.[28] In addition, as the inflation in the country decreased and as the new, more efficient legal system was put into place, analysts predicted wider acceptance of credit cards. Furthermore, the size of Poland's population was quite large (40 million people). It was predicted that by 2003 about 25 per cent of the population would have direct access to the Internet, which represented about 10 million potential e-customers.

There was another important aspect of the future of e-business in Poland. The country had a large number of software engineers and information technology specialists. Unfortunately, there was also a mass exodus of qualified personnel as

Polish companies simply could not compete in salary terms with the Western European and North American firms. However, the government of Poland recognized the problem and was anxiously trying to address it.[29] But until those changes became a reality, people in Poland would probably remain fascinated by the Internet, but shop elsewhere.

THE WAY AHEAD?

The Polish government had decided to privatize TPSA and to introduce more competition in the telecom market, but at the same time it wished to maintain control over many aspects of this vital sector. France Telecom, as well as others, wished to purchase a controlling interest in TPSA, but the price required by the government seemed to be excessively high. The TPSA infrastructure might be obsolete in the context of rapid technological change, and the employee skills and attitudes might be an increasingly severe burden.

In a nation that was shifting dramatically from communism to free enterprise, there might be a vast array of new entrepreneurial opportunities in e-business. Future EU membership and traditional linkages with other formerly communist nations could make Poland a gateway between western and eastern Europe. However, as Poland entered the 21st century the new economy and e-business had scarcely made an appearance. Necessary improvements in the telecom infrastructure remained in the future. For all the stakeholders and potential stakeholders in Poland's telecom industry, the way ahead seemed quite confusing.

NOTES

1. See the TPSA website at: http://www.tpsa/pl/english/index.html

2. Note: TPSA financial information is presented in Appendix 1.

3. Annual Report, TPSA-1998.

4. This section was written by Rick Ironside, Clive MacKay, Connie Martin and Maureen O'Brien.

5. Note Exhibit 1—Polish Economic Statistics.

6. The New Poland, *Time Magazine,* May 3, 1999.

7. Studia nad integracja Europejska, Telekomunikacja, Warszawa, 1997.

8. See Exhibit 2—Polish Telecommunications Providers—Overview.

9. Studia nad integracja Europejska, Telekomunikacja, Warszawa, 1997.

10. The Polish Electronic and Telecommunication Industry, PIAZ 1999.

11. Studia nad integracja Europejska, Telekomunikacja, Warszawa, 1997.

12. The Polish Electronic and Telecommunication Industry, PIAZ 1999.

13. Projekt Emisyjny Akcji Netia Holdings, Warsaw 2000.

14. Projekt Emisyjny Akcji Netia Holdings, Warsaw 2000.

15. Studia nad integracja Europejska, Telekomunikacja, Warszawa, 1997.

16. Ministry of Communication, Interview, May 2000.

17. The Polish Electronic and Telecommunication Industry, PIAZ 1999.

18. Annual Report , UPC 1999.

19. Annual Report, TPSA 1998.

20. Annual Report, TPSA 1998.

21. The Polish Electronic and Telecommunication Industry, PIAZ 1999.

22. Annual Report, TPSA 1998.

23. Studia nad integracja Europejska, Telekomunikacja, Warszawa, 1997.

24. Computer World Polska, Top 2000, Polski Rynek Informatyczny i Telekomunikacyjny, May 2000.

25. Ibid.

26. The Polish Electronic and Telecommunication Industry, PIAZ 1999.

27. Computer World Polska, Top 2000, Polski Rynek Informatyczny i Telekomunikacyjny, May 2000.

28. Computer World Polska, Top 2000, Polski Rynek Informatyczny i Telekomunikacyjny, May 2000.

29. Nowa Trybuna Opolska, May 2000-06-20.

APPENDIX 1

Telekomunikacja Polska Consolidated
Balance Sheets as at 31 December 1999 and 1998

Translation of the report originally issued in Polish

TELEKOMUNIKACJA POLSKA
CONSOLIDATED BALANCE SHEETS AS AT 31 DECEMBER 1999 AND 1998

	Note	31 December 1999	1998
Assets		*(in PLN millions)*	
Current assets			
Cash and cash equivalents	6	783	3,642
Marketable securities	26(d)	16	—
Receivables	7	2,651	2,162
Current income taxes		313	258
Inventories	8	150	205
Current assets		3,913	6,267
Fixed assets			
Property, plant and equipment	9	21,555	17,230
Intangible assets	10	950	475
Investments	11	152	217
Fixed assets		22,657	17,922
Non-current receivables		2	1
Assets		26,572	24,190
Liabilities and shareholder's equity			
Current liabilities			
Loans and other borrowings	12	721	3,329
Accrued expenses and other payables	13	3,801	2,849
Provisions	24(e)	90	—
Deferred income	14	195	224
Current liabilities		4,807	6,402
Non-current liabilities			
Loans and other borrowings	12	10,337	7,209
Accrued expenses and other payables	13	490	329
Deferred income	14	271	264
Deferred income taxes	15	288	576
Non-current liabilities		11,386	8,378
Minority interest	16	270	274
Shareholders' equity	17		
Common stock		4,200	4,200
Share premium		832	832
Revaluation reserve		2,332	2,332
Retained earnings		2,745	1,772
Shareholders' equity		10,109	9,136
Liabilities and shareholders' equity		26,572	24,190

The notes to the financial statements are an integral part of these Consolidated Balance Sheets

1

Source: Annual Report, TPSA 1998.

Telekomunikacja Polska Consolidated
Profit and Loss Accounts for the
Years Ended 31 December 1999 and 1998

Translation of the report originally issued in Polish

**TELEKOMUNIKACJA POLSKA CONSOLIDATED PROFIT AND LOSS
ACCOUNTS FOR THE YEARS ENDED 31 DECEMBER
1999 AND 1998**

	Note	12 months ended 31 December	
		1999	*1998*
		(in PLN millions)	
Revenues	18	**13,160**	**10,887**
Employee related expenses		(3,048)	(2,723)
Depreciation and amortisation		(2,357)	(1,891)
Payments to other operators		(1,383)	(1,037)
Purchased services		(1,910)	(1,673)
Goods purchased for resale		(382)	(314)
Other operating expenses, net		(1,240)	(965)
Operating expenses		**(10,320)**	**(8,603)**
Operating profit		**2,840**	**2,284**
Interest and other charges, net	19	(1,345)	(883)
Profit before income tax		**1,495**	**1,401**
Income tax	15	(572)	(654)
Minority interest	16	106	27
Net income before obligatory dividend		**1,029**	**774**
Obligatory dividend	20	—	(160)
Retained income		**1,029**	**614**
Earnings per share (in PLN):			
Net income before obligatory dividend		0.74	0.55
Obligatory dividend		—	(0.11)
Retained income per share		0.74	0.44
Weighted average common stock outstanding (millions)		1,400	1,400

The notes to the financial statements are an integral part of these Consolidated Profit and Loss Accounts

2

Source: Annual Report, TPSA 1998.

MALAYSIA'S MULTIMEDIA DEVELOPMENT CORPORATION

*Prepared by Joel Thompson and Sylvie Weeks
under the supervision of Professor David W. Conklin*

Version: (A) 1998-01-27

Malaysia is offering the world a special greenfield environment designed to enable companies to collaborate in new ways and reap the rich rewards of the Information Age. There are no legacies of artificial constraints created and perpetuated by entrenched interests through the laws. The role of the government will be to remove any administrative encumbrances and to provide an environment where the full energies of the private sector can be unleashed.

—Dato' Seri Anwar Ibrahim,
Deputy Prime Minister of Malaysia

INTRODUCTION

Dr. Arif Nun, chief operating officer with the Multimedia Development Corp. (MDC), was reviewing the proposals of some 30 multimedia companies which wished to assist in refining the Multimedia Super Corridor (MSC) concept, setting priorities for development and establishing standards. It had been nearly two years since the government announced the project in 1995, and a decision had to be made soon. A committee would be meeting at the end of January (1997) to select the privileged few, and Dr. Arif Nun wanted to be prepared.

MALAYSIA

Malaysia is divided between the peninsula and the Island of Borneo, separated by the South China Sea. The peninsula is divided into 13 states, and the states of Sabah and Sarawak are located on the island. The Island of Borneo is divided between Malaysia and Indonesia. Approximately two-thirds of Borneo is under Indonesian control.

From the 9th to the 13th century, the Malay Peninsula had been dominated by the Buddhist Malay Kingdom of Srivijaya. In the 14th century, the Hindu Kingdom of Majapahit, which ruled the island of Java (now part of Indonesia), gained control of the peninsula and introduced the Hindu religion to the area.

The 15th century saw the rise of the Muslim state of Malacca, and conversion to Islam began. The state of Malacca ruled the peninsula until the Portuguese conquered Malacca in 1511.

From 1511 until Malaysian Independence in 1957, the peninsula had been dominated by European occupation. European interest in the peninsula was due to its geographical position. The peninsula, with the South China Sea on one side and the Malacca Strait leading into the Indian Ocean on the other side, provided important access to commercial and military sea routes between Europe, the Middle East, Africa and Asia.

The first to conquer the region were the Portuguese, who would later be defeated by the Dutch in 1641. The British occupation of the Island of Penang, just off the west coast of Malaysia, began in 1786. Britain's East India Company occupied Penang as a trading settlement. British expansion onto the mainland began in 1795. Kuala Lumpur, the national capital, was founded as a trading post for tin in 1857. Throughout the 1850s, thousands of Chinese were imported to the region to work in the tin mines.

British rule of the peninsula was interrupted during World War II when the Japanese invaded and occupied the region from 1942 to 1945. The Chinese bore much of the Japanese hostility during their occupation.

Demand for independence began during the Japanese occupation and continued after British rule resumed. The Federation of Malaya was created by the British in 1948. On Aug. 31, 1957, Malaya became an independent nation, and the city of Kuala Lumpur was declared the national capital. Through negotiations with Britain, the colonies of Sabah, Sarawak, and Singapore were granted the right to join the federation in 1962, forming Malaysia. However, Singapore withdrew from Malaysia and became an independent republic in 1965.

The historical influx of various cultures produced a multicultural society within Malaysia. By 1996, the population was a combination of Malay (61 per cent), Chinese (30 per cent), Indian (7 per cent) and Indigenous Tribes (2 per cent), with five key religions represented: Islam, Buddhism, Taoism, Christianity, and Hinduism.

EXTERNAL RELATIONSHIPS

Due to Malaysia's cultural mix, it had enjoyed close ties with many countries in the region, including China and India.

Malaysia's long land and sea borders as well as its separation between the peninsula and the island made policing boundaries difficult. The thinly patrolled border between Thailand and Malaysia attracted smugglers and bandits. In 1996, a Malaysian-Thai military alliance stepped up activities along the border in an attempt to bring back order.

Due to strong ethnic and religious ties, relations with Indonesia had been strong. But a large influx of illegal migrant workers from Indonesia caused increased tension as workers had migrated to the plantations. Low unemployment rates and rising wage rates throughout the 1990s forced plantation owners to seek cheap labor.

Relations with Singapore had been more sensitive. Singapore's population had traditionally been the mirror opposite of Malaysia. While Malaysia traditionally had a Malay majority and a Chinese minority, Singapore had a Chinese majority (77 per cent) and a Malay minority (14 per cent). In the past, the minority in one country had tended to turn to the majority in the other country in order to promote its interests. Ethnic conflicts were the reason for Singapore's withdrawal from the federation in 1965.

The continuous underlying tension was illustrated in March 1997 when Senior Minister Lee Kuan Yew (Prime Minister 1965 to 1990) made an unflattering comment about a Malaysian state. Comments in Malaysian newspapers and online Internet discussions included threats of reclaiming Singapore. Mr. Lee was later forced to retract the statement.

Large infrastructure projects undertaken by the Malaysian government as the country entered the late 1990s added fuel to the fire. Projects included new sea ports in order to ship exports directly instead of through Singapore; a new airport in Kuala Lumpur designed to be the biggest in the region; and a multimedia super corridor to house information technology businesses.

Malaysia had been active in regional and international bodies. Malaysia was one of the founding members of the Association of South East Asian Nations (ASEAN) which by 1996 included Indonesia, The Philippines, Singapore, Thailand and Vietnam. Malaysia also joined the Asian-Pacific Economic Co-operation (APEC) forum, which not only included Asian countries but also Australia, New Zealand and the United States. APEC was established to assist in the formation of a free trade zone between its members. Malaysia had remained a member of the commonwealth, and in 1994 Kuala Lumpur won the right to host the 1998 Commonwealth Games.

POLITICAL CONDITIONS

Since independence, the Malay majority held political power in Malaysia while the Chinese minority held much of the economic power. The economic disparity helped to foster Malay nationalism. Malay political domination had resulted from Malay solidarity, while the Chinese tended to be more divided.

Founded in 1946 as part of the independence movement, the United Malays National Organization (UMNO) had won the most number of parliamentary seats in general elections from 1955 to 1995. However, in order to promote independence in the 1950s, UMNO built a coalition with political parties from other racial groups. This coalition group became known as the Alliance. The Alliance consisted of UMNO, the Malaysia Chinese Association (MCA), and the Malaysian Indian congress (MIC). In the first national election in 1955, the alliance won 80 per cent of the popular vote.

After the general elections in 1969, serious ethnic riots erupted between the Malays and the Chinese. Many people were killed in the riots. In order to resolve the ethnic tension, the Alliance broadened its political base and became known as the Barisan Nasional (BN— "National Front"). UMNO remained the dominant party. In the 1995 general election, BN consisted of 14 parties and won 164 out of a possible 194 seats.

SOCIAL CONDITIONS

After intense ethnic riots in 1969, the New Economic Policy (NEP) was formed. The goal was to bring greater economic equality between Malaysia's ethnic groups. Specific hiring quotas were established, and Malays were given preferred land rights and special access to training and higher education. Despite preferential treatment given to Malays and increased industrialization and education, the Chinese continued to hold economic control.

At the same time the NEP was formed, Malay was declared the national language and would be the only language taught in the educational system. However, Malay was not widely accepted or adopted in business. Criticism of the language policy peaked in the late 1980s with the statement that the inability of Malaysians to communicate in English would hinder Malaysia's economic progress. In 1990, Prime Minister Dr. Mahathir Mohamad opened the door for English to be taught in the educational system, particularly in the fields of medicine, science and technical subjects.

ECONOMIC CONDITIONS

Historically, the Malaysian economy depended on exports of rubber, palm oil, tin, timber, pepper and cocoa. However, in the mid-1980s, through government incentives, a shift towards manufacturing was achieved. In 1996, manufactured goods accounted for 70 per cent of exports.

The period from 1985 to 1995 was one of rapid industrialization in Malaysia. In 1986, agriculture and manufacturing represented equal portions of the national GDP. But by 1995 manufacturing accounted for twice as much as agriculture.

Electronic goods was the fastest growing manufacturing sector during this period. The growth in this sector was concentrated on the Island of Penang, due to its establishment by the government as a custom-free industrial zone. This enabled manufacturers to import components for assembly in Penang. Another region that attracted manufacturing was the Klang Valley which was established as a general manufacturing area.

During this period of rapid growth, the Malaysian government had held tight fiscal controls with budgets close-to-balance throughout the decade. Substantial surpluses were recorded in a number of years. The Bank Negara Malaysia, the central bank, had maintained strict management over interest rates, inflation, and currency exchange.

Malaysia had also benefited from one of the world's highest savings rates. In 1996, the savings rate of Malaysia was 38.8 per cent of GDP. Government savings programs had produced these levels.

As of January 1997, Malaysia could no longer export into the U.S. duty free. Certain manufactured goods had been allowed to enter the U.S. under the Generalized System of Preference (GSP). But, due to Malaysia's rapid development, the U.S. had withdrawn this preferential treatment.

Also, in January 1997, Malaysia agreed to sign the U.S. International Trade Agreement on computer and related products. The agreement would attempt to establish free world trade on computers and all related products.

LABOR MARKET

The population grew at an annual rate of 2.8 per cent throughout the 1980s but declined in the 1990s to 2.2 per cent. In 1995, only 35 per cent of the population was below 14 years of age. Government concerns about the size of the labor pool affecting the growth potential of Malaysia had resulted in the introduction of incentive programs to encourage births. This came at a time when other Asian countries were operating programs to lower the birth rate.

Labor shortages in the mid-1990s resulted in inflationary pressure. By 1996, Malaysia had 1.2 million foreign workers which represented 10 per cent of the labor force. The seventh Five Year Economic Plan introduced in May 1996 placed an emphasis on attracting capital intensive technology industries and automation to reduce labor demands.

The tight labor market through the 1990s had forced wages to increase faster than productivity, which adversely affected industries which relied on cheap labor. However, labor shortages were not limited to low skill groups. The large migrant workforce had helped to fill gaps at the lower end while companies had to import high skilled workers to fill gaps at the other end of the labor pool.

Labor laws had limited the formation of trade unions. Throughout Malaysia's development, the government had held the belief that unions caused unwanted wage increases and therefore inflationary pressure that would not be beneficial to Malaysia in the long term.

Traditionally, strong emphasis had been placed on education. Government programs had provided universal access to all Malaysians up to secondary education levels. Several public and post secondary schools were available, as well as private schools which were mostly foreign run.

INFRASTRUCTURE

Years of rapid growth had placed a strain on the existing infrastructure of Malaysia. In August 1996, the peninsula suffered a major power failure that caused the national power grid to shift down for nearly 15 hours. Equipment failure was the cause of the blackout.

Major road and port expansion projects began in 1994 as well as rail upgrades. Telecommunication and power upgrades began in 1996, including the launch of Malaysia's first satellite. In 1995, work began on the Petronas Twin Towers, designed to be the world's tallest building at 450 metres. The towers signified the beginning of the Kuala Lumpur City Centre project.

The telecommunications industry in Malaysia was deregulated and licensed for open competition. By 1996, the Association of the Computer Industry Malaysia (PIKON) found that seven per cent of all IT spending was in the telecommunications sector. Tele-density was estimated at 17 per cent and targeted for 50 per cent by the year 2000.

MULTIMEDIA SUPER CORRIDOR

The government sought the help of several industries with expertise as well as consultants such as McKinsey & Co. to help define the visionary concept of the Multimedia Super Corridor (MSC) and strategy to ensure its success.

The MSC was officially announced by the government of Malaysia in 1995. It was defined as a greenfield project, 15 kilometres wide by 50 kilometres long, stretching from Kuala Lumpur City Centre at the Petronas Twin Towers south to the new airport. It would cover an area larger than all of Singapore and had been designed to contain the new national capital (Putrajaya), the "intelligent city" (Cyberjaya), and the new Multimedia University. The goal of the MSC was to turn Malaysia into the Asian hub for information technology: creation, distribution, and integration of both products and services.

The new national capital of Putrajaya, designed within the corridor, would be completed by 1998 and have a population of 75,000 by the year 2000. The city had been established to house the new electronic government.

Cyberjaya, located next to Putrajaya, had been created not only as an enterprise zone for offices and business facilities but as a full community with residential housing, shopping and schools. Located in the heart of Cyberjaya was the Multimedia University. The university, being funded by Telekom Malaysia, would offer educational programs in hi-tech fields as well as conduct research in multimedia areas.

The Malaysian government had set a goal to reach developed nation status by 2020. The government had declared that the only way to reach this status was to shift the economy from a labor-based to a service-based economy. The MSC had been selected as the means to achieve this goal. The government would have to target international companies involved in the multimedia industry for assistance. The government committed RM$48 billion towards the physical infrastructure that would be required to make the corridor a success. In 1996, the installation of the telecommunications backbone began with state-of-the-art, fully-digital fibre optics.

Special incentives were announced to encourage companies to apply for MSC status and thus locate within the corridor. They included exemption from local foreign ownership rules, unlimited influx of expatriates, up to 10 years tax holiday or 100 per cent investment tax allowance, duty-free imports on multimedia equipment, special telecommunication rates, and protection of intellectual property rights.

In order to speed up the project's development, the government had identified seven flagship applications that would receive priority: electronic government, smart schools, telemedicine, R&D clusters, national multipurpose card, borderless marketing centres, and worldwide manufacturing webs. The government also established the Multimedia Development Corporation (MDC) to be the "one-stop shop" for investors.

MULTIMEDIA DEVELOPMENT CORPORATION

Ensure world's best environment for multimedia.

—Mission of MDC

The Multimedia Development Corporation was established to promote the MSC and provide client services, quality control as well as award MSC status. With a staff of approximately 50 people, the MDC would act as a facilitator between foreign and local companies as well as between investors and the government. The MDC would not only act as the MSC's marketer but as an advisor to the government.

In order to obtain MSC status, a company had to meet specific criteria: be a provider or a heavy user of multimedia products and services; employ a substantial number of knowledge workers; specify how it would transfer technology and/or knowledge to Malaysia or otherwise contribute to the development of the MSC and the Malaysian economy; establish a separate legal entity within Malaysia; and locate within designated areas.

Companies that met the selection criteria and were interested in obtaining status had to submit an application to the MDC outlining their business concept and plans. The MDC guaranteed a response within 30 days. If a company did not receive a response within 30 days, the company was awarded automatic acceptance. If a company was rejected, it could resubmit a proposal within six months. Companies already established in Malaysia who were looking solely to re-establish existing operations within the corridor were not granted approval. Such companies had to submit proposals that included additional multimedia operations, such as an R&D facility, before they could enter the corridor.

During the initial phase of the MSC, the preference was for companies referred to as "web shapers." Web shapers were companies which were defining the multimedia industry and its standards throughout the world, and included such companies as Intel or Microsoft. The rest were simply web adopters, companies that utilized the existing standards to develop commercialized products.

Preference was also extended to up-and-coming domestic companies. With the help of the MDC, such companies could obtain venture financing through special funds such as the Malaysian Technology Development Corporation. Recognizing the need these companies would have for future capital, Masdaq, a stock exchange similar to the Nasdaq in the U.S., had been approved for operation in late 1997.

INTELLECTUAL PROPERTY RIGHTS

Concerns expressed by the industry internationally had focused on intellectual property rights and particularly computer software piracy, in Malaysia. While the percentage of illegal software used in Malaysia had declined, the value had increased. The U.S.-based Business Software Alliance (BSA) estimated that in 1994 to 1995 the proportion of illegal software in Malaysia declined from 82 per cent to 77 per cent, but the value increased from RM$165.6 million to RM$201.3 million. In January 1997, Microsoft was able to obtain an injunction against a Malaysian software company which had infringed on Microsoft's copyright laws. The government had promised that protection would be provided under the new "cyberlaws" bill.

Five new cyberlaws were introduced for government approval to ensure protection. The laws included the digital signatures cyberlaw, the multimedia intellectual property cyberlaw, the computer crime cyberlaw, the telemedicine development cyberlaw, and the electronic government cyberlaw. In addition, the Multimedia Convergence Act would be established to govern the new communication framework.

CHALLENGES AHEAD

The MSC faced many challenges as it progressed. Challenges included cross border issues regarding cyberlaws, standards, censorship, as well as the possible impact on relationships with neighboring companies. Due to Malaysia's limited IT expertise, reliance on foreign expertise and international firms had exposed the government to domestic perceptions of preferential treatment to foreigners while excluding Malaysians. The limited scope of the corridor in terms of geographical coverage had only intensified the perception that the benefits to the Malaysian population were limited.

Malaysia had entered uncharted waters, and the social implications of creating an IT society were unknown. Questions surrounding the future social structure were beginning to arise. Due to the dominance of the U.S. in the multimedia industry, would "western" thinking shape Malaysia's future or would some new Asian thinking emerge? How would the general public accept the government position on no censorship of the Internet and no domestic content policies? Could the government continue on its present course without addressing local concerns?

Dr. Arif Nun believed these challenges had to be taken into account during the selection of the flagship advisory companies. The companies selected would have to work with MDC and the government to help refine the MSC concept, set priorities for development and define the standards. Once the standards were set they would influence all future projects within the MSC. Dr. Nun knew it was important to select a balance of companies from around the world so no one region would dominate the outcome. It was also important to select company representatives who were willing to set aside their own company interest and work in the best interest of the MSC. The representatives had to be visionaries and shapers. Selection of the flagship advisory companies would be one of the most important decisions he would be involved in.

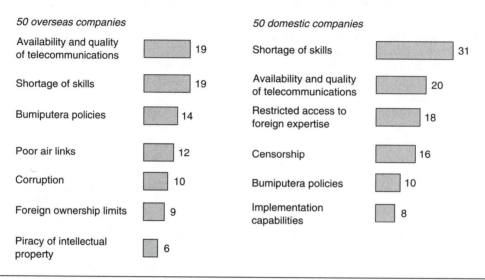

50 overseas companies

Availability and quality of telecommunications	19
Shortage of skills	19
Bumiputera policies	14
Poor air links	12
Corruption	10
Foreign ownership limits	9
Piracy of intellectual property	6

50 domestic companies

Shortage of skills	31
Availability and quality of telecommunications	20
Restricted access to foreign expertise	18
Censorship	16
Bumiputera policies	10
Implementation capabilities	8

Exhibit 1 Perceived Obstacles to Malaysia's Success in 1994 (number of mentions)

▒ Critical issue

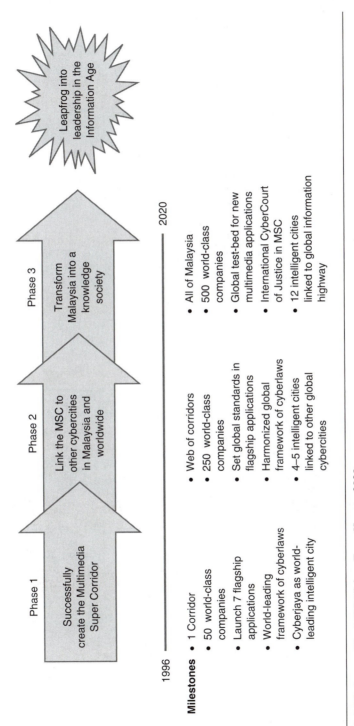

Exhibit 2   The MSC Vision: From Here to 2020

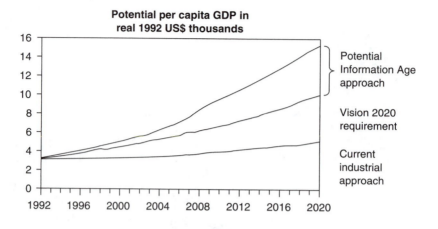

Exhibit 3   Creating Wealth and Achieving Vision 2020

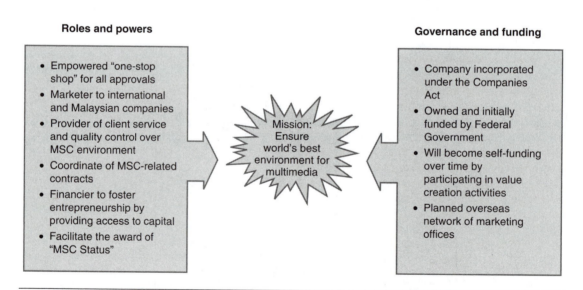

Exhibit 4   MDC Will Act as a One-Stop Super Agency to Ensure Success of MSC and Its Clients

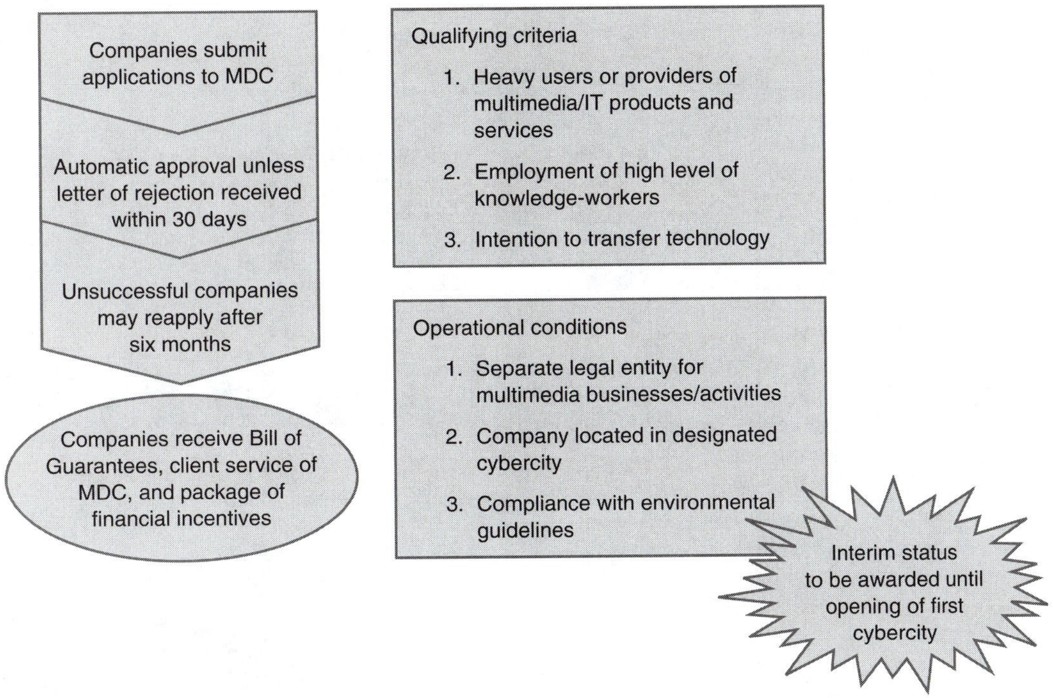

Companies submit applications to MDC

Automatic approval unless letter of rejection received within 30 days

Unsuccessful companies may reapply after six months

Companies receive Bill of Guarantees, client service of MDC, and package of financial incentives

Qualifying criteria

1. Heavy users or providers of multimedia/IT products and services

2. Employment of high level of knowledge-workers

3. Intention to transfer technology

Operational conditions

1. Separate legal entity for multimedia businesses/activities

2. Company located in designated cybercity

3. Compliance with environmental guidelines

Interim status to be awarded until opening of first cybercity

Exhibit 5   Approach to Awarding MSC Status

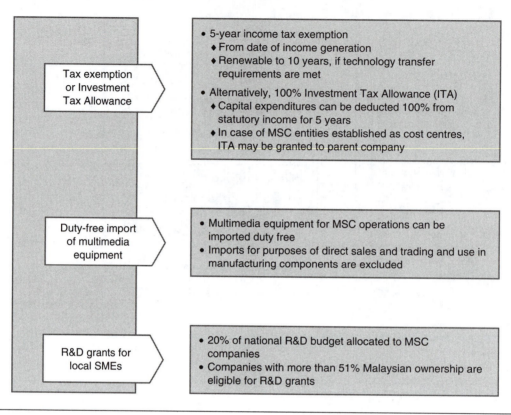

Exhibit 6   Financial Incentives

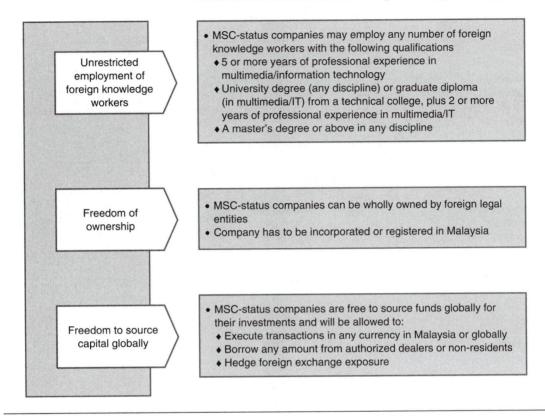

Exhibit 7   Non-Financial Incentives

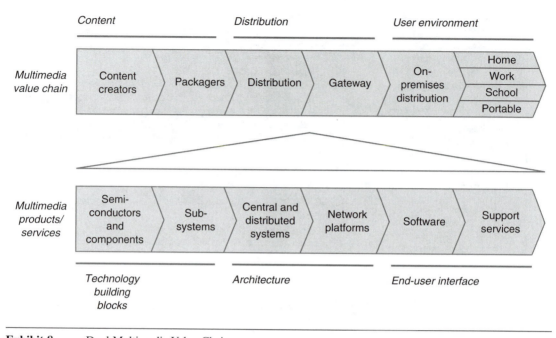

Exhibit 8   Dual Multimedia Value Chain

---

1. Provide a world class physical and information infrastructure;
2. Allow unrestricted employment of local and foreign knowledge workers;
3. Ensure freedom of ownership by exempting companies with MSC status from local-ownership requirements;
4. Give MSC the freedom to source infrastructure capital and the right to borrow funds globally;
5. Provide competitive financial incentives, including no income tax for up to 10 years, or an Investment Tax Allowance, and no duties on the importation of multimedia equipment;
6. Become a regional leader in terms of intellectual property protection and cyberlaws;
7. Ensure no censorship of the Internet;
8. Provide globally competitive telecommunication tariffs;
9. Tender key MSC infrastructure contracts to leading companies who are willing to use the MSC as their regional hub;
10. Provide a high-powered agency to act as an effective one-stop super shop (MDC).

Exhibit 9   Bill of Guarantees

Financial Incentives

1. Five-year exemption from Malaysian income tax, renewable to 10 years or a 100 per cent Investment Tax Allowance (ITA), on new investments made in MSC cybercities;

2. Duty-free importation of multimedia equipment;

3. R&D grants for local small- and medium-size enterprises (SMEs).

Non-Financial Incentives

1. Unrestricted employment of foreign knowledge workers;

2. Freedom of ownership;

3. Freedom to source capital globally for MSC infrastructure and the right to borrow funds globally;

4. Intellectual property protection;

5. Globally competitive telecommunication tariffs and service;

6. No censorship of the Internet;

7. Green environment protected by strict zoning.

Exhibit 10   Incentives for MSC Status Companies

Phase I (1996 to 2002)

- establish the MSC (creation)
- introduce initial 50 companies
- introduce cyberlaws
- create Cyberjaya

Phase II (2002 to 2020)

- link the MSC to other cybercities in Malaysia and in the world
- operate 250 world class companies operating within the MSC
- harmonize cyberlaws globally
- establish four to five "intelligent" cities within Malaysia

Phase III (2020 and beyond)

- transform Malaysia into a knowledge society
- operate 500 companies within the MSC
- use MSC as a global test bed for new multimedia applications
- establish the Cybercourt of Justice within the MSC
- establish 12 intelligent cities within Malaysia

Exhibit 11   Development Phases

GLOBAL WARMING AND THE KYOTO PROTOCOL: IMPLICATIONS FOR BUSINESS

*Prepared by Darcy Jones under the
supervision of Professors David Conklin and Alan Davenport*

Copyright © 2001, Ivey Management Services

Version: (A) 2001-12-14

Except for nuclear war or a collision with an asteroid, no force has more potential to damage our planet's web of life than global warming. It's a "serious" issue, the White House admits, but nonetheless George W. Bush has decided to abandon the 1997 Kyoto treaty to combat climate change—an agreement the U.S. signed but the new President believes is fatally flawed. His dismissal last week of almost nine years of international negotiations sparked protests around the world and a face-to-face disagreement with German Chancellor Gerhard Schröder.[1]

INTRODUCTION

Through the Kyoto Protocol, many nations are collaborating to restrain global warming by restricting greenhouse gas emissions. These new restrictions will place a heavy financial burden on corporations—and their shareholders and customers. With the threat of global warming, businesses confront a two-sided challenge: without political interventions, such as the Kyoto Protocol, an increase in the number and intensity of natural disasters will create new business risks and costs, yet compliance with new regulations to limit this damage will also increase their costs substantially.

In response to this two-sided challenge, business will need to develop new strategies—in terms of technologies, societal image, political lobbying and investment location decisions. At the same time, dramatic environmental changes—as well as new government regulations—will create new business opportunities, most notably in emissions trading and the creation of "environmental sinks."

The Kyoto Protocol is a model for other agreements to address various global pollution problems. Because issues of pollution impact almost every industry, the nature and content of international environmental agreements will be of significant interest to all.

The costs of any additional global warming are predicted to be enormous. The United Nations' financial services initiative has stated that losses due to more frequent tropical cyclones, loss of land as a result of rising sea levels and damage to fishing stocks, agriculture and water supplies could annually cost about US$304.2 billion.[2] Human costs may be even higher, in terms of increased illness and loss of life and possessions, as a result of increases in natural disasters.

Human activities are changing the world's climate. Burning coal, oil and natural gas to power the industrial activities of modern society has resulted in an increase of carbon dioxide in the atmosphere from 275 parts per million to 360 parts per million since the start of the industrial revolution. It is estimated, unless action is taken to reduce the emission of carbon dioxide and other greenhouse gases, that by 2050 this concentration will approach 550 parts per million.[3] Further confounding the difficulty is that at least half of the increase can be attributed to deforestation and land clearing. Forests and plant life are able to transform carbon dioxide into oxygen, limiting the accumulation of carbon dioxide in the atmosphere; deforestation and land clearing reduce this regenerative capacity.[4]

Carbon dioxide and other greenhouse gases, produced as a result of human industrial activity increase the world's average temperature. The latest Intergovernmental Panel on Climate Change report (IPCC), sponsored by the United Nations Environment Programme and the World Meteorological Organization, predicts that average temperatures across the world could climb by 1.4°C to 5.8°C over the coming century.[5] Average temperatures are already increasing. It has been proposed by some that these changes have been a natural development, but extensive research has determined that the existence of greenhouse gases in the atmosphere is responsible for the majority of the increase.

Although 85 per cent of the increase in human-induced carbon dioxide can be attributed to North Americans and Europeans, the costs of this increase will not be borne in the same proportions.[6] It has been estimated that the United States, responsible for 25 per cent of worldwide emissions, will face a loss of a few tenths of one per cent of gross domestic product each year. However, small island states, such as Micronesia, may face losses that far exceed 10 per cent of the gross domestic product of the island.[7]

Natural disasters have been increasing worldwide. The frequency of catastrophes averaged 35 per year from 1989 to 1995 versus 25 per year during the period from 1950 to 1988.[8] Increasingly, research is pointing to global warming, due to increased concentrations of greenhouse gases in the atmosphere, as the cause. The costs of these disasters are, likewise, increasing. Between 1989 and 1995, total insured losses from earthquakes, hurricanes and other natural disasters amounted to US$75 billion, compared to a total of $51 billion for the entire period between 1950 and 1988.[9] The increase in cost, however, is not entirely attributable to the number of disasters themselves. Since 1950, there has been a substantial increase in the population and an even larger increase in the proportions of people living in high-risk areas. At present, 50 per cent of the population of North America lives within 80 km of a coastline.[10] This proportion will continue to grow over the next century. Because the percentage of wealthy people living near the coastline is greater than in the less disaster-prone regions, the value of the property subject to increased risk of destruction through natural disasters is even higher than the population would indicate. Paul Kovacs, director of the Canadian Institute for Catastrophic Loss Reduction (ICLR) has stated that the problem is "more storms, more people and more stuff in more dangerous regions."

Although the number of insured losses has increased dramatically, the costs to a nation are even higher than these numbers would indicate. Many of the costs of natural disasters will not be borne by the insurance industry. All property is not insured. Infrastructure costs and reductions in gross domestic product (GDP) from agricultural losses, etc. will have to paid by private individuals and government. However, there is debate over the proportions of these costs each group ought to bear. Overreliance on insurance mechanisms has resulted in complacency in addressing the problems and reducing the costs. For example, the National Flood Assistance Program provided by the United States federal government for property owners in at-risk areas, has resulted in buildings being built in unsafe areas.[11] A large number of structures have been destroyed and reconstructed multiple times, with the program paying the costs of each rebuilding in the same location. There is no incentive to build in safer regions, or to build to a higher resistance standard when the homeowner bears little, or none of the costs of these decisions.

At present, there appear to be two approaches for addressing the issue of global warming. Certain groups have advocated efforts to mitigate the costs of natural disasters. Lobbying for more stringent building codes, more effective mechanisms for responding to the results of natural disasters and better urban planning are a few of the proposals of these groups.

Other groups believe that the answer is to address the root cause by reducing or eliminating greenhouse gas emissions, requiring an international concerted effort. The Kyoto Accord on Greenhouse Gas Emission is the product of these initiatives.

The implications of climate change and the Kyoto Protocol depend highly on the views, interests and abilities of the various stakeholder groups.

Mitigation Efforts

Private Insurance Companies

The group most obviously bearing many of the costs of the property damage created as a result of climate change and the resulting increase in natural disasters is the insurance industry. Insurance allows a large group of individuals to contribute small sums of money (in the form of premiums), that when pooled, are available to cover the costs for those members of the group who experience large, improbable losses. Although life and liability insurers will feel some of the costs of the increase in natural disasters, by far the property and casualty sector of the insurance industry will be responsible for the majority of the costs, because it is this sector that ensures the personal and real property vulnerable to the effects of natural disasters.

The attitude of this group towards natural disasters is that an increase is inevitable, and that the role of the insurance company is to promote actions that reduce the potential for damage as a result of this increase.[12] To that end, the Insurance Bureau of Canada (representing property and casualty insurers and auto insurers) has been a vocal advocate of programs to ensure that Canadian structures are built to a standard that optimally minimizes the costs of floods, storms, etc. The Institute for Catastrophic Loss

Reduction at The University of Western Ontario is a research body, jointly promoted by the federal government and the Insurance Bureau to uncover the best methods of mitigating disaster. In the United States, studies of the attitudes of property and casualty insurers revealed that this group does not feel it has the ability or the scientific knowledge to assist in efforts to reduce the rate of global warming of the atmosphere.

Despite the efforts to keep property damage to a minimum, the insurance industry will, certainly, face substantially increased costs as a result of the additional number of natural disasters. However, this industry believes that this will not be a direct concern for the industry because premiums will be raised to reflect the higher losses. It would appear that a major natural disaster, in which insurance companies may be held contractually liable for policies priced at levels less than necessary to cover the damage, has the potential to bankrupt an insurance company. However, the industry has addressed this concern through the use of reinsurance. Insurance companies are, themselves, able to purchase insurance from large, well-capitalized reinsurance companies. The largest and most prominent of these companies are General RE: and Standard RE:. The reinsurer, in exchange for the insurance company's premium, agrees to cover the costs of a natural disaster. Because a large number of insurance companies operating in diverse geographic locations purchase insurance from the reinsurer, the reinsurer has a large customer base that any disaster impacting a few insurance companies will have a relatively small impact on the overall reinsurer's profitability. Due to competition in the market, the cost of reinsurance is currently low, relative to previous time periods.

One of the difficulties that property and casualty insurers face is in pricing premiums for unanticipated events. Actuaries set premiums using pooled historical data for large groups with similar characteristics to determine the probability and average cost of an insurable event. The premium will be set at a level that is believed to cover the anticipated costs of coverage and the cost of administering the insurance contract. The actuary must determine the time period to consider when calculating probabilities. For example, should a 10-year period be considered in which it is less likely that a major disaster will take place? If yes, it could be assumed the probability of a major disaster is close to zero. Or is it more appropriate to consider a 100-year span when it is more likely that there will be major disasters? The premiums charged will depend on this decision.

At present, very little data exists that can be used to accurately predict the probability of a natural disaster taking place in a certain geographical area. Hence, there may be a shortfall in the pool of premiums available to cover the costs of natural disasters. Reinsurers will absorb a portion of these costs, but will ultimately increase prices to compensate. In areas where it is difficult to exit markets (for example, a number of U.S. states have restrictions that make it difficult, if not impossible, to exit certain markets) or to increase premiums to reflect the actual risk to a region, certain risks may become uninsurable. Flood insurance in Florida may become unavailable. The costs of flooding will not disappear, but will have to be borne by either individuals or government. Where coverage remains available and guaranteed affordable by government legislation, there will be a disincentive to use prudent building standards if there is no financial incentive for doing so.

Overreliance on the insurance industry can foster blind complacency. Because each insurance contract differs in the risks it covers, many home and business owners do not know exactly which risks are covered and which are not. For example, certain policies cover fire, but will not cover the cost of flooding. This creates the danger of individuals facing large, unexpected costs for uninsured losses arising from events that policyholders assumed were covered by the insurance contract. If the individual is not able to cover the costs, tax revenue may need to be contributed to pay for those losses. Governments have made attempts to standardize coverage, but

as of yet, this has not been well received by the insurance industry.

The Reinsurance Industry

This group accepts that the number and frequency of natural disasters will continue to increase and has made substantial efforts to record and analyse the trends and patterns of these increases. This data, while primarily compiled to allow the reinsurers to better price risk, has been shared with the scientific and legislative community. Much of this data has been the basis on which national and international efforts have been spearheaded in order to address the root causes of the increase. Hence, while the reinsurers intend to prepare their own industry for additional increases in risk, they have been extremely important in the effort to reduce greenhouse gas emissions worldwide. Because these groups operate on an international basis, they have been able to contribute the data to demonstrate that global warming is a global issue that impacts all nations.

Although overall premiums will increase for reinsurance based on the increase in natural disasters, reinsurers will not be vulnerable to any one natural disaster. Because of the international spread of their insured insurance companies and the vast number of companies using reinsurance, the repercussions of a single disaster will have little impact on the vulnerability of the overall corporation. Currently, it is believed that insurance companies, in general, and reinsurance companies in particular, have financial reserves available that are well in excess of the worst-case loss scenario. In addition, reinsurers have the option of minimizing their risk by purchasing catastrophe-based financial instruments.

Financial Markets

It is now possible to purchase securities that are contingent upon a natural disaster. For example, bonds are available that pay a premium coupon to investors who agree to forfeit the principal should an agreed-upon disaster occur. Other derivative securities exist in which the buyer agrees to purchase shares in a company at an agreed-upon price should a catastrophe occur. Using these securities enables those subject to loss to access the large pool of capital available in the financial markets. Because the depth of the financial markets is far greater than the reserves available to insurance and reinsurance companies, this is a viable means of reducing the individual risk to a corporation.

Thus far, these securities have been in strong demand. The superior yields available to investors and the relatively unlikely event of a payout make these securities extremely attractive. When Warren Buffet was offered the opportunity to purchase a portion of J.P. Morgan's first offering, he opted to purchase the entire offering. So far, the largest issuers of these securities (usually referred to as "cat-bonds") have been large, public corporations who have found the cost of acquiring adequate insurance to be greater than the costs of covering their risks. Potential issuers are large insurance companies and the reinsurers themselves. However, the currently low cost of reinsurance makes cat-bonds more expensive for insurance companies to issue than obtaining a similar degree of coverage using reinsurance. As the data on the frequency of natural disasters begins to emerge, it is believed that reinsurance prices will experience a dramatic increase and cat-bonds may become an attractive alternative for insurance companies.

Corporations

While corporations will likely also be required to reduce their greenhouse gas emissions through government action, they already face the reality that natural disasters have increased. Hence, this group must decide how to address the additional risk they are facing. For example, an individual company must decide how to insure against losses. If the company is large enough, it may consider selling catastrophe-bonds as an alternative to traditional property insurance, or it may decide to band together with other companies facing similar risks to self-insure. In this scenario,

each company agrees to cover the losses of a member of the group, to a certain maximum. Typically, a loss threshold must be reached before the group member suffering the loss is able to access the pool.

In building new facilities, companies must decide on the degree of natural force they want to be able to withstand. Building codes are the minimum levels acceptable by the government, however, for certain businesses, these levels will not be adequate. Despite owning insurance, certain companies will experience losses from natural disasters that are not covered by insurance. For example, companies attempting to develop new products that need patent protection would find time delays (as a result of a natural disaster) intolerable; during the delays, their competitors' similar products could reach the market first. Hence, these companies may elect to build facilities that are above average in resilience.

Other corporations may elect to make detailed contingency plans for disasters, either independently or in concert with other companies. For example, All State Insurance has all data backed up at numerous locations that can be accessible if a disaster strikes a given location. This way, the company will be able to provide service to customers without experiencing the interruptions that disasters frequently create. Other companies in a given industry are able to unite to prepare for natural disasters. Newspaper companies form consortiums that purchase spare machinery in the event of an irreparable breakdown. Although these companies possess insurance, there is a five-year wait for a new printing press. Being unable to publish for five years would almost certainly destroy the paper's market share and result in bankruptcy. To deal with this situation, groups of 10 to 12 publishers share in the cost of a spare printing press that contributors are able to use during the waiting period.[13]

Ultimately, however, the observed and expected increase in the severity of natural disasters will impose significant costs on corporations. Each of the methods of preparation for weather-related damage will create additional costs that would not have existed in previous decades.

Because these increases in costs will be passed along to consumers, the purchasing power and productivity of the nations in which these corporations operate will be negatively impacted as a result.

Governments

A large share of property owned by the citizens of a country is not covered by private insurance. In wealthy countries, up to 70 per cent of private property is uninsured. If this property is damaged, the loss falls to the owner. However, many owners do not have the resources available to rebuild following disasters. Because of this situation, many governments and charitable organizations find themselves granting resources to repair private property. Should governments elect not to provide disaster financing, many families will find themselves without adequate shelter. Because most governments attempt to ensure adequate housing for their residents, substantial costs will be incurred in order to provide this housing. In addition, displaced individuals have a need for emergency food and shelter that compassionate governments will attempt to provide. Medical costs are incurred as a result of direct injury and disease that spreads through groups of people sharing inadequate housing. Because few countries have universal private health insurance, many of these costs will have to be covered by government.

While government-run insurance schemes guarantee coverage for residents of risk-prone areas, unless these programs create incentives for risk reduction, the overall costs can be greater than if these programs did not exist. An example of this dilemma is the previously discussed U.S. National Flood Insurance Program.

In addition, there exists extensive property that is publicly owned. Roads, sewers, public buildings and other infrastructure are held in the public domain and are not insured. If this uninsured property is damaged, the loss will have to be borne by the public purse. This will eventually result in less disposable income within a country and the stifling of economic growth.

The problem of the vulnerability of infrastructure is even greater than it would appear. Much of the public infrastructure in developed nations is aging and in poor repair. The building standards used to construct sewers and other systems are not able withstand the weather-related demands created by the increase in natural disasters. Magnifying the problem, any loss of capacity is a great blow to an economy. Much of this infrastructure was built using the capacity needs of the much smaller population of 50 years ago, but is currently operating at full capacity to meet the demands of a much increased population.

The combined costs of maintaining both private and public property have already placed a substantial financial burden on current governments. Despite the actions these governments are taking to address the root causes of climate change, these costs are expected to continue to increase. The funding for this maintenance will have to be raised through one of two means. First, taxes could be raised. This would decrease the disposable income of the economy and stifle growth. A second option would be to decrease the services currently offered by a government. Health care, education and other human services would suffer, as would government initiatives to spur technological development. The costs of these reductions would negatively impact productivity and total wealth. Wealthy individuals will continue to have access to education and health care, but less well-off individuals would be at a disadvantage.

Developing Nations

The costs of climate change will not be borne in a uniform manner across nations. For a number of reasons, developing nations will face more severe consequences of existing and additional climate changes than will more developed nations.

First, the geographical location of developing nations will result in greater vulnerability to the effects of climate change. It has been predicted that countries in North America and Europe will actually experience increased crop yields, while countries located in more southern locations will experience either drought (in landlocked regions) or flooding (in regions bordering the oceans). The increase in storms predicted over the next century will likely hit developing nations harder than developed nations. This will have devastating effects on the subsidence industries of these countries. Because many developing nations are located in regions already suffering from inadequate agricultural resources, the growth and development of these nations will be hampered. It has been predicted that land losses due to flooding will result in a contraction of the economy of Micronesia totaling over 10 per cent of the Gross Domestic Product.[14]

Second, increases in natural disasters in developed nations will reduce the pool of capital available for international aid.[15] If North America is using greater resources to deal with domestic disasters, there may be less aid available to countries that depend on international aid during periods of disaster. Studies of how countries deal with natural disasters have indicated that developing countries hold far less private insurance than developed nations and depend on international aid as a means of stemming the human and financial losses from disasters. For example, China, with a poorly developed insurance industry, depends heavily on international aid to address disasters. By contrast, Britain uses private insurance to a much greater degree to cover these losses. Hence, losses in other countries will have far less of an impact on Britain than on China.[16]

Third, much of the infrastructure in developing nations is built to very low standards. Sewage systems and telephone networks are far more vulnerable to damage than if they had been built to the standards of the developed world. Because infrastructure will not be able to withstand the effects of a disaster, and because the governments have few resources available to rebuild, a disaster has the potential to significantly stifle economic development in a nation.[17]

The population of developing nations is growing while the population of developed nations is leveling off. If the majority of the world's population suffers a disproportionate share of the damage from climate change, overall development will be impeded. Technology developments will not be possible if the majority of the population is preoccupied with addressing the devastation from increased natural disasters.

PREVENTION

Although there is a definite need for mitigation of the impacts of natural disasters, ultimately, this approach will entail heavy costs, and disasters will continue to intensify. Eventually, the only solution that prevents the upward spiral of costs will be one capable of stemming the causes of disaster-causing climate change. Although in the past there has been a certain degree of denial (most notably by George W. Bush), it is now generally accepted that the cause of climate change is global warming resulting from human-generated greenhouse gases.

THE KYOTO ACCORD

The Kyoto Accord, initially negotiated in 1997, is an international agreement that grew out of the United Nations Convention on Climate Change in 1992. The initial 1992 agreement was established to regulate the level of greenhouse gases emitted into the atmosphere. It outlines each country's responsibilities for reducing these gases. The Kyoto Protocol goes one step further, by outlining the legally binding amounts of greenhouse gases permitted to be emitted for the 160 participating nations. Reductions in emissions were established for 38 developed nations and countries in transition. It specifically excludes developing nations from reduction requirements. Each country has a different target level. Overall, reductions will average 5.2 per cent lower than 1990 levels. It allows the countries to average emissions over the period from 2008 to 2012. Each individual country may determine how to reach its target. Some countries may elect to compel industry and individual reductions in emissions, while others may elect to undertake projects that will count towards the reduction targets. Still other countries may simply elect to continue emitting greenhouse gases and purchase credits from other nations in order to fulfill the agreement. The review process is not to be intrusive. However, specifics of how this will be carried out have not been determined.

Initially, the United States was part of the Kyoto agreement, but has since opted to withdraw. Nevertheless, many nations did agree to the treaty in July of 2001, after a number of alterations to the original treaty. For example, Canada was now granted additional credit for existing forests that served as a "sink" for carbon dioxide. Each signatory country would now take the agreement back to its domestic legislature for ratification. The principles of the treaty had been agreed to, however, the operation and enforcement details had yet to be written.

One of the key features of this treaty is the "emissions credit" trading system. Each country will be awarded a certain number of credits entitling them to produce a certain amount of greenhouse gases. Activities undertaken that reduce the concentration of greenhouse gases (for example, forestation initiatives or implementation of clean technology) will result in greater credits towards the target reductions. Countries will be able to trade or sell credits. In this way, countries that are unable to meet targets will be able to purchase credits for additional gas creation than would otherwise have been allowed. The rationale behind this system is that it allows reduction of overall greenhouse gas emission in the most economically efficient manner. Concern has been raised that wealthier countries, that traditionally have produced the lion's share of emissions will continue to do so by purchasing credits from nations that have a surplus as a result of economic contraction.

The treaty has not specified penalties for countries not able to meet targets, nor has it specified either enforcement mechanisms or regulations for trading systems. The World Trade Organization (WTO) has traditionally found it difficult to resolve disputes over environmental issues. Perhaps a new international organization will be required to mediate and resolve these issues. At present, despite the agreement reached in Bonn, there is a great deal of uncertainty over the effectiveness and implications of the new treaty. The implications, without a doubt, will differ for the different groups affected. Individual nations will find implementation more or less costly depending on a number of factors: the country's dependence on fossil fuels for energy creation, the current industries making up the economy, resources needed for additional industries, regulations, relationships with other nations and the agreed to targets. These considerations will have significant effects on the degree of difficulty in adhering to the agreement. In addition, the penalties imposed for non-adherence will also impact a country's willingness to dishonor the agreement.

The Kyoto Protocol is the first time binding, international coordination has been attempted to address global warming; its impacts are largely unknown and will differ for each stakeholder group affected.

Governments

Each developing nation that is a party to the Kyoto Protocol has committed to greenhouse gas reduction targets. For example, Canada has agreed to reduce total greenhouse gas emissions to six per cent below the 1990 levels. The average of the years from 2008 to 2012 will be calculated to determine compliance, reducing the costs of an abnormal year.

The methods to obtain the targets will be left up to the countries involved. Nations (and individuals) have the possibility of purchasing credits from other nations (or individuals) that have benefited from greater than expected success in meeting their targets. The correct proportion of credit purchase to actual reductions will need to be determined and the criteria for this determination are not clear. It could be that the objective is to merely meet the targets at minimum cost. If this is the case, wealthy nations would likely find it less expensive to purchase credits, than to undertake changes that have the potential to stifle the domestic economy. This had been the view of the United States prior to their withdrawal from the protocol. If the objective is to reduce emissions, in keeping with the spirit of the agreement, countries will undertake to change their economic base to one that does not produce the same volume of emissions. This was the view of many of the European participants in the Kyoto Protocol. These countries viewed the credit trading system as a means of adhering to the agreement during periods when emissions may be impossible to reduce. For example, should a country experience severely cold weather, it could be expected to produce larger quantities of emissions until new methods of adapting to colder conditions could be put into place.

Greenhouse gas emissions are created through the activity of both industries and consumers. Although less responsible for total emissions, consumers directly contribute over 30 per cent of all carbon dioxide emissions into the atmosphere.[18] For a government to be able to meet its commitments to reduce national emissions, one or both groups must be compelled to reduce emissions. Decisions must be made to determine which groups will be compelled to reduce, which members of each group will be compelled to reduce and how the government intends to compel adherence. These decisions are vital to achieving compliance.

The combinations of strategies for meeting reduction targets are limitless. One solution might be to mandate a uniform reduction in emissions for both consumers and industries. Another alternative might be to mandate a uniform reduction for industry only. Quotas for emissions could be granted to industries and consumers, however, certain industries may require larger quotas than others. Certain industries may be deemed to be so important that reduction efforts will not be required. New corporations and industries will need to be specifically addressed because it will be impossible to impose percentage reductions on companies that presently do not exist. If the government awards all credits to existing corporations, there is the danger of stifling new development because emission credits will not be available to be distributed. In addition, financial or credit incentives could be introduced for the companies that attempt to implement cleaner technologies.

Unless the selected method of meeting target reductions includes penalties in excess of the costs of complying, corporations or individuals may opt to merely accept the penalty and continue to create excess emissions. In addition, the way in which corporations and individuals react to the imposition of restrictions will also depend on the ability of each to purchase credits. If individual corporations, as well as nations, are able to buy and sell credits, purchasing a credit may be the most economical means of adhering to government restrictions. If, however, the penalty for non-compliance is lower than the cost of purchasing credits, it will be less costly to simply continue to produce excess emissions.

In addition, there is a concern that countries will stockpile (or sell) credits for reductions achieved solely through economic contraction. For example, the Russian economy has experienced substantial contraction since the 1990-pegged period. Because considerably less industrial activity is taking place, fewer emissions are being released. Hence, Russia has an excess of credits, despite taking little or no effort to make meaningful reductions by changing technologies. Because these credits will have value to more wealthy nations, they can be bought and used to create additional emissions that would not have been possible had the economy of Russia not experienced this contraction.

Old Economy Industries

Because the majority of the greenhouse gases in the atmosphere are produced through industrial activity, it is expected that the industries producing the largest emissions will be the industries most required to make adaptations. The added costs required to meet the reductions will create a strain for these industries. Ultimately, some may cease to exist, as new, cleaner technologies are developed capable of replacing the old industry. However, there is likely to be a period in which there is a great upheaval as economies change their major industry groups. Old industries, such as oil and gas, may experience decline, while new industries, such as wind and solar power, may replace the old.

Because the decline of the older industries will result in significant job losses while people adapt and train to meet the needs of the new industries in operation, the economy may suffer some temporary downturns. These may create public resentment towards the international efforts to limit global warming. Governments, responsive to the will of citizens, may become indifferent to international commitments.

However, there is the potential that these better managed old economy industries will adapt to the changes and adopt new, more efficient technologies. Productivity has the potential to increase. Forcing industry into innovation by imposing penalties and additional costs for greenhouse gas emissions may direct research activities in new areas that stem the need to produce these gases.

Overall, there will almost certainly be a period of adaptation that will result in significant financial costs to the economy. However, it is hoped that compelling cleaner technologies will result in sustainable innovation and productivity increases.

New Industry Groups

The enactment of the Kyoto Protocol creates a number of new business opportunities. First, as previously mentioned, there will likely be new industries capable of meeting society's needs for food, energy and other products, without the greenhouse gas emissions of former providers of these products. Second, the Protocol, by itself, creates a number of opportunities in law, regulation, enforcement and administration of the treaty and the credit trading system.

Because modern society has been extremely dependent upon the carbon-based energy techniques that have resulted in the production of carbon dioxide, the development and implementation of alternative and cleaner methods of energy production have the potential to greatly reduce the world's emissions of greenhouse gases. In addition, because carbon-based resources are finite, development of renewable energy sources has the potential to contribute significantly to productivity. Although the prevention of further global warming is the impetus for a government shaping behavior towards cleaner technology, the side benefit has the potential to create an economic boom not unlike that seen in the early 1990s.

Solar, hydro and wind energy have the potential to produce large quantities of energy. Almost every major oil company has recognized the inevitable need to reduce dependency on oil reserves for energy and has undertaken significant research efforts towards developing new technologies. By proactively identifying new opportunities to replace declining industries, these companies seek to secure future growth. Shell has been one of the major leaders in the search to develop new energy producing technologies.

One concern raised is the use of nuclear power to reduce greenhouse gas emissions. Although there have been no new nuclear power plants built in the last 20 to 30 years, there has been a renewed interest; nuclear power has the potential to allow countries to meet energy needs without meaningfully changing the lifestyle of the average consumer and industry. Nuclear power does not produce greenhouse gas emissions and is not believed to contribute to global warming, however, it raises a number of other environmental concerns that have not been adequately addressed. For example, in addition to energy, the products of nuclear power are radioactive used fuel cells. There is no known method of reducing this radioactivity and, thus far, the only method of dealing with this radioactive waste is to store it in uninhabited areas. Although this is a satisfactory temporary solution, the long-run consequence of this material on the earth's environment is unknown. Several well-known nuclear power accidents have resulted in a great deal of human illness and suffering. Expansion of the nuclear power industry without addressing with these concerns may ultimately produce greater human suffering than if global warming continued unabated. However, if the issues of storage and safety are adequately addressed, nuclear power does have the potential to meet the earth's energy needs without the corresponding release of greenhouse gases that is seen with carbon-based energy production.

Another major research effort currently underway is the development of new, renewable fuel cells capable of powering vehicles. Because a great deal of the greenhouse gases in the atmosphere is produced by transportation vehicles using carbon engines, cleaner methods of powering vehicles ought to have a significant impact on the level of greenhouse gas emissions. The auto industry has been extremely active in this area. Alliances have been formed by auto manufacturers entering into co-operative ventures to produce the first fuel cell powered vehicles.[19] Toyota, GM, Ford and Honda have all funneled substantial resources into this effort. Thus far, vehicles have been produced that release fewer emissions, but other than Toyota's Primus, there has not been widespread availability of these vehicles.

The Kyoto Protocol will need to be implemented and monitored for effectiveness. The credit trading system will need to be administered. These functions will provide new business opportunities. Already, corporations are attempting to secure a dominant position in these areas. Two consulting companies, Accenture and Ernst & Young, are attempting to develop brokerage capabilities for the trading of credits. Because so little is known about how the system will operate, these consulting companies will likely find a large volume of business advising other corporations on how best to prepare for the impact of the Protocol. Lawyers who gain familiarity with the regulations as they develop will likely experience the same boon in their practices.

Insurance programs will likely develop to cover the costs of well-intentioned failure to meet standards. Alliances may develop between countries and corporations to facilitate the trading of credits. There will likely be a significant role for businesses that are able to bring together potential credit trading partners. Monitoring systems will need to be developed and it is likely that those corporations that establish an early role in the system will be rewarded with the right to continue those roles.

As knowledge and experience are gained, the number of participants will likely decrease to the point where a few, large corporations are able to entrench their positions. However, over the short term, there may be significant opportunity costs as these systems are set up, before they begin to show equilibrium returns. Governments will likely have to commit sizable resources to get the systems up and running and this may reduce the dollars available to meet the human and social services requirements expected by their citizens. Over the longer term, however, the new industry will put money back into the economy in the form of taxes, to enhance the services available to the citizens of the nations involved. However, there is likely to be short-term displeasure with the costs of the Protocol, especially given that the dangers of global warming are in the future and not, in the minds of many, an immediate emergency. Education efforts may be needed to convince a skeptical population of the need to reduce emissions. Employment opportunities created by this education initiative, will ultimately translate into greater economic benefits for the country involved.

Developing Nations

The average citizen of India produces 1/25 or four per cent of the greenhouse gas emissions produced by the average citizen of the United States.[20] Of the accumulated greenhouse gases in the atmosphere that can be attributed to human activities, only a small percentage has been contributed by the developing nations of the world. These nations rely less on the internal combustion engine and have less dependence on carbon-based energy for daily life and industrial activities. Hence, the problem of global warming has been created by the developed world.

The Kyoto Protocol specifically exempts developing nations from the first round of emission reductions. The rationale behind this exclusion is twofold. First, these nations produce only a small proportion of the greenhouse gases on a per capita basis. Second, these countries are only now developing their industrial capabilities and restrictions based on greenhouse gas emissions have the potential to stymie the economy's transition to developed nation status. To place target reduction quotas on these nations has the potential to permanently assign these nations to Third World status. Because these nations have little surplus purchasing power to enable them to purchase credits, they are left with having to implement the most costly technology in order to meet reduction quotas. Since these countries are struggling to provide the necessities of life for their residents, any economic disadvantage will cause disproportionate hardship. Developed nations, it is argued, were given the opportunity to develop using the most economical technology. To deny these opportunities to developing nations will doom their citizens as a permanent underclass.

Although the per capita production of greenhouse gases by developing nations is low, their vast population size and growth projections mean that the overall emissions are sizable and growing. Population predictions for this century indicate that developing nations will experience a population growth surge, while developed nations will see their populations decline. As the populations of the developing world grow, overall emissions will likely increase if these countries are not held to the same standard as the rest of the world.

In addition, there has been a great deal of objection by potential signatory developed nations (in particular, the United States) that exclusion of these countries will not result in any meaningful reductions in the total greenhouse gases in the atmosphere. The biggest concern of these nations, however, has more to do with national competitiveness. The United States has vocally argued (and subsequently rejected the treaty on these grounds), that because developing nations will not bear the costs of adherence to the protocol targets, businesses located there will have a significant advantage over businesses located in

countries that are party to the protocol. The damage to the U.S. economy, as a result, would be too great to permit the United States to commit to the treaty.

Signatory Countries

After gaining a number of concessions, Canada has agreed to be party to the treaty. Although the federal government's delegation has made the commitment to the rather general terms of the treaty, it now must take the agreement back to Parliament to gain ratification before the nation is officially bound. Under the Constitution Act of 1867, §91, the federal government is responsible for international trade and has the authority to negotiate international treaties, however, the power over industry falls to the provinces under §92. Hence, unless the federal government can claim that emissions fall under federal jurisdiction, a great deal of co-operation will be required by the two levels of government. The federal government could claim that the jurisdiction over natural resources grants authority to implement this treaty. Failing that, the peace, order and good government provisions under the national concern doctrine will likely suffice.

Canada, a nation highly dependent on natural resources, requires substantial energy resources for their extraction and refinement into saleable products. In addition, the cold climate and large geographic distances that goods must travel add to the energy requirements of the country. Given its energy source dependence, Canada will find it difficult to meet the target requirements of the treaty. Canada, however, has vast quantities of uninhabited forests that act as "carbon sinks" for greenhouse gases. Because these forests are capable of converting carbon dioxide into oxygen, Canada has argued for and been granted additional credit for these forests. One argument against this concession is that these forests have existed for centuries and represent no incremental effort to reduce the production of greenhouse gases.

Canada is in a difficult trade position. It's largest trading partner, the United States, has rejected the Kyoto Protocol. Trade groups have argued that this places Canadian industries at a sizable disadvantage to U.S. competitors. U.S. companies will not be forced to bear the costs of changing to cleaner technologies; so they will be able to reap cost advantages that Canadian companies will not be able to match. Some countries may find that by making real reduction attempts, they will find themselves at a trade disadvantage. In order to avoid this situation, they may view the credit trading system as the most economical (and trade favorable) method of adherence to the treaty. This will create an incentive to minimize the cost of adherence, through the use of cheaply purchased credits, rather than making meaningful reductions that contribute to the fight against global warming.

Given the globalization of trade, this is a serious concern for all nations trading internationally. In addition, the industries operating in countries party to the agreement will be forced to devote substantial resources to research and development of new, cleaner technologies. While these new circumstances have the potential to create substantial economic opportunities in the future, once developed and part of the accepted practices for an industry, the advantage over other companies will be short lived. In essence, industries forced to innovate will subsidize the innovation of companies operating in non-party countries.

Non-Signatory Nations: The United States

There are many reasons why certain countries rejected the Kyoto Protocol. The greatest contributor to greenhouse gases in the atmosphere, the United States, has officially rejected the treaty.[21] Although President George W. Bush has stated that the United States intends to pursue its own program of emission reductions, the effectiveness of the Kyoto treaty without this significant player has come into question.

The main reason why the United States rejected the treaty has much to do with protecting the U.S. trade position. Although it has stated

that other reasons exist for the rejection of the treaty (for example, the lack of recognition of the U.S. need for increased emissions due to the country's unique role as a worldwide military power), the major stumbling block to U.S. agreement has been the issue of exemption of developing nations from the initial round of reduction targets. The fear is that exempting these nations will result in the United States being disadvantaged in trade because it faces the additional costs required for adherence, when developing nations are exempt from efforts incurring these costs. Although there has been some vocal domestic displeasure with the U.S. withdrawal from the treaty, the recent energy crisis in California has added to the public fear of energy shortages. This fear has resulted in greater public support for withdrawing from the Protocol negotiations.

It has been suggested that the importance of their international trade position will result in U.S. corporations voluntarily adopting more environmentally friendly practices. There has been the concern that trading partners who adhere to the requirements of the Protocol will reject alliances with corporations that do not meet the same standards. For that reason, some have speculated that the U.S. non-signatory status will be irrelevant. U.S. corporations operating in multiple markets will determine that the most efficient choice is voluntary compliance. Adding to the pressure on U.S. corporations to comply is the fact that many of these corporations are multinational and will simultaneously be operating in signatory nations. Because different standards will be difficult to administer, uniform compliance will be the result.

Multinational Corporations

Many multinational corporations will find themselves producing products in two different regulatory environments: signatory countries and non-signatory countries. Many of the products produced will be transferred from division to division. Nations adhering to the protocol may reject trade with partners not meeting the same environmental standards. Hence, it may be infeasible to maintain Protocol standards in one country while eschewing them in another. In addition, technologies developed to reduce emissions may be implemented in all locations because they may be more efficient and cost-effective than current emission producing technologies. If the corporation devotes resources to develop more efficient processes in one market, it may tend to adopt those processes in another.

Multinational corporations are in an enviable position because they will be able to transfer credits between national sites. For example, if it becomes unlikely that a certain manufacturing plant will be able to meet the targets set by the domestic government, it will be possible to transfer credits from plants that have met or exceeded their targets. In addition, these corporations will be able to use the policies of more lenient governments that have been more liberal with the granting of credits, to offset the requirements of more stringent governments. This may allow multinational corporations to minimize the costs of adherence to the treaty and be at a cost advantage compared to single nation corporations. Hence, growth in the size and number of multinational corporations could be the result.

The alternative to multinationals adhering to the Protocol requirements in all national locations is to concentrate production in those nations with few regulatory emission standards. However, the public backlash from this strategy could result in a sullied reputation for these firms. The reputation impact may make it difficult to obtain the governmental support in signatory companies necessary to operate efficiently. If a government is displeased with the lack of co-operation by a particular multinational corporation, tax and regulatory issues in non-environmental areas could make it difficult for that corporation to operate.

CONCLUSION

Human activity producing greenhouse gas emissions is causing the earth's atmosphere to become warmer. The costs of this warming will be substantial over the course of this century if nothing is done to address the issue. Certainly, it will be important to mitigate the existing and expected impacts of climate change through better building standards and through more efficient mechanisms for paying for the damage caused by climate. In the long term, only efforts that stem the problem at the root cause, the emission of greenhouse gases, have the potential to permanently contain these costs. Many groups will be impacted in the quest to mitigate the loss from climate change and through the efforts to permanently quell the problem. There will be short-term costs and opportunities created as societies adapt to the realization that current energy production techniques cannot continue unabated and as new methods of energy creation are implemented. The international community has selected one method, the Kyoto Protocol, to reduce the problems created by global warming. Whether or not this solution is the most efficient—or whether it is even feasible will only be determined over time. Certainly, there will be unanticipated consequences of the agreement that will serve to shape future international environmental initiatives.

KYOTO'S LESSONS FOR BUSINESS

Although the issue of global warming attributable to increases in the concentration of greenhouse gases in the atmosphere is, of itself, vitally important, the examination of this issue and proposed solutions provide a useful starting point for identifying solutions to other global environmental problems. In situations where no one nation is able to legislate to limit or stem environmental damage to its citizens, international co-operation will be required. The difficulties encountered in securing the Kyoto Protocol agreement and the uncertainty surrounding implementation of the signed agreement illustrate what can be expected in future environmental negotiations.

One example of the difficult nature of multi-nation negotiation over environmental problems is the situation that has been observed along the Mexico-U.S. border. As a result of incentives created through multilateral trade agreements, it is economically advantageous for American companies to assemble products in the border region of Mexico. The result of the increased manufacturing activity in Mexico has been the production of significant volumes of hazardous waste. This waste was supposed to be returned to the United States for safe disposal, however, this has not happened. Hazardous waste has not been adequately stored and has leaked into the groundwater, affecting both Mexicans and Americans. The reasons for this are numerous. First, although Mexico does have stringent environmental regulations, the implementation and monitoring of the adherence to these regulations is, at best, lax. Fines for non-compliance are often significantly less than the costs of adhering to the regulations. The economic benefit these American factories provide the people of Mexico make it undesirable for the Mexican government to come down hard on Americans who have violated the regulations. To lose investment in these regions would risk putting a great number of Mexican workers into poverty. Second, the legal system in Mexico does not hold the offending parties responsible for their actions. Individual lawsuits brought against companies for environmental damage are rare and class-action lawsuits are virtually non-existent. Mexican companies contract with trucking services to dispose of hazardous waste, but are not held liable if those contractors dump the hazardous material inappropriately. Given the costs involved with appropriate disposal, it is only reasonable for these contractors to disregard regulations and use illegal dumping locations.

The problem of American-owned Mexican factories polluting the environment would, at first glance, appear to be solely within Mexican control. However, the United States is also impacted in a number of ways. First, its companies are responsible for much of the pollution problem. As long as it is cheaper to produce in Mexico because it is less costly than adhering to U.S. environmental standards, the U.S. companies will continue to contribute to the problem.

Second, and most pressing, is that the health of U.S. residents has been placed in jeopardy as a result of the Mexican pollution seeping into the groundwater that eventually flows into U.S. soil. The incidence of birth defects in Texas has increased drastically in the past few decades and this increase has been attributed to the pollution produced in the Mexican border regions.

Because the issue of the pollution along the Mexican-U.S. border involves two different nations, the solution will involve the co-operation of both nations. However, because trade issues form a significant component of both the creation of the problem, and its eventual solution, the resolution of this problem will be of interest to all nations, particularly as trade becomes more global in the future. Agreements, enforcement and monitoring of any international agreements should be considered with reference to what has been achieved with the Kyoto Protocol, with further refinements being considered to improve on past experience. Herein lies the value of understanding and questioning the Kyoto Accord and the greenhouse gas emissions.

Alternative Models for Environmental Trade Agreements

Although the Kyoto Protocol is an important example of an international agreement on environmental issues, it is not groundbreaking in the sense of being the first such agreement. The Montreal Protocol on Substances that Deplete the Ozone Layer, signed in 1992, is an important alternative model to consider when drafting future environmental agreements. The impetus for the Montreal Protocol was the thinning of the ozone layer over the earth that was allowing increased levels of cancer-causing ultraviolet light to penetrate the earth's atmosphere. This protocol is of interest because it addressed several of the weak points currently existing in the Kyoto Protocol. First, the Montreal Protocol provided for specific sanctions for nations not meeting their objectives. Second, it built in major incentives for developing nations to join the pact. Lastly, it ensured that there were no economic incentives available for nations violating the pact.

On the surface, the Montreal Protocol appears to have been extremely successful. Between 1986 and 1993, world chlorofluorocarbon (CFC) production fell 60 per cent, from 0.9 million tonnes to about 0.4 million tonnes.[22] It would appear as though CFC levels are easier to regulate than greenhouse gases, because CFCs can be eliminated completely, while total eradication of greenhouse gas emissions is unlikely. Despite the apparent success of the protocol, during the same time period (1986 to 1993), production of CFCs by developing nations increased 87 per cent.[23] Exports from developing nations to developed nations increased 17-fold, despite the restrictions on exports and imports stated in the agreement. An underground market has developed, with estimates that 20 per cent of sales are illegal, many originating in developing countries.[24] It has been speculated that one of the reasons is that the incentives allocated to encouraging developing nations to adhere to the pact were not fully provided. Another concern that arises over the Montreal Protocol is its perceived inconsistency with the export/import provisions set out in General Agreement on Tarriffs and Trade (GATT) and the World Trade Organization (WTO). When the treaty comes up for review, it is expected many nations participating in the underground economy will argue that trade restrictions make the Protocol invalid.

Despite the drawbacks of the Montreal Protocol, the treaty may provide useful lessons as the finer points of the Kyoto agreement continue to be resolved. The reduction of acid rain provides an additional example of government intervention to protect the environment. Many analysts have been very positive in evaluating the success of these programs.

The greatest environmental success story of the past decade is probably America's sulphur dioxide scheme, aimed at reducing acid rain. . . .

The key was the introduction of tradable rights, combined with a credible threat of punishment for non-compliance. This spurred the development of

a vibrant market and lowered emissions beyond expectations.[25]

It appears that each environmental concern may have to be addressed individually, based on the particular environmental problem and existing treaty obligations, and with an understanding of the incentives and disincentives for adherence for each stakeholder group. This individualized approach to agreements on environmental issues will create a myriad of both challenges and opportunities for business.

NOTES

1. "Feeling the heat—Special Report—Global warming," *Time Magazine,* April 9, 2001, p. 16.

2. "BUSINESSWORLD (PHILIPPINES): Global impact of climate change to cost $300B a yr," *BusinessWorld*, Manila; Feb. 8, 2001, p. 1.

3. Ibid.

4. Virginia H. Dale, "Climate change and forest disturbances," *Bioscience*, Sept. 2001; Vol. 51, No. 9, p. 723.

5. Antonio Regalado, "Weighing the Evidence of Global Warming—MIT study calculates odds of higher temperatures, indicates need for action," *Wall Street Journal*, Eastern Edition, Mar. 22, 2001.

6. Martin Bartlam, "Understanding the greenhouse gas debate," *Power Economics*, June 2001, Vol. 5, No. 6, p. 21.

7. "The climbing cost of climate change," *Earth Island Journal*, Summer 2001, Vol. 16, No. 2, p. 19.

8. Stanley A. Changnon, "Human factors explain the increased losses from weather and climate extremes," *Bulletin of the American Meterological Society*, Mar. 2000, Vol. 18, No. 3, p. 437.

9. Dan R. Anderson, "Catastrophe insurance and compensation: Remembering basic principles," *Society of Chartered Property and Casualty Underwriters. CPCU Journal,* Summer 2000, Vol. 53, No. 2, p. 76.

10. Amanda Levin, "Insurers see disaster risks rising in 21st century," *National Underwriter*, Dec. 1999, Vol. 103, No. 51, p. S34.

11. Dan R. Anderson, "Catastrophe insurance and compensation: Remembering basic principles," *Society of Chartered Property and Casualty Underwriters. CPCU Journal,* Summer 2000, Vol. 53, No. 2, p. 76.

12. Amanda Levin, "American insurers decried as cool on global warming," *National Underwriter,* Mar. 8, 1999, Vol. 103, No. 10, p. 3.

13. Eve Patterson, Insurance Bureau of Canada.

14. "The climbing cost of climate change," *Earth Island Journal*, Summer 2001, Vol. 16, No. 2, p. 19.

15. Nora Lustig, "Broadening the agenda for poverty reduction: Opportunity, empowerment, security," *Finance & Development*, Dec. 2000, Vol. 37, No. 4, p. 3.

16. David C. Marlett et al., "Managing flood losses: An international review of mitigation and financing techniques: Part II," *Society of Chartered Property and Casualty Underwriters. CPCU Journal,* Fall 2001.

17. "Aging infrastructure key link to disasters," *Canadian Underwriter,* Jan. 2001, Vol. 68, No. 1, p. 58.

18. Ken Conca, "American environmentalism confronts the global economy," *Dissent*, Winter 2000, Vol. 47, No. 1, p. 72.

19. David Welch, Lorraine Woellert, "The eco-cars: As Detroit stalls, Japan drives in with appealing new hybrid models," *Business Week,* Aug. 14, 2000, No. 3694, p. 62.

20. Michael B. McElroy, "Perspectives on environmental change: A basis for action," *Daedalus,* Fall 2001, Vol. 130, No. 4, p. 31.

21. Robert U. Ayres, "How economists have misjudged global warming," *World Watch,* Sept./Oct. 2001, Vol. 14, No. 5, p. 12.

22. Ivan Lerner, "Fluorocarbon industry adapting to regulations," *Chemical Market Reporter,* Sept. 10, 2001, Vol. 260, No. 10, p. 10.

23. Peter Powell, "The refrigerant issue: Is the debate cooling off?" *Air Conditioning, Heating & Refrigeration News,* Mar. 5, 2001, Vol. 212, No. 10, p. 13.

24. John Wickham, "International trade and climate change policies," *Journal of Environment & Development*, Sept. 2001, Vol. 10, No. 3, p. 298.

25. "Economic man, cleaner planet," *The Economist,* Sept. 29, 2001, p. 74.

Enron Wind Corporation: Challenges and Opportunities in the 21st Century

Prepared by Erich Ossowski under the supervision of Professor David Conklin

Version: (A) 2004-06-04

An Expansion Strategy

As it entered the 21st century, Enron Wind Corporation (EWC) was considering building a wind farm in Fortaleza, Brazil, a region on Brazil's northeastern coast that had experienced strong industrial growth and where the increase of power consumption in the region had exceeded all expectations. This project could provide Enron Wind with an opportunity to enter the Latin American wind energy market. However, Brazil had a history of political and economic instability.

On December 31, 2001, the U.S. Renewable Energy Production Tax Credit (PTC) would expire if it were not extended by the Bush administration (see Exhibit 1). Although Bush had included the PTC extension in his budget, he had also made it clear in March 2001 that the United States would not honor its commitment to the Kyoto Protocol. It was uncertain what effect this would have on the U.S. domestic wind energy industry, but this political situation seemed to favor a strategy of pursuing projects in foreign markets. In addition to this, the long-term annual growth in demand for electricity in the United

In 1992, the Energy Policy Act was signed into law and included enactment of a Production Tax Credit (PTC) under Section 45 of the Internal Revenue Code of 1986. This credit was available to corporate entities building new renewable energy production facilities such as solar, biomass, wood chip, geothermal and wind electric power production plants. The tax credit at inception of the law was $0.015 per kilowatt-hour (kWh) produced by the facility, increased each year by the official rate of inflation from the previous year, for the first 10 years of operation of the equipment. The credit was available to new renewable energy facilities placed into commercial service after enactment of the law and prior to December 31, 2001.

A key benefit of the PTC was that it provided substantial incentive for wind turbine manufacturers to improve the reliability and efficiency of their equipment. Poor turbine availability, high operations and maintenance costs, and/or substandard power production for a given wind regime would quickly eliminate a turbine from consideration for installation on a project planning to utilize the PTC. Competition between manufacturers was intense, with market pressures resulting in warranties consisting of five-year, 100 per cent parts and labor for any turbine malfunction, and guarantees that the turbines would achieve 95 per cent of their projected power curve at the site or the manufacturer would reimburse the owner for the lost revenue. This combination of high quality equipment and hefty manufacturer warranties had removed much of the wind project risk for the project finance community.

As a direct result of the availability of the PTC and major improvements in equipment reliability, during the last three years of the 1990s, over $3 billion in capital investment in wind energy projects had been made in the United States alone. From 2000 until the deadline for projects qualifying for the PTC in December 2001, $2 billion was projected to be invested in wind projects in the United States.

Exhibit 1   The U.S. Renewable Energy Production Tax Credit[1]

1. This information was sourced from www.worldlinkinsurance.com/windpro/ptc.

States was expected to remain at only 1.2 per cent. In developing economies, however, there was expected to be a much more rapid growth in demand for electricity.

Robert Gates, senior vice-president (VP) of Enron Wind, summarized the firm's expansion strategy in the following words:

The market sizes in the world are No. 1, Germany; No. 2, Spain; and No. 3, the United States—and those are the markets we're strong in. Currently, we need to get into—and we're working on getting into—markets other than Germany on the European side; and on the America's side, the same thing: expand outside the United States. We have been working in Central America and Latin America for years, and I think it will begin to bear fruit in the next year or two—I've been saying that for six or seven years now and it hasn't happened.

In April 2002, GE Power Systems acquired Enron Wind Corp.:

"The acquisition of Enron Wind represents GE Power Systems' initial investment into renewable wind power, one of the fastest growing energy sectors," said John Rice, president and CEO of GE Power Systems. The wind energy industry is expected to grow at an annual rate of about 20 per cent, with principal markets in Europe, the U.S. and Latin America.

GE Power Systems (www.gepower.com) is one of the world's leading suppliers of power generation technology, energy services and management systems with projected 2001 revenues exceeding $20 billion. The business has the largest installed base of power generation equipment in the global energy industry. GE Power Systems provides equipment, service and management solutions across the power generation, oil and gas, distributed power and energy rental industries.[1]

Enron Wind and its new owner GE Power Systems faced the questions: In what proportions should they divide their future investments and sales activities among the United States and other countries, and what criteria should it use in evaluating investment opportunities? Was wind energy about to really take off?

THE IMPACTS OF DEREGULATION

Power generation markets were consistently in the news in 2001, mainly due to the growing power crisis in California. In 1998, California, like many other American states and other countries, had opened its electricity industry to competition. The resulting industry uncertainty inhibited investment in new power capacity, which—combined with the severe increase in the price of natural gas, used in many electricity generating plants—caused price spikes and blackouts in California. In addition, regulatory change placed California's two largest electricity utilities on the verge of bankruptcy, causing many to reconsider the rationale behind breaking up the traditional power monopoly.

According to Gates, deregulation had the following implications for the wind energy industry:

> Deregulation in general will allow people to choose their sources of electricity. That's good, because we think, over time, some portion of the population will say, "I'd like to have some of my energy come from renewable." If people can't choose, and the choice is by middle management in the utility, they will choose cheap, and cheap is coal or gas. It is not wind. If gas prices go up, wind can be in there, but it'll never be as cheap as marginal coal. The only time wind would have a chance against coal is if you've got emissions limitations and you need a new plant. But as long as there's surplus capacity, marginal coal will always be cheaper than anything really. So deregulation is good because it gives people a choice, and they can choose wind.

Deregulation of electricity markets was not confined to the United States. By 2001, several other countries had also deregulated, or had intentions to do so. In the European Union (EU) for example, the United Kingdom was the first country to deregulate its electricity market, beginning in 1989. By 1996, Sweden, Norway and Finland had all initiated the deregulation process and had the intention of integrating their electrical systems. The ultimate goal in the EU was to create a unified internal electricity market, which would be open to competition and allow for cross-border electricity sales among all member countries. Elsewhere, deregulation was under way in two Canadian provinces, in Argentina and in Brazil.

ALTERNATIVE SOURCES FOR ELECTRICITY GENERATION

In general, energy sources were either renewable or non-renewable, and each of these could generate electricity through either a thermal or a non-thermal process. Thermal generation was accomplished through the combustion of non-renewable fossil fuels, such as oil, natural gas or coal, or through the combustion of renewable biomass fuels such as wood. Nuclear power was also a thermal generation process, accomplished through the fission of non-renewable uranium. Geothermal energy was a renewable form of energy whereby heat from the earth's core was used to thermally generate electricity.

Non-thermal generation consisted primarily of hydroelectric power, but also included solar photovoltaic and wind power. All non-thermal generation methods used renewable energy sources. In 1997, globally, 64 per cent of power was generated through the combustion of fossil fuels, 16 per cent was derived from nuclear, and the remaining 20 per cent came from renewable sources. Of the renewable sources of electricity, the vast majority came from hydropower.

Natural Gas

Natural gas was increasingly becoming the fuel of choice for new power plant projects around the globe.[2] World natural gas use in electricity generation was expected to more than double by 2020. Strong growth was particularly expected in North America, Western Europe and in Central and South America.

Natural-gas-fired generation was becoming increasingly efficient, and capital costs were falling, making gas more cost-competitive relative to other fuels, including coal. For example, the capital cost per kilowatt-hour of capacity for a new gas-powered plant was $449 (1998 U.S. dollars), compared with $1,102 for a similar coal unit. The difference in capital cost became more significant when interest rates were higher.

Between 1997 and 2020, natural gas was expected to grow from 17 per cent to 25 per cent of the global electricity fuels market. This growth in part resulted from increased confidence in the future availability of natural gas supplies. Other factors contributing to the growing popularity of gas-fired generation were the significant improvements in natural gas turbine technology and the environmental advantage of natural gas over other fossil fuels. The increasing availability of liquefied natural gas (LNG) was also expected to lead to more use of natural gas in power generation. Although it accounted for only five per cent of world gas consumption in 2000, LNG exports had grown by 40 per cent since 1992. In 2000, Algeria, Indonesia and Malaysia were the largest exporters of LNG; Japan, South Korea and France were the largest importers.

Pipeline trade in natural gas, which was nearly three times as large as LNG trade, was also an industry experiencing rapid growth. In the 1990s, exports of natural gas from Canada into the United States, from Norway and Russia into Western Europe, and from Algeria into Italy and Spain contributed to the increase in world trade. A number of pipeline projects had also been recently completed in South America. These were expected to make Argentina and Bolivia major exporters of natural gas, with Chile and Brazil becoming major importers.

Nuclear Power

While it had once been touted to form a significant share of global power generation, nuclear power's share of the electricity market was expected to drop from 17 per cent in 1997 to 10 per cent by 2020. The reasons for the decline in new nuclear power capacity included past cost overruns in the construction of nuclear facilities, the high costs of plant decommissioning and spent fuel retirement, and safety and environmental concerns. In Sweden and Germany, years of public opposition had led to a government commitment to gradually phase out nuclear power programs in both countries. In Germany, the nuclear phase-out was expected to begin in 2002. The United Kingdom also intended to reduce its reliance on nuclear power from 34 per cent of its electricity supply in 1997 to 18 per cent in 2020. Globally, only France and Japan were expected to maintain their reliance on nuclear power to the extent that they had in the past. In Japan however, some doubt was cast on the future of the nuclear industry after a 1999 accident at a nuclear fuel facility. In most other industrialized nations, a gradual reduction in the reliance on nuclear power was expected. In North America, neither Canada nor the United States was expected to generate more than 10 per cent of their electricity from nuclear sources by 2020.

Hydro Generation

Hydroelectricity, while renewable, was not without its social and environmental problems. These frequently led to public opposition to the development of new hydroelectric plants. In China, for instance, the Three Gorges project would require 1.2 million people to relocate due to the flooding of their homes. Damming rivers for hydroelectricity also resulted in depletion of fish stocks, which used the rivers as spawning grounds. In the United States, this led to competing economic interests between natives and fishers, whose livelihood depended on healthy fish stocks, and farmers, who needed the dams for irrigation during times of drought. In 2000, environmental groups were pressing for the breaching of dams on the Columbia River, hoping that this would replenish spawning grounds for salmon. A further environmental concern was the silting effect, whereby the depth of hydro reservoirs decreased due to a gradual build-up of silt behind the dam. The resulting decrease in depth had adverse effects on the hydropower generating capacity and on the flood-control ability of a dam. This inevitably led to additional costs and environmental concerns when future dredging was required.

Coal

Coal was expected to maintain a dominant share of electricity fuel markets in the future, as it had since the 1980s. Part of the reason for coal maintaining a large share of the electricity fuel market lay in coal's global abundance. Coal was the most abundant and widely distributed of the fossil fuels. Based on 1999 global consumption, known reserves were projected to last for 220 years. Electricity generated through the combustion of coal was expected to decrease from 36 per cent of the global total in 1997 to 34 per cent in 2020. The world's highest growth rate for coal demand was in China, where the share of world coal consumption for electricity generation was projected to increase from 15 per cent in 1997 to nearly one-third in 2020. China had been the leading consumer of coal in the world since 1982, followed by the United States, whose coal consumption was expected to increase by roughly one-third by 2020. India was also projected to experience rapid growth in coal consumption, despite the government's desire to increase natural gas use for electricity production.

The largest factor against coal as a fuel for electricity generation was its high carbon intensity, leading to the highest carbon dioxide output of any fossil fuel. Carbon dioxide was acknowledged to be the primary pollutant responsible for global warming. While combustion of coal was used in many different industrial processes, combustion for the purpose of generating electricity

was the single-largest contributor to the emission of global warming gases into the atmosphere.

Renewable Sources

The problems associated with traditional technologies had created a market for the so-called "new renewables": solar, wind, biomass and geothermal. Although these technologies formed only a miniscule percentage of global electrical generating capacity in 2001, they were the most rapidly growing. Solar energy technology consisted of thermal applications, for home heating, and photovoltaic (PV), which was used to generate electricity. While the cost of energy generated by solar PV had decreased substantially since the 1970s, it was still not competitive with wind energy on a kilowatt-hour basis. The cost of electricity generated by utility-scale photovoltaic systems was approximately $0.218 per kilowatt-hour in 1995. This cost was projected to drop to $0.131 in 2005, and to $0.087 in 2010. However, like wind energy, solar PV was particularly attractive in developing regions of the world, where there was a need for electrical capacity that could be implemented rapidly.

The Kyoto Protocol

Except for nuclear war or a collision with an asteroid, no force has more potential to damage our planet's web of life than global warming.[3]

In 1997, representatives from more than 160 nations met in Kyoto, Japan, to negotiate an agreement that would limit greenhouse gas emissions in the developed nations, pursuant to the objectives of the Framework Convention on Climate Change of 1992. The result of this meeting was the Kyoto Protocol—an agreement among the developed nations to limit their greenhouse gas emissions, relative to the levels emitted in 1990. Under the protocol, 38 industrialized countries—but not the less developed countries—agreed to reduce their overall emissions to between six per cent and eight per cent below 1990 levels by

2012, with a range of specific reduction requirements for different countries.

The United States had signed the protocol in 1998, but by 2001, was refusing to ratify it. Since the United States generated 20 per cent of the world's global warming gases, without U.S. ratification, many feared the protocol would die. The European Union countries however had expressed their intention to meet their Kyoto obligations. For the Kyoto Protocol to be successful, a greater emphasis on renewable energy sources would be required, since fossil fuels were a major contributor to global warming.

THE FUTURE OF WIND ENERGY

According to Enron's senior vice-president, Robert Gates:

> Wind looks likes it could really start to take off. Our costs are coming down. Gas prices are going down, but can gas prices continue to go down? Everybody in the whole world, particularly in North America, is building infrastructure that is going to use cheap, plentiful natural gas. This can't go on forever. You can't keep building 1000 megawatts gas-fired power generating plants and use gas in homes. At some point there are no more dinosaurs, so there's some limit . . . who knows what it is. But we had a philosophy that said, at two cents, how much cheaper can it get? So we said if wind is going to take off, because we're coming down and they're coming up, there's some point out there in the future where the cost curves cross and there is a huge market.

By the fall of 2000, Robert Gates' prediction that natural gas prices would rise had come true. Natural gas prices had tripled in less than a year, driving up electricity prices in California, as power plants competed with industry and consumers for the available supply. Wind-generated electricity, which was now significantly cheaper than gas-generated on a kilowatt-hour basis, suddenly looked like a very attractive alternative.

The idea of harnessing the power in the wind was not a new one. The most obvious—and earliest—method of deriving power from wind was through the sailboat. Indeed, later sail-type windmills were derived from the technology used at the time in sailboat sails. The power derived from these early windmill types was used to automate the process of grinding grain or to pump water from underground wells. These early windmills were usually of the vertical-axis type. The first horizontal-axis windmills were used in Western Europe until the early 1900s.

While several experimental wind turbines were developed for electricity generation throughout the 1900s, large-scale government research and development (R&D) efforts did not begin until the global oil crisis of 1973. These R&D efforts were focused on developing larger wind turbines, with the aim of achieving greater economies of scale. Development of large-scale wind energy projects did not begin in earnest until the late 1970s, when governments began to develop incentives for wind-generated electricity. In the United States, this took the form of the National Energy Act, which encouraged the conservation and development of the domestic energy resources. In total, the federal tax credits combined with California state tax incentives resulted in a tax reduction of 50 per cent. This spawned the California wind energy boom of the early 1980s.

During the 1990s, wind energy began to be developed on a more accelerated and geographically diverse basis. Other countries such as Germany, Spain and India had also experienced rapid growth in installed wind energy generating capacity. By 2001, wind energy projects had been developed in close to 50 countries around the world. Wind energy was the fastest growing energy technology in the world, with global installed capacity reaching 17,000 megawatts and growing at between 25 per cent and 35 per cent per year.[4]

In its short history, three major influences had driven the wind energy industry: *political* drivers, *environmental* drivers, and *commercial* or *cost* drivers. There had been no concrete transition from one driver to the next; rather, one could speak of a gradual transition from *political* to *environmental* to *cost* drivers of wind energy development. In emerging markets, such as China and India, the situation was unique in that new wind energy development was driven solely by rapidly increasing *demand* for power.

During the early years of its development, wind energy was not cost-competitive with conventional power generation technologies. The driver of wind energy development in these years was political, by way of government support, through tax concessions and accelerated depreciation. Indirect political support, through government-sponsored research programs, also aided development in the early years. The motivation for this political support was often a belief in the need to diversify energy sources. In Denmark for instance, the 1970s oil crisis exposed that country's dependence on foreign fossil fuels, due to its own lack of reserves.

Wind energy was also attractive due to its minimal land space requirements. The land space occupied by a wind farm could be simultaneously used for agricultural or other purposes. This was of particular concern in nations of high population density, such as in Europe or Japan, where land costs were relatively high. However, even in nations with low population densities, such as the United States, a wind farm could bring significant royalty income to the owner of the land on which the wind farm was situated. Depending on the strength of the wind resource, a single one megawatt wind turbine could earn a landowner between $2,000 and $5,000 in royalty income per year, with only an insignificant effect on crop yield.

During the 1990s, political support became more progressive for the wind energy industry. In the United States, the Production Tax Credit allowed investors participating in wind energy projects to realise tax credits for wind-generated electricity. These tax credits last for 10 years from the commissioning of the project. While the PTC was set to expire at the end of 2001, the Bush administration had included an extension of the PTC in its first budget. Expectation was that the legislation would be passed. George W. Bush had clearly supported greater North American exploration for oil and gas, particularly in environmentally sensitive areas such as the Arctic National Wildlife Refuge in Alaska. In order to offset adverse public reaction to such exploration, Bush was also expected to fully support incentives for further renewable energy development, such as the PTC. As governor of Texas, Bush had supported the Texas Renewable Portfolio Standard (RPS), which had mandated that 2,000 megawatts of new renewable electric generating capacity be installed by 2009. Through the RPS mechanism, governments in an increasing number of developed countries were introducing legislation that mandated electrical utilities to provide a minimum proportion of electrical energy generated by renewables (see Exhibit 2). The United States, for instance, set specific plans to achieve a level of five per cent of its electricity generation from wind by 2020. The EU was aiming for a 10 per cent wind energy proportion over the same period.

Political support for wind energy development also existed in many other countries. In Canada, the new Canadian Renewable and Conservation Expense regulations gave wind energy developers preferential tax treatment on expenses related to the development of projects, as well as accelerated depreciation on installed equipment. The German government in 1991 instituted its Renewable Energy Feed-In Tariff, which guaranteed a set price for electricity generated from wind. In the United Kingdom, wind energy development had been driven by the Non Fossil Fuel Obligation, a law passed under the 1989 Electricity Act. This legislation obligated regional electricity companies to purchase specified amounts of renewable energy.

A further environmental driver of wind energy was that of market demand. The deregulation of the power generation industry worldwide was forcing consumers to increase their knowledge of how electricity was generated. Where consumers had increased knowledge of generation sources, and a choice between those sources, they were more likely to choose clean electricity from renewable sources such as wind. In North America, this had spawned green-power marketing programs; in the United States, there

The Renewables Portfolio Standard (RPS) was a flexible, market-driven policy that could ensure that the public benefits of wind, solar, biomass and geothermal energy would continue to be recognized as electricity markets became more competitive. The policy ensured that a minimum amount of renewable energy was included in the portfolio of electricity resources serving a state or country, and—by increasing the required amount over time— the RPS could put the electricity industry on a path toward increasing sustainability. Because it was a market standard, the RPS relied almost entirely on the private market for its implementation. Market implementation, it was argued, would result in competition, efficiency and innovation that would deliver renewable energy at the lowest possible cost.

How the RPS Worked

Renewable energy credits, or "credits," were central to the RPS. A credit was a tradable certificate of proof that one kilowatt-hour of electricity had been generated by a renewable-fuelled source. Credits were denominated in kilowatt-hours and were a separate commodity from the power itself. The RPS required all electricity generators (or electricity retailers, depending on policy design) to demonstrate, through ownership of credits, that they had supported an amount of renewable energy generation equivalent to some percentage of their total annual kilowatt-hour sales. For example, if the RPS were set at five per cent, and a generator sold 100,000 kilowatt-hours in a given year, the generator would need to possess 5,000 credits at the end of that year.

Efficiency Advantages of the RPS Approach

First, the RPS avoided the administrative dissemination of funds by government agencies, which could be bureaucratic and inefficient. In addition, government-administered programs almost always imposed artificial constraints of various types, which increased costs.

Second, under the RPS, no renewable energy project was guaranteed a place in the market. Unlike a one-time competition for funds, each project had to continually compete to keep its place in the market created by the standard. For example, existing projects and technologies had to compete with new ones, and project enhancements had to compete with greenfield projects.

Third, the certainty and stability of the renewables market created by a properly designed RPS would enable long-term contracts and financing for the renewable power industry, which would, in turn, lower renewable power costs.

Fourth, least-cost compliance was encouraged through the flexibility provided to generators who were subject to the standard: they could compare the cost of owning a renewables facility to the cost of a credit/renewable power purchase package and to secondary-market credits. Those who were most efficient at generating renewable power would end up producing it, and those who could not efficiently produce it would purchase credits on the competitive market.

Finally, and perhaps most importantly, since large generation companies would be looking to improve their competitive position in the market, they would have an interest in driving down the cost of renewables to reduce their RPS compliance costs. They could do this by lending their own financial resources to a renewables project, by seeking out least-cost renewables applications, or by entering into long-term purchasing commitments. This fostered a "competitive dynamic" that was not achieved with policies and that involved direct subsidies to renewable generators without involving the rest of the electric industry.

Exhibit 2   The Renewables Portfolio Standard (RPS)[1]

1. This information was sourced from www.awea.org/policy/rpsbrief.

were over 150 utilities offering consumers wind-generated electricity at a premium price.[5] The high demand for green power placed further demands on utilities for new wind-generating capacity. According to Gates, this increased environmental consciousness was also demographically driven:

> One of the things that I think helps wind in the United States and in the world is the demographics. People of the baby boomer generation, including me, have aged to the point where they're in positions of responsibility. We look at it more holistically. We should be using renewable energy—that is a correct thing to say. And I think that's going even further, you know, we say sure there's a differential but . . . it costs you more to take care of waste than to dump it in rivers, and that's what we do. It costs more to buy a car with a catalytic converter but we've already decided everybody gets a catalytic converter. Clean is OK. It's OK to pay a little bit more for clean; that's how we're going to run the world. So, I think we are going through a demographic change in generation with a fairly significant differential and perspective as it pertains to energy and the environment, to the benefit of wind energy. And I think as my generation passes out of it and my kids come in, it will be stronger still.

Although environmentally driven market demand for wind energy development was somewhat limited, it was supported through increasing international pressure to curb greenhouse gas emissions. It was expected that the Kyoto Protocol would place a cost on electricity generators for emissions of carbon dioxide. Wind energy development could decrease carbon dioxide emissions. A single one megawatt wind turbine displaced over 2,000 tonnes of carbon dioxide every year from the average U.S. electricity generation mix.[6]

According to Gates, however, cost was still the most important driver in the industry:

> Our view was, and continues to be, that the heart of the issue is cost of energy—that the environmental benefits are nice, but if you are out of the ballpark economically wherever that turns out to be, there is

not a large business to be had. We thought that, in wind, if you have the cost of energy from the wind curve coming down, and if the alternative cost of generation curve is going up over time—now in the 80s it was going down because gas was going down—but if you could get the curves to cross, to where all in cost of wind was equal to or less than the marginal cost of conventional generation, you'd have, for practical purposes, an almost unlimited market for wind—and that's Nirvana.

With increasing implementation, wind energy by the turn of the century was cost-competitive on a kilowatt-hour basis with all other generating methods, if average wind speeds exceeded six metres per second (m/s) (see Exhibits 3 and 4). At the Fortaleza site, wind speeds were between eight and 8.5 m/s. Since the early 1980s, the cost of generating electricity from wind energy had declined more than 80 per cent. Where the levelized cost[7] of wind energy was 38 cents per kilowatt-hour in the early 80s, by 2000, it had fallen to a range of between three cents and six cents. Wind looked particularly competitive when compared with gas-fired generation, given the high price of natural gas in 2001. In January 2001, the high cost of natural gas had driven the cost of generating electricity from a gas plant to between 15 and 20 cents per kilowatt-hour in some markets.[8]

The cost of wind-generated electricity, however, was sensitive to the size of the project. In general, a project with a greater capacity could realize economies of scale, which would decrease the cost of energy. The cost of energy was also very sensitive to the average wind speed of the development site. Since the energy contained in the wind was proportional to the cube of its speed, a site with marginally higher wind speed would result in a large increase in energy output, and corresponding decrease in cost of energy.

Another significant sensitivity was the prevailing interest rate. The upfront capital cost of a wind energy project was about twice as high as that of an equal capacity gas-fired power plant (see Exhibit 5). This meant that a higher interest rate would adversely affect the cost of energy

Wind Energy Costs

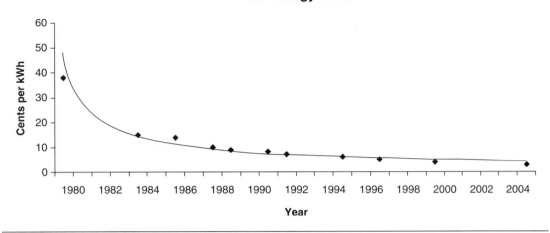

Exhibit 3   Cost of Wind Generated Electricity 1980 to 2005[1]

1. AWEA, 1999.

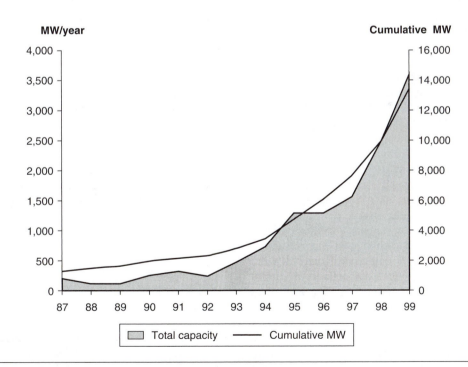

Exhibit 4   Annual Wind Power Capacity Installed—World[1]

1. BTM Consult, 1999.

Technology Type	1996	2000	2010	2020
Advanced Combustion Turbine	459	300	256	251
Conventional Combustion Turbine	325	299	296	295
Advanced Gas/Oil Combined Cycle	572	442	324	315
Conventional Gas/Oil Combined Cycle	440	437	431	431
Gas/Oil Steam Turbine	992	984	982	982
Scrubbed Coal New	1,080	1,080	1,053	1,029
Integrated Gas Combined Cycle	1,796	1,644	1,644	1,644
Fuel Cells	2,185	2,185	2,185	2,185
Advanced Nuclear	2,357	2,357	2,357	2,357
Biomass	3,368	3,361	3,092	2,190
Solar Photovoltaic	4,488	4,378	2,705	2,599
Wind	1,013	795	750	732

Exhibit 5   Capital Costs by Technology (1996 US$ per kilowatt of capacity)[1]

1. www.eia.doe.gov/oiaf/archive/aeo98/ov98/elec.

from a wind power facility. Wind energy advocates also argued that a "social discount rate" should be used when comparing the costs of various forms of electricity generating capacity, rather than the market rate of interest. While it could not be calculated precisely, the social discount rate would be no higher than the rate a government would pay on long-term bonds. Perhaps the interest rate used in cost comparisons should be less in order to reflect the heavy costs future generations would incur as a result of the global warming caused by fossil fuels.

Despite the current global boom in wind energy development, there were still many risks to investment in this industry. While it brought obvious environmental benefits, ironically, wind energy also brought with it some environmental concerns. The most significant of these was the threat posed by large wind farms on migratory bird populations. This issue first came to light in the late 1980s, when a study commissioned by the California Energy Commission determined that as many as 160 birds had died, or had been killed, within the vicinity of California wind farms. This study showed that one of the affected species was the golden eagle, a protected species in the United States since 1963.

As is often the case with such an environmental issue, the project risk inherent in the threat to bird life was a result of the potential for public opposition to specific project developments. This risk could not been taken lightly; in 1999 the Andalusia government in Spain had passed legislation limiting wind energy development in Tarifa, Spain, over concerns that too much wind development would have a hazardous effect on birds at a nearby wildlife area. Enron Wind Corp. itself had also made an agreement with the National Audubon Society in 1999 to terminate its lease on a potential wind farm site in California, in favor of another site nearby.[9] It had been feared that the original site, if developed, would interfere with the flight patterns of the endangered California condor.

In general, industry practice had evolved to mitigate this risk. All projects were required to undergo an environmental assessment, which usually precluded any wind farm development in migratory bird paths. Additionally, the industry trend toward larger turbines necessitated the use of tubular towers. Research had shown that birds could not perch on tubular towers like they could on the original lattice-structure towers, so they were more likely to avoid the development area altogether.

Public opposition to wind farms had also inhibited the development of many projects, based on their appearance, which many felt cluttered the landscape. In addition, early wind energy projects had met with opposition due to the noise emitted from the turbine gearing mechanism. While the technology had advanced to the point that wind turbines were barely audible from a distance of 200 metres, the appearance issue remained. This issue was location specific—in some countries, such as Germany, wind farms were regarded as a symbol of environmental friendliness, while in others, such as the United Kingdom, the opposition had been strong enough at times to cancel projects. Robert Gates stated the following about public opposition:

I think wind turbines are beautiful—beauty is in the eye of the beholder. I think that they're beautiful; I think that they're symbolic of what we should be doing. We should be doing proper, prudent stewardship of the world. That is our job during the time in history when we are in those positions. It's irresponsible, in my opinion, not to use wind. To say that they're unsightly . . . you know, I think that freeway is unsightly, I think those transmission lines are unsightly, but I like the electricity coming on when I turn on the light. I think the road is unsightly, but I want to drive to work.

The visual impact issue was also related to the cultural attitude toward property. In the United States, there was a strong sense of property ownership and the individual property owner's right to choose what he wished to do with that property. This made it relatively easy to win approval for wind power projects, without experiencing the "not in my backyard" problem that arose elsewhere, such as in the United Kingdom. The United States, of course, was not as densely populated, so a wind farm was less likely to intrude on another property owner's rights. In other countries, such as China, the nature of the planned economy created a completely different attitude toward property. In this case, the individual had very little capacity to object to the development of a wind or other energy project.

One way of mitigating public opposition to the visual impact of wind power projects was to locate them offshore. In 2000, Enron Wind had completed one of the world's first offshore wind parks on the Utgrunden shoal in southeastern Sweden. The size of the global offshore wind energy resource, however, would depend greatly on technology, since current technology limited economic exploitation to relatively shallow waters. The increased cost of offshore construction and connection to land-based transmission lines was expected to be offset by more favorable winds and lower site acquisition costs. Offshore costs were projected to be roughly the same as moderately good land-based sites—about five cents per kilowatt-hour. Denmark had embarked on an ambitious wind power development program whereby much of the expansion would be through offshore wind parks. While siting wind power plants offshore minimized land and visual impacts, it was not certain what the environmental impact on marine ecosystems would be.

On the technical side, wind suffered from the fact that it was an intermittent source of power. This characteristic was more significant in power markets that had undergone deregulation. Unlike other sources of power, wind could neither be scheduled, nor could it be stored. In deregulated markets, power generators who wished to participate in the spot market, where prices were usually higher, needed to be able to deliver a definite amount of capacity for a fixed period of time. Since wind was variable, this was not possible. According to Gates:

You can't schedule wind. In the electric industry, the whole supply infrastructure is set up on dependable power, dispatchable power. People schedule to deliver power. They either deliver it or they pay liquidated damages. It is really straightforward, and really right-angled—a real square hole, and we are a round peg, because we just show up. So the easy answer on the electrical system, is to say, "wind doesn't fit." The challenge that we and others in the industry have, is to say, well wait a minute, we just have to do this.

The intermittency of wind meant that wind farm developers had to secure a long-term (usually 20 to 30 years) power purchase agreement (PPA) with an electricity retailer, who agreed to purchase all the electricity produced by the wind farm over its lifetime, at a set price. The intermittency drawback to wind-generated electricity also meant that wind farms had lower capacity factors[10] than other forms of electricity generation. Typically, sites with average wind speeds in the 7 to 8 m/s range resulted in capacity factors of 30 per cent to 40 per cent. By comparison, gas-fired power plants could achieve capacity factors over 80 per cent, since they needed to be shut down only for routine maintenance or safety reasons.

It was also feared that the intermittency of wind could ultimately limit the amount of wind-generated electricity that could be incorporated into a power grid.

A further challenge to wind project development was the nature of the electrical transmission system. Under a regulated electrical industry, the utility aimed to build new power generation capacity close to a metropolitan centre in order to minimize the costs of connecting to the power grid. Gates stated:

> The way the transmission system evolved was you had centralized generators, and a spider web going out to feed load. Almost by definition, the really good wind sites are where people *aren't*, because they're usually in really crummy places to live. People started near the sea, near harbors and towns and rivers. And mountain ridges are where the wind is really good. So almost by definition, there's not much transmission where there's really good wind. And if there is, it's spotty. So how do you plug in new generation into an electric system that wasn't set up to do that at all? The easy answer is you put in giant new wires, but that adds to the cost, which brings the cost of wind up.

The trend in deregulated electricity markets had been toward distributed generation—small-scale stationary applications of electric generating technologies. Distributed generation aimed to move away from the traditional practice of building large-scale, centralized power plants. This would minimize the transmission losses associated with transporting power over large distances. Wind energy suffered from both the lack of transmission infrastructure in windy areas and the loss of electricity from long-distance transmission.

Ironically, the very nature of prime wind energy locations was such that it made construction of wind farms difficult and risky. Where there were high winds, there was potential for a wind energy project. However, the larger a wind turbine became, the more difficult it became to transport it to a construction site and to lift it into position for installation. The largest wind turbine capacity had grown from under 500 kilowatts in the late 1980s to over 1.5 megawatts by 2000. Since there were economies of scale to be realized through manufacture of larger turbines, the capacity was expected to grow to as high as five megawatts in the foreseeable future. Larger turbines could not be transported in a normal shipping container—this necessitated special transportation arrangements that added to project cost.

ENRON CORPORATION[11]

Although it was headquartered in Houston, Texas, Enron was a global player and one of the world's leading electricity, natural gas and communications companies. In the year 2000, Enron had assets of $53 billion and revenues of $101 billion. The company was formed in July 1985, when InterNorth Inc. of Omaha Nebraska merged with Houston Natural Gas Corporation.

Houston Natural Gas had existed since the 1920s, concentrating its resources in Texas and the upper Midwest. Northern Natural Gas, which would go on to become InterNorth in 1980, was formed in 1930 to transport gas from the Texas Panhandle to the Midwest. Three years later, Northern had a pipeline network stretching from Texas to Minnesota.

In the decades leading to their merger, Northern and Houston grew through acquisitions and through expansion of their operations from distribution to exploration and production, natural gas liquids processing, marketing and transportation. When InterNorth and HNG merged to form Enron in 1985, the new firm had the largest natural gas pipeline system in the United States. Enron proceeded to expand its core exploration and production business to marketing of physical gas, and by 1990, it was the largest integrated gas company in the United States.

During the 1990s, Enron continued to grow into one of the world's premiere natural gas and electrical energy providers. Indeed, Enron experienced its most profound changes during this decade: In 1990, 80 per cent of its revenues came from the regulated gas pipeline business. Ten years later, Enron derived 95 per cent of revenues and 80 per cent of operating profits from the buying and selling of gas and electricity. In addition to these trading activities, Enron engaged in related risk management and finance services worldwide, and in the late 1990s had begun its foray into communications, through the construction of its own broadband network.

Enron Wind Corp.[12]

According to Kenneth L. Lay, chairman and chief executive officer of Enron Corp.,

> Renewable energy will capture a significant share of the world energy market over the next 20 years, and Enron intends to be a world leader in this very important market. We believe wind energy is one of the most competitive renewable energy resources, and we believe this acquisition clearly positions Enron as a leader in this business.[13]

Enron Wind Corp. was created in 1997 with the acquisition by Enron of Zond Corp. Zond had been developing, building and operating wind power stations since 1981. In the early 1980s, Zond's strategy had been to develop wind power projects in which it—and other individual investors—could maintain an equity interest. This strategy paid off until the end of 1985, when the tax credits that had attracted investors to

wind energy projects were not renewed. As a result, Zond began to explore ways to develop projects for institutional investors rather than individual investors. These efforts led to the initiation of the largest U.S. wind power project in the world, the 77 megawatts Sky River project, a $150 million project which, for the first time, brought in institutional debt and equity.

Why Invest Internationally?

Enron Wind's most significant foray into the international wind energy market was through its acquisition of Tacke Windenergie in 1997. Since then, Enron had created a European division that had the second largest share of the German wind energy market, the largest market in the world. While 2001 was expected to be a high-growth year in the U.S. wind energy market, international investment was attractive for several reasons:

- Higher growth rates were still being experienced elsewhere, mainly in the European Union, where these were driven by greater political support for newly installed wind energy capacity. Since 1993, the European wind energy market had grown by 40 per cent per year.
- The U.S. market had been characterized by a boom-and-bust nature since its beginnings in the late 1970s. This was partially the result of inconsistent tax concessions for wind energy development. The original wind energy Production Tax Credit in the United States had been extended to the end of 2001. It was expected that the Bush administration would further extend the PTC; however, it was uncertain whether this legislation would be passed by the U.S. Senate. Investment in foreign markets had the benefit of smoothing out the variations in the U.S. market.
- Power prices were generally higher in foreign markets. This generally meant wind energy could be competitive with alternative forms of generation, even in less-than-ideal wind sites.
- Although certain countries did not yet have significant installed wind energy capacity, due to their geography, they had sites with excellent

wind energy potential. Investment now could lead to a first-mover advantage, which would greatly aid future investment when growth rates were expected to be higher.

Ideally, Enron Wind hoped to remain at the forefront of the global wind energy industry. While the global installed wind energy capacity had expanded by 3,500 megawatts in 2000, the U.S. market had accounted for less than two per cent of this total. The U.S. market was expected to increase in 2001, however Enron Wind needed to gain a foothold in international markets with greater potential. There were many countries with non- or under-developed wind energy prospects: Brazil to be sure, but in addition to that, Argentina, Chile, Nicaragua, Honduras, Ireland and Japan. Since it was relatively easy to determine which locations around the globe had prime wind energy development potential, there was a certain urgency to acquire such prime sites, even if the intent was to hold them for future development.

BRAZIL: A NATION OF ECONOMIC AND POLITICAL UNCERTAINTY

With a population of 172 million, Brazil had experienced an "economic miracle" at the end of the 1960s, with high rates of growth, combined with relatively low inflation, industrial diversification and some trade liberalization. However, the combination of a repressive military regime and the oil price shock of 1973 brought an end to this miracle. "In looking at the Brazilian economy, over all, economists and other academics began to refer to the 1980s as Brazil's 'lost decade.'"[14] During the 1980s, annual inflation rates ranged from 65 per cent in 1986 to 1,783 per cent in 1989. Two more decades of economic instability followed. In spite of several attempts to introduce stabilization programs, Brazil continued to experience severe cycles of government fiscal deficits, money supply expansion, inflation, currency devaluation, and high and volatile interest rates.

A noteworthy stabilization attempt was made with the introduction in 1990 of the Collor plan by newly elected president Fernando Collor de Melo.

The plan undertook large scale currency reform, wage and price controls, and fiscal and trade adjustments. Collor's currency reform replaced the novo cruzado with the cruzeiro. Unlike the novo cruzado, the cruzeiro was subject to a floating exchange rate. In an even more radical move, the Minister of Economics, Zélia Cardoso de Mello, froze for a period of 18 months all saving and chequing accounts of over US$1,000 and "overnight" accounts of over US$500.[15]

Under the Collor plan, inflation decreased temporarily, but by the end of 1990 was on the rise again. By 1992, after two years of recession and high inflation, Collor and his associates faced allegations of corruption, and with waning popular opinion, he was impeached by Congress. When vice-president Itamar Franco replaced Collor as president, the economy still did not stabilize until Fernando Henrique Cardoso was appointed finance minister in 1993. Cardoso's economic plan, which saw the introduction of a new currency, the Real, in 1994, was initially successful in reducing inflation and boosting real incomes. This success was enough to win Cardoso the presidency in 1994.

Upon taking office in 1995, Cardoso's first move was to win approval for constitutional amendments to deregulate the economy. The Congress however resisted his proposed structural reforms to the public sector and reforms to the tax and social security systems. Despite the continuation of painful cycles, Cardoso was re-elected in 1998.

The second term of the Cardoso administration was further marred by political corruption, this time involving government officials close to the president. This made it increasingly difficult to win support for new legislation. When Congress rejected crucial measure in the IMF-supported fiscal adjustment package, the markets were once again thrown into turmoil. The Central

	1996	*2000*
GDP at market prices (R$ billion)	779	1,139
GDP (US$ billion)	775	622
Real GDP growth (per cent)	2.8	4.0
Consumer price inflation (average; per cent)	15.8	7.0
Population (millions)	158	166
Exports of goods fob (US$ millions)	47,851	55,086
Imports of goods fob (US$ millions)	53,304	55,783
Current-account balance (US$ millions)	−23,248	−25,080
Foreign-exchange reserves excl gold (US$ millions)	58,323	32,488
Total external debt (US$ billion)	181	235
Debt-service ratio, paid (per cent)	41	64
Exchange rate (average; R$:US$)	1.01	1.83

Exhibit 6   Brazil Economic Indicators[1]

1. EIU Country Report, March 2001.

Bank attempted to alleviate pressure on the currency by widening the trading margins early in 1999; however, when this failed, they were forced to float the Real. Within two weeks, the currency had lost 37 per cent of its value. Fortunately, the currency devaluation caused neither a resurgence in inflation nor a deep economic recession—both mainly due to the strength of the financial sector and the hedging of foreign exchange risk by the private sector. It did, however, cause a drop in Cardoso's popularity, which made it increasingly difficult to achieve legislative progress. Despite this, the remaining tax measures contained in the IMF-backed fiscal plan were approved in the first half of 1999.

In 2000, Cardoso's popularity strengthened, as Brazil's debt was upgraded, GDP grew by four per cent, and unemployment continued to fall. The trade deficit narrowed in 2000, and by early 2001 returned to surplus. Net capital inflows rose sharply, as foreign firms began to invest in Brazil (see Exhibit 6).

In looking towards the future the Economist Intelligence Unit report on Brazil was quite pessimistic: Corruption scandals, an energy crisis and a slowing economy have weakened the popularity of the ruling coalition and diverted attention from the reform agenda in Congress. Tepid external demand, tighter fiscal policy and high interest rates will push the economy into recession in the second half of 2001. Continuing concerns about Argentina and the uncertainty in the wake of terrorist attacks on the United States on September 11th will sustain risk aversion towards Brazil and dampen capital inflows. The Real will bear the brunt of this uncertainty, forcing the authorities to retain tight economic policies to preserve economic stability.[16]

The Brazilian Electricity Sector

As of 1998, Brazil had installed electric capacity of 62.4 million kilowatts, 87 per cent of which was hydropower. Together with Paraguay, Brazil maintained the world's largest operational hydroelectric complex, the Itaipu facility on the Paraná River, which had a capacity of 12,600 megawatts. The remainder of Brazil's electricity generation capacity came from coal and a rapidly increasing amount from natural gas. Brazil's small northern and larger southern electrical grids were interconnected in January 1999 to form a unified grid that served 98 per cent of the country.

Growth in electricity demand in Brazil had exceeded GDP growth in recent years, and many analysts were concerned that construction of new generation facilities would not keep pace with demand, resulting in shortages. Construction of new generation capacity had not been occurring as quickly as government officials had hoped. In the southern part of the country, hydro sources were considered to be mostly exploited, and heavy reliance on hydropower had left the country's electricity supply vulnerable to drought and water shortages. Further expansion of the existing hydroelectric capacity was considered uneconomical and could not be realized without significant environmental consequences. In an attempt to meet growing power demand, Brazil had begun importing electricity from neighbouring Argentina. In April 2000, plans to import electricity from Venezuela proceeded when Venezuela announced its intention to construct 500 kilometres of electric transmission lines to join the two countries, after reaching agreements with indigenous peoples living along the border area.

Privatization of the electricity sector in Brazil began in 1995, although it stalled slightly following the January 1999 currency devaluation. Generation was in the process of changing over to private control, distribution was mostly in private hands, and transmission was expected to remain under government control in the near term. Eletrobras, the federal utility company, controlled 50 per cent of the country's installed capacity and most of the large transmission lines. Eletrobras had been unable to divest the three largest generation companies, and the federal government had instead announced in 2000 that its priority was to focus on the construction of new capacity. There were no plans to sell the transmission assets. Eletrobras co-ordinated and supervised the expansion and operation of the generation, transmission and distribution systems, as well as assisting in financing the expansion of the power sector, making it one of the largest agencies for long-term financing in the country.

To facilitate the purchase of electricity both in the domestic market and from its neighbors, Brazil had begun the process of creating a wholesale energy market. Under such a system, generation, consumption and prices would follow free market conditions, allowing for quicker responses to the fluctuations of supply and demand. The Brazilian Wholesale Electric Energy Market Administrator (ASMAE) announced in April 2000 intentions to create an Internet-based electric trading system. The system was expected to be operational by late autumn 2000 or early winter 2001.

One factor that had the potential of increasing cross-border sales in electricity was the MERCOSUR common market (see Exhibit 7), which had existed between Brazil, Argentina, Paraguay and Uruguay since December 1994. This market would allow for cross-border sales of electricity and the equipment used to generate that electricity. Since Brazil favored energy developers who also had a local manufacturing presence, this introduced the possibility of manufacturing certain wind turbine components in Brazil. For instance, Enron Wind could assemble its wind turbines in Brazil or another MERCOSUR country and have open access to the whole MERCOSUR trade area.

Foreign firms that had successfully bid for Brazilian generation facilities included U.S.-based Duke Energy, which, in July 1999, purchased Paranapanema, part of the former Sao Paulo Energy Company, with installed capacity of 2,300 megawatts. By January 2000, Duke owned about 95 per cent of Paranapanema. In September 1999, U.S.-based CMS Energy announced plans to buy a controlling stake in Grupo Companhia Paulista de Energia Electrica (CPEE), a group of electricity distribution companies. At the same time, U.S.-based El Paso Energy commissioned the 158-megawatts Rio Negro power plant, which supplied Eletronorte, an Eletrobras subsidiary. El Paso was also in the process of completing the 409-megawatts Termonorte project, which would supply western Brazil with natural gas sources from the Urucu

Mercosur emerged from a bilateral integration agreement, originally between Argentina and Brazil, that signed a Treaty on 29 November 1988 establishing a 10-year timetable for the creation of a common economic area. In July 1990, the two countries decided to shorten this time period and set 1 January 1995 as the date for achieving their common market.

The process being opened to other countries, Paraguay and Uruguay joined Argentina and Brazil in signing the Treaty of Asunción on 26 March 1991, which marked the official birth of Mercosur.

Brazil represented 80 per cent of the population and a little less than 70 per cent of overall GDP. Brazil and Argentina together represented around 95 per cent of the population and of the GDP.

Integration of Energy

Energy constituted a very important element in the integration process, and the region had already carried out some bi-national projects such as the Salto Grande dam between Argentina and Paraguay and the Itaipu dam between Brazil and Paraguay.

Hydro-electric power was Mercosur's major energy resource, accounting for 52 per cent of the region's total production, followed by coal (16 per cent) and uranium (12 per cent)—these last two fuels being produced mainly in Brazil—followed by biomass energy (nine per cent), oil (six per cent) and gas (five per cent). With regard to consumption, however, 43 per cent was satisfied by oil.

The energy integration process consisted of two elements:

- The closer alignment of legislations regarding prices, taxation, the environment or technical standards;
- Physical exchanges of energy and networks.

Closer Alignment of Legislations

Traditionally, there had been major differences between the various energy legislations—these were now being reduced. Argentina had carried out a liberalizing process whereby the energy sector was opened up and privatized, whereas Brazil had retained a rigid structure characterized by the predominance of two national companies, Petrobras and Electrobras. The situation in Brazil was beginning to change—a privatization process had been set in motion in order to attract foreign investment.

As a result, the distributing companies dependent on Electrobras had either been privatized, or were about to be privatized and in July 1995, the Brazilian Parliament passed a law opening the way to private initiatives in the electricity sector.

Mercosur's Sub-Committee on Energy carried out a comparative analysis of legislation on energy in the various countries and submitted a report in November 1994. Their work revealed a lack of uniformity in the legislations of the various member countries and examined to what extent such differences could represent a hindrance to integration.

The Sub-Committee identified no major obstacles to integration in the electricity sector. While clear differences between the legislations existed, they did not entail distortions in trade. This was hardly surprising given the bi-national experience acquired in this area. The Sub-Committee merely noted the absence of any legislation concerning the supply of electricity from one country to another through the network of a third and suggested that various arbitration procedures be introduced to solve conflicts between the countries regarding the purchase and sale of electricity.

While progress had been made to integrate the electrical grids between MERCOSUR countries, exchanges of electricity between the countries were still very limited for technical reasons (different frequencies and voltages) and financial reasons (delays in payments). Above all, the interconnection between the Argentinian and Brazilian electrical systems had not yet been carried out.

The integration of the electrical systems would, however, have some advantages:

- It would enable the hydroelectric sources located in areas with different rainfalls to complement each other;
- It would optimize the use of a country's secondary hydraulic energy and permit the setting up of large installations. This would be particularly true in the case of Brazil.

Exhibit 7   Mercosur[1]   *(Continued)*

> Such interconnections were hampered not only by legal or financial problems but also by technical difficulties. Brazil's system had an alternating current of 60 Hertz while the other three countries of Mercosur used a 50-Hertz system. When interconnecting, therefore, provision would have to be made to install either frequency convertors or direct current lines.
>
> The borderlands, particularly Chile and Bolivia, were potential producers and/or consumers of gas and electricity. In addition, either one of them could join the new economic area. It was therefore essential to take these two countries into account in order to establish a regional scheme for the integration of networks.

Exhibit 7   Mercosur[1]

1. This information was sourced from http://europa.eu.int/en/comm./dg17/27casa2.

basin. Once complete, the Termonorte project would make El Paso the largest independent power producer (IPP) in Brazil.

Despite foreign firms' attraction to thermal power plants in the Brazilian market, Brazil's wind power potential had seen little attention. While there were sites in Brazil with excellent potential for wind power projects, by the beginning of 2001, only 20 megawatts of capacity existed. Over all, the Brazilian wind energy resource was estimated to be over 10,000 megawatts.

While there were certain incentives to investing in wind energy projects in Brazil, these incentives were neither transparent, nor were they automatically granted. Enron Wind would have to fight for them in each project, based on the fact that they had been offered to previous such projects. In each case, the amount of the tax deduction would be subject to negotiation. The possible incentives were offered at each of the three levels of government:

Municipal Level

Enron could request a deduction on the Imposto Sobre Serviços—ISS. This was a five per cent municipal service tax on all services provided to the wind farm.

State Level

Since the electricity sold by the wind farm was considered a good, it was subject to the ICMS (imposto sobre circulaç o de mercadorias e serviços), a sales and services tax of 18 per cent. This tax was also applied to any imported equipment, such as wind turbines, which Enron would be importing from the United States. Enron could request a deduction on this tax.

Enron could also negotiate with the state government to pay certain infrastructure costs related to a project. For example, transmission lines above 69 kilovolts, and other communication based infrastructure could be covered by the state government.

Federal Level

The value-added excise tax, or IPI (imposto sobre produtos industrializados), was applied to most imported goods, at a rate of between 10 per cent and 15 per cent. Enron could ask for a deduction on this tax.

Brazil also had two government agencies to encourage development in poorer regions of the country—SUDENE for the Northeast, and SUDAM for the Amazon region. If Enron could get approval from either of these agencies, it would mean a 75 per cent reduction in income tax.

Investment in Brazilian wind energy projects, as with any international investment, also introduced several risks. The political risk could be mitigated to some degree by using OPIC insurance (see Exhibit 8). However, the

The Overseas Private Investment Corporation was a self-sustaining U.S. government corporation created in 1971 to promote private-sector investment in foreign economies through loans, loan guarantees and political risk insurance. The organization had supported investments worth $84,000 million in 140 countries by 1996.

OPIC financed U.S. business expansion overseas by providing long-term, limited recourse project financing to ventures involving significant equity participation by U.S. businesses. The financing was available for new ventures, as well as expansion or moderation of existing successful operations.

Loan guarantees were typically used for larger projects and ranged in size from $10 million to $200 million. Direct loans were reserved for projects involving small businesses and co-operatives and generally ranged from $2 million to $30 million.

OPIC could provide project financing in countries where conventional financial institutions were reluctant or unable to lend on such a basis. Rather than relying on sovereign or sponsor guaranties, OPIC looked for repayment from the revenues generated by the project itself. OPIC required that there be a projected cash flow sufficient to pay all operational costs, service all debt and provide an adequate return on the investment. Sponsors pledged their own general credit for loan repayment through project completion. In ventures where project financing was impractical, OPIC would consider more conventional lending techniques.

OPIC protected U.S. investors against political risks overseas by offering insurance for American investments in new ventures and expansions of existing enterprises. OPIC insured against the following political risks:

1. Currency Inconvertibility—deterioration in an investor's ability to convert profits, debt service, and other remittances from local currency into U.S. dollars and transfer those dollars out of the host country;

2. Expropriation—loss of an investment due to expropriation, nationalization or confiscation by a foreign government;

3. Political Violence—loss of assets or income due to war, revolution, insurrection or politically motivated civil strife, terrorism or sabotage.

Exhibit 8   OPIC Insurance[1]

1. This information was sourced from www.usembassy-israel.org.il.

---

risk of devaluation of the Real was not so easy to mitigate.

ENRON'S INVESTMENT STRATEGY

In the fall of 2000, it became clear that Enron Corp. intended to follow a strategy that concentrated on trading and communications, while moving away from equity ownership in large-scale power plant projects, gas-fired, wind or other types. For 2001, this meant Enron Wind could not count on its parent's support for the Fortaleza project. Gates wondered what this change in the parent corporation's strategy meant for Enron Wind Corp. Should Enron Wind pursue the Brazilian wind energy market on its own? Should Enron Wind be at all involved in equity ownership of wind power facilities? Where was the money in the wind energy value chain?

In the short term, Enron Wind had plenty of investment alternatives in the United States. According to Gates:

The really big growth market for wind is the United States. You've got the money, you've got the people attitude that paying a little more for green is OK. If gas prices remain where they are, we think it will be OK without the PTC.

The PTC is a mixed blessing—it brings down the cost because part of the revenue comes from tax. But it is a very small market to use that tax credit. So as wind grows, you have more and more supply of investment chasing, at some point a finite amount of tax-credit-available capital to invest.

Robert Gates gazed out his office window at the array of wind turbines in the Tehachapi Pass. These wind farms were the heart of the U.S. wind energy industry. Gates wondered, however, how long the U.S. industry would remain strong. What would be the impact if the PTC were not extended? What effect would it have if the United States didn't support Kyoto? Should Enron Wind pursue Brazilian and other international opportunities now to mitigate the risk of a United States downturn?

NOTES

1. GE Power Systems news release. "GE Power Systems signs agreement to acquire Enron Wind's business," www.gepower.com/corporate/en_us/aboutgeps/releases/022002.pdf, February 20, 2000.

2. Material in this section was sourced from www.eia.doe.gov.

3. "Feeling the Heat—Special Report—Global Warming," *Time Magazine*, April 9, 2001, p. 16.

4. "Wind energy's costs hit new low," *AWEA news release*, March 6, 2001.

5. WEW, Vol. 19, No. 903, June 30, 2000.

6. "Large wind projects seeing all-time low costs," *Wind Energy Weekly,* Vol. 20 #936, March 9, 2001.

7. The levelized cost of energy is defined as the cost in current dollars of all capital, fuel, operating and maintenance expenses associated with a generating plant over its lifetime, divided by the estimated output in kilowatt-hours over its lifetime.

8. "As demands for energy multiply, windmill farms stage a comeback," *Wall Street Journal*, January 26, 2001.

9. "National Audubon applauds Enron Wind Corp. decision to pursue alternate site for wind power development," *National Audubon Society Press Release*, November 3, 1999.

10. The capacity factor represents the total number of kilowatt-hours generated by an electricity plant in one year, divided by the total kilowatt-hours which could have been generated if the plant had been operating at full capacity for the entire year.

11. More information on Enron Corp. can be found at www.enron.com.

12. More information on Enron Wind Corp. can be found at www.wind.enron.com.

13. "Enron forms Enron Renewable Energy Corp.; Acquires Zond Corp., Leading developer of wind energy power," Enron Corp. press release, January 6, 1997.

14. Lada do Brasil. Harvard Business School Case #9-392-122, June 1993.

15. Ibid.

16. Country Report: Brazil. *The Economist Intelligence Unit,* October 2001.

EUROGRAIN (PHILIPPINES) AND HYBRID CORN

Prepared by Professor Don Lecraw

Version: (A) 2002-10-18

Dr. David Surgiss, director of seed hybridization for Asia for Eurograin, opened the meeting in Eurograin's offices in the Citibank Tower in Manila:

Since 1991 we've come a long way with our hybrid corn seed operations in the Philippines. Over the past four years we have increased our market share from four to 25 per cent. Pioneer still is the market leader with 60 per cent of the market, but we are well on track. Cargill has 15 per cent of the market. The question now is what, if anything, should we do relative to the emerging dynamics of the corn market in the Philippines?

As I see it, there are three major, on-going developments that could have a substantial impact on the corn industry in the Philippines over the next five years. First, the government has announced its intention to relax its stringent import quotas on corn and replace them over time with tariffs. These tariffs will then be reduced over time leading to a substantial liberalization of the corn market in the Philippines. Second, the government, under the Gintong Ani (Golden Harvest) program has instituted a number of measures to assist farmers to increase their productivity—encouraging the use of hybrid seeds, financial support for input purchases and research into the development of single-cross hybrid seeds suitable for the Philippines—so that they can meet the challenge of more intense international competition in the future. Third, the government is slowly proceeding toward introducing laws on Plant Variety Protection (PVP) to give the developers of new hybrid seeds protection against anyone who tries to copy new hybrids once they have been developed.

The final outcome, and the time horizon of all three of these government initiatives, is still uncertain. How should Eurograin respond to this emerging policy environment? Should we act now in a major way to commit substantial resources to our seed operations in the Philippines, or should we wait until the policy environment becomes clearer over time?

Eurograin and the Philippines

Eurograin started operations in the Philippines in 1978. By 1996, it had operations in Lucena City, traded sugar and soya beans, engaged in financial trading and developed and supplied hybrid corn seeds. Eurograin (Philippines) was a relatively small subsidiary of Eurograin (Europe), one of the largest grain traders in the world. Although Eurograin's (Philippines) operations were relatively small in terms of profits and revenues, the success of its operations was important to the parent company in achieving its goal of developing a major strategic presence in the Asia-Pacific region. Eurograin's hybrid corn seed operations were still small relative to its other activities in the Philippines.

From 1981 to 1991, Eurograin had developed its own hybrid corn seeds, produced them

through contract farmers, and distributed them itself. By 1994, however, Eurograin's competitive position was weak and its market share was low and declining, as it had lagged behind Pioneer, the market leader, and Cargill in developing hybrids that were suitable to conditions in the Philippines. In 1991, Eurograin had downsized and reorganized its corn operations drastically by turning over production, distribution and marketing of its seeds to Asia Agricultural Development Company (AADC) on a five year agreement. Eurograin concentrated on developing a competitive advantage in corn seeds through intensive R&D in hybridization so that its seeds would be appropriate to the soil and climatic conditions in the Philippines. Starting in 1992, Eurograin's corn operations had begun to expand. They had grown rapidly, however, over the past four years. Depending on developments in the corn industry in the Philippines, they had the potential for further substantial growth.

Development of hybrid corn was not a substantial part of Eurograin (Europe) operations. Eurograin (Europe) had only been developing hybrid seed corn for the past 20 years. It had about four per cent of the U.S. market, compared to Pioneer, whose sole business was seeds, with 43 per cent of the market and the next largest competitor with only eight per cent of the market. Outside the United States, Eurograin had a substantial share (45 per cent) of the hybrid corn seed in Europe. But Pioneer's dominant share of the huge U.S. market made it the largest producer of hybrid corn seeds in the world. Eurograin (U.S.) wanted to change this situation by increasing its share of the U.S. market, on the one hand, and by becoming the major producer of hybrid corn outside the United States on the other. Operations in Asia were a key part of this strategy.

The Corn Industry in the Philippines

In 1995, corn production in the Philippines had reached about 4.5 million metric tonnes, up from three million metric tonnes in 1990. Planted area was about 3.3 million hectares located in two regions: the Cagayan Valley in northern Luzon (53 per cent of production) and in Mindanao in the south (47 per cent of production).[1] Productivity (output per hectare) was relatively low, however. Only 17 per cent of production used three-way cross hybrid seeds, the remainder was from open pollination; there was no production from single-cross hybrid seeds.[2] Yields from three-way cross hybrid seeds were about 4.5 metric tonnes per hectare per crop cycle with two crops per year in the Philippines. Yields from non-hybrid seeds were 1.0 to 1.5 metric tonnes per hectare. For single-cross hybrids, yields were about 20 higher than for three-way cross hybrids. In the United States, yields were about 10 metric tonnes per hectare, but there was only one crop per year. In the Philippines there were two crops: a dry season crop and a wet season crop. In Thailand, a major competitor in corn trade in the region, over the past three years, all production had changed from open pollination and three-way cross hybrids to single-cross hybrids with yields of about 5.5 metric tonnes per hectare.

There were several problems in the corn industry in the Philippines. Corn prices fluctuated widely and averaged between five and six pesos ($0.20 to $0.25) per kilogram to farmers.[3] These prices were typically 20 to 30 per cent above world prices. Domestic demand for corn in the Philippines was between five and 5.5 million metric tonnes per year; production was only 4.5 million metric tonnes. Each year government regulators in the Department of Agriculture estimated supply and demand and authorized importation of corn to meet the estimated supply-demand gap. Within this quota, imported corn faced tariffs of 30 per cent. Imports of corn outside this quota faced tariffs of 100 per cent. When government estimates were not correct, the resulting supply/demand imbalance had led to significant price fluctuations. Over the past five years, corn prices had been as high as 10 pesos per kilogram to as low as four pesos per kilogram.

Post-harvest support—drying, storage, transportation and distribution—was poor resulting in substantial wastage (25 to 30 per cent of the crop). Since the Philippines is made up of 7,000 islands, transportation costs were high, especially for production in Mindanao to the millers located in the Manila area of central Luzon. About 90 per cent of yellow corn production was used for animal feed—and most animal feed operations were located in central Luzon, near Manila.[4] Shipping costs from Mindanao to Manila were roughly one peso per kilogram, about the same cost as shipping corn from Bangkok to Manila. Although recent government policies had substantially liberalized inter-island passenger shipping operations, as yet inter-island cargo shipping was still highly regulated and controlled by only a few companies. As a consequence, farmers in Mindanao received one peso less per kilogram to cover the transportation costs to the Manila millers compared to farmers in the Cagayan Valley who were connected to Manila by fairly good roads. In the Philippines, yellow corn was used for animal feed and white corn was used for human consumption. Only one per cent of white corn was produced from hybrid seeds.

As in many low income countries, rural credit was a major problem in the Philippines. In 1986, the "rediscounting window" for low-interest rate loans to small-scale farmers was closed by the Central Bank due to problems with its administration that had led to these loans being directed to inappropriate persons. Under the new "Agri Agra" Law, the government had recently mandated that banks allocate 25 per cent of all loans to agriculture. There were a number of provisions in this law that enabled banks to circumvent it, and its impact on credit to small farmers was uncertain. Most farmers obtained credit from the traders from whom they purchased their inputs of fertilizers, pesticides, and seeds and sold their production of corn at harvest time. The traders covered the costs of these credits in the margins they charged on the inputs and the prices they paid for the corn. Under this arrangement, the traders bore the risks of non-payment due to crop failures and non-delivery.

The prices of fertilizers and other agricultural chemicals were higher in the Philippines than in other neighboring countries by 10 per cent compared to Indonesia and five per cent compared to Thailand. For three-way cross seeds, input costs were 10,000 to 12,000 pesos per hectare and seed costs were 800 to 900 pesos per hectare, about 50 pesos per kilogram of three-way cross seeds. For open pollination, most farmers used little or no fertilizers or other chemicals and the seed cost was about 140 pesos for the 20 kilograms per hectare of seed required.

In Mindanao, land quality is generally lower than in the Cagayan Valley. Rainfall in Mindanao averages 700 millimeters per year compared to 1,400 millimeters in the Cagayan Valley. Mindanao is outside the typhoon belt, and its rainfall is more uniformly distributed over the year. The Cagayan Valley is squarely within the typhoon belt, and rainfall is concentrated in the June to October months. Several typhoons per year directly affect the Cagayan Valley, sometimes with devastating results for agricultural products due to the high winds and flooding. In general, both productivity and returns to farmers were higher in the Cagayan Valley. As a consequence, hybrid usage was higher there as well.

Income in both areas was below the national average, and there was an active Muslim insurgency in Mindanao. The government had an active policy to raise incomes in both regions. As one of its initiatives to achieve this goal, the government had instituted a number of programs to increase corn yields and production. In 1993, the government had purchased three-way cross hybrid seeds and distributed them to some farmers so that they would learn the advantages of the use of hybrid seeds. Initially this program did not offer support for other inputs, the major cost of hybrid seed production. But if hybrid seeds were used without fertilizers and other chemicals, yields would be far below potential (only about 2,000 kg per hectare). In 1995, the government began financial support for fertilizers and pesticides. It also began to develop better post-harvest support facilities, such as drying and farm-to-market support. In part, these government programs had led to the increase in usage of hybrid seeds in the Philippines from eight to nine per cent in 1993 to 17 per cent in 1995/1996.

In 1995, the government also had begun research on developing a single-cross hybrid that

would be suitable for conditions in the Philippines. As part of this project, it had provided funding to the Institute of Plant Breeding at the University of the Philippines at Los Banos, the site of the development of the "miracle rice" hybrids that brought the "Green Revolution" in the 1960s. The first hybrids from this program were expected to be available to farmers in 1996. As of mid-1996, however, only 300 tonnes (20,000 of the planned 40,000 bags) had been produced. Neither the effectiveness of this hybridization program nor the extent of the usage of whatever hybrids that were developed was known.

As of 1995, the two government policies most relevant to the corn industry had been its assistance programs, on the one hand, and trade protection on the other. In 1996, the government announced its intentions for a radical change in the policy environment of the corn industry. As a member of the General Agreement on Tariffs and Trade (GATT) and the WTO, the Philippines had made undertakings during the Uruguay Round of trade negotiations to liberalize its trade regime substantially. For trade in corn, this liberalization would involve three measures. First, over time it would increase the within quota amount for imports. It would initially charge a 30 per cent tariff on within minimum access volume. Second, it would reduce tariffs on imports outside the quota to 60 per cent by the year 2004. Third, over time, it would reduce the tariffs on both within quota and outside quota imports, possibly to zero. The speed of the reductions had not been specified. Other liberalization initiatives in trade in poultry and pork were also announced.

Even this general announcement of intent had led to a strong adverse reaction in the often outspoken Philippine Senate and House of Representatives and in the usually vociferous press. If liberalization did occur, the death of the corn industry was widely predicted due to "dumping" of subsidized corn from the United States and Thailand. On the other side, chicken and hog producers also predicted the demise of their industry if trade in chicken and pork products were liberalized as it was slated to be, unless they could access corn and feeds at the lower world prices.

Mindanao

In Mindanao, armed rebellions by some of the Muslims (called Moros) against the central government had been going on for decades—at an estimated cost of about 100,000 lives on both sides. The problems between the Muslims and the Christians were deeply rooted in history. When the Spanish first came to the Philippines 400 years previously, all of the southern Philippines, up through parts of southern Luzon, had been Muslim, in part by conversion of the people and in part by migration from lands that are now Indonesia and Malaysia. The Spanish landing in 1521, and later fortification in Cebu in 1565, and their capture of Manila in 1571, effectively blocked the northward expansion of the Islamic religion.[5] The Sulu Islands and most of Mindanao remained outside the direct control of the Spanish, although they did claim sovereignty over these lands.

In August 1896, the Philippine independence movement broke out in earnest and spread throughout much of the country, with Philippine independence declared in 1898. In 1898, as part of the Spanish American War over Cuba, Admiral Dewey decisively defeated the Spanish navy in Manila Bay. The Philippine independence fighters supported the United States against Spain. At the end of the Spanish American War, however, the United States paid Spain $20 million for the Philippines; the Philippines became an American colony; and the president of its revolutionary government, General Aguinaldo, was not recognized by the United States. Instead, the United States found itself engaged in an increasingly vicious fight with Filipino revolutionaries. Over the next 40 years, the United States gradually transferred increasing authority to the people of the Philippines. President Roosevelt recognized a newly drawn up Philippine constitution, and Manuel L. Quezon was sworn in as the first president of the Philippines. During World War II, the

Philippines was occupied by the Japanese. In 1946, the Philippines was granted full independence.

The course of Philippine history had important implications for the Muslims of Mindanao. They had never accepted Spanish sovereignty nor that of the United States. For example, when Spain ceded the Philippines to the United States, they had hoped that their traditional lands in Mindanao would be returned to their own sovereign government. They were not—and the most bitter and prolonged fighting of the war was in the south. In fact, some areas of Mindanao and the Sulu Islands were never subdued by American forces. Again, when the Philippines was granted independence in 1946, the provinces of Mindanao and the Sulu Islands demanded that they, too, be granted independence from the central government in Manila, which they regarded as colonial oppressors in the same vein as the Spanish and the Americans.

Over the course of the 20th century, two developments further exacerbated the problems between the Muslim south and the central government. Despite the large domain in which Muslims were the dominant religious group, population density on Mindanao was low. Mindanao was endowed with substantial forest, fishery, and mineral natural resources. Low population density and plentiful natural resources led to massive immigration from the more populated northern provinces to settle its land, on the one hand and to exploit its natural resources on the other. At one time, Mindanao was largely covered in forests. By the mid-1970s, except in inaccessible areas, it had been totally logged and was covered with grasses and coconut trees. As well, in most of the provinces of Mindanao, Christians enjoyed a substantial majority over the Muslims. Not surprisingly, the Muslims felt that they had been despoiled of their resources and deprived of their lands.

The Muslims of Mindanao had had a 400 year history of fighting for independence. In the 1970s, they received substantial political, financial, and military aid from certain Islamic countries and from the Organization of Islamic States. In 1976, President Marcos signed the Tripoli

Agreement, which was to make Mindanao an "autonomous region" within the Philippines. This agreement was not implemented. After the fall of President Marcos in 1986, the government, in an effort to end the rebellion in Mindanao, agreed to allow the people of all the provinces in Mindanao to vote on whether they wanted to be part of an autonomous Islamic region. Given the demographic shifts that had occurred over the previous one hundred years, only four of 21 provinces voted to form this region. Not surprisingly, this outcome did not satisfy the Muslims in Mindanao—and the armed struggle continued.

There were three major Moro liberation groups. The largest and least radical was the Moro National Liberation Front (MNLF) led by Nur Misauri, the original signer of the Tripoli Agreement. Using the good offices of Indonesia, in 1995, the Philippine government had entered intensive negotiations with Mr. Misauri to resolve the conflict. By mid-1996, a draft agreement had been worked out and both sides had announced that the peace process was so far advanced that it could not be derailed. The two sides had agreed to set up a Southern Philippines Council for Peace and Development (SPCPD) headed by Mr. Misauri. Initially, this council would have jurisdiction over 14 of the 21 provinces of Mindanao. MNLF cadres would be disarmed and integrated into the Philippine National Police and Armed Forces to serve in these areas. The SPCPD would have a limited budget and would have some limited authority over education in Islamic schools and cultural activities. After three years, a vote would be taken on whether the SPCPD would become permanent and its powers increased. As well, the number of provinces within the autonomous region of Muslim Mindanao might be expanded, if this expansion were approved by a vote by the people of these areas.

The second largest group, the Moro Islamic Liberation Front (MILF), was more extreme in its demands and had not been a party to the negotiations. This group demanded that negotiations be in relationship to a change in government to a federal system in which Mindanao and the Sulu Islands would have total control over their own internal affairs within a Federation of Philippine States. Finally, the most radical, and by far the smallest, group was Abu Sayyaf. This group was particularly strong in the southern island of the Philippines. It demanded total independence from the Philippines. Both groups had denounced the SPCPD, branded Mr. Misauri a traitor to their cause and vowed to continue fighting until their position prevailed.

Catholic residents in Mindanao felt betrayed by the agreement. They believed that their democratic rights had been abrogated by the government: the Muslim minority had been given control over their lives, not by democratic vote, but by government fiat. They felt that the government in Manila wanted peace at any cost to polish the image of the Philippines and neither understood nor cared about their problems. Some groups had threatened to take up arms to defend their rights. Since Catholics formed a substantial majority in most of the provinces, they believed they could prevail by arms and take back what had been unfairly taken from them.

The hope of the Philippine government was that the SPCPD would satisfy Muslim demands for more control over affairs in the provinces in which they had historically lived and that there would be peace in Mindanao. The initial budget for the SPCPD was projected as being quite small, about $10 million. With the cadres of the MNLF brought into the police and armed forces units stationed in the south, there was hope that these fighters could be integrated into these units, on the one hand, and used to fight against the other Muslim insurgent groups on the other. The majority of the people in Mindanao, however, were against the SPCPD. They felt that their democratic rights to have a government of their own choosing and to determine their own fate had been grossly violated in a "rush for peace" by the central government for its own political purposes. They saw the SPCPD as the "thin wedge" that would be used by Mr. Misauri to expand Muslim influence over all their lives. As well, they were skeptical of the ability and the will of the proposed integrated police and armed forces to deal with the MILF and Abu Sayyaff. Instead, they felt that over time both the SPCPD and the central government would give away more and more of their rights to appease these two groups.

FOREIGN INVESTMENT RESTRICTIONS

Foreign investors in the Philippines faced a number of restrictions that limited the scope of their operations. A foreign-owned company (defined as one with 40 per cent or more foreign equity) could not own land. As well, foreign companies were barred from retail sales operations. Relaxing the ban on retail sales was under consideration by the Philippine congress. The outcome was clear: the ban would be lifted. There was still a great amount of uncertainty over what minimum size of foreign investment—either in total or per store—would be allowed. Together, these two regulations encouraged Eurograin to work through independent farmers who owned their own land to produce its hybrid seeds and to use independent retailers as the final link in the distribution chain.

EUROGRAIN AND CORN IN THE PHILIPPINES: DR. SURGISS' PRESENTATION

As you know, in 1991 hybrid corn seed operations were a very minor part of Eurograin's operations here in the Philippines. And we were not doing an adequate job on the little we did. We had only four per cent of a very small market. Our hybrids were not well-adapted to conditions in the Philippines; our seed quality was low; and our delivery system was not good. We had the wrong seeds; our seeds were poor quality; and we delivered them to the wrong place, at the wrong time. At that time, Eurograin decided that the opportunities were there in hybrid seeds if our operations could be improved.

I joined Eurograin at this time as seeds manager after 11 years at Pioneer in the position of regional research director. As you know, producing a new hybrid takes time, five to seven years. Since it involves successive crosses to obtain the desired result, and each cross takes one crop season, it cannot be rushed.

Even in this short time, our program has been quite successful. At present, our hybrids are at least equal to those of Pioneer, and for some specific areas and conditions they are significantly better. For example, we have developed a hybrid with a strong stalk for use in the Cagayan Valley to reduce damage from typhoons. We transfer our hybrid seeds to AADC who in turn arranges for their production by selected farmers. Sales and marketing of the seeds is also handled by AADC, a subsidiary of the huge Asia Group conglomerate. We provide support for both AADC's production and marketing operations, but the investment cost in these operations is borne by AADC. Large-scale production of our three-way cross hybrid seeds only commenced in 1994, and as of now we have 25 per cent of the market. This gain has been based on quality, not price. Farmers tend to equate lower price with lower quality, so price-cutting is self-defeating. Instead, we have helped in the selection of key farmers in each region to try our seeds in small quantities. When the results are positive, they expand usage of our seeds and other farmers imitate them. Our current goal is to get 50 per cent of the market within two years.

One of the questions we must address is what to do about the single cross hybrid seeds. Two years ago, we began the development process. This research did not require substantial investment. We simply added it to our on-going hybrid development programs with three-way cross seeds. The first single cross hybrids should be ready in 1997. Until that time, however, we will not know how good our single cross seeds are relative to those being developed by Pioneer or the government. There are also several new entrants into the hybrid seed business, such as Bioseed, Asian Hybrid, Philippine Corn, and, yes, even AADC, who are also working to develop their own single-cross hybrids.

Production costs of single-cross hybrid seeds are projected to be two and a half times higher than for three-way cross seeds, about 50 pesos per kilogram compared to 20 pesos. We estimate that the sales price for the single-cross seeds will be about 100 pesos per kilogram, with yields about 15 to 20 per cent higher than for three-way cross seeds. Put another way, the farmer will be paying 900 pesos more for seeds for one hectare. Output will be about one metric tonne per hectare higher—and the farmer can get about 5,000 pesos for this additional tonne. Input usage also needs to be higher for single-cross seeds and will add 1,000 pesos to costs. But overall, the farmer nets more income per hectare.

The usual progression for hybrid seeds has been from open pollination to two-way cross to three-way cross to single-cross seeds. In Thailand, however, the farmers jumped directly from open pollination and three-way cross seeds to single-cross seeds. In Thailand, unlike in the Philippines, the farmers seem to be more open to change. As well, they see the results of the change to hybrids more quickly since they reap more of the gains from the change. In Thailand transportation and post-harvest facilities are better and lower cost. Fertilizer and other chemical inputs are also somewhat lower cost there compared to the Philippines. And the government agricultural credit system and financial assistance are better. Farm size is also somewhat larger in Thailand, so there is an opportunity for farmers to experiment with hybrids on the additional land, with less risk, than in the Philippines. Our estimate is that in the Philippines, most of the initial usage of single-cross seeds will be by farmers who are already using three-way cross hybrids.

We have another problem with the single-cross hybrid: it is much easier to copy than a three-way cross. At present, there is no Plant Variety Protection (PVP) laws in the Philippines. We have great concerns that if Eurograin develops a superior single-cross and commercializes it, it will be copied quickly. As you know, for corn, the output from a hybrid seed is **not** a hybrid itself but commercial grain. So at least we don't have to worry about corn producers using hybrid seed to produce and sell hybrid seeds themselves once they get our initial hybrid.

The government is currently considering introducing laws on PVP. We expect to have a clearer idea of how this process will come out in about a year.

Now in Thailand, there is no PVP either—and Eurograin and other companies have developed, produced, and marketed single-cross seeds. But the situation is different there. In Thailand, there are several established companies in the industry and each one has developed its own single-cross hybrids. Since we are all in the same situation in Thailand, there is little incentive to steal each other's hybrids. Here, there are only two established companies, us and Pioneer, and several new ones, with no experience developing hybrids in the Philippines. The danger of pirating is high. There is a real question of when, or even if, we should go into full-scale production of our single-cross seeds once they have been developed in 1997 unless PVP laws are in place.

A second, and related, question involves how we should be involved in single-cross hybrids, and with three-way cross hybrids as well. As I said before, development of hybrid seeds is time-consuming and represents a major investment. An even bigger investment comes in three areas: production, sales, and post-harvest support services. Since 1991, we have used AADC for both production and sales. Post-harvest support, such that it is in this country, has been left to the traders and to some extent the government.

This strategy may not be the best way to go for two reasons. First, AADC is also undertaking development of hybrids. Second, if we had our own sales and warehouse facilities, we could increase our effectiveness with the farmers, on the one hand, and not be entirely dependent on AADC on the other. On the other hand, AADC has been very effective in promoting our product, even when our hybrids were not satisfactory. With AADC our market share and sales rose substantially. AADC has a wide distribution network which would be expensive to replicate. Even if we were to decide once again to develop our own production and distribution systems, our relationship with AADC might be maintained, but on a non-exclusion basis. It's really up to us since the agreement with AADC expires this year—and AADC has indicated that they do not want to extend it.

Finally, if post-harvest services were improved, wastage would be reduced, and farmers would receive a higher return for switching to hybrid seeds, especially Eurograin's hybrids. Pioneer already has its own seed production operations and its own sales and distribution network.

Another factor to bear in mind is the generally conservative nature of the Philippine farmer. Switching to hybrid seeds is seen as risky, even if the promised benefits are achieved. It is relatively straightforward to demonstrate the value of switching from open pollination to a hybrid or from a three-way cross to a single-cross. Although there are some differences between the seeds of different producers of the same type of hybrid, these differences are much smaller and more difficult to demonstrate. The differences may take several growing cycles to become clear. Hence, it is quite difficult to induce a farmer to switch to another company's hybrid once the farmer is satisfied with the hybrid being used. This gives a strong first-mover advantage to a company that first introduces a hybrid. Most of our gain in market share over the past few years has been with farmers who have decided to move from open pollination to hybrid seeds. Pioneer's "orange sack" has given it a powerful competitive advantage among producers who had initially started using Pioneer's hybrid seeds.

If Eurograin decides to develop its own production and sales operations, development will take time: time to select and train farmers to produce our hybrid seeds; time to recruit and train sales representatives, and time to build and equip two warehouses (one in the Cagayan Valley and one in Mindanao) in which to store our seeds and from which to distribute them; time to line up sales agents among the traders in these two regions; and time to recruit and train agricultural extension agents to work with the farmers to demonstrate to them the value of our seeds and the proper way to use them. And, of course, all these activities will require substantial funds for their operations even before we introduce our single-cross hybrids.

Finally, let me end with a more general observation. To my mind, the world of international trade is changing rapidly, driven by two forces. First, the amount of information available to traders, and business has increased enormously. Through the spread of international and national telecommunications networks this information has become ever more widely available. Just a year ago, we could not phone our plant outside Lucena City. Now, we talk many times a day by phone and e-mail. Traders in Manila have instant access to corn prices in Chicago and have the potential to negotiate landed prices in Manila, without ever leaving their offices. Whenever the landed price of imported corn in Manila is cheaper than domestic prices, traders will know this instantly, and they will exert pressure on the government to allow imports. Some may try to resist these changes, but the pressure will always be there and will mount year-on-year as long as free trade is impeded by trade barriers.

Second, the GATT and the WTO have been a great boon to traders in their drive to increase international trade. The GATT and the WTO give institutional sanction to freer trade and provide a mechanism by which pressure can be brought to bear on governments. President Ramos has shown that he is basically in favor of market liberalization and deregulation across the board. Even such a sensitive industry as oil is soon to be liberalized. Now, in 1998, under the Constitution, there will be a new president. Chances are this will be Joseph Estrada. The *Economist* has called Estrada an outspoken nationalist, protectionist and populist. The *Economist* also states that even if Estrada is elected, his advisers in the government bureaucracy will continue to push for further liberalization—as it is the only way that the Philippines can become competitive. If Estrada turns toward protectionism, the pressure from the business community and from abroad will be intense, and I believe he will have to give in to this pressure.

There is one other factor. Given the volatile situation in Mindanao, much of the attention of the government is directed toward reaching a peaceful solution to the conflict. Yet, corn production is a major source of farm income, and many farmers are Muslims. If trade barriers were dropped on corn too quickly, the economy of Mindanao might suffer. This outcome would be directly contrary to government policy to foster rapid economic development in Mindanao as part of its pacification strategy toward the province.

So trade liberalization will come, even if its speed is uncertain. The biggest question is how the Philippines and the Filipino farmer will respond to this liberalization. Increasingly over time, agricultural production will take place in the country and area where productivity (yield per hectare) is highest. The first question for the long term is whether the Philippines can raise its productivity in corn to world standards. If it can, then the corn industry will flourish; if it cannot, then corn production will ultimately decline. At this time, we cannot know whether the Philippines can indeed do this. The second question is what is the best strategy for Eurograin given the evolution of the corn industry in the Philippines over time?

If we go ahead aggressively now, the investment will be substantial compared to Eurograin (Philippine) resources. But the returns could be very high—if things work out. If we hold back and don't start now, then we may miss the boat and, in two or three years we may find ourselves trying to gain market share against entrenched competitors who were more aggressive than we were.

NOTES

1. One hectare is 10,000 square meters, approximately 2.4 acres.
2. Unlike wheat and rice, the corn seeds produced from hybrid seeds were not hybrids themselves. Under "open pollination" non-hybrid corn seeds were held back from sale and consumption and used as seeds for the next crop.
3. In 1995/1996 the peso traded at about 26 pesos against the U.S. dollar.
4. About 60 per cent of U.S. yellow corn production was used for animal feed.
5. Some commentators have asserted that if the Spanish had arrived 50 years later, all of what is now the Philippines would have been Muslim.

SHIRE PHARMACEUTICALS GROUP'S ACQUISITION OF BIOCHEM PHARMA: BROADENING PRODUCT PORTFOLIO AND ACHIEVING ECONOMIES OF SCALE IN PHARMACEUTICALS[1]

Prepared by Professor David Conklin

Version: (A) 2003-08-18

INTRODUCTION

This is a very positive strategic move for BioChem and its shareholders. The pharmaceutical industry is rapidly consolidating, and new leaders are emerging. In this environment, scale and leadership are increasingly important. We are excited by the prospects of the combined company: our two companies complement each other extensively and the combined pipeline and financial strength are impressive. The combined company is on track to become one of the world's leading specialty pharmaceutical companies.[2]

—Francesco Bellini, Chief Executive Officer (CEO) of BioChem

BioChem Pharma's recognition of a need to achieve greater size in order to compete led to a merger with Shire Pharmaceuticals (Shire) in May 2001. In order to maintain competitive momentum, both companies needed to grow. Attaining adequate financial resources to fund research and development was one of the most significant ongoing issues in the pharmaceutical industry. The escalating investment in pharmaceutical research and development was one of the chief reasons behind the acceleration in pharmaceutical mergers and acquisitions. Companies would need enhanced abilities to develop and formulate drugs in order to remain competitive.

> The wave of M&A activity in the late 1990's has radically altered the landscape of the pharmaceutical market, putting intense presence on other players to keep up. . . . The three-year wave of high profile mergers from 1997–2000 formed mega-pharmaceutical companies on a scale never seen before, sweeping past the smaller pharmaceutical players . . . the remaining rivals floundering to make a dent in markets dominated by products with far more resources behind them. The smaller players must look towards their own mergers and acquisitions to maintain their place in the pharmaceutical industry.[3]

The "Hollowing-Out" Debate

As Canada entered the 21st century, foreign acquisitions of Canadian corporations received considerable public attention. A central concern was that this takeover process might eliminate important business functions and employment opportunities within Canada, leaving the Canadian entity "hollowed out." Commentary focused on the degree to which head offices might be shifted out of Canada to the country of parent corporations. It was feared that this restructuring of head offices might reduce the purchase of certain services—such as legal, research or marketing services—from other Canadian corporations, and the business community as a whole might experience a hollowing-out impact. A job function of particular concern was the role of the board of directors. In the context of hollowing-out of head offices, Canadian board members might now be playing a lesser role than in the past, and this trend might reduce opportunities for participation by Canadians in corporate strategic management.

A series of issues was involved in the view that foreign takeovers were causing the "hollowing-out" of corporate Canada. These included:

- Loss of corporate head office and managerial functions;
- Loss of strategic decision-making opportunities;
- Loss of higher value-added functions;
- Reduced responsibilities for international operations;
- Enhanced tendencies to source more outside Canada;
- Reduced availability of RRSP-eligible shares;
- A thinning of the TSE as companies were delisted;
- The requirement for Canadians to leave Canada to further their careers and
- A general thinning of the Canadian business environment.

At the same time, the Canadian sellers could use the proceeds of the sale to start new businesses, thereby reintroducing into Canada strategic decision-making, high-level positions and, in some cases, new listings on either traditional Canadian exchanges or venture exchanges. This domestic investment process could create significant benefits for the Canadian economy. A series of such issues could counterbalance the hollowing out perspective, including:

- Access to capital for growth;
- Enhanced access to export markets and marketing networks;
- Increased efficiencies in production, marketing, distribution, research or other functions: due to economies of scale, international distribution network or some other factor and
- Increased sales and employment.

Assessment of "net benefit" or "net loss" for Canadians and the Canadian economy involved the analysis of each of these issues, and the assessment could be complex and the conclusions might be somewhat uncertain. Nevertheless, the hollowing-out debate had become an important subject, both in terms of understanding the basic changes that were accruing, and also in considering the appropriate role of government in the foreign investment process.

The Investment Canada Act (ICA)

From 1974 until 1985, the Canadian Foreign Investment Review Agency (FIRA) analysed investment proposals by foreign firms. FIRA had the right to reject applications, and it negotiated with applicants in an attempt to maximize the benefits Canada would gain from each foreign investment. In 1985, Canada replaced its Foreign Investment Review Act with the Investment Canada Act (ICA), which remained in effect at the time of the takeover. Investment Canada's mission included the positive role[4] of encouraging both foreign and Canadian investments in Canada that would contribute to economic growth and job opportunities. The ICA stated:

> Recognizing that increased capital and technology would benefit Canada, the purpose of this Act is to encourage investments in Canada by Canadians and non-Canadians that contribute to economic growth and employment opportunities and to provide for the review of significant investments in Canada by non-Canadians in order to ensure such benefit by Canada.[5]

Initially, Investment Canada was charged with this new responsibility of investment promotion. When this agency ceased to exist, however, the investment promotion function was passed to Investment Partnerships Canada (IPC), jointly run by Industry Canada and the Department of Foreign Affairs and International Trade. Foreign takeovers of large Canadian businesses still required government approval, and the review process was the responsibility of the Investment Review Division of Industry Canada.

The burden of proving net benefit under the Investment Canada Act fell upon the foreign investor.[6] The investor had to provide the director of investment with data and submissions that would enable the director to make a recommendation to the minister, who had the ultimate authority to rule on a given takeover. Should this review determine that a takeover of a Canadian company by a non-Canadian investor was not likely to be of net benefit to Canada, the Industry Canada Minister had the right to either impose conditions for the takeover or absent an agreement to those conditions, to disallow the transaction.

In assessing whether the burden of net benefit had been met, the legislation set out a number of issues that should be considered:

1. For the purposes of section 21, the factors to be taken into account, where relevant, are

   a. the effect of the investment on the level and nature of economic activity in Canada, including, without limiting the generality of the foregoing, the effect on employment, on resource processing, on the utilization of parts, components and services produced in Canada and on exports from Canada;

   b. the degree and significance of participation by Canadians in the Canadian business or new Canadian business and in any industry or industries in Canada of which the Canadian business or new Canadian business forms or would form a part;

   c. the effect of the investment on productivity, industrial efficiency, technological development, product innovation and product variety in Canada;

   d. the effect of the investment on competition within any industry or industries in Canada;

   e. the compatibility of the investment with national industrial, economic and cultural policies, taking into consideration industrial, economic and cultural policy objectives enunciated by the government or legislature of any province likely to be significantly affected by the investment; and

   f. the contribution of the investment to Canada's ability to compete in world markets.

BioChem Pharma

In 1986, Dr. Francesco Bellini co-founded BioChem Pharma, an innovative, fast-growing, biopharmaceutical company based in Quebec. By 2001, BioChem Pharma employed approximately 500 workers and had annual revenues in excess of $300 million. BioChem operated from three sites: two in Canada and one in the United States. For years, BioChem Pharma was Canada's most profitable drug developer, as the inventor of the blockbuster AIDS drug, 3TC. BioChem Pharma was dedicated to the development and commercialization of innovative products, with a focus on the prevention and treatment of specific human diseases, including HIV/AIDS and cancer. BioChem's first therapeutic product, 3TC, also known as Epivir, became the cornerstone of HIV/AIDS combination therapies. 3TC/Epivir is a nucleoside analogue reverse transcriptase inhibitor whose anti-HIV activity was discovered by BioChem in 1989. It is the most widely prescribed anti retroviral for HIV/AIDS and is available in more than 100 countries. This product was also launched as part of GlaxoSmithKline's Trizivir therapy and BioChem received substantial royalties from GlaxoSmithKline on 3TC/Epivir's worldwide sales.[7] BioChem also received royalties from GlaxoSmithKline on its worldwide sales of Zeffix, an oral treatment for chronic hepatitis B. Zeffix had been proven to improve liver function and reduce progression to cirrhosis in chronic hepatitis B patients.

Dr. Francesco Bellini

> I don't like big organizations. I think science is always my first love. . . . This company was getting too big for me.[8]

Italian-born Dr. Francesco Bellini came to Canada in 1967. The respected scientist and successful entrepreneur completed a B.Sc. in chemistry at Loyola College in Montreal in 1972, and then a PhD in organic chemistry at the University of New Brunswick in 1977. In 1984, he set up the biochemistry division of the Institut Armand-Frappier of the Université du Québec, and two years later, co-founded BioChem Pharma and turned it into a worldwide biopharmaceutical leader.

Prior to BioChem, most drug research in Canada was done by branch plants of companies based in the United States and Europe. "I take my hat off to Mr. Bellini, he was one of the first," said analyst Laurence Rouleau of Yorkton

Securities.[9] Rouleau further commended Bellini on his efforts:

> The Canadian biotechnology industry wasn't what it is today. It had a lot less credibility, there were a lot fewer people interested in investing in the sector, so BioChem was the first Canadian success story in a much more difficult context.[10]

Nevertheless, as chairman and CEO of BioChem, Bellini had been criticized for not expanding the company through acquisition. Bellini was a researcher at heart and often felt bogged down in the administration of the large company. Even though he had succeeded over the years in keeping investor interest high with his public relations skills, some remained skeptical of his conservative decisions. Claude Camiré of Dundee Securities admired Bellini's public relations skills but said, "He was less successful in finding new products for its pipeline and this is what forced BioChem to seek a partner." Camiré believed BioChem could have undertaken a $1 billion acquisition on its own, instead of selling the company:

> But (Mr.) Bellini has always been very slow, careful and conservative at looking at new ventures. Acquisitions have not been part of the corporate culture. They have a staff of very bright scientists and have been more willing to develop drugs internally or through collaborations.

> That go slow approach . . . forced Mr. Bellini to entertain offers to acquire the company . . . at least a half dozen major drug companies had a look at BioChem this year.[11]

Bellini had actually begun the search for a partner three years prior to considering U.K.-based Shire Pharmaceuticals. Although Bellini would have preferred to have the company remain in the hands of Canadians, he and his shareholders couldn't resist the Shire offer. "Francesco Bellini . . . had dreamed of creating a Canadian drug research, development and manufacturing group with its own marketing, but said he lacked the resources and Shire was the best merger fit."[12]

	1999	1998
Assets		
Current Assets:		
Cash and cash equivalents	68,791	53,801
Temporary investments	81,460	120,295
Accounts receivable	83,331	64,871
Inventories	3,236	2,312
Prepaid expenses	3,089	2,464
Current assets of discontinued operations	89,620	123,586
	329,527	367,329
Long-term investments	110,324	103,746
Capital assets	137,988	98,778
Other assets	12,880	10,846
Non-current assets of discontinued operations	33,998	51,863
	624,717	632,562
Liabilities		
Current Liabilities:		
Bank indebtedness	—	2,276
Accounts payable and accrued liabilities	45,314	25,122
Current portion of long-term debt	600	942
Current liabilities of discontinued operations	42,558	67,906
	88,472	96,246
Long-term debt	124,614	12,470
Non-current liabilities of discontinued operations	34,767	45,225
	247,853	153,941
Shareholder's Equity		
Capital stock	382,174	408,365
Contributed surplus	9,451	10,199
Retained earnings	(14,582)	45,813
Foreign currency translation adjustment	(179)	14,244
	376,864	478,621
	624,717	632,562

Exhibit 1   BioChem Pharma Consolidated Balance Sheets (for years ending December 31) (in Cdn$000s)

Source: BioChem Annual Report 1999.

SHIRE PHARMACEUTICALS GROUP PLC

Founded in 1986, Shire was an international specialty pharmaceutical company based in the United Kingdom, with a strategic focus in four main therapeutic areas: central nervous system disorders, metabolic diseases, oncology and gastroenterology. Shire's strong acquisition strategy

	1999	1998	1997
Operating Revenue			
Sales	23,412	22,094	20,172
Royalties	172,588	154,122	124,130
Research and development contracts	79,923	33,718	4,004
Interest	7,528	9,869	10,458
Other	6,824	5,162	4,096
	290,275	224,965	162,860
Expenses			
Cost of sales	14,223	11,812	10,491
Selling and administrative	26,081	31,250	30,163
Research and development	87,498	49,116	33,175
Financial	(918)	(114)	(796)
	126,884	92,064	73,033
Earnings before depreciation, amortization and other	163,391	132,901	89,827
Depreciation and amortization	(8,282)	(6,952)	(3,349)
Earnings before income taxes and other	155,109	125,949	86,478
Gain on sale of long-term investments	24,181	—	—
Income taxes	(12,091)	(9,479)	(4,000)
Non-controlling interest	—	1,428	1,797
Share of loss of a company subject to significant influence	—	—	(6,595)
Earnings From Continuing Operations	167,199	117,898	77,680
Earnings (loss) from discontinued operations	(18,097)	(3,124)	2,158
Net Income	149,102	114,774	79,838
Basic Earnings per Common Share			
Continuing operations	1.59	1.09	0.72
Net income	1.42	1.06	0.74
Fully Diluted Earnings per Common Share			
Continuing operations	1.57	1.09	0.72
Net income	1.41	1.06	0.74

Exhibit 2   BioChem Pharma Consolidated Statements of Earnings (for years ending December 31) (in Cdn$000s, except per share amounts)

Source: BioChem Annual Report 1999.

led to six mergers and acquisitions in six years, making it Britain's fastest growing pharmaceutical company.

Shire's expansion has been phenomenal—in seven years its sales have risen from $3M to $500M and its market value has jumped 177-fold to £3.6bn. Last month Shire leapt into the FTSE 100 index as the country's fourth largest drug firm.

Shire (has been built) to a large extent on the back of drugs to pacify disruptive American children. The company is market leader in medicines for attention deficit hyperactivity disorder (ADHD).

Shire's two treatments, Adderall and Dextrostat, have a 36% share of the market for treating ADHD, reaping revenue of $103M in the first half of this year. They account for nearly half the company's overall sales.

Mr. Stahel describes drug discovery as "molecular roulette," pointing out that only one in 10,000 discovery projects typically yields a marketable drug. This, he says is a flaw in the dream of building any biotech company into a multinational corporation. "Statistically, you can't do it, you need to be lucky. Amgen (a leading U.S. biotech company) were lucky but there aren't many Amgens around."

The solution is for biotech firms to license out programs in early clinical trials, allowing bigger players—such as Shire—to share the risk.[13]

Stahel discussed Shire's focus on specialty drugs for specific aliments:

> The company will remain concentrated on specialty diseases, making drugs prescribed by hospital consultants, rather than GPs. This smaller target group means the firm needs fewer salesmen.

> Mr. Stahel says: "The dream is to become the top specialty pharmaceuticals company in the world. I'm not promising that, but we could become one of the top three worldwide within five years."[14]

History of Shire

1986	Founded
1987	Began trading
1995	Acquired Imperial Pharmaceutical Services
1996	Floated on the London Stock Exchange
1997	Acquired Pharmavene Inc.
1997	Acquired Richwood Pharmaceutical Company, Inc.
1998	Listed on Nasdaq
1999	Acquired subsidiaries of Fuisz Technologies in France, Germany and Italy
1999	Merged with Roberts Pharmaceutical Corporation
2001	Merged with BioChem Pharma[15]

These acquisitions enabled Shire to build an expanded global marketing infrastructure, leading to Shire's direct marketing capability in the United States, Canada, United Kingdom, the Republic of Ireland, France, Germany, Italy and Spain. Shire also covered other significant pharmaceutical markets indirectly through distributors. However, the company had come under fire from analysts for relying too heavily on one product, its Adderall treatment for hyperactive children.

THE PHARMACEUTICAL INDUSTRY

Mergers within the last decade between large pharmaceutical companies had created leading enterprises with global market access and sales forces capable of servicing huge product launches. The Shire/BioChem Pharma merger was an example of this continued consolidation. Yet, it was predicted that antitrust concerns would weigh heavily in the future against mega-mergers. "The creation of GlaxoSmithKline, for example, took over 11 months to complete and required some significant product disposals."[16] Nonetheless, the wave of mergers and acquisitions rolling through the biotech sector was still expected to accelerate with the main driving force being competition for new products. As patents expired over the next few years, billions in annual revenues were set to disappear, and pharmaceutical companies were attempting to buy new drugs through acquisitions in efforts to strengthen performance.

The industry in Canada was competing well and was recognized globally as a leader in the field. The Canadian government had seen the importance of the biotech industry and had made financial commitments to aid potential growth. In 2002, an analyst described the significance of Canada's biotech industry:

> About $1.3 billion will be spent in Canada this year on research and development in biotech, an amount that is growing about 24% annually, or four times the average for the whole economy. The Canadian biotech industry ranks second only to that of the

	Consolidated		Company	
	1999	1998	1999	1999
Fixed Assets:				
Intangible assets—Intellectual property	214,856	7,938	—	31
Intangible assets—Goodwill	469,531	—	—	—
Tangible assets	23,256	4,671	874	1,101
Fixed asset investments	1,617	—	881,091	234,942
	709,260	12,609	881,965	236,074
Current Assets:				
Stocks	24,532	6,652	—	—
Debtors				
– due within 1 year	45,488	17,560	1,920	264
– due after 1 year	1,392	—	—	—
Investments	49,850	21,435	708	17,522
Cash at bank and in hand	36,038	8,230	9,814	1,362
	157,300	53,877	12,442	19,148
Creditors: amounts falling due within 1 year:	(107,140)	(14,384)	(19,785)	(1,473)
Net Current Assets	50,160	39,493	(7,343)	17,675
Total Assets Less Current Liabilities	759,420	52,102	874,622	253,749
Creditors: amounts falling due after more than 1 year:	(80,133)	(1,508)	(1,861)	—
Net Assets	679,287	50,594	872,761	253,749
Capital and Reserves				
Called-up share capital	12,226	7,055	12,226	7,055
Share premium	839,026	228,537	839,026	228,537
Capital reserve	2,755	2,755	1,674	1,674
Other reserves	24,247	24,247	18,079	18,079
Profit and loss account	(198,967)	(212,000)	1,756	(1,596)
Equity Shareholders' Funds	679,287	50,594	872,761	253,749

Exhibit 3   Shire Pharmaceuticals Group PLC Balance Sheets (for years ending December 31) (in £000s)

Source: Shire Annual Report 1999.

U.S. in number of firms (about 400), people employed (about 62,000) and annual revenues (projected to be more than $3 billion this year).[17]

Some analysts were concerned that mergers of Canadian companies would result in a negative impact on the Canadian industry as global superpowers gradually took control, but in the Shire case there were expected to be significant benefits for Canada.

Many analysts, including Ernst & Young's Morrison, see Shire's acquisition of BioChem as a positive thing for Canada. "A company getting gobbled up usually leads to a lot of offshoots of new companies," Morrison says, "because a lot of

	1999	1998
Turnover		
Existing operations	131,544	80,328
Acquisitions	2,334	—
Continuing operations	133,878	80,328
Cost of sales and operating expenses	(103,506)	(72,449)
Operating profit		
Existing operations	30,894	7,879
Acquisitions	(522)	—
Continuing operations	30,372	7,879
Costs of a fundamental restructuring of continuing operations	(11,516)	—
Profit on ordinary activities before interest	18,856	7,879
Bank interest receivable	2,334	1,434
Interest payable and similar charges	(181)	(214)
Profit on ordinary activities before taxation	21,009	9,099
Tax on profit on ordinary activities	(8,439)	(2,852)
Profit on ordinary activities after taxation	12,570	6,247
Earnings per share—basic	8.7p	4.5p
Earnings per share—diluted	8.3p	4.3p

Exhibit 4   Shire Pharmaceuticals Group PLC Consolidated Profit and Loss Account (for years ending December 31) (in £000s)

Source: Shire Annual Report 1999.

people with successful track records start their own companies." That's exactly what happened at BioChem. Since the merger, many of the top BioChem managers have left to start new businesses in the greater Montreal area, adding further to the city's growing reputation in the field.[18]

THE STRATEGIC RATIONALE
FOR THE TAKEOVER

In December 2000, Shire Pharmaceuticals plc announced intentions to acquire Canadian-based BioChem Pharma in an all-share deal. The $5.9 billion deal was expected to be completed by the end of March 2001 but was delayed pending

review by Investment Canada, the investment review division of Industry Canada.

The purpose of the takeover was to broaden and enhance the product portfolio as well as deepen its pipeline by acquiring products in all stages of development. "With BioChem, Shire had 25 products in development and targeted 50 in five years."[19] BioChem's early stage programs complemented those at a later stage at Shire. Additionally, opportunity existed to market BioChem's development stage products using Shire's direct sales infrastructure. Overall, the deal was expected to generate strong cash flow for re-investment in the enhanced group's search and development strategy.

Although the takeover would mark the end of a purely Canadian success story, BioChem shareholders voted 99.8 per cent in favor of the deal. With the March 2001 vote, BioChem shareholders would exchange each of their shares for part of a Shire share, valuing each BioChem share at US$37. BioChem shareholders were entitled to receive new Shire shares or new Shire ADSs (American Depository Securities) in exchange for their BioChem shares. Ultimately, Shire shareholders owned 53 per cent of the company and BioChem shareholders owned the remaining 47 per cent. Rolf Stahel, chief executive of Shire Pharmaceuticals Group, said:

> This merger is another important step in building one of the strongest specialty pharmaceutical companies in the world. We see significant benefits from combining these two companies. It will further broaden and diversify our revenue base, strengthen our early phase project pipeline and provide greater financial strength to capitalize on our search and development capability.[20]

The BioChem press release issued May 11, 2001 outlined the details of the closing transaction:

> The merger has been effected by way of a share-for-share exchange, pursuant to which each BioChem shareholder had the choice of receiving as consideration for each BioChem common share held:
>
> - a number of Shire Ordinary Shares equal to the exchange ratio referred to below in respect of the merger;
> - provided that the BioChem shareholder is a Canadian resident, a number of Exchangeable Shares of Shire Acquisition Inc. equal to the exchange ratio divided by three, which are exchangeable into Shire Ordinary Shares or Shire ADSs at a rate of 1 Exchangeable Share for 3 Shire Ordinary Shares or 1 Exchangeable Share for 1 Shire ADS;
> - a number of Shire ADSs equal to the exchange ratio divided by three; or
> - a combination of the above.

As set out in the announcement dated May 8, 2001, the exchange ratio is 2.2757 Shire Ordinary Shares for each BioChem common share held. As a result of completion of the merger, and further to elections made by BioChem shareholders, 67,319,773 Shire Ordinary Shares, 17,292,148 Exchangeable Shares and 37,375,952 Shire ADSs in aggregate were issued to BioChem shareholders at closing.[21]

Under the deal, BioChem's stock, which had performed strongly since first issued in 1986, would cease to exist. Shire shares would be traded on the Toronto Stock Exchange, as well as Nasdaq and London.

> BioChem shareholders and analysts who follow the company, looking at the 40% premium Shire agreed to pay for the Montreal company's shares, heartily applauded the takeover. Besides securing a top price, it was thought that the deal avoided layoffs to its 500-odd staff which would have come from virtually any other sale and also gave BioChem shareholders a near-equal stake in the merged entity.[22]

Shire planned to build on BioChem's research and development and would continue its commitment to the Technology Partnerships Canada agreement, under which the Canadian government and would support Canadian vaccine research and manufacturing. It was expected that Shire's Canadian headquarters were to remain in Quebec with minimal elimination of existing BioChem employees, and no reduction in BioChem's current operations.

The Shire-BioChem merger was approved in May 2001 by Industry Canada Minister Brian Tobin, who believed that the merger would unite two profitable companies that would complement each other. He commented:

> BioChem will benefit from Shire's commercial and clinical expertise, late-stage product pipeline and significant global reach. . . .
>
> Shire will benefit from BioChem's research and development capabilities and its strength in early-stage products. The result of this merger will be enhanced global orientation of the Canadian company's activities.[23]

After analysing the deal's effect on employment, Canadian sourcing, export, competition,

Canada's ability to compete internationally, the participation by Canadians in decision-making and the impact on research and development, Investment Canada concluded that the merger should go ahead as it would be of net benefit to Canada.

In the Shire-BioChem deal, Shire had no intention of hollowing the Canadian head office. Shire was not expected to reduce any operations. Rather, it intended for the merger to add to its existing strengths. BioChem's North American location was an advantage in the 21st century pharmaceutical business, and Shire had contemplated a stronger North American presence for some time.

A merger last year with Roberts Pharmaceuticals of New Jersey boosted the firm's presence in America and there is a temptation for Shire to move across the Atlantic entirely. Mr. Stahel says: "Our U.S. people suggest that regularly but my preference is to stay here. I want to strengthen our position in Europe and Japan."[24]

Over the past five years, the hub of world pharmaceutical R&D has shifted more markedly from Europe to the United States.

While the European pharmaceutical market as a whole is roughly comparable in size to the U.S. market in terms of the number of prescriptions written, it ranks well below the United States in terms of sales, profitability, and growth. This primarily reflects government-controlled healthcare systems in Europe, which dictate which drugs are eligible for reimbursement and at what prices. Operating under constrained budgets, European agencies generally emphasize lower-cost generics and other relatively inexpensive drugs.

Healthcare bureaucracies are also much more cumbersome in Europe and Japan than in the United States. In most European countries, after a drug is cleared for safety and efficacy, the sponsor company usually has to wait up to a year for pricing and reimbursement protocols to be completed before it can commence marketing. By comparison, after a drug receives FDA approval in the United States, it is usually ready for immediate commercialization.

Although the European Union has transformed Europe into a single economic market with the elimination of tariffs and trade barriers, the pharmaceutical industry has not benefited to the degree other industries have. While the creation of the European Agency for the Evaluation of Medicinal Products has simplified and harmonized the new drug evaluation and approval process, products still cannot be sold in individual countries until their respective governments approve pricing and reimbursement. Such red tape often holds up marketing for as long as a year after the drug is approved for safety and efficacy.[25]

THE FUTURE

In explaining the rationale for this merger, Stahel pointed to several important factors:

What the merger brings together is first a major royalty income from antivirals, which BioChem Pharma brings us through their marketing arrangements with GlaxoSmithKline and in the future, subject to government approval, again a major income stream, royalty based from our Alzheimer's drug, Reminyl that will be marketed in most countries by Johnson & Johnson. Secondly, the two companies bring together two strong therapeutic areas for Shire's direct sales, meaning sales through Shire's own marketing infrastructure that already exists in most key markets. These two therapeutic areas are central nervous system disorders (CNS) and oncology/haematology, The third exciting point is that BioChem brings to the combined company very interesting opportunities in the vaccine area, its vaccine R&D. I see this as offering the combined company a long-term growth opportunity. Perhaps last but not least, it brings together two experienced pharmaceutical management teams, and therefore together, we finish up with what I believe is quite an impressive broad management force. If you look at it simply in strategic terms, the combined company follows the following focused strategy. At the business level, we are focusing on innovation rather than on generic or OTC products. We are targeting specialty pharmaceutical doctors rather than general practitioners. Functionally, we are focusing on search, development and marketing. Geographically, we already have in Shire, a presence of seven of the eight key markets in the world. The only one we are not yet covered in is Japan. In terms of therapeutic areas, as I have indicated before, CNS and oncology/ haematology is for direct marketing, antiviral is royalty income, and vaccines offer us long term upside potential. . . .

The two companies bring together enhanced R&D capabilities. They have complementary skills. BioChem is particularly strong in lead optimization. They have a fantastic chemistry team. Shire is perhaps stronger at the clinical end of the development process and in marketing. So in early phase support, we can expect substantial strengthening through the merger with putting BioChem and Shire together. Shire then adds strength at the later phase development and specifically at the marketing end. In terms of numbers, if we look at it from pre-clinical phase one to last phase, phase three and registration, the following figures emerge. Overall, the combined company will have 24 projects. Twelve will be in pre-clinical and phase I, five will be in phase II, and seven will be in phase III and in registration. We are particularly delighted that in putting the two companies together, you finish overall with a more balanced portfolio.[26]

The future looked bright for Shire BioChem, the company resulting from the deal. This was also the case for its biologics business, Shire Biologics. Early in 2002, Health Canada approved for commercialization Shire's meningitis vaccine (NeisVac-C). The implications for this vaccine were huge, as it could even be administered to infants (unlike many other vaccines). Shire Biologics had acquired the rights to sell it in a deal with Baxter International Inc., a U.S. pharmaceuticals company. Ironically, BioChem Pharma once owned the worldwide rights to market the vaccine, but sold them to Baxter. Randall Chase, president of Shire Biologics commented on being given the go-ahead to sell the vaccine:

It is unclear what impact the approval would have on Shire BioChem's sales. . . . Canada has seen a surge in the number of meningitis cases in recent years, with 101 confirmed cases reported in 2000 and 87 in the first six months of last year. Provincial

health departments would be the prospective buyers of the vaccine should they decide to undertake a province-wide immunization.[27]

Another perk for Shire Biologics' balance sheet was the pandemic readiness contract the federal government signed with the company in 2001. Shire had agreed to provide 32 million doses of flu vaccine within 16 weeks of being asked by the government. The cost of providing the vaccine would be in addition to the contract amount. "Shire said the value of the full agreement—pandemic readiness and annual flu vaccine—could exceed $300 million."[28]

CONCLUSION

Canada's federal minister of industry received assurances that Shire would maintain BioChem's investment in research, federally backed vaccine development and production and job levels. These assurances calmed worries that the Shire takeover could harm Canada's science base, and the deal progressed. Rolf Stahel claimed the merger had almost doubled Shire's business. "We've hitched BioChem's product pipeline to our global marketing capacity and we may yet have a blockbuster with annual sales of US$1 billion or more in BioChem's Zeffix oral treatment for hepatitis B."[29]

Shire Pharmaceuticals claimed to have taken only four days to integrate BioChem. "Mr. Stahel said the two companies have worked on the integration while waiting for the deal to be approved by the Canadian government."[30] The deal announced in December was approved by shareholders of both companies in March and was given final approval in May 2001.

As Shire anticipated the deal's closing, it decided to lay off 54 BioChem staff, write down US$85 million of BioChem investments and begin a review of its product portfolio. "The writedowns were part of the US$177 million merger charge, which also included about US$40 million in advisor's fees, US$40 million in stamp duty and US$10 million in severance."[31] Sales for the new merged company rose 32 per cent,

	*Shire**	*BioChem**
Revenues	380.6	156.8
Net Income**	62.0	77.0
Net Assets	681.1	433.4
Net Cash	41.8	186.5

BioChem as % of Shire BioChem	
Revenues	29.2%
Net Income	55.4%
Net Assets	38.9%
Net Cash	81.7%

Exhibit 5   Unaudited Financial Results (for the nine months ending September 30, 2000) (US$ millions)

Source: www.shire.com, accessed June 11, 2003.

* Shire reports in U.S. GAAP, BioChem in Canadian GAAP.

** Net income stated prior to charges and gains.

driven by sales of Shire's best-selling drug for hyperactive children, Adderall. However, while overall company profits rose, some uncertainty existed. "The risk with BioChem's drugs is that Shire will not be able to use its famous marketing prowess because GlaxoSmithKline has the license to sell them."[32]

The Shire takeover did involve some uncertainties, but the future looked brighter for Canadians than continuation of BioChem on its own. The structure of the pharmaceutical industry had evolved to the point where BioChem needed further financial resources to fund the research and development that would be necessary to maintain its competitive momentum. The takeover also provided a stronger global distribution network, which had also become a prerequisite for success.

NOTES

1. This case has been written on the basis of published sources only. Consequently, the interpretation and perspectives presented in this case are not necessarily those of Shire Pharmaceuticals Group or any of its employees.

2. "Merger of Shire Pharmaceutical Group plc with BioChem Pharma Inc. to Form a Leading Global Specialty Pharmaceutical Company," *Canadian Press Newswire*, December 11, 2000.

3. "Is M&A the Key to Survival in the New Pharma Landscape?," *Datamonitor*, November, 2001.

4. B. Little, "New Agency Strives to Erase FIRA's Memory," *Globe and Mail*, July 8, 1985, B1–2.

5. S. 2. Investment Canada Act, 1985. c. 20.

6. Ibid., s.17(1).

7. 3TC, Epivir and Zeffix are trademarks of GlaxoSmithKline.

8. "BioChem Pharma Shareholders Vote Thursday on Takeover by British Drug Maker," *Canadian Press Newswire*, March 28, 2001.

9. Ibid.

10. Ibid.

11. Leonard Zehr, "Shire Merger Only Way Out for BioChem's Bellini," *Biotechnology Reporter*, December 12, 2000.

12. Robert Gibbens, "Shire Plans Fresh Growth after BioChem Purchase: British Drug Firm to Use Acquisition as Global Springboard," *Financial Post (National Post)*, October 15, 2001, FP4.

13. Andrew Clark, "The Man who Sold America Calmer Kids," *The Guardian*, November 18, 2000.

14. Andrew Clark, "The Man who Sold America Calmer Kids," *The Guardian*, November 18, 2000, www.guardian.co.uk, accessed May 27, 2002.

15. Shire Pharmaceuticals Web site, www.shire.com, accessed March 28, 2002.

16. Anderson Consulting, "Deal survey 2000/2001 Health Care," 2001, p. 15.

17. Steven Frank, "The Stuff of Life: Special Report/Biotechnology," *Time*, May 20, 2002, p. 45.

18. Ibid., p. 46.

19. Robert Gibbens, "Shire Plans Fresh Growth after BioChem Purchase: British Drug Firm to Use Acquisition as Global Springboard," *Financial Post (National Post)*, October 15, 2001, FP4.

20. "Merger of Shire Pharmaceutical Group plc with BioChem Pharma Inc. to Form a Leading Global Specialty Pharmaceutical Company," *Canadian Press Newswire*, December 11, 2000.

21. BioChem Press Release, May 11, 2001.

22. Paul Brent, "Toothless Agency Gums up Works: Why the Sudden Interest in BioChem Acquisition?," *Financial Post (National Post)*, April 27, 2001, C2.

23. "Ottawa Okays British Firm's Acquisition of Montreal-based BioChem Pharma," *Canadian Press Newswire*, May 8, 2001.

24. Andrew Clark, "The Man who Sold America Calmer Kids," *The Guardian*, November 18, 2000, www.guardian.co.uk, accessed May 27, 2002.

25. Standard & Poor's, *Industry Surveys—Healthcare: Pharmaceuticals*, December 12, 2002, p. 8.

26. "CE of Shire Pharmaceuticals Speaks About the Exciting Merger with BioChem Pharma in Wall Street Transcript Interview," *Twist.com*, http://twst.com/notes/articles/kaq060.html, accessed May 27, 2002.

27. Paul Vieira, "Shire Unit's Meningitis Vaccine Wins Approval: Made-in-Canada Treatment Can be Given to Infants," *Financial Post (National Post)*, January 15, 2002, FP7.

28. Mark Kennedy, "Concerned about Looming Flu Pandemic, Feds Sign Contract for Vaccine," *Canadian Press Newswire*, October 30, 2001.

29. Robert Gibbens, "Shire Plans Fresh Growth after BioChem Purchase: British Drug Firm to Use Acquisition as Global Springboard," *Financial Post (National Post)*, October 15, 2001, FP4.

30. Francesco Guerrera, "Shire Says BioChem Integration Going Well: But Merger Leads to Expensive Writedowns," *Financial Post (National Post)*, July 24, 2001, C6.

31. Ibid.

32. Ibid.

6

INTEGRATIVE CASES

I n this chapter, the objective is to discuss cases that draw on the frameworks and perspectives developed throughout the casebook and that include important issues from each of the earlier chapters.

GM IN CHINA

For GM China, the year 2004 brought a wide variety of new challenges that added to an already complex business environment. The industry structure was changing quickly. Demand and supply projections for motor vehicles had promised substantial increases in sales and profits, but suddenly the optimism faded. China's new membership in the World Trade Organization (WTO) created expectations of "a level playing field" for foreign investors, but—at least in the short run—major barriers remained. Government intervention persisted, particularly the requirement of a joint venture partner, competition from government-owned assembly firms, and arbitrary rules such as sector-specific credit restrictions. Violation of intellectual property, with the copying of foreign automobile designs and the false branding of parts, was an ongoing threat. Meanwhile, inflation was increasing, and the government was unsure whether and how to use monetary and fiscal policies. Of great importance, the government had purposely kept the renminbi undervalued for many years. Pressures were building for the government to change its foreign exchange rate policy, but a higher renminbi would suddenly decrease GM China's international competitiveness.

INTEL'S SITE SELECTION DECISION IN LATIN AMERICA

Intel decided to locate its next assembly and testing plant in Latin America. Four countries had made the short list: Brazil, Chile, Mexico, and Costa Rica. Ted Telford, International Site Selection Analyst for Intel, needed to recommend a final site. There were two key issues that had to be resolved first: (a) What kind of business environment was most suitable to Intel's needs, and (b) how could Intel leverage its bargaining advantages most effectively? The case illustrates the advantages for a high-technology company such as Intel, with its strong need to operate in a country with stable, predictable rules of business and to invest in a fully consolidated democracy.

THE ACER GROUP'S CHINA MANUFACTURING DECISION

The Acer Group is one of the world's largest PC and computer component manufacturers. The vice president of global operations was pondering whether the timing and environment were conducive for Acer, based in Taiwan, to commence full-scale manufacturing operations on the Chinese mainland. Students are asked to examine the criteria on which Acer should base its decision to manufacture overseas and, in so doing, create the framework for a corporation's global manufacturing strategy. The teaching objectives also include having students consider the political, economic, and societal environments of a global manufacturing strategy.

GM IN CHINA[1]

Prepared by Danielle Cadieux under the supervision of Professor David Conklin

Version: (A) 2004-12-09

We have an enviable position in the world's fastest-growing automotive market, China, where investments in the mid- and late 1990s have paid dividends far larger and sooner than anyone predicted. Our unit sales in that market increased 46 per cent last year, and we increased our market share.[2]

A leap over the cliff: are the big profits to be made in China blinding foreign carmakers to the risks ahead? A flood of investment is causing concern that the industry will soon be vulnerable to overcapacity. There are also longer term doubts about the rules by which Beijing expects manufacturers to play.[3]

CHALLENGES IN CHINA

Founded in 1908, GM was the world's largest vehicle manufacturer, with 15 per cent of the global vehicle market and manufacturing operations in 32 countries. Beginning in 1992, GM created many joint ventures with Chinese government-owned enterprises, and by 2004, GM had attained outstanding profit levels. However, by the fall of 2004, a series of issues threatened GM in China, and several of these issues raised doubts about GM's strategy. China's entry into the WTO had led many to hope that the government's interventionist policies would come to an end. However, in 2004, the government of China promulgated a series of rules in regard to the motor vehicle sector, making it clear that intervention would be ongoing. Of particular concern was the continuing requirement that foreign ownership of assembly factories would be limited to 50 per cent, requiring a government-owned enterprise as an equal partner. Meanwhile, intellectual property was not being protected in the way that automakers had come to expect in other countries, causing concerns about Chinese competitors copying the models and designs of foreign corporations.

While sales growth had been truly exceptional, there were many reasons to doubt that the rapid pace could continue. Furthermore, huge investments by competing firms would result in substantial increases in production volumes, threatening a reduction in prices and consequently in gross margins and profits. As part of its macroeconomic policies, the government of China arbitrarily imposed restrictions on automobile financing as a way of restraining inflation, but this sector-specific intervention introduced a wild card into demand projections. Having kept the foreign exchange rate at an overvalued level for many years, it now appeared that the government might allow the exchange rate to rise substantially, and this could severely reduce the international competitiveness of China's vehicle manufacturers. The degree to which Chinese production facilities could be used as a low-cost export base remained an important and related question.

At the same time, the government faced a series of questions in regard to the policies it should put in place for the motor vehicle sector. Through its regulations, the government had consistently played a major role in directing the growth of the sector. In particular, its requirement for 50 per cent Chinese ownership of each manufacturing investment constrained investment and managerial decisions by foreign firms. However, it was not clear what rules could best provide for China's future economic success. Many developing countries had imposed foreign ownership restrictions, but had later reduced or eliminated these restrictions in order to stimulate investment and economic growth. Perhaps China would also follow this path. By 2004, inflationary pressures were building, and the government imposed credit limitations to restrain purchases of vehicles, raising the question of the appropriate role for sector-specific intervention as a component of China's macroeconomic policies.

Meanwhile, air pollution was becoming extremely severe, and the road system was becoming increasingly inadequate. These developments, as well, meant that government interventions to limit pollution and to expand the road system would be important determinants of future motor vehicle sales.

Going to China

By 2004, GM had about 10,000 employees in China, and it operated six joint ventures and two wholly owned foreign enterprises. GM had participated with its joint venture partners in investments of over $2 billion in China. With a combined manufacturing capacity of 530,000 vehicles, GM and its joint ventures offered the widest portfolio of products among foreign manufacturers in China. GM's major joint venture partner, SAIC, had been founded in 1956, and, by 1997, had grown to become China's largest manufacturing plant. As presented in GM company reports, these joint ventures consisted of the following:

Shanghai General Motors Co. Ltd. (Shanghai GM)

Shanghai GM was a Shanghai-based 50-50 joint venture with Shanghai Automotive Industry Corporation Group (SAIC). The largest automotive joint venture in China, Shanghai GM was formed in June 1997 with an initial planned investment of $1.3 billion and an annual production capacity of 200,000 vehicles while operating on three shifts. Shanghai GM assembled and distributed a family of Buick midsize sedans, the Buick GL8 executive wagon and the small-size Buick Sail. Shanghai GM began producing engines in 1998. Its powertrain facility had an annual production capacity of 180,000 V-6 engines, 75,000 L-4 engines and 100,000 automatic transmissions.[4] Shanghai GM was supported by a network of sales, aftersales and parts centres.

SAIC-GM-Wuling Automobile Co. Ltd. (SAIC-GM-Wuling)

SAIC-GM-Wuling was a $99.6 million joint venture launched in November 2002 and capable of producing up to 180,000 vehicles per year. GM held a 34 per cent stake, while SAIC held 50.1 per cent and Wuling Automotive 15.9 per cent. This joint venture was situated in Liuzhou, in western China, and it manufactured a range of mini-trucks and minivans.

Shanghai GM Dong Yue Motors Co. Ltd.

Dong Yue Motors Co. Ltd. was a $108 million joint venture manufacturing facility situated in Yantai, Shandong. Shanghai GM held a 50 per cent stake, with GM China and SAIC each holding 25 per cent stakes. The facility began production of the Buick Sail in April 2003 and had an annual designed production capacity of 100,000 units while operating on two shifts.

Shanghai GM Dong Yue Automotive Powertrain Co. Ltd.

Dong Yue Automotive Powertrain Co. Ltd. was located in Yantai, Shandong in northeastern China. The joint venture was the former Shandong Daewoo Automotive Engine Co. Ltd., which began production in August 1996. Under an agreement signed in 2004, Shanghai GM would own 50 per cent of the new joint venture, while GM China and SAIC would each own 25 per cent. The facility would have an annual manufacturing capacity of 300,000 engines, providing engines for vehicles manufactured in China by GM and SAIC's joint ventures.

Jinbei General Motors Automotive Co. Ltd. (Jinbei GM)

Jinbei GM manufactured the Chevrolet Blazer SUV. In 2004, a new shareholder structure was put in place, with Shanghai GM holding a 50 per cent stake, while GM China and SAIC each held 25 per cent stakes. Located in Shenyang,

Liaoning, Jinbei GM's production capacity was 50,000 vehicles.

Pan Asia Technical Automotive Center (PATAC)

PATAC was a $50 million, 50-50 joint venture between General Motors and SAIC. It provided automotive engineering services including design, development, testing and validation of components and vehicles. Among its achievements was the reengineering of the Buick Regal, Buick Excelle and other products for Shanghai GM.

GM Warehousing and Trading (Shanghai) Co. Ltd.

GM Warehousing and Trading was located in Shanghai's Waigaoqiao Free Trade Zone and represented a $3.2 million investment by GM. The wholly owned parts distribution centre (PDC) officially started operation in August 1999. It was established to ensure the quick delivery of genuine GM and AC Delco parts to customers in mainland China. The PDC featured a fully computerized management and inventory control system and stocked about 25,000 different parts.

GM (China) Investment Corporation

GM China was a wholly owned venture based in Shanghai. It housed all of GM's local staff and was the investor in GM's vehicle joint ventures in China.

Sales, marketing and aftersales services were key functions of GM China. Cadillac, Opel and Saab products were imported from GM facilities worldwide and were marketed in China. GM China also supported a network of authorized service centres and parts distributors across China.

GM-Shanghai Jiao Tong University Technology Institute

GM-Shanghai was a co-operative institution established by GM and Shanghai Jiao Tong

University, focusing on joint research and development and on technical training.

General Motors Acceptance Corporation (GMAC)

GMAC was one of the world's largest automotive financing companies, serving more than eight million customers in 35 countries. In 2004, the government of China gave it permission to operate in China, and it was actively seeking to develop local partnerships.

ACDelco

ACDelco, the world's leading aftermarket brand, operated a growing network of more than 100 ACDelco service centres in mainland China. The facilities, which stocked genuine ACDelco parts, provided repair and maintenance services for all makes and models of vehicles.

Allison Transmission Division (ATD)

ATD was the world's largest producer of automatic transmissions for medium- and heavy-duty trucks, buses and specialty vehicles. ATD was working with Chinese original equipment makers and end-users to upgrade the quality of its medium and heavy commercial vehicles.

Electro-Motive Division (EMD)

EMD was recognized as a world leader in the design and manufacture of locomotive equipment and technology. EMD operated a representative office in Beijing that established links with China's railway industry.[5]

Shanghai GM had introduced a series of new products in China:

- In April 1999, Shanghai GM began regular production of three models of midsize luxury sedans: the Buick Xin Shi Ji (New Century), Buick GLX and Buick GL.
- In May 2000, Shanghai GM launched the driver-oriented Buick GS sedan and the first executive wagon made in China, the Buick GL8.

- In August 2000, a sedan with a smaller engine, the Buick G, was added to the portfolio.
- In December 2000, Shanghai GM's first small car, the Buick Sail, came off the production line.
- In October 2001, Shanghai GM began exporting the GL8-based Chevrolet Venture to the Philippines.
- In November 2001, Shanghai GM introduced the Buick S-RV recreational vehicle.
- In November 2002, Shanghai GM announced that it had secured a contract with GM's CAMI joint venture in Canada to export engines beginning in 2003.
- On December 26, 2002, the Buick Regal midsize sedan was introduced.
- On April 19, 2003, Shanghai GM unveiled the Buick Excelle, its first lower-medium sedan.[6]

INDUSTRY STRUCTURE: COMPETITION AND PROFITABILITY

In 2004, sedans represented 44 per cent of motor vehicle sales in China, with trucks at 30 per cent and buses at 26 per cent. In was in the sedan component that growth promised to be most rapid and where profits appeared to be most substantial. In 2003, Volkswagen had dominated the sedan market with a 36 per cent share. However, by June 2004, GM and its joint venture partners were selling more sedans than Volkswagen, with their joint ventures accounting for 40 per cent of the total sedan market.

By 2004, GM was earning exceptionally high profits from its China operations:

China is no longer merely a market of great potential.

It's now the real McCoy, where global companies with the right partners and strategies can and do reap huge profits.

The proof is on page 37 of General Motors Corp.'s 2003 report to the federal government called a 10-K under the heading "Investment in Nonconsolidated Affiliates." Right there, for the first time ever, GM publicly revealed how much profit it is raking in from its vehicle-making ventures in China.

The number was a big one: $437 million last year. And that's only half of the profit from GM's four joint-venture plants in China, which sold 386,710 vehicles. The other half of the profits went to the Detroit automaker's Chinese partners.

For some perspective, look at the numbers this way:

Figure that GM and its Chinese partners had a combined net profit of nearly $875 million, or about $2,267 per vehicle sold in China.

In North America, GM's net profit last year was only $811 million on sales of 5.6 million cars and trucks in the United States, Canada and Mexico, or about $145 per vehicle.

That means GM China was nearly 15 times more profitable, per vehicle sold, than GM North America.

"GM is making money hand over fist in China, selling cars as fast as they can make them, at very attractive prices," says Kenneth Lieberthal, a University of Michigan professor and China expert who was senior director for Asian affairs on the National Security Council under President Bill Clinton. "All of the other car markets of the world are either mature or they're poor."[7]

While GM had achieved outstanding results to date, nevertheless a plethora of competitors were fighting for market share. In 2004, China had more than 200 carmakers. Most were relatively small Chinese firms, and these domestic firms, solely owned by the government, had a 40 per cent market share. Exhibit 1 indicates market shares as of June 2004. The government was reluctant to see its motor vehicle manufacturers eliminated by the new joint venture firms. How to support their existence while also attracting foreign technology and managerial skills posed serious challenges at this point in time. As one analyst saw the strategy of domestic firms:

With Japanese and U.S. technology battling it out for the top, the only hope for domestic carmakers without joint venture partners is to capture the bottom end of the market, then begin the slow ascent up the price-and-sophistication ladder. That's the path chosen by BYD, the former bombmaker. The Flyer retails for about $4,700, making it affordable to the 50 million Chinese earning at least $7,000 a year, whom the government considers middle class. "Look around my office," says Liu, the BYD general manger. He has one dusty filing cabinet, bare whitewashed walls and a view overlooking the decrepit former bomb factory. "We can get by on the slimmest profits."[8]

This industry structure created great uncertainty about future prices. The domestic firms did not have shareholders demanding certain profit levels, and so they might strive to maintain their market share by cutting prices. Furthermore, an ongoing temptation for them was simply to copy the designs and technologies that were being introduced by the new joint venture firms. Meanwhile, foreign competitors were jostling to increase their investments in this fast-growing market, a process that would further intensify price competition. Already, over the 2001–2004 period, prices had fallen 25 per cent. Analysts

Shangahi VW	15%
Shanghai GM	11%
FAW VW	11%
GZ Honda	5%
Tianjin FAW	5%
Changan Suzuki	5%
Beijing Hyundai	4%
Geely	5%
Chery	4%
Dongfeng Citroen	4%
Others	31%

Exhibit 1   Market Shares by Manufacturer

Source: "China's Automotive and Components Market 2004," KPMG, September 2004.

expected prices to continue to fall at a rate around 10 per cent a year.[9]

UNCERTAINTIES OF DEMAND AND SUPPLY PROJECTIONS

Some analysts extrapolated the exceptionally high growth rates of the 1999–2003 period to arrive at projections of enormous sales volumes. China's auto sales had climbed from some two million units in 2000, to more than three million units in 2002, to 4.4 million vehicles in 2003. China's rapid economic growth supported the view that an increasing number of Chinese would be able to purchase cars in the future. Exhibit 2 presents data in regard to China's

economic growth, and Exhibit 3 indicates the very unequal income distribution as a result of which the top 20 per cent of China's population would soon be able to afford automobiles.

Based on this optimism, some analysts predicted:

China is on track to overtake Japan "in a couple of years" to become the world's second biggest vehicle market, according to John Devine, General Motors' chief financial officer, in the U.S. vehicle maker's latest bullish assessment of the mainland.

Mr. Devine said GM expected the market to maintain double-digit growth "for some time" on the back of continuing economic growth, cheaper cars and the approval of vehicle financing for three foreign manufacturers.

	1999[a]	2000[a]	2001[a]	2002[a]	2003[a]
GDP at market prices (Rmb bn)	8,206.60	8,946.80	9,731.50	10,479.10	11,975.80
GDP (US$ bn)	991.4	1,080.7	1,175.7	1,266.1	1,446.9
Real GDP growth (%)	7.1	8.0	7.5	8.0	9.3
Consumer price inflation (av; %)	(1.5)	0.4	0.7	(0.8)	1.2
Population (m)	1,250.50	1,261.80	1,273.10	1,284.30[b]	1,295.20[b]
Exports of goods f.o.b. (US$ bn)	194.7	249.1	266.1	325.7	438.3
Imports of goods f.o.b. (US$ bn)	(158.7)	(214.7)	(232.1)	(281.5)	(393.6)
Current-account balance (US$ bn)	21.1	20.5	17.4	35.4	45.9
Foreign-exchange reserves excl gold (US$ bn)	157.7	168.3	215.6	291.1	408.2
Total external debt (US$ bn)	152.1	145.7	170.1	168.3	189.1[b]
Debt-service ratio, paid (%)	11.7	9.3	7.8	8.1	4.6[b]
Exchange rate (av) Rmb; US$	8.3	8.3	8.3	8.3	8.3
Inward FDI (US$ bn)	38.8	38.4	44.2	49.3	53.5

Exhibit 2   China Annual Indicators

Source: EIU Report, China, September 2004.

a. Actual.
b. Economist Intelligence Unit estimates.

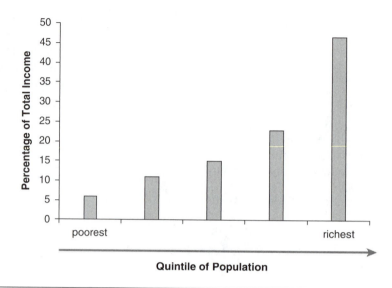

Exhibit 3   China, Income Distribution

GM China sold 386,710 vehicles in China last year (2003) through its various joint ventures, up 46 per cent on 2002. Saloon car sales increased 82 per cent year-on-year.[10]

For the motor vehicle sector, the year 2004 witnessed an abrupt end to the 50 per cent annual sales growth of the previous years. Some of the best-selling models experienced particularly sharp decreases, as customers shifted to less expensive automobiles. For some models, September 2004's sales dropped more than 50 per cent from the September 2003 level. Analysts pointed to a series of new forces: a loss of consumer confidence, expectations of further vehicle price decreases, the threat of oil shortages and higher gasoline prices, government rationing of power supplies, and the government's abrupt imposition of credit restrictions for automobile financing. Long-term constraints included a very poor highway system—in fact, one analyst suggested that "China has no national highway system."[11] Driving was basically restricted to the roads within each city. Air pollution had become a major concern, and this could also limit China's motor vehicle growth. "According to the World Bank, China has 16 of the world's 20 most polluted cities,"[12] resulting in 300,000 premature deaths annually due to respiratory disease. As a result of these new developments and long-term constraints, analysts claimed that foreign investments that had once appeared to be enormously successful might now be open to question.[13] In the third quarter of 2004, GM saw its profits in China drop 44 per cent to US$80 million.[14]

Over-capacity will be a major factor within two years, with the passenger car market—already the single most important sector within the Chinese vehicle market—likely to be at the forefront.

Paul Brough (managing partner of KPMG's financial advisory services practice in China) continued: "We are already seeing the first outward signs of the pending over-capacity. Average car prices in China have already fallen by seven per cent between January and June this year (2004). A lot of this can be attributed to manufacturers looking to grab early market share through aggressively low pricing. In addition, rising inventory levels are also forcing price reductions on older models as businesses look to clear stock levels."

"Further over-capacity will see increased price pressures on sedans as well as lower prices and margins. Taking the reasoning to its ultimate extreme also raises the fear of some new production facilities becoming real white elephants as capacity is inevitably scaled back at some point."[15]

As noted above, the intensification of competition was resulting in price cuts that would inevitably reduce profit margins. Furthermore, it was not clear whether certain supply constraints might limit the expansion plans of China's automakers. In August 2004, a Financial Times article pointed to a decrease in car production of 20 per cent compared with the previous month, and noted that, "This is forcing a rethink among multinational and local carmakers about their multibillion-dollar expansion plans in China."[16]

FIRST MOVER ADVANTAGE IN CREATING A VALUE CHAIN

The industry structure of parts suppliers had a similar dual nature. On the one hand, the joint venture enterprises initiated by foreign parts suppliers brought modern technologies and managerial practices. On the other hand, domestic firms pursued traditional practices that resulted in poor quality components and that lacked innovation and ongoing product development. A persistent temptation for domestic firms was to label their parts falsely, claiming them to be the genuine products of firms with brand-name recognition. A foreign assembler had to create an efficient value chain capable of creating vehicles that would be consistently high quality. Just-in-time delivery practices faced real challenges in China.

> The joint venture operations many of the Tier 1 suppliers have set up vary little in terms of technological sophistication and part quality between what they do in China and the rest of the world, says Guy Bouchet, a vice-president with A.T. Kearney. He recently returned to Chicago after spending five years in China. The rest of the local supply base is a different story. It's fragmented,

and there's a wide spectrum of capabilities, qualifications and quality, he says. Some of these suppliers understand the multinationals' requirements and are ready to play the game. Others aren't so willing or able.

> "Late-comers run the risk of not being able to lock in business relationships, in whatever form, with the highest-capability guys," says Bouchet. "You have to tap into a second tier who are not as good, which means that your investment in terms of training, in terms of revamping the assets, are higher, which has an impact on your return on investment and your short-term competitiveness."[17]

NEW OPPORTUNITIES WITH SALES FINANCING

In 2004, China's four state-owned banks held more than 80 per cent of China's outstanding automobile loans, while the automobile manufacturers had been prohibited from extending loans as part of their sales programs. In August 2004, General Motors became the first overseas automaker in China to be allowed to issue car loans to its purchasers. GM had created a new joint venture for its financing operations, with 60 per cent owned by General Motors Acceptance Corporation (GMAC) and 40 per cent owned by SAIC. Analysts expected that this expansion would greatly increase GM sales. Other automakers had also applied for permission to offer auto loans, but GM had a head start. Overseas banks such as Citigroup Inc. and HSBC faced a delay of several years before they would be allowed to offer loans denominated in yuan to Chinese purchasers. GM now enjoyed a brief window of limited competition.

However, GM's finance operations faced certain restrictions. Initially, GM could lend as much as 90 per cent of the car's price tag, but this percentage could be reduced by government regulation as a mechanism for restraining demand in time of inflation. Furthermore, China's central bank determined the interest rates to be charged on local currency loans; GM would not be allowed to set its own rates.

POST-WTO CHALLENGES:
THE PERSISTENCE OF GOVERNMENT
REGULATIONS, TRADE AND INVESTMENT
RESTRICTIONS, AND VIOLATION OF
INTELLECTUAL PROPERTY PROTECTION

WTO Provisions

Prior to joining the World Trade Organization (WTO), China had imposed exceptionally high tariffs on motor vehicles and components, and has also imposed import quotas for certain products. China was granted a transition period in tariff reductions, with a decrease from levels of 80 per cent to 100 per cent down to 25 per cent by 2006. Import quotas were to be phased out by 2005. In the past, the government had also imposed local content requirements in order to support domestic suppliers of components, but these also were to be eliminated. In addition, the government had intervened to dictate the types of vehicles that foreign companies manufactured, with production licences as a requirement. With the WTO, foreign companies received greater independence in production decisions, and by 2004, they were free to distribute whatever products they wished. While China maintained its 50 per cent domestic ownership requirement for assembly plants, the government did eliminate its joint venture requirements for the production of engines.

Some analysts predicted that these WTO reforms would give foreign companies valuable new opportunities. In particular, foreign companies would be able to import certain segments of their product mix, while focusing their China production on a limited product range, thereby capturing greater economies of scale. This would mean that foreign companies could rationalize their product mix globally, and China's place in global production would depend on its inherent competitiveness. Meanwhile, the domestic firms would face heightened import competition, as would component manufacturers.

These market-opening commitments are expected to bring considerable challenges—and opportunities—for both Chinese and foreign automakers. For Chinese companies, the challenges will likely outweigh the opportunities. Reduced tariff and non-tariff barriers will allow high-quality, inexpensive foreign vehicles to flood the domestic market. China's small and inefficient auto companies will probably be unable to compete with well-established multinational competitors.[18]

Persistent Government Intervention

In June 2004, the government of China proclaimed its new version of rules concerning foreign investment in China's vehicle sector. Exhibit 4 presents KPMG's summary of these rules and their implications. Some rules were unchanged from the past, but overall the June 2004 proclamation represented an ongoing intervention that carried uncertainty with it. For example, in discussions about formulating these rules, analysts had warned of the possibility that the government might impose new rules to support technology development in domestic companies. In particular, a policy option being debated was that 50 per cent of all sales in China by 2010 would have to come from domestic companies that would own 100 per cent of a vehicle's technology. An additional proposal was that any foreign company that owned 10 per cent or more of a Chinese company would be compelled by law to share its expertise in research and development, production and sales. The 2004 rules did not include these provisions, but the possibility remained that similar provisions might be imposed in the future to enhance Chinese ownership of technology.[19]

CHALLENGES OF THE
JOINT VENTURE REQUIREMENT

China's requirement that foreign investors enter joint ventures with domestic firms was a position held by many developing country governments in the mid-to-late 20th century. It was generally accepted throughout the world that foreign direct investment (FDI) led to some degree of loss of control by host country governments over their economies. This loss of control was seen as a

Policy	Policy Maker	Impact
Foreign Ownership	Foreign Ownership will remain limited to 50 per cent	Although China obtained an exemption from the WTO on rules that ban limits placed on foreign investment, many auto manufacturers were hoping China would eventually relent: this does not appear to be the case
Number of Joint Ventures	The number of joint ventures a manufacturer is allowed to establish remains at two per vehicle segment (sedan, bus and truck)	This regulation gives domestic manufacturers more opportunity to develop their own technology and production bases by increasing the barrier for foreign manufacturers
Minimum Investment Size	A minimum investment of RMB2 billion (US$241 million) is required	The restriction on investments increases the market entry barrier in China
Manufacturing Licence Transfer	Licence transfer from existing vehicle production companies to non-automotive enterprises is not permitted	The policy makes it more difficult for non-automotive companies to diversify their business into the fast growing automotive market in China
Domestic Sourcing and Production	From 2005 (no specific date mentioned), imported vehicles can no longer be stored in bonded warehouses in China Certain imported parts will be subject to the same level of import tariffs as complete vehicles (currently, tariffs on imported cars are 30 per cent to 38 per cent, while tariffs on parts range from 10 per cent to 23 per cent) Cars with major subassemblies (e.g. chassis, engine) that are imported may be taxed as imported vehicles	Import duty on vehicles will be payable upon entry to China An increase in local manufacturing and sourcing is expected, foreign automotive manufacturers are likely to continue to step up efforts to identify local sources of parts in order to have price competitive products This is already forcing some automakers to further localize their vehicles
Research & Development (R&D)	R&D expenses will be tax deductible in the future	This policy is expected to continue to encourage foreign companies to establish domestic R&D centres as well as encourage local R&D activities and the development of local intellectual property, for example • GM has already established its own R&D centre in Shanghai • At present, Nissan and Dongfeng Motors are building a new R&D centre in Guangzhou, which will be ready at the end of 2005

Exhibit 4   KPMG Summary of 2004 Motor Vehicle Rules

cost to the host country and to its government. Transnational corporations (TNCs), with international production and distribution networks, had the flexibility to respond more quickly to changing conditions in all the countries in which they operated than did domestically owned firms. If, for example, a host country's real exchange rate rose, a TNC could reallocate production to a cheaper source of supply in another country. A domestically owned firm might not have this option, or, if it did, it might exercise it less quickly. A similar situation existed with many of the major policy variables under government's command. Governments might lose control over their ability to raise taxation rates, wage rates and labor conditions, interest rates and so on for the fear of the reaction of TNCs in their investment and production decisions.

Many believed that TNCs had very different goals for their operations in host countries than did the host country governments. TNCs could also be subject to pressures from a number of sources, and these sources might be outside the influence of host country governments. Consequently, a degree of tension was introduced when foreign investors were permitted to enter the private enterprise system. Not only were TNCs seen as trying to control the operations of their firms in the best interests of their stockholders, but these stockholders were located outside the host country. Put another way, foreign investment implied that some form of direct control was exercised from outside the country. As well, those for whose benefit the control was being exercised also resided outside the host country. Moreover, TNCs were seen as being responsive to the policies and goals of the government in their home country (and other countries in which they operated) and these goals and policies might not be in the best interests of the host country.

Based on all these rationales, host country governments wished to be able to exercise a degree of control over foreign investors relative to domestic investors in order to align their operations more closely with the goals of the country. General restrictions on foreign investors were an attempt to lodge some degree of control with domestic entities, either host country nationals or, in some cases, the government itself. However, being the foreign partner in a joint venture raised many difficult challenges.

> Under the best of circumstances, joint ventures can be difficult to manage. They've gone out of fashion among U.S. auto companies because the interests of the individual parties frequently diverged before the ventures had run their course. What's worse is that SAIC owns 50% of each joint venture by government regulation and gets half the votes when decisions are made. That's normally a recipe for frustration and deadlock.

> Asked how disputes get resolved when neither party has a tie-breaking vote, SAIC president Hu says: "When we have different ideas, we close doors and argue against each other. It is okay to lose your temper as long as the door is closed." He adds that he has learned a few things about conflict resolution between different nationalities. "Americans have more flexibility than the Germans, who are very serious once they make up their mind," he says.[20]

Of central concern was the risk that the domestic partner might create an alternative production facility and compete against the joint venture. Or the government of China might arbitrarily dissolve the joint venture and encourage SAIC to purchase GM's interest in the joint venture. Nationalization of GM's interest seemed an extreme possibility but one that could not be completely ruled out. If any of these developments were to occur, GM might now be creating its own worst enemy—and not just in China, but perhaps globally. Nothing would prevent SAIC from exporting to GM's markets throughout the world.

> Some China experts believe the joint ventures will be unwound once the Chinese are capable of competing on their own. "Foreign automakers should be afraid of domestic competition—very afraid," wrote economist Kroeber. "In sector after sector, foreign manufacturers have piled into China only to see their technology copied and their prices

undercut with alarming speed by domestic competitors operating with government support. Chinese firms have picked up technology much faster and kicked foreign competitors out of the market far faster than anyone predicted."[21]

And by 2004, SAIC had already shifted into initial stages of competition against GM:

The boldest plans belong to SAIC. In the next three years, SAIC aims to make 50,000 vehicles bearing its own brand; in 2003, the company produced fewer than 3,000 of its own vehicles. By 2010, SAIC wants to be among the world's top 10 auto makers, according to Xiao Guopu, a vice-president of SAIC.[22]

In 1978, China had begun its gradual transition from central planning and state-owned enterprises to private ownership in a market economy. It was possible that the joint venture requirement with a government-owned partner might be eliminated in the future. If so, GM would face the strategic issue of whether to attempt to purchase the domestic partner's interests in the joint ventures. The government would face the strategic issue of how to privatize and whether it should retain a "golden share" with veto rights over certain managerial decisions. In Germany, for example, the state of lower Saxony held a "golden share" in Volkswagen that gave it power to override the board should it decide to shift jobs out of Germany.

Protection of Intellectual Property

A major conflict between GM and Chery illustrated the threat that domestic firms could copy designs and technologies of the foreign investors. GM created production facilities for a new small car, the Chevrolet Spark, with a planned price of $7,500 and a production date of December 2003. However, before it could begin its sales campaign, one of the local Chinese automakers, Chery, began selling a $6,000 version with many similar features. GM was faced with an important challenge in protecting its intellectual property.

The dispute drags GM into the murky waters of intellectual property-rights protection in China, an arena that has snagged makers of sneakers and other goods that saw Chinese companies mimic their wares. The GM complaint is complicated by the fact that Chery is 20% owned by GM's main joint venture partner in China, Shanghai Automotive Industrial Corp. GM and SAIC make Buick sedans in Shanghai, as well as cars at two other plants elsewhere in China.

Yet, as GM's dispute shows, these companies could face a vexing battle.

GM was not alone in seeing a clone suddenly appear from a domestic manufacturer. Toyota also experienced this challenge:

When Geely, China's largest private carmaker, launched its Meiri saloon, it made certain to advertise one of the vehicle's big selling points—its Toyota engine, installed under licence from the Japanese company.

Toyota perhaps could have lived with that, but not with the Geely logo plastered on the Meiri's front grill, which it considered, looked suspiciously like the stylized T-shape that brands the Japanese company's vehicles globally.

Similar—but not so much that potential purchasers would be misled—ruled Beijing's Second Intermediate Court this week, throwing out legal action mounted by Toyota for alleged trademark infringement.[23]

ONGOING RISKS IN CHINA

A KPMG Survey in 2004 revealed serious concerns held by foreign investors in China. These ongoing risks threatened GM as well as foreign investors in other sectors:

- Forty per cent of those surveyed agree that government regulations posed a significant challenge to their expansion plans.
- Eighty per cent of companies surveyed said that Intellectual Property Rights infringement posed a significant threat to their businesses in China.

- Nearly 25 per cent of those surveyed agree that they overestimated the potential of the Chinese market, and a further 16 per cent even admitted they wrongly believed they would get rich quick.[24]

KPMG listed the most prominent mistakes made when investing in China. By working with a joint venture partner, GM had been able to avoid many of these mistakes, and this reality placed a strong positive value on GM's relationship with SAIC.

1. Failure to appreciate the differences in the Chinese market. Companies that focus solely on the largest, high-profile coastal cities may miss out.

2. Failure to appreciate the ferocity of domestic competition. Before 1949, the Chinese were known for entrepreneurship. Since 1978, these trading talents have been reviving, and local companies will go head-to-head with foreign concerns.

3. Investment information can be difficult to get and may not be reliable.

4. Failure to appreciate and understand cultural differences. In China many common Western cultural and economic paradigms do not apply. . . . Contracts are certainly not worthless in China, but their significance is not as great as they are in the West.[25]

MACROECONOMIC POLICIES

As Exhibit 2 indicates, China had experienced five years of very rapid growth, ranging from seven per cent to over nine per cent annually, without experiencing any significant inflation. In fact, in the years 1999 and 2002, China's general price level appears to have fallen. However, with the year 2004, analysts throughout the world became increasingly concerned about the possibility of rapid inflation in China, and the government of China shared this concern. Essentially, there was a substantial increase in aggregate demand due to higher consumer incomes, increased levels of exports and substantial foreign investment. At

the same time, there appeared to be new constraints on global capacity to produce natural resources necessary for the burgeoning Chinese manufacturing sector. World prices for natural resources, and particularly oil, were skyrocketing, and this threatened to drive up cost levels and, therefore, prices in China.

> Inflation in China has become a growing concern to bankers, corporate executives and monetary officials around the world.[26]

> Rapid growth—especially with regard to infrastructure improvements—has turned China into a major oil and commodity importer. With commodity prices rising, and its currency pegged to the low-flying dollar, China's import costs have soared. Overall, prices for raw materials and energy in China jumped 8.3 per cent in the first quarter of 2004, while overall input costs for China's manufacturing increased by 4.8 per cent. Other inflationary pressures facing China are its rapidly growing money supply and a new generation of hyperactive consumers whose spending drove up retail sales by 10.7 per cent in the first quarter of 2004.[27]

In response to these pressures, the government of China instituted policies to restrain demand in specific sectors that seemed to be overheating. The motor vehicle sector became one of the targets for this restraint, and the government imposed restrictions on loans made to finance the purchase of motor vehicles.

In other nations, inflationary pressures were often met with monetary and fiscal policies, but the government of China felt constrained in its ability to use these economy-wide measures. The government lacked experience in both fiscal and monetary policies and had not yet developed the many systems on which these policies relied. To raise taxes as a means of restraining aggregate demand, for example, would be a novel exercise with unclear results. It seemed to be an inappropriate time to reduce government expenditures, when the growth process had been so successful. China required new infrastructure expenditures, particularly for the rapidly growing cities along the coast, but also for huge inland projects like the Three Gorges project that would be necessary to generate hydro-electric power. At the same time, tens of millions of people were drifting into unemployment, both with a shift of population from rural areas to the cities and also with extensive employee lay-offs as enterprises strove to increase efficiency—both publicly owned enterprises and the increasing number of privatized firms. The threat existed of both inflation and unemployment, creating a difficult choice in macroeconomic policy direction.

Monetary policy offered limited hope because of the fragile state of the banking system and because of the loss-making, state-owned enterprises. To restrain credit and raise interest rates on an economy-wide basis might cause a financial and business collapse. In October 2004, the government did experiment in monetary policy by raising interest rates 27 basis points (a basis point is one one-hundredth of a per cent). The world's media immediately erupted with concerns. The Financial Times ran a front-page headline that read, "China rate rise sends markets into a spin. Central Bank's first move in nine years hits commodity prices and stocks around the world."[28]

> The government's short-term priority is to slow the current rapid rates of GDP growth without triggering a damaging hard landing for the economy. To this end, tightening measures have been targeted rather than broad-based, aimed at cooling particular types of spending in individual industries—notably investment expenditure in the real-estate, steel, aluminum and cement sectors—rather than the economy as a whole. Specifically, the government has raised reserve requirements for banks, and imposed administrative limits on lending to and investment in the offending sectors.

> This focus on the ability of banks to supply funds is sensible. China's capital markets are still immature, so it is largely banks that are financing the current bout of overheating. Of course, the authorities could try to ease demand for funds by raising interest rates, but this would probably not just be ineffective but even counter-productive. The sharp rise in bank credit to particular sectors appears to be based not purely on the low cost of capital but on relationships at local levels between government officials, banks and companies. Arguably, a sharp rise in interest rates would end even some of this lending, but such a change would also discourage investment in sectors that are not currently overheated.[29]

Another force underlying the inflationary pressures was the decision of the government to peg the renminbi to the U.S. dollar. As Exhibit 2 indicates, China was experiencing a positive current account balance as well as huge capital inflows. In a freely floating foreign exchange market, the demand for the Chinese currency would have driven up the value of the renminbi. However, the government wished to maintain an undervalued currency in order to stimulate its exports and restrain imports. Here again, the basic motivation was a political need to create millions of jobs and to expand the economy. The government was able to keep the renminbi pegged to the U.S. dollar by selling the renminbi on the foreign exchange market in return for U.S. dollars and other currencies that it then accumulated as an increase in its reserves.

As Exhibit 2 indicates, China's foreign exchange reserves increased from US$158 billion in 1999 to US$408 billion in 2003. The government of China used these reserves to buy bonds, to a large degree in the United States, a process that enabled the United States to maintain low interest rates in spite of its large US$400 billion to US$500 billion fiscal deficit. This process also increased China's money supply and thereby created an additional inflation threat. Other nations that followed a policy of maintaining an undervalued currency could deal with the resultant inflationary threat through a tight money policy that would restrain aggregate demand. But, as noted above, there were political and economic reasons for being concerned about the impacts of such monetary restraint.

Some analysts felt that China's macroeconomic policies had painted the country into a precarious position in terms of impending inflation and the difficulties and dangers of fiscal and monetary restraint. An additional element in this situation was the concern of other governments that China's policy in maintaining an undervalued currency was causing job losses in their countries. This was a widespread concern in the United States, where it seemed that China's macro-economic policies were causing the "offshoring" of U.S. jobs at a time of relatively high U.S. unemployment. Some administration officials—particularly the U.S. Treasury Secretary, John Snow—publicly urged the government of China to allow its currency to rise in value. By the fall of 2004, the U.S. dollar had devalued substantially against the euro, and this meant that the Chinese renminbi had devalued by a similar percentage against the euro. Consequently, it was likely that European government leaders would soon add their voices to that of the United States in calling for an upward revaluation of the renminbi. Without such action, it was possible that governments in North America and Western Europe might impose new import restrictions on goods from China in order to protect their nations' jobs.

For GM and other foreign investors in China, the undervaluation of the renminbi had offered protection against competitive imports. In this sense, the undervaluation of the renminbi had acted as the tariff, supporting their initial business enterprises. By the fall of 2004, however, the threat of the revaluation of the renminbi and/or the threat of new protectionist measures on the part of foreign governments had created new concerns about the appropriate China strategy. The danger of a financial crisis and economy-wide depression, though remote, seemed a possibility.

> All this though, has raised a burning question. Is China's boom, like those in 19th century America, merely the precursor of an imminent bust? Or is it the harbinger of a more sustainable economic take-off? The lack of consensus is striking.

> Despite the optimism that attends China's foreseeable economic future, there are a couple of scenarios under which Beijing's best laid plans could be thrown off-course.

> The first concerns the possibility of shortages of coal, electricity, raw materials, port and rail capacity

coalescing into an inflationary trend. If this happened, the central bank would have to raise interest rates and the renminbi would probably appreciate.

> Eventually, either an ill wind or a surfeit of domestic success will cause China's stellar phase of growth to abate or crumble—just as it has in every emerging economy in history. When that day comes, the fallout may be spectacular.[30]

CHINA AS AN EXPORT BASE

Analysts were pointing to China's low labor costs and rapidly improving skill levels as the basis for motor vehicle exports. Many saw China as a new global player in the sector at a time when there was already a world glut of production facilities. China had the potential to disrupt existing global production and marketing patterns. Here as well, GM was quickly approaching a crossroads. Should it stand by while its partner SAIC and others created a vibrant export base, becoming GM competitors throughout the world? Or should GM take the initiative and use its China facilities to export to North America and Europe? How should China fit in GM's global strategy? It appeared that Honda had already made the strategic decision to use China as an export base:

> First, the home market. Next, the world. China is poised to become a significant car exporter as production standards rise and costs fall.

> With Honda's new plant, there's a difference: The cars rolling off its assembly lines by early next year are heading not for the Chinese market, but to Europe—the first big push by a foreign carmaker to produce in China for export.

> If successful, Honda's Guangzhou venture will be a significant demonstration of the ability of China-based manufacturing to climb the value chain. Specifically, it would signal China's debut as a car exporter, based on what Tim Dunne of Automotive Resources Asia, a car industry consultancy, describes

as the "marrying of Japanese manufacturing efficiency with cheap labor in China." Production costs at Honda's Guangzhou plant are expected to be 20% lower than those in Japan, say factory officials.[31]

THE WAY AHEAD

The government of China had created a motor vehicle strategy that had attained outstanding initial success. Domestic firms lacked design capability, modern technologies and managerial capabilities. Allowing foreign investors to create joint ventures with domestic firms had quickly overcome these challenges. By 2004, the question had arisen as to whether this strategy should be modified. What should be China's next steps in its motor vehicle strategy?

For GM, predicting these next steps would be critical in determining its corporate strategy. In many respects, the business environment it faced was changing dramatically. New competitors from abroad and heightened competition from domestic firms were influencing the industry structure. Demand and supply projections seemed subject to great uncertainties. Its joint ventures with SAIC had been extremely profitable for both partners, but should GM trust this relationship to continue indefinitely? In Thailand, where GM had substantial assembly operations, there were no joint venture requirements. Meanwhile, India had a population nearly as large as China's, as well as low wages and optimistic growth forecasts. Should GM diversify its China risks by investing heavily in India and other Asian countries?

NOTES

1. This case has been written on the basis of published sources only. Consequently, the interpretation and perspectives presented in this case are not necessarily those of General Motors or any of its employees.

2. General Motors Corporation Annual Report 2005.

3. J. Mackintosh and R. McGregor, "A Leap Over the Cliff," *Financial Times,* August 25, 2003, p. 13.

4. www.autointell-news.com/News-2002/November-2002/November-2002–1/November-06–02-p10.htm, accessed October 20, 2004.

5. www.gmchina.com/english/news/background/inchina.htm, accessed October 20, 2004.

6. www.gmchina.com/english/operations/shgm.htm, accessed October 20, 2004.

7. T. Walsh, "GM's China Bonanza," *Detroit Free Press,* accessed March 30, 2004. http://www.freep.com/money/business/walsh30_20040330.

8. M. Forney, "Moving too Fast? *Time,* V. 163, I. 8, February 23, 2004, A6.

9. "Here Be Dragons," *The Economist,* September 4, 2004, p. 10.

10. Richard McGregor, "GM to Focus on Growing China Market," *Financial Times,* February 12, 2004, p. 20.

11. Mark Graham, "Paddy Fields to Full Production," *Industry Week,* November 6, 2000.

12. "Special Report on China's Environment: A Great Wall of Waste," *The Economist,* August 21, 2004, p. 56.

13. Peter Wonnacott, "Slower Growth Fuels Anxiety," *The Wall Street Journal,* October 21, 2004, B13.

14. Richard McGregor, "Carmakers Changing Plans as Chinese Sales Fall Off," *Financial Times,* October 16, 2004, p. 2.

15. "Significant Over-capacity to Hit Chinese Car Market within Two Years," www.kpmg.com/search/index.asp?cid=753, accessed August 27, 2004.

16. Richard McGregor, "Chinese Car Output Falls by 20%," *Financial Times,* August 25, 2004, p. 13.

17. David Drickhamer, "Balancing Act," *Industry Week,* February 2004 V. 253, I. 2, 49.

18. Allan Zhang, "China's WTO Accession: Implications for the Auto Sector," www.pwc.com/servlet/printFormat?url=http://www.pwc.com/extweb/newcloth.nsf/docid/F117 826, accessed May 14, 2004.

19. Leslie P. Norton, "A Bumpy Road for Foreign Auto Makers in China," *Barron's,* June 23, 2003, V. 83, I. 23, MW12.

20. Alex Taylor III, "Shanghai Auto Wants to Be the World's Next Great Car Company," *Fortune,* October 4, 2004, V. 150, I. 7, 103.

21. Ibid.

22. Peter Wonnacott, "Global Aims of China's Car Makers Put Existing Ties at Risk," *Wall Street Journal,* August 24, 2004, B1.

23. Richard McGregor, "Chinese Law Courts Make Their Marque," *Financial Times,* November 28, 2003, 20.

24. www.kpmg.ca/en/news/pr20040608.html, accessed July 2, 2004.

25. "Consumer Markets in China—the Real Deal?" KPMG international, 2004, www.kpmg.com.cn/pub .htm?id=669.

26. "Inflationary Pressures Rising Fast in China," *Taipei Times,* April 10, 2004, 12.

27. J. Kurtzman, "Is China Going the Way of Brazil?" European Business Forum, Summer 2004, I. 18, 95.

28. Alexandra Harney, "China Rate Rise Sends Markets into a Spin," *Financial Times,* October 29, 2004, 1.

29. "China Country Report," *EIU Report,* August 2004, www.eiu.com.

30. J. Kynge, "The Chinese Boom Is Bound to End in Tears. But It Might Not End for Another 10 Years . . . With Bumps Along the Way," *Financial Times,* March 24, 2004, 13.

31. David Murphy, "Driving Ambition," *Far Eastern Economic Review,* May 27, 2004, V. 167, I. 21, 28.

THUNDERBIRD
THE GARVIN SCHOOL OF INTERNATIONAL MANAGEMENT

INTEL'S SITE SELECTION DECISION IN LATIN AMERICA

Prepared by Professor Roy Nelson based on his interviews and field research in Costa Rica, Brazil, Chile and Mexico in Fall 1998

Ted Telford faced a dilemma. As the only full-time member of Intel Corporation's worldwide site selection team, he had to make a recommendation about where Intel should locate its first manufacturing plant in Latin America.[1] After months of analysis, involving both desk research and numerous field trips to potential country locations, the site selection team had narrowed the choice to four countries: Brazil, Chile, Mexico, and Costa Rica. All were attractive in different ways, but now it was October 1996, and Ted had to write his final report for the headquarters office in Santa Clara. Headquarters would want his recommendation and evidence to support it. He shifted uneasily in his chair. At stake was a long-term investment decision involving $300–$500 million, a substantial amount

of money even for a company like Intel, with over $20 billion in annual revenues. Ted hunched over his files, and began reviewing the data one more time.

INTEL AND THE SEMICONDUCTOR INDUSTRY

Microprocessors are the brains of personal computers. They are composed of millions of microscopically small transistors—essentially, tiny electronic switches—grouped and interconnected with each other on individual chips of silicon to store and manipulate data.[2] This is why microprocessors are often referred to as chips, as in "the Pentium II chip." Computer software enables microprocessors to perform specific functions with the stored data. As a result, microprocessors today are found not just in computers, but in virtually any inanimate object that can "think" (be programmed to perform certain tasks): traffic lights, cars, cellular telephones, airplanes, etc.

This enormous range of applications for microprocessors spawned a huge industry—the semiconductor industry—with well over $120 billion in sales in 1995, and a projected growth rate of over 20% per year.[3] Intel, as the first company in the world to introduce microprocessors in 1971, quickly established a dominant position in this industry and, in 1996, remained the dominant player with over 85% of microprocessor sales worldwide.

Although Intel had a number of competitors, the company invested billions each year in Research and Development (R&D) in order to retain its lead in innovation and design of new chips. As a result, Intel was constantly introducing faster and more powerful microprocessors in order to stay ahead of the competition. Intel's former CEO, Andy Grove, noted that in a high-technology industry such as semiconductors, "only the paranoid survive."[4]

The contrast between Intel's first microprocessor, the 4004, with only 2,300 transistors, and the one it planned to assemble and test in the proposed Latin American plant, the Pentium II—with over 7.5 million transistors—illustrated this dramatic rate of growth in computing power. Gordon Moore, one of Intel's founders, highlighted the fast-paced nature of competition and innovation in the semiconductor industry when he devised his famous "Moore's Law": driven by competitive market forces, the power of microprocessors will double every 18 months. This law had been fairly consistent with developments in the industry, and Intel had been leading the way since the beginning.

Given the speed of developments and growth in the industry, Intel needed to open a new plant at a rate of almost one every nine months.[5] Doing this, as well as maintaining high levels of spending on R&D, was very expensive—a serious disadvantage when the company had to deal with competitors who could imitate its product designs, then offer similar products at lower cost. Clearly,

if Intel wanted to remain competitive, it could not pass on these costs to consumers in the form of higher prices. Early on, then, Intel's management realized that the company would have to build at least some plants in countries where costs (especially labor costs, which in assembly and testing facilities amount to between 25–30% of total costs) would be lower than in the United States.[6]

Intel's first overseas plant was built in Malaysia in 1972. Later plants followed in Israel, the Philippines, Ireland, and mainland China. But now, in 1996, Ted knew that there was a sense among management that the next plant should be in Latin America. Excessive investment in one region could create risks. For example, although Intel's plant in Malaysia had been productive for many years, in 1996 the plant faced problems resulting from a shortage of qualified labor. As a result, turnover among employees was approaching 30–40%, training was becoming expensive and difficult, and salaries were rising. It made sense to diversify the geographic location of the plants. The company already had a number of plants in Asia, but absolutely none in Latin America. The region offered relatively low labor costs, as well as logistical advantages for exporting production to the U.S. or Europe.[7]

INTEL'S PROPOSED LATIN AMERICAN PLANT: CHARACTERISTICS

Ted knew that the plant Intel had in mind would be an assembly and testing facility, rather than a more sophisticated fabrication plant ("fab"). Still, when it came to making microprocessors, assembly and testing was an involved, complex process, requiring significant technical and engineering expertise, clean rooms, advanced knowledge of chemical processes, and considerable expense. The site selection committee already knew that the plant or plants would employ about 2,000 technicians and engineers initially; this number would eventually increase to 3,500. It would also require the participation of significant numbers of expatriate personnel for extended periods, at least during the startup phase.

While all of these considerations would influence the site selection process, the size of the selected country's market would be irrelevant. This was because Intel planned to export 100% of the product assembled and tested at the plant; almost all of that would be going to the United States.

THE SITE SELECTION PROCESS, PHASE 1: DESK RESEARCH—AND COSTA RICA MAKES THE SHORT LIST

As Ted reviewed the data before him, he reflected on the long, highly systematic site selection process. It had all started with several weeks of desk research. During that time, a group of Intel employees had gathered as much information as they could on a long list of countries in Latin America. The group gathered data on such issues as political and economic stability, labor unions and labor regulations (a particular concern of Intel's), infrastructure, and the availability of an educated workforce (after all, the plant would need trained technicians and engineers).

After this desk research, Ted had been able to eliminate some countries altogether. Venezuela, for example, seemed to be too unstable financially; the desk research phase quickly ruled it out as a serious candidate. But three countries stood out as seeming to have necessary conditions for Intel's planned investment: Mexico, Chile, and Brazil. Costa Rica was added later.

Ted recalled that Costa Rica had *not* been on the original short list. It was only after officials at *Coalición Costarricense de Iniciativas para el Desarrollo* (CINDE, Costa Rica's Investment Promotion Agency) had given presentations to Silicon Valley executives in late 1995 about Costa Rica's potential as a center for high technology investment that Intel executives in California had considered this possibility.

CINDE had been created in 1982 with financial assistance from the United States Agency for International Development (USAID). Its original purpose was to serve as a private, nonprofit export promotion center. Its Board of Directors was (and still is) composed almost entirely of businessmen from the Costa Rican private sector. CINDE was a collaborative effort between USAID and civic-minded businessmen in Costa Rica to promote nontraditional exports (in Costa Rica, this meant anything that was *not* bananas or coffee) and enhance economic development in Costa Rica.

At the time CINDE was created, the Reagan administration was hoping to strengthen the private sector in Central America and the Caribbean to prevent the spread of political instability in these regions. The Administration's Caribbean Basin Initiative (giving preferential access to the U.S. market for manufactured goods from Central America and the Caribbean) was one way to do this. USAID's creation of CINDE was a separate policy but was consistent with the overall strategy.[8]

Over the years, especially after the end of the Cold War in the early 1990s and the fall of the Sandinista regime in Nicaragua in 1990, USAID reduced its funding to Costa Rica and finally closed its offices in the country in 1996. CINDE, with new funding from the World Bank and a trust fund of its own to finance its activities, continued—but with a different emphasis.

Following advice from a consultant with the highly successful Irish Development Authority (IDA)—Ireland's investment promotion agency— as well as from the World Bank, CINDE's directors realized that they should focus on promoting investment from specific firms in specific industries.[9] Professors at the *Instituto Centroamericano de Administración de Empresas* (INCAE), Costa Rica's premier business school, gave CINDE similar advice. Founded by Harvard University, INCAE was influenced by Harvard professor Michael Porter, a frequent visitor to the school and a close adviser to Costa Rica's president, Jose Maria Figueres (himself a Harvard graduate). INCAE recommended that CINDE pursue Porter's idea of promoting clusters of firms in particular industries as a way to accelerate national economic development.[10]

In a detailed study, the World Bank recommended to CINDE that it should target the electronics industry.[11] The Bank argued that the level of technical education in Costa Rica, and the number of electronics firms already located there, made it a suitable location for attracting a number of companies and creating clusters of firms in this industry. Others in CINDE had already made similar arguments, but the World Bank study confirmed these views.[12]

While not a government organization itself, CINDE was fortunate that it had support for its plans at the highest levels of government. Costa Rica's President, Jose Maria Figueres (1994–98), was very interested in promoting high-technology investment in Costa Rica.[13] Educated at West Point (with later graduate study at Harvard), Figueres had a vision of making Costa Rica a haven for high-technology investment. He believed very strongly that the country would be left behind in its quest for economic development if it remained principally an exporter of bananas and coffee, with only some manufacturing investment in low-tech, low-wage, low-value-added industries such as textiles. Costa Rica's gradual increase in Gross Domestic Product (GDP)/capita, education levels, and living standards, combined with the end of political unrest in neighboring Central American countries, had already resulted in a migration of investment out of Costa Rica's textile sector. New investment in this industry was going to countries like Nicaragua, where wages were much lower.

Clearly, changes in the world economy meant that Costa Rica would have to change its strategy, as well. As Figueres explained his government's plan:

> We wanted to incorporate Costa Rica into the global economy in an intelligent way. Globalization was more than simply opening the country to foreign trade. We needed a national strategy not based on cheap labor or the exploitation of our natural resources. We wanted to compete based on productivity, efficiency and technology . . . many textile firms [had] left the country, and the government received severe criticism for not trying to sustain the maquila industry . . . [but] the foreign investment attraction strategy had changed. We wanted to attract industries with higher value-added, that would allow Costa Ricans to increase their standard of living.[14]

All of these factors, including the high level of support from the Figueres administration, made CINDE eager to approach Intel when they heard, in 1995, that the company was planning to put a plant somewhere in Latin America. CINDE officials paid a special visit to Intel's headquarters in Santa Clara and were able to persuade management there that Costa Rica should be on the list. During the actual country visits, the site selection team decided to visit Costa Rica on their way to Brazil.

THE SITE SELECTION PROCESS, PHASE 2: INITIAL COUNTRY VISITS

Actually visiting the countries on the short list was crucial to get a sense, beyond all the data and statistics the team already had, of whether a plant would be a viable investment for a given country. For example, would the country's roads and airport facilities be adequate to transport the product quickly and efficiently to foreign markets? Did the country pose a security risk, to expatriate personnel or to the product? After all, silicon wafers containing hundreds of chips were very valuable—indeed, they were literally "worth more than their weight in gold." (Intel executives used this phrase often in interviews when referring to silicon wafers.) If trucks transporting hundreds or thousands of these on a daily basis were likely to be robbed, the site should be ruled out.

Other questions Intel wanted answered were even more difficult to glean from secondhand written reports. For example, would Intel executives be able to negotiate effectively with government offcials in the country in question? Could a good working relationship be established? Finally, would expat managers be happy living in the country?

Ted was in charge of making the initial contacts with the relevant government officials in each of the countries the site selection team planned to visit. In setting up the visits for the team, he wrote detailed letters explaining what the team hoped to learn during its visit. Central concerns, he stressed, included the following:

- availability of technical personnel and engineers to staff the proposed plant;
- labor unions and labor regulations;

- transportation infrastructure and costs (roads and airports only, since Intel would export all of its product via air);
- the availability and reliability of the electrical power supply;
- the government's corporate taxation rates—and, more specifically—whether the government offered any tax incentives for investments of the kind Intel proposed to make.

Ted had been confident in asking about incentives, for he knew that his requests for meeting with the relevant government officials would be well received. In the past, governments in Latin America had adhered to ideas of protectionism and economic nationalism, but by the late 1990s those ideas were a thing of the past. The proposed investment was something that would be attractive to almost any government in Latin America. After all, Intel's $300–$500 million investment would bring with it thousands of good jobs for technically trained workers and engineers.

In addition, rather than displacing indigenous producers by selling in the domestic market, Intel's product would be 100% exported. This would also contribute to the country's balance of payments. Finally, there was the possibility that Intel would use at least some locally produced components or products, thus creating so-called "linkage effects" and contributing to local economic development. If anything, Ted knew, Intel's proposed plant was the kind of project that countries would compete with one another to attract.

As it had turned out, the site selection team's initial experiences in each of the four countries were very important in making their decision. The team's first visit was to Costa Rica, then Brazil, Chile, and Mexico. Ted opened the first file, and began reviewing what he had learned.

Costa Rica

At first, despite CINDE's lobbying, Costa Rica had seemed an unlikely prospect. The country was simply too small. With only 3.5 million people and a tiny (if reasonably healthy) economy, the Intel executives feared that their investment would overwhelm the small nation. As Bob Perlman said, they were concerned that if Intel did invest in Costa Rica, it would be like "putting a whale in a fish bowl."[15] But the CINDE officials had been persistent, and the site selection team was willing to give the country a closer look.

When it came to luring foreign investors, Costa Rica had many advantages. One was its well-deserved reputation for political stability and democratic government. Surrounded by other countries that had been engulfed in political turmoil and war for much of the 1980s, Costa Rica, in contrast, had abolished its military in 1948 and had been stable, peaceful, and democratic ever since. Costa Rican President Oscar Arias (1986–90) won the Nobel Peace Prize for brokering a peace among the warring Central American nations, thus enhancing Costa Rica's reputation as a center of peace and stability in a chaotic region. Since 1948, the nation had devoted its main government activities toward providing social welfare for the populace and improving education and health care. The government had even set aside over 25% of its national territory as national parks in order to preserve its astonishingly rich biodiversity (and to promote ecotourism).

But for Intel, more important than any of this was the role CINDE played in attending to their concerns. CINDE, autonomous from the government and administered by private business people, was by the mid-1990s a streamlined, efficient, flexible organization. One factor in CINDE's success was that its private status allowed it to pay its employees far more than they could have made working for the government. As a result, CINDE had bright, highly competent employees who were able to pursue Intel aggressively and creatively.

During the visit to Costa Rica, the site selection team was deeply impressed with how prepared CINDE was to receive them and answer their questions quickly and efficiently. The CINDE officials had clearly done their homework. For the harried team, trying to get information as quickly as possible so that a decision could be made and a plant could be built fast, this quality made a very favorable impression indeed.

Following specific advice from Michael Porter, and also from the World Bank's Foreign Investment Advisory Service (an agency at the World Bank that provides less-developed countries with advice on investment promotion), CINDE knew that for a high-tech company like Intel, quick, speedy responses to questions were essential. Therefore, Enrique Egloff, CINDE's General Director, assigned three investment promotion specialists to the task of working exclusively on the upcoming Intel visit. Rather than waiting for the site selection team to arrive and then responding to questions, each of these CINDE officials researched potential questions *in advance* to *anticipate* what Intel might ask. Then, if asked, they were exceptionally well prepared with facts, figures, etc. Also, together the three organized visits for the Intel executives with all of the key government officials that they knew the team would want to meet.[16]

When Ted and his colleagues arrived in Costa Rica, CINDE had a well-planned, extensive agenda already laid out for them. During this and later visits, the Intel team was able to have in-depth discussions on relevant issues with, among others, the head of the ICE (the Costa Rican Electric Utility Company, still state-owned); the Minister of Transport and Public Works; the Minister of Education; the Minister of Science and Technology; the Dean of the *Instituto Tecnológico de Costa Rica* (ITCR); two separate accounting and consulting firms; and a number of other high-technology companies already established in Costa Rica, including Motorola, DSC Communications, and Baxter Healthcare. (Although Baxter had nothing to do with microprocessors, Intel found that it was useful to consult with this company during site selection. Like Intel, Baxter had operations all over the world and had similarly high standards in its production processes, such as the use of clean rooms.)

During the site selection team's initial visit to the country, CINDE officials arranged a visit with Jose Rossi, Minister of Foreign Trade, and President Figueres himself. Figueres impressed the team with his level of personal interest in the company, and his willingness to get involved in details of the negotiating process. But Figueres' level of personal involvement really hit home when the team casually mentioned that they were interested in getting to know Costa Rica's central valley better, since that was where the proposed plant would be located. Figueres said that if they could show up at 7:00 am the next day, he could arrange a helicopter tour. When Ted and his colleagues showed up early the next morning, they were astonished to find Figueres himself at the controls.

Despite the high level attention and the apparent willingness the government had to work with Intel, the site selection team still had several very serious concerns about Costa Rica. The main issues were:

Education

Although Costa Rica appeared to have a sufficient number of engineers, it was lacking in mid-level technicians, crucial for staffing the assembly and testing plant. While the engineers needed to keep the plant operating might number in the several hundreds, the need for mid-level technicians would be in the thousands. Finding enough people with the right training was clearly going to be a problem in Costa Rica.

In discussing this problem with Figueres, the Minister of Education, and the Dean of the Costa Rican Technological Institute (ITCR), the virtues of Costa Rica's small size quickly became evident. All of these officials made clear that they could adapt to Intel's needs, modifying the curriculum of the ITCR and even creating a special certification program to produce the requisite numbers of technicians.

Adapting to Intel's need in this way raised a potential problem. The site selection team had emphasized from the beginning that Intel did not want special treatment, no matter how much Costa Rica wanted its investment project. A major concern was that any special deals or special incentives offered by the Figueres government, and not done in a transparent, legal way, would create problems for Intel in the future, should the next president want to withdraw this special support. Intel was very explicit from the beginning, therefore, that the government not try to offer anything like this.

But the Costa Rican government took care to make sure that the agreement to modify the ITCR's curriculum did not fall into this category. Although the new curriculum would be created in direct response to Intel's concerns, adapting the ITCR's curriculum to Intel's rigorous standards would make the school's graduates better-trained overall, and thus better-equipped to work for *any* high technology firm. The modifications were not just for Intel—they were strengthening the ITCR generally.

In addition to investigating the technical preparedness of Costa Rica for the proposed plant, Ted and his colleagues also observed the level of English language proficiency in the general population, which they perceived to be much higher than it was in other Latin American countries. Ted and his colleagues observed that in Costa Rica, even cab drivers seemed to have a high degree of proficiency in English. Clearly, the general population was relatively well educated, and this was just one indication of that. In addition, the team noted that the current government had made English a required subject in the public school system. While a relatively minor point, English proficiency would be important when expatriates arrived to train local workers, especially since most technical manuals were in English.

Labor Issues

Labor unions were a major concern of Intel's. It did not want them in any of its plants, anywhere in the world, even if they were weak or labor unions in name only. In large part this had to do with the company's complex, highly technical production processes, which simply could not function properly with work stoppages or other kinds of union-related disruptions. These kinds of issues appeared to present few problems

for Intel in Costa Rica. In fact, only about 7% of Costa Rica's private-sector workers belonged to labor unions.[17]

Labor unions had not had much power in Costa Rica since the end of the civil war in the late 1940s, when the new government banned the largest labor confederation in the country because of its affiliation with the Communist Party. Later, when the *Partido Liberación Nacional* (PLN) government was elected in the 1950s, it established *Solidaridad* (Solidarity), a government-sponsored movement to create special voluntary associations as an alternative to more confrontational, industry-wide unions.

Workers who belonged to these *solidarista* associations received numerous benefits, including participation in special savings plans (with contributions made by employers as well as employees), low-interest loans, and profit-sharing. (The profit-sharing was with the association, not the company.) *Solidarista* associations were quite different from labor unions in that they allowed management as well as workers to participate, and had no negotiating power of their own. Some believed that this system had contributed greatly to "labor peace" in the workplace.[18] Over 19% of multinational corporations in Costa Rica, including Firestone, McDonalds, and Colgate-Palmolive, had *solidarista* associations.[19]

In addition to the Solidarity movement, other factors also prevented the development of more traditional, combative labor unions in Costa Rica. One was the government's establishment of a national collective bargaining system, using wage boards to establish wage levels—thereby eliminating an important role for such unions. Still another was the law stating that unions could call a strike only if 60% of affected members signed a petition in favor of doing so, and a judge decided that the reason for the strike was valid. While the judge was deciding, the employer could fire any workers who were involved.[20]

Clearly, labor unions in Costa Rica would not be a major concern for Intel. Moreover, wages in Costa Rica were low in comparison with those in the United States, even for technical workers or skilled technicians. However, this was also true of the other countries on Intel's short list, with the exception of Chile (more on that below).

Transportation

While the roads from most potential sites for the plant to the airport were in excellent condition, and San Jose's international airport was acceptable, Intel's main concern was that the airport did not offer sufficient daily flights. This presented a very serious problem, because Intel would need to export all of its chips by air. After discussing the problem at length with Intel's executives, Costa Rica's Ministry of Transportation and Public Works was willing to be flexible in creating an "open skies" program. It began issuing more licenses and encouraging many other airlines to use the national airport. Again, while this might have seemed a special concession to Intel, it benefited other companies and other industries, especially the tourism industry, as well.

Electrical Energy

Because Costa Rica was not accustomed to industrial projects of the size Intel proposed, it did not have adjusted rates for heavy industrial users. The rate for industrial users varied only between $0.07 and $0.09 per kilowatt-hour—much more expensive, for example, than Mexico's rate of about $0.02 per kilowatt-hour.[21]

After discussion of this issue, ICE agreed to create a new rate for especially heavy users of electricity: $0.05 per kilowatt-hour. This rate would apply to any company using more than 12 megawatts of electricity (more than any other user of electricity in the country). Again, this was *not* a special concession to Intel—because *any* large industrial user that chose to invest in Costa Rica could also take advantage of this heavy use rate.

Investment Incentives

Costa Rica already offered generous incentives to companies located in its eight industrial parks with free trade zone status. Companies in the *Zona Franca* not only did not pay duties on imported parts or components, but were also completely exempt from income tax for eight years, and 50% exempt for four years after that. Intel wanted even more than this and the Costa Rican government was willing to negotiate. After all, other multinational corporations operating in the free trade zones, such as Baxter and Conair, had expressed concern about paying the higher tax rate at the end of their eight-year exemption, even if they planned to reinvest in the country.

Jose Rossi, the Minister of Foreign Trade, agreed to lobby the Costa Rican legislature for a change in the legislation. The new law would give a company a 75% exemption after eight years, provided that it reinvested more than 25% of its initial investment after the fourth year. Again, this would benefit not just Intel but other multinational corporations as well. Jose Rossi emphasized to Intel executives that he would do his best to push for the new policy to become law, but that he could promise no more than that.[22] Working its way through the slow but democratic legislative process, this law finally passed in 1998.

Clearly, there were reasons to be concerned about putting the plant in Costa Rica. But the government did seem willing to work with Intel without breaking any of its own laws by offering special deals. The prospects at least looked promising. But the next country the team planned to visit, Brazil, seemed potentially to offer a lot more.

Brazil

The site selection team's experience in Brazil was in marked contrast to what had happened in Costa Rica. Brazil's size alone was an enormous contrast: 160 million people in contrast to Costa Rica's relatively puny 3.5 million. Also, unlike Costa Rica's simple, unitary political system, where power was centered in the national legislature and the president, Brazil offered another layer of complexity: it had a federal system. This meant that Intel could pick and choose among Brazil's 26 states for just the right investment deal. Under Brazil's decentralized system, states and even municipalities had some control over taxation policy and could offer individual incentives in order to lure investment. This practice had grown to such an extent that in Brazil it had come to be known as the *guerra fiscal* or "taxation war." Some states had actually driven themselves to the point of bankruptcy in their efforts to compete with other states in offering the most generous exemptions from the state value-added tax, the ICMS.[23]

At the federal level, Brazil provided a tax incentive specifically directed toward the computer industry through the *Processo Produtivo Básico* (PPB), or Basic Productive Process law. In order to receive this incentive (which included a reduction of up to 50% of corporate income tax, as well as reductions in some other taxes), companies had to invest 5% of total revenue in research and development. At least 2% of this had to be invested in universities or other government-approved institutions; the rest could be invested internally.[24]

While the PPB potentially seemed interesting, the fiscal incentives at the state level turned out not to be very relevant. The site selection team had already decided that the best location for a plant would be in the state of São Paulo—where the governor, Mario Covas, had explicitly rejected offering any special tax incentives.[25] In any case, the ICMS tax itself would not apply to Intel, since this tax was not levied on exported products.[26]

Covas's reason for not being generous about incentives was that São Paulo did not need to do much to lure investment. For after Brazil had finally stabilized its economy with the implementation of the *Plano Real* in 1994, billions of dollars of foreign investment were flowing into the country every year. And the lion's share of this investment went to São Paulo, the most heavily populated and economically developed state in the entire country.

What intrigued Intel about São Paulo was that the state had already succeeded in attracting numerous high technology firms. In fact, within a couple hours' drive from the capital, the megacity of São Paulo (population: 16 million people), were the much smaller cities of São Jose dos Campos and Campinas. In these cities, hundreds of high-technology firms had already established themselves. São Jose dos Campos was the home of EMBRAER and many other high-technology firms. Campinas, of particular interest to Intel, had managed to attract IBM, Compaq, Hewlett Packard, DEC, and Texas Instruments, to name just a few. Significantly, while São Paulo state did not offer any special tax incentives, Campinas's municipal government did provide them. Specifically, it granted exemption from city property and service taxes for any high-technology companies that established manufacturing plants in either of two industrial parks in the city, both specifically oriented toward high-technology firms.[27]

Clearly, Brazil had a lot to offer. In terms of *adequate numbers of technical personnel*, there was no question that the numbers in Campinas (home of the famed technological university, the *Universidade Estadual de Campinas*, or UNICAMP) would be far superior to what Intel could find in Costa Rica. *Infrastructure* was more than adequate; electrical power was readily available at reasonable costs, and the airports were already capable of meeting Intel's needs.

But other issues worried Intel's site selection team. *Security* was of some concern; according to some reports, hijacking of trucks in the São Paulo area was on the rise.[28] Another concern was *labor unions*, which, while not as powerful as they were in some Latin American countries, could be more militant than those in Costa Rica. In Brazil, all workers paid union dues, whether they were formal union members or not (of Brazil's total workforce, about 20–25% was unionized). A single union represented all workers in a particular industry in a given geographic area. These unions were organized at the federal level into labor federations. The *Central Única dos Trabalhadores* (Central Workers' Union, or CUT), the more combative of Brazil's two principal labor federations, was linked to the *Partido dos Trabalhadores* (Workers' Party, or PT), which controlled some state and municipal governments in Brazil. While workers' base wages were relatively low, overall labor costs in Brazil tended to be higher than in other Latin American countries because mandatory benefits for full-time employees, such as paid vacations, lengthy maternity (also paternity!) leaves, and social security taxes, added 50–80% to the total cost.[29]

But perhaps the biggest problem that the site selection team encountered in their visit to Brazil was that, after their highly favorable experience with CINDE, and all the personal attention to their concerns lavished upon them from Figueres, Brazilian government officials seemed indifferent to their concerns. Foreign firms were so eager to get into Brazil to get access to its huge internal market that state and national government officials did not need to concern themselves with addressing special concerns of individual corporations—even of an industry giant like Intel. Moreover, on balance, the federal government's policies did not seem all that favorable. While the federal government did offer the specific PPB incentive for firms investing in R&D, it offered no general exemption from corporate income tax—and it had a high rate of taxation.

After the Costa Rica experience, all of this left a negative impression. Certainly Brazil did have a huge and very attractive domestic market. But for this particular project, Intel had no interest whatsoever in the domestic market of the country where its plant would be located. 100% of the product manufactured in the plant would be exported.

In addition to the lack of special incentives in São Paulo state, and the required income tax at the federal level, there were still more additional costs associated with doing business in Brazil. There seemed to be numerous other taxes, such as the infamous tax on financial transactions, and other expenses that all added up to what expatriate executives referred to as "the Brazil cost"— the extra cost of doing business in Brazil. Extra costs might be worth enduring if the tradeoff was access to a huge local market. But when a company intended to produce exclusively for export, as in Intel's case, these costs could be prohibitive. After all, aside from the (at the time) overvalued exchange rate, the "Brazil cost" was one of the chief reasons Brazilian firms themselves had difficulty exporting and why Brazil's current account deficit was so large.

Chile

After Brazil, the site selection team visited Chile. The team was very impressed with Chile's modern infrastructure and the country's technical training programs. But they immediately encountered four problems: distance, labor costs, capital controls, and lack of government incentives.

Distance

The site selection team was struck by the sheer amount of travel time to get from the United States to Santiago, Chile (almost 12 hours, given the scarcity of direct flights). Aware of the number of expatriate executives who would have to be traveling to the plant, at least in the startup phase, the team saw that this could present a problem. Costa Rica, in contrast, was only a three-hour flight from Texas or California.

Labor Costs

One legacy of the dictatorship of General Augusto Pinochet in Chile (1973–89) was a labor code that inhibited the development of powerful, confrontational labor unions. Only about 12% of the workforce was unionized. Unions that included members from more than one company were allowed to engage in collective bargaining only if the company in question agreed to this arrangement—which few companies ever did.[30]

Partly as a result of these rules, labor costs for unskilled workers were low in Chile, even though the country had one of the highest GDPs/capita in all of Latin America. However, salaries for technically trained personnel, which Intel needed most, were relatively high. The starting salary for an engineer in Chile was between $30,000–$40,000—not very different from what it would be in the U.S. Intel could hire engineers in Costa Rica or Mexico for almost half that amount.

Capital Controls

At the time of Intel's visit in 1996, Chile's Central Bank had a policy designed to control capital flight during times of market volatility. This policy stated that for portfolio capital investments (*not* for direct foreign investments, such as what Intel planned), investors would be restricted from withdrawing their investment from Chile for one full year. In addition, investors would be required to deposit an amount, called the *encaje,* equivalent to 30% of their overall investment in a special account at Chile's Central Bank during that time period.[31]

This policy was a legacy of an earlier era, when capital controls were common throughout Latin America. Most Latin American countries had already eliminated this kind of policy, considering it to be counterproductive, in line with the overall "Latin American consensus" in favor of market-oriented policies. Even though Intel presumably would not be affected, since the proposed plant would be a *direct* foreign investment (as opposed to portfolio investment, e.g., investment in the Chilean capital markets), Intel executives were spooked by this policy. One government official was struck with how often the Intel executives brought up this issue, in meeting after meeting.[32]

Government Incentives

Beyond these other concerns, the Chilean government simply was not able to offer any significant investment incentives to Intel. Government officials at *Corporación de Fomento de la Producción* (CORFO), Chile's government development agency, explained to the site selection team that the market-oriented "Chilean model" was designed not to interfere with market forces, i.e., *not* to give special incentives for investment in selected industries.[33]

CORFO *was* authorized to offer incentives if the investment were to be located in an especially poor region of the country in need of economic development. CORFO officials went so far as to suggest a location for Intel's plant that would meet these criteria, a poor region of Chile not far from Valparaiso. But the site selection team made very clear to CORFO that they did not want to be outside of the general vicinity of Santiago.[34]

Mexico

The final country on the team's itinerary, Mexico, offered an especially promising location for Intel's plant: the Silicon Valley of Mexico, Guadalajara. The second-largest city in the country, Guadalajara had by the mid-1990s established itself as a center for high technology firms, particularly in the electronics sector. Beginning with Motorola and IBM in the 1960s, hundreds of electronics firms had established plants in and around Guadalajara, the capital of the relatively prosperous Mexican state of Jalisco.

The site selection team was highly impressed with Guadalajara. They talked to a number of executives in high-technology firms, including Motorola and Lucent, which were already there. The *Secretaría de Promoción Económica* (SEPROE), or Jalisco State Economic Development Agency, was extremely well prepared with eye-catching brochures and detailed information that rivaled what the Intel executives had encountered at CINDE. SEPROE, too, prepared a detailed agenda, just as CINDE had done; and the site selection team had plenty of opportunities to speak to several expatriate executives on their own, just as they had done in Costa Rica.

The response from all of the site selection team's interviews was highly favorable about Guadalajara.[35] As part of Mexico's fabled "Golden Triangle," infrastructure in the city and surrounding area was more than adequate. The airport's number of flights and capacity was sufficient. Labor costs were low, yet there appeared to be a relatively large supply of skilled engineers and technicians. Finally, energy in Mexico, produced from abundant supplies of natural gas, was relatively inexpensive. As mentioned before, electrical power in Mexico was only about $0.02 per kilowatt-hour—significantly cheaper than Costa Rica's rate, even after implementation of the ICE's new policy granting special rates to heavy industrial users.

Unlike the indifference the site selection team had encountered in São Paulo, the Jalisco state government was eager to work with Intel. SEPROE officials explained that, in collaboration with the governor of Jalisco (renowned for his honesty and effectiveness), the agency was actively pursuing a strategy of encouraging high-technology investment. It was doing this indirectly by subsidizing numerous technical training schools so that there would be an adequate supply of skilled labor in the region. Also, like CINDE in Costa Rica, SEPROE officials traveled frequently (sometimes accompanied by the governor) to spread the word about Guadalajara overseas and encourage foreign investment by high-technology firms, particularly in the electronics sector. The governor, Alberto Cardenas, was a member of the *Partido de Acción Nacional* (PAN), a business-friendly political party with market-oriented economic views.

SEPROE had a complex formula that it used to determine the number of jobs a company's investment project would be likely to produce, and the capital that the project would bring to the state. On the basis of this formula, SEPROE was prepared to offer Intel free land for the plant's site, and subsidized training for Intel employees for an extended period. But despite all of these positive factors, Intel had two serious concerns.

Lack of Government Incentives at the Federal Level

For all of the incentives the Jalisco state government was prepared to offer at the state level, the federal government of Mexico refused to budge on giving income tax exemptions at the federal level. Also, the extreme centralization of the budget process in Mexico meant that, while the states could provide incentives such as free land and subsidized training for employees, state officials had no ability to offer fiscal incentives of their own, even if the federal government had allowed them to do so. As one top SEPROE official remarked in frustration, "The federal government receives 100% of the tax revenues, but then only redistributes about 20% of that revenue to the states."[36]

Labor Unions

Mexican federal law also contained certain rules about unions that worried the site selection team. Intel had a policy about not having unions anywhere in the world. But Mexico's federal law stated that if a minimum of 20 employees in a given company decided to form a union, the company would be required to recognize it. If only two employees chose to affiliate with a union from outside the company, the company would be required to recognize and work with that union, provided that it was already recognized by the Mexican labor authorities. However, the workers would have to decide which form of representation they wanted, because only one union was allowed to represent the workers in a specific company. Most workers belonged to unions that were members of Mexico's nine largest national labor confederations, which had close ties to the dominant *Partido Revolucionário Institucional* (PRI) party.[37]

Although companies were not required to have unions, in practice union organizers from outside the company would often work with company employees to organize a union or recruit them to affiliate with outside unions. This meant that most large companies in Mexico had to deal with unions, and that the country had a high rate of unionization. Of Mexico's total workforce, nearly 40% was unionized; of industrial workers in companies with more than 20 employees, the figure was closer to 80%.[38]

Many companies in Mexico ensured harmonious labor relations by working with company unions referred to as *sindicatos blancos* ("white unions"). In some cases, these unions were not really representative of the workers, but served only to comply technically with Mexico's legal requirements. Outside organizers would not be able to come in and form a more combative union (unless a majority of the workers voted for this), because the company would technically already have union representation. Other white unions were more genuinely representative of the workers, but worked in a collaborative way with management. In any case, white unions were much easier to work with than the more combative, confrontational unions that existed in many industries in Mexico.

But even if Intel were able to negotiate an agreement with a white union, this would still go against Intel's worldwide policy not to have unions in its plants. Intel would no longer be able to tell its employees elsewhere that the company had no unions whatsoever, at any plant in the world.

IBM managed to get around this problem at its own plant in Guadalajara by contracting out the majority of its workforce. Although 10,000 people worked at the IBM plant in Guadalajara, only about 500, all nonunionized management-level personnel (engineers and executives), were actually IBM employees. The rest worked *at* the IBM plant but were actually employed by other companies that were contact manufacturers, doing specific projects on a temporary basis for IBM. (Of course, all of these companies had unions.) This arrangement gave IBM flexibility in terms of its payroll, because during times of slack demand it could simply hire fewer contract manufacturers without having to worry about dismissing its own personnel and dealing directly with Mexican labor law issues.

Knowing about these different ways of working around Mexico's labor laws, SEPROE officials told Intel's site selection team not to worry. The company would not need to have a labor union. Intel could very easily be an exception to the general norm in Mexico.

But this very willingness on the part of government officials in Mexico even potentially to make an exception in Intel's case alarmed the site selection team even more. If the rules were not clear-cut, objective, and adhered to in a straightforward manner, then this created an unpredictable, nontransparent environment. This potential for lack of predictability and transparency in the rules of the game was of grave concern to Intel. It smacked of the "special deals" that the company had tried so much to avoid in Costa Rica.

Ted closed the last file and rubbed his eyes. He really had to finish that report.

Notes

1. The principal members of the site selection team were Ted Telford, International Site Selection Analyst; Chuck Pawlak, Director, New Site Development; and Bob Perlman, Vice President for Tax, Customs, and Licensing. Telford and Pawlak worked out of Intel's Chandler, Arizona, office; Perlman was based at the headquarters office in Santa Clara, California. Beyond these three members, there was an extended group of about 15 Intel employees all over the world who participated in detailed assessment of countries on issues such as energy availability, construction, operations, security, etc. Frank Alvarez, Vice President of the Technology and Management Group, was also based in Santa Clara and ultimately had final say over the site selection decision, along with Mike Splinter, Vice President of Worldwide Manufacturing and, of course, Craig Barrett, Intel's CEO.

2. Silicon is used because it is a semiconductor. Semiconductors are materials that can be altered either to be conductors of electricity or insulators—a useful quality in a material used for constructing the complex electronic circuitry of microprocessors. "Silicon Valley" is a nickname for the region around Stanford University, which includes many towns that serve as a home to important high-technology companies (including Santa Clara, where Intel headquarters were located).

Using sophisticated chemical processes and engineering techniques, microprocessors are manufactured by the hundreds on extremely thin layers of silicon known as wafers. Each wafer is about 6–8 inches in diameter. The microprocessors are tested while they are still on the silicon wafer. Later, these wafers are cut into individual pieces or chips, each containing one microprocessor. The microprocessors are then tested again, packaged, and sent to customers for installation in many different kinds of automated devices.

3. World Bank, Foreign Investment Advisory Service, *FDI News,* December 1996, p. 5.

4. Grove later wrote a book with this title.

5. Debora Spar, "Attracting High Technology Investment," Foreign Investment Advisory Service, World Bank, Occasional Paper #11, April 1998, p. 4.

6. Ibid., p. 8.

7. Interview with Ted Telford, Site Selection Analyst, Intel, Glendale, Arizona, September 10, 1998.

8. Mary A. Clark, "Transnational Alliances and Development Policy in Latin America: Non Traditional Export Promotion in Costa Rica," *Latin American Research Review,* Vol. 32, No. 2, 1997, p. 91.

9. Interviews with CINDE officials, San Jose, Costa Rica, October–November 1998.

10. Thomas T. Vogel, "Costa Rica's Sales Pitch Lures High-Tech Giants Like Intel and Microsoft," *Wall Street Journal,* April 2, 1998, p. A-18; interviews with CINDE officials, San Jose, Costa Rica, October–November 1998.

11. The World Bank, "Costa Rica: A Strategy for Foreign Investment in Costa Rica's Electronics Industry" (Washington, D.C.: The World Bank), 1996.

12. Interview with Rodrigo Zapata, former Vice President of CINDE (now General Manager for GE–Costa Rica), San Jose, Costa Rica, October 1998. The study was conducted by the World Bank's Foreign Investment Advisory Service. Although the final version was published in 1996, CINDE was well aware of its main points long before that time.

13. Jose Maria Figueres was the son of Jose (Pepe) Figueres Ferrer, who led a civil war in 1948 when the Costa Rican legislature had nullified the outcome of a presidential election for a candidate who had won a legitimate election victory. During a brief period as interim president immediately following the war, Pepe Figueres succeeded in writing a new constitution and abolishing Costa Rica's military entirely, an unprecedented feat in Latin America (or virtually anywhere else, for that matter). He then turned power over to the rightful victor in the 1948 presidential election. He was elected president of Costa Rica himself several years later (1953–57).

14. Excerpt from interview with Jose Maria Figueres, quoted in Nils Ketelhohn, "The Costa Rican Electronics and information Technology Cluster," unpublished manuscript, 1998, p. 6.

15. Telephone interview with Bob Perlman, Intel's Vice President for Tax, Customs, and Licensing, August 1998.

16. Interviews with all three individuals in San Jose, Costa Rica, October–November 1998.

17. Bruce M. Wilson, *Costa Rica: Politics, Economics, and Democracy* (Boulder, CO: Lynne Rienner Publishers, 1998), p. 70.

18. CINDE Web site, www.cinde.or.cr.

19. Ibid.

20. Wilson, *Costa Rica,* pp. 69–70.

21. Interview with Danilo Arias, former CINDE investment promotion specialist, San Jose, Costa Rica, October 1998.

22. Interview with Jose Rossi, former Minister of Foreign Trade, San Jose, Costa Rica, November 1998.

23. I use only the acronym for the state value-added tax here because the full name is quite a mouthful. ICMS stands for *Imposto sobre as operações relativas a Circulação de Mercadorias e sobre a prestação de Serviços de transporte intermunicipal e de comunicação.*

24. Renato Bastos, U.S. Department of Commerce, "Computer Hardware and Peripherals," Industry Sector Analysis for Brazil, São Paulo, Brazil, October 1998, p. 15.

25. Although São Paulo did allow an exception for the computer industry by reducing its relatively high ICMS from 18% to 12% for computer products only, this was still a high rate. See Bastos, p. 15.

26. American Chamber of Commerce–São Paulo, "How to Undertstand Corporate Taxation in Brazil" (informational pamphlet), São Paulo, 1999, p. 17.

27. Município de Campinas, Lei N. 8003 de agosto de 1994, in "Incentivos Fiscais do Município de Campinas–SP," provided by Prefeitura Municipal de Campinas, November 1998.

28. Interview with Intel executive, Glendale, Arizona, October 1998.

29. "Brazil: Investing, Licensing, and Trading," *The Economist Intelligence Unit* (London: The Economist Intelligence Unit), January 1999.

30. Matt Moffett, "Pinochet's Legacy: Chile's Labor Law Hobbles Its Workers and Troubles the U.S.," *Wall Street Journal,* October 15, 1997, p. A-10.

31. Technically, the policy still exists. However, currently, the rate is set at 0%—so portfolio investors do not have to put any money in this special account. Some in Chile, and all foreign investors, would like to see the end of this policy once and for all. The fact that the policy still remains, even if the rate is set at 0%, means that a higher percentage could be re-imposed at any time.

32. Interview with Francisco Troncoso, Director, International Relations Division, CORFO, Santiago, Chile, December 1998.

33. Interview with Mario Castillo, Deputy Director, Strategic Planning Division, CORFO, Santiago, Chile, December 1998.

34. Ibid.

35. Interview with Ted Telford, Phoenix, September 1998. Information from this section is also based on my interviews with officials at SEPROE, with executives at Lucent, Motorola, SCI, and IBM, and with others in Guadalajara, Mexico, December 1998, and August 1999.

36. Comments by SEPROE official, Guadalajara, Mexico, August 1999.

37. Edward G. Hinkelman (ed.), *Mexico Business: The Portable Encyclopedia for Doing Business with Mexico* (San Rafael, CA: World Trade Press), 1994, p. 15.

38. "Mexico: Investing, Licensing and Trading," *The Economist Intelligence Unit* (London: The Economist Intelligence Unit Limited), September 1998.

THE ACER GROUP'S CHINA MANUFACTURING DECISION

Prepared by Donna Everatt under the supervision of Professors Terence Tsai and Borshiuan Cheng

Version: (A) 1999-08-25

In the late summer of 1998, M.Y. Lin, the vice-president of the Acer's Global Operations Centre for manufacturing operations, was reviewing the brief he had prepared for a meeting with senior management. Specifically, the brief provided background information on which to base the decision of whether the time was right to commence full-scale manufacturing operations on the Chinese mainland, and if so, where and how should he recommend that Acer begin?

THE ACER GROUP

The Acer Group was one of the world's largest PC and computer component manufacturers. Associated Acer companies included the world's third-largest PC manufacturer, and Acer's mobile computers, network servers and personal computers were ranked in the world's top 10 most popular brands in their respective product categories. Acer was the market leader in 13 countries around the world, and was ranked in the top five in more than 30 nations globally. Sales of the six million PCs and almost four million monitors

Acer produced in 1997 topped US$6.5 billion with earnings of US$89 million due to the strength of its core businesses (see Exhibit 1). Besides being a top PC supplier in Africa, the Middle East and Southeast Asia, Acer had a lucrative US$500 million operation in OEM manufacturing. With more than 23,000 employees, half of whom were located outside of Taiwan, and 120 enterprises in 44 countries supporting dealers and distributors in over 100 countries throughout the world, Acer was a truly global organization.

Acer's global mission statement was "fresh technology enjoyed by everyone, everywhere." This was the philosophy on which Acer had grown, and the firm was widely regarded as a worldwide pioneer in delivering high-performance PCs at accessible prices. Based on this principle, in 1997 Acer introduced the low-cost multimedia PC, the Acer Basic II, for just under US$1,000, the much-talked-about price point in the U.S. Media and observers in the PC industry had been widely expecting that a PC at this price would initiate the next generation of PCs to be introduced into the marketplace. This focus on price

Acer Group financial highlights
Combined
Excluding TI-Acer*

Unit: US $ Million

For the year	1993		1994		1995		1996		1997	
	Combined	Excl. TI-Acer	Combined	Excl. TI-Acer	Combined	Excl. TI-Acer	Combined	Excl. TI-Acer	Combined	Excl. TI-Acer
Total Revenue	1,883	1,651	3,220	2,901	5,825	5,262	5,893	5,346	6,509	6,132
Revenue Growth %	49.4%	38.4%	71.0%	75.7%	80.9%	81.4%	1.2%	1.6%	10.5%	14.7%
Net Earning	86	22	205	103	413	163	188	150	89	262
Net Earning %	4.6%	1.3%	6.4%	3.6%	7.1%	3.1%	3.2%	2.8%	1.4%	4.3%
Total Equity	497	316	703	420	1,450	939	2,008	1,321	2,065	1,638
ROE	18.5%	7.0%	34.2%	28.1%	38.4%	23.9%	10.9%	13.3%	4.4%	17.7%
Total Assets	1,584	1,143	2,082	1,520	3,645	2,340	4,192	3,156	4,758	3,608
ROA	5.7%	2.0%	11.2%	7.8%	14.4%	8.4%	4.8%	5.5%	2.0%	7.7%
Net Investment in Property, Plant and Equipment	497	181	538	197	963	284	1,347	418	1,470	616
Working Capital	173	149	288	280	767	758	996	995	875	974
No. of Stockholders	70,000	44,000	70,000	69,000	90,000	89,000	123,000	122,000	155,000	154,000
No. of Employees	7,200	6,348	9,700	8,612	15,352	13,947	16,778	15,272	22,948	21,307

Exhibit 1   Sales Chart

*Due to the drastic drop in the market price of DRAM during 1996–97, the Acer Group's financial results excluding TI-Acer operations are provided to more accurately reflect the economic status of non-DRAM Acer Group operations.

competition was restructuring the PC industry, and PC firms worldwide were struggling for ways to manage eroding margins by lowering costs. The Acer Basic II was initially to be introduced in Acer's domestic market, followed by Greater Asia, mainland China, India, Russia and the U.S. Features varied from country to country; however, the standard configuration was equipped with an Intel Pentium processor, at least 16 MB of RAM and Microsoft Windows 95. In countries further along the technology adoption curve, the Acer Basic II would also include an 8x CD-ROM drive and 33.6 k fax/modem for express connection to the Internet.

LEADING ACER TO THE NEXT MILLENNIUM

Stan Shih, the founder and chairman of the Acer group and widely regarded as a high-tech visionary, had a long-term vision for Acer to transform the Group into a global high-tech corporation. Though fully committed to aggressively pursuing ever-growing segments of the PC market, Acer began to shift a sizable portion of its attention and resources to the "3E" market—education, entertainment, and e-commerce. Newly created ventures in the realm of semiconductors, communications and consumer electronics were expected to play an integral role in Acer's strategic growth. In keeping with Acer's style of growth to date, these interests capitalized on prior technological competencies, while complementing the development of the existing PC business.

With a view to creating an organizational structure that would support this new vision and enhance global competitiveness, in 1998, the Acer group was re-engineered (see Exhibit 2). The modified organizational structure resulted in the creation of several new corporate functions and business development teams.

This reorganization was adopted to fortify Acer's overall competitiveness in light of what industry analysts saw as a disintegration of the PC industry in 1998, meaning that almost every product was based on an "open standard," resulting

in competition in market niches where companies were fighting for market segment leadership. Whereas PCs had historically been Acer's core business, and continued to be in 1998, the disintegration of the entire IT industry forced Acer into developing strategic new business divisions. In 1998, Acer continued to develop its technological expertise in components for mainstream PC systems as well as peripheral markets, while seriously exploring dynamic new opportunities in the consumer electronics, communication and semiconductor industries.

DECENTRALIZATION—WITH A CENTRALIZED CORE

Each Acer Group member company operated independently, while at the same time working together to take full advantage of the resources available from a global US$8 billion multinational. The glue that bound the associated Acer Group of companies together was the Acer brand name and the technological development brought about by Acer's R&D activities. Over the last several years, however, it became clear that centralization of some common corporate functions would be a more effective method of managing the Acer Group. To that end, in January 1998, the Acer Group centralized four functions, which were consequently controlled by Acer Group's global operations: Brand Management, Global Logistics, Customer Service and Information Technology Infrastructure. These divisions provided the strategic direction, planning, integration and implementation of all related Acer businesses throughout the world.

Acer's decentralized organizational structure delegated responsibility to management to involve employees in the decision-making process. This was considered their strategic advantage in the fast-moving, ever-changing world of computers. It was expected that this approach would occasionally involve conflicts that would be assuaged through open discussion and persuasion. Head office management recognized that it was unreasonable to ask their managers to follow various

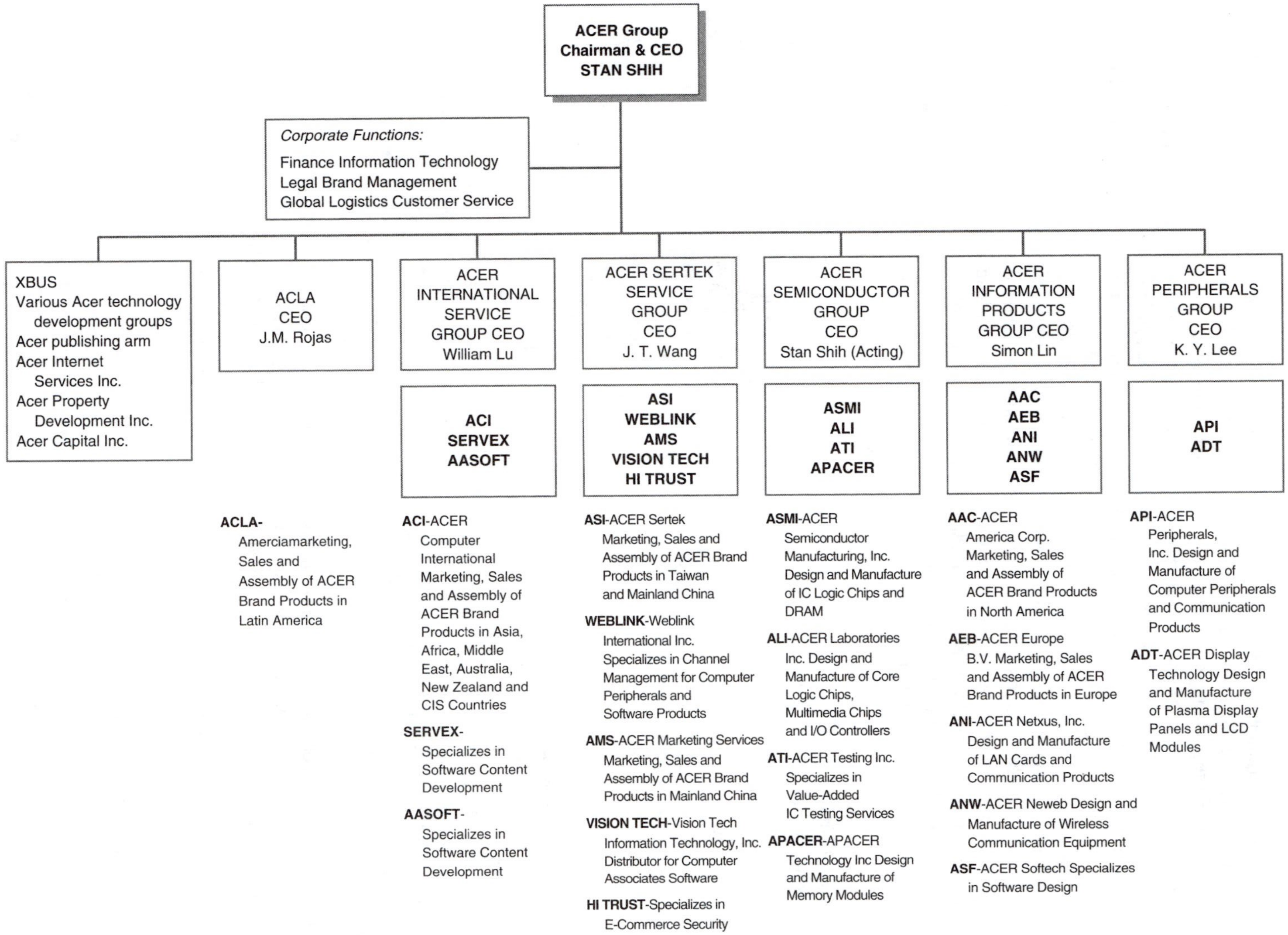

ACER Group Chairman & CEO STAN SHIH

Corporate Functions:
Finance Information Technology
Legal Brand Management
Global Logistics Customer Service

XBUS
Various Acer technology
development groups
Acer publishing arm
Acer Internet
Services Inc.
Acer Property
Development Inc.
Acer Capital Inc.

ACLA
CEO
J.M. Rojas

ACER INTERNATIONAL SERVICE GROUP CEO William Lu

ACI
SERVEX
AASOFT

ACER SERTEK SERVICE GROUP CEO J. T. Wang

ASI
WEBLINK
AMS
VISION TECH
HI TRUST

ACER SEMICONDUCTOR GROUP CEO Stan Shih (Acting)

ASMI
ALI
ATI
APACER

ACER INFORMATION PRODUCTS GROUP CEO Simon Lin

AAC
AEB
ANI
ANW
ASF

ACER PERIPHERALS GROUP CEO K. Y. Lee

API
ADT

ACLA- Amerciamarketing, Sales and Assembly of ACER Brand Products in Latin America

ACI-ACER Computer International Marketing, Sales and Assembly of ACER Brand Products in Asia, Middle East, Australia, New Zealand and CIS Countries

SERVEX- Specializes in Software Content Development

AASOFT- Specializes in Software Content Development

ASI-ACER Sertek Marketing, Sales and Assembly of ACER Brand Products in Taiwan and Mainland China

WEBLINK-Weblink International Inc. Specializes in Channel Management for Computer Peripherals and Software Products

AMS-ACER Marketing Services Marketing, Sales and Assembly of ACER Brand Products in Mainland China

VISION TECH-Vision Tech Information Technology, Inc. Distributor for Computer Associates Software

HI TRUST-Specializes in E-Commerce Security

ASMI-ACER Semiconductor Manufacturing, Inc. Design and Manufacture of IC Logic Chips and DRAM

ALI-ACER Laboratories Inc. Design and Manufacture of Core Logic Chips, Multimedia Chips and I/O Controllers

ATI-ACER Testing Inc. Specializes in Value-Added IC Testing Services

APACER-APACER Technology Inc Design and Manufacture of Memory Modules

AAC-ACER America Corp. Marketing, Sales and Assembly of ACER Brand Products in North America

AEB-ACER Europe B.V. Marketing, Sales and Assembly of ACER Brand Products in Europe

ANI-ACER Netxus, Inc. Design and Manufacture of LAN Cards and Communication Products

ANW-ACER Neweb Design and Manufacture of Wireless Communication Equipment

ASF-ACER Softech Specializes in Software Design

API-ACER Peripherals, Inc. Design and Manufacture of Computer Peripherals and Communication Products

ADT-ACER Display Technology Design and Manufacture of Plasma Display Panels and LCD Modules

Exhibit 2   Organization Chart

593

courses of action without reason. According to the associate vice-president of the Acer Institute of Education, Alan Chang, management at corporate headquarters were willing to explain and justify policies to local managers, and were willing to "take the time to convince the manager, and importantly, were willing to be convinced."

Although there were several advantages in the autonomy of individual business units, senior management's biggest challenge at Acer was to consolidate the strength of the decentralized structure—to find the balance between Acer's core concept of "symbiotic common interest," which fostered personal commitment toward Acer's goals, and another core concept of adopting a highly decentralized, delegated management system that encouraged the head of each business unit to interpret and implement the corporate culture according to their own ideas and to achieve their specific mandates in the way they considered most effective. In this way, it was Shih's belief that Acer would achieve a "global vision with a local touch."

"LOCAL TOUCH"

A "local touch" was achieved in several ways. For example, Acer's foreign market entry strategy involved forming joint ventures to establish distribution systems and marketing and promotional activities in the local market. This "local touch" involved partners, who had intimate knowledge of the market, well-established relationships with local businesses and local distribution networks. Advertising and brand name support (marketing communications and promotion) costs were shared equally.

Acer's "local touch" was also achieved through product adaptation to suit local market language, tastes, trends, conditions and technological innovation. Also, Acer took an active attitude toward its local social responsibilities, left to the judgment of regional managers, which helped Acer integrate into foreign cultures with a long-term view. Workers were hired locally and, over a period of several years, Acer gradually replaced

Taiwanese managers with local managers. Local managers were encouraged to be entrepreneurial and to feel like owners, and as such were invited to participate in stock options, purchasing stock in their SBUs at book value.

In the future, another way that "local touch" would be attained was in the creation of a global coalition of highly autonomous Acer companies that would be owned predominantly by local investors and managed by local employees. Acer's strategy of floating various SBUs on stock exchanges throughout the world would allow not only institutional and retail investors to buy into Acer's success in a less intimidating way than purchasing shares in Taiwan (where most investors did not follow the market) but also allowed participation from local distributors who would have a built-in incentive to promote Acer computers to local buyers.

This "borderless network of companies" would be achieved with listings of a total of 21 Acer SBUs on stock exchanges throughout the world before the end of the 21st century. In Acer parlance, this program was referred to as "21 in 21." The program began in the summer of 1998, with the public listing of five Acer companies. The first listing outside of Taiwan where Acer Inc. was listed was in 1995 when Acer Computer International (which oversaw the distribution of Acer products throughout Asia, Africa, the Middle-East and Russia) was floated on the Singapore stock exchange. Other companies in the Acer Group that were listed on international stock exchanges included Acer Peripherals, which manufactured color monitors and keyboards, as well as Acer Sertek, a distributor of a full range of Acer products in Taiwan. Acer was intent on becoming a global player not only through international stock market listings, but also through the global expansion of its manufacturing operations.

ACER'S GLOBAL MANUFACTURING STRATEGY

The Acer Group had 17 production sites and 30 assembly plants located in 24 countries around the world that manufactured computers, peripherals and related high-tech components. In addition to the company's home base in Hsinchu Science-Based Industrial Park, Acer had established production facilities in: Penang, Malaysia; El Paso, Texas; Tilburg, Netherlands; Subic Bay, Philippines; Mexicali and Juarez, Mexico; and Cardiff, South Wales. Additional production facilities were planned in North America, Europe and Latin America. Acer was one of the few IT companies in the world that had the manufacturing capabilities to produce complete product lines.

Acer's global manufacturing strategy involved not only expanding manufacturing plants throughout the world, but also shifting the assembly of computers from Taiwanese plants to areas where the computers would be distributed. These so-called "uniload" plants assembled Acer-brand computers as well as computers for Acer's OEM customers. This "fast food" business model ensured reduced inventory plus a faster time to market and was more responsive to changes in local market conditions (see Exhibit 3). Moreover, being closer to the market meant that distribution logistics were more manageable and highly flexible.

ACER'S "FAST FOOD" MODEL

This approach involved moving the assembly of PCs to local sites, using components supplied by

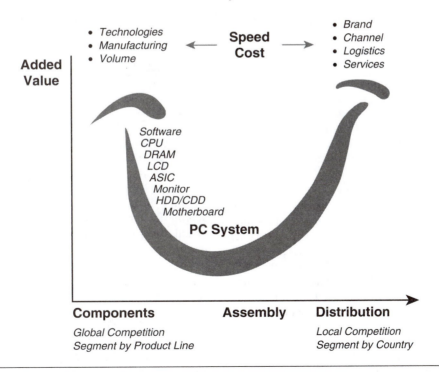

Stan Shih's Smiling Curve

PC Industry Value Curve

Exhibit 3 Acer's Fast Food Model

SBUs. Components themselves were referred to as "perishable," determined by how much was at risk if the part was kept in inventory or not available. Perishability was also used to describe how sensitive the component was to either changing technology or fluctuations in market price. These components were shipped via air freight to manufacturing sites worldwide to keep them "fresh," and the most "perishable" components (such as CPUs) were sourced locally. Non-perishable components, such as PC housings and power supplies, were shipped via sea transport because their "freshness" was not as much of an issue.

The analogy could also be used to describe Acer's "central kitchens," which were located in Asia and produced components such as motherboards, housings and monitors. This included Acer factories in Hsinchu, Taiwan and Subic Bay in the Philippines. A major thrust of Acer's globalization strategy involved setting up "central kitchens" closer to the world's fastest-growing markets. In response to this, Acer was in the process of building manufacturing sites in Juarez, Mexico, to expand market share in NAFTA markets, which were slated for opening before the end of 1998. These strategically located facilities were designed to help shorten the time from component production to final product delivery.

Success on a global scale in the manufacturing realm was due in part to the customized systems Acer had established that transferred knowledge from R&D to manufacturing. For example, Acer's manufacturing management had developed fully documented procedures for project management, similar to a project flow of critical events from the conception stage through development on to the marketing of the final product. Acer had also developed a fully documented system to facilitate the phasing out of various products in the marketplace. This system provided a step-by-step guide for such procedures as how to phase out inventory of parts and product in question, how many spare parts were required for servicing, and so on.

Pursuant to Acer's fundamental principle of decentralization, the autonomy of overseas manufacturing operations was evidenced through local control of many functions such as human resource recruitment and management (under a set of general guidelines set out by head office) as well as all operational decisions, and ensuring compliance with local legal and administrative matters. Although vendor contracts were centrally negotiated, quantities and timing were decided by local managers to ensure their specific needs were met while capitalizing on head office's purchasing power.

Vendor contracts were secured at head office also so that Acer could guard its ISO 9000 Certification, which was partially dependent on the quality of inputs. ISO 9000 series certifications ensured the highest standards of quality and were recognized throughout the world. In July 1997, Acer plants were also awarded ISO 14000 Certification, which ensured that plants adhered to local environmental standards. Different countries applied the ISO regulations independently. For example, in Australia, Acer could not ship using wooden pallets, and deliveries to European companies could not be packed in polyform. Although logistics to ensure global ISO compliance was a formidable task, Acer faced many other more daunting challenges in the management of its global operations, such as multinational inventory management.

GLOBAL INVENTORY MANAGEMENT

One of the most significant challenges associated with being a global manufacturing company was inventory management. Inventory levels were predicated on market forecasts, which in the rapidly changing computer industry were difficult enough to predict accurately domestically, and were far more complicated in international markets. Inventory levels that were too high created cash flow problems, downward pressure on prices, and delayed the launch of leading-edge products when older and obsolete products piled up in inventory; this could create a chain reaction of further difficulties, including a loss of market share and brand erosion. In 1997, inventory miscues contributed strongly to Acer's loss in the U.S. market of US$75 million on sales of US$1 billion.

In his book, *Me-Too is not My Style,* Shih used the following analogy to illustrate the challenges in multinational inventory management:

> This is like adjusting the water temperature when taking a shower. If the distance between the water faucet and the water heater is very long, it is more difficult to adjust the water temperature to a perfect level. Increasing the temperature may need 20 seconds, but one is already impatient after 10 seconds so you adjust it further again. Twenty seconds later the water will be too hot, and one has to make the adjustment again. When the product supply is far away from the market, there will always be the problem of a time lag.

Despite varying levels of efficiency in logistics and forecasting between locations, being close to the market allowed significantly greater opportunity to adjust supply to market conditions. Significantly, inventory turnover levels lowered from 100 days to 50 days after Acer implemented the "fast food" model.

The Strategy Behind the Decision to Explore Mainland China

Traditional thinking with regard to seeking economies of scale dictated that concentrating on large markets supported volume production and, therefore, reduced operating costs. Acer's thinking to date had been that securing a firm footing in niche markets was invaluable in gaining a footing in large markets. This was Acer's "surrounding the cities from the countryside" strategy, extracted from Sun Tzu's *The Art of War.* This war strategy involved winning large cities by overtaking numerous surrounding villages, much like the popular Chinese board game *"GO,"* where players with the most markers in the smaller cities surrounding large cities won the battle for the region by besieging the larger city. The impetus behind Acer's adoption of *"GO"* game strategy was predominantly due to the size of Acer's "home base." Taiwan's domestic market size and country strengths were no match for the enormous resources and size of other global players, such as the U.S.

"GO" Game Strategy

The *"GO"* game analogy as applied to Acer's corporate philosophy was that Third World markets represented the villages, and markets such as the U.S. and Japan were major "cities" to be besieged through the storming of smaller villages. Acer's logic was that taking hold of these "villages" or smaller territories would create a strong foundation on which to base Acer's assault into larger markets. Thus, development of Third World markets would actually act as a catalyst to Acer's capabilities to compete in the developed markets rather than diverting its efforts.

"GO" game strategy included another concept that would be considered in Acer's decision whether or not to enter the mainland Chinese market—the concept of "long breath," a Chinese term referring to stamina and perseverance. For a company to maintain "long breath," certain factors such as operational efficiency and high morale contributed; however, it was also contingent on giving up other activities to conserve energy for "catching the big dragon." Though highly diversified, Acer was careful to pursue only those businesses that were inter-related and developed competencies transferable to other operations.

Acer's competitive strategy was based on the development of various core competencies as a necessary prerequisite to tackling its largest competitors on their home turf for a share of the largest market in the world, accounting for over a third of the sales of PCs globally—the U.S. Acer suffered heavy losses with its foray into the U.S. market where Acer's major competitors held a distinct competitive advantage—the playing field was their home turf. Acer was more familiar with marketing in Third World countries and had a more developed understanding of both the Chinese culture and the Chinese market. This was a prime consideration for Acer in its decision whether to pursue a higher profile in China. However, Acer management was particularly concerned with the history of strained political relations between Taiwan and China and the risks Taiwan faced in investing in the mainland.

TAIWAN'S POLITICAL STRUCTURE AND ITS RELATIONSHIP WITH CHINA

Shortly after the Second World War, civil war in China between the Nationalists and the Communists resulted in the rise of the Communists to power in 1949. The Nationalists fled to Taiwan and, protected by the U.S. navy, developed the region based on a more democratic form of government. Over the years, Taiwan's governments became increasingly more democratic and by 1998, Taiwan's political system, business ideology and culture more closely resembled western principles than those of traditional Chinese origin.

In 1998, Beijing continued to emphatically assert that the small island was not an independent state as Taiwan had declared, but rather a province of China. This point of view was tacitly accepted by many other nations and world governing bodies as China's economic might had the power to sway countries in the West who, despite an ideology closer to Taiwan than China, saw immense opportunity in the Chinese market. And with China incrementally opening its economy, compared to the tiny island of Taiwan, lucrative opportunities appeared to be closer at hand than they ever had in the past.

In Taiwan, however, the Economic Affairs Ministry advocated a slow and patient policy toward economic ties with China. Their official policy restricted direct investment on the mainland, and strongly discouraged large, high-profile investments by Taiwanese businesses on the mainland. One of the most publicized cases exemplifying the seriousness of the Taiwanese government was their efforts to enforce their mainland investment policy on Formosa Plastics, a Taiwanese firm which, despite restrictions

placed upon it by the government and the risks associated with a large capital investment in China, went ahead and constructed a US$3.2 billion power plant in China's Fujian province, only to have the Taiwanese government force it to sell the plant. Despite the risks, the mainland market remained so attractive that Taiwanese firms had invested US$35 billion indirectly in China by 1998 (see also Exhibit 4).

Commercial ties with China were not only limited by Taiwanese government policy, which discouraged investment in China, but also by restrictions on transport links across the East China Sea. It was only during the summer of 1998 that shipping links were re-established directly between Taiwan and the mainland after a 48-year history of diverting shipments south to Hong Kong before having them enter the mainland. Although by mid-1998, Taiwanese regulations allowed Chinese ships to enter Taiwan's harbor for the first time in 48 years, they still prohibited goods shipped directly from China to pass through their customs and prohibited Taiwanese goods from being shipped directly to China. This meant that while the shipping link was permitted, Taiwan could only use it for goods that were destined for international ports other than China. With regard to air traffic, all flights from Taiwan to any city on the mainland were diverted through Hong Kong, thus adding several hundred kilometres for travel between the two regions.

However, there was some reason for optimism among Acer and other Taiwanese companies planning to increase their profile on the mainland that these restrictions would be eased in the coming years. Unlike the United Nations and the World Bank, the World Trade Organization did not require statehood for membership; thus Taiwan was seeking WTO membership.

Despite a somewhat encouraging outlook, Lin could not be certain of the risks his people or the capital investments faced in China in the event that relations between China and Taiwan deteriorated further. Deciding on the recommendation to put forward to senior management was made more complicated in this environment of political uncertainty. Lin considered other factors that

Taiwan's decentralized economic model was considered an integral contributing factor in its success. While Japan and Korea were dominated by giant firms, Taiwan's businesses were characterized by their manufacturing focus and resultant agility. Whereas Hitachi manufactured everything from nuclear reactors to electric razors, and Samsung everything from semiconductors to automobiles, the majority of the thousands of entrepreneurial Taiwanese firms focused on one or two products.

Other factors had contributed to the success of the Taiwanese technological industry. Taiwan had benefited greatly from the trend in the PC industry of outsourcing. The growing market for a sub-$1,000 PC had contributed to the trend in outsourcing. For example, IBM had purchased $300 million in computer hardware from Taiwan in 1994, and that figure was expected to reach $1.8 billion in 1998. It was anticipated that Compaq would surpass this amount. Moreover, Dell Computer was expected to source all of its notebook computers from Taiwan manufacturers in 1998.

However, over the past several years, Taiwanese firms had emerged as more than simply manufacturing agents. Increasingly, Taiwanese partners were becoming involved higher up in the value chain, contributing to design, engineering, production, inventory management and worldwide logistics, making Taiwanese firms ideal partners for Silicon Valley firms.

This evolution helped protect Taiwan's economy during the Asian financial crisis. Moreover, the high-tech industry, which had so firmly established itself during the PC boom over the last four to five years was thought to have buoyed the economy. During the Asian financial crisis, Taiwan's economic growth was forecast to top five per cent. However, in other parts of Asia, companies were struggling to manage the fallout of the economic crisis: more volatile foreign exchange rates, higher interest rates, a more close-fisted lending environment, and falling input costs. For example, labor costs on the mainland were one-tenth of those in Taiwan.

Exhibit 4   Taiwan's Manufacturing Base

would determine the success of an R&D lab in China, some of which he was aware of through his experiences with co-ordinating projects between the Taipei and the Silicon Valley R&D labs.

Although Acer did not face such high profile political issues at other global manufacturing sites, there were many other issues that Acer would face in the mainland manufacturing site that it had experienced previously in the implementation of its global manufacturing strategy. An example of how Acer faced another significant challenge, that of sourcing inputs regionally, could be found in Acer's experience at its Juarez, Mexico facility.

THE JUAREZ MANUFACTURING SITE

The site in Juarez was chosen because of its proximity to the huge U.S. market as well as the fact that it was a twin city with El Paso, Texas. Moreover, Juarez was located in a maquiladora, a special economic zone (SEZ) created by the Mexican government, which offered tax incentives, favorable business conditions and the infrastructure to attract multinationals to the region.

Originally, Acer had been planning to import inputs from Taiwan for the Juarez plant; however, it quickly became clear that this strategy did not allow the necessary degree of responsiveness and would make inventory management more complicated, and less flexible. It would also add precariously to lead times in ordering parts. Instead, Acer, who in many cases was its suppliers' biggest customer, was able to persuade many of its vendors to join it in Mexico. This arrangement was attractive to Acer's suppliers due to the volume of business Acer could guarantee and the fact that the arrangement allowed the suppliers to manufacture for other customers. Acer's well-managed long-term vendor relationships meant that suppliers were considered family and were willing to partner with Acer throughout the world, contributing to Acer's, and in turn their own, success. Whether or not this practice could be applied in China was still unclear.

HUMAN RESOURCE MANAGEMENT AT ACER'S MANUFACTURING SITES

Another major resource that would be sourced locally at the China plant was the workforce of several hundred people. It was expected that the human resource management (HRM) policy for workers at a mainland China manufacturing facility would most closely resemble the profile of workers at Acer's Hsinchu factory in Taiwan, where almost a third of the workers were from another region (in this case, the Philippines), predominantly female, with an average age of 21 years. In China, workers migrated from urban communities in China to seek factory work in industrialized regions. They would most likely sign two-year contracts as the Filippino workers had at the Hsinchu plant; there were government restrictions with regard to mobility in China just as there were Taiwanese-enforced immigration laws with regard to foreign workers at Hsinchu. Motivation for working in the plant would be based on the financial rewards such work offered. For example, working in Taiwan was an attractive proposition for Filipino workers. At NT$20,000[1] per month in Taiwan, a factory worker's salary was approximately four times that in the Philippines.

The common practice in many large-scale Taiwanese factory operations of providing dormitory-style housing and meals as well as transportation and basic medical care to workers from other regions would be implemented in China as well, where it was also common practice. Lin expected that Acer could leverage its favorable reputation to attract the best workers, as employees from other regions could be assured of fair treatment and were guaranteed a reasonable standard of living and a competitive wage working with Acer. However, it was expected that training the workforce to standard efficiency levels in a timely manner could generate significant challenges.

A highly disciplined and flexible workforce was critical for success at any of Acer's manufacturing locations. This meant that during peak production periods workers would be asked to work diligently and commit to overtime. Conversely, during periods when orders slowed, such as the summer months, workers would work light shifts. In western manufacturing plants, such as El Paso, this was fairly easy to arrange with incentives such as overtime pay for workers, because they were familiar with adjusting for capacity in manufacturing environments. In Taiwan, workers also would adjust their schedules, but for a slightly different reason. In Taiwan, workers at all levels were considered family by their employers. This meant that they were treated well and found a higher degree of job security than in North America. This relationship was reciprocal in that personal time would be sacrificed to a degree for the sake of the company. Of course, workers were given overtime pay as well; however, their motivation was partly financial and partly to aid the "family" when their services were required. However, in China this degree of flexibility could not reasonably be assured, despite overtime pay, due to the ideology of many Chinese workers.

The communist doctrine and the environment of the state-owned enterprise (SOE) had a strong influence on the attitudes of Chinese workers. For example, a worker's pay in an SOE was guaranteed, regardless of the performance of the company or of the individual employee. The SOE system had inherently discouraged creativity and initiative, and indeed, showing these traits could create resentment and hostility among one's peers. Thus, the underlying concept behind incentives or reward programs was not fully understood by Chinese workers. Therefore, Lin felt that creating a disciplined workforce who were willing to "go the extra mile" for Acer when required would be a significant challenge awaiting any management team in mainland China.

Beyond these training and cross-cultural issues, Acer had experienced other significant challenges at some of its overseas manufacturing plants. For instance, the Subic Bay site posed many challenges. Local authorities there were strongly recommending the hiring of local workers, despite their unsuitability in some cases. Also, transportation logistics proved challenging. Although there were regular cargo flights right into Subic Bay, they were operated by Purolator who did not have the expertise or capacity to handle the type and volume of shipping Acer required, forcing managers to arrange ground transportation from Subic Bay to the Manila airport. Other challenges at Subic Bay included managing in an environment of political uncertainty. Finally, Acer's usual management succession plan, replacing expatriate managers with local hires, was not feasible at the Subic Bay manufacturing facility. In the Philippines, well-educated, highly experienced local managers were particularly scarce. However, at least one manager was local (the personnel manager) and there was a succession plan in place that involved the training and development of line supervisors to eventually assume a managerial capacity, which was expected to take several years. A similar, though less pronounced, succession pattern was anticipated in China, but it meant that expatriate managers could be required to relocate to the mainland for at least five years.

A critical success factor for the mainland China factory in the realm of human resources would be Acer's ability to persuade highly skilled managerial and technical Taiwanese expatriates and their families to relocate to the site for such a prolonged period of time. This was expected to be a great challenge because many Taiwanese were hesitant to relocate themselves and their families to mainland China.

First, the ideology that was taught in the schools in China was fundamentally different from that which the students learned in Taiwan. Moreover, many families did not wish to take their children out of the school system in Taiwan, where the education the children would receive would be of a higher caliber. Once children left the Taiwanese school system, it was impossible to integrate them back into the system without being set back a year or two. Providing their children with a good education, from the very beginning, was important to parents in

Taiwanese culture, so much so that it was not unusual for professionals in Taiwan to move their families to the West for schooling, while they remained in Taiwan to make the money to support the family abroad.

Second, a repatriated manager often found that upon his return to Taiwan, positions of equal opportunity and status were difficult to find, and being away reduced a manager's profile. Thus, other executives quickly perceived that an international posting was, more often than not, a career-limiting move. Consequently, repatriated executives often were recruited by competing companies to serve as their overseas business heads. Combined, these two factors resulted in not only a loss of valuable talent to Acer, but also a void in experienced overseas executives. Several years ago, Acer had extended the term of its management postings overseas to five years or more, but it was difficult to persuade skilled executives to move themselves and their families abroad for that period of time, especially to countries where Taiwanese and their families were less than eager to relocate.

Other difficulties, such as cultural differences, were expected to affect long-term relocation to mainland China, and it would prove challenging to recruit experienced, highly-skilled Taiwanese management. Despite the fact that Mandarin was spoken by both Taiwanese and Chinese, the two cultures were very different. Indeed, many Taiwanese considered their culture, background and experience to be more similar to the West than to that of China. This would mean great adjustment on the part of both the manager and his family.

Another adjustment to life on the mainland would be the fact that many amenities freely available in Taiwan were scarce in China; consequently, in addition to adapting to a new and diverse culture away from their extended families and network of friends, employees and their families would also have to adjust to a lower standard of living. Thus, many employees did not have the desire to move anywhere that took them away from their parents and other family members because family ties were strong in the Taiwanese culture. Finally, the security of the Taiwanese was not fully guaranteed in China due to the political and regional social unrest.

A critical part of the location strategy for Lin was to pick a location that would be safe for expatriate workers and their families who would be required to relocate there for a period of several years:

> Though input costs, distribution logistics and tax incentives are, of course, fundamental factors in my decision, the most important factor is the safety of my employees. For example, during my tour of Shenzhen, I noticed that all the taxi cabs had bullet-proof shields to protect the drivers.

The safety of the Taiwanese in China had received much media attention in recent weeks. The kidnapping and murder of a city council-woman from Taiwan in a northeastern coastal city in China, and the mainland's subsequent handling of the event, caused Taiwanese busi-nessmen to take extra precautions in their busi-ness dealings in China. The quasi-official Straits Exchange Foundation (SEF), which had tracked almost 200 cases involving Taiwanese business-people's personal safety in China over the last several years, discovered attacks, robberies and extortion as well as kidnapping and occasionally even murder. The most recent case had involved a Taiwanese investor in Shenzhen who had been beaten to death on July 27, 1998. This prompted calls from the Taiwanese public for the Mainland Affairs Council (MAC), which charted Chinese policy, to establish a warning system for Chinese-bound businesspeople and travellers, as well as a rating system that gauged the extent of the risk in various cities and regions within China based on the general crime rate and the proportion of inci-dents that involved Taiwanese expatriates.

THE BRIEFING TO SENIOR MANAGEMENT

Lin had prepared an analysis of these factors, but exactly how China would fit into Acer's global manufacturing strategy would require further exploration. Lin saw validity in both sides of the argument. On the one hand, the economies of a move to the mainland were apparent. Moreover, a manufacturing operation could be a platform on which to expand Acer's presence in the huge China market for either existing or new product lines. On the other hand, there were serious issues that could adversely affect Acer's economic return on any investment on the mainland. For example, uncertainty regarding cross-strait political rela-tions created a risky business environment for Taiwanese companies investing heavily in China. Was the infrastructure sufficient to ensure effec-tive logistics? And what about the opportunity costs associated with such a large investment—was Acer missing out on more lucrative opportu-nities or were there alternative locations that would better suit its manufacturing needs? Other critical factors on which the decision would be based involved the safety and difficulties involved in the transfer of the expatriate workforce, the disparity between the two cultures, as well as environmental certification concerns.

For Lin, this dilemma could be distilled into one principal question—had Acer secured enough "villages" to enter China, or was it too soon and would Acer risk being surrounded by opponents and falling to its competitors in battle?

NOTE

1. US$1 was equivalent to 33.2 New Taiwan dollars.

REFERENCES

Acocella, N. (1998). *Foundations of economic policy: Values and techniques.* New York: Cambridge University Press.

Adamantopoulos, K. (Ed.). (1997). *An anatomy of the World Trade Organization.* London: Kluwer Law International.

Brandenburger, A. M., & Nalebuff, B. J. (1995, July/August). The right game: Use game theory to shape strategy. *Harvard Business Review,* pp. 57–71.

Bulik, B. S. (2002, July). Can CEOs defend corporate America's image? *Chief Executive,* pp. 54–58.

Chambers, B. (Ed.). (2001). *Inter-linkages: The Kyoto Protocol and the international trade and investment regimes.* New York: New York University Press.

Chrystal, A., & Pennant-Rea, R. (Eds.). (2000). *Public choice analysis of economic policy.* New York: St. Martin's.

Conklin, D., & Lecraw, D. (1997). *Foreign ownership restrictions and liberalization reforms.* Aldershot, UK: Ashgate.

Conklin, D., & Tapp, L. (2000). The creative web. In S. Chowdhury (Ed.), *Management 21C: Someday we'll all manage this way* (pp. 220–234). Mahwah, NJ: Prentice Hall/Pearson Education.

Donaldson, T. (1996). Values in tension: Ethics away from home. *Harvard Business Review, 74*(75), 4–12.

Dragsbaek Schmidt, J., & Hersh, J. (2000). *Globalization and social change.* New York: Routledge.

Eltis, W. (2000). *Britain, Europe and the EMU.* Hampshire, UK: Macmillan.

Greenspan, A. (1993). Centrally planned economies & capitalist market economies: The process of transition and the lessons learned. *The World of Banking, 12*(4), 26–31.

Grundfest, J. A. (1997). The board as a portfolio. *Directors and Boards, 21*(1), 28.

Hartman, L. (2002). *Perspectives in business ethics.* Boston: McGraw-Hill.

Hatcher, T. (2002). *Ethics and HRD: A new approach to leading responsible organizations.* Cambridge, UK: Perseus.

Held, D., & McGrew, A. (2002). *Globalization/anti-globalization.* Malden, MA: Blackwell.

Hufbauer, G. C., & Schott, J. J. (1993). *NAFTA: An assessment* (Rev. ed.). Washington, DC: Institute for Entrepreneurial Economics.

Hughes Hallett, A., & Piscitelli, L. (2002). Does one size fit all? A currency union with asymmetric transmissions and a stability pact. *International Review of Applied Economics, 16*(1), 71–96.

International Institute for Management Development (IMD). (2002). *The world competitiveness yearbook.* Lausanne, Switzerland: Author.

Keating, M., & Loughlin, J. (1997). *In the political economy of regionalism.* Portland, OR: Frank Cass & Co.

Kennedy, P. (2000). *Macroeconomic essentials: Understanding economics in the news* (2nd ed.). Cambridge: MIT Press.

Krueger, A. (Ed.). (1998). *The WTO as an international organization.* Chicago: University of Chicago Press.

Kynge, J. (1999, November 17). Fears for banks over China entry into WTO. *Financial Times,* p. 1.

Kynge, J. (2002, January 3). China's burden. *Financial Times,* p. 10.

Loong, P. (2000, July/August). What WTO means for Chinese banking. *Asiamoney,* p. 23.

McNutt, P. (2002). *The economics of public choice.* Cheltanham, UK: Elgar.

Mitchell, W. (1994). *Beyond politics: Markets, welfare, and the failure of bureaucracy.* Boulder, CO: Westview.

Modigliani, F., Fitoussi, J.-P., Lindbeck, A., Moro, B., Snower, D., Solow, R., et al. (1998). An economists' manifesto on unemployment in the European Union. *BNL Quarterly Review, 206,* 327–361.

North, D. (1990). *Institutions, institutional change, and economic performance.* Cambridge, UK: Cambridge University Press.

Oestreich, J. (2002). What can businesses do to appease anti-globalization protestors? *Business and Society Review, 2,* 207–220.

O'Leary, G. (Ed.). (1998). *Adjusting to capitalism: Chinese workers and the state.* New York: M. E. Sharpe.

Organization for Economic Cooperation and Development (OECD). (1999). *Action against change: The Kyoto Protocol and beyond.* Paris: Author.

Ougaard, M. (2004). *Political globalization: State, power and social forces.* New York: Palgrave Macmillan.

Pardo, J. P., & Schneider, F. (Eds.). (1996). *Current issues in public choice.* Cheltanham, UK: Elgar.

Peacock, A. (1992). *Public choice analysis in historical perspective.* New York: Cambridge University Press.

Porter, M. (1979, March/April). How competitive forces shape strategy. *Harvard Business Review,* pp. 137–145.

Porter, M. (1990, March/April). The competitive advantage of nations. *Harvard Business Review,* pp. 73–91.

Rayport, J. E., & Jaworski, B. (2001). *E-commerce.* Boston: McGraw-Hill.

Rosser, J. B. (1996). *Comparative economics in a transforming world economy.* Chicago: Irwin.

Rugman, A. (Ed.). (1994). *Foreign investment and NAFTA.* Columbia: University of South Carolina Press.

Sachs, J. (1991). *The economic transformation of Eastern Europe: The case of Poland.* Acceptance paper, P. K. Seidman Foundation, Memphis, TN.

Smith, D. (1999). *Will Europe work?* London: Profile Books.

Special report: Lots of it about—corporate social responsibility. (2002). *The Economist, 365*(8303), 74.

Special report: The way we govern now—corporate boards. (2003). *The Economist, 366*(8306), 62.

Stiglitz, J. (2002). *Globalization and its discontents.* New York: Norton.

Stiles, P. (2001). *Boards at work: How directors view their roles and responsibilities.* New York: Oxford University Press.

Torres, R. (2001). *Towards a socially sustainable world economy: An analysis of the social pillars of globalization.* Geneva, Switzerland: International Labor Organization.

Weimer, D. L. (1999). *Policy analysis: Concepts and practice.* Upper Saddle River, NJ: Prentice Hall.

ABOUT THE EDITOR

David W. Conklin is the James D. Fleck Professor in International Business at the Richard Ivey School of Business, London, Ontario, Canada. He earned a Ph.D. in Economics from the Massachusetts Institute of Technology. His research and teaching interests include the global environment of business, trade agreements, international competitiveness, and public policy. He has designed several university courses dealing with international business, including a macroeconomics course that analyzes the challenges and policy options faced by countries throughout the world, and the implications for trade and investment decisions. He has also taught in economics and political science departments and in Canada's Foreign Service Institute.

Prior to joining the Richard Ivey School of Business, Dr. Conklin had extensive experience in research institutes, corporations, and governments. He has consulted for governments in the design and enforcement of legislation and regulations and has consulted for corporations in developing strategies, influencing public policies, and complying with government legislation and regulations. He has organized many conferences dealing with international business issues, involving participation of business leaders from around the world.

His depth of international experience is reflected in the publication of more than 135 articles, book chapters, and cases, and he has also written or edited more than 30 books. His courses are based on case teaching that involves students in lively discussions concerning international business decisions. He has taught in universities in Latin America, Europe, and Asia.